Gender in

Cross-Cultural

Perspective

FIFTH EDITION

Gender in Cross-Cultural Perspective

Edited by

Caroline B. Brettell

and

Carolyn F. Sargent

Southern Methodist University

PEARSON

Prentice
Hall

Upper Saddle River, New Jersey 07458

Library of Congress Cataloging-in-Publication Data

Gender in cross-cultural perspective / edited by Caroline B. Brettell and
Carolyn F. Sargent. – 5th ed.
   p. cm.
 Includes bibliographical references.
 ISBN-13: 978-0-13-606132-8
 ISBN-10: 0-13-606132-X
 1. Sex role–Cross-cultural studies. I. Brettell, Caroline. II. Sargent,
Carolyn Fishel
 GN479.65.G4634 2008
 305.3–dc22

2008014543

Publisher: Nancy Roberts
Editorial Director: Leah Jewell
Editorial Assistant: Nant Varoqua
Marketing Manager: Lindsey Prudhomme
Marketing Assistant: Craig Deming
Production Liaison: Fran Russello
Permissions Supervisor:
   Sherith H. Pankratz/
   Kathleen Karcher
Operations Specialist: Ben Smith
Cover Design: Marganet Kenselaar
Cover Illustration/Photo: Leon
   Zemitsky/Images.com.
Director, Image Resource Center: Melinda
   Patelli

Manager, Rights and Permissions:
   Zina Arabia
Manager, Visual Research: Beth Brenzel
Manager, Cover Visual Research &
   Permissions: Karen Sanatar
Image Permission Coordinator: Nancy Seise
Photo Researcher: Rachel Lucas
Composition/Full-Service Project
   Management: Laserwords/Karen Berry;
   Pine Tree Composition
Printer/Binder: RRDonnelley & Sons
   Company

Credits and acknowledgments borrowed from other sources and reproduced, with permission, in this textbook appear on appropriate page within text

Pearson Education Ltd., London
Pearson Education Singapore, Pte. Ltd
Pearson Education Canada, Inc.
Pearson Education-Japan
Pearson Education Australia PTY, Limited

Pearson Education North Asia, Ltd., Hong Kong
Pearson Educación de Mexico, S.A. de C.V.
Pearson Education Malaysia, Pte. Ltd.
Pearson Education Upper Saddle River,
   New Jersey

10 9 8 7 6 5 4
ISBN-(13): 978-0-13-606132-8
ISBN-(10): 0-13-606132-X

For Richard Brettell and David Freidel, men who have given new meaning to the gendered division of labor, with gratitude for the intellectual and emotional support that they have provided for many years.

Contents

IX. **Gender, Ritual, and Religion** 395

X. **Gender, Politics, and Reproduction** 449

XI. **Culture Contact, Development, and the Global Economy** 505

Preface

The initial idea for this reader came from the experience of teaching undergraduate courses in gender and anthropology. In reviewing the textbooks available for an introductory course, we came to the conclusion that there was a need for a readable text that built on the classic contributions of the 1970s while incorporating the more recent and diverse literature on gender roles and ideology around the world. Although a number of sophisticated theoretical works devoted to this subject existed, we felt there was a dearth of classroom material available in one volume and appropriate for less advanced students, whether undergraduates or beginning graduate students.

We have had six goals in mind as we selected materials for the fifth edition. First, as in previous editions, we want to introduce students to the most significant topics in the field of the anthropology of gender. These include the study of men and women in prehistory; the relationship between biology and culture; the cultural construction of masculinity, femininity, sexuality, personhood, and the body; variations in the sexual division of labor and economic organization; women's involvement in ritual and religion; and the impact on gender issues of various forces of change such as colonialism, the rise of the state, the global economy, and migration.

Second, we think it is important to maintain the broad cross-cultural coverage evident in earlier editions. This breadth encourages comparative analysis of the themes under discussion and allows us to address issues of gender in industrial society as well as in developing societies.

Third, we consider it important to have authors who have written original pieces for this book to update their work from time to time. In this edition, Lucinda Peach has updated her work on gender and war, and Guenther and Freidel have updated their work on Maya royal women. Susan Rasmussen has revised her essay on the Tuareg, and Josephine Caldwell Ryan has updated her essay "Encountering the State." Several new essays are included in the fifth edition.

Fourth, we have expanded our efforts to complement research on women's lives with essays that deal with masculinity and male gender roles. Feminist theory is increasingly being applied to the study of men, and we have tried to represent some of this research in our volume.

Fifth, we have always been committed to combining theoretically and ethnographically based essays in each section of the book. We hope that we have compiled a volume that can stand alone or, if the instructor so desires, can be complemented by the use of full ethnographies.

Sixth, in every edition we have included introductions to each section that review as clearly as possible some of the significant issues debated in particular subject areas in the anthropology of gender. These introductions, updated for the current edition, are intended to orient students to the essays in the section and to provide a context in which readers can more fully understand each essay. Each introduction concludes with a list of references that can be used by teachers and students to examine further the questions raised in that section.

We do not expect all instructors to assign the sections in the order that they appear in the text, although for this edition we have rearranged the sections slightly. The order makes sense to us, but our ultimate goal is to provide for maximum flexibility in teaching. Indeed, there are essays in some sections that can be related to essays in other sections. We also have no intention of imposing a particular theoretical perspective, although our own predilections may be apparent to some readers. We include readings that reflect a variety of theoretical orientations to enable instructors to emphasize their own approach to the subject.

ACKNOWLEDGMENTS

Many people have contributed substantially to the preparation and development of this book over its multiple editions. For the first edition, Andrew Webb provided invaluable clerical and organizational assistance. The undergraduate students in Professor Sargent's course "Gender and Sex Roles: A Global Perspective" have consistently offered valuable criticisms of selected essays. Their opinions continue to influence us enormously in the final selection process. John Phinney acted as an invaluable library of knowledge for obscure references; Sue Linder-Linsley offered indispensable computer advice and tirelessly scanned in text to save us time in the preparation of the second edition; and Sue Racine and Scott Langley contributed clerical assistance. Tim Benner and Louann Miller worked conscientiously to help us complete the third edition; Melissa Nibungco helped us with the fourth edition. We are also grateful to Southern Methodist University for various forms of support over the years.

We want to thank the reviewers of the original manuscript and the professors around the world who have used previous editions and offered valuable suggestions for improvements to the fifth edition. Finally, we wish to acknowledge Sharon Chambliss, formerly with Prentice Hall, who worked with us on the first four editions, and Nancy Roberts, who first recognized the importance of this project and whose confidence in our judgment and constant support are much appreciated. We have a wonderful partnership!

Caroline B. Brettell
Carolyn F. Sargent

About the Authors

Caroline Brettell received her B.A. degree from Yale University and her M.A. and Ph.D. degrees from Brown University. She joined the faculty of the Department of Anthropology at Southern Methodist University in 1988, and in 2003 was named Dedman Family Distinguished Professor. From 1989 to 1994, she served as Director of Women's Studies, and from 1994 to 2004 she served as Chair of the Department of Anthropology. From 2006 to 2008, she served as Interim Dean of Dedman College, the Humanities and Sciences College at Southern Methodist University. Her research interests are in the areas of immigration, gender roles, European ethnography, and anthropology and history. She is the author of *Men Who Migrate, Women Who Wait: Population and History in a Portuguese Parish* (1986), *We Have Already Cried Many Tears: The Stories of Three Portuguese Migrant Women* (1982, 1995), *Writing against the Wind: A Mother's Life History* (1999), and *Anthropology and Migration: Essays on Transnationalism, Ethnicity and Identity* (2003); coauthor with Richard Brettell of *Painters and Peasants in the 19th Century* (1983); editor of *When They Read What We Write: The Politics of Ethnography* (1993) and *Constructing Borders/Crossing Boundaries: Race, Ethnicity, and Immigration* (2007); coeditor of *International Migration: The Female Experience* (1986), *Gender in Cross-Cultural Perspective* (Prentice Hall 1993, 1997, 2001, 2005), *Gender and Health: An International Perspective* (1996), *Migration Theory: Talking Across Disciplines* (2000, 2007), *Citizenship, Political Engagement, and Belonging: Immigrants in Europe and the U.S* (2008), and *America's Twenty-First Century Immigrant Gateways: Immigrant Incorporation in Suburbia* (2008). She is also the author of numerous book chapters, and articles. Professor Brettell has served as a member of National Institutes of Health (NIH) Study Section-SNEM 3 and several selection panels for the Social Science Research Council and the National Endowment for the Humanites (NEH). She has served as President of the Society for the Anthropology of Europe and of the Social Science History Association. She has conducted field research in France, Portugal, and Canada and is currently engaged in a long-term study of new immigrants into the Dallas–Fort Worth metropolitan area with funding from the National Science Foundation and the Russell Sage Foundation.

Carolyn Sargent received her B.A. degree from Michigan State University, her M.A. degree from the University of Manchester, and her Ph.D. from Michigan State University. She joined the faculty of the Department of Anthropology at Southern Methodist University in 1979. She served as Director of Women's Studies from 1994 through 2007. She is currently a research fellow at the University of Paris 13 (CRESP) and the University of Paris 5 (POP-INTER). Her research interests are in the areas of global health, gender and reproduction, and bioethics. Sargent is the author of *The Cultural Context of Therapeutic Choice: Obstetrical Decisions among the Bariba of Benin* (1982), and *Maternity, Medicine and Power: Reproductive Decisions in Urban Benin* (1989); and coeditor of *Medical Anthropology: A Handbook of Theory and Method, Gender in Cross-Cultural Perspective* (Prentice Hall 1993, 1997, 2001, 2005), *Gender and Health: An International Perspective* (1996), *Childbirth and Authoritative Knowledge* (1997), and *Small Wars: The Cultural Politics of Childhood* (1999). In addition to several book chapters, she has also authored numerous articles, many of them published in *Medical Anthropological Quarterly* and *Social Science and Medicine*. She has conducted fieldwork in West Africa and the Caribbean and is currently engaged in a long-term study of West African immigrants in France funded by the Wenner Gren Foundation and the National Science Foundation. She has served on a Senior Advisory Panel of the National Science Foundation and on the Executive Board for the Society for Medical Anthropology. In 2007 she assumed the role of President of the SMA. In Dallas she serves as a Community Representative for both Parkland and Baylor Hospitals.

1

Biology, Gender, and Human Evolution

What is the role of biology in human behavior? To what extent are differences between men and women explained by biology, by culture, or by an interaction between the two? Is there a biological basis for the sexual division of labor? These questions are hotly debated in the United States as we struggle with such issues as why men dominate the fields of math and science, whether women are equipped for war and combat, and the implications for child development of female participation in the labor force (Blum 1998; Gallagher and Kaufman 2005; Geary 1998; Udry 2000). In this chapter, we consider issues of gender in a cross-cultural context, and we explore whether women are universally subordinated to men and to what extent biological differences explain the allocation of roles and responsibilities between men and women.

The relative importance of biology, or nature, versus culture, or nurture, is an enduring dilemma. This issue was addressed by anthropologist Margaret Mead early in the twentieth century. Using data drawn from her fieldwork in Samoa and New Guinea, Mead (1928, 1935) set out to establish the significance of culture or environment in molding gender differences. She wanted to offer an alternative to the powerful intellectual principles of biological determinism and eugenics (biological engineering) that dominated academic circles in the 1920s. She also hoped to demonstrate to North American women that a range of possibilities was open to them and that the social roles of housework and childrearing were not their inevitable lot. In her view, anatomy was not destiny.

Mead's work was challenged in the 1980s by Derek Freeman (1983). Freeman accused Mead of cultural determinism (that is, giving priority to culture over biology) and opened a lively debate within academic and nonacademic circles (Holmes 1987; Leacock 1993; Orans 1996; Rensberger 1983; Scheper-Hughes 1987; Schneider 1983). For some, Freeman's book was taken (erroneously) as new support for the sociobiological approach to an understanding of human behavior, an approach formulated by Edward Wilson (1975) that contends that there is a genetic basis for all social behavior.

Although few people deny the anatomical and hormonal differences between men and women, they disagree about the importance of these differences for gender roles and personality attributes. A significant body of research, much of it conducted by psychologists, suggests that male and female infants cannot be significantly distinguished by their degree of dependence on parents, their visual and verbal abilities, or their aggression as measured by activity level (Bleier 1984; Fausto-Sterling

1985; Renzetti and Curran 1989). These characteristics tend to emerge later in the development process, indicating the importance of environment.

One controversy centers on how the brain is organized and to what extent brain lateralization is related to sex differences. One position holds that women are left-brain dominant, giving them superior verbal skills, whereas men are right-brain dominant, giving them superior visual-spatial skills. While research on variations in the structure and development of male and female brains continues, there are those who contend that to date "there is little evidence indicating that the sexual differentiation of the brain, if it occurs in humans, consequently predisposes males and females to behave in gender-specific ways" (Renzetti and Curran 1989: 33; see also Fausto-Sterling 1985: 44–53). However, there are equally those who suggest that sex hormones affect brain organization very early in life, resulting in brains that are differently wired in boys and girls (Geary 1998).

Within anthropology the role of biology in explaining differences between men and women, including social behaviors such as the division of labor and the tendency for women to be subordinated to men, has been explored within an evolutionary framework. Evolutionary theories fall roughly into four categories: male strength hypotheses, male aggression hypotheses, male bonding hypotheses, and women's childbearing hypotheses. Male strength hypotheses argue that men are physically stronger than women and this gives them superiority. They are larger, and they have stronger muscles and less fat, a pelvis better adapted for sprinting, larger hearts and lungs, and so forth. These physical differences between the males and females of a species are referred to as sexual dimorphism.

Several anthropologists have studied both fossil and nonhuman primates in order to explore the evolutionary origins of sexual dimorphism (differences in morphology, such as weight and body dimensions) and, by analogy, sexual asymmetry, the sexual division of labor, and the emergence of the nuclear family (Fedigan 1992; Leigh 1995; Plavcan and van Schaik 1997a, 1997b; Zihlman 1993). This research with nonhuman primates is part of a large body of literature that uses animals as models for understanding human behavior. One of the earliest statements was Leibowitz's (1975) discussion of the evolution of sex differences. Leibowitz challenged the tendency to link sexual dimorphism to particular sex role patterns by demonstrating enormous variations among different species of primates. Rather than explaining greater male size and strength solely as an adaptation to the roles of protection and provisioning associated with hunting, Leibowitz urged consideration of the reproductive advantage to women of the cessation of growth soon after sexual maturity is reached. In the process, she asked us to reconsider what we mean by strength. She also cautioned that our stereotypes of human male attributes have been drawn from one of the most sexually dimorphic species of nonhuman primates, the plains baboon. As Sperling observed, "This use of the baboon troop as model for ancestral human populations was very influential in forming both sexist and anthropomorphic views of monkeys in popular culture" (1991: 210). Sperling, Fedigan (1986), and Leibowitz have all emphasized the inappropriateness of the "baboonization" of early human life, given the distant relationship between humans and baboons. If we are going to draw comparisons with nonhuman primates, it would be preferable to draw analogies with the great apes, particularly the chimpanzees.

In this book, biologist Marlene Zuk takes up the question of animal models in gender studies, exploring the biological roots of sex differences. She argues forcefully that we should not succumb to stereotypes that would make us pawns of our evolutionary heritage. She cites current research that supports the idea of female preference for particular types of males as a major force in evolution. But she also stresses that there is a great deal of diversity and variation in sexual selection in the animal world and that this variation should offer lessons for how we understand the biological basis of sex differences and mating practices in humans. Even the non-human primate world is characterized by this variation.

A second line of argument attempts to explain male dominance with reference to the biological basis of aggression. Many studies of aggression contend that men are more aggressive than women (Wilson 1975; see Fedigan 1992: 71ff for a critique of this position) and often link this difference to levels of male hormones (testosterone). According to Fausto-Sterling (1985: 126), "Many societies, including our own, have tested this belief by castrating men who have a history of violent or antisocial behavior." Scientific research has demonstrated that there is no connection between castration and aggression.

It has also been argued that male aggressive tendencies are an adaptation to the male role in defense (Keeley 1996; Martin and Voorhies 1975) among both human and nonhuman primates. The problem with any line of argument that links male dominance or male social roles to male aggression is that it ignores the wide variation in behaviors and personalities not only between the sexes, but also within them (Renzetti and Curran 1989: 38). This is certainly true of nonhuman primates. Smuts (1986), for example, argues that both males and females in various species are capable of opportunistic alliances and defense of victims, depending on the circumstances.

Cross-cultural ethnographic data indicate that human societies also differ in culturally appropriate levels of aggression expressed by men and women (Burbank 1994; Counts, Brown, and Campbell 1992; Daly and Wilson 1990). Richard Lee's (1979) study of conflict and violence among the !Kung San, a relatively egalitarian and peace-loving people, addresses the issue of aggression among men and women. He lends support to the argument that both men and women are aggressive in different ways. !Kung women engage in verbal abuse, but homicides are disproportionately committed by men. Lee compares trends in !Kung violence to those in several other societies. Although his statistics are from the 1950s and 1960s, more recent research indicates that the patterns remain similar. Statistics on criminal activity in the United States indicates that while violent offenses committed by women increased between the mid-1970s and the mid-1980s, they were still predominantly committed by men (Morris 1987: 35). Between 1986 and 1991, the proportion of violent offenses among female prison inmates declined from 40.7 percent to 32.2 percent. Corresponding figures for males were from 55.2 percent and 47.4 percent (U.S. Department of Justice 1991). In 1991, 24 percent of male prison inmates and 20 percent of female prison inmates in England and Wales were incarcerated for "violence against a person" (Lynch et al. 1994). In 2000 in the United States, 83 percent of convicted criminals were male and 17 percent were female. In the United Kingdom the comparable figures were 82 percent and 18 percent. While there has been a convergence in recent years between men and women in theft offenses, there is little convergence for violent offenses (Austin 1993). A comparison between the !Kung and modern industrial societies suggests that the reasons for gender differences in aggressive behavior are complex. In addition to biological factors, access to weapons, culturally approved expressions of hostility, and the role of the state in the evolution of social control should also be considered.

Among the !Kung the victims of violent crimes tend to be other men, a finding that supports Maccoby and Jacklin's (1974) observation that primate males in general demonstrate more aggression against one another than against females (Daly and Wilson 1990). Dominance of men over women through aggression is thereby brought into question, as is the concept of aggression itself. As Fedigan (1992: 89) suggests, aggression "is such a heterogeneous category of behaviors and interactions that 'amount of aggression' is not a very useful concept." Fausto-Sterling (1985: 129) concurs and points to the fact that no studies on hormone levels and aggression use female subjects or compare men and women. She raises fundamental questions regarding the causal relationship between testosterone levels and aggression.

A third body of evolutionary theory attempts to explain male domination in terms of their supposedly greater ability to form social bonds among themselves (Tiger 1969). This ability is presumed to be genetically programmed and associated with the evolutionary adaptation to hunting. Women, conversely, are thought to lack the genetic code for bonding and are therefore unsuited to the kinds of cooperative and political endeavors that give men power and prestige.

Margaret Ehrenberg (in this book) explores this bonding issue in its relation to the development of the sexual division of labor among early humans. She suggests that women were often the social center of groups. They fostered sociability and sharing. Ehrenberg also addresses a much wider debate about the relative contributions of men and women to human evolution. She provides an alternative to what has been labeled the "coattails theory" of biological evolution—"Traits are selected for in males and women evolve by clinging to the men's coattails" (Fedigan 1986: 29). The male bias reflected in this approach has been equally evident in analyses of cultural development, especially in the emphasis on hunting, a male activity, as the distinctive human activity (Lee and DeVore 1968). In her reevaluation of a discussion that essentially omitted half of humanity from the story of evolution, Ehrenberg suggests that hunting probably evolved from the physical, technological, and social innovations associated with gathering (a female activity).

In this book, Lucinda J. Peach explores how the ideas about male strength, male bonding, and male aggression have shaped the debate in the United States about women in the military. While women in the U.S. military are now "seeing combat," U.S. policy continues to exclude them from the majority of combat roles. Peach suggests that such exclusions are based on assumptions and stereotypes about female "nature" rather than on verifiable gender differences that clearly demonstrate women's inability to perform competently specific combat duties such as operating offensive, line-of-sight weapons or participating in ground fighting. Warfare is a masculine arena; women need to be protected; women lack the necessary physical and psychological strength to perform adequately; the presence of women in combat units would undermine unit cohesion by disrupting male bonding—these are some of the arguments that are put forward to justify the banishment of women from specific military activities. One result, by extension, is that women are denied certain opportunities for promotion that are predicated on active combat service.

A fourth body of theory linking biology to gender difference and gender hierarchy explains the absence of women from cooperative and political activity in the nondomestic sphere (hence their subordination) in terms of their reproductive roles. A corollary of this argument is the idea that women possess a maternal instinct. The fact that women bear children and lactate has been the basis of assertions that women innately experience an attachment to their children that forms the foundation of effective mothering, while men lack a similar capacity to nurture (Peterson 1983; Rossi 1977, 1978). This attachment may be the result of such factors as hormone levels (O'Kelly 1980: 30) or the experiences of pregnancy, labor, and nursing (Whitbeck 1983: 186).

In contrast, Collier and Rosaldo (1981: 315) have argued that "there are no facts about human sexual biology that, in and of themselves, have immediate social meanings or institutional consequences. Mothering is a social relation, much like fathering, judging, or ruling, whose meaning and organization must be understood with reference to a particular configuration of relationships within a complex social whole."

The article by Nancy Scheper-Hughes (in this book) illustrates this assertion. She examines the inevitability of maternal–infant attachment among mothers in the shantytowns of northeast Brazil. In an environment of poverty, chronic hunger, and economic exploitation, Scheper-Hughes finds that mothers adopt a strategy of delayed attachment and neglect of weaker children thought unlikely to survive. Such attitudes of resignation and fatalism toward the death of children are documented in historical studies of other cultures as well; for example, Ransel's account of child abandonment in Russia relates the passive attitude toward childhood death to child death rates in the 50 percent range (1988: 273; see also Boswell 1988). Parental attitudes are reflected in an entire category of lullabies with the motif of wishing death on babies; women sang these lullabies to infants who were sickly, weak, or crippled (Ransel 1988: 273). Thus, mother love seems less a "natural and universal maternal script" than a luxury reserved for the strongest and healthiest children. In the context of frequent infant death, maternal attachment means grief, and mother love emerges as culturally and socially constructed, rather than as an innate emotion.

Barry S. Hewlett (in this book) offers a somewhat different perspective on the question of maternal instinct by exploring the role of fatherhood among the Aka pygmies, a group of foragers who live in the tropical forest regions of central Africa. Aka fathers spend a significant portion of their day caring for and nurturing their children. A good father, among the Aka, is a man who stays near his children, shows them affection, and assists the mother with her work. Indeed Aka male–female relations are very egalitarian. Women and men each contribute significantly to subsistence; while Aka men hold all the named positions of status, women challenge men's authority regularly and play a decisive role in all kinds of decision making; physical violence is infrequent, and violence against women is rare (Hewlett 1991). Hewlett suggests that strong father–infant attachment among the Aka can be explained by a range of ecological, social, ideological, and demographic factors. The implications of the Aka example, especially for alternate parenting models in the United States, are clear. As Hewlett argues, "The Aka demonstrate that there are cultural systems where men can be active, intimate and nurturing caregivers" (Hewlett 1991: 171).

Research on nonhuman primates has shown that role variability and plasticity are deeply rooted in the evolutionary history of primates. Cross-cultural data suggest a similar plasticity among humans. The evidence from this section should support the argument that biology merely sets the parameters for a broad range of human behaviors. Thus, biological differences between men and women have no uniform and universal implication for social roles and relations. Biology, for humans, takes on meaning as it is interpreted in human culture and society (Rosaldo and Lamphere 1974: 4).

REFERENCES

Austin, Roy L. 1993. "Recent Trends in Official Male and Female Crime Rates: The Convergence Controversy," *Journal of Criminal Justice* 21: 447–466.

Bleier, Ruth. 1984. *Science and Gender: A Critique of Biology and Its Theories on Women.* New York: Pergamon Press.

Boswell, John. 1988. *The Kindness of Strangers: The Abandonment of Children in Western Europe from Late Antiquity to the Renaissance*. New York: Pantheon Books.

Burbank, Victoria Katherine. 1994. *Fighting Women. Anger and Aggression in Aboriginal Australia*. Berkeley: University of California Press.

Collier, Jane E., and Michelle Z. Rosaldo. 1981. "The Politics of Gender in Simple Societies." In Sherry S. Ortner and Harriet Whitehead (eds.). *Sexual Meanings*, pp. 275–330. Cambridge, UK: Cambridge University Press.

Counts, D, J. Brown, and J. Campbell (eds.). 1992. *Sanctions and Sanctuary: Cultural Perspectives on the Beating of Wives*. Boulder, CO: Westview Press.

Daly, M., and M. Wilson. 1990. "Killing the Competition: Female/Female and Male/Male Homicide," *Human Nature* 1: 81–107.

Fausto-Sterling, A. 1985. *Myths of Gender*. New York: Basic Books.

Fedigan, Linda Marie. 1986. "The Changing Role of Women in Models of Human Evolution," *Annual Review of Anthropology* 15: 25–66.

———. 1992. *Primate Paradigms: Sex Roles and Social Bonds*. Chicago: University of Chicago Press.

Freeman, Derek. 1983. *Margaret Mead and Samoa: The Making and Unmaking of an Anthropological Myth*. Cambridge, MA: Harvard University Press.

Geary, David C. 1998. *Male, Female: The Evolution of Human Sex Differences*. Washington, DC: American Psychological Association.

Hewlett, Barry S. 1991. *Intimate Fathers: The Nature and Context of Aka Pygmy Paternal Infant Care*. Ann Arbor: University of Michigan Press.

Holmes, Lowell D. 1987. *Quest for the Real Samoa: The Mead/Freeman Controversy and Beyond*. South Hadley, MA: Bergin Garvey.

Keeley, L. H. 1996. *War before Civilization: The Myth of the Peaceful Savage*. New York: Oxford University Press.

Leacock, Eleanor. 1993. "Women in Samoan History: A Further Critique of Derek Freeman." In Barbara Diane Miller (ed.). *Sex and Gender Hierarchies*, pp. 351–365. Cambridge, UK: Cambridge University Press.

Lee, Richard. 1979. *The !Kung San: Men, Women, and Work in a Foraging Society*. Cambridge, UK: Cambridge University Press.

Lee, Richard S., and Irven DeVore (eds.). 1968. *Man the Hunter*. New York: Aldine.

Leibowitz, Lila. 1975. "Perspectives on the Evolution of Sex Differences." In Rayna Rapp (ed.). *Toward an Anthropology of Women*, pp. 20–35. New York: Monthly Review.

Leigh, S. R. 1995. "Socioecology and the Ontogeny of Sexual Size Dimorphism in Anthropoid Primates," *American Journal of Physical Anthropology* 97: 339–356.

Lynch, James P., Steven K. Smith, Helen A. Graziadei, and Tanutda Pittayathikhun. 1994. "Profiles of Inmates in the United States and in England and Wales," U.S. Department of Justice, Office of Justice Programs, Bureau of Justice Statistics, NFJ-145863.

Maccoby, E. E., and C. N. Jacklin. 1974. *The Psychology of Sex Differences*. Stanford, CA: Stanford University Press.

Martin, M. Kay, and Barbara Voorhies. 1975. *Female of the Species*. New York: Columbia University Press.

Mead, Margaret. 1928. *Coming of Age in Samoa*. New York: Dell.

———. 1935. *Sex and Temperament in Three Primitive Societies*. New York: Dell.

Morris, Allison. 1987. *Women, Crime and Criminal Justice*. Oxford, UK: Basil Blackwell.

O'Kelly, Charlotte. 1980. *Women and Men in Society*. New York: D. Van Nostrand Co.

Orans, Martin. 1996. *Not Even Wrong: Margaret Mead, Derek Freeman and the Samoans*. New York: Chandler and Sharp.

Peterson, Susan Rae. 1983. "Against 'Parenting'." In Joyce Trebilcot (ed.). *Mothering: Essays in Feminist Theory*, pp. 41–62. Totowa, NJ: Rowman and Allanheld.

Plavcan, J. M. and C. P. van Schaik. 1997a. "Interpreting Hominid Behavior on the Basis of Sexual Dimorphism," *Journal of Human Evolution* 32: 345–374.

——— 1997b. "Intrasexual Competition and Body Weight Dimorphism in Anthropoid Primates," *American Journal of Physical Anthropology* 103: 37–68.

Ransel, David L. 1988. *Mothers of Misery: Child Abandonment in Russia.* Princeton, NJ: Princeton University Press.

Rensberger, Boyce. 1983. "Margaret Mead: The Nature-Nurture Debate: From Samoa to Sociobiology," *Science* 83: 28–46.

Renzetti, Clair M., and Daniel J. Curran. 1989. *Women, Men and Society: The Sociology of Gender.* Needham Heights, MA: Allyn and Bacon.

Rosaldo, Michelle Z., and Louise Lamphere (eds.). 1974. *Woman, Culture, and Society.* Stanford, CA: Stanford University Press.

Rossi, Alice. 1977. "A Biosocial Perspective on Parenting," *Daedalus* 106: 1–31.

———. 1978. "The Biosocial Side of Parenthood," *Human Nature* 1: 72–79.

Scheper-Hughes, Nancy. 1987. "The Margaret Mead Controversy: Culture, Biology and Anthropological Inquiry." In Herbert Applebaum (ed.). *Perspectives in Cultural Anthropology,* pp. 443–454. Albany: State University of New York Press.

Schneider, David. 1983. "The Coming of a Sage to Samoa," *Natural History* 92(6): 4–10.

Smuts, Barbara. 1986. "Gender, Aggression, and Influence." In Barbara Smuts, Dorothy L. Cheney, Robert Seyfarth, Richard Wrangham, and Thomas Struhsaler (eds.). *Primate Societies,* pp. 400–412. Chicago: University of Chicago Press.

Sperling, Susan. 1991. "Baboons with Briefcases vs. Langurs in Lipstick. Feminism and Functionalism in Primate Studies." In Micaela di Leonardo (ed.). *Gender at the Crossroads of Knowledge: Feminist Anthropology in the Postmodern Era,* pp. 204–234. Berkeley: University of California Press.

Tiger, Lionel. 1969. *Men in Groups.* New York: Random House.

Trebilcot, Joyce (ed.). 1983. *Mothering: Essays in Feminist Theory.* Totowa, NJ: Rowman and Allanheld.

Udry, J. Richard. 2000. "Biological Limits of Gender Construction," *American Sociological Review* 65: 443–457.

U.S. Department of Justice. 1991. *Women in Prison,* Bureau of Justice Statistics, Special Report. Washington, DC: U.S. Department of Justice.

Whitbeck, Caroline. 1983. "The Maternal Instinct." In Joyce Trebilcot (ed.). *Mothering: Essays in Feminist Theory,* pp. 185–192. Totowa, NJ: Rowman and Allenheld.

Wilson, Edward O. 1975. *Sociobiology: The New Synthesis.* Cambridge, MA: Harvard University Press.

Zihlman, Adrienne L. 1993. "Sex Differences and Gender Hierarchies among Primates: An Evolutionary Perspective." In Barbara Diane Miller (ed.). *Sex and Gender Hierarchies,* pp. 32–56. Cambridge, UK: Cambridge University Press.

Animal Models and Gender

Marlene Zuk

The notion that biology, particularly evolutionary biology, can explain much about gender differences in humans raises hackles in many people. The fear is that science will be used to justify sexism, so that men are "naturally" dominant and women submissive, men natural phi-

Marlene Zuk, *Sexual Selections: What We Can and Can't Learn About Sex from Animals.* © 2003 University of California Press, Berkeley.

landerers and women naturally inclined to stop them from straying. These stereotypes are often said to arise from the animal kingdom, apparently leaving us with no other choices than to accept our evolutionary heritage and resign ourselves to a life of oppression, or reject the idea that biology has any relevance to explaining gender in modern day humans.

In this chapter I hope to counter this impression, both by explaining how biologists view the evolution of sex differences in animals and by showing how understanding the connection between our sexual behavior and that of other species can be liberating rather than restrictive. It is possible to use evolution to inform us about gender without either succumbing to the old stereotypes or substituting new ones; a caricature of a nature-girl is just as damaging as one that stays barefoot and pregnant. Much of the material here is discussed in more detail in Zuk (2002). Numerous other authors have attempted to link feminism and evolutionary biology, and provide feminist critiques of biology from a scientific perspective, perhaps most notably Patricia Gowaty (1997, 2003), but also including Hrdy (1986, 1997, 1999), Keller (1985), Fausto-Sterling (1987, 2003), Liesen (1995), and many others. Here I focus on studies from animals, rather than examining the field of biology as a whole, and examine the use of animal models in studies of gender.

SEXUAL SELECTION

Sex differences in animals are of much interest to biologists, and the body of theory commonly accepted as the explanation of how these differences evolve is called sexual selection. Like its relative natural selection, sexual selection relies on individual differences in the likelihood of leaving genes in succeeding generation, but unlike natural selection, the differential reproduction due to sexual selection occurs because of an individual's ability to acquire the best and/or most mates, not because of survival ability. Thus a bird with a long ungainly tail that attracts more females than his shorter-tailed counterparts is at a sexual selection advantage, even if he has a harder time flying and cannot escape predators as easily.

Also like natural selection, the theory of sexual selection has its origin in the work of Charles Darwin. When Darwin began to develop his ideas about the origin of species, he attempted to explain the evolution of traits that differ between the sexes, but are not necessary for the physical act of reproduction,

such as the mane on male lions or the antlers of male deer. Darwin devoted an entire book, *The Descent of Man and Selection in Relation to Sex,* published in 1871, to explaining such traits, which he called secondary sexual characters, and noted that in many cases they simply could not seem to have arisen through natural selection because they are often costly to produce and make their bearers more conspicuous to predators.

Darwin suggested that secondary sexual characters could evolve in one of two ways. First, they could be useful to one sex, usually males, in fighting for access to members of the other sex. Hence, the antlers and horns on male ungulates, such as bighorn sheep, or on the aptly named male rhinoceros beetles. These are weapons, and they are advantageous because better fighters are presumed to get more mates and have more offspring. The second way was more problematic. Darwin noted that females often pay attention to traits like long tails and elaborate plumage during courtship, and he concluded that the traits evolved because the females preferred them. Peahens find peacocks with long tails attractive, just like we do. The sexual selection process, then, consisted of two components: male–male competition, which results in weapons, and female choice, which results in ornaments.

While competition among males for the rights to mate with a female seemed reasonable enough to Darwin's Victorian contemporaries, virtually none of them could swallow the idea that females—of any species, but especially the so-called dumb animals—could possibly do anything so complex as discriminating between males with slightly different plumage colors. Alfred Russell Wallace, who also independently arrived at some of the same conclusions about evolution and natural selection that Darwin did, was particularly vehement in his objections (Wallace 1889). He, and many others, simply found it absurd that females could make the sort of complex decision required by Darwin's theory; it would require the female to possess an aesthetic sense like that of humans, an idea they were unwilling to accept. According to the thinking of his time, even among humans only those of the upper social classes could appreciate aesthetic things like art and music, so it seemed ridiculous to imagine that animals could do something many humans—particularly non Englishmen—could not.

Largely because of this opposition to the idea of female choice, sexual selection as a theory lay dormant for several decades. This time lag meant that while sexual selection and natural selection were introduced at about the same time, sexual selection has not received the same continuous scrutiny by scientists. In some ways, therefore, the study of sex differences is a younger science than the study of species origin and diversity. It was not until the late 1960s that interest in the evolution of sex differences was revived, and the most important contribution to the new theory was a 1972 paper by Robert Trivers, who argued that selection acts differently on males and females because of how they allocate resources into succeeding generations. Females are limited by the number of offspring they can successfully produce and rear. Because they are the sex that supplies the nutrient-rich egg, and often the sex that cares for the young, they have an upper limit set at a relatively low number. They leave the most genes in the next generation by having the highest quality young they can. Which male they mate with could be very important, because a mistake in the form of poor genes or no help with the young could mean that they have lost their whole breeding effort for an entire year.

Males, on the other hand, can leave the most genes in the next generation by fertilizing as many females as possible. Because each mating requires relatively little investment from him, a male who mates with many females sires many more young than a male mating with only one female. Hence, males are expected to compete among themselves for access to females, and females are expected to be choosy, and to mate with the best possible male they can. In addition, females were often referred to as "coy," with the implication that the impetus for sex came largely from males, who fought among themselves to get to the females and allow the choices to occur.

This, of course, is the same division of sexual selection that Darwin originally proposed, and Trivers had given it a new rationale. What he did, too, was bring female choice back to the forefront of sexual selection, and suggest a more modern underlying advantage to it. Furthermore, ideas about the evolution of behavior had advanced enough that scientists no longer worried about an "aesthetic sense" in animals; it didn't matter how females recognized particular males, just that if they did, and it was beneficial, the genes associated with the trait females were attracted to would become more common in the population than the genes of less-preferred traits. Evolutionary biologists, therefore, could ignore questions about motivation and get to the more testable issue of how discrimination among males might result in the evolution of ornamental traits that did not function either in day-to-day life or in male combat.

Current work on female behavior in many species of animals has confirmed Trivers'—and Darwin's—basic idea about female preference for particular types of males being a major force in evolution (Andersson 1994). Again and again, females have been shown to be able to distinguish small differences among available mates, and to prefer to mate with those individuals bearing the most exaggerated characters. In some cases those males are also more healthy and vigorous, so that ornaments appear to indicate not just attractiveness but the ability to survive.

One of the most well-known examples can be found in peacocks, often used as the symbol of sexual selection with their huge elaborate tails. English gentry have kept peacocks (more correctly, peafowl, as the term peacock strictly speaking refers only to the male) for many years, and British biologist Marion Petrie studied the behavior of flocks that were allowed to range freely in a park in England (Petrie 1994, Petrie and Halliday 1994). She discovered that females did indeed prefer males with greater numbers of eyespots on their tail feathers, and that this preference could be manipulated by cutting the eyespots off of some males' tails and gluing them onto others; females lost interest in the dubbed peacocks, and became attracted to the augmented ones. Even more interesting, she allowed females to mate with males that had variable numbers of eyespots, and then reared all of the offspring in communal incubators to control for differences in maternal care. The chicks fathered by the more ornamented males weighed more than the other chicks, an attribute usually connected with better survival in birds. Indeed, when the individually marked chicks were then released into the park and recaptured the following year, the ones with the more attractive fathers also were more likely to evade predators and survive in the seminatural conditions.

The notion that females are "coy" has not survived so well, as it has been amply demonstrated that females frequently seek out matings with multiple males, and that they often take an active part in many kinds of sexual interactions (Andersson 1994; Jennions and Petrie 2000, 1997; Gowaty and Buschhaus 1998). The reasons behind such behaviors are the subject of intensive study by biologists, and ideas are changing all the time. Nevertheless, the concept of sexual selection, and the core ideas of reproductive competition and mate choice, appears to explain a great deal about animal sexual differences.

The Philandering Male, the Coy Female, and Other Myths

What about humans? Does this mean that males are designed by evolution to be indiscriminate in seeking sex, and females are forever conscribed by the need to raise children alone? The answer is an emphatic no, and to understand why it is important to understand how animal models are used in biology.

First of all, even among animals a great deal of variation exists in the manifestation of the basic principles of sexual selection. For example, male elephant seals come ashore at isolated beaches along the Pacific coast during late summer. The males can weigh up to three tons, more than twice the size of females, and spend several weeks fighting among themselves for dominance. Females arrive after the males, and after they come ashore the dominant males attempt to sequester groups of females and keep them from rival males; the

females themselves, although they do exert some degree of choice, are constrained in their movements by the males (Le Boeuf and Reiter 1988; Galimberti et al. 2002). The male competition aspect of sexual selection appears to prevail in this species.

In contrast, female bowerbirds have virtually total control over mating. This group of several species of birds is found in Australia and New Guinea. The males construct elaborate structures out of twigs, grass and other objects, and then decorate them with ornaments that can include plastic items as well as fruit, flowers, bones, and shells (Borgia 1995; Uy et al. 2001; Madden 2003). Each species has a characteristic bower type. After the bowers are made, males wait for females to visit; the bowers are generally rather widely separated, so males cannot hear or see each other when they are tending their bowers. A female generally visits the bowers of several males before choosing one of them. When a female arrives, the male courts her with elaborate vocal and visual displays, but he cannot prevent a female from leaving to sample additional males, something the females commonly do. Eventually a female selects a male, mates with him, and leaves to lay her eggs and rear her chicks alone. The bower is not a nest, and males take no part in rearing offspring. Female choice, rather than male competition, is paramount among bowerbirds.

These two systems illustrate completely different "solutions" to the same problem of reproduction faced by all species. Other examples, including substantial male contributions to offspring, extreme female aggression and competition, and sexual behavior outside the fertile period, could also be cited. Among bonobos, small relatives of chimpanzees, sexual activity occurs between virtually all members of a social group, including members of the same sex. This point is an important one: although male competition and female choice are the basic elements of sexual selection, even among animals tremendous diversity exists in how they are implemented. Those unfamiliar with the behavior of animals in the wild often do not realize that animal family life, or lack of it, is not a simplified version of human existence, even human existence in an imaginary early hunter–gatherer society. It is simply incorrect to suggest that finding a link between our gender-related behavior and that of other animals would inevitably mean a link to a male-dominated social system. A single animal model for the origin of sex roles does not exist, even if we were to accept that finding such a model would make it impossible to act outside of it.

Note that this diversity also precludes claiming that women are naturally caring, verbal, peace loving, or sexually adventurous. Substituting one stereotype, of a strong Amazon, for the more traditional one of a coy stay at home mom uninterested in sex, does not solve the problem. We may like the previously unappreciated female bonobo, with her overt sexuality, more than another animal model, but it is important to remember that the animals are model systems for understanding a range of behaviors, and not role models.

How, then, can we learn from animals about gender and sex roles? Below I detail two examples of topics that are often discussed in the context of animal behavior, maternal instinct and mate fidelity. I hope to show that we can learn from biology without either succumbing to old stereotypes or substituting new ones for them.

MATERNAL INSTINCT AND MOTHER LOVE

One of the cornerstones of popular belief in a biological basis for gender-based behavior is that females instinctively care for their young. If maternal care-giving behavior is natural, then presumably all women want to do it, know how to do it without learning how, and feel deprived if they do not. A modern version of the maternal instinct is the mother–infant bond, this mysterious connection that supposedly naturally occurs between a woman and her child soon after birth.

How fixed is this bond, and how ingrained in a female's psyche is the ability—and even the desire—to care for her young? It would seem reasonable to assume that animals should

show a behavior that women are supposed to have inherited, and it is therefore instructive to look at research from the 1950s and 1960s using rhesus macaques, the monkeys used in numerous medical and behavioral studies; the "Rh" in Rh-positive or Rh-negative blood types comes from the name of this species. Two psychologists named Harry and Margaret Harlow were interested in understanding the effects of social deprivation on humans, the kind of deprivation that arises through abuse, neglect, and warfare. The Harlows wanted to know how these problems arose and thus perhaps gain insight into correcting them. They could not, of course, perform controlled experiments on human children, and so they used an animal model and manipulated the early rearing environment of groups of macaques so that deprived youngsters could be compared to more normally raised controls. The Harlows' research is expertly analyzed by Deborah Blum (2002), who also raises some of the interesting ethical issues that arise from the treatment of the monkeys.

The infant macaques were taken from their mothers at birth, and raised under one of several different sets of conditions. For example, some were allowed access to a monkey-sized, wire-covered model that had a bottle attached to it approximately where the nipple of a mother monkey might be. The bottle was filled with milk and the cages cleaned at appropriate intervals by human caretakers who had no contact with the monkeys. Other baby macaques had the wire-covered model with the food, and in addition were given another model covered with terrycloth. In some instances, the monkeys saw or contacted other equally deprived infants during their development, while in others they were kept in isolation. As the monkeys grew up, they were used in a variety of tests to examine their social behavior and eventually their ability to mate and have offspring of their own.

To the surprise of few, the socially deprived monkeys did not exhibit normal behavior. They were more fearful when new stimuli were introduced to their cages, they did not interact with other juvenile monkeys the way that babies raised with their mothers did, and they showed numerous other signs of psychological abnormality. Interestingly, however, the babies given the cloth-covered model "mother" were better adjusted than those given only the wire model, and when a novel and potentially frightening object was introduced into the cage, they ran not to the source of food but to the source of what the Harlows called "contact comfort." In other words, clinging to a soft object is more soothing than returning to the place where essential nourishment is found.

The Harlows went on from these studies to discuss a number of fascinating theories about the need for this contact comfort and its potential value in helping children with minimal resources develop more normally. Their ideas have been thoroughly dissected—and in some cases debunked—by developmental psychologists. For my purposes here, however, a more relevant finding was the discovery that females raised with the models had difficulties in mating with male monkeys once they reached sexual maturity. They simply did not know how to have sex—they didn't know the postures, the signals, the responses. Even more significant, if they were artificially inseminated and became pregnant, they were incapable of caring for the resulting young, and their infants had to be removed from their mothers lest they be seriously injured. The mothers did get better with experience, so that subsequent young fared better, but the early babies were as foreign as extra-terrestrials to their mothers.

These results seem to flatly contradict the notion of a simple maternal instinct. Even mother monkeys, animals very similar to ourselves, do not automatically feel bonded to their infants, much less know how to take care of them. The mystical mother–child relationship is shattered when the mother is raised without others of her kind. This situation is clearly unusual, of course. The monkeys are not usually raised by wire models, and under natural circumstances they can relate to their offspring perfectly well. This, however, is precisely my point: even a behavior supposedly as sacrosanct at the love a mother will have for her child depends on the environment. And therefore it is also clear that the evidence does not support assuming a particular behavior in

humans is "natural," even one as supposedly biological as mothering.

The consequences of acknowledging this fact are many. If one is freed from the idea of the maternal instinct, one is also freed from equating being female to being a mother, as if no other role was possible or important. Examining female behavior, in humans or animals, is therefore enriched by abandoning the stereotype. Females can exhibit all kinds of behavior, and females, human or not, are not only defined by their relationship to their offspring. One can also start dissecting maternal behavior itself, asking questions about what kind and how much of an investment would benefit mothers under different circumstances. The "maternal-infant bond" becomes a malleable behavior rather than a fixed biological entity.

The idea of variable mothering leads to some interesting and sometimes startling predictions. For example, the eminent anthropologist Sarah Blaffer Hrdy has found that infanticide can be adaptive for monkeys and other mammals that exhibit it (Hausfater and Hrdy 1984). While I hasten to point out that this hardly justifies the behavior in humans, it does suggest that an analysis that does not focus exclusively on the stereotypical nurturing mother can be enlightening.

ADULTERY AND PHILANDERING MALES

Infidelity, again whether in humans or animals, is a topic of great interest to those wanting to understand whether animals show us our own biologically based behaviors. The classic stereotype of male nature is of the man seeking multiple sexual partners while the woman is content to remain with a single partner for her entire life. Infidelity has also recently become a subject of interest to scientists, because the advent of genetic testing has allowed us to sample the DNA from a set of chicks in a nest and compare it to the DNA of the male and female associated with the young. As it turns out, so-called extra-pair paternity is quite common among birds; estimates of the proportion of offspring sired by males other than the one attending a female and her nest range from 0 in snow geese to a whopping 90% in a species of fairy wren, brilliantly colored tiny birds from Australia (Griffith et al. 2002, Griffith and Montgomerie 2003). Although frequently only one male and one female are seen associating, including feeding and protecting the young, it has become apparent that additional males fathered offspring in the nest. In mammals that have multiple young in a litter, the young may also have more than one father, though mammals are less likely to appear to be monogamous in the first place.

This discovery was quite a shock to scientists, because outwardly it had appeared that most birds were monogamous. If this was not the case, many questions arose. What are the advantages to females of having multiple fathers for her brood? Do males attempt to deter females from such multiple mating, since it is costly to them to help rear offspring not their own? Why, given the apparent disparity of investment of males and females in offspring, should females pursue quantity rather than quality of mates? Questions like these are currently the subject of ongoing research in a variety of species.

The occurrence of extra-pair mating is also rather surprising to non-scientists, perhaps because the birds unwittingly had served as something of a role model for human marriage. It is tempting to conclude that if warblers, robins, and other models of monogamy are doing it, we should admit that extra-pair copulation, or adultery—or whatever term you prefer—is natural, expected, and maybe we should stop making such a fuss about it and resign ourselves to our evolutionary heritage.

But the problem is that the birds are not "cheating," they are just doing what they do, and they did not invent the rules about the pair bond between a male and female, we did. It isn't cheating if there are no rules to break. Some animals are monogamous, some are not, and one mating system is no more "natural," or "biological," than the other. Certainly multiple mating appears to be favored in many species, more species than had previously been believed, but that does not argue for the death

of fidelity. Instead, it suggests a reexamination of sexual selection theory, something that is already occurring among scientists. This brings up an important point about the use of animal models for human behavior. Animals are useful for showing us what kinds of solutions exist to the common biological problems involved in survival and reproduction. How does the environment influence the costs and benefits of multiple mating? This is an interesting and relevant question—whether human males are biologically destined to cheat on their wives is not. As with maternal behavior, in mating systems multiple solutions are virtually always the norm, and there is no single natural male or female role.

What about the primates, our closest relatives? Here too, the sex role stereotypes are crumbling. Male dominance was viewed as the major force in primate societies when most monkeys and apes were studied in the middle of the twentieth century (Strum and Fedigan 2000), with females viewed as relatively uninterested in sex outside the time when they were most likely to become pregnant. However, probably not coincidentally with the growing numbers of women entering primatology, as more species were studied more intensively, it soon became clear that male-female relationships were more complex and furthermore that females often sought out sex (sometimes with both males and females) outside the period of maximum fertility (Smuts 1999, Strum and Fedigan 2000). In olive baboons, some males and females became what primatologist Barbara Smuts called "friends," with bonds of association that went beyond the brief act of sex itself (Smuts 1999). This complexity argues against the caricature of sex-crazed males and demure females that people sometimes thinks constitutes our heritage from other animals.

Studying a diversity of human cultures is also of interest once we recognize this multiplicity of solutions in other animals. What patterns of courtship and marriage seem to be universal, and what patterns depend on environmental attributes such as food availability and distribution?

Model Systems and Role Models

It is also important to remember not to substitute one stereotype for another; it would be just as fallacious to conclude that all women are sexual adventuresses as to adhere to the old model of the frigid female. Deciding that biology is relevant to understanding gender does not mean that we imitate the species we prefer; model systems like the fruit flies used in genetics are useful tools for generalizing because we understand a great deal about them, but, as I mentioned earlier, they should not be confused with role models. Animals tell us that females can be assertive, but perhaps more important they tell us that females are variable. Furthermore, like many other biologists, I urge caution in interpreting nature. The naturalistic fallacy holds that what is natural is good, but what is natural can't be inherently "good" any more than it can be inherently amusing, inherently painful, or more likely to keep your hair shiny. Finding out that some animals eat their young says no more about the ethics of infanticide than finding out that some animals are yellow says about fashion trends.

As a scientist studying animals, not humans, I am also concerned about how our verdict of cheating affects our views of the animals themselves. Some of the early papers on extra-pair paternity in birds are interestingly divided in whom is portrayed as the active party in the behavior. Initially, there seemed to be two approaches, neither one particularly favorable to females. Either the males were roaming around taking advantage of hapless females waiting innocently in their own territories for the breadwinner males to come home with the worms, or else females were brazen hussies, seducing blameless males who otherwise would not have strayed from the path of moral righteousness into turpitude. One scientist refers rather peevishly to "female promiscuity" in blackbirds. Several papers, including one published in the prestigious journal *Nature*, call young birds fathered by males not paired with the mother as "illegitimate," as if their parents had tiny avian marriage licenses and chirped their vows (Gyllensten et al. 1990, Hassequist et al. 1995; Bjornstad and Lifjeld 1997). Scientists, of course, are subject to social influences just like other people, but we should try not to allow our prejudices to influence our interpretation of what we see the animals doing. A paper on Tasmanian native hens, birds with a rather complex set of relationships between the sexes, discussed what appears to be polyandry, multiple males associated with a single female (Maynard Smith and Ridpath 1972). The paper refers to this behavior as "wife-sharing," but I have never seen multiple females associated with a male, its mirror image, and a common mating pattern, called "husband-sharing." Making the males the active parties (they "share" the female, as if she were a six-pack of beer) may reduce the likelihood of noticing what the females do, of seeing things from their point of view. Similarly, if we only see female baboons as mothers, we are less likely to notice that in fact their relationships, not those of males, determine troop structure and movement (Smuts 1999).

CONCLUSIONS

It is no surprise that many people get twitchy when they hear about any so-called "biological" explanations of behavior in humans. They are also nervous when scientists study behaviors in animals that seem to occur in humans, for the reasons I described above. Here I have tried to ameliorate this fear, though at least in part it should be replaced with caution and awareness. Biology has great potential for harming women, but it is through our misbehavior, not the science itself. Biology can extend the boundaries of our thinking about gender as it can for so many other ideas. Contrary to popular belief, biology does not set limits, it demolishes them.

It is also important to remember that discoveries of mate fidelity, male tenderness or female sexual violence do not argue for a human nature that includes or excludes them. Evolution is an important explanation for the origin and diversity of life on earth, including human life. It helps us understand how organisms are related to each other, how the species that occur on a coral reef got there, whether a reed warbler female is likely to have any surviving young in a given year, how the members of chimpanzee groups sometimes benefit by being kind to one another, and why diet may help determine the probability of getting heart disease. Suggesting that evolutionary biology is irrelevant to human lives is as foolish as suggesting that it is irrelevant to the lives of fruit flies. Men and women are not the same, both from the standpoint of physiology and evolution. Neither are male and female goldfish, or fruit flies, or weasels. But this does not mean that men and women inherit templates of irreversible behavior.

REFERENCES

Andersson, M. 1994. *Sexual Selection.* Princeton University Press, Princeton.

Bjornstad, G. and Lifjeld, J. T. 1997. High frequency of extra-pair paternity in a dense and synchronous population of Willow Warblers *Phylloscopus trochilus.* *J. Avian Biol.* 28 (4): 319–324.

Blum, D. 2002. *Love at Goon Park.* Perseus Publishing, New York.

Borgia, G. 1995. Why do bowerbirds build bowers? *Amer. Sci.* 83: 542–547.

Fausto-Sterling, A. 1987. *Myths of Gender: Biological Theories about Women and Men.* Basic Books, New York.

Fausto-Sterling, A. 2003. Science matters, culture matters. *Perspec. Biol. Med.* 46: 109–124.

Galimberti, F., Fabiani, A. and Sanvito, S. 2002. Measures of breeding inequality: a case study in southern elephant seals. *Can. J. Zool.* 80: 1240–1249.

Gowaty, P. A. and Buschhaus, N. 1998. Ultimate causation of aggressive and forced copulation in birds: Female resistance, the CODE hypothesis, and social monogamy. *Amer. Zool.* 38: 207–225.

Gowaty, P. A. (ed.) 1997. *Feminism and Evolutionary Biology: Boundaries, Intersections, and Frontiers.* Chapman and Hall, New York.

Gowaty, P. A. 2003. Sexual natures: How feminism changed evolutionary. *Signs* 28: 901–921.

Griffith, S. C., Owens I. P. F., and Thuman K. A. 2002. Extra pair paternity in birds: a review of interspecific variation and adaptive function. *Molec. Ecol.* 11: 2195–2212.

Griffith S. C. and Montgomerie, R. 2003. Why do birds engage in extra-pair copulation? *Nature* 422: 833–833.

Gyllensten, U. B., Jakobsson, S., and Temrin, H. 1990. No evidence for illegitimate young in monogamous and polygynous warblers. *Nature* 343: 168–170.

Hasselquist, D., Bensch, S. and von Schantz, T. 1995. Low frequency of extrapair paternity in the polygynous great reed warbler *Acrocephalus arundinaceus.* *Behav. Ecol.* 6: 27–38.

Hausfater, G. and Hrdy, S. B. (eds.) 1984. *Infanticide: Comparative and Evolutionary Perspectives.* Aldine de Gruyter, New York.

Hrdy, S. B. 1986. Empathy, polyandry, and the myth of the coy female. In: *Feminist approaches to science,* R. Bleier, ed. Pergamon Press, New York.

Hrdy, S. B. 1997. Raising Darwin's consciousness—Female sexuality and the prehominid origins of patriarchy. *Human Nature* 8:1–49.

Hrdy, S. B. 1999. *Mother nature.* Pantheon, New York.

Jennions, M. D. and Petrie, M. 2000. Why do females mate multiply? A review of the genetic benefits. *Biol. Rev. Cam. Phil. Soc.* 75: 21–64.

Jennions, M. D. and Petrie, M. 1997. Variation in mate choice and mating preferences: A review of causes and consequences. *Biol. Rev. Cam. Phil. Soc.* 72: 283–327.

Keller, E. F. 1985. *Reflections on gender and science.* Yale University Press, New Haven.

Le Boeuf, B. J. and Reiter, J. 1988. Lifetime reproductive success in northern elephant seals. Pp. 344–362 in *Reproductive Success: Studies of Individual Variation in Contrasting Breeding Systems,* T. H. Clutton-Brock, ed. University of Chicago Press, Chicago.

Liesen, L. T. 1995. Feminism and the politics of reproductive strategies. *Politics Life Sci.* 14: 145–162.

Madden, J. R. 2003. Male spotted bowerbirds preferentially choose, arrange and proffer objects that are good predictors of mating success. *Behav. Ecol. Sociobiol.* 53 (5): 263–268.

Maynard Smith, J. and Ridpath, M. G. 1972. Wife sharing in the Tasmanian native hen, *Tribonyx mortierii:* a case of kin selection? *Amer. Nat.* 106: 447–452.

Petrie, M. 1994. Improved growth and survival of offspring of peacocks with more elaborate trains. *Nature* 371: 598–599.

Petrie, M. and Halliday, T. 1994. Experimental and natural changes in the peacock's (*Pave cristatus*) train can affect mating success. *Behav. Ecol. Sociobiol.* 35: 213–217.

Smuts, B. B. 1999. *Sex and Friendship in Baboons.* 2nd ed. Harvard University Press, Cambridge, MA.

Strum, S. C. and Fedigan, L. M. (eds.) 2000. *Primate encounters: Models of Science, Gender, and Society.* University of Chicago Press, Chicago.

Trivers, R. L. 1972. Parental investment and sexual selection. Pp 136–179 In B. Campbell, ed., *Sexual Selection and the Descent of Man, 1871–1971.* Heinemann, London.

Uy, J. A. C., Patricelli, G. L., and Borgia, G. 2001. Complex mate searching in the satin bowerbird *Ptilonorhynchus violaceus. Amer. Nat.* 158: 530–542.

Wallace, A. R. 1889. *Darwinism: An Exposition of the Theory of Natural Selection with Some of Its Applications.* MacMillan Press, London.

Zuk, M. 2002. *Sexual Selections: What We Can and Can't Learn about Sex from Animals.* University of California Press, Berkeley.

The Role of Women in Human Evolution

Margaret Ehrenberg

Human evolution has traditionally been discussed in terms of the role which "Man the Hunter" played in devising weapons and tools for catching and slaughtering animals for food, how he needed to walk upright on two feet to see his prey above the tall savanna grass, and how he was more successful than other species in his hunting exploits because he teamed up with other men and learnt the value of co-operation. And what of "woman," meanwhile? Was she sitting at home, twiddling her thumbs, waiting for "man" to feed her and increase his brain capacity and abilities until he became "*Homo sapiens sapiens*"? The argument went that as human evolution progressed, more and more time was needed to look after infants, so females no longer had time to hunt, and male co-operative hunting became essential in order that the men could bring enough food home to feed the family. As a result, male-female bonding in monogamous unions was an essential and a very early development. While most accounts of human evolution have assumed that all the advances in human physical and cultural development were led by men, a number of recent studies suggest alternative possibilities and have pointed out the vital role which must have been played by women.

Research into the earliest stages of human evolution is based on three strands of evidence. Physical anthropologists study the remains of early human skeletons, to assess the way in which they developed. For example, it is possible to tell from the structure of the legs and back whether an individual would have walked upright on two legs, or used the forearms for balance. Changes in the size of the skull through time give an indication of brain capacity. Secondly, the study of the behavior of other animals, and especially primates, particularly those species closest to humans such as apes and chimpanzees, reveals some patterns that may have been shared by the earliest humans before cultural norms began to play an overriding part. For example, chimpanzees may be studied to see if males and females eat or collect different foods, or to find out whether they share any of the differences in child-care practices seen in human women and men. Thirdly, archaeological evidence for tools, settlements, environment and diet sheds light on the social and cultural development of the earliest humans.

Some scholars within all these three areas have turned away from the traditional male-dominated view of evolution and have begun to formulate an alternative model, allowing that female primates and hominids have played an important part, if not the key role, in the development of human behavior. Different authors have stressed different factors in this development. Adrienne Zihlman[1] argues that changes in the environment were crucial in necessitating social and economic changes in human populations in order to exploit this environment efficiently. Sally Slocum[2] points out that the only division of labor by sex amongst other primates is that females take primary care of their young, while males tend to dominate in protecting the group. She argues that a division of labor in food collecting is therefore unlikely to have been a key feature of early human behavior. Other feminist writers[3] suggest that the female's choice of a co-operative and gentle mate was a critical factor in human evolution, as the chances of survival were improved by caring more closely for near relatives; in all mammals, and especially in primates, this is much more a female task or trait.

Among the physical changes which took place in the early stages of human evolution were increases in the size of the brain and the teeth; a decrease in sexual dimorphism (difference in size between males and females); increased hairlessness over the body; and bipedalism, or walking on two feet, rather than using the forelimbs for support, as chimpanzees and apes do. While an infant chimpanzee can cling to its mother's cover of body hair, leaving her hands free for walking or carrying food, a young human or early hairless hominid would need to be carried by the mother: this seems a much more likely stimulus both to bipedalism and to the invention of tools for carrying the infant as well as food than is the need to see prey animals over tall savanna grass and to throw simple weapons at them, which has been the traditional explanation for these changes.

A key aspect of the debate about the evolution of sex-role behavior centers on food collection, and the way in which females and males may have foraged for different foods. Many discussions, including those written by some feminist anthropologists, assume that from a very early stage in evolution females primarily gathered plant foods, while males mainly hunted animals, the pattern usual in modern hunter-gatherer societies. Many recent arguments about other aspects of the role played by females in human social and technological evolution depend on this belief, even though it is rarely argued out fully. At one end

of the scale other primates show little evidence for differences in food collecting behavior between females and males, while at the other all modern foragers apparently divide subsistence tasks on the basis of sex. The question, therefore, is when and why this difference came about, and whether looking after young offspring would have a limiting effect on hunting by females. One view[4] suggests that although males unburdened by young might have caught meat more often than females, a regular division of labor would probably have come quite late in human evolution, as the physical differences between females and males are insufficient to make one sex or the other more suitable for either task. Recent work has also questioned whether meat actually filled a significant part of the early human diet, suggesting that this would have been far more like that of other primates, based almost entirely on a wide range of plant foods. What meat was eaten in the earliest phases of the Paleolithic was probably scavenged, rather than hunted. Both these factors are problematic for the traditional view, as they suggest that hunting was neither an important factor in physical evolution, nor in the social and economic balance between female and male activities. Both sexes would have obtained vegetable foods and occasional meat, and brought some of their day's collection back to the homebase for sharing.

If there was little division of labor in the earliest phase of human development, when and why did it become usual? Two chronological points may have provided possible contexts. Initially, hominids would have been content to catch small game or to scavenge meat caught by other animals, or to collect those that had died naturally, but perhaps around 100,000 years ago they developed suitable tools and techniques for hunting large animals. While hunting small game would not have been hazardous, big-game hunting might often have resulted in death or injury to the hunter rather than the hunted. In small societies, such as these early human groups and present-day forager societies, every unexpected death is a serious blow to the viability of the community, particularly the death of women of child-bearing age. Mobility would also have been more important in hunting large game; the hunter would have to move rapidly and quietly, with hands free to throw a spear or shoot an arrow. It would not be possible to do this while carrying a bag or basket of gathered food, nor a young child, who might cause an additional hazard by making a noise at a crucial moment. Thus gathering and hunting become incompatible as simultaneous occupations; pregnant women and those carrying very small infants would have found hunting difficult, though gathering is quite easily combined with looking after young children. It is therefore possible that at this stage women began to hunt less, until a regular pattern of dividing subsistence tasks was established.[5]

Another possible context for the origin of the division of labor[6] is the change in environment which hominids found when they first entered Europe. It is argued that this spread could not have occurred until the perceptual problems of coping with a new environment had been resolved, by splitting food foraging into separate tasks. During the Lower Paleolithic in East Africa, plants and animals would have been abundant, so vegetable foods and small game would have provided plenty of easily obtainable food with only the occasional large game caught to supplement the diet. As the hominid population increased and went in search of new territory, some hominids moved north into Europe. There they encountered colder conditions in which plant foods were harder to come by, so meat would have formed a more significant part of their diet. If this problem was not serious enough to necessitate a solution when hominids first moved into Europe, it would have become so with the onset of the last glaciation when conditions became very much colder and vegetation more sparse (this period equates archaeologically with the Upper Paleolithic). The time and danger involved in hunting large animals became more worthwhile, but would not have provided a regular, guaranteed source of food, and would have been more dangerous. A solution might have been for only part of the community to concentrate on hunting, while the rest continued gathering plants and small animals. It is likely that this division would

usually have been on a female-male basis for the reasons already suggested.

On the other hand, more detailed studies of chimpanzee behavior suggest that there may be slight differences in the food collecting behavior of females and males of non-human primates, which could argue for an early gathering/hunting division.[7] Although chimpanzees eat very little animal flesh, males make nearly all the kills and eat more of the meat; however, termite fishing, involving the use of sticks as fishing rods to poke into the termite mounds, a skilled task requiring patience and simple tool use, is far more commonly carried out by females. Whether the "changing environment" theory or the latter argument is preferred, both hypotheses suggest that a division of labor on the basis of sex would have been an early development in human history.

Tool-using was once thought to be a distinctly human attribute, but in simple form it is now known to be shared with several of the higher primates, and even other animals and birds. Most early theories suggested that tool-using by humans was intimately linked with hunting, which in turn was assumed to be a male task, and that the earliest tools would have been spears for hunting animals and stone knives or choppers for butchery. This idea was partly encouraged by the archaeological evidence of the early stone tools, most of which are thought to have had such functions. However, this is partly a circular argument, as on the one hand the function of these tools is far from certain, and many would have been just as useful for cracking nuts or digging roots, and on the other, the very earliest tools would almost certainly have been made of wood, skins, or other perishable material. Artifacts such as digging sticks, skin bags, nets, clubs and spears can be made entirely of organic materials, and would not have survived, so the extant stone tools are probably quite late in the sequence of hominid tool use. The evidence of tool use by other primates and by modern foragers, combined with a more balanced theoretical view, suggests that other factors and possibilities need to be considered.

One of the most significant human tools must be the container. Whether it be a skin bag, a basket, a wooden bowl or pottery jar, it allows us to carry items around or store them safely in one place. The container may have been one of the earliest tools to be invented, though unfortunately there is little archaeological evidence to demonstrate this. Chimpanzees can carry things in the skinfold in their groin, but when hominids became bipedal this skin was stretched and the fold was lost. The use of a large leaf or an animal skin, carried over one arm or the developing shoulder, or tied to the waist, might have replicated this lost natural carrier.[8] One of the most important things that a female hominid would need to carry would be her young offspring. The complex interaction of bipedalism, food gathering, the loss of hair for the infant to cling to, and changes in the structure of the toes which made them useless for clinging to its mother would have made it necessary for the mother to carry the child. The development of a sling for supporting the infant, found in almost all modern societies, including foraging groups, is likely to have been among the earliest applications of the container.

The first tools to aid in foraging and preparing foodstuffs are perhaps more likely to have been used in connection with plant foods and small animals than in the hunting of large mammals. The tools and actions required for termite fishing, for example, are not unlike those required for digging up roots more easily. Modern foraging groups often choose a particularly suitable stone to use as an anvil for cracking nuts, which they leave under a particular tree and then return to it on subsequent occasions. Higher primates also use stones for cracking nuts, so it is very likely that early hominids would have done this even before tools were used for hunting. The role of women as tool inventors, perhaps contributing many of the major categories of tools that are most essential even today, cannot be dismissed.

The introduction of food gathering, as opposed to each individual eating what food was available where it was found, was another significant advance which would both have necessitated and been made possible by the invention of the container. More food might be gathered than was needed immediately by one individual, either for giving to someone else or for later consumption. With the exception of parents feeding very young offspring, this behavior is unusual among other animals and presumably would not have been common amongst the very earliest hominids, but gradually developed to become a hallmark of human behavior. Another change would have involved carrying this food to a base, which would imply both conceptual and physical changes, made possible by the use of containers, and may also have made it necessary to walk on two legs, leaving the hands free to carry the food, either directly or in containers. The development of consistent sharing, not only with offspring but also with others in the group, and exchanging food brought from different environments of savanna and forest would have been a stage towards living in regular social groups.

Environmental changes would also have led to social changes within early hominid groups. In savanna grassland, as opposed to forest, it would have been more difficult to find safe places to sleep overnight, and water would have been harder to obtain. Once a suitable location was discovered, there would have been a greater tendency to remain there as long as possible rather than sleeping in a different place each night, thus introducing the idea of a homebase.

Women also played a key role in social development. A major difference between human development and that of other animals is the greater length of time during which infants need to be cared for and fed: this has probably contributed to a number of human characteristics, including food sharing and long-term male–female bonding. The sharing of food between mother and offspring would necessarily have continued for longer in early hominids than in other primates, and it is argued that when a mammal too large to be consumed by the hunters alone was killed, the males would have shared it with those who had shared with them in their youth, that is their mothers and sisters, rather than with their sexual partners. This argument is supported by a primate study[9] that shows that banana sharing almost always takes place within matrifocal groups rather than between sexual partners. This has important implications for the primacy or otherwise of monogamy and marriage. Several scholars have also pointed out that in this situation the female would choose to mate with a male who was particularly sociable and willing to share food with his partner while she was looking after a very young infant. As well as preferring those most willing to share, females would choose those males who appeared to be most friendly. Not surprisingly, female chimpanzees will not mate with males who are aggressive towards them. The more friendly-looking males would probably have been smaller, or nearer in size to the female, and would have had less pronounced teeth, and therefore have been less aggressive-looking. Over thousands of years this female sexual preference would have led to gradual evolutionary changes in favor of smaller, less aggressive, males.

The stronger tie between mother and offspring caused by the longer period of time during which human infants need to be cared for would have resulted in closer social bonds than are found in other species. The primary bond between mother and offspring would be supplemented by sibling ties between sisters and brothers growing up together. Older offspring would be encouraged or socialized to contribute towards the care of younger siblings, including grooming, sharing food, playing and helping to protect them. The natural focus of such a group would clearly be the mother rather than, as is so often supposed, any male figure. Moreover, this group behavior would lead to increased sociability in the male as well as in the species in general. The role of the female, both in fostering this increased sociability in the species and as the primary teacher of technological innovations during this long period of caring, must be recognized.

An increase in human sociability, and particularly female sociability, would have had a number of other positive side-effects. As a result of a mutual willingness to share food and food resources, each individual would have had more access to overlapping gathering areas when a particular resource was abundant. This in turn might greatly increase the chances of the offspring being well fed and

therefore surviving, and thus of the survival of the species in general. As the ability to communicate precisely increased with the development of language, it would have become possible for humans to have ordered social relationships with more individuals and other groups. This would have evolved into a pattern very similar to that found in modern foraging groups, many of which include distant relations who regularly meet up with other groups in the course of their annual movements. Males who had moved out of the matrifocal group in order to mate would have learnt a pattern of friendly contact with their ancestral females when they met them in the course of their foraging.

It can therefore be argued that the crucial steps in human development were predominantly inspired by females. These include economic and technological innovations, and the role of females as the social center of groups. This contrasts sharply with the traditional picture of the male as protector and hunter, bringing food back to a pair-bonded female. That model treats masculine aggression as normal, assumes that long-term, one-to-one, male–female bonding was a primary development, with the male as the major food provider, and that male dominance was inherently linked to hunting skills. None of these patterns, however, accords with the behavior of any but the traditional Western male. Other male primates do not follow this pattern, nor do non-Western human groups, in particular those foraging societies whose lifestyle in many ways accords most closely with putative early human and Paleolithic cultural patterns.

REFERENCES

Dennell, R. 1983. *European Economic Prehistory.* London: Academic Press.

Friedl, E. 1975. *Women and Men: An Anthropologist's View.* New York: Holt, Rinehart and Winston.

———. 1978. "Society and sex roles." *Human Nature* 1: 68–75.

Goodall, J. 1986. *The Chimpanzees of Gombe: Patterns of Behavior.* Cambridge, MA: Harvard University Press.

Isaac, G. and Crader, D. 1981. "To what extent were early hominids carnivorous?" In Teleki, G. (ed.).

Omnivorous Primates: Gathering and Hunting in Human Evolution. New York: Columbia University Press.

Martin, M. K. and Voorhies, B. 1975. *Female of the Species.* New York: Columbia University Press.

McGrew, W. 1981. "The female chimpanzee as a human evolutionary prototype." In Dahlberg, Frances (ed.). *Woman the Gatherer.* New Haven: Yale University Press.

Slocum, S. 1975. "Woman the gatherer: male bias in anthropology." In Reiter, Rayna R. (ed.). *Toward an Anthropology of Women.* New York: Monthly Review Press.

Tanner, N. 1981. *On Becoming Human.* Cambridge: Cambridge University Press.

Tanner, N. and Zihlman, A. 1976. "Woman in evolution. Part 1: Innovation and selection in human origins." *Signs* 1(3): 585–608.

Zihlman, A. 1978. "Women in evolution. Part 2: Subsistence and social organization among early hominids." *Signs* 4: 4–20.

———. 1981. "Woman as shapers of human adaption." In Dahlberg, Frances (ed.). *Woman the Gatherer.* New Haven: Yale University Press.

NOTES

1. Zihlman, 1981.
2. Slocum, 1975.
3. For example, Tanner, 1981; Martin and Voorhies, 1975.
4. Zihlman, 1981; Isaac and Crader, 1981.
5. Zihlman, 1978; the same arguments are used by Friedl, 1975 and 1978, who explains in more detail than here why present-day foragers divide food collecting tasks along gender lines.
6. Dennell, 1983, 55.
7. McGrew, 1981; Goodall, 1986.
8. Tanner and Zihlman, 1976.
9. McGrew, 1981, 47.

Gender and War:
Are Women Tough Enough for Military Combat?

Lucinda J. Peach

INTRODUCTION

"Women are not supposed to be in combat. The fact of the matter is they are in combat" (Army Captain Kevin Hanrahan, quoted in Little 2005: 1). As the traditional boundary between "the front line" and "behind the front line" vanishes in the face of the kinds of combat tactics and military technologies now being used to wage war in the twenty-first century, more soldiers, including women, are facing dangerous and life threatening situations. This fact has been made starkly evident with the current Iraq war, where guerilla tactics have put women soldiers constantly in the line of fire. They have routinely participated in convoy missions where they have been at risk of being hit. Women at times even have been

Original material prepared for this text. Reprinted by permission of the author.

assigned as "gunners," positioned at the machine gun on the top of the Humvee during such convoys, while their fellow soldiers of both sexes use their weapons when the convoy stops to "pull a perimeter" and protect the area from hostile fire. As one female Iraqi vet put it, "That may not be hand-to-hand combat, but if it isn't combat, I don't know what is" (Martineau and Wiegand 2005: 6).

In addition, whenever a unit is ambushed, any women in that unit are of necessity "in combat" (Little 2005: 1). Women soldiers in Iraq also regularly serve as military police and at checkpoints, where they are indispensable to search women because of cultural notions regarding women's modesty, but which put them at higher risk of being fired upon (*see* Cox 2006). Despite this indisputable evidence that women serving in the American military are "seeing combat," often on a daily basis, official US policy has been, and continues to be, that women are prohibited from serving in the majority of combat roles.[1]

Even before being highlighted because of the striking number of deaths of female soldiers during the seemingly interminable Iraq War which began in 2003 (see, e.g., Cox 2006), the issue of whether women *should* participate in military combat has been debated sporadically by military personnel, government officials, public policy makers, and members of the public since women's military service in the Persian Gulf War was given high profile media attention in the early 1990s.

A number of arguments have been made over the years to justify excluding women from what has been considered the "heart" of warmaking: combat, and especially ground combat. Although certain positions in the military designated as "combat" were opened up to women by the Clinton Administration following the Persian Gulf War, especially on combat aircraft and naval vessels (except for submarines), the majority of combat positions—including all ground combat positions—remain closed to them.

The definition of "direct ground combat" that was adopted in 1993 bars women from units that engage the enemy with weapons on the ground while exposed to hostile fire and which involve substantial probability of direct physical contact with hostile forces (see Lancaster 1994: A1; Pine 1994: A5; Schmitt 1994a; Schmitt 1994b: A18). Under this policy, exposure to risk, alone, is an insufficient ground for excluding women from a particular assignment. Nevertheless, women are barred from almost all assignments that involve operating offensive, line-of-sight weapons, and from all positions involving ground fighting. This includes armor, infantry, and field artillery, the three specialties that are considered the core of combat (see Schmitt 1994b; Schmitt 1994: A7). It also has included combat support positions, such as those providing fuel, food, ammunition, etc., to units which are engaged in combat, called "collocation," which literally means "to place side by side (see Martineau and Wiegand 2005: 5).

The combat exclusions have become an ~lly vexed issue in the past couple of years as the Iraq War has continued, putting increasing strain on the military to find adequate numbers of service*men* available and qualified to perform all of the combat and combat support roles. Both the Army and Marines have been using women in combat support positions since the beginning of the Iraq War (Katz 2005: 1). Yet in January 2005, President Bush reaffirmed that there would be no change of policy regarding "No women in combat" (Scarborough and Curl 2005: 1).[2]

The consequence of these combat restrictions is that servicewomen have been excluded from certain benefits and opportunities for promotion and advancement within (and outside) the military that are available only to those with combat experience. The exclusion also functions to limit the numbers of women who can participate in military service because of the relatively small percentage of positions that are available to them. (As of June 2007, over 200,000 women—about 15 percent of those recruited to active duty—are on active duty in the U.S. armed services and an additional 150,000 serve in the National Guard and Reserves. However, this comprised only approximately 19 percent of the Navy, 15 percent of the Army, 20 percent of the Air Force and 24 percent of the Army Reserve (Martineau and Wiegand 2005)). In addition, the exclusion of women from combat contributes to other forms of discrimination against women, both within and outside of the military.

In this essay, I will argue that all of these arguments have been based more on "gender ideology"—that is, on assumptions, prejudices, stereotypes and myths about male and female "natures" and "natural" or "proper" sex roles and behaviors (see Code 1991: 196)—than on empirically verifiable gender differences that demonstrate women's inability to competently perform combat roles in the U.S. military (see also Gold and Solaro 2005: 1).

Two ideological myths about gender in particular underlie many of the arguments against according combat positions to women. First, identification of the military as masculine makes males the standard by which females are assessed. The male standard operates, sometimes explicitly, but more often implicitly, to perpetuate the stereotype that women are out of place in the military, particularly in combat. Throughout history, war has been a theater in which men could prove their masculinity, and in which masculinity has been deemed a necessary prerequisite to success. During his 1992 presidential election campaign, for example, Bill Clinton's lack of military experience received a lot of attention, some of it based on the view that Clinton's lack of exposure to war made him unfit for presidential leadership. The perception that the virtues of "manliness" are necessary for effective combat soldiering, and that women are incapable or ill-suited to the development of these virtues, has contributed to the maintenance of women's exclusion from most combat assignments.

The second myth used as a rationale to exclude women from combat duty suggests that the purpose for which men fight is to protect women (see Stiehm 1989: 6–7; Kornblum 1984). Women, according to the myth, are the weaker sex and need to be protected by strong men; they are victims dependent upon men rather than autonomous agents who are competent to defend themselves. Members of the military have expressed "a special regard for women who must be protected as the symbolic vessel of femininity and motherhood" (Karst 1991: 536). An example of this perspective is implicit in the rationale of Republican Duncan Hunter, the chairman of the House Armed Services Committee, in support of a congressional bill restricting combat roles for women (which was defeated) in 2005:

> I think one of the marks of civilization is we have not had our women in direct ground combat. In fact, we have decried the enemy when they have pushed women into the frontlines and into combat situations, and utilized women to attack combat forces. We have said that is wrong. That is not something that civilized nations do (Ho 2005: 1).

The fact of "civilization" alone was apparently a sufficient reason for the prohibition in the Congressman's mind, without the need to explain specifically what made women's participation in combat uncivilized, although he also added that the "lack of privacy," and the fact that combat is "brutal and grim" were additional reasons (Ho 2005: 1). In the absence of an underlying gender ideology that women are supposed to be protected, not do the protecting, none of these reasons, either alone or together, provides any explanation of *why* women should be excluded from combat.

Such myths are bolstered by arguments that integrating women into combat would be deleterious to combat effectiveness and the military's ability to mobilize in time of war (Hooker 1989: 36; Kelly 1984: 103; Mitchell 1989: 159; Marlowe 1983: 194; Rogan 1981: 21). Women's supposed physical, physiological, and psychological characteristics are offered as the basis for this argument. Although none of these rationales, alone or combined, provides an adequate ethical basis for maintaining the combat restrictions for women, their popularity and prominence makes it important to note how each of them is based on ideological notions of gender that frequently are inconsistent with the realities of gender difference.

The most common arguments in support of the view that the inclusion of women would diminish combat readiness and effectiveness are that: (1) women lack the necessary physical and psychological strength to perform adequately; (2) their capacity for pregnancy and childbearing makes them inappropriate combatants; and (3) women's participation in combat units would reduce unit cohesion by disrupting male bonding and promoting sexual fraternization. Let us examine each of these arguments in greater detail.

PHYSICAL AND PSYCHOLOGICAL STRENGTH

Military effectiveness is often said to be compromised by women's lack of physical and psychological strength and stamina relative to men (Mitchell 1989: 156–62; Kantrowitz 1991; Gordon and Ludvigson 1991: 20–22; D'Amico 1990: 6). Regarding the physical strength issue, military personnel have testified before Congress that few women would meet the physical standards for combat duty

(Hackworth 1991: 25; United States Senate Appropriations Hearings 1991; Cramsie 1983: 562). Women's purported inferior physical capability is voiced especially loudly by enlisted men, who deny that women have the strength necessary for fighting on the front lines (see Kantrowitz 1991: 23). For example, one of the reasons integrated basic training was ended in the Army in 1982 was because of enlisted men's complaints that women were holding them back (see Coyle 1989; Stiehm 1985b: 209; Rogan 1981: 27). A study of enlisted service personnel's attitudes toward women in the Army in 1975 indicated that only about 50 percent of men interviewed thought women had the physical strength for combat (see Mitchell 1989: 157–58; Stiehm 1989: 102).

There is no question that, in general, most men are physically stronger than most women. Military studies document that men have some advantages in upper body and leg strength, cardiovascular capacity, and lean muscle, which make men "more fitted for physically intense combat" (see Mitchell 1989: 157; Kelly 1984: 100–101; Marlowe 1983: 190; Hooker 1989: 44). However, these tests generally do not also indicate the fact that some women are capable of meeting the standards established for men. Nor do they typically take into consideration the disparities in prior physical training and physical conditioning that men and women have undergone. Army reports reveal that some women do have the requisite upper body strength to qualify for combat. In addition, some women are stronger than some men. Women have performed well in the limited number of combat-type situations in which they have been tested. However, because the combat exclusion has precluded the possibility of obtaining data about women's physical performance under actual combat conditions, gender-based assumptions and prejudices have dominated policy discussions.

The assumption that women lack the physical strength necessary for combat is ideological because it often persists in the face of direct evidence to the contrary. The nature of modern combat, with its emphasis on high-technology

equipment, makes the issue of physical strength far less important than it was in an era when war involved primarily hand-to-hand combat. Physical size and strength are of minimal, if any, consideration, when weapons are being fired at the touch of a button from a location far removed from the combat theatre. As Judith Stiehm argues, the question should not be "how strong women are, but how strong they need to be" (1989: 219). The positive experiences with using women in traditionally all-male fields, such as police and fire fighting forces, which require similar skills to combat, support the conclusion that women are capable of performing satisfactorily in physical defense of self and others in situations involving the use of lethal force (see McDowell 1992; Segal 1982: 286; Karst 1991: 539; Kornblum 1984: 392–93).

Nonetheless, skeptics point out that "there is no real evidence that technology has in fact reduced the need for physical strength among military men and women. What evidence there is shows that many military jobs still require more physical strength than most women possess" (Mitchell 1989: 157). To the contrary, although there are some combat positions that most women are unable to perform satisfactorily because of inadequate physical strength, there is a considerable range of combat positions that many, if not most, women are qualified to perform. Although sheer physical strength may occasionally be an issue when technology fails to function properly, more often than not, the physical strength issue is no longer a legitimate reason for excluding women from combat duty. In addition, physical strength is only one of many factors that needs to be assessed in determining the capability of persons for military combat.

Several proposals have been forwarded, by military personnel and others, to assign combat positions on the basis of the physical strength required to perform them, as at least one of several relevant criterion, rather than exclusively on the basis of gender (Coyle 1989: 31; Nabors 1982: 51; Proxmire 1986: 110; Rogan 1981: 306; Roush 1990: 11–12; Segal 1983: 110; Segal 1982: 270–71; U.S. Senate

Hearings 1991: 865).[3] Such proposals would result in a fairer and more accurate measure of "fit" between persons and assignments than the current reliance on gender difference. The main rationale used by military officers for their failure to implement such a gender-neutral scheme is that it may not be "cost-effective" (see Association 1991: 54; Rogan 1981: 20). However, the military's failure to demonstrate how gender-neutral standards for assignments would be financially infeasible suggests that the maintenance of the combat exclusion is based more on the continuing force of gender ideology than on financial expense or damage to military effectiveness.

Sometimes the protection myth serves to reinforce the physical strength argument by portraying women as "the weaker sex" who need to be protected from the risks of being raped and physically violated in war. It is sometimes argued that the presence of women in combat would cause male soldiers to respond by becoming more concerned about protecting them than fighting the enemy, thus compromising combat effectiveness (see Barkalow 1990: 260 (quoting Colonel Houston's comment that men's emotional commitment to recapture POW women would be so intense and extreme as to cause fighting to escalate); Beecraft 1989: 43; Van Creveld 1993).

Such arguments are ripe for resurgence as a result of the Iraq war, where unprecedented numbers of American women soldiers are being killed, most of them in combat situations (see Martineau and Wiegand 2005: 6). Although the total number is still less than one-thirtieth of the number of male soldiers killed, it is still larger than the number of military women killed in Korea, Vietnam and the Persian Gulf War combined (Schleicher 2006).

The notion that women in the military are in need of protection is based on stereotypes of male machismo and female weakness and vulnerability. Further, the assumption that males are able to protect military women is itself a myth, since women are too integrated throughout the armed forces to be protected by their exclusion from combat. (Providing women soldiers with arms and training in self-defense would provide a measure of protection against sexual violence that they would not otherwise have.) The rationale that women need to be protected from becoming POWs because of the risk that their torture would include sexual abuse ignores the reality that men as well as women are raped in war, and that women are already subject to such sexual violence at home or by their fellow soldiers on or near the field of combat. In addition, military women are susceptible to being captured and raped during war, regardless of whether they are themselves engaged in combat.

Regarding women's alleged psychological lack of fitness for military combat, during the Gulf War, the press raised the argument that women soldiers would be psychologically unable to handle being taken as prisoners of war, especially because of the greater possibility that they would be raped and otherwise sexually abused (see Nabors 1982: 59; Rogan 1981: 26). Here, the assumption is that women are less stable than men emotionally, and are thus less well equipped to handle the extreme psychological stresses of combat (Mitchell 1989: 7, 182–92; Marlowe 1983: 195).

There is no factual basis for the conclusion that female combatants would be any weaker or more vulnerable than men under such circumstances. To the contrary, the experience of military women such as Air Force Major Rhonda Cornum, a flight surgeon whose aircraft was shot down during the Gulf War, reveals a very matter-of-fact attitude about survival in the face of physical injury and sexual abuse at the hands of her captors. Cornum's response stands as a testament to the ability of military women to cope as POWs (see Cornum 1992).

A relatively new psychological argument has begun to emerge with the Iraq War in view of the unprecedented numbers of women soldiers who have been directly exposed to combat. Since studies have shown that *civilian* women suffer from PTSD at rates nearly twice as high as that of *civilian* men, an inference can be made that women soldiers may also suffer higher rates of post-traumatic stress disorder (PTSD) (Cox 2006). The specter of women vets flooding the health care system upon returning from their tours in Iraq have concerned some health care providers (see Martineau and Wiegand 2005: 1). However, there is little evidence from studies of the U.S. military to bear out this hypothesis. In fact, one Army study released in 2005, indicates that rates of mental health problems among returning male and female soldiers are similar (Cox 2006).

Also related to the physical and psychological strength arguments is the assumption that men are naturally more aggressive than women, and that the "natural aggressiveness" of males would be "softened" by women's participation in battle (Marlowe 1983: 191; Mitchell 1989: 7; Tuten 1982: 255).

More recently, some scholars have challenged the argument that women are innately less aggressive than men (see Marquit 1991; Rosoff 1991; Sunday 1991), while others observe the lack of evidence regarding women's psychological weakness (see Dillingham 1990: 227–28; Gordon and Ludvigson 1991; Kornblum 1984: 398–99). Many of those who conclude that men are "naturally" more aggressive than women rely on incomplete studies of primates, not humans, conducted by anthropologist Lionel Tiger. Tiger observed that male primates in the wild spend much of their time in groups organized to fight with outsiders, whereas female primates were engaged in grooming activities in pairs. Tiger's research has since been largely discredited by further research. Subsequent studies have revealed that females also engaged in collective aggressive action to protect their young, and that both males and females spend much of their time grooming (see United States Senate Hearings 1991: 981; Holm 1982: 95).

The evidence to support the claim of women's lesser aggression is very tenuous, especially after women soldiers demonstrated their competence in performing the psychologically demanding tasks required in combat duty during the Gulf War. But even assuming that women are less aggressive than men, there is still no evidence that it stems from biological causes rather than culture and socialization, which are malleable. The military has not offered empirical evidence to demonstrate that women cannot be trained to exhibit the same degree of aggressiveness that men exhibit. Nonetheless, the assumption that women are less aggressive continues to strengthen the myth of combat as a masculine institution of which only men are capable.

PREGNANCY AND MOTHERHOOD

One specific aspect of women's physiology that some have argued disrupts unit cohesion and consequently hampers combat effectiveness is pregnancy (Nabors 1982: 56–58; see Barkalow 1990: 238–41; Rogan 1981: 256; Shields 1988: 108; Stiehm 1985b: 226). The Army has expressed concern with the effects of pregnancy on "readiness," "mission accomplishment," and "deployability" (Mitchell 1989: 6, 166–71; Rogan 1981: 26; Stiehm 1985a; see Tuten 1982: 251). Until 1975, women were automatically discharged from the military as soon as their pregnancy was discovered. This contributed to high attrition rates for women in the armed services. In 1975, the Department of Defense (DOD) made such discharge for pregnancy voluntary (see Segal 1983: 207; Treadwell 1954: 200).

Pregnancy also arguably interferes with the ability of the armed forces to rapidly mobilize troops for combat, since it cannot be predicted in advance which women will be pregnant, and thus unavailable for deployment. Pregnancy continues to be an issue of concern, both in the military and among the public. A *Newsweek* poll conducted in 1991 revealed that 76 percent of the public is concerned about military women becoming pregnant and putting the fetus at risk (Hackworth 1991: 27). Pregnancy does account for a significant percentage of women's lost time, although military women lose less service time overall than do men for illness, drug and alcohol abuse, and disability (see Coyle 1989: 39; D'Amico 1990: 8; Kornblum 1984: 417–18; Shields 1988: 109).

Because of the way military units are currently structured, pregnancy does present a genuine difficulty in the full integration of all women into combat forces. Since military policy, at least in the Army, does not provide temporary replacements for pregnant personnel, the presence of pregnant women in a unit increases everyone else's work load, and consequently brings with it the risk of breeding resentment among coworkers. In addition, although there is no certainty that women desiring to get pregnant will be successful, some opponents of women combatants contend that enlisted women will use pregnancy as a means of avoiding combat duty.

Therefore, pregnancy may be a legitimate reason to exclude women from actually engaging in some forms of combat. However, excluding all women from all positions designated as combat is far too extreme a response. Most women are not pregnant most of the time. Only about ten percent of servicewomen are pregnant at any given time (see Gordon and Ludvigson 1991: 22–23; Hackworth 1991: 27). There has been no surge of pregnancies in the military since the initiation of the Iraq war (Gold and Solaro 2005: 1). Further, the experience of pregnancy varies widely in affecting a woman's job performance. Some women are able to carry on their normal activities into the latter stages of pregnancy. Most logistical problems relating to pregnancy, such as deployment plans, etc., can be satisfactorily surmounted by careful planning.

The protection myth also operates here to call into question the propriety of risking the safety of the nation's child bearers by exposing them to the risks of combat. As with the lack of data on gender-integrated units, there have been no studies of the actual impact of pregnancy on military effectiveness because the combat exclusion has precluded the possibility of gathering data. Pregnancy is one consideration that needs to be factored into the analysis of how and whether to integrate women into certain combat roles. But it does not justify the stringency of the current restrictions.

Related to the pregnancy issue is the symbolic, if not actual, role of women as mothers. Motherhood and women's responsibilities to their families are viewed as antithetical to effective combat soldiering. The assumption

underlying this view is that women's proper role is to be the center of family life. According to this perspective, women not only bear the children, but are also primarily responsible for their care and nurture (see Costin 1983: 305; Mitchell 1989: 6, 171–76; Rogan 1981: 26; Segal 1982: 274–75, 281–82). The media's promulgation of images of women soldiers kissing their infants goodbye before going off to the Gulf War, and its stories about fathers left at home to care for children emphasized the unnaturalness of female soldiers going off to combat (see Enloe 1993: 201–27).

The influence of gender ideology on this issue is evident in the view of Alexander Webster, a chaplain for the Army National Guard, who speculates about the "identity confusion that must confront any would-be woman warrior who pauses for a moment to consider her potential for motherhood." Webster also surmises that the paradigm of the citizen soldier may have been destroyed by the "social disruption and havoc among families wreaked by the mobilization and deployment of mothers of young children to the theater of operations in the Persian Gulf" (1991: 29). Webster continues: "Disturbing images on television and in the print media of mothers wrenched from their offspring may be the most enduring from the Persian Gulf War" (24–25). According to these ideological notions of gender, women need special protection because they are responsible, in turn, for protecting their children. Notably missing from this assessment is consideration of the consequences of *fathers* being "wrenched from their offspring," thus perpetuating the identification of women as the primary parent. Such testimony assumes that mothers are more responsible for family life than are fathers, so that it is women's military involvement that is questionable, not men's, whenever families are concerned.

Such ideological assumptions about the gender of parenthood are widespread. Surveys reveal that the public continues to be more willing to send young fathers into combat than young mothers. Even supporters of combat roles for women have assumed that mothers would be more reluctant to risk their lives in combat than would men (see Campbell 1992: 18; Lieberman 1990: 219). Attrition and reenlistment data for women indicate that motherhood is a primary reason why women leave the military. And surveys indicate that the large majority of service women do want to have children (see Shields 1988: 109). Former Secretary of Defense Richard Cheney argued that exempting all single parents and dual-service career couples from deployment would weaken military capability (see Campbell 1992: 18, 20). This problem impacts more heavily on women, who comprise the larger percentage of single parents in the military. Women's family obligations may thus present a practical problem for women's ability to carry out combat assignments, particularly for single mothers.

Several other factors need to be considered, however. Many military women are not mothers, and have no plans to become mothers. Most women entering the military are not (yet) mothers. The belief that women are essentially mothers is an outdated ideological assumption. It leads to the irrational result that men who are fathers can be required to participate in combat whereas women who are not mothers cannot (see Association of the Bar of the City of New York 1991: 25; Segal 1982: 283). Such beliefs underlie the former Army prohibition on the enlistment of women who had children in certain age groups (see Treadwell 1954: 496).[4]

Further, although most women traditionally *have* taken primary responsibility for protecting and providing for their children, not all mothers are primary caretakers. Many families include alternative arrangements for childcare that do not make the mother primarily responsible. Finally, tradition should not determine who *should* be responsible for national defense in time of war. Fathers have equal responsibility for protecting and providing for their children. Yet, since the Korean War, they have not been exempted from combat duty. In addition, the legislation mandating women's exclusion from combat does not exempt them from military service in time of war. Children of military parents are just as much in need of care and protection during wartime, regardless of

whether their mothers are assigned to combat duty or some other position. In the absence of evidence indicating that combat jobs are more incompatible with being a wife and mother than a husband and father, families should be entitled to make their own decisions about child care in the event that the mother is called to serve in combat duty. Current military policy provides that if both parents are in the services, one can claim an exemption in the event that troops are deployed. There is no rational basis for the government to preempt the parents' right to choose based on a set of assumptions about motherhood.

UNIT COHESION AND MALE BONDING

Unit or troop "cohesion" is a function of interpersonal relationships between military leaders and their troops, and the leader's ability to create and sustain "those interpersonal skills that allow him to build strong ties with his men" (Gabriel 1982: 172–73). The argument that male soldiers will lose the camaraderie and team spirit necessary for unit cohesion if they are required to share their duties with women has been advanced as a reason to exclude women from military combat. For example, former Marine Corps Commandant Robert Barrows defends the notion of male bonding as a "real . . . cohesiveness," a "mutual respect and admiration," and a "team work" that would be destroyed by the inclusion of women. "If you want to make a combat unit ineffective," he said, "assign some women to it" (United States Senate Hearings 1991: 985–96).

Although the argument about the indispensability of cohesion to effectiveness is persuasive, the view that the presence of women will damage the "male bonding" linked to that cohesion is exaggerated by the influence of gender ideology. This "influence" is often supported by outdated and anecdotal evidence, such as Tiger's largely discredited research (Mitchell 1989; Golightly 1987; Rogan 1981: 25; Hooker 1989: 45). In addition, the military has not studied the impact that integration of the forces has had on "male bonding" in actual combat for the past several years, nor has it made efforts to instill male–female or female–female bonding in its soldiers (see Stiehm 1989: 236; Stiehm 1985a: 172).

There is also anecdotal evidence that there is a lack of gender integration that harms troop cohesion (and by extension, combat effectiveness). For example, after seven years in the Army and another seven in the Reserves, retired servicewoman Elizabeth Vasquez opined: "I think we have every right and capability to be on the front lines. . . . But you need that sense of unity, and I don't think it's possible in integrated units. Its hard to do your job to your fullest capability when you're thought of as less than what I wanted to be—a soldier" (Martineau and Wiegand 2005: 8). However, the experience with female soldiers in the Iraq and Persian Gulf Wars, as well as the limited studies that have been done in simulated combat and field conditions, indicate that the presence of women in combat units does not adversely affect combat effectiveness (see Gold & Solaro 2005: 1). The Army Research Institute conducted two of these studies, labeled "REFWAC" and "MAXWAC" (Johnson et al. 1978; United States Army Research Institute 1977). MAXWAC results showed that female ratios varying from 0 to 35 percent had no significant effect on unit performance. REFWAC results similarly showed that the presence of 10 percent female soldiers on a REFORGER ("Return of Forces to Germany") ten-day field exercise made no difference in the performance of combat support and combat service support units.

In addition, Navy Commander Barry Boyle, participating in Navy squadron preparations, Charles Moskos, observing an Army exercise in Honduras, and Constance Devilbliss, participating in rigorous Army exercises, reached similar conclusions that integrated units performed as effectively, if not more so, than all-male units (see Coyle 1989; Moskos 1985; Devilbliss 1985). Experience with women in combat in other nations, as well as the successful integration of women into police and other traditionally male-only professions, also provides useful analogies indicating that the participation of American military women in combat would not hamper unit or troop cohesion (Association 1991; United States Senate Hearings 1991; Goldman 1982a, b).

FRATERNIZATION

Women in uniform represent an anomaly to traditional social ordering based on traditional sex-gender distinctions, and thus to traditional sexual morality. Thus, in addition to their supposedly detrimental effect on male bonding, including women in combat roles is sometimes alleged to diminish troop effectiveness because of the inevitable sexual attraction and behavior that would follow from having mixed-gender units. Some express a fear that men will be preoccupied with winning the sexual favors of women rather than concentrating on their mission (Donnelly 2006: 2; Mitchell 1989: 176–78; Golightly 1987: 46; Rogan 1981: 27).

The fraternization argument ignores the capability of the sexes to interact with one another in nonsexual ways, particularly under the exigent circumstances of combat. The limited studies that have been conducted under simulated combat conditions indicate that fraternization does not hamper combat readiness or troop effectiveness. Studies show that gender-integrated combat units are as effective as all-male units, and that members of gender-integrated units develop brother-sister bonds rather than sexual ones.

Fraternization is most likely to be a problem where there is ineffective leadership. It is likely that unit bonding depends more on shared experiences, including sharing of risks and hardships, than on gender distinctions (see Karst 1991: 537, 543; Devilbliss 1985: 519; Opinion 1988: 138). Experience has shown that actual integration diminishes prejudice and fosters group cohesiveness more effectively than any other factor. It is thus likely that women's integration into combat forces would parallel that of black men into previously all-white forces during the 1950s and 1960s (see Moskos 1990: 74; Kornblum 1984: 412, 422; Segal 1983: 203–04, 206; Holm 1982: 257).

CONCLUSION

It is a fact that U.S. servicewomen are involved in military combat despite the lack of official recognition they are given. As the preceding discussion reveals, none of the primary rationales that have been forwarded to exclude women from being able to "officially" serve in combat roles provides a legitimate basis for maintaining the current restrictions on women's participation in combat. The analysis of these rationales suggests that the resistance of Congress, the courts, the military, and the public to removing the combat restrictions results more from gender ideology than from demonstrated evidence of women's inability to perform combat roles effectively.

Once outdated stereotypes and myths about women's capabilities and deficiencies are eliminated from consideration of the ethics of women in military combat, the current restrictions on combat roles for women are revealed to lack persuasive foundations. Certainly, differences in physical strength and other physiological distinctions between men and women need to be taken into consideration, but these can be accommodated without the need to exclude women from combat roles. Only when the military begins assigning women to positions on the basis of gender-neutral standards for evaluating the degree of physical strength, psychological fortitude, bonding and troop cohesiveness necessary to perform combat roles can the issue of women in combat be addressed without the undue influence of ideological notions of gender.

REFERENCES

Association of the Bar of the City of New York, "The Combat Exclusion Laws: An Idea Whose Time Has Gone," *Minerva*, Vol. 9, No. 4 (Winter, 1991), pp. 1–55 (Association).

Barkalow, Carol, *In the Men's House* (New York: Poseidon Press, 1990).

———. "Women Have What It Takes," *Newsweek* (August 5, 1991), p. 30.

Beecraft, Carolyn, "Personnel Puzzle," *Proceedings* (*of the U.S. Naval Institute*), Vol. 115, No. 4 (April, 1989), pp. 41–44.

Campbell, D'Ann, "Combatting the Gender Gulf," Temple Political and Civil Rights Law Review, Vol. 1, No. 2 (Fall, 1992), reprinted in *Minerva*, Vol. X, Nos. 3–4 (Fall/Winter 1992), pp. 13–41.

Code, Lorraine, *What Can She Know? Feminist Theory and the Construction of Knowledge* (Ithaca, NY: Cornell University Press, 1991).

Cornum, Rhonda, *She Went to War: The Rhonda Cornum Story* (Novato, CA: Presidio Press, 1992).

Costin, Lela, "Feminism, Pacifism, Nationalism, and the United Nations Decade for Women," in Judith Stiehm (ed.), *Women and Men's Wars* (Oxford: Pergamon Press, 1983), pp. 301–16.

Cox, Amy, "Women at War: Mental Health Toll Unknown," *CNN.com* (posted May 22, 2007; originally published May 2006), http://www.cnn.com/2006/US/05/26/ch.women.vets/index.html (accessed June 20, 2007).

Coyle, Commander Barry, U.S. Navy, "Women on the Front Lines," *Proceedings* (*of the U.S. Military Institute*), Vol. 115, No. 4 (April, 1989), pp. 37–40.

Cramsie, Jodie, "Gender Discrimination in the Military: The Unconstitutional Exclusion of Women From Combat," *Valparaiso Law Review*, Vol. 17 (1983), pp. 547–88.

D'Amico, "Women at Arms: The Combat Controversy," *Minerva*, Vol. 8, No. 2 (1990), pp. 1–19.

Devilbliss, M. C., "Gender Integration and Unit Deployment: A Study of G.I. Jo," *Armed Forces and Society*, Vol. 11, No. 3 (1985), pp. 523–52.

Dillingham, Wayne, "The Possibility of American Military Women Becoming Prisoners of War: Justification for Combat Exclusion Rules?" *Federal Bar News and Journal*, Vol. 37, No. 4 (1990), pp. 223–30.

Donnelly, Elaine, "Rumsfeld Dithers on Women in Combat," *Center for Military Readiness* (June 16, 2006), online at http://www.cmrlink.org/WomenInCombat.asp?docID=273 (accessed June 21, 2007).

Enloe, Cynthia, *The Morning After: Sexual Politics at the End of the Cold War* (Berkeley, CA: University of California Press, 1993).

Gabriel, Richard, *To Serve With Honor: A Treatise on Military Ethics and the Way of the Soldier* (Westport, CT: Greenwood Press, 1982).

Gold, Philip and Erin Solaro, "Facts About Women in Combat Elude the Right," *Seattle Post-Intelligencer*

(May 18 2005), online at http://seattlepi
.nwsource.com/opinion/22465_womenincom
bat18.html (accessed June 21, 2007).

Goldman, Nancy Loring (ed.), *Female Soldiers—
Combatants or Noncombatants? Historical and Con-
temporary Perspectives* (Westport, CT: Greenwood
Press, 1982a).

———. *The Utilization of Women in Combat: An His-
torical and Social Analysis of Twentieth-Century
Wartime and Peacetime Experience* (Alexandria, VA:
U.S.A.R.I., 1982b).

Golightly, Lieutenant Neil L., U.S. Navy, "No Right
to Fight," *Proceedings (of the U.S. Naval Institute)*,
Vol. 113, No. 12 (1987), pp. 46–49.

Gordon, Marilyn and Mary Jo Ludvigson, "A Constitutional Analysis of the Combat Exclusion
for Air Force Women," *Minerva: Quarterly
Report on Women and the Military*, Vol. 9, No. 2
(1991), pp. 1–34.

Hackworth, Colonel David, "War and the Second
Sex," *Newsweek* (August 5, 1991), pp. 24–28.

Ho, Stephanie, "US House Debates Role of Women
in Combat," *VOA News.com*, http://www.voanews
.com/english/archive/2005-05/2005-05-22-voa38
.cfm?CFID=165219291&CFTOKEN=53222921
(accessed June 21, 2007).

Holm, Maj. Gen. Jeanne, U.S.A.F. (Ret.), Women
in the Military (Novato, CA: Presidio Press,
1982).

Hooker, Richard, "Affirmative Action and Combat
Exclusion: Gender Roles in the U.S. Army,"
Parameters: U.S. War College Quarterly, Vol. 19,
No. 4 (1989), pp. 36–50.

Johnson, Cecil, et al., *Women Content in the Army:
REFORGER (REFWAC 77)* (Alexandria, VA:
U.S.A.R.I., 1978).

Kantrowitz, Barbara, "The Right to Fight,"
Newsweek (August 5, 1991), pp. 22–23.

Karst, Kenneth, "The Pursuit of Manhood and the
Desegregation of the Armed Forces," *U.C.L.A.
Law Review*, Vol. 38, No. 3 (1991), pp. 499–581.

Katz, Amy, "The Future of Women Serving in Combat Being Debated," *VOA News.com* (May 23,
2005), on line at http://www.voanews.com/
english/archive/2005-05/2005-05-23-voa16
.cfm?CFID=91000318&CFTOKEN=87046523
(accessed June 21, 2007).

Kelly, Karla, "The Exclusion of Women From
Combat: Withstanding the Challenge," *Judge
Advocate General Journal*, Vol. 33, No. 1 (1984),
pp. 77–108.

Kornblum, Lori, "Women Warriors in a Men's
World: The Combat Exclusion," *Law and
Inequality*, Vol. 2 (1984), pp. 351–445.

Lancaster, John, *Washington Post* (January 13,
1994), pp. A1, A7.

Lieberman, Jeanne, "Women in Combat," *Federal Bar
News and Journal*, Vol. 37, No. 4 (1990), pp. 215–22.

Little, Vince, "Debate Aside, Women in Uniform
Know Combat Roles," *Stars and Stripes* (June 15,
2005), online at http://www.estripes.com/
article.asp?section=104&article=26903&archive
=true (accessed June 21, 2007).

Marlowe, David, "The Manning of the Force and
the Structure of Battle: Part 2—Men and
Women," in Robert Fullinwider (ed.), *Conscripts
and Volunteers: Military Requirements, Social Justice, and the All-Volunteer Force* (Totowa, NJ: Rowman & Allanheld, 1983), pp. 189–99.

Marquit, Doris and Erwin Marquit, "Gender Dif-
ferentiation, Genetic Determinism, and the
Struggle for Peace," in Anne E. Hunter (ed.),
*Genes and Gender VI: On Peace, War, and Gender:
A Challenge to Genetic Explanations* (New York:
Feminist Press, 1991), pp. 151–62.

Martineau, Pamela and Steve Wiegand, "Women at
War," *Sacramento Bee* (March 6, 2005).

McDowell, Jeanne, "Are Women Better Cops?"
Time (February 17, 1992), pp. 70–72.

Mitchell, Brian, *The Weak Link: The Feminization of
the American Military* (Washington, DC: Regnery
Gateway, 1989).

Moniz, Dave, "Public Backs Female Troops in Iraq,
But Not in Ground Force," *USA Today* (May 25,
2005), online at http://www.usatoday.com/
news/world/iraq/2005-05-25-women-combat_x
.htm (accessed June 21, 2007).

Moskos, Charles, "Female GI's in the Field," *Society*,
Vol. 22, No. 6 (1985), pp. 28–33.

———. "Army Women," *Atlantic Monthly*, Vol. 266,
No. 2 (August, 1990), pp. 70–78.

———. "How Do They Do It? *The New Republic*
(August 5, 1991), pp. 16–20.

Nabors, Major Robert, "Women in the Army: Do
They Measure Up?" *Military Review* (October,
1982), pp. 50–61.

Opinion, "No right to Fight?" *Proceedings of the U.S.
Naval Institute* 114(5):134–39, May 1988.

Pine, Art, "Women Will Get Limited Combat Roles,"
Los Angeles Times (January 14, 1994), p. A5.

Proxmire, Senator William, "Three Myths About
Women and Combat," *Minerva*, Vol. 4, No. 4
(Winter, 1986), pp. 105–19.

Rogan, Helen, *Mixed Company: Women in the Modern
Army* (New York: G.P. Putnam's Sons, 1981).

Rosoff, Betty, "Genes, Hormones, and War," in
Hunter (ed.), *Genes and Gender VI: On Peace, War,
and Gender: A Challenge to Genetic Explanations*
(New York: Feminist Press, 1991), pp. 39–49.

Roush, Paul, "Combat Exclusion: Military Necessity or Another Name For Bigotry?" *Minerva*, Vol. 13, No. 3 (Fall, 1990), pp. 1–15.

Scarborough, Rowan and Joseph Curl, "Despite Pressure, Bush Vows 'No Women in Combat'" (Jan. 12, 2005), online at http://www.washingtontimes.com (accessed June 20, 2007).

Schmitt, Eric, "Generals Oppose Combat by Women" *Newsweek* (June 17, 1994a) pp. A1, A18.

Schmitt, Eric, "Army Will Allow Women in 32,000 Combat Posts" *New York Times* (July 28, 1994b), p. A5.

Segal, Mady Wechsler, "The Argument for Female Combatants," in Goldman (ed.), *Female Soldiers—Combatants or Noncombatants? Historical and Contemporary Perspectives* (Westport, CT: Greenwood Press, 1982), pp. 267–90.

———. "Women's Roles in the U.S. Armed Forces: An Evaluation of Evidence and Arguments for Policy Decisions," in Robert Fullinwider (ed.), *Conscripts and Volunteers: Military Requirements, Social Justice, and the All-Volunteer Force* (Totowa, NJ: Rowman & Allanheld, 1983), pp. 200–13 .

Shields, Patricia, "Sex Roles in the Military," in Charles Moskos and Frank Wood (eds.), *The Military—More Than Just a Job?* (Washington, DC: Pergamon Basseys, 1988), pp. 99–111.

Stiehm, Judith Hicks, "Women's Biology and the U.S. Military," in Virginia Sapiro (ed.), *Women, Biology, and Public Policy* (Beverly Hills: SAGE Publications, 1985a), pp. 205–32.

———. "Generations of U.S. Enlisted Women," *Signs: Journal of Women in Culture and Society*, Vol. 11, No. 1 (1985b), pp. 155–75.

———. *Arms and the Enlisted Woman* (Philadelphia: Temple University Press, 1989).

Sunday, Suzanne R., "Biological Theories of Animal Aggression," in Hunter (ed.), *Genes and Gender VI: On Peace, War, and Gender: A Challenge to Genetic Explanations* (New York: Feminist Press, 1991), pp. 50–63.

Treadwell, Mattie, *The Women's Army Corps, in World War II Special Studies*, Vol. 8 (Washington, DC: Office of the Chief of Military History of the Army, 1954).

Tuten, Jeff, "The Argument Against Female Combatants," in Goldman (ed.), *Female Soldiers—Combatants or Noncombatants? Historical and*
Contemporary Perspectives (Westport, CT: Greenwood Press, 1982), pp. 237–66.

United States Army Research Institute, *Women Content in Units Force Deployment Test* (MAXWAC) (Alexandria, VA: U.S.A.R.I., 1977).

United States Senate, Hearings before the Committee on Appropriations, DOD Appropriations, 102d Cong., 1st Sess., H.R. 2521, Pts. 4 & 6, *Utilization of Women in the Military Services* (Washington, DC: Government Printing Office, 1991) (Appropriations Hearings).

Van Creveld, Martin, "Why Israel Doesn't Send Women into Combat," *Parameters*, Vol. 23, No. 1 (Spring, 1993), pp. 5–9.

Webster, Alexander, "Paradigms of the Contemporary American Soldier and Women in the Military," *Strategic Review* (Summer 1991), pp. 22–30.

NOTES

1. Interestingly, this parallels the findings of a recent *USA Today*/CNN/Gallup public opinion poll, which found that "Americans overwhelmingly favor the use of female troops in Iraq, including having them serve in support jobs that often put them in or near combat. . . . A majority of those polled, however, oppose women serving as ground troops" (Moniz 2005).

2. However, a House of Representatives bill to codify the combat exclusions (which up until then had been military policy rather than congressionally mandated), as well as further limit the military positions open to women, was defeated in May 2005 (Moniz 2005: 1; Ho 2005: 1) Instead, a measure was passed instead that requires the Defense Department to notify Congress 60 days in advance of any policy change that would put women in new direct combat roles (id.).

3. A standard based on physical strength rather than gender could be waived in emergency situations where rapid mobilization is necessary and individual testing would be inefficient (see Segal 1982: 270–71).

4. This policy was reversed in *Crawford v. Cushman*, 531 F.2d 1114 (2d Cir. 1976).

Lifeboat Ethics:
Mother Love and Child Death in Northeast Brazil

Nancy Scheper-Hughes

I have seen death without weeping.
The destiny of the Northeast is death.
Cattle they kill.
To the people they do something worse.

Anonymous Brazilian singer (1965)

"Why do the church bells ring so often?" I asked Nailza de Arruda soon after I moved into a corner of her tiny mud-walled hut near the top of the shantytown called the Alto do Cru-zeiro (Crucifix Hill). I was then a Peace Corps volunteer and a community development/ health worker. It was the dry and blazing hot summer of 1965, the months following the military coup in Brazil, and save for the rusty, clanging bells, of N. S. das Dores Church, an eerie quiet had settled over the market town that I call Bom Jesus da Mata. Beneath the quiet, however, there was chaos and panic. "It's nothing," replied Nailza, "just another little angel gone to heaven."

Nailza had sent more than her share of little angels to heaven, and sometimes at night I could hear her engaged in a muffled but passionate discourse with one of them, two-year-old Joana. Joana's photograph, taken as she lay propped up in her tiny cardboard coffin, her eyes open, hung on a wall next to one of Nailza and Zé Antonio taken on the day they eloped.

Nailza could barely remember the other infants and babies who came and went in close succession. Most had died unnamed and were hastily baptized in their coffins. Few lived more than a month or two. Only Joana, properly baptized in church at the close of her first year and

placed under the protection of a powerful saint, Joan of Arc, had been expected to live. And Nailza had dangerously allowed herself to love the little girl.

In addressing the dead child, Nailza's voice would range from tearful imploring to angry recrimination: "Why did you leave me? Was your patron saint so greedy that she could not allow me one child on this earth?" Zé Antonio advised me to ignore Nailza's odd behavior, which he understood as a kind of madness that, like the birth and death of children, came and went. Indeed, the premature birth of a stillborn son some months later "cured" Nailza of her "inappropriate" grief, and the day came when she removed Joana's photo and carefully packed it away.

More than fifteen years elapsed before I returned to the Alto do Cruzeiro, and it was anthropology that provided the vehicle of my return. Since 1982 I have returned several times in order to pursue a problem that first attracted my attention in the 1960s. My involvement with the people of the Alto do Cruzeiro now spans a quarter of a century and three generations of parenting in a community where mothers and daughters are often simultaneously pregnant.

The Alto do Cruzeiro is one of three shantytowns surrounding the large market town of Bom Jesus in the sugar plantation zone of Pernambuco in Northeast Brazil, one of the many zones of neglect that have emerged in the shadow of the now tarnished economic miracle of Brazil. For the women and children of the Alto do Cruzeiro the only miracle is that some of them have managed to stay alive at all.

The Northeast is a region of vast proportions (approximately twice the size of Texas) and of equally vast social and developmental problems. The nine states that make up the region are the poorest in the country and are representative of the Third World within a dynamic and rapidly industrializing nation. Despite waves of migrations from the interior to the teeming shantytowns of coastal cities, the majority still live in rural areas on farms and ranches, sugar plantations and mills.

Life expectancy in the Northeast is only forty years, largely because of the appallingly high rate of infant and child mortality. Approximately one million children in Brazil under the age of five die each year. The children of the Northeast, especially those born in shantytowns on the periphery of urban life, are at a very high risk of death. In these areas, children are born without the traditional protection of breast-feeding, subsistence gardens, stable marriages, and multiple adult caretakers that exists in the interior. In the hillside shantytowns that spring up around cities or, in this case, interior market towns, marriages are brittle, single parenting is the norm, and women are frequently forced into the shadow economy of domestic work in the homes of the rich or into unprotected and oftentimes "scab" wage labor on the surrounding sugar plantations, where they clear land for planting and weed for a pittance, sometimes less than a dollar a day. The women of the Alto may not bring their babies with them into the homes of the wealthy, where the often-sick infants are considered sources of contamination, and they cannot carry the little ones to the riverbanks where they wash clothes because the river is heavily infested with schistosomes and other deadly parasites. Nor can they carry their young children to the plantations, which are often several miles away. At wages of a dollar a day, the women of the Alto cannot hire baby sitters. Older children who are not in school will sometimes serve as somewhat indifferent caretakers. But any child not in school is also expected to find wage work. In most cases, babies are simply left at home alone, the door securely fastened. And so many also die alone and unattended.

Bom Jesus da Mata, centrally located in the plantation zone of Pernambuco, is within commuting distance of several sugar plantations and mills. Consequently, Bom Jesus has been a magnet for rural workers forced off their small subsistence plots by large landowners wanting to use every available piece of land for sugar cultivation. Initially, the rural migrants to Bom Jesus were squatters who were given tacit approval by the mayor to put up temporary straw huts on each of the three hills overlooking the town. The Alto do Cruzeiro is the oldest, the largest, and the poorest of the shantytowns. Over the past three decades many of the original migrants have become permanent residents, and the primitive and temporary straw huts have been replaced by small homes (usually of two rooms) made of wattle and daub, sometimes covered with plaster. The more affluent residents use bricks and tiles. In most Alto homes, dangerous kerosene lamps have been replaced by light bulbs. The once tattered rural garb, often fashioned from used sugar sacking, has likewise been replaced by store-bought clothes, often castoffs from a wealthy *patrão* (boss). The trappings are modern, but the hunger, sickness, and death that they conceal are traditional, deeply rooted in a history of feudalism, exploitation, and institutionalized dependency.

My research agenda never wavered. The questions I addressed first crystallized during a veritable "die-off" of Alto babies during a severe drought in 1965. The food and water shortages and the political and economic chaos occasioned by the military coup were reflected in the handwritten entries of births and deaths in the dusty, yellowed pages of the ledger books kept at the public registry office in Bom Jesus. More than 350 babies died in the Alto during 1965 alone—this from a shantytown population of little more than 5,000. But that wasn't what surprised me. There were reasons enough for the deaths in the miserable conditions of shantytown life. What puzzled me was the seeming indifference of Alto women to the death of their infants, and their willingness to attribute to their own tiny offspring an aversion to life that made their death seem wholly natural, indeed all but anticipated.

Although I found that it was possible, and hardly difficult, to rescue infants and toddlers from death by diarrhea and dehydration with a simple sugar, salt, and water solution (even bottled Coca-Cola worked fine), it was more difficult to enlist a mother herself in the rescue of a child she perceived as ill-fated for life or better off dead, or to convince her to take back into her threatened and besieged home a baby she had already come to think of as an angel rather than as a son or daughter.

I learned that the high expectancy of death, and the ability to face child death with stoicism and equanimity, produced patterns of nurturing that differentiated between those infants thought of as thrivers and survivors and those thought of as born already "wanting to die." The survivors were nurtured, while stigmatized, doomed infants were left to die, as mothers say, a mingua, "of neglect." Mothers stepped back and allowed nature to take its course. This pattern, which I call mortal selective neglect, is called passive infanticide by anthropologist Marvin Harris. The Alto situation, although culturally specific in the form that it takes, is not unique to Third World shantytown communities and may have its correlates in our own impoverished urban communities in some cases of "failure to thrive" infants.

I use as an example the story of Zezinho, the thirteen-month-old toddler of one of my neighbors, Lourdes. I became involved with Zezinho when I was called in to help Lourdes in the delivery of another child, this one a fair and robust little tyke with a lusty cry. I noted that while Lourdes showed great interest in the newborn, she totally ignored Zezinho who, wasted and severely malnourished, was curled up in a fetal position on a piece of urine- and feces-soaked cardboard placed under his mother's hammock. Eyes open and vacant, mouth slack, the little boy seemed doomed.

When I carried Zezinho up to the community day-care center at the top of the hill, the Alto women who took turns caring for one another's children (in order to free themselves for part-time work in the cane fields or washing clothes) laughed at my efforts to save Zé, agreeing with Lourdes that here was a baby without a ghost of a chance. Leave him alone, they cautioned. It makes no sense to fight with death. But I did do battle with Zé, and after several weeks of force-feeding (malnourished babies lose their interest in food), Zé began to succumb to my ministrations. He acquired some flesh across his taut chest bones, learned to sit up, and even tried to smile. When he seemed well enough, I returned him to Lourdes in her miserable scrap-material lean-to, but not without guilt about what I had done. I wondered whether returning Zé was at all fair to Lourdes and to his little brother. But I was busy and washed my hands of the matter. And Lourdes did seem more interested in Zé now that he was looking more human.

When I returned in 1982, there was Lourdes among the women who formed my sample of Alto mothers—still struggling to put together some semblance of life for a now grown Zé and her five other surviving children. Much was made of my reunion with Zé in 1982, and everyone enjoyed retelling the story of Zé's rescue and of how his mother had given him up for dead. Zé would laugh the loudest when told how I had had to force-feed him like a fiesta turkey. There was no hint of guilt on the part of Lourdes and no resentment on the part of Zé. In fact, when questioned in private as to who was the best friend he ever had in life, Zé took a long drag on his cigarette and answered without a trace of irony, "Why my mother, of course!" "But of course," I replied.

Part of learning how to mother in the Alto do Cruzeiro is learning when to let go of a child who shows that it "wants" to die or that it has no "knack" or no "taste" for life. Another part is learning when it is safe to let oneself love a child. Frequent child death remains a powerful shaper of maternal thinking and practice. In the absence of firm expectation that a child will survive, mother love as we conceptualize it (whether in popular terms or in the psychobiological notion of maternal bonding) is attenuated and delayed with consequences for infant survival. In an environment already precarious to young life, the emotional detachment of mothers toward some of their babies contributes even further to the spiral of high mortality—high fertility in a kind of macabre lock-step dance to death.

The average woman of the Alto experiences 9.5 pregnancies, 3.5 child deaths, and 1.5 still-births. Seventy percent of all child deaths in the Alto occur in the first six months of life, and 82 percent by the end of the first year. Of all deaths in the community each year, about 45 percent are of children under the age of five.

Women of the Alto distinguish between child deaths understood as natural (caused by diarrhea and communicable diseases) and those resulting from sorcery, the evil eye, or other magical or supernatural afflictions. They also recognize a large category of infant deaths seen as fated and inevitable. These hopeless cases are classified by mothers under the folk terminology "child sickness" or "child attack." Women say that there are at least fourteen different types of hopeless child sickness, but most can be subsumed under two categories— chronic and acute. The chronic cases refer to infants who are born small and wasted. They are deathly pale, mothers say, as well as weak and passive. They demonstrate no vital force, no liveliness. They do not suck vigorously; they hardly cry. Such babies can be this way at birth or they can be born sound but soon show no resistance, no "fight" against the common crises of infancy: diarrhea, respiratory infections, tropical fevers.

The acute cases are those doomed infants who die suddenly and violently. They are taken by stealth overnight, often following convulsions that bring on head banging, shaking, grimacing, and shrieking. Women say it is horrible to look at such a baby. If the infant begins to foam at the mouth or gnash its teeth or go rigid with its eyes turned back inside its head, there is absolutely no hope. The infant is "put aside"—left alone—often on the floor in a back room, and allowed to die. These symptoms (which accompany high fevers, dehydration, third-stage malnutrition, and encephalitis) are equated by Alto women with madness, epilepsy, and worst of all, rabies, which is greatly feared and highly stigmatized.

Most of the infants presented to me as suffering from chronic child sickness were tiny, wasted famine victims, while those labeled as victims of acute child attack seemed to be infants suffering from the deliriums of high fever or the convulsions that can accompany electrolyte imbalance in dehydrated babies.

Local midwives and traditional healers, praying women, as they are called, advise Alto women on when to allow a baby to die. One midwife explained: "If I can see that a baby was born unfortuitously, I tell the mother that she need not wash the infant or give it a cleansing tea. I tell her just to dust the infant with baby powder and wait for it to die." Allowing nature to take its course is not seen as sinful by these often very devout Catholic women. Rather, it is understood as cooperating with God's plan.

Often I have been asked how consciously women of the Alto behave in this regard. I would have to say that consciousness is always shifting between allowed and disallowed levels of awareness. For example, I was awakened early one morning in 1987 by two neighborhood children who had been sent to fetch me to a hastily organized wake for a two-month-old infant whose mother I had unsuccessfully urged to breast-feed. The infant was being sustained on sugar water, which the mother referred to as soro (serum), using a medical term for the infant's starvation regime in light of his chronic diarrhea. I had cautioned the mother that an infant could not live on soro forever.

The two girls urged me to console the young mother by telling her that it was "too bad" that her infant was so weak that Jesus had to take him. They were coaching me in proper Alto etiquette. I agreed, of course, but asked, "And what do you think?" Xoxa, the eleven-year-old, looked down at her dusty flip-flops and blurted out, "Oh, Dona Nanci, that baby never got enough to eat, but you must never say that!" And so the death of hungry babies remains one of the best-kept secrets of life in Bom Jesus da Mata.

Most victims are waked quickly and with a minimum of ceremony. No tears are shed, and the neighborhood children form a tiny procession, carrying the baby to the town graveyard where it will join a multitude of others. Although a few fresh flowers may be scattered over the tiny grave, no stone or wooden cross will mark the place, and the same spot will be reused within a few months' time. The mother will never visit the grave, which soon becomes an anonymous one.

What, then, can be said of these women? What emotions, what sentiments motivate them? How are they able to do what, in fact, must be done? What does mother love mean in this inhospitable context? Are grief, mourning, and melancholia present, although deeply repressed? If so, where shall we look for them? And if not, how are we to understand the moral visions and moral sensibilities that guide their actions?

I have been criticized more than once for presenting an unflattering portrait of poor Brazilian women, women who are, after all, themselves the victims of severe social and institutional neglect. I have described these women as allowing some of their children to die, as if this were an unnatural and inhuman act rather than, as I would assert, the way any one of us might act, reasonably and rationally, under similarly desperate conditions. Perhaps I have not emphasized enough the real pathogens in this environment of high risk: poverty, deprivation, sexism, chronic hunger, and economic exploitation. If mother love is, as many psychologists and some feminists believe, a seemingly natural and universal maternal script, what does it mean to women for whom scarcity, loss, sickness, and deprivation have made that love frantic and robbed them of their grief, seeming to turn their hearts to stone?

Throughout much of human history—as in a great deal of the impoverished Third World today—women have had to give birth and to nurture children under ecological conditions and social arrangements hostile to child survival, as well as to their own well-being. Under circumstances of high childhood mortality, patterns of selective neglect and passive infanticide may be seen as active survival strategies.

They also seem to be fairly common practices historically and across cultures. In societies characterized by high childhood mortality and by a correspondingly high (replacement) fertility, cultural practices of infant and childcare tend to be organized primarily around survival goals. But what this means is a pragmatic recognition that not all of one's children can be expected to live. The nervousness about child survival in areas of northeast Brazil, northern India, or Bangladesh, where a 30 percent or 40 percent mortality rate in the first years of life is common, can lead to forms of delayed attachment and a casual or benign neglect that serves to weed out the worst bets so as to enhance the life chances of healthier siblings, including those yet to be born. Practices similar to those that I am describing have been recorded for parts of Africa, India, and Central America.

Life in the Alto do Cruzeiro resembles nothing so much as a battlefield or an emergency room in an overcrowded inner city public hospital. Consequently, morality is guided by a kind of "lifeboat ethics," the morality of triage. The seemingly studied indifference toward the suffering of some of their infants, conveyed in such sayings as "little critters have no feelings," is understandable in light of these women's obligation to carry on with their reproductive and nurturing lives.

In their slowness to anthropomorphize and personalize their infants, everything is mobilized so as to prevent maternal overattachment and, therefore, grief at death. The bereaved mother is told not to cry, that her tears will dampen the wings of her little angel so that she cannot fly up to her heavenly home. Grief at the death of an angel is not only inappropriate, it is a symptom of madness and of a profound lack of faith.

Infant death becomes routine in an environment in which death is anticipated and bets are hedged. While the routinization of death in the context of shantytown life is not hard to understand, and quite possible to empathize with, its routinization in the formal institutions of public life in Bom Jesus is not as easy to accept uncritically. Here the social production of indifference takes on a different, even a malevolent cast.

In a society where triplicates of every form are required for the most banal events (registering a car, for example), the registration of infant and child death is informal, incomplete, and rapid. It requires no documentation, takes less than five minutes, and demands no witnesses other than office clerks. No questions are asked concerning the circumstances of the death, and the cause of death is left blank, unquestioned and unexamined. A neighbor, grandmother, older sibling, or common-law husband may register the death. Since most infants die at home, there is no question of a medical record.

From the registry office, the parent proceeds to the town hall, where the mayor will give him or her a voucher for a free baby coffin. The full-time municipal coffinmaker cannot tell you exactly how many baby coffins are dispatched each week. It varies, he says, with the seasons. There are more needed during the drought months and during the big festivals of Carnaval and Christmas and São Joao's Day because people are too busy, he supposes, to take their babies to the clinic. Record keeping is sloppy.

Similarly, there is a failure on the part of city-employed doctors working at two free clinics to recognize the malnutrition of babies who are weighed, measured, and immunized without comment and as if they were not, in fact, anemic, stunted, fussy, and irritated starvation babies. At best the mothers are told to pick up free vitamins or a health "tonic" at the municipal chambers. At worst, clinic personnel will give tranquilizers and sleeping pills to quiet the hungry cries of "sick-to-death" Alto babies.

The church, too, contributes to the routinization of, and indifference toward, child death. Traditionally, the local Catholic church taught patience and resignation to domestic tragedies that were said to reveal the imponderable workings of God's will. If an infant died suddenly, it was because a particular saint had claimed the child. The infant would be an angel in the service of his or her heavenly patron. It would be wrong, a sign of a lack of faith, to weep for a child with such good fortune. The infant funeral was, in the past, an event celebrated with joy. Today, however, under the new regime of "liberation theology," the bells of N. S. das Dores parish church no longer peal for the death of Alto babies, and no priest accompanies the procession of angels to the cemetery where their bodies are disposed of casually and without ceremony. Children bury children in Bom Jesus da Mata. In this most Catholic of communities, the coffin is handed to the disabled and irritable municipal gravedigger, who often chides the children for

one reason or another. It may be that the coffin is larger than expected and the gravedigger can find no appropriate space. The children do not wait for the gravedigger to complete his task. No prayers are recited and no sign of the cross made as the tiny coffin goes into its shallow grave.

When I asked the local priest, Padre Marcos, about the lack of church ceremony surrounding infant and childhood death today in Bom Jesus, he replied: "In the old days, child death was richly celebrated. But those were the baroque customs of a conservative church that wallowed in death and misery. The new church is a church of hope and joy. We no longer celebrate the death of child angels. We try to tell mothers that Jesus doesn't want all the dead babies they send him." Similarly, the new church has changed its baptismal customs, now often refusing to baptize dying babies brought to the back door of a church or rectory. The mothers are scolded by the church attendants and told to go home and take care of their sick babies. Baptism, they are told, is for the living; it is not to be confused with the sacrament of extreme unction, which is the anointing of the dying. And so it appears to the women of the Alto that even the church has turned away from them, denying the traditional comfort of folk Catholicism.

The contemporary Catholic Church is caught in the clutches of a double bind. The new theology of liberation imagines a kingdom of God on earth based on justice and equality, a world without hunger, sickness, or childhood mortality. At the same time, the church has not changed its official position on sexuality and reproduction, including its sanctions against birth control, abortion, and sterilization. The padre of Bom Jesus da Mata recognizes this contradiction intuitively, although he shies away from discussions on the topic, saying that he prefers to leave questions of family planning to the discretion and the "good consciences" of his impoverished parishioners. But this, of course, sidesteps the extent to which those good consciences have been shaped by traditional church teachings in Bom Jesus, especially by his recent predecessors. Hence, we can begin to see that the seeming indifference of Alto mothers toward the death of some of their infants is but a pale reflection of the official indifference of church and state to the plight of poor women and children.

Nonetheless, the women of Bom Jesus are survivors. One woman, Biu, told me her life history, returning again and again to the themes of child death, her first husband's suicide, abandonment by her father and later by her second husband, and all the other losses and disappointments she had suffered in her long forty-five years. She concluded with great force, reflecting on the days of Carnaval '88 that were fast approaching:

> No, Dona Nanci, I won't cry, and I won't waste my life thinking about it from morning to night. . . . Can I argue with God for the state that I'm in? No! And so I'll dance and I'll jump and I'll play Carnaval! And yes, I'll laugh and people will

wonder at a pobre like me who can have such a good time.

And no one did blame Biu for dancing in the streets during the four days of Carnaval— not even on Ash Wednesday, the day following Carnaval '88 when we all assembled hurriedly to assist in the burial of Mercea, Biu's beloved *casula*, her last-born daughter who had died at home of pneumonia during the festivities. The rest of the family barely had time to change out of their costumes. Severino, the child's uncle and godfather, sprinkled holy water over the little angel while he prayed: "Mercea, I don't know whether you were called, taken, or thrown out of this world. But look down at us from your heavenly home with tenderness, with pity, and with mercy." So be it.

The Cultural Nexus of Aka Father–Infant Bonding

Barry S. Hewlett

Despite a steady increase in the quantity and quality of studies of infants, young children and motherhood in various parts of the world (e.g., LeVine et al. 1994), we know relatively little about the nature of father–child relations outside of the U.S. and Western Europe (see Hewlett 1992 for some exceptions). In general, mother-oriented theories of infant and child development have guided cross-cultural research. The majority of these theories view the mother–infant relationship as the prototype for subsequent attachments and relationships (Ainsworth 1967, Bowlby 1969, Freud 1938, and Harlow 1961). According to Freud and Bowlby, for instance, one had to have a trusting, unconditional relationship with his or

Adapted for this text from Barry S. Hewlett, *Intimate Fathers: The Nature and Context of Aka Pygmy Paternal-Infant Care* (Ann Arbor: University of Michigan Press, 1991). Copyright © 1991 by the University of Michigan Press.

her mother in order to become a socially and emotionally adjusted adult. These influential theorists generally believed that the father's role was not a factor in the child's development until the Oedipal stage (3–5 years old). The field methods to study infancy reflected this theoretical emphasis on mother. Observations were either infant or mother-focused and conducted only during daylight hours; father-focused and evening observations were not considered. Also, standardized questionnaires and psychological tests were generally administered only to the mother. One consistent result from the cross-cultural studies was that fathers provided substantially less direct care to infants than mothers. In fact, all cross-cultural studies to date indicate that a number of other female caretakers (older female siblings, aunts, grandmothers) provide more direct care to infants than do fathers. Since fathers are not as conspicuous as mothers and other females during daylight hours researchers tend to emphasize a "deficit" model of fathers (Cole and Bruner 1974); that is, fathers are not around much and therefore do not contribute much to the child's development.

Given the paucity of systematic research outside of the U.S. on father's interactions with children, it is ironic that this variable (i.e., the degree of father vs. mother involvement with children) should be so consistently invoked as an explanatory factor in the literature. It is hypothesized to be related, for example, to gender inequality (Chodorow 1974), universal sexual asymmetry (Rosaldo and Lamphere 1974), and the origin of the human family (Lancaster and Lancaster 1987).

FATHER–INFANT BONDING

Bowlby's (1969) theory, mentioned above, suggested that an early secure attachment (or "bonding") between infant and caregiver (usually mother) was crucial for normal development. Lack of bonding between mother and infant led to the infant's protest, despair, detachment, and eventual difficulty in emotional and social development. Most studies of attachment have focused on mother–infant bonding, but an increasing number of studies in the U.S. and Europe have tried to understand if and when infants become attached to fathers. Numerous psychological studies now indicate that infants are attached to their fathers and that the infants become attached to fathers at about the same age as they do to mothers (8–10 months of age) (Lamb 1981). But how does this bonding take place if infant bonding to mother is known to develop through regular, sensitive, and responsive care? American fathers are seldom around to provide this type of care. The critical factor that has emerged in over 50 studies of primarily middle-class American fathers is vigorous play. The physical style of American fathers is distinct from that of American mothers, is evident three days after birth, and continues throughout infancy. The American data have been so consistent that some researchers have indicated a biological basis (Clarke-Stewart 1980). The idea

is that mother–infant bonding develops as a consequence of the frequency and intensity of the relationship, while father–infant bonding takes place because of this highly stimulating interaction. British, German, and Israeli studies generally support this hypothesis. This chapter examines the process of father–infant bonding among the Aka, a hunter–gatherer group living in the tropical forest of central Africa.

THE AKA

There are about 30,000 Aka hunter–gatherers in the tropical rain forests of southern Central African Republic and northern Congo-Brazzaville. They live in camps of 25–35 people and move camp every two weeks to two months. Each nuclear family has a hut, and each camp generally has 5–8 huts arranged in a circle. The circle of huts is about 12 meters in diameter and each hut is about 1.5 meters in diameter. Each hut has one bed of leaves or logs on which everyone in the family sleeps. The Aka have patriclans and many members of a camp belong to the same patriclan (generally a camp consists of brothers, their wives and children, and unrelated men who are doing bride service for the sisters of the men in camp). The Aka have high fertility and mortality rates: A woman generally has five to six children during her lifetime, and one-fifth of the infants die before reaching 12 months and 43 percent of children die before reaching 15 years.

Life in the camp is rather intimate. While the overall population density is quite low (less than one person per square kilometer), living space is quite dense. Three or four people sleep together on the same 4-feet-long by 2-feet-wide bed, and neighbors are just a few feet away. The 25–35 camp members live in an area about the size of a large American living room. The Aka home represents the "public" part of life, while time outside of camp tends to be relatively "private." This is the reverse of the American pattern (i.e., home is usually considered private). The camp is relatively young as half of the members of the camp are under 15 and most women have a nursing child throughout their childbearing years.

The Aka use a variety of hunting techniques, but net hunting, which involves men, women, and children, is the most important and regular hunting technique. Women generally have the role of tackling the game in the net and killing the animal. Game captured is eventually shared with everyone in camp. Some parts of the game animal are smoked and eventually traded to Bantu and Sudanic farmers for manioc or other domesticated foods. The Aka have strong economic and religious ties to the tropical forest. The forest is perceived as provider and called friend, lover, mother, or father.

Sharing and cooperation are pervasive and general tenets of Aka camp life. Food items, infant care, ideas for song and dance, and material items such as pots and pans are just some of the items that are shared daily in the camp. An Ngandu farmer describes Aka sharing:

> Pygmies [the Ngandu use the derogatory term Babinga to refer to the Aka] are people who stick together. Twenty of them are able to share one single cigarette. When a pygmy comes back with only five roots she shares them all. It is the same with forest nuts; they will give them out to everybody even if there are none left for them. They are very generous.

The Aka are also fiercely egalitarian. They have a number of mechanisms to maintain individual, intergenerational, and gender equality. The Ngandu villager mentioned above describes his concerns about Aka intergenerational egalitarianism:

> Young pygmies have no respect for their parents; they regard their fathers as their friends. . . . There is no way to tell whether they are talking to their parents because they always use their first names. Once I was in a pygmy camp and several people were sitting around and a son said to his father "Etobe your balls are hanging out of your loincloth" and everyone started laughing. No respect, none, none, none. . . . It's real chaos because there is no respect between father and son, mother and son or daughter. That's why pygmies have such a bad reputation, a reputation of being backward.

Three mechanisms that promote sharing and egalitarianism are prestige avoidance, rough joking and demand sharing. The Aka try to avoid drawing attention to themselves, even if they have killed an elephant or cured someone's life-threatening illness. Individuals who boast about their abilities are likely to share less or request more from others in the belief that they are better than others. If individuals start to draw attention to themselves, others in the camp will use rough and crude jokes, often about the boastful person's genitals, in order to get the individuals to be more modest about their abilities. Demand sharing also helps to maintain egalitarianism: if individuals like or want something (cigarettes, necklace, shirt) they simply ask for it, and the person generally gives it to them. Demand sharing promotes the circulation of scarce material goods (e.g., shoes, shirt, necklaces, spear points) in the camp.

Gender egalitarianism is also important. For instance, there are male and female roles on the net hunt, but role reversals take place daily and individuals are not stigmatized for taking the roles of the opposite sex. If one does the task poorly, regardless of whether it is a masculine or feminine task, then one is open to joking and teasing by others (e.g., when the anthropologist chases the game in the wrong direction).

The rough joking mentioned above is also linked to another feature of Aka culture— playfulness. There is no clear separation between "work" and "play" time. Dances, singing, net hunting, male circumcision, sorcery accusations all include humorous mimicking, practical jokes, and exaggerated storytelling. Aka life is informal because of egalitarianism and the playful activity that occurs throughout the day by both adults and children. Play is an integral part of both adult and child life and contributes to enhanced parent–child and adult–child communication. Parents and adults have an extensive repertoire of play, and can and do communicate cultural knowledge to children through their playful repertoire.

Greater ethnographic detail on the Aka can be found in Hewlett (1991) or Bahuchet (1985).

AKA INFANCY

The infant lives with a relatively small group of individuals related through his or her father (unless the infant is the first born in which case the family is likely to be in the camp of the wife for the purposes of bride service) and sleeps in the same bed as mother, father, and other brothers and sisters.

Cultural practices during infancy are quite distinct from those found in European and American cultures. Aka parents are indulgent as infants are held almost constantly, nursed on demand (breast-fed several times per hour), attended to immediately if they fuss, and are seldom, if ever, told "no! no!" if they misbehave (e.g., get into food pots, hit others, or take things from other children). An Aka father describes Aka parenting and contrasts it with parenting among his Ngandu farming neighbors:

> We, Aka look after our children with love, from the minute they are born to when they are much older. The villagers love their children only when they are babies. When they become children they get beaten up badly. With us, even if the child is older, if he is unhappy, I'll look after him, I will cuddle him.

Older infants are allowed to use and play with knives, machetes, and other "adult" items. They are allowed to crawl into a parent's lap while the parent is engaged in economic (e.g., butchering animal, repairing net) or leisure (e.g., playing a harp or drum) activity. While older infants are given considerable freedom to explore the house and camp, parents do watch infants to make sure they do not crawl into the fire.

Extensive multiple caregiving of 1- to 4-month-old infants (Hewlett 1989) exists, especially while the Aka are in the camp. Individuals other than mother (infant's father, brothers, sisters, aunts, uncles, grandmothers) hold the infant the majority of the time (60 percent) in this context, and the infant is moved to different people about seven times per hour. Mothers' holding increases to 85 percent and the transfer rate drops to two transfers per hour outside of the camp (i.e., on net hunt or in fields).

Infancy is very active and stimulating. Infants are taken on the hunt and are seldom laid down. They are held on the side of the caregiver rather than on the caregiver's back as in many farming communities so there are opportunities for caregiver–infant face-to-face interaction and communication. The infant can also breast feed by simply reaching for the mother's breast and can nurse while mother walks. While out on the net hunt the infant sleeps in the sling as the caregiver walks, runs, or sits.

THE STUDY

I started working with the Aka in 1973 so by the time I started the father–infant study in 1984 I was familiar with specific Aka families and Aka culture in general. Since I wanted to test some of the psychological hypotheses regarding father–infant relations, I incorporated psychological methods into my research. The quantitative psychological methods consisted of systematically observing 15 Aka families with infants from 6 A.M. to 9 P.M. (the observations focused either on the father or the infant). This enabled me to say precisely how much time Aka versus American fathers held or were near their infants and precisely describe how American versus Aka styles of interaction were similar or different. Informal discussions while on the net hunt and in camp were also utilized to develop structured interviews. Men and women, young and old, were asked about their feelings regarding relations with their mothers, fathers, and other caregivers.

The study focused on two domains important for trying to understand father–infant bonding: the degree of father involvement and mother's versus father's parenting style. For degree of father involvement I wanted to know: How often do fathers actually interact with their infants, how often are fathers available to their infants, if fathers are not involved with infants what other activities are they involved in, how do children characterize the nature of their involvement with their father? Questions regarding paternal versus maternal parenting style included: Are there distinctions between the mother's and the father's play behavior with their infants, do mothers and fathers hold their infants for different purposes, what do mothers and fathers do while they hold the infant, do infants show different types of attachment behavior to mothers and fathers, how do children view their mother's and father's parenting styles?

WHY ARE AKA FATHERS SO INVOLVED WITH THEIR INFANTS? THE CULTURAL NEXUS OF FATHER–INFANT BONDING

Although few cross-cultural studies of father–child relations have been conducted, Aka father involvement in infancy is exceptional, if not unique. Aka fathers are within an arm's reach (i.e., holding or within one meter) of their infant more than 50 percent of 24-hour periods. Table 1.1 demonstrates that Aka fathers hold their very young infants during the day at least five times more than fathers in other cultures, while Table 1.2 indicates Aka fathers are available to their infants at least three times more frequently than fathers in other cultures. American and European fathers hold their infants, on average, between 10 and 20 minutes per day (Lamb et al. 1987) while Aka fathers, on average, hold their infants about one hour during daylight hours and about 25 percent of the time after the sun goes down. At night fathers sleep with mother and infant, whereas American fathers seldom sleep with their infants. While Aka father care is extensive, it is also highly context dependent—fathers provide at least four times as much care while they are in the camp setting than they do while out of camp (e.g., out on the net hunt or in the villagers' fields). What factors influence this high level of paternal emotional and physical involvement among the Aka?

Aka father–infant bonding is embedded within a cultural nexus—it influences and is influenced by a complex cultural system. This brief overview describes some of the cultural facets linked to Aka father–infant bonding.

Like many other foragers, the Aka have few accumulable resources that are essential for survival. "Kinship resources," the number of brothers and sisters in particular, are probably the most essential "resource" for survival, but are generally established at an early age. Food resources are not stored or accumulated, and Aka males and females contribute similar percentages of calories to the diet. Cross-cultural studies have demonstrated that in societies where resources essential to survival can be accumulated or where males are the primary contributors to subsistence, fathers invest more time competing for these resources and, consequently, spend less time with their children. In contrast, where resources are not accumulable or men are not the primary contributors to subsistence, men generally spend more time in the direct care of their children. Katz and Konner (1981: 174) found that father–infant proximity (degree of emotional warmth and physical proximity) is closest in

Table 1.1 Comparison of Father Holding in Selected Foraging Populations

POPULATION	AGE OF INFANTS (MOS.)	FATHER HOLDING (PERCENT OF TIME)	SOURCE
Gidgingali	0–6	3.4	Hamilton (1981)
	6–18	3.1	
!Kung	0–6	1.9	West and Konner (1976)
	6–24	4.0	
Efe Pygmies	1–4	2.6	Winn et al. (1990)
Aka Pygmies	1–4	22.0	Hewlett (1991)
	8–18	14.0	

NOTE: All observations were made in a camp setting (Table from Hewlett 1991).

Table 1.2   **Comparison of Father Presence with Infants or Children among Selected Foraging and Farming Populations**

POPULATION	LOCATION	SUBSISTENCE	PERCENT TIME FATHER PRESENT/ IN VIEW	PRIMARY SETTING OF OBSERVATIONS	SOURCE
Gusii	Kenya	farming	10	house/yard & garden	1
Mixteca	Mexico	farming	9	house/yard	1
Ilocano	Philippines	farming	14	house/yard	1
Okinawan	Japan	farming	3	public places & house/yard	1
Rajput	India	farming	3	house/yard	1
!Kung	Botswana	foraging	30	camp	2
Aka Pygmies	Central African Republic	foraging	88	forest camp	3
Logoli	Kenya	farming	5	house/yard	4
Newars	Nepal	farming	7	house/yard	4
Samoans	Samoa	farming	8	house/yard	4
Carib	Belize	farming	3	house/yard	4
Ifaluk	Micronesia	farm-fish	13	house/yard	5

Sources (Table from Hewlett 1991):
1. Whiting and Whiting 1975
2. West and Konner 1976
3. Hewlett 1991
4. Munroe and Munroe 1992
5. Betzig, Harrigan, and Turke 1990

gathering-hunting populations (gathered foods by females are principal resources, meat is secondary) and most distant in cultures where herding or advanced agriculture is practiced. In the latter cultures, cattle, camels, and land are considered the essential accumulable resources necessary for survival. These findings are consistent with Whiting and Whiting's (1975) cross-cultural study of husband–wife intimacy. They found husband–wife intimacy to be greatest in cultures without accumulated resources or capital investments. While there are other factors to consider (the protection of resources and the polygyny rate), there is a strong tendency for fathers/husbands to devote more time to their children/wives if there are no accumulable resources.

Three additional factors seem to be especially influential in understanding the extraordinarily high level of Aka paternal care. First, the nature of Aka subsistence activity is rather unique cross-culturally. Usually mens' and womens' subsistence activities take place at very different locations. The net hunt and other subsistence activities, such as caterpillar collecting, involve men, women, and children. If men are going to help with infant care on a regular basis they have to be near the infant a good part of the day. The net hunt makes this possible. The net hunt also requires that men and women walk equal distances during the day. In most foraging societies, females do not travel as far from camp as males. Older siblings are not useful for helping their mothers because of the extensive labor involved in walking long distances with an infant. If a mother is to receive help on the net hunt, it needs to come from an adult. Most of the other adult females carry baskets full of food and have their own infants or young children to carry since fertility is high. Fathers are among the few alternative caregivers regularly available on the net hunt to help mothers. While fathers do carry infants on the net hunt, especially on the return from the hunt when the mothers' baskets are full of meat, collected nuts, and fruit, father–infant caregiving is much more likely to occur in the camp.

Another influential factor is the nature of husband–wife relations. The net hunt contributes substantially to the time husband and wife spend together and patterns the nature of that time spent together. Observations in the forest and village indicate husbands and wives are within sight of each other 46.5 percent of daylight hours. This is more time together than in any other known society, and it is primarily a result of the net hunt. This percentage of course increases in the evening hours. But, husbands and wives are not only together most of the day, they are actively cooperating on the net hunt. They have to know each other well to communicate and cooperate throughout the day. They work together to set up the family net, chase game into the net, butcher and divide the game and take care of the children. Husbands and wives help each other out in a number of domains, in part because they spend so much time together. Husband–wife relations are many-stranded; that is, social, economic, ritual, parenting, and leisure activities are shared and experienced in close proximity. When they return to camp the mother has a number of tasks—she collects firewood and water, and prepares the biggest meal of the day. The father has relatively few tasks to do after returning from the hunt. He may make string or repair the net, but he is available to help with infant care. He is willing to do infant care, in part, because of the many-stranded reciprocity between husband and wife. In many societies men have fewer tasks to do at the end of the day, while women have domestic tasks and prepare a meal. Men are available to help out with childcare, but seldom provide much assistance, in part, due to the more distant husband–wife relationship.

The third important factor in understanding Aka fathers' involvement with infants is father–infant bonding. Father and infant are clearly attached to each other. Fathers seek out their infants and infants seek out their fathers. Fathers end up holding their infants frequently because the infants crawl to, reach for, or fuss for their fathers. Fathers pick up their infants because they intrinsically enjoy being close to their infants.

They enjoy being with them and carry them in several different contexts (e.g., out in the fields drinking palm wine with other men).

While the factors described above are especially influential, other cultural factors also play a part. Gender egalitarianism pervades cultural beliefs and practices: Men do not have physical or institutional control over women, violence against women is rare or nonexistent, both women and men are valued for their different but complementary roles, there is flexibility in these gender roles, and holding infants is not perceived as being feminine or "women's work." Sharing, helping out, and generosity are central concepts in Aka life; this applies to subsistence and parenting spheres. Aka ideology of good and bad fathers reiterates the importance of father's proximity—a good father shows love for his children, stays near them, and assists mother with caregiving when her workload is heavy. A bad father abandons his children and does not share food with them. There is no organized warfare and male feuding is infrequent, so men are around camp and help with subsistence rather than being away at battle. Fertility is high, so most adult women have nursing infants and there are few other adult women around to help out. Finally, the Aka move their camps several times a year and consequently do not accumulate material goods that need to be defended.

The point here is that Aka father-infant relations have to be viewed in a complex cultural nexus. Some cultural factors are somewhat more influential than others—net hunting, husband–wife relations, for instance—but even these cultural features take place in a web of other cultural beliefs and practices that contribute to the intimate nature of Aka father–infant relations.

FATHER–INFANT BONDING IN THE AKA AND UNITED STATES

Over 50 studies of European and American fathers indicate that father's interactions with infants and young children are clearly distinguished from mother's interactions in that fathers are the vigorous rough and tumble playmates of infants and young children, while mothers are sensitive caregivers. The American literature suggests that this rough and tumble play is how infants become attached to fathers ("bond") and develop social competence (Lamb et al. 1987). The Aka father–infant study is not consistent with the American studies that emphasize the importance of father's vigorous play. Aka fathers rarely, if ever, engage in vigorous play with their infants; only one episode of vigorous play by a father was recorded during all 264 hours of systematic observation. Informal observations during more than 10 field visits over the last 20 years are also consistent with this finding. The quantitative data indicate that by comparison to mothers, Aka fathers are significantly more likely to hug, kiss, or soothe a fussy baby while they are holding the infant.

While Aka fathers do not engage in vigorous play with their infants, they are slightly more playful than mothers; fathers are somewhat more likely to engage in minor physical play (e.g., tickling) with their one- to four-month-old infants than are mothers. But characterizing the Aka father as the infant's playmate would be misleading. Other caretakers, brothers and sisters in particular, engage in play with the infant while holding much more frequently than fathers or mothers. Mothers have more episodes of play over the course of a day than fathers or other caretakers because they hold the infant most of the time. The Aka father–infant relationship might be better characterized by its intimate and affective nature. Aka fathers hold their infants more than fathers in any other human society known to anthropologists, and Aka fathers also show affection more frequently while holding than do Aka mothers.

So how can vigorous play be a significant feature in American studies of father–infant bonding, but not among the Aka? Four factors appear to be important for understanding the process of Aka father–infant bonding: familiarity with the infant; knowledge of caregiving practices (how to hold an infant, how to soothe an infant); the degree of relatedness to the infant; and cultural values and parental goals.

First, due to frequent father-holding and availability, Aka fathers know how to communicate with their infants. Fathers know the early signs of infant hunger, fatigue, and illness as well as the limits in their ability to soothe the infant. They also know how to stimulate responses from the infant without being vigorous. Unlike American fathers, Aka wait for infants to initiate interaction. Aka caregivers other than mothers and fathers are less familiar with the infants and the most physical in their play, suggesting a relationship between intimate knowledge of the infant's cues and the frequency of vigorous play while holding. Consistent with this is the finding that working mothers in the U.S. are more likely to engage in vigorous play than are stay-at-home mothers.

Second, knowledge of infant caregiving practices seems to play a role in determining how much play is exhibited in caretaker–infant interactions. Child caretakers were the most physical and the loudest (singing) in their handling of infants. Children were not restricted from holding infants, but they were closely watched by parents. While "other" caretakers were more playful than mothers or fathers, younger fathers and "other" caretakers were more physical than older ones, probably because they did not know how to handle and care for infants as well as adult caretakers.

A third factor to consider is the degree of relatedness of the caretaker to the infant. If vigorous play can assist in developing attachment, more closely related individuals may have a greater vested interest in establishing this bond than distantly related individuals. Attachment not only enhances the survival of the infant, but it can potentially increase the related caretaker's survival and fitness. Aka mothers and fathers establish attachment by their frequent caregiving; vigorous play is not necessary to establish affective saliency. Brothers and sisters, on the other hand, might establish this bond through physical play. Aka brothers and sisters, in fact, provided essentially all of the physical play the focal infants received; cousins and unrelated children were more likely to engage in face-to-face play with the infant instead of physical play.

Finally, cultural values and parental goals of infant development should be considered. American culture encourages individualistic aggressive competition; Aka culture values cooperation, nonaggression, and prestige avoidance (one does not draw attention to oneself even, for instance, if one kills an elephant). Apparently, Americans tolerate—if not actually encourage—aggressive rough-and-tumble types of play with infants. Also, due to the high infant mortality rate, the primary parental goal for Aka is the survival of their infants. The constant holding and immediate attention to fussing reflect this goal. In the United States, infant mortality rates are markedly lower and, as a result, parental concern for survival may not be as great. The Aka infant is taken away from a caretaker who plays roughly with the infant, in part because it could be seen as aggressive behavior, but also because the pervasive aim of infant care practices is survival of the infant, and rough-and-tumble play could risk the infant's safety.

These factors tentatively clarify why Aka fathers do not engage in vigorous play like American fathers, but do participate in slightly more physical play than Aka mothers (but not more than other caretakers). American fathers infrequently participate directly in infant care and consequently are not as familiar with infant cues. To stimulate interaction and (possibly) bonding, they engage in physical play. Aka brothers and sisters are also much less physical in their play with infants than American fathers (Aka never tossed infants in the air or swung them by their arms), again suggesting that Aka children know their infant brother or sister and the necessary infant caregiving skills better than American fathers. These observations are obviously speculative and need further empirical study.

Sociologists LaRossa and LaRossa (1981) also describe stylistic differences between American mothers' and fathers' interactions with their infants. They list a number of male–female role dichotomies that reflect different parenting styles. One distinction they make is role distance versus role embracement. Fathers are more likely to distance themselves from the parenting role while mothers are more likely to embrace the parenting role. American women generally want to remain in primary control of the children, and while fathers may show interest in caregiving, they are more likely to distance themselves from caregiving while embracing their roles as the breadwinners. LaRossa and LaRossa also suggest that fathers generally have low intrinsic value and relatively high extrinsic value, while mothers have the reverse.

> The intrinsic value of something or someone is the amount of sheer pleasure or enjoyment that one gets from experiencing an object or person. The extrinsic value of something or someone is the amount of social rewards (e.g., money, power, prestige) associated with having or being with the object or person. (64)

They use this dichotomy to explain why fathers are more likely to carry or hold an infant in public than in private. Fathers receive extrinsic rewards from those in public settings, while this does not happen in the home. According to LaRossa and LaRossa,

> Fathers will roughhouse with their toddlers on the living-room floor, and will blush when hugged or kissed by the one-year-olds, but when you really get down to it, they just do not have that much fun when they are with their children. If they had their druthers, they would be working at the office or drinking at the local pub. (65)

These role dichotomies may be useful for understanding American mother–father parenting styles, but they have limited value in characterizing Aka mother–father distinctions. Aka mothers and fathers embrace the parenting role. Generally, mothers and fathers want to hold their infants, and certainly they derive pleasure from infant interactions. As indicated earlier, fathers were in fact more likely to show affection while holding than mothers. Fathers also offered their nipples to infants who wanted to nurse, cleaned mucus from their infants' noses, picked lice from their infants' hair, and cleaned their infants after they urinated or defecated (often on the father). Fathers' caregiving did not appear any more or less perfunctory than mothers'. Aka fathers are not burdened with infant care; if a father does not want to hold or care for the infant he gives the infant to another person. Overall, Aka fathers embrace their parenting role as much as they embrace their hunting role.

The intrinsic–extrinsic role dichotomy does not fit well with Aka mother–father parenting styles either. Again, both Aka mothers and fathers place great intrinsic value and little extrinsic value on parenting. The fathers' intrinsic value is demonstrated above, but the lack of extrinsic value among the Aka can best be seen by comparing Aka and Ngandu fathers (the Ngandu are the horticulturalist trading partners of the Aka). When a Ngandu father holds his infant in public he is "on stage." He goes out of his way to show his infant to those who pass by, and frequently tries to stimulate the infant while holding it. He is much more vigorous in his interactions with the infant than are Aka men. The following experience exemplifies Ngandu fathers' extrinsic value towards their infants. An Ngandu friend showed me a 25-pound fish he had just caught, and I asked to take a photograph of him with his fish. He said fine, promptly picked up his nearby infant, and proudly displayed his fish and infant for the photograph. His wife was also nearby but was not invited into the photograph. Aka fathers, on the other hand, are matter-of-fact about their holding or transporting of infants in public places. They do not draw attention to their infants. Aka fathers also hold their infants in all kinds of social and economic contexts.

CONCLUSION

This paper has examined the cultural nexus of Aka father–infant bonding and has made some comparisons to middle-class American father–infant relations. American fathers are characterized by their vigorous play with infants, while Aka fathers are characterized by their affectionate and intimate relations with their infants. Aka infants bond with their fathers because they provide sensitive and regular care, whereas American infants bond to their fathers, in part, due to their vigorous play. The purpose of this paper is not to criticize American fathers for their style of interaction with their infants; physical play is important in middle-class American context because it is a means for fathers who are seldom around their infants to demonstrate their love and interest in the infant. Vigorous play may also be important to American mothers who work outside the home; studies indicate they are also more likely than stay-at-home mothers to engage in vigorous play with their infants. The Aka study does imply that father–infant bonding does not always take place through physical play, and it is necessary to explore a complex cultural nexus in order to understand the nature of father-infant relations.

Aka fathers are very close and affectionate with their infants, and their attachment processes, as defined in Western bonding theory, appear to be similar to that of mothers. While Aka mother– and father–infant relations are similar they are not the same. Fathers do spend substantially less time with infants than do mothers, and the nature of their interactions is different. Aka and American fathers bring something qualitatively different to their children; father's caregiving pattern is not simply a variation of mother's pattern. More research is needed on the unique features of father involvement so we can move away from a "deficit" model of fathering.

Finally, this paper identifies cultural factors that influence father–infant bonding; biological forces are not considered. This is unusual in that mother–infant bonding generally mentions or discusses the biological basis of mother's attachment to the infant. The release of prolactin and oxytocin with birth and lactation is said to increase affectionate feelings and actions toward the infant. These same hormones exist in men but endocrinologists generally believe they have no function in men. Is there a biology of fatherhood, or is motherhood more biological and fatherhood more cultural? This is a complex question as both men and women probably have evolved ("biological") psychological mechanisms that influence their parenting, but if one just focuses on endocrinology, few data exist on the endocrinology of fatherhood. For instance, Gubernick et al. (unpublished paper) found that men's testosterone levels decreased significantly two weeks after the birth of their children; the decrease was not linked to decline in sexual behavior, increased stress, or sleep deprivation. Another small study of American fathers indicated significant increases in plasma prolactin levels after fathers held their 3-month-old infants on their chest for 15 minutes (Hewlett and Alster, unpublished data). The few biological studies that do exist suggest that biology can and does influence fatherhood. More studies of the biocultural nexus of fatherhood are needed.

While biology probably influences both mothers' and fathers' parenting to some degree, this chapter has demonstrated that the cultural nexus is a powerful force that profoundly shapes the nature and context of father–infant bonding. Aka father–infant bonding takes place through regular and intimate (i.e., hugging, kissing, soothing) care while American father–infant bonding takes place through vigorous play. American fathers often do not know their infants very well and try to demonstrate their love and concern through vigorous play. American mothers that work outside the home also tend to be more vigorous with their infants. American fathers are not necessarily "bad" fathers because they do not do as much direct caregiving as the Aka fathers. Fathers around the world "provide" and enrich the lives of their children in diverse ways (e.g., physical and emotional security, economic well-being). The Aka data do suggest that there are alternative processes by which father–infant bonding can and does take place and that Americans and others might learn from this comparative approach as policy decisions about parental leave and other topics are considered.

REFERENCES

Ainsworth, M. D. S. 1967. *Infancy in Uganda: Infant Care and the Growth of Love*. Baltimore: Johns Hopkins Press.

Bahuchet, S. 1985. *Les Pygmées Aka et la Fôret Centrafricaine*. Paris: Selaf.

Betzig, L., A. Harrigan, and P. Turke. 1990. "Childcare on Ifaluk." *Zeitscrift fur Ethnologie* 114.

Bowlby, J. 1969. *Attachment and Loss Vol. 1: Attachment*. New York: Basic Books.

Chodorow, N. 1974. "Family Structure and Feminine Personality." In *Woman, Culture, and Society*, ed. Michelle Zimbalist Rosaldo and Louise Lamphere. Stanford, CA: Stanford University Press.

Clarke-Stewart, K. A. 1980. "The Father's Contribution to Children's Cognitive and Social Development in Early Childhood." In *The Father–Infant Relationship*, ed. S.A. Pedersen. New York: Praeger.

Cole, M., and J. S. Bruner. 1974. "Cultural Differences and Inferences about Psychological Processes." In *Culture and Cognition*, ed. J.W. Berry and P. R. Dasen. London: Methuen.

Freud, S. 1938. *An Outline of Psychoanalysis*. London: Hogarth.

Gubernick, D. J., C. M. Worthman, and J. F. Stallings. "Hormonal Correlates of Fatherhood in Men." Unpublished paper.

Hamilton, A. 1981. *Nature and Nurture: Aboriginal Child-Rearing in North-Central Arnhem Land*. Canberra: Australian Institute of Aboriginal Studies.

Harlow, H. F. 1961. "The Development of Affectional Patterns in Infant Monkeys." In *Determinants of Infant Behavior*, Vol. 1, ed. B. M. Foss. London: Methuen.

Hewlett, B. S. 1989. "Multiple Caretaking Among African Pygmies. *American Anthropologist* 91: 186–191.

———. 1991. *Intimate Fathers: The Nature and Context of Aka Pygmy Paternal-Infant Care*. Ann Arbor, MI: University of Michigan Press.

———. 1992 (ed.). *Father-Child Relations: Cultural and Biosocial Perspectives*. NY: Aldine de Gruyter.

Hewlett, B. S., and D. Alster. "Prolactin and Infant Holding among American Fathers." Unpublished manuscript.

Katz, M. M., and Melvin J. Konner. 1981. "The Role of Father: An Anthropological Perspective." In *The Role of Father in Child Development*, ed. Michael E. Lamb. New York: John Wiley and Sons.

Lamb, M. E., ed. 1981. *The Role of the Father in Child Development*, 2nd ed. New York: John Wiley & Sons.

Lamb, M. E., J. H. Pleck, E. L. Charnov, and J. A. LeVine. 1987. "A Biosocial Perspective on Paternal Behavior and Involvement." In *Parenting Across the Lifespan*, ed. J. B. Lancaster, J. Altmann, A. Rossi, L. R. Sherrod. Hawthorne, NY: Aldine.

Lancaster, J. B., and C. S. Lancaster. 1987. "The Watershed: Change in Parental-Investment and Family Formation Strategies in the Course of

Human Evolution." In *Parenting Across the Life Span*, ed. J. B. Lancaster, J. Altmann, A. S. Rossi, and L. R. Sherrod. Hawthorne, NY: Aldine.

LaRossa, R., and M. M. LaRossa. 1981. *Transition to Parenthood: How Infants Change Families*. Beverly Hills: Sage Publications.

LeVine, R. A., S. Dixon, S. LeVine, A. Richman, P. H. Leiderman, C. H. Keefer, and T. B. Brazelton. 1994. *Child Care and Culture: Lessons from Africa*. New York: Cambridge University Press.

Munroe, R. H., and R. L. Munroe. 1992. "Fathers in Children's Environments: A Four Culture Study." In *Father-Child Relations: Cultural and Biosocial Contexts*, Barry S. Hewlett, ed. New York: Aldine de Gruyter.

Rosaldo, M. Z., and L. Lamphere, eds. 1974. *Woman, Culture and Society*. Stanford, CA: Stanford University Press.

West, M. M., and M. J. Konner. 1976. "The Role of Father in Anthropological Perspective." In *The Role of the Father in Child Development*. 2nd ed., M. E. Lamb, ed. New York: John Wiley & Sons.

Whiting, B. B., and J. W. M. Whiting. 1975. *Children of Six Cultures*. Cambridge, MA: Harvard University Press.

Winn, S., G. A. Morelli, and E. Z. Tronick. 1990. "The Infant in the Group: A Look at Efe Caretaking Practices." In *The Cultural Context of Infancy*, J. K. Nugent, B. M. Lester, and T. B. Brazelton, eds. Norwood, NJ: Ablex.

II

Gender and Prehistory

A popular introductory archaeology text began its career thirty-four years ago with the title *Men of the Earth* (Fagan 1974). For the last twelve editions (Fagan 1977–2006) it has been called *People of the Earth*. This change is deliberate and illustrates a growing sensitivity on the part of archaeologists to the importance of considering the contribution of women, as well as men, to the history of our species (Adavasio, Soffer, and Page 2007; Ardren 2002; Claassen and Joyce 1997; Gero and Conkey 1992; Hays-Gilpin and Whitley 1998; Joyce 2000; Seifert 1991; Wright 1996; Wylie 1991, 1992). An archaeological focus on gender provides a lens for reassessing modern myths about the past that single out men as the prime movers of cultural change. As some archaeologists seek to reinstate women as agents and as subjects, widely held assumptions about "mankind" and "man's past" are challenged by a focus on women's involvement in production, politics, ritual performance, and the generation of symbol systems in past societies. In contrast to earlier archaeological orientations (see Hays-Gilpin and Whitley 1998 and Gero and Conkey 1991 for a review of archaeological approaches) an "engendered" archaeology proposes that the process of adaptation throughout human history has of necessity involved a collaborative effort between men and women. Those who advocate a feminist-informed archaeology have explored such issues as women's participation in the creation of wealth (for example, women's production of textiles or ceramics and power relations among craft producers), women's roles in the dynamics of state formation, representations of powerful women in prehistoric art in relation to gender inequality and identity, and women's roles in the development of agriculture (see Wright 1996 for a collection of articles representing a range of methodologies and theoretical orientations applied to the "archaeologies of gender"; also Spielmann 1995; Simon and Ravesloot 1995).

Questions of fundamental importance regarding the sexual division of labor in past societies can only be resolved from an archaeological perspective that includes explicit methods of identifying the material traces of women's political interests. Rather than assuming that it is simply a natural given that the "earliest human groups were conscious of and elaborated sex differences into differentially valued, gender-exclusive task groups," Spector and Whelan (1989: 73) suggest that an archaeology of gender needs to begin by raising questions about the origins of a sexual division of labor and by determining what gender differentiation might have accomplished among early human populations (Spector and Whelan 1989: 72–73; see also Ehrenberg 1989).

As Margaret W. Conkey (in this book) suggests, in the study of gender in archaeology, we are reminded of the importance of confronting presuppositions and values that guide our work, however "scientific" we presume our methodologies to be. Conkey outlines a number of challenges for future archaeological research. First, archaeologists must recognize and eliminate biased reconstructions of past gender roles that derive from our own cultural assumptions. Second, they must pay more attention to theories about gender in analyzing their data. Third, archaeologists need to use their data to make explicit inferences about men and women in prehistory. Finally, Conkey points out biases not only in analysis but also in the very practice of archaeology. Eliminating gender bias from archaeology, as Conkey suggests, will require a major commitment to the same critical reflection that has characterized other branches of anthropology. As Nelson and Kehoe (1990: 4) observe, "disentangling our culture-bound assumptions from the actual archaeological record will be a long and wrenching procedure."

Nelson's discussion of Upper Paleolithic "Venus" figurines in archaeology textbooks (1990) illustrates the potential for distortion in the archaeological record when cultural values affect archaeological analysis. She demonstrates that most textbooks convey the same ideological message in their treatment of Venus figurines—adult male humans are and have always been fascinated by women's bodies and view them as signs of fertility. The widely held assumption that Upper Paleolithic figurines possibly depicting human females are fertility fetishes is, according to Nelson, poorly founded. Feminist analysis of the figurines suggests alternative explanations regarding their production, functions, and symbolism, and serves as a warning that "reinforcing present cultural stereotypes by projecting them into the past allows whole generations of students to believe that our present gender constructs are eternal and unchanging" (Nelson 1990: 19; see also Rice 1991; Wright 1996: 9).

Similarly, J. M. Adavasio, Olga Soffer, and Jake Page (in this book) present a scenario representing the division of labor in a European village 26,000 years ago. Based on recent scholarship, they observe that it is now evident that female humans "have been the chief engine in the unprecedentedly high level of human sociability, were the inventors of the most useful of tools (called the String Revolution), have shared equally in the provision of food for human societies, almost certainly drove the human invention of language, and were the ones who created agriculture" (2007: 3). Like Nelson, they assess the meanings attributed to a famous figurine, which came to be known as the "Vestonice Venus." In contrast to the conventional views Nelson describes, Adavasio, Soffer, and Page note that it is most likely that this figurine was carved by a woman, probably the "priestess" who used it. They then turn to the important but overlooked "Fiber" or "String Revolution," referring to the gendered development of fiber arts (weaving, basketry, cordage). The String Revolution, they contend, is a technological breakthrough with profound effects on human destiny. Although ethnographic accounts of fiber arts among contemporary bands indicates that making things such as baskets, clothing, sandals, or other fiber items is not the exclusive prerogative of either sex, in such societies both men and women know the production techniques. Further, weaving is practiced primarily by women in the tribal world today. Thus they present their "default" position: most ceramics, weaving, basketry was done by women in the time frame of the Vestonice Venus, 26,000 years ago. Hence they conclude that the concept of gender, and some division of labor, was already in place at that time.

The provocative argument concerning the String Revolution reflects the dramatic changes in archaeology since the mid-1970s, as archaeologists have uncovered increasing evidence of women's work and women's roles in everyday social life. In an innovative exploration of gender, social organization, and settlement patterns, Galloway (1997) argues that ethnocentric bias has shaped archaeological interpretations of structures found in late prehistoric Southeastern Indian societies. She suggests that archaeologists have neglected the importance of menstrual houses in these societies and proposes that the search for evidence of menstrual practices is a direct route to finding women in the archaeological record. Menstrual seclusion may be an important correlate of social organization, indicating the probability of matrilineal kinship. Accordingly, investigation of menstrual structures may provide a means of testing for matriliny archaeologically. In spite of the likelihood that there are thousands of menstrual structures in the Southeast, so far none has been reliably reported from an archaeological context. Galloway argues that discomfort with the topic has produced its erasure from scientific discourse, and she urges archaeologists both to reinterpret existing data and search for new evidence to identify these "women's houses" and the artifactual evidence of ritual elements and requirements of daily life associated with them.

In an effort to better explain contemporary gender relations, archaeological evidence has offered a means of understanding the present by reconstructing our evolutionary past. Scholarly and public imaginations have been drawn to the possibility that archaeological data might document the existence of a matriarchal society in which women occupied a privileged position as rulers. If powerful women could be found in history or prehistory, this would serve as evidence that male dominance is not inevitable.

Myths of past matriarchy exist in both western and nonwestern societies. Nineteenth-century evolutionists such as J. J. Bachofen (1967) described a history of humankind that passed from a state of primitive communal marriages, through mother right, or a rule of women, to patriarchy. Similar myths of matriarchy have been recorded in several South American societies (Bamberger 1974: 266). According to Bamberger, these myths share a common theme, that of women's loss of power through moral failure. The myths describe a past society in which women held power; however, through their incompetence, the rule of women was eventually replaced by patriarchal leadership.

Rather than representing historical events, the myths of matriarchy serve as a tool to keep "woman" bound to her place. They reinforce current social relations by justifying male dominance (Bamberger 1974: 280). There is no historical or archaeological evidence of matriarchal societies in which women systematically and exclusively dominated men. In spite of the absence of such evidence the idea remains popular, precisely because it conveys the possibility of a future society characterized by female dominance that is reminiscent of the matriarchal past.

We can avoid projecting our common assumptions and wishful fantasies about gender roles in the past by paying more careful attention to a range of sources at our disposal in the archaeological record. The reconstruction of gender roles and relations in ancient societies may be facilitated by representations of women and men in burials, images, and written texts. The oldest writing tradition in the world is found in the cities of the Sumerian civilization in southern Iraq. Four-thousand-year-old literary texts pertaining to early Sumer portray women in supportive, nurturing roles, acting to further the interests of male political rulers or heroes (Pollock 1991). In some texts, women are also described as political officeholders, or queens. Pollock concludes that some women seem to have had significant political and economic power, although few of them were written about compared to the number of men in such positions whose lives were more fully recorded. Sumerian women also held offices in the temple hierarchy as priestesses; it is possible that these were the primary positions of power available to women. An informative example is that of the priestess Enheduanna, installed at Ur by her father King Sargon. Literary texts suggest that she acted to further her father's political ambitions as well as her own authority (Pollock 1991). These texts, as well as burials and images, suggest that Sumerian women were not pawns to be manipulated by men, but were able to attain positions of high status and power.

Similarly, recent access to Maya history by decipherment of glyphic texts on public monuments has shown that some royal women played politically central roles in their kingdoms. Hypogamy, or the marriage of higher-status women to lower-status men, insured the alliance of these lower-status men to higher-status men of their wives' families. Hypergamy, or the marriage of lower-status women to higher-status men, also occurred. More importantly, the women involved in marriage alliance and royal politics were anything but passive pawns in the games of men. Stanley Guenter and David Freidel (in this book) look at the lives and exploits of powerful Maya women, demonstrating that Maya royal women were important political players. The translation of glyphic texts has also shown that royal women can emerge as extraordinarily heroic figures and great politicians when their stories are known. Guenter and Freidel review the exploits of several Classic period royal women who had central roles in the unfolding history of their civilization. For example, they present the saga of one of these women, a queen at Yaxchilan, who rose to full partnership with her king in matters of war and statecraft and saw to it that her son succeeded to the throne despite the rivalry to a younger queen's child. The queen's success resulted not only from a forceful personality, but from religious and political currents in Maya culture that thrust women into the forefront of regional struggles for imperial power.

Whether as queens, daughters of kings, mothers of kings, or political envoys, Maya royal women wielded considerable power. The various forms of power exercised by these women suggest that although there were no matriarchies in the past, women could control important resources and influence the course of public events. Breakthroughs in the translation of Maya texts correlated with archaeological findings are now yielding important information relevant to gender relations and meanings among ancient royal Maya. Little is known about the lives of commoner women, whose exploits are less visible in texts and other representations. The limited information available on commoner Maya women highlights the need for innovative conceptual and methodological approaches to the archaeological record that will help reconstruct gender roles in past societies.

Conkey and Spector discuss the general problem of the prehistoric "archaeological invisibility" of women (1984: 5), which, they contend, is more the result of a false notion of objectivity and of the gender paradigms archaeologists use than of an inherent invisibility of such data (Conkey and Spector 1984: 6). Questions that would elicit information about prehistoric gender behavior or organization are too infrequently asked, while researchers "bring to their work preconceived notions about what each sex ought to do, and these notions serve to structure the way artifacts are interpreted"—for example, the presumption of linkages between projectile points with men and pots with women (Conkey and Spector 1984: 10). In contrast, goals for feminist archaeologies would include gender-inclusive reconstructions of past human behavior, the development of a specific paradigm for the study of gender, and an explicit effort to eliminate androcentrism in the content and mode of presentation of archaeological research (Conkey and Spector 1984: 15). As Brian Fagan has observed, "an engendered archaeology ventures into new territory, using innovative approaches to present the multiple voices of the past . . . " (2006: 23).

REFERENCES

Adavasio, J. M., O. Soffer, and J. Page. 2007. *The Invisible Sex. Uncovering the True Roles of Women in Prehistory*. Smithsonian Books. New York: Harper Collins.

Ardren, Traci. 2002. *Ancient Maya Women*. Lanham, MD: Rowman and Littlefield.

Bachofen, Johann. 1967. *Myth, Religion and Mother Right* [Die Mutterrecht 1861 orig.]. London: Routledge and Kegan Paul.

Bamberger, Joan. 1974. "The Myth of Matriarchy: Why Men Rule in Primitive Society." In Michelle Z. Rosaldo and Louise Lamphere (eds.). *Woman, Culture, and Society*, pp. 263–281. Stanford, CA: Stanford University Press.

Claassen, Cheryl, and Rosemary A. Joyce (eds.) 1997. *Women in Prehistory*. Philadelphia: University of Pennsylvania Press.

Conkey, Margaret W., and Janet Spector. 1984. "Archaeology and the Study of Gender." In Michael B. Schiffer (ed.). *Advances in Archaeological Method and Theory*, Vol. 7, pp. 1–29. New York: Academic Press.

Ehrenberg, Margaret. 1989. *Women in Prehistory*. Norman, Oklahoma: University of Oklahoma Press.

Fagan, Brian. 1974. *Men of the Earth*. Boston: Little, Brown and Co.

———. 2006. *People of the Earth*. Upper Saddle River, NJ: Prentice Hall.

Galloway, Patricia. 1997. "Where Have All the Menstrual Huts Gone? The Invisibility of Menstrual Seclusion in the Late Prehistoric Southeast." In Claussen, C. and R. Joyce (eds.). *Women in Prehistory: North America and Mesoamerica*, pp. 47–62. Philadelphia: University of Pennsylvania Press.

Gero, J. M., and Margaret W. Conkey (eds.). 1991. *Engendering Archaeology: Women in Prehistory*. Oxford, UK: Basil Blackwell.

Hays-Gilpin, K., and D. Whitley. 1998. *Reader in Gender Archaeology*. London: Routledge.

Joyce, Rosemary. 2000. *Gender and Power in Prehispanic Mesoamerica*. Austin: University of Texas Press.

Nelson, Sarah M. 1990. "Diversity of the Upper Paleolithic Venus Figurines and Archeological Mythology." In Sarah M. Nelson and Alice B. Kehoe (eds.). *Powers of Observation: Alternative Views in Archeology*, pp. 11–23. *Archeological Papers of the American Anthropological Association*, Number 2.

Nelson, Sarah M., and Alice B. Kehoe. 1990. "Introduction." In Sarah M. Nelson and Alice B. Kehoe (eds.). *Powers of Observation: Alternative Views in Archeology*, pp. 1–10. *Archeological Papers of the American Anthropological Association*, Number 2.

Pollock, Susan. 1991. "Women in a Men's World: Images of Sumerian Women." In Joan Gero and Margaret Conkey (eds.). *Engendering Archaeology: Women and Prehistory*. Pp. 366–388 Oxford: Basil Blackwell.

Rice, Patricia. 1991. "Prehistoric Venuses: Symbols of Motherhood or Womanhood?" *Journal of Anthropological Research* 37(4): 402–414.

Seifert, Donna J. (ed.). 1991. "Gender in Historical Archaeology." *Historical Archeology* (special issue) 25(4): 1–132.

Simon, Arleyn W., and John C. Ravesloot. 1995. "Salado Ceramic Burial Offerings: A Consideration of Gender and Social Organization." *Journal of Anthropological Research* 51(2): 103–124.

Spector, Janet D., and Mary K. Whelan. 1989. "Incorporating Gender into Archaeology Courses." In Sandra Morgen (ed.). *Gender and Anthropology: Critical Reviews for Research and Teaching*, pp. 65–95. Washington, DC: American Anthropological Association.

Spielmann, Katherine A. 1995. "Glimpses of Gender in the Prehistoric Southwest." *Journal of Anthropological Research* 51(2): 91–102.

Wright, Rita P. (ed.) 1996. *Gender and Archaeology*. Philadelphia: University of Pennsylvania Press.

Wylie, Alison, 1991. "Feminist Critiques and Archaeological Challenges." In D. Walde and N. Willows (eds.). *The Archaeology of Gender*, pp. 17–23. Calgary: The Archaeological Association of Calgary.

———. 1992. "The Interplay of Evidential Constraints and Political Interests: Recent Archaeological Research on Gender." *American Antiquity* 57(1): 15–35.

The Archaeology of Gender Today:
New Vistas, New Challenges

Margaret W. Conkey

The *entire village* left the next day in about 30 canoes, leaving us alone with the *women and children* in the abandoned houses.

> Levi-Strauss 1936, *as cited by Michard-Marshale and Ribery 1982, in Eichler and Lapointe 1985: 11.*

When we close our eyes and think about the human societies and individuals who lived thousands of years ago, what kinds of people do we "see"? What are they doing? What kinds of roles and relationships do we imagine? Is everyone clearly identifiable as either a man or a woman, or are there other social persons, as well? If one really thinks about this, it should be apparent that there must have been many different roles and relationships, ones that even shifted during the course of any one person's lifetime, or with varied circumstances. There must have been men and women of power, men with children, women as decision-makers, men making pots, women making stone tools, men and women working together in the fields or elsewhere, men in trance, and women as healers. And in many societies it was likely that there were other social persons; perhaps ritual undertakers who were neither "just" men or women, but those who served to mediate between the living and the dead (Hollimon 1997), or perhaps pre-adolescent young people who did not yet bear the social signifiers of any one more particularly gendered person (Joyce 2000a). Yes, we must recognize that a "two genders" system is not likely to have been everywhere and throughout time.

Yet all too often archaeological accounts, and especially the popular reconstructions of past societies that appear in magazines or coffee table books, suggest a much simpler picture: only men hunt while women gather plants or

hover in the background; the men are making the tools, and, if women are depicted at all, they are almost always the ones with children, carrying out a limited range of activities: bringing firewood or scraping hides (Gifford-Gonzalez 1993). Why do we have such simple and yet rather familiar kinds of reconstructions? Certainly part of the explanation is that, until relatively recently, archaeologists had not done much that explicitly asked about gender, yet we had developed models or reconstructions that implicate or involve gender. These reconstructions derive from a variety of problematic sources: from ethnographic accounts that are gender-biased (such as the opening quote from Levi-Strauss) or from the beliefs that twentieth century (mostly western, white, male) archaeologists hold about gender, about men and women, about sexuality and about the division of labor, and about how prehistoric societies "worked" and changed.

We are all, of course, understandably susceptible to our own cultural ideals, ideas, and ideologies, although its not very anthropological to just dismiss certain general activities from being plausible—such as women performing as ritual artists in a past society—based on our presuppositions and cultural biases and beliefs. Most North American archaeologists have taken somewhat longer to be as reflexive and self-critical about this than some of their anthropological colleagues.

Thus, to think about the people of prehistoric societies and to think about their gender roles, gender ideologies, engendering practices, and gender relations raises several archaeological challenges. First, there is the challenge of recognizing and stripping away as much as possible the biased or implied gender reconstructions. It has been said about the study of gender in archaeology that it is not so much a matter of adding gender but of re-gendering the narratives or re-thinking gender. Second, there is the matter of understanding more explicitly what gender is about so we can develop theories of gender—or, as some would argue, theories about identity and difference—that are useful in archaeological research. Third, there is the challenge of making explicit inferences about gender, and about men and women, using archaeological data to help answer questions concerning what might have happened in prehistory and in the historical past. For some, this is a methodological challenge: after all, how can we infer gender and social relations if we cannot "see" the people in action, or talk to them about what their lives are like, what their rituals and symbols might mean, or how they conceptualize what might be "gender" and other aspects of personal identity and social practice?

While archaeologists clearly came late to the field of gender studies and to using insights from feminist theory, the past fifteen years have been explosive in the amount and diversity of studies and literature that explicitly take up aspects of gender in the human past. The first major paper that reviewed archaeology and the study of gender (Conkey and Spector 1984) came more than ten years after the first major books in sociocultural anthropology, but even then it was clear that archaeological accounts were already "saturated" with gender, albeit accounts that were androcentric (male-centered). Furthermore, these were accounts with a delimited notion of "gender," one that considered gender to be simply another variable or an attribute that could be straightforwardly lined up with being male or being female, rather than the current views that approach gender as a much more fluid, complex, even performative process that is entangled with other aspects of social personhood. Ten years ago, one might have said that at least half of the task of thinking about men and women in prehistory was to question the gendered accounts that pervaded our reconstructions of past societies. And while today we must still be very attentive to the ways in which androcentric (male-centered) and gynecentric (female-centered) accounts are perpetuated, there are, nonetheless, many explicit archaeologies of gender and abundant archaeological

studies that have taken on critical and insightful analyses of all sorts of social practices and processes—from craft-specializations, to rock art, to trading systems, to mortuary practices, to queenships, among others—with an explicit concern for their gendered natures and gendered effects.

Twenty years ago, it would have been a challenge to "find" many women in our accounts of the prehistoric past, or, if there, they were usually depicted in a passive way: they were rarely the ones who had made or used the "fancy" ritual objects, even if the objects had been found in a female's grave (Winters 1968). Indeed, the first impulse of a gender-aware archaeology was to "find" the women of the past who had been missing, to make women visible. Today, there are dozens of studies about women and prehistory, women in prehistory, women and production in prehistory. But there are also studies that have pushed archaeological scholarship in other directions as well: archaeologies of sexuality, of mothering, of childhood, of gender transformations, and of the inter-sectionalities of gender with other dimensions of identity, such as race, class, and ethnicity. Many of these studies have taken up topics that were unimagined by the scholars who first proposed a more gender sensitive, critical and feminist-informed archaeology, but this is a good indicator of a healthy and robust field of inquiry.

In the following brief essay, I will try to give something of a historical account of how, despite the many challenges, the archaeological study of gender has come to be so robust and so prevalent in contemporary archaeology. As one author has noted, in referring to the 1991 collection of papers on engendering archaeology (Gero and Conkey 1991), this was "possibly the most influential book published on archaeological theory in the last decade" (Johnson 1999). That the archaeological study of gender could "come from behind" with such success is a testimony to the ways in which dozens of scholars have succeeded in not just providing compelling critiques of previous archaeological work but primarily by engaging in theoretically-informed and empirically-substantiated ways with archaeological materials that can allow valid and insightful inferences about many dimensions of "gender" in the human past.

In writing a short essay like this more than ten years ago (Conkey 1992), the main headings for the essay were: "Challenging Gender Bias" and "Making Gender Explicit in Archaeological Research." Here the two headings will be: "Why an Archaeology of Gender has Emerged" and "Why Gender Matters." In both sections, the challenges that have been faced and that archaeologists continue to grapple with will be highlighted. But one thing is for sure, not only has the concern for gender in archaeological studies opened all sorts of perspectives on the human past, but also, it has promoted (if not initiated) a genuine concern with the everyday lives, the on-the-ground *people* of the past instead of the more abstract concerns with prehistoric "cultural systems" "groups" or "societies."

WHY AN ARCHAEOLOGY OF GENDER HAS EMERGED

Although it was not immediately apparent to most archaeologists of the 1970s, just a little bit of critical work made it painfully obvious that our archaeological accounts were androcentric, highlighting topics of research that were gendered male in contemporary societies, such as technological innovations and achievements, politics and rulers, warfare and conquest. Hunting (by males) was said to have "caused" the evolutionary success of humans as a species, and the "male-provisioning" of stay-at-home females with children was pushed back to our earliest hominid ancestors (Lovejoy 1981), millions of years ago. At a more subtle level, the ways in which archaeologists represented the males and females of the past was readily shown to be androcentric as well. Men were described with more detail and in more active terms, using active verbs, while women, if portrayed or mentioned, were presented as passive, and by the use of more passive language.

As the substantive critiques of archaeological accounts accumulated, and as studies of language, of the illustrations used to show the people of the past, and of the preferred research topics pointed out all sorts of biases and omissions, over and over again, no one could deny that we had been producing differential representations of men and women in the human past. Our accounts were very archaeo-*logical* because they "made sense" and were logical, given, of course, a certain specific western male-centered point-of-view. Furthermore, by ascribing considerable antiquity to such things as a sex-based division of labor—with active risk-taking adventurous males, and passive, "home-making," maternally-restricted females—these social relations and arrangements were legitimated and naturalized. Even though it was admitted that women might have had, for example, more to do, as a group, with plants (as in "woman the gatherer"), when it came to explaining the "origins of agriculture"—considered to be one of the most significant transformations in human history—some scholars went to great lengths to disassociate women from the acts and processes of plant domestication (Watson and Kennedy 1991), suggesting, for example, that (male) shamans cultivated the gourds they needed for their rattles, or that the plant seeds that accumulated in refuse heaps around living sites basically domesticated themselves.

It became clear that bias can creep into archaeological (and other) accounts when the analysts do not consciously reflect upon their assumptions nor explicitly use some theoretical models about gender and social identity. Archaeology, like all other research, is influenced by and embedded in the social and political worlds within which it is practiced. There is now a very well established body of literature that shows how the values, cultural assumptions, and social contexts of the researchers can and do strongly affect the kind of science that is practiced; the production of knowledge is always situated (Haraway 1988). All sciences are social; every fact has a factor, a maker, who is a person of a certain identity, a certain nationality, race, class, gender, ethnicity, status, experience and perspective within their profession or field of research. In addition to the substantive critiques of the archaeological accounts as primarily androcentric—and androcentric in many different dimensions—early studies in the practice of archaeology that looked at *who* it is that produces archaeological accounts showed the gender differentials and inequities that had favored males.

It is not just Indiana Jones who is the archaeologist-hero; children's drawings of who an archaeologist is confirm the deep-seated assumptions that men are archaeologists (and scientists). One archaeologist once said there were two types of archaeologists: the "hairy chested" or the "hairy chinned" (Ascher 1960). The statistics about who actually is an archaeologist would show that until well into the 1980's archaeology in North America was a predominantly white male enterprise. Although there has been a notable increase in women archaeologists (Zeder 1997), the ethnic diversification of the discipline is slower to take place. Throughout the past two decades of explosive work on gender in archaeology, concerns with equity issues have been side-by-side with the archaeological research. Of course, it was not merely the case that there were many more male archaeologists, but it was shown that they received many more of the major research grants to carry out the highly-valued fieldwork and excavation projects, while women archaeologists, as Gero (1994) has shown, had been more relegated to the "housework" of archaeology, such as in the lab, or carrying out the specialist studies rather than directing the "big dig." In other research, Gero has shown (1993) how the studies of American Paleoindian cultures have been dominated by male archaeologists and how the primary picture of Paleoindian lifeways is one that focuses almost exclusively on activities presumed to be male, especially the hunting of big game, with all the associated tools and strategies.

The point of studies like Gero's is not merely to "expose" and critique androcentric thinking and practice. It is, of course, a serious charge to note that the nature of archaeological (or any other) knowledge is directly created by the topics that are given research priority and that these can be influenced by the gender, race, class, ethnicity and nationality of the practitioners (and of those who fund archaeology). Rather, the point of such studies is to understand how such factors work, how they do or might bias our archaeological understandings, and to ask critical questions, such as "where *do* archaeologists get assumptions about gender and social life that underlie their interpretations?"

While these studies exposed bias and enhanced a critical reflection about archaeological research and the structure of the discipline, these alone were not enough to bring a genuine concern for gender into archaeology. In addition, of course, we needed to show that we could make inferences about gender, about men and women, and even about other gender systems and roles, that were based on archaeological evidence, or "evidential constraints" (Wylie 1992). This continues to be a genuine challenge. On the one hand, we could not just replace a male-centered view with a female-centered one, even though some of these have been crucial in revealing the biases of the androcentric accounts (e.g., Slocum 1975). On the other hand, this could not be accomplished by merely "adding women" to the story somehow, or by finding some methodological breakthrough that would enable us to "see" gender in the human past. Many researchers have made important and productive contributions by pursuing how we might attribute gender to certain artifacts or burials or living spaces (such as identifying men's houses, or women's work spaces, or women's artifacts), but others have argued that while this was an important step in the re-gendering of archaeology, there were many additional studies and perspectives to take.

For example, while using ethnohistoric information that associated Aztec women with cooking and weaving, Brumfiel (1991) not only made these women more "visible" in the archaeology by drawing on relevant texts and not on our modern assumptions about women's work, but she also considered the ways in which women's labor was being used and deployed in the service of the functioning of the Aztec state. The required cloth tribute, it appears, was provided either directly by women weavers or indirectly by those women who purchased cloth using the funds they raised by selling large amounts of food at the markets, as inferred by the large size of the cooking vessels in archaeological contexts. For Brumfiel, the question at hand is not so much that of doing a remedial archaeology that makes "women visible" but how do systems of social inequality work and how do they draw upon and structure the daily and gendered practices of local people?

Within twenty years or less, the literature that has critiqued gender biases, made women visible, and inquired into the gendered nature of past human cultural lives and processes is rich and diverse: studies have looked at rock art sites as likely female initiation sites, or as bearing heretofore undiscussed images that relate to women's mythologies and social statuses (Hays-Gilpin 2003); all sorts of aspects of gendered power relations have been identified and discussed in a wide variety of past societies (e.g., in Sweely 1999); human skeletal remains have been used to make valid inferences about gendered work practices (e.g., Peterson 2002), and, for example, about violence and skeletal trauma among women, men and "other genders" in the archaeological record of the northern Plains (USA) (Hollimon 2001). The ambiguity of gender in many prehistoric settings (e.g., Klein 2001; Crass 2001; Schmidt 2000) or at certain points in human lifecycles (Joyce 1996, 2001) has shown how we can not really look only for "men" or "women"; rather that gender is more of a process (always being performed, always in the process of becoming) or a relation (one "becomes" gendered in the context of relationships to others or to certain cultural events and practices) than a stable, unchanging given "fact" of life. But this is to jump ahead a bit to talk about why gender matters in our archaeological accounts.

The overall trajectory of gender research in archaeology, then, over the past few decades has been first, to critique our biased accounts and the disciplinary practices of archaeology that might have promoted or at least tolerated such biases. This work must still go on, but we have been building on this necessary foundation. The next major spurt of research was to indeed "make women visible," given that the single most apparent gender bias was against the active presence of women in the human past. Many studies for many parts of the world are still concerned with "finding" women and demonstrating not only their presence but their active contributions to the archaeological record—their tools, spaces, accomplishments—and thus, to the human societies of the past. But in addition, what this quest has brought forth has been a spate of all sorts of new questions, new perspectives, and perhaps even some new archaeologies, both in terms of what questions we ask, what accounts we can give of the human past and various events, and how we therefore "do" archaeology.

As one archaeologist once noted, when he had the "ah ha" experience of realizing that gender was a crucial aspect of human life that, as an explicit and theoretically informed concept, had been quite missing from archaeology, much—he actually said "most"—of the archaeological record must have been in all or in large part the work of women, especially when one is working with the remains of residences, work patios, ceramics, and such. While we no longer can assume that "the domestic" exists as a separate space (as had been the case among Victorian societies and later anthropologists, see Lamphere, this volume, and Rosaldo 1980), there is no doubt that the hearths, the residential refuse, and many of the day-to-day activities of human societies that were carried out in the sites that are most often more visible to and more substantial in contents for archaeologists most likely contain evidence of gendered work and gendered life, often gendered predominantly female. When we have very complete archaeological records due to exceptional preservation (e.g., Hamlin 2001), we can get a much more nuanced understanding of the various activities and tasks carried out at sites of everyday life, including the recognition of not just "men" and "women" but also sub-adults, children, and even infants. In fact, if there is one major contribution of a gender-sensitive archaeology, it has been to augment and expand our understandings of everyday life, and the micro-scale level of archaeology. When added to the often prevalent interests in macro-scale archaeology that seeks to understand large scale cultural processes, such as population expansions, state-formation, or the origins of certain technologies (metals, agriculture), this refined micro-scale archaeology and archaeology of the everyday makes for a more complete archaeology, a veritable multi-scalar archaeology.

WHY GENDER MATTERS

Just as we note that social and political concerns can affect our science and our anthropology, couldn't it be said that this robust interest in gender and in reclaiming women as active agents in the making of culture and culture history is primarily a political and social act, set in the wake of the second and third wave feminist movements of western society? Is this archaeology of gender of such interest because gender issues are (or at least ought to be, given persistent inequities) among some of more important and widespread interests of our times, in our societies? Perhaps this is partly true, and, to the extent that our research has almost always been influenced by what our interests are and what resonates with our concerns and social needs are, then the engagement with, and even the passion for an engendered archaeology can be accounted for in terms of our present-day interests. Is it no surprise that, for the most part, the scholars who have really focused on gender in archaeology have been women? Does this, however, tend to make this subfield something of a marginalized "ghetto" of scholars or at least more liable to be marginalized? These are long-standing concerns, and have led some archaeologists of gender (e.g., Stig-Sorenson 2000) to distance themselves, and the field of gender archaeology, from any politics at all. We could go much further in discussing this topic, and it is one well worth discussing, but in the short space that remains, I would like to emphasize instead what an engendered archaeology has led to, and what, no matter what the inspiration for the research, a concern with gender can do and has done for our archaeology and for our understandings of the human past.

First, as noted above, the "gender focus" has led not only to even more emphasis on the micro-scale and the archaeology of everyday life, it has also allowed for/encouraged a link with other theoretical interests that have been re-shaping archaeological inquiry. In particular, a concern with gender has fit well with and enhanced the adoption of some aspects of what is called "practice theory" by archaeologists, in which, simplistically put, the concern is for understanding the everyday, often unacknowledged social practices that not only constituted the social formations and "cultures" of the past, but that also constituted the identities and social personae of the people of the past. How our practices inform our identities and notions of self and how these might have worked in the past are fascinating, somewhat new questions. They are fundamental questions if we want to understand even the large-scale events or processes that shaped past societies. Some of the most exciting and provocative of studies in an engendered archaeology have drawn explicitly from practice and performance theories (e.g., Joyce 1998, 2000b).

Second, we can perhaps better understand "gender" as a phenomenon in the contemporary world not by assuming it has always been there or always been more-or-less the same, but by explicitly questioning the concept, and by accepting that perhaps—as archaeologists are beginning to show—"our" understandings of gender and our ways of using gender ideologies to structure social relations are not the only possibilities. As Henrietta Moore once said (1995: 53), "it is the archaeologists [rather than the post modernists] to whom we look to sustain our awareness of the plurality of social times." That is, archaeological inquiry into "gender"—if it existed, how it was practiced, what it might have signified, how it was defined and performed, what varieties of gender might have been "at work" in past societies—has shown some of the ways in which a single notion of gender—usually that there are 2 biological sexes who perform associated gender roles (those of men and those of women)—cannot be sustained for all human societies. For those who do have political concerns about inequality in the present, this is important evidential information that can be helpful in challenging some of the "givens" of present day society. If there is one "fact" about gender that archaeologists have shown, it is that gender is mutable, and, as a distinct social concept, may not have existed in the same terms as today, if it even existed at all.

Furthermore, what a concern with gender also facilitated was an increasing archaeological interest in and engagement with broader social processes that archaeologists had heretofore often considered in simplistic terms. For example, some feminist archaeologists (e.g., Meskell 2001, 2003) would suggest that archaeological concerns are thus with "identity" and difference, how this was constructed in the past, and how gender, as third wave feminists demonstrated (e.g., Moraga and Anzaldua 1981), cannot be understood as distinct from other dimensions of identity and social position and practice. For many contemporary researchers, their concerns have been with the intersections among gender, race, class, ethnicity (e.g., Collins 1999). These may not always be the relevant "categories" for societies in the past, but it is increasingly clear that aspects of one's identity, such as age, social positions (but not necessarily socioeconomic class, as in capitalist societies), kinship, wealth, sexual orientations, experience, as well as something we might broadly consider to be "genders," were integral to how one's social status was determined and how societies "worked." Many of these processes, how they worked, changed, and shaped societies are crucial even to understanding large scale sociopolitical processes and cultural change, long the favorite topics of archaeologists.

If one really wants to better understand how human systems—social, political, economic, etc.—work and changed, the workings of such phenomena as "gender, class and faction" (Brumfiel 1992), and their intersections, are of enormous relevance: that it was the work of women making *chicha* (corn-based beer) that "fed" the politics of the Inka state (Hastorf 1991); that it was the net-making knowledge and practices, most likely by women, that allow us to infer their role in making the famous Ice Age female figurines (Soffer et al. 2000); that certain stone tool making practices were crucial to the redefinition of Aboriginal masculinities and the maintenance of a viable identity in the face of colonial impacts (Harrison 2002); that there were many possible ways in which women gained legitimate as well as covert political powers (Marcus 2001). These are all examples of how archaeological work has not only made women visible, but added to the more nuanced understandings of how gender and social relations are at work in social stability and transformation. These archaeologies add to the evidence that has toppled the once-prevalent notion that we could talk about "the" cross-cultural status of women, which is now shown to be so variable in its forms, processes, and practices.

Gender, or something akin to what we mean by gender, almost has to be in existence in some forms or another in many human societies since the appearance of symbol-using, socially-bound modern humans. If archaeology does not consider how gender, age and other factors have been instrumental in the formation and definition of such fundamental human social practices as the division of labor and the construction of identity-consciousness by individuals and social groups, we will surely miss a lot about how human societies worked, "got on" and changed, changing others on the way.

Looking at gender has also prompted more engaged attention to other dimensions of human life that have rarely been in the archaeological focus, such as sexuality, children, and mothering. After all, all of these were surely part of prehistoric life and societies; without them, there would be no us, no descendants! Yet, some may ask, how can we ever "see" sexuality, or "find" the activities of children? These have become some of the new archaeological challenges, now that much archaeology has turned its attention to the people of the past, as much as to the cultural processes. Of course, these are not likely to be aspects of life that we can make inferences about in every situation, with every archaeological record, for every site or "culture." But we now know more about such things as the African-American midwife and mothering practices in the late 19th century southern United States (Wilkie 2003), or about the strategies of women and their female partners in forging identities in a colonial women's prison in Tasmania (Casella 2000), or about how the imposition of new architectures and uses of space on native Californians by colonizing Spaniards must have re-structured their intimate interpersonal lives (Voss 2000).

Even if one makes the move, then, from what might have started out as a somewhat straightforward inquiry into the archaeology of (just two?) genders, especially by "adding women," into some of the multiple related domains of social life—sexual orientation and identity; the construction of difference of all sorts and in varying contexts; the practices of mothering; the place, roles and practices of children; a more intense look at the everyday lives; the micro-scale; the household lives and labors of everyone—archaeology has gained in our understandings of not just past social life, social formations, social transformations and change. We also gain a more expanded understanding of what these social processes, categories and practices are about in contemporary life and in human societies more broadly. Archaeologists have expanded their theoretical resources beyond a good grasp on how humans and their environments inter-relate to how social life is enacted and could be defined and how humans not only develop a sense of difference, but institutionalize and challenge such differences, at many scales of their lives. This then is an archaeology that continues to have challenges; after all, it is not easy to make valid inferences about issues that we have difficulty with even when we can participate in a living society or interview selected informants. And it is not easy to change the persistence of biases, the disciplinary structures that prefer and reward certain kinds of research over others, and that are part of wider institutional and social settings that are still marked by inequities and differential access to resources and social value.

What we have seen is that once made aware of just some of the more blatant androcentric archaeologies, in content and in practice, many archaeologists not only re-assessed their own work and interpretations, but took up the challenges of "finding women," then questioning the concepts of "gender," trying to infer aspects of sexuality, mothering, and other gendered practices, and using gender as a stepping stone in concept and method to broaden our

archaeological horizons, contribute to defining what we now see to be richly varied tableau of human social arrangements and cultural ways of being in the world.

REFERENCES

Ascher, Robert. 1960. Archaeology and the public image. *American Antiquity* 25(3): 402–403.

Brumfiel, Elizabeth. 1991. Weaving and cooking: Women's production in Aztec Mexico. In Joan Gero and Margaret Conkey (eds). *Engendering Archaeology: Women and Prehistory*, pp. 224–254. Oxford: Basil Blackwell.

———. 1992. Breaking and entering the ecosystem: Gender, class and faction steal the show. *American Anthropologist* 94(3): 551–567.

Casella, Eleanor. 2000. Bulldaggers and gentle ladies: Archaeological approaches to female homosexuality in convict-era Australia. In Robert Schmidt and Barbara Voss (eds.). *Archaeologies of Sexuality*, pp. 143–159, London and New York: Routledge.

Collins, Patricia Hill. 1999. Moving beyond gender. Intersectionality and scientific knowledge. In M. M. Ferree, Judith Lorber, and B. B. Hess (eds.). *Revisioning Gender*, pp. 261–284. Thousand Oaks, CA: Sage.

Conkey, Margaret. 1992. Men and women in prehistory: An archaeological challenge. In Caroline Brettell and Carolyn Sargent (eds.). *Gender in Cross-Cultural Perspective*, pp. 41–50, Englewood Cliffs, NJ: Prentice-Hall.

Conkey, Margaret and Janet Spector. 1984. Archaeology and the study of gender. In Michael B. Schiffer (ed.) *Advances in Archaeological Method and Theory*, Vol. 7, pp. 1–38, New York: Academic Press.

Crass, Barbara A. 2001. Gender and mortuary analysis: What can grave goods really tell us? In Bettina Arnold and Nancy L. Wicker (eds.). *Gender and the Archaeology of Death*, pp. 105–118, Walnut Creek, CA: Alta Mira Press.

Eichler, Margrit and Jeanne Lapointe. 1985. *On the Treatment of the Sexes in Research*. Ottawa: Social Sciences and Humanities Research Council of Canada.

Gero, Joan. 1993.The social world of prehistoric facts: gender and power in Paleoindian research. In Hilary du Cros and Laurajane Smith (eds.). *Women in Archaeology, A Feminist Critique, Occasional Papers in Prehistory*, No. 23, pp. 31–40, Canberra: Australian National University, Department of Prehistory.

———. 1994. Excavation bias and the woman-at-home ideology. In Margaret Nelson, Sarah M. Nelson, and Alison Wylie (eds.). *Equity Issues for Women in Archaeology, Archaeology Papers of the American Anthropological Association, Number 5*, pp. 37–42, Washington, DC: American Anthropological Association.

Gero, Joan and Margaret Conkey (eds.). 1991. *Engendering Archaeology: Women and Prehistory*. Oxford: Basil Blackwell.

Gifford-Gonzalez, Diane. 1993. You can hide, but you can't run. Representations of women's work in illustrations of Paleolithic life. *Visual Anthropology Review* 9(1): 3–21.

Hamlin, Christine. 2001. Sharing the load: Gender and task division at the windover site. In Bettina Arnold and Nancy L. Wicker (eds.). *Gender and the Archaeology of Death*, pp. 119–136, Walnut Creek, CA: Alta Mira Press.

Haraway, Donna. 1988. Situated knowledges: The science question in feminism and the privilege of partial perspective. *Feminist Studies* 14(3): 575–599.

Harrison, Rodney. 2002. Archaeology and the colonial encounter: Kimberly spearpoints, cultural identity and masculinity in the north of Australia," *Journal of Social Archaeology*, 2(3): 352–377.

Hastorf, Christine. 1991. Gender, space and food in prehistory. In Joan Gero and Margaret Conkey (eds.). *Engendering Archaeology: Women and Prehistory*, pp. 132–162, Oxford: Basil Blackwell.

Hays-Gilpin, Kelly. 2003. *Ambiguous Images: Gender and Rock Art*. Walnut Creek, CA: Alta Mira Press.

Hollimon, Sandra. 1997. The third gender in California: Two-spirit undertakers among the Chumash and their neighbors. In Cheryl Claassen and Rosemary Joyce (eds.). *Women in Prehistory. North America and Mesoamerica*, pp. 173–188, Philadelphia: University of Pennsylvania Press.

———. 2001. Warfare and gender in the northern Plains: Osteological evidence of trauma reconsidered. In Bettina Arnold and Nancy L. Wicker (eds.). *Gender and the Archaeology of Death*, pp. 179–194, Walnut Creek, CA: Alta Mira Press.

Johnson, Matthew. 1999. *Archaeological Theory*. Oxford: Basil Blackwell.

Joyce, Rosemary. 1996. The construction of gender in classic Maya monuments. In Rita B. Wright (ed.). *Gender and Archaeology*, pp. 167–198, Philadelphia: University of Pennsylvania Press.

———. 1998. Performing the body in prehispanic Central America. *Res: Anthropology and Aesthetics* Vol. 33 (spring): 147–165.

———. 2000a. Girling the girl and boying the boy: The production of adulthood in ancient Mesoamerica. *World Archaeology* 31(3): 473–483.

———. 2000b. *Gender and Power in Prehispanic Mesoamerica*. Austin, TX: University of Texas Press.

———. 2001. Negotiating sex and gender in Mesoamerican society. In Cecelia Klein (ed.). *Gender in Pre-hispanic America*, pp. 109–142, Washington, DC: Dumbarton Oaks Research Library and Collection.

Klein, Cecelia. 2001. None of the above: Gender ambiguity in Nahua ideology. In Cecelia Klein (ed.). *Gender in Pre-hispanic America*, pp. 109–142, Washington, DC: Dumbarton Oaks Research Library and Collection.

Levi-Strauss, Claude. 1936. Contributions á l' étude de l'organization sociale des Indiens Bororo. *Journal de la Société des Americanistes de Paris* 28: 269–304.

Lovejoy, Owen. 1981. The origin of man. *Science* 211: 341–350.

Marcus, Joyce. 2001. Breaking the glass ceiling: The strategies of royal women in ancient states. In Cecelia Klein (ed.). *Gender in Pre-hispanic America*, pp. 305–340, Washington, DC: Dumbarton Oaks Research Library and Collection.

Meskell, Lynn. 2001. Archaeologies of identity. In Ian Hodder (ed.). *Archaeological Theory Today*, pp. 187–211, Cambridge: Polity Press.

———. 2003. Feminist archaeologies of identity and difference. In special feature: Revisiting Feminism and Anthropology Across the Four Fields. *VOICES: A Publication of the Association for Feminist Anthropology*, volume 6(1): 5, 13, 14.

Michard-Marshale, Claire and Claudine Ribery. 1982. *Sexisme et Science Humaine*. Lille: Presses Universitaires de France.

Moore, Henrietta. 1995. The problems of origins: Poststructuralism and beyond. In Ian Hodder, Michael Shanks, Alexandra Alexandri, Victor Buchli, John Carman, Jonathan Last, and Gavin Lucas (eds.). *Interpreting Archaeology: Finding Meaning in the Past*, pp. 51–53. London and New York: Routledge.

Moraga, Cherrie and Gloria Anzaldua (eds.). 1981. *This Bridge Called My Back. Writings by Radical Women of Color*. Watertown, MA: Persephone.

Peterson, Jane. 2002. *Sexual Revolutions: Gender and Labor at the Dawn of Agriculture*. Walnut Creek, CA: Alta Mira Press.

Rosaldo, Michelle. 1980. The use and abuse of anthropology. Reflections on feminism and cross-cultural understanding, *SIGNS: Journal of Women in Culture and Society*, 5(3): 389–417.

Schmidt, Robert. 2000. Shamans and northern cosmology: The direct historical approach to Mesolithic sexuality. In Robert Schmidt and Barbara Voss (eds.). *Archaeologies of Sexuality*, pp. 220–235. London and New York: Routledge.

Slocum, Sally. 1975. Woman the gatherer: Male bias in anthropology. In Rayna Rapp Reiter (ed.). *Toward an Anthropology of Women*, pp. 36–50, New York and London: Monthly Review Press.

Soffer, Olga, James Adovasio and D. C. Hyland. 2000. The "Venus" figurines: Textiles, basketry, gender and status in the Upper Paleolithic. *Current Anthropology* 41(4): 511–537.

Stig-Sorenson, Marie-Louise. 2000. *Gender Archaeology*. Cambridge: Polity Press.

Sweely, Tracy L. (ed.). 1999. *Manifesting Power. Gender and the Interpretation of Power in Prehistory*. London and New York: Routledge.

Voss, Barbara. 2000. Colonial sex: Archaeology, structured space, and sexuality in Alta California's Spanish-colonial missions. In Robert Schmidt and Barbara Voss (eds.). *Archaeologies of Sexuality*, pp. 35–61. London and New York: Routledge.

Watson, Patty Jo and Mary C. Kennedy. 1991. The development of horticulture in the eastern woodlands of North America: Women's role. In Joan Gero and Margaret Conkey (eds.). *Engendering Archaeology: Women and Prehistory*, pp. 255–275, Oxford: Basil Blackwell.

Wilkie, Laurie. 2003. *The Archaeology of Mothering. An African-American Midwife's Tale*. London and New York: Routledge.

Winters, Howard. 1968. Value-systems and trade cycles of the late archaic in the Midwest. In S. R. Binford and L. R. Binford (eds.). *New Perspectives in Archaeology*, pp. 175–222. Chicago: Aldine.

Wylie, Alison. 1992. The interplay of evidential constraints and political interests: Recent archaeological research on gender. *American Antiquity* 57(1): 15–35.

Zeder, Melinda. 1997. *The American Archaeologist: A Profile*. Walnut Creek, CA: Alta Mira Press.

The Fashioning of Women

J. M. Adovasio, Olga Soffer, and Jake Page

In which we visit a pleasant encampment full of Brooks Brothers–style weaving and other womanly creations, the first fireworks, mammoth non-hunts, and people who could be your neighbors.

THE PLACE: A camp on the gentle, grassy slope of a hill in today's Pavlov Hills, from which three limestone outcrops rise above the broad south Moravian plain in the eastern region of today's Czech Republic. The view to the north, south, and east stretches for miles over grassland and forest: a broad valley that served people and wildlife as a highway from the flatlands of the mighty Danube into northern Europe. The Pavlov Hills lie along the right bank of a river that flows into the Morava River, a major tributary to the Danube. To the north, a month's march away, lies the great wall

of glacial ice. Equally far to the southwest, ice blankets the great mountains known today as the Alps. The village is not far above a swampy area fed by the river that courses through the plains, its moisture supporting a variety of deciduous trees—alder, ash, birch, groves of willows, the occasional oak, and beyond, in drier soils, the conifers, pines, spruce, and others. Off in the distance, a few clusters of reindeer and small herds of horses head south. Beyond, a group of female mammoths and their young plod northward.

THE TIME: 26,000 years ago. The summer has ended, and the nightly temperatures in these early autumn weeks reach near freezing. It will get colder as the winter comes on, but for now the days are relatively warm once the sun rises above the hills.

THE VILLAGE: This is where several groups of people have come together to spend the long fall, winter, and early spring, just as they and their ancestors have done since longer than anyone can remember or compute. The camp is about 200 yards upslope from the river at a place where natural mineral licks attract nutrient-starved animals

J. M. Adovasio, Olga Soffer and Jake Page, "The Fashioning of Women," in *The Invisible Sex: Uncovering the True Roles of Women in Prehistory*, by J. M. Adovasio, Olga Soffer and Jake Page, pp. 169–193. © 2007 by James M. Adovasio, Olga Soffer and Jake Page. Reprinted by permission of HarperCollins.

in the spring months, especially mammoth females and their young. There the weaker ones die, leaving their bones for the people to use. Over the eons, people have made use of their bones and tusks as raw materials to build dwellings and make tools and other objects. Now they have erected five tentlike structures over depressions in the ground they have cleaned out, throwing away last year's broken flint and bone and broken tools and other household trash. Walls and roofs of skins sewed together are held up by wooden poles, their edges held down against the force of the cold winds with rocks. In the largest of these structures, sitting in the middle of the camp, five hearths have been delineated with circles of rocks. The others contain single hearths. Upslope from the camp about 80 yards sits another structure, with limestone slabs holding down walls of hide on three sides. Inside this structure are layers of ashes and ceramic fragments.

On this particular morning, just as the eastern sky is beginning to lighten, a woman emerges from one of the tents and nods to the sleepy youth who is tending the fire in the middle of the camp that burns through the night as a warning to predators. She walks slowly and painfully up the slope to this small structure. Taking sticks of wood from a pile she ordered her young grand-children to make yesterday, she builds a fire. The flames lick hungrily at the pine sticks, reaching into the cold air. Not pausing to warm herself, she piles more sticks, larger ones, on the flames, and then retreats down the slope to her dwelling. Moments later, she reemerges, carrying a tightly woven basket filled with water and a cloth carrying bag filled with dusty brown soil. By now the fire has rendered the fuel into glowing hot coals. She nods approvingly, then sits down beside the kiln with a grunt about her complaining knee joints. Making clay by mixing the fine dusty soil with water, she fashions a tiny bear's head and body. She sets that aside, fashions legs, and presses them into the body. She intones some words and throws the bear into the fire. In minutes, the bear explodes with a sharp *Crack!* and a cascade of sparks and pieces of the bear rattle off the walls of the kiln. Thus does the old woman's day begin, rendering their world as safe as she can for the rest of the people.

By now people are stepping outside their dwellings into the cold, scratching, yawning, looking up at the sky for signs of the weather for this day. Young children begin darting here and there, yelping and shouting, parents hissing at them to be quiet. Two women, each suckling a new baby, stand together talking. Some of the group's men stand in a circle, chewing on narrow strips of rabbit jerky, glancing out to the horse herds moving across the plains far away, making plans. From up the hillside at the kiln, the sharp pops of the old woman's fireworks are reassuring sounds. As the sun rises over the hills, casting long shadows that reach down the slope, activity in the camp begins to pick up. Innumerable chores need doing. Several men are soon engaged in replacing the tiny old blades affixed to the ivory foreshafts of their wooden spears with newly knapped flint blades, renewing the lethally sharp array. These weapons are for hunting horses and the small red deer out on the plains, a task that could take several men an entire day and night and still result in failure.

Another man grinds a piece of gray slate into a pendant to replace the one that shattered the day before when he fell onto some rocks while running. An older man, his hands now gnarled and crooked, slowly opens up a long hunting net, unrolling it on the ground. He then inspects it from one end 40 feet to the other end, seeing that the knots are still all secure. Satisfied, he rolls it back up and places it on the ground near a lone tree that stands a few feet from the dwelling where he, with his family, sleeps.

Inside, his daughter boils a mush of various wild seeds in a tightly plaited basket with hardened clay inside. The thickening gruel bubbles, some of it slopping over the edge of the basket and falling into the hearth. The young woman has been feeding this to her four-year old daughter for a week now, weaning her from the breast. Earlier, she and three other mothers sent their daughters off to collect the nettles that grow in the disturbed soil around the camp and are now ready to be processed. The girls and their mothers will set about soaking the nettles to remove the outer cover and free up the finer fibers inside. The fibers will then be twisted into string of various plies.

The Old Woman, the oldest person in camp, though she is still vigorous, will supervise the making of the string and will take the finest as warps and wefts for her own work on her loom. Last year, she taught the young girls five of the eight ways of twining, some for making baskets and floor mats, some for making the wall hangings that helped keep out the icy winds of winter, and yet others for the fine mysteries of creating loom-woven fabric to sew together into form-fitting warm-weather clothes. The Old Woman, who is a bit scary for the girls because she is so powerful, has chosen one of the girls as a special student: she will learn to sew the seams of ceremonial shirts. She will show another girl the arts of the loom, and one day perhaps this girl will become the Old Woman, the weaver who makes the finest fabric for clothing for whoever in her lifetime emerges as the leader.

As the day goes on, several of the men set out for the plains below, bristling with flint knives and spears of wood tipped with ivory and stone blades, sweating in the midday sun, their hide shirts hanging from their belts. They will be on the march most of the day, camping near a place on the river favored by horses and some of the local deer. Other men stay in camp, a few telling exaggerated tales of hunting to the boys, a few others digging up the loose dusty soil and carrying it up the hill in bags made of fiber to the old woman at the kiln. In the shade of one of the free-standing trees, three young women gossip and laugh as they grind the small tough seeds of certain prairie grasses. It is a good day for a feast to celebrate the coming together here of these related families for the season.

By late afternoon, each family's net has been unrolled and carefully inspected, and tied together to form two long nets, each some 80 feet across. Now the children, some of the women and men, and a few elders set out with the nets. The children carry sticks, which they brandish bravely as they run along behind the adults. Several of the adults carry clubs fashioned from fallen branches. Led by the oldest in the party, they pause after a half hour's walk on the slopes that are covered by underbrush. Carefully the oldsters unfurl the nets, unwinding them from the carrying poles, which are then used to anchor the nets to the ground. Several of the younger women, the men, and all the children silently circle around upslope until they reach nearly to the top of the hill. There they form into a wide arc and on a signal begin the charge down the hill, shrieking wildly, whacking trees as they go by, setting up a terrifying din. Rabbits, foxes, and other small mammals emerge from the underbrush and dart back and forth, trending downhill to escape the mayhem coming their way. Within minutes several dozen of these creatures have leaped into the nets to be quickly dispatched by people swinging their clubs. As the sun drops down to the western horizon, the people head back with more meat and fur than they will be able to use for days.

The camp bustles with activity as preparations for the feast get under way—skinning the animals, starting the hearth fires and the outdoor fire that will burn all night, and performing innumerable other chores. Meanwhile, the old woman who was first to greet the day has returned to the kiln up the slope with one of her youthful apprentices. She has kneaded into existence a few dozen small clay pellets, several animal figurines, and, most elaborate, a figurine of a woman with broad hips and buttocks and pendulous breasts, faceless, footless, with lines etched into her back that suggest ample flesh, which bespeaks a prosperous woman. Carefully, she places all these objects into her basket except for the figurine, which she hands to the older of her two apprentices. The girl grins widely at the honor and holds the figurine carefully in her hand, and they set out for the camp below. As the feasting proceeds into the night, a few couples slip off into the dark, heading for courting camps a short walk away in a copse of trees. Others dance and chant, while the old woman throws an occasional pellet or animal figure into the fire as she sings a special song to herself in a high keening voice and the clay figurines explode. Toward the end of the festivities, she instructs the sleepy apprentice to throw the figurine of the woman into the flames. Most of the people in camp stop to watch as the girl flips the figurine into the fire, and they wait silently for a minute or so until a loud crack signifies the end of the ritual, of the feast, of the day.

With that, the people settle down for the night, eyelids drooping, stomachs full, ceremonies properly done to celebrate the successful hunt—a good day indeed.

WHAT'S RIGHT ABOUT THAT PICTURE

How much of this scenario is guesswork and how much is certain? What is the evidence that lies behind this view of a day spent at a site that would come to be known as Dolni Vestonice I? This site has been excavated and examined by numerous archaeologists over the last three quarters of a century and, over this time, has yielded up several startling discoveries. Among the first such was the figurine of the woman that we saw tossed into the central fire of the camp at the end of the feast. She was subsequently discovered on July 13, 1925, during the Moravian Museum's excavation under the leadership of Karel Absolon. The workers found her in two unequal pieces less than a foot apart. The Vestonice Venus, as she came to be known, became famous as the earliest ceramic object ever found. A picture soon emerged—indeed, an actual illustration by Zdenek Burian—showing an elderly man with disheveled white hair, wearing a sleeveless shirt of some animal skin, with a necklace of teeth and other no doubt meaningful objects around his neck, carefully sculpting the figurine with a stick of animal bone. It is more likely that the figurine was carved by a woman, probably the "priestess" who used it.

At the time of its discovery, one member of the crew noted what appeared to be a fragmentary fingerprint left on the Venus's spine before firing. Recently this fingerprint was analyzed microscopically to determine such features as the breadth of ridges, which correlate with the age of the originator of the print. It turns out that the person who held this figurine was between 7 and 15 years old, and almost surely was not the maker of the figurine, since it is unlikely that a beginner or a child could have made it.

On the other hand, it was possible to call into question the actual ceramic skill of this "first" ceramicist. The site of the kiln upslope was first looked into by archaeologists in the 1950s. It yielded fragments of a total of 707 animal figurines and 14 human figurines, all fired clay. In addition there were some 2,000 small pellets. This suggests two possibilities. One, the ceramicist(s) were extremely incompetent. Two, they knew just what they were doing and had no interest in creating objects that would remain intact but instead were making objects that would, by design, harden in the flames and explode. This can be achieved by, among other things, adjusting the wetness of the clay. The building of three walls of the kiln suggests that they knew full well that the figurines would explode, adding to the suggestion that a deliberate effort was going on—not only the first ceramic objects ever known, but also perhaps the first example of a kind of fireworks. Our description of this as embodying some sort of ritual is something of an imaginative leap, but it seems unlikely that such onerous activity would be done out of sheer frivolity at a time when survival was a full-time job.

THE CRUCIAL ROLE OF THE FIBER ARTS

More important probably than the presumably ritual use of ceramics in Dolni Vestonice is the discovery that by 26,000 years ago, these Upper Paleolithic people of Eurasia were well along in what has been called the String Revolution, a technological breakthrough (better thought of as the Fiber Revolution) that had profound effects on human destiny—probably more profound effects than any advance in the technique of making spear points, knives, scrapers and other tools out of stone. The term String Revolution was evidently the original idea of Elizabeth Wayland Barber of Occidental College in California. She wrote a lovely book, *Women's Work*, suggesting what a remarkable invention string was, whenever it first was used. String's invention, she wrote, "opened the door to an enormous array of new ways to labor and improve the odds of survival . . . " Comparing it to the steam engine, she mentioned the need of string for weaving and said that on a far more basic level, "string can be used simply to tie things up—to catch, to hold, to carry. From these notions come snares and fishlines, tethers and leashes, carrying nets, handles, and packages, not to mention a way of binding objects together to form more complex tools." Indeed, she thought, so powerful was string "in taming the world and to human will and ingenuity" that it may well have made it possible for humans to populate virtually every niche they could reach. So the fiber artifacts found in those old Moravian sites were far more important than their humble appearance would have suggested.

Three certainties exist about fiber artifacts. Compared with things made out of stone, bone, antler, shell, and even (in some cases) wood, fiber items are highly perishable. Because of this, there simply aren't as many fiber artifacts remaining in the ground as other kinds. And there are even fewer fiber artifacts in the archaeological record than have persisted in the ground because practically all archaeologists have not been trained to see them in the ground, much less recover them (often an extremely delicate and technical task). There remain only a handful of archaeology departments here and abroad where such training is available, particularly at the graduate level. The other certain thing about fiber artifacts is that, in dry caves and other places where they do not deteriorate and disappear, they have been found to outnumber stone artifacts by a factor of 20 to 1. In several other situations (places covered with water where aerobic bacteria cannot get to the artifacts, and in permafrost), fiber and wood artifacts have been found to account for 95 percent of all artifacts recovered. That amounts to a tremendous amount of information that archaeologists have missed in most parts of the world, including Late Pleistocene Eurasia.

A third certainty about fiber artifacts such as baskets is that, unlike stone or bone artifacts or even pottery, the method by which the artifact was made is apparent in the artifact itself. Modern stone-knappers who like to replicate old spear points, for example, can do so with considerable skill, and of course they know the steps they took to get to the finished product.

But the earlier steps made are not necessarily present in the point. By contrast, a practiced eye can perceive which of a finite number of logical steps the basket maker took. Indeed, no weaver of baskets and fabrics and other items makes such things exactly as anyone else does, so one can actually glimpse a bit of the living individual craftswoman. At the same time, most basket makers of prehistory operated within an identifiable cultural framework, just as one sees tribal distinctions in the baskets, say, of Apache women as distinct from Paiute women. And within such a tribal tradition, one can also see what appears to be one generation, or even one basket maker, who taught those who came along afterward.

If one takes modern ethnographic studies of hunter-gatherer societies as not wholly unrepresentative of Late Paleolithic societies, the work of most human beings—especially women—has been overlooked. One result, which we noted in Chapter One, was that this left room for the picture to emerge of Upper Paleolithic society and economics dominated by the mighty hunters setting out to slaughter mammoths and other large animals—though mammoths especially caught the imagination of those reconstructing these ancient lifeways. There was some evidence for this, but only a smidgin. Most notably, in a few places archaeologists found stone points among huge mammoth bone assemblages in Eurasia (and also North America, where we will go in a later chapter). It appeared to many that astonishingly efficient and daring hunters were taking on entire herds and killing them for food.

But there was a problem here of specialization. Paleontologists, whose interest lay in the realm of prehistoric zoology rather than in the affairs of humans and hominids, found numerous similar assemblages of mammoth bones in Eurasia (and smaller assemblages in Siberia and North America) that had no stone points. And even in those assemblages where stone points and other tools were found, butchering marks were few and far between. In other words, over thousands of years and in various places (such as mineral licks, as at Dolni Vestonice, where the remains of a hundred or so mammoths were found), proboscidians died and created boneyards from which the people made what use they could.

Ethnographic studies of modern people have turned up practically no instances of deliberate elephant hunting before the advent of the ivory trade in modern times. There is no evidence of Upper Paleolithic assemblages of enough hunters (maybe 40 or so) to take down a mammoth, much less the number needed to wipe out a herd. It is dangerous enough, in fact, to go after any animal the size of a horse or a bison if one is armed with a spear. Only the foolhardiest would attempt to kill an animal that stands 14 feet high and has a notoriously bad temper when annoyed. A statement that has been assigned to multiple originators suggests that it is more likely that every so often a Paleolithic hunter brought down an already wounded mammoth (or one slowed down a bit in the mud of a swamp) and then talked about it for the rest of his life. The picture of Man the Mighty Hunter is now fading out of the annals of prehistory. By far, most of the animal remains found strewn about places like Dolni Vestonice consists of the bones of small mammals like hares and foxes.

The finds of perishable artifacts in Dolni Vestonice I and several other sites in Moravia have done much to blow the old picture of Upper Paleolithic life out of the water, and with it the dominant figure of the mighty male hunter, and replaced it with a picture something like the one with which this chapter began. The first of these finds was made in 1993, consisting of mysterious impressions in strange clay fragments in Dolni Vestonice I, which turned out to be the imprints of basketry and textiles made from wild plants. These were the earliest forms of the fiber arts known— indeed, some 10,000 years earlier than anything found before. Just what the fragments themselves were is not clear. They might have been pieces of flooring on which items of weaving or basketry had been impressed, and turned into hard evidence when the place burned down. In any event, they and subsequent finds in these sites showed that people here were already weaving and making basketry with at least eight different styles of twining, some of which remain common today. Some of the fabrics

were as fine as a Brooks Brothers shirt. People had to have been weaving textiles on looms and making free-standing basketry for a very long time to have developed such ability and diversity and sophistication of technique.

Just exactly what those people were making from all this weaving, basketry, and cordage is impossible to say with certainty, but given the excellence of technique there is reason to think that they were making baskets of various kinds and possibly mats for sleeping and wall hangings, and clothing of various kinds such as shawls, skirts, sashes, and shirts. They used whipping stitches like those used today to sew two pieces of fabric together and that no doubt served the same end 26,000 years ago.

In addition to knots and other signs of weaving, numerous tools were turned up over the many times these sites were examined that can now be seen as tools for weaving and other steps in the production of such materials. One puzzling artifact made of mammoth ivory was shaped something like a boomerang but without the curve. It makes perfect sense as a weaving batten (and in fact is nearly identical to the battens still in use today among Navajo weavers). Another tool, basically a rod with a doughnut-shaped end, has been fairly commonly found throughout the world dating from later times, and has puzzled archaeologists, whose best idea for them is that they were used somehow to straighten spear and arrow shafts. But when they are thought about in the context of Moravian weaving, it seems that they would have been useful in the spinning of threads into string or yarn for weaving. Fairly large ivory needles were already known from such places, and the assumption was that they were used for sewing together skins and furs for clothing, but the proliferation of smaller needles found across Eurasia could not have been conveniently used for stitching such tough and unforgiving materials—except for the thinnest of leather. They are the right size, however, for stitching together pieces of woven fabric. Some of the ivory needles found are so fine that they would have permitted embroidery.

The very diversity of styles and workmanship that emerges from all these perishable artifacts and their associated tools, plus the fact that

Figure 8-1. Fragment of netting at Zaraisk showing (clock-wise from top-left) positive impression of the cast, microphotograph of the netting structure, and schematic of the structure.
O. Soffer, J. M. Adovasio, and Stephanie Snyder

most of the stone used to make stone tools was not local, all suggests that these were people who assembled here for part of the year (perhaps a large part) and separated into smaller groups—probably near-nuclear family groups—at other times. It is reasonable to speculate that each such household might well have its (her) own favored techniques and brought them to the larger group, thus accounting for much of the remarkable diversity of products.

GROUP HUNTING

Four of the fragments examined had impressions of cordage tied into sheet bends or weaver's knots and this (along with what appear to be tools for measuring the spaces between knots) strongly suggests that they were making nets for hunting relatively small mammals, as well as string bags. Earlier workers had noticed the abundance—indeed, prevalence—of bones of such small mammals as hares and foxes in Upper Paleolithic camps in eastern

and central Europe, but came up with fairly weak suggestions for the means of hunting them. Anyone who has watched these animals race and dart when threatened will find it implausible in the extreme to imagine people chasing them down in the open and clubbing them, or even throwing little spears at them, both of which have been offered as serious explanations (of course by male archaeologists). The use of nets, on the other hand, as well as cordage snares, easily explains the peoples' success. They could, obviously, have made nets of wider mesh and thicker cordage for hunting larger animals as well, but no evidence of this has been found. At the same time, the large bone needles that were assumed to be used for sewing skins together would have also been handy tools for making the nets.

What then are the social implications of all this? First of all, we know from such modern hunter-gatherer societies as the Pygmies of the Ituri Forest in Africa's Congo region that net hunting is a communal affair involving women, children, and elderly people as well as adult males. It engages essentially everyone in the group as beaters, clubbers, or net holders and makes the acquisition of high-energy and high-protein food (meat) much less dangerous and more dependable. By adjusting the mesh, they could have caught even smaller forms of life—birds, even insects. This would ease the problems involved in feeding a relatively larger aggregation of people by providing a mass harvest in a short time—a surplus beyond their immediate need that in turn would make ceremonial feasts possible. Such behavior is noted ethnographically.

Making things out of fiber is not the sole prerogative of either sex in ethnographic accounts of small bands or larger tribal societies. More often than not, for example, men make sandals for themselves and their families, and it is also fairly clear that in such societies both men and women *know how* to produce sandals and other items that use basketry techniques and materials. In many cases, men probably do make things like baskets that they need for their own purposes, but throughout the tribal world, today women make most basketry. But loom or frame weaving is a craft practiced almost exclusively by women in the tribal world, as is the gathering and processing of plant products for such weaving. This is the case in virtually all tribal societies where textiles and basketry are produced for domestic and communal needs, and typically it breaks down only when such perishable products enter the domain of market exchange. One rare exception to this among American Indian tribes is the Hopi of northeastern Arizona (an agricultural society) whose men do all the weaving—restricted to ceremonial wear such as sashes and kilts and costumery of brides made by their paternal uncles. Next door to the Hopi, as it were, Navajo women do all the weaving—almost entirely rugs—though the looms are often built by the husbands, and a weaver's son-in-law is expected to supply her with some of the weaving tools.

In addition, from cross-cultural studies throughout the world, the making of ceramic items, especially pottery, in many societies that we are familiar with is chiefly the province of women. There are, to be sure, innumerable variations that people have invented over time for all such matters, but even in the face of some scholarly quibbles, it is safe to assume what could be called the default position: that most if not all of the ceramics, weaving, basketry, and clothing was made by women in the years that Dolni Vestonice and the other Moravian sites were inhabited. And from that and other evidence—notably the Venus figures—it is safe to assume that the *idea* of gender—the separate category with its associated roles and identities was now present. In other words, we see here the malleable social notion of gender, as opposed to (and in addition to) the clear biological function of sex. It is not clear from any particular archaeological evidence at these Moravian sites that the *idea* of man as opposed to male was prevalent. There is virtually no iconography that suggests otherwise, but Thurber's war of the sexes (read gender) would presumably soon begin. In any event, it is safe to say that some division of labor was in place, and with it probably a set of family relatives with whom one identified and by whom one identified oneself on a permanent intergenerational basis, a group in which every segment—children, men, women, elders—stood to gain. The population explosion that took place in this period seems to bear this out. In other words, here is one of the most vivid examples yet discovered of what we can safely call thoroughly, recognizably, behaviorally modern humans.

Does this seem to be a great deal to read into these fragments of perishable items and ceramics along with a few intact tools? In fact, it isn't, and new, closer looks at those enigmatic Venus figurines that are so fascinating a feature of this Upper Paleolithic Eurasian society tend to strengthen this hypothesis and round out our picture of life in those days.

VENUSES

Some 200 Venus figurines and figurine fragments from across Europe are the most representational three-dimensional images made in the Gravettian period some 27,000 to 22,000 years ago, which, of course, includes the Moravian sites described above. Nothing is their equal before this period from anywhere in the world, and thousands of years go by before anything comparable appears again. As a result, they have claimed the attention of amateurs and professionals alike with almost the same continuing fascination certain scholars and most kids have for dinosaurs. As we said in Chapter Six, the Venus of Willendorf is surely the best known of all these sculptures. They remain in many ways enigmatic, mysterious, even confusing. They serve many purposes today, including as Rorschach emblems for some of today's hangups. They obviously mean "female," and they probably mean "woman," which suggests that they are not simply representations of the reproductive function of the female human, or gynecological and obstetrical "textbooks," as one scholar put it. At the

same time, there is simply no denying that the sculptors of these figurines went to a great deal of trouble to show off the sexual and secondary sexual features of the female human, even to the point of leaving the rest of the figure—face, feet, arms, and so forth—either abstract or absent altogether. (There are exceptions to this, of course, but no exception in the entire matter is more obvious than the fact that there are only one or two examples of clearly male figurines from this region and period. There are many figurines that are androgenous, without visible sex.)

What escaped many observers, both male and female, for many years was that some of these figurines were partly clad. The Venus of Willendorf's head, for example, though faceless, did have hair, it seemed, braided and wrapped around her head. Others had little bits of decorations—body bands, bracelets, minor bits and pieces of material of some

Figure 8-2. Front and back views of the female figurine in ivory from Kostenki I.
O. Soffer

0   5
cm

sort. But never mind—they were largely naked and had to represent fertility, menstruation, the godhead (as goddess), or (giggle) paleoporn.

Then in 1998, coming off their discovery of the many fiber artifacts from Moravian sites, which many of their colleagues considered an important rearrangement of the picture of Upper Paleolithic society in Europe, Adovasio and Soffer turned their attention to these figures. To begin with, a close inspection of the braids of the Venus of Willendorf showed that her "hair" was, on the contrary, a woven hat, a radially hand-woven item of apparel that was probably begun from a knotted center in the manner of certain coiled baskets made today by Hopi, Apache, and other American Indian tribes in which a flexible element is wrapped with stem stitches as the spiral grows. Seven circuits encircle the head, with two extra half-circuits over the nape of the neck. Indeed, so precise is the carving of all this stitchery that it is not unreasonable to think that, among the functions involved in this Upper Paleolithic masterpiece, it served as a blueprint or instruction manual showing weavers how to make such hats. Indeed, anyone who has done any sculpting in stone or wood can tell you that the fashioning of the body, while extremely closely realized, would have been easy compared with the astounding control and staying power needed to render the stitching (even a few splices) of this hat so true and precise. The carver had to have spent more time on just the hat than on the rest of the entire figurine.

Of all the scholars who have examined these figurines over the decades (and there must be hundreds), only one other, Elizabeth Barber, ever took notice of the fiber accoutrements some of them wore. One British scholar who studied the Venuses in his youth never noticed any clothing because, he recalled, he "never got past the breasts."

Several other such figurines from central and eastern Europe wear similarly detailed radial or spiral woven hats as well as some begun by interlacing grids. Western European figurines tend to be more schematic, such as the Venus of Brassempouy, whose hair may be covered, in a more abstract rendering, by some sort of hairnet or snood. One thing that seems fairly common to all the partly clad figurines is that when they wear hats or caps, the facial details are absent. This suggests a social importance to the headgear, rather than an individual statement of personal identity. In other words, these various forms of headgear may speak to a particular status or rank enjoyed by at least some women.

Other forms of clothing or cloth decorations found on Venuses of this Gravettian period include straps wrapped around the figure, often above the breasts, and sometimes held there with over-the-shoulder straps. Yet others wear belts, often low on their hips, sometimes connected to skirts of string. The Venus of Lespugue, for example—she of the

Figure 8-3. Close-up of the coiling start of the basket hat depicted on the head of the Venus of Willendorf
S. Holland, Courtesy of O. Soffer

0   5
|___|___|___|___|___|
         cm

0   5
cm

Figure 8-4. Left, right, and top views of the plaited start of the basket hat depicted on the marl head of the female figurine from Kostenki I.
S. Holland, Courtesy O. Soffer

truly overwhelming hips—wears a back skirt carved with a remarkable attention to detail. It consists of eleven cords attached to a base cord that serves as a belt. The cords are secured to the belt by looping both ends of a single-ply string over the belt and twisting the ends together with a final Z twist. On several of the cords, the carver made 30 and 40 separate incisions to show the individual twists, and she took great care to depict the progressive changes in angle of twist. At the bottom of the skirt, the angle of twist is much looser, clearly suggesting that the cords were unraveling or fraying at the hem.

What is to be made of all this? An important thing to note is that, except for one sexually ambiguous fragment that has a belt, such apparel appears only on figurines that are female. Clearly, as well, the garments so carefully portrayed are not the normal daily wear of women in these times, since they lived in climates where such clothing would be utterly insufficient against the cold—except of course

Figure 8-5. The Venus of Brassempoy, carved from ivory.
S. Holland, Courtesy O. Soffer

0   3
cm

for the woven hats. In the few known burials of the time, people were interred fully clothed. The body bands, belts, string skirts, and so forth could have been for ritual purposes, or they could have been signs of status, perhaps worn over one's daily clothing—or not, in the case of ceremonial use. Indeed, they might have been imagined, as with the halos depicted on icons of saints. What they do suggest is that such apparel was a woman thing, not worn by males, and that it served to immortalize at some great effort the fact that such apparel set women (or at least certain women) apart in a social category of their own. Much of the woven material from this period that was found imprinted on ceramic fragments is as finely done as anything done later in the Bronze and Iron Ages, and equal to much of the thin cotton and linen garments worn today. Given the amount of effort involved in weaving such cloth and also in carving a replica of it in stone, one can reasonably conclude that the pieces of apparel found on so many of the Gravettian Venuses were symbols of achievement, or prestige. And it is also fair to say that, for those who were weavers or ceramicists, the workaday world was more complex, the daily round of chores, tasks, and roles more intense. Who were they?

The precision with which the carvers of the Venuses represented woven items leads almost inevitably to the conclusion that they were created by the weavers themselves, or at least under the sharp-eyed tutelage of the weavers. That it was almost surely women who did most of this fine weaving and basketry is one matter to which the ethnographic record appears to be a reliable guide.

Warriors and Rulers: Royal Women of the Classic Maya

Stanley P. Guenter and David A. Freidel

INTRODUCTION

The Classic Maya civilization of southern Mexico and northern Central America, encompassed some 80,000 sq km of tropical lowland country at its height in 750 AD. With only stone tool technology and no beasts of burden, Maya men and women created dozens of cities with towering pyramids and sprawling palaces. They turned forested swamps and rolling hills into flourishing agricultural fields capable of feeding millions and also producing vast quantities of cotton and cacao for export trade. Most importantly, the Maya recorded their religion, histories, and advanced astronomical knowledge in their unique hieroglyphic writing system. Although all but a handful of

Maya paper books perished centuries before modern scholars could read them, texts sculptured on stone monuments, painted on walls and pottery vases, and incised on bone, shell, and jade, have survived to reveal the outlines of the Pre-Columbian world's only literate society.[1] While most archaeologists have to construct models of past gender relations without the aid of writing, the Classic Maya elite themselves now provide insight into how they conceived of women's roles at the pinnacles of power.[2]

The Roles of Women

There are many millions of people today in Mexico and Central America who speak a Mayan language and are culturally related to the ancient Maya who lived in this country. The great majority of these contemporary people reckon kinship through the male line and men generally dominate public affairs. Women, however, can have important roles in the preparation of religious festivals and in the performance of ritual activities in homes. Moreover, there are numerous women curers, midwives, and diviners, specialists with access to supernatural powers that make them deeply respected and influential in their communities.[3] While the Maya world was and remains quite patriarchal, in that men controlled greater access to power and resources, and most Pre-Columbian Classic royal women merit mention in glyphic texts only as mothers of kings, it is clear that noble women were barred from few, if any, principal courtly roles. For example, a text painted upon a fine ceramic vessel informs us that the mother of a sixth century king of the great lowland capital of Tikal was a "scribe,"[4] indicating that at least some women were literate in the hieroglyphic writing system. Recent analyses by Marc Zender and Alfonso Lacadena suggest that some Maya women played priestly roles in the ecclesiastical hierarchy,[5] honoring and caring for the gods on behalf of their subjects as did their male counterparts.

Female variants of most royal titles have been found. Thus we read of "Lady First-of-the-Earth," "Lady Ruler" and "Lady Supreme Warlord."[6] We should note at this point that the on-going decipherment of ancient Mayan texts reveals a hodge-podge of titles and names, some still nick-names where the experts do not yet agree on a Mayan decipherment, and others in ancient Mayan where they do agree. For the sake of simplicity and clarity in this introductory level review of gender issues, we will use as few Mayan words as possible. However, scholarly integrity requires us to use agreed-upon decipherments when available. Most experts read the last title, Lady Supreme Warlord, or *kaloomte'* in Mayan, as "emperor" because it is a political status clearly superior to that of king and is only applied to rulers governing kingdoms beyond their own dynastic realm. It clearly had military connotations and one variant of the glyph portrays the storm god wielding an axe. So another fair reading of this title is thus "supreme warlord" and a number of important queens took this title. Lady

K'ab'el, a seventh century princess of Calakmul, a huge city in present-day Campeche, Mexico, was one of these, and as Supreme Warlord she actually held a higher status than her husband, the king of El Peru-Waka' in northwestern Petén, Guatemala.

Lady Warlords: A Case Study from Yaxchilan

Classic Maya history is dominated by the political and military competition between *kaloomte'* level lords. On the other hand, the site of Yaxchilan, situated above the Usumacinta River in the western Maya lowlands in present-day Chiapas, Mexico, provides one of the most intriguing stories of the competition between aspiring Supreme Warlords both male and female, *within* the same kingdom. Yaxchilan had languished underneath the domination of its northern neighbor down river on the Guatemalan side of the Usumacinta, Piedras Negras, throughout the late sixth and entire seventh centuries. In 713 AD, however, in the 32nd year of his long reign, king Itzamnaaj B'ahlam III reasserted Yaxchilan's independence in battle, and was thus in later years referred to as the kingdom's "first supreme warlord."[7]

Structure 23, the first great construction of Itzamnaaj B'ahlam III's reign was built ten years later yet extolled not his own great feats, but those of his principal wife, Lady K'ab'al Xook. Like her husband, she took the title "western supreme warlord," a title reflecting the pretension of Yaxchilan's king to political and military dominance of the western Maya lowlands. Structure 23 contained three beautifully carved lintels featuring the queen performing in a related series of rituals, apparently associated with her role as a Lady supreme warlord. The lintels are large stone slabs that held up the heavy masonry over the doorways. The carved surfaces could only be viewed by the gods and the privileged few nobility who paused and looked up as they passed through the doors. Carved lintels were a typical way that the Maya elite used to dedicate buildings. The first, Lintel 24, shows the queen on the day of her husband's coronation, performing self-sacrifice by pulling a thorn-studded rope through her tongue. Her husband, the new king, is shown as an attendant, raising a flaming torch above her to illuminate the gruesome scene.

The second, central doorway, lintel (Lintel 25) portrays Lady K'ab'al Xook experiencing a vision of a serpent, out of whose open mouth emerges a warrior. Until recently, everyone thought that the warrior was a male, an ancestor of the king. However, a closer reading of the accompanying text shows that this is actually the queen herself[8] emerging as a goddess named "Lady Heart of the *Wite' Naah*."[9] *Wite' Naah* is an enigmatic place associated with royal dynasties and the city of Teotihuacán in Mexico. It appears to refer to a sacred fire temple deeply infused with political and religious symbolism of Teotihuacan.[10]

It is important to note here that the warrior figure emerging armed with battle shield and spear, the elementary symbols of Maya warfare, is said in the inscription to be the queen herself and not her husband. We may never know if royal women actually went to battle, but Lady K'ab'al Xook is certainly given credit in this temple for the religious and political legitimacy of war prosecuted by her husband. The final lintel in this series, Lintel 26, highlights the queen's role as source of military power, as a Lady supreme warlord, by depicting Lady K'ab'al Xook handing her husband his war gear, including shield, spear and jaguar-headed, feather-crested battle helmet.

Lady K'ab'al Xook's position as the Lady western supreme warlord of her kingdom secured her power as leading lady and primary queen, positions she held throughout the reign of her husband. She may well have given birth to his heir, king Yopaat B'ahlam II. This king remains a shadowy figure as he in turn was succeeded by another son of Itzamnaaj B'ahlam III, a famous king name Yaxuun B'ahlam IV. Yaxuun B'ahlam IV was born in the 28th year of his father's reign and when his mother, a princess of Calakmul named Lady Uh Chan[11] was at least 38 years old. Certainly a very junior member of the royal family, Yaxuun B'ahlam was a great warrior and struggled long and hard, likely against Yopaat B'ahlam II, to finally secure the throne ten years after his father died.

By this time his mother and, more importantly, her co-wife Lady K'ab'al Xook, had also passed away. In his retrospective history, Yaxuun B'ahlam portrayed his mother as a primary queen during the reign of Itzamnaaj B'ahlam III. Lady Uh Chan, who is said to have been a courtesan,[12] is also accorded the title of eastern supreme warlord, in reference to her coming from Calakmul, northeast of Yaxchilan. While we have no contemporary records of Lady Eveningstar, a junior wife of Itzamnaaj B'ahlam, she left a lasting impression with her son who went to great pains once he had finally secured the kingship for himself to credit his mother as not only a great queen but also a Lady supreme warlord on par with Lady K'ab'al Xook.

Foreign Princesses: Lady Six Sky at Naranjo and Lady Batz' Ek' at Caracol

It can thus been seen that certain remarkable and forceful women appeared as the ultimate wielders of power within their kingdoms. Lady Six Sky of Dos Pilas, a small but highly strategic and famous royal capital in southern Peten, Guatemala, is another of these. She was the daughter of a great Dos Pilas warrior-king and she established herself at the city of Naranjo to the northeast where she appears on monuments with all the prerogatives of sole ruler in the early eighth century AD. Her son, born five years after her arrival at Naranjo, became the next king of this city. While Lady Six Sky herself never claimed the title of ruler of that city (she was always referred to as a princess of Dos Pilas), she was certainly the *de facto* ruler until her son was old enough to take command of the armies himself. The father of her son was apparently never mentioned in the site's history but her son did regularly pair his own monuments with ones dedicated to his mother.

The tropical environment and the vagaries of history have destroyed or damaged most of the historical records that the Classic Maya left to posterity and our current understanding of their past still remains, and always shall remain, fragmentary. What information that has survived the passage of centuries, the heat and humidity, and looters, both ancient and modern, provides but random facts and insights into Classic Maya individual lives. Thus, while we know a lot about Lady Six Sky's actions at Naranjo as dowager queen, we cannot even state how old she was when she arrived at her new home, nor how long she lived and ruled there as neither her tomb nor a mention of her death having yet been found.[13]

In order to arrive at a fuller view of the lives of Classic Maya royal women we must compare the snippets of biographical information for various queens and princesses to come up with cultural norms. Lady Batz' Ek', who married into the royal family of Caracol, a huge city in the Maya mountains of Belize and Naranjo's arch-rival for dominance of the eastern Peten, provides a close parallel to the life of Lady Six Sky. Lady Batz' Ek' was born in 566 AD as a princess of a little known dynasty related to that of the powerful Snake Kingdom, then with its capital apparently at Dzibanche, in southern Quintan Roo state, Mexico. At the age of 18 she journeyed to Caracol to marry its king. He was a relatively old man and he had already been on the throne for 31 years, during which time he had switched his allegiance from the powerful city of Tikal in Peten, Guatemala, to its arch-rival, Calakmul in Mexico. His new princess bride, Lady Batz' Ek', was proof of his newfound allegiance in flesh and blood. Marriage alliances of this sort were common throughout the Classic period and undoubtedly in both the periods preceding and following this, periods for which we do not have written records.

Lady Batz' Ek' was not her husband's first wife. As we saw in the case at Yaxchilan, the polygamous marriages of Maya kings often lead to competition between their wives for the position of primary queen and the ability to place one of their children on the throne. Providing the king with children, especially sons, was one of the keys to success for his wives. Lady Batz' Ek' gave birth to a son, Sak Witzil B'aah ("White Mountain Gopher"), four years after her arrival. In 599 the king died and was succeeded by his elder son, Knot Ajaw. Prince Sak Witzil B'aah was only eleven years old at the time and while Lady Batz' Ek' bided her time,

she groomed her son for the throne. This must have taken considerable skill and intelligence, as Sak Witzil B'aah was a threat and rival to his half-brother, the new king. We will never know the full story of this tense situation but after a reign of 18 years, Knot Ajaw disappears from the historical record and Sak Witzil B'aah finally gained the throne as king K'an II, arguably the greatest king of Caracol.

Our vision of Lady Batz' Ek' guiding her son to the throne and being his major backer is not merely modern speculation. It is the portrait that K'an II wished painted of the foundation of his rule. One of the major monuments of his reign is largely devoted to recording her personal history and mentions the crucial information that she was a "witness" to his accession, a position usually associated with political authority and agency. The devotion of K'an II to his mother extended even in death. Her probable tomb, bearing a painted date of 634, was located deep inside Temple B–19, the central pyramid atop the largest building at Caracol and the tallest ancient structure in all of Belize. That this foreign princess should be accorded such incredible honor in her adopted home bespeaks the success of her life, the love of her son and subjects, and provides an excellent example of just how lofty the achievements of Classic Maya royal women could be.

An Assertive Queen: Lady Winikhaab' Ajaw at Piedras Negras

On the other side of the Maya world, at Piedras Negras on the Usumacinta River, we read of the story of Lady Winikhaab' Ajaw,[14] a princess from the small, neighboring kingdom of Maan. Texts on monumental carved stone stelae tell us that at the age of twelve she was married to the Piedras Negras heir who shortly thereafter succeeded his father as king. This king had a long reign but appears to have been a weak ruler. While he raised many monuments at his home city, texts from foreign centers document the failures in warfare that Piedras Negras suffered during his reign. Within twenty years, this king's realm consisted of little more than the immediate vicinity of his capital. Gradually in the course of his reign, his wife took an increasingly prominent role. Finally, the text on the rear of Stela 3 records that on the occasion of the king's 25th anniversary of accession his wife "took (possession of) the throne." Just what this seizure of power entailed is hard to discern from archaeology, but the recording of it in public history is quite remarkable.

Lady Winikhaab' Ajaw's source of power is unknown but the birth of her daughter, Lady Juntahn Ahk is given special prominence on the same monument recording her seizure of power and the events may be linked. The king does not appear to have had a son, and Lady Juntahn Ahk may have been his first (and possibly only) child and, hence, heir. The future husband of this princess stood to gain a kingdom and by overseeing the marriage of her daughter, Lady Winikhaab' Ajaw became very influential and the source of considerable power over the future of Piedras Negras. Although living in a patriarchal society, Classic Maya women could adroitly use the system to achieve success and positions of power.

The Ruling Queens of Palenque

When situations arose in which no clear male heir was available to assume the throne it was possible, at least in certain kingdoms, for royal women to assume the status and position of actual ruler. At Palenque in the far west of the lowlands, we have chronicles that record the accession of a Lady Yohl Ik'nal in 584. She went on to reign for two decades and was considered so important by her illustrious descendant, K'inich Janaab' Pakal I (the Great), that she was given two portraits on the latter's famous sculptured sarcophagus, an honor otherwise reserved only for the king's parents. Unfortunately, no contemporary evidence of her reign has survived to the present and we are left with only Pakal's retrospective accounts as a document to this woman.

The reason for the lack of any records from the reign of Lady Yohl Ik'nal, or from any reign prior to that of Pakal the Great, is that for a decade (and perhaps even longer) following this great woman's reign, the site of Palenque was subject to a series of devastating attacks by its neighbors and foreign enemies. The worst of these took place in 611 when the king of Calakmul marched his army hundreds of kilometers to the west to sack Palenque. The Temple of the Inscriptions at Palenque records the results of these military disasters in poetic form: "lost is the queen, lost is the king,"[15] an apparent reference to the capture or even (sacrificial?) deaths of the royal family.

In the aftermath of this dynastic catastrophe a new lineage came to the throne of Palenque. Curiously, the first new ruler who acceded in 612 AD took the same name as that of the local variant of the Maize (Corn) God, Muwaan Mat. Mythological texts from Palenque record that Muwaan Mat was born in 3121 BC and gave birth to the site's triad of patron deities before acceding in 2325 BC. This primordial accession is recorded as Muwaan Mat's "first," the implication being that the Muwaan Mat who acceded in 612 AD was a reincarnation of the deity.

There has been considerable controversy among epigraphers as to who the human behind the divine façade of Muwaan Mat really was. As the Maize God is normally portrayed in Classic Maya art as a male, some scholars have sought a male to fill this role. However, maize is traditionally conceived of by modern Maya as female and one portrait of the Maize Deity in the Dresden Codex, identified by this god's distinctive name glyph, is clearly a woman complete with an exposed breast. In fact, the Maize "God" now appears to best be described as a hermaphroditic Maize Deity.[16]

If one accepts that as Maize Deity Muwaan Mat was both male and female, there can no longer be any objection to seeing a woman behind this ruler. In fact, the most common costume for Maya royal women was as the Maize Deity, a costume also worn by men (a fact which has led to considerable confusion in the study of Classic Maya concepts of gender). The most likely candidate for Muwaan Mat is the mother of Pakal I, Lady Sak K'uk' ("White Quetzal"). She is the one shown on the Oval Palace Tablet (set behind the royal throne) passing the royal crown to her son at his accession, which took place only three years after the accession to the throne of the reincarnated Muwaan Mat. Pakal's Sarcophagus

Lid, which provides an account of the deaths of all of this king's predecessors, includes that of his mother in the royal position expected for the ruler/deity Muwaan Mat.

It can thus be seen that Lady Sak K'uk', likely a princess from the earlier dynastic line whose primary members had been "lost" in the wars of the early seventh century, came to the throne under the guise of Muwaan Mat, to "divinely" restart the dynasty. After three years as sole ruler she elevated her 12-year old son, Pakal I, as king and co-ruler. Lady Sak K'uk' was undoubtedly the driving force in this royal duo throughout the early years of his reign and it is not until after her death that we really see Pakal emerging as a ruler in his own right.

Queens as Viceroys

While at least one Maya queen seems to have seized control of her adopted home city, and others assumed the throne peacefully in the absence of male heirs, still others appear to have been sent by imperial kings to vassal cities to rule in the name of their royal families. The Dallas Panel, from the ancient vassal city of *Sak Nikte'* (the modern site of La Corona) in north-western Guatemala records the "arrivals" (the establishment in authority) of three royal women of the Snake Kingdom over a period of two centuries beginning in 520 AD. The Snake Kingdom, *Kan*, one of the mightiest of the ancient Maya polities, had successive capitals at the sites Dzibanche in southeastern Quintana Roo, and then Calakmul in southern Campeche, during the course of the Classic period. The mightiest Snake King of the Classic period, Yuhknoom Ch'een the Great (who ruled from 636–686) celebrated his 20-year anniversary in power at *Sak Nikte'* and he may have used it as a southern base-of-operations in his long and ultimately successful war of imperial expansion against his arch-enemy, the kingdom of Tikal. His daughter was one of the royal Snake women mentioned on the Dallas Panel (she married the local lord, a vassal of her father's).

The rituals that she and the other royal women from *Kan* are said to have carried out at *Sak Nikte'* include those usually reserved for the ruler himself. Indeed, evidence suggests that the Dallas Panel was originally placed in a wall of a throne room where the queens ruled. The images on the panel show women standing in front of their thrones framed by gods and war beasts. It may well be that these women actually ruled in place of their husbands and it is interesting that during their time, there is little evidence for the actions of any local rulers, who were likely preempted by these foreign queens.

A similar practice may be in evidence at Calakmul's great enemy, the kingdom of Tikal. Altar 5 of that city portrays two lords dressed in deathly costumes and kneeling to either side of a stack of bones and a skull. The text on this monument has long puzzled scholars, but clearly revolves around a woman, Lady Tuunte' Kaywak. She is said to have accompanied Tikal's king to the small island site of Topoxte, southeast of Tikal. This island was in the jurisdiction of Yaxha's capital city on the other side of the same lake. The kingdom of Yaxha was allied with Tikal and Lady Tuunte' Kaywak may have been a wife of the Tikal king sent by her husband to govern a vassal royal court. We have reason to suspect that the skull and bones prominently displayed on this altar are hers, retrieved from the kingdom of Yaxha because they were threatened with desecration by the king of Narjano, son of Lady Six Sky. Archaeologists discovered a skull and long bones underneath the stela portraying the Tikal king next to the altar. These may well be the re-interred bones of the queen whose burial dedicated and sanctified these monuments.

CONCLUDING THOUGHTS

The study of Maya texts and their correlation with archaeology is just beginning to yield information relevant to gender studies in this civilization. It is already clear to us, however, that Maya royal women were major players on their historical stage. As role models for other elite women of their world, powerful royal women may well have encouraged a certain gender parity among the nobility that does not yet seem evident to us among the commoner classes. However, 50 years ago, no Maya archaeologists believed that royal women wielded such power. Future breakthroughs in research may show that ordinary Maya women enjoyed modest versions of the religious and political roles of noble women, analogous to the women shamans, healers, and midwives of the modern Maya peoples.

NOTES

1. However, there is a price to be paid for the unique window on the past that textual information can afford. In order to discuss these historical figures, their names, titles, and achievements, we cannot avoid using the actual Mayan words. Where we can, we use glosses in English for the titles, and sometimes the decipherment of the texts has not progressed sufficiently to yield actual names and experts are still using "nicknames" for some people. But just as historians use the actual names of people in ancient Egypt, Greece, Rome, Mesopotamia, and China, so we must use the actual names of Maya women, their husbands, and children. To do otherwise is not only poor scholarship, but also a disservice to these people, who played important roles in shaping the history and destiny of their world. So we encourage readers not to get hung up on the pronunciation of the names or their exotic character and concentrate on the exploits of their owners. Someday, just as people accept Cleopatra VI and her consort Julius Caesar as named historical figures, perhaps they will accept the names of the great women of Maya civilization as part of common knowledge among educated Americans.

2. There are many recent publications on gender roles in ancient Maya civilization. Rosemary Joyces's *Gender and Power in Prehispanic Mesoamerica* (2000) is a clearly written introduction to the general theme with special chapters on the Maya. *Ancient Maya Women* (2002) is an edited book with more technical and advanced discussions covering important aspects of the topic.

3. See Barbara Tedlock's *Time and the Highland Maya* 1992, chapter 3, for a good review of Maya men and women specialists in the supernatural.

4. The term scribe is *aj tz'ihb'* in ancient Mayan.

5. The *ajk'uhuun* title, carried by a few Maya royal women, was a priestly title according to Alfonso

Lacadena (personal communication, 2002) and Marc Zender, 2003, *A Study of Classic Maya Priesthood,* unpublished Ph.D. dissertation, University of Calgary.

6. Maya scribes formed female titles by simply prefixing the female agentive *ix* to the title itself. Thus we read of *ix b'akab'* ("Lady First-of-the-Earth," *ix ajaw* ("Lady Ruler"), and *ix kaloomte'* Supreme Warlord.

7. The phrase is *natal kaloomte* in ancient Mayan.

8. Personal communication from Marc Zender, 2001.

9. *Ix Yohl Wite' Naah* in ancient Mayan.

10. Karl Taube (1999) makes the argument that the *Wite' Naah* is a fire temple. See also the article by David Stuart (1999).

11. Her name translates likely as "Lady Moon Sky." In earlier articles and texts she is referred to by the nickname of "Lady Eveningstar."

12. *ix ajk'uhuun* in ancient Mayan.

13. An hieroglyphic bench from Lady Six Sky's hometown of Dos Pilas has long been thought to mention her death in 741. However, a closer analysis by Stanley Guenter and Federico Fahsen has noted that the eroded name of a Dos Pilas princess on this monument only resembles in part that of Lady Six Sky and is almost certainly another woman, perhaps a sister of Lady Six Sky and probably the wife of Dos Pilas Ruler 3.

14. Traditionally known as Lady Katun Ahau.

15. *satay k'uhul ixik satay ajaw,* in ancient Mayan.

16. See Mathew Looper "Women Men (and Men-Women): Classic Maya Rulers and the Third Gender," in Ancient Maya Women, T. Adren, editor, 2002, for a related argument on the Maize god and the Moon goddess.

REFERENCES

Ardren, Traci, 2002, *Ancient Maya Women.* Walnut Creek, CA: AltaMira Press.

Joyce, Rosemary, 2002, *Gender and Power in Prehispanic Mesoamerica.* Austin: University of Texas Press.

Looper, Mathew, 2002, "Women Men (and Men-Women): Classic Maya Rulers and the Third Gender." In T. Ardren, ed. *Ancient Maya Women.* Pp. 171–202. Lanham, MD: AltaMira Press.

Stuart, David, 1999, "Arrival of strangers: Teotihuacan and Tollan in Classic Maya History." *In Mesoamerica's Classic Heritage: Teotihuacán to the Aztecs. David Carrasco, Lindsay Jones, and Scott Sessions, eds. pp. 465–513.* Boulder, CO: University Press of Colorado.

Taube, Karl A., 1999, Turquoise hearth: Fire, self-sacrifice, and the Central Mexican Cult of War. *In Mesoamerica's Classic Heritage: Teotihuacán to the Aztecs. David Carrasco, Lindsay Jones, and Scott Sessions, eds. pp. 269–340.* Boulder, CO: University Press of Colorado.

Tedlock, Barbara, 1992, *Time and the Highland Maya.* Albuquerque: University of New Mexico Press.

Zender, Marc, 2003, *A Study of Classic Maya Priesthood.* Unpublished Ph.D. dissertation, University of Calgary.

III

Domestic Worlds and Public Worlds

In 1974, in an attempt to document a universal subordination of women, Michelle Rosaldo (1974: 18) proposed a paradigm relating "recurrent aspects of psychology and cultural and social organization to an opposition between the 'domestic' orientation of women and the extradomestic or 'public' ties, that, in most societies, are primarily available to men." The domestic–public model led Rosaldo to suggest that women's status is highest in societies in which the public and domestic spheres are only weakly differentiated, as among the Mbuti pygmies. In contrast, "women's status will be lowest in those societies where there is a firm differentiation between domestic and public spheres of activity and where women are isolated from one another and placed under a single man's authority, in the home. Their position is raised when they can challenge those claims to authority . . ." (Rosaldo 1974: 36). According to this argument, women may enhance their status by creating a public world of their own or by entering the men's world. In addition, the most egalitarian societies will be those in which men participate in the domestic domain.

Correspondingly, writing in the same volume (Rosaldo and Lamphere 1974), Sanday (1974) suggested that women's involvement in domains of activity such as subsistence or defense may be curtailed because of their time and energy commitment to reproduction and mothering. Men, on the other hand, are free to form broader associations in the political, economic, and military spheres that transcend the mother–child unit. While the linkage of women with the domestic and men with the public domains may imply a biological determinism based on women's reproductive roles, Rosaldo (1974: 24) argued that the opposition between domestic and public orientations is an intelligible but not a necessary arrangement.

One aspect of women's domestic responsibilities is that it is women who primarily raise children. Nancy Chodorow (1974) developed a theory linking adult sex role behavior to the fact that children's early involvement is with their female parent. Chodorow contended that girls are integrated through ties with female kin into the world of domestic work. Age, rather than achievement, may define their status, while boys must "learn" to be men. Unlike girls, boys have few responsibilities in childhood and are free to establish peer groups that create "public" ties. To become an adult male a boy is often obliged to dissociate himself from the home and from female kin. According to Rosaldo (1974: 26), "the fact that children virtually everywhere grow up with their mothers may well account for characteristic differences in male and female psychologies" as well as set the stage for adult organization of activities.

As scholarship devoted to an understanding of gender issues has evolved, the influential domestic–public model has been the focus of considerable controversy, revolving around three related issues: whether male domination is universal, whether male domination is explained by the domestic-public dichotomy, and whether—and under what conditions—the concept of domestic-public has relevance.

Louise Lamphere (in this book) reviews the formulation of the domestic–public model, and discusses the subsequent critiques of its validity and applicability. Rosaldo herself, rethinking her original position, said that although male dominance appears widespread, it does not "in actual behavioral terms assume a universal content or a universal shape. On the contrary, women typically have power and influence in political and economic life, display autonomy from men in their pursuits, and rarely find themselves confronted or constrained by what might seem the brute fact of male strength" (1980: 394). Although the domestic–public opposition has been compelling, Rosaldo suggested that the model assumes too much rather than helping to illuminate and explain.

As Lamphere observes, it has become increasingly clear that the domestic–public opposition is the heir to nineteenth-century social theory rooted in a dichotomy contrasting home and woman, with a public world of men, and reflecting an understanding of political rights based on sex. The domestic–public dichotomy emerged from the industrial revolution and the separation of home and workplace. Conceptualizing social life as dichotomized into domestic and public domains does not make sense in societies in which management of production occurs within the household and in which household production itself involves the management of the "public" economy (Leacock 1978: 253).

In contrast, in an industrial society, where home and workplace are clearly demarcated, the domestic–public opposition may have explanatory value. For example, Anne Murcott (in this book) analyzes one domestic task, cooking, as part of an exploration of economic relations in the family and of the division of labor between spouses. Interviews with Welsh housewives indicate that ideas about home cooking reflect understandings of the relationship between domestic and paid labor. An analysis of the production of meals illuminates the allocation of responsibility for different domestic tasks, the gendered control of decision making and the distribution of power and authority in marriage. The informants shared the view that proper eating must occur at home and that a cooked dinner is necessary to family health and well-being. Murcott suggests that the emphasis on having a proper dinner waiting for the husband when he comes in from work underscores the symbolic importance of the return home: "the cooked dinner marks the threshold between the public domains of school or work and the private sphere behind the closed front door" (Murcott, this volume).

In his analysis of fatherhood in the United States, Nicholas W. Townsend (in this book) contends that in the United States, an industrialized society, it is often assumed that parenting represents a simple division of labor in which men are engaged in the public sphere of paid labor and politics, while women are involved in the domestic sphere of childcare and reproduction. His research demonstrates, however, that the domestic and public spheres interpenetrate and that arrangements made in one sphere influence behavior in another. Parenting, he argues, is deeply gendered. This means not only that fathers and mothers "do" different things, but that fatherhood has different meanings for men and women. Men interviewed in his research claimed to want greater involvement as fathers than their own fathers had experienced. They saw "marriage and children" as a package deal; for these men, a relationship with a woman was necessary for a man to see himself as a father. Correspondingly, Townsend shows that women are often influential in men's decisions about when to have children. Women are the "default parent" while men are in a more "optional" position with their role as disciplinarian or "fun dad" shaped by the interests of their children's mother. Thus women, as wives and mothers, mediate and facilitate fatherhood. Moreover, the structural division of labor placing men in the labor force and women at home has been maintained by strong cultural themes that continue to emphasize women's involvement in their children's lives, even with women's increasing labor force participation.

Townsend shows that in the United States, an ideological association of men with the public and women with the domestic does not accurately represent the interpenetration of these spheres. Similarly, in Andalusia, in southern Spain, women are ideologically associated with the home, and men with public places, yet the reality is more complex (Driessen 1983). According to widely held ideals, the woman should be virtuous, docile, and devoted to husband and children; the ideal man is the head of the household, tough, but seldom at home. However, in actuality, the involvement of men in the private sphere and women in the public sphere varies according to social class. Among agricultural laborers, women's labor is critical to the household economy. It is common for women to be employed, while their men are unemployed. This contradiction produces tensions that are reflected in men's sociability patterns. The bar offers men the opportunity to display their masculinity by heavy drinking and sexual banter. Men's sociability is best understood as a response to the vulnerability of unemployed men to women who contribute substantially to the family income through wage labor. This results in blurred idealized distinctions between male and female identities and responsibilities.

Research on the public–private distinction has implications for the interplay among gender, status, and power. Whereas traditional conceptions of power emphasized formal political behavior and authority associated with a status conferring the "right" to impose sanctions (Lamphere 1974: 99), informal power strategies such as manipulation and maneuvering are also important aspects of political activity. Cynthia Nelson (1974) examined the concept of power, focusing on images of women and power in the domestic and public domains in the societies of the Middle East. Ethnographies of this region have commonly differentiated two social worlds, a woman's private world and a man's public world. Women's concerns are domestic, men's political. Nelson argues that the assignment of private and public reflects the imposition of western cultural categories on the Middle East; the meaning of power is influenced by these categorizations, as well as by the limitations of data obtained by male ethnographers from male informants.

This is a point made forcefully by Annette Weiner (1976) in her reanalysis of Trobriand exchange. She argues that "we unquestioningly accept male statements about women as factual evidence for the way a society is structured. . . . Any study that does not include the role of women—as seen by women—as part of the way the society is structured remains only a partial study of that society. Whether women are publicly valued or privately secluded, whether they control politics, a range of economic commodities, or merely magic spells, they function within that society, not as objects, but as individuals with some measure of control" (228).

Similarly, Nelson argues that by asking such questions as "How do women influence men?" "Who controls whom about what?" "How is control exercised?" it becomes apparent that women exercise a greater degree of power in social life than is often appreciated. In addition, she challenges the idea that the social worlds of men and women are reducible to private and public domains, with power limited to the public arena. Nelson's review of ethnographies addressing the role and position of women in Middle Eastern society indicates that women play a crucial role as structural links between kinship groups in societies in which family and kinship are fundamental institutions. Women are in a position to influence men through ritual means, to channel information to male kin, and to influence decision making about alliances; consequently, women do participate in "public" activities, and women's exclusive solidarity groups exercise considerable social control and political influence. The conceptions of power as defined by the Western observer are particularly challenged by literature on women written by women who offer multiple perspectives on the experiences of Middle Eastern women, derived from the actors themselves.

In the course of her critique of the application of the domestic-public opposition to social organization in the Middle East, Nelson challenges longstanding assumptions regarding women's subordination and male dominance and calls into question the association between political power and a public domain that excludes women. Similarly, in studies of peasant societies Rogers (1975) and others (Friedl 1967; Riegelhaupt 1967) contend that the sector of life over which peasant women have control—the household—is in fact the key sphere of activity, socially, politically, and economically. Men occupy public and prestigious positions of authority within the village sphere, but these activities do not have the impact on daily life that household activities have. In light of these analyses demonstrating women's power and influence, we are reminded that the universality of male dominance appears untenable.

Similarly, Brenner (1995) questions the value of totalizing models of gender-based power and prestige in her study of gender ideologies in Java. Her analysis critiques the stereotyped, male-centered visions of male power pervasive in Javanese cultural representations and in ethnographic accounts. The ethnographic record has emphasized male-focused gender ideologies while neglecting alternative conceptions of gender voiced by women. She shows that the home and market, both associated with women in Javanese thought, are not only sites of economic production, but also sites where conflicting understandings of male and female nature are symbolically negotiated. According to the gendered division of domestic power, the wife should defer to her husband as head of the household but in reality, women's power may far outweigh that of their husbands. Moreover, the dominance of women in the household is often linked to economic power within and outside the home. Yet in spite of their economic power, central ideologies devalue women precisely because of their commercial pursuits, which are held to detract from prestige. This analysis suggests that although women are identified with the domestic, their activities are central to the production of the family's status in the broader society.

In "Cities of Women," Mary Weismantel (in this book) also explores the interpenetration of domestic and public spheres, using the case of Andean women's domination of the produce market. Weismantel challenges the universality of an opposition between a feminine private domain and a masculine outside world, although some scholars have asserted that this dichotomy characterizes Latin America. Rather, she contends that the market exists as a highly gendered institution, a public space that is dramatically feminine, in spite of the idealized boundary between domestic and commercial work. Men find women's domination of this public space unnerving, in contrast to the generalized masculinization of public life in Andean communities. This study also demonstrates that market women are not merely "women serving men," but are social actors engaged in pursuing their own needs and goals, as well as those of other women. For these women, home and domesticity do not necessarily represent a private female domain but rather, a patriarchal territory. Market work is both domestic and commercial, generating income for the vendors while producing food for housewives, thus shaping the workload for women in the home. Weismantel's analysis of Andean market women illustrates how the line between work and family, the public and domestic, is erased in conjunction with the domesticity of the market and the commodification of private life.

In reflecting on feminist research in anthropology, Rosaldo critiqued the very tendency to look for universal truths and origins. Rather, anthropologists need to develop theoretical perspectives that analyze the relationships of men and women in a broader social context (Rosaldo 1980: 414), involving inequality and hierarchy. As Henrietta Moore emphasizes, although women in many societies share some experiences and problems, women have had very different encounters with racism, colonialism, the penetration of capitalism, and international development. We need to move from assumptions of the shared experience of "women" to a critical analysis of the differences among them (1988: 9). Assuming the universality of dichotomous domestic and public spheres constrains our exploration of gendered social space and the interconnections between home and workplace. Yet although there is now a consensus that public and private are not universal and timeless absolutes, these concepts remain powerful signifiers of how our social worlds are ordered (Davidoff 1995). We continue to confront the challenges posed by the need to critically examine the relevance of the distinctions between domestic and public in particular historical moments and diverse social and economic conditions.

REFERENCES

Brenner, Suzanna A. 1995. "Why Women Rule the Roost: Rethinking Javanese Ideologies of Gender and Self-Control." In Aihwa Ong and Michael Peletz (eds.). *Bewitching Women, Pious Men: Gender and Body Politics in Southeast Asia.* Berkeley: University of California Press.

Chodorow, Nancy. 1974. "Family Structure and Feminine Personality." In Michelle Z. Rosaldo and Louise Lamphere (eds.). *Woman, Culture, and Society,* pp. 43–67. Stanford, CA: Stanford University Press.

Davidoff, L. 1995. "Regarding Some 'Old Husbands' tales': Public and Privaate in Feminist History." In *Worlds Between: Historical Perspectives on Gender and Class,* pp. 227–75. Cambridge: U. K. Polity Press.

Driessen, Henk. 1983. "Male Sociability and Rituals of Masculinity in Rural Andalusia." *Anthropological Quarterly* 56(3): 125–133.

Friedl, Ernestine. 1967. "The Position of Women: Appearance and Reality." *Anthropological Quarterly* 40: 97–108.

Lamphere, Louise. 1974. "Strategies, Cooperation, and Conflict Among Women in Domestic Groups." In Michelle Z. Rosaldo and Louise Lamphere (eds.). *Woman, Culture, and Society,* pp. 97–113. Stanford: Stanford University Press.

Leacock, Eleanor. 1978. "Women's Status in Egalitarian Society. Implications for Social Evolution." *Current Anthropology* 19(2): 247–275.

Moore, Henrietta L. 1988. *Feminism and Anthropology.* Minneapolis: University of Minnesota Press.

Nelson, Cynthia. 1974. "Public and Private Politics: Women in the Middle Eastern World. *American Ethnologist* 1(3): 551–563.

Riegelhaupt, Joyce. 1967. "Saloio Women: An Analysis of Informal and Formal Political and Economic Roles of Portuguese Peasant Women." *Anthropological Quarterly* 40: 109–126.

Rogers, Susan Carol. 1975. "Female Forms of Power and the Myth of Male Dominance: A Model of Female/Male Interaction in Peasant Society." *American Ethnologist* 2: 727–756.

Rosaldo, Michelle Z. 1974. "Theoretical Overview." In Michelle Z. Rosaldo and Louise Lamphere (eds.). *Woman, Culture, and Society*, pp. 17–43. Stanford, CA: Stanford University Press.

———. 1980. "The Use and Abuse of Anthropology: Reflections on Feminism and Cross-Cultural Understanding." *Signs* 5(3): 389–418.

Rosaldo, Michelle Zimbalist and Louise Lamphere, eds., 1974, *Women, Culture & Society*. Stanford: Stanford University Press.

Sanday, Peggy R. 1974. "Female Status in the Public Domain." In Michelle Z. Rosaldo and Louise Lamphere (eds.). *Woman, Culture, and Society*, pp. 189–207. Stanford, CA: Stanford University Press.

Weiner, Annette B. 1976. *Women of Value, Men of Renown: New Perspectives in Trobriand Exchange*. Austin: University of Texas Press.

The Domestic Sphere of Women and the Public World of Men:
The Strengths and Limitations of an Anthropological Dichotomy

Louise Lamphere

Since 1974 there has been a burgeoning interest within anthropology in the study of women, sex roles, and gender. Anthropology has long been a discipline that contained important women (Elsie Clews Parsons, Ruth Benedict, and Margaret Mead among the most famous) and a field in which women have been studied as well (e.g., Kaberry 1939, 1952; Landes 1938, 1947; Leith-Ross 1939; Paulme 1963; and Underhill 1936). However, with the publication of *Woman, Culture, and Society* (Rosaldo and Lamphere 1974) and *Toward an Anthropology of Women* (Reiter 1975a), women scholars, many of whom were identified as feminists, began to critique the androcentric bias in anthropology, to explore women's status in a wide variety of societies, and to provide explanatory models to understand women's position cross-culturally.

One of the most powerful and influential models was proposed by Michelle Rosaldo in her introductory essay to *Woman, Culture, and Society* (1974). Her argument began by asserting that although there is a great deal of cross-cultural variability in men's and women's roles, there is a pervasive, universal asymmetry between the sexes. "But what is perhaps most striking and surprising," Rosaldo writes, "is the fact that male, as opposed to female, activities are always recognized as predominantly important, and cultural systems give authority and value to the roles and activities of men" (Rosaldo 1974: 19).

One of the quotes we chose to appear at the beginning of the book, a passage from Margaret Mead's *Male and Female*, sums up what we saw in 1974 in all the ethnographies and studies we examined. "In every known society, the male's need for achievement can be recognized. Men may cook, or weave, or dress dolls or hunt hummingbirds, but if such activities are appropriate occupations of men, then the whole society, men and women alike, votes them as important. When the same occupations are performed by women, they are regarded as less important" (Mead 1949: 125). Not only were there differential evaluations of women's activities, but, Rosaldo argues, "everywhere men have some authority over women, that [is] they have culturally legitimated right to her subordination and compliance" (1974: 21).

Having argued for a pervasive sexual asymmetry across cultures, not just in terms of cultural

Original material prepared for this text. Reprinted by permission of the author.

values, but also in terms of power and authority, Rosaldo accounted for this difference between men and women in terms of a dichotomy.[1] She argued that women are associated with a "domestic orientation," while men are primarily associated with extradomestic, political, and military spheres of activity. By "domestic" Rosaldo meant "those minimal institutions and modes of activity that are organized immediately around one or more mothers and their children." In contrast, the "public" referred to "activities, institutions, and forms of association that link, rank, organize, or subsume particular mother-child groups. Put quite simply, men have no single commitment as enduring, time-consuming, and emotionally compelling—as close to seeming necessary and natural—as the relation of a woman to her infant child; and so men are free to form those broader associations that we call 'society,' universalistic systems of order, meaning, and commitment that link particular mother–child groups."

Rosaldo, along with Sherry Ortner and Nancy Chodorow, who also wrote essays in *Woman, Culture, and Society,* insisted that the connection between women's role in reproduction (the fact that women everywhere lactate and give birth to children) and their domestic orientation is not a necessary one. In other words biology is not destiny. Women's domestic orientation was structurally and culturally constructed and "insofar as woman is universally defined in terms of a largely maternal and domestic role, we can account for her universal subordination" (Rosaldo 1974: 7).

"Although" Rosaldo writes, "I would be the last to call this a necessary arrangement or to deny that it is far too simple as an account of any particular empirical case, I suggest that the opposition between domestic and public orientations (an opposition that must, in part, derive from the nurturant capacities of women) provides the necessary framework for an examination of male and female roles in any society" (Rosaldo 1974: 24).

For Rosaldo, then, women were involved in the "messiness" of daily life; they were always available for interruption by children. Men could be more distanced and may actually have separate quarters (such as men's houses) away from women's activities. Men could thus "achieve" authority and create rank, hierarchy, and a political world away from women. The confinement of women to the domestic sphere and men's ability to create and dominate the political sphere thus accounted for men's ability to hold the greater share of power and authority in all known cultures and societies.

At the time Rosaldo wrote her overview and in the introduction we both wrote, we were faced with building a framework where none existed. Despite the number of monographs on women, Margaret Mead's work and that of Simone de Beauvoir (1953) were the most provocative, and perhaps the only, theoretical works we knew.[2] The argument for universal sexual asymmetry followed in a long tradition in anthropology where scholars have sought to look for what is broadly "human" in all cultures. In addition to language, anthropologists have discussed the universality of the incest taboo, marriage, and the family. The notion that women might be universally subordinate to men thus made sense as a first attempt at theory building in this newly revived "subfield" within anthropology.

Although Rosaldo argued for universal subordination, she was careful to make clear that women are not powerless. They exercise informal influence and power, often mitigating male authority or even rendering it trivial (Rosaldo 1974: 21). In addition, there are important variations in women's roles in different cultures, and variation was discussed in most of the rest of the articles in the collection. For example, Sanday and Sacks compared women's status in a number of different societies, while Leis examined the structural reasons why women's associations are strong in one Ijaw village in Nigeria, yet absent in another. Finally, in my own article I examined the differences in women's strategies within domestic groups in a number of societies, which related to the relative integration or separation of domestic and political spheres.

Since 1974 the hypothesis of universal subordination of women and the dichotomous relationship between women in the domestic sphere and men in the public sphere have been challenged and critiqued by a number of feminist anthropologists. As appealing as this dichotomy seemed in the abstract, it turned out to be difficult to apply when actually looking at examples of women's activities in different cultures. For example, in an important article written about the same time as Rosaldo's introduction, Rayna Reiter (now Rayna Rapp) described women's and men's distinct lives in a small French village in the south of France. "They inhabited different domains, one public, one private. While men fraternized with whomever they found to talk to in public places, women were much more enmeshed in their families and their kinship networks" (Reiter 1975b: 253). However, two categories of public space fell into women's domain: the church and three shops, including the local bakery. Men tended to avoid women's places, entering the bakery, for example, only when several men were together and joking, "Let's attack now" (Reiter 1975b: 257).

Reiter argues that men and women use public space in different ways and at different times. "The men go early to the fields, and congregate on the square or in the cafes for a social hour after work. Sometimes they also fraternize in the evenings. These are the times when women are home cooking and invisible to public view. But when the men have abandoned the village for the fields, the women come out to do their marketing in a leisurely fashion. The village is then in female hands. In the afternoon, when the men return to work, the women form gossip groups on stoops and benches or inside houses depending on the weather" (Reiter 1975b: 258). Despite the powerful imagery—women associated with the private or domestic domain and men with public space—the description also shows that the dichotomy is not neat. After all women are in public a great deal; they have taken over, in some sense, the Church and the shops and even the public square in the middle of the day.

In Margery Wolf's description of women in a Taiwanese village based on data she collected in the late 1950s, she emphasizes that because researchers have focused on the dominance of patrilineal descent in the family, they have failed to see women's presence. "We have missed not only some of the system's subtleties but also its near-fatal weaknesses" (Wolf 1972: 37). Women have different interests than men and build uterine families—strong ties to their daughters, but primarily to their sons who give their mothers loyalty and a place in the patrilineal extended family. Outside the family in the community women formed neighborhood groups—around a store, at a platform where women washed their clothes in the canal, or under a huge old tree. In a village strung out between a river and a canal, there was no central plaza dominated by men as in the South of France.

In Peihotien Wolf did not describe a cultural geography where women were in a private sphere and men in the public one; rather there was more of a functional separation—men and women had different activities and interests. They were often located in the same places but had a different relationship to the patrilineal extended family and the male-dominated community. Women's lack of power led them to different strategies, different tactics that often undermined male control of the household and even the community. As Sylvia Yanagisako (1987: 111) has pointed out, the notion of domestic-public entails both a spatial metaphor (of geographically separated or even nested spaces) and a functional metaphor (of functionally different activities or social roles) in the same conceptual dichotomy. Analysts often "mix" these different metaphors in any particular analysis—sometimes using domestic–public spatially and at other times functionally.

Even in the Middle East, the association of women with a private domain (and a lack of power) and men with a public domain (and the center of politics) was too simple, as Cynthia Nelson pointed out in her article, "Public and Private Politics: Women in the Middle Eastern World" (1974). Because they are born into one patrilineal group and marry into another, women are important structural links between social groups and often act as mediators. Because there are segregated social worlds, all-female institutions are important for enforcing social norms: Women fill powerful ritual roles as sorceresses, healers, and mediums; women are important sources of information for their male kin; and women act as "information brokers," mediating social relations within both the family and the larger society.

From Rosaldo's point of view, these aspects of women's power are primarily "informal" and very different from the public, legitimate roles of men. Nevertheless, even though Nelson affirms the separation of male and female worlds (both spatially and functionally), what is "domestic" has public ramifications (the arrangement of a marriage, the transmission of highly charged political information) and the shadow of the family and kin group (the "domestic") is present in even the most "public" of situations. What at first seemed like a simple straightforward dichotomy, in light of actual case material seems very "slippery" and complex.

Furthermore, in many cultures, particularly those with an indigenous band or tribal structure, a separation of "domestic" and "public" spheres makes no sense because household production was simultaneously public, economic, and political. Leacock pointed out the following after reviewing the literature on the Iroquois during the seventeenth and eighteenth centuries:

> Iroquois matrons preserved, stored, and dispensed the corn, meat, fish, berries, squashes, and fats that were buried in special pits or kept in the long house. Brown (1970: 162) notes that women's control over the dispensation of the foods they produced, and meat as well, gave them de facto power to veto declarations of war and to intervene to bring about peace. . . . Women also guarded the "tribal public treasure" kept in the long house, the wampum quill and feather work, and furs. . . . The point to be stressed is that this was "household management" of an altogether different order from management of the nuclear or extended family in patriarchal societies. In the latter, women may cajole, manipulate, or browbeat men, but always behind the public facade; in the former case, "household management" was itself the management of the "public economy." (Leacock 1978: 253)

Sudarkasa has made much the same point about women in West African societies such as the Yoruba. She argues that many of the political and economic activities anthropologists discuss as public are actually embedded in households (Sudarkasa 1976, as quoted in Rapp 1979: 509). Furthermore, "in West Africa, the 'public domain' was not conceptualized as 'the world of men.' Rather, the public domain was one in which both sexes were recognized as having important roles to play" (Sudarkasa 1986: 99).

A more appropriate conception would be to recognize two domains, "one occupied by men and another by women, both of which were internally ordered in a hierarchical fashion and both of which provided 'personnel' for domestic and extradomestic (or public) activities" (Sudarkasa 1986: 94).

Furthermore, a careful examination of "domestic domain" indicates that the categories of "woman" and "mother" overlap in Western society, but the meaning of motherhood may be vastly different in another society. Women may not be exclusively defined as mothers and childrearers in terms of their status and cultural value (see Moore 1988: 20–29 for a discussion of this point).

In addition to the issue of whether the domestic–public dichotomy can provide an adequate *description* of men's and women's spatial and functional relationships in our own and other societies, the model has problems as an *explanation* of women's status. One of these problems is the inherent circularity of the model. A central point is to account for the nature of these domains, yet they are already assumed to exist widely and are treated as categories in terms of which women's activities (such as food preparing, cooking, childcare, washing) can be classified (as opposed to male hunting, warfare, political councils). Comaroff says that the model "can only affirm what has already been assumed—that is, that the distinction between the domestic and politico-jural is an intrinsic, if variable, fact of social existence" (Comaroff 1987: 59). When the model is used to explain women's positions in different societies in relation to these two orientations, the reasoning is equally circular. To put it in the words of Yanagisako and Collier, "The claim that women become absorbed in domestic activities because of their role as mothers is tautological given the definition of 'domestic' as 'those minimal institutions and modes of activity that are organized immediately around one or more mothers and their children'" (Yanagisako and Collier 1987: 19).

Finally, we have come to realize that the concepts of domestic and public were bound up in our own history and our own categories grounded particularly in a Victorian heritage. Rosaldo, in a thoughtful reevaluation of her model, came to argue this position herself.

> The turn-of-the-century social theorists whose writings are the basis of most modern social thinking tended without exception to assume that women's place was in the home. In fact, the Victorian doctrine of separate male and female spheres was, I would suggest, quite central to their sociology. Some of these thinkers recognized that modern women suffered from their association with domestic life, but none questioned the pervasiveness (or necessity) of a split between the family and society. (Rosaldo 1980: 401–402)

Rosaldo traced the historical roots of domestic–public from the nineteenth-century evolutionists through twentieth-century structural functionalists to her own work. Instead of two opposed spheres (different and apart), Rosaldo suggested an analysis of gender relationships, an examination of inequality and hierarchy as they are created particularly through marriage (Rosaldo 1980: 412–413).

The dichotomy has been usefully employed in several ways since 1974. First, several authors have shown us how it works in Western societies (e.g., France and the United States, where it arose historically and still has an important ideological function) (Reiter 1975b; Collier, Rosaldo, and Yanagisako 1982). In a related way, analysts have explored the meanings surrounding domestic activities of women, putting together a much more complex picture of women's relation to men in this sphere (Chai 1987; and Murcott 1983, reprinted in this book). Second, anthropological analysis has helped us to understand the historical development of domestic–public spheres in societies under colonialism. John Comaroff's analysis of the Tshidi chiefdom in South Africa during the early twentieth century is an excellent example of this approach (1987: 53–85). Finally, some analysts have used the cultural concepts of other societies to critique our own model of domestic–public orientations. Sylvia Yanagisako's essay on the clear separation of "inside–outside" domains (a spatial metaphor) and "work–family" activities (a functional dicho-tomy) in Japanese American culture demonstrates how the anthropological model of domestic–public mixes these metaphors, which has made analysis confusing and difficult (Yanagisako 1987).

Despite these useful attempts at examining women's lives through the lens of a domestic-public opposition, many of us would agree with Rayna Rapp's 1979 summary of the problems with this dichotomy.

> We cannot write an accurate history of the West in relation to the Rest until we stop assuming that our experiences subsume everyone else's. Our public/private conflicts are not necessarily the same as those of other times and places. The specific oppression of women cannot be documented if our categories are so broad as to decontextualize what "womanness" means as we struggle to change that definition. A Tanzanian female farmer, a Mapuche woman leader, and an American working-class housewife do not live in the same domestic domain, nor will the social upheavals necessary to give them power over their lives be the same. We must simultaneously understand the differences and the similarities, but not by reducing them to one simple pattern. (Rapp 1979: 511)

Thus, many of us have tired of the domestic-public dichotomy. We feel it is constraining, a "trap," while new approaches try to get away from dichotomous thinking. These approaches do one of several things. Often they take history seriously, examining women's situation as it has evolved, often in a colonial context. Furthermore, they treat women as active agents and following Collier (1974), as people who have interests, often divergent from men, and who act on them. Third, they often focus on gender relationships, rather than only on women. Finally, they do not treat all women as part of a single universal category of "woman." Rather women are usually analyzed in terms of their social location. Age, class, race, ethnicity, and kinship are all likely to divide women, so newer analyses examine women's strategies and identities as they are differently shaped. Several examples will illustrate some of the different approaches taken in recent years.

Collier's examination of Comanche, Cheyenne, and Kiowa gender relationships (1988) illustrates the recent focus on gender and on the multiple positions that men and women hold in societies in which the domestic–public dichotomy seems inappropriate. This is because these "spheres" are integrated, and there is no firm line between domestic and public space (see Lamphere 1974 and Leacock 1978).

The Comanche are an example of a bride service society in which, like many hunter–gatherer societies, men and women were relatively autonomous, the concept of femininity was not elaborated, and the greatest status differences were between unmarried and married men. Marriage established men as having something to achieve (e.g., a wife), leaving women without such a cultural goal. Young men, through providing meat for their in-laws (bride service), become equal adults, and older men, through egalitarian relations and generosity, become the repositories of wisdom and knowledge. Politics focused on the issue of sexuality and on male–male relationships, which often erupted in conflict and violence. Women celebrated their health and sexuality, and hence the roles of "woman the gatherer" or even "woman the mother" did not emerge as cultural themes.

Among the Cheyenne, an equal bride-wealth society, and among the Kiowa, an unequal bridewealth society, marriage relationships were structured in a much different way in the nineteenth century, so gender relationships had a much different content, politics were more hierarchical, and ideology played a different role. Collier's interest is not in the subordination of women in these three societies, because in all three there are several kinds of inequality: between men and women, between older women and girls, between unmarried men and married men, and between kin and affines. An interest in "spheres" and "domains" has been replaced by an emphasis on relationships and an analysis that focuses on the ways in which inequality gets reproduced through marriage transactions, claims on the labor of others, and giving and receiving of gifts. Dominance and subordination become a much more layered, contextualized phenomenon—more interesting than the simple assertion that women are universally subordinated. The processes through which women's inequality (and that of young

men) is constructed are laid bare, rather than flatly asserted.

Mary Moran's study of civilized women (1990) explores the historical beginnings and present-day construction of the category "civilized," which does confine educated women among the Glebo of southeastern Liberia to a "domestic sphere." The dichotomy between "civilized" and "native" (or even tribal or country) is a result of missionization and has created a status hierarchy differentially applied to men and to women. Men, once educated and with a history of paid wage work, never lose their status as "civilized," while women, even though married to a "civilized man," may lose their status if they do not dress correctly, keep house in specific ways, and refrain from farming and marketing. Native women, who market or have farms, are more economically independent but occupy positions of lower prestige. Here we see not only the importance of historical data in examining how cultural categories evolve, but also the ways in which both civilized and native women actively manage their status positions. Civilized women, through the practice of fosterage, recruit younger women to their households to carry out the more elaborate household routines in which they must engage and to train these fostered daughters to become civilized themselves.

The civilized–native dichotomy represents the juxtaposition of two systems. One is a parallel-sex system in which native men and women are represented by their own leaders in two linked but relatively autonomous prestige hierarchies (as suggested by Sudarkasa 1986). The other is a single-sex system (based on a Western model) in which men in political positions represent both sexes, and women have little access to prestige except through their husbands. Thus, this is a much more complex system than one based on a domestic–public dichotomy. There are dichotomous categories—civilized–native, male–female—but they do not fit neatly together. Moran speaks of categories as "gender sensitive" and suggests that "the Glebo have inserted gender into the civilized/native dichotomy to the point that women's status is not only more tenuous and vulnerable than men's but also very difficult to maintain without male support." In some respects civilized women trade off dependency for prestige, but Moran provides a sympathetic picture of how both civilized and native women manage their lives.

Lila Abu-Lughod's study (1986) of Bedouin women's ritual poetry gives us further insights into the complexity of women who in 1974 we would have simply thought of as "confined to a domestic sphere." Among the Bedouin, women's marriages are arranged; wives wear black veils and red belts (symbolizing their fertility); and women must behave within a code of behavior that emphasizes family honor and female modesty and shame. When confronted with loss, poor treatment, or neglect, the public discourse is one of hostility, bitterness, and anger. In the case of lost love the discourse is of militant indifference and denial of concern. In contrast, Bedouin poetry, a highly prized and formally structured art, expresses sentiments of devastating sadness, self-pity, attachment, and deep feeling (Abu-Lughod 1986: 187). Although both men and women recite poetry for women, it may express conflicting feelings concerning an arranged marriage, a sense of loss over a divorce, or sentiments of betrayal when a husband marries a new wife. The poems are used to elicit sympathy and get help, but they also constitute a dissident and subversive discourse. Abu-Lughod sees ritual poetry as a corrective to "an obsession with morality and an overzealous adherence to the ideology of honor. . . . Poetry reminds people of another way of being and encourages, as it reflects, another side of experience. . . . And maybe the vision [offered through poetry] is cherished because people see that the costs of this system, in the limits it places on human experiences, are just too high" (Abu-Lughod 1986: 259). Bedouin women in this portrait are not simply victims of patriarchy confined to a domestic sphere; they are active individuals who use a highly valued cultural form to express their deepest sentiments, acknowledge an alternative set of values, and leave open the possibility of subverting the system in which they are embedded.

A large number of studies have been conducted in the United States that loosely focus on what used to be termed the domestic sphere and the public world of work. As in the Native American, African, and Middle Eastern cases cited previously, when one begins to examine a topic in detail, global notions like domestic–public seem too simple to deal with the complexities of women's lives. Clearly work and home are distinctly separated spheres in the United States. Women who have been employed in the paid labor force have experienced the disjunction of spending eight or more hours of the day in a place of employment where they are "female workers" and the rest of their time in the home where they are daughters, wives, and/or mothers. With this comes responsibilities for cooking, cleaning, and providing nurturance, care, and intimacy for other family members. Several recent studies have examined the contradictions women face when combining work and family, the impact of paid employment on family roles, and vice versa. I will refer to only three examples of this growing literature.

Patricia Zavella's research on Chicana cannery workers examines women's networks that link the workplace and the family (Zavella 1987). Calling these "work-related networks," Zavella describes groups of friends who saw each other outside work and who were members of a kin network employed in the same cannery. Women used work-related networks as sources of exchange for information, baby sitters, and emotional support. Networks operated in more political ways as workers organized a women's caucus and filed a complaint with the Fair Employment Practices Commission. Women's cannery work was seasonal and had relatively little impact on power relations in the family or the household division of labor. On the other hand, work-related networks of friends or kin were an important "bridging mechanism" helping women to deal with the contradictions and demands that came from two different spheres.

Karen Sacks' study of hospital workers at the Duke Medical Center examines the ways in which black and white women brought family notions of work, adulthood, and responsibility to work with them and used these values to organize a walk out and subsequent union drive (1988). Sacks focuses on the activities of "center women"—leaders in the union drive. Unlike the men who were often the public speakers at rallies and events, the center women organized support on an interpersonal, one-to-one basis. Rather than emphasizing the bridging aspect of women's networks, Sacks shows how the family is "brought to work" or in the old terminology how the "domestic" influences the "public."

In my own research I have traced the changes in the relationship between women, work, and family historically through the study of immigrant women in a small industrial community, Central Falls, Rhode Island (Lamphere 1987). Using the twin notions of productive and reproductive labor, I examined the rise of the textile industry in Rhode Island and the recruitment of working daughters and later of working mothers to the textile industry and to the other light industries that have replaced it since World War II. Rather than seeing production and reproduction as a rigid dichotomy (like public and domestic), I have used these categories to study relationships and to examine the kinds of strategies that immigrant women and their families forged in confronting an industrial system where wage work was a necessity and where working-class families had no control over the means of production. Such an approach revealed a great deal of variability both between and within ethnic groups—the Irish, English, French-Canadian, and Polish families who came to Central Falls between 1915 and 1984 and the more recent Colombian and Portuguese immigrants. Examination of strikes and walkouts in the 1920s and 1930s and my own experience as a sewer in an apparel plant in 1977 led me to emphasize the strategies of resistance the women workers used on the job, as well as the impact of women's paid labor on the family itself. When daughters were recruited as workers in textile mills, the internal division of labor within the household did not materially change because wives and mothers continued to do much of the reproductive labor necessary to maintain the household. Fathers, teenage sons, and daughters worked for wages. In the current period, in contrast, as more wives have become full-time workers, immigrant men have begun to do some reproductive labor, particularly child care. Immigrant couples often work different shifts and prefer to care for children themselves rather than trust baby sitters from their own ethnic group. In my study I argue that "the productive system as constituted in the workplaces has shaped the family more than issues of reproduction have shaped the workplace" (Lamphere 1987: 43).

More recently, Patricia Zavella, Felipe Gonzalez, and I have found that young working mothers in sunbelt industries have moved much further than Cannery women or New England industrial immigrant women in changing the nature of the household division of labor (Lamphere, Zavella, Gonzalez, and Evans 1993). These new committed female workers have been employed since high school and do not drop out of the labor force for long periods of time to have children. Thus, they and their husbands construct a family life around a two-job household. Although some couples have a "traditional" division of housework (women do the cooking and the majority of the cleaning and husbands take out the garbage, do minor repairs, and fix the car), many husbands participate in "female chores" and do substantial amounts of childcare (often caring for children while the wife is at work). Here we see the impact of what we used to call the "public sphere" on the domestic one, but in our analysis we have focused more on the varied ways that Anglos and Hispanics (including single mothers) have negotiated household and childcare arrangements, viewing husbands and wives as mediating contradictions. Subtle similarities and differences among and between working class Anglo and Hispanic women have emerged from this analysis, making it clear that the impact of work in the public world is not a monolithic but a variegated process.

In summary the dichotomy between the public world of men and domestic world of women was, in 1974, an important and useful starting point for thinking about women's roles in a cross-cultural perspective. As anthropologists have written more detailed and fine-grained studies of women's lives in a wide variety of other cultures and in our own society, we have gone beyond the use of dichotomies to produce analyses of the complex and layered structure of women's lives. We now treat women more historically, viewing them as social actors and examining the variability among women's situations within one culture and in their relationship to men.

REFERENCES

Abu-Lughod, Lila. 1986. *Veiled Sentiments: Honor and Poetry in a Bedouin Society.* Berkeley and Los Angeles: University of California Press.

Brown, Judith. 1970. "Economic organization and the position of women among the Iroquois." *Ethnohistory* 17(3/4): 131–167.

Chai, Alice Yun. 1987. "Freed from the elders but locked into labor: Korean immigrant women in Hawaii." *Women's Studies* 13: 223–234.

Collier, Jane. 1974. "Women in politics." In Michelle Z. Rosaldo and Louise Lamphere (eds.). *Woman, Culture, and Society.* Stanford, CA: Stanford University Press.

———. 1988. *Marriage and Inequality in Classless Societies.* Stanford, CA: Stanford University Press.

Collier, Jane, Michelle Rosaldo, and Sylvia Yanagisako. 1982. "Is there a family? New anthropological views." In Barrie Thorne and Marilyn Yalom (eds.). *Rethinking the Family: Some Feminist Questions.* pp. 25–40. New York and London: Longman.

Comaroff, John L. 1987. "Sui genderis: Feminism, kinship theory, and structural 'domains'." In Jane Fishburne Collier and Sylvia Junko Yanagisako (eds.). *Gender and Kinship: Essays Toward a Unified Analysis.* pp. 53–86 Stanford: Stanford University Press.

de Beauvoir, Simone. 1953. *The Second Sex.* New York: Alfred A. Knopf. Originally published in French in 1949.

Kaberry, Phyllis M. 1939. *Aboriginal Women, Sacred and Profane.* London: G. Routledge.

———. 1952. *Women of the Grassfields.* London: H. M. Stationery Office.

Lamphere, Louise. 1974. "Strategies, cooperation, and conflict among women in domestic groups." In Michelle Z. Rosaldo and Louise Lamphere (eds.). *Woman, Culture, and Society.* pp. 97–113 Stanford, CA: Stanford University Press.

———. 1987. *From Working Daughters to Working Mothers: Immigrant Women in a New England Industrial Community.* Ithaca, NY: Cornell University Press.

———. 1989. "Feminist anthropology: The legacy of Elsie Clews Parsons." *American Ethnologist* 16(3): 518–533.

Lamphere, Louise, Patricia Zavella, Felipe Gonzales, and Peter Evans. 1993. *Sunbelt Working Mothers: Reconciling Family and Factory.* Ithaca, NY: Cornell University Press.

Landes, Ruth. 1938. *The Ojibwa Woman, Part 1: Youth.* New York: Columbia University. Contributions to Anthropology, Vol. 31.

———. 1947. *The City of Women: Negro Women Cult Leaders of Bahia,* Brazil. New York: Macmillan.

Leacock, Eleanor. 1978. "Women's status in egalitarian society: Implications for social evolution." *Current Anthropology* 19(2): 247–275.

Leith-Ross, Sylvia. 1939. *African Women: Study of the Ibo of Nigeria.* London: Faber and Faber.

Mead, Margaret. 1949. *Male and Female.* New York: William Morrow and Co.

Moran, Mary H. 1990. *Civilized Women: Gender and Prestige in Southeastern Liberia.* Ithaca, NY: Cornell University Press.

Moore, Henrietta L. 1988. *Feminism and Anthropology.* Minneapolis: University of Minnesota Press.

Murcott, Anne. 1983. "'It's a pleasure to cook for him': Food, mealtimes and gender in some South Wales households." In Eva Gamarnikow, D. H. J. Morgan, June Purvis, and Daphne Taylorson (eds.). *The Public and the Private.* London: Heinemann Educational Books.

Nelson, Cynthia. 1974. "Public and private politics: Women in the Middle East." *American Ethnologist* 1: 551–563.

Parsons, Elsie Clews. 1913. *The Old Fashioned Woman.* New York: G. P. Putnam's Sons.

———. 1914. *Fear and Conventionality.* New York: G. P. Putnam's Sons.

———. 1915. *Social Freedom: A Study of the Conflicts Between Social Classifications and Personality.* New York: G. P. Putnam's Sons.

Paulme, Denise (ed.). 1963. *Women of Tropical Africa.* Berkeley: University of California Press.

Rapp, Rayna. 1979. Anthropology. *Signs* 4(3): 497–513.

Reiter, Rayna (ed.). 1975a. *Toward an Anthropology of Women.* New York: Monthly Review Press.

———. 1975b. "Men and women in the South of France: Public and private domains." In Rayna Reiter (ed.). *Toward an Anthropology of Women.* pp. 252–283 New York: Monthly Review Press.

Rosaldo, Michelle. 1974. "Woman, culture and society: A theoretical overview." In Michelle Z.

Rosaldo and Louise Lamphere (eds.). *Woman, Culture, and Society*. pp. 17–43 Stanford, CA: Stanford University Press.

———. 1980. "The uses and abuses of anthropology." *Signs* 5(3): 389–417.

Rosaldo, Michelle Z., and Louise Lamphere (eds.). 1974. *Woman, Culture, and Society*. Stanford, CA: Stanford University Press.

Sacks, Karen. 1988. *Caring by the Hour: Women, Work, and Organizing at the Duke Medical Center*. Urbana and Chicago: University of Illinois Press.

Sudarkasa, Niara. 1976. "Female employment and family organization in West Africa." In Dorothy McGuigan (ed.). *New Research on Women and Sex Roles*. Ann Arbor, MI: Center for Continuing Education of Women.

———. 1986. "The status of women in indigenous African Societies." *Feminist Studies* 12: 91–104.

Underhill, Ruth. 1936. *Autobiography of a Papago Woman. Supplement to American Anthropologist* 38(3), Part II. Millwood, NY: American Anthropological Association.

Wolf, Margery. 1972. *Women and the Family in Rural Taiwan*. Stanford, CA: Stanford University Press.

Yanagisako, Sylvia Junko. 1987. "Mixed metaphors: Native and anthropological models of gender and kinship domains." In Jane Fishburne Collier and Sylvia Junko Yanagisako (eds.). *Gender and Kinship: Essays Toward a Unified Analysis*. pp. 86–119 Stanford, CA: Stanford University Press.

Yanagisako, Sylvia Junko, and Jane Fishburne Collier. 1987. "Toward a unified analysis of gender and kinship." In Jane Fishburne Collier and Sylvia Junko Yanagisako (eds.). *Gender and Kinship: Essays Toward a Unified Analysis*. pp. 14–53 Stanford, CA: Stanford University Press.

Zavella, Patricia. 1987. *Women's Work and Chicano Families: Cannery Workers of the Santa Clara Valley*. Ithaca, NY: Cornell University Press.

NOTES

1. Rosaldo says that "the opposition does not *determine* cultural stereotypes or asymmetries in the evaluations of the sexism, but rather underlies them, to support a very general . . . identification of women with domestic life and of men with public life" (Rosaldo 1974: 21–22). Thus, I would argue, Rosaldo did not attempt to *explain* women's subordination through the dichotomy, but saw it as an underlying structural framework in any society that supported subordination and that would have to be reorganized to change women's position.

2. It is interesting that we did not know of Elsie Clews Parsons's extensive feminist writing during 1910 to 1916, much of which is reminiscent of the kind of position we took in *Woman, Culture, and Society*. In another article I have noted the similarities between Shelly's prose and that of Parsons (see Lamphere 1989 and Parsons 1913, 1914, 1915).

"It's a Pleasure to Cook for Him":
Food, Mealtimes, and Gender in Some South Wales Households

Anne Murcott

INTRODUCTION

I think it lets him know that I am thinking about him—as if he knows that I am expecting him. But it's not as if "oh I haven't got anything ready." . . .

Reprinted with permission from Eva Gamarnikow, David H. J. Morgan, June Purvis, and Daphne Taylorson (eds.), *The Public and the Private* (London: Heinemann Educational Books, Ltd., 1983), pp. 78–90. Copyright © 1983 British Sociological Association.

Fair play, he's out all day . . . he doesn't ask for that much . . . you know it's not as if he's been very demanding or—he doesn't come home and say "oh, we've got chops again," it's really a pleasure to cook for him, because whatever you . . . oh I'll give him something and I think well, he'll like this, he'll like that. And he'll always take his plate out . . . and he'll wash the dishes without me even asking, if I'm busy with the children. Mind, perhaps his method is not mine.

Every now and then an informant puts precisely into words the results of the researcher's analytic efforts—providing in the process a quotation suitable for the title! The extract reproduced above, explaining the importance of having the meal ready when her husband arrives home, comes from one of a series of interviews on which this paper is based.[1] The discussion starts by remembering that "everyone knows" that women do the cooking: all the women interviewed—and the few husbands/boyfriends or mothers who came in and out—took it for granted that cooking was women's work. Informants may not enjoy cooking, or claim not to be good at it; they may not like the arrangement that it is women's work, or hanker after modifying it. But all recognize that this is conventional, some volunteer a measure of approval, most appeared automatically to accept it, a few resigned themselves and got on with it.

Studies of the organization of domestic labor and marital role relationships confirm that cooking continues to be a task done more by women than men; this is also the case cross-culturally (Stephens, 1963; Murdock and Provost, 1973). Emphasis in the literature has shifted from Young and Willmott's (1975) symmetrical view of sharing and marital democracy. Now rather more thoroughgoing empirical study suggests their assessment is little more than unwarranted optimism (Oakley, 1974a and b; Edgell, 1980; Leonard, 1980; Tolson, 1977). This work improves on earlier studies of the domestic division of labor by going beyond behaviorist enquiry about "who does which tasks" to consider the meanings attached to them by marital partners. The distribution of work turns out not to correlate neatly with assessments of importance or allocation of responsibility (Oakley, 1974b; Edgell, 1980).

Part of this effort (in particular, Oakley, 1974a and b) has in addition attempted to analyze domestic work as a "job like any other," considering housewives' work satisfaction, routines, supervision and so on. While this line of enquiry has undoubtedly made visible much of women's lives conventionally rendered invisible, it has perhaps not gone far enough. The study of housework as an occupation needs to attend in addition to features such as quality control, timekeeping, client as well as worker satisfaction, and perhaps further consideration of who, if anyone, is a housewife's boss. As will be seen, each of these is implicated in the discussion that follows.

These occupational aspects of housework provide, moreover, additional means of examining the relationship of the domestic division of labor to the economic structure as a whole. Recent commentary has also proposed that the view of the family as stripped of all but the residual economic function of consumption is ill-conceived and over-simplified. Domestic laborers refresh and sustain the existing labor force and play a key part in reproducing that of the future—as well as providing a reserve of labor themselves. The precise manner in which the political economy is to be accounted continues to be debated (West, 1980; Fox, 1980; Wajcman, 1981). For the moment, however, the general drift of that discussion can be borne in mind by recalling the everyday terminology of eating; food is consumed, meals have to be produced. The language favored in cookbooks echoes that of industry and the factory (Murcott, 1983a). Homecooking may nicely embody the terms in which the family and household's place in the division of labor has to be seen. It may also provide a convenient arena for the further exploration of the economic and labor relations in the family and the relation of the marital partners to the means of production of domestic labor (Middleton, 1974).

Examination of the household provision of meals in these terms is, however, some way in the future. This paper does no more than offer some empirical foundation on which such study might build. It brings together informants' ideas about the importance of cooking, their notions of propriety of household eating, and indicates their relation to gender. It starts with views of the significance of good cooking for home life, and goes on to deal with the place of cooking in the domestic division of labor. The familiar presumption that women are the cooks is extended to show that their responsibility in this sphere is tempered with reference to their husband's, not their own, choice. The paper concludes with brief comment on possible ways these data may illuminate some of the questions already raised.

HOME COOKING

> Aside from love, good food is the cornerstone of a happy household . . . (Opening lines of a 1957 cookbook called *The Well Fed Bridegroom*)

Right through the series of interviews three topics kept cropping up; the idea of a proper meal, reference to what informants call a "cooked dinner" and the notion that somehow home is where proper eating is ensured. Moreover, mention of one like as not involved mention of another, sometimes all three. The composite picture that emerges from the whole series suggests that these are not merely related to one another in some way, but virtually equated.

It first needs to be said that informants seemed quite comfortable with a conception of a proper meal—indeed the very phrase was used spontaneously—and were able to talk about what it meant to them. Effectively a proper meal is a cooked dinner. This is one which women feel is necessary to their family's health, welfare and, indeed, happiness. It is a meal to come home to, a meal which should figure two, three, or four times in the week, and especially on Sundays. A cooked dinner is easily identified—meat, potatoes, vegetables and gravy. It turns out that informants displayed considerable unanimity as to what defines such a dinner, contrasting it to, say, a "snack" or "fried." In so doing they made apparent remarkably clear rules not only for its composition but also its preparation and taking. I have dealt with their detail and discussed their implications in full elsewhere (Murcott, 1982). But in essence these rules can be understood as forming part of the equation between proper eating and home cooking. And, as will be noted in the next section, they also provide for the symbolic expression of the relationship between husband and wife and for each partner's obligation to their home.

The meal for a return home is, in any case, given particular emphasis—a matter which cropped up in various contexts during the interviews. Thus, for some the very importance of cooking itself is to be expressed in terms of homecoming. Or it can provide the rationale for turning to and making a meal, one to be well cooked and substantial—not just "beans on toast . . . thrown in front of you."

The actual expression "home cooking"—as distinct from "cooking for homecoming"—received less insistent reference. Informants were straightforward, regarding it as self-evident that people preferred the food that they had at home, liked what they were used to and enjoyed what they were brought up on. Perhaps untypically nostalgic, one sums up the point:

> When my husband comes home . . . there's nothing more he likes I think than coming in the door and smelling a nice meal cooking. I think it's awful when someone doesn't make the effort. . . . I think well if I was a man I'd think I'd get really fed up if my wife never bothered. . . .

What was prepared at home could be trusted—one or two regarded the hygiene of restaurant kitchens with suspicion, most simply knew their chips were better than those from the local Chinese take-away or chippy. Convenience foods had their place, but were firmly outlawed when it came to a cooked dinner. In the ideal, commercially prepared items were ranged alongside snacks, and light, quick meals: lunches and suppers in contrast to proper dinners. Informants talked about home cooking, but used this or some such phrase infrequently; the following is an exception:

> I'd like to be able to make home-made soups and things, it's just finding the time and getting organized, but at the moment I'm just not organized. . . . I think it would probably be more good for us than buying. . . . I suppose it's only—I'd like to be—the image of the ideal housewife is somebody who cooks her own food and keeps the household clean and tidy.

The sentiments surrounding her valuation of home-made food are not, however, an exception. Time and again informants linked not only a view of a proper meal for homecoming, but a view of the proper parts husband and wife are to play on this occasion. So cooking is important when you are married.

> You must think of your husband . . . it's a long day for him at work, usually, . . . even if they have got a canteen at work, their cooking is not the same as coming home to your wife's cooking. . . . I think every working man should have a cooked meal when he comes in from work. . . .

Cooking is important—though not perhaps for everybody "like men who don't cook"—for women whose "place [it is] to see the family are well fed."

In this section, I have indicated that informants virtually treat notions of proper meals, home-based eating, and a cooked dinner, as equivalents. The stress laid on the homecoming not only underlines the symbolic significance attached to both the meal and the return home. It simultaneously serves as a reminder of the world beyond the home being left behind for that day. Put another way, the cooked dinner marks the threshold between the public domains of school or work and the private sphere behind the closed front door. In the process of describing these notions of the importance of cooking in the home, it becomes apparent that the familiar division of labor is assumed.

COOKING IN THE DOMESTIC DIVISION OF LABOR

As noted in an earlier section, all those interviewed took it for granted that it is the women who cook. What they had to say refers both to conventions in general, and themselves and their circumstances in particular.[2] There are two important features of their general presumption that women are the cooks; one indicates the terms in which it is modifiable, the other locates it firmly as a matter of marital justice and obligation. The upshot of each of these is to underline the manner in which the domestic preparation of meals is securely

anchored to complementary concepts of conduct proper to wife and husband.

To say that women cook is not to say that it is only women who ever do so. It is, however, to say that it is always women who daily, routinely, and as a matter of course are to do the cooking. Men neither in the conventional stereotype nor in informants' experience ever cook on a regular basis in the way women do.[3] Husband/boyfriends/fathers are "very good really"; they help informants/their mothers with carrying the heavy shopping, preparing the vegetables, switching the oven on when told, doing the dishes afterwards (cf. Leonard, 1980). Such help may be offered on a regular enough basis, notably it is available when the women are pregnant, dealing with a very young infant, unwell or unusually tired. But none of this is regarded as men doing the cooking.

More significantly, it is not the case that men do not cook—in the strict sense of taking charge of the transformation of foodstuffs to some version of a meal. They may make breakfast on a Sunday, cook only "bacon-y" things, can do chips or "his" curries: all examples, incidentally, of foods that do not figure in the proper cooked dinner (Murcott, 1983c).

For some, however, competence in the kitchen (and at the shops) is suspect: he'll "turn the potatoes on at such and such a time . . . but leave him he's hopeless" and another just "bungs everything in." For others, it is men who make better domestic cooks than women, are more methodical, less moody. Another couple jokingly disagree: she "not taken in" by Robert Carrier on TV, he claiming that "the best chefs are men." The point is that either way, of course, informants do regard gender as relevant to the question of who is to cook.

It is not even the case that all men cannot cook the proper, homecoming meal. One or two, when out of work for a while, but his wife still earning (this only applied to those having a first baby) might start the meal or even have it ready for her return. But once he is employed again he does not continue to take this degree of responsibility, reverting either to "helping" or waiting for her to do it. Now and again, wives have learned to cook not at school or from their mothers, but from their husbands.

But it was still assumed that it was for the woman to learn. This was even so in one instance where the informant made a "confession . . . my husband does the cooking." But now that she was pregnant and had quit paid work she would take over; "it would be a bit lazy not to." Like others for whom the cooking may have been shared while both were employed, cooking once again became the home-based wife's task (cf. Bott, 1957, p. 225; Oakley, 1980, p. 132).

The issue is, however, more subtle than an account of who does what, or who takes over doing what. Men and women's place involve mutual obligation. "I think a woman from the time she can remember is brought up to cook . . . Whereas most men are brought up to be the breadwinner." The question of who does the cooking is explicitly a matter of justice and marital responsibility. A woman talks of the guilt she feels if she does not, despite the greater tiredness of late pregnancy, get up to make her husband's breakfast and something for lunch—"he's working all day." Another insists that her husband come shopping with her so he knows the price of things—he's "hopeless" on his own—but she has a clear idea of the limits of each person's responsibility: each should cook only if the wife *has* to earn rather than chooses to do so.

Here, then, I have sought to show that informants subscribed in one way or another to the convention that it is women who cook. In the process it transpired that it is certain sorts of cooking, i.e., routine, homecoming cooking, which are perennially women's work. The meal that typically represents "proper" cooking is, of course, the cooked dinner. Its composition and prescribed cooking techniques involve prolonged work and attention; its timing, for homecoming, prescribes when that work shall be done. To do so demands the cook be working at it, doing wifely work, in time that corresponds to time spent by her husband earning for the family (Murcott, 1982). This is mirrored in Eric Batstone's (1983) account of the way a car worker's lunch box prepared by his wife the evening before is symbolic of the domestic relationship which constitutes the rationale for his presence in the workplace; he endures the tedium of the line in order to provide for his wife and family. It transpired also that men do cook in certain circumstances, but such modification seems to reveal more clearly the basis for accounting cooking as part of a wife's responsibility (to the family) at home corresponding to the husband's obligation (to the family) at work, i.e., their mutual responsibilities to each other as marriage partners.

WHO COOKS FOR WHOM?

At this point I introduce additional data which bear on cooking's relation to the question of marital responsibility. Repeatedly informants indicated that people do not cook for themselves; evidently it is not worth the time and effort.[4] But the data suggest implications beyond such matters of economy. Two inter-related features are involved: one is the distinction already alluded to in the previous section, between cooking in the strict sense of the word and cooking as preparation of a particular sort of meal. The other enlarges on the following nicely. To observe that people do not cook for themselves can mean two things. First it can imply that a solitary person does not prepare something for themselves to eat while on their own. But it can also imply that someone does not do the cooking on their own behalf, but in the service of some other(s). Examination of the transcripts to date suggests that not only could informants mean either or both of these, but also that each becomes elided in a way that underlines the nuances and connotations of the term cooking.

The question of a lone person not cooking themselves a meal unsurprisingly cropped up most frequently with reference to women themselves, but men, or the elderly, were also thought not to bother.

Informants are clear, however, that not cooking when alone does not necessarily mean going without. Women "pick" at something that happens to be in the house, have a bar of chocolate or packet of crisps later in the evening or a "snack." Men will fry something, an egg or make chips. No one said that a man would go without altogether (though they may not know), whereas for themselves—and women and girls in general—skipping a meal was thought common enough. Men—and occasionally women—on their own also go back to their mother's or over to their sister's for a meal. One informant was (the day of my interview with her) due to go to her mother's for the evening meal, but fearful of being alone in the house at night, she was also due to stay there for the next few days while her husband was away on business.

The suggestion is, then, that if a person is by themselves, but is to have a proper meal, as distinct from "fried" or a "snack" then they join a (close) relation's household. The point that it is women who cook such meals receives further emphasis. Indeed, when women cook this particular meal, it is expressly for others. In addition to the temporary lone adults just noted who return to mothers or sisters, women in turn may cook for the older generation, as well as routinely cooking for children or for men home at "unusual" times if unemployed or temporarily or a different shift.

This conventional requirement that women cook for others is not always straightforward in practice. At certain stages in an infant's life the logistics of producing meals for husband and child(ren) there as well meant the woman felt difficulties in adequately meeting the obligations involved. And not all informants enjoyed cooking; most just accepted that it needed doing, though there were also those who took positive, creative pleasure in it (cf. Oakley, 1974b). Part of this is expressed in the very satisfaction of providing for others something they should be getting, and in turn will enjoy.

More generally cooking can become tiresome simply because it has to be done day-in, day-out. The pleasure in having a meal prepared for you becomes all the more pointed if routinely you are cooking for others.[5] In the absence of any data for men, it can only be a guess that going out for a meal is thus specially enjoyable for women. But for those who on occasion did eat out this clearly figures in their pleasure. Even if it rarely happened, just the idea of having it put in front of you meant a treat: "it's nice being spoiled."

The question "who cooks for whom?" can now begin to be answered. Apparently it is women who cook for others—effectively, husbands and children. If husbands and children are absent, women alone will not "cook," indeed many may not even eat. It is the others' presence that provides the rationale for women's turning to and making a proper meal—that is what the family should have and to provide it is her obligation. Men—and children—have meals made for them as a matter of routine: but for women it is a treat. That solitary men do not "cook" for themselves either, and may go to a relative's for meals (cf. Rosser and Harris, 1965; Barker, 1972), or that a woman on her own may also do so does not detract from the main proposal that it is women who cook for others. For it is not only that informants or their husbands will go temporarily back to their mother's, not their father's, home-cooking. It is also that both men and women revert to the status of a child for whom a woman, a mother, cooks. The mother may actually be the adult's parent, but they—and I with them—may stretch the point and see that she may be mother to the adult's nieces or nephews or indeed, as in the case of cooking for the elderly, she may be mother to the adult's grandchildren.

The appreciation that it is women who cook for others elaborates the more familiar convention, discussed above, that in the domestic division of labor cooking is women's work. First of all it indicates that this work is service work. Cooking looks increasingly like a task quite particularly done for others. Second, when cooking for others women are performing a service to those who are specifically related (sic) rather than for a more generalized clientele known only by virtue of their becoming customers. The marital—and parental—relationship defines who is server, who served.

That said, there remains the question of deciding what the server shall serve. As already discussed in an earlier section, the conventional expectation shared, it seems, by both woman and man, is that meals shall be of a certain sort—a cooked dinner for a certain occasion, most commonly the return home from work, or the celebration of Sunday, a work-free day. The "rules" involved are not entirely hard and fast, or precisely detailed. Cooked dinners are neither daily nor invariable affairs (Murcott, 1982). And the cooked dinner itself can properly comprise a number of alternative meats (and cuts) and range of different vegetables. What then, determines the choice of meat and vegetables served on any particular day? Some of the factors involved, as will be seen in the next section, once again echo ideas of responsibility and mutual obligation.

DECIDING WHAT TO HAVE

A number of factors feature in deciding what to have for a particular day's meal.[6] First, a question of cost was taken for granted. This does not necessarily mean keeping expenditure to a minimum—eating in the customary manner despite hard times was highly and expressly valued by some. Second, the conventional provision of proper dinners itself contributed to the determination of choice. These two factors present themselves as marking the limits within which the finer decisions about what the precise components of the day's dinner are to be. Here reference to their husband's—and, to a lesser extent, children's—preferences was prominent in informants' discussion of such detailed choices.

It was indicated earlier that in an important sense women's cooking is service work. This sort of work has two notable and interrelated aspects affecting decisions and choice: is it the server or served who decides what the recipient is to want? Exploring the mandate for professionals' work, Everett Hughes (1971, p. 424) highlights a key question: "professionals do not merely serve: they define the very wants they serve." Servants, and service workers such as waitresses (Whyte, 1948; Spradley and Mann, 1975) compliantly provide for the wants identified by the served. On the face of it, then, the professional has total and the waitress nil autonomy. Examples reflecting this sort of range occurred among informants, varying from one woman apparently always deciding, through to another always making what he wants for tea. But in the same way that the

maximum autonomy of the professional is continually, to a certain degree, a matter of negotiation and renegotiation with clients, and that, similarly, the apparent absence of autonomy is modified by a variety of more or less effective devices waitresses use to exert some control over customers, so a simple report of how meal decisions are reached can, I propose, either conceal negotiations already complete, or reveal their workings.

Thus informants interested in trying new recipes still ended up sticking to what they usually made because their husbands were not keen. Others reported that "he's very good" or "never complains" while some always asked what he wanted. A non-committal reply however did not necessarily settle the matter, for some discovered that being presented with a meal she had then decided on could provoke adverse and discouraging remarks. But it was clear that even those who claimed not to give their husbands a choice were still concerned to ensure that he agreed to her suggestion. It is almost as if they already knew what he would like, needed to check out a specific possibility every now and then but otherwise continued to prepare meals within known limits. Deciding what to have already implicitly took account of his preferences so that the day-to-day decision seemed to be hers.

The material presented in this section provides only a glimpse of this area of domestic decision-making. Other aspects need consideration in future work. For instance, what degree of importance do people attach to the matter (cf. Edgell, 1980, pp. 58–9)? Attention also needs to be paid to wider views of the legitimacy of choice in what one eats. In what sense do restaurant customers choose and mentally subnormal patients not? Does a child that spits out what it is fed succeed in claiming a choice or not? And in apparently acquiescing to their husband's choice, are wives circumscribing their own? But it looks as if deciding what to have is of a piece with a shared view of marital responsibility whereby he works and so deserves, somehow, the right to choose what she is to cook for him.

GENDER AND THE PRODUCTION OF MEALS

> I know a cousin of mine eats nothing but chips, in fact his mother-in-law had to cook him chips for his Christmas dinner and she went berserk . . .

This "atrocity story" recapitulates various elements of the preceding discussion. Such unreasonableness is, no doubt, unusual but its artless reporting emphasizes a number of points already made. Not only do chips break the rules of what should properly figure in a Christmas meal, superior even to the Sunday variant of a cooked dinner, but it remains, however irksome, up to the woman to prepare what a man wants. The burden of this paper, then, may be summarized as revealing allegiance to the propriety of occasion such that a certain sort of meal is to mark home (male) leisure versus (male) work-time, and that such meals are cooked by women for others, notably husbands, in deference, not to the woman's own, but to men's taste.

This examination of cooking, mealtimes and gender within the household has implications for the continuing analysis of domestic work as work. While it does not shed light on why such work is women's, only reasserting that conventionally this is so, it clearly casts the work of meal provision as service work.

The everyday way of describing dishing up a meal as serving food is embedded in a set of practices that prescribe the associated social relationships as of server and served. As already observed this involves two interrelated matters: control over the work, and decisions as to what are the "wants" the worker shall serve, what the work shall be. Each is considered in turn.

Oakley (1974a and b) reports that one of the features of housewifery that women value is the feeling of autonomy. Care is needed, though, not to treat such attitudes as tantamount to their analysis. Just because housewives express their experiences in terms of enjoying being their own boss does not mean that their conditions of work can be analyzed in terms of a high degree of autonomy. The material presented in this paper suggests that doing the cooking is not directed by the woman herself, but is subject to various sorts of control.

First of these is the prescription for certain kinds of food for certain occasions. The idea of the cooked dinner for a homecoming is just such an example of cultural propriety. Related to this is a second control, namely that the food is to be ready for a specific time. Mealtimes construed in this way may exert just the same sort of pressure on the cook as any other production deadline in industry. Third, control is also exerted via the shared understanding that it is the preferences of the consumer which are to dictate the exact variant of the dinner to be served. What he fancies for tea constrains the cook to provide it. These kinds of control in the domestic provision of meals find their counterpart in the industrial concerns of quality control, timekeeping and market satisfaction. A woman cooking at home may not have a chargehand "breathing down her neck" which is understandably a source of relief to her. But this does not mean to say that she enjoys autonomy—simply perhaps that other controls make this sort of oversight redundant. Evidence either way is extremely sparse, but Ellis (1983) suggests that failing to cook according to her husband's wishes can contribute to a wife's battering.

Linked to the issue of control of domestic cooking is the question of decision-making. Edgell (1980) has drawn attention to the degree of importance couples attach to different aspects of family living about which decisions have to be made. He distinguishes assessments of importance from, first, whether the decision is mainly the wife's or husband's responsibility and second, from the frequency with which the decision has to be made. So, for instance, moving is the husband's decision, perceived to be very important and infrequent, a contrast to the matter of spending on food. What Edgell does not make clear, however, is quite what either his informants or he mean by "importance." As an analytic device, the idea does not distinguish between family matters which partners may identify as both important and somehow major or permanent such as moving, and those identified as mundane, or fleeting but important nonetheless, such as daily eating. Like refuse collection or sewage work which is regarded as vital but low-status, the importance attached to meals may not be remarked in the general run of things, though noticed particularly if absent. But that does not necessarily mean that both husband and wife regard it as unimportant. And, harking back to the question of autonomy in decision-making, reports such as Edgell's that food spending, cooking or whatever is regarded as the wife's responsibility, cannot, of itself, be seen as evidence of her power and freedom from control in those areas. For as Jan Pahl (1982, p. 24) has so cogently observed, "being able to offload certain decisions and certain money-handling chores on to the other spouse can itself be a sign of power." The delegate may be responsible for execution of tasks, but they are answerable to the person in whom the power to delegate is originally vested.

The preliminary analysis offered in this paper has theoretical and political implications concerning power and authority in marriage and the relation between domestic and paid work. The exploration of ideas about cooking and mealtimes starts to provide additional approach to detailing the means of domestic production. And the sort of work women are to do to ensure the homecoming meal provides a critical instance of the juncture between the control of a worker and the (his) control of his wife. The meal provides one illustration not only of a point where the public world of employment and the private world of the home meet one another; it also shows how features of the public take precedence within the private. For the stress informants lay on this mealtime offers an interesting way of understanding how the industrial rhythms which circumscribe workers are linked to the rhythms which limit women's domestic work (cf. Rotenberg, 1981). And women's continual accommodation to men's taste can also be seen as a literal expression of wives' deference to husbands' authority (Bell and Newby, 1976; Edgell, 1980, p. 70). This acquiescence to his choice provides the cultural gloss to the underlying economic relationship whereby industry produces amongst other things both the wage, and the raw materials it buys, for the domestic to produce what is needed to keep the industrial worker going. Part of the conjugal contract that each in their own way provide for the other, it does indeed become "a pleasure to cook for him."

ACKNOWLEDGMENTS

I am very grateful to all those necessarily anonymous people who made the research possible and who generously gave their time to answer my questions. I should like to record my appreciation of conversations with Tony Coxon, Sara Delamont, Robert Dingwall, Rhian Ellis, Bill Hudson and Phil Strong at various stages during the preparation of this paper and of the computing help and advice Martin Read provided. Only I and not they are to blame for its deficiencies. And I must thank Lindsey Nicholas, Joan Ryan, Sheila Pickard, Myrtle Robins and Margaret Simpson very much, despite flu all round, and an unusually scrawly manuscript, for their help in typing both drafts.

REFERENCES

Barker, D. L. 1972. "Keeping close and spoiling," *Sociological Review*, 20(4), 569–590.

Batstone, E. 1983. "The hierarchy of maintenance and the maintenance of hierarchy: Notes on food and industry," in A. Murcott (ed.), *The Sociology of Food and Eating*, Gower.

Bell, C. and Newby, H. 1976. "Husbands and wives: The dynamics of deferential dialectic," in D. L. Barker and S. Allen (eds.), *Dependence and Exploration in Work and Marriage*, Longmans.

Bott, E. 1957. *Family and Social Network*, Tavistock.

Edgell, S. 1980. *Middle Class Couples: A Study of Segregation, Domination and Inequality in Marriage*, Allen and Unwin.

Ellis, R. 1983. "The way to a man's heart . . .," in A. Murcott (ed.), *The Sociology of Food and Eating*, Gower.

Fox, B. (ed.). 1980. *Hidden in the Household*, Toronto: Women's Press.

Hughes, E. C. 1971. "The humble and the proud," in *The Sociological Eye: Selected Papers*, Aldine-Atherton.

Leonard, D. 1980. *Sex and Generation,* Tavistock.

Middleton, C. 1974. "Sexual inequality and stratification theory," in E. Parkin (ed.), *The Social Analysis of Class Structure,* Tavistock.

Murcott, A. 1982. "On the social significance of the 'cooked dinner' in South Wales," *Social Science Information,* 21(4/5), 677–695.

———. 1982a "Menus, meals and platefuls," *International Journal of Sociology and Social Policy* 2(4):1–11.

———. 1982a. "Women's place: Cookbook's image of technique and technology in the British Kitchen," *Women's Studies International Forum,* 6(1): 33–40.

———. (ed.) 1983b. *The Sociology of Food and Eating,* Gower.

———. 1983c. "Cooking and the cooked," in A. Murcott (ed.), *The Sociology of Food and Eating,* Gower.

Murdock, G. P. and Provost, C. 1973. "Factors in the division of labour by sex: A cross-cultural analysis," *Ethnology,* XII(2), 203–225.

Oakley, A. 1974a. *Housewife,* Penguin.

———. 1974b. *The Sociology of Housework,* Martin Robertson.

———. 1980. *Women Confined: Towards a "Sociology of Childbirth,"* Martin Robertson.

Pahl, J. 1982. "The allocation of money and the structuring of inequality within marriage," *Board of Studies in Social Policy and Administration,* University of Kent, mimeo.

Rosser, C. and Harris, C. 1965. *The Family and Social Change,* Routledge and Kegan Paul.

Rotenberg, R. 1981. "The impact of industrialisation on meal patterns in Vienna, Austria," *Ecology of Food and Nutrition,* 11(1), 25–35.

Spradley, J. O. and Mann, B. J. 1975. *The Cocktail Waitress: Women's Work in a Man's World,* John Wiley.

Stephens, W. N. 1963. *The Family in Cross-Cultural Perspective,* Holt, Rinehart and Winston.

Tolson, A. 1977. *The Limits of Masculinity,* Tavistock.

Wajcman, J. 1981. "Work and the family: Who gets "the best of both worlds?"" in Cambridge Women's Studies Group, *Women in Society,* Virago.

West, J. 1980. "A political economy of the family in capitalism: Women, reproduction and wage labour," in T. Nichols (ed.), *Capital and Labour: A Marxist Primer,* Fontana.

Whyte, W. F. 1948. *Human Relations in the Restaurant Industry,* McGraw-Hill.

Young, M. and Willmott, P. 1975. *The Symmetrical Family,* Penguin.

NOTES

1. In order to begin remedying sociology's neglect (Murcott, 1983b) of food beliefs and of the social organization of eating, I conducted a single-handed exploratory study (supported by a grant from the SSRC) holding unstructured tape-recorded interviews with a group of 37 expectant mothers attending a health center in a South Wales valley for antenatal care (22 pregnant for the first time), 20 of whom were interviewed again after the baby's birth. No claim is made for their representativeness in any hard and fast sense, though they represent a cross-section of socioeconomic groups. For present purposes the data are treated as providing a composite picture. The prime concern here is to indicate the range and variety of evidence gathered. An instance that occurs once only thus becomes as interesting as one occurring 30 times. This is reflected in the discussion by the deliberate use of phrases such as "some informants" rather than "6 out of 37." In any case reference to numbers of instances is no more exact, and risks implying a spurious representativeness.

   These qualifications are most important. But for the sake of a tolerably readable account I do not hedge every other sentence with reminder of these limitations. Yet they do actively have to be taken as read.

2. Informants referred not only to themselves but also to mothers, sisters, sisters-in-law and women friends doing cooking.

3. No informant who had children old enough to cook currently shared the household with them.

4. Market researchers know how to trade on such reports. During the period of interviewing a TV commercial was running which sought to persuade busy housewives not to neglect themselves but have a frozen ready-cooked meal at lunchtime.

5. Interestingly, no one talked of hospital meals put in front of them as a treat. (None had a home delivery.) Rather it was the quality of the food provided which informants concentrated on. Institution cooking could not be home cooking.

6. It might have been expected that nutritional criteria would figure in these decisions. Analysis so far suggests that cultural prescriptions for proper eating at home override what is known about healthy eating (Murcott, 1983d).

Fatherhood and the Mediating Role of Women

Nicholas W. Townsend

In this chapter I confront an apparent paradox in men's accounts of fatherhood. Men say they want to be involved fathers, but they do not seem to be acting that way.

Nearly all the men I talked to in my research said they wanted to be more involved as fathers than their own fathers had been, and this stated desire is very common for men in the United States. But men in the United States do not put much time into domestic work or child care (Coltrane 1996), and after divorce many men in the United States pay very little or nothing in child support and frequently maintain no contact with their children (Furstenberg and Cherlin 1991; Arendell, 1995). I argue that we can understand some of this paradox if we consider what men do as fathers as well as what they do not do, and if we listen to what they have to say about being fathers.

Parenting is deeply gendered. And by this I do not mean only that fathers and mothers do different things, though that is clearly the case, but also that being a parent means different things to mothers and fathers, and that being a father means different things to men and women. Parenting is also gendered in other ways, such as men's stated preference for sons and the ways they treat daughters and sons differently. I have discussed these aspects of fatherhood elsewhere (Townsend 2002). In this chapter, I am focusing on the gendered relationship between fathers and mothers. Seeing men and their accounts as gendered in this way helps us to understand how men think about being fathers and about relationships in general.

In the first section below I describe how men see "marriage and children" as elements of a "package deal" which cannot be easily separated.

Original material prepared for this text. Reprinted by permission of the author.

Conceptually, a relationship with a woman is necessary for a man to see himself as a father or "family man." In the subsequent sections, I show how women are often the "driving force" behind men's decisions about when to have children; that a structural division of labor that places men in the labor force and women at home is maintained and supported by cultural work in the face of women's increasing labor force participation; and that parenting itself is gendered, with women being the "default parents" who maintain schedules and routines, while men are in a more "optional" position, with their participation as "fun dads" or "enforcers" mediated by their children's mothers.

It has been easy to see the gendered division of labor in parenting as a simple division in which men are engaged in the public sphere of paid work and politics and women are involved in the domestic sphere of child care and reproduction.[1] What my description shows, however, is that these two spheres interpenetrate, and that arrangements made in one sphere influence behavior in another. For instance, we shall see that cultural ideas about the division of paid labor and about who should provide for families have an impact on ideas about who should do what for children.

My discussion in this chapter is based on talking to men who graduated from the same high school in 1972 and were in their late thirties when I interviewed them.[2] Because they all graduated from the same high school, I was able to learn a lot about the community in California in which they grew up, the events of their youth, and the opportunities they faced as adults. I can speak with confidence about the attitudes these men shared, and about the differences between them, and I would argue that these men are in many ways typical of men in the United States, but these men's experiences and meanings cannot be used to support universal or essential ideas about "male" experience or fathering as a universal pattern of behavior.[3]

What emerged from my conversations is that, for the men I talked to, the father–child relationship could not be described or thought about independent of the relationship between husband and wife. When I ask men about their parents, they talk mostly about their fathers, but when I ask them about becoming fathers they talk about their wives. Some of the paradoxes of men's relations to their children may be resolved by understanding the relative positions of men, women, and children, and specifically the crucial linking or mediating role of women.

Appreciating the linking role of women is not the same as saying that men do not care about children, or that they think that children are entirely women's business. Certainly becoming a parent is more separated from biological reproduction for men than for women. One can scarcely imagine a woman saying, as one of my male informants did: "Actually I have had a child before, although through very strange circumstances I didn't know I had a child before he was a year old and someone sent me a Christmas card saying: 'This is your baby.'" Equally certainly, men consider childbearing and child rearing to be predominantly women's responsibility. This is not to say that men are indifferent to having children. They have strong feelings about the number, timing, and kind of children they want, but at crucial points in their lives they find that their paternity depends on the cooperation of women. The men are not passively dependent on women's motivations—they actively select and try to persuade, pressure, and coerce women, but the mediating link provided by women remains crucial.

It is not just that men need, and realize that they need, a woman's physical cooperation in order to become fathers. There is also an asymmetry in the ways that men and women think about becoming parents. For instance, many women are prepared to think about single parenthood as a possible, though usually less desirable, route to motherhood; the men I talked to, on the other hand, do not even register it as a possibility. Many single, childless women are able to think and talk directly about whether they want to have children. In doing so, and in reading the advice and examples they are offered in books and magazines, it is clear that they see having a child on one's own as an option. It is an option with definite emotional, social, and financial drawbacks as well as opportunities, and it is an option that they may well reject, but it remains a possibility. That having a child on her own is a possibility to be considered means that women are able to weigh and articulate their specific desire for children outside the matrix of family and relationship with a man. The relationship between mother and child, the activity of mothering, and the transformation of self into a mother, are things women can think about directly and in isolation. The men I talked to could not talk about having children without talking about "having a family" or "being a family man." For these men, "having children" is part of "being married and having a family." They can only conceptualize the relationship between father and children within the matrix of family relationships.

Of course, the relationships between men and their wives are very important in their own right, but my interest here is in the way that marital relationships are structurally important for men's relationships with their children. Women, as wives and mothers, mediate and facilitate fatherhood. The word "mediate" describes women's role in the relationship between men and children because it captures, in its various meanings, some of the complexity of that role. Women are in the middle of this relationship, they frequently do mediate in the most literal sense of operating as go-betweens or negotiators between their husbands and their children, and their presence and activity makes possible the reproduction, both biological and social, that is at the heart of fatherhood.

For men, having children is a reproduction of fatherhood—a patrilineal process of the movement of males through the statuses of son, father, and grandfather and of child, adult, and old man (Townsend 1998). There are five moments, phases, or aspects of reproduction at which women's mediating role is most apparent: at marriage, when decisions are made about the timing and number of children, in the structural division of labor after children are born, in gendered parenting, and after divorce.

MARRIAGE AND CHILDREN: WIFE AND MOTHER

"We always knew we wanted to get married and have a family" was a frequent comment of men who married women they had known in high school. For my informants, marriage is almost always considered to be a relationship that will involve having children. In most first marriages, husbands say they either "knew" or "assumed" that their wives would want children. For the men, marriage meant getting a "wife and family" as a sort of package deal.

As is often the case, it is when obstacles to meeting a norm arise that its existence is made most clear. Several men told me that they did not marry women with whom they had "good relationships" because those women did not want or could not have children. Conversely, men who had actually wanted to have children told me that they had ended relationships with women they did not want to marry by telling them that they did not want to have children. That this was an excuse is made clear by the rapidity with which they subsequently met, married, and had children with other women. Regardless of whether the particular men or women in any relationship or marriage really wanted children or not, the point is that the cultural idea that marriage and children go together was so clear to all that it could be used as a reason to end a relationship without rejecting the other person by saying: "I don't want to marry you." Men are making a simultaneous decision about "a wife and a mother to my children."

Greg, an earnest man with two children who worked as a programmer in a software company, had married at age twenty-nine, a fact that was very significant to him and to which he returned repeatedly. To him, twenty-nine

was old to be getting married, and he did not want to be too old to be a vigorous father to his children. He felt, however, that waiting until he was twenty-nine had not been a bad thing:

> I kind of got everything out of my system before I got married. And then, when I did get married I wanted it to be forever, as they say, and I was ready to have kids. When I got married I was ready to have kids. I probably had it planned in my mind. "We'll get married and we'll have children."

Although Greg linked marriage with having children, he said that he and his wife had not talked explicitly before their marriage about having children, but that it was "Just something you kind of know."

> I had seen a lot of women over a period of years. You see all kinds of women out there. I mean, there are some smart ones, but most of them are—they don't know if they're coming or going, you know. Maggie's very intelligent, which I like, very kind, and very funny. That's very important to me, a sense of humor. It is kind of hard to explain exactly why you know that that's the person, but she had all the factors that I was looking for. I remember telling myself: "I can live with this girl for the rest of my life. I mean I can actually do it through the day to day." I just had the inner feeling that I could be comfortable with her for basically the rest of my life.

Greg's choice of a wife was, however, not based simply on personal compatibility: "If I knew that she did not want to have children," he added, "I would not have married her."

Gordon, an engineer with three sons, had married his wife two years after they met, and two years later, while he was still in college, his first son was born. Gordon told me early on that: "Before we got married we had a goal of three and when we finally got three, I just said: 'I don't have enough for any more.'" Later, when I asked him if he had always wanted children, he replied, after a pause: "I never felt that I would not have children. But, you know, up until I found the person I wanted to marry and live with, I never thought 'I really want kids.' I don't think I consciously said that." And when I asked him if children are needed to complete a family, he immediately responded: "That's not the reason we had children, but I believe that's a true statement. Not to say that a couple is incomplete, but I think you're *more married* if you have children." His predisposition to have children, and his liking for children (he taught Sunday school before he was married) had not gelled into a firm plan to have children of his own until he met the person he wanted to marry. Marriage and children were inextricably linked in his thinking, as they were in another man's comment that "Getting married and not having kids at all, seems kind of incomplete. I can see you being a single person and not having kids. I can understand that more now. If you're married it would be odd not having children."

A deliberately childless marriage is definitely a thing to be negotiated beforehand. At least normatively, inability to bear children is not grounds for divorce, but one partner's unwillingness to have them might cause the other partner to hesitate or to refuse to enter into marriage in the first place. Several men said that in order to marry a woman who did not want children "you would have to love her a lot." There is an implication here that a marriage without children requires a stronger love than a marriage with children. But I think it is closer to these men's meanings that children provide structure and cohesion to a marriage, and that romantic love alone, without the cement of shared parenting and the economic partnership of working to support home and family, is a slender thread on which to hang a lifetime together.

During the 1970s and early 1980s, when the men I interviewed were aged between eighteen and thirty, the divorce rate for childless couples was higher than for couples who had children (Wienberg, 1988). Divorces of childless couples also proceeded more rapidly than the divorces of couples with children (White et al. 1986). Conversely, the birth of a first child within marriage drastically reduced the divorce rate for the next year (Waite et al. 1985). Although subsequent births did not have this effect, the presence of children in a marriage did appear to slow the process of divorce (White et al. 1986).[4] Of the men I talked to, those who had been through divorces in which

children had been involved reported more protracted divorces, with separations and reconciliations, whereas the divorces that did not involve children were more rapid and clearcut. The direction of causation in these relationships between fertility and divorce is not always clear. It may be that having children makes a marriage less likely to end in divorce, but it may also be that couples who think their marriage is in trouble are less likely to embark on childbearing.

The men I talked to recognized that having a child may both strengthen and undermine the relationship between husband and wife. On the one hand, they appreciated the problems of fatigue, busy schedules, and restrictions on shared leisure that children create for marriages. On the other hand, they stressed the responsibility they felt toward maintaining an intact family and also mentioned the new connections with their wives that came from enjoying their children and from sharing activities with them. Having children certainly made divorce harder to think about. They would, they said, stay married through hard times and routine times.

The comments I heard are consistent with the statistical picture that fertility within marriage reduces the incidence and slows the process of divorce. They also indicate that childlessness within marriage is not a common goal, and would demand of a marriage something qualitatively different than is expected in a reproductive union. Several men described a couple they knew who were married soon after high school graduation but deliberately had no children. After their divorce, both partners remarried and had children. The interpretation put on this by their friends is that the marriage without children could not sustain itself, but that subsequent marriages to people with whom they were ready to have children were likely to be satisfying and successful. Childlessness, in this account, is presented as both a consequence of doubts about the marriage and a cause of its failure.

The men I spoke to depend on a marital relationship with a woman for a paternal relationship with children. In the contemporary United States, the availability of effective contraception and a relaxation of the standard of sexual chastity for brides means that a man's girlfriend, his premarital sexual partner, the woman he lives with, and his wife may all be the same person, but are not necessarily so—the roles and the individuals filling them are uncoupled. A wife, however, is unique in the formalization of her social position and in the way that she links a man to other social persons by virtue of that social position and not merely by virtue of her personal qualities and associations.

Barry, balding and hospitable, lived in a new house in a new subdivision. As we sat on his deck, watching his young children from his second marriage play in the wading pool, he told me a story that encapsulated the connection between marriage and children:

> It's funny, I knew this one girl that I worked with. She was living with her boyfriend. She never took any birth control. For probably years, she never did. Never got pregnant. But they finally got married, and like their wedding night, she got pregnant. It was kind of a psychological thing, you know? Like: "Geez, I can't get pregnant, I'm not married. Well, now I'm married, it's OK."

In both his own marriages, Barry had drawn the same distinction between living together (and therefore not having children) and being married (and having or planning children).

> The first time, you just get married because it was the thing to do, so to speak. The second time you're a little bit wiser and more cautious. The first time I was twenty-one and my wife had just turned nineteen. We were married for a couple of years. And what's interesting is that she was raised in a very strict Catholic background so living together was kind of taboo. So we never lived together. We basically got married and we found out that what she wanted and what I wanted were really different. We talked about children. Nothing real serious, but like: "Down the road here, we should have children." So it's a good thing that we didn't. We were using birth control. It wasn't to the point where we decided "Let's try" and we weren't successful. We weren't ready at that time.

The second time he got married, Barry proceeded very differently. Even his sentence structure and word choice when telling me about it expressed his greater deliberation:

> We both had our own separate homes and lifestyles when we first met and we spent a lot of time together. We decided we had a pretty lasting relationship going and that we should live together and consolidate. That way we could really tell, by living together, whether or not we could live together forever. Because you just don't know people until you actually live with them. So we lived together for a while. And then we decided to get married and have children. In fact, that was kind of interesting. My wife—one of her comments that kind of surprised me was: "Geez, we don't need to get married to have children." And that really kind of took me by surprise because I've kind of had different morals than that. If you're going to have children, at least plan children, then you need to be married. Obviously there are times when things are not planned and you're not married. But the way I believe, if you're going to plan to have children, you should be married. She was very insistent that that didn't need to be the case. . . . She likes children, and I like children, so it was kind of a—We discussed it and decided "Let's get married and we'll have children" instead of just having children and not getting married.

Barry attributed his surprise at his wife's suggestion that they did not need to get married to have children to "different morals," but when his comments are taken as a whole, we can see that his association of children and marriage is not so much moral as conceptual. His picture of family life, his conceptual framework for social relationships, was one that included the possibility of living together and that separated sexual relations from procreation, but equated having children with being married. In this, and in the difference between him and his wife, Barry was typical. In order to be a father, he had to be married. His fatherhood, therefore, conceptually depends on his having a marital relationship with a woman. Once married, the timing of his children's births would depend on his wife's willingness and initiative.

"THE DRIVING FORCE": WOMEN, TIMING, AND BIRTH CONTROL

In general, the men I talked to assumed that, in their own lives, conception and birth were events that could be controlled. They assumed that sexual intercourse without pregnancy was a reasonable expectation, so that premarital sex, a space of time between marriage and their first birth, a controlled space between their children's births, and a cessation of childbearing were all things to be reasonably expected and planned for. Their confidence in their ability to plan was, to a certain extent, justified by the technological innovations of the birth control pill, the IUD, and safe and easy techniques for male and female sterilization.

Previous fertility declines and control, at the level of populations and of couples, have depended on a mix of methods, including heavy reliance on abstinence and withdrawal (Schneider and Schneider 1996). These are methods that involve at least the participation, if not the active initiation, of men. The Pill and the IUD, by contrast, are methods that are used by women and that do not require contraceptive action by men or women at the time of intercourse. They are, particularly for men, much less psychically costly than withdrawal or abstinence. For men in the United States, these methods have had the double effect of enabling a conceptual and physical separation between sexual activity and reproduction and of moving control over reproduction to women. Control over reproduction was seen as not only technically, but also morally, women's responsibility.

Barry, for example, does not say the decision about when to have children was his wife's alone, but he does put the primary responsibility on her.

She was probably the driving force. Again, I wanted children too. So it wasn't like: "OK, I'll just give in. If you want children, we'll have children." But she was probably more the driver of that issue than myself. I could have been content to wait a couple years. But again, we both wanted children. It wasn't just because she wanted children. If she would have been very insistent against it, it would have been something we probably would have had to talk about. It's really hard to say, but I think I wanted to have children also, but not to the same degree as she did. It would have been nice to have them, but if I didn't, I could have lived without them. It wouldn't have been a decision I may have regretted.

Notice that while she is the "driving force" behind the timing, he also makes it clear that he too wanted children. But he then questions his own desire when he says "I think I wanted to have children" and "I could have lived without them." In the face of this uncertainty, he placed the initiative with his wife.

The norm expressed by all the men I talked to is that there should be a period at the beginning of married life when the couple have "time for themselves as a couple." This norm may be violated by early conception, or by a period of living together followed by marriage and rapid subsequent conception.

Marvin, a large, easygoing man, who worked in purchasing, told me that he and his wife had children sooner than he would have liked. His plan had been to graduate from college and buy a house before having children. His wife had taken the initiative and had persuaded him that they should have children while he was still in college.

I wasn't all that hot about the idea. I was not sure I could handle all the responsibilities. I probably thought, in fact I did think, about how they develop and how you grow along with them. It's "Oh gosh, what am I gonna do when they're teenagers?" that sort of thing. So I wasn't all that hot about having kids. My wife convinced me that yeah, it's probably not all that tough. I should say now I know how tough it is. It's very hard. It's a never-ending challenge. But we finally agreed that we'd go ahead and have kids. And so we did. I wanted to make sure I had a house, which we didn't at the time. And go ahead and have college for me, which I didn't. So that was a kind of unsettling thing, to go from following this nice neat path to success. And here's the time to have kids. Here's the time to do this, to do that. I couldn't do that. So that kind of bothered me.

In the event, Marvin had not finished college, but he told me that had not been a real obstacle in his career, and he and his wife had bought a house with help from his wife's parents.

Men discuss their decisions about timing in terms of their "readiness" to become fathers.[5] Readiness is presented as a psychological state that does not necessarily coincide with the birth of the first child. Men may realize that they are "ready" when their first child is born, but they may also feel "not ready," causing personal anxiety and strain on their marriage. Several men told me that they only became ready to be fathers some time after the birth of their first child, usually at a point when they felt they could relate to their children.[6] On the other hand, other men have reported "being ready" before their wives were, and then embarking on campaigns to persuade them to become pregnant. For these men, it was not women's enthusiasm that drove the decision, but their reluctance or hesitation that put women in a position to control the realization of men's plans for fatherhood.

The men I talked to discussed the timing of births as if they were under perfect control, and difficulties getting pregnant, as well as unplanned pregnancies, were seen as surprising. From my perspective as an observer who knows something about the variability of human biology, this sense of being in perfect control was itself surprising. But being in control is a central organizing element of my informants' stories in all areas. Being out of control is an explanation for the bad things that happen, and a good deal of rhetorical effort is expended to create a life story characterized by control and the realization of intentions.[7] Men are actively involved in decisions about timing, but contraception during the childbearing years is overwhelmingly by female methods and men are dependent on the cooperation of their wives. But their dependence is not inevitable or driven simply by the use of female contraceptive methods. These men are actually *relinquishing* control and presenting the situation as if their wives were the only ones responsible.

Alfred, for instance, had wanted only one child, but he delayed his vasectomy after the birth of his first child. He reported that his wife then "surprised" him with a set of twins, but he delayed his vasectomy again. He only got around to sterilization after she "surprised" him with a second set. He is an exceptional example only because of the extreme personal and demographic consequences of his dependence on imperfect methods and his reluctance to assume responsibility for birth control. Alfred's position, however, underlines the centrality of effective birth control for the realization of these men's fertility plans and life plans in general. With five children under the age of six, he found himself living in too small a house, with bills higher than he had expected, and with no financial leeway. He worked as a skilled technician, but his skills were being made obsolete by technological change, and he was not in a position to make the expenditure, or take the cut in pay, necessary to acquire new skills or to move into a job with prospects of promotion. His high fertility, in fact, had effects on his work, his place of residence, and the division of labor in his marriage, and will continue to have effects in the future.

MEN AT WORK, WOMEN AT HOME: THE STRUCTURAL DIVISION OF LABOR

The archetypical picture of family life in the United States has been of a nuclear household, composed of a married heterosexual couple and their children, in which the man is the breadwinner and the woman is the homemaker. This has not, of course, been an accurate picture of the family lives of many people, but it has been a cultural archetype, or hegemonic image, that shapes people's perceptions even when it does not represent their reality.[8] Even when they become very common, however, behaviors that do not conform to hegemonic cultural norms continue to be perceived as "exceptions." When people's lives diverge from cultural norms they have to do cultural work to deny, explain, or reinterpret, this divergence. Some husbands of employed women who wanted to emphasize that they were the primary providers for their families explained that their wives' incomes were used for "extras" or "luxuries." Others described their wives' work as something they did mainly for variety, social contacts, or to "get away from the kids." But in either case they were doing cultural work to interpret their arrangements as conforming to a hegemonic picture of the structural division of labor in marriage. In support of this division of labor, the men I talked to made three interlocking arguments: that they liked or chose the arrangement, that it was best for the children, and that it was natural.

Gordon, the engineer with three sons who felt "more married" once he had children, expressed very clearly the structural division of labor between parents: one parent should stay home to raise the children, and it should be the mother.

> I think it's wrong to have kids and then lock them in daycare centers while you're working. That's why I'm really grateful that my wife can stay home. And although at times we were real tight for money, and I told her she might have to start looking for a job if we were going to make ends meet, I was grateful when things worked out and she didn't have to. Because this is really the place the kids need a full-time mother, to watch them.

This arrangement works, Gordon says, because "She's not the working type." This gendered division of labor between husband and wife is a reproduction of his parents' pattern. His father had been a skilled machinist, his mother, with a college degree, had stayed home and not worked outside the home until her children were in high school. Gordon explains the arrangement he has with his wife as the result of their "choice" and in accord with his wife's personality. Although Gordon described both the division of labor and the fact that he followed his father into working on machines as "natural," this couple is an instance of a social fact: in the overwhelming number of cases where one of a couple works full time, it is the husband.

Like Gordon, Marvin attributes the division of labor in his marriage to his wife's preference. She has worked off and on, he says, selling products from the home and working as a teacher's aide for the local school district, which "gives her a lot of flexibility." When I asked him if she had ever wanted to work full-time, he said:

> She seems to have wanted more to be a good mother. And she was the type of person that when we got married, she had this view of herself

as not "Super Mom," but "Nice Mom" that does the things that Moms do and takes the kids and gets involved in things. And that was a really big thing to her.

Marvin is articulating what Garey (1999) points to as a dominant cultural image of mothers as oriented either to work or to family. Garey argues that many employed mothers downplay their aspirations to "career"or to being "Super Mom" and practice "maternal visibility" by making a point of being seen as doing "the things that Moms do."

Paul went a step beyond Gordon and Marvin in his defense of a structural gendered division of labor, turning it into a timeless and natural pattern. Paul is a serious, almost intense man who talks quietly but displays a fierce protectiveness of his family. He works a night shift with lots of overtime and shift differential pay. He and his wife, who was employed full time, lived with their two sons, ages six and eight, in a townhouse near his work. The children were cared for by his wife's mother during the day, but she was about to move away and Paul's plan was for his wife to reduce her hours of employment and work part time.

> I was thinking about trying to buy a [single family] house over here, but if it's going to cause me to be away from the family, or cause [my wife] to have to work all the time, I think we're gonna back out. If I can't afford a house on my pay alone, and make it, if we can't do it on my paycheck alone, we're not gonna do it. Because that's just basic. It's just the way it's been since time began. Women stay home. I'm not trying to be chauvinist by any—but if you're gonna have a family, that's the way it works best.

The gendered division of labor, then, puts women in the home as the mothers of men's children, and this division of labor is reinforced by cultural work that emphasizes men's responsibility as providers and women's involvement in their children's lives. Such a division of labor is presented as natural and equal, but it is a product of a particular economic structure and social organization of work, and it works to the advantage of men in giving them more control over their leisure time (though less over the large amount of their lives they spend at work). The gendered division of labor at the structural level also has profound implications for the daily activity of parenting.

DISCIPLINE, CARING, AND PROVIDING: GENDERED PARENTING

In parenting and child rearing men once again place women between themselves and their children. Their interactions with their children are controlled, arranged, or supervised by their wives. Women have most of the responsibility for arranging and enforcing children's activities, with men exerting their influence through their wives. Some men do put a lot of energy into their children's activities, especially into their athletic activities, and even more express the desire to do so, especially to do more with their children than their fathers did with them. But studies of time use continue to find differences between working husbands and wives in the total number of hours worked when paid labor, childcare, and housework are combined.[9]

Not only is there a difference in the number of hours men and women spend in child rearing, but fathers and mothers approach parenting very differently. The men I talked to express the belief that mothers are the "default parent." They act on this belief and by their actions make it true. Being the default parent means being on terms of greater intimacy, being the one to whom a child turns first, and being the one with the responsibility for knowing what the child's needs and schedules are. The default parent, ultimately, is the one who has to be there, to whom parenting is in no sense optional (Walzer, 1998). For example, fathers may go to meetings at their children's schools or take their children to sports practice, but it is usually mothers who keep track of when the meetings and practices are, and who are, therefore, the default parents. Lareau (2000a, 2000b) reports that fathers are very vague and general in their accounts of their children's daily routine, in contrast to the detailed and specific responses of mothers. In general, my informants indicated that it was their wives who kept the mental and physical calendar, and I would simply add that the person who keeps track of scheduling has a good deal of control over what is scheduled.

Even in the area of discipline and punishment, where it would seem that the father's position as ultimate authority was secure, mothers are the gatekeepers or mediators. Consider the proverbial threat of mothers to their children: "Just you wait until your father gets home!" This expression was used as an example by a number of men to express that they were deeply involved in their children's lives. It was meant to indicate that they were the source of discipline even if they were not in a position of direct supervision most of the time. On closer examination, however, the expression indicates a very different relationship, for it is the mother who decides when and what the father is told, and thus when he can act. Rather than being in an immediate disciplinary relationship with his children, he is a resource to be mobilized by his wife in her dealings with the children, and thus in a relationship mediated by his wife.

The disciplinary dynamic in families can take several forms, but two are common. While they may seem very different, in both of them the wife and mother is ultimately responsible for discipline. In the first, the husband is an authority figure and disciplinarian who sees himself as supporting or backing up his wife. In the second, the husband is allowed to be fun because his wife is the disciplinarian.

Both Ralph and Terry used the word "enforcer" to describe their role in their children's discipline. Neither of them liked this, though both accepted it as their responsibility to support their wives. Ralph had two children and was one of the most impressive men I met doing this research. He had had a troubled adolescence, but since then he had worked his way to a highly responsible job in public service and was universally admired by his former classmates. Ralph told me that there had been one disciplinarian in his family when he was growing up, and that it was the same in his marriage:

> One parent seems like the disciplinarian and the other one is not. And in my family I am. And my wife doesn't understand: "Why won't the children listen to me?" Because it's always: "I'm gonna tell your father." She had to call me here [at work]. I've had to talk to them on the phone. And they straighten right up.

Ralph felt that his wife should be more consistent in her discipline so that the children would not ignore her threats and make her lose her temper. She, on the other hand, sometimes felt overwhelmed and told him that if she were to hit the children instead of threatening: "I'd beat them to death. I'd be constantly hitting them."

Terry, the father of two boys, is also critical of his wife's treatment of the children, but he too accepts his role as enforcer.

> The thing is, you've gotta be the enforcer. The man has to be the enforcer and that's the only thing that sometimes irritates me. I come home from working a hard day and my wife right off "Terry, he's done this, he's done that." And I get mad and I go in there and yell at him. That's where a lot of times I would like to say "You're the mother. Handle it. If you want to restrict him, restrict him. If you want him to be whupped, do it." She's home every day. She knows exactly what's going on. I think she ought to handle it more herself.

For both Ralph and Terry, the structural division of labor, their position at work, and their wives' presence at home, means that their wives are the ones who determine what is expected of their children and who know what they are doing. The women then decide what to tell their husbands and so determine the kinds of interactions fathers and children will have. Terry yells at his children and Ralph spanks his, but their wives, as the default parents, mediate the flow of information and expectation between fathers and children. Women's mediation should not, however, be seen as deliberately manipulative. The gendered division of discipline is not an individual choice or decision, but part of a whole gendered system of division of labor.

Gordon's situation is a rather different manifestation of the same gendered system. In Gordon's family, he is the one who can relax and have fun with his sons because his wife is protective and strict. When it comes to parenting, he says:

> My wife does a better job. Although she is very protective of the kids. Like my eleven-year-old, she won't drop off at baseball practice. She'll stay and wait until it's over. And even though sitting in a car, she's always there. She won't leave the kids anywhere alone. . . . I think she's just worried about something happening to them. Not having an accident, like falling off of something, but with all the crazies out there, she's just worried about losing one of them. Which is—I mean, it's a real-life concern. I can't blame her for that, but it gets a little excessive sometimes. And she does discipline them better, they mind her better, she's more sensitive to their feeling and that kind of thing. It's the insensitive dad, sometimes. . . . I don't treat my kids the way [my father] treated us. He was a very heavy disciplinarian and we were afraid of him when we grew up. I don't want my kids to be afraid of me.

Partly because he does not want his children to fear him as he feared his father, and partly because his wife is watching over them, protecting them, and disciplining them, he feels he can let them run a little wild: "When they're just goofing off and it's Friday night, I'm not going to crack the whip and put them to bed." He laughs, "It wouldn't work anyway."

Edward's position as a "fun dad" to his three children is also mediated by his wife, who ran a child care business in her home when the youngest was a toddler and now teaches at the private school the children attend. She is very involved in the lives of children in general and her own children in particular, and part of her involvement is in scheduling her husband's time with his children. Edward says that: "When there are three there, it's tough. They're all vying for your attention." So his wife intervened and he now says to his children: "'Your Mom says it's your turn.' So each time I do something I take a different child with me. And it works out two ways. It's a lot cheaper for one. And also I get that one-on-one with my kids." Many of the things he does with his children are recreational activities that he enjoys, such as baseball and basketball games. While his wife is orchestrating this activity, Edward gets to be the fun father, spending quality time with his children doing something they can enjoy together. Edward also gets to be spontaneous with the whole family. Several times he told me that he would, "on the spur of the moment," sweep the family up and drive to the beach:

> Like I get them going at seven in the morning up to Santa Cruz and I'll bring my camping stuff and we'll cook breakfast and we'll just have breakfast and when other people are coming, we're leaving and coming back home. We do stuff off the wall like that. Spur-of-the-moment type things. On Friday afternoon I'll tell everyone to pack their suitcase and we'll go to Monterey for a night and things like that. I think that's pretty neat.

Overall, Edward emphasized the fun and spontaneity of his relations with his children: "Age wise, I'm probably considered an adult, but you talk to my kids and I'm probably the biggest kid around. I'm not kidding. I'm a big kid at heart. I love sports. I love my kids." It is important to notice that Edward's ability to be spontaneous and to have fun with his children, just like his one-on-one time with his children, is dependent on the routine, day-by-day, planned, and conscientious work of his wife.

The gendered division of labor in parenting not only distributes work and fun differentially between fathers and mothers, it also distributes who gets taken for granted, and who gets the credit for what they do. Hochschild shows how couples negotiate not only a material division of labor, but also an economy of gratitude (1989): people do not just want to be appreciated, they want to be appreciated for the contributions they think are important. Psychologists Carolyn and Philip Cowan (1999) observed that, for men, paid employment "counts" as childcare—when men work they are seen as doing something for their children. In addition, wives see their husbands' attention to their children as contributions to the marriage relationship. Women's employment, on the other hand, is seen as detracting from their mothering, and their husbands do not see the care mothers give their children as

couple time or as building the marriage. For the men I talked to, their fathers' employment was remembered and appreciated, while their mothers' employment was minimized or forgotten. In addition, their mothers' parenting was taken for granted, while their fathers' more occasional attention was treasured.

Even though he said his father did not spend much time with him—"Dad was working. I remember when my father worked three jobs"—Edward appreciated the hard work his father had done to build a financially stable foundation for his family: "My Dad's helped me out financially, he's helped every single one of his kids out. Financially and every other way." Edward also remembered "the few vacations we had" with his father. His fond memories of those rare occasions was one motivation for his own spontaneous family trips. But his memories of his mother are less precise and more matter-of-fact. I asked him if his mother had worked:

> I know she worked off and on because she worked at [an electronics company] for the longest time. Yeah, she did work. I'm just trying to remember. There was a time when I know she didn't because I know when I was in elementary school I remember coming home at lunchtime and she would have lunch for me. So maybe when the kids were smaller she didn't work. And then she started working. I remember her working at [the electronics company] a long time. Then went to [a computer manufacturer] and retired from there.

In fact, his mother had also worked full-time before the family moved to Orchardtown when Edward was six, but the point to notice is not so much whether she worked or not as that her son did not see her work as part of her identity, and certainly not as part of her parenting, which was represented by that daily routine of having lunch ready. On the other hand, for her husband work was central to his being a father. The financial help Edward received from his parents (both of whom were working full time when he was a young man) is reported as coming from his father, and the family activities he points to are a handful of family vacations with his father.

Mothers who are supervising and caring for their children may well know more about those children, about their hopes and insecurities, than fathers who are there to have occasional fun. They are then in a position to relay or to hold back knowledge about their children, and mothers are the ones who both fathers and children talk to about the other. Edward told me a typical story of an incident between him and his daughter about which both of them had, independently, talked to his wife. Their communication about the event, and its resolution in Edward's mind, was very directly mediated by the mother.

> I just talked to my wife the other night. My oldest daughter, somehow I felt like she wasn't communicating with me lately, the last couple weeks. I was asking my wife if there was anything wrong. What particular things had happened at school. I went to pick up my son and she was gonna go somewhere else and I saw her and I know she saw me, but she didn't acknowledge me being there. So I was kind of hurt because usually they'll come up "Hi Dad!" And my wife goes "It had nothing to do with her not wanting—" What it was, I guess, her friends were wearing makeup and she knows I'm against girls at this age wearing makeup and I guess that was why she didn't come and talk to me. So that's fine. I can see why she didn't want to talk to me.

These examples illustrate that the structural division of labor, in which men are seen as providers and women as homemakers, is connected to a gendered division of parenting. Mothers not only do more child care and domestic work, they also know more about what their children are doing and feeling, they talk to them more, and they control the flow of information between fathers and children. They also schedule their children's lives and the interactions they have with their fathers. As part of this gendered system, the relationship that mothers have with their children even influences the quality of the interactions men have with their children. Mothers may invoke their husbands as disciplinarians and enforcers, so that the fathers are stricter or sterner than they might otherwise be. Or mothers may maintain the structure of family life, giving men the space to be spontaneous and fun.

Within this gendered system of parenting, men and women act out and reinforce gender stereotypes. Men are expected to play more actively with children than women do, and as a general rule they do so. Mothers, so I was told, control male exuberance, calming people down and discouraging dangerous or overexuberant play. It is mothers, I am told, who set limits on the activity of men and children. By doing so, they constrain themselves or, rather, are constrained by an entire system of expectations from being "fun" in quite the same way that men are. Men's playfulness and men's anger, their distance and their sense of inadequacy, are reproduced in the daily interactions of family life. A crucial element of these interactions is the mediating position of women, as wives and mothers.

CONCLUSION

The question arises of whether women jealously guard their control over the family or whether men relegate women to the less prestigious area of domestic work and childcare. At the level of family life and the lives of individual men and women, clearly both are going on (Coltrane 1989; Cowan and Cowan 1999; Hertz 1986: 64–65; Walzer 1998: 45 ff). The gendered division of labor in parenting is part of an "arrangement between the sexes" (Goffman 1977)—a constructed and continually reinforced division of being between men and women. Men certainly develop a learned or deliberate incompetence in certain areas. It is a joke among both men and women that after a man has once done the laundry with mixed whites and coloreds and turned everything pink, or fixed a meal and turned the kitchen into a disaster area, or looked after the children for a weekend during which they ate nothing but pizza and never bathed, it is easier for women to do these things themselves. But men also develop different ways of doing things—playing more aggressively, teasing, and challenging children to take risks or break out of routines. Both men and women live out and perform stereotypes, frequently performing them while acknowledging that, in some sense at least, they should not do so. So a woman who says: "I know I should learn how to check the oil in the car, but I let my husband do it," or a man who, like me, sheepishly excuses himself from making social arrangements because "My wife keeps track of the calendar," is perpetuating a particular gendered division of labor at the same time that his words are explicitly criticizing it.

This process of negotiating gender, which is often referred to as "doing gender" (West and Zimmerman 1987) to describe gender as an activity rather than an intrinsic quality that people have, is complex and often internally contradictory. In this chapter I have shown how the cultural norm of men's public labor force participation and their role in the domestic sphere as family providers is maintained by cultural work done by men (and women) to emphasize the importance of fathers' earnings although mothers are also playing vital roles in the work force and public sphere. I have also shown that, within the domestic area, there is a gendered division of parenting, and of the meaning of being a parent, that continues to be very important even when both parents are involved in the day-to-day activities of their children. Fathering, like all human activity, is both a pattern of behavior and a set of meanings. Behavior and meaning sometimes reinforce each other, sometimes contradict each other, and sometimes work together to cover over contradictions or to make sense of changing circumstances.

In family life in the United States, as men, women, and children move back and forth between the public areas of employment and school and the domestic areas of home life and care giving, cultural ideas of what is gender-appropriate function to make sense of change and to provide meaningful continuity and coherence.

REFERENCES

Arendell, Terry. 1995. *Men and Divorce*. Thousand Oaks, CA: Sage.

Billy, John H. G., Nancy S. Landale, and Steven D. McLaughlin. 1986. "The Effect of Marital Status at First Birth on Marital Dissolution Among Adolescent Mothers." *Demography* 23: 329–349.

Coltrane, Scott. 1989. "Household Labor and the Routine Production of Gender." *Social Problems* 36: 473–490.

———. 1996. *Family Man: Fatherhood, Housework, and Gender Equity*. New York: Oxford University Press.

Cowan, Carolyn Pape, and Philip A. Cowan. 1999. *When Partners Become Parents: The Big Life Change for Couples*. Mahwah, NJ: Lawrence Erlbaum.

Ehrensaft, Diane. 1990. *Parenting Together: Men and Women Sharing the Care of Their Children*. Urbana: University of Illinois Press.

Ferree, Myra Marx. 1991. "The Gender Division of Labor in Two-Earner Marriages: Dimensions of Variability and Change." *Journal of Family Issues* 12: 158–180.

Furstenberg, Frank F., and Andrew Cherlin. 1991. *Divided Families: What Happens to Children When Parents Part*. Cambridge, MA: Harvard University Press.

Garey, Anita Ilta. 1999. *Weaving Work and Motherhood*. Philadelphia: Temple University Press.

Goffman, Erving. 1977. "The Arrangement Between the Sexes." *Theory and Society* 4: 301–336.

Hansen, Karen V. 1994. *A Very Social Time: Crafting Community in Antebellum New England*. Berkeley: University of California Press.

Hernandez, Donald J. 1993. *America's Children: Resources from Family, Government, and the Economy*. New York: Russell Sage Foundation.

Hertz, Rosanna. 1986. *More Equal Than Others: Women and Men in Dual-Career Marriages*. Berkeley: University of California Press.

Hochschild, Arlie. 1989. *The Second Shift: Working Parents and the Revolution at Home*. New York: Viking.

Langer, Ellen J. 1983. *The Psychology of Control*. Beverly Hills: Sage.

Lareau, Annette. 2000a. "Vague Answers: Reflections on Studying Fathers' Contributions to Children's Care." Paper presented at "Work and Family, Expanding the Horizons," University of California, Berkeley.

———. 2000b. "Social Class and the Daily Lives of Children: A Study from the United States," *Childhood* 7 (2): 155–171.

Leone, Catherine L. 1986. "Fairness, Freedom, and Responsibility: The Dilemma of Fertility Choice in America," Unpublished Ph.D. dissertation in Anthropology, Washington State University.

Martin, Teresa Castro, and Larry L. Bumpass. 1989. "Recent Trends in Marital Disruption." *Demography* 26: 37–51.

Pleck, Joseph. 1985. *Working Wives/Working Husbands.* Beverly Hills, CA: Sage.

Schneider, Jane C., and Peter Schneider. 1996. *Festival of the Poor: Fertility Decline and the Ideology of Class in Sicily, 1860–1980.* Tucson: University of Arizona Press.

Schor, Juliet B. 1991. *The Overworked American: The Unexpected Decline of Leisure.* New York: Basic Books.

Shelton, B. A. 1992. *Women, Men, Time.* New York: Greenwood.

Townsend, Nicholas W. 1998. "Fathers and Sons: Men's Experience and the Reproduction of Fatherhood." In Karen V. Hansen and Anita Ilta Garey (eds.). *Families in the U.S.: Kinship and Domestic Politics,* pp. 363–376. Philadelphia: Temple University Press.

———. 1999. "Fatherhoods and Fieldwork: Intersections Between Personal and Theoretical Positions." *Men and Masculinities* 2(1): 89–99.

———. 2002. *The Package Deal: Marriage, Work, and Fatherhood in Men's Lives.* Philadelphia: Temple University Press.

Waite, Linda, and Gus Haggstrom, and David Kanouse. 1985. "The Consequences of Parenthood for the Marital Stability of Young Adults." *American Sociological Review* 50: 850–857.

Walzer, Susan. 1998. *Thinking About the Baby: Gender and Transitions Into Parenthood.* Philadelphia: Temple University Press.

West, Candace, and Don H. Zimmerman. 1987. "Doing Gender." *Gender & Society* 1(2): 125–151.

White, Lynn, Alan Booth, and John Edwards. 1986. "Children and Marital Happiness: Why the Negative Relationship?" *Journal of Family Issues* 7: 131–148.

Wienberg, Howard. 1988. "Duration Between Marriage and First Birth and Marital Stability." *Social Biology* 35: 91–102.

NOTES

1. A large amount of human activity is carried on in an area that is neither strictly domestic nor public. Areas of life such as friendship, visiting, kinship, and socializing cut across the public/domestic divide. In a study of community in nineteenth-century New England, Hansen (1994) proposes the term "social" for this third sphere of action.

2. The interviews involved an interaction between my personal situation, the perceptions of the men I talked to, and my conclusions (Townsend, 1999). I refer to all the men by pseudonyms. The quotations are taken from the transcripts of tape-recorded interviews. I have not changed or added to what men said, but because I do not want to distract attention from the content of what they told me, I have not presented all the "ers," "ums," and "you knows" with which real speech is studded. In the quotations, a dash (—) indicates an incomplete sentence or change of topic, ellipsis (. . .) indicates that I have omitted words or sentences from a quotation.

3. I do not mean to imply that all men, or all women, think and feel alike. Certainly, fatherhood means something different to men in the contemporary United States than it does to men in India, in the Congo basin, or in New Guinea. Fatherhood also has different meanings to men in the United States now than it did to men in the nineteenth century or in the colonial period. Fatherhood also means different things to different groups of men in the contemporary United States. Fathers in the upper classes, for instance, have concerns about inheritance and family status that are very different from those of fathers in the middle class who are worried about their children's college education and the dangers of downward mobility, or from working class fathers whose positions in families are being transformed by declining real wages and an increasing family dependence on two incomes.

4. The birth of children before marriage is associated with a marital disruption rate 57 to 80 percent higher than for couples without premarital births for cohorts of white women married between 1970 and 1985 (Martin and Bumpass, 1989: 42). This association may be because of greater strains on the early marriage, because couples who have a child before marriage have less normative commitment to marriage, or because some of the births were the biological children of men other than the husband and so do not have an "own children" effect on his behavior. My assertion of the connectedness of marriage and children is bolstered, however, by the lack of association between premarital conception and marital disruption (Billy et al., 1986).

5. Leone's (1986) discussion of the key values invoked by middle class white women in the United States to describe and explain their childbearing decisions reveals the importance of "readiness" for women as well as for men.

6. Ehrensaft (1990: 119–122) interviewed couples who had decided to share the work of parenting their children. She describes the men's reactions of "falling in love with" their children. For women, "the gap between the anticipation and the reality

[of children] was smaller" and the major surprise was the absorbing day-to-day reality of parenthood. For men, the anticipation was more anxious and the realization of parenthood marked a greater break. In the terms of my discussion, the paternal relationship, the paternal sentiment, and the sense of being a father is something that is brought about, that happens, and that is not taken for granted or inevitably linked to the biological events of conception or birth. (In an absolute sense, the same is true of women. "Maternal bonding" is a cultural event also, but it is an unquestioned event of our culture in a way that "paternal bonding" is not.)

7. Langer (1983) has analyzed the psychology of "perceived control" and its importance for both a sense of well-being and the actual outcome of events.

8. The "father breadwinner, mother homemaker" family has been both historically recent and short-lived as a dominant pattern. From 1850 until the Second World War, the decline of farm families was matched by an increase in the percentage of children in "father breadwinner, mother homemaker, nonfarm families" which reached almost 60 percent by 1930 and then fluctuated around that level until 1960, when it began a rapid drop to 27 percent by 1989. From 1950 onward, the declines in farm and father breadwinner families has been matched by a rise in the percentage of children in dual-earner and one-parent families, which was approaching 70 percent by 1990. Since 1970, less than half of the children in the United States have been in families of the father breadwinner, mother homemaker type (Hernandez, 1993: 103).

9. Hochschild (1989: 3–4 and 271–273) summarized studies that concluded that there was a difference of ten to twenty hours of total work between working husbands and wives. Other studies have found that men and women spend approximately equal amounts of time on the combination of housework and paid work (Ferree, 1991; Pleck, 1985; Schor, 1991), but certain domestic tasks continue to be overwhelmingly women's work (Coltrane, 1996; Shelton, 1992), and men's contribution to housework still tends to be thought of, by both husbands and wives, as helping (Coltrane, 1989; Walzer, 1998). When married couples have children, the division of domestic labor tends to become more traditionally gendered (Cowan and Cowan, 1999) and women spend less time in the paid labor force while men spend more (Shelton, 1992).

Cities of Women

Mary Weismantel

INTRODUCTION: SEXING THE MARKET

In her influential essay "Democracy for a Small Two-Gender Planet," Mexican anthropologist Lourdes Arizpe surveys a wide range of politically active women, including "Bolivian peasant[s] . . . Chilean trade unionists, mothers . . . in Argentina . . . and the women leaders of the poor neighborhoods and shanty towns in São Paolo, Lima, and other Latin American cities" (1990:xvi), and finds one underlying commonality. All of these women struggled to gain

access to the public life of their societies. Regardless of class, race, or nationality, she asserts, the opposition between a feminine private domain and the masculine outside world is fundamental to the social geography of the continent. Arizpe goes on to provide an illuminating analysis of political activism at the end of the century; but the gendered geography from which she begins is not as universal as she claims. Throughout the Andean nations of Ecuador, Peru and Bolivia, (and elsewhere in Latin America as well, including some regions of Arizpe's own Mexico), every small town and big city is home to one kind of public space dominated by women—the produce market.

The Andean marketplace is unmistakably female. Men drive the trucks, buses and taxis that move sellers and products in and out of the market, and they control the wholesale end of the business, where most of the money is made. But by far the largest numbers of people who work in the market are vendors, and almost all of these are women. In my own research on markets in the Ecuadorian city of Cuenca, at least ninety percent of the vendors in the two central markets were women. Ownership of the prized interior stalls was almost 100% female. Similar patterns obtain throughout the highlands. Bromley found that eighty-five to ninety-five percent of the retailers of fresh fruits, vegetables, meat and fish in the highland Ecuadorian markets in the early 1970s were women (1981). Blumberg and Colyer, too, estimated that eighty-five percent of the vendors in the Saquisilí main market in the late 1980s were women (1990:255), results that I confirmed throughout the 1980s and 1990s for all of the major markets of Cotopaxi Province. In Peru, women comprised seventy percent of all vendors in metropolitan Lima in 1976 (Bunster and Chaney 1985) and eighty percent of all sellers in the Huaraz market in the 1980s (Babb 1989). In Bolivia, this occupation has been "almost exclusively" female throughout the latter half of the century (Buechler and Buechler 1996:223).

That such a large, old and well-established institution could remain invisible to analysts like Arizpe, allowing her to speak unconditionally of Latin America as a society without public spheres for women, illustrates just how anomalous the market is within dominant sexual geographies. The markets are flamboyantly female and unabashedly public, yet they exist within a larger world in which the public sphere is masculine, while feminine realms are enclosed and hidden away from the intrusive eyes of strangers. The existence of this highly gendered institution highlights the masculinity of other public spaces, even as, for market women themselves, it reverses the gendering of both public and private space. And for every household that consumes its products, the market, and the variety of cooked and uncooked foods it provides, troubles the boundary between domestic and commercial work—between a labor of love and working for money.

THE TWO PLAZAS

The incompatibility between femininity and public space is, of course, inflected by race and class. For the most part, working-class women have not been afforded the protection—or suffered the imprisonment—of seclusion within the private domain to the same extent as elite and middle-class women. Ethnicity, too, changes how South Americans think about women's mobility. In the rural Quichua-speaking community of Zumbagua, in Cotopaxi province, Ecuador, where I have done fieldwork for ten years now, the sunburnt farmwomen of the parish spend most of their waking hours outdoors, among the sheep and the barleyfields. Their physical presence within the parish—the way in which they move, work, and talk in public—is strikingly masculine by comparison with other Latin American social contexts.

The cities are different. Gender is deeply inscribed in the plan of the Latin city, which exalts the difference between public and private. Traditional homes are often walled, turned inwards to protect family life within a generous but totally enclosed space. Public life occurs within a city plan dominated by a central square, typically bearing a name like "Plaza de Armas," "Plaza de la República," or "Plaza de la Independencia." As a physical representation of victories by and for European men, the Plaza de Armas defines itself against those it excludes: Indian leaders dethroned and banished to the peripheries of empire, Africans deracinated and forced into slavery, and women of all races disenfranchised and contained within houses and convents.

The central plaza is designed to present a visually overwhelming image of the power of the state, the glory of the wealthy, and the honor of men. It is clean and barren and masculine, an open space surrounded by the closed and forbidding architecture of state power. But the Plaza de Armas is not the only plaza to be found in Andean cities. Each of them also boasts another plaza: the messy and feminine space where the produce markets are held. In rural towns, these two different plazas occupy the same space: once a week the market takes over the civic plaza, temporarily re-defining its purpose. In larger cities, civil authorities try to keep the two spaces separate, designating specific squares, streets, and buildings around the periphery of the city as officially sanctioned markets, and sending the police to cleanse the main plaza of vendors and *ambulantes*. The public authorities in Andean cities and towns are perpetually at work to contain the constant, organic growth of this feminine, vernacular space within spatial and temporal limits, and so to protect the dignity of the city's public persona.

The masculinity of the public sphere, we are told, is everywhere under attack. In the global society occupied by the professional classes, it has become a commonplace to speak of women's success in entering the worlds of business and politics. But the inclusion of women as full-fledged members of such communities remains tentative and incomplete, giving rise to a popular discourse about glass ceilings and a legal wrangle over hostile environments. These architectural metaphors are apt: the buildings erected by governments, banks and corporations, like the central plazas around which these buildings are arrayed, are white male spaces, within which femininity continues to be a stigma that marks the interloper. Inside the markets, it is elite men who are made to feel peripheral, like women and the poor in the "other" public spaces. They enter with hesitation and leave quickly, afraid that people are laughing at them behind their backs. The market is made up of individual stalls, row upon row piled with fresh food. Whether the display of food is simple or elaborate, at its center sits the marketwoman herself, a rounded vertical form rising from flat rectangles piled with goods. Repeated again and again across the open expanse of the plaza, or under the enormous metal roofs of the municipal market building, the female bodies of the vendors take on an almost architectonic function. Stationary in the midst of the tumult, these are the pivotal figures who give the market its shape and purpose. This public visibility of the female form, on display not for male delectation but for other purposes entirely, presents a symbolic inversion of the dominant sexual order that some men find profoundly unsettling.

When travel writer Henry Shukman entered the municipal market building of a small town on the altiplano, he was stung by the silent stares of the sellers. They appeared indifferent to him; even their clothing— "absurd, wide, ballerina-like skirts and derby hats"—expressed an apparent unconcern with attracting masculine desire that he found frankly terrifying. Nonplussed, he translated what he saw there into a total reversal of the patriarchal order. These women "hold a frightening dominion over the men" of the town, he asserts hyperbolically. Upset by their unreadable expressions, appalled by the absence of other men, he hastened to leave. "[T]hey didn't want me here," he writes, apparently astonished at the notion (1989:53).

Constrained by the bold gaze of a myriad of women, men in the markets temporarily lose what they have previously taken for granted: the freedom to move about in public with relative unself-consciousness. The sight of so many women so completely at ease in a public sphere of their own making, creates a corresponding unease in men momentarily bereft of a hitherto unquestioned privilege.

This unease has its origins not merely in the fact that this space is dominated by women, but in its dedication to "women's work"—activities normally hidden from view. The visual impression created by the market mimics the intimate spaces and informal organization of domestic life; rather than the empty formality of the masculine plaza, here impromptu constructions criss-crossed with ephemeral passageways fill every available space. This is a haphazardly vernacular architecture, with hand-made, open-walled structures that invite the passerby to look, touch, and taste. The atmosphere is redolent with the smells of food and cooking, as well as of garbage and ordure.

Public life derives its masculine air of dignified display, from its contrast with the secluded existence of its necessary complement: the private world of the family. In erasing this opposition, the placeras' daily activities undermine the plaza's self-importance, making low comedy of high drama. The sight of bloody carcasses and dirty potatoes, the sound of voices calling out "Escobas! Escobas!", "Chochoooos! Chochoooos!", the loudspeakers extolling Jesus or toilet paper, the bustle of women cooking dinner, washing dishes, emptying the slop bucket—all of these bring the mundane and even the unmentionable into open view.

Nor can the activities here be subsumed under the category of women serving men, for the women at work here are very publicly engaged in serving their own needs and one another's needs as well—including the bodily needs that are strictly excluded from other public spaces. In Cuenca, I saw market women urinating in a public park, using their full skirts to hide their genitals, but completely unabashed about the nature of the act itself. In this, they resemble country women; in Zumbagua, too, women squat down unashamedly to urinate beside a road or a path, just as men turn their backs to do the same. (It is a surprisingly modest act for individuals of either sex wearing traditional clothing: women's full skirts cover them from exposure just as men's long ponchos do.) This matter-of-factness about a physical need that bourgeois women never acknowledge in public, may enable us to see that their attitude towards another bodily function, eating, is also rather extraordinary.

Market women eat in public with gusto. Older women, especially, display a self-congratulatory indulgence in the physical pleasures of eating that is more reminiscent of eighteenth century English novels like Tom Jones, than of prevalent attitudes towards public consumption today. In contrast to the manners thought appropriate to fine dining—not to mention the epidemic of disorders that make it impossible for many American women to eat in public at all—public eating in the markets is a proud display of financial success and physical well-being. In a public display of power, important women eat with relish, licking their fingers, sucking on ripe mangoes or greasy chicken bones—even, in one memorable scene in a Quito market last year, eating the brains out of a goat's head with a spoon.

The unequal relationships between older and younger, richer and poorer women take on physical form in the plates of food that move between stalls. Established vendors—big women with rolls of flesh—sit behind their piles of merchandise and watch while younger, thinner women who approach them timidly with plates of food. "Por si acaso . . ." the young women offer timidly, "If perhaps this might please you a little. . . ." Grudgingly, the older woman accepts, and sit back eating slowly and with relish while her younger associates wait on customers. Occasionally the she stops her meal to make change for her helpers, pulling out an enormous roll of bills of different denominations.

The overall impression is not one of comic vulgarity, however: the women who gossip, eat, and take naps in public, shell beans and make soup, clean fish and fry pork, do so with a dignified self-confidence that makes it difficult to take them lightly. When travel writer Eric Lawlor was brought to the La Paz markets by a Bolivian women friend, he had a series of alarming encounters with the women working there, which culminated when he accidentally knocked over a pail of *refresco* belonging to a vendor who specialized in these flavored beverages. "The woman glared with such ferocity that, before I quite knew what I was doing, I had pressed all my money into her hand and fled," he recalled. "To be frank, marketwomen unnerved me" (1989:32).

This surface appearance of the market as an independent city of women can mislead. Relationships with men and with masculine institutions set invisible boundaries everywhere. Socially, women live within neighborhoods and extended families dominated by men; in their businesses, marketwomen depend upon the male wholesalers, truckers and drivers who bring them their merchandise; politically, the relentless intervention of the state wears a masculine face and uniform—that of the policeman. The many faceted and heavy-handed effort by all the Andean states to control the markets, which includes draconian measures to limit their growth economically and spatially, as well as abusive police tactics against individual vendors, is itself an indication that, however limited the freedoms it offers to women, the market nevertheless offers a profound threat to the social order. The market provides the women who work there not only with a job, but with a vantage point from which to critique, to reject—and even to transform—the domestic unit that is the building block of civil society.

REJECTIONS

Travelers' impressions of the Andean marketplace as a profoundly female, even an anti-masculine zone, are supported by a recent life history, *In The World of Sofia Velasquez: The autobiography of a Bolivian market vendor* (1996), published by anthropologists Hans and Judith-Maria Buechler. Unlike the alienating sea of identical female faces described by male writers, the market in Sofia's book is a richly heterogeneous territory. She speaks with affection, antagonism, familiarity and irritation of many different kinds of women: her fellow vendors, with whom she must negotiate for room to sell; the female restaurant owners who buy her pork, eggs and cheeses; the women who loan her money and those who are indebted to her. While men—especially her brother Pedro— are never entirely absent from the story of her life, they are far overshadowed by the dozens if not hundreds of female partners, competitors, customers, relatives, neighbors, friends and enemies who populate Sofia's busy world.

The working lives of professional women in offices are still largely defined by their relationships with men, whether as subordinates or colleagues. But Sofia, asked about what it means to be a woman, emphasizes the opportunities for homosociality that the produce market provides:

> I see friendships between women sitting next to one another. They become friends or comadres. I frequently see them talk to one another or go and drink together. They lend one another money and they are concerned about what is happening in each other's lives.

For women who work in such intimacy with other women, the home has a different meaning than it does for women who work in male-dominated contexts—or who do not work outside the home at all. For market vendors, domesticity does not appear as the one definitively and unambiguously female domain, where women can feel at home and in control; far from it. In a radical inversion of this gender paradigm, domestic life with husbands, fathers and brothers appears in market women's testimonies as an ominously patriarchal territory controlled and dominated— often violently—by men.

In Sofia Velasquez's account, domesticity and the market are twin magnetic poles pulling women in opposite directions, towards men and away from them. Throughout her story, two family members stand for these opposite worlds. Her mother represents a happily feminine life of buying and selling, while her brother Pedro emerges as a repressive figure, forever attempting to shape her behavior to conform to masculine ideals which Sofia does not attempt to refute, but which she nevertheless refuses to live by. When she first became an ambulante, conflict with Pedro erupted almost immediately.

> [O]ne afternoon, my brother Pedro saw me selling on the street . . . [and] said, 'I will tell my sister that she is no longer my sister. It is shameful for her to be selling on the street.' . . . He said that it was unseemly for me to sit in the street and that his friends would criticize him. . . . But . . . I liked to sell. Selling was pleasant. I could go and sell whenever I wanted and I was earning money. (20–21)

At this young age, Sofia's turn to marketing involved staking out her gender loyalties, rejecting male authority and looking to other women for support. "I won't stop, Mother," I told her. 'Let him go ahead and say that I am not his sister. It's fine with me. They (the other vendors) will help me.' And so I continued to sell . . . (21)."

To Pedro, as to other working-class men of La Paz, it is especially inappropriate for married women to sell. Sofia repeatedly tells of women leaving the market at the behest of husbands, especially newlyweds (often to reappear when family finances dictate). One of her most richly enjoyed victories over Pedro's meddling, occurs when his own finances take a downturn and his wife joins Sofia selling on the street.

If family life sometimes pulls women from the marketplace, it has just as often pushed them into it. This feminine workplace not only provides women with an income when male wages are insufficient; it also acts as a refuge when a home falls apart, or becomes too dangerous. Sociologists Bunster and Chaney, in their 1985 study of working-class women in Lima, heard many tales of domestic tragedy when they interviewed recent immigrants from the highlands. Some women had been abandoned, like Alicia, who said, "I had separated from my husband because he ran off with another woman. That was the reason I came to Lima. In the sierra I couldn't support myself . . . I came alone. . . ." Or Edelmira, who explained that "I didn't have anything, my husband went off with another woman. I came here when I was two months pregnant." Another woman fled "the sexual advances of her stepfather after her mother's death" (1996:40–41). Anthropologist Leslie Gill, who wrote an engaging study of domestic workers in La Paz, also met many young immigrants escaping family violence: "Six-year-old Zenobia Flores fled to La Paz with her mother in 1972 to escape the drunken rages of her father, who regularly beat up his wife and children" (1994:65).

The opposition between the market and the home in these accounts is strikingly gendered; while some women described fleeing an abusive stepmother, most were escaping fathers and husbands. Inasmuch as it provides them with a source of income, the market clearly gives women some independence. Perhaps as importantly, it places them within a collectivity of other women, one that, in the central markets, is highly organized. This position enables them to pass collective judgment about what goes on within the domestic sphere, and even to intervene. When married women work in the market, their co-workers claim the right to protest marital abuse, speaking on behalf of marketwomen in general. Sofia Velasquez recalled: "My secretary of organization, Rosa Espinosa, was beaten by her husband. One day, I called her husband and told him that I didn't like the fact that he was beating his wife." But

Sofia admits that the vendor's ability to protect one another is limited. The story of one woman, Ventura, ends tragically: "We [the market women's union] dealt with the matter, but the man killed her anyway, by beating her."

In the Mercado 10 de Agosto, a municipal market in the center of Cuenca, most of the socias [members] had inherited their professions, and sometimes even their stalls, from mothers, aunts or grandmothers. Rosa Loja, for example, who sells peppers, has been a market vendor for forty-four years. Her mother was a *frutera*, a seller of fruit, in the now-defunct Mercado San Francisco. Women who do not inherit this job have little chance of joining an association like the 10 de Agosto's, but they still come to the markets by the thousands trying to develop a successful career as a vendor. Economic, political and military upheavals have driven record numbers of rural peasants to the cities in recent decades, but this migration takes gender-specific forms. Women make their way to the markets along well-established routes, one of the most common of which is an initial flight from one's own rural family, followed by a second escape from the oppressive life of a domestic. "The sexual harassment and abuse of household workers is one of the enduring features of female domestic service in La Paz" (Gill 74). Speaking to Bunster and Chaney in Peru, and to Gill in Bolivia, market women explained their choice of occupation by describing themselves as psychologically unable to bear the repressive and abusive situations they had encountered previously as domestics. In another life history from the Andes, Gregorio Condori Mamami's wife Asunta, a vendor of cooked food in the Cuzco market in the 1970s, recalled her earlier employment as a domestic with distaste. The husband of the woman who employed her, she said, was "un diablo" who tried to rape her whenever he found her alone in the house (1977).

The market can offer temporary respite from the violent excesses of male violence, or a permanent escape from patriarchal domination. While some vendors suffer execrable relationships with men, others terminate relationships that are abusive, seek transitory rather than permanent alliances, or insist upon more egalitarian relationships with husbands and lovers. Some women reject heterosexual partnerships with men completely.

My interest in the domestic arrangements of women who work in the markets was first aroused by two women who had succeeded in opening establishments not in the market square itself, but in small buildings on its periphery. Heloisa Huanotuñu was the owner of a tiny but much-frequented tavern on the edge of the square where the Zumbagua weekly market is held; her friend Elena had turned her kitchen into a lunch room popular with the white school teachers, doctors, and nurses who worked in the parish school and clinic. The two were inseparable, Heloisa's tall black-clad figure a counterpoise to stout little Elena, who always wore one of the frilly shawls that the Irish nuns had taught local women to crochet. Heloisa and Elena were well-respected businesswomen by the standards of the town, and both were popular there; their establishments were central clearing houses for news, as well as crucibles where public opinion was forged—Heloisa's a gathering place for indigenous farmers, as Elena's was for the town's tiny white bourgeoisie.

The two were interesting personalities in their own right, but I was especially fascinated because they did not conform to the image of rural Andean women promulgated in social-science textbooks, in which heterosexual marriage is described as mandatory (see for example Bolton and Mayer 1977). Neither had ever been married. Although they maintained separate (but adjacent) households, it was Elena who provided Heloisa with companionship, in the early morning, at meals, in the slow hours of the afternoon, and at night in bed. (In the cold mountain towns of the Andes, sleeping together in the same bed is a common practice and does not necessarily imply sexual intimacy. It is extremely unusual for either children or adults to sleep alone, and the need for a sleeping companion for warmth and to prevent loneliness is universally acknowledged. Nevertheless, people in town speculated that the two were indeed lovers.)

I never heard either woman express the slightest desire for adult male companionship beyond that of their brothers—indeed, quite the reverse. They spoke of the married women they knew in voices that mixed sympathy, pity, and a slight but unmistakable contempt.

Far to the south in Bolivia, living in a bustling capital city rather than in a remote rural periphery, Sofia Velasquez grew up knowing women like Heloisa and Elena. As a child, Sofia was resentful of her older brothers' control over her, and quick to note that some of her friends lived in all-women households. As though to foreshadow the adult relationships between women that would be so important to her later on, the first page of Sofia's life story introduces a childhood friend, Yola, who lived in an exclusively female household:

> She doesn't have a father. [Her mother] lived with a friend called Agustina Quiñones. They came from Peru together. . . . To this day, neither one of them is married and they are still living together. They are inseparable friends. (1996:1)

Later in the text, she describes them as Yola's "two mothers."

Explaining her decision to work in the market, Sofia begins by stating that she had never had any desire to marry, or to live with men. In drawing the connection between working in the market and escaping domestic life with men so explicitly, she inadvertently makes her brother's relentless opposition to her marketing more understandable. Like Sofia, Pedro sees the market as the antithesis of patriarchal domesticity—and thus as a direct threat to his own attempts to control the women in his life, both sisters and wives.

There appears to be a popular recognition that the markets make these alternative domesticities possible. Consider the words of Bolivian working-class men in the early 1990s, who repeatedly described market women to anthropologist Robert Albro as "varonil," manlike, or the traditional belief, widespread in parts of Bolivia as well as in southern Ecuador, that market women lived in "matriarchal" households. Or the exchanges between Cuzco market vendors and other working-class women recorded by Linda Seligman a decade earlier. In one argument, a market woman snapped at a customer, "Watch out or I'll slap you one." The other woman replied, "And you? Who are you to have to slap me? Don't I already have a husband who slaps me? Perhaps you [formal] don't have one who would slap you" (Seligman 1993:196).

Despite the provisional freedoms it permits from male domination, hierarchies of other kinds permeate the markets; relationships between market vendors and their employees can be as exploitative and abusive as the domestic situations that initially brought young women to the market looking for work. Zenobia Flores, for example, who ran away from employment as a child maid, told Leslie Gill that she was

> taken home by a chola woman, who saw her crying and walking aimlessly down a street, and for a year Zenobia worked for this woman, grinding chilies into powder and selling in a small dry-goods store. She was never paid and frequently went hungry, and the woman eventually abandoned her on a street corner. (Gill 63)

But without patriarchal or legal pressures binding the parties together, poor women are more easily able to leave oppressive situations if better opportunities arise; indeed, other women often urge them to do so.

> Julia Yapita came to La Paz with her female cousins when she was twelve years old. For over a year, she lived with an older sister, who resided in one of the sprawling immigrant neighborhoods in the Alto. The sister sold food on the street and knit sweaters for tourists. Julia assisted her in these tasks but resented always being ordered about. "My sister bossed me around a lot", Julia explained, "and my aunts, who lived next door, told me to find a job, because my sister was never going to buy me clothes. They knew of a chola . . . who wanted a maid and took me to meet her. She wore a pollera . . . and sold salteñas. I started working for her that day." (Gill 68–9)

Without men to define the limits of female behavior, Julia is free to become like the older, more independent women she sees around her—and to successfully resist their attempts to control her.

This independence explains why Pedro considered his sister's work to be indecent, calling it "shameful" and "disgraceful." The source of this immorality lies in an apparent rejection of domesticity, an act which, Arizpe tells us, would place them outside of the norm for Latin American women of all classes and races. However, this marginality does not render their understanding of the home as a patriarchal space, irrelevant. Don Kulick observes that such marginality can allow members of a subculture to "distill and clarify" aspects of sexuality and gender of profound and pervasive importance in Latin America (1997:582). Like the prostitutes with whom Kulick worked, market women are not alone in their perceptions, but their perspective gives them a greater clarity of vision.

In recent Peruvian fiction by two very different male authors, Mario Vargas Llosa and Jaime Bayly, childhood memories of well-to-do homes are characterized by an all-pervasive and terrifyingly violent paternal order (Ellis 1998). Nor do working-class homes appear to be domains controlled by women: the title of Wendy Weiss's doctoral dissertation sums up working-class Quiteños domesticity with the phrase, "Es El Que Manda." But while women of wealth and poor women alike resent the autocratic behavior of husbands and fathers, they imagine themselves to be without alternatives. Male authors, too, write of vaguely imagined temporary refuges, such as an escape into nature or a few hours in a whorehouse. In contrast, the markets are full of women who slammed the door on oppressive domestic lives, in active pursuit of viable permanent alternatives. When wealthy Bolivian girls, sent away to college in the United States or Europe, began coming home in the 1970s filled with new feminist ideas about living outside of marriage, they found that such a move had meanings within the Andes that it did not have elsewhere. To reject sexist domestic arrangements would not be seen as a radical innovation, but as a scandalous abandonment of one's class and race position: an educated woman choosing to live like a market vendor (Gill 1994:87).

AT HOME IN THE MARKET

Market vendors, then, are public scandals: women without men, working the streets. Many of the women who work in the market are in fact married, or live in consensual unions with men; most of them are mothers; and all of them, except the truly destitute, have homes. But market women, even when earning money to support their husbands, fathers, and sons, evoke images of wicked women rather than of the good wife. The negativity that attaches to the woman of the plaza, is a measure of the positive valuation given to the woman at home.

The only problem with this picture, is that the street market is less an antithesis to the domestic kitchen, than its raucous twin. The public market exists in close economic symbiosis with the unseen interiors of the private homes that surround it, and which it daily provisions. The home and the home-maker are the market to which produce vendors sell their goods: The world of the plaza exists to provide services for the domestic sphere. "Casera," "casera," shout the market-women to potential customers: "homemaker," "homemaker."

Visitors from other countries are often charmed and surprised by the incongruous domesticity of scenes in the market: a man sits at his sewing machine, ready to patch your trousers or catch up a fallen hem; a woman spreads a wooden table with a bright-colored plastic tablecloth, and offers to sell you anything from a Coca-cola to a four-course *almuerzo,* complete with dessert. Nor is this commercial domesticity a mirage: workmen and students cultivate special relations with particular market women, eating at their stalls day after day, taking comfort in the familiarity of the woman's voice, her steady supply of gossip, and her knowledge of their particular tastes and appetites. Real and fictitious family relationships abound. Some customers are distant relatives—perhaps the son of a country cousin, sent to the city to attend high school with a strict enjoinder to eat all his meals "*donde su tía*" [where your aunt is]. No one who eats at a particular stall for any length of time remains a stranger; regular customers are inexorably drawn into the domestic dramas between the women who work there, and are ruthlessly—albeit sympathetically—interrogated about their own lives and kin.

Cooking is not the only housewifely work that market women do. Like women who shop for their families, they bring the products of male producers and wholesalers into a feminine realm where these can be transformed into meals for individual families. Babb observes that market women's labor is wrongly characterized as strictly distributive in nature. In fact, many kinds of food processing take place in the market that would readily be interpreted as productive if done in a factory. Vendors break down bulk quantities into smaller portions; shell beans and peas; peel fruit and vegetables; chop herbs and grate onions. They even make small ready-to-cook soup packages, filled with combinations of raw legumes, herbs and vegetables in exact proportions. Many stalls feature a single product offered in every stage of preparation, from unpeeled and dirty, to washed and sliced, to cooked and ready to eat.

Heloisa's trago shop is a case in point. She buys contraband cane alcohol in large quantities from the men who bring it up from the western jungle by mule and llama train. The little caravans arrive at her home in the early hours of the morning, and she and the men pour the alcohol from saddlebags into big plastic containers that once held kerosene. Customers occasionally buy entire barrels of the stuff for weddings or funerals, or to bootleg over the mountains for resale in the white towns to the east. Most people bring smaller containers—gallon jars, empty liquor bottles—that are filled by a hose and closed with a fragment from a plastic bag. As the morning wears on, other customers appear looking for a shot to be consumed on the spot. Heloisa or another family member is ready to oblige, siphoning the liquor directly from a fifty-gallon drum into a tiny glass.

Sometimes a group of people makes an impromptu celebration there; in that case, Heloisa can provide soft drinks for the children, and stale bread for everyone. She does not cook for her customers, but can always use her extensive social network to rustle up snacks or cooked food, as well as a variety of other services: a child to run an errand or deliver a message, a decoy to keep enemies away—and, not least in importance, her own physically and psychologically imposing presence to prevent the arguments that develop among drunks, from getting out of hand.

If work done in the market strikes economists as somehow too informal, too feminine, too unimportant to be recognized as productive, it is at the same time too commercial in nature to be properly domestic. The same activities, done inside the home, do not count as labor at all; in economic terms, they become invisible. But for housewives, the existence of inexpensive market labor radically re-shapes the work load within the home. Women come to buy big quantities of corn already cooked into *mote* for a family dinner, or a little bag of it with hot sauce on top for immediate snacking. They may purchase a whole cooked pig or a single slice of roast pork. Some vendors sell enormous wheels of *panela* [turbinado sugar] dark and strong-smelling, wrapped in banana leaves; but they will also cut you off a little chunk to eat like candy.

Histories of the American consumer describe the advent of ready-to-eat foods as a recent innovation made possible by enormous technological advances. The willingness of working women and their families to eat prepackaged food, or to dine in restaraunts, is described as a fundamental change in twentieth century social life. Arizpe describes this as a pernicious penetration of the capitalist market into women's traditional sphere of authority, one that has usurped their most valuable "function" and left them "empty handed" (xv). These visions of history are too narrow in both class and geographical perspectives. In Latin America, the presence of the markets, with their abundance of pre-cooked foods, is old rather than new. Some industrial technologies have filtered into the plaza: many factory-made foods are sold there; beverage stall counters are lined with electric blenders; the small stores that ring the market occasionally invest in a refrigerator for milk and cheese. But for the most part, this enormous system of provisioning works through the simplest of technologies: knives to slice and peel, ropes to carry bundles, cooking pots and wooden spoons to boil and stir. The fact that it is human labor,

not capital investment or technological innovation, that adds value to the products there, is transparently obvious. The fact that this labor is predominantly feminine, has limited the ability of scholars and policy-makers to understand, or even perceive it.

Working-class women depend upon the ready availability of meals and ingredients from the markets; in small cities and towns this attitude extends to professional women as well. Travelling the back roads of Cotopaxi Province with a car full of Ecuadorian anthropologists, I was surprised when one passenger insisted that we drop in for lunch on an old school friend he had not seen in some time. Her feelings would be hurt, he insisted, when she found out he had been in the town and had not let her give his friends a midday meal. How, I wondered, could this unknown woman cope with a half dozen unexpected lunch guests? The market provided the answer: our hostess disappeared within minutes of our arrival, then returned to usher us in with fanfare to a dining room laden with local specialties: potato pancakes, roast pork, tomato salad, fresh corn. Beaming, she boasted of knowing all the best market stalls in town: without her, she insisted, we would never have been able to eat well in a strange place.

The willingness of market women to perform any sort of food preparation, and the eagerness of housewives and domestic servants to avail themselves of these services, mediates the boundary between the loving work of caring for a family, and the paid labor of strangers. Men and children eating a meal within the house, consume the work not only of their own wife and mother, but of other women as well. In order to be the ideal housewife who knows how to provision her family, women must create and keep good relations with the women of the market and of the small shops that surround it. Thus even for women who do not work there, the markets demand a degree of female homosociality which customers find alternately maddening and rewarding. Market women foster affective relations with their customers, capturing their loyalty, blurring the line between business and friendship. An expatriate American scholar who lives in Cuenca spoke to me fondly about "her egg ladies," whose stall was a regular stop on her Saturday morning excursions around town. But personal relationships are always risky. When Sofia Velasquez, an "egg lady" herself, got on the wrong side of one of a restaurant owner who bought large quantities of eggs from her on a weekly basis, she found herself scrambling for new customers—and missing the tasty sandwiches the woman's husband used to sell her, as well.

The relationship between a market woman and her customers has its own arcana. Many a gringa who has lived in the Andes for an extended period of time, recalls with pride her first "yapa"—the first time that, as a repeat customer, she earned a little "extra" scoop of flour or beans, poured into her bag after it has been weighed and the price figured. Marketwomen who sell to Indians often keep a bag of cheap, brightly colored candies with which they "yapa" their customers, preferring to offer these treats rather than any of the more expensive dry goods or produce they sell. The result is a subtle insult, masked as a kindness: are these candies for the purchaser's children, or is the Indian woman herself being treated as a child? Why is it that the seller, pretending friendship, nevertheless insists that Indians—unlike their white customers—pay full price for every ounce of merchandise?

I vividly remember archaeologist Clark Erickson and his wife Kay Chandler's return to the United States, after spending almost three years in a small, isolated community on the Peruvian Altiplano near Lake Titicaca. They ruefully recalled to me their first attempts at creating good relations with local shopkeepers. Anxious not to offend, the couple had tried to alternate making purchases between each of the two small stores that sold dry goods—the only source of food on the days in between the weekly market. The women who owned the shops, miffed that Kay had not cultivated a special friendship with one or the other of them in accordance with local mores, responded by refusing to sell them anything at all—and temporarily succeeded in turning the market women against them as well. Within a few months, however, Kay had learned to behave

appropriately enough to create a completely different relationship with "her" chosen shop owner: by the end of their stay, the woman carefully tucked away specially chosen eggs and cheeses for "her" special gringa to buy.

From the market woman's perspective, maintaining the proper degrees of intimacy with customers is among the most complicated and delicate of tasks—and the one that separates an inept from a successful entrepreneur. My landlady in Zumbagua, Rosa Quispe, operated a cooked-food stall in the Saturday market there for a while, but gave it up in disgust. "It costs me more than I earn," she explained to me. "The entire family comes to the market and expects me to feed them for free, but I have to buy all my ingredients in Latacunga the day before, and there I pay cash."

Successful market women, too, find the boundary between market and domestic relations impossible to maintain. What distinguishes professional women like the stall-owners in the Cuenca municipal markets from amateurs like Rosa is their ability to make profit out of their personal relationships, while using their commercial ties to benefit themselves and those they care about. For the true professional, the line between public and private, commercial and familial disappear almost completely. The Buechlers comment about Sofia Velasquez, that she and her co-workers, unlike the Bolivian middle class, eat out all the time. The domestic expertise upon which mothers and wives pride themselves, is among market women translated into knowledge of especially tasty or reasonably-priced meals cooked by others. They collect coveted relationships with restaurant owners who give free meals, wholesalers who add on a generous yapa "just for the family," and growers who reserve choice produce for friends and intimates.

Sofia Velaquez, for example, reminisces about sharing meals with her daughter, but not because she had stayed home and cooked for her. Rather, returning home after a long overnight journey to make purchases at a rural fair, she recalls that "We would always arrive hungry and would go to eat salchipapas together" at a favorite stall that stayed open late into the night (Buechler and Buechler 1996: 204).

CONCLUSIONS: COOKING
FOR LOVE AND MONEY

In the late afternoons, when the market is quiet, the market in Cuenca is a drowsy place. There are almost no customers. The big metal doors of the market are pulled down part-way, making the interior dim and cool. Young assistants and relatives have been sent home; only the older women, owners of the stalls, lounge in them half-asleep, reading newspapers or taking naps as though in their own living rooms. They take out their reading glasses, their crocheting, and their slippers, wrap themselves in their shawls and prop their feet up on a sack of potatoes or noodles.

If the market is literally a domestic space for these women, whose work brings them there seven days a week from the middle of the night till mid-afternoon, their homes, in turn, become staging sites for commercial and productive operations. Sra. Loja, the rocoto seller, didn't mind that her daughters had not followed exactly in the footsteps of their mother and grandmother. They sell clothing rather than food, and recently began to manufacture some items at home. "They have turned the house into a factory," she remarked with satisfaction.

In La Paz, Pedro complains that Sofia uses the family home, inherited from their mother, as a source of income. He doesn't mind that she has filled the bedrooms with boarders, as her mother had done before her. What upsets him is that Sofia rents out the courtyard to her fellow vendors as storage space. It is stacked with folding tables, portable stoves, piles of raw produce, and even—much to Pedro's disgust, and eliciting complaints from the long-suffering tenants—loads of freshly slaughtered meat.

Heloisa Huanotuñu lives in her trago shop. The counter and shelves, table and chairs serve both as her kitchen and the bar's furniture. Her bed, partly curtained with a sheet of plastic, and the small storage areas above and below it, are the only semi-private spaces within the one-room building. Much of her emotional life is centered elsewhere, in the family farmstead up above town, where her brothers and sisters and nieces and nephews live. She spends many hours there, cooking and eating, listening to complaints and giving advice, loaning money and demanding help. But she does not sleep there. She, too, then, has arranged working, sleeping, eating, and loving in ways that cannot readily be reduced to a single dichotomy of public and private.

Henry Shukman and Pedro Velasquez are separated by race, class, and nationality, but united in their embrace of the idea that family life, the home and domesticity should be a single unit, defined by its contrast to the public spheres of work, business and politics. In rejecting this pattern, market women do not challenge universal or essential sexual patterns, or even Hispanic or Mediterranean cultural patterns. Rather, they are rejecting a pattern specific to modern capitalism, which fetishizes the home as the realm of affective relations (Moore 1988:23). Market women, although they live completely within the commercial and urban spheres of capitalism, are as resistant to this, its central tenet, as are the Indian peasants who live on its fringes. Women vendors do not merely leave the realm of the domestic in order to enter commercial life; they drag domesticity into public in order to make money, and embrace a commodification of private life that is more unnerving still to a bourgeois sensibility.

The domesticity of the market stall and the industrialization of the home erase the line between work and family. If some market vendors have unconventional domestic partnerships, all of them create intergenerational relationships that violate bourgeois notions about love. It is in their relations with children—the individuals with whom vendors typically form their most enduring and intimate relationships—that market women violate the norms of bourgeois capitalism most egregiously.

Their intergenerational relationships are manifestly as commercial and industrial as they are emotional and social. In Cuenca, young women helped older ones in relationships that were either actually or fictively the kinship relations of mother and daughter, or aunt and niece—but were also those of employer and employee, banker and debtor, investor and fledgling entrepreneur. Sofia Velasquez provides a detailed, decades-long account of how such relationships develop. She began life as her mother's dependent, but quickly became her employee, then her partner. In her eyes, there is no contradiction between financial and emotional investment—and no shame in the expectation of both immediate and long-term return. Remembering the loans her mother made to get her started as in her own independent business, and the careful accounting of interest payments each night, she says fondly and with pride, "She made a really good profit from me in those years."

Today, she explains her love for her own daughter—and her daughter's love for her—by detailing the girl's labors as her employee.

> Rocio is helping me at home for two years now. . . . She gets up at 4:30, dresses warmly and goes out to light the kerosene stoves and prepares the food. . . . I get up at 5:00 just to see what she has done. At 6:30 she packs up the food and has it transported with the stevedore to my sales site on the street . . . at 7:30 she leaves for school. (Buechler and Buechler 1996:210–11)

Here, the bourgeois convention of cooking as an expression of female affection for loved ones, is translated into a commercial proposition. In Sofia's experience, mothers and daughters cook for one another, not in intimate, lovingly-produced meals removed from the uncaring relations of the commercial world, but in bulk, as cheaply and efficiently as possible, because they are business partners hoping to turn a profit.

The market, then, challenges the sexual geography of the Americas on several fronts at once. It brings women and women's work into the public sphere; and it allows some women to reject the patriarchal domination exerted over the private sphere as well. The most profound challenge it offers, however, is to the very separation of private and public spaces, and of commercial and familial relations. It threatens to create a domesticity without walls, drawing household members outside into the plaza for the satisfaction of their social, emotional and bodily needs, while invading the domestic kitchen with commoditized relationships between the marketwomen who work for money, and the housewives who buy their labor when they might have done the work themselves.

As Sofia Velasquez' brother Pedro seems all too aware, the market undermines the foundations of Andean patriarchy, including the authority and privilege extended to men within the home—an authority backed up, when necessary, with violence. More unsettling still is the erosion of a distinction between highly valued male wage labor, and the unpaid domestic labor performed by women. And worst of all is the market woman's insistence on defining her emotional work in raising children, as well as her remunerative work in the commercial sphere, not as selfless giving for the good of her family, but as activities from which she herself enjoys multiple returns—in love and friendship, money and security, and in the immediate physical pleasures of eating and drinking, talking and laughing in the company of other women.

Today, large American-style supermarket chains are beginning to undermine the importance of the open-air produce market in the Andes, a process that will no doubt accelerate in years to come. Many of the daughters of Cuenca's market women are abandoning not only the plazas where their mothers sell, but the city, the nation, and the region as a whole, emigrating to the United States in droves. These girls grew up in households in which the lines between profit and pleasure, domesticity and public life, friendship and commerce were configured in defiance of the dominant sexual geographies of the Americas; what they will do with this intimate and embodied knowledge as they move into spheres far removed from the produce markets of the Andes, we can only wait to discover.

REFERENCES

Arizpe, Lourdes
1990   Democracy for a small two-gender planet. Forward *to Women and Social Change in Latin America*. Pps. xiv–xix. London: Zed Books.
Babb, Florence
1989   *Between Field and Cooking Pot: The political economy of marketwomen in Peru*. Austin: University of Texas Press

Bolton, Ralph and Enrique Mayer, eds.
1977   *Andean Kinship and Marriage.* Washington, D.C.: American Anthropological Association. Special Publication Number 7.

Blumberg, Rae Lesser and Dale Colyer
1990   Social Institutions, Gender and Rural Living Conditions. Pps. 247–266 in *Agriculture and Economic Survival: The Role of Agriculture in Ecuador's Development.* Morris D. Whitaker and Dale Colyer, eds. Boulder: Westview Press.

Bromley, Ray
1981   Market Center and Market Place in Highland Ecuador: A Study of Organization, Regulation, and Ethnic Discrimination. Pp. 233–259 in *Cultural Transformations and Ethnicity in Modern Ecuador.* Norman E. Whitten, Jr., editor. Urbana: University of Illinois Press.

Buechler, Hans and Judith-Maria Buechler
1996   *The World of Sofía Velasquez: The Autobiography of a Bolivian Market Vendor.* New York: Columbia University Press.

Bunster, Ximena and Elsa M. Chaney
1985   *Sellers and Servants: Working Women in Lima, Peru.* New York: Praeger.

Condori Mamani, Gregorio and Asunta Quispe Huaman,
1977   *Gregorio Condori Mamani: Autobiografía.* Ricardo Valderrama Fernandez and Carmen Escalante Guetierrez, editors and translators. Cuzco: Centro de Estudios Rurales Andinos "Bartolome de las Casas."

Ellis, Robert
1998   The Inscription of Masculinity and Whiteness in the Autobiography of Mario Vargas Llosa. *Bulletin of Latin American Research* 17(2).

Gill, Leslie
1994   *Precarious Dependencies: Gender, Class and Domestic Service in Bolivia.* New York: Columbia University Press.

Kulick, Don
1997   The Gender of Brazilian Transgendered Prostitutes. *American Anthropologist* 99(3): 574–585.

Lawlor, Eric
1989   *In Bolivia: An adventurous odyssey through the Americas' least-known nation.* New York: Vintage Press.

Moore, Henrietta L.
1988   *Feminism and Anthropology.* Minneapolis: University of Minnesota Press.

Seligman, Linda J.
1989   To Be In Between: The Cholas as Marketwomen. *Comparative Studies in Society and History* 31(4):694–721.
1993   Between Worlds of Exchange: Ethnicity among Peruvian Market Women. *Cultural Anthropology* 8(2):187–213.

Shukman, Henry
1989   *Sons of the Moon: A Journey in the Andes.* New York: Charles Scribner's Sons.

Valderrama Fernandez, Ricardo and Carmen Escalante Gutierrez
1977   *Gregorio Condori Mamani: Autobiografía.* Cuzco: Centro de estudios rurales andinos bartolomé de las casas.

IV
Equality and Inequality:
The Sexual Division of Labor and Gender Stratification

In most societies certain tasks are predominantly assigned to men while others are assigned to women. In European and American cultures it used to be considered "natural" for men to be the family breadwinners; women were expected to take care of the home and raise the children. An underlying assumption of this division of labor was that men were dominant because their contribution to the material well-being of the family was more significant than that of women. Women were dependent on men and therefore automatically subordinate to them.

The "naturalness" of this division of labor has been called into question as women increasingly enter the labor force. However, has this significantly altered the status of women within their families and in the wider society? Or has it simply meant that women are now working a double day, performing domestic tasks that are negatively valued and not considered work once they get home from their "real" day's work? If employment enhances the social position of women, why is it that women still earn less than men earn for the same work? Why is there still a high degree of occupational segregation by gender? What precisely is the relationship between the economic roles of women and gender stratification? Cross-cultural research on the sexual division of labor attempts not only to describe the range of women's productive activities in societies with different modes of subsistence, but also to assess the implications of these activities for the status of women.

In many parts of the world women contribute significantly, if not predominantly, to subsistence. This is perhaps most apparent among hunting and gathering or foraging populations, and for this reason such groups have been labeled the most egalitarian of human societies. Hunters and gatherers used to form the bulk of the human population, but today only a small number remain. They are found in relatively isolated regions; they possess simple technology and therefore make little effort to alter the environment in which they live. They tend to be characterized by a division of labor whereby men hunt and women gather. Friedl (1975: 18) outlines four reasons for this division: the variability in the supply of game, the different skills required for hunting and gathering, the incompatibility between carrying burdens and hunting, and the small size of seminomadic foraging populations. Friedl (1975) further argues that in foraging societies in which gathering contributes more to the daily diet than hunting, women and men share equal status (see also Lee 1979; Martin and Voorhies 1975). Conversely, in societies in which hunting and fishing predominate (such as among the Inuit), the status of women is lower. It seems that female productive activities enhance the social position of women in society, but Sanday (1974) cautions that participation in production is a necessary but not sufficient precondition. Control over the fruits of their labor and a positive valuation of this labor are other factors to consider, as is the extent to which women are involved in at least some political activities. In addition, the absence of a sharp differentiation between public and private domains (Draper 1975) and the fact that there is no economic class structure and no well-defined male-held political offices (Leacock 1975) have been cited as explanations for the relative egalitarianism in foraging societies compared to more complex societies.

Despite the common assumption that men hunt and women gather, in some foraging societies the division of labor is not sharply defined. This often provides the basis for the highest degree of egalitarianism. Among the Tiwi, Australian aborigines who live on Melville Island off the coast of northern Australia, both men and women hunt and gather. Goodale (1971) demonstrates that resources and technology, rather than activities, are divided into male domains and female domains. Although the big game that Tiwi men hunt provides most of the meat to the group and therefore gives them a dominant position in the society, Tiwi women, who hunt and gather, provide more than half of the food consumed; they share in both the comradery and the spoils of their endeavors. As major provisioners, women are economic assets and a source of wealth and prestige for men in this polygynous society. Despite the fact that their opportunities for self-expression may be more limited than those of men, with age women acquire social status and can be politically influential. In general Goodale suggests that Tiwi culture emphasizes the equality of men and women in society.

Among the Agta Negritos of northeastern Luzon, the Philippines, women enjoy even greater social equality with their men than among the Tiwi. This is a society in which the division of labor and the battle of the sexes appear to be virtually absent. Agta women hunt game animals and fish just as men do. Not only do they make significant contributions to the daily food supply, but they also control the distribution of the foods they acquire, sharing them with their families and trading them in the broader community. The Griffins (Agnes Estioko-Griffin and P. Bion Griffin, in this book) argue that these roles are clearly the basis for female authority in decision making within families and residential groups.

The Agta case challenges the widely held notion that pregnancy and child care are incompatible with hunting in foraging societies (Friedl 1978: 72). Agta women have developed methods of contraception and abortion to aid them in spacing their children. After becoming pregnant, they continue hunting until late in the pregnancy and resume hunting for several months after the birth of the child. There are always some women available to hunt, during which time children may be cared for by older siblings, grandparents, or other relatives. Reproduction is clearly not a constraint on women's economic roles in this society.

In horticultural societies, in which cultivation is carried out with simple hand-tool technology and slash-and-burn methods of farming, women also play important roles in production (Boserup 1970; Bossen 1989). One theory argues that the economic importance of female production in horticultural societies emerged from women's gathering activities in foraging groups. Horticultural societies vary in the degree to which men participate in crop cultivation as well as whether this cultivation is supplemented by hunting, fishing, and raising livestock. In addition, many horticultural societies are matrilineal (reckoning descent through the female line), and in these societies women tend to have higher status than in patrilineal societies. Maria Lepowsky (in this book) points to gender egalitarianism among the horticultural and matrilineal people of the Pacific island of Vanatinai. In this society, men are not dominant over women either in practice or ideologically. Like men, women on this island can gain both prestige and power through engaging in exchange activities and the sponsorship of feasts where valuable goods are distributed. As a result of these activities, they can become "big women" as men can become "big men." Thus, Lepowsky argues that "the prominent positions of women in Vanatinai exchange and other activities outside of household and subsistence indicate as well as reinforce generally egalitarian relations between women and men. Vanatinai women have access to power both through their control of the economic capital of land and the subsistence and surplus production of yams and through their accumulation of symbolic capital in exchange and mortuary ritual" (1993: 38).

Despite descent systems and economic roles that enhance the status and power of women among horticulturalists such as the people of Vanatinai, Friedl (1975) cautions that women's status is not universally high in such societies. Male control of valued property and male involvement in warfare (an endemic feature in many of these societies) can be mitigating factors that provide the basis for male dominance over women. For example, among horticulturalists in highland New Guinea, women raise staple crops but men raise prestige crops that are the focus of social exchange. This cultural valuation is the foundation for gender stratification that is then reinforced by gender ideologies of male superiority and a high degree of sexual antagonism between men and women (Brown and Buchbinder 1976; Herdt and Poole 1982; Strathern 1988). Among the Hua, for example, Meigs (1990) describes a "chauvinistic" ideology that is rooted in men's roles as warriors.

Among the Mundurucú, an Amazonian horticultural society who were also once involved in fierce warfare (Murphy and Murphy 1985), the division is such that men hunt, fish, and fell the forest area for gardens while women plant, harvest, and process manioc. In their daily tasks women form cooperative work groups, have authority, and are the equals of men. To the extent that their work "draws women together and isolates them from the immediate supervision and control of the men, it is also a badge of their independence" (Murphy and Murphy 1985: 237). However, according to a male-dominated ideology, women are subservient to men. Despite the contributions that Mundurucú women make to subsistence, what men do is assigned more value. As Murphy and Murphy state, "Male ascendancy does not wholly derive from masculine activities but is to a considerable degree prior to them" (234). Male domination among the traditional Mundurucú is symbolic. As the Mundurucú become increasingly drawn into a commercial economy based on the rubber trade, men, with their rights to rubber trees and to trading, may gain a more complete upper hand. "The women may well discover that they have traded the symbolic domination of the men, as a group, over the women, as a group, for the very real domination of husbands over wives" (238).

Although women's labor is clearly important in horticultural societies, it has been argued that it becomes increasingly insignificant relative to that of men with the development of intensive agriculture. Intensive agriculture is based on the use of the plow, draft animals, fertilizers, and irrigation systems. In a survey of 93 agricultural societies, Martin and Voorhies (1975: 283) demonstrate that 81 percent delegate farming to men who then achieve primacy in productive activities. One explanation for the decline in female participation in agriculture is that the female domestic workload tends to increase when root crops are replaced by cereal crops and when animal labor replaces manual labor (Martin and Voorhies 1975). Cereal crops require more extensive processing, and field animals must be cared for. Both these activities fall to women. In addition, the kin-based units of production and consumption become smaller, and this too adds to the burden on individual women.

Concomitant with the presumably declining importance of women in agricultural activities is a supposed decline in social status (Boserup 1970). Women's value is defined by their reproductive abilities rather than by their productive activities. It has been suggested that the lesser status of women in some agricultural societies, particularly those of Eurasia, compared to some horticultural societies, as in sub-Saharan Africa, is reflected in the contrast between systems of bridewealth and systems of dowry (Goody 1976). Bridewealth is a compensation to the bride's parents or her kin for the productive and reproductive rights of the bride; dowry, as a form of inheritance, provides a bride with land and other wealth and helps her to attract a husband (see Caroline James and Linda Stone, Section 7 in this book).

Despite arguments describing a decline in women's status and their relegation to the domestic sphere in association with the emergence of intensive agriculture, cross-cultural data indicate that women in agricultural societies lead much more diverse and complex lives than some theories suggest (Bossen 1989). In northwestern Portugal women do most of the agricultural activity, inherit property equally, and are often the recipients of a major inheritance that generally includes the parental household (Brettell 1986). This division of labor has emerged because men have been assigned the role of emigrants. Another exception is rural Taiwan, where, despite the patriarchal and patrilineal character of Chinese society, women construct a familial network that gives them a good deal of power and influence in later life (Wolf 1972). Finally, in rural Ireland today, women have become active partners in the farm business (O'Hara 1998).

Another economic adaptation is that of pastoralism or herding. Some pastoralists are fully nomadic, moving their entire communities in accordance with the demands of the herd. Others are involved in cultivation and are therefore transhumant. They engage in seasonal migration. Among pastoralists the ownership, care, and management of herds are generally in the hands of men. Though there are exceptions, male domination of herding tends to be reflected in other aspects of social organization—the near universality of patrilineal descent and widespread patrilocal residence. Pastoral societies are also generally characterized by patriarchy and a dichotomization of the sexes, both symbolically and socially. Segregation of the sexes and gender stratification, in other words, are fundamental attributes of many pastoral societies.

The symbolic opposition between men and women is apparent among the Sarakatsani, a group of transhumant shepherds who live in the mountainous regions of the province of Epirus in Greece. According to Campbell (1964), the life of pastoral Sarakatsani revolves around three things: sheep, children (particularly sons), and honor. "The sheep support the life and prestige of the family, the sons serve the flocks and protect the honour of their parents and sisters, and the notion of honour presupposes physical and moral capacities that fit the shepherds for the hard and sometimes dangerous work of following and protecting their animals" (18). Gender ideology is embedded in these three valued items, especially in the parallel oppositions between sheep and goats on the one hand and men and women on the other. The practical division of labor parallels this symbolic opposition. Women give assistance in the care of animals and make major contributions to their families. The economic roles of husband and wife are complementary. Nevertheless, Sarakatsani husbands have ultimate authority over their wives; obedience to a husband is a moral imperative for a wife. As among the Mundurucú, ideology assigns women to a lesser status, in spite of their economic complementarity.

Susan Rasmussen (in this book) reviews many of these aspects of men's and women's roles among pastoralists, but her essay focuses most closely on the Tuareg, a seminomadic, Islamic, socially stratified people who live in Niger, Mali, Burkina Faso, and Algeria. The Tuareg, in her view, offer variations to standard interpretations of gender in pastoral nomadic societies. For example, the frequent absence of Tuareg men from home (in raiding activities in the past and in separatist warfare against the central state governments of Mali and Niger more recently) as well as men's peaceful trading activities have necessitated women's independence in work and the education of children. Tuareg women are not sequestered, they do not veil their faces (although Tuareg men do), and they do not engage in gestures of subservience to their husbands such as kneeling or bowing their heads. Men and women regularly meet and socialize in public and women regularly entertain male visitors (although not necessarily lovers) when their husbands are absent. Although Tuareg women are generally consulted by men about matters that affect the life of the camp or village, there are contexts in which women defer to men—before Islamic scholars, important chiefs, and elders on the patrilineal side. Much of the status of Tuareg women is sustained by their rights of ownership in livestock.

Rasmussen concludes with a discussion of the impact of increasing sedentarization on the roles of Tuareg men and women. Sedentarization has increased women's workloads and altered their bases of property. A shift to virilocal patterns of residence (living with the husband and his kin) has increasingly isolated women from the support of their own kin networks. And, for all Tuareg, sedentarization has reduced autonomy as it has opened new opportunities for work in cooperative agencies.

In more recent years anthropologists have begun to exam the roles of poor urban men and women in a variety of developing countries (Nelson 1979; Smith 1989). Bossen (1989: 348) points out that most of this research shows "that men have a distinct advantage in obtaining a variety of formal, higher paying jobs, while women are concentrated in the less profitable informal service sectors, where the competition is intense." Often these women are involved in small-scale trading and marketing activities (Babb 1985; Mary Weismantel, Section 3 of this volume). Florence E. Babb's chapter in this volume takes up the subject of women's roles in the urban economy, examining their participation in several urban cooperatives as well as in home production and petty sales in the barrios of Managua. She describes the challenges that women have faced in keeping cooperative enterprises going, as well as the competing demands on their time that result from their income-producing and domestic responsibilities. She observes that while poor urban Nicaraguan women contribute virtually all their income to collective household needs, men do not, and that it is women who help to absorb the shocks to household finances generated by economic and political instability. Indeed, Babb demonstrates how men and women in Nicaragua have been differentially impacted by the international economy, by internal conflicts such as the Contra War of the 1980s, and by post-War structural adjustments that have eroded many of the gains of the Sandinista period.

Generalizations are often made about the status of women according to different modes of adaptation. However, the readings in this section demonstrate that there is a great deal of diversity within each subsistence strategy. For example, in foraging societies women may hunt as well as gather; in intensive agricultural and pastoral societies not all women are powerless, dependent, and relegated to the domestic sphere. Although women's contributions to subsistence are important to gender stratification, a number of other factors need to be considered. These include leadership roles in family and kinship units and in the wider community; inheritance of property; control of the distribution and exchange of valued goods; authority in childrearing; and participation in ritual activities. In addition, the ideological definitions of women's roles and valuations of their economic activities are often powerful determinants of status.

To fully understand gender stratification, both ideology and participation in production must be taken into account. As Atkinson (1982: 248) states, "It is too facile to deny the significance of sexual stereotypes or to presume that women's influence in one context cancels out their degradation in another. Just as we know that women's status is not a unitary phenomenon across cultures, we need to be reminded that the intracultural picture is equally complex."

REFERENCES

Atkinson, Jane. 1982. "Review: Anthropology." *Signs* 8: 236–258.

Boserup, Esther. 1970. *Women's Role in Economic Development*. London: G. Allen and Unwin.

Bossen, Laurel. 1989. "Women and Economic Institutions." In Stuart Plattner (ed.). *Economic Anthropology*, pp. 318–350. Stanford, CA: Stanford University Press.

Brettell, Caroline B. 1986. *Men Who Migrate, Women Who Wait: Population and History in a Portuguese Parish*. Princeton, NJ: Princeton University Press.

Brown, Paula, and Georgeda Buchbinder (eds.). 1976. *Man and Woman in the New Guinea Highlands*. Washington, DC: American Anthropological Association.

Campbell, John K. 1964. *Honour, Family and Patronage*. Oxford, UK: Oxford University Press.

Draper, Patricia. 1975. "!Kung Women: Contrasts in Sexual Egalitarianism in Foraging and Sedentary Contexts." In Rayna Reiter (ed.). *Toward an Anthropology of Women*, pp. 77–109. New York: Monthly Review Press.

Friedl, Ernestine. 1975. *Women and Men: An Anthropologist's View*. New York: Holt, Rinehart and Winston.

———. 1978. "Society and Sex Roles." *Human Nature* April: 68–75.

Goodale, Jane C. 1971. Tiwi *Wives: A Study of the Women of Melville Island, North Australia*. Seattle: University of Washington Press.

Goody, Jack. 1976. *Production and Reproduction*. Cambridge, UK: Cambridge University Press.

Herdt, Gilbert, and Fitz Poole (eds.). 1982. "Sexual Antagonism, Gender, and Social Change in Papua New Guinea." *Social Analysis* (special issue), Volume 12.

Leacock, Eleanor. 1975. "Class, Commodity, and the Status of Women." In Ruby Rohrlich-Leavitt (ed.). *Women Cross-Culturally: Change and Challenge*, pp. 601–616. The Hague: Mouton.

Lee, Richard. 1979. *The !Kung San*. Cambridge, UK: Cambridge University Press.

Lepowsky, Maria. 1993. *Fruit of the Motherland: Gender in an Egalitarian Society*. New York: Columbia University Press.

Martin, M. Kay, and Barbara Voorhies. 1975. *Female of the Species*. New York: Columbia University Press.

Meigs, Anna. 1990. Multiple Gender Ideologies and Statuses. In Peggy Sanday and Ruth Goodenough (eds.). *Beyond the Second Sex: New Directions in the Anthropology of Gender*, pp. 99–112. Philadelphia: University of Pennsylvania Press.

Murphy, Yolanda, and Robert F. Murphy. 1985. *Women of the Forest*. New York: Columbia University Press.

Nelson, Nici. 1979. "How Women and Men Get By: The Sexual Division of Labour in the Informal Sector of a Nairobi Squatter Settlement." In Ray Bromley and Chris Gerry (eds.). *Casual Work and Poverty in Third World Cities*, pp. 283–302. New York: John Wiley & Sons.

O'Hara, Patricia. 1998. *Partners in Production? Women, Farm and Family in Ireland.* New York: Berghahn Books.

Sanday, Peggy Reeves. 1974. "Female Status in the Public Domain." In Michelle Z. Rosaldo and Louise Lamphere (eds.). *Woman, Culture, and Society*, pp. 189–206. Stanford, CA: Stanford University Press.

Smith, M. Estellie. 1989. "The Informal Economy." In Stuart Plattner (ed.). *Economic Anthropology*, pp. 292–317. Stanford, CA: Stanford University Press.

Strathern, Marilyn. 1988. *The Gender of the Gift: Problems with Women and Problems with Society in Melanesia.* Berkeley: University of California Press.

Wolf, Margery. 1972. *Women and the Family in Rural Taiwan.* Stanford, CA: Stanford University Press.

Woman the Hunter:
The Agta

Agnes Estioko-Griffin and P. Bion Griffin

Among Agta Negritos of northeastern Luzon, the Philippines, women are of special interest to anthropology because of their position in the organization of subsistence. They are substantial contributors to the daily subsistence of their families and have considerable authority in decision making in the family and in residential groups. In addition, and in contradiction to one of the sacred canons of anthropology, women in one area frequently hunt game animals. They also fish in the rivers with men and barter with lowland Filipinos for goods and services.[1]

In this chapter, we describe women's roles in Agta subsistence economy and discuss the relationship of subsistence activities, authority allocation, and egalitarianism. With this may come an indication of the importance of the Agta research to the anthropology of women and of hunter–gatherers in general. . . .

Women, especially women in hunting-gathering societies, have been a neglected domain of anthropological research. The recent volume edited by Richard Lee and Irven DeVore (1976) and *The !Kung of Nyae Nyae* (Marshall 1976) begin to remedy the lack but focus solely on the !Kung San of southern Africa. Other works are either general or synthetic (Friedl 1975; Martin and Voorhies 1975), or report narrowly bounded topics (Rosaldo and Lamphere 1974). Sally Slocum, writing in *Toward an Anthropology of Women* (Reiter 1975), has provided impetus for the Agta study. Slocum points out a male bias in studying hunter–gatherers, showing how approaching subsistence from a female view gives a new picture. From the insights of Slocum we have sought to focus on Agta women, to compare the several dialect groups, and to begin investigating the nature and implications of women as not "merely" gatherers but also hunters.

THE AGTA

The Agta are Negrito peoples found throughout eastern Luzon, generally along the Pacific coast and up rivers into the Sierra Madre interior. . . . Although perhaps fewer in numbers, they are also located on the western side of the mountains, especially on the tributary rivers feeding the Cagayan. In general terms, the Agta of Isabela and Cagayan provinces are not dissimilar to other present and past Philippine Negritos. (See Vanoverbergh 1925, 1929–30, 1937–38; Fox 1952; Garvan 1964; and Maceda 1964 for information on Negritos outside the present study area.) In the more remote locales, hunting forest game, especially wild pig, deer, and monkey, is still important. Everywhere, collection of forest plant foods has been eclipsed by exchange of meat for corn, rice, and cultivated root crops. Fishing is usually important throughout the dry season, while collection of the starch of the caryota palm (*Caryota cumingii*) is common in the rainy season. An earlier paper (Estioko and Griffin 1975) gives some detail concerning the less settled Agta; both Bennagen (1976) and Peterson (1974, 1978*a*, *b*, n.d.) closely examine aspects of subsistence among Agta in the municipality of Palanan.

A brief review of Agta economic organization will be sufficient for later discussion of women's activities. Centuries ago all Agta may have been strictly hunter-gatherers. Since at least A.D. 1900 the groups near the towns of Casiguran (Headland and Headland 1974) and Palanan have been sporadic, part-time horticulturalists, supplementing wild plant foods with sweet potatoes, corn, cassava, and rice. The more remote, interior Agta, sometimes referred to as *ebuked* (Estioko and Griffin 1975), plant small plots of roots, a few square meters of corn, and a banana stalk or two. They usually plant only in the wet season, harvesting an almost immature crop when staples are difficult to obtain by trade. *Ebuked* neglect crop production, preferring to trade meat for grains and roots.

Lee and DeVore (1968:7) argue that women produce much of the typical hunter–gatherers' diet and that in the tropics vegetable foods far outweigh meat in reliability and frequency of consumption. The Dipagsanghang and Dianggu-Malibu Agta strikingly contradict this idea. They are superb hunters, eat animal protein almost daily, and, as noted above, may have both men and women hunting. (The Tasaday, to the south in Mindanao, may represent an extreme non-hunting adaptation, one in which plant food collection is very dominant [Yen 1976].) Hunting varies seasonally and by techniques used among various groups, but is basically a bow and arrow technology for killing wild pig and deer, the only large game in the Luzon dipterocarp forests. Monkey, although not large, is a reliable rainy season prey. Among Agta close to Palanan and Casiguran, hunting is a male domain. Many hunters pride themselves on skill with bow and arrow; less able hunters may use traps. Dogs to drive game are very desirable in the dry season when the forest is too noisy for daylight stalking of animals.

The collecting of wild plant food is not a daily task. Most Agta prefer to eat corn, cassava, and sweet potatoes, and neglect the several varieties of roots, palm hearts, and greens procurable in the forest. . . . Forest foods are difficult to collect, necessitate residence moves over long distances, and do not taste as good as cultivated foods. Emphasis of trade networks with lowland farmers favors deemphasis of forest exploitation of plants. Only in the rainy season do Agta actively process a traditional resource, the sago-like caryota palm. Fruits are often picked on the spur of the moment; seldom do parties leave camp solely for their collection.

Trade with farmers is practiced by all Agta known to us. Rumors of Agta "farther into the mountains" who never trade (or cultivate) seem to be without substance. In the report of the Philippine Commission (1908:334), evidence of lowland-Agta trade around 1900 indicates the *ibay* trade partner relationship to have some antiquity. As the lowlander population has increased since World War II, trade has also increased. Agta are more and more dependent on goods and foodstuffs gained from farmers; adjustments of Agta economic behavior continue to be made, with labor on farms being one aspect of change. Agta formerly simply traded meat for carbohydrates. Around Palanan they may now work for cash or kind when residing close to farmers' settlements. Hunting decreases as the demands of cultivation are met. A cycle is created, and further withdrawal from forest subsistence occurs. Farmers live in areas once solely owned by Agta. Debts to farmers increase with economic dependence; freedom of mobility and choice of activity decrease; and Agta in farming areas become landless laborers.

At the same time, Agta seek to get out of the cycle by emulating the farmers. Many Agta within ten kilometers of Palanan Centro are attempting to become farmers themselves. While the success rate is slow, the attempt is real. Again, when questioned by an early American anthropologist, Agta close to Palanan Centro claimed to be planting small rainy season plots with corn, roots, and upland rice (Worcester 1912:841). Living informants confirm the long practice of cultivation, but suggest a recent expansion of Agta fields and commitment to abandoning forest nomadism (especially over the last fifteen years). Around the areas of Disuked-Dilaknadinum and Kahanayan-Diabut in Palanan, Agta are well known for their interest in swidden cultivation. Even the most unsettled Agta farther upriver claim small fields and sporadically plant along the rivers well upstream of lowland farmsteads.

The horticultural efforts of the Agta appear less than is the case, since the social organization and settlement patterns are very different from those of the farmers. Agta throughout Isabela and Cagayan are loosely organized into extended family residential groups. A group, called a *pisan*, is seldom less than two nuclear families and very rarely more than five (in the dry season—perhaps slightly higher average during the wet season). The nuclear family is the basic unit of Agta society, being potentially self-sufficient under usual circumstances. The residential group is organized as a cluster of nuclear families united either through a common parent or by sibling ties. Non-kin friends may be visitors for several weeks, and any nuclear family is able to leave and join another group of relatives at will.

As is typical of hunting–gathering societies, no formal, institutionalized authority base exists. The nuclear family is the decision maker concerning residence, work, and relations with other people. Older, respected individuals, often parents and grandparents of group members, may be consulted, but their opinions are not binding. Often group consensus is desired; people who disagree are free to grumble or to leave.

The settlement pattern is determined, in part, by the seasonal cycle of rains and sunny weather, and by these influences on the flora and fauna exploited for food. Rainy season flooding restricts forest travel, brings hardships in exchange, but is compensated by good condition of the game animals. The dry season permits travel over greater distances and into the remote mountains. Predictable fish resources enhance the advantages of human dispersal; only the need to carry trade meats to farmers inhibits distant residence placement.

WOMEN'S ACTIVITIES

Women participate in all the subsistence activities that men do. Women trade with farmers, fish in the rivers, collect forest plant foods, and may even hunt game animals. Tasks are not identical, however; a modest sexual division of labor does exist. Furthermore, considerable variation is found among the groups of Agta of Isabella and Cagayan provinces. These differences may possibly be ascribed to the degree of adjustment of Agta to lowland Filipino culture. Some differences may be due to unique culture histories and to little contact.

Although in Isabela most Agta women do not hunt with bow and arrows, with machetes, or by use of traps, most are willing to assist men in the hunt. Not uncommonly, women help carry game out of the forest. Since mature pig and deer are heavy and the terrain is difficult, this is no small accomplishment. Even in areas around Palanan and Casiguran, women are known to accompany men and dogs into the forest and to guide the dogs in the game drive. Some women are famous for their abilities to handle dogs; one informant, a girl about fifteen years of age, was especially skilled. In Palanan and Casiguran, women and men laugh at the idea of women hunting. Such a practice would be a custom of wild, uncivilized Agta (*ebuked*) far in the mountains, they say. Many of the attributes of ebuked seem to be old-fashioned customs still practiced by interior groups.

Two groups studied as part of the present research do have women who hunt. Among the Dipagsanghang Agta, several mature women claim to have hunting skills; they learned these in their unmarried teen years. They only hunt under extreme circumstances, such as low food supplies or great distances from farmers and a supply of corn. All these Agta are found in southern Isabela between Dipagsanghang and Dinapiqui.

In the northernmost section of Isabela and well into Cagayan province, women are active and proficient hunters. While we have termed the Agta here as the Dianggu-Malibu group, we are actually referring to speakers of the southeast Cagayan dialect who live on the river drainage areas of the Dianggu and Malibu rivers.[2] Both the dialect and women who hunt are found over a considerably greater territory, according to informants, reaching north to Baggao, Cagayan, and at least to the Taboan River.

Among the Dianggu-Malibu women some variation, perhaps localized, perhaps personal, is found. On the Dianggu, some of the women questioned, and observed hunting, carried machetes and were accompanied by dogs. They claim to prefer the machete to the bow and arrow, allowing dogs to corner and hold pigs for sticking with the knife. Our sample of actual observations is too small to argue that only immature pigs are killed, but we do know that in the dry season adult male pigs are dangerous in the extreme. Dogs may be killed during hunts. Since Agta dogs are seldom strong animals, we wonder if mature pigs are acquired only occasionally. On the other hand, so many dogs are owned by these Agta that sheer numbers may favor large kills. We have observed two Agta women with as many as fifteen dogs. Other Dianggu women prefer the bow.

On the Malibu River, Agta women are expert bow and arrow hunters. On both of our brief visits to this group, women were observed hunting. They claim to use bows always, and they seek the full range of prey animals. Wild pig is most desired, while deer are often killed. Future work must quantify the hunting details, but women seem to vary slightly from men in their hunting strategies. Informants say they hunt only with dogs. On closer questioning they admit to knowing techniques that do not involve dogs—for example, they may climb trees and lie in wait for an animal to approach to feed on fallen fruit. Among all Agta, hunting practices vary considerably between the rainy and dry seasons. Our fieldwork in Malibu has been confined to the dry season, when dogs are important. In the rainy season solitary stalking is practiced. Field observations should eventually provide quantitative data on women hunting in this season; we must stress that our data are primarily from interview and brief observation. We have not resided among Cagayan Agta long enough to advance quantitatively based generalizations.

Women not only hunt but appear to hunt frequently. Like men, some enjoy hunting more than others. The more remotely located Agta seem most to favor hunting. Even among Agta certain males and females are considered lacking in initiative, a fault that may not be confined to hunting.

Informant data indicate that while women may make their own arrows, the actual blacksmithing of the metal projectile points is a male activity. More field research is necessary to confirm the universality of this detail. Other items of interest pertain to the composition of hunting parties. Most people in any one residence group are consanguineally or affinely related. We have observed several combinations of hunting parties. Men and women hunt together or among themselves. Often sisters, or mother and daughter, or aunt and niece hunt together. At Malibu, two sisters, co-wives of one male, hunt together, and either or both sisters join the husband to hunt. When young children exist, one of the two wives may stay at the residence while the husband and the other wife hunt and fish. Also, sisters and brothers cooperate on the hunt. A woman would not hunt with, for example, a cousin's husband unless the cousin were along.

The only real argument, in our opinion, that has been advanced to support the contention that women must gather and men hunt relates to childbearing and nurture. Among the Agta, during late pregnancy and for the first few months of nursing, a woman will not hunt. In spite of the small size of each residential group, however, some females seem always to be around to hunt, although one or more may be temporarily withdrawn from the activity. Women with young children hunt less than teenagers and older women. On the occasion of brief hunts—part of one day—children are cared for by older siblings, by grandparents, and by other relatives. Occasionally a father will tend a child. Only infants are closely tied to mothers.

Girls start hunting shortly after puberty. Before then they are gaining forest knowledge but are not strong. Boys are no different. We have no menopause data, but at least one woman known to us as a hunter must have passed childbearing age. She is considered an older woman, but since she is strong, she hunts. The pattern is typical of men also. As long as strength to travel and to carry game is retained, people hunt. Our best informant, a young grandmother, hunts several times a week.

Both Agta men and women fish. In fact, from early childhood until the infirmity of old age all Agta fish. If most adults are gone on a hunting trip for several days, the remaining adults and children must obtain animal protein by themselves. Only women in late pregnancy, with young infants, or into old age, withdraw from fishing, which makes considerable demands of endurance as well as skill. Some men excel at working in rough, deep, and cold waters. The everyday techniques for fishing are limited to underwater spear fishing. Glass-lensed wooden goggles, a heavy wire spear or rod varying according to size of fish sought, and an inner-tube rubber band complete the equipment. To fish, people simply swim underwater, seeking fish in the various aquatic environments known for each species. Girls in their teens are very capable at fishing. When fishing individually, women may be major contributors to the daily catch.

When group fishing is undertaken, a drive is conducted. In this operation, a long vine is prepared by attaching stones and banners of wild banana stalks. Two people drag the vine, one on each end and on opposite sides of the river, while the people in the water spear fish startled by the stones and stalks. Women join men in the drives, with older men and women dragging the vine while all able-bodied youths and adults work in the water.

Difficulty of fishing may be characterized as a gradient upon which men and women become less and less able as age and debilities increase. The elderly, when mobile, may still be productive, but instead of true fishing, their activities may be termed collecting. Both the coastal reef areas and freshwater rivers and streams have abundant shellfish, shrimp, and amphibians that may be caught by hand. Elderly women and grandchildren are especially eager to harvest these resources. Older men are not ashamed to follow suit, although the enthusiasm of others for the task seldom gives old men incentive. Men are much less eager to give up riverine fishing after middle age than are women. Clearly some emphasis on males securing protein is found among Agta. Women, however, seem to have traditionally been active in fishing. Interestingly, as a few Agta adopt lowland fishing technology, especially nets, women seldom participate. Like their female counterparts in lowland society, women are deemed not appropriate in net fishing.

One might expect that, on the basis of worldwide comparison, tropic hunters would really be gatherers, and that women would be the steady and substantial providers. Agta do not fit the generalizations now accepted. Few Agta women regularly dig roots, gather palm hearts, seek fruit, or pick greens. Most Agta daily consume domesticated staples grown by the farmers. Women are, however, very knowledgeable concerning flora and its use, and among the less settled Agta, young girls are still taught all traditional forest lore. Brides-to-be among these Agta are partially evaluated on the basis of their knowledge, skill, and endurance in collecting jungle plant foods.

Roots are collected by women whenever more desirable food is unobtainable, when several wild pigs have been killed and the men want to eat "forest food" with pig fat, or when a visit to relatives or friends calls for a special treat. The interior groups may actually combine meat and wild roots for weeks when camped so far from farmers that exchange for corn is impossible. Downriver Agta consider such a practice a real hardship, not to be willingly endured. Men are known to dig roots, even though they say it is women's work. On long-distance hunts men do not as a rule carry food, and they may occasionally dig roots to alleviate the all meat-fish diet.

As hunting is thought of as a "sort of" male activity among many Agta (in Isabela), processing the starch of the caryota palm is a female activity. Women cruise the forest searching for trees containing masses of the starch; they also chop down the trees, split the trunks, adze out the pith, and extract the flour. Often parties of women and girls work together, speeding up the laborious task. On occasion, men will assist. Extracting the flour starch is moderately heavy work, and tiring. Husbands may help when wives have a pressing need to complete a task quickly. Since much of the final product is given in gift form, the need for haste occurs frequently. Perhaps most important to note is the male participation. Sexual division of labor is tenuously bounded among all Agta. Emphases may exist, but a man can even build a house (i.e., tie the fronds to the frame—a female task).

As noted at the beginning, trade, exchange, and horticulture are not new to Agta. Informants, early photographs, and writings indicate that all but the most remote Agta were not "pure" hunter-gatherers after about A.D. 1900. Since the mountains have been a final retreat—from the earliest Spanish attempts to conquer the Cagayan Valley until the present— Agta must have been in contact with former farmers/revolutionaries in hiding. Keesing (1962), summarizing the peoples of northern Luzon, documents several societies of pagan swiddeners adjacent to or in Negrito territory. The Palanan River drainage area was inhabited by farmers before Spanish contact in the sixteenth century. Doubtless, Agta have participated in economic exchange and social intercourse for centuries. Agta now have institutionalized trade partnerships, at least in Palanan and Casiguran municipalities. Trade partners are called ibay (Peterson [1978a, b] discussed the *ibay* relationship in detail), and partnerships may last between two families over two or more generations. *Ibay* exchange meat for grains and roots, or meat for cloth, metal, tobacco, beads, and other goods. Services may be exchanged, especially in downriver areas.

Fields may be worked by Agta, who then borrow a carabao, receive corn or rice, and satisfy any of a number of needs. What is important in relation to this chapter is that Agta women may engage in *ibay* partnerships. Among the lowland farmers almost all *ibay* are males. An Agta woman may be an *ibay* with a lowland man. According to our data, an Agta husband often is not also *ibay* with his wife's *ibay*, but he must treat the farmer as he would his own *ibay*. Of course Agta men and women trade with any farmer they choose, but such exchange is without the consideration given to an *ibay*. (Considerations include credit, acts of friendship, and first choice/best deal on goods.) Not only do women have *ibay*, but they very frequently are the most active agents of exchange. In areas where the trade rests mostly on meat and where men do most of the hunting, women are likely to carry out the dried meat and bring back the staple. They therefore gain experience in dealing with the farmers. We should note that many farmers attempt to cheat the Agta by shortchanging them on counts or weights, but they do so on the basis of gullibility or naiveté of the Agta, not on the basis of sex. Agta women are actually more aggressive traders than are men, who do not like confrontation.

Among the Dipagsanghang Agta, women seldom hunt today, and infrequently dig roots. They do carry out meat to trade. They seem to have an easier life, with emphasis on corn, rice, and roots instead of gathering wild foods. However, downriver, close to farmers, Agta women have reversed this trend, and are working harder and longer hours.[3] Intensification of the ibay relationship and need to own and cultivate land has forced women to become horticulturalists and wage laborers for farmers. On their own family plots (family-owned, not male- or female-owned) they, together with adult males and youths, clear land, break soil, plant, weed, and harvest. When clearing virgin forest of large trees, women do not participate. They do clear secondary growth in fallowed fields.

In the families that reside close to Palanan . . . men and women work almost daily in the fields of farmers. Women go to the forest to collect the lighter raw materials for house construction, mats, betel chews, medicines, and so on. Men follow a similar pattern, giving up hunting for field labor and a corn and sweet potato diet supplemented by small fish. Again we see a remarkable parallel in the activities of males and females.

Looking more closely at specialized women's activities, one may suggest increasing importance in downriver areas. Women have several domains that they use to gain cash or kind income. As just stated, income from labor in fields adds to the economic power of women. A small-scale traditional pursuit, shared by men and women, is the gathering of copal, a tree resin common to trees (*Agathis philippinensis*) found scattered in the Sierra Madre. Women often collect and carry the resin out to lowland "middlemen," who sell it to the depot in town. While corn and cash may be sought in exchange, cloth is desired in order to make skirts. Medicine and medical treatments for ailing children may be paid for by copal collection. Another example of entrepreneurship by females is a small-scale mobile variety store effort. After working in fields for cash and building a surplus, families may cross the Sierra Madre to the towns of San Mariano, Cauayan, and Ilagan. There Agta, often women, purchase in markets and stores goods for use and resale in Palanan. Palanan Centro itself has no real market, only several small general stores selling goods at highly marked up prices. Since no road reaches Palanan, all manufactured supplies must enter town by airplane from Cauayan or boat from Baler. Freight costs are high. Some Agta women are very eager to hike outside to get tobacco, which always commands a high price and a ready market.

DISCUSSION

The role of women in Agta economic activities has been reviewed. Assessment of an hypothesized egalitarian position of women may be more difficult, and rests on assertions and interpretations drawn from the economic roles. First, drawing in part from Friedl (1975), an argument can be made that women in Agta society have equality with men because they have similar authority in decision making. The authority could be based on the equal contribution to the subsistence resources. Working back, we see that among many Agta, women do contribute heavily to the daily food supply, do perform maintenance tasks with men, and may initiate food acquisition efforts through their own skills. They do control the distribution of their acquired food, sharing first with their own nuclear family and extended family, then trading as they see fit. They may procure nonfood goods as they desire. Men may do the same; generally spouses discuss what work to do, what needs should be satisfied, and who will do what. Whole residential groups frequently together decide courses of action. Women are as vocal and as critical in reaching decisions as are men. Further examples could strongly validate the hypothesis that women do supply a substantial portion of foods, and the assertion that women have authority in major decision making. Two questions arise. May we accept a causal relationship between percentage of food production and equality? Certainly there are cases to the contrary. According to Richard A. Gould (personal communication), Australian Aboriginal women in various areas collected the bulk of the food, yet remained less than equal (as we will define equality). Second, we may ask if Agta males and females are actually "equal."

Two avenues may suffice in answering this question. First, one might explore a definition of equality, surely a culturally loaded concept. Since Agta women have authority or control of the economic gain of their own labor, they may be equal in this critical domain. Equality must surely be equated with decision-making power and control of one's own production. The second avenue of equality validation by the scientist may be to examine the female's control over herself in noneconomic matters. These could include selection of marriage partner, lack of premarital sexual intercourse proscription, spacing of children, ease of divorce, and polygyny rules.

In marriage, two forms are typical of Agta. One, the less common, is elopement by young lovers. While such marriages admittedly are fragile, elopement is not uncommon. In this case both partners must be willing. Rape and abduction are rare. Rape by Agta men is not known to the authors. Abduction must involve a slightly willing female, and is not done by young people. A mature man might abduct a married woman, crossing the mountains to a safe locale. To abduct a young girl would be difficult. Parents of eloping couples may be enraged, but usually reconcile themselves to the marriage. If the newlyweds stay together, no more is made of it.

The proper form of marriage is one arranged by customary meetings and discussions, as well as exchange of goods between two families. Often neither the bride nor the groom has had much say in the matter, although serious dislike by either would probably kill the negotiations before the marriage. Mothers are the most important in choosing who will marry whom. Even when their children are young, they are looking about for good partners. Word filters around when a young girl is marriageable, and efforts are made to get the appropriate young man and his family into negotiations before an undesirable family appears. Once any family with a prospective groom formally asks, a rejection is given only for strong and good reasons, since the denied family loses considerable face and may be angry enough to seek revenge.[4]

Criteria for choice of a marriage partner are varied. Often a young man in his early twenties marries a girl about fifteen. Girls entering marriage before puberty are not uncommon. In such cases the husband may help raise the girl until the time the marriage is consummated and full wifehood is recognized. Other combinations are seen. One much discussed case was the marriage of a woman in her forties to a man in his mid-twenties. The couple seemed very happy, with the wife paying rather special attention to her husband. The man's mother, a friend of the wife's, decided that the marriage was peculiar but acceptable.

Premarital female chastity is not an idea of much currency. Agta close to farmers will pay lip service to the idea, but should a girl become pregnant she will take a husband. There are no illegitimate Agta children, although an occasional rape of an Agta by a lowland male may produce a child. Since by the time a girl is fertile she likely will be married, illegitimacy is not the issue. Although some data are difficult to collect concerning sex, almost certainly girls are able to engage in sexual activity with relative ease; promiscuity is not favored in any circumstance. Males may have as little or great difficulty in engaging in sex as females. The Agta are widely dispersed in extended family groups; hence appropriate sexual partners are seldom seen. No homosexuality is known to exist.

Agta gossip suggests that many Agta, male and female, married and unmarried, constantly carry on extramarital sexual relations. This may be a function of gossip and a gross exaggeration. Whatever reality, neither males nor females seem to be especially singled out for criticism.

Women say they space their children. The practice certainly varies hugely from person to person, as does fecundity and luck in keeping children alive. The Agta use various herbal concoctions that supposedly prevent conception, cause abortions shortly after conception, and have several functions related to menstruation. These medicines are known to all Agta and are frequently used. Our census data indicate that some women seem to be successful in spacing births. Other cases note high infant mortality yet no infanticide, female or male. All Agta abhor the idea.

Divorce is infrequent among Agta, with elopement being more prone to failure than are arranged marriages. Divorce does happen often enough, however, for us to look at the causes and relate them to an inquiry into female equality. First, either sex may divorce the other with equal ease. Agta have no possessions. Some gift giving between the two families establishes the marriage, but most of the gifts are food. Cloth, kettles, and minor items make up the rest. Return of marriage gifts is unlikely. Spouses simply take their personal possessions and return to the residential group of close relatives.

Causes for divorce are mainly laziness or improvidence, excessive adultery, or personality clashes and incompatibility, usually caused by a combination of the first two conditions. Skill and success in subsistence activities is of primary importance to marriage. While some

Agta are less industrious and less skilled than others, all Agta expect a mate to work hard at all appropriate tasks. Should a male fail, divorce is likely. Occasionally, very young couples experience extra difficulties. These may be accentuated by displeased parents of either party.

Polygamy is not found in most of Isabela. Census data collected to date reveal only monogamy or serial monogamy. That is, spouses may be divorced or widow(er)ed several times in a lifetime. In Cagayan the data are incomplete but startling. Probably some of the strongest support for the equality of women hypothesis, when added to the facts of women as hunters, comes from a study of Agta polygamy. We noted earlier that two co-wives, sisters, hunted together in Malibu. South of Malibu at Blos, another husband and two sisters/co-wives arrangement was found. In the same residential unit we recorded a woman residing with her two co-husbands. They were not brothers; one was older than the wife, one younger. The other women considered this arrangement as humorous, but acceptable. An insight into the male sexual jealousy found in many societies worldwide is the comment of a Palanan Agta man. This old man, when told of the polyandrous marriage to the north, thought for a moment and commented, "Well, perhaps one man with two wives is OK, but a woman with two husbands? I find that totally bad." The women laughed at him.

REFERENCES

Bennagen, Ponciano. 1976. Kultura at Kapaligiran: Pangkulturang Pagbabago at Kapanatagan ng mga Agta sa Palanan, Isabela. M.A. thesis, Department of Anthropology, University of the Philippines, Diliman, Quezon City.

Estioko, Agnes A., and P. Bion Griffin. 1975. The Ebuked Agta of northeastern Luzon. *Philippines Quarterly of Culture and Society* 3(4):237–44.

Fox, Robert B. 1952. The Pinatubo Negritos, their useful plants and material culture. *Philippine Journal of Science* 81:113–414.

Friedl, Ernestine. 1975. *Women and men: an anthropologist's view*. New York: Holt, Rinehart and Winston.

Garvan, John M. 1964. *The Negritos of the Philippines*, ed. Hermann Hochegger, Weiner beitrage zur kulturgeschichte und linguistik, vol. 14. Horn: F. Berger.

Headland, Thomas, and Janet D. Headland. 1974. *A Dumagat (Casiguran)–English dictionary*. Pacific Linguistics Series C. No. 28. Australian National University, Canberra: Linguistics Circle of Canberra.

Keesing, Felix. 1962. *The ethnohistory of northern Luzon*. Stanford, Calif.: Stanford University Press.

Lee, Richard B., and Irven DeVore. 1968. Problems in the study of hunters and gatherers. In *Man the Hunter*, ed. Lee and DeVore. Chicago: Aldine.

———. 1976. *Kalahari hunter-gatherers: studies of the !Kung San and their neighbors*. Cambridge, Mass.: Harvard University Press.

Maceda, Marcelino M. 1964. *The culture of the mamanuas (northeast Mindanao) as compared with that of the other Negritos of Southeast Asia*. Manila: Catholic Trade School.

Marshall, Lorna. 1976. *The !Kung of Nyae Nyae*. Cambridge, Mass.: Harvard University Press.

Martin, M. Kay, and Barbara Voorhies. 1975. *Female of the species*. New York: Columbia University Press.

Peterson, Jean Treloggen. 1974. An ecological perspective on the economic and social behavior of Agta hunter-gatherers, northeastern Luzon, Philippines. Ph.D. dissertation, University of Hawaii at Manoa.

———. 1978a. Hunter-gatherer farmer exchange. *American Anthropologist* 80:335–51.

———. 1978b. The ecology of social boundaries: Agta foragers of the Philippines. *Illinois Studies in Anthropology No. 11*. University of Illinois, Urbana–Champaign, Ill.

———. n.d. Hunter mobility, family organization and change. In *Circulation in the Third World*, ed. Murray Chapman and Ralph Mansell Prothero. London: Routledge & Kegan Paul.

Philippine Commission. 1908. *8th Annual Report of the Philippine Commission: 1907*. Bureau of Insular Affairs, War Department. Washington, D.C.: Government Printing Office.

Reiter, Rayna R., ed. 1975. *Toward an anthropology of women*. New York: Monthly Review Press.

Rosaldo, Michelle Zimbalist, and Louise Lamphere, eds. 1974. *Woman, culture, and society*. Stanford, Calif.: Stanford University Press.

Vanoverbergh, Maurice. 1925. Negritos of northern Luzon. *Anthropos* 20:148–99.

———. 1929–30. Negritos of northern Luzon again. *Anthropos* 24:1–75, 897–911; 25:25–71, 527–656.

Worcester, Dean C. 1912. Head-hunters of northern Luzon. *National Geographic* 23(9):833–930.

Yen, D. E. 1976. The ethnobotany of the Tasaday:
III. Note on the subsistence system. In *Further
studies on the Tasaday,* ed. D. E. Yen and John
Nance. Makati, Rizal: PANAMIN Foundation
Research Series No. 2.

NOTES

1. Although the authors have worked among the
Agta about fourteen months, visits to the
northerly group in the Dianggu-Malibu area have
been brief. The practice of women hunting was
first observed during a survey trip in 1972. We
again visited the Dianggu group in 1975. In
August 1978 we returned for one week to Dianggu
and Malibu, where we verified in greater detail
the subsistence activities of women. Data were collected using the Palanan Agta dialect and Ilokano.
2. Dianggu and Malibu are river names used by Agta
and nearby Malay Filipinos. On the Board of
Technical Surveys and Maps (Lobod Point, Philippines), the Dianggu is named the Lobod and the
Malibu is named the Ilang.
3. Peterson (n.d.) argues that "downriver" Agta
women are highly variable in their devotion to
labor, older women being hardworking and
young mothers not at all industrious.
4. Thomas Headland tells us that rejection of a
prospective spouse may be a less serious matter
among Casiguran Agta than among those we
know.

Gender, Horticulture, and the Division
of Labor on Vanatinai

Maria Lepowsky

GENDER AND HORTICULTURE

"Women are the owners of the garden," Koita
said, early one morning. I probably looked startled, because she added, emphatically, "That is
our custom; it's the way of the ancestors." Koita
was my neighbor, a respected female elder on
the small Pacific island of Vanatinai. She was stating, with no prompting from me, a fundamental
principle of island gender ideologies, part of
their overall worldview, their outlook on life.

I was studying relations between women and
men in what I suspected would be at least a fairly
egalitarian society. I chose the island for my
research in part because I had read that cultures
in this region of small islands had matrilineal
kinship systems. People belonged to their mothers' clans. Matrilineality meant, I reasoned, that
women were central to kinship systems, control
of communally held lands, and inheritance patterns. This might translate, on Vanatinai, into
egalitarian relations between the sexes.

Original manuscript prepared for this text. Reprinted by
permission of the author.

The people of Vanatinai and their neighbors are primarily horticulturalists, practicing
a nonintensive form of agriculture, which anthropologists sometimes refer to as gardening. The
islanders actually have a mixed economy, fishing, hunting, and gathering wild plant foods
as well as planting and harvesting crops. Horticulturalists rely especially on root and tree
crops. They use simple tools, such as digging
sticks, rather than spending time and caloric
energies on intensive, plow-based farming that
uses draft animals (horses, mules, water buf-
falo) or machinery.

Social relations in horticultural societies
vary, but they tend to be more gender egalitarian than in other agricultural societies or in
large-scale industrial societies. Horticultural
societies are often smaller in scale, with fewer
people dependent on the resources of a particular territory. This leads to more possibilities
for face to face negotiation, personal influence,
consensus formation, and conflict resolution.
All of these factors can make for more egalitarian social relations overall: less hierarchy,
fewer specialized roles and positions based on

age, sex, rank, and/or training; and a greater overlap between the kinship system and the political system. Leaders or influential persons within an extended family or clan tend to be the political leaders as well, the most influential people in the community or region. Gender relations, the interactions between men and women and the ideologies that shape them, are a key aspect of the potentially more egalitarian social relations found in many small-scale societies, where people make their living by horticulture, foraging, or a mixture of the two.

Vanatinai (whose European name is Sudest Island) is the largest island of an archipelago, a chain of islands, in a remote part of the Southwest Pacific, southeast of the great island of New Guinea by 200 miles, and 700 miles northeast of Australia. The island had never previously been studied by an anthropologist. I had hypothesized that the roles of women and men, and cultural ideologies of gender, were largely egalitarian. If so, women and men would have reasonably equal rights, privileges, personal autonomy, and influence over the actions of others. Women as well as men would be involved in prestige-generating activities. Here, that would mean exchanging ceremonial valuables and hosting elaborate feasts in honor of the dead. The region has been famous to anthropologists since the pioneering research of Bronislaw Malinowski (1922) on Trobriand Island kula. Kula is a remarkable system for the ceremonial exchange of shell valuables and stone axe-blades. These prized objects circulate hundreds of miles among islanders who speak a dozen different languages and travel by sailing canoe to visit their exchange partners. They trade yams, pigs, clay pots, and other, more obviously practical goods at the same time. But in the Trobriands, kula is almost entirely a male prestige activity. Trobrianders also have chiefs, and they too are almost always male. Years later, anthropologist Annette Weiner (1976) showed that Trobriand women have their own system of wealth exchange, based on banana-leaf skirts and the hosting of memorial feasts, and that it was closely articulated with kula.

On Vanatinai, 300 miles southeast, I found that there were no chiefs and no commoners. Women as well as men gained regional fame in the same way as men, by successfully exchanging the ceremonial valuables that circulate in kula as far as the Trobriands. Vanatinai women as well as men could, and did, host large-scale feasts commemorating the dead that drew hundreds of visitors from a half dozen islands.

Both Vanatinai women and men, it turned out, describe island women as *ghuma tanuwa-gai*, owners, or bosses, of gardens. This is a philosophical statement. In actuality, men and women, sisters, brothers, mothers, maternal grandmothers, mother's brothers, held land in common as matrilineal property. But it was a senior woman, or women, who tended to get everyone organized. Married men usually made gardens on their wives' matrilineal land, not that of their mothers, even though they retained the right to do so.

To a remarkable extent, the tasks considered appropriate for males and females, and for people of varying ages, were much the same. In other words, the sexual division of labor (sometimes called the gendered division of labor) was largely overlapping. This kind of overlap is a characteristic that anthropological theorists have long suggested is characteristic of a gender egalitarian society.[1] On Vanatinai, women and men alike plant weed, and harvest the large, white tropical yams that are one of the islanders' staple foods. Yams are the only annual crop, harvested just before the bright, tightly clustered stars of the Pleiades are visible once more on the eastern horizon. This marks the start of the new year. Both sexes also tend taro and banana patches, and plant and harvest the easy-to-grow, drought-resistant sweet potatoes and manioc that were introduced in the colonial era. Every stage of the process of yam gardening is hedged with garden magic and ritual. I found that only a few people had the magical knowledge, derived from ancestor spirits and handed down from elders, to officiate at communal garden rituals. But these few people included both women and men.

Women and men, sisters and brothers, wives and husbands have to agree on which clan lands they are going to use for a garden. Sometimes this is a challenge. A big woman or big man, either for powerful emotional reasons or to enlarge a regional reputation, may want to host a feast the following year to commemorate someone who has died. That means clearing an especially big garden—cutting and then burning a clearing in the rainforest canopy—so as to have plenty of high-quality yams to feed off-island visitors, who may end up camped out in the hamlet for weeks.

It is the men, young and middle-aged, who do the work of cutting old-growth hardwood trees, while women cut understory trees and shrubs. A senior woman usually supervises the burning, which takes place about a month later when the slash has had a chance to dry out. The ashes then fertilize the soil of the new garden. (This technique, characteristic of tropical horticulture, is called swidden, or slash and burn.) The population density on Vanatinai is quite low, only about four persons per square miles. In many parts of the island, land lies fallow for up to forty years before it is again made into a garden. By then it resembles mature, closed-canopy rainforest.

Men are the ones, I was told, who use eight-foot long wooden poles to loosen and aerate the soil of the new garden, forming it into mounds ready to receive yam seed. It is true that men do it most of the time. But women perform this hard labor as well. I saw a couple of my women neighbors hard at it, and took their photo. The other villagers, men and women, commented admiringly that they were *ivurigheghe*, strong. They meant both physically and socially, a reference to their good reputations and influence over others.

Women do much of the preparation and planting of seed yams, removing them from storage in small, stilted houses adjacent to the gardens, slicing off their growing tips, and stockpiling them in woven, coconut-leaf garden baskets. The rest of each seed yam is boiled with coconut cream in a clay cooking pot and served for lunch to the communal working group. Women also tend to take primary responsibility for maintaining gardens. But this is only a general rule. Some men take great pride in their gardens. And some women are less ambitious gardeners, making more of their subsistence contribution by gathering shellfish or forest fruits rather than weeding under the tropical sun.

Women do much of the harvesting of garden produce, often several times a week. There is no refrigeration, and thin-skinned tubers will go rotten in a few days. The best way to store them is by keeping them under the soil, digging them up as needed for daily subsistence, feeding visiting in-laws, or contributing food to feasts. Yams are the only annual crop. Because of their tough, thick skins, these tropical yam varieties are the only root crop it is possible to store for many months, in baskets on high shelves in house rafters, or in a small yam house. Harvesting is an individual affair, private and secret. The gardener offers prayers to ancestor spirits as she or he digs loose the tubers from the tropical soil with a long digging stick, piling them into a garden basket. Inviting acquaintances and neighbors to observe could be unwise: it might arouse envy if the garden was especially prolific. Some islanders are said to know a special kind of magic that persuades tubers growing in a neighboring garden to travel underground to the garden of the magician. People know not to appear uninvited in someone's garden for another reason as well. A garden house or shelter (a wall-less, palm-thatch roofed structure on wooden stilts) is where islanders take a work break, get out of the midday sun, and cook lunch, but also the only place where a married couple have enough privacy during the daytime for sexual relations, after lunch while it is too hot to work.

Men are strongly identified in island ideology with the production of sago, the almost pure starch extracted from the trunk of a mature female palm. Sago is the other principal food in the island diet. Extensive sago palm groves grow wild in the swamps, dim, almost primeval-looking places that are home as well to voracious clouds of mosquitoes. Islanders throughout the region count the sago swamps of Vanatinai as a source of great wealth. This is an enormous reservoir of potential food, not planted (although the occasional palm is transplanted closer to a village) but wild. The sago groves, and the tracts of swamp, are communally owned by island matrilineages.

Sago processing is not horticulture but a form of plant management. It is hard, concentrated work over the course of two or three days. But it requires far less time, caloric energy, and risk than planting a yam garden, guarding it from wild boars, dealing with drought or flooding by using weather magic to petition ancestors and place spirits, then digging up unknown numbers and sizes of tubers nine months later.

Men do most of the pounding of sago pith—the fibrous insides of the split-open palm—and the sluicing out the starch in a wooden trough, but the work party is usually mixed. Women supervise the drying of cakes of sago starch over a low fire, the cutting of long green sago leaves to use for wrapping the fresh bricks of starch, and the actual wrapping. The bundles are hung in pairs over long poles, then each is carried by two men or youths back to the village. Everyone who has joined the work party gets a share, and lines of sago bundles hang in pairs from the rafters in each house. They are ready for use at a moment's notice: to throw a chunk in a boiling pot of vegetables, prepare a sago and grated coconut dumplings or pancakes, grilled on a broken shard of clay pot over the fire, or a sago and green coconut pudding. Bundles of sago are major items to barter to people who sail to Vanatinai from the smaller coral islands to obtain sago or yams for clay cooking pots or the smoked meat of giant clams.

Vanatinai women, men, and children are all diligent foragers, studying the growth patterns, seasons, and locations of a wide array of wild nuts, legumes, tubers, fruits, ferns, and edible leaves. The large grubs that live in decaying sago palms are a special treat, usually eaten on the spot. They are also a fine source of protein. In general, I observed that women spent more time foraging than men. Foraging, and being in the forest more generally, is something that men and women alike enjoy more than the tedious, sweaty work of weeding gardens.

Shellfish collecting is another subsistence activity practiced equally by men, women, and older children. It too is something people enjoy: going down to the shore, alone or with friends or relatives, to gather the small, tasty oysters that cling to aerial roots of mangroves; hunting for blue mangrove crabs (taking care to avoid getting pinched by their giant front claws), or prying clams loose from the reef at low tide. Anyone who feels like it may fish in the lagoon, from a canoe, from shore, or by wading in the shallows. Men sometimes use metal-tipped spears to fish in the shallows, either from a canoe or on foot at low tide. The metal is often scavenged, washing ashore after a storm from some distant place.

Whole hamlets full of people troop down to the lagoon at neap tide, the lowest tides of the year. They use derris root, from a forest plant that contains a potent neurotoxin, to temporarily stun the fish that have collected in shallow pools in the coral, left behind by the falling sea. The fish are scooped up by hand, strung on a piece of cord made from a forest vine, and carried home. (Fortunately, stunning fish this way does not affect the human diner, although eating derris root directly would be fatal.) The islanders nowadays use monofilament for line fishing. But both men and women use to fish collectively, using nets woven by men from the fibrous aerial root of pandanus, a wild palm that grows in the rainforest.

Occasionally young men, and less often young women, dive in the lagoon for blacklip pearlshell, or the larger, glowing goldlip pearl that is used in other countries to make mother of pearl buttons. Shell can, in theory, be sold at the tradestore at the end of the island, but the commodity price for it, set on the London market, has been extremely low for several decades now, a result of competition from the plastic button industry. Goldlip pearlshell is rarer and harder to obtain, as it lives on reefs in deeper lagoon waters. Goldlip shell is used by islanders themselves to make the translucent pendants that are attached to ceremonial shell-disc necklaces. Young or vigorous men and women sometimes take a canoe to certain reefs where they dive for bagi, the red-rimmed shells used to make the discs for shell necklaces. The shells can be bartered or given to relatives. Discs to string into necklaces are manufactured, using pump drills with a metal bit, by island men and women, often middle-aged, who have chosen to specialize in this form of labor. Necklaces are strung together on bush cord, with mother of pearl pendants added to the larger ones. The deep reddish color of the shell discs should be set off pleasingly by the glossy black of wild banana seeds. These are bartered by visitors arriving by sailing canoe from larger islands near the mainland of New Guinea, 200 miles away; wild banana does not grow on or near Vanatinai. Newly made shell necklaces circulate through sets of exchange partners from island to island for hundreds of miles, as far as the Trobriand Islands, joining necklaces and other valuables that are 100 years and more old in the kula system of interisland exchange that Malinowski made famous.

Sometimes islanders successfully land a sea turtle by wrestling it into a canoe. Or they find a lonely beach where the female is laying eggs in the sand, turn her over, and drag her off. The eggs are scooped up as well. Once in a while, men spear a dugong, a sea mammal, cousin to the manatee of Florida and tropical South America, that grazes on the sea grasses of the lagoon. (Luckily for the dugong, they swim remarkably fast and often elude the hunters.) The islanders fish the inland streams for little silvery fish, sweet reddish prawns, and giant black eels. Every so often, parties of men, accompanied by the occasional young woman, hunt crocodiles late at night, using coconut-leaf torches and black palm, metal-tipped spears.

It is up to the individual to decide how much time she or he wishes to spend fishing or collecting shellfish versus other kinds of subsistence activities such as gardening, gathering, or hunting. The variation in time and effort expended varies based on personal preference, not by sex.

Almost every adult, and some older children and adolescents, is the proud owner of at least one pig. Big women and big men own whole herds of them, and they snuffle around the hamlet scavenging scraps of food. More dedicated owners cook their pigs a meal of sago pith (the part that is inedible to humans) at dusk, after the family dinner has been taken care of. Pigs go unfenced on Vanatinai, wandering into the forest to forage on their own during the day. They not infrequently find their way to someone's garden, where they enthusiastically dig up the sweet potatoes or yams the gardener has been carefully cultivating. Gardens too are unfenced. Islanders are always complaining about the serious damage done to gardens by both wild and domestic pigs. But it would be too much work, they say, to fence off a whole garden. They have a point. Fences have to be made from tree limbs, laboriously cut in the forest, carried to the garden, then roped together with cord made from forest vines to form a sort of corral. Since wild and domestic pigs routinely commingle in one giant, island-wide herd, the wild boars are the ones that sire the piglets. In the hamlet, juvenile males are castrated. Domestic pigs often show affection for their owners. They also serve as watchpigs, growling menacingly and sometimes charging at strangers and visitors, who shout in alarm, on entering a hamlet, "Call off your pigs!"

There is one dramatic restriction on Vanatinai subsistence activities that is based on sex. It is taboo for women to hunt using spears. In earlier times it was taboo for women to make war using spears, or using greenstone axeblades as hatchets. Young, unmarried women did go into battle, elders told me, handing spears to their brothers and dragging them to safety if they were wounded. Mature women knew the special magic—petitions to powerful ancestor and place spirits—that was used to make war and to make peace. Senior women negotiated truces as experts in diplomacy.

Whenever I asked someone, of either sex, why women were not supposed to hunt with spears, or use weapons of war, the answer was always the same.

"Women are the life givers, and men are the death givers."

"And," the speaker usually added, "life giving is more important."

"But women hunt on Vanatinai," I would argue. "And some women are witches, or even sorcerers." In the supernatural domain of the island division of labor, most but not all witches are women, and most but not all sorcerers are men.

At this point, though, the elder I was talking would add emphatically,

"Ighabubu." It is taboo.

That always ended the conversation.

I learned first-hand from this conundrum that Vanatinai gender ideologies are multi-layered and occasionally contradictory. As is the case in all cultures, ideological statements of how people are supposed to behave are sometimes contradicted by individual actions.

Women do hunt on Vanatinai; they just don't hunt with spears.[2] They climb tall tropical hardwoods and coconut palms to capture opussum, flying foxes, and fruit bats. Young women are supposed to be the best at catching the slow-moving, four-foot-long monitor lizards that resemble miniature Komodo dragons and frequent the tall mangroves lining the estuaries. Girls and women either climb the trees or set traps for them. The rough skins of monitor lizards, stretched by men and used for drum heads, are dark gray and whitish, abstractly patterned in a way that resembles the geometric designs of the fine coconut-leaf baskets that island women weave, whose traditional colors are also gray (from being dipped in swamp water overnight) and off-white.

The climbing of trees by Vanatinai women and girls is telling in itself. In many Pacific societies, it is taboo for women to climb, or for her genitals to be higher than a man's head. Here, island women not only climb to hunt, but agile younger women and girls routinely climb areca and tall coconut palms to cut betel nuts (used daily as a stimulant and exported to other islands), brown ripe coconuts, and green drinking nuts. (The only issue, women told me jokingly, is to make sure there are no men or boys standing directly below a palm tree looking up their skirts.)

This is another aspect of Vanatinai women's physical mobility, their freedom to roam around as they wish, just as men do. Island women are manifesting their freedom of movement when they disappear of their own accord, unchaperoned, into the forest or down the shore on some vague errand. Women also paddle and pole canoes, on subsistence tasks or to visit other coastal hamlets, and some are expert sailors. A few women know how to navigate a sailing canoe between islands single-handed, although navigating and crewing sailing canoes are mostly done by men and male youths.

Woodworking is a male specialization: chopping down hardwoods in the tropical forest to clear a garden, cutting down a mature sago palm, hauling a dense log of false mahogany out of the forest to carve out a canoe hull, or cutting and hauling timbers for housebuilding. The island houses are perched on tall hardwood stilts to catch cooling sea breezes, help defeat mosquitoes, and keep the pigs from wandering in the door. The walls, flooring, and roof come from the bark and leaves of the nipa and sago palms. Women gather sago leaves and weave them into panels that will overlap on the roof, and weave sago leaves together for a particular kind of wall. They also prepare cooked yams and other food to the male housebuilders.

Vanatinai men's woodworking specialty continues with the carving of large wooden, mushroom-shaped ceremonial spatulas, decorated with shell discs, another form of ceremonial valuable used in exchange and feasting. This kind of carving is done by only a few men, middle-aged or older, as is carving narrow ebony lime spatulas incised with representations of bird's heads. These master carvers also produce large, 7-shaped ceremonial axe handles from tropical hardwoods, featuring a stylized bird's head at the apex and abstract designs at the handle. These are valuable items in interisland exchange. Vanatinai men also carve tortoise-shell into the rows of earrings worn by both sexes, as well as into smaller, mushroom-shaped lime spatulas, whose intricate curvilinear designs are outlined in the brilliant white of powdered coral lime.

Vanatinai island women are admired regionally for their fine, soft, tightly woven coconut-leaf baskets, whose zigzag and chevron patterns are picked out in contrasting colors. These small, round open baskets are used daily as purses by men and women. They are also essential objects at memorial feasts, circulating in interisland exchange. Women weave wild pandanus-leaf sleeping mats and larger, coarse garden baskets of coconut leaf, and make skirts out of dried, shredded coconut fronds. The skirts too play a key role in the ceremonial exchanges of feasts honoring the dead.

The tasks of daily household maintenace are ideologically considered by islanders to be the domain of women: cooking, washing, fetching water from spring or creek, fetching salt water from the lagoon for seasoning food, gathering firewood, and sweeping the hamlet clean of debris and pig excrement each morning with a coconut-rib broom. The house itself is considered to be a woman's house, and the pigs are usually her pigs. It is a common sight every day, though, to see a man or boy performing one or more of these tasks, with the exception of sweeping the hamlet grounds.

Childcare is the primary responsibility of women, who customarily breastfeed on demand for up to three years. (A baby's diet is supplemented with other foods starting at around six months.) But it is common to see fathers, uncles, grandfathers, and older brothers carrying babies and toddlers around. Vanatinai women also make full use of that ancient institution, the babysitter, calling on older siblings—boys as well as girls—grandparents, and neighbors to watch a child while they are weeding a garden, collecting nuts in the forest, or gathering shellfish. Both fathers and mothers are loving and indulgent parents; island childrearing is remarkably permissive. If a small child is frustrated and crying, that is, denied its desires, it may become angry and leave us, people say, meaning it might die and rejoin the ancestors. Fathers as well as mothers often take an older girl or boy to the garden, gathering, or even on a long exchange voyage.

EXCHANGE AND THE LIFE COURSE

In Vanatinai ideologies of gender, I learned, there is no principle of male superiority or female weakness or inferiority, no idea that women are supposed to defer to men. In fact, in customary and daily life, leaving aside colonial and postcolonial government and legal systems, no adult has the right to tell another adult what to do. The only options are to persuade, influence, shame, or work magic or witchcraft or sorcery on someone to get them to behave in a certain way: join a work party planting a large yam garden, agree to have sexual relations, offer a fine red shell-disc necklace to an exchange partner, or attend a feast, bringing a giant, tusked boar as a contribution.

Vanatinai women and men are valued for the same qualities. The most admired individuals of both sexes were described to me as strong, wise, and generous. By strong, people mean hardworking, morally powerful, and successful in producing large gardens, obtaining valuables from their many exchange partners, hosting feasts, and persuading kinspeople and neighbors to work with them. Wise means practical knowledge, insight, and judgment, but also good relations with powerful ancestor spirits and place spirits, who are petitioned through magic and ritual learned over a lifetime from one's elders. Generous refers directly to giving things away—shell-disc necklaces, greenstone axeblades, pigs, yams—especially as contributions offered at the sequence of three to four feasts, increasingly large and elaborate, that honor the dead. These generous people, men and women alike, were called the *giagia*, a gender-neutral term which literally means the givers. In other societies of the Southwest Pacific, this kind of influential and respected person is referred to by anthropologists as a big man. On Vanatinai, there are both big women and big men.

Neither every man nor every woman, aspires to become known as a *gia*. But each person, from youth to elder, is expected to honor kinship obligations and respect the dead—who become powerful ancestor spirits—by contributing labor, valuables, or both at the increasingly elaborate feasts that mark a person's death. Death is an all too familiar visitor to every family: women die in childbirth, babies die suddenly, toddlers are carried off in a day by cerebral malaria, and strong, healthy adults are stricken with pneumonia or tuberculosis (Lepowsky 1990). This means each person learns first-hand from youth about mortuary obligations of the matrilineal kin group. The ceremonial rules are complex; there are different expectations depending on whether the deceased is a member of one's own matrilineage, an in-law's, or the father's. Some of the heaviest responsibilities come at the death of the father himself, who in a matrilineal society is not a kinsman, but a member of another matrilineage. His heirs need to be compensated—given valuables—by the deceased man's own children and widow. The father's kin bear the heaviest ceremonial burden at the death of the mother, his wife.

To document whether Vanatinai society is gender egalitarian, in ideology and practice, we have to compare experiences, ideological principles, and expectations for each life stage, for girls and boys, men and women. Given islanders' cultural emphasis on ceremonial exchange, our comparison should highlight the ceremonial division of labor and access to the most important island domains of prestige and influence.

The life course on Vanatinai is not strongly marked by age categories. A person is referred to as child (*gama*) from birth to around puberty. There are no rituals of initiation for either males or females. A girl begins to be known as *gamaina* (literally, child woman) when her breasts start to show. She begins to menstruate a couple of years later, at around age 15 or 16, and to observe the taboo of not going to the garden during her period. Otherwise, people say, birds and animals, attracted by the blood, will eat the growing food plants (she is not considered unclean or polluting, and she may prepare and share food with others). An adolescent boy, around the time of his growth spurt and voice change, becomes known as *zeva*, or youth. The period of youth, for both sexes, extends into the late twenties, well into what Westerners consider adulthood. (This cultural pattern of extended youth is traditional in many Pacific Island societies; see Lepowsky 1998). A person on Vanatinai is generally considered an adult (*wevo*, or woman; *ghomoli*, or man) when she or he is in a stable marriage and has a child. This is a gradual transition, as many early marriages end in divorce. Respected adults can soon earn the title of female or male elder (*laisali* for females and *amalaisali* for males), even as young as their mid-thirties. But most individuals addressed as female or male elder range in age from their fifties to their eighties. The rights, privileges, constraints, and degrees of personal autonomy of both sexes are largely congruent throughout the life course, even though they are not perfectly symmetrical. This is a hallmark of a gender egalitarian society, a society that tends toward equality (Lepowsky 1993).

Girls or boys as young as ten or so may get their start in the interisland ceremonial exchange system with a parent's gift of a piglet to care for. When it is a portly, swaying adult, it is valuable enough to be exchanged for an impressive quantity of shell-disc necklaces, greenstone axeblades, or other shell valuables. The owner of the pig, regardless of age or sex, is the one who decides whether or not to accept a request for it from a kinsperson, or new or existing exchange partner. She or he alone decides whether to contribute the pig at a feast commemorating a deceased relative or in-law. People sometimes cry over the death of the beloved pig they have offered, sacrificed, to honor the deceased and the feast host. The owner never eats the meat from her or his own pig, but instead eats pork from someone else's animal, a form of ritual sharing that emphasizes the close identity among human owner, deceased, and valued pig.

Youths of both sexes also earn a name as a hard worker and respected young person by producing yams, bundles of sago, skirts, baskets, and other goods to contribute to an upcoming feast. Some young adults go to kin, or a parent's exchange partner, to request a valuable to contribute. Eventually, they will have to replace it with another wealth object. Young people are expected to devote much of their energy to courtship and sexual intrigue: this is the stage of life for them to enjoy the cultural expectation of full premarital sexual freedom. But a young person who becomes known as lazy will be gossiped about, shamed by older kin, and spurned as a potential marriage partner.

Young people are enthusiastic attendees at feasts, working hard at the labor of provisioning hundreds of guests as directed by the host and food magician. They are sometimes gifted with a valuable, such as a greenstone axeblade, by the appreciative host. The last and largest feast, the *zagaya*, features at least one, and sometimes many, all-night sessions of drumming, singing, and traditional dancing. It is the perfect time for unmarried youths from small hamlets on far-flung islands to meet. They are expected to slip away discreetly and meet a lover in some dark corner of beach or forest.

The final feast celebrates the lifting of the final mourning taboos, and the renewal and regeneration of life, the mending of ties of kinship and exchange after a death. Youthful sexuality is part of this celebration. Many marriages begin with flirtations and romances at feasts.

At feasts or occasions of communal labor such as planting a new yam garden, or raising or re-roofing a house, men and women, girls and boys work diligently at the many tasks necessary to provide food and shelter for up to several hundred people for days or weeks, fetching huge quantities of firewood and water, grating mounds of coconut, cooking, and cleaning. Women are in charge of roasting vegetable food in the earth ovens, using superheated round river rocks wrapped in soft forest leaves. Men are responsible for preparing the ritual sago and coconut pudding, stirred with a special, eight foot long carved wooden paddle. Men also take charge of spearing, butchering, and boiling the pigs that visitors and exchange partners have brought to add to those of the feast host. There is generally one man who knows the secret magical spell for making the meat multiply itself to feed the multitudes. Women and men alike know some kinds of food magic, but a few individuals are experts. A senior female or male expert is selected by the feast host to say magical spells over piles of donated yams and bundles of sago—hidden in, or underneath, the host's house—so that they will extend far enough to feed the visitors and still have food left over. The food magician is simultaneously an experienced "kitchen" manager, directing all the food workers of both sexes for the duration of the feast.

Mature adults, male and female, are equally expected to honor ceremonial obligations. Rarely, individuals, scorned and feared as antisocial sorcerers or witches, refuse to participate. Some adults, of both sexes, contribute the bare minimum of labor or ceremonial valuables. The most common path is to work especially hard at ritual obligations when a spouse's parent, or one's own parent or matrilineal aunt or uncle, dies.

A minority of adult men and women whose children are already youths or adults (or who are childless), strive to exceed others in ceremonial exchange. They accumulate valuables, garden produce, sago, and other goods; host feasts, and contribute lavishly and publicly, in acts of ritual generosity, at the numerous feasts of exchange partners, kin, or in-laws. These people seek regional fame, prestige, and influence over others; striving to be admired as *giagia*, givers, big men or big women. This is a matter of individual personality and desire. It is also related to life stage. Along with the obvious childcare issues, children are placed at risk of death or illness by the destructive magic of a parent's envious rival, so it is unwise to strive for the status of *gia* when one has young children. Mature adults also have more supernatural and practical knowledge, and greater stores of social capital through personal ties and exchange partners.

Established or aspiring *giagia* set off, on foot or by canoe, accompanied by kin or spouse, to request valuables from exchange partners. They attend and contribute to all the feasts in the region. They are admired but also feared, for their supernatural knowledge: without the power of ancestor and place spirits, exercised through magic, witchcraft, or sorcery, a person cannot be successful in ceremonial exchange.

Vanatinai women as well as men can build personal fame and renown through active participation in the prestige and ritual economy of exchange and feasting. But they may also choose to gain respect in other ways: by nurturing families and gardens, practicing food magic or weather magic, or helping kin and neighbors through the spirit-directed practices of healing. Women and men have equivalent access to supernatural powers: to apprentice with an elder knowledgeable about certain kinds of magic and ritual. Choosing to do so is up to the seeker, not limited by sex or inherited position.

Vanatinai ideologies validate powerful beliefs in personal autonomy, control of one's own actions, and wide tolerance of personal idiosyncrasies. When I asked why a person behaved a certain way, people said, "We can't know their *renuanga*, their thoughts, emotions. It's up to them." This principle applies to both sexes. Yet, in this small-scale subsistence society, people must be persuaded to cooperate, to share food, wealth, and knowledge, in order that all, or at least many, will survive and thrive. This ideological and practical tension underlies island life. Still, island ideologies grant all adults, female and male, equal opportunities to manage their own lives, and to influence others. The same personal qualities, strength, wisdom, and generosity, are valued in women and men.

REFERENCES

Bacdayan, Albert. 1977. "Mechanistic Cooperation and Sexual Equality Among the Western Bontoc." In Alice Schlegel (ed.). *Sexual Stratification: A Cross-Cultural View*, pp. 271–291. New York: Columbia University Press.

Brightman, Robert. 1996. Biology, Taboo, and Gender Politics in the Sexual Division of Foraging Labor. *Comparative Studies in Society and History* 38 (4): 687–729.

Du, Shanshan. 2002. *Chopsticks Only Work in Pairs: Gender Unity and Gender Equality Among the Lahu of Southwest China*. New York: Columbia University Press.

Estioko-Griffin, Agnes, and P. Bion Griffin. 1981. "Woman the Hunter." In Frances Dahlberg (ed.). *Woman the Gatherer*, pp. 121–140. New Haven, CT: Yale University Press.

Estioko-Griffin, Agnes, and P. Bion Griffin. 1985. "Women Hunters: The Implications for Pleistocene Prehistory and Contemporary Ethnography." In Madeleine Goodman (ed.). *Women in Asia and the Pacific: Towards an East-West Dialogue*, pp. 61–81. Honolulu: Women's Studies Program, University of Hawaii.

Goodale, Jane. 1971. *Tiwi Wives*. Seattle: University of Washington Press.

Kaberry, Phyllis. 1939. *Aboriginal Woman: Sacred and Profane*. London: Routledge.

Landes, Ruth. 1938. *The Ojibwa Woman*. New York: Columbia University Press.

Leacock, Eleanor. 1978. "Women's Status in Egalitarian Society: Implications for Social Evolution." *Current Anthropology* 19: 247–276.

Lederman, Rena. 1990. "Contested Order: Gender and Society in the Southern New Guinea Highlands." In Peggy Reeves Sanday (ed.) *Beyond the Second Sex: New Directions in the Anthropology of Gender*, pp 43–74. Philadelphia: University of Pennsylvania Press.

Lepowsky, Maria. 1990. "Sorcery and Penicillin: Treating Illness on Papua New Guinea Island." *Social Science and Medicine* 30(10): 1049–1063.

Lepowsky, Maria. 1993. *Fruit of the Motherland: Gender in an Egalitarian Society*. New York: Columbia University Press.

Lepowsky, Maria. 1998. "Coming of Age on Vanatinai: Gender, Sexuality, and Power." In Gilbert Herdt and Stephen Leavitt (eds.). *Adolescence in Pacific Island Societies*, pp. 123–147. ASAO Monograph 18. Pittsburgh: University of Pittsburgh Press.

Malinowski, Bronislaw. 1922. *Argonauts of the Western Pacific*. New York: Dutton.

Murphy, Yolanda, and Robert Murphy. 1974. *Women of the Forest*. New York: Columbia University Press.

Ortner, Sherry. 1996. "Gender Hegemonies." In *Making Gender: The Politics and Erotics of Culture*, pp. 139–172. Boston: Beacon Press.

Sanday, Peggy. 1974. "Female Status in the Public Domain." In Michelle Rosaldo and Louise Lamphere (eds.). *Woman, Culture and Society*, pp. 189–206. Stanford, CA: Stanford University Press.

Sanday, Peggy. 1981. *Female Power and Male Dominance: On the Origins of Sexual Inequality*. Cambridge, UK: Cambridge University Press.

Sanday, Peggy. 2002. *Women at the Center: Life in a Modern Matriarchy*. Ithaca, NY: Cornell University Press.

Schlegel, Alice. 1990. "Gender Meanings, General and Specific." In *Beyond the Second Sex: New Directions in the Anthropology of Gender*, pp. 21–42. Philadelphia: University of Pennsylvania Press.

Weiner, Annette. 1976. *Women of Value, Men of Renown: New Perspectives on Trobriand Exchange*. Austin: University of Texas Press.

NOTES

1. In a now classic set of writings, Peggy Sanday (1974, 1981) hypothesized that if both sexes contributed equally to subsistence in a particular society, women's status would be higher. She was the first to suggest that when the sexes commingle in the labor of everyday life, this worked against the rise of male dominance. Albert Bacdayan (1977) suggests that what he labels "task interchangeability" between men and women is a key indicator of egalitarian gender relations. See Lepowsky (1993) for further discussion of characteristics that scholars have hypothesized are associated with gender egalitarian societies. After research with the Lahu, matrilineal horticulturalists living in Yunnan, China, Shanshan Du (2002) has proposed that there are several different types, or cultural "schemas," of gender egalitarian societies worldwide. She argues, for example, that the cultural emphasis in Lahu is "dyadic," organized

around the wife and husband in subsistence and divine sister-brother twins in mythology. On Vanatinai, she continues (relying on my ethnographic reports), the cultural "schema," is, in contrast, based on "individual autonomy" and "collective cooperation." In other words, there are different, viable ways to organize a gender egalitarian society.

2. Female hunting is relatively rare worldwide, compared to hunting by males, but it has been documented in many societies. Examples include foragers such as Australian aborigines (Goodale 1971; Kaberry 1939), the horticultural Agta of the Philippines (Estioko-Griffin and Griffin 1981, 1985), and the Ojibwa, Montagnais-Naskapi, and Rock Cree, who hunt large game such as moose and caribou in the eastern woodlands and boreal forests of Canada (Brightman 1996; Landes 1938; Leacock 1978). In some, but not all, cases cross-culturally, women are ideologically restricted from hunting certain animals, using particular killing

technologies (such as spears and greenstone axe-blades in the Vanatinai example), or hunting when they are menstruating. See Brightman (1996) for a detailed discussion.

The existence of contradictions between levels of gender ideology, the ideological positions of each sex, or between the ideal and the real, has long been pointed out by gender theorists (for example Lederman 1990; Murphy and Murphy 1974; Ortner 1996; Sanday 2002; Schlegel 1990). The strands of gender ideology on Vanatinai are more congruent than those of most societies. I found no categorical difference between what men and women stated about gender philosophies, and not much individual or situational variation. This degree of congruence, I suggest, and the lack of a major gap between gender ideologies and social life as experienced, is characteristic of societies that tend toward gender egalitarian (Lepowsky 1993: 34–35).

Do Tents and Herds Still Matter?
Pastoral Nomadism and Gender among the Tuareg in Niger and Mali

Susan Rasmussen

INTRODUCTION: TUAREG GENDER CONSTRUCTS IN ANTHROPOLOGICAL PERSPECTIVE

After the divorce of Aghaly and Mariama (pseudonyms), Aghaly retained his male-owned adobe mud house, and Mariama retained her female-owned tent, both of which stood inside the same courtyard surrounded by its compound walls, on the same land, in their rural Tuareg village in northern Niger. At first, the ex-husband adamantly refused to leave his house inside this compound. The couple took their case to the secular courts in the nearby town of Agadez, which ruled a compromise: each party changed the door on his or her respective residential structure, so that the buildings faced away from, rather than

Original material prepared for this text. Reprinted by permission of the author.

toward the interior courtyard of their compound. Aghaly ate his meals at his mother's home. This solution divided the property, and also saved the divorced couple from daily contentious interaction. Eventually, Aghaly moved back into his older house adjacent to his parents' compound in a neighboring village, where he worked in an oasis garden. Mariama retained her tent, near her own parents' compound, and continued to herd goats and donkeys with her mother.

There are multiple forces impinging upon gender and pastoralism among the Tuareg, a seminomadic, Islamic, socially stratified people. This is a discussion of women's perceived economic contributions in relation to property ownership, status, prestige, and division of labor in a traditionally pastoral nomadic, stockbreeding society, the Tuareg, also known as Kel Tamajaq ("People who speak Tamajaq"), after their language, who live in Niger, Mali, Burkina Faso, and Algeria. I also offer a critique of some interpretations of gender and pastoralism in predominantly seminomadic communities. I draw upon data from my research among the Kel Ewey Tuareg in the Air Mountains near the town of Agadez in northern Niger, and more recently, among the Ifoghas and Iwllemeden Tuareg in and around the Adragh-n-Ifoghas Mountains and the town of Kidal in northern Mali.[1]

Seminomadism and agropastoralism are widely practiced by many Tuareg today, and this process brings challenges, but also offers opportunities for women, who enjoy traditionally-high social prestige and, along with men, independent property ownership of livestock: In seminomadic Tuareg communities, the presence of men's houses competes with women's tents. Men's houses, which have sprung up in many Tuareg Saharan communities and along its Sahelian fringes, complicate property disputes upon divorce, particularly in more settled agropastoral communities where predominantly men own houses and oasis gardens. By contrast, in more nomadic camps, men are guests in their wives' tents, and may be left homeless when their wives eject them from that residence upon quarrels or divorce.

The issue arising here is, to what extent do livestock herds and tents still empower women? Some, though not all Tuareg communities are moving toward sedentarization, oasis gardening, and migrant labor. Many also face wider global processes: neo-liberal economic policies of structural adjustment and privatization, and national policies, in Niger and Mali, of decentralization and semiautonomy for some northern regions following the peace accords ending the 1990–1996 Tuareg Rebellion against the central governments of these countries.

Gender is socially and culturally constructed, and can usefully be understood as a comparative, relational concept (Di Leonardo 1990; Butler 1990: 6; Davison 1997; Wood 1999). Critical to gender structuring are intertwined modalities: social variables such as ethnicity, class, religion, and age, among many (Ortner and Whitehead 1981; Di Leonardo 1990). Regional and rural–urban variations may also impinge on inter-and intragender identities

and relationships (Meena 1992; Gaidzanwa 1985; Mannathoko 1992; Davison 1997). Constructions of gender therefore depend heavily upon positionality.[2]

In recent years, a number of scholars have called for studies that treat gender dynamically, as occurring in processes generated by discrete locales and through particular histories; they assert that gender is not fixed either across time or in location (di Lauretis 1984; Scott 1988, 1992; Kondo 1990; Probyn 1990; Butler 1990; Flax 1993; Barlow 1996). Thus although I use the term "women," I also try to make clear that the Tuareg women about whom I write do not constitute an undifferentiated category of "essentialized woman." They interact with men, and are defined by their age, social origins, occupations, kinship roles, and other locations in Tuareg society. Gender and pastoral arrangements must be understood against the backdrop of seminomadism, sedentary oasis gardening, migrant labor, and some residence in towns, albeit with continuing rural social and economic ties, and interaction with larger, multiethnic nation-states experiencing ecological disaster, economic crisis, and political tensions.

THE TUAREG CASE

Tuareg Gender Constructs and Relations between the Sexes: Women's Status and Prestige

Tuareg pastoral nomads today are predominantly seminomadic and practice, to varying degrees, mixed subsistence patterns. Most Tuareg live in the central Sahara and along its borders, in the Sahel. More nomadic Tuareg herd camels, sheep, goats, cattle, and donkeys. Although Tuareg converted to Islam between the eighth and eleventh centuries C.E., different groups vary in their degree of adherence to Qur'anic law and extent of Arabic cultural influences (Norris 1972, 1975, 1990). Some Tuareg trace their origins to the Fezzan region of Libya; others trace this to Yemen. Allied descent groups comprise a drum group or confederation under the power of a drum chief called *ettebel*, a legitimate male successor from the dominant noble group within it. In each region, the large political unit, the confederation, is socially stratified into noble and vassal named groups. Eight politically distinct descent groups (drum groups) all speak mutually intelligible dialects of their Berber-derived language, Tamajaq, and are designated by geographic region. Two of these, Kel Ajjer and Kel Ahaggar, are the northern Tuareg in Algeria. The other six—Kel Adar, Kel Air, and Kel Geres, Iwllemmeden Kel Dennek, and Iwllemmeden Kel Ataram, and Kel Tademaket—live on the southern fringes of desert in Mali, Niger, and Burkina Faso, and are the southern Tuareg. Within the Kel Adar is the political confederation of Ifoghas, who live in and around the Adragh-n-Ifoghas mountains and the town of Kidal in northern Mali. Within the Kel Air are the political confederations of Kel Ewey, Kel Ferwan, and Kel Fadey, who live in and around the Air Mountains and the town of Agadez in northern Niger. Precolonial social organization was divided into nobles, Islamic religious scholars, tributaries, smiths/artisans, and servile peoples. In most regions, slavery was abolished by the mid-twentieth century.

In general, many Tuareg women enjoy considerable rights and privileges. They are not sequestered, do not veil their faces (although Tuareg men do), and have much social and economic independence and freedom of movement. Separation of the sexes is relatively minimal. Men and women regularly meet and socialize in public. Women are singers and musicians, and organizers of many social events, such as drum playing and dance gatherings, which feature much flirting and courtship. Throughout their lives, many Tuareg women enjoy freedom of choice in sexual involvement and actively pursue romantic preferences (King 1903: 280; Rodd 1926: 174–175). They may regularly have male visitors, though not always lovers, when their husbands are absent (Rodd 1926: 174–175); Nicolas 1946: 225; Lhote 1955: 335; Murphy 1964; Claudot-Hawad 1993).

Although many of these gender constructs and relationships apply to most Tuareg, there is the need to refine and specify, rather than generalize, interpretation of some aspects of Tuareg

women's status. Many Tuareg groups display variation in gender arrangements according to relative degrees of nomadism and sedentarization, religious devotion, regional and confederational, and rural–urban differences, as well as age, kinship roles, and social stratum origins. The Kel Ewey *ineslemen* clans of maraboutique Islamic scholars, for example, attempt to control their women slightly more by placing greater emphasis upon virginity and application of Qur'anic inheritance laws. Even among these clans, however, women own property, are not secluded, and go about unveiled and relatively freely visit and receive male visitors, and although extramarital affairs are less tolerated, men, not women, are fined or punished in reprisals (Rasmussen 1994, 1998a, 1998b). In some Iwllemeden Tuareg maraboutique clans in the Azawagh region in Niger, Walentowitz (in Claudot-Hawad 1993: 47–48) reports unusual restrictions: contrary to most Tuareg women who go unveiled, these women hide the face before men of equal or higher status, particularly potential marriage partners, and conceal their bodies by wrapping large mats around themselves while traveling on foot. Yet as their travel and visiting suggest, these women are not strictly secluded, and they own property independently.

There are also gender transformations over the life course. Older women enjoy security as mothers-in-law and grandmothers. Many specialize in herbal medicine, divination, and bone-setting healing specialties. A widow or divorcee may become a household head in advanced age; if younger, she usually returns to her parental household.

In rural seminomadic Kel Ewey caravanning villages in the Air Mountains, men are often gone from five to seven months a year on caravan trade and migrant labor. Young, unmarried girls and older post-childbearing-age women often go out and establish temporary camps with their herds, intermittently for four months during the dry season; elderly women in the rainy season leave for several weeks to gather leaves and roots and grasses for sauces and medicines from trees on Mount Bagzan (Rasmussen 2006).

During the cold, dry caravanning season, women construct their tent doors to face outward, toward the compounds of their female relatives, the more matrifocal or matricentric space reflecting these women's greater cooperation and sharing at this time. In contrast, in the hot and rainy seasons while many men are at home, the women close these doors and construct doors opening onto the interior courtyard of the nuclear-household compound; the emphasis here is more patrifocal, and patricentric, reflecting greater focus within the nuclear household.

Most women prefer monogamous unions, and polygyny is a rare occurrence, except among some prominent chiefs, Islamic scholars, and prosperous, more sedentarized gardeners and merchants. Polygynous men try to minimize co-wives' jealousy by installing wives in separate compounds and even distant villages. Co-wives never share cooking facilities or sleep in the same compound.

Tuareg women do not engage in any extreme gestures of subservience to their husbands. Husbands and wives may eat together in private, though not usually at public rites of passage. Name avoidance does not entail wife-to-husband deference among the Tuareg as Schlegel (1975: 167–168) inferred from the data available on Tuareg through the HRAF (Human Relations Area Files). The use of teknonymy and sobriquets is symmetric, applying to both sexes. Direct expression of anger on the part of a man toward his wife is considered shameful, and in rural areas, at least, rape and wife-beating are extremely rare. Since the end of the Tuareg rebellion, however, some men returning from refugee flight and political exile have brought back alien ideas concerning gender and relations between the sexes: in order to restore their damaged masculine pride from economic unemployment and military defeat, some men value virgins upon marriage, heretofore not an important local cultural value.

Tuareg women receive their nuptial tent (*ehan*) as part of their dowry. It is constructed communally on the evening of the wedding by elderly female relatives of the bride, and torn down and reconstructed to be larger on each successive evening of the seven-day wedding ritual (Ramussen 1997). In many dialects of Tamajaq, "to make a tent" idiomatically denotes "to

marry." The nuptial tent, which after the wedding will be the married couple's residence, is erected near the compound of the bride's parents. Later, the couple may decide to remain there or move with this tent to the husband's family's camp or village. Because descent is bilateral and the tent is matrilineally defined and transmitted, the tent also becomes a metaphor for matriliny and an allegory for maternity (Prussin 1995: 92). The married woman owns the tent.

The nuptial tent is therefore women's property, but also much more: it symbolizes the traditional ideal of monogamy. Recently, however, many men have been constructing adobe mud houses that the married man owns. These houses now often stand next to the tent owned by a married woman within the married couple's household compound (Rasmussen 1994, 1996, 1997). The more nomadic Tuareg groups still count women as owners of compounds, as well as tents, in identifying the household compounds. But the semisedentarized Kel Ewey in the Air region of Niger have begun to identify compounds by the names of husbands, as belonging to men, as they do the men's adobe mud houses in many of these compounds, standing next to the women's tents. These processes indicate some important changes in gender roles, status, and power upon sedentarization, which disrupts the property balance between the sexes. To what extent, then, does the tent confer women's control? The key issue, as Moore (1988: 52–53) points out, is the relationship between women's productive and reproductive roles, in the descent and inheritance system.

LEGAL/JURAL RIGHTS, PROPERTY, DESCENT, AND INHERITANCE

The Tuareg official political structure is male-dominated. Among the more nomadic groups, the camping group (*eghiwan*) is an extended family headed by a male elder (*amghar*). In more sedentarized, seminomadic groups this term *eghiwan* refers to the village or hamlet, which may include a number of families, many of whom are related, and today often also includes households whose members vary in occupation and degree of nomadism, sometimes combining or alternating between several different subsistence forms (for example, a man of diverse social stratum origins might practice caravan trade, herding, oasis gardening, and migrant labor within a single lifetime, in different seasons).

Most Tuareg descent groups are bilateral, combining influences from Arabic and Qur'anic patriliny with local matriliny. Many descent groups trace their origins matrilineally to female ancestresses or culture heroines, although some more devoutly Muslim groups and men in general tend to downplay these ancestresses and emphasize patrilineal descent and male ancestors or culture heroes. For example, many Kel Ewey Tuareg men and marabouts in rural Air communities where I conducted research mentioned Boulkhou, a patrilineal ancestor of the current *ettebel*, as their important founder (Rasmussen 1997). He had sunk the first well, built a mosque, and resisted enemies in battles in that region. By contrast, many women tended to emphasize Tagurmat, the female ancestor of the Kel Igurmaden descent group within the Kel Ewey confederation, who in a myth gave birth to twin daughters who founded the professions of herbalism and Islamic/Qur'anic healing (Rasmussen 2006). The Kel Fadey say their people descend from two sisters who came from the east, bringing with them livestock, herds, and a large wooden drum (the drum, kept by the chief's wife, is used to call the tribal sections together for political or military action) (Worley 1992: 56).

A recurring question in Tuareg ethnography has been the extent to which Tuareg practice matrilineal inheritance and descent and succession. In matriliny, theoretically, mothers and sisters of heirs enjoy status. A problem here is the use of the term to mean certain institutions, or "society" and "culture" in general (Oxby 1978, 1990). Also often ignored are variations and changes among the different Tuareg groups and according to social context. Thus the issue becomes, which kin links are most important and what factors other than kinship are important in determining relationships between the generations and the sexes? Descent

group (*tawsit*) allegiance is, in practice, through the mother. Ideally, however, political office passes from father to son in all groups but the Kel Geres, where it goes from maternal uncle to sister's son. Hence both matrilateral and patrilateral kin ties are important. There are also important criteria apart from kinship in political leadership: for example, wealth and personal qualities of leadership.

Women's property is passed down mainly from mother to daughter; men's, from father to son. Objects acquired by women before marriage include jewelry, blankets, a bed, other household items, and sometimes cloth and sandals. In the past, noble women brought a slave to their married household; today, some rural noble women still inherit an attached smith/artisan client family. But this client–patron relationship is increasingly flexible. Inheritance of livestock is predominantly Qur'anic: daughters receive one-third to one-half of sons' shares. Children are considered, among most Air Tuareg, more important heirs than spouses and siblings. If there are only daughters, a brother receives the son's share. The mother's brother is a more significant figure in some groups than in others, but everywhere the mother's brother/sister's son tie features, at minimum, affection, and frequent gifts, and security in assistance. The sibling tie sometimes competes with the husband-wife tie. Each spouse, regardless of postmarital residence, if possible spends much time during the day (for example, eating meals) at the residence of his/her own kin. Individuals often try to return to maternal kin in latter years of life. Brothers often look out for sisters' legal and other interests, support sisters upon the divorce, and contribute to the support of widowed sisters' children. The father's sibling group is equated with the father, as a source of authority and possible conflict; the mother's sibling group, by contrast, is a source of love and aid, generosity, and support (Nicolaisen 1997).

Some Tuareg say, "It is the stomach that colors the child." Among the Ifoghas Tuareg in northern Mali where I conducted research, matrilineally-related "children of the stomach" can be depended upon more than other relatives for future care in illness and old age. Women therefore attempt to remain close to, and surround themselves with, "children of the stomach" for affection and security. By contrast, some other Tuareg tend to place less emphasis upon these maternally-based kin ties; the Kel Ewey Tuareg in northern Niger, for example, often go into business with those they call "children of men," persons—usually men—who share a common father. Significantly, Kel Ewey also tend to be more sedentarized and also practice polygyny to a greater extent than the Ifoghas. Kel Ewey men explain that additional wives and more children are advantageous in the work of oasis gardening. Many Tuareg believe that the maternal nephew inherits intelligence from his maternal uncle. But Kel Ewey do not use separate kinship terms for a maternal versus paternal nephew; they refer to both as *tegazay*.

In some legal contexts, the concept of maternal kinship identity tends to be submerged in Qur'anic and patrilineal influence: for example, in naming, ideas about children's affiliation and identity, and marriage. Some more sedentarized Kel Ewey Tuareg men in Niger tend to disparage an older form of naming a girl "daughter of" (*welet* or *oult*), still actively practiced by the Ifoghas Tuareg in Mali, as "only done with an illegitimate child." Many urban women are now called Madame plus the name of husband's father as surname, in postal addresses, clinic rosters, and school registration. Illegitimacy is considered shameful, antisocial, and greatly stigmatizing to the mother. Some men insist that the secret, Tamajaq name which older female relatives bestow on the child in the unofficial naming ritual the evening before the official Islamic naming by the father and marabout at the mosque, is "not important, it means nothing," but women dispute this, saying the latter name is as important to the child's identity as the Arabic, Qur'anic name. Women's property is sometimes subject to dispute and challenge in Qur'anic-based rulings by marabouts. For example, although a woman has the right to eject her husband from her tent, a woman's bridewealth is only reimbursed to the person the marabout rules is not at fault in divorce; many marabouts rule the woman at fault if she requests divorce to protest polygyny.

Nonetheless women's opinions are highly valued, and they are normally consulted by men on decisions that affect the life of the camp or village (Bernus 1981: 146–147). Yet there are some contexts in which women defer to some men: namely, before Islamic scholars and important chiefs, and toward elders in general, particularly those on the patrilineal side. Female herbal medicine women, for example, referred patients to marabouts for diagnosis of illness, more often than vice versa (Rasmussen 2006).

A number of authors (Bernus 1981; Casajus 1987; Claudot-Hawad 1993; Keenan 1977; Lhote 1955; Murphy 1964) have described a Tuareg endowment known as *akh hudderan*, which allows an individual to make a pre-inheritance gift of livestock to female relatives, usually daughters, sisters, and nieces, which they then own and control corporately. This property cannot be sold or otherwise disposed of. Additionally, Tuareg women accumulate livestock through important gifts (*alkhalal*) from both parents and other relatives after birth, which form the basis of their own herds. Women may receive outright gifts of livestock from consanguine kin throughout their lives, and in all marriages after the first, it is usually the wife herself who accepts the bridewealth (*taggalt*). Women's livestock herds therefore constitute their traditional source of wealth. There has been much property loss in droughts and wars since the mid-twentieth century. Women in particular suffer here; for although these losses affect both sexes, gardens are easier than herds to reconstitute after disasters. Some non-governmental organization (NGO) and United Nations (UN) agencies are trying to compensate women and men for lost herds, in some cases by replacing them, or in other cases, by encouraging Tuareg to settle down and practice oasis gardening and other newer occupations, such as tailoring and artisan work, more extensively. There is evidence that women's bases of property are increasingly altered by all these processes. For example, much property in the Saharan town of Agadez is not independently owned by the married woman, but merged together with that of her husband in civic records. In semisedentarized communities, men's houses complicate property disputes on

divorce. Some married women residing virilo-
cally (with the husband's family near his oasis
garden) are more isolated from their own kin
and more dependent upon the husband and
his family.

SEXUAL DIVISION OF LABOR

Domestic work varies according to region,
nomadic/sedentarized, and rural/urban differences. In more nomadic groups, this takes
a minimum of women's time. In some regions,
for example in northern Mali where the water-
table is too low for oasis gardening, many rural
Tuareg there still practice nomadic stockbreeding, and women are discouraged from
performing heavy physical labor, reflecting
past noble disdain for household, herding,
and gardening labor formerly performed by
servile and client peoples. There, women are
encouraged to limit their bodily motility and
perform tasks locally-defined as "light," such as
tent-repair and light herding. In other regions,
for example, in northern Niger on gardening
oases, women do much more arduous tasks:
going to the well, crushing grains, and increasingly, assisting with crop harvesting—the latter encouraged by NGO and aid agencies in
that region. In these more sedentarized communities, women's time is taken up more
extensively with food-processing work within
the compound.

In semisedentarized and urban communities, some women are now described as "housewives" (called by the French term *menageres*) in
response to this researcher's query concerning
their work. These women have given up herding (though not always herd ownership), or
have relegated this task to kinspersons. A few
gardeners' wives have even given up their tents.
Very few women individually own gardens,
which are traditionally inherited and owned
mostly by men, though a few women have date-
palms through matrilineal *akh huderan* endow-
ments. Until the recent establishment of
women's gardening cooperatives in the rural
Air region by NGO and aid agencies, planting
was traditionally done by men, and harvesting
was done only by elderly women. By 1998, a

development agency had established a women's
garden cooperative in an Air Mountain region
Kel Ewey community, and some women had
begun enclosing and gardening in this designated space, known as the "women's garden
(enclosure)" (*afarag n tchidoden*), and traded
millet on the market in Agadez. In order to
prevent erosion, a fence was being constructed:
each woman is paid an amount to participate
in the work party, provide wood, and construct
the fence. A female "president" supervises this
project, in which the women take up a collection (250 CFA or approximately 50 cents each)
from each household to build a well (cost:
25,000 CFA, approximately $50). When the
well was completed, the project organization
gave the group an animal. Alternative occupations to gardening are increasingly available:
some women own small shops and restaurants,
and some belong to women's sewing and leatherwork cooperatives.

Smith/artisan men and women derive
much income from arts and crafts. Metal and
woodworking are smith men's work; most
leatherworking is smith women's work. Women
of diverse social origins tan hides, but mostly
smith/artisan women cut and embroider
them. Smith/artisan women in rural areas
obtain cash and food gifts through leather-
working and rites-of-passage services for
nobles. In Saharan towns, women smiths continue to do leatherwork, but with fewer raw
materials, which cost more in the sedentarized
setting, and also fewer customers; for there is
less demand for leatherwork than in rural communities. Recently, some aid organizations in
France have assisted by bringing art objects
made in workshops (by both men and women
specialists) to sell in France.

COMPARATIVE AND THEORETICAL
DISCUSSION: WOMEN AND MEN
IN PASTORAL NOMADISM

Some researchers (Barth 1961; Martin and
Voorhies 1975: 332–366) view pastoralism as
one extreme on a continuum of dependence
upon herd animals and cultivation for subsistence, in which segments of sedentary tilling

communities may, during periods of scarce resources (i.e., droughts, overpopulation) come to depend increasingly on the products of their herd animals for subsistence. Many Tuareg have been pressured during difficulties of drought to become more sedentary, and to depend increasingly on products of their oasis gardens rather than herd animals for subsistence. Despite this, however, a pastoralist ideology persists. Many Tuareg yearn to return to pastoral nomadism, but realize the necessity today for mixing subsistence modes of herding, oasis gardening, caravan and other itinerant trading, and migrant labor, and among the more specialized artisan social strata, arts/crafts production (Rasmussen 1992, 1994, 1996; Claudot-Hawad 1993). Martin and Voorhies also observe that during periods of plenty, when the size of herds becomes cumbersome or provides the wherewithal for purchase of arable land, pastoral segments may be repatriated to villages. Most Tuareg remain predominantly rural, but often alternate between nomadic camps, sedentarized oasis villages, and large towns according to seasonal needs and more long-term stresses, such as ecological disaster of drought and political violence of war. In the 1960s, the central government of Mali pressured many Tuareg in the northern region to come to the towns for food relief distribution. Many migrated south during droughts of 1969–1971, 1984, and 2001. In the 1990s, there was massive refugee flight of many Tuareg from northern Niger and Mali during the armed rebellion. In more peaceful times, during the rainy season, nomads often congregate at wells and other water-points for special festivals. During the cold dry season, some men travel on caravan trading expeditions. Many Tuareg families are also dispersed in both town and countryside at different times of the year; for example, some children board with relatives in town to attend school, and return to the countryside to assist with herding and gardening tasks during the rainy season.

Tuareg patterns therefore suggest the need to modify or refine some prevalent representations of the cyclical pattern of pastoralism (Martin and Voorhies 1975: 334). They offer contradictions, or at least variations, of some previous interpretations of gender in pastoral nomadic societies, and show the need to deconstruct concepts in both pastoralist and gender studies. In a classic study, Martin and Voorhies (1975: 351) make several tentative generalizations. They note that the sexual division of labor seems related to the degree and nature of mobility required for the successful execution of subsistence activities (Martin and Voorhies 1975: 352). They argue that gender variations among pastoralists are influenced by at least three factors: (1) their specific adaptation to a given environment (settlement pattern, interaction of herding and cultivation); (2) cultural history of society (common culture areas such as sedentary community origins in Africa south of the Sahara correlate with economic independence, the hoe, polygyny, and sexual freedom; those in the Middle East and of agricultural origins display the opposite pattern); and (3) recent diffusion of ideas rather than cultural origins (Islam, for example— although the Tuareg are an exception to other Muslim pastoralists, in demonstrating less emphasis on the patriarchal family and on gender inequalities) (Martin and Voorhies 1975: 365–366).

From their study of forty-four pastoral societies, Martin and Voorhies conclude that the female contribution to the diet of herders is small. Men do almost all herding and women dairy in only about one-third of societies. Men also do most of the cultivation in half of their sample, however, where cultivation is based on horticultural techniques, women are either the exclusive cultivators, or men and women share equally in cultivation (Martin and Voorhies 1975: 339–343; O'Kelly and Carney 1986: 66). O'Kelly and Carney (1986: 66) argue that gender division of labor within many pastoral societies is "tipped toward male dominance" of economically productive tasks. These authors explain this in terms of the strength required to handle large animals. Males tend to be exclusive herders of large animals. Females may, however, herd smaller animals and serve as dairy maids for large and small species. Women and children contribute by gathering food, carrying water, and processing byproducts such as milk, wool, hides, and dung. But the lack of firm differentiation between domestic and public spheres encourages gender egalitarianism. Where women have some economic control, women's status may be raised. Tuareg women make important contributions to subsistence; most of the rural diet derives from products of small animals, and Tuareg women, unlike women in some other pastoralist societies, own herds, milk them, and control their products.

Boulding (1976: 288–299) argues that women participate more fully in the total life of these societies than they do in settled agricultural communities. But Martin and Voorhies (1975) argue that male dominance of economic production gives rise to male dominance in the wider culture and social structure of pastoral societies. Lois Beck, on the other hand, found a flexible division of labor, economic interdependence between genders, and a low degree of gender segregation among the Qashqai of Iran (Beck in Beck and Keddie 1978: 365–367). Furthermore, because of the small size of independent households of these pastoralists, males and females were partners in economically independent units, and neither males nor females formed strong separate solidarity groups.

Many authors agree that, however diverse the forms it takes, the division of labor among herders does not create a sharp dichotomy between domestic and public spheres. Women's tasks are more likely to take place in camp than men's tasks, but they do not isolate women in the household (Wood 1999). Much women's work is done in cooperation with other women. Both men and women participate in collective work patterns with other members of the same gender. Camps are typically divided into women's spaces and men's spaces, but almost all activities are carried out in the open, avoiding development of private domestic spheres for women versus public spheres for men (O'Kelly and Carney 1986: 67). Women's work may be household work, but it is public household work; public/domestic domains thus emerge as overly rigid and bound to western cultures.[3]

In many pastoral nomadic societies, ownership and control over the disposition of livestock appear to be predominantly in male hands. However, females are sometimes at least nominal owners of some livestock through inheritance, dowries, or purchase (O'Kelly and Carney 1986: 68; Hutchinson 1996). But even owners of livestock cannot usually dispose freely of their animals: they are bound by an intricate web of kinship-based exchanges, which requires giving periodically large numbers of animals to close kin, as bridewealth to the bride's family, dowries to the groom, and as compensation for violation of certain rules, for example, homicide (Evans-Pritchard 1956; Hutchinson 1996) and adultery (Rasmussen 1998a). Males who control large herds thus do not necessarily derive significant economic power from these herds; rather, use rights are important considerations. But large herds bring prestige and influence to owners.

Other factors influencing gender are the defense needs and warfare practices of herders and patricentric kinship systems. In terms of Peggy Sanday's (1981: 181) typology, many pastoralists, such as the Gabra of the Chalbi Desert on the Kenyan-Somalian border (Wood 1999), appear to fall under the rubric of "real male dominance," because in most cases the environment is sufficiently dangerous for the society to depend on the strength and aggressiveness of their men for survival. Sanday argues that under such conditions of stress, for the sake of social and cultural survival, women "accept real male dominance." The Tuareg data suggest modifications of this hypothesis. Tuareg men's frequent absence from home in past raiding and more recent separatist warfare against the central state governments of Mali and Niger, and also men's peaceful trading, have encouraged, indeed necessitated women's independence in some domains of activity (education of children and work). However, some high-status men remain at home and control official political decisions. Thus a warrior aristocracy does not produce gender inequality in all respects; rather, there is a mixed bag here. In fact, some authors report legends of "warrior queens" in Tuareg and other pastoralist nomadic cultures (Boulding 1976: 303–312; Brett and Fentress 1997; Rodd 1926: 170; Worley 1988, 1992).[4] While difficult to verify, they suggest that women's elevated position in the class structure may modify their gender roles; thus class cross-cuts gender (Ortner and White-head 1981; di Leonardo 1990). The pastoral-nomadic/gender relationship is therefore complex, and defies facile generalizations or typologies.

CONCLUSIONS: DO TENTS AND HERDS STILL MATTER?

Summary of Socioeconomic and Political Changes; Implications

One of the key changes affecting the organization of nomadic pastoralism is the nomads' loss of autonomy after incorporation into sedentary nation-states, in the wake of the military advantage of sedentary states and revolutions in transportation technology during the past century (Barfield 1993: 207). Upon sedentarization, there is disruption of traditional ties and undermining of important sources of defense and security. As men are increasingly obliged to travel as migrant laborers and children are sent to school, the workload of women extends from their traditional routines to a heavier involvement in supplementary tasks. In Niger and Mali, colonial and postcolonial eras saw pastoralist border zones farmed, depleting the soil and disrupting ecological and socio-economic balance and relations between groups and lands. Mobility has been curtailed, censuses, schools and taxes imposed by colonial and postcolonial central state governments. Sometimes these have imposed a patrilineal bias. Tuareg are unique among pastoralists in the enduring significance their matrilineal institutions have for gender and relations between the sexes. But there is evidence that matriliny is under duress. This is shown by the transformations in property balance described in this article and elsewhere (Oxby 1990; Figueiredo in Claudot-Hawad 1996: 113–137; Rasmussen 1994, 1996, 1997, 1998, 2006). It is also shown in Gast's (1992: 151–172) description of Tuareg cultural encounters with more powerful neighbors: nation-state policies toward Tuareg nomads brought many workers, functionaries, soldiers,

and tourists into rural Tuareg communities. Often, they were ignorant of and disrespectful toward traditional beliefs and practices; for example, they misunderstood evening festival and courtship customs as opportunities to seduce women, whereas traditionally, Tuareg cultural values emphasize music, poetry, flirting, visits, and conversation without necessarily including sexual intercourse. In some respects, then, Tuareg women appear to have become the wards of men in encounters with outside males, and in national systems of registration/naming, food relief and medical distribution programs, taxation and census counts. However, as shown, there are also new opportunities—in new cooperative agencies and projects offering some benefits for women, as well as men.

The question raised is how nomadic pastoral Tuareg women actively respond to forces of sedentization, urbanization, and nationalism. Do they gain or lose? How? Women can use the urban setting to escape from an extended household ruled over by a mother-in-law. They can also gain access, in more sedentarized centers, to new jobs, thereby benefiting from emerging economic opportunities not available in more remote rural areas. Finally, they often alternate back and forth between locations and occupations over long-term, and/or combine different strategies at the same time. It is therefore hazardous to generalize too sweepingly about pastoralism, women, and gender—some urban Tuareg women still own livestock, but keep them in the countryside with relatives, and some rural Tuareg women have given up herding. Hence the importance of not solely structural, but also situational meanings and practices. Rather than building models and typologies, anthropologists need to deconstruct and refine pastoral and gender-related categories and processes.

REFERENCES CITED

Barfield, Thomas J. 1993. *The Nomadic Alternative.* Upper Saddle River, NJ: Prentice Hall.
Barlow, Tani. 1996. "Theorizing Women: Funu, Guojia, Jiating. (Chinese Women, Chinese State,

Chinese Family)." In Joan W. Scott (ed.). *Feminism and History*, pp. 48–59. Oxford: Oxford University Press.

Barth, Fredrik. 1961. *Nomads of South Persia: The Basseri Tribe of the Khamseh Confederacy.* Oslo, Norway: Oslo University Press.

Beck, Lois. 1978. "Women among Qashqai Nomadic Pastoralist in Iran." In Lois Beck and Nikki Keddie (eds.). *Women in the Muslim World*, pp. 351–374. Cambridge, MA: Harvard University Press.

Bernus, Edmond. 1981. *Touaregs Nigeriens: Unité Culturelle et Diversité Regionale d'un Peuple Pasteur.* Paris: Office de la Recherche Scientifique et Technique Outre-Mer.

Boulding, Elise. 1976. *The Underside of History.* Boulder, CO: Westview Press.

Brett, Michael and Elizabeth Fentress. 1997. *The Berbers.* Oxford, UK: Blackwell.

Butler, Judith. 1990. *Gender Trouble.* New York: Routledge.

Casajus, Dominique. 1987. *La Tente dans l'Essuf.* London and Paris: Cambridge.

Claudot-Hawad, Hélène 1993. *Les Touaregs: Portrait en Fragments.* Aix-en-Provence, France: Edisud.

Davison, Jean. 1997. *Gender, Lineage, and Ethnicity in Southern Africa.* Boulder, CO: Westview Press.

di Lauretis, Teresa. 1984. *Alice Doesn't: Feminism, Semiotics, Cinema.* Bloomington: Indiana University Press.

Di Leonardo, Michaela. 1990. *Gender at the Crossroads of Knowledge.* Berkeley: University of California Press.

Evans-Pritchard, E.E. 1956 *Nuer Religion*, Oxford, UK: Oxford University Press.

Figuereido, Christina. 1996. "Identite et concitoyennete: La reelaboration des relations entre homes et femmes aux marges de la societe Kel Adagh (Mali)." In Helene Claudot-Hawad (ed.). *Tuaregs et autres Sahariens entre plusieurs mondes*, pp. 113–137. Aix-en-Provence, France: Edisud.

Flax, Jane. 1993. *Disputed Subjects: Essays on Psychoanalysis, Politics, and Philosophy.* New York: Routledge.

Gaidzanwa, R. B. 1985. *Images of Women in Zimbabwean Literature.* Harare, Zimbabwe: College Press.

Gast, Marcel. 1992. "Relations Amoureuses chez les Kel Ahaggar." In Tassadit Yacine (ed.). *Amour, Phantasmes, et Sociétés en Afrique du Nord et au Sahara*, pp. 151–173. Paris: L'Harmattan-Awal.

Hutchinson, Sharon. 1996. *Nuer Dilemmas.* Berkeley: University of California Press.

Keenan, Jeremy. 1977. *Tuareg: People of Ahaggar.* New York: St. Martin's Press.

King, William J. Harding. 1903. *A Search for the Masked Tawaraks.* London: Smith, Elder and Co.

Kondo, Dorinne. 1990. *Crafting Selves.* Chicago: University of Chicago Press.

Lhote, Henri. 1955. *Les Touaregs du Hoggar.* Paris: Payot.

Mannathoko, C. 1992. "Feminist Theories and the Study of Gender in Southern Africa." In R. Meena (ed.). *Gender in Southern Africa*, Harare, Zimbabwe: SAPES Books.

Martin, M. Kay, and Barbara Voorhies 1975. *Female of the Species.* New York: Columbia University Press.

Meena, R. 1992. "Gender Research/Studies in Southern Africa: An Overview." In R. Meena (ed.). *Gender in Southern Africa: Conceptual and Theoretical Issues* Harare: SAPES Books.

Mernissi, Fatima. 1987. *Beyond the Veil: Male-Female Dynamics in Modern Muslim Society.* Bloomington: Indiana University Press.

Mohanty, C.T. 1992. "Feminist Encounter: Locating the Politics of Experience." In M. Barrett and A. Phillips (eds.). *Destabilizing Theory: Contemporary Feminist Debates*, pp 74–93. Palo Alto, CA: Stanford University Press.

Moore, Henrietta. 1988. *Feminism and Anthropology.* Minneapolis: University of Minnesota Press.

Murphy, Robert. 1964. "Social Distance and the Veil." *American Anthropologist* 66: 1257–1274.

Nicolaisen, Ida and Johannes. 1997. *The Pastoral Tuareg.* Copenhagen: Rhodos.

Nicolas, Francis. 1946. *Tamesna: Les Ioullemmeden de l'Est, ou Tuareg Kel Dinnik, Cercle de T'awa—Colonie du Niger.* Paris: Imprimerie Nationale.

Norris, H. T. 1972. *Saharan Myth and Saga.* Oxford, UK: Clarendon Press.

———. 1975. *The Tuaregs: Their Islamic Legacy and its Diffusion in the Sahel.* Warminster, UK: Aris and Phillips.

———. 1990. *Sufi Mystics of the Niger Desert.* Oxford, UK: Clarendon.

O'Kelly, Charlotte G, and Larry S. Carney 1986. *Women and Men in Society: Cross-Cultural Perspectives on Gender Stratification.* Belmont, CA: Wadsworth Publishing Company.

Ong, Aihwa. 1987. *Spirits of Resistance and Capitalist Discipline: Factory Women in Malaysia.* Albany: State University of New York Press.

Ortner, Sherry, and Harriet Whitehead (eds.). 1981. *Sexual Meanings.* Cambridge, UK: Cambridge University Press.

Oxby, Clare. 1978. *Sexual Division and Slavery in a Tuareg Community.* Ph.D. dissertation, London School of Economics.

———. 1990. The 'Living Milk' Runs Dry: The Decline of a Form of Joint Ownership and Matrilineal

Inheritance among the Twareg (Niger.) In P. T. W. Baxter and R. Hogg (eds.). *Property, Poverty, and People: Changing Rights in Property and Problems of Pastoral Development*, pp. 222–228. Manchester, UK: Manchester University Press.

Probyn, Elspeth. 1990. "Travels in the Postmodern: Making Sense of the Local." In Linda J. Nicholson (ed.). *Feminism/Postmodernism*, pp. 176–190. New York: Routledge.

Prussin, LaBelle. 1995. *African Nomadic Architecture: Space, Place, and Gender.* Washington, DC: Smithsonian Institution Press.

Rasmussen, Susan. 1992. "Disputed Boundaries: Tuareg Discourse on Class and Ethnicity." *Ethnology* 31: 351–366.

———. 1994. "Female Sexuality, Social Reproduction, and Medical Intervention: Kel Ewey Tuareg Perspectives." *Culture, Medicine, and Psychiatry* 18: 433–462.

———. 1995. *Spirit Possession and Personhood among the Kel Ewey Tuareg.* Cambridge, UK: Cambridge University Press.

———. 1996. "Tuareg Tent as Field Space and Cultural Symbol." *Anthropological Quarterly*, 69: 14–27.

———. 1997. *The Poetics and Politics of Tuareg Aging: Life Course and Personal Destiny in Niger.* DeKalb, IL: Northern Illinois University Press.

———. 1998a. "Within the Tent and at the Crossroads: Travel and Gender Identity among the Tuareg of Niger." *Ethos* 26: 153–182.

———. 1998b. "Only Women Know Trees: Medicine Women and the Role of Herbal Healing in Tuareg Culture." *Journal of Anthropological Research* 54: 147–171.

———. 2006. *Those Who Touch: Tuareg Medicine Women in Anthropological Perspective.* DeKalb: Northern Illinois University Press.

Rodd, Francis, Lord of Rennell. 1926. *People of the Veil.* London: MacMillan and Co.

Rosaldo, Michele, and Louise Lamphere (eds.). 1974. *Women, Culture, and Society.* Stanford, CA: Stanford University Press.

Sanday, Peggy. 1981. *Female Power and Male Dominance: On the Origins of Sexual Inequality.* Cambridge, UK: Cambridge University Press.

Schlegel, Alice. 1975. "Three Styles of Domestic Authority: A Cross-Cultural Study." In Dana Raphael (ed.). *Being Female: Reproduction, Power, and Change,* The Hague, Paris: Mouton Publishers.

Scott, Joan W. 1988. *Gender and the Politics of History.* New York: Columbia University Press.

Scott, Joan W. 1992. "Experience." In Judith Butler and Joan W. Scott (eds.). *Feminists Theorize the Political,* pp. 22–41 New York: Routledge.

Walentowitz, Saskia. 2002. "Partir sand quitter: Rites et gestes autour des deplacements feminines chez les Ineslimen de l'Azawagh." In Helene Claudot-Hawad (ed.). *Voyager d'un point de vue nomade*, pp. 37–53. Helene Hawad, Paris: Editions Paris-Mediterranee de l'IREMAM.

Wood, John. 1999. *When Men Are Women.* Madison: University of Wisconsin Press.

Worley, Barbara. 1988. "Bed Posts and Broad Swords: Tuareg Women's Work Parties and the Dialectics of Sexual Conflict." In Richard R. Randolph, David M. Schneider, and May N. Diaz (eds.). *Dialectics and Gender: Anthropological Approaches*, pp. 273–288. Boulder, CO: Westview Press.

———. 1992. "Where All the Women Are Strong." *Natural History* 101(11): 54–64.

NOTES

1. In these projects—on spirit possession, aging and the life course, herbal healers, divination, rural and urban smith/artisans, gender, and verbal art performance, I gratefully acknowledge assistance from Fulbright Hays (1983, 1998, 2001); Wenner Gren Foundation for Anthropological Research (1991, 1995, 1998, 2006); Social Science Research Council (1995); National Geographic Society for Research and Exploration (1995, 1998); Indiana University (1983), and University of Houston (1991).

2. For example, Mohanty (1992) criticizes Western feminists for essentializing women's experience regardless of race, class, or nationality. Mohanty faults Western feminists for universalizing women's oppression, as well. She argues that western feminists psychologize complex and often contradictory historical and cultural realities that mark differences among women. Differences among women need to be engaged rather than transcended. She also warns against globalizing women as victims; there is the need to acknowledge women's active agency. Yet feminists in these areas are diverse; they come from various schools of thought depending on their national and cultural orientations.

3. Pastoralist societies therefore break down the assumed dichotomy of private/public or domestic/public domains, a tenacious concept in some early feminist anthropology (Rosaldo and Lamphere 1974) later critiqued in more recent anthropology of gender studies (Ong 1987).

4. These observations of female battle warriors in mythico-history raise interesting issues. There is a

paucity of data on women's roles in the recent armed rebellion. Traditionally, most women have participated indirectly in fighting because men's honor depended upon women's praise music upon their victorious return from battles; thus women control men's reputations. Women's praise songs of men often welcomed them after successful raids or migrant labor or caravan trade, but women could also mock and scorn men who returned less victorious or without money. Women still hold power over men's reputations,

but many men have not returned victorious or wealthy in recent years. Some men have attempted to find social recognition through participation in the 1990–1995 nationalist/separatist military conflict. Much new music of the Tuareg rebellion composed by both sexes, as well as women's traditional songs, perhaps is responding to these new predicaments and in effect, conveys men's and women's efforts to reconstruct social prestige and independent socioeconomic status in Tuareg gender-role relationships.

Women and Work in a Postrevolutionary Society:
Urban Cooperatives and the Informal Economy in Nicaragua

Florence E. Babb

Throughout Latin America, governments introduced economic stabilization and structural adjustment programs during the 1980s in an effort to bring rampant inflation under control. In Nicaragua, the Sandinista revolutionary government implemented adjustment programs late in the decade, but harsher measures mandated by the International Monetary Fund and the World Bank came more recently, after the 1990 elections ushered in the government of Violeta Chamorro de Barrios. A debate emerged in the country over the consequences of these measures for the most vulnerable social groups. In Nicaragua as elsewhere, the poor, women, and children were hit hardest by these policies. Yet in Nicaragua the recent history of social mobilization prepared these sectors in distinct ways to confront the harsh effects of these economic programs, setting the country apart from others in Latin

America. Low-income urban women have been among those affected most by the political change of the past fifteen years, and they have responded by actively confronting difficult conditions both at work and at home.

In this essay, I first consider some of the general consequences of structural adjustment policies for Third World women and men and then turn to examine the effects these policies have had in Nicaragua, particularly for women in formal and informal work in small industries and commerce in the capital city of Managua. I concentrate on the situation of women in several urban cooperatives I followed over the years of my research, and then discuss the growing number of women conducting informal activities, often out of the front rooms of their homes in the city's working-class and poor barrios.

Several authors have led the way toward a critical and gendered perspective on the recent effects of development policies that rely on stabilization and adjustment measures (e.g., Elson 1991; Benería and Feldman 1992; Afshar and Dennis 1992). They have called for attention to the household, where women are functioning

This essay is adapted from chapter five of [Florence E. Babb's] book, *After Revolution: Mapping Gender and Cultural Politics in Neoliberal Nicaragua* (University of Texas Press 2001).

as shock absorbers for these measures, and they have argued that adjustment plans extend women's unpaid work in the home in ways that must be assessed. I suggest that while turning to the household and women's unpaid work—the emphasis of most feminist research in this area—has brought about a needed transformation in our thinking about economic development, it is equally important at this point to assess the gender-specific ways that women are experiencing adjustment and absorbing the shock through their paid work in and outside the home. Indeed, women's unpaid and paid work are highly interconnected, and just as women's expanding work in the household may constrain their participation in the labor force, their increasingly difficulties in earning a livelihood make the new demands at home that much harder to meet. In taking this position, I hope to complement other feminist analyses of economic policy based on structural adjustment, demonstrating through the Nicaraguan case the need for greater attention to forms of women's economic and political participation that extend beyond the home.

WOMEN AND THE INTERNATIONAL ECONOMY

In her examination of male bias in the development process, Diane Elson (1991: 164) writes that "macro-economic problems, such as large balance of payments deficits, high inflation rates and very low growth rates, have devastated many countries in Asia, Africa, Latin America and the Caribbean." She notes that these problems stem from both internal and external problems and that many countries have no choice but to look to the International Monetary Fund (IMF) and the World Bank for financial assistance. Elson was among the first to challenge the supposedly gender-neutral programs of economic stabilization and structural adjustment that are introduced as conditions of international assistance. These include plans to reduce inflation, privatize industry, increase export production, decontrol prices, and cut public expenditures.

As Elson and others (Benería and Feldman 1992; Afshar and Dennis 1992) have noted, adjustment programs that are designed to streamline economies and enhance competitiveness are based on macroeconomic concepts that apply to economies overall rather than to particular enterprises or households. Therefore, they rarely examine the disproportionate number of women who are located in the small industries and informal businesses that are apt to suffer most from the new policies. Nor are they likely to notice that when unemployment rises, food costs go up, and health care and education become less widely available, it is women who must adjust to meet pressing family needs. Because the work of stretching household budgets, caring for the ill, and in general managing to get along under conditions of economic and psychological stress are unpaid services that do not apparently affect the market, they are overlooked by development planners. Yet there is increasing evidence that women's ability to cushion the blow of economic adjustment is not without limits, and many households are suffering serious consequences from the crises produced by recent policies.

Research has shown that where men are present as contributors to households in Third World countries, they typically offer a smaller portion of what they earn to meet family expenses and keep more for personal spending than women, even though their incomes are generally higher; in contrast, whether or not women are the sole providers in their families, they tend to turn almost all their income to collective needs (Blumberg 1991). Gender inequality in unpaid service to families is even more apparent, with women performing far more of the work of family maintenance. Unequal economic power is frequently accompanied by domestic conflict and violence against women, a serious social problem that is now coming to public attention largely because of women's activism. Thus, if we are interested not only in aggregate measures of economic development but also in social justice, we need to disaggregate the household to discover patterns of resource allocation, the gender division of labor, and gender relations in the home (Tinker 1990).

In an analysis that considers the microdynamics of class and gender as households respond to structural adjustment at the macroeconomic level, Benería (in Benería and Feldman 1992: viii) describes the deepening inequalities that are emerging. While she notes the significant absence of proposed alternatives to structural adjustment, she judges that, given women's key roles in the household and beyond, they will be instrumental in efforts to resolve current problems. In fact, she and others (e.g., Elson 1992; Pérez-Alemán et al. 1992) point to evidence of women's organizing in grassroots social movements in ways that may ultimately transform societies. In the Nicaraguan case, women contributed significantly in the period of social revolution and they have demonstrated a determination to play a similar role even under drastically changed circumstances since 1990.[1]

THE NICARAGUAN ECONOMY IN THE SANDINISTA PERIOD

When the Sandinistas came to power in 1979 following their long struggle against the Somoza dictatorship, they faced almost insurmountable problems of underdevelopment, among them an impoverished population, poorly managed resources, and inadequate health care and education. In their first few years in government they carried out a broad program of agrarian reform, created a mixed economy and improved working conditions, made medical care and education widely available, and addressed issues of gender inequality as perpetuated through the media, the law, and other social institutions. Through the Nicaraguan Women's Association (AMNLAE), they worked with women in both the rural and the urban sectors to promote social participation in support of the revolution.

Within a few years, however, the conflict known as the Contra War required the development of a wartime economy that left little in the budget to sustain the development that was under way. Analysts have described the Sandinista period as a decade of both enormous hope and deep disappointment as the country struggled to bring about structural change while defending itself against internal and external aggression.[2] Until 1983, the economy experienced growth and social services expanded, but the strain produced by the war and by a U.S. economic embargo became great enough that by 1985 an economic adjustment was imposed to try to stabilize the economy. As the formal economy crumbled, the informal sector of unregulated small enterprises expanded, serving as a safety valve for rising unemployment.

The high cost of defending the country and continuing to subsidize social services such as health care and education had contributed to spiraling inflation and a large deficit. Attempting to reverse the trend, the government implemented the 1988 Stabilization and Adjustment Program—shifting from domestic production and consumption to export-oriented production, devaluing the currency, laying off thousands of workers in the public sector (a measure known as *compactación*), and drastically cutting social services. The government continued to provide food packages of sugar, beans, and rice to state employees, as well as subsidies for basic needs such as transportation, electricity, and water. Even so, the social cost of the adjustment was high and women were affected most adversely by the measures both as workers in less secure jobs and as family members responsible for child care and household maintenance (Brenes et al. 1991).

During this period of economic crisis, when households needed income earners, more women sought to enter the labor market. As the formal sector shrank, many urban women sought employment in the informal sector, where they found increased competition. As early as 1985, 60 percent of employed women were in the informal sector, compared with 49 percent of employed men (Pérez-Alemán et al. 1992: 245). Women continued to experience higher levels of unemployment and lower wages and other earnings than men, an especially critical disparity given the large proportion of female-headed households (conservatively estimated at about 45 percent in Managua). Women were also hit harder as artisans and as workers in small industries, since most available inputs were directed to large private and state industries, and credit was tightened.

Thus, when the Sandinista government brought about a devaluation of the national currency and massive cuts in the public sector, the results were severe for the majority of the population and especially for low-income women. This accounts in significant part for the Sandinistas' electoral loss two years later and for the gender gap in the vote, with more women than men supporting the opposition. Nevertheless, the adjustment programs adopted by the postrevolutionary governments since 1990 have had even more severe consequences. Privatization, cuts in social spending, and a reduction of the state sector are familiar by now as key elements in the structural adjustment program, but in Nicaragua, the rate at which these measures have been implemented has been crushing—particularly for a country that had grown accustomed to the state providing a safety net for those most vulnerable in the society.

THE POST-SANDINISTA PERIOD

Soon after taking power, the Chamorro government embraced the structural adjustment model in an effort to stabilize the economy. Key components of the program have included reducing government spending (cutting back state sector employment and eliminating government subsidies of food, public utilities, and transportation), increasing the sales tax (affecting the poor most, since they spend a greater proportion of their income on goods that are taxed), devaluing the currency, increasing interest rates and reducing access to credit, privatizing state enterprises, promoting assembly plants in the free trade zone (largely textiles), and eliminating import tariffs (allowing cheaper imported goods to undercut national production). As a result of these harsh measures, 700,000 Nicaraguans left the country to seek work elsewhere, whenever possible sending home remissions to allow their families to escape the worst economic hardship.[3]

A new monetary plan in 1991 included a major currency devaluation that caused sharp socioeconomic dislocations as real wages fell and prices of many basic goods rose out of reach for the majority. That year, the Occupational Conversion Plan, funded by the Agency for International Development (AID), offered up to US$2,000 in severance pay to state-sector workers who would give up their jobs "voluntarily." Some 30,000 left by 1993 (25 percent of the total, and disproportionately women) and many more did so in the next couple of years. Some paid off debts and many more began selling food and other household items informally from their homes—having the intended effect of shifting workers from the public to the private sector.[4] By 1992, the "Year of Reactivation," privatization of industries and export-oriented production were proceeding apace. Inflation was brought under control, yet all indicators showed that Nicaragua had never had a worse depression, with levels of unemployment and poverty unprecedented in the country's history. Formal-sector employment dropped 18 percent in two years, with many workers leaving jobs in health, education, and other public services. Unemployment rose to 19 percent and underemployment to 45 percent (*Envío* 1992a: 18–20). The figures reached 20 percent and 54 percent respectively by 1995, making the unemployment rate twice that of 1990 and ten times that of 1984 (Arana 1997: 84).

An agreement known as the ESAF (Enhanced Structural Adjustment Facility) was signed in 1994 with the International Monetary Fund (IMF). In return for balance of payment stability, broad and stringent conditions had to be met. At the macroeconomic level there were signs of growth and recovery, but new problems emerged a year later when the country could not meet the requirements set by the IMF. The foreign debt reached over $11 billion, the highest per capita debt in the world. Furthermore, the wide gap between rich and poor remained, with poverty conditions unabated, and the high social cost of the plan came to be viewed as a key political issue.

With the rapid entry of competing foreign industries and products, cuts in credit available to national industry, and the removal of subsidies and some price controls, small producers and sellers faced a shortage of the primary materials needed in their work and a declining demand for the items they offer for sale. The strategy of establishing free-trade zones and favoring large industries that are more competitive in the world market, as well as sharply reducing protective tariffs on imported goods, has driven out many small industries and threatens to weaken many more in Nicaragua. As a result, the informal sector has expanded to absorb displaced workers from industries and from the shrinking, "more efficient" state sector.

Viewed by Western development analysts, the Nicaraguan government, and even some critics as inevitable, structural adjustment has curbed inflation while contributing to high levels of unemployment, declining real wages, and a sharply falling standard of living. Access to basic health care and education, available to all during the Sandinista period, became a privilege for the middle class. Although many new products, including luxury items, have entered the market, few people have the resources to buy them.

Once widely considered gender-neutral, structural adjustment has had particularly harsh consequences for women—something that has received attention in Nicaragua (Fundación Internacional para el Desafío Económico Global—FIDEG 1991a). Researchers have noted that the redistributive impact has been largely at the expense of women (Stahler-Sholk 1997; Metoyer 1997). Often, when men made up the majority of the newly unemployed, women were more numerous among the underemployed (Renzi and Agurto 1993). Since women made up the majority of state workers, they were disproportionately affected by cuts in the public sector, which sent many of them into the informal sector (Evans 1995). At work and in the family, women have often provided the cushion needed when resources are in short supply. Women seek new sources of income, stretch household budgets, and take up the slack by offering services that are no longer provided by the government. Thus, any success that structural adjustment may have in contributing to "productivity" and "efficiency" depends on a longer working day for women, who carry the major responsibility for maintaining their families. And this, of course, leaves in place the underlying structural basis of economic crises and gender inequality.

WOMEN AND URBAN COOPERATIVES

Changes in economic policy in Nicaragua have had particularly adverse consequences for low-income women. Throughout the country, women have worked harder to earn a livelihood and support their families, and in the capital city of Managua many have turned to small industries and commerce, organized formally or informally and based outside or within their homes. The government offered little assistance to small and medium-size enterprises or the informal sector, where the majority of Nicaraguans find employment, and instead relied on market forces which favored larger industries. When assistance was offered to small enterprises, the impact was limited.

During the Sandinista period, many small-scale producers were organized into cooperatives in the urban sector, just as in the rural, agricultural sector. The cooperatives were part of the state project to formalize and collectivize small industries to increase production and build class unity among workers. These co-ops benefited from the distribution of low-cost materials and from the state's assistance in marketing their products. Women were drawn into the newly formed cooperatives for the same reasons men were, but also as part of the deliberate effort to include women in the revolutionary process.[5] Unfortunately, while women were drawn into cooperatives as well as mass organizations, traditional gender relations persisted at home, making it difficult for women to carry out many new responsibilities and avoid men's criticism that they were not fulfilling their family "duty." Many men, even those who in principle supported women's right and responsibility to engage in the wider economy, feared that their wives were beyond their control as they gained access to space in the public sphere. Implicit or explicit was the traditional invocation of women's proper place in the home (*en la casa*) and not in the "street" (*en la calle*). Some women bowed to the challenge to their propriety as wives and mothers and left work in cooperatives, but many others actively engaged in economic and political work that took them outside the household. Unfortunately, economic policy in the postrevolutionary period generally has not favored small industry, instead encouraging foreign investment and larger industries that can better compete in the global market. As a result, many small industries (estimated at over half nationwide) failed in the early 1990s, and those that remained have struggled in the new political economic context (*Barricada Internacional* 1993).

My ethnographic research in Managua sought to provide in-depth local-level studies of working women as a window through which to view the effects of the dramatically shifting policy and the responses of women to these changes. Although women working in small industries and commerce form the majority of employed urban women in the country, they have rarely been the focus of research. The four urban cooperatives I discuss here formed after the Sandinista victory, one as late as 1991. Two of the co-ops were made up exclusively of women, while women figured prominently in the other two. Two involved women in traditional gender roles, in the preparation of clothing and food, and the others in nontraditional ones, in welding and artisanry. All felt the impact of the changing economic policies, and the women interviewed noted the adjustments that they themselves were making at work and at home in order to get by. These are frequently viewed as coping or survival strategies, but they should also be understood as women's response to economic policies that are transferring work from the public to the private sector. In their workplaces and in the household, women absorb the shock of the economic crisis, and in so doing they underwrite the very policies that adversely affect them.

WOMEN'S UNITED TEXTILE COOPERATIVE

The Women's United Textile Cooperative formed in 1982 as a service co-op, made up of women sewing clothing at home who came on a rotating basis to sell their clothes from a small store in Managua's Mercado Oriental (Eastern Market) district. Like other service co-ops formed under the Sandinista government, they benefited from the availability of lower-priced materials, in their case fabric and thread. They enjoyed the friendships they made with other women workers, and along with many other cooperatives they joined the National Chamber of Medium-and Small-Scale Industry (CONAPI), which allocated supplies and offered other support.

The co-op began with 68 members, but by 1991 its membership had declined to 29. Many of the remaining women were among the founders, now middle-aged or older women, who regarded the co-op as a sort of family to which they owed their loyalty. Like others in small industries, they identified the problems they were experiencing as stemming from postrevolutionary government support of large industries and elimination of assistance to small industries in the name of the "free market." The garment producers were particularly hard hit, however, as imported new and used clothing from the United States and elsewhere began flooding the market and underselling them. For those who retained active membership in the co-op, the altered conditions and slower sales stalled their production, and many sought other sources of income. Some began selling soft drinks or other items from their homes, and some, ironically, entered in the business of selling used clothing. As one woman put it, "The *compañeras* understand that I do it out of necessity."

The first half of 1992 saw an even more serious downturn for this cooperative. Its store, which had displayed racks of clothing made at home by members, stood nearly bare, and almost no customers came to make purchases. The women continued taking turns coming to the store but mainly to safeguard their property and to share a midday meal that they prepared together; everyone ate, regardless of ability to pay, and they had each other's company at a time when the mood was grim. Some expressed resentment that CONAPI had used them as a "battle horse" for the organization, praising the women's relatively long history and commitment, but saying nothing when times were hard. They were particularly bitter because the new president of CONAPI had been in the garment industry himself but changed to another business in time to avoid the problems they were facing. They felt that he had had a responsibility to advise them but instead had only looked out for his own interests.

The cooperative dealt in isolation with the difficult question of whether to sell its store and dissolve the co-op or to hang on a while longer. On my last visit to the store that year, I found the women in low spirits, feeling defeated, with a single rack of clothing for sale. Sadly, the items were imported second-hand clothing from the United States. One woman summed up the situation by saying, "The truth is, our chances of surviving here are slim." Indeed, when I returned to Nicaragua early in 1993 I was surprised to find that the store had simply vanished. Upon questioning, I learned that the co-op members had sold the store to a neighboring clothing retailer, who had absorbed the space to enlarge his own establishment. It took me several weeks to locate members who still identified actively with the cooperative and worked on some basis from their homes or in the streets. These women spoke of trying to find a new space in which to work together again, but in the meantime they were changing leadership and preparing to carry out business from the new coordinator's home.

Although the co-op's clothing production has dropped off sharply since that time, some members have put more time into attracting sales by selling to clients from their homes and from market stalls in the streets. Some have added shoes or other merchandise to their offerings. Still others concentrate on working to meet the seasonal demand for new school uniforms or Easter dresses. Those who continue to sew find that locating acceptable-quality fabric and thread at reasonable prices is more difficult, and therefore more time is put into searching for supplies. Several women travel regularly to other Central American countries to purchase sewing supplies or ready-made apparel at lower prices.

If economic policies that favor large garment factories and imported clothing have not yet put the women of this cooperative out of business, they are nonetheless struggling harder to retain sales. They extend their hours of work, diversify their production and their market, and travel greater distances to purchase materials and to make sales. In all these ways, they not only support themselves and their families but also underwrite the process of structural adjustment through their resolve to work harder and withstand its force. In spite of all their efforts, the women who continue to identity as members of the cooperative are still threatened with the prospect of failure.

INDUSTRIAL BAKERS OF MANAGUA

The largest service cooperative of bakeries, Industrial Bakers of Managua, was established in 1979. More men than women became members, but many had wives who worked closely with them, and a number of women owners of bakeries were represented as well. As members of the trade union organization CONAPI, they benefited from the co-op's provision of basic materials such as flour at lower cost. The co-op owned ample office space in a working-class neighborhood, where meetings were held regularly by the leadership.

Bread producers would seem to have the advantage of engaging in a business that would have a constant demand. Yet, as more bakeries open there is more competition, with larger enterprises having more chance of success. Some bakers reported changing with the times to offer popular items like pizza or sweet pastries. In one bakery where I conducted interviews, the family is proud of its college-educated daughter, who handles the bookkeeping and manages the enterprise, no doubt contributing to its success. Another family in the bakery business has cornered the market in one city neighborhood, with the mother doing business near a major traffic circle and her daughter managing her own bakery just a block away. The daughter has space for a half-dozen tables where customers can sit down to enjoy pastry and something to drink, thus drawing more people to the bakery. But even in these more fortunate enterprises production was declining sharply and the loss of income was threatening families' economic survival.

In early 1992, the cooperative ceased to function, having been driven out of operation when suppliers of flour began selling directly to the bakeries at favorable prices. Unable to compete, the co-op put its offices up for sale, and the bakeries I visited began viewing their enterprises as independent. They saw little advantage in affiliating with a trade-union organization that was itself struggling for survival. A year later the co-op's property remained unsold, and the formerly active secretary came periodically to sell a small quantity of bread there, half hoping that the co-op could be revived—a prospect that looked less and less likely. Bakery owners in general were divided between those who adopted the government attitude regarding the desirability of open competition and others who looked back nostalgically on the more protective policies of the Sandinista goverment. All appeared critical of CONAPI, noting its lack of support for the co-ops, whether or not they favored the continuation of the bakery cooperative. And all were demoralized by the economic situation that further reduced bread consumption as many families bought tortillas and even bananas as cheaper substitutes.

This cooperative's experience suggests that while some individuals place responsibility for their present difficulties on CONAPI or on the bakers' co-op itself, their problems stem from increasing competition and lack of government support in the market-driven economy. Like the garment producers, the bakers are highly resourceful, yet both are reporting that production is being cut dramatically, often by 50 percent, as sales dwindle.

FRANCISCO ESTRADA COOPERATIVE

Five jewelry makers and five bark-work artisans came together in 1987, working out of the home of one woman, a German who had come to Nicaragua in solidarity with the revolution during its early years. They founded the Francisco Estrada cooperative, named for an artisan and national hero, and became active within CONAPI. The men and women who made up their workshop included experienced jewelers who worked with silver, malachite, and black coral, resources found in the country, as well as a woman who specialized in making ornamental wall hangings and other items from the bark of trees found on the Atlantic coast. The latter trained several other women who became part of the co-op, though she herself left to work independently. Despite the high quality of their work, sales have remained low, limited to foreigners in Nicaragua seeking unusual artisans' crafts and the small number of Nicaraguans who can afford ornamental items. Two men, jewelry makers, left the co-op in 1992, and the other members explained their departure by saying that the men could not accept the crisis conditions that they were collectively facing. In response to these conditions, members began slowing down production and seeking new markets to increase sales.

As in the sewing cooperative described above, members of this co-op substituted time spent in marketing their products for production time. Often, several members would take an afternoon off to visit hotels or shops that might sell their jewelry or bark items. They also explored possibilities of exporting their work to European markets; however, these efforts did not result in many opportunities to expand their sales. Another strategy has been to try new techniques and designs to capture the interest of the buying public. This has sometimes backfired, however, as when two of the women invested many hours and costly materials to create several folding room screens with detailed bark work—and then the client, who had commissioned the work with a down payment, failed to come up with the remaining money owed. The co-op considered whether the bark workers should be apprenticed as jewelers (one already had been), since jewelry sales were somewhat better.

By 1993, however, the two remaining bark workers had left the co-op to return to their homes. Both said that the needs of their husbands and children demanded more of their time. Certainly another factor in the women's decisions was the very low level of their sales. They had virtually been subsidized by the jewelry makers for some time and may have considered themselves a liability to the co-op. In better times they might not have faced this difficult decision. More recently, the cooperative sought and received financial support to build a separate workshop and expand its productive capacity. Following months of effort requiring many visits to various offices, CONAPI and a Norwegian nongovernmental organization (NGO) gave the co-op the loan they needed for the construction. The artisans hope that as their visibility and their productive capacity grow, so will their sales. They have apprenticed several new women in jewelry making and have stepped up efforts to find markets outside Nicaragua. They acknowledge that they are taking a risk in incurring debts as they expand production, but morale has improved as they enjoy their spacious new workshop and the new equipment they have acquired.

As in the first two cooperatives described, this one has had some internal problems, but in general members have worked hard to build a successful working environment and viable business. The artisans in the Francisco Estrada co-op are recognized for the high quality and design of their products, but sales are down at a time when international travel to Nicaragua is low, few Nicaraguans purchase ornamental items, and those who do find better buys in imported jewelry and other artisanry from neighboring countries. While some government officials claim that so many small industries are failing because of the poor quality of their products and poor managerial skills, the examples offered here suggest ways in which new policies favoring larger industries and imported goods undermine the best efforts of many small producers.

WELDERS' COOPERATIVE

Finally, a fourth cooperative is one of welders that formed in 1991 after a group of ten formerly unemployed women completed a trade-school course. The women's preparation included not only ten months of technical training in welding but also consciousness-raising workshops organized by the vocational program INATEC (National Technical Institute) to ready them as women for nontraditional work. A sample of their work was displayed at an International Women's Day festival and soon afterward they inaugurated their workshop with a gala opening in one of Managua's women's centers, sponsored by AMNLAE. In high spirits, the women began their work with support from local organizations, making wrought-iron chairs and tables, plant stands, and security bars for windows and doors.

Jobs kept them busy in the early months, but then work tapered off and interpersonal problems developed over how work was shared. Some felt that the co-coordinators were lacking in necessary leadership skills. Other differences emerged when CONAPI sought their participation and the director of the AMNLAE center where they worked resisted this decision on feminist grounds, saying that the women would lose their autonomy under the male-dominated leadership. By mid 1992 only two welders from the original group remained active in the co-op. One of the co-coordinators, judged by others to be too much of an individualist for the cooperative, left to work in partnership with a male welder. Lack of work and heavy family responsibilities kept some women away, including a few who hoped to resume their work later. Eight new women began a training course, but within a few months only three remained. The continuing coordinator of the co-op surmised that the cost of transportation to the training center was prohibitive when the women lacked paid employment.

Despite these setbacks, the remaining welders devised several strategies for the survival of their co-op. Besides training new women, they consulted with several individuals regarding the promotion of their work. One woman, the designated advertising manager, polled the others concerning ways of becoming better-known around the city. The women continued to receive a few jobs by word of mouth and through INATEC. Given the competitive nature of work in welding and the discrimination against women in the field, the future looked uncertain. Those remaining in the co-op depended, for the most part, on other sources of family support to get through that difficult period. The women talked about refashioning the co-op as a microenterprise—a legal entity of up to five workers promoted by the government—to increase their likelihood of receiving a loan. During this time, two Peace Corps volunteers became involved with the welders, offering them workshops designed for women in small businesses and encouraging them to apply for development grants. To take this suggestion, however, they would have needed to invest more unpaid time before seeing a return, something they could ill afford.

By 1993 the welders' co-op had disbanded. Citing the family obligations of the other women, the former coordinator (the only single woman among them) expressed disappointment at their failure to continue working together. The lack of work and an unresolved disagreement over the use of space in the women's center surely entered into the decision of the women to return home, though the coordinator emphasized the "jealousy of husbands." Her own passionate commitment to welding led her to join briefly with several male welders, but the relationship was a tenuous one. Her outlook during our last meeting was grim.

In this cooperative, the only one of the four discussed here that had ceased to function by 1993, family needs and expectations were often cited as drawing women back home and away from their paid work. This was also the case for the two women doing bark work in the last co-op mentioned. While this might be interpreted as the result of individual circumstances rather than changing economic and political conditions, I would maintain that the two are intertwined. As I have noted, structural adjustment has often resulted in heavier responsibilities for women at home when social services are cut, health care and education costs rise, and household incomes drop. The competing demands on women's time and energy, often divided between the family and the workplace, become especially acute when conditions of austerity and adjustment combine with a conservative social ideology. At a certain point the day can be stretched no farther and women must negotiate "personal" solutions to their collective problems.

WOMEN IN THE URBAN INFORMAL SECTOR

As women in cooperatives and other formal-sector employment are losing ground in Managua, many are turning to a precarious livelihood in the urban informal sector. There, small-scale production and commerce, often based in the home, do not benefit from protective legislation or the representation of a trade-union organization. While earnings are typically quite low, there is great diversity within the informal sector in terms of economic activities and the individuals who perform them (Chamorro, Chávez, and Membreño 1991).

The urban informal sector has for some time included over half of Managua's economically active population, but there has been significant growth in recent years. Under the Sandinista government, some informal workers were "formalized" as they joined cooperatives and state enterprises. Now that these are being reduced in the interest of streamlining the economy, people are falling back on independent and informal activities. Recent policy has had the effect of transferring even more workers from the public to the private sector. The Plan for Occupational Reconversion, mentioned before, was introduced to encourage public-sector employees to leave their jobs and set up small businesses. Many who left public-sector jobs were Sandinistas, considered undesirable by the new government, or women, viewed as appropriately turning their attention back home. Home is no refuge, however, when women must work double time to take care of families and earn incomes by undertaking a host of small-scale informal activities in manufacturing and commerce. Far from supporting sustainable enterprises, one result of the plan was an abundance of freezer purchases allowing people to sell drinks or ice out of their homes.

The Managua barrio where I stay is known for its high concentration of artisans and sellers and a smaller number of professionals. I have found city blocks in which a majority of households are also small commercial establishments, operating both informally and formally. Small restaurants, barbershops, and carpenters', tailors', and mechanics' workshops are among the most visible. Less obvious from the street are the many households engaged in selling small quantities of fruit, vegetables, soft drinks, or other goods out of their homes' front rooms. In the poorest families, children add to the family income by selling in the streets or by asking for tips for guarding parked cars.

Interviews with people in this barrio often led from conversations about declining business and deteriorating standards of living to discussions of how women are attempting to survive crisis conditions. The stories told in people's homes were often poignant. A young woman I spoke with one morning as her two children sat nearby was employed as a teacher but seeking other sources of income to support her family. Her husband's business had failed four years before, around the time her second child was born. Under the Sandinistas they had received the package of support for state workers that included rice, beans, and sugar. Now they received no such benefits. Her husband had been deeply affected by his unemployment, consulting a psychologist and later converting to an evangelical faith that had finally brought him some peace of mind.

Another young woman I visited lived with her three children, selling ice cream, soap, and chlorine from her home to support them. Her brother, who had once lived with them, had taken his life two months earlier out of despair over the economic situation they faced. The woman talked on for a time, distraught and clearly needing to unburden herself. She blamed privatization and other changes in the country for her brother's suicide, adding that women were the most affected, especially because many did not have the support of men at home.

A visit with another woman in the barrio led to a conversation with a number of family members. In all, 30 people were living in the four rooms of her home. Besides her husband and five children, her mother and several sisters and their husbands shared the household, as did their many children. This woman had been an active Sandinista and her husband had been part of the revolutionary insurrection. Their hardship by the early 1990s was clearly demonstrated by their surroundings and their dress. When I visited, they had no water or electricity, since they could not pay the bills. Their lack of a functioning refrigerator affected not only their eating habits but also their ability to sell food or drink items from their home. Their close quarters were unbearably hot, with no fan to relieve them, and they had to carry water in pails from a park a few blocks away. As they took me through their very crowded house, they indicated the number of people who slept in each of the beds and joked self-consciously about the sorry state of their inexpensive shoes.

The sources of family income in this household included the husband's low salary as a police officer, a son-in-law's employment as a typographer, another son-in-law's earnings as a market porter, and a daughter-in-law's sales of cooked ears of corn, candy, and gum in the street in front of their home. A teen-aged daughter who worked part-time helping in meal preparation and cleaning in the home of a neighbor may have been the top income-earner in the family, making just over $100 a month; she lost the job soon after my visit, however, when she was caught stealing from her employer. While three of the older children in the family attended college, most of the children had dropped out of school because of new fees and the rising cost of uniforms and shoes.

With little money even for food, the family sometimes had nothing to eat. They tried to feed the youngest ones first, when possible. In the morning, they generally had coffee; when there was no milk, the children drank sugared water. Other foods they bought included rice, eggs, cheese, and tortillas, but rarely beans since the price had risen so high. In the past they had shopped in a supermarket to save money, but by this point they were purchasing just a little at a time at a corner market to save on transportation costs and because they had little cash on hand at any given time. With medical costs rising, they made few trips to see doctors, and their general level of health appeared rather poor.

Like many in the barrio, members of this family expressed the view that things were far better before the Sandinistas lost the elections in 1990. They mentioned the distribution of basic foods, the better employment situation, and the active part they had played in neighborhood politics. "Now there is nothing," they said. When I asked if men and women were affected differently, they first said no, but then the senior woman added that women suffered more because they cared for the children and had to see that low incomes stretched to meet family needs.

Another woman who had lived in the barrio for many years was in somewhat better circumstances. Several adults, including her grown children, contributed income to her household. She herself managed a front-room store, selling items that she advertised with a number of makeshift signs displayed outside her door along with Sandinista campaign posters left over from the 1990 elections. The signs suggested the range of goods that she had sold at one time or another: cheese, cream, beans, bread, and snacks, ice and ice cream, soft drinks, *chicha*, black dye, used clothes. She smiled when I asked if she sold all of these items, saying that she was currently selling just a few things, including bread, cheese, cream, eggs, soft drinks, and beer.

Beginning in 1960, she and her husband sold materials for shoemaking, but the business was declining by the late 1970s. With the "Triumph" in 1979, they started the store she has today and during the next decade they expanded to sell basic grains. Yet by 1988–1989, this business was also suffering, and by 1993 they were even worse off. She attributed the economic problems of the Sandinista government to the war and the blockade and said that at least people had had something to eat, since the government had provided basic foods at lower prices. Before, there were loans for small businesses, but now those who could get them had to pay high interest rates for short-term loans. With no money circulating and high unemployment caused by the poor leadership of the new government, she told me, the situation was critical.

This woman described for me how she and her family got along during a recent "difficult time" when her sales were low. Although she is skilled as a seamstress and still has a sewing machine in her front room where she used to sew for clients, she now sews mainly for family. Her husband's small retirement income helped, as did the food and other needed supplies brought by friends from time to time. Much of the personal support that she counted on, however, came from her long-time political commitment to a group of women whose relatives had been killed or disappeared during the revolutionary insurrection. As a community leader she had a wide network of friends and acquaintances who met often, and she told me that this helped relieve some of the psychological pressure that is prevalent in the country as a consequence of the economic crisis. Her story suggests the importance of women's organizing to confront current political and economic conditions and to maintain a safety net of social support.

STRUCTURAL ADJUSTMENT OR STRUCTURAL CHANGE?

Women in Managua's barrios did not all share the same political views, but many of them sounded critical of the postrevolutionary government as they commented on the ways in which they were coping at home and at work with low earnings, rising prices, and inadequate services. Many noted that their families' eating habits had changed; instead of waking up to large meals of rice, beans, eggs, and cheese, they just had a bit of *gallopinto* (mixed rice and beans) and coffee. Instead of having three abundant meals, including meat, each day, they included meat in their diet only about once a week. They looked longer and harder for less expensive foods. Other women cut back on transportation costs, opting to walk to places where they had formerly taken buses. Some who had had the resources in the past to hire other women to wash and iron their clothes were doing this work themselves. Those who had always done this work themselves were restricting it to once or twice a week to save on soap and electricity. In addition, with an apparent deterioration of physical and mental health in the country, women were taking on the care of family members in ill health. These household responses to the crisis conditions brought on by adjustment policies in Nicaragua have parallels in a number of other Third World countries.

What is distinct about Nicaragua is the way in which the fast pace and devastating effects of these policies have eroded the gains brought about with the Sandinista revolution. Yet, also distinct is the readiness of the population to mobilize in opposition to these policies. The decade of broad participation left a legacy of expectations that has been challenged but not eliminated since 1990. The persistent determination of Nicaraguans to take part in the political process and to retain their hard-won rights is expressed in everyday strategies of resistance to the economic crisis, as well as through organized social protests.

I suggested at the beginning of this essay that we need to reexamine women's strategies for confronting crisis conditions in their paid work as well as at home. By offering examples of women working in urban cooperatives and in the urban informal sector, I have shown that even in instances where production and sales have slowed down, working women often step up their efforts to get by. They often work longer hours to find affordable materials, to acquire the skills they need, and to gain access to markets for their products. The strain of surviving under conditions that are driving many small industries and commercial enterprises out of business surely affects their ability to carry out family responsibilities, too. Therefore, we need to examine the interconnectedness of women's unpaid and paid work as both are extended in response to current economic policies.

Almost half of the households in Nicaragua's cities are headed by women, and women make up at least 44 percent of the economically active population. Policies that do not take gender into account stand to have serious effects on the health and well-being of these women and their children. My work and that of others (Afshar and Dennis 1992; Benería and Feldman 1992; Elson 1991) presents evidence that structural adjustment is cushioned by women whose discretionary time and energy are already extremely limited. The human cost of recent policies will be seen in the long term if the consequences of these policies are not considered now.

Structural adjustment, by introducing new competition and reducing national demand, has led to the decline of many urban cooperatives and small industries established under the Sandinistas in Nicaragua. A report by CONAPI (*Barricada Internacional* 1993) indicated that some 7,000 small and medium-sized industries and services closed in 1992 alone, leaving just 3,000 shops registered with the Ministry of Economy. Since women have been disproportionately represented in the co-ops and industries, the decline has hit them particularly hard.

Some writers have argued that more enlightened approaches to structural adjustment would lower the high cost exacted among the most vulnerable sectors in Third World countries (Cornia, Jolly, and Stewart 1987; UNICEF 1989). However, they overlook the adverse effects of adjustment programs on both men and women in broad sectors of the population and the ways in which structural inequalities of gender, class, and race serve to underwrite economic "stabilization." We have seen that women, in particular, subsidize the cost of national development through their extended workdays. Other analysts more in line with the view presented here have been more critical of structural adjustment and have called for discussion of more far-reaching structural transformation (Gladwin 1991). Such discussion should be informed by the experiences of countries such as Nicaragua that have broken away—for a time—from the dominant economic development models.

In Nicaragua, a nation that has seen the structural transformation of the 1980s rolled back to a significant degree since the 1990 election, discussion of alternatives to the current economic model has begun (*Envío* 1992b). During a brief period, the country went through two major transitions, from a market economy dominated by the Somoza family dictatorship to a state-regulated economy under the Sandinistas and back to a market-driven program under postrevolutionary governments. These were not simple shifts between capitalist and socialist models, however, but rather negotiated processes that often allowed for unexpected economic juxtapositions. While state intervention in the market characterized the Sandinista period, the current period is also marked by a significant degree of market regulation by the government (Spoor 1994). The political lines from the 1980s to the present have been no less complicated. Just as some Sandinistas became critical of the party and adopted a supportive stance in relation to government policy, some business elites supported the Sandinistas in the past and currently oppose undercutting national production through structural adjustment. While it was widely expected that the gains of the revolution would be dismantled in the post-Sandinista period, the transition has been considerably more complex (Spalding 1994: 157).

Not surprisingly, women are among the most vocal in questioning the current economic model and pressing for substantive change. As active participants in the Nicaraguan revolution, they claimed a space in which to assert their rights to full citizenship. In the late 1980s these women found new ways to organize and confront difficult conditions as the demands on their time increased both in the labor force and at home. Although women's participation in political organizations declined in the 1990s, their engagement in the labor movement grew stronger (Pérez-Alemán et al. 1992: 250). In the postrevolutionary period, there have been new openings for women's activism despite the deepening problems the country is facing. While AMNLAE no longer plays a strong leadership role, emergent feminist and women's organizations are growing along with NGOs and social movements. Thus, while women in Managua's urban cooperatives and informal economy are experiencing tough economic conditions in their workplaces and their homes, through their struggle for better lives and livelihoods these women are also challenging Nicaraguans to seek alternative national policies that will benefit all of society.

REFERENCES

Afshar, Haleh and Carolyne Dennis (eds.). 1992. *Women and Adjustment Policies in the Third World.* New York: St. Martin's Press.

Arana, Mario. 1997. "General Economic Policy." In *Nicaragua without Illusions: Regime Transition and Structural Adjustment in the 1990s.* Thomas Walker, ed. Pp. 82–96. Wilmington, DE: SR Books.

Babb, Florence E. 1996. "Women's Movements and Feminism." In *Cross-Cultural Research for Social Science.* Carol R. Ember and Melvin Ember, eds. Pp. 23–40. Englewood Cliffs, NJ: Prentice Hall.

———. 2001. *After Revolution: Mapping Gender and Cultural Politics in Neoliberal Nicaragua.* Austin, TX: University of Texas Press.

Barricada Internacional. 1993. "Recession decimates small businesses." 13 (January): 7.

Benería, Lourdes and Shelley Feldman, eds. 1992. *Unequal Burden: Economic Crises, Persistent Poverty, and Women's Work.* Boulder, CO: Westview Press.

Blumberg, Rae Lesser. 1991. "Income under female versus male control: hypotheses from a theory of gender stratification and data from the Third World." In *Gender, Family, and Economy: The Triple Overlap.* Rae Lesser Blumberg, ed.. Pp. 97–127. Newbury Park, CA: Sage.

Booth, John A. 1985. *The End and the Beginning: The Nicaraguan Revolution.* Boulder, CO: Westview Press.

Brenes, Aria Julia, Ivania Lovo, Olga Luz Restrepo, Sylvia Saakes, and Flor de Maria Zuniga. 1991. *La Mujer Nicaragüense en los Años 80.* Managua, Nicaragua: Nicarao.

Chamorro, Amalia, Mario Chávez, and Marcos Membreño. 1991. "El Sector Informal en Nicaragua." In *Informalidad Urbana en Centroamérica: Entre la Acumulación y la Subsistencia.* J.P. Pérez Sáinz and R. Menjívar Larín, eds. Pp. 217–257.

Collinson, Helen, ed. 1990. *Women and Revolution in Nicaragua.* London: Zed Books.

Cornia, Giovanni Andrea, Richard Jolly, and Frances Stewart (eds.). 1987. *Adjustment with a Human Face.* New York: Oxford University Press.

Criquillon, Ana. 1995. "The Nicaraguan Women's Movement: Feminist Reflections From Within." *The New Politics of Survival: Grassroots Movements in Central America.* Minor Sinclair, ed. Pp. 209–237. New York: Monthly Review Press.

Elson, Diane. 1992. "From Survival Strategies to Transformation Strategies: Women's Needs and Structural Adjustment." In *Unequal Burden: Economic Crises Persistent Poverty and Women's Work.* Lourdes Benería and Shelley Feldman, eds. Pp. 26–48. Boulder, CO: Westview Press.

Elson, Diane, ed. 1991. *Male Bias in the Development Process.* Manchester, England: Manchester University Press.

Envío. 1992a. "Economic takeoff: the little train that couldn't." 11 (October): 18–20.

———. 1992b. "A national project." 11 (December): 31–40.

Evans, Trevor. 1995. *La transformación neoliberal del sector público.* Managua, Nicaragua: CRIES (Coordinadora Regional de Investigaciones Económicas y Sociales).

Fernández Poncela, Anna M. 1996. The Disruptions of Adjustment: Women in Nicaragua. *Latin American Perspectives* 23(1): 49–66.

Gladwin, Christina (ed.). 1991. *Structural Adjustment and African Women Farmers.* Gainesville, FL: University of Florida Press.

Kampwirth, Karen. 2002. *Women and Guerrilla Movements: Nicaragua, El Salvador, Chiapas, Cuba.* University Park, PA: The Pennsylvania State University Press.

Metoyer, Cynthia Chávez. 1997. "Nicaragua's Transition of State Power: Through Feminist Lenses." In *The Undermining of the Sandinista Revolution* Gary Prevost and Harry Vanden, eds. Pp. 114–140. New York: St. Martin's Press.

———. 2000. *Women and the State in Post-Sandinista Nicaragua.* Boulder, CO: Lynne Rienner.

Molyneux, Maxine. 1986. "Mobilization without emancipation? Women's interests, state, and revolution," in Richard R. Fagen, Carmen Diana Deere, and José-Luis Coraggio (eds.), *Transition and Development: Problems of Third World Socialism* pp. 280–302. New York: Monthly Review Press.

Montoya, Rosario. 1996. *Fractured Solidarities: Utopian Projects and Local Hegemonies among a Sandinista Peasantry, Nicaragua, 1979–1995.* Ph.D. dissertation, University of Michigan.

Padilla, Martha Luz, Clara Murguialday, and Ana Criquillon. 1987. "Impact of the Sandinista Agrarian Reform on Rural Women's Subordination." In *Rural Women and State Policy: Feminist Perspectives on Latin American Agricultural Development.* Carmen Diana Deere and Magdalena León, eds. Pp. 124–141. Boulder, CO: Westview Press.

Pérez-Alemán, Paola. 1990. *Organización, identidad y cambio.* Managua, Nicaragua: Editorial Vanguardia.

Pérez-Alemán, Paola. 1992. Economic Crisis and Women in Nicaragua. In *Unequal Burden: Economic Crises, Persistent Poverty, and Women's Work.* Lourdes Beneria and Shelley Feldman, eds. Pp. 239–258. Boulder, CO: Westview Press.

Randall, Margaret. 1981. *Sandino's Daughters: Testimonies of Nicaraguan Women in Struggle.* Vancouver, BC: New Star Books.

Renzi, María Rosa, and Sonia Agurto. 1993. *Que hace la mujer nicaragüense ante la crisis económica?* Managua, Nicaragua: FIDEG (Fundación Internacional para el Desafio Económico Global).

Spalding Rose J. 1987. *The Political Economy of Revolutionary Nicaragua.* Boulder, CO: Westview Press.

———. 1994. *Capitalists and Revolution in Nicaragua: Opposition and Accommodation, 1979–1993.* Chapel Hill: University of North Carolina Press.

Spoor, Max. 1994. "Issues of state and market: from interventionism to deregulation of food markets in Nicaragua." *World Development* 22 (4): 567–578.

Stahler-Sholk, Richard. 1997. "Structural Adjustment and Resistance: The Political Economy of Nicaragua under Chamorro." In *The Undermining of the Sandinista Revolution.* Gary Prevost and Harry Vanden, eds. Pp. 74–113. New York: St. Martin's Press.

Tinker, Irene (ed.). 1990. *Persistent Inequalities: Women and World Development.* New York: Oxford University Press.

UNICEF. 1989. *The Invisible Adjustment: Poor Women and the Economic Crisis.* Santiago, Chile: UNICEF.

Walker, Thomas W. 1986. *Nicaragua: The Land of Sandino.* Boulder, CO: Westview Press.

Walker, Thomas W. (ed.). 1991. *Revolution and Counterrevolution in Nicaragua.* Boulder, CO: Westview Press.

———. 1997. *Nicaragua Without Illusions: Regime Transition and Structural Adjustment in the 1990s.* Wilmington, DE: SR Books.

NOTES

1. For further discussion of the impact of structural adjustment on women in Nicaragua since 1990, see Babb 1996, 2001, Metoyer 2000, and Fernández Poncela 1996.
2. A number of writers have offered extensive analyses of this decade of revolutionary government in Nicaragua (e.g., Booth 1985; Spalding 1987; Walker 1986, 1991). A few have considered the situation of women in the revolutionary process (Randall 1981; Molyneux 1986; Padilla, Murguialday, and Criquillon 1987; Collinson 1990; Kampwirth 2002). See Babb 1996 and Criquillon 1995 for discussion of emergent feminism in Nicaragua in the postrevolutionary period.
3. A summary of the effects of neoliberalism and structural adjustment is offered by Nicholson in the newsletter *Nicaraguan Developments* 7(1): 4–5 (1999).
4. In his discussion of structural adjustment programs under the Sandinista and post-Sandinista

governments, Stahler-Sholk (1997) indicates that while Violeta Chamorro de Barrios's government made some attempt to soften the blow of adjustment by offering limited support for employment, this barely offset the growing rate of unemployment.

5. See Montoya 1996 for a useful discussion of women's involvement in two rural cooperatives organized during the Sandinista period and the mixed success they had due to difficulties faced by many cooperatives as well as persistent male bias against women's participation in the economy and society beyond the household. Her work examines the general problems women faced as they made claims to public space usually controlled by men. See also Pérez-Alemán 1990 for discussion of women's participation in rural cooperatives in the Sandinista period and the difficulty of carrying the burden of housework and childcare as women performed more agricultural work.

V

The Cultural Construction of Gender and Personhood

We all live in a world of symbols that assign meaning and value to the categories of male and female. Despite several decades of consciousness raising in the United States, advertising on television and in the print media perpetuates sexual stereotypes. Although "house beautiful" ads are less prominent as women are increasingly shown in workplace contexts, "body beautiful" messages continue to be transmitted. In children's cartoons, women are still the helpless victims that the fearless male hero must rescue. Toys are targeted either for little boys or little girls and are packaged appropriately in colors and materials culturally defined as either masculine or feminine (see Jacqueline Urla and Alan C. Swedlund in Section 6 of this book).

To what extent are these stereotypes of men and women and the symbols with which they are associated universal? If they are universal, to what extent are they rooted in observed differences in the biological nature of men and women that are made culturally significant? These questions have interested scholars as they have attempted to account for both similarity and difference among the people of the world. Making the assumption that the subordination of women exists in all societies—a "true universal"—Ortner (1974: 67) sought to explain the pervasiveness of this idea not in the assignation of women to a domestic sphere of activity, but in the symbolic constructions by which women's roles are evaluated. Ortner argues that women, because of their reproductive roles, are universally viewed as being closer to nature while men are linked with culture. She defines culture as "the notion of human consciousness, or . . . the products of human consciousness (i.e., systems of thought and technology), by means of which humanity attempts to assert control over nature" (72). That which is cultural and subject to human manipulation is assigned more worth than that which is natural; hence, women and women's roles are denigrated or devalued, whether explicitly or implicitly.

The nature–culture dichotomy is a useful explanatory model in the United States where, according to Martin (1987: 17), "Women are intrinsically closely involved with the family where so many 'natural,' 'bodily' (and therefore lower) functions occur, whereas men are intrinsically closely involved with the world of work where (at least for some) 'cultural,' 'mental,' and therefore higher functions occur. It is no accident that 'natural' facts about women, in the form of claims about biology, are often used to justify social stratification based on gender."

Although this model may be applicable in some cultures, its universality has been challenged not only by those who point out that nature–culture is a dichotomy of western thought in particular (Bloch and Bloch 1980; Jordanova 1980; Moore 1988), but also by those who provide ethnographic data to indicate its lack of salience in other cultures around the world (Strathern 1980). Similarly, the assumption that women are universally subordinated while men are dominant (Ortner 1974: 70) appears questionable when viewed through the lens of recent ethnographic analysis. The critique of the concepts of universal subordination and of the nature–culture dichotomy has stimulated significant research on how gender identity and gender roles are constructed in particular cultural contexts (Errington and Gewertz 1987; Ortner and Whitehead 1981; Weiner 1976). Whether and under what conditions social asymmetry between men and women emerges in the process of this construction is open to empirical investigation.

The cultural construction of gender in a particular society involves definitions of what it means to be masculine or feminine, and these definitions vary cross-culturally. In this book, David D. Gilmore takes up the question of how masculinity is culturally constructed by describing his encounter with machismo in the southern Spanish region of Andalusia. He outlines three components of Andalusian "manhood"—virility, valor, and virtue. Men must live up to the anatomical equipment with which they are born—to enact their virility. There are certain rites of passage—including the activity of *abuchear*—associated with this enactment. Real manhood implies seduction. But it also requires bravery, heroism, and hard work—the elements of valor or *hombria*. Finally, being honorable, a person of rectitude, decency, and generosity, is essential to Andalusian manhood. The behavior of Spanish men in bars (Driessen 1983) must be viewed in this light. As Gilmore argues, to stay away from the bars and to hold back one's purse is considered unmanly and effeminate.

Gilbert H. Herdt (in this book) also focuses on the manhood, examining how it is constructed in the context of ritual among the Sambia of New Guinea. The Sambia, like many other societies in New Guinea (Biersack 2001; Brown and Buchbinder 1976; Herdt 1982; Meigs 1984; Roscoe 2001), are characterized by a high degree of segregation and sexual antagonism between men and women, both of which are reinforced by powerful taboos. These taboos, and other facets of Sambian male identity including that of the warrior, are inculcated during a series of initiation rituals whereby boys are "grown" into men. As Herdt observes, the Sambia "perceive no imminent, naturally driven fit between one's birthright sex and one's gender identity or role" (1982: 54). Indeed, Sambian boys and men engage in what some societies would label homosexual activity, yet they do it to create masculinity. It is precisely for this reason that an analytical distinction is often made between "sex" as a biological classification and "gender" as a set of learned social roles.

Through the rituals of manhood Sambian boys are progressively detached from the world of women, a world they occupied for the first six or seven years of their lives and which they must now learn to both fear and devalue. This process of detachment has been identified by Chodorow (1974) as a major phase of human male development. If it is unmarked and therefore ambiguous in most western cultures, it is marked in many nonwestern cultures and often associated with male circumcision. Among the Mende of Sierra Leone (Little 1951), for example, boy initiates are seized from their homes by the force of spirits—men wearing masks and long raffia skirts. In this act they are dramatically and suddenly separated from their childhood, and carried into the bush where they will spend several weeks in seclusion and transition before they reemerge as men.

Gilmore (1990: 11) sums up the importance of these rituals to construct manhood by identifying a recurring cross-cultural notion: that "real manhood is different from simple anatomical maleness, that it is not a natural condition that comes about spontaneously through biological maturation but rather is a precarious or artificial state that boys must win against powerful odds" (1990: 11). He examines a post-Freudian understanding of masculinity as a category of self-identity, showing how boys face special problems in separating from their mother. A boy's separation and individuation is more perilous and difficult than a girl's, whose femininity is reinforced by the original unity with her mother. Thus, to become separate the boy must pass a test, breaking the chain to his mother.

Initiation rituals that prepare girls for their roles as women and instruct them in what it means to be a woman in a particular cultural context can also be found in various societies around the world (Brown 1963; Richards 1956). However, the transition to womanhood is often part of a more subtle and continuous process of enculturation and socialization. In a description of Hausa socialization, Callaway (1987) demonstrates how girls in this society learn how to behave in culturally appropriate ways. The Hausa are an Islamic people who live in northern Nigeria. Historically, ruling-class Hausa women had significant authority and social standing, but with the expansion of Islam this position was eroded and a sexually segregated society characterized by female subordination emerged. Hausa girls marry young, generally upon reaching puberty. At that time they enter kulle, or seclusion. In seclusion, the social roles of women are specifically defined and their sexual activities are limited. Though a Hausa woman becomes part of her husband's family, her place is secured only by bearing sons, and all her children belong to her husband. Hausa women are taught the expected life course from early childhood. In Hausa society, Callaway (1987: 22) claims, "the reproduction of 'masculine' and 'feminine' personalities generation after generation has produced psychological and value commitments to sex differences that are tenaciously maintained and so deeply ingrained as to become central to a consistent sense of self." This self is defined by reproductive roles and by deference to men; thus a good daughter-in-law gives her first-born child to her husband's mother, an act that strengthens family ties.

Conceptions of the self or personhood are, as Henrietta Moore (1988: 39) has observed, "cross-culturally as variable as the concepts of 'woman' and 'man.'" Personhood is constituted by a variety of attributes. In addition to gender, it may comprise age, status in the family and in the community, and physical appearance or impairment. In many cultures naming is also an important mechanism for constructing personhood. In the United States, for instance, the use of Ms. to replace Mrs. and Miss is an acceptable option. It is increasingly common for married women to retain the name that they were born with rather than replace it with one that only gives them an identity in relation to someone else—their husband.

Among the Chambri of New Guinea, initial identity or personhood is gained through a totemic name given by a child's patrilineal and matrilateral relatives. According to Errington and Gewertz (1987: 32, 47), "these names both reflect and affect the transactions which constitute a person's fundamental social relationships and identity. . . . Totemic names allow both men and women to pursue respectively their culturally defined preoccupations of political competition and the bearing of children. The totemic names available to men, however, convey different sorts of power and resources than do those available to women. . . . Men seek to augment their own power through gaining control of the names of others. . . . The power conveyed by [women's] names cannot shape social relationships as does the power of names men hold, but, instead, ensures reproduction."

Women's names among the Chambri work in different ways from those of men, but they nonetheless enable women to claim personhood in Chambri society. The married Chinese women described by Rubie S. Watson (in this book) have an entirely different experience. They are denied individuating names, and through this denial their personhood is in question. They remain, says Watson, "suspended between the anonymous world of anybodies and the more sharply defined world of somebodies." In contrast with the namelessness of Chinese women, men in Chinese culture acquire numerous names as they pass through the life cycle. Nowhere is the difference more apparent than at marriage—a time when a man acquires a name that symbolizes his new status and public roles and a woman loses her girlhood name and becomes the "inner person." Like the Hausa women who assume an identity with respect to their husbands, Chinese women begin newly married life by learning the names and kinship terms for all their husbands' ancestors and relatives. Namelessness follows them to the grave—anybodies in life, they become nobodies at death.

Personhood is also encoded in the language that men and women use. Indeed anthropologists and others have focused on the relationship between language and gender, building on the pioneering work of Lakoff (1975) and, more recently, Deborah Tannen (1990). In many cultures around the world, speech styles differ between men and women while in others there are no distinctions (Keenan 1974; Sherzer 1987). Sometimes these differences are associated with the relative equality/inequality between the sexes, and hence with power. As Susan Gal (1991: 177) has written, "some linguistic strategies and genres are more highly valued and carry more authority than others." Bonnie McElhinney (this book) takes up the topic of gendered language and its relation to authority and personhood in her research on the Pittsburgh police department. She links gender to race and class, offering a complex analysis of how police officers talk about the use of physical force and how this has affected the integration of women into the police profession, a traditionally male occupation. Equally at issue is the extent to which women police officers use "tough talk" and whether this usage results in them being described as more masculine or less feminine, as well as more or less competent as police officers.

In many societies, personhood for women is also associated with conceptions of the body (Conklin 2001; Diemberger 1993). Sarah Lamb (in this book) addresses the gendered nature of the body and how it makes and unmakes the social ties of Bengali Indian women over the life course. Purity among Bengalis is associated with touching and the controlled exchange of bodily fluids. Women are considered more impure than men and hence must bathe more often and must observe cultural practices that discipline their bodies—spatial seclusion, cloth covering, and so on. Their bodies are more open and hence more vulnerable; menstruation marks the beginning of openness—a sign of readiness for marriage and reproduction. At her wedding, a time when her personal identity is changing, a Bengali woman must absorb substances originating from her husband's body and household. This also represents a severing of ties with her natal family and a forging of ties with her husband's family. Similarly later in life, and as a widow, women begin to unmake ties. When a woman loses her husband she becomes half a person and if young, Lamb tells us, "not merely a sexual hazard, but also a repulsive anomaly." In old age, when they are past reproduction, their bodies close and cool and they regain purity. Postmenopausal women become "like men" and enjoy many of the freedoms that men enjoy.

The readings in this section of the book all emphasize that the biological categories of male and female are foundations upon which culturally defined and culturally appropriate gender roles and gender identities are constructed by both men and women in any society. What it means to be masculine or feminine varies across cultures, across social locations defined by such factors as class, ethnicity, or employment sector, and over the life course.

REFERENCES

Biersack, Aletta. 2001. "Reproducing Inequality; The Gender Politics of Male Cults in the Papua New Guinea Highlands and Amazonia." In Thomas A. Gregor and Donald Tuzin (eds.). *Gender in Amazonia and Melanesia,* pp. 69–90. Berkeley: University of California Press.

Bloch, Maurice, and Jean Bloch. 1980. "Women and the Dialectics of Nature in Eighteenth-Century French Thought." In Carol MacCormack and Marilyn Strathern (eds.). *Nature, Culture and Gender,* pp. 25–41. Cambridge, UK: Cambridge University Press.

Brown, Judith K. 1963. "A Cross-Cultural Study of Female Initiation Rites Among Pre-Literate Peoples." *American Anthropologist* 65(4): 837–853.

Brown, Paula, and Georgeda Buchbinder. 1976. *Man and Woman in the New Guinea Highlands.* Washington, DC: American Anthropological Association, Special Publication, number 8.

Callaway, Barbara J. 1987. *Muslim Hausa Women in Nigeria: Tradition and Change.* Syracuse, NY: Syracuse University Press.

Chodorow, Nancy. 1974. "Family Structure and Feminine Personality." In Michele Z. Rosaldo and Louise Lamphere (eds.). *Woman, Culture, and Society,* pp. 43–67. Stanford, CA: Stanford University Press.

Conklin, Beth. 2001. "Women's Blood, Warriors' Blood, and the Conquest of Vitality in Amazonia." In Thomas A. Gregor and Donald Tuzin (eds.). *Gender in Amazonia and Melanesia,* pp. 141–174. Berkeley: University of California Press.

Diemberger, Hildegard. 1993. "Blood, Sperm, Soul and the Mountain. Gender Relations, Kinship and Cosmovision among the Khumbo (NE Nepal)." In Teresa del Valle (ed.). *Gendered Anthropology,* pp. 88–127. London and New York: Routledge.

Driessen, Henk. 1983. "Male Sociability and Rituals of Masculinity in Andalusia." *Anthropological Quarterly* 56: 125–133.

Errington, Frederick, and Deborah Gewertz. 1987. *Cultural Alternatives and a Feminist Anthropology: An Analysis of Culturally Constructed Gender Interests in Papua New Guinea.* Cambridge, UK: Cambridge University Press.

Gilmore, David. 1990. *Manhood in the Making.* New Haven, CT: Yale University Press.

Herdt, Gilbert. 1982. *Rituals of Manhood: Male Initiation in Papua New Guinea.* Berkeley and Los Angeles: University of California Press.

Jordanova, L. J. 1980. "Natural Facts: A Historical Perspective on Science and Sexuality." In Carol MacCormack and Marilyn Strathern (eds.). *Nature, Culture and Gender,* pp. 42–69. Cambridge, UK: Cambridge University Press.

Keenan, Elinor Ochs. 1974. "Norm-Makers and Norm-Breakers: Uses of Speech by Men and Women in a Malagasy Community." In Richard Bauman and Joel Sherzer (eds.). *Explorations in the Ethnography of Speaking,* pp. 125–143. Cambridge: Cambridge University Press.

Keesing, Roger. 1985. "Kwaio Women Speak: The Micropolitics of Autobiography in a Solomon Island Society." *American Anthropologist* 87: 27–39.

Lakoff, Robin. 1975. *Language and Women's Place.* New York: Harper and Row.

Little, Kenneth L. 1951. *The Mende of Sierra Leone: A West African People in Transition.* London: Routledge and Kegan Paul.

Martin, Emily. 1987. *The Woman in the Body: A Cultural Analysis of Reproduction.* Boston: Beacon Press.

Meigs, Anna S. 1984. *Food, Sex, and Pollution: A New Guinea Religion.* New Brunswick, NJ: Rutgers University Press.

Moore, Henrietta. 1988. *Feminism and Anthropology*. Minneapolis: University of Minnesota Press.

Ortner, Sherry. 1974. "Is Female to Male as Nature to Culture?" In Michelle Z. Rosaldo and Louise Lamphere (eds.). *Woman, Culture, and Society*, pp. 66–87. Stanford, CA: Stanford University Press.

Ortner, Sherry, and Harriet Whitehead. 1981. *Sexual Meanings: The Cultural Construction of Gender and Sexuality*. Cambridge, UK: Cambridge University Press.

Powers, Marla. 1986. *Oglala Women*. Chicago: University of Chicago Press.

Richards, Audrey I. 1956. *Chisungu: A Girls' Initiation Ceremony among the Bemba of Northern Rhodesia*. London: Faber and Faber.

Roscoe, Paul. 2001. "Strength and Sexuality: Sexual Avoidance and Masculinity in New Guinea and Amazonia." In Thomas A. Gregor and Donald Tuzin (eds.). *Gender in Amazonia and Melanesia*, pp. 279–308. Berkeley: University of California Press.

Sherzer, Joel. 1987. "A Diversity of Voices: Men's and Women's Speech in Ethnographic Perspective," In S. Philips, S. Steel, and C. Tanz (eds.). *Language, Gender and Sex in Comparative Perspective*, pp. 95–120. Cambridge: Cambridge University Press.

Strathern, Marilyn. 1980. "No Nature, No Culture: The Hagen Case." In Carol MacCormack and Marilyn Strathern (eds.). *Nature, Culture and Gender*, pp. 174–222. Cambridge, UK: Cambridge University Press.

Tannen, Deborah. 1990. *You Just don't Understand. Women and Men in Conversation*. New York: William Morrow.

Weiner, Annette. 1976. *Women of Value, Men of Renown*. Austin: University of Texas Press.

My Encounter with Machismo in Spain

David D. Gilmore

Let me begin with a disclaimer. When I first went to Spain as a novice anthropologist in 1972, I did not choose machismo to study. On the contrary, machismo chose me: I had no choice. This happened during my dissertation fieldwork in the southern region of Andalusia. Being a child of the 60s and influenced by the then-fashionable mix of Marxism and do-goodism, I originally went to Spain with the intention of studying (and possibly ameliorating) the "objective realities" of what I saw as oppression under the Franco dictatorship. I envisioned a scholarly thesis on weighty matters like class consciousness and workers' rights, with an emphasis on the clandestine labor organizations that were springing up as Franco breathed his last (he died in 1975 and the dictatorship fell soon afterwards). However, while collecting data, I soon ran into a practical problem. While conducting informal discussions and interviews,

Original material prepared for this text. Reprinted by permission of the author.

I was constantly bombarded by verbal static emanating from my subjects. By "static" I mean background noise, chatter—talk about tangential topics. Since this noise struck me as irrelevant, rather like radio interference, I largely ignored it. As I soon learned this was a mistake.[1]

One's person's noise can be another's symphony. When interviewed, people would get bored talking about politics, and to liven things up would launch into gratuitous pronouncements about more interesting subjects. The most common detour was the subject of sex, perhaps not surprisingly since most of my informants were unmarried youths. Usually these impromptu digressions would lead to colorful accounts about the nature of male and female, about what a "real man" should be, "being macho" and so on. Often the talk would segue into mild boasting about how they, the Andalusians, were superior to other Spaniards in matters romantic, and certainly better than benighted foreigners such as myself. As often happens to tyro anthropologists—and despite my intentions—I became sidetracked by the "subjective reality" of sex talk and eventually the static took on a life of its own. After returning to the U.S., and for years afterwards I tried to avoid thinking too hard about it, dismissing it all as youthful braggadocio. But after having written some dull treatises on politics, I retuned to what had imposed itself upon me so urgently in the field. In what follows I will explain how—and what—I learned about Andalusian "machismo."

Of course I learned other things. For example, I learned to appreciate the good old anthropological "culture concept," about which I had been indoctrinated in graduate school. While this hoary tenet has been questioned recently by some postmodernists (see Abu-Lughod 1993), it has withstood the test of time. As anthropologists have said, culture consists of shared understandings and standards held by a group: a body of mutually-agreed upon values, norms and beliefs that work as a non-verbal grammar and also as a source of identity, of ethnic pride, and of group unity. As I quickly learned in Andalusia, people's notions of manhood (and of its converse, femininity, too, of course), were very different from my own, and indeed contrasted starkly with what I had read about other cultures elsewhere. Moreover, these ideas about gender were not only widespread, but they were enthusiastically shared by both sexes, were consensual among all ages, and were repeated by different people in different settings. Ideas about what a "real man" was, especially, were cherished by virtually all the men I knew and by many women as well. These ideas made up a very substantial part of Andalusian culture.

It is also important to point out that whatever discrepancies might exist between these ideas and my own cannot be ascribed to differences in social-class between me and my informants, as a critic has meretriciously alleged (Pina-Cabral 1989). Nor are these differences due to a deficient understanding about working-class culture in my own native America. I can say this because most of my informants in Spain were not in fact working class at all. Rather, they were similar to me in status, being mainly middle-class professionals,

and they possessed an impressive vocabulary to articulate their ideas. Some were college graduates; one or two, like me, were in graduate school. Among them was a sprinkling of high-school teachers, menial workers and farmers. A few were peasants, and one or two were illiterate landless laborers who joined our almost nightly talk sessions. So I was dealing with a decidedly cross-sectional sample, with an emphasis, if anything, on the middle classes—a social setting rather analogous to my own in America.

As these nightly gabfests would gather steam, many of these friends and acquaintances would join in until we were often twenty or more guys chewing the rag, or "cutting the cloth," as they say in Spain. The conversations took place during long walks in the village park or in the bars where village men relax for hours, sipping wine or coffee, playing cards or dominoes and of course chatting. Sometimes, the men who were absent at one occasion would confirm my written notes later. All this continual affirmation led me to conclude I was dealing with a "cultural fact," because when one encounters a point of view so widely and repetitively expressed, it constitutes something objectively real, a fact. There was of course some variation of opinion as there is in any society, but such variations were of degree, not of kind. Agreement on the main principles of a proper manhood was virtually unanimous.

VIRILITY, VALOR, VIRTUE

Let me provide some ethnographic context. The largest region of Spain, Andalusia makes up most of the southern part of the country. In many ways it is similar to America's "Deep South" or the Mezzogiorno of Italy, being a largely agrarian region, socially and culturally conservative compared to the rest of the country, and having its own distinctive accent, a "southern drawl," and well known for cultural peculiarities, in this case peculiarities from which other Spaniards often disassociate themselves as being backward or dubious. In the northern regions of Castile or Catalonia for example, many people say that Andalusians are lazy, carefree, given over to wine, song and sloth—the usual prejudices about "southerners" one encounters in Europe and America. Andalusia is also the region most closely identified with the stereotypical Spain of the travel posters: bullfights, flamenco music, raven-haired maidens with roses in their teeth, perfumed gardens, mantillas, and, of course, don Juanism. Remember that the original don Juan story was set by Tirso de Molina (1571–1648), in Seville—the unofficial capital of Andalusia.

First, before recounting my experiences, let me emphasize my main point: *machismo* and *manliness* are not synonymous in Andalusia. Although this region has been identified in some accounts as the epicenter of so-called "Hispanic machismo," and supposedly transported thence throughout the Spanish-speaking world by Andalusian emigrants (see Gonzalez-Lopez and Gutmann 2005), nevertheless the manhood code here is complex and cannot be reduced to a single factor. What I propose to do here is to explain how the bundle of manhood traits imposed itself on my ethnographic radar in Spain, then to describe the components of the manhood code, "machismo" being just one, and, finally, to compare this package briefly with such codes elsewhere. The reader will immediately gather that the so-called "machismo" so tirelessly invoked in social science in actuality represents a wide diversity of forms all of which have something in common and are therefore amenable to comparative analysis. What is needed here is what Ward Goodenough, borrowing from descriptive linguistics, has called the method of "componential analysis." This method involves breaking down a semantic category into its constituent parts and analyzing each independently before putting the whole together again as an over-all pattern, a Gestalt. Goodenough explains (1970: 72):

> . . . a linguistic expression may be said to *designate* a class of concepts or images. It may be said to *denote* a specific image or subclass. . . . And it may be said to *signify* the criteria by which specific images or concepts are to be included or excluded from the class of images or concepts that the expression designates. What is signified consist of the definitive attributes of the class, the

ideational components from which the class is conceptually formed. Componential analysis is a method for forming and testing hypotheses about what words signify.

Briefly put: the main components of Andalusian "manhood" (that is, the subclasses constituting native ideas) are three, which I will here gloss as: *virility, valor,* and *virtue.* Each has its own linguistic label in standard Castilian, which will discussed in turn as we proceed. I begin by describing some eye-opening experiences from my first few months in the rural town of Fuentes de Andalucía—my research site in Spain since 1972. Fuentes is small farming pueblo (population 7,500) located in Seville Province, about equidistant between the provincial capitals of Seville and Cordoba. The ethnographic present used here is the decade between 1972 and 1982. Since then, of course, it has all changed with modernization—but that is a subject for another study.

VIRILITY: THE MACHO

Attending to my original research program, I made friends with a number of young men (and a few women), usually seeking them out in their favorite bars or taverns. When one meets regulars in any bar in Spain, one very soon is introduced to a large coterie of friends and friends-of-friends—a kind of spontaneous expanding network that makes fieldwork in Spain both easy and pleasurable. I found that very often my queries about subjects of concern to me would be sidetracked by more immediate interests of my friends, as I suppose is true in any social setting. But I found this to be true especially where a comparison or analogy, often invidious, could be drawn between what their own self-image and what they attributed to "*forasteros,*" (outsiders). The latter term included not only strangers from other parts of Spain, but also foreigners from what they referred to as "the north," meaning northern Europe and North America. Such exotics were referred to as "*nórdicos*" (Nordics) in what anthropologists nowadays call an invocation of "the other," that is, the formulation of a stereotype as a straw man. Although not a *nórdico* by ethnic persuasion, I became their resident representative from this mysterious world, which was to them an unofficial sounding board to their native Andalusian habits and customs.

One evening I was sitting in a bar with about ten friends, talking as usual about why Spain "is different" as the travel posters say, when the conversation turned to the influx of European tourists on the Costa del Sol, that is, the Spanish beach resorts—a hot topic and one that gave grist to the mill for judgmental comparison. The ensuing conversation turned on the point of supposed characterological differences between the nórdicos and the Andalusians. Something they had noticed keenly was the behavior of the foreign men on the crowded resort beaches. The nórdicos, they observed, would sit quietly amongst scantily-dressed tourist women and "do nothing"—an egregious act of omission which proved the inherent superiority of the Andalusians. The logic went as follows.

My friends noted that the northerners who visit the Costa del Sol beach resorts (mainly British, Germans and Scandinavians) go out to take the sun and swim in the company of beautiful blonde women who wear virtually nothing. "Those men," he scoffed, "do nothing. Are they men?" This lack of any reaction at all to the unclothed female he found both notable and bizarre. An Andalusian man would not let such an opportunity pass. A real man must "do something," a real man answers the call of his manhood. My friend repeated: some remark must be said, some sort of pass made, "something, anything" must be done to acknowledge the opportunity for a *lio*, or romantic connection.

Now, occasionally, the Spanish men observing all this at the beach resorts would converse in broken English with the foreigners in some bar and this subject would come up. My friends said that the nórdicos would explain that they were "just friends" with these naked girls, a concept that incited incredulity and scorn from the Andalusians. To get the point across my friends would recite one of their favorite aphorisms. "A man and a woman," they would say,

"cannot be friends, unless the woman is very, very ugly and the man very, very foolish (*tonto*)." Explanation: to neglect one's manhood not only qualifies a man for contempt as inert, but also, as my comrades emphasized stupid, "foolish." A shy man is not only unmanly but also brainless and unnatural. Another term they used in this context is significant: weak men are called *flojo*. In Spanish *flojo* means inadequate, flaccid, weak, or soft. Literal dictionary definitions also include flabby, lax, loose, slack and sluggish. Andalusians of both sexes use *flojo* liberally to describe a flat tire, a broken tool, or anything that does not work, often with derisory connotations of debility and perversity. The analogy to sexual impotence is of course obvious: a man who "can't get it up," like a dead battery or a punctured tire, is *flojo*. But more, such a man is said to neglect his natural duty to inspire romance and make a *lio*. So even more than merely signifying inadequacy or inutility, *flojo* carries with it a strong whiff of moral disapproval and opprobrium. I detected in all this not only contempt for the moribund nórdicos, but also an invidious judgment and a not-so-hidden self congratulation. There were nationalistic overtones to all this. This piqued my curiosity and naturally provoked further discussions.

I learned that the quality being adjudged here is "being macho" (*ser macho*). Although *machismo* is a perfectly good Spanish word (Castilian nouns take an *-ismo* ending as with the cognate *-ism* in English) it is never used in everyday speech in Spain, except nowadays as an epithet by university feminists. As elsewhere in Hispanic countries "macho' simply means "male" (Gonzalez-Lopez and Gutmann 2005). It connotes explicitly anatomical maleness, the possession of a penis and testicles. When a child is born, or a farm animal calved, for example, the first thing people ask is, "Macho o hembra?" (male or female?). "Hembra" means both female and, literally, womb; so the sexes here are initially distinguished by reproductive physiology, as is the case in many societies. But for a postpubescent male in Andalusia to "be macho" (*ser macho*) has a special the connotation of living up to the qualities attributed to the male physiology. In Andalusia, being macho means using your anatomical equipment in the expected ways; or at least giving the impression of doing so. Further concrete examples and some colorful illustrations flowed from my friends. Telling the poor deluded nórdico anthropologist about "being macho" was becoming a cottage industry in Fuentes.

A few days later, I was out walking at dusk with a few friends. We came upon a group of about twelve boys, 13 or 14 years old, milling about in one of the central squares of the pueblo. These youth packs are called *pandillas* (cliques or gangs). While nothing unusual in that male *pandillas* are often seen lurking outdoors at any time of day or night, my ethnographic alarm bell went off and told me this group was poised for some mischief which might be of interest. So I made inquiry to my companions. They told me the following. What I was witnessing was the first stage of a traditional adolescent activity called the "*abuchear*," a word I later found translated loosely as shouting, jeering, or hooting. My informants immediately understood what was going on because they had participated in such rituals themselves in their teens. The boys were in fact lying in wait for some unsuspecting and, more importantly, unaccompanied, young girl to pass by. When one did, they would rush after her, hollering obscenities, jeering and grasping at her clothing, driving her crying to her home, at which point they would relent and reorganize to repeat the process with another victim. The boys did not physically molest the girls (physical abuse is against the rules), but their victims were usually shaken up and frightened. In one famous case of abuchear, I was told, a girl ran home in tears, her clothes in tatters, and told her father that she recognized the persecutors. Angry and insulted, her father then went to the boy's house to extract an apology from the boy's father; some words were exchanged. But the response of the hooting boy's father remains a classic piece of folklore in the pueblo. Rather than being chagrined or apologetic, the father coolly replied, "Why thank you for telling about this: that means my boy must be a real macho." He took it as a compliment.

Obviously, the central theme in "ser macho" is the erotic element: by *virility* here I mean

pure sexual potency, sexual assertiveness. Ser macho implies an adventurous, probing, phallic sexuality that is both predatory and peremptory. My friends consistently defined "macho" in terms of a quantifiable energy stemming from the *cojones,* testicles. When I asked a friend what macho meant in a fly-specked bar (he was a university-educated youth) he pointed to two copulating flies on the counter and said, "You see that fly, the one on top? That's what we mean by *macho.*" A refrain I heard often touted in these discussions was this: we Andalusians are more highly sexed than forasteros— this was offered often as a scientific fact. Andalusians are more potent, more irrepressibly sexual than others; they have larger penises and heftier balls (a legacy some said proudly of the Moorish occupation of Andalusia). Indeed, this was the only instance I heard anything complementary said about "los moros," the generic term Andalusians use for Arabs and Muslims. One of my friends added, "You know, don David, that's how we Spaniards conquered the Americas: one hand waving the sword, the other the penis!" (I learned later this was a common saying in Spain). So macho, then, means being a sexual conquistador.

THE PIROPO

Further conversations ensued as my friends continued amplifying on what they meant by *macho.* I heard many other local sayings, for example: "Dress a shovel in a dress and we *fontaniegos* [male residents of Fuentes] will gladly make love to it: that's macho." Then there is the venerable tradition called *el piropo,*" which remained strong in both rural and urban Andalusia until very recently (Pitt-Rivers 1971: 92). This requires a brief digression. The word *piropo* means a complement or an offering given by a man to a passing woman in public (literally it means a ruby). It can mean a gift or a gallantry of any sort, but in modern-day usage it refers to a linguistic tradition of cavalier flirtatiousness. In Andalusia, the piropo is a verbal "something," "a spoken gift" or symbolic acknowledgement that a man offers to a comely woman passing by. If a good-looking girl walks by unaccompanied by a man (piropos are off-limits when the girl has a man with her for obvious reasons of prudence), her sexual allure must be commented upon, even in some abstract sense, "something, anything," as my informants repeated, "must be done." To fail to do something is to be egregiously *flojo*, to be deficient in masculinity. Piropos are expected especially when men are in groups, as each outdoes the other in expressing appropriate lust. I recorded some of these piropos from Fuentes and some from other pueblos; they range from the chivalrous and polite to the ugly and vulgar. For example, a youth, bowing slightly or raising his cap, will say to a passing girl: "I salute your mother, to create such a beauty as you." He may then pucker up and offer a kiss, make lurid lip-smacking noises, or pantomime a dance step. Or, if less courtly, he may shout "Hooray for the brunette (or blonde, or whatever), let me hold you in my arms, let me make passionate love to you." The girl always ignores the comment and walks on. If the boy feels he has been insufficiently forceful, he may pursue the girl down the street issuing further pronouncements, and these can get aggressive and lewd (see Suarez-Orozco and Dundes 1984 for some crude Latin American examples).

Sometimes, when boys from Fuentes traveled to the next town or to a big city where they were less known, their terminology would indeed degenerate into aggressive witticisms and obscenities. However, whatever the words, the symbolic communication of the piropo was always the same. The men told me that the verbal dart was not directed so much at the woman, who, unless an actual prostitute, was always immune and never reacted, as to the general *male* audience: its purpose was to "show that you are a man," to demonstrate virility. A man, they said, needs to show his manhood constantly, to show that he never fails to appreciate feminine pulchritude and that he has no hesitations about it. Otherwise there may be doubt.

Another American anthropologist, Irwin Press, who was working in the city of Seville at about the same time I was in Fuentes, found much the same thing among relatively sophisticated urbanites. Press notes that a man in

Seville feels it necessary to make a piropo in order to express his masculinity publicly, to show "his nature verbally" (1979: 133). Other anthropologists in Spain have collected hundreds of these pronouncements once again from the poetic to the uncouth. Press collected some colorful examples in his entertaining book on Seville (1979: 133–134). His remarks on this subject are worth repeating at some length:

> Traditionally, the piropo was a statement of admiration to a woman as she walked by. Piropos ranged from the elegant ("The stars and moon are at your feet, along with I, your slave, my pretty!") to the ludicrous ("I worship the mushroom that grows in the shade of the tree which you grace with your presence, beautiful!"), from the simple ("I salute your mother, my beauty!") to the complex. Today's [1979] piropos are more direct. . . .
>
> Jose Maria the painter, thirty-seven years old, married but a year, stands with his buddies at the bar when two shapely but very heavy young women walk by, arm in arm. "Wow!" Look at this!" he cries to his friends. "Real juicy!" They run to the door of the bar and José Maria calls out to the girls, "Oh, how sweet this meat is, fitting sepulcher in which to bury myself!" The girls continue on, pretending to hear nothing. "Ooooooo, but I'd like to suck your cunts," he hisses loudly after them, and returns to the bar stool with his approving friends, whereupon the conversation shifts to the vulval virtues of fat versus thin women.

The corollary to such lechery is recognized outside Spain as don Juanism, personified in the image of Latin Lover, a deathless stereotype which figures prominently in folklore about all the Mediterranean peoples (for vicissitudes of the Italian variant, see Reich 2004). Stereotype it may be, but it nevertheless reflects a real, self-appointed and certainly unapologetic aspect of the masculine self-image in Andalusia. My friends insisted that a real man takes advantage of sexual opportunities regardless of context, and he does so because this is his god-given nature as a man, which he has a sacred duty to heed. So it is often said that one is not a real man who does not at least attempt to seduce an available (unattached) woman, and thus, in consequence, a man and a woman cannot be Platonic friends, unless, as they say, the girl is very ugly or the boy is very foolish. My friends adhered to these sexist sentiments without any self-doubt or squeamishness.

While in Fuentes, my friends would often resort to the abundant local poetry to get certain points across when I was being obstinate or dense. There is an old tradition in Andalusia of reciting oral poetry to hammer home a point, especially those that reflect community themes and concerns. In Fuentes, for example, many local bards (all the poets are men) composed raunchy ditties every year to be sung during February carnival, and they would march around the village with accompanists and shout their lyrics in exchange for drinks. So, in keeping with this tradition, my friends decided it would help illustrate local attitudes by reciting salacious carnival songs. I repeat one such exemplary poem below, composed in the 1960s by a most famous carnival poet. In it, a nameless everyman encounters an unchaperoned young girl, called Isabel, out at dusk seeking to buy milk. Confronted by such a rare opportunity, and being too wily to settle for a mere piropo and too mature for the abuc-hear, the hero of the piece performs what is expected, maneuvering the maiden into sex in a dark doorway:

Y en la Alameda me preguntó una criada,
Me dijo que si vendía
La leche merengada,
Y yo le dije: 'eso no lo vendo yo,
Pero aquí tengo un tubito
Que apretándole un poquito
Echa leche pa' los' dos.
Vamos ligero que aquí no estamo' mojando;
Vamos a una cada puerta y me la sigues topando.
Y ella me dijo, dice la niña Isabel:
"¡¿Porque me siento un chorrito
Que me coje del ombligo
Hasta la punta de los pies!?"

Once in the park I happened upon
A serving girl, who asked me
If I sold fresh milk.
I answered no, this I do not sell,
But better still, I have little spigot here
Which when squeezed a little bit,
Will make "milk" enough for both of us.

So let's not tarry here, we might get wet.
Let's go to some doorway
So I can give you what you need."
And then she cries out, does the maiden Isabel:
"Oh why do I feel a gushing that
Shakes me from the navel to the toes?!"

The song repeats a common analogy made between male "milk" (semen) and breast milk. Perhaps it also reflects the universal male fantasy of the willing rape victim; but despite the crude metaphors the ditty evoked amusement and approval among my male friends. The innocent young maiden Isabel, not knowing what she wants, must be seduced by the cunning, tricky male. His high-voltage sexuality is uncontainable—a life-force that gushes and spurts. It is no coincidence that the original Don Juan story is entitled "the Trickster of Seville" ("El Burlador de Sevilla"). For the macho, any means, fair or foul, are acceptable to make a conquest.

A final anecdote will conclude this account; then we will look at other ingredients in Andalusian manhood. When I first went to Spain I was with my wife, and she frequently accompanied me during fieldwork. One week early in our stay in Fuentes, she returned briefly to the States. She was gone only for about a week. During this time I was conspicuously alone in the pueblo. My friends regarded this as a trial, for it is thought that without a woman to take care of him, a man is helpless and pathetic. Soon my friends became concerned for my wellbeing. They conferred among themselves, debated and finally sent a delegation to my house one evening. "Don David," they said, "now that your wife has been away all this time [three days], you must need a woman. So we have agreed to take you to Carmona [the nearest big town] and to get you a nice clean whore." When I told them this was unnecessary, they professed disbelief: "No grown man can last for more than one day without a woman. Come on, we'll take you in your car, you drive." They were being merry of course, but not facetious.

This erotic fixation is the phallic component of manhood, and for simplicity's sake, I call it *virility*. It constitutes the first and most flamboyant symbol of manliness. As well as providing a unitary and global theme to the subject in Andalusia—a shared understanding—it deviates somewhat from other instances of "machismo" such as the North American, so far as I understand it. For most Andalusians, physical power, feats of strength and bravery are not considered part of "being macho." Indeed, pugilistic prowess, fighting, issuing challenges, or taking silly risks with life and limb, and so on are highly devalued. In Andalusia, men cherish a deep culture of civility which preludes displays of bravado or belligerence. Similarly, toughness and athleticism, which seem to loom large in America, are scorned as childish and vulgar. Rarely does one see physical confrontations among Andalusians—a fact that other ethnographers working in the area have noticed. In the pueblo of Almonaster (Huelva Province), there exists "a total proscription on all expression of overt hostility. There are no angry shouts, scuffles, offenses to property, or even stumbling drunks on the streets" (Aguilera 1990: 13). In Santaella (in neighboring Cordoba Province), "the actual use of fighting is rare and people strongly devalue fighting" (Driessen 1983: 129). The same is true in Fuentes. In twenty years of working there I never witnessed a single physical fight or even a brief scrap among men. The idea of a "barroom brawl" is anathema to these genteel, courteous folk.

OTHER "MACHISMOS"

Given the above, we should perhaps pause here to take note of the very salient discontinuities between Spanish machismo and the so-called machismos of other places and times. First of all we have a semantic problem. In my opinion, the ethno-label "machismo," like other sociological words such as "unilinear" or "matrilocal" is in danger of becoming reified aprioristically into a pigeonhole, an example of lexical "butterfly collecting." There are many variants of hyper-masculinity codes throughout the world. All of them have something in common, perhaps (because men have to "do something" to prove themselves; there are tests of manliness, etc.); but all have widely different emphases and nuances. It is true that cognate forms have been reported throughout the Spanish-speaking world, especially in Mexico, and so a supposedly monolithic "Hispanic machismo" has been held up as a kind of classic model for comparative purposes (see, for example, Lewis 1961; Ingham 1964: 96). One must point out, however, that even the model of Mexican machismo has been subject to its own critical scrutiny lately and come in for a drubbing as being ethnocentric (Gutmann 1996, 1997). There is also, for example, the Sicilian *maschio* or manliness code (Giovannini 1987: 66) and the *rajula* complex of swaggering Moroccan youths (Mernissi 1975; Geertz 1979), the violent *wand-nat* concept of Ethiopian tribesmen, and the bellicose *pwara* masculinity cult of the Trukese islanders in the South Pacific (Marshall 1979; for more examples, see Gilmore 1990; Guttman 1997). Most of these male codes have been explicitly likened to "Mexican machismo" by their observers; and indeed the ubiquitous use of the Spanish term tends to conflate variants under that vague rubric (for a review, see Gilmore and Uhl 1987).

In most of these variants of machismo, of course, fighting and violence play a big role. For example in the Truk case, the youths demonstrate their manly *pwara* by Kung Fu combat and in weekend fistfights, and some Ethiopians show their *wand-nat* in whipping battles and by beating each other up (Levine 1966; Reminick 1982). In Sicily, Sardinia, and Greece, men may engage in violent vendettas and feuds, and may they steal each others sheep or compete in singing and dancing contests, or engage in verbal duels, and so on (Campbell 1964; Herzfeld 1985; Sorge 2007). But in the Andalusian variety, for whatever historical reasons, violence is specifically excluded from the ideal, and as we have seen "ser macho" is fixated purely upon erotic prowess and is directed only at women (possibly the same historical actors have militated also against the violent mafias that one finds, for example in southern Italy). In other words, an Andalusian man cannot act "macho" with *only* other men present. To be macho in Andalusia needs a woman as sexual object, a *tertium pro quid*. All this brings us to the second component in manliness, which I call "valor." Here, physical bravery, and in some extreme cases, even fighting, may play a role. But such behaviors are not part of the Andalusian meaning of "macho."[2]

VALOR: BRAVERY

An emphasis on civility limits belligerence in Andalusia to a degree unknown among men in many places. But, civility notwithstanding, men in Andalusia are expected to stand up for what they believe in and to show determination in the face of danger, even if this means a fight. But this is a different matter from machismo. It constitutes a totally distinct semantic subclass of manliness, one analogous to what we might call "heroism." In Spain, in casual conversation they call a man "strong" (*un hombre fuerte*), if he stands up for himself and specifically, protects his dependents. When a man shows moral courage, they call it "valiant" (*valiente*). Valor constitutes our second component of masculinity. The qualities connoted add up to charisma. Together these criteria have their own name: *hombría*, or simply, "manhood." A man can be valorous and thus have hombría and not be a "macho" and vice versa. *Hombría* was a subject that men were somewhat less enthusiastic to talk about, but it came up in discussions later in my fieldwork; some of which are described below.

First, when my friends and I began conversations relating to courage as opposed to machismo, many resorted to a concrete example of the bullfighter (matador). One must note the matador does not fight other men, but shows—as Hemingway put it in his Spanish stories—grace under pressure. Perhaps the difference between North American machismo, as I understand it, is that for most Andalusians, bravery is not played out in contests with rivals, but rather against the inimical forces of nature, against injustice, or against adversity in the workplace. An important ingredient here is the sense of duty or obligation. This theme is often conveyed when my friends (male and female) would say that a "real man" was one who worked hard under harsh or perilous conditions and who never complained,

never ran away, who was "a hard worker" and who made "sacrifices" for his family. When I spoke to women about masculinity, they often referred to this abstract quality: a real man works hard, they said, never complains, and brings home the bacon. We hear such sentiments in working-class cultures in America also, and in many other places around the world where men are expected to do their duty (a man's gotta do what a man's gotta do). The word "dignity" (*dignidad*) is often invoked in this context.

Men sometimes compete about *hombría*; so it can indeed involve contests between men. As a form of heroism, hombría is shown off in multitudinous ways. For instance, in Fuentes, a group of young men, usually after a few late drinks at a bar, will meander down to the municipal cemetery to exhibit their disdain for ghosts and goblins. On their way the boys will acquire a hammer and a nail or a metal spike pinched from some garbage heap or borrowed from someone's toolbox. After arriving at the cemetery and climbing over the five-foot high wall, they posture drunkenly for a while, then one of them pounds the spike into the cemetery's stucco wall, while reciting the following formula:

Aqui hinco clavo	Here I drive in a spike
Del tio monero	Before goblin or sprite
Venga quien venga,	And whoever appear,
Aqui lo espero!	I remain without fear!

The last man to flee wins the laurels as the bravest. Occasionally, I was told, young men may challenge one another to spend the night in the cemetery, but otherwise hombría is non-confrontational, as in the above instance in which the threat is displaced onto a supernatural object. Men and boys do not fight each other in shows of athletic prowess or even compete much in aggressive sports or games, although young boys do play soccer. One-on-one competition among older men is confined largely to dominoes, cards, competitive drinking and, ironically, generous barroom "inviting," as we saw above. The Hollywood "tough-guy" had little resonance in Andalusia. "Only Americans and Germans shove each other around like that," the men told me dryly. Of course, Spaniards slaughtered each other during the Civil War, but a line is drawn between the unavoidable violence of war and the civility of peacetime.

HOMBRÍA AND "HONOR"

Julian Pitt-Rivers, who worked in Andalusia in the 1940s and 1950s, has perhaps depicted this quality of valor/hombría best: "The quintessence of manliness is fearlessness," he writes, "a readiness to defend one's own pride and that of one's family" (1971: 89). Perhaps the best way to get the idea across is to quote an old Andalusian saying which conveys the image both metaphorically and ironically in a typical Andalusian inversion: "El hombre como el oso, lo mas feo, lo mas hermoso." A rough translation: "Men are like bears, the uglier they are, the handsomer." What this means is that, unlike women, men are not supposed to be pretty or charming. Rather, a man should be strong, resolute, and determined, and even perhaps a little feisty (I call this "The beauty of the beast").[3] Masculine "beauty" is a moral, not an aesthetic, value, consisting of a man's ability to inspire respect—even fear—in the observer, rather than sympathy or love.

Unfortunately, the emphasis on valor has sometimes been, mistakenly I believe, conflated with the obsolete notion of a belligerent "honor." For Pitt-Rivers for example, honor in Andalusia as elsewhere in the Mediterranean World is a gender-bound quality, or "sex-linked." Only men have honor. The most important attribute of honor, in this traditional view, is that it forms the main public arena for a competitive masculinity based upon the sexual modesty of one's kinswomen. As Pitt-Rivers (1977: 45) remarks, "The honor of a man is involved . . . in the sexual purity of his mother, wife, and sisters." Another expert on Andalusian male norms and the author of *Metaphors of Masculinity* (1980), Stanley Brandes seems to concur in his study of a pueblo in nearby Jaen Province. He points out (1980: 75) that "a woman's sexual purity must be maintained lest her entire family's image be tainted. It is the husband's prime responsibility to control the conduct of his wife and daughter. If the females should go astray, their behavior reflects as much on him as on them." I found that in Fuentes, it was the mother, not the father, who policed the sexual morality of her daughter, but no matter. One finds similar statements in virtually all the works on Andalusia, rural and urban. Men are like bears in this regard: fierce in defense of self and kin. Most important in all this is the defense of ones' women. This is the one arena in which violence may be acceptable. One recent and well-reported incident will perhaps illustrate this.

In February of 2000, hundreds of men in and around the Andalusian pueblo of El Ejido (Almería Province) went on a violent rampage, attacking immigrant north Africans who had come to their district to take low-paying jobs in agriculture that the newly affluent Spaniards had rejected. This riot was not altogether spontaneous. The men had organized their attack days before, and armed with sticks and clubs chased, beat and pummeled Africans throughout the region. The depredations went on savagely for three days: one Moroccan man was beaten to death and many others injured before the national police intervened to stop the riot. What triggered the incident, according to local accounts, was the rape and murder of Spanish woman a few days earlier, after which a Moroccan immigrant had been arrested and charged with the crime. Interestingly enough, tensions had been running high between the Spaniards and the north Africans for months, even years, before the riot, but these had never erupted into a full-scale lynch mob attack. Interviewed later, some of the rioters spoke openly about their motives, saying that economic competition played no role in their anger, but that it was the violation of a local woman by the outsiders that caused them to react. "They can't abuse our women and get away with it," one of the men said with heat, "we're men: we have to do something." Apparently, such motives still play a role in Andalusian male culture.[4]

I finish this section with a final comment about manliness-as-valor. In Andalusia, hombría has one additional element, which is probably a political legacy of the Franco dictatorship.

In the waning years of Franco, hombría could be demonstrated by active defiance of the regime, by standing up to the secret police or the paramilitary Civil Guard. It was often shown among workers who organized the clandestine unions and who refused to back down in labor disputes—these acts were praised not only as politically correct, but also as manly. Heroes of the labor movement (of whatever class) were called *valiente* and were said to be *muy hombre* (very manly). Charismatic labor leaders, especially those jailed and tortured under Franco, like Marcelino Camacho, the head of the underground Communist Party, were highly praised in this regard, almost as icons of hombría. I found it of interest that, no matter what a man's political viewpoint, most would admit the manliness of an opponent who showed courage in the face of overwhelming odds.

One concrete instance from Fuentes may help. During the years after the Civil War (1936–1939) a famous ex-Republican lived in Fuentes, and was known throughout the village by his nickname "El Robustiano (his real name was never used as far as I knew). Literally this moniker means "the Robust One, but can best be rendered as "Hero" or perhaps more colloquially as "The Big Guy." He was so called for his height (he was almost six feet tall in a land of smallish people), and known his for political savvy and physical courage. After serving in the Loyalist Army and serving a prison term afterwards, Robustiano returned to Fuentes and began the militant labor agitation that made him famous ever since. Even while he suffered fierce persecution during the Franco dictatorship, he continued to defy the police again and again, serving numerous prison terms, undergoing torture both physical and mental. But all the beatings, threats and blackballing had no effect on him. After each jail term he returned martyr-like to the struggle. He was also known never to have betrayed a comrade, to have taken beatings with equanimity, and indeed he won admiration from all sides, including his jailors, one of who I actually met, who effused about his erstwhile victim. Robustiano developed a huge and active following in the town until his death in 1969 and is remembered to

this day (2007) as a "man among men." My friends told me he represented the ideal of hombría and it was great pity that I never got to meet him (I arrived in Fuentes three years after his death). It also helped his reputation that his wife and three daughters were beyond reproach—chaste and virginal respectively. Also in his favor was that he had fathered nine children in all, and most importantly, six sons—a sure sign of virility, because having many sons is—for reasons always unclear to me—a crowning glory of manhood. So here, the man personified both attributes of Andalusian masculinity discussed so far: the sexual and the moral, a paragon of both the machismo and valor components of manhood.

VIRTUE: MANHOOD AND COURTESY

Finally we come to the third and last ingredient in the Andalusian masculinity ideal, which I will call for simplicity's sake *virtue*. As I mentioned above, the notion of a classical "honor" has little resonance with men in Andalusia today. Nevertheless, townsmen do speak of an analogous criterion, a moral formality, which they reckon to be as important to a man's status as being virile and valiant. This final quality is what they call being "honrado," which literally means honorable, but having the connotation in Fuentes of rectitude and personal probity; that is, it means taking one's obligations seriously and paying back one's debts, and doing so with promptness and dignity. It relates to character and also what we might call "attitude." For example, early in my fieldwork, when I asked my friends if a certain man I knew in town was "honorable" (using the term that Pitt-Rivers made so much of), I was informed that if I meant "honest," then yes, this man measured up. They said as far as they knew, he paid his debts and he returned favors reliably and courteously. Going further, they noted that, for example, in his regular bar, this man would routinely enter into exchanges of drinks and do his fair share of what they call "*invitas*" (invitations); that is, if someone bought him a drink, he would reciprocate ("invite") them back sooner or later. Honesty of this sort is crucially important to man's standing and especially in his circle of peers, wherein lies community judgment. The true measure of virtue in this sense is communicated in what Brandes calls "the estimates of personal decency" (1980: 48). In this sense it differs little from the standard English "honest" or "creditable." It has little to do with one's sexual prowess and nothing to do with bravery. Nevertheless it is intimately bound up with manliness and forms a third, independent variable of the Andalusian manhood jigsaw puzzle. The negative pole of honorability is *vergüenza*, or "shame." If a man has the requisite quality of shame, that is, has a decent respect for the opinion of others, he complies with expectations and is therefore honorable. The unethical, dishonest, man has no shame and callously ignores obligations, thumbing his nose at public opinion. He has a "hard face" (*cara dura*), they say. In this regard, Andalusian notions of decency can be elaborated further as an integral aspect of character. Its internal mechanism and social (thus measurable) manifestation is a punctilious reciprocity, which is usually balanced and predictable. Whether monetary or not, repayments of goods and services are often calculated to an amazing degree of exactitude, but just as often they are vague and approximate. In any event, returns of favors are carried out on the community public stage, in public places like streets and bars, conspicuously, but always in the spirit of nonchalance, without ostentation, as though the matter were but a trifle. Obviously reference should be made here to what Michael Herzfeld and others have called "Mediterranean hospitality" (Herzfeld 1989), a common denominator around the Mediterranean and known to the ancient Greeks and modern Arabs. These rituals of generosity are exclusively male. Women never enter the bars except for holidays and are always accompanied by a man. Women do not "invite" in bars or anywhere else; given the conservative sexual code in rural villages like Fuentes, women are not "invited" by unrelated men. Bar invitations are thus entirely male, and an integral part of a man's "connectedness" to society and his public face.

Having observed these exchanges and begun to participate in them, I soon became aware that there were many contexts in which men were expected to get involved, and in so doing to publicly demonstrate trustworthiness. The main context is the arena of the public house (bars, taverns, coffee houses, casinos, and clubs). Every man in Fuentes has a neighborhood dive where he hangs out for at least three or four hours a day, meets with cronies, palavers incessantly, and does business. Thus comfortably ensconced, he participates in the requisite rituals of exchange. These exchanges look and "feel" casual to the first-time observer, yet are deadly earnest. Always accompanying bar conviviality are serious rounds of what anthropologists call "tournaments of value," (Appadurai 1986). In Spain, these tournaments of value consist of offerings of drinks and cigarettes, usually accompanied by much backslapping and glad-handing. Although seemingly disinterested, barroom exchanges are governed by a subtle, but iron-clad etiquette. While no one would ever say so openly, it is a crass transgression to accept more than a drink or two without reciprocating. As the evening proceeds, everyone makes out more or less evenly in the long run. In the circular movement of commodities, what counts most is the display of disinterested generosity and "playing the game," that is, not holding back. For a man to withhold, to hesitate, to stint, or to respond grudgingly, is to court opprobrium as a cheat and a rogue. If a man continually fails to play his part, he is quickly labeled a *sinvuergüenza*, a shameless guy. Worse is the *sinvergüenzón* (a big flagrant shameless), someone who is notorious for toadying, no better than a thief. Considering the pervasiveness of bar gossip, such labeling quickly leads to general censure, and this can sometimes result in social ostracism. Hence, most men voluntarily abjure a calculus of personal aggrandizement in bar society for it can lead to economic paralysis, since no one wants to cooperate with a *sinvergüenzón*. If a man is niggardly in bars, the logic goes, he will be equally if not more untrustworthy in business deals. How all this relates to judgments about manliness is explained below.

When I inquired about what motivated all these little offerings, I was told that the point was not the object given to another, but the generosity so evidenced, and that indeed generosity was the gold standard by which character was judged. The operative principle involved is "personality." The *fontaniegos* evaluate a man's personality once again on a binary scale as either *abierto* ("open") or *cerrado* ("closed"). Although there can be degrees, I quickly noticed that most men considered the open/closed measure in absolute and oppositional terms, either/or. So when speaking of an absent party, people would usually say that he was either of an "open" or "closed" personality. Such judgments were, again, often consensual, rigid, and immutable. One of course could be "very open" or "very closed," but not slightly open or closed. (Incidentally, women were never judged by this idiom, as these words would have devastating sexual connotations for a woman in a pueblo). An "open fellow" (*un tio abierto*) is generous to a fault, convivial, gregarious, rapidly reciprocating a favor. A closed guy is sour, stingy, evasive, furtive, louche. Decisions were based largely on simple degree of *social participation*. A man who "gets involved" in the raucous conviviality of the bars and who pays back debts was open; one who kept himself apart, refused to engage, or failed to reciprocate was closed.

All of this may seem axiomatic: one finds similar judgments in most societies where men cooperate. However, it soon became clear to me that such evaluations went deeper than character assessment and touched upon a man's reputation as manly or not. A man who stayed away from the bars, or who held back his purse, or who spent "too much time" indoors avoiding male society, was regarded not only as closed and delinquent, a *sinvergüenza*, squalid, but also as unmanly, as effeminate. One unhappy example will demonstrate this connection between personality and manliness.

There lived an odd fellow in Fuentes named Alfredo Tissot, a commercial broker. I got to know him rather well, since he lived on my street, but he was scorned by my other friends as a recluse and a miser (the Catalan-sounding name did not help). What made him really repugnant was his avoidance of the bars and of men's circles in general. Alfredo was that rarity in Andalusia: an uxorious homebody, a sit-by-the-fire. In consequence he was a virtually friendless man. Although aware of men's expectations, he resisted them, because, as he confided to me, such goings-on were not only a waste of time, but also expensive: he watched his pennies and hated the profligacy of the barroom. So he preferred staying at home with his family—a wife and two adolescent daughters—reading books, watching television, or going over his accounts. I should add that he was a relatively successful businessman, indeed quite affluent by local standards, and therefore all the more susceptible to demands and expectations for generosity.

Walking past his house one day with a coterie of my friends, I was treated to a rare tirade that intensified into a crescendo of abuse. "What kind of man is he anyway," said one, nodding at his sealed and cloistered home, "Spending every second at home like that?" The others took up the cue, savaging the loner for his defects, likening him to a "brooding hen" and to a "mother cow" and other female animals. They insinuated a number of character flaws, most egregiously stinginess and furtiveness, misanthropy and avarice; but beyond these surface defects they alluded to something worse: a failure at man-acting. Intensifying the character assassination, my friends left the domain of the observable and ventured into the realm of speculation, which is common when a man is judged faulty. We proceeded up the street and the men offered their suspicions about this pathetic scapegoat. It all boiled down, they said, to his failure to be a man. This was demonstrated by his shadowy introversion, his hermit-like, withdrawn lifestyle. When I asked if his self-removal could be attributable to business requirements, I was hooted down with denunciations of "a guy who will not invite, who never goes to the bars!" "He's the worst closed," they continued, "hoarding, never participating; selfish, petty." The others seconded this and began scurrilous speculations as to the deviant's sexual preferences, some insinuating homosexuality or some sordid clandestine perversion which might explain his evasion of manliness. In all this, Tissot was paying the price for his withdrawal from the man's world. Being "closed," he must also be self-protective, introverted, guarded—traits associated with women, who must protect their chastity by social withdrawal and evasion; hence the comparison to hens and cows. One may, of course, appreciate the Freudian symbolism here of the open-closed metaphors with their anatomical suggestiveness without being psychologically reductive about it.

SUMMARY AND CONCLUSIONS

When I first went to Spain, like many foreigners, I was duly impressed by displays of machismo. I soon noted however that Andalusian machismo differed from notions of masculinity in my culture (middle-class America) and in many others in its erotic intensity. But the main lesson I learned is not that machismo defines manhood in Spain, but, ironically, that one cannot speak of "manhood" in Andalusia by reference just to machismo. Machismo is a necessary but not sufficient ingredient in the Andalusian code of the real man. As I have tried to show, being a real man signifies (in Goodenough's term) a complex bundle of behavioral subclasses, the interplay of which results in a carefully cultivated dynamic—a multi-layered system of checks and balances. As I came to understand it, the measure of manliness in Andalusia is a three-fold package, a triumvirate of do's and don't's.

The first component is *virility* (this is what the Andalusians themselves mean when they speak of macho). It connotes sexual potency—a sexual fire in the belly. Although Americans might call this "machismo" and leave it at that, in Spain it has none of the American overtones of belligerence and risk taking. The second component is what I have called *valor*. Valor implies intestinal fortitude and tenacity—doggedness in the face of adversity. The final piece in the jigsaw puzzle is a more ambiguous concept which I call *virtue*. In Andalusia, this is measured by a man's enthusiasm in public dealings: his generosity, his honesty, his courtesy and his participation in masculine pursuits. If a man wants to be truly manly, seducing women is not enough. He must adhere strictly to rules of civility and must

engage in lavish public generosity. These rules tend to prohibit or at least limit confrontations among men and they put a damper on sexual competitions and misdeeds, and so there are built-in inhibitors against antisocial behavior. Each of the three components, virility, valor, and virtue, plays its own necessary role in the evaluation a "manly man." Each component operates alongside, and in tandem with, the others.

What all this complexity shows, perhaps, is the obvious conclusion that gender evaluations in places like Spain are part of a broader moral calculus which men negotiate on an everyday basis and in a variety of contexts. From this we can conclude that in many societies, Hispanic or otherwise, anyone who wants to understand gender codes must be aware of the context in which judgments are made, and must also understand the rules governing personality assessment. Even in a famously macho land like Spain, men do not live by machismo alone.

NOTES

1. My fieldwork in Spain, conducted intermittently between 1971 and 2003, was supported by grants and fellowships from the following institutions: the National Science Foundation, the National Endowment for the Humanities, the H. F. Guggenheim Foundation, the J. S. Guggenheim Foundation, the American Philosophical Society, the Council for Exchange of Scholars, and the Program for Cultural Cooperation between Spain's Ministry of Culture and U.S. universities. I thank these agencies for their generosity.

2. The best monograph on Andalusian machismo is that of Stanley Brandes (1980). For a comparative view from neighboring southern Portugal, see the interesting book by Vale de Almeida (1992). Matthew Gutmann attempts to debunk "Hispanic machismo" as an ethnocentric fantasy or a sexist conspiracy with varying degrees of success (1996, 1997).

3. For more on the notion of masculine "beauty" and its relationship to concepts of manliness in various cultures, see Gilmore (1994).

4. The riots were reported in all local papers, in the Malaga paper *Correos de Andalucia*, in the Madrid daily *El Pais*, and in the *New York Times*.

The quotation is excerpted from interviews taken by the author in October 2006 in El Ejido.

REFERENCES

Abu-Lughod, Lila. 1993. *Writing Women's Worlds*. Berkeley CA: University of California Press.

Aguilera, Francisco. 1990. *Santa Eulalia's People: Ritual, Structure and Process in an Andalusian Multicommunity*, 2nd edition. Prospect Heights, IL: West Publishing Co.

Appadurai, Arjun. 1986. "Introduction: Commodities and the Politics of Value." In Arjun Appadurai (ed.). *The Social Life of Things*, pp. 3–63. Cambridge, UK: Cambridge University Press.

Brandes, Stanley. 1980. *Metaphors of Masculinity: Sex and Status in Andalusian Folklore*. Philadelphia: University of Pennsylvania Press.

Campbell, John. 1964. *Honour, Family and Patronage*. Oxford, UK: Clarendon Press.

Corbin, John, and M. Corbin. 1984. *Compromising Relations: Kith, Kin, and Class in Andalusia*. Aldershot, UK: Gower.

Driessen, Henk. 1983. "Male Sociability and Rituals of Masculinity in Andalusia." *Anthropological Quarterly* 56: 125–133.

Geertz, Hildred. 1979. "The Meanings of Family Ties." In Clifford Goertz et al. (eds.). *Meaning and Order in Moroccan Society*, pp. 315–386. New York: Cambridge University Press.

Gilmore, David. 1990. *Manhood in the Making*. New Haven, CT: Yale University. Press.

———. 1994. "The Beauty of the Beast: Male Body Imagery in Anthropological Perspective." In M. G. Winkler and L. B. Cole (eds.). *The Good Body: Asceticism in Contemporary Culture*, pp. 191–214. New Haven, CT: Yale University Press.

———, and Sarah Uhl. 1987. "Further Notes on Andalusian Machismo." *Journal of Psychoanalytic Anthropology* 10: 341–360.

Giovannini, Maureen. 1987. "Female Chastity Codes in the Circum-Mediterranean: Comparative Perspectives." In David Gilmore (ed.). *Honor and Shame and Unity of the Mediterranean*, pp. 60–73. Washington DC: American Anthropological Association, special publication no. 22.

Gonzalez-Lopez, Gloria, and Matthew C. Gutmann. 2005. "Machismo." In M. C. Horowitz (ed.). *New Dictionary of Ideas*, Volume 4, pp. 1328–1330. New York: Thomson Gale.

Goodenough, Ward. 1970. *Description and Comparison in Cultural Anthropology*. Chicago: Aldine.

Gutmann, Matthew. 1996. *The Meanings of Macho: Being a Man in Mexico City*. Berkeley: University of California Press.

———. 1997. "Trafficking in Men: The Anthropology of Masculinity." *Annual Reviews in Anthropology* 26: 385–409.

Herzfeld, Michael. 1985. *The Poetics of Manhood*. Princeton, NJ: Princeton University Press.

———. 1989. *Anthropology through the Looking Glass*. Cambridge, UK: Cambridge University Press.

Ingham, John. 1964. "The Bullfighters." *American Imago* 21: 85–102.

Levine, Donald. 1966. "The Concept of Masculinity in Ethiopian Culture." *International Journal of Social Psychiatry* 12: 17–23.

Lewis, Oscar. 1961. *The Children of Sanchez*. New York: Random House.

Marshall, Mac. 1979. *Weekend Warriors*. Palo Alto, CA: Mayfield.

Mernissi, Fatima. 1975. *Beyond the Veil: Male-Female Dynamics in a Modern Muslim Society*. New York: Schenkman.

Pina-Cabral, João. 1989. "Mediterranean Studies." *Current Anthropology* 30: 399–406.

Pitt-Rivers, Julian, 1971. *The People of the Sierra*. Chicago: University of Chicago Press.

———. 1977. *The Fate of Shechem, or the Politics of Sex: Essays in the Anthropology of the Mediterranean*. Cambridge, UK: Cambridge University Press.

Press, Irwin. 1979. *The City as Context: Urbanism and Behavioral Constraints in Seville*. Urbana: University of Illinois Press.

Reich, Jackie. 2004. *Beyond the Latin Lover*. Bloomington: Indiana University Press.

Reminick, Ronald. 1982. "The Sport of Warriors on the Wane." In William Morgan (ed.). *Sport and the Humanities*, pp. 31–36. Knoxville, TN: Bureau of Educational Research.

Sorge, Antonio. 2007. *The Free Highlands: Honour, Identity, and Change in Central Sardinia*. Calgary: Department of Anthropology, University of Calgary. Unpublished Ph.D. Dissertation.

Suarez-Orozco, Marcelo, and A. Dundes. 1984. "The Piropo and the Dual Image of Women in the Spanish-Speaking World. *Journal of Latin Lore* 10: 111–133.

Vale de Almeida, Miguel. 1992. *The Hegemonic Male: Masculinity in a Portuguese Town*. Providence, RI: Berghahn.

Rituals of Manhood:
Male Initiation in Papua New Guinea

Gilbert H. Herdt

Sambia are a mountain-dwelling hunting and horticultural people who number some 2,000 persons and inhabit one of New Guinea's most rugged terrains. The population is dispersed through narrow river valleys over a widespread, thinly populated rain forest; rainfall is heavy; and even today the surrounding mountain ranges keep the area isolated. Sambia live on the fringes of the Highlands, but they trace their origins to the Papua hinterlands; their culture and economy thus reflect a mixture of influences from both of those areas. Hunting still predominates as a masculine activity through which most meat protein is acquired. As in the Highlands, though, sweet potatoes and taro are the staple crops, and their cultivation is for the most part women's work. Pigs are few, and they have no ceremonial or exchange significance; indigenous marsupials, such as possum and tree kangaroo, provide necessary meat prestations for all initiations and ceremonial feasts (cf. Meigs 1976).

Sambia settlements are small, well-defended, mountain clan hamlets. These communities comprise locally based descent groups organized through a strong agnatic idiom. Residence is patrivirilocal, and most men actually reside in their father's hamlets. Clans are exogamous, and one or more of them together constitute a hamlet's landowning corporate agnatic body. These men also form a localized warriorhood that is sometimes allied with other hamlets in matters of fighting, marriage, and ritual. Each hamlet contains one or two men's clubhouses, in addition to women's houses, and the men's ritual life centers on their clubhouse. Marriage is usually by sister exchange

Reprinted with permission from Gilbert H. Herdt, *Rituals of Manhood: Male Initiation in Papua New Guinea* (Berkeley, University of California Press, 1982), pp. 50–57. Copyright

or infant betrothal, although the latter form of prearranged marriage is culturally preferred. Intrahamlet marriage is occasionally more frequent (up to 50 percent of all marriages in my own hamlet field site) than one would expect in such small segmentary groupings, an involutional pattern weakened since pacification.

Sambia male and female residential patterns differ somewhat from those of other Highlands peoples. The nuclear family is an important subunit of the hamlet-based extended family of interrelated clans. A man, his wife, and their children usually cohabit within a single, small, round hut. Children are thus reared together by their parents during the early years of life, so the nuclear family is a residential unit, an institution virtually unknown to the Highlands (Meggitt 1964; Read 1954). Sometimes this unit is expanded through polygyny, in which case a man, his cowives, and their children may occupy the single dwelling. Girls continue to reside with their parents until marriage (usually near the menarche, around fifteen to seventeen years of age). Boys, however, are removed to the men's clubhouse at seven to ten years of age, following their first-stage initiation. There they reside exclusively until marriage and cohabitation years later. Despite familial cohabitation in early childhood, strict taboos based on beliefs about menstrual pollution still separate men and women in their sleeping and eating arrangements.

Warfare used to be constant and nagging among Sambia, and it conditioned the values and masculine stereotypes surrounding the male initiatory cult. Ritualized bow fights occurred among neighboring hamlets, whose members still intermarried and usually initiated their sons together. At the same time, though, hamlets also united against enemy tribes and in staging war parties against them.

Hence, warfare, marriage, and initiation were interlocking institutions; the effect of this political instability was to reinforce tough, strident masculine performance in most arenas of social life. "Strength" (*jerundu*) was—and is—a pivotal idea in this male ethos. Indeed, strength, which has both ethnobiological and behavioral aspects, could be aptly translated as "maleness" and "manliness." Strength has come to be virtually synonymous with idealized conformity to male ritual routine. Before conquest and pacification by the Australians, though, strength had its chief performative significance in one's conduct on the battlefield. Even today bitter reminders of war linger on among the Sambia; and we should not forget that it is against the harsh background of the warrior's existence that Sambia initiate their boys, whose only perceived protection against the inconstant world is their own unbending masculinity.

Initiation rests solely in the hands of the men's secret society. It is this organization that brings the collective initiatory cycle into being as jointly performed by neighboring hamlets (and as constrained by their own chronic bow fighting). The necessary feast-crop gardens, ritual leadership, and knowledge dictate that a handful of elders, war leaders, and ritual experts be in full command of the actual staging of the event. Everyone and all else are secondary.

There are six intermittent initiations from the ages of seven to ten and onward. They are, however, constituted and conceptualized as two distinct cultural systems within the male life cycle. First-stage (*moku*, at seven to ten years of age), second-stage (*imbutu*, at ten to thirteen years), and third-stage (*ipmangwi*, at thirteen to sixteen years) initiations—bachelorhood rites—are collectively performed for regional groups of boys as age-mates. The initiations are held in sequence, as age-graded advancements; the entire sequel takes months to perform. The focus of all these initiations is the construction and habitation of a great cult house (*moo-angu*) on a traditional dance ground; its ceremonialized building inaugurates the whole cycle. Fourth-stage (*nuposha*: sixteen years and onward), fifth-stage (*taiketnyi*), and sixth-stage (*moondangu*) initiations are, conversely, individually centered events not associated with the confederacy of interrelated hamlets, cult house, or dance ground. Each of these initiations, like the preceding ones, does have its own ritual status, social role, and title, as noted. The triggering event for the latter three initiations, unlike that for the bachelorhood rites, is not the building of a cult house or a political agreement of hamlets to act collectively but is rather the maturing femininity and life-crisis events of the women assigned in marriage to youths (who become the initiated novices). Therefore, fourth-stage initiation is only a semi-public activity organized by the youths' clansmen (and some male affines). Its secret purificatory and other rites are followed by the formal marriage ceremony in the hamlet. Fifth-stage initiation comes at a woman's menarche, when her husband is secretly introduced to additional purification and sexual techniques. Sixth-stage initiation issues from the birth of a man's wife's first child. This event is, de jure, the attainment of manhood. (The first birth is elaborately ritualized and celebrated; the next three births are also celebrated, but in more truncated fashion.) Two children bring full adulthood (*aatmwunu*) for husband and wife alike. Birth ceremonies are suspended after the fourth birth, since there is no reason to belabor what is by now obvious: a man has proved himself competent in reproduction. This sequence of male initiations forms the basis for male development, and it underlies the antagonistic tenor of relationships between the sexes.

It needs stating only once that men's secular rhetoric and ritual practices depict women as dangerous and polluting inferiors whom men are to distrust throughout their lives. In this regard, Sambia values and relationships pit men against women even more markedly, I think, than occurs in other Highlands communities (cf. Brown and Buchbinder 1976; Meggitt 1964; Read 1954). Men hold themselves as the superiors of women in physique, personality, and social position. And this dogma of male supremacy permeates all social relationships and institutions, likewise coloring domestic behavior among the sexes (cf. Tuzin 1980 for an important contrast). Men fear not only pollution from contact with women's vaginal fluids and menstrual blood but also the depletion of their semen, the vital spark of maleness, which women (and boys, too) inevitably extract, sapping a man's substance. These are among the main themes of male belief underlying initiation.

The ritualized simulation of maleness is the result of initiation, and men believe the process to be vital for the nature and nurture of manly growth and well-being. First-stage initiation begins the process in small boys. Over the ensuing ten to fifteen years, until marriage, cumulative initiations and residence in the men's house are said to promote biological changes that firmly cement the growth from childhood to manhood. Nature provides male genitals, it is true; but nature alone does not bestow the vital spark biologically necessary for stimulating masculine growth or demonstrating cold-blooded self-preservation.

New Guinea specialists will recognize in the Sambia belief system a theme that links it to the comparative ethnography of male initiation and masculine development: the use of ritual procedures for sparking, fostering, and maintaining manliness in males (see Berndt 1962; Meigs 1976; Newman 1964, 1965; Poole 1981; Read 1965; Salisbury 1965; Strathern 1969, 1970). Sambia themselves refer to the results of first-stage collective initiation—our main interest—as a means of "growing a boy"; and this trend of ritual belief is particularly emphatic.

Unlike ourselves, Sambia perceive no imminent, naturally driven fit between one's birthright sex and one's gender identity or role.[1] Indeed, the problem (and it is approached as a situation wanting a solution) is implicitly and explicitly understood in quite different terms. The solution is also different for the two sexes: men believe that a girl is born with all of the vital organs and fluids necessary for her to attain reproductive competence through "natural" maturation. This conviction is embodied in cultural perceptions of the girl's development beginning with the sex assignment at birth. What distinguishes a girl (*tai*) from a boy (*kwulai'u*) is obvious: "A boy has a penis, and a girl does not," men say. Underlying men's communications is a conviction that maleness,

unlike femaleness, is not a biological given. It must be artificially induced through secret ritual; and that is a personal achievement.

The visible manifestations of girls' fast-growing reproductive competence, noticed first in early motor coordination and speech and then later in the rapid attainment of height and secondary sex traits (e.g., breast development), are attributed to inner biological properties. Girls possess a menstrual-blood organ, or *tingu,* said to precipitate all those events and the menarche. Boys, on the other hand, are thought to possess an inactive *tingu.* They do possess, however, another organ—the *kere-ku-kereku,* or semen organ—that is thought to be the repository of semen, the very essence of maleness and masculinity; but this organ is not functional at birth, since it contains no semen naturally and can only store, never produce, any. Only oral insemination, men believe, can activate the boy's semen organ, thereby precipitating his push into adult reproductive competence. In short, femininity unfolds naturally, whereas masculinity must be achieved; and here is where the male ritual cult steps in.

Men also perceive the early socialization risks of boys and girls in quite different terms. All infants are closely bonded to their mothers. Out of a woman's contaminating, life-giving womb pours the baby, who thereafter remains tied to the woman's body, breast milk, and many ministrations. This latter contact only reinforces the femininity and female contamination in which birth involves the infant. Then, too, the father, both because of postpartum taboos and by personal choice, tends to avoid being present at the breast-feedings. Mother thus becomes the unalterable primary influence; father is a weak second. Sambia say this does not place girls at a "risk"—they simply succumb to the drives of their "natural" biology. This maternal attachment and paternal distance clearly jeopardize the boys' growth, however, since nothing innate within male maturation seems to resist the inhibiting effects of mothers' femininity. Hence boys must be traumatically separated—wiped clean of their female contaminants—so that their masculinity may develop.

Homosexual fellatio inseminations can follow this separation but cannot precede it, for otherwise they would go for naught. The accumulating semen, injected time and again for years, is believed crucial for the formation of biological maleness and masculine comportment. This native perspective is sufficiently novel to justify our using a special concept for aiding description and analysis of the data: masculinization (Herdt 1981: 205 ff). Hence I shall refer to the overall process that involves separating a boy from his mother, initiating him, ritually treating his body, administering homosexual inseminations, his biological attainment of puberty, and his eventual reproductive competence, as *masculinization*. (Precisely what role personal and cultural fantasy plays in the negotiation of this ritual process I have considered elsewhere: see Herdt 1981: chaps. 6, 7, and 8.)

A boy has female contaminants inside of him which not only retard physical development but, if not removed, debilitate him and eventually bring death. His body is male: his tingú contains no blood and will not activate. The achievement of puberty for boys requires semen. Breast milk "nurtures the boy," and sweet potatoes or other "female" foods provide "stomach nourishment," but these substances become only feces, not semen. Women's own bodies internally produce the menarche, the hallmark of reproductive maturity. There is no comparable mechanism active in a boy, nothing that can stimulate his secondary sex traits. Only semen can do that; only men have semen; boys have none. What is left to do, then, except initiate and masculinize boys into adulthood?

REFERENCES

Berndt, R. M. 1962. *Excess and Restraint: Social Control among a New Guinea Mountain People.* Chicago: University of Chicago Press.

Brown, P., and G. Buchbinder (eds.). 1976. *Man and Woman in the New Guinea Highlands.* Washington, D.C.: American Anthropological Association.

Herdt, G. H. 1981. *Guardians of the Flutes: Idioms of Masculinity.* New York: McGraw-Hill.

Meggitt, M. J. 1964. Male-female relationships in the Highlands of Australian New Guinea. In New Guinea: The Central Highlands, ed. J. B. Watson, *American Anthropologist,* 66, pt. 2 (4): 204–224.

Meigs, A. S. 1976. Male pregnancy and the reduction of sexual opposition in a New Guinea Highlands society. *Ethnology* 15 (4): 393–407.

Newman, P. L. 1964. Religious belief and ritual in a New Guinea society. In New Guinea: The Central Highlands, ed. J. B. Watson, *American Anthropologist* 66, pt. 2 (4): 257–272.

———. 1965. *Knowing the Gururumba.* New York: Holt, Rinehart, and Winston.

Poole, F. J. P. 1981. Transforming "natural" woman: female ritual leaders and gender ideology among Bimin-Kuskumin. *In Sexual Meanings,* ed. S. B. Ortner and H. Whitehead pp. 116–165 New York: Cambridge University Press.

Read, K. E. 1954. Cultures of the Central Highlands, New Guinea. *Southwestern Journal of Anthropology* 10 (1):1–43.

———. 1965. *The High Valley.* London: George Allen and Unwin.

Salisbury, R. F. 1965. The Siane of the Eastern Highlands. In *Gods, Ghosts, and Men in Melanesia,* P. Lawrence and M. J. Meggitt, pp. 50–77. Melbourne: Melbourne University Press.

Sears, R. R. 1965. *Development of gender role. In Sex and Behavior,* ed. F. A. Beach, pp. 133–163. New York: John Wiley and Sons.

Stoller, R. J. 1968. *Sex and Gender.* New York: Science House.

Strathern, A. J. 1969. Descent and alliance in the New Guinea Highlands: some problems of comparison. Royal Anthropological Institute, *Proceedings,* pp. 37–52.

———. 1970. Male initiation in the New Guinea Highlands societies. *Ethnology* 9(4): 373–379.

Tuzin, D. F. 1980. *The Voice of the Tambaran: Truth and Illusion in Ilahita Arapesh Religion.* Berkeley, Los Angeles, and London: University of California Press.

NOTES

1. I follow Stoller (1968) in adhering to the following distinctions: the term *sex traits* refers to purely biological phenomena (anatomy, hormones, genetic structure, etc.), whereas *gender* refers to those psychological and cultural attributes that compel a person (consciously or unconsciously) to sense him or herself, and other persons, as belonging to either the male or female sex. It follows that the term gender role (Sears 1965), rather than the imprecise term sex role, refers to the normative set of expectations associated with masculine and feminine social positions.

The Named and the Nameless:
Gender and Person in Chinese Society

Rubie S. Watson

In Chinese society names classify and individuate, they have transformative powers, and they are an important form of self-expression. Some names are private, some are chosen for their public effect. Many people have a confusing array of names while others are nameless. The theory and practice of personal naming in Chinese society is extremely complex and unfortunately little studied.

For the male villagers of rural Hong Kong, naming marks important social transitions: the more names a man has the more "socialized" and also, in a sense, the more "individuated" he becomes. To attain social adulthood a man must have at least two names, but most have more. By the time a male reaches middle age, he may be known by four or five names. Village women, by contrast, are essentially nameless. Like boys, infant girls are named when they are one month old, but unlike boys they lose this name when they marry. Adult women are known (in reference and address) by kinship terms, teknonyms, or category terms such as "old woman."

In Chinese society personal names constitute an integral part of the language of joking, of boasting, and of exhibiting one's education and erudition. The Chinese themselves are fascinated by personal names: village men enjoy recounting stories about humorous or clumsy names, educated men appreciate the elegance of an auspicious name, and all males worry about the quality of their own names and those of their sons. To a large extent women are excluded from this discourse. They cannot participate because in adulthood they are not named, nor do they name others. Until very recently the majority of village women were illiterate and so could not engage in the

intellectual games that men play with written names. Women were not even the subjects of these conversations.

The namelessness of adult women and their inability to participate in the naming of others highlights in a dramatic way the vast gender distinctions that characterize traditional Chinese culture. The study of names gives us considerable insight into the ways in which gender and person are constructed in Chinese society. Judged against the standard of men, the evidence presented here suggests that village women do not, indeed cannot, attain full personhood. The lives of men are punctuated by the acquisition of new names, new roles, new responsibilities and new privileges; women's lives, in comparison, remain indistinct and indeterminate.

In his essay "Person, Time, and Conduct in Bali," Clifford Geertz argues that our social world "is populated not by anybodies . . . but by somebodies, concrete classes of determinate persons positively characterized and appropriately labeled" (1973:363). It is this process by which anybodies are converted into somebodies that concerns me here. Do men and women become "somebodies" in the same way? Are they made equally determinate, positively characterized and labeled?

Although this discussion is based primarily on field research carried out in the Hong Kong New Territories, examples of naming practices have been drawn from other areas of Chinese culture as well. It is difficult to determine the extent to which the patterns described in this paper are indicative of rural China in general.[1] Available evidence suggests that there is considerable overlap between Hong Kong patterns of male naming and those of preliberation Chinese society and present-day rural Taiwan (see for example Eberhard 1970; Kehl 1971; Sung 1981; Wu 1927). Unfortunately, there have been no studies that specifically examine the differences between men's and women's naming, although brief references in Martin Yang's study of a Shantung village (1945: 124) and in Judith Stacey's account of women in the People's Republic (1983:43, 131) suggest that the gender differences discussed here are not unique to Hong Kong. In making these statements I do not wish to suggest that there are no substantial differences in personal naming between rural Hong Kong and other parts of China. A general survey of personal naming in China, especially one that takes the postrevolution era into account, has yet to be done.

This paper draws heavily on ethnographic evidence gathered in the village of Ha Tsuen, a single-lineage village located in the northwest corner of the New Territories. All males in Ha Tsuen share the surname Teng and trace descent to a common ancestor who settled in this region during the 12th century (see R. Watson 1985). For most villagers postmarital residence is virilocal/patrilocal. The Ha Tsuen Teng practice surname exogamy, which in the case of a single-lineage village means that all wives come from outside the community. These women arrive in Ha Tsuen as strangers and their early years of marriage are spent accommodating to a new family and new community. The Teng find this completely natural; "daughters," they say, "are born looking out; they belong to others."

Patrilineal values dominate social life in Ha Tsuen. Women are suspect because they are outsiders. As Margery Wolf points out, Chinese women are both marginal and essential to the families into which they marry (1972:35). They are necessary because they produce the next generation, yet as outsiders their integration is never complete. Women are economically dependent on the family estate, but they do not have shareholding rights in that estate. Half the village land in Ha Tsuen is owned by the lineage (see R. Watson 1985:61–72), and the other half is owned by private (male) landlords. Women have no share in this land; they do not own immovable property nor do they have rights to inherit it. Few married women are employed in wage labor, and since the villagers gave up serious agriculture in the 1960s, most women are dependent on their husbands'

paychecks for family income. At the time I conducted my research (1977–78) Ha Tsuen had a population of approximately 2500—all of whom are Cantonese speakers.

NAMING AN INFANT

Among the Cantonese a child's soul is not thought to be firmly attached until at least 30 days after its birth. During the first month of life the child and mother are secluded from all but the immediate family. After a month has passed, the child is considered less susceptible to soul loss and is introduced into village life. The infant is given a name by his or her father or grandfather at a ceremony called "full month" (*man yueh*). If the child is a son, the "full month" festivities will be as elaborate as the family can afford; if, on the other hand, a girl is born, there may be little or no celebration (except, perhaps, a special meal for family members). The naming ceremony for a boy normally involves a banquet for neighbors and village elders, along with the distribution of red eggs to members of the community. The first name a child is given is referred to as his or her *ming*.[2]

This name (*ming*) may be based on literary or classical allusions. It may express a wish for the child's or family's future, or it may enshrine some simple event that took place at or near the time of the child's birth. Examples of this kind of naming are found not only in Ha Tsuen but in other areas of China as well. Arlington, in an early paper on Chinese naming, describes how the name "sleeve" was given to a girl of his acquaintance who at the time of her birth had been wrapped in a sleeve (1923:319). In the People's Republic of China, people born during the Korean War might be called "Resist the United States" (Fan-mei) or "Aid Korea" (Pang-ch'ao). Alternatively, children may be given the name of their birthplace, for example, "Born in Anhwei" (Hui-sheng) or "Thinking of Yunnan" (Hsiang-yun). In the past girl babies might be named Nai ("To Endure"). This name was given to infant girls who survived an attempted infanticide. One way of killing an infant was to expose it to the elements.

If a girl survived this ordeal, she might be allowed to live. In these cases the name Nai commemorated the child's feat of survival.[3]

A child's name may express the parents' desire for no more children. For instance, in Taiwan a fifth or sixth child may be named Beui, a Hokkien term meaning "Last Child." Alternatively, a father may try to ensure that his next child will be a son by naming a newborn daughter "Joined to Brother" (Lien-ti). There are several girls with this name in Ha Tsuen. A father or grandfather might express his disappointment or disgust by naming a second or third daughter "Too Many" (A-to)[4] or "Little Mistake" (Hsiao-t'so) or "Reluctant to Feed" (Wang-shih). A sickly child might be given the name of a healthy child. My informants told me that a long-awaited son may be given a girl's name to trick the wandering ghosts into thinking the child had no value and therefore could be ignored (see also Sung 1981:81–82). For example, a Ha Tsuen villager, who was the only son of a wealthy family (born to his father's third concubine), was known by everyone as "Little Slave Girl" (in Cantonese, Mui-jai).

In most cases the infant receives a *ming* during the full month ceremony but this name is little used. For the first year or two most children are called by a family nickname ("milk name" or *nai ming*). Babies are sometimes given milk names like "Precious" (A-pao), or A-buh (mimicking the sounds infants make) or "Eldest Luck," or "Second Luck," indicating sibling order.

Some care and consideration is given to a child's *ming*, especially if it is a boy. By referring to the Confucian classics or by alluding to a famous poem, the name may express the learning and sophistication of the infant's father or grandfather. The name, as we will see, may also save the child from an inauspicious fate. Commonly girls' names (*ming*) are less distinctive and less considered than are boys' names. And, as we have seen, girls' names may also be less flattering: "Too Many" or "Little Mistake." Often a general, classificatory name is given to an infant girl; Martin Yang reports from rural Shantung that Hsiao-mei ("Little Maiden") was a "generic" girls' name in his village (1945:124).

Most Chinese personal names are composed of two characters, which follow the one character surname (for example, Mao Tse-tung or Teng Hsiao-ping). One of the characters of the *ming* may be repeated for all the children of the same sex in the family or perhaps all sons born into the lineage during one generation (for example, a generation or sibling set might have personal names like Hung-hui, Hung-chi, Hung-sheng, and so on). Birth order may also be indicated in the child's name. In these cases part of the name indicates group affiliation and sibling order. However, one of the characters is unique to the individual and so the child is distinguished from his siblings. A variation on this theme occurs when a parent or grandparent selects a name for all sons or grandsons from a group of characters that share a single element (known as the radical—a structured component found in every Chinese character). For example, Margaret Sung (1981:80) in her survey of Chinese naming practices on Taiwan notes that in some families all son's names may be selected from characters that contain the "man" radical (for example, names like "Kind" [Jen], "Handsome" [Chun], or "Protect" [Pao]).

Individuation of the name, Sung points out, is very strong in Chinese society (1981:88). There is no category of words reserved specifically for personal names and care is taken to make names (particularly boys' names) distinct. The Chinese find the idea of sharing one's given name with millions of other people extraordinary.[5] In Taiwan, Sung notes that individuation of one's name is so important that the government has established a set of rules for name changes (1981: 88). According to these regulations a name can be changed when two people with exactly the same name live in the same city or county or have the same place of work. "Inelegant" names or names shared with wanted criminals can also be changed.

In Ha Tsuen a boy might be named, in Cantonese, Teng Tim-sing, which translates Teng "To Increase Victories"; another person could be called Teng Hou-sing, "Reliably Accomplish" (Teng being the shared surname). Parents, neighbors, and older siblings will address the child or young unmarried adult (male or female) by his or her *ming* or by a nickname. Younger siblings are expected to use kin terms in addressing older siblings. It should be noted that, in contrast to personal names, Chinese surnames do not convey individual meaning. When used in a sentence or poem, the character *mao* (the same character used in Mao Tse-tung) means hair, fur, feathers, but when it is used as a surname it does not carry any of these connotations.

THE POWER OF NAMES: NAMES THAT CHANGE ONE'S LUCK

Names classify people into families, generational sets, and kin groups. Ideally, Chinese personal names also have a unique quality. Personal names carry meanings; they express wishes (for more sons or no more daughters), mark past events ("Sleeve" or "Endure"), and convey a family's learning and status. Beyond this rather restricted sense there is, however, another level of meaning. According to Chinese folk concepts each person has a unique constitution—a different balance of the five elements (fire, water, metal, earth, and wood). When the child is about one month old a family will usually have a diviner cast the child's horoscope. The horoscope consists of eight characters (*pa tzu*)—two each for the hour, day, month, and year of birth. The combination of these characters determines in part what kind of person one is (what kind of characteristics one has) and what will happen in future years. However, the *pa tzu* do not represent destiny; one is not bound to act out this fate.

By means of esoteric knowledge a person's fate can be changed. Perhaps the most common method of accomplishing such a change is through naming. For example, if one of the five elements is missing from a person's constitution or is not properly balanced with other elements, the name (*ming*) may then include a character with the radical for that element. In the event of illness the diviner may suggest that the patient suffers from an imbalance of wood and that the radical for this element be added to the child's name. In such a case the character *mei* (plum), for example, may replace one of the original characters of the ming and thus save the child from a bad fate, illness, or perhaps death. *Mei* achieves this astounding feat not because there is anything intrinsically wood-like about *mei* but because the written character *mei* has two major components: *mu*, the radical for wood and another symbol that is largely phonetic. It is the written form of the character that is important here; in spoken Chinese there is nothing that suggests that *mei* has within it the element wood. I will return to this point later.

Significantly, it is not only one's own horoscope that matters; one must also be in balance with the horoscopes of parents, spouses, and offspring. It is particularly important that the five elements of mother and child be properly matched to ensure mutual health.[6] If conditions of conflict arise and nothing is done to resolve this conflict, the child may become ill and even die. A name change, however, can rectify the situation. It is obvious that Chinese personal names *do* things: they not only classify and distinguish but also have an efficacy in their own right.

GENDER DIFFERENCES AND THE WRITTEN NAME

As noted above, even in childhood there are important gender distinctions in naming. Girls nearly always have less elaborate full month rituals than their brothers, and less care is taken in choosing girls' names. The greatest difference between the sexes, however, pertains not to the aesthetics of naming but to the written form of the name.

Until the 1960s in Ha Tsuen and in rural Hong Kong generally births were seldom registered with government agencies. Except in cases of a bad fate, there was no compelling reason for girls' names ever to appear in written form. There was rarely any need to attach their names to legal documents. Girls did not inherit land, they had no rights in property, and their given names were not entered in genealogies (on this point see also Hazelton 1986) or on ancestral tablets (see below). Until the 1960s girls rarely attended primary schools.

Consequently, nearly all village women born prior to 1945 cannot write or recognize their own names.

Commenting on the role of nicknames, Wolfram Eberhard makes the point that in spoken Chinese with its many homonyms, a two-word combination may fail to express clearly what the speaker wants to convey. The intended meaning of a name (that is, the two-character *ming*) is only apparent when it is written. Nicknames, Eberhard notes, are not normally meant to be written and, hence, are usually longer (often three or four characters) than a person's *ming* (1970: 219). Given the ambiguities, a great deal of play is possible with the spoken form of names. For example, Hsin-mei can mean "New Plum" or "Faithful Beauty" depending on the tones that one uses in pronouncing the characters. In the written form the meaning of this name is perfectly clear, but in the spoken form it can be misunderstood or misconstrued, sometimes with disastrous consequences. The Manchu (Ch'ing) authorities played the naming game when they changed the written form of one of Sun Yat-sen's many names. During Sun's long political career, he used a variety of names and aliases (see Sharman 1934), one being Sun Wen (*wen* translates as "elegant," "civil," "culture"). In Manchu attacks on Sun the character *wen* pronounced with a rising tone (elegant, culture) was replaced by another character *wen* pronounced with a falling tone (which translates as "defile"). The change was effected simply by adding the water radical to the term for elegant. *Wen* (defile), it should be noted, was also the name of a famous criminal in southern China during the last years of Manchu rule.

Upon seeing a person's written name, the beholder may comment on the beauty, the refinement, the auspicious connotations of the characters. As long as it is simply spoken, however, it is in a sense "just a name." Although women have names, these do not convey as much information as do men's names, for the obvious reason that the former were rarely written. Until recently New Territories women were not given names with a view to their written effect. The written form of "Too Many" may be offensive or unpleasant in a way that the spoken form is not.

Given that it is the written form of names that has force, that informs, that can be used to change a bad fate, there is justification for thinking that those whose names are rarely or never written are at some disadvantage. Girls, it would appear, did not have names in the same way that boys did.[7] It is also clear that girls' names are less expressive, less individuating than their brothers' names are. Fathers strove to make son's names distinctive, unique—whereas girls' names tended to classify (for example, Endure, Little Maiden) or to be used as a vehicle for changing circumstances external to the girl herself (for example, Joined to Brother). Many girls of course had names like Splendid Orchid, Morning Flower, Resembling Jade, but in general they were more likely than were their brothers to be given negative names, stereotypic names, or goal-oriented names. These gender distinctions are significant, but the contrast between men and women becomes even more dramatic when we consider adult naming practices.

MEN'S NAMING

When a Ha Tsuen man marries, he is given or takes (often he chooses the name himself) a marriage name, or *tzu*. Considering the importance of the written name it is significant that *tzu* is the same character that is commonly used for "word" or "ideograph." The marriage name is given in a ceremony called *sung tzu*, which literally means "to deliver written characters." This ceremony is an integral part of the marriage rites and is held after the main banquet on the first day of wedding festivities.

In Ha Tsuen, the marriage name (always two characters) is written on a small rectangular piece of red paper and is displayed in the main reception hall of the groom's house (alternatively, it may be hung in the groom's branch ancestral hall). This name is chosen with regard to its effect in the written form. Great care is taken in choosing the characters; they often have origins in the Confucian classics. In Ha Tsuen one of the two characters of this marriage name is usually shared by a lineage generational set. In some kin groups a respected scholar may be asked to choose a poem or aphorism to be used in generational naming. Each generation will then take in turn one character of the poem as part of their (*tzu*) name. Of course, this makes the selection of an auspicious, learned name more difficult and also more intellectually challenging. Naming at this level can become a highly complicated game.

In choosing a marriage name (*tzu*) the groom demonstrates his sophistication, learning, and goals. Among the people I studied, the possession of a marriage name is essential for the attainment of male adulthood, which gives a man the right to participate in important lineage and community rituals. In Ha Tsuen the correct way to ask whether a man has full ritual rights in the lineage is to inquire, "Does X have a *tzu*?" not "Is X married?" Marriage names are not used as terms of address; they may, however, appear in lineage genealogies and in formal documents.

By the time a man is married he will have acquired a public nickname (*wai hao*, literally an "outside name"). This is usually different from the family nickname he had in infancy or the "school name" given to him by a teacher.[8] Nicknames are widely used as terms of address and reference for males in the village; in fact, a man's birth and marriage names may be largely unknown.

In a discussion of naming among the Ilongot, Renato Rosaldo emphasizes the process by which names come into being (1984:13). Rosaldo argues that names are negotiated, and that naming, like other aspects of Ilongot social life, is a matter of give and take, challenge and response (1984:22). Rosaldo's approach is particularly useful for understanding Chinese nicknaming. *Ming* (birth names) are formally bestowed by one's seniors, one chooses the *tzu* (marriage name) and, as we will see, the *hao* (courtesy name) oneself. Nicknames (*wai hao*), however, are negotiated; both the namer and the named play the game. By setting up this dichotomy between nicknames and other given names, I do not mean to suggest that these two categories have no common features or that *ming*, marriage names, and courtesy names are simply the consequence of a set of rigidly applied rules and structures. It is clear, however, that nicknames fit into the transactional world of local politics, friendship, and informal groups more comfortably than do formal names.

In Chinese society, one can gain a reputation for cleverness by giving nicknames that are particularly apt or make witty literary allusions. Chinese nicknames are highly personalized and often refer to idiosyncratic characteristics. They may also be derogatory or critical, whereas one's formal names would never be intentionally unflattering (especially for a man). Nicknames may refer to a physical quality (for example, "Fatty") or a personal quality ("Stares at the Sky" for someone who is a snob). Nicknames may also protect ("Little Slave Girl") or they may equalize, at least temporarily, unequal relationships. The richest and most powerful man in one New Territories village was nicknamed "Little Dog." In one respect this was a useful nickname for an extremely wealthy man whose political career depended on being accepted by everyone in the community. Rather than rejecting his derogatory nickname he embraced it.

In Ha Tsuen when a man reaches middle age or when he starts a business career, he usually takes a *hao*—"style" or "courtesy" name. A man chooses this name himself. Sung notes that such names are "usually disyllabic or polysyllabic, and [are] selected by oneself bas[ed] upon whatever one would like to be" (1981:86). Some people have more than one courtesy name. The *hao* is a public name par excellence. Such names, Eberhard points out, are often used on occasions when a man wants "to make his personal identity clear without revealing his personal name (*ming*)" (1970:219). In the past, and to some extent today,[9] the *ming* was considered to be too intimate, too personal to be used outside a circle of close friends and kin (Eberhard 1970:218). "The Chinese I know hide their names," writes Maxine Hong Kingston in *Woman Warrior;* "sojourners take new names when their lives change and guard their real names with silence" (1977:6).

Sung notes that *hao* names are no longer popular in present-day Taiwan except among high government officials (1981:86). However, in Hong Kong *hao* are still widely used; they are commonly found, for example, on business cards, and of course many painters or writers sign their work with a *hao*.

In one sense courtesy names are different from birth and marriage names. One achieves a courtesy name. They are a mark of social and economic status, and a poor man who gives himself such a name may be accused of putting on airs. Any man may take a *hao* but if he is not a "man of substance," the *hao* is likely to remain unknown and unused. With poor men or politically insignificant men these names, if they have them at all, may appear only in genealogies or on tombstones.

Some Ha Tsuen men have posthumous names (*shih-hao*) that they take themselves or have conferred upon them by others. Among the imperial elite posthumous names or titles were given to honor special deeds. In the village, however, taking or giving a *shih-hao* is left to individual taste. The practice has declined in recent years.

The preceding discussion suggests that names mark stages in a man's social life. The possession of a birth name, school name, nickname, marriage name, courtesy name, and posthumous name attest to the fact that a man has passed through the major stages of social adulthood. By the time a man reaches middle age he has considerable control over his names and naming. He names others (his children or grandchildren, for example) and he chooses his own marriage, courtesy, and posthumous names. He also has some control over the use of these names. This is especially true of a successful businessman or politician whose business associates may only know his courtesy name, his drinking friends one of his nicknames, his lineage-mates his birth name, and so on. The use of names is situational and involves some calculation both on the part of the named and those with whom he interacts.

Beidelman, in an article on naming among the Kaguru of Tanzania, emphasizes the point that the choice of name reflects the relation between the speaker and the person to whom he speaks (1974:282; see also Willis 1982). The choice of one name or another, or the use of a kin term rather than a personal name, is a tactical decision. In Ha Tsuen the use of nicknames,

pet names, birth names, courtesy names is, like the use of kin terms, highly contextual. Intimates may address each other by a nickname when they are among friends but not when strangers are present; family nicknames may be used in the household but not outside of it; birth names and surnames with titles may be used in formal introductions but not in other settings. A man might be addressed by a kin term or a nickname depending on the speaker's goals. One can give respect by using a courtesy name or claim intimacy by using a nickname. In a single lineage village like Ha Tsuen, where all males are agnatic kinsmen, the strategic use of kin terms and personal names provides a fascinating glimpse into social relationships.

Surprisingly, however, this flexibility does not continue into old age. When a man reaches elderhood at age 61, his ability to control his names diminishes just as his control over his family and corporate resources weakens. In Ha Tsuen and in China generally men often hand over headship of the family when they become elders. The village code of respect requires that male elders be addressed by a kin term (for example, in Cantonese *ah baak*, FeB, or a combination of the given name and kin term, for example, *ah Tso baak*). Only an exceptional man, a scholar or wealthy businessman, will continue to be called by one of his personal names after his 60th birthday. For example, no villager would dare refer to or address the 93-year-old patriarch of the wealthiest family in Ha Tsuen as *ah baak*. In general, however, with advancing age the playful aspects of names and naming are taken away as is a man's power to transact his name. In old age a man has little control over what he is called, and in this respect his situation is similar to that of a married woman. As with wives, old men have left (or are leaving) the world of public and financial affairs to become immersed in the world of family and kinship where they are defined not by a set of distinctive names but by their relationship to others.

"NO NAME" WOMEN

At one month a Ha Tsuen girl is given a name (*ming*); when she marries this name ceases to be used. Marriage is a critical rite of passage for both men and women, but the effect of this rite on the two sexes is very different. Just as a man's distinctiveness and public role are enhanced by his marriage and his acquisition of a marriage name, the marriage rites relegate the woman to the inner world of household, neighborhood, and family. On the one hand, the marriage rites seek to enhance the young bride's fertility, but on the other hand, and in a more negative vein, they also dramatize the bride's separation from her previous life and emphasize the prohibitions and restrictions that now confine her. When the young bride crosses her husband's threshold, what distinctiveness she had as a girl is thrust aside. It is at this point that she loses her name and becomes the "inner person" (nei jen), a term Chinese husbands use to refer to their wives.

While the groom is receiving his marriage name on the first day of marriage rites, his bride is being given an intensive course in kinship terminology by the elderly women of Ha Tsuen. Marriage ritual provides a number of occasions for the formal, ritualized exchange of kin terms (for a description of marriage rites in Ha Tsuen see R. Watson 1981). These exchanges, which always feature the bride, instruct the new wife and daughter-in-law in the vast array of kin terms she must use for her husband's relatives. The prevalence of virilocal/patrilocal residence means that the groom remains among the kin with whom he has always lived. It is the bride who must grasp a whole new set of kin terms and learn to attach these terms to what must seem a bewildering array of people. Two women residents in the groom's village (called in Cantonese *choi gaa*, "bride callers") act as the bride's guides and supporters during the three days of marriage rites, and it is their responsibility to instruct the bride in the kin terminology she will need in order to survive in her new environment.

These ritualized exchanges of kin terms do more, however, than serve as a pedagogic exercise; they also locate and anchor the bride in a new relational system. As the groom acquires his new marriage name—a name, it should be noted, that denotes both group or category

membership *and* individual distinctiveness— the bride enters a world in which she exists only in relation to others. She is no longer "grounded" by her own special name (*ming*), however prosaic that name might have been; after marriage she exists only as someone's eBW or yBW or as Sing's mother, and so on. Eventually even these terms will be used with decreasing frequency; as she approaches old age, she will be addressed simply as "old woman" (*ah po*) by all but her close kin.

When I first moved into Ha Tsuen, I quickly learned the names of the male residents (mostly nicknames). But for the women I, like other villagers, relied on kin terms or category terms. Significantly, the rules that govern the use of these terms are not dependent on the age of the women themselves, but rather are a function of the lineage generation of their husbands. Women married to men of an ascending generation to the speaker (or the speaker's husband) may be addressed as *ah suk po* (a local expression meaning FyBW) or by the more formal *ah sam* (also meaning FyBW). For women married to men of one's own generation (male ego) the terms *ah sou* (eBW) or, if one wanted to give added respect, *ah sam* (FyBW) may be used.

A woman may also be referred to by the nickname of her husband plus "leung" (for example, ah Keung leung), or by a teknonym. For their part married women ordinarily use kin terms for their husbands' agnates and for other women in the village. I was told that a woman must use kin terms for men older in age or generation than her husband. Between husband and wife teknonyms are often used so that the father of Tim-sing might address his wife as *ah Sing nai* (ah is a prefix denoting familiarity, *Sing* is part of the son's *ming*, nai is "mother" or, literally, "milk"). In addressing their husbands, women might use nicknames; my neighbor always called her husband "Little Servant."[10]

Although there is some flexibility in deciding what to call a woman, the reference and address terms used for women in Ha Tsuen are very rigid compared to those employed for men. Furthermore, among women there is no possibility of self-naming. Men name themselves, women are named by others. Similarly, Ha Tsuen women are more restricted than their husbands in the tactical use they can make of names and kin terms. Whereas a man may refer to or address his neighbor by his nickname ("Fatty"), his *ming* (*ah Tim*), or by a kin term, decorum dictates that his wife use either a kin term appropriate to her husband's generation or one appropriate to her children. In Cantonese society, and presumably in China generally, adults often address and refer to each other by a version of the kin term their children would use for that person. I suspect, but at this point cannot document, that women are far more likely to do this than are men.

While it is true that a man has little choice in the reference or address terms he uses for women, he does have considerable freedom in distinguishing among his male acquaintances, friends, and kin. Women, as outlined previously, have a restricted repertoire for both sexes. In this sense adult women may be said to carry a particularly heavy burden for guarding the kinship and sexual order. No adult woman is free to act alone or to be treated as if she were independent. The terms by which she is addressed and the terms she uses to address others serve as constant reminders of the hierarchical relations of gender, age, and generation.

As men grow older, as they become students, marry, start careers, take jobs, and eventually prepare for ancestorhood, their new names anchor them to new roles and privileges. These names are not, however, only role markers or classifiers. Ideally, they assign people to categories and at the same time declare their uniqueness. The pattern of naming in Chinese society presents an ever changing image of men. Viewed from this perspective Chinese males are always growing, becoming, accumulating new responsibilities and new rights.

Peasant women, on the other hand, experience few publicly validated life changes, and those that they do undergo link them ever more securely to stereotyped roles. Women's naming leaves little room for individuation or self-expression. Unlike males, whose changes are marked by both ascribed (for example, elderhood) *and* achieved criteria (such as

student, scholar, businessman, writer, politician), a woman's changes (from unmarried virgin to married woman, from nonmother to mother, from reproducer to nonreproducer) are not related to achievement outside the home. Instead of acquiring a new name at marriage or the birth of a first child, women's changes are marked by kin terminology or category shifts. At marriage the bride loses her *ming* and becomes known by a series of kin terms. At the birth of a child she may add a teknonym ("Sing's mother"), and as she approaches and enters old age more and more people will address her simply as "old woman" (*ah po*).

The most dramatic changes that women make are the shift from named to unnamed at marriage and the gradual shift from kin term to category term as their children mature and marry.[11] It would appear that as a woman's reproductive capacity declines, she becomes less grounded in the relational system. She becomes, quite simply, an "old woman" much like any other old woman. Of course, family members continue to use kin terms for these elderly women, especially in reference and address, but gradually their anonymity increases. Unlike men, women do not become elders. There is no ceremony marking their entry into respected old age. They move from reproductively active mother to sexually inactive grandmother with no fanfare and with little public recognition of their changed status.

Even in death a woman has no personal name. On the red flag that leads the spirit of the deceased from the village to the grave is written the woman's father's surname (for example, *Lin shih*, translated "Family of Lin"); no personal name is added. For men, the deceased's surname plus his courtesy and/or posthumous name is written on the soul flag. Neither do women's personal names appear on the tombstone where, here again, only the surname of the woman's father is given ("Family of Lin"). In Ha Tsuen women do not have separate ancestral tablets; if they are commemorated at all, they appear as minor appendages on their husbands' tablets. And, once more, they are listed only under the surnames of their fathers. In subsequent generations whatever individuating characteristics a woman might have had are lost—not even a name survives as testimony of her existence as a person.

CONCLUSIONS

If one were to categorize Ha Tsuen villagers on a social continuum according to the number and quality of their names, married peasant women would stand at the extreme negative pole.[12] To my knowledge they share this dubious distinction with no other group. In the past even male slaves (*hsi min*) and household servants had nicknames (see J. Watson 1976:365). They may not have had *ming* or surnames as such but they did possess names that distinguished them from others. It is important to note that it is not only the possession of multiple names that matters but also the fact that, at one end of the continuum, people have no control over their own names while, at the other end, they name themselves and others.

At marriage women find themselves enmeshed in the world of family and kinship. It is a world, as noted in the introduction, that they belong to but do not control. In Ha Tsuen brides arrive as outsiders but quickly, one might even say brutally, they become firmly entrenched in their new environment. Village women can only be identified within the constellation of male names or within the limits of kinship terminology. Unlike their husbands and brothers, women—having no public identity outside the relational system—are defined by and through others.

In Ha Tsuen women are excluded from participation in most of the formal aspects of lineage or community life and they are not involved in decision making outside the home. Ha Tsuen women do not inherit productive resources; they are also restricted in the uses to which they can put their dowries (R. Watson 1984). Furthermore, women in Ha Tsuen cannot become household heads and, even today, they do not vote in local elections. They do not worship in ancestral halls nor do they join the cult of lineage ancestors after death. Although individual peasant women may attain considerable power within their households,

they are said to have gained this power by manipulation and stealth. Women by definition cannot hold positions of authority.

In a discussion of male and female naming among the Omaha Sioux, Robert Barnes writes: "The names of Omaha males provide men with distinctive individuality, while also linking each unmistakably to a recognized collectivity. The possibility of acquiring multiple names in adulthood enhances individual prominence for men" (1982:220). Barnes goes on to say that women's names "barely rescue them from a general anonymity, neither conferring uniqueness nor indicating group membership" (1982:22). As among the Sioux, personal naming among Chinese men is a sign of both individual distinctiveness and group membership, while naming practices among village women simply confirm their marginality.

In Ha Tsuen the practice of personal naming reflects and facilitates the passage from one social level to another. Names establish people in social groups and give them certain rights within those groups. With each additional name, a man acquires new attributes. Maybury-Lewis has argued that among many Central Brazilian societies names give humans their "social persona and link [them] to other people" (1984:5; see also Bamberger 1974). Names, Maybury-Lewis writes, "transform individuals into persons" (1984:7). Naming may not be as central to Chinese social organization and ideology as it is among the societies of Central Brazil, yet there is no doubt that, for Chinese men, names have a transformative power that binds them as individuals to society.

In Ha Tsuen the ultimate goal of all males is to produce an heir, to have a grandson at one's funeral, to leave property that guarantees the performance of one's ancestral rites. The possession of many names testifies to the fact that a man has completed the cycle of life. Full personhood is not acquired at birth, at marriage, or even at the death of one's father. It is a process that continues throughout life and is punctuated by the taking and bestowing of names. One might argue that it is a process that extends even beyond death as the named ancestor interacts with the living. If, as Grace

Harris suggests, personhood involves a process of social growth "in the course of which changes [are] wrought by ceremony and ritual" (1978:49), then Chinese women never approximate the full cycle of development that their menfolk experience.[13] In stark contrast to men, women become less distinct as they age. The changes they undergo remain largely unrecognized and unnoticed.

In Chinese society, as in other societies, there is a tension between the notion of the unique individual (the individual as value) and the notion of the person tied to society.[14] In some sense the great philosophical systems of Taoism and Confucianism represent these two poles. Among men, naming involves a dual process through which they achieve personhood by being bound to society, while at the same time they acquire an enhanced sense of individuality and distinctiveness. The peasant women described in this paper seem to have been largely excluded from the individuating, individualizing world of personal naming. The situation with regard to personhood is, however, another matter. It would be wrong to say that peasant wives are nonpersons; rather, they are not persons in the same sense or to the same degree as are husbands and sons. Viewed from the perspective of names, peasant women are neither fully individuated nor "personed." In life as in death they remain suspended between the anonymous world of anybodies and the more sharply defined world of somebodies.

ACKNOWLEDGMENTS

The research for this study was conducted in 1977–78 and was made possible by a grant from the Social Science Research Council (Great Britain) and by the University of London Central Research Fund. An earlier version of this paper was presented at the 1984 American Anthropological Association Annual Meetings. Versions of this paper were also presented at the University of London Intercollegiate Anthropology Seminar and at the University of Rochester's Anthropology Colloquium. I thank the members of those seminars for their suggestions and criticisms. I owe a special debt to Jack Dull, Hsu Cho-yun, Sun Man-li, Roderick MacFarquhar, and James Watson, all of whom have helped in this project. Deborah Kwolek, Judy Tredway, and Martha Terry of the Asian Studies Program at the University of Pittsburgh helped in the preparation of the manuscript and I thank them for their assistance.

Cantonese terms are in Yale romanization and Mandarin terms follow the Wade-Giles system.

This paper is dedicated to the memory of my friend and fellow anthropologist Judith Strauch (1942–85).

REFERENCES

Arlington, L. C. 1923. The Chinese Female Names. *China Journal of Science and Arts* 1(4):316–325.

Bamberger, Joan. 1974. Naming and the Transmission of Status in a Central Brazilian Society. *Ethnology* 13:363–378.

Barnes, Robert B. 1982. Personal Names and Social Classification. In *Semantic Anthropology*. David Parkin, ed., pp. 211–226. London: Academic Press.

Beidelman, T. O. 1974. Kaguru Names and Naming. *Journal of Anthropological Research* 30:281–293.

de Bary, William Theodore. 1970. Individualism and Humanitarianism in Late Ming Thought. In *Self and Society in Ming Thought*. Wm. Theodore de Bary, ed., pp. 145–247. New York: Columbia University Press.

Eberhard, Wolfram. 1970. A Note on Modern Chinese Nicknames. In *Studies in Chinese Folklore and Related Essays*. Wolfram Eberhard, ed., pp. 217–222. Indiana University Folklore Institute Monograph Series, Vol. 23. The Hague: Mouton.

Elvin, Mark. 1985. Between the Earth and Heaven: Conceptions of the Self in China. In *The Category of the Person*. Michael Carrithers, Steven Collins, Steven Lukes, eds., pp. 156–189. Cambridge: Cambridge University Press.

Geertz, Clifford. 1973. Person, Time, and Conduct in Bali. In *The Interpretation of Cultures*. pp. 360–411. New York: Basic Books.

Harris, Grace. 1978. *Casting Out Anger: Religion among the Taita of Kenya*. Cambridge: Cambridge University Press.

Hazelton, Keith. 1986. Patrilines and the Development of Localized Lineages: The Wu of Hsiuming City, Hui-chou, to 1528. In *Kinship*

Organization in Late Imperial China. Patricia B. Ebrey and James L. Watson, eds., pp. 137–169. Berkeley: University of California Press.

Kehl, Frank. 1971. Chinese Nicknaming Behavior: A Sociolinguistic Pilot Study. *Journal of Oriental Studies* 9:149–172.

Kingston, Maxine Hong. 1977. *The Woman Warrior: Memories of a Girlhood among Ghosts.* New York: Vintage Books. (Originally published in hardcover by Alfred Knopf, 1976.)

La Fontaine, Jean. 1985. Person and Individual: Some Anthropological Reflections. In *The Category of the Person.* Michael Carrithers, Steven Collins, and Steven Lukes, eds., pp. 123–140. Cambridge: Cambridge University Press.

Maybury-Lewis, David. 1984. Name, Person, and Ideology in Central Brazil. In *Naming Systems.* Elisabeth Tooker, ed., pp. 1–10. 1980 Proceedings of the American Ethnological Society. Washington, DC: American Ethnological Society.

Munro, Donald (ed.). 1985. *Individualism and Holism: Studies in Confucian and Taoist Values.* Ann Arbor: University of Michigan Press.

Rosaldo, Renato. 1984. Ilongot Naming: The Play of Associations. *In Naming Systems.* Elisabeth Tooker, ed., pp. 11–24. 1980 Proceedings of the American Ethnological Society. Washington, DC: American Ethnological Society.

Shiga, Shuzo. 1978. Family Property and the Law of Inheritance in Traditional China. In *Chinese Family Law and Social Change.* David Buxbaum, ed., pp. 109–150. Seattle: University of Washington Press.

Stacey, Judith. 1983. *Patriarchy and Socialist Revolution in China.* Berkeley: University of California Press.

Sung, Margaret M. Y. 1981. Chinese Personal Naming. *Journal of the Chinese Language Teachers Association* 16(2):67–90.

Topley, Marjorie. 1974. Cosmic Antagonisms: A Mother-Child Syndrome. In *Religion and Ritual in Chinese Society.* Arthur Wolf, ed., pp. 233–249. Stanford, CA: Stanford University Press.

Watson, James L. 1976. Chattel Slavery in Chinese Peasant Society: A Comparative Analysis. *Ethnology* 15:361–375.

Watson, Rubie S. 1981. Class Differences and Affinal Relations in South China. *Man* 16:593–615.

———. 1984. Women's Property in Republican China: Rights and Practice. *Republican China* 10(12):1–12.

———. 1985. *Inequality Among Brothers: Class and Kinship in South China.* Cambridge: Cambridge University Press.

Willis, Roy. 1982. On a Mental Sausage Machine and other Nominal Problems. In *Semantic Anthropology.* David Parkin, ed., pp. 227–240. London: Academic Press.

Wolf, Margery. 1972. *Women and the Family in Rural Taiwan.* Stanford, CA: Stanford University Press.

Wu, Ching-chao. 1927. The Chinese Family: Organization, Names, and Kinship Terms. *American Anthropologist* 29:316–325.

Yang, Martin C. 1945. *A Chinese Village: Taitou, Shantung Province.* New York: Columbia University Press.

NOTES

1. There are bound to be regional, temporal, urban-rural, and class differences in Chinese naming practices. A general discussion of Chinese naming awaits further research.

2. In Taiwan the *ming* is the legal name (it appears in the official household register) and is sometimes called the *cheng ming* (correct name) (Sung 1981:70). In Hong Kong this name may or may not be the name used on legal documents.

3. I am grateful to Professor Jack Dull for pointing out to me the significance and frequency of the personal name Nai among Chinese women.

4. In a similar vein a fifth or sixth child might be named "To End" or "To Finish." One can find such names in the Hong Kong and Taipei telephone directories (see also Sung 1981:81).

5. In China there are no given names like John that are shared by millions of people; on this point see Sung 1981:85.

6. In a discussion of the cosmic relationship between mother and child Marjorie Topley writes of her Cantonese informants:

    The constitutional imbalance of a child with a queer fate may also involve other parties. First, the child may be polarized in the same direction as someone with whom it has a continuous relationship. Then both parties may suffer from continual illness. This may be corrected by adding an element to the child's name so it is compatible with that of the other party [1974:240].

7. This is changing now that girls go to school and their births are registered.

8. In the past when village boys started school at age five or six (girls did not attend school until the 1960s), the schoolmaster gave each student a school or "study name" (*hsueh-ming*). School names are no longer very important in the New Territories.

9. In the past officials' *ming* could not be used except by intimates (see Eberhard 1970 and Sung 1981).
10. After I gained some insight into the micropolitics of my neighbor's household, the name seemed well chosen.
11. Once a son marries reproduction becomes a matter for the younger generation, and in Ha Tsuen it was considered shameful for the mother of a married son to become pregnant.
12. It should be noted here that men do not constitute a uniform category in this regard. Highly literate men make up one extreme but many poorly educated or uneducated men fall somewhere between the two extremes. Like the names of their sisters, their names may be inelegant and rarely seen in written form, but unlike adult women, they do retain their names after marriage.
13. On this point see also LaFontaine 1985:131.
14. For discussions of the concept of the individual as value and the self in Chinese society see for example de Bary 1970; Shiga 1978:122; and more recently Elvin 1985; Munro 1985 (especially essays by Hansen, Yu, Munro, and de Bary).

Gender and the Stories Pittsburgh Police Officers Tell about Using Physical Force

Bonnie McElhinny

When most people think of work on language and gender, they probably think of works like linguist Deborah Tannen's *You Just Don't Understand* or perhaps even psychologist John Gray's *Men are From Mars, Women are from Venus,* studies of "miscommunications" between women and men in heterosexual couples. Despite an increasing number of different approaches, in studies of language and gender in North America the focus on cross-sex miscommunication remains influential and, at its best, insightful.[1] There are, however, a number of increasingly controversial theoretical assumptions about gender often implicitly embedded in this approach, including the notions that the study of gender is closely wedded to the study of heterosexual relations, that gender is an attribute rather than a practice, and that the study of gender is the study of individuals (McElhinny 2003). Studying gender in heterosexual dyads can suggest that "gendered talk is mainly a personal characteristic or limited to the institution of the family" (Gal 1991:185). It also draws attention away from the importance of studying the ways that gender is a structural principle organizing social institutions such as workplaces, schools, courts, and the state and the patterns they display in the recruitment, treatment, and mobility of different men and women (Gal 1991). Gender, like class and racialized ethnicity, nationality, age and sexuality, is an axis for the organization of inequality, a principle for allocating access to resources, though the way each of these axes work may have their own distinctive features (Scott 1986:1054). In this chapter, I talk about how gender structures policing, a type of work that has been traditionally reserved in the United States for men, especially working-class White men. In 1991–1992 I spent twelve months patrolling with the Pittsburgh police department, and recorded 182 hours of police officer interaction. This department was, at the time of my resarch, one of the most racially and sexually diverse big-city police departments in the United States, with 25% female officers and 25% Black officers. This was largely due to a court-enforced affirmative

Adapted from Bonnie McElhinny, "Fearful, Forceful Agents of the Law: Ideologies about Language and Gender in Police Officers' Narratives about the Use of Physical Force," *Pragmatics* 13 (2003): 253–284. Reprinted with permission of publisher.

action program in place from 1975–1991 which mandated the hiring of gender and ethnic quotas: each time the department hired a class of recruits, the class was 25% Black women, 25% White women, 25% Black men and 25% White men. The Pittsburgh police force, like many other public sector jobs, was also shaped by a veterans' hiring preference program. Each veteran who took the civil service exam for policing had ten percent added to the score achieved. This practice tended to benefit men, perhaps especially White men (see McElhinny 2000). Even though this workplace was increasingly diverse, it was still perceived as "men's work." The gender of a workplace is determined not only by the presence, or even predominance, of women or men in it but also by cultural norms and interpretations of gender that dictate who is best suited for different sorts of employment. Female police officers routinely found themselves addressed as "sir." My research investigates what the dominant kind of masculinity was in this workplace, and the ways that different officers adopted, adapted or rejected this way of defining policing.

In this chapter, I examine narratives told by male and female, Black and White police officers in Pittsburgh about moments when they found it necessary to use physical force. Policing is a job predominantly staffed by men, and the dominant style of policing is understood as masculine. Nonetheless, in this study I do not assume that men and women are different. Rather, I ask what advantages and disadvantages accrue to men and women embracing different interactional strategies at different moments, when these are associated with gender, and the ways they are associated with dominant institutional norms and practices. I believe that, "interpretations of maleness, manhood, or masculinity are not neutral, but rather all such attributions have political entailments. In any given situation, they may align men against women, some men against other men, some women against other women, or some men and some women against others. In short, the processes of gendering produce difference and inequality" (Cornwall and Lindisfarne 1994:10).

"ACTING CRAZY" AS A THEORY OF AGENCY AND MODEL OF PERSONHOOD

Many male and some female police officers in Pittsburgh understand themselves as fighting a "war" on crime. These police officers believe that the only way to earn respect from citizens is by "acting crazy," a phrase they use to describe their efforts to instill fear in others so that they will not try to push them around. Acting crazy is also a useful strategy for gaining control over an interactional situation since it entails a refusal to negotiate. The construction of authority by using displays of anger raises certain dilemmas that "acting crazy," as a theory of agency and model of personhood, is meant to solve. First, police officers find it important to distinguish between acting crazy and being crazy.

> **You're not really a hard person, but you have to act that way**, because they'll brick you. [PO 30A, Black male, 30, 2 years on the job]

(For details on the transcription conventions used for these recordings, please see Appendix A.) Certain officers, often portrayed as male and older, are seen as "going off," or "blowing their tops" that is, breaking out into unexpected rages that they are not in control of. Though the suddenness of their anger is similar to "acting crazy," other officers distinguish their actions by suggesting that some of these older male officers ARE crazy, rather than ACTING crazy. The difference, then, is that police officers portray other officers as out of control even when they are in control, while understanding themselves as in control even when out of control. Second, in order to justify fear-inspiring actions which they fully realize are controversial, police officers describe the wild, dirty, terrifying world of "the streets" which they must react to. Some officers themselves come to seem inordinately fearful as they tell these stories. As a result, at the very moments when police officers exercise the most force they portray themselves as most helpless: "What else could I do?" "Acting crazy" is thus a way of simultaneously claiming and denying responsibility for action.

Although the necessity for "acting crazy" is not extensively challenged by police officers in Pittsburgh, not all police officers support or value this style of interaction. Some officers perceive themselves more like bureaucrats or social workers than street fighters, and these beliefs lead to different models of agency and personhood (McElhinny 1995). Nonetheless a focus on fighting crime, often called the *crime control* model of policing (Walker 1977) predominates. The *crime-control* model, also known as the crime fighter or militarized model, "characterizes the typical police officer as a crime fighter extraordinaire, a seasoned, well-armed, professional soldier in an unending and savage war on crime" (Appier 1998:160). Between World War II and the early 1970s, women were not seen as appropriate for policing jobs because they were thought incapable of being combat soldiers. The ideal police officer was aggressive and tough, authoritative and male. However, with the advent of affirmative action hiring programs in police departments in the early 1970s (McElhinny n.d.), the gendered ideal shifted a bit. For this reason, not all proponents of a crime-fighting ideology are men: we will look at the narratives of several women below too. A far greater percentage of men, however, embraced such a model, for a variety of complex historical and institutional reasons. At the end of this chapter, I consider what the implications of how police officers talk about the use of physical force are. I am particularly interested in understanding whether and how the integration of women into a traditionally masculine occupation like policing leads to the reinscription or transformation of certain ideologies about how interaction should proceed.

USING NARRATIVES TO STUDY GENDER AND IDEOLOGY

Analyzing narratives is particularly helpful for elucidating how police officers' make sense of their experiences in particular. First, narratives are *event-centered*, that is, they focus on human action and interaction. Second, narratives are *experience-centered*, and thus allow us to infer something about what it feels like to be in the story world. Third, narratives are *performative, seductive, and evocative.* That is, narratives do not merely refer to past experience but create experiences for their audience, and they try to persuade listeners by seducing them into the world portrayed. Narratives make an argument about what happened as part of describing what happened (Mattingly 1998:31). Analyses of narratives helps us to understand how stories are given shape by their tellers but also how stories shape the way tellers see and experience themselves, how people become the stories they tell about their lives. Police officers who embrace a crime control model frequently rehearse how they will behave in certain situations if confronted with a recalcitrant husband, or drunken prisoner, or fleeing burglar. They also frequently review the moments in which they have found themselves embroiled in such situations. Narratives allow officers to simultaneously present their own views on past conflicts, shape the on-going interaction (here, with an anthropologist), and rehearse how they would, ideally, talk in the future. The very reiteration of these stories serves to keep alive for these officers the need to be prepared, always, to use force. Stories thus can provide crucial insights into how ideologies around certain styles of policing are forged or reinforced on the ground by police officers.

ALL OF A SUDDEN: RAPID ACTION, REASONABLENESS, AND ROBOCOP

Rapid, perhaps unpredictable, behavior is a central feature of most police officers' stories about the use of force. In the following narrative, a White female officer is describing the actions of a towering young Black officer ("David") who has come to be called "Robocop" by some of the people in the neighborhood, in part because of his weight-lifter's physique, in part because he's six foot three inches tall, and in part because of his policing style.[2]

I was working behind a desk last um, last SPRING. . . . David's brought these two people in, a guy and a girl and the guy he had handcuffed to a chair and the girl he had handcuffed to the other chair and the guy's . . . was talking and ta::lking and talking and talking and David's like "SHUT UP." He told him like twenty times and Zellini's sitting behind me . . . singing these little songs like <<in song-song voice>> "You better shut u:::p, David's gonna get ma:::d." (LAUGHS) and like right when he says that **all of a sudden** David PICKED this guy up, chair and all and just like **slammed** him down to the ground. He's like "I told you to SHUT THE FUCK UP. NOW SHUT UP." (LAUGHS) and then he comes over to me afterwards he goes <<she mimics him mumbling under his breath>>, "I'm sorry. I lost my temper." He goes "I can't—I can't stand when I do that you know." (LAUGHS) I'm like, "That's cool David y::—you don't have to apologize." He's like "I didn't mean to swear that much in front of you." He's like real polite and stuff too you know but- They call him Robocop. [PO 25A, White female, 28, 3 years on the job]

Although the narrator concludes by suggesting that David's size and strength alone are enough to intimidate the public, the story suggests otherwise. He (even he) needs to construct a police persona. This female officer portrays him as being unpredictable, crazy, wild. "All of a sudden" is an adverbial phrase which marks Robocop's transition from one condition to another, and which describes him as being out of control. "Slammed", with its connotations of violence, noise and unexpectedness, is used to similar effect, as are the profanity and shouting in David's reported speech. Although David's action is portrayed as perhaps being sudden from the handcuffed man's point of view, it is also portrayed as intelligible and even predictable from a police officer's point of view. The narrator manages this by portraying the actions of the handcuffed man as unreasonable (*"he was talking and ta::lking and talking and talking"*).

What, however, is the point of this story? Skillful narratives often include an evaluation that indicates why a story was told and what the narrator was getting at. Evaluations may be external (in which the point is made explicitly) or internal (in which the narrative dramatizes

this information). Here the narrator's laughter throughout the story draws our attention to the hilarious juxtaposition of the fearsome giant with the pussycat who then apologizes to the young female officer. The juxtaposition itself implicitly suggests that David's actions are not an intrinsic part of his character, but part of a display. Indeed the narrator, here relying on the U.S. folk ideology which associates people's real selves with those they display to family and friends, may even be suggesting that the real man is the "real polite" man and not the real angry man. Such a story thus minimizes the actions that "Robocop" takes while acting out his violent role.

ARMED ROBBERS AND AGENCY

If this story begins to illustrate the theory of personhood associated with acting crazy, the stories of Jay, a White officer in his mid-20s from a policing family (his Dad and his wife are also officers) elucidate the interactional and professional dilemmas for which "acting crazy" is a solution. One of Jay's principal fears—and it was a fear he articulated repeatedly even in the few days I rode with him—was that his firearm would be wrestled from him in a fight, or that the firearm of another officer would be taken and used against him. Even if most policing doesn't require guns or physical force, Jay repeatedly pointed out that it only takes one incident to get him killed. Jay justifies police force by describing it entirely in terms of self-defense, as a reaction to other actions. Portraying the use of force as self-defense contributes to a siege mentality. Any struggle between a police officer and another person is seen merely as a fight between individuals rather than one between an individual and an institution. Jay offers one example of series of events which were, he says, distorted by the "liberal media."

I caught an armed robber on Polka Street. Guy runs out. "Hey some black guy—" had a big knife, runs at the car. I say, "Hey, what the fuck are you doing?" Andy sees <the robber> hiding between these homes, crouched down. I hear

Andy yell. Guy was supposed to be armed so Andy had his gun on him. Guy could have gone straight up on this porch. Andy couldn't see his hands—he said, "Show me your hands, real slow, or you're gonna get whacked." **Now we're in a fist fight, he got his ass beat,** <community members> saw this brutal act, by a police man, was a bunch of shit. This brutal police man. Man falsely accused. He was the guy that robbed the place. He wouldn't show Andy his hands. Community leaders saw it, and they said it's wrong. "You police man are wrong." [PO 114B, White male, 26, 5 years on the job]

In the part of the narrative where Jay is catching the robber, he regularly uses historic present tense ("*I say,*" "*Andy sees,*" "*I hear*") and leaves "guy" unmodified by a definite or indefinite article. This iconically captures and conjures up the breathless rapidity with which events happen and with which officers must make decisions about appropriate actions. The suddenness of the movement from threat to force ("*Now we're in a fist fight*") emphasizes the danger of police work, and justifies the rapidity with which he too must make a transition from one emotional state to another. Most surprising here is the vagueness at a crucial moment: Who exactly initiated the fist fight? Although police officers have a kind of discretionary power over others' freedom that would justify a portrayal of themselves as super agents, they often downplay their own agency. "Now we're in a fist fight" and "He got his ass beat" leave unmarked the agent or agents of the acts. Jay consistently blames the other person for escalating interactions from a polite to an impolite one, from a verbal interaction to one which is physically threatening, from an interaction in which a physical threat is implicit to one in which it is explicit.

If Jay accounts for his actions in terms of the activities he must respond to, Frank, a burly man who looks like Hollywood's stereotype of an Irish policeman, justifies his actions in terms of the character of the people he must deal with. He half-jokes, "Anymore when someone asks me what I do for a living, I say garbageman" [9A]. He uses other metaphors for criminals ("vermin" and "maggots") which serve to downplay the agency and humanity of those

he interacts with. He portrays his actions as inevitable, as entirely determined by the situation rather than his own agency.

> I don't usually confess up to too many things, but the one time I did beat a man I didn't really have to, whereas we get a call for child molestation. We could look in the window we could see this little girl about four years old bleeding from the vagina-area. This maggot's in the corner, crying. I hit him. More than once. **What am I supposed to do**. [PO 9B, White male, 39/40, 13 years on the job]

Frank offers no apologies for actions that he sees as natural, in the circumstances. Like Jay, he sees his role as reaction, not action.

Even in seemingly frank descriptions of the emotional distress the job causes him, Frank uses agency-masking grammatical devices. After he described this child abuse call, I ask if it was difficult not to take the job home.

> Not to sound like a wimp, but more than once I've gone home and cried. I don't see myself as a wimp but . . . **it catches up to you**. One time I had to take little girls, I didn't actually take them, I helped carry them out of the fire, they'd died. That bothered me. Thinking of those girls— nobody gets a break on a fire hydrant. [PO 9B, White male, 39/40, 13 years on the job]

Though he does say "I've cried," "it catches up to you" doesn't even give him the relative passive role of experiencer (compare "I felt"). Frank also moves quickly away from a discussion of how the job affects him to describing the sort of tough professional action he takes as a result (writing tickets for people illegally parked near fire hydrants).

"BETWEEN A ROCK AND A HARD PLACE": THE DILEMMAS OF BEING A BLACK POLICE OFFICER

So far the stories considered here have been stories told by White officers, but a crime fighter ideology is not limited to these officers. Doug, a young African-American officer, came on the job with a college degree but no street experience.

He notes that when he first became a police officer, he tried to be polite and nice (a strategy he calls being "Officer Friendly"), but these strategies did not work. He says that police officers cannot simply let others tell them what to do. Instead, he says, police officers need to take control of situations:

> **If you more or less yell at them**, tell them "Get the hell outta here, we're not gonna have this," they'll get real quiet, they'll get real soft, and everything else [PO 30A, Black male, 30, 2 years on the job]

"If you more or less yell at them" uses a hedge to downplay the police officer's action. The use of impersonal "you" ("*If you more or less yell . . .*") rather than "I" has a similar effect.

Doug uses many military metaphors to describe his work. He describes the drug trade in Pittsburgh as a "drug war", and says that the job of policing sometimes becomes so overwhelming that police men become "just like Vietnam vets—they need to get away." He describes his own style of policing as aggressive. In the accounts of officers like Doug, there often seems to be a surprisingly thin edge between displays of anger and aggression and accounts of fear. Doug himself is most aware of this when discussing other officers. As part of his training period, he worked with a White officer who was tense every time he found himself around a group of Blacks. Though Doug is critical of such White officers' actions, he also excuses them to some extent by suggesting that they're not "mean," just "scared." He reserves his harshest critique for the supervisors who deploy their officers without sensitivity to what they can and cannot do.

Like Jay, Doug argues that people's critiques of cops arise because they do not fully understand what it is like "out here", not because people might have different moral or legal views about force. Doug's comments arose when we were talking about his reaction to the beating of African-American motorist Rodney King by white police officers in Los Angeles. He quickly noted that he believed the L.A. police officers were wrong, but followed that with comments on the ways that people tend to misinterpret police actions. His comments condense a number of the strategies discussed thus far in this paper.

> Say for instance you would like be in a window and you would see me run up on some kids you seen right across the street. And you—they don't look like they're doing anything to you. But I go up and choke one of them, just running out of my car and and I go up and choke one of them. It seems like for no reason at all. It would be hard for me to explain that I told them to get off the street, I knew they were dealing drugs, I wouldn't have it, I told them if I came back, you know. Now if they would have pulled him out of the car and somebody would have shot that saying that "Oh they just beat him." Now how do they know he didn't have a gun or whatever? Now like I said, that <<the beating of Rodney King>> was excessive force, and that was ridiculous, to beat a guy like that. But I mean if they would have beat him a couple times or whatever and that was filmed, it would look kinda one-sided. See as a police officer, you have enough problems worrying about yourself (pause) being all—getting, you know, being shot, being—existing out on the street. But to worry about if you're gonna get sued, if your family's gonna, you know if you're gonna lose your house and all that stuff. Every time you question something, or move you make, it could cost you your life. If you're afraid that someone is watching you, you're afraid you don't want to hit this guy or snatch him up, and then he turns around and stabs you, and kills you. You're between a rock and a hard place. [PO 30A, Black male, 30, 2 years on the job]

Doug is torn. He wants to critique what happened in L.A., but reserve the right to use force for himself. He wants to critique outsiders' views of policing at the same time that he is an outsider to what happened in L.A. In this brief passage a cluster of grammatical features mark anxious preoccupation and serve to heighten the officer's message about his double bind, how immobilized he feels by needing to balance a need for self-defense with a concern for citizens' rights. There is a cluster of verbs and adjectives that describes worry and fear, though note that here again the officer does not construct himself as the agent or actor or even the experiencer ("*to worry about if you're gonna get sued, if you're afraid*"). The author also piles up the potential consequences of any act, with a series of "if" clauses that together imagine the worse that could happen: *if you're gonna get sued, if your family's gonna, if you're afraid.* Finally, impersonal "you" serves to distance these concerns from him in the second half of his account: "*if you're afraid,*" "*you're between a rock and a hard place.*" If Jay largely emphasizes the physical dangers of policing, Doug adds to these concerns a preoccupation with the moral and legal hazards of the job. This spiral of panic may reflect the particular dilemmas that being Black and being a police officer pose.

Girls Who Freak: Turning Rapport Talk on Its Head

After having repeatedly heard how masculine Cissy was, I was eager to meet her. I was startled to find she was a short, plump White woman with long, curly black hair. Though following department regulations would have meant pulling her hair up into a bun, she wore it loose down on her shoulders. It was the week before Halloween and she was wearing a pumpkin tie pin. Though regulation socks are dark blue, her socks had pumpkins on them. She looked like a PTA mother. My surprise at the fact that she was perceived as masculine reflects some dominant gender ideologies that link femininity and masculinity to appearance. For police officers, however, it is interaction which is a more salient characteristic, in part because interactions are so carefully scrutinized by the public and by supervisors, but also because interactions shape the work environment for other officers. Cissy's enthusiasm for "acting crazy" led to her being perceived as masculine, and is evidence that the crime control ideology is gendered as masculine, regardless of who embraces it. There was, however, a stronger negative connotation in labelling her as masculine than in labelling male officers as such. Other officers saw Cissy as an impatient, impetuous officer who did not treat people right. More than any of the other officers I rode with, Cissy's image of the kind of police officer she was differed from my observations and from the perceptions of other officers. Cissy repeatedly painted herself as an active officer who was interested in helping people,

and who had a knack for establishing rapport with the public. She describes the way people in a racially-mixed, lower-to-middle income neighborhood reacted to her and her female partner.

> [I]t was funny cause they would see two females come down in the car and it was like, "We're not afraid of you" so you kinda had to get real hard-nosed with them at first, but it was funny cause after you like really got out of the car and you show them this is the way it's gonna be, they kinda like you. **You got a rapport going** with them, where when they would see your car, they would just leave. We have worked out **such a good rapport** with those people down there. I've NE:VER had no problems. Those other officers they go down there and they give them a real hard time. . . . I had one problem and after that. "I'm not moving, you're not nothing." I'm like, "Oh yeah. We're something. Let's go." And we were out of the car. And it was like, "**Those girls are CRA:zy.** They'll actually make you move." [PO 11A, White female, mid-30s, 2 years on the job]

In the literature on language and gender, seeking rapport has been largely associated with women's talk. Tannen (1990:77) defines rapport-talk as a way of establishing connections and negotiating relations in which emphasis is placed on displaying similarities and matching experiences. She contrasts this with report-talk, in which she maintains many men display knowledge or skills as a way to preserve independence and status in a hierarchical social order. Cissy's definition of rapport is much more like Tannen's definition of report-talk. For her, rapport seems to be understood as everyone recognizing her right and ability to use verbal and physical force, and fearing that possibility.

The extent to which women officers are licensed to use physical force and tough talk is at least partly linked to the class and ethnic persona they present, and to stereotypes about White and Black femininity in the U.S. Though Cissy was seen in a negative light, as "too masculine," Ayanna, a young Black woman who was seen as ready, willing, and able to use force, did not receive similar sanctions. Ayanna was one of the few young female police officers who received the accolade of "knows her way around out there" from older White male officers. She was in her mid-20s and had been on the force for 2 years. She was a slight African-American woman (weighing about 100 pounds, she confessed, and trying to gain more), with tightly cropped hair. Though many smaller women were ignored or babied by male officers, Ayanna was, at the time I rode with her, being actively recruited by the City's Drug Task Force, which at the time of my field-work had no female officers. She tells stories about fights with relish.

> We had to chase this guy . . . when I first came on. We had to chase him cause they were going on a drug bust . . . and they wanted him and Jimmy Baker. . . . We got a tip right, we had to chase these boys, they were supposed to be armed. . . . We really didn't know if they were armed or not. Police officers been chasing them for months and they been lying to them, blowing them off. Me and my partner caught these guys. . . . When I finally caught them I had these fake nails on. I used to go and get my nails done every week. Broke my nail. Fifty dollars. When I seen he broke my nail, I **freaked.** I said, "You broke my nail!" I **pounded** him in his head, **acting like I was crazy.** "I can't believe you broke my nail!" I'm **tripping** over my nail right. I'm still huffing and puffing from the run. Was fun. We had a great time that day. [PO 58A, Black female, early 20s, 2 years on the job]

In a curious reversal of feminine stereotypes, here a broken fingernail does not reduce a woman to ineffectiveness, but rather leads to the use of physical force. Though a fake fingernail is a symbol of femininity, perhaps especially a symbol of a certain kind of Black femininity, her physical reaction is precisely that of other officers whose authority is questioned in any way. Again verbs mark a sudden change of state ("*was tripping*," "*freaked*," "*pounded*"). Like the male officers above, she describes her actions as a masquerade ("*acting like I was crazy*"). Ayanna also invoked the necessity for "acting crazy" in other, rather different circumstances. She was on her way to a call that had been described by the dispatcher as "complainant says her boyfriend's on the way over to her house and she expects trouble." As Ayanna drove to the largely White working-class area she said that this was an area where people were known for fighting police officers, and for their dislike of Black officers. She described the strategy she would try to adopt to handle the call ("*First I'll try to start off nice*"), but points out that sometimes "you gotta act crazy" to be recognized as an authority in such a neighborhood.

It is clear from these descriptions that women, too, can embrace a crime control ideology, and that younger women in particular are likely to do so. They are not trying to establish a distinctively feminine or womanly style of policing as a way of creating space for themselves in this predominantly masculine workplace, as women did at the turn of the century when they saw policing as an extension of social work (Appier 1998). Instead, these younger women choose to assimilate to, and reinscribe the power of, the dominant ideology of how to act, and interact, as a police officer, in ways that end up allying them with certain male officers, and against older female officers who often adopt a more critical stance towards the crime control model. Indeed, younger women argue that older women may have been qualified for the job, but they took it for the wrong reasons: "they only do it for the money." Many of the older women did enter policing at times of financial hardship (e.g. a divorce, a husband's loss of a job in a steel mill), and they do not describe policing as a job they had always dreamed of doing. Because they "only took the job for the money" they are not seen as professional. Younger women distance themselves from the problems faced by the first female officers, many of whom are still on the job, understanding them as difficulties faced by particular individuals rather than challenges linked to breaking down the barriers to women working on this job. They tend to see measures such as affirmative action as unnecessary. Young women therefore tend to overestimate the extent to which simply being a "good" police officer allows them to succeed on the job, and to under-estimate the ways that their presence on the job was and is supported by certain institutional measures (like affirmative action). Their views do not allow them to see the ways that gender remains linked to the definition of what being a good police officer is, albeit in a less marked way that when women were seen as incapable of becoming police officers.

CONCLUSIONS

The wide distribution of the ideology of police officer as crime fighter among Pittsburgh police officers is partial evidence for its dominant status among Pittsburgh police officers. Police officers who espouse it may be White or Black, men or women. Some have college educations and others have high school educations, some are veterans and some are not, some are rookies and some have been on the force for close to fifteen years. Among those who espouse the ideology there is, perhaps, an unusually high cluster of people who come from policing families. And yet the crime fighter ideology remains associated with a certain kind of masculinity, irrespective of the people who hold it. This makes it difficult for women, and men who have not traditionally been police officers, to be perceived as competent, and thus gives them a tenuous foothold within the job. In addition, those who challenge the dominant ideology may not be judged as policing effectively. Rather than "acting crazy" some officers focus on constructing another persona, that of the rational, calm, cool bureaucrat. Officers who orient towards this way of thinking about policing tend to be women (especially older women), or Black men, or White men with college educations. These officers may be portrayed by others as unwilling or unable to do "real" police work. Still, those who fall in with dominant norms may not be seen as effective police officers either. As affirmative action hiring plans have been rolled back in police departments in recent years, hirings of women and (to a lesser extent) minority men have immediately dropped because they still are not seen by administrators as fully capable of doing the job. Recent redefinitions of policing as community policing, or as "social work in combat boots" do offer a significant challenge to the crime-fighter ideology, and may create more permanent niches for women and minority men in policing. In Pittsburgh, however, community policing has not been embraced by either administrators or police officers.

When the police officers tell stories, to themselves or to the public or to me, about moments when the use of force was necessary, they are not merely describing those experiences, but recreating them, seducing themselves and others into believing that the sequence of events that they describe was not only justified, but inevitable. Given the emotional power of these stories, simply instructing officers to behave in other ways, where their actions are perceived as inappropriate, seems unlikely to be a productive strategy for changing the way they approach these scenarios. Activists have repeatedly found that in numerous settings presenting research which suggests to people that their beliefs are "false" is not sufficient for engendering support for change, or even agreement that the activists are right. One needs, instead, to find a way of restructuring these ways of feeling.

The discursive strategies which accompany these officers' descriptions of and justifications for their use of force focus on the ways they elicit respect and fear by acting crazy, and by acting in abrupt and unpredictable ways. These narrators also (with attentiveness to public perceptions of the use of force) often de-emphasize their own role as agents of the law. This denial of agency may be one of the defining features of legal and medical institutional talk in many settings, and one of the key ways that authority and power not only justified but disguised (see also Briggs 1997). Many of these officers' stories about the use of force are accompanied by sheer fear about the potential crumbling of their police power. By emphasizing the danger they face "out here", they justify the use of force in self-defense. Other working class jobs—mining, construction, agriculture—are, in fact, more dangerous than police work but police officers' constant sense of fear distinguishes them from these workers (Reuss-Ianni 1983:19–20). The discourse on fear here shares with studies of colonial violence, where talk about fear of the dominated was used to justify suppression, as well as a way of bargaining with other elites for resources and support needed to face down the purported threat (see

Abu-Lughod and Lutz 1990:14). It does not seem inconsequential for understanding the particular stances towards violence expressed here that veterans of the U.S. military receive preference in hiring as police officers (McElhinny 2000), or that my fieldwork was conducted during a period when the U.S. government saw itself as waging a "war on drugs" both in the U.S. and in Latin and South America. Perhaps what is most striking about the worldview of police officers is precisely the ways in which they assume that social interactions are built around conflict and mayhem. They repeatedly insist that the world is violent and that no one is trustworthy. Though some may lament the loss of innocence and trust that comes with repeatedly dealing with violence, most police officers were convinced that the Hobbesian view of human nature which this led them to have was much more accurate than the blinkered and rosier view of others. The stories they tell about instances in which they use physical force, and the justifications which they offer for it, are built around this linguistic and social ideology. For them, instances of lying, conflict and violence are not extraordinary, but ordinary, everyday occurrences. Indeed, for many police officers, violence and deception define humanity.

ACKNOWLEDGMENTS

Research and writing were supported by the National Science Foundation (NSF Graduate Fellowship and NSF Dissertation Improvement Grant), the Mellon Foundation, the Wenner Gren Foundation for Anthropological Research (Pre-Doctoral Grant, and Richard Carley Hunt Post-doctoral Grant), the Stanford Humanities Center, the University of Pittsburgh Women's Studies Program, the Stanford Center for the Study of Conflict and Negotiation, and the Department of Anthropology at the University of Toronto.

APPENDIX A. TRANSCRIPTION CONVENTIONS

Each transcribed example is followed by information about the tape that the example can be found on, as well as the police officer's sex (male or female), ethnicity (Black, White, Mixed ethnicity) and years of work on the Pittsburgh police force (where available). For example, [PO 11A, White female, mid-30s, 2 years on the job] indicates that the transcribed example is on side A of PO 11. The officer is White, female, and in her mid-30s. She has worked as a police officer for two years. This paper also draws on the following transcription conventions:

(pause)	**All pauses are marked between parentheses.**
We were walk—	A dash marks a word or phrase broken off before it is finished.
LOUD	Capital letters indicate increased volume.
eve::ry	Semi-colon marks lengthened sound.
(laughs)	Laughter is marked between single parentheses.
" quote "	Indicates quoted speech.
<text>	Parentheses surround barely audible speech for which the transcription is uncertain.
....	Three or four dots indicate that some material from the original transcript has been omitted.
<<comment>>	Double brackets enclose transcriber comments.
bold	Part of transcript highlighted for analyst's purposes.

REFERENCES

Abu-Lughod, Lila and Catherine Lutz. 1990. Introduction: Emotion, discourse and the politics of everyday life. In Catherine Lutz and Lila Abu-Lughod (eds.), *Language and the politics of emotion*. Cambridge: Cambridge University Press, 1–23.

Appier, Janis. 1998. *Policing women: The sexual politics of law enforcement and the LAPD*. Philadelphia: Temple University Press.

Briggs, Charles (1997) Introduction: From the ideal, the ordinary, and the orderly to conflict and violence in pragmatic research. Special issue of *Pragmatics* on "Conflict and violence in pragmatic research." Volume 7(4): 451–459.

Cornwall, Andrea and Nancy Lindisfarne. 1994. Dislocating masculinity: Gender, power, and anthropology. In Andrea Cornwall and Nancy Lindisfarne (eds.), *Dislocating masculinities: Comparative ethnographies.* New York: Routledge 11–47.

Gal, Susan. 1991. Between speech and silence: The problematics of research on language and gender. In Micaela di Leonardo (ed.), *Gender at the crossroads of knowledge.* Berkeley: University of California Press, 175–203.

Mattingly, Cheryl. 1998. *Healing dramas and clinical plots: The narrative structure of experience.* Cambridge: Cambridge University Press.

McElhinny, Bonnie. 1995. Challenging hegemonic masculinities: Female and male police officers handling domestic violence. In Kira Hall and Mary Bucholtz (eds.), *Gender articulated: Language and the socially constructed self.* New York: Routledge, 217–243.

McElhinny, Bonnie. 2000. Affirmative action and veterans' hiring preferences: Two quota systems. *Voices: Newsletter of the association for feminist anthropology.* July, 4(1): 1–6.

McElhinny, Bonnie. 2003. Theorizing gender in sociolinguistics and linguistic anthropology. In Janet Holmes and Miriam Meyerhof (eds.), *Handbook of language and gender.* Oxford: Basil Blackwell. pp. 21–42.

McElhinny, Bonnie. n.d. *Policing language and gender.* Unpublished ms.

Reuss-Ianni, E. 1983. *The two cultures of policing: Street cops and management cops.* New Brunswick, NJ: Transaction Books.

Scott, Joan. 1986. Gender: A useful category of historical analysis. *American Historical Review.* 91(5): 1053–75.

Tannen, Deborah. 1990. *You just don't understand: Women and men in conversation.* New York: William Morrow.

Walker, Samuel. 1977. *A critical history of police reform: The emergence of professionalism.* Lexington, MA: Lexington Books.

NOTES

1. It is perhaps significant that Deborah Tannen's later work, focusing on men and women at work, did not receive the same public attention as her work on men and women in couples. This suggests that work which matches certain prevailing assumptions about how gender works is amplified and widely circulated, while other kinds of research are not.

2. I have chosen to use the terms *Black* and *White* throughout this paper because they are the terms which police officers usually use. Female officers tend to use *policeman* or *police officer* to describe their own role; male officers tend to use *policeman*. I have opted to use *police officer* as the default term throughout, adding a description of gender where it seems relevant.

The Making and Unmaking of Persons:
Gender and Body in Northeast India

Sarah Lamb

A principal theme in sociocultural studies of South Asia[1] over the past several decades has been the investigation of South Asian notions of what a "person" or "self" is.[2] One of the most interesting insights of much of this research has been the suggestion that Indians view

"The Making and Unmaking of Persons: Notes on Aging and Gender in North India." *Ethos* 25(3): 279–302. Used with permission.

persons as relatively fluid and open in nature. Research produced by McKim Marriott, Ronald Inden, and E. Valentine Daniel, for instance, has suggested that Indian persons are not thought to be bound and self-contained individuals, but rather connected *substantially* with the other people, places, and things of their lived-in worlds. By means of transactions with other persons, such as through sex, childbirth, living together, feeding, touching, and exchanging words, people are thought to absorb and give out parts of themselves. Thus it is possible—indeed, inevitable—for persons to establish substantial relations with other people (such as sexual partners, household and community members) and with the places (land, village, houses) in which they live. It may then make sense to describe Indian or South Asian persons as composite and hence "dividual" or divisible in nature, Marriott and later other scholars suggested; by contrast, Europeans and Americans view persons as relatively closed, contained and solid "*in*dividuals."[3]

One deficiency in early studies of personhood in South Asia, however, was the relatively scant attention paid to gender. This was true not only of the work on the person in South Asia, but also of the wider anthropological literature on personhood. What is striking is that although anthropological interest in personhood developed contemporaneously with the anthropology of gender (from about the 1970s on), there has been little attempt to bring these two fields of inquiry together. As Henrietta Moore observes: "Indigenous concepts of the person and self are presented, most often, as gender neutral, but on closer examination it is clear that the implicit model for the person in much ethnographic writing is, in fact, an adult male" (1994:28). This gives the misleading impression that person and self are ontologically prior to and separate from gender identity.

This chapter explores gendered aspects of personhood[4] for Bengali Indians, focusing on the gendered nature of the body and its implications for the making and unmaking of women's ties over the life course. Although Bengalis regard both men and women as relatively fluid and open in nature, they view women as being significantly more so, especially during their postpubertal and premenopausal years. This has important implications both for the ways women manage their daily interactions, and for the ways women's ties are made, unmade and remade over the course of their lives.

The chapter draws primarily on fieldwork done in the village of Mangaldihi in the northeast Indian state of West Bengal, where I lived for a year and a half in 1989–90 and for a brief revisit in 2003. Mangaldihi is a large, predominantly Hindu village of about 1,700, in the gently undulating terrain of the Birbhum District, about 150 kilometers northwest of Kolkata.

OPEN PERSONS AND SUBSTANTIAL EXCHANGES

The people I know in Mangaldihi (consistent in many ways with previous models of South Asian personhood) do feel themselves to be inherently relational, each person functioning as a nexus within a "net" (*jal*) of ties shared with people (especially kin), places, and things. By sharing and exchanging bodily and other substances through acts such as sex, touching, living together, sharing food, owning things, and eating the fruits of village soil, people see themselves as forming substantial-emotional bonds with their kin, homes, possessions, and land—all of which together make up a "person" (or *lok*).[5] Bengalis commonly refer to these kinds of relations as *maya,* a polyvalent term often translated by scholars as "illusion," but locally more often equated with affects like attachment, affection, compassion, and love.[6] The concept of maya entails integrally both material and what we might call emotional or sentimental dimensions. Maya is often imaged as a "net" (*jal, mayajal*), the strands of which are constituted both of shared bodily substance, as well as of emotional attachments such as affection, love, and compassion.

Such an understanding of persons as relatively open and unbound was at first especially apparent to me in practices surrounding "mutual touching" (*choyachuyi*) and the management of "impurity" (*asuddhata*) in daily life. People in Mangaldihi are concerned about whom and what they touch because touching involves a mutual transfer of substantial qualities from one person or thing to the next. High-caste Hindus avoid touching low-caste Hindus; Hindus avoid touching Muslims; and people of all castes frequently avoid touching those who are in states of "impurity" because of recent activities (e.g., defecating, visiting a hospital, or riding on a crowded bus of mixed castes and unknown substances). To be sure, people often touch one another in the course of their daily affairs. But when they do, each considers that substantial properties from the other have permeated his or her own body, and the person who is in the "higher" or more "pure" position will often feel it necessary to change clothes and bathe to rid him or herself from the effects of the contact. Further, some forms of contact—such as regularly sharing food or living together—are regarded as being so intimate and extensive that they cannot be erased simply by bathing: a person's substance and nature will have changed. (This is, in fact, how some relations of kinship are formed.)

As I happened to reside in a neighborhood of Brahmans—the highest Hindu caste and those tending to be most concerned about matters of purity—I was taught early on as part of my bodily training as an anthropologist to carefully manage my own touching, or bodily influxes and outflows. I was pressed to be careful about whom and what I interacted with, and to bathe and change my clothes after coming into contact with "impure" (*asuddha*) persons and things. On some days it seemed I had to bathe almost continuously—after I defecated (which unfortunately could happen more than once, especially when suffering from mild dysentery), or visited a lower-caste neighborhood, or came into contact accidentally with some dog-doo, or returned from a bus trip, or accidentally touched the outside panel of a truck carrying a dead person to the cremation ground, and on and on—so that I felt I could get almost nothing else done.

I am chagrined to confess, however, that for my first several months in the village, I did not notice that women were much more vulnerable than men to such daily impurities, and thus more frequently subjected to bathing rituals. Then one day quite by chance as I was having a casual conversation with an older Brahman man, he told me that, in fact, men (Brahman or otherwise) do not have to bathe after coming into cursory contact with impure things. They can if they *wish* to, that is if they desire to be particularly "pure" for the purposes of

entering a temple or some such; but they do not *have* to—no harm (*dos*) will occur if they do not. It is only *women* who must so often bathe. I was astounded, not only because I realized that a male anthropologist in Mangaldihi would not have had to spend so many seemingly futile hours bathing, but also because I had been so oblivious to this crucial difference in men's and women's daily practices. I spent the next several weeks asking everyone, men and women, why it is that women are more vulnerable to impurity than men, and their answers led me to some crucial differences in the ways people conceive of men's and women's bodies and personhoods.

GENDERED BODIES AND EVERYDAY PRACTICES

Key here are differences perceived in the biologies of the two sexes. In the predominant patrilineal discourses of Mangaldihi, women's bodies are taken to be naturally more "open" (*khola*) than men's—especially because of their involvement in the processes of menstruation, marriage, sexuality, and childbirth—all processes that entail, for women, substances going into and out of the body. This means that women can be viewed as more dangerously vulnerable to impurity, sexual violations, and receipts from the outside than are men, and also as more exudative.

For instance, a woman is especially open, and also impure (*asuddha*), during her menstrual period. A girl's first menstruation marks the beginnings of a state of openness, and thus her readiness for marriage, sexual relations, and pregnancy. Many women practice closing and containing techniques during their periods, such as refraining from touching household deities and food intended for superiors, and binding their hair tightly in a braid or bun. Sexual intercourse also involves opening a woman, and virgins are sometimes described as *bandha*, or closed. Intercourse, say Bengalis, takes place within the woman and outside the man. Sexual fluids leave the man at the moment of ejaculation to enter and permeate the woman: once she has slept with a man, a woman contains some of his substance within her permanently, although a man can sleep with a woman with no real lasting effect. A woman's sexual "heat" also makes her open (to sexuality, fertility, and other mixings); and many across India say that women have even more sexual heat and desire than men (unlike popular American conceptions).[7] Childbirth as well makes women impure and leaves them dangerously open for a period of one month after they give birth or experience a late miscarriage or abortion. To remedy this condition—to close and "dry out" (*sukote*) her body and womb—a woman has to undergo a drying, self-containing, and separative period of birth impurity (*asauc*), similar to that occurring after a death in the family.[8]

Village women themselves express clear ideas about the relative openness and impurity of women's bodies. A married Brahman woman, Subradi, told me: "Women are always impure (*apabitra*), because everything happens to them—menstruation, childbirth. These don't happen to men. For this reason if men touch a Muslim[9] or defecate, no harm (*dos*) happens to them, and they don't have to wash their clothes or bathe. But harm happens to a woman." My closest companion Hena (then soon to be married, in her early twenties) offered similar comments: "Men are always pure. They don't menstruate or give birth. Women menstruate, give birth—all that happens to them. Men only defecate, and nothing else." As Subradi and Hena both put it, things "happen" to women—menstruation, childbirth, defecation, and so on. As passive receivers of action, women have a greater vulnerability to outside agents. One common north Indian saying illustrates this notion of the openness or permeability of women particularly vividly: Women are like unglazed earthen water jugs, which are permeable and become easily contaminated to such depth that they cannot be purified. Men are like impermeable brass jugs, which are difficult to contaminate and easy to purify (cf. Dube 1975:163, 1988:16; Jacobson 1978:98).

A final point made to me about women's relative openness emphasized not their receptivity but their diffusion. It is women, people told me, who nurse children, cook, fetch water, feed and care for household gods, and handle on a daily basis all sorts of household things. That is why women, rather than men, must take the most care in regulating their mixings with others, lest they exude impurity or unwanted substances onto the household things and members they feed and care for.

Because of the perceived potential dangers of their openness, women and girls in the Mangaldihi region are taught by their senior kin to discipline their bodies—to attempt selectively (in certain contexts, especially in public and around men) to close themselves. They rely not only on bathing, but also on spatial seclusion, cloth coverings, binding the hair, and the like. These disciplining techniques seem to aim primarily at controlling and channeling a woman's powers toward desired ends within a patrilineage. Dominant discourses indicate that a woman's body is in most need of control or containment between the onset of puberty and marriage, as well as during the early years of marriage, because a woman is most vulnerable to violations—sexual and otherwise—of her body and household during these times. So women, when possible, confine their movements to the home, sending men or young children to the store for needed goods instead of going themselves, refraining from attending the entertaining plays and videos that periodically come through the village, and traveling only when accompanied by close male kin to visit natal homes or married daughters. They also cover their bodies carefully with saris, modestly pull a sari end over their heads when around senior and unknown men, and keep their hair bound (for "open" hair signifies looseness, in morality and body).

Not all women accept such expectations fully or without critique. For instance, I have known village women to venture out with friends to see a play or take a trip to town, or embark on a pilgrimage while (impurely) menstruating, or engage in an extra-marital romances (see Lamb 2000:194–197). Others speak of women's impurity and openness with an air of critical sarcasm, indicating a sense of the system's injustice. For instance, Mona exclaimed sarcastically, when I asked about women's need to bathe, "A Brahman man can even drink alcohol and sleep with a Leather-working woman [the lowest Hindu caste in Mangaldihi], and no harm happens. A woman never could! This is just the human [or male] system (*manuser bidhan*)."[10] Nonetheless, dominant understandings across genders and castes in Mangaldihi are that women are more "open" than men and need thus to practice some containment.

Such notions about the relative openness of women's bodies are not uncommon cross-culturally. Thus Carol Delaney (1991:38) finds that in Turkish society the male body is viewed as self-contained whereas the female body is relatively unbounded. Renee Hirschon (1978: 76–80) writes about the ambiguous nature of female "openness" in Greek society, while Jean Comaroff (1985:81) notes the relative lack of closure of female bodies among the Tswana of South Africa. But we must remember that in this community of northeast India, even the male body is not usually considered to be wholly bound; it is only *relatively* bound compared to the greater openness of the female body.

GENDERED LIFE COURSES

The same traits of openness and permeability that mean that women are dangerously open to impurities also impact the ways women's bodily-emotional ties—of kinship, love, attachment, or maya—are made and unmade over the life course. The main argument I wish to make here is that women's personhood is unique, in that their ties are disjoined and then remade, while men's ties are extended and enduring. Feminist theorists such as Nancy Chodorow (1978) and Carol Gilligan (1982) have challenged the adequacy of models of the autonomous individual to explain women's experiences (in the United States, at least), arguing that American women's self-conceptions tend to focus more on connectedness to others than men's do. Such a contrast, however, does not really hold for Bengalis. *Both* men and women in Mangaldihi define themselves strongly in terms of their relations with

others. But there are significant differences in the way women and men find themselves to be constituted via relational ties over their lives.

These contrasts can be said to begin with the differences perceived in the biologies of the two sexes, differences magnified by practices in upbringing and marriage. The contrasts can also be said to derive from patrilineality and virilocal postmarital residence, which favor the continuity of men and the transformation of incoming women. These perceptions and practices continually lead to contrary treatments of the genders: the most important connections of males are made but once and intended to endure throughout and beyond their lifetimes, while those of females are repeatedly altered—first made, then unmade and remade, then often again unmade. Women are said to be capable of such changes because of the natural "openness" of their bodies. One piece of proverbial wisdom states that a woman will fare best if she is malleable like clay, to be cast into a shape of his choice by the potter (her husband), discarding earlier loyalties, attributes, and ties to become absorbed into her husband's family.

Infants of both sexes are marked and initially connected with their kin and the village by a first feeding of rice ceremony (*annaprasana*). Males are differentiated, however, by the greater scale and elaboration of that ceremony, and among Brahmans by several other subsequent ceremonies of "marking" or "refining" (*samskara*). Among Brahmans, marriage thus might be the eighth connection-making ceremony for a boy, but only the second for a girl. In many castes, the male child is identified as a growing node of his enduring patrilineage (*bamsa*, literally a "bamboo"), while a girl might be spoken of as a mere temporary sojourner awaiting her departure in marriage. A phrase I would often hear was, "A daughter is nothing at all. You just raise them for a few days, and then to others you give them away." People speak of daughters as "belonging not to us but to others" (cf. Dube 1988; Jeffery and Jeffery 1996; Narayan 1986:69–70).

Among the many urban Bengali families who have settled in Kolkata apartments upon fleeing East Pakistan (now Bangladesh) at the time of partition between India and Pakistan, or moved abroad to the United States for work, *men* also speak of having been forced painfully to cut apart the ties of their maya prematurely— like a woman does in marriage—viewing the "modern" era following partition and globalization as a very "separate," "independent," and "maya-reducing" time (c.f. Lamb 2002). However, men in Mangaldihi and other nearby villages still usually reside—save perhaps for brief periods of urban work—within the same community and on the same soil where they were born. That is why, some men say, it is so difficult for them to loosen their ties of maya at the end of a lifetime when facing death; for they have become so deeply embedded within a family, community, home, soil.

For girls in Mangaldihi, it is through marriage that they receive their most markings and that the ties of their personhood are substantially unmade and remade. Throughout the three-day wedding, the bride is made to absorb substances originating from her husband's body and household. She rubs her body with turmeric paste with which he has first been anointed, she eats leftover food from his plate, she absorbs his sexual fluids (which are described as permeating her body), she moves to his place of residence, and there mingles with his kin and mixes with the substances of his soil. The bride's surname and patrilineal membership (*bamsa*) are also formally changed to those of her husband. In this way, her marriage is generally interpreted as obscuring and greatly reducing, although not obliterating, the connections she once enjoyed with her natal home. She will no longer refer to persons of her natal family as her "own people" (*nijer lok*), but rather as her husband does—as her "relatives by marriage" (*kutumb*s), for she is said to have become by marriage the "half body" (*ardhangini*) of her husband.

For a girl, then, preparing to marry is like a first confrontation with mortality. Anticipating the pain of cutting so many ties with their natal families, homes, and friends, young brides spoke to me with dread, not comprehending how they would ever survive such an ordeal. These conversations struck me as resembling the ways I heard older people speak of impending separations at death. During the months before her wedding, my companion Hena would say to me through tears, "Your father gives you away. He makes you other. He wipes out the relation." She would also purposefully pick quarrels with me and other friends and kin in Mangaldihi in order, she said, "to cut the maya" of bodily-emotional ties before her actual departure.

Mothers at least as much as fathers in Mangaldihi stress the transience of a daughter's connections with her natal place. Most mothers have known such separations from personal experience, and at each visit after marriage— their own or others'—they might relive their earlier feelings. Many tell of feeling always the pain of having the ties of their girlhood and family downgraded or ignored in their husbands' homes. Yet all agree that however disused, violated, or abused their earlier ties might be after marriage, a connection does remain forever between mother and child. Most said they continue to "feel a pull (*tan*) of maya," "of blood," or "of the womb."

A WIDOW'S BONDS

High-caste families' responses to the deaths of husbands often do even more than marriages to unmake women, and do so again mainly through stopping their interpersonal connections. Having lost many earlier relationships in marriage, most women rightly dread widowhood as another, similar phase of disconnection that will occur in their later lives. They expect such a phase since girls are married at younger ages, generally outlive their husbands, and usually do not remarry.

The legal option of remarriage for widows in West Bengal was sanctioned by British legislation in 1856 and has been exercised by widows in cities, but never by a high-caste widow in Mangaldihi. On the other hand, a man who loses his wife is usually encouraged to remarry, unless already senior with grown children. Thus in Mangaldihi's 335 households in 1990 there were only 13 unremarried widowers, but 69 unremarried widowed women. Childless young widows of Mangaldihi's lower castes are generally remated swiftly by a simpler ritual called "joining" (*sanga kara*), which does not require or attempt their removing the marks and ties of their first husbands; for even among these groups, a woman can ordinarily go through a true marriage ceremony (*biye*) but once.

Women of the higher castes who are widowed in Mangaldihi are pressed by their husbands' kin to minimize their transactions. While varying in strictness from group to group, this set of restrictive practices includes wearing white clothing, avoiding "hot" foods (such as fish, onions, garlic), limiting rice intake to only once a day (an amount considered almost equivalent to fasting), living in celibacy, avoiding participation in any auspicious ceremony, and often (because of their other dietary restrictions) cooking their food separately. Until recently, most families also required their widows to keep the head shaved (a practice some of the most senior Mangaldihi widows still observe) and to sleep on the ground.

One hears these practices recommended because they will reduce the widow's sexual desires and thus also reduce the husband's family's vulnerability to the slander and sexual marking that would occur were the widow to engage in liaisons with others. It is also striking that these are the very same practices that persons suffering death impurity (*asauc*) observe when a family member dies. Death impurity, however, lasts for just a limited period, whereas the widow's condition persists forever.

I first began to compare the condition of widows with that of others suffering death impurity because of their many similarities. Like a widow, persons suffering death impurity are expected to remain celibate; avoid "hot," non-vegetarian food; limit intake of boiled rice; restrict sharing of food with others; and avoid participating in auspicious rituals. Males suffering from death impurity, like older, more traditional widows, also have their heads shaved. These are all practices that reduce the likelihood that personal properties will be transferred among people.[11] During the transitional phase of death impurity, the survivors

limit their interactions, both in order to separate themselves from the deceased person and to avoid infecting others in the community with their condition. The aim is to cut the lingering bodily emotional connections between the survivors and the deceased, so that both the departed spirit and the survivors can move on to form new relationships. For other survivors, the practices of impurity end with the final funeral rites after 10 to 30 days (cf. D. Mines 1990).

But the incapacity and inauspicious (*asubha*) condition of the widow is permanent due, it appears, to her having become, through her putatively indissoluble merger with him in marriage, the "half body" (*ardhangini*) and life-long soul mate of her husband. When he is dead, her living bodily presence makes her, if young, not merely a sexual hazard, but also a repulsive anomaly. Until her own death, she can be seen as either the remnant, leftover half-body of a corpse, or as a faithless companion who has abandoned her husband by remaining on earth. She is also sometimes spoken of as a deficient wife whose lapses must have hastened her husband's death. Feared then for her defects as a devouring witch by some (as in Bandyopadhyay 1990), or as a vulture, she is often peripheralized within the family, if not expelled.

The asymmetry generally thus assumed in the high-caste marital relation is extreme, for the husband is not considered to be the wife's half-body, and unlike her, is not said to be diminished by (or responsible for) his partner's death. If she dies first, his person remains whole and free to remarry, his temporary incapacity of death impurity lasting no more than that of other close survivors. On the other hand, people tell me that even if the woman dies first, then although her surviving husband may be free, *her* spirit still remains bound to him and wanders around near him until the time of his funeral, when her soul will be merged under his name into the line of his male ancestors.

If people in Mangaldihi view persons, then, to be constituted of networks of relations, then women are in a peculiar position because their connections are made, remade, and unmade at several critical junctures over their lives: in girlhood, marriage, widowhood, and death. A daughter has to attenuate painfully ties with her natal family and place, so that she can move on to form new ties within her husband's home. A woman's ties to others as an ancestor are also uncertain, as she is ritually merged indistinguishably with her husband after death. The only tie for a high-caste woman that seems to be unambiguously unseverable, within the dominant patrilineal discourse of Mangaldihi, is the one she shares with her husband. This bond, which defines a woman's very bodily substance and identity, is one that a married woman cannot cut, even if her husband dies. This underlies why the majority of women in Mangaldihi endure such singular existences as widows as the last phase of their lives.

THE CHANGES OF AGE

Old age, however, brings important changes to the bodies and social identities of both widows and married women. Anthropological studies of women, in South Asia and elsewhere, have tended to focus on women in their married, domestic and reproductive years, with very little attention paid to how women's bodies may be perceived to change in old age. Although I have described female bodies as relatively open—making possible the somatic-social conditions that women must contend with, such as impurity and the capacity to mix profoundly with a husband—women's bodies are believed to become much cooler, dryer and more contained as they grow old.

According to villagers, it is as women enter into post reproductive phases of life that they experience a relative closing and cooling of the body. Women say that after menopause, their bodies become cool and dry and they no longer feel the heat of sexual desire. The cessation of childbearing entails an important bodily closing as well; and it is expected that women, like men, will become celibate as they age and their children marry, a further closing. An older widowed Brahman woman, Mejo Ma, described: "When you get old, everything becomes closed or stopped (*bandha*). That which happens between husband and wife stops. Menstruation stops. And then when your husband dies, eating all hot food stops as well. This is so that the body will dry out and not be hot." Bhogi Bagdi, an elderly lower caste widow, spoke as well of the cooling and drying of her body. She enjoyed sitting in the narrow, dusty lane in front of her house talking about sex, using vulgar language, and teasing the young people who visited her about their sexual practices. So I asked her one day if *she* still had sexual desire. She answered quickly, "No, of course not! After the blood stopped, my body dried out. Even if I wanted to [have sex], I wouldn't be able to. I had four kids, then my blood dried up, and then my body dried up. Now I have desire only for food."

Such somatic transitions bring women to a state of increased purity and boundedness, making them similar in some respects, people say explicitly, to men. The perception that postmenopausal women are in significant ways "like men" can also be found elsewhere in India (e.g., Flint 1975) and in other societies, such as the Kel Ewey Tuareg of northeastern Niger (Rasmussen 1987) and the Bedouins of Egypt (Abu-Lughod 1986:131, 133). When I would ask *why*, village women would explain that old women no longer menstruate, no longer give birth, no longer have sex, and (especially if they are upper-caste widows) no longer eat hot, non-vegetarian foods. This makes them relatively closed and "pure" (*suddha*) like men ordinarily are. Upper caste *widowed* women are further at times described as *so* "pure" (*suddha*) that they are "like gods" (*thakurer moto*), presumably because they are categorically free from the hot and female activities of sexuality and wifehood, and observing for life a radically cooling, separative, and minimally transacting code for conduct. It might warrant explaining here that daily impurities due to mixing and openness (*asuddhata*) are *not* the same as the death impurity that kin experience following a death (*asauc*), although the two terms are both traditionally glossed by Indologists as "impurity." In fact, by observing the set of minimally transacting practices prescribed for death-impure persons and widows, a person can become highly "pure" (*suddha*) in the everyday sense, because he or she will be made quite separate from others.

Young and older women alike in Mangaldihi speak of the processes of aging, stopping menstruation and becoming more like a man as a positive one. These somatic transitions mean that older women can take on some of the freedoms and privileges that men enjoy throughout their lives, such as exposing their calves and even chests on hot days, their saris simply wrapped around the waist in the style of a man, and wandering freely beyond the home—to visit friends or daughters, play cards on open temple platforms, watch village plays, dance freely with young men at festivals, and sit on front stoops gossiping and watching the passers-by. Because their bodies have become naturally cool and dry, older widows are not even compelled to follow the strict widow's code for conduct, some say; because these restrictions are meant especially to curb the heat, sexual desire and openness of a *young* widow's body. The older widows I know nonetheless observe such restrictions—out of habit, fear of slander, and/or a desire to respect "tradition" or their husbands—but many do enjoy the other "male-like" freedoms of old age. Thus, suspended amid the countervailing currents of restraint and freedom, inauspiciousness and auspiciousness, the greater portion of Mangaldihi women live the last phases of their lives.

CONCLUSION

We have seen, then, that for those in Mangaldihi, understandings of personhood are profoundly gendered and intricately tied to the body. This ethnographic material challenges the tendency—which has been widespread in anthropological literature on personhood—to examine person and self as ontologically prior to or separate from gender identity. Conceptions of personhood, I would argue, cannot be understood in isolation from conceptions about gendered selves.

We also see how a focus on age and the life course can illuminate our understandings of gendered personhood. For Bengalis, contrary to assumptions found in much existing literature, gender is not a constant determined by dichotomous and fixed physical differences between men and women. Instead, the qualities of openness and permeability that all bodies and persons possess to relative degrees fluctuate significantly over the life course. This means that what it is to be a woman—the nature of a woman's body, personhood, and ties with others—is profoundly different at different life phases. By paying attention to age, we can train our gaze on this kind of flux in the ways the body is used to create gendered identities, and thereby gain a much more nuanced and complex understanding of the plural and evolving nature of gender and personhood conceptions.

REFERENCES

Abu-Lughod, Lila. 1986. *Veiled Sentiments: Honor and Poetry in a Bedouin Society.* Berkeley: University of California Press.

Bandyopadhyay, Tarashankar. 1990. "The Witch." In Kalpana Bardhan (trans. and ed.). *Of Women, Outcastes, Peasants and Rebels: A Selection of Bengali Short Stories,* pp. 110–123. Berkeley: University of California Press.

Bennett, Lynn. 1983. *Dangerous Wives and Sacred Sisters: Social and Symbolic Roles of High-Caste Women in Nepal.* New York: Columbia University Press.

Chodorow, Nancy. 1978. *The Reproduction of Mothering: Psychoanalysis and the Sociology of Gender.* Berkeley: University of California Press.

Comaroff, Jean. 1985. *Body of Power, Spirit of Resistance: The Culture and History of South African People.* Chicago: University of Chicago Press.

Daniel, E. Valentine. 1984. *Fluid Signs: Being a Person the Tamil Way.* Berkeley: University of California Press.

Delaney, Carol. 1991. *The Seed and the Soil: Gender and Cosmology in Turkish Village Society.* Berkeley: University of California Press.

Dissanayake, Wimal, ed. 1996. *Narratives of Agency: Self-Making in China, India, and Japan.* Minneapolis: University of Minnesota Press.

Dube, Leela. 1975. "Woman's Worlds—Three Encounters." In A. Beteille and T.N. Madan (eds.). *Encounter and Experience: Personal Accounts of Fieldwork,* pp. 157–177. Delhi: Vikas.

———. 1988. "On the Construction of Gender: Hindu Girls in Patrilineal India." *Economic and Political Weekly* 23(18): 11–19.

Dumont, Louis. 1980. *Homo Hierarchicus.* Chicago: University of Chicago Press.

Ewing, Katherine P. 1990. "The Illusion of Wholeness: Culture, Self, and the Experience of Inconsistency." *Ethos* 18: 251–278.

———. 1991. "Can Psychoanalytic Theories Explain the Pakistani Woman? Intrapsychic Autonomy and Interpersonal Engagement in the Extended Family." *Ethos* 19: 131–160.

Flint, Marcha. 1975. "The Menopause: Reward or Punishment?" *Psychosomatics* 16: 161–163.

Geertz, Clifford. 1983. "'From the Native's Point of View': On the Nature of Anthropological Understanding." In *Local Knowledge: Further Essays in Interpretive Anthropology,* pp. 55–70. New York: Basic Books.

Gilligan, Carol. 1982. *In a Different Voice: Psychological Theory and Women's Development.* Cambridge, MA: Harvard University Press.

Gold, Ann Grodzins. 1991. "Gender and Illusion in a Rajasthani Yogic Tradition." In Arjun Appadurai, Frank Korom, and Margaret Mills (eds.). *Gender, Genre, and Power in South Asian Expressive Traditions,* pp. 102–135. Philadelphia: University of Pennsylvania Press.

———. 1992. *A Carnival of Parting: The Tales of King Bharthari and King Gopi Chand as Sung and Told by Madhu Natisar Nath of Ghatiyali, Rajasthan.* Berkeley: University of California Press.

———. 1999. "Maya." In Serinity Young (ed.). *Encyclopedia of Women and World Religion* 2: 635–636. New York: Macmillan.

Hirschon, Renee. 1978. "Open Body/Closed Space: The Transformation of Female Sexuality." In Shirley Ardener (ed.). *Defining Females: The Nature of Women in Society,* pp. 66–88. London: St. Martin's Press.

Jacobson, Doranne. 1978. "The Chaste Wife: Cultural Norm and Individual Experience." In Sylvia Vatuk (ed.). *American Studies in the Anthropology of India,* pp. 95–138. New Delhi: Manohar.

Jeffery, Patricia and Roger Jeffery. 1996. *Don't Marry Me to a Plowman! Women's Everyday Lives in Rural North India.* Boulder, Colo.: Westview Press.

Lamb, Sarah. 1997. "The Making and Unmaking of Persons: Notes on Aging and Gender in North India." *Ethos* 25(3): 279–302.

———. 2000. *White Saris and Sweet Mangoes: Aging, Gender, and Body in North India.* Berkeley: University of California Press.

———. 2002. "Intimacy in a Transnational Era: The Remaking of Aging among Indian Americans." *Diaspora* 11(3): 299–330.

Marglin, Frederique Apffel. 1985. "Female Sexuality in the Hindu World." In Clarissa W. Atkinson,

C. H. Buchanan, and M. R. Miles (eds.). *Immaculate and Powerful: The Female in Sacred Image and Social Reality,* pp. 39–60. Boston: Beacon Press.

———. 1996. "Rationality, the Body, and the World: From Production to Regeneration." In Frederique Apffel Marglin and Stephen A. Marglin (eds.). *Decolonizing Knowledge: From Development to Dialogue,* pp. 142–181. Oxford: Clarendon Press.

Marriott, McKim. 1976. "Hindu Transactions: Diversity without Dualism." In Bruce Kapferer (ed.). *Transaction and Meaning: Directions in the Anthropology of Exchange and Symbolic Behavior,* pp. 109–142. Philadelphia: Institute for the Study of Human Issues.

———. 1990. "Constructing an Indian Ethnosociology." In McKim Marriott (ed.). *India through Hindu Categories,* pp. 1–39. Delhi: Sage Publications.

Marriott, McKim and Ronald Inden. 1974. "Caste Systems." *Encyclopedia Britannica, Macropaedia* 3: 982–991. Chicago: H. Benton.

———. 1977. "Toward an Ethnosociology of South Asian Caste Systems." In Kenneth David (ed.). *The New Wind: Changing Identities in South Asia,* pp. 227–238. The Hague: Mouton Publishers.

McHugh, Ernestine. 1989. "Concepts of the Person among the Gurungs of Nepal." *American Ethnologist* 16: 75–86.

Mines, Diane Paull. 1990. "Hindu Periods of Death 'Impurity.'" In McKim Marriott (ed.). *India through Hindu Categories,* pp. 103–130. New Delhi: Sage Publications.

Mines, Mattison. 1988. "Conceptualizing the Person: Hierarchical Society and Individual Autonomy in India." *American Anthropologist* 90: 568–579.

———. 1994. *Public Faces, Private Voices: Community and Individuality in South India.* Berkeley: University of California Press.

Moore, Henrietta. 1994. *A Passion for Difference: Essays in Anthropology and Gender.* Bloomington: Indiana University Press.

Nabokov, Isabelle. 2000. *Religion against the Self: An Ethnography of Tamil Rituals.* New York: Oxford University Press.

Narayan, Kirin. 1986. "Birds on a Branch: Girlfriends and Wedding Songs in Kangra." *Ethos* 14: 47–75.

Ortner, Sherry B. 1995. "The Case of the Disappearing Shamans, or No Individualism, No Relationism." *Ethos* 23: 355–390.

Ostor, Akos, Lina Fruzzetti, and Steve Barnett, eds. 1982. *Concepts of Person: Kinship, Caste, and*

Marriage in India. Cambridge, MA: Harvard University Press.

Parish, Steven M. 1994. *Moral Knowing in a Hindu Sacred City: An Exploration in Mind, Emotion, and Self*. New York: Columbia University Press.

Parry, Jonathan P. 1989. "The End of the Body." In Michel Feher, with Ramona Naddaff and Nadia Tazi (eds.). *Fragments for a History of the Human Body, Part Two*, pp. 490–517. New York: Zone.

Rasmussen, Susan. 1987. "Interpreting Androgynous Woman: Female Aging and Personhood among the Key Ewey Tuareg." *Ethnology* 26: 17–30.

Shweder, Richard A., and Edmund J. Bourne. 1984. "Does the Concept of the Person Vary Cross-Culturally?" In Richard A. Shweder and Robert A. LeVine (eds.). *Culture Theory: Essays on Mind, Self, and Emotion*, pp. 158–199. Cambridge: Cambridge University Press.

Strathern, Marilyn. 1988. *The Gender of the Gift: Problems with Women and Problems with Society in Melanesia*. Berkeley: University of California Press.

Vatuk, Ved Prakash, and Sylvia Jane Vatuk. 1979. "The Lustful Stepmother in the Folklore of North-Western India." In Ved Prakash Vatuk (ed.). *Studies in Indian Folk Traditions*, pp. 190–221. New Delhi: Manohar.

NOTES

1. The subcontinent of South Asia includes the contemporary nations of India, Nepal, Pakistan, Bangladesh, Sri Lanka, Assam, and Bhutan. Sometimes Afghanistan—also part of British "India"—is included as South Asia, as well. Work on India has often dominated South Asian studies, and some scholars use "India" and "South Asia" somewhat interchangeably.

2. Studies of person or self in South Asia include Daniel 1984; Dissanayake 1996; Dumont 1980; Ewing 1990, 1991; Lamb 1997, 2000; Marriott 1976, 1990; Marriott and Inden 1974, 1977; McHugh 1989; M. Mines 1988, 1994; Nabakov 2000; Ortner 1995; Ostor et al. 1982; Parish 1994; Parry 1989; Shweder and Bourne 1984.

3. Marriott (1976) was the first to posit more or less "open" persons whose capacities for exchanging properties make them composite and "*dividual*" (rather than individual)—a suggestion that has spread in Melanesian as well as in South Asian studies (see also Marriott 1990; Strathern 1988:13, 15, 348–349n). Clifford Geertz suggests that the Western notion of the bounded and autonomous "individual" is, in fact, "a rather peculiar idea within the context of the world cultures" (1983:59).

4. "Personhood" refers to beliefs and practices surrounding what it is to be a person, or human being. Conceptions about personhood vary profoundly cross-culturally, and are constituted via a variety of elements. These elements might include some or all of the following: a subjective sense of self; the nature of the body, mind, emotions, and/or spirit; forms of power and status; age and the shape of the life course; relationships with others; karma or fate (perhaps ingrained in or written on the body or soul in some way); and significantly in most, if not all, contexts—sex and gender. For those living in the northeastern Indian state of West Bengal, gender is a very salient dimension of personhood.

5. The Bengali (and Sanskrit) term *lok* can also mean "world." These overlapping meanings of "world" and "person" connote the openness and nonindividuality of persons, as well as the common notion of the person as a microcosm of the world.

6. Among the Newars of Nepal, maya similarly refers to "love" or the "web of relatedness" (Bennett 1983:39; Parish 1994:156 ff). Gold (1991, 1992, 1999) also compellingly explores the complex, intertwining meanings of maya as "illusion" and as love for women, creative divine grace, delusive magicians' skills, and binding attachments to the relationships of this world.

7. For perspectives on the comparative sexual heat and capacities of women and men in various parts of India, see Daniel 1984:171–72, Lamb 2000:187–92, Marglin 1985:60, Vatuk and Vatuk 1979:215.

8. For more on menstrual, birth, and death impurities (which are distinct), see Lamb 2000:183–87, 164–69, 229–31; Marglin 1996; and D. Mines 1990.

9. Hindus in Mangaldihi commonly use the example of "touching a Muslim" to describe how people become impure (*asuddha*). Although Mangaldihi is a predominantly Hindu village, it is surrounded by smaller Muslim villages, and the Hindus there are especially concerned with preserving their own separateness.

10. As in English, the Bengali term for "man" (*manus*) can refer either to males in particular or to humankind in general.

11. Together these practices constitute what McKim Marriott (1976) would call a "minimal transactional strategy."

VI

Culture, Sexuality, and the Body

The study of sexuality in anthropology is a relatively recent research emphasis but one that has drawn increasing attention. Ethnographic, theoretical, and policy-related research on sexuality is now central to the field and significant in its contributions to our understandings of gender, health, and the body (Browner and Sargent 2007; Day 2007; Farmer 1992; Kulick 1998; Lewin 2006; Padilla 2007; Sargent and Brettell 1996; Weeks et al. 1996). In contrast to contemporary studies that take sexuality as their core focus, classic anthropological monographs reported exotic sexual practices in the course of "holistic" ethnographic description. For example, we learn in Malinowski's *The Sexual Life of Savages in Northwestern Melanesia* (1929) that the Trobriand islanders may bite each others' eyelashes in the heat of passion, but other than occasional esoterica, the naturalistic, biological bias dominated the study of sexuality.

However, as Vance observed in her classic volume *Pleasure and Danger: Exploring Female Sexuality* (1984: 8), "although sexuality, like all human cultural activity, is grounded in the body, the body's structure, physiology, and functioning do not directly or simply determine the configuration or meaning of sexuality." Rather, sexuality is in large part culturally constructed. Moreover, the body itself has been the focus of feminist analysis. Feminist theorists have argued that historical, social, and political influences "produce" the body; the lived experience of the body is gendered and culturally diverse. Just as we may inquire into the culturally variable meanings of masculinity and femininity, we may examine the ways in which sexuality and the body are invested with meaning in particular societies (Ortner and Whitehead 1981: 2).

Sexuality, as a topic of analysis, links the personal and the social, the individual and society. To Americans sex may imply the body, medical facts, Freud, and erotic techniques, but all of these aspects of sexuality are socially shaped and sexual activity is inevitably curbed. Within every culture there are measures for the management of sexuality and gender expression (Ortner and Whitehead 1981: 24–25) and sanctions for those who break the rules.

These sanctions may be imposed at the level of the family, the lineage, the community, or the state. Indeed, Foucault (1981) has suggested that a feature of the recent past is the increasing intervention of the state in the domain of sexuality. In this regard Ross and Rapp (1981: 71) conclude that it is not accidental that contemporary Western culture conceptualizes sex as a thing in itself, isolated from social, political, and economic context: "The separation with industrial capitalism of family life from work, of consumption from production, of leisure from labour, of personal life from political life, has completely reorganized the context in which we experience sexuality. . . . Modern consciousness permits, as earlier systems of thought did not, the positing of 'sex' for perhaps the first time as having an 'independent' existence." However, Caplan (1987: 24) warns that while western culture may have a concept of sexuality divorced from reproduction, marriage, or other social domains, it is not possible to analyze sexuality without reference to the economic, political, and cultural matrix in which it is embedded.

A comparative perspective informs us that the attributes of the body seen as sexual and erotic vary cross-culturally. For example, scarification, the corseted waist, bound feet, and the subincised penis are admired and provocative in particular cultures. Such attributes as these are not only physical symbols of sexuality, but indicators of status. Similarly, Sudanese women practice infibulation, a form of female genital cutting, causing serious pain and health risks to young women, for the honor of the family and as a sign of virtue. In the name of power, young men applied as recruits to the palace eunuch staff in Imperial China carrying their genitals in jars (Ortner and Whitehead 1981: 24). These examples are reminders of the impact of social concerns and cultural meanings in the domain of sexuality.

Lila Abu-Lughod (in this book) explores the cultural construction of sexuality and local meanings of Islam through an analysis of wedding rituals in a Bedouin community in Egypt's Western Desert. Weddings produce and transform people's experiences of sexuality and gender relations and serve as a marker of cultural identity. Whereas sexuality in North America is considered something essentially private, separate from society and social power, to these Bedouin the wedding involves sexuality that has a public and participatory element. The defloration of the bride is a ritualized encounter between the bride and groom and including the women and men who congregate around them. Central to the ritual is the bride's virginity, which represents her family's honor; her body and the emphasis on opening the bride's vagina thus become a matter of public interest. Connections to kin and control of the kinship group are symbolized in these wedding rites. The sexual politics of gender relations were formerly portrayed in women's wedding songs and dances that represented the encounter between male and female as a contest of wills. Changing power relations have led to a deemphasis of this mechanism for challenging male power. As Bedouins are drawn into the wider Egyptian state and economy, weddings increasingly are seen as entertainment and spectacle rather than as the ritual reproduction of the social and political dynamics of the community, symbolized in the sexual contest surrounding the bride's virginity.

Research in hunting and gathering societies also shows that sexual intercourse, while personal, can be a political act. In such societies, claims to women are central to men's efforts to achieve equal status with others (Collier and Rosaldo 1981: 291). Through sexual relations with women, men forge relationships with one another and symbolically express claims to particular women. Shostak (1981) presents the perspective of a !Kung woman, Nisa, on sex, marriage, and fertility in the broader context of a hunting and gathering society in which women have high status.

The !Kung believe that without sex, people can die, just as without food, one would starve. Shostak observes that "talk about sex seems to be of almost equal importance [to eating]. When women are in the village or out gathering, or when men and women are together, they spend hours recounting details of sexual exploits. Joking about all aspects of sexual experience is commonplace" (1981: 265). According to Nisa, "If a woman doesn't have sex . . . her thoughts get ruined and she is always angry" (Shostak 1981: 31). Nisa's characterization of sexuality among the !Kung suggests that for both men and women, engaging in sex is necessary to maintaining good health and is an important aspect of being human.

In contrast, for the past 150 years Anglo-American culture has defined women as less sexual than men. This represents a major shift from the widespread view prior to the seventeenth century that women were especially sexual creatures. By the end of the nineteenth century the increasingly authoritative voice of male medical specialists argued that women's bodies were characterized by sexual anesthesia (Caplan 1987: 3). Victorian ideas about male sexuality emphasized the highly sexed and baser nature of men. In contrast, Muslim concepts of female sexuality (Mernissi 1987: 33) cast the woman as aggressor and the man as victim. Imam Ghazali, writing in the eleventh century, describes an active female sexuality in which the sexual demands of women appear overwhelming, and the need for men to satisfy them is a social duty (Mernissi 1987: 39). Women symbolize disorder and are representative of the dangers of sexuality and its disruptive potential.

The example of the Kaulong of New Guinea further illustrates the extent to which understandings of male and female bodies and sexual desires are cultural products (Goodale 1980). Both sexes aspire to immortality through the reproduction of identity achieved through parenting. Sexual intercourse, which is considered animal-like, is sanctioned for married people. Animals are part of the forest and nature, so the gardens of married couples are in the forest. The only sanctioned purpose of sex and marriage is reproduction; sex without childbearing is viewed as shameful. Suicide was formerly considered an acceptable recourse for a childless couple. Sexual activity is thought to be dangerous to men and women in different ways: polluting for men and leading to dangers of birth for women. Goodale notes that girls are encouraged to behave aggressively toward men, to initiate sex, and to choose a husband. In contrast, men are reluctant to engage in sex, are literally "scared to death of marriage," and rarely take the dominant role in courtship (1980: 135). Thus, the Kaulong view seems to reverse the Western idea of the passive woman and the active man (Moore 1988: 17).

For the Kaulong, as among numerous groups in New Guinea, men's anxiety about contact with the body of a woman is heightened by the understanding that menstrual blood is dangerously polluting. A man who had sexual contact with a menstruating woman would risk serious physical and mental harm. Men engage in a range of symbolic behaviors—for example, tongue scraping and smokehouse purification—to cleanse themselves of what they believe are the harmful effects of contact with women's bodies. The Mae Enga, for instance, believe that "contact with [menstrual blood] or a menstruating woman will, in the absence of appropriate countermagic, sicken a man and cause persistent vomiting, turn his blood black, corrupt his vital juices so that his skin darkens and wrinkles as his flesh wastes, permanently dull his wits, and eventually lead to a slow decline and death" (Meggitt 1964: 207).

Concern about the symbolic dangers of women's bodies is not limited to New Guinea, but rather, has been documented in diverse cultures (Buckley and Gottlieb 1988). Research on such symbolic dangers and the body as ritually polluting has often focused on menstruation. Buckley (1982) has addressed male bias and the female perspective on menstruation in his discussion of menstrual beliefs and practices among the Yurok Indians of North America. In his reanalysis of Yurok data, Buckley found that while precontact Yurok men considered women, through their menstrual blood, to be dangerous, Yurok women viewed menstruation as a positive source of power. Rather than looking on the forced monthly seclusion as isolating and oppressive, women viewed it as a source of strength and sanctuary.

In her essay in this book, Alma Gottlieb notes that most early anthropological writings on menstruation were overly simplistic in assuming that menstrual blood was necessarily a source of mystical contamination. Works such as Buckley's study of Yurok menstruation and Buckley and Gottlieb's 1988 classic collection on menstrual practices cross-culturally were groundbreaking in furthering our understanding of the diversity of women's bodily experiences and how body practices are shaped by culture and history. Gottlieb describes the growing feminist literature that focuses on menstruation and on the body in general. Recent scholarship includes accounts by anthropologists who gained first-hand knowledge of women's menstrual houses by means of participant observation. In addition, scholars have emphasized the agency of menstruating women—for example, their use of menstrual blood to engage in magical procedures to deceive their husbands or to attract sexual advances, the use of herbal and other methods to regulate menstruation, or the use of diverse techniques to induce abortions. Gottlieb's analysis reminds us that women shape their own menstrual experiences and are not bound to a solely biological or cultural script.

Such biological or cultural scripts are equally influential in whether a society defines two, and only two gender identities, the masculine and the feminine, leaving little room for culturally defined variance. This is true in popular thought in the United States, but other cultures provide for alternative gender constructs as well as acknowledgement of physical variation. Some research suggests at least three phenotypic sexes in human cultures: female, male, and androgynous or hermaphroditic individuals. This classification refers to characteristics observable to the naked eye rather than to medical classifications of sex types based on chromosomal evidence (Jacobs and Roberts 1989: 440). Linguistic markers for gender reveal culturally specific epistemological categories (Jacobs and Roberts 1989: 439). Accordingly, in English one may distinguish woman, lesbian, man, or gay male. The Chuckchee counted seven genders—three female and four male—while the Mohave reportedly recognize four genders—a woman, a woman who assumes the roles of men, a man, or a male who assumes the roles of women (Jacobs and Roberts 1989: 439–440). Thus, cross-cultural research suggests that we need to use categories of sex and gender that reflect the evidence of diversity rather than rigid classification systems.

In any culture gender, sex, and body are recognized, named, and given meaning in accordance with the culture's rules or customs (Jacobs and Roberts 1989: 446). When a baby is born, people generally rely on the appearance of the infant's external genitalia to determine whether that child will be treated as female or male. As a child grows, more criteria come into play, such as the phenotypic expression of sex—facial hair, voice, and breast development. In some societies, social and sexual identities may be created by means of modifying the physical body. One such example is the *hijras* of Indian society. The *hijra* role attracts people who in the West might be called eunuchs, homosexuals, transsexuals, transvestites, or hermaphrodites. *Hijras* are primarily phenotypic men who have chosen to sacrifice their genitalia in return for the power to bless or curse others with fertility or infertility.

The *hijra* role is deeply rooted in Indian culture, and it accommodates a variety of sexual needs, gender behaviors and identities, and personalities. Gayatri Reddy and Serena Nanda (in this book) show that Hinduism encompasses ambiguities and contradictions in gender categories without trying to resolve them. *Hijras,* have been identified as a "third sex" or "intersexed" identity—in Nanda's terms, "neither men nor women" (1990), situated within a larger continuum of sexual and gender configurations. In Hindu myths, rituals, and art, the theme of the powerful man–woman is significant; mythical figures who are androgynous figure in popular Indian culture.

Islam also reinforces the construct of alternative genders by means of the historical role of the eunuch in the Muslim court culture of India. Although the popular understanding of *hijras* is as an alternative sex and gender, their identities are also constructed through spirituality, religious affiliation, and political action. As political candidates, some *hijras* have used their sexual and physical ambiguities as a symbolic asset in their campaign platforms.

Additional examples of cultures that tolerate gender ambiguity are found in Native American societies, in which a male who felt an affinity for female occupation, dress, and attributes could choose to become classified as a two-spirit, sometimes known as a berdache. Williams (1986) discusses alternative gender identities for Native American women whom he calls amazons. According to Williams's use of the term, an amazon is a woman who has manifested an unfeminine character from infancy, has shown no interest in heterosexual relations, and might have expressed a wish to become a man. Such women were known for their bravery and skill as warriors. For example, Kaska Indians would select a daughter to be a son if they had none; after a transformation ritual the daughter would dress like a man and be trained for male tasks. Ingalik Indians also recognize such a status; in this society the amazons even participated in male-only sweat baths. The woman was accepted as a man on the basis of her gender behavior (Williams 1986).

The assignment of this changed gender "operates independently of a person's morphological sex and can determine both gender status and erotic behavior" (Williams 1986: 235). In some societies a woman could choose to be a man, as among the Kutenai Indians. The "manlike woman" was greatly respected, although the Kutenai did not recognize a similar status for men. A tribe with an alternative gender role for one sex did not necessarily have one for the other, and the roles were not seen as equivalent. The Mohave also recognized this alternative, subjecting these women to a ritual that authorized them to assume the clothing, sexual activity, and occupation of the opposite, self-chosen sex. It is sometimes believed that such women do not menstruate because menstruation is a crucial part of the definition of a woman. However, the category of amazon is distinct from that of men or women. It is another gender status. Thus, some Native American cultures have a flexible recognition of gender variance, and they incorporate fluidity in their world view.

In American society sexuality is an integral part of identity on a personal and a social level. Sexuality not only classifies one as male or female but is an aspect of adult identity. In the United States, where heterosexual relations are the norm, the dominant ideology suggests that heterosexuality is innate and natural. Correspondingly, lesbianism may be threatening to male dominance, while male homosexuality threatens male solidarity and the sense of masculine identity. The linkage of sexual identity and gender leads to an identification of gay men and lesbians in terms of their homosexuality, although they do not necessarily change their gender. In the United States, a lack of fit among sexual anatomy, gender, and sexuality may cause suspicion. In other cultures, however, gender and sexuality are conceptually separate. For example, Shepherd (1987) shows that for Swahili Muslims of Mombasa, Kenya, being in a homosexual relationship does not change one's gender, which is essentially assigned by biological sex.

If some scholars, through their cross-cultural research, are attempting to show us significant variation in gender identities as well as attitudes toward sexuality and the body, others have focused on the heightened standardizing and regulation of the "ideal" woman's body in industrialized societies. This is precisely the question that Jacqueline Urla and Alan C. Swedlund (in this book) address in their exploration of how images of the ideal body in twenty-first-century North America are represented and shaped by the popular and controversial cultural icon, the Barbie doll. Barbie symbolizes the appropriately gendered female body, and conveys the significance of appearance for success in the "rituals of heterosexual teenage life." As the first teen fashion doll, Barbie personifies the sexy girl but at the same time the clean-cut teen who does not actually have sex. Barbie, her wardrobe, and other accessories exemplify the commodification of the body and of gender itself. To achieve the feminine ideal that Barbie represents requires constant vigilance and endless financial investments, physical adornments, and interventions. The glamorous doll serves as a reminder that women—and even young girls—often experience their bodies as defective and embark on lifelong quests in pursuit of an inaccessible ideal. Urla and Swedlund describe attempts to scientifically define an "average" U.S. female body in the late nineteenth and early twentieth centuries in relation to an implicit male prototype. Conforming to gendered norms of fitness and weight are now identified with social and moral worth. The disciplined body, beautiful, sexually appealing, and embedded in consumerism, exists in the fantasy world of Barbie.

The articles in this section reveal that there are multiple culturally acceptable gendered and sexual identities (Caplan 1987: 22) as well as diverse constructs of the ideal gendered body. Although Western categorizations impose a particular rigidity on concepts of gender, sexuality, and the body, cross-cultural data demonstrate that these identities are not fixed and unchangeable. This realization necessitates a critique of these Western classifications and provokes a number of stimulating questions: Are heterosexuality and homosexuality equally socially constructed? Is there cross-cultural variation in the extent to which sexuality represents a core feature of human identity? Is there a timeless, universal, normative body?

REFERENCES

Browner, C., and C. Sargent. 2007. "Engendering Medical Anthropology." In Francine Saillant and Serge Genest (eds.). *Medical Anthropology: Regional Perspectives and Shared Concerns,* pp. 233–252. London: Blackwell.

Buckley, Thomas. 1982. "Menstruation and the power of Yurok Women: Methods in Cultural Reconstruction." *American Ethnologist* 9: 47–60.

Buckley, Thomas, and Alma Gottlieb (eds.). 1988. *Blood Magic: The Anthropology of Menstruation.* Berkeley: University of California Press.

Caplan, Pat. 1987. "Introduction." In Pat Caplan (ed.). *The Cultural Construction of Sexuality,* pp. 1–31. London: Tavistock.

Collier, Jane E., and Michelle Z. Rosaldo. 1981. "Politics and Gender in Simple Societies." In Sherry Ortner and Harriet Whitehead (eds.). *Sexual Meanings: The Cultural Construction of Gender and Sexuality,* pp. 275–330. Cambridge, UK: Cambridge University Press.

Day, Sophie. 2007. *On the Game. Women and Sex Work.* London: Pluto Press.

Farmer, Paul. 1992. *AIDS and Accusation. Haiti and the Geography of Blame.* Berkeley: University of California Press.

Foucault, Michel, 1981. *The History of Sexuality.* Harmondsworth, UK: Penguin.

Goodale, Jane C. 1980. "Gender, Sexuality and Marriage: A Kaulong Model of Nature and Culture." In Carol P. MacCormack (ed.). *Nature, Culture and Gender,* pp. 119–143. Cambridge, UK: Cambridge University Press.

Jacobs, Sue-Ellen, and Christine Roberts. 1989. "Sex, Sexuality, Gender, and Gender Variance." In Sandra Morgen (ed.). *Gender and Anthropology: Critical Reviews for Research and Teaching,* pp. 438–462. Washington, DC: American Anthropological Association.

Kulick, Don. 1998. *Travesti. Sex, Gender and Culture among Brazilian Transgendered Prostitutes.* Chicago: The University of Chicago Press.

Lewin, Ellen (ed.). 2006. *Feminist Anthropology: A Reader.* London: Blackwell.

Malinowski, Bronislaw. 1929. *The Sexual Life of Savages in Northwestern Melanesia.* New York: Harvest Books.

Meggitt, M. J. 1964. "Male–Female Relationships in the Highlands of Australian New Guinea," *American Anthropologist* 66(4, Part 2): 204–227.

Mernissi, Fatima. 1987. *Beyond the Veil: Male–Female Dynamics in Modern Muslim Society.* Bloomington and Indianapolis: Indiana University Press.

Moore, Henrietta L. 1988. *Feminism and Anthropology.* Minneapolis: University of Minnesota Press.

Nanda, Serena. 1990. *Neither Man Nor Woman: The Hijras of India.* Belmont, CA: Wadsworth, Inc.

Ortner, Sherry B., and Harriet Whitehead. 1981. "Introduction: Accounting for Sexual Meanings." In Sherry Ortner and Harriet Whitehead (eds.). *Sexual Meanings: The Cultural Construction of Gender and Sexuality,* pp. 1–29. Cambridge, UK: Cambridge University Press.

Padilla, Mark. 2007. *Caribbean Pleasure Industry: Tourism, Sexuality, and AIDS in the Dominican Republic.* Chicago and London: University of Chicago Press.

Ross, E., and R. Rapp. 1981. "Sex and Society: A Research Note from Social History and Anthropology," *Comparative Studies in Society and History* 20: 51–72.

Sargent, Carolyn, and Caroline Brettell 1996. *Gender and Health.* Upper Saddle River, NJ: Prentice Hall.

Shepherd, Gill. 1987. "Rank, Gender, and Homosexuality: Mombasa as a Key to Understanding Sexual Options." In Pat Caplan (ed.). *The Cultural Construction of Sexuality,* pp. 240–271. London: Tavistock.

Shostak, Marjorie. 1981. Nisa: *The Life and Words of a !Kung Woman.* Cambridge, MA: Harvard University Press.

Vance, Carole S. 1984. "Pleasure and Danger: Toward a Politics of Sexuality." In Carole S. Vance (ed.). *Pleasure and Danger: Exploring Female Sexuality,* pp.1–29. Boston: Routledge and Kegan Paul.

Weeks, Margaret et al. 1996. "Gender Relations, Sexuality, and AIDS Risk among African American and Latina Women." In C. Sargent and C. Brettell (eds.). *Gender and Health,* pp. 338–370. Upper Saddle River, NJ: Prentice Hall.

Williams, Walter L. 1986. *The Spirit and The Flesh.* Boston: Beacon Press.

Is There a Muslim Sexuality?
Changing Constructions of Sexuality in Egyptian Bedouin Weddings

Lila Abu-Lughod

The project of defining the nature of Muslim Arab sexuality—what it is or what it should be—has engaged many people with different stakes and interests. Western discourses have tended to contrast the negative sexuality of "the East" with the positive sexuality of the West. French colonial settlers in Algeria depicted Algerian

Original material prepared for this text. Reprinted by permission of the author.

women in pornographic postcards that suggested a fantastic Oriental world of perverse and excessive sexuality (Alloula 1986). Western feminists concerned with global issues dwell on veiling and other practices like clitoridectomy found in the Muslim Arab world as signs of the repressive control over or exploitation of women's sexuality (e.g., Daly 1978).

From the Muslim world itself come other discourses on Arab Muslim sexuality. These include religious and legal texts and pronouncements, but also, more recently, some critical studies by intellectuals and scholars. How different the understandings can be is clear from two important books. One, by a Tunisian scholar with a background in psychoanalytic thought, argues that the misogynist practices of sexuality in the Muslim world are corruptions of the ideals of the Quran and other religious texts (Bouhdiba 1985). The second, by a Moroccan sociologist, argues from a feminist perspective that the legal and sacred texts themselves, like the erotic texts that flourished in the medieval period, carry negative messages about and perpetuate certain consistent attitudes toward the bodies and behavior of Muslim women (Sabbah 1984).

What these various discourses on Arab Muslim sexuality, by outsiders and insiders, defenders and critics, share is the presumption that there is such a thing as a "Muslim sexuality." An anthropologist like myself, familiar with the tremendous variety of communities to be found in the regions composing the Muslim Arab world, would have to question this presumption. Neither Islam nor sexuality should be essentialized—taken as things with intrinsic and transhistorical meanings. Rather, both the meaning of Islam and the constructions of sexuality must be understood in their specific historical and local contexts.[1]

To show why I argue this, I will analyze wedding rituals in a community of Awlad 'Ali Bedouin in Egypt's Western Desert—a community I worked in over a period of twelve years. Weddings are the highlight of social life, awaited with anticipation and participated in with enthusiasm. Each wedding is different. And each wedding is a personal affair of great moment for the bride and groom, even if only one dramatic event in what will be their marriage, lasting for years. Yet public rituals in face-to-face societies are also arenas where people play out their social and political relations. There are other discourses and practices related to sexuality in this Bedouin community but none so powerfully seek to produce, and are now transforming, people's experiences of sexuality and gender relations as weddings do. Without pretending that a symbolic analysis exhausts the meaning of weddings for the individuals involved, I would still insist that such an analysis of Awlad 'Ali weddings is useful: It reveals both how sexuality is constructed by the symbols and practices of members of particular communities and how these symbols and practices themselves are open to change and political contestation. Islam, it will be seen, figures not so much as a blueprint for sexuality as a weapon in changing relations of power.

SEXUALITY AND CULTURAL IDENTITY

In the twelve years between 1978 and 1990 that I had been regularly returning to this community of Arab Muslim sedentarized herders in Egypt, the same questions had been asked of me, sometimes even by the same people, as were asked in the first month of my stay. Usually in the context of a gathering of older women, one old woman would lean toward me and ask if I were married. After a short discussion of the fact that I was not, she or another older woman would ask me the next intense question: "Where you come from, does the bridegroom do it with the finger or with 'it'?" The first time they asked me this, I did not know what they meant by "it" and they had a good laugh. The question that followed inevitably in such conversations was, "And do they do it during the daytime or at night?" They were asking about weddings and particularly about the defloration of the virgin bride, which is for them the central moment of a wedding.[2]

In the obsessive concern with whether they do it with the finger or "it," at night or during the daytime, is a clue to one of the things the discourse on this aspect of sexuality has become as the Awlad 'Ali Bedouins have greater contact and interaction with outsiders, primarily their Egyptian peasant and urban neighbors. Whatever its former or current meaning within the community, meanings I will analyze in the following section, the central rite of weddings has now also become a marker of cultural identity—essential to the Awlad Ali's self-defining discourse on what makes them distinctive.

Individuals vary in how they evaluate their differences from their compatriots. When I met the Bedouin representative to the Egyptian Parliament, a sophisticated man in sunglasses whose long contact with other Egyptians showed in his dialect, he assured me that there were a few Bedouin practices that were wrong: One was that they used the finger in the daytime. But he defended the practice by saying that it reminded girls to be careful. Another respected man of the community explained to me that "entering" with the finger was wrong. "We're the only ones who do it this way," he noted. Then he added, "Nothing in our religion says you should." By way of excuse, though, he said, "But the faster the groom does it, the better—the more admired he is because it means he wasn't timid or cowardly." Even women occasionally complained that it was stupid how the female wedding guests waited and waited, just to see that drop of blood. But they too defended the ceremony, saying that the defloration had to take place in the afternoon so that everyone could see and there would be no doubts about the reputation of the girl. Their horror at the idea that the groom would use "it" came from their fear that it would be more painful for the bride.

Besides asking whether they do it with the finger or "it," day or night, the women I knew often asked whether, where I came from, there was anyone with the bride to hold her down. They were surprised to hear that she needed no one and marveled that she wasn't afraid to be alone with the man. Among themselves, they almost always had a few older women, usually aunts or close neighbors of the groom and bride, in the room with the bride when the groom came to her. There in theory to hold the bride, these women also end up giving advice to the groom and making sure that he knew what to do so that everything—the display of the blood on the cloth—would turn out right.

For their part, somewhat like most Europeans and Americans, non-Bedouin Egyptians and assimilated Awlad 'Ali from the agricultural areas find Bedouin weddings scandalous and distasteful. Bedouin women are not unaware of these views and the men discussed

previously were probably reacting defensively to them. These outsiders may laugh at some customs but they are embarrassed by others. After one wedding in the community in which I was living, the bride's aunt, who had spent most of her life in a non-Bedouin provincial town, talked about the wedding and some of the customs she had witnessed that made her laugh "until her stomach hurt." She obviously considered her new in-laws backward.[3]

What seemed to disturb her most was the public nature of what she felt should be private. She thought it humiliating, for example, that at night, the young men from the community (peers of the bridegroom) hung around the room, listening, shining a flashlight under the door and through the window, and generally being disruptive. More horrible to her was the public display of the blood-stained cloth. "It was incredible," she exclaimed. "After the defloration didn't you hear my son saying to his aunt when she went to hang the cloth on the tent ropes, 'It's shameful, my aunt, it's shameful to put the cloth out for people to see.'" Like other urban and rural Egyptians, she thought that the bride and groom should be brought together at night and left alone.

Although other Egyptians and Americans might feel that such privacy is more civilized, the Awlad 'Ali women I knew did not see it that way. Bedouin women were scandalized by the secrecy of night deflorations, the immediate and explicit link such weddings make between marriage and sexual intercourse, and what they view as either the total vulnerability of the poor bride forced to be alone with a man or, even worse, the bride's immodest desire for a man. They knew that instead of struggling, the Egyptian bride has her photo taken with her husband-to-be, she sits with him at weddings where the sexes mix, and she dresses in makeup and fancy clothes for all to see. Because poorer Bedouin men sometimes marry young women from peasant areas, whether they are of Egyptian stock or long-sedentarized Bedouin involved in agriculture, the Bedouin women also knew that unmarried sisters accompanied the bride. They interpreted this practice as a shameful attempt to display and "sell" marriageable daughters. They also knew that such brides sometimes arrived bringing a cooked duck or goose to feed a new husband; they took this as a sign of the bride's unseemly eagerness to please the groom.

Egyptian weddings, much like American ones, construct the couple as a separate unit, distinct from families or ties to members of the same gender group. At their center is a sexual joining that is private and intimate. For the Awlad 'Ali, this is a strange thing. The secrecy of private sex, in the dark, behind closed doors, and preferably in the foreign or anonymous setting (for the honeymoon) produces sexuality as something personal, intensely individual, apparently separate from society and social power. It produces sexuality as something belonging in an inviolable private sphere—the bedroom—a sphere in which others cannot interfere with whatever pleasure or violence and coercion accompanies it. One of the consequences of this construction of sexuality is that we, and perhaps Egyptians, come to think there is a part of oneself that is not social or affected by the prevailing power relations in society.[4]

The three crucial elements in the Bedouin discourse on differences between their weddings and those of other groups are (1) whether the defloration is public and participatory, (2) whether it involves sexual intercourse, and (3) whether it is seen as a contest, especially between bride and groom. These elements also had meaning within the local context. In Bedouin weddings the ways in which sexuality is related to power relations and the social order were clear. Marriages have been the occasion for people to collectively enact and reproduce this social order and the individual's place in it. And the individual's place was, until recently, very much a part of the group—whether the kin group or the group defined by gender.

WEDDINGS AS PUBLIC RITES: THE POWER OF KINSHIP AND GENDER

The participants in Awlad 'Ali Bedouin weddings instantiate, by means of a bride and groom, the relations between families or kin groups on the one hand, and the relations between men and women on the other. A symbolic analysis of the central rite, the defloration, enacted in a homologous fashion on the bodies of the bride and groom and on the collective bodies of the gathered kin and friends, reveals that it produces an understanding of sexuality as something public and focused on crossing thresholds, opening passages, and moving in and out. There are no strong messages of mingling or joining or even interchange in a private sexual act. The emphasis is on opening the bride's vagina by breaking the hymen and bringing out or making visible what was in there. And although people say that deflorations should be done during the daytime so everyone can see the cloth, the fact that in the rhythm of daily life morning and daytime generally are times of opening and going out from home or camp, while evening is a time of returning inward, cannot but reinforce the auspiciousness of this time for opening and taking outward.[5]

That this opening is a prelude to the insemination which should eventuate in childbirth is suggested by some practices associated with the blood-stained virginity cloth. It is taken out of the room by the groom and thrown to the women gathered just outside. It is said that if the cloth is then brought back into the room without the bride having exited first—if, as they say, the cloth enters upon her—it will block her from conceiving.[6] Young women are told to save their virginity cloths; if they have trouble conceiving, they must bathe in water in which they have soaked the cloth.

Everything in the rites and the songs that accompany them suggests that the individuals engaged in this opening and being opened, taking out and showing, and having something taken out and shown, embody both their kin groups and their gender groups. The connection to kin, and control by the kin group, is clear in the key role they have in arranging and negotiating marriages and is reflected in the songs the groom's female relatives sing as they go to fetch the bride from her father's household. It is also reinforced in the songs the bride's female kin sing to greet these people. Most of the songs compliment the social standing of the families of the bride and groom.

Even the practices and movements of the wedding itself perpetuate the identifications with kin groups. Most brides, even today, are brought from their fathers' households completely covered by a white woolen woven cloak (*jard*) that is the essential item of men's dress. The cloak must belong to the girl's father or some other male kinsman. So, protected and hidden by her father's cloak, she is brought out of her father's protected domain and carried to her husband's kin group's domain. There she is rushed, still hidden, into the room (or in the past, the tent) which she will share with her husband. Although nowadays the woven cloak is usually removed once she enters the room, in the past the bride remained under her father's cloak and was not revealed even to the women gathered around her until after the defloration.

The virginity of the bride is also constructed as something inseparable from her family's honor. Although one unmarried girl explained the importance of the blood-stained cloth in terms of her own reputation, she stressed the effect it would have on others.

> For us Bedouins, this is the most important moment in a girl's life. No matter what anyone says afterward, no one will pay attention as long as there was blood on the cloth. They are suspicious of her before. People talk. "She went here, she went there." "She looked at So-and-so." "She said hello to So-and-so." "She went to the orchard." But when they see this blood the talk is cut off. . . . When they see the cloth, she can come and go as she pleases. They love her and everything is fine.

The best way to get a sense of who has a stake in the girl's virginity and why is to listen to the conventional songs sung wildly outside the door of the bride's room as the defloration is underway. Unmarried girls and some young married women clap and sing rhyming songs that refer to the effect of the proof of the bride's virginity on various members of her family and community.

> Make her dear Mom happy, Lord
> Hanging up her cloth on the tent ropes
> O Saint 'Awwaam on high
> Don't let anyone among us be shamed

Older women sing more serious songs that take up similar themes:

> When the people have gathered
> O Generous One favor us with a happy ending
> . . . Behind us are important men
> who ask about what we are doing . . .

Relatives of the bride show their support and faith in the bride in songs like this:

> I'm confident in the loved one
> you'll find it there intact . . .

Even the groom's behavior during the defloration reflects on his relatives. One song a relative of his might sing as he arrives or is inside with the bride is the following:

> Son, be like your menfolk
> strong willed and unafraid . . .

After the virginity cloth is brought out by the groom and thrown to the women, a different set of songs is sung. These praise the cloth and the honor of the girl who had remained a virgin. The songs reflect on who is affected by her purity and who is proud. At one wedding a female relative of the bride sang to a nephew nearby:

> Go tell your father, Said
> the banner of her honor is flying high . . .

About the bride a woman might sing:

> Bravo! She was excellent
> she who didn't force down her father's
> eyelashes . . .

Given this group investment in the bride's virginity, the central rite of the wedding becomes a drama of suspense and relief that must powerfully shape people's experiences of sexuality as something that belongs to the many, and especially to one's family. The wedding is also, importantly, an occasion when families find themselves in some rivalry, the honor of each at stake. This was more apparent in the past when the young men celebrated all night on the eve of the wedding and expressed the rivalry through singing contests that sometimes broke out into actual fights between lineages.

Kinship is not the only power-laden aspect of social life that finds itself reflected and reinforced in the wedding. The second set of power relations weddings play with are those of gender. The bride and groom in the wedding rite enact the charged relations between men and women as distinct genders in a kind of battle of the sexes. Although most activities in the community are informally segregated by gender, at weddings—in part because there are non-family members present—the sexual segregation is more obvious and fixed, women and men forming highly separate collectivities for nearly all events.

Given this separation of the sexes, the defloration, taking place in the middle of the day when all are gathered in their distinct places, becomes a ritualized and extreme form of encounter between both the bride and groom and the women and men who surround each of them. The movements of the groom and his age-mates as they penetrate the crowd of women surrounding the bride mirror the groom's penetration of his bride, who forms a unit with the women in the room with her. The young men stand just outside the door, sometimes dancing and singing, ready to fire off guns in celebration when the groom emerges. They rush him back away from the women. This mirroring is expressed in the ambiguity of the term used for both moments of this event: the entrance (*khashsha*) refers both to the entry with the finger and the whole defloration process when the groom enters the bride's room, which can be thought of as his kin group's womb.

The encounter between male and female takes the form of a contest. The groom is encouraged to be fearless. He is expected to finish the deed in as short a time as possible. The bride is expected to try valiantly to fight him off. Taking the virginity she has been so careful to guard and thus opening the way for his progeny is the groom's victory; the bride doesn't give it up without a struggle. Calling this, as the literature often does, a virginity test is a misnomer in that it misses this combative dimension of the ritualized act. The way people describe what happens even on the wedding night suggests again that the groom and bride are involved in a contest. The rowdy young men who listen outside the marital chamber want to know "who won." They know this, some adolescent girls informed me, not just by whether the groom succeeds in having intercourse with his bride (a rare event), but by whether the groom succeeds in making his bride talk to him and answer his questions. This is, perhaps, another kind of opening up.

There is other evidence that weddings provoke a heightened attention to issues of gender and sexual mixing. One of the most revealing and intriguing is the spontaneous cross-dressing that sometimes happens at weddings. At several weddings I attended one woman in our community actually put on men's clothes, a fake mustache and beard, and covered her head in a man's headcloth. Amidst much hilarity she came out to dance in front of the bride. Others expressed some disapproval and called this woman a bit mad. But they laughed riotously anyway. One woman who thought it excessive described someone else who she thought was quite funny: All she did was dance in front of the bride with a shawl bunched up in front like male genitalia. Sometimes it was reported that the unmarried men and young boys had celebrated the night before the wedding by dressing up a boy with women's bracelets and a veil and dancing in front of him as if he were a bride.

SEXUAL TRANSFORMATIONS

Many Awlad 'Ali claim that their rituals are changing. In this final section, I want to explore how in these changed wedding practices we can begin to track changes in the nature of power and social relations. This is further support for my initial argument that constructions of sexuality cannot be understood apart from understandings of particular forms of social power. Most people talked about changes in weddings over the last twenty years or so in terms of what had been lost. Many said weddings were not fun any more. As far as I could determine, the main element that seems to have been lost is the celebration the night before the wedding (*saamir*). Not only do the young men no longer sing back and forth, but no longer is it even thinkable that a young woman from the community would come out to dance in front of them. This is what used to happen and the change is crucial for Bedouin gender relations.

What happened in the past was that an unmarried sister or cousin of the groom would be brought out from among the women by a young boy. She would dance amidst a semi-circle of young men. Her face veiled and her waist girded with a man's white woven cloak, like the one the bride would come covered in the following day, she danced with a stick or baton in her hands. According to one man who described this to me, the young men tried to "beg" the stick from her, sometimes using subterfuges like pretending to be ill; she would often bestow the stick, he said, on someone she fancied. But according to the women I spoke with, the young men would sometimes try to grab the stick from her and she would, if they were too aggressive, get angry with them and leave. The young men took turns singing songs that welcomed the dancer and then described her every feature in flattering terms. The standard parts praised in such songs were her braids, her eyes, her eyebrows, her cheeks, her lips, her tattoos, her neck, her breasts, her arms, her hands, and her waist—most of which, it should be remembered, because of the way she was dressed were not actually visible. Thus in a sense the dancer was, through men's songs, made into the ideal woman, attractive object of men's desires.

The dancer must be seen as the bride's double or stand-in, an interpretation supported by the other occasion on which a young woman danced in front of men. In the days before cars, brides were carried from their fathers' households to their husbands' on camel-back, completely cloaked and sitting hidden inside a wooden litter (*karmuud*) covered in red woven blankets. Another woman always preceded her on foot, dancing as young men sang to her and shot off guns near her.

In both cases, the dancer as bride and as ideal womanhood went out before men who complimented and sought her. What is crucial to notice is how the women described the dancer. They attributed to her a special bravery and described her actions as a challenge to the young men. One wedding in which a young woman was accidentally wounded by a poorly aimed gun was legendary. The wedding went on, the story went, as a second dancer who had been near her merely wiped the blood from her forehead and continued to dance. More telling is the ritualized struggle over the stick, which one anthropologist who worked with a group in Libya has argued is associated with virginity (Mason 1975). A woman explained to me, "If the dancer is sharp they can't take the stick from her. They'll be coming at her from all sides but she keeps it."

But perhaps some of the short songs traditionally exchanged between the women (gathered in a tent some distance away from the young men standing in a line near the dancer) and the young men, make clearest the ways in which a challenge between the sexes was central to weddings. One especially memorable competitive exchange was the following. As her sister danced a woman sang of her:

A bird in the hot winds glides
and no rifle scope can capture it . . .
A man responded with the song:
The heart would be no hunter
if it didn't play in their feathers . . .

In the loss and delegitimation of this whole section of the wedding ritual, an important piece of the construction of Bedouin sexual relations has disappeared. Today, all that is left in a ritual that was a highly charged and evenly matched challenge between the sexes is the enactment of the men's hunt. The groom is the hunter, the bride his prey. Decked out in her make-up and white satin dress, she is brought from her father's house and her "virginity" taken by her groom in a bloody display.

Wedding songs, only sung by women now, reinforce this construction of the bride as vulnerable prey. They liken the bride to a gazelle. This is a compliment to her beauty but also suggests her innocence and defenselessness. Other songs liken the groom to a falcon or hunter.

This is no longer balanced by women's former powers to create desire but elude capture.

The disappearance of the female dancer can thus be seen to have shifted the balance such that women's capacities to successfully challenge men have been de-emphasized. Although the sexes are still pitted against each other, the contest is no longer represented as even.

There is a second important point to be made about the dancer that relates to some transformations in constructions of power and sexuality. For it is not completely true that women no longer dance in front of men at Awlad 'Ali weddings. It has become unacceptable for respectable young kinswomen to dance, but there are now some professional dancers. They accompany musical troupes hired to entertain at weddings of the Bedouin nouveau riche. These women may or may not be prostitutes but they are certainly not considered respectable.[7] In that sense, and in the fact that ordinary women go nowhere near the areas where these musicians and dancers perform, one cannot any longer claim that the dancer represents Woman or enacts women's challenge of men. The opposite may be true. This new kind of wedding may be introducing a new view of women, one quite familiar to us in the United States but quite strange to the Awlad 'Ali: women as sexual commodities stripped of their embeddedness in their kin groups or the homosocial world of women.

The professionalization of weddings as entertainment and spectacle (spectacles that retain vestiges of the participatory in that young men seize the microphone to sing songs) may also be signaling a fundamental shift in the relationship of the construction of sexuality and the construction of the social order. What seems to be disappearing is the participation of the whole community in the responsibility of ritually reproducing the fundamental social and political dynamics of the community. Does this indicate the emergence of a new kind of power? One that works differently? One whose nexus is perhaps the individual rather than the kin group or gender group? This new form of wedding is not being adopted universally in the Bedouin region since the poor cannot afford it and the respectable condemn it as undignified and inappropriate for pious Muslims. Nevertheless, as a public discourse it must enter and shape the field of sexuality for all.

The third and final historical shift I will discuss comes out in the comments women made about what had happened to weddings. One old woman reminisced about weddings of the past. She shook her head and laughed, "No, the things they did before you can't do anymore. Nowadays weddings are small, like a shrunken old man. People used to really celebrate, staying up all night, for days! But they have become like the Muslim Brothers now." The younger woman she was talking to had explained for me. "They say it is wrong. Now everything is forbidden. People before didn't know. They were ignorant." She used a term with connotations of the pre-Islamic era.

These women's invocations of Islam and the proper behavior of the pious in the contexts of weddings mark some significant changes in power relations. It has always been important to the Awlad 'Ali that they are Muslims and that they are good Muslims. And these two women themselves were devout. They prayed regularly and the old one had been on the pilgrimage to Mecca. Yet when they and other women brought up the religious wrongness of their traditional wedding practices, it was with some ambivalence since they were also nostalgic for the richer days of the past. After one wedding there was a hint of disapproval in women's gossip about one aunt in the community. Someone with a good voice who usually sang at weddings, she had just returned from the pilgrimage to Mecca and had refused this time. "It is wrong," she told them. They thought she was being self-righteous—and selfish.

What is really at stake comes out clearly from women's discussions of a happy wedding that had taken place in my absence. I was told that, as usual, for days before the wedding the women and girls had been celebrating by themselves every evening, drumming and singing. The older men of the community wanted them to stop and instructed them that at least once the guests (non-relatives) had begun to arrive, they would have to stop. It was shameful to sing in front of people, the men insisted. On the eve of the wedding as the women and girls gathered and began to sing and dance in celebration, the groom's father came in to greet his visiting female relatives. He also wanted to try to silence the group of women. When he entered the tent, he saw his own older sister, a dignified woman in her sixties, dancing. "Hey, what's this?" he said. "Rottenest of days, even you, Hajja?" He called her by the respectful title reserved for those who have performed the pilgrimage to Mecca. "That's right," she answered definitely, "even me!" Everyone laughed then and each time they retold the story.

Women still refuse to be stopped from celebrating weddings. But the older men, armed with religious righteousness, are clearly trying to assert authority over them in domains that were previously inviolable. Weddings, like the discontinued sheep-shearing festivities to which they are often likened, were always before classified as occasions where young men and young women could express desires. Elder men were not to interfere. At sheep-shearing festivities young men used to sing with impunity oblique sexual songs to flirt with the women present. The songs often insulted the patriarch whose herds the young men were shearing. Similarly, at weddings young men sang to women, not just the dancer. Even more important, women sang back—songs of love and desire. Older men made sure they were not in the vicinity.[8]

Now, not only have the exchanges between young men and women stopped but older men seem to be trying to assert control over the separate women's festivities. Their motives for this intervention are irrelevant. They may genuinely believe they are encouraging their families to live up to an interpretation of Islam that denounces such frivolity as impious. The effect, however, on women and young men, is that by means of this discourse of Islamic propriety wielded by older men, they are being displaced as the prime actors in the rites that produced and reproduced Bedouin constructions of sexuality and desire.

If, as I have tried to show, in a small Bedouin community in Egypt, sexuality can come to be a crucial marker of cultural identity, and if the construction of sexuality is so closely tied to the organization of kinship and gender and changes as the community is transformed by such broad processes as its incorporation into the wider Egyptian nation and economy, then it seems impossible to assert the existence of a Muslim sexuality that can be read off texts or shared across communities with very different histories and ways of life. Instead, we need to think about specific constructions of sexuality and, in the case of the Muslim Arab world, about the variable role discourses on religion can play in those constructions.

AUTHOR'S NOTE

Most of the research in Egypt on which this article is based was supported by an NEH Fellowship for College Teachers and a Fulbright Award under the Islamic Civilization Program. I am grateful to Samia Mehrez for inviting me to present an early version at Cornell University. I am more grateful to the women and men in the Awlad 'Ali community who shared their lives, including their weddings, with me.

REFERENCES

Abu-Lughod, Lila. 1993. *Writing Women's Worlds: Bedouin Stories.* Berkeley and Los Angeles: University of California Press.

Alloula, Malek. 1986. *The Colonial Harem.* Myran and Wlad Godzich, trans. Minneapolis: University of Minnesota Press.

Boddy, Janice. 1989. *Wombs and Alien Spirits: Women, Men, and the Zar Cult in Northern Sudan.* Madison, WI: University of Wisconsin Press.

Bouhdiba, Abdelwahab. 1985. *Sexuality in Islam.* London and Boston: Routledge & Kegan Paul.

Bourdieu, Pierre. 1977. *Outline of a Theory of Practice.* Cambridge: Cambridge University Press.

Caplan, Patricia, ed. 1987. *The Cultural Construction of Sexuality.* London and New York: Tavistock Publications.

Combs-Schilling, M.E. 1989. *Sacred Performances: Islam, Sexuality and Sacrifice.* New York: Columbia University Press.

Daly, Mary. 1978. *Gyn/ecology, the Metaethics of Radical Feminism.* Boston: Beacon Press.

Foucault, Michel. 1978. *The History of Sexuality: Volume 1: An Introduction.* New York: Random House.

———. 1985. *The Use of Pleasure.* Vol. 2 of *The History of Sexuality.* New York: Pantheon.

Mason, John. 1975. "Sex and Symbol in the Treatment of Women: The Wedding Rite in a Libyan Oasis Community." *American Ethnologist* 2: 649–61.

Peters, Emrys. 1990. *The Bedouin of Cyrenaica.* Edited by Jack Goody and Emanuel Marx. Cambridge: Cambridge Univeristy Press.

Sabbah, Fatna A. 1984. *Woman in the Muslim Unconscious.* New York and Oxford: Pergamon Press.

Vance, Carole. 1984. *Pleasure and Danger: Exploring Female Sexuality.* Boston and London: Routledge & Kegan Paul.

Van Nieuwkerk, Karin. 1995. *"A Trade Like Any Other": Female Singers and Dancers in Egypt.* Austin, TX: University of Texas Press.

NOTES

1. The literature, especially the feminist literature, on sexuality has become vast in the last decade or two. A helpful early text is Vance (1984). Anthropologists have recently begun to pay more attention to constructions of sexuality and their cross-cultural perspective should contribute to our understanding of the way that sexuality is constructed. For a good introduction to some of that work, see Caplan (1987).

2. For this reason the weddings of divorcees or widows are not celebrated with as much enthusiasm and are considered somewhat ordinary affairs.

3. For example, she described what is known as the *dayra* (the circling). On the evening of the wedding day, they had seated the bride and groom on a pillow, back to back. A neighbor carrying a lamb on his back, holding one foreleg in each of his hands, had walked around and around them—seven times. She mimicked the audience counting: "Hey, did you count that one? One, two, three, four." "Thank God," she said at one point, "there were no outsiders (non-relatives) from back home with us. How embarrassing it would have been."

4. The theorist who has most developed this notion of the effects on subjectivity and sense of individuality of the Western discourses on sexuality is Michel Foucault (1978, 1985).

5. For an analysis of similar kinds of symbolic constructions of gender and sexuality, see Bourdieu's (1977) work on Algerian Kabyles. My analysis of the meaning of this rite differs significantly from that of Combs-Schilling (1989), who worked in Morocco.

6. For more on rituals related to fertility and infertility, see my *Writing Women's Worlds* (1993). Boddy (1989) has analyzed for Muslim Sudanese villagers the extraordinary symbolic stress on women's fertility over their sexuality.

7. As Van Nieuwkerk (1995) has documented, this is generally true about professional dancers in Egypt.

8. Peters (1990) describes a similar avoidance by elders of wedding celebrations among the Bedouin of Cyrenaica in the 1950s.

From Pollution to Love Magic:
The New Anthropology of Menstruation

Alma Gottlieb

Consider this story: A college student—we'll call him Eddie—is having difficulty in his love life. Girls are so keyed into feminism these

"Bloody Mess, Blood Magic, or Just Plain Blood? Anthropological Perspectives on the Menstrual Experience" (adaptation/elaboration of "Afterword," *Ethnology* 41 (4): 381–390).

days, Eddie's concluded, that they rarely consider boys worthy of their affection. How to seduce a girl of this feminist generation? One day, our frustrated student is inspired: Even the staunchest feminist might be excited at the thought of a prospective boyfriend who himself professes an interest in feminist theory, he ventures. Eddie decides to make use of campus resources and scours the bookstores for the most unabashedly, even outrageously feminist book he can find. He chooses a scholarly tome called *Blood Magic: The Anthropology of Menstruation,* a collection of essays about the ways that women around the world experience their periods (Buckley and Gottlieb 1988a). Eddie buys the volume, brings it home, and places the unread prop strategically on his coffee table before inviting his next date to his apartment, then hopes for the book to have its anticipated effect.[1]

In planning his strategy, the model Eddie used was an old one, although he was undoubtedly unaware of its pedigree: he was relying on menstrual blood—or its textual representation— as a seduction technique, a form of "love magic." This use of menstrual blood to secure sexual favors (or fidelity) is well documented in other cultural contexts (Hoskins 2002a, & b); in fact, a (semi-fictionalized) folk example from southen Illinois is even mentioned in the introduction to the very book Eddie was displaying on his coffee table.

However, most previously documented forms of menstrual-blood-as-love-magic involve women manipulating the substance either to seduce men, or to bind straying husbands or lovers to them; Eddie had reversed the more usual gender pattern. Using cunning and deceit, he had acted as the initiator of the sexual relationship. In his plan, he upheld the usual patriarchal structure of Western gender relations of men taking advantage of women by exercising differential access to power of one sort or another. Thus if Eddie's unexpected use of a feminist book about menstrual experiences spoke to a documented ethnographic practice, it also represented a violation of the feminist intention of the analytic project of understanding those practices. Eddie's story signals how far scholars still have to go in

furthering the widespread understanding of feminism and how it can lead us to understand women's lives and bodily-based experiences.

When the book Eddie was using as a quasi-fetish in his flirtation repertoire was first published (Buckley and Gottlieb 1988b), anthropological works about menstruation were few and far between. Moreover, most early anthropological writings on menstruation tended to confirm a simplistic agenda suggesting that menstrual blood is generally taken as a source of what anthropologists call symbolic pollution (Douglas 1966). In other words, menstrual blood was assumed to be seen as mystically contaminating, hence something to be avoided at all costs by anyone who is not menstruating— and especially by men.[2] Feminism had not yet made serious inroads into the comparative, cultural study of women's bodies in general. And systematic cross-cultural fieldwork with consultants concerning the topic of menstruation, let alone with menstruating women themselves about their own perspectives on their somatic lives, was still a rarity. In assembling our collection of anthropological essays about menstrual practices cross-culturally, Buckley and I hoped to be followed by a new generation of writings that would both add new data to our existing knowledge of women's experiences of their bodies, and that would pose a range of new models inspired in one way or another by feminist theory. These future works would, we thought, investigate how women's experiences of the menstrual cycle—as with other body practices—are profoundly shaped by culture and history. For this to occur, we needed to be followed by a new generation of ethnographers committed to conducting fieldwork-based studies on somatic processes such as menstruation that seemed to belong exclusively to the domain of biology but that were nevertheless deeply defined by systems of cultural values and historical factors alike.

---

[1] The story was shared with me by my husband, writer Philip Graham, who heard it from a writing student of his who was "Eddie's" roommate. The writing student was visiting our home for a class party and, after noticing a copy of *Blood Magic* on my bookshelf, relayed the above narrative to his amused professor.

[2] For a critical review of earlier works informed by this and other problematic perspectives, see Buckley and Gottlieb (1988a).

During the fifteen years that have elapsed since *Blood Magic* appeared, feminism has indeed made exciting inroads into the comparative, cultural study of women's bodies in general. Accordingly, systematic cross-cultural fieldwork with consultants concerning the topic of menstruation in particular, and with menstruating women themselves about their own perspectives on their somatic lives, is no longer such a rarity. Indeed, in the past decade-and-a-half, there has been a groundswell of published work, both within and outside anthropology, that focuses on menstruation as well as other aspects of reproduction in particular and the body in general. Originally, these writings emphasized *women's* bodily experiences. In many ways launched by Emily Martin's award-winning work, *The Woman in the Body* (1987), a host of books and articles have brilliantly explored the culturally and historically produced nature of a wide gamut of reproduction experiences previously assumed to be regulated by biology alone.[3] Increasingly, scholars have begun to explore cultural and historical constructions of *men's* bodily experiences as well (e.g. Gardiner 2002, Gutmann 1996, Kimmel 1987, Lugo and Maurer 2000). Contemporary authors now writing about the menstrual experience cross-culturally are thus in conversation with a larger cohort of colleagues bringing fresh perspectives to the dynamic interface between body, person, gender identity, and society.

In this chapter, I will especially focus on one recent collection of essays that offers an especially rich selection of practices, beliefs and values concerning menstrual cycle cross-culturally (Hoskins 2002a). Some important themes run through the essays in that collection.

---

[3] For an excellent review of earlier work, see Ginsburg and Rapp (1991). More recent works include: Bledsoe and Banja (2002), Davis-Floyd (1992), Davis-Floyd and Sargent (1997), Davis-Floyd, Cosminsky and Pigg (2002), Davis-Floyd and Dumit (1997), Feldman-Savelsberg (1999), Franklin and Ragoné (1998), Ginsburg and Rapp (1995), Handwerker (1990), Héritier (1994, 1996), Inhorn (1994, 1995), Jordan (1993), Morgan (1999), Nourse (1999), Owen (1993), Ragoné (1994), Rapp (1999), Roth (2002), Sargent (1989), and M. Strathern (1992).

For example, the in/famous *menstrual hut* is drastically revisioned in this new writing. Long conceived as an architectural instantiation of female oppression, the "menstrual hut" in much classic anthropological literature was usually described as a lonely and flimsy structure in which women were consigned to spend their menstruating days alone—bored, self-loathing (allowed only to scratch an itch on their contaminated bodies using the infamous "scratching sticks" to avoid auto-pollution), and in virtual (if temporary) exile. This anthropologically vaunted, somewhat mystical space was surrounded by decades of disciplinary speculation that was, however, rarely based on relevant fieldwork. The menstrual buildings described in current anthropological writings inhabit an entirely different universe.

Janet Hoskins (2002b) occupies an especially privileged position from which to understand the experiences of women while inside a menstrual residence. While living among the Huaulu people in eastern Indonesia, Hoskins herself was expected to spend time in the menstrual hut every month while she had her period. Her account runs parallel to that of another ethnographer, Wynne Maggi, who has recently conducted participant observation research in menstrual houses every month over the course of fieldwork with the (largely non-Muslim) Kalasha community in Pakistan and has written a first-person account of her experiences (Maggi 2001: 125–133). Having conducted fieldwork in societies with active menstrual shelters and a number of explicit menstrual expectations, both Hoskins and Maggi were afforded rare opportunities to gain firsthand knowledge of the occupants' activities and the general atmosphere inside the houses, and thus to demystify women's actual experiences.

Perhaps the greatest challenge posed by both the Huaulu and the Kalasha to the infamous image of the menstrual-hut-as-prison concerns the personnel. Due to the now fairly well documented but still-little-understood phenomenon of menstrual synchrony—the likelihood of co-resident women starting their periods on the same day each month (often at the new moon or full moon)[4]—there is usually a lively gathering of several simultaneously menstruating women inside both Huaulu and Kalasha menstrual huts, rather than the stereotyped single, lonely woman. Moreover, among the Huaulu, beyond the menstruating women themselves, one is also likely to find some of their young children—both boys and girls—and on occasion some visiting women friends as well. Hoskins intrigues us with her account of all manner of pleasurable female activity occurring inside the collectivity temporarily inhabiting the hut. Singing and playing instruments, telling stories, doing craftwork, relaxing, breastfeeding, caring for young children—all these occur each month inside the menstrual residence. Indeed, the sociable nature of the chamber lends itself to charismatic personalities: one Huaulu woman even turned the hut into a performance space in which she recounted lively stories, building up political reputations village-wide from her narrative skills.

Elsewhere, women do not maintain a complete monopoly over the menstrual residence. Among the Pangia of the New Guinea highlands, such buildings may also legitimately shelter *men* (Stewart and Strathern 2002). This occurs on the rare occasion that a man is said by members of the local community to be pregnant because he inadvertently ingested menstrual blood. In such a disastrous situation, the unfortunate man is said to be cured by a ritual that he undergoes inside the menstrual hut shelter—now empty of women. Writing of less legitimate cases elsewhere in New Guinea, Stewart and Strathern (ibid.) also mention in passing the possibility of *menstrual adultery* occurring in the private space of the menstrual hut. This is an under-discussed but surely fruitful topic for comparative inquiry, especially where menstrual seclusion is practiced. Both these Melanesian cases serve as a powerful reminder to the outsider that, as anthropology so often teaches us about nearly every other aspect of social life, nothing may be assumed: in this case, in any

given menstrual residence, even the gender of the occupants may be variable.

In Indonesia, Hoskins (2002b) further notes that the Huaulu menstrual building shelters women not only when they are menstruating but also while they are in labor. Such dual-use structures—for both menstruation and childbirth—are reported elsewhere as well (e.g., Maggi 2001). In such cases where the menstrual shelter also serves as the birth clinic, perhaps even the term "menstrual hut" (or "house") is misleading and ought to be replaced by a more culturally inclusive term—"women's reproduction house" or even just "women's house," echoing the "men's houses" that are documented among many groups in Melanesia, Africa and South America. Such a semantic shift would be in keeping with the fact that menstruation may not always be singled out for special treatment in complete contrast to all other bodily fluids and processes.

The emphasis on *agency* in contemporary works about menstruation extends beyond the menstrual shelter to the experience of menstruating women, whether or not they inhabit a special building reserved for the occasion. Thus, the agency of the individual woman-as-menstruator is stressed in several recent essays. From Hoskins (2002b), for example, we learn of Kodi women on Sumba in eastern Indonesia who deploy menstrual blood to deceive their husbands in a variety of disempowering ways, effectively manipulating the secret powers of menstrual blood at the expense of their men. The flip side to such actions is exercised by Huaulu women, who manage the more public powers of menstruation for the *protection* of their men.

Elsewhere in Indonesia, Balinese women may make use of menstrual blood in manufacturing more friendly forms of "love magic". At the same time, in a provocative narrative, Pedersen (2002) illustrates how the individual menstruator's own perceptions of her state can complicate seemingly simple ideologies of menstruation-as-pollution when she cites a Balinese consultant who claims that sitting on a garbage heap while menstruating makes her feel royal. Other Balinese women knowingly violate menstrual taboos by illicitly entering a

---

[4] For ethnographic and historic examples of menstrual synchrony, see Buckley (1988), Knight (1988, 1991); and Lamp (1988).

temple while menstruating but apparently feel no remorse or guilt. As analyzed by Pedersen, such women employ psychological techniques to counterbalance the spiritual pollution they should in theory cause by their violation. Here we see how ideologies of pollution, where they exist, should be the beginning—not the end—of ethnographic analysis. Women's own views of a patriarchal ideology can strikingly offer an alternative reading of that ideology, sometimes affording women a form of personal resistance to a degrading cultural script, or allowing them to reinterpret it entirely.

The agency of the individual is explicitly stressed by Phyllis Morrow writing about the native American Yupik of central Alaska. Morrow (2002) explores how the Yupik generally emphasize individual responsibility in maintaining cultural expectations. Thus the Yupik allow latitude for individuals to find their own comfort level in adhering to rules, or "teachings" (as Morrow sometimes translates the Yupik word), for personal behavior—including those that pertain to menstruation. This is an apt case of an indigenous or "folk" model of social life pointing productively to an appropriate analytic model. The conjunction between indigenous and analytic models serves as a humble reminder that local systems of knowledge exist on the same level as do "scientific" ones, and each can speak productively to the other (cf. Rosaldo 1989).

Another means to deploy agency in the menstrual experience involves the use of *emenagogues:* herbal and other practical methods that women throughout the world and throughout history have devised to regulate the timing of their periods. Sometimes these techniques have been used to promote fertility, at other times, they have been used (usually furtively) to induce abortions. In either case, using such techniques may constitute a more secular effort by women to regulate their menstrual flow, thereby allowing them to exercise general control over their bodies.

Writing of Bali, for example, Pedersen (2002) mentions that women may prepare a dish with uncooked pig's blood to hasten the onset of their menstrual periods. This observation echoes abundant information contained in a new collection of essays (Renne and van der Walle 2001) reporting an impressive variety of emenagogues cross-culturally and historically. Once again, we encounter the theme of agency, as women deliberately shape their own menstrual experience rather than seeing themselves as scripted actors reading from either a biologically *or* culturally mandated text.

All these cases demonstrate how close attention to individual perspectives deconstructs the classic, monolithic view of menstrual taboos and cultural expectations as preprogrammed models from which actual subjects may never diverge. Such testimonies are theoretically critical insofar as they challenge the image that anthropologists have long held of menstrual culture—perhaps as an extension of a more general model inherited from such early scholars as Lucien Lévy-Bruhl (1985) and others, that cultural traditions in general exert a certain deadening, conservative force. This is a perspective that is very much challenged in the recent work on menstruation.

The individual manipulation of menstrual taboos and expectations speaks at another level to intracultural variation via subgroups with structurally divergent agendas or even ambiguity or ambivalence among members of a given society regarding women's menstrual activities. When Buckley (1988) first suggested that among the native North American Yurok of California, men and women, as well as aristocrats and commoners, may perceive menstruation differently from one another, it was a somewhat novel proposal. Several recent essays provide extended studies of situations that are likewise complex in their own ways. Menstruation emerges from these societies as a process that is perceived differentially according to multiple subject positions.

Writing of Bali, for example, Pedersen charts how the deeply structured system of rank adapted from the Hindu caste system has a significant impact on how girls and women experience their periods. Whereas high-ranking Balinese women may find menstrual taboos to be empowering, low-ranking girls and women may experience menstrual taboos as simply one more painful sign of their inferior status. Social change adds further layers to the entanglements of rank. Pederson notes that "'modern' working women are more prone than any to 'take advantage' of the leverage provided by the exempting options." If such options are more available to higher-ranked women than to lower-ranked ones, this would perpetuate, and perhaps even magnify, the divide between women at different ends of the system of social hierarchy. Here we see the complexity of class and gender as they work against each other. Ironically, women's bodies—which might (seemingly) serve as a foundation for female solidarity—can be culturally manipulated in such a way as to divide rather than unite women of diverse class and prestige backgrounds. The menstrual experience speaks here to broader feminist concerns: sadly, the empowerment of some women often comes at the expense of the oppression of others.

Ironically, the opposite effects of the relationship between class and menstrual symbolism are found in Bengal. In this region of Hindu India, as analyzed by Hanssen (2002), the Brahmanic view is that menstrual blood is polluting. However, when men and women of the low-ranked leatherworker caste become "renouncers" through a particular religious sect—the Vaishnava Baul group—they embrace a major precept of the sect: that menstrual blood contains a life force or "seed" within it— as with other bodily fluids in the Baul scheme of life, but even more so. Taking into account such symbolic potency, some of the "renouncers" with whom Hanssen conducted research may on occasion ingest menstrual blood so as to regain spiritual strength. Here we see the symbolic potency to menstrual fluid being harnessed not for nefarious goals, as is reported in much of the classic literature, but for regenerative purposes. Again, the menstrual pollution model is effectively challenged.

Another subgroup meriting particular attention is that of *unmarried girls*. The menstrual blood of this group—defined variously as virgins and/or unmarried—is held up for special ritual treatment in several societies that are the focus of the articles I have been discussing. For example, Stewart and Strathern (2002) report that the Duna people of Melanesia addressed societal disruptions that were said to be caused by a mis-chievous spirit by offering the spirit the menstrual blood of a virginal girl. The consequences to the girl chosen to supply this critical ritual ingredient were drastic: as an adult, she was not allowed ever to bear children. In exploring the individual nuances of such cases here and elsewhere, there may be a subject ripe for new, comparative analysis.

Indeed, the experiences of girls undergoing menarche in general are still underreported by anthropologists. Scholars in history, cultural studies, nursing, journalism, and other disciplines are embarrassingly ahead of anthropologists here, inasmuch as the menarcheal histories of girls in the U.S. are now well documented by scholars in adjacent fields (e.g., Golub 1992, Houppert 1999, Lee and Coen 1996). A few current works by anthropologists do address the issue, however. Thus Pedersen (2002) recounts intriguing menarcheal histories of Balinese women that are at great variance from those reported for contemporary North American girls. Whereas in the U.S., many women and girls still feel great shame concerning their first periods (and regarding menstruation in general), and they attest to the continuing existence of a virtual taboo against discussion of the subject in most contexts, this is not the case in Bali. Intriguingly, Pederson reports that Balinese of all ages and both genders feel comfortable in discussing menstruation quite casually, and all females with whom Pederson conversed about the subject recalled that they enjoyed their first periods, even when they were surprised by or afraid of their first flow. Such discussions of the menarcheal experiences of non-Western girls reminds us that the more negative experiences of contemporary North American and other Western girls, while now well reported, cannot be taken as universal.

Surely it is time for more anthropologists to conduct systematic fieldwork with menstruating— as well as pre-menarcheal—girls to hear their own perspectives on this crucial life passage. At a more structural level, such discussions may enable us to think about *deconstructing* the category of "menstrual blood" itself. Are we talking about a unified semantic field when we analyze the blood flow of young girls and that of married women in the same way, if a given society singles out the menstrual blood of unmarried/virginal girls as harboring special capacities that the menstrual blood of adult women does not bear?

In short, from recent work it is clearer than ever that we can no longer talk of "the" (single or hegemonic) view or model of menstruation in a particular society. Rather, it is now clear that before assuming generality, we must interrogate the *range* of views and experiences that menstruation may produce across the social divides that structure women's lives.

Related to the previous points, one notices in the essays I have been discussing an insistence that the meanings of menstrual blood and menstruating women are decidedly *plural* in a given locale depending on the particular context. The classic menstrual-blood-as-pollution model that permeated so much early writing by anthropologists is definitively discarded here in favor of much more situationally nuanced understandings. In particular, the symbolically constituted relation of menstrual blood to both *fertility and infertility*, as well as to other cultural matrices, emerges as an especially critical theme in these papers (for an earlier example, see Gottlieb 1988).

Thus Stewart and Strathern (2002) propose a dramatic re-visioning of the hegemonic, disciplinary model of menstruation-as-pollution as it was foundationally conceptualized. Taking us to the heartland of classical anthropological thinking about menstruation—the highlands of Papua New Guinea—they draw on A. Strathern's recent, stimulating book, *Body Thoughts* (1996) to ground their discussion of menstruation in broader issues relating the body and society. Their description (from Sainsbury) of the menarcheal Siane girl who is celebrated and courted for her induction into life as a menstruator is at striking odds with the classic pollution model that permeated much early anthropological writing about gender relations in New Guinea. Stewart and Strathern then produce in effect a counterfactual model, imagining what regional ethnography might have been like over the past three decades had Sainsbury's ethnography—rather than that of other Melanesianists such

as Mervyn Meggitt—prevailed as the orienting study.[5]

But Stewart and Strathern's *What if . . . ?* line of thinking is not purely conjectural: they argue that the Siane would indeed serve as a more appropriate model for the New Guinea highlands. Drawing on additional Melanesian ethnography, Stewart and Strathern (2002) propose that a complementary rather than antagonistic model of gender relations is more relevant to much of Melanesia than previous ethnography suggested. Stewart and Strathern's disarmingly reorienting survey should serve to reinscribe the anthropological imagining of that cultural region with new models steeped in subtlety well beyond the classic statements. Moreover, their proposed model of complementary gender relations resonates with contemporary discussions of complementary and egalitarian models of gender being developed for a variety of independent, non-Western groups elsewhere before state conquest (e.g., Du 2002). Here we see how menstruation theory can speak to, and even inform, gender theory more broadly. This is the case insofar as menstruation is deeply implicated in a wide array of social matrices, from religion (most obviously) to such disparate spheres as architecture, political economy and beyond.

Indeed, the necessity for a contextual approach highlighting what anthropologist Victor Turner might have called *positionality*—an approach that would produce a wide-ranging analysis of how menstrual practices relate to other ritual and social forces at play in a given society—becomes quite pressing from all the work I have been discussing. Most of the societies that are the subject of the articles I have discussed—the Yupik of Alaska, several Melanesian groups, the eastern Indonesian Huaulu, and the Balinese—expect women to adhere carefully to culturally delimited menstrual restrictions; at the same time, the members of

[5] Their fantasy reminds one of Mary Douglas' long-ago published wondering what Africanist ethnography would look like had the British scholar, Sir E. Evans-Pritchard, studied the Dogon of francophone West Africa and the French scholar, Marcel Griaule, studied the Nuer of anglophone northeast Africa (Douglas 1975).

these societies orient these practices around conceptual models that are far from a simple pollution framework. Thus all the authors of the works I have discussed remind us that menstrual restrictions are best seen as one of many types of ritual and/or somatic restrictions in the lives of all who practice them. Depending on the society, the proper context for understanding menstrual restrictions may necessitate understanding comparable restrictions in the lives of both males and females, old and young, laypersons and ritual specialists alike. The language of pollution misleads here, these authors all observe; as Morrow (2002) points out, Mary Douglas' early hypothesis that menstrual pollution indexes underlying sociological ambiguity concerning women does not necessarily apply.

At the same time, writing of the Kodi, Hoskins (2002b) points out that the *absence* of menstrual taboos belies a deep-seated conviction that menstrual blood is exceedingly *potent*. Her insight signals that a lack of explicitly religious *taboos* concerning menstrual practice does not necessarily signal a lack of culturally shaped thinking about menstruation. The current outpouring of ethnographies of modern urban life speaks powerfully to this point: secular culture is still culture, these ethnographies remind us—even science is grounded in a set of cultural assumptions that appeal to deeply held but unverifiable beliefs about the nature of reality.[6] As Clifford Geertz cautioned some time ago (1983), what passes for "common sense" is not necessarily common, as peoples everywhere forge their own distinctive notion of common sense as the basis for reality. A contextual approach to social life borrowed from Turner, highlighting positionality, offers a fruitful method for teasing out local nuances that seeming similarities across cultures might otherwise conceal.

As with other taboos, the longstanding anthropological and popular images alike of menstrual taboos is that they have somehow existed since time immemorial and that their origins

are untraceable. In the recent writings I have been discussing, we learn otherwise. In taking into account the press of *history and social change*, it becomes clear that menstrual practices engage with a variety of modernities. Earlier studies tended to treat the body either as an artifact of biology—i.e., more or less immutable, hence anthropologically boring—or, more recently, as cultural constructions that were nevertheless conceived as static. More recent discussions have taken up the insistence—persuasively argued by the French scholar, Michel Foucault, and others—that bodily regimes are as much subject to historical shifts as are political regimes. In keeping with this productive direction for scholarly research, in the essays I have been considering, the authors offer discussions of how menstrual practices have—or in some surprising instances have not—transformed within the recent past. Indeed, in some places, rather than insistent continuity, radical changes in menstrual practices have been documented.

Not only may their histories be knowable, but menstrual practices have weakened in some places whereas—in contrast to what modernization theory would have predicted—they have intensified in other regions. Among the Pangia in Melanesia, for example, Stewart and Strathern (2002) inform us that menstrual huts, far from having existed since some primeval *ur*-time, were first introduced to the group along with performances dedicated to a regional female spirit cult. This spirit is widely respected as promoting fertility; Stewart and Strathern treat it as an index of a more general model of gender complementarity. The traceable co-introduction of female spirit cult performances and the practice of menstrual seclusion raises fascinating questions about changing gender roles during an earlier era of Pangia history. The case suggests that we might question the seemingly unchanging history of other menstrual practices elsewhere. Assuming that contemporary menstrual practices are a permanent feature of a given social landscape makes no more sense than assuming that any other aspect of a society—say, its political structure, or its economic base—has existed unchanged for millennia.

[6] For some examples of ethnographic accounts of contemporary scientific culture, see Gusterson (1996), Haraway (1990), Martin (1994), and Toumey (1996).

Moreover, in those cases where cultural continuity *is* demonstrable, its meanings are not necessarily transparent. On Bali, Pedersen (2002) tells us, menstrual taboos continue in strong force even in the face of available new menstrual technologies (industrially produced sanitary pads and tampons). However, the continuity of menstrual restrictions does not imply a thoroughgoing neglect of, or resistance to, modernity; the practices of menstrual culture can also acknowledge and even adapt to changing medical science. Thus nowadays, some Balinese women take birth control pills in order to delay the onset of their periods; precisely timing the menstrual cycle in this way can allow women to participate in traditional temple rituals from which menstruating women are still actively banned. In this menstrual culture that persists in the face of active engagement with the Western world, even tourists are subject to regulations . . . as the English-language signs at Balinese temples forbidding entrance by menstruating women remind foreign visitors. The Balinese case teaches us that apparent cultural conservatism may be maintained self-consciously for reasons engaging with modernity. Contemporary factors such as ethnic pride and nationalism in the face of international pressure to Westernize may become as relevant as insistent maintenance of tradition might have been in a previous era.

In short, tracing menstrual histories can serve to remind us that, as with other current social practices, what we observe at any given moment in the field *may* represent continuity— but it may also be an aberration, a variation, or a rejection of what has occurred in the recent or distant past. In the colonized world in particular, the ravages brought by the triple invasion of soldiers, traders and missionaries likely produced upheavals in the way that the body is culturally read and produced. *Precolonial* somatic regimes will of course be much more of a challenge to reconstruct, but oral histories, and in some cases colonial records, should help us to understand pivotal moments in history when the gendered body may have been re-thought and re-experienced. Through such records, can we begin to account for *why* menstrual taboos have relaxed in some areas whereas they have rigidified in others under varying colonial and post-colonial regimes, as indigenous populations endeavor to forge their own futures in the face of an increasingly engulfing modernity? This question contains a promising set of issues for researchers to continue to pursue.

THE FUTURE OF MENSTRUAL STUDIES

For over fifteen years, a pedagogical engagement with menstruation has allowed me to construct a classroom-based ethnographic portrait that affords some insight into contemporary U.S. college students' perceptions and experiences of the menstrual cycle. At my home university, I have regularly taught an undergraduate course on "Cultural Images of Women" which always includes a section on menstrual practices in cross-cultural perspective. Learning of the obfuscatory terms by which American female students (who are largely but not exclusively female) still refer to their periods ("the curse," "Aunt Flo," "on the rag," and so on)—which are typically identical to terms that have been documented for the U.S. for much of the twentieth century—is a depressing exercise. For the striking continuity in such terms speaks to the continuing existence of strong menstrual taboos and a polluting image of menstruation at the heart of the supposedly rationalized and secular (and, dare one hope, decreasingly patriarchal) mainstream North American society.

However, another student exercise in this course often reveals a different, and more hopeful, portrait of the current generation of American students' attitudes towards toward menstruation. In choosing among several options for final exam essays, the most popular choice is often the essay question that invites students to design a new menstrual ritual for an imagined future daughter or niece, based on what students know from the menstrual experiences of their friends, relatives, and themselves, as well as what they have learned about women's menstrual experiences elsewhere from class readings. In writing their final essays, students year after year have proposed empowering rituals that harness the menstrual cycle to inspire menarcheal girls to feel pride rather than shame at their new somatically acquired status. One student, for example, envisioned a long ritual process of educating her not-yet-conceived daughter into the wonders of the menstrual cycle. During one portion of the imagined ritual, the author and her future husband would, she planned, "throw confetti into the air in celebration" (Schroeder 2001:2). This and other festive acts would serve to teach their future daughter to feel comfortable with her menstrual identity: "She would never once feel she had to hide the box of tampons in her bathroom or avoid the clerk's gaze while purchasing pads at the local grocery store" (ibid.:6–7).

Year after year, imagined rituals such as these have testified to a hunger by my students to revision menstruation in general, and menarche in particular, from a stigmatized to a celebrated event in contemporary North America. If my students' responses are typical, menstrual experiences offer a rich site from which to understand the embodied subject as a place in which gender, power and representation intersect in personally forceful ways. In particular, my students' writings suggest that at least some of the contemporary generation of young women is motivated to rethink their own menstrual histories and enjoys imagining menstrual futures offering ritualized revelry rather than secrecy and shame.

Meanwhile, current anthropological writings offer a range of models of menstrual practices that some of the world's women have forged. Together, these work constitute an exceedingly provocative set of writings that point to the exciting state that characterizes current comparative research into menstruation and that signal the fresh, *multiple* intellectual roads down which the anthropology of menstruation—as an exemplar of the embodied subject—is now traveling.

ACKNOWLEDGMENTS

A short version of this chapter was first presented at the 99th Annual Meeting of the American Anthropological Association (San Francisco, 2000), and a somewhat different version was published in *Ethnology* 41(4) (2002) (special issue: "Blood Mysteries: Beyond Menstruation as Pollution," ed. Janet Hoskins). Many thanks to Janet Hoskins for comments on the earlier version.

REFERENCES

Bledsoe, Caroline with Fatoumatta Banja
2002   *The Contingent Life Course: Reproduction, Time and Aging in West Africa.* Chicago: University of Chicago Press.
Buckley, Thomas
1988   Menstruation and the Power of Yurok Women. In *Blood Magic: The Anthropology of Menstruation*, ed. Thomas Buckley and Alma Gottlieb. Berkeley: University of California Press, pp. 187–209.
——— and Alma Gottlieb
1988a   A Critical Appraisal of Theories of Menstrual Symbolism. In *Blood Magic: The Anthropology of Menstruation*, ed. Thomas Buckley and Alma Gottlieb. Berkeley: University of California Press, pp. 1–53.
——— and ———, eds.
1988b   *Blood Magic: The Anthropology of Menstruation.* Berkeley: University of California Press.
Davis-Floyd, Robbie E.
1992   *Birth as an American Rite of Passage.* Berkeley: University of California Press.
———, Sheila Cosminsky and Stacy Leigh Pigg, eds.
2002   Daughters of Time: The Shifting Identities of Contemporary Midwives. Special issue of *Medical Anthropology* 20 (3).
——— and Joe Dumit, eds.
1997   *Cyborg Babies: From Techno Tots to Techno Toys.* New York: Routledge.
Davis-Floyd, Robbie E. and Carolyn F. Sargent, eds.
1997   *Childbirth and Authoritative Knowledge: Cross-Cultural Perspectives.* Berkeley: University of California Press.
Douglas, Mary
1966   *Purity and Danger: An Analysis of Concepts of Pollution and Taboo.* New York: Praeger.
1975   [1967]If the Dogon . . . ? In *Mary Douglas, Self-Evidence: Essays in Anthropology.* London: Routledge & Kegan Paul, pp. 124–141.
Du, Shanshan
2002   *"Chopsticks Always Work in Pairs": Gender Unity and Gender Equality among the Lahu of*

Southwest China. New York: Columbia University Press.

Feldman-Savelsberg, Pamela
1999 *Plundered Kitchens, Empty Wombs: Threatened Reproduction and Identity in the Cameroon.* Ann Arbor: University of Michigan Press.

Franklin, Sarah and Helena Ragoné, eds.
1998 *Reproducing Reproduction: Kinship, Power, and Technological Innovation.* Philadelphia: University of Pennsylvania Press.

Gardiner, Judith Kegan, ed.
2002 *Masculinity Studies and Feminist Theory: New Directions.* New York: Columbia University Press.

Geertz, Clifford
1983 [1975] Common Sense as a Cultural System. In Clifford Geertz, *Local Knowledge: Further Essays in Interpretive Anthropology.* New York: Basic Books, pp. 73–93.

Ginsburg, Faye and Rayna Rapp
1991 The Politics of Reproduction. *Annual Review of Anthropology* 20: 311–343.

Ginsburg, Faye and Rayna Rapp, eds.
1995 *Conceiving the New World Order: The Global Politics of Reproduction.* Berkeley: University of California Press.

Golub, Sharon
1992 *Periods: From Menarche to Menopause.* London: Sage.

Gottlieb, Alma
1988 Menstrual Cosmology among the Beng of Ivory Coast. In *Blood Magic: The Anthropology of Menstruation,* ed. Thomas Buckley and Alma Gottlieb. Berkeley: University of California Press, pp. 55–74.

Gusterson, Hugh
1996 *Nuclear Rites: A Weapons Laboratory at the End of the Cold War.* Berkeley: University of California Press.

Gutmann, Matthew C.
1996 *The Meanings of Macho: Being a Man in Mexico City.* Berkeley: University of California Press.

Handwerker, W. P., ed.
1990 *Births and Power: Social Change and the Politics of Reproduction.* Boulder: Westview Press.

Hanssen, Kristen.
2002 "Ingesting Menstrual Blood: Notions of Health and Bodily Fluids in Bengal," *Ethnology* 41(4): 365–380.

Haraway, Donna
1990 *Primate Visions: Gender, Race and Nature in the World of Modern Science.* New York: Routledge.

Héritier, Françoise
1994 *Les deux soeurs et leur mère.* Paris: Editions Odile Jacob.
1996 *Masculin/féminin: La pensée de la différence.* Paris: Editions Odile Jacob.

Hoskins, Janet
2002a "Blood Mysteries: Beyond Menstruation as Pollution." *Ethnology,* special issue, Volume 41, No 4.

Hoskins, Janet
2002b "The Menstrual Hut and the Witch's Lair in Two Indonesian Societies" *Ethnology* 41(4), 317–334.

Houppert, Karen
1999 *The Curse—Confronting the Last Unmentionable Taboo: Menstruation.* New York: Farrar, Straus, Giroux.

Inhorn, Marcia
1994 *Quest for Conception: Gender, Infertility, and Egyptian Medical Traditions.* Philadelphia: University of Pennsylvania Press.
1995 *Missing Motherhood: Infertility, Patriarchy and the Politics of Gender in Egypt.* Philadelphia: University of Pennsylvania Press.

Jordan, Brigitte
1993 [1978] *Birth in Four Cultures: A Cross-Cultural Investigation of Childbirth in Yucatan, Holland, Sweden and the United States.* Robbie Davis-Floyd, ed. 4th ed. Prospect Heights, IL: Waveland Press.

Kimmel, Michael S., ed.
1987 *Changing Men: New Directions in Research on Men and Masculinity.* Beverly Hills, CA: Sage.

Knight, Chris
1988 Menstrual Synchrony and the Australian Rainbow Snake. In *Blood Magic: The Anthropology of Menstruation,* ed. Thomas Buckley and Alma Gottlieb. Berkeley: University of California Press, pp. 232–255.
1991 *Blood Relations: Menstruation and the Origins of Culture.* New Haven: Yale University Press.

Lamp, Frederick
1988 Heavenly Bodies: Menses, Moon, and Rituals of License among the Temne of Sierra Leone. In *Blood Magic: The Anthropology of Menstruation,* ed. Thomas Buckley and Alma Gottlieb. Berkeley: University of California Press, pp. 210–231.

Lee, Janet and Jennifer Sasser-Coen
1996 *Blood Stories: Menarche and the Politics of the Female Body in Contemporary U.S. Society.* New York: Routledge.

Lévy-Bruhl, Lucien
1985 [1922] *How Natives Think.* Lilian A. Clare, transl. Princeton: Princeton University Press.

Lugo, Alejandro and Bill Maurer, eds.
2000   *Gender Matters: Rereading Michelle Z. Rosaldo.* Ann Arbor: University of Michigan Press.
Maggi, Wynne
2001   *Our Women Are Free: Gender and Ethnicity in the Hindukush.* Ann Arbor: University of Michigan Press.
Martin, Emily
1987   *The Woman in the Body: A Cultural Analysis of Reproduction.* Boston: Beacon Press.
1994   *Flexible Bodies: Tracking Immunity in American Culture—From the Days of Polio to the Age of AIDS.* Boston: Beacon Press.
Morgan, Lynne, ed.
1999   *Fetal Subjects, Feminist Positions.* Philadelphia: University of Pennsylvania Press.
Morrow Phyllis
2002   "The Woman's Vapor: Yupik Bodily Powers in Southwest Alaska," *Ethnology* 41(4): 335–348.
Nourse, Jennifer W.
1999   *Conceiving Spirits: Birth Rituals and Contested Identities Among Laujé of Indonesia.* Washington, D.C.: Smithsonian Institution Press.
Owen, Lara
1993   *Her Blood Is Gold: Celebrating the Power of Menstruation.* San Francisco: Harper San Francisco.
Pedersen, Lene
2002   "Ambiguous Bleeding: Purily and Sacrifice in Bali," *Ethnology* 41(4): 303–316.
Ragoné, Helena
1994   *Surrogate Motherhood: Conception in the Heart.* Boulder: Westview Press.
Rapp, Rayna
1999   *Testing Women, Testing the Fetus: The Social Impact of Amniocentesis in America.* New York: Routledge.

Renne, Elisha and Etienne van der Walle, eds.
2001   *Regulating Menstruation: Beliefs, Practice, Interpretations.* Chicago: University of Chicago Press.
Rosaldo, Renato
1989   *Culture and Truth: The Remaking of Social Analysis.* Boston: Beacon Press.
Roth, Denise.
2002   *Managing Motherhood, Managing Risk: Fertility and Danger in West Central Tanzania.* Ann Arbor: University of Michigan Press. In press.
Sargent, Garolyn
1989   *Maternity, Medicine, and Power: Reproductive Decisions in Urban Benin.* Berkeley: University of California Press.
Schroeder, Annica
2001   A "Rite" ful Passage into Womanhood for Little Gabriella. Paper for ANTH 262, University of Illinois at Urbana-Champaign, December 6, 2001. Unpublished manuscript.
Stewart, Pamela J. and Andrew Strathern
2002   "Power and Placement in Blood Practices," *Ethnology* 41(4): 349–367.
Strathern, Andrew
1996   *Body Thoughts.* Ann Arbor: University of Michigan Press.
Strathern, Marilyn
1992   *Reproducing the Future: Anthropology, Kinship, and the New Reproductive Technologies.* New York: Routledge.
Toumey, Christopher P.
1996   *Conjuring Science: Scientific Symbols and Cultural Meanings in American Life.* New Brunswick, NJ: Rutgers University Press.

Hijras:
An "Alternative" Sex/Gender in India

Gayatri Reddy and Serena Nanda

In much of the current literature on sexual difference, hijras are represented as the principal

"The Evolution of Third-Sex Constructs in Ancient India: A Study in Ambiguity" In *Invented Identities: The Interplay of Gender, Religion and Politics in India.* Julia Leslie and Mary McGee, eds., New Delhi: Oxford University Press; pp. 99–132.

"alternative" sex/gender identity in India—the so-called "third sex," "eunuch-transvestite," or "intersexed" identity—a cultural definition that emphasizes hijras' status as "neither men nor women," as the title of Serena Nanda's (1999) book indicates. For the most part, hijras are phenotypic men who wear female clothing, and ideally renounce sexual desire and practice by undergoing a physical emasculation known as the *nirvan* or rebirth operation. This operation entails the sacrifice of male genitalia to the goddess Bahuchara or Bedhraj Mata, one of the many incarnations of Devi [Goddess] worshipped throughout India, in return for the divine power to bless or curse with fertility/infertility. As vehicles of this divine power, hijras engage in their "traditional" occupations of performing at the birth of a child, at marriages, and as servants of the goddess at Bedhraj Mata's temple (Vyas and Shingala 1987; Sharma 1989; Nanda 1999; Hall, 1995, 1997; Reddy 2001, 2003).

In addition to this idealized asexual role and in apparent contradiction to it, hijras also engage in prostitution or sex work with men. Those who engage in this activity, however, legitimize it through a life-cycle trajectory; according to them, all hijras start out as sex workers and it is only when their bodies and/or desires change that they become sexual renouncers and ritual performers. Whatever their occupation, unlike the commonly understood ascetic ideal, hijras lead their daily lives as a social group, inexorably tied to the [person]-in-the-world, to paraphrase Louis Dumont (1960). Hijras' position in Indian society thus shares features of both a caste within society, complete with rules of comportment, exchange, and hierarchies of moral value, as well as of (marginal) renouncers outside it. As individuals however, it is important to note that hijras represent a wide variety of desires, abilities, identities, and gender characteristics, and also vary widely in their constructions of self in relation to their culturally defined identity.

Since Serena Nanda's work, first published in 1990, much has been written about hijras in the context of sexual difference. Drawing on the anthropological fieldwork of both authors among hijras in South India, this article traces the construction of this category through three different lenses—sex/gender, religion, and politics. It challenges existing accounts of hijras that see them solely as a "traditional" sexual category, rather than a contemporary, politically engaged

identity that is crosscut by a range of axes that shape their lives. As such, this article introduces readers to hijras with a descriptive account of them as the so-called "third sex" of India, as well as provides an introduction to the theoretical and methodological issues in the analysis of gender, sexuality, and identity construction in India.

HIJRAS AS A "THIRD" SEX AND GENDER

The popular understanding of hijras as an alternative sex and gender is predicated on a model of intersexuality—most typically, a *male* model of physical or functional anomaly of the reproductive and sexual system, although theoretically, women who do not menstruate can also become hijras. The word "hijra" is a masculine noun, widely translated into English as either "eunuch" or "hermaphrodite" (intersexed). Both these terms emphasize sexual impotence and are commonly understood in India to mean a physical defect impairing sexual function, both in the act of intercourse and in reproductive ability.

In much of the predominant literature, hijras are represented as sexually anomalous or impotent men who lack desire for women, an attribute often ascribed to their impaired reproductive capacity, or more specifically, their sexual organ. If a hijra is not born with a "defective" organ (and most are not), s/he must ideally make it so by emasculation, an act that is interpreted as a "rebirth"—from male to hijra. Whether hijras are "born" or "made," their identity is primarily envisioned in terms of a loss of virility, or as Wendy O'Flaherty (1973) puts it, they are "men minus men." But importantly, they are "men minus men" who perform many aspects of a female-gendered identity: they wear women's clothes, embody "feminine" gestures, movements and performative attributes, and adopt women's names. Importantly, this understanding is accompanied by the significant corollary that hijras are also 'not women,' their inability to bear children being the most significant marker of this construct. Hijras, in this scenario are therefore both 'not-women' and 'not-men,' often, though not always, identifying as an identity outside of the binary frame of gender (see

Cohen (1995) for an alternative view that troubles the desire to locate hijras as an undeniably "third" category).

HIJRAS AND OTHER "NOT-MEN"

While hijras are clearly the most visible "alternative" sex/gender, they locate themselves within a larger spectrum of sexual and gender configurations in India. This spectrum, with its own social categories, lexicon, and criteria of membership, is indexed at the broadest level by the labels *kothi, panthi* and *naran* (cf. Hall, 1995; see Reddy, 2005, for an elaboration of this complex spectrum). In this conceptualization of sex/gender, *narans* are an undifferentiated category based primarily on gendered practice and the patriarchal naturalization of femaleness as reproductive capacity—that is, *all* women, in other words; *kothis* are those men who "like to do women's work" and desire the receptive position in same-sex encounters with other men; and *panthis* (or *giriyas* as they are referred to in north India) are the partners of *kothis* and/or *narans*, bounded both by their desire for penetrative sexuality, as well as their lack of desire for the constellation of "female" practices typically embodied by *kothis* and *narans*. In other words, the gender system in India appears to be divided on the basis of practice rather than anatomy, into "men" [*panthis*] and to use Don Kulick's phrase, "not-men" [*kothis* and *narans*] (Kulick 1998; Reddy 2005).

Within this sex/gender system, hijras identify themselves as one 'category' or branch of a broader spectrum of identities they refer to as their *kothi* "family." Hijras rank themselves as the most authentic of *kothis*, deserving of the most respect (*izzat*) in the community. They base this ranking on their formal kinship affiliation with hijra lineages and houses, their absence of sexual desire, their modes of self-presentation including the kind of dress they wear, and their religious practice (Reddy 2001).

Perhaps one of the most important of these authenticating criteria for hijras is kinship. In this context, kinship is the affiliation and social obligation to one of the hijra houses or lineages

in the community.[1] By engaging in a specific hijra kinship ritual, individuals not only acquire a *guru* or teacher within the community, but also signify their membership in the particular house/lineage to which the teacher belongs. This ritual not only denotes formal membership in the community, but also hierarchizes *kothis* along this axis of kinship. There are *kothis* (such as hijras) who are "official" kin—those who have engaged in this ritual kinship act—and those *kothis* who have not undertaken this formal ritual and therefore are only informally or unofficially related. While this does not prevent the latter from identifying/being identified as *kothis*, it places them lower in the *kothi* prestige hierarchy, according to hijras.

In addition to kinship, hijras' claim to asexuality—lacking sexual desire for either women or men—is another key element in their definition of themselves in relation to other *kothis* and *gandus* (a pejorative label applied to men who enjoy anal [*gand*] sex, a category which includes self-identified "gay" men). Such *gandus* are defined not only by the *form* of their sexual desire, but more importantly, by its *excess*. Excessive sexual desire is a marker of inauthenticity that apparently defines *gandus* and by that token, separates them from the supposedly asexual hijras. An active symbol of hijras' essential *a*sexuality that is deployed for this purpose is the physical excision of their reproductive organs or the nirvan operation. One becomes resolutely and irrevocably a "real hijra" following this operation, serving by this token to separate hijras from their libidinous fellow—*kothis*.

As mentioned earlier, hijras serve as the most strikingly visible dimension of *kothi* identity. For the most part, they are identifiable as "men" who grow their hair long, are clean-shaven, often adopt exaggerated "feminine" gestures and styles of self-presentation, and

---

[1] Hijras are organized into formal groupings or lineages, each with its own leader (or *nayak* Kinship obligations within these lineages are built on hierarchical principles of seniority, similar in some respects to that of Indian joint families (see Nanda 1999; Reddy forthcoming for elaborations on hijra kinship rules and obligations).

most importantly, wear saris, the most common dress worn by women in India. So important is this criteria that some hijras refer to themselves, in their own terminology, as sari-wearing *kothis* (*chatla kothi*) as opposed to other, non-sari-wearing (or *kada-chatla*) *kothis.*

Finally, in addition to sexual desire, kinship and sartorial presentation, religious practice is also a key dimension of hijras' self-image as the *kothis* most deserving of respect. Whether they identify as Hindu or Muslim (see below), most hijras claim to be blessed by (Hindu) gods/goddesses. Thereby, as vehicles of divine authority, hijras see themselves as having more respect (or *izzat*) than some of the other *kothi* identities, who they see as motivated solely by sexual desire rather than religious authenticity.

HIJRA RELIGIOUS AFFILIATION/PRACTICE

In addition to constructing identity through sex/gender difference, hijras also emphasize religious mythology and practice as an integral aspect of their identity-formation. Contrary to popular opinion, which identifies hijras as devotees of Bedhraj Mata and therefore as Hindus, many hijras in India also identify as Muslim. They do not see these identities as necessarily mutually contradictory, each identification in their eyes, providing different, contextually specific referents.

Hinduism and Hijra Mythology

In Hinduism, the complementary opposition of male and female, man and woman, represents a key symbolic referent. The interchange of male and female qualities, transformations of sex and gender, and alternative sex and gender roles, both among deities and humans, are meaningful and positive themes in Hindu mythology, ritual and art, and are often drawn on in everyday constructions of self in India.

Hijras also draw on these mythological and divine themes and images to construct and present themselves, identifying with various gods and goddesses in this process. As "eunuch-transvestites" (Vyas and Shingala 1987), hijras identify most closely with Arjun, hero of the epic Mahabharata, who lives for a year in the guise of a "eunuch," wearing bangles, braiding [his] hair like a woman, dressing in female attire, and teaching the women of the King's court singing and dancing. In this gendered performance as a "eunuch-transvestite," Arjun participates in weddings and births, providing legitimacy for the ritual contexts in which hijras perform (Hiltebeitel 1980). The portrayal of Arjun in popular enactments of the Mahabharata in a vertically divided half-man/half-woman form highlights this identification.

This representation of Arjun resonates with the 'creative ascetic' Shiva, another key mythological/divine figure hijras identify with, especially in his appearance as Ardhanarisvara, a vertically divided half-man/half-woman (representing Shiva united with his female power or shakti). Shiva is one of the most important sexual/asexual figures in Hinduism, incorporating both male and female characteristics. He is an ascetic—one who renounces sex—and yet he appears in many erotic and procreative roles (O'Flaherty 1973). His most powerful symbol and object of worship is the *linga*, or phallus, but the phallus is almost always set in the *yoni*, the symbol of the female genitals. The generative power of the phallus severed from the body is another important point of identification between Shiva and hijras, highlighting the latters' self-identification as ascetics or *sannyasis;* those who renounce sexuality and yet have the power to confer fertility.

Other Hindu deities, such as Vishnu, also have dual gender representations that are drawn on in public enactments of (hijra) self. In one myth, the basis of a festival in South India attended by thousands of hijras, Vishnu comes to earth as a woman to marry a prince, who is, by this marriage, granted success in battle by the gods. However, although the prince is destined to win the battle against his enemies, it is also well known that he will be martyred in this process, rendering marriage to the prince undesirable for would-be brides, thereby necessitating Vishnu's performance of this role. During the festival, hijras enact the role of women who marry, and later, as widows, mourn the death of their husband, represented by the prince/god Koothandavur. Similarly, an important ceremony at the Jagannatha temple in Orissa involves a ritual in which Balabhadra, the ascetic older brother of the deity Jagannatha (commonly identified with Shiva), is seduced by a young man dressed as a female temple dancer (Marglin 1985). Ancient Hindu texts and origin myths likewise refer to androgynous, intersexed or "alternative" sexes and genders both among humans as well as deities (Bullough 1976; O'Flaherty 1980). The Kama Sutra, the classic Hindu "treatise on love," also specifically refers to those of a "third nature" and the particular sexual practices prescribed for them. In fact, as some authors contend, Hinduism is sometimes characterized as having a "propensity towards androygynous thinking" (Zwilling and Sweet 2000).

Islam and Hijra Practice

The Hindu religious context of alternative genders that provides a positive meaning for hijras is reinforced by the historical role of the "eunuch" in the five hundred year history of Muslim court culture in India. This historical role has merged with those described in Hindu texts as a source of contemporary hijra identification. Indeed, while identifying with religious figures in Hinduism, hijras also identify as Muslims. The apparent paradox of hijras identifying with Hindu religious figures while also identifying as Muslim, is partly resolved by context, with claims to Muslim religious identity being constructed mainly through practice: through the acts that hijras employ, the proscriptions they are subject to, and the festivals that they celebrate. Although some hijras maintain that "religion does not matter for us, all can join," many of them also say that when hijras join the community they "become Muslims." In many regions of India, hijras approximate the Islamic ideal in their custom of praying, using prescriptive Muslim greetings such as 'salam aleikhum,' undertaking the pilgrimage to Mecca, celebrating Muslim festivals, as well as engaging in certain commensal practices, sartorial prescriptions, circumcision rites, and (Muslim) burial practices. Clearly, however, hijras are not strictly "orthodox" religious practitioners. Apart from their worship of a Hindu goddess, hijras also blur the gender boundary in their practice of Islam, following rules of comportment specified by the shari'at for *both* men *and* women. Sometimes, in addition to the female names they choose at initiation, they may also choose male Muslim names. Hijra leaders (or *nayaks*) almost invariably are called by their Muslim names. Further, although not all hijras go on the Haj or pilgrimage to Mecca, those who do, go unescorted by male relatives, a prescription for post-pubescent and pre-menopausal women. In addition to these so-called "male" practices, hijras also follow Islamic practices enjoined on women, such as wearing the *burqa* on occasion (a garment that covers the entire body except for parts of the face), though they never wear this item of clothing when performing or entertaining. Though hijras also wear saris like all Indian women, for special occasions they wear green saris, as green is the color of Islam. Also, like some orthodox Muslim women, hijras are not permitted to wear *bindis* (the dot Hindu women wear on their foreheads).

Hijra practice reveals a pluralistic form of religion, which is arguably typical rather than unusual in Indian religious practice. Both Hindus and Muslims in India are characterized by an enormous diversity of communities, traditions, and customs, and religious pluralism has a long history in India. This pluralistic tradition, along with the ability to "compartmentalize" potentially conflictual beliefs and practices (Ramanujam 1990; Shweder and Bourne 1984), allows for a continuum rather than a dichotomy of religious thought, empowering hijras, amongst others, to practice their religion(s) without experiencing significant cognitive dissonance.

HIJRAS AND CONTEMPORARY POLITICS

The association of hijras with the power of (dis)embodied generativity is clearly related to their cultural identity as ritual performers at marriages and the birth of a child. It is these "traditional" roles for which they gain their respect or *izzat* in society. But recently, hijras have also gained visibility in another role, one that on the surface would seem to be in contrast to their marginalization in Indian society and culture.

This "new" role for hijras is in contemporary Indian politics. As one hijra stated during recent fieldwork, "Within this *kaliyug* (current cosmic period), hijras will become kings and rule the world. That is what [the god] Rama decreed thousands of years ago when he blessed us." Although hijras have not become kings, they have achieved notable political success. In recent years, hijras have been standing for and winning public election to local, state and even national office, and have been actively courted by mainstream political parties for these positions. Significantly, they are entering these new spheres as hijras, explicitly highlighting their identity as gender-neutral, asexual figures.

In the past few years, at least six hijras have been elected to public office at the local and state level, defeating more prominent candidates from national political parties such as Congress (I) and the Bharatiya Janata Party, and it is their transcendant morality *as* hijras that has been central to their success at the polls. Explicitly constructing themselves as individuals without the encumbrances of a family, gender, or caste affiliation, hijras emphasize that they are free from the impetus for nepotism, and therefore are the perfect antidotes to the rampant corruption and immorality of Indian politics. And indeed, the election of hijras can be viewed, at the most obvious level, as a revolt against upper-caste privilege, nepotism and corruption. In one of these elections, the hijra candidate was enthusiastically supported by an emerging political party formed to protect lower-caste and Dalit (formerly untouchable caste) interests, with her victory being hailed by the lower castes and Dalits as a victory over the corrupt and exploitative upper castes. Hijras are also viewed as being more sensitive to issues of poverty and social stigma, and the electorate does seem to perceive hijras as more approachable and effective than other politicians. However, in the past year, the election of at least one hijra has been overturned by the lower courts in the north Indian state of Madhya Pradesh, on the grounds that hijras

are in fact *men* (masquerading as women), and therefore cannot stand for election from seats reserved for women. This case is currently being appealed in the Supreme Court.

In their political campaigns, hijras selectively highlighted their resonance with the traditional *sannyasi* or ascetic identity, emphasizing religious and sexual renunciation as the source of their authenticity and *izzat* (Reddy 2003), even as this image marginalizes them in Indian society. This emphasis—on the connection between sexual renunciation and politics—has a long history in India, most prominently expressed by early Indian nationalists, Swami Vivekananda, and Mahatma Gandhi, but also by many contemporary Hindu politicians (cf. Basu 1995). The hijra political candidates also remained conspicuously silent in public on their Muslim identity, a seemingly paradoxical silence, given their articulated embrace of Islam.

An important question raised by the success of hijras in contemporary politics is what it heralds for the transformation of hijras from a culturally and socially marginalized community to a new position in Indian society (Reddy 2003). Indeed, we may look at this as part of the larger question of whether—or to what extent—gender ambiguous roles in all societies are a form of resistance that disrupts the gender and cultural status quo (Nanda 2000). Does this new role for hijras herald a "new chapter of enfranchisement in the history of India's eunuchs" as one news columnist claimed (Jacinto 2000)? Will it reformulate not only hijras' place in Indian society, but also prevailing constructions of Indian citizenship, sexuality, gender, and politics?

The answers are perhaps more ambiguous than the initial media enthusiasm suggests. Not only has the recent legal verdict located hijras as inexorably *male*, a position that precludes the possibility of a more fluid identity and presentation of self, but a closer analysis suggests that rather than remaking normative institutions, hijra political campaigns and their subsequent election appear to have subtly played with "traditional" cultural values, thereby reinscribing the dominant status quo. Indeed, contrary to popular representations, it seems to us that hijras were elected precisely because they did not disrupt the status quo, and in fact reinforced the prevailing politics of Hindu nationalism. This not only questions the emancipatory and subversive potential of the hijras, but in fact might actually reinforce the majoritarian (Hindu) view of politics and society. If, as one hijra campaign slogan contends, "you don't need genitals for politics," incorporating those without genitals in the "new" political order might not necessarily herald a radically new or liberal social and moral order in India (Reddy 2003).

Certainly at the most basic level, the initial mandate of the hijras did not emphasize their radical potential, but rather the public's denigration of their sexual ambiguity, viewing them as symbols of politicians' impotence and the publics' disillusionment with existing (male) politicians (who are often referred to as "eunuchs"). Their election therefore might have highlighted precisely the hijras' marginality—as a caricature of virile masculinity and the lack of political capability that this apparently symbolizes. By emphasizing the renunciate aspect of their identity, hijras are complicit in this construction—a construction that equates virile (hetero)masculinity with political competence—ultimately reinforcing rather than undercutting their marginalization in society (Reddy 2003).

HIJRAS AND CULTURAL CHANGE

Despite their marginalization, hijras have demonstrated a remarkable ability to survive throughout their long history in India. With the advent of British rule, the position of the hijras not only began to lose its traditional royal patronage, with the British ultimately removing this community from any state protection (Preston 1987), but hijras were also classified in the colonial hierarchy along with other "criminal castes," resulting in the confiscation of much of their property and the vilification of their status in society (Ayres, 1992; Reddy, 2005). Building on this colonial history, laws criminalizing sodomy and emasculation, specifically targeting hijras, were incorporated into

the criminal code of independent India. While these state policies appear to have had little deterrent effect, combined with the declining opportunities and cultural interest in traditional performances of many kinds, hijras have had to creatively adapt to new situations to maintain their visibility and legitimacy in Indian society. Their entry into contemporary politics is perhaps one such creative re-crafting of themselves in response to changing historical and political circumstances. Despite the ambivalent feelings toward hijras, and the stigma, fear and ridicule that continues to surround them, their survival and vibrant identity is perhaps yet another powerful recognition of the *multiplicity* of differences and the complex history that goes to construct humanity, including, and perhaps especially, hijra identity.

REFERENCES

Ayres, Alyssa C.
1992. A Scandalous Breach of Public Decency: Defining the Decent—Indian Hijras in the 19th and 20th Centuries. B.A. Honor's thesis. Harvard University.

Basu, Amrita
1995 "Feminism inverted: the gender imagery and real women of Hindu nationalism. In T. Sarkar and U. Butalia, eds., Women and the Hindu Right. Pp. 158–80. New Delhi: Kali for Women.

Bullough, Vern
1976. *Sexual Variance in Society and History.* Chicago: University of Chicago Press.

Cohen, Lawrence
1995. "The Pleasures of Castration: The Postoperative Status of Hijras, Jankhas and Academics." In *Sexual Nature, Sexual Culture.* (eds.) P. Abramson, and S. Pinkerton. Chicago: University of Chicago Press.

Dumont, Louis
1960. "World Renunciation in Indian Religions." *Contributions to Indian Sociology* 4: 33–62.

Hall, Kira
1995. Hijra/Hijrin: Language and Gender Identity. Ph.D diss., University of California, Berkeley.

Hall, Kira
1997. "Go Suck Your Husband's Sugarcane!" Hijras and the Use of Sexual Insult. In Anna Livia and Kira Hall (eds.), *Queerly*

Phrased: Language, Gender, and Sexuality. New York: Oxford University Press. 430–460).

Hiltebeitel, Alf
1980. "Siva, the Goddess, and the Disguises of the Pandavas and Draupadi." *History of Religions*: 147–174.

Jacinto, Leela
2000. "Political Outing: Once Ostracized, India's Secretive Eunuchs Get Enfranchized." ABCNews.com, 30 November. <http://abcnews .go.com/sections/world/dailynews/india_ eunuch001129.html>

Kulick, Don
1998. *Travesti: Sex, Gender, and Culture Among Brazilian Transgendered Prostitutes.* Chicago: University of Chicago Press.

Marglin, Frederique A.
1985. *Wives of the God-King: The Rituals of the Devadasis of Puri.* Delhi: Oxford University Press.

Nanda, Serena
2000. *Gender Diversity: Cross-Cultural Variation.* Prospect Heights, IL:Waveland Press.

1999 *Neither Man nor Woman: The Hijras of India*: Belmont, CA:Wadsworth Press.

O'Flaherty, Wendy Doniger
1973. *Asceticism and Eroticism in the Mythology of Siva.* London: Oxford University Press.

1980. *Women, Androgynes, and Other Mythical Beasts.* Chicago: University of Chicago Press.

Preston, Laurence W.
1987. "A right to exist: Eunuchs and the state in nineteenth-century India. "*Modern Asian Studies,* 21 (2), pp. 371–387.

Ramanujam, A. K.
1990. "Is There an Indian Way of Thinking? An Informal Essay." In *India Through Hindu Categories.* M. Marriott (ed.), Delhi: Sage Publications.

Reddy, Gayatri
2005. *With Respect to Sex: Charting Hijra Identity in Hyderabad, India.* Chicago: University of Chicago Press.

2003. "'Men' Who Would Be Kings: Celibacy, Emasculation and the Re-Production of Hijras in Contemporary Indian Politics." *Social Research,* 70 (1): 163–200.

2001 "Crossing 'Lines' of Subjectivity: The Negotiation of Sexual Identity in Hyderabad, India," Special Issue 'Sexual Sites, Seminal Attitudes: Sexualities, Masculinities and Culture in South Asia,' *South Asia* vol. XXIV: 91–101.

Sharma, Satish. K.
1989. *Hijras: The Labelled Deviants.* New Delhi: Gian Publishing House.

Shweder, R. and E. J. Bourne
1984. Does the Concept of a Person Vary Cross-culturally? In *Culture Theory: Essays of Mind, Self, and Emotion.* Cambridge: Cambridge University Press.

Vyas, S. and D. Shingala
1987. *The Life Style of the Eunuchs.* New Delhi: Anmol Publications.

Zwilling, Leonard and Michael J. Sweet
2000. "The Evolution of Third-Sex Constructs in Ancient India: A Study in Ambiguity" In *Invented Identities: The Interplay of Gender, Religion and Politics in India.* Julia Leslie and Mary McGee, eds., New Delhi: Oxford University Press; pp. 99–132.

Measuring Up to Barbie: Ideals of the Feminine Body in Popular Culture

Jacqueline Urla and Alan C. Swedlund

It is no secret that thousands of healthy women in the United States perceive their bodies as defective. The signs are everywhere: from potentially lethal cosmetic surgery and drugs, to the more familiar routines of dieting, curling, crimping, and aerobicizing, women

Adapted for this text from Jacqueline Urla and Alan C. Swedlund, "The Anthropometry of Barbie: Unsettling Ideals of the Feminine Body in Popular Culture." In Jennifer Terry and Jacqueline Urla (eds.). *Deviant Bodies:*

Critical Perspectives on Difference in Science and Popular Culture (Bloomington: Indiana University Press, 1995). pp. 277–313. Reprinted by permission of the authors.

seek to take control over their unruly physical selves. Every year at least 150,000 women undergo breast implant surgery (Williams 1992), while Asian women have their noses rebuilt and their eyes widened to make themselves look "less dull" (Kaw 1993). Studies show the obsession with body size and sense of inadequacy starts frighteningly early; as many as 80% of 9 year old suburban girls are concerned about dieting and their weight (Bordo 1991:125). Reports like these, together with the dramatic rise in eating disorders among young women are just some of the more noticeable fall-out from what Naomi Wolf calls "the beauty myth." Fueled by the hugely profitable cosmetic, weight loss, and fashion industries, the beauty myth's glamorized notions of the ideal body reverberate back upon women as "a dark vein of self hatred, physical obsessions, terror of aging, and dread of lost control" (Wolf 1991:10).

It is this paradox—that female bodies are never feminine enough, that they require deliberate and oftentimes painful refashioning to be what "nature" intended—that motivates our inquiry into the feminine ideal. Neither universal nor changeless, idealized notions of both masculine and feminine bodies have a long history that shifts considerably across time, racial or ethnic group, class, and culture. Body ideals in twenty-first century North America are influenced and shaped by images from classical or "high art," the discourses of science and medicine, as well as a multitude of commercial interests, ranging from mundane life insurance standards, to the more high-profile fashion, fitness, and entertainment industries. Each have played contributing and sometimes conflicting roles in determining what counts as a desirable body for us today. In this essay, we focus our attention on the domain of popular culture and the ideal feminine body as it is conveyed by one of pop culture's longest lasting and most illustrious icons: the Barbie doll.

Making her debut in 1959 as Mattel's new teenage fashion doll, Barbie rose quickly to become the top selling toy in the United States. Several decades and a women's movement later, Barbie dolls remain one of Mattel's biggest selling items netting over one billion dollars in revenues worldwide (Adelson 1992), or roughly one Barbie sold every two seconds (Stevenson 1991).[1] By the nineties, Mattel was estimating that in the U.S. over 95% of girls between the ages of 3 and 11 own at least one Barbie and that the average number of dolls per owner is seven (Shapiro 1992). Barbie is clearly a force to contend with, eliciting, over the years, a combination of critique, parody, and adoration. A legacy of the post-war era, she remains an incredibly resilient visual and tactile model of femininity for pre-pubescent girls.

It is not our intention to settle the debate over whether Barbie is a good or bad role model for little girls. Though that issue surrounds Barbie like a dark cloud, we are more concerned with how Barbie has been able to survive and remain popular in a period marked by the growth of consumer society, intense debate over gender and racial relations, and changing notions of the body. Our aim, then, is not to offer another rant against Barbie, but to explore how this doll crystallizes some of the predicaments of femininity and feminine bodies in late twentieth-century North America.

A DOLL IS BORN

> Parents thank us for the educational values in the world of Barbie. . . .They say that they could never get their daughters well groomed before— get them out of slacks or blue jeans and into a dress . . . get them to scrub their necks and wash their hair. Well that's where Barbie comes in. The doll has clean hair and a clean face, and she dresses fashionably, and she wears gloves and shoes that match. (Ruth Handler 1964, quoted in Motz 1983:130)

Legend has it that Barbie was the brainchild of Mattel owner Ruth Handler, who first thought of creating a three dimensional fashion doll after seeing her daughter play with paper dolls. As an origin story, this one is touching and no doubt true. But Barbie was not the first doll of her kind nor was she just a mother's invention. Making sense of Barbie requires that we look to the larger socio-political and cultural milieu that made her genesis both possible and meaningful. Based on a German prototype, the "Lili" doll, Barbie was from "birth" implicated in the ideologies of the cold war and the research and technology exchanges of the military-industrial complex. Her finely crafted durable plastic mold was, in fact, designed by Jack Ryan, well known for his work in designing the Hawk and Sparrow missiles for the Raytheon Company. Conceived at the hands of a military weapons designer-turned-toy inventor, Barbie dolls came onto the market the same year as the infamous Nixon–Khrushchev "kitchen debate" at the American National Exhibition in Moscow. There, in front of the cameras of the world, the leaders of the capitalist and socialist worlds faced off, not over missile counts, but over "the relative merits of American and Soviet washing machines, televisions, and electric ranges" (May 1988:16). As Elaine Tyler May has noted in her study of the Cold War, this much celebrated media event signaled the transformation of American-made commodities and the model suburban home into key symbols and safeguards of democracy and freedom. It was thus with fears of nuclear annihilation and sexually charged fantasies of the perfect bombshelter running rampant in the American imaginary, that Barbie and her torpedo-like breasts emerged into popular culture as an emblem of the aspirations of prosperity, domestic containment, and rigid gender roles that were to characterize the burgeoning post-war consumer economy and its image of the American Dream.

Marketed as the first "teenage" fashion doll, Barbie's rise in popularity also coincided with and no doubt contributed to the post-war creation of a distinctive teenage lifestyle.[2] Teens, their tastes and behaviors, were becoming the object of both sociologists and criminologists, as well as market survey researchers intent on capturing their discretionary dollars. While J. Edgar Hoover was pronouncing "the juvenile jungle" a menace to American society, we have retailers, the music industry, and movie-makers declaring the 13 to 19 year old age bracket "the seven golden years" (Doherty 1988:51–52).

Barbie dolls seemed to cleverly reconcile both of these concerns by personifying the good girl who was sexy, but didn't have sex, and was willing to spend, spend and spend. Amidst the palpable moral panic over juvenile delinquency and teenagers' new found sexual freedom, Barbie was a reassuring symbol of solidly middle-class values. Popular teen magazines, advertising, television and movies of the period painted a highly dichotomized world divided into good (i.e. middle class) and bad (i.e. working class) kids: the clean-cut college-bound junior achiever versus the street corner boy; the wholesome American Bandstander versus the uncontrollable bad seed (cf. Doherty 1988; and Frith 1981 for England). It was no mystery where Barbie stood in this thinly disguised class discourse. As Motz writes, Barbie's world bore no trace of the "greasers" and "hoods" that inhabited the many grade B films about teenage vice and ruin. In the life Mattel laid out for her in story books and comics, Barbie, who started out looking like a somewhat vampy, slightly Bardot-esque doll, was gradually transformed into a "'soc' or a 'frat'—affluent, well-groomed, socially conservative" (Motz 1983:130). In lieu of back-seat sex and teenage angst, Barbie had pajama parties, barbecues, and her favorite pastime, shopping.

Every former Barbie owner knows that to buy a Barbie was to lust after Barbie accessories: that matching pair of sandals and handbag, canopy bedroom set, or country camper. Both conspicuous consumer and a consumable item herself, Barbie was surely as much the fantasy of U.S. retailers as she was the panacea of middle class parents. For every "need" Barbie had, there was a deliciously miniature product to fulfill it. As Paula Rabinowitz has noted, Barbie dolls, with their focus on frills and fashion, epitomize the way that teenage girls and girl culture in general have figured as accessories in the historiography of post-war culture; that is as both essential to the burgeoning commodity culture as consumers, but seemingly irrelevant to the historical events defining cold war existence (Rabinowitz 1993).

Perhaps what makes Barbie such a perfect icon of late capitalist constructions of femininity is the way in which her persona pairs endless consumption with the achievement of femininity and the appearance of an appropriately gendered body. By buying for

Barbie, girls practice how to be discriminating consumers knowledgeable about the cultural capital of different name brands, how to read packaging, and the overall importance of fashion and taste for social status (Motz 1983:131–132). Being a teenage girl in the world of Barbie dolls becomes quite literally a performance of commodity display requiring numerous and complex rehearsals. In making this argument, we want to stress that we are drawing on more than just the doll. "Barbie" is also the packaging, spin-off products, cartoons, commercials, magazines, and fan club paraphernalia, all of which contribute to creating her persona. Clearly, as we will discuss below, children may engage more or less with those products, subverting or ignoring various aspects of Barbie's "official" presentation. However, to the extent that little girls *do* participate in the prepackaged world of Barbie, they come into contact with a number of beliefs central to femininity under consumer capitalism. Little girls learn, among other things, about the crucial importance of their appearance to their personal happiness and ability to gain favor with their friends. Barbie's social calendar, like her closet, is constantly full, and the stories in her fan magazines show her frequently engaged in preparation for the rituals of heterosexual teenage life: dates, proms, and weddings. A perusal of Barbie magazines, and the product advertisements and pictorials within them, shows an overwhelming preoccupation with grooming for those events. Magazines abound with tips on the proper ways of washing hair, putting on make-up, and assembling stunning wardrobes. Through these play scenarios little girls learn Ruth Handler's lesson about the importance of hygiene, occasion-specific clothing, knowledgeable buying, and artful display as key elements to popularity and a successful career in femininity.

Barbie exemplifies the way in which gender has become a commodity itself, "something we can buy into . . . the same way we buy into a style" (Willis 1991:23). In her insightful analysis of the logic of consumer capitalism, cultural critic Susan Willis pays particular attention to the way in which children's toys like Barbie and the popular muscle-bound "He-Man" for boys link highly conservative and narrowed images of masculinity and femininity with commodity consumption (1991:27). Being or becoming a teenager, having a "grown-up" body, observes Willis, is presented as inextricably bound up with the acquisition of certain commodities, signaled by styles of clothing, cars, music, etc. In play groups and fan clubs (collectors are a whole world unto themselves) children exchange knowledge about the latest accessories and outfits, their relative merit, and how to find them. They become members of a community of Barbie owners whose shared identity is defined by the commodities they have or desire to have. The articulation of social ties through commodities is, as Willis argues, at the heart of how sociality is experienced in consumer capitalism. In this way, we might say that playing with Barbie serves not only as a training ground for the production of the appropriately gendered woman, but also as an introduction to the kinds of knowledge and social relations one can expect to encounter in late capitalist society.

BARBIE IS A SURVIVOR

For anyone tracking Barbie's history, it is abundantly clear that Mattel's marketing strategies have been sensitive to a changing social climate. When the women's movement gained momentum in the seventies, Barbie dolls became a target of criticism (Billyboy 1987; Lord 1994). Mattel responded by giving Barbie new outfits to "reflect the activities and professions that modern women are involved in" (quoted in *Harpers*, August 2, 1990, p. 20). Just as Barbie graduated from Candy Striper and ballerina to astronaut and doctor, Mattel also tried to diversify her lily-white image beginning in 1967 with Barbie's first Black friend, "Colored Francie." With the expansion of sales worldwide, Barbie has acquired multiple national guises (Spanish Barbie, Jamaican Barbie, Malaysian Barbie, etc.).[3] In addition, her cohort of "friends" has become increasingly ethnically diversified, as has Barbie advertising, which now regularly feature Asian, Hispanic and Afro-American little girls playing with Barbie. Today, Barbie pals include a smattering of brown and yellow plastic friends, like Teresa, Kira, and Miko who appear on her adventures and, very importantly, can share her clothes.

Perhaps Mattel's most glamorous concession to multiculturalism was Shani who premiered at the 1991 Toy Fair with great fanfare and media attention. Unlike her predecessors who were essentially "brown plastic poured into blond Barbie's mold," Shani, together with her two friends, Asha and Nichelle (each a slightly different shade of brown), and boyfriend Jamal created in 1992, were decidedly Afro-centric, with outfits in "ethnic" fabrics rather than the traditional Barbie pink (Jones 1991). The packaging also announced that these dolls' bodies and facial features were meant to be more realistic of African American women, although as we will see, the differences, while meaningful, don't preclude interchanging clothes with Barbie. Now, Mattel announced, "ethnic Barbie lovers will be able to dream in their own image" (*Newsweek* 1990:48). Multiculturalism cracked open the door to Barbie-dom and diversity could walk in as long as she was big busted, slim hipped, had long flowing hair, tiny feet, and was very very thin.[4]

In looking over the course of Barbie's career, it is clear that part of her resilience, continuing appeal and profitability stems from the fact that her identity is constructed primarily through fantasy and is consequently open to change and reinterpretation. As a fashion model, Barbie continually creates her identity anew with every costume change. In that sense, we might want to call Barbie emblematic of the restless desire for change that permeates postmodern capitalist society (Wilson 1985:63). Not only can her image be renewed with a change of clothes, Barbie is also seemingly able to clone herself effortlessly into new identities— "Malibu Barbie"; "Totally Hair Barbie"; "Teen Talk Barbie"; even Afro-centric Shani—without somehow suggesting a serious personality disorder. Furthermore, as a perpetual teenager, Barbie's owners are at liberty to fantasize any number of life choices for her; she might be a high-powered fashion executive or she just might marry Ken and "settle down" in her luxury condo. Her history is a barometer of changing fashions, changing gender and race relations, and a keen index of corporate America's anxious attempts to find new and more palatable ways of selling the beauty myth and commodity fetishism to new generations of parents and their daughters.

What is striking, then, is that while Barbie's identity may be mutable—one day she might be an astronaut, another a cheerleader—*her hyper-slender, big-chested body has remained fundamentally unchanged over the years*—a remarkable fact in a society that fetishizes the new and improved. Barbie, of course, did acquire flexible arms and legs as we know, her face has changed significantly, and her hair has grown by leaps and bounds (Melosh and Simmons 1986). But her body measurements, pointed toes, and proportions have not altered significantly. It is to that body and to the results of our class experiment in the anthropometry of Barbie that we now turn. But before taking out our calipers on Barbie and her friends to see how their bodies measure up, we want to offer a very brief historical overview of anthropometry to help us understand how the notion of the "average" American female body was debated in post-war United States.

THE MEASURED BODY: NORMS AND IDEALS

> The paramount objective of physical anthropology is the gradual completion, in collaboration with the anatomists, the physiologists, and the chemists, of the study of the normal white man under ordinary circumstances.
>
> *Ales Hrdlicka, 1918*

Anthropometry, the science of measuring human bodies, belongs to a long line of techniques of the 18th and 19th centuries— craniometry, phrenology, comparative anatomy—concerned with measuring, comparing, and interpreting variability in the physical dimensions of the human body. Early anthropometry shared with these early sciences the expectation that the body was a window into a host of moral, temperamental, racial, or gender characteristics. It sought to distinguish itself from its predecessors, however, by being more rigorous and standardized in its techniques (Hrdlicka 1939:12). Head shape (especially cranial capacity) was a constant source of special fascination, but by the early part of this century, physical anthropologists, together with anatomists and medical doctors were developing a precise and routine set of measurements for the entire body that they hoped would permit systematic comparison of the human body across race, nationality, and gender.[5]

Anthropometry developed in the United States under the aegis of Ernest Hooton, Ales Hrdlicka, and Franz Boas, located respectively at Harvard, the Smithsonian, and Columbia University. Their main areas of interest were (1) identifying the physical features of racial and or national types, (2) the measurement of adaptation and "degeneracy," and (3) a comparison of the sexes. As is well documented by now, women and non-Europeans did not fare well in these emerging sciences of the body which held white males as the pinnacle of evolution (see the work of Blakey 1987; Gould 1981, Schiebinger 1989; Fee 1979; Russett 1989). Hooton, in his classic book *Up from the Ape* (1931), regularly likened women and especially non-Europeans of both sexes to non-human primates. Similarly Hrdlicka's 1925 comparative study of male and female skulls went to rather extraordinary lengths to argue that women's brains (presumed at the time to be a sign of intelligence) were actually *smaller* than men's even though his measurements showed females to have a relatively *larger* cranial capacity than that of males.[6]

When it came to defining racial or national types, men, not women were the most commonly studied.[7] Although Hrdlicka and others considered it necessary to measure both males and females, early physical anthropology textbooks reveal that more often than not it was the biologically male body that was selected to visually represent a particular race or humanity as a whole. Males were, in short, the unspoken prototype, while women's bodies were understood as a sexual subset. Women's bodies were frequently described as deviations from the generic or ideal type: their body fat "excessive";

their pelvis maladaptive to a bipedal (i.e. more evolved) posture; their musculature weak. Scientists seem to agree that what most dictated a woman's physical shape was her reproductive function. All other features were subordinated to and could be explained by this capacity to bear children. Not surprisingly, given this assumption, it was women's, particularly African or non-European women's, reproductive organs, genitalia and secondary sexual characteristics, that were the most carefully scrutinized and measured (see Fausto-Sterling 1995).

In the United States, we begin to find an attempt to scientifically define a normative "American" female body in the late 19th and early twentieth centuries. By the 1860s, Harvard as well as other universities had begun to regularly collect anthropometric data on their male student populations, and in the 1890s comparable data began to be collected from the East Coast women's colleges as well. It was thus upper class, largely WASP, young people who were the basis of some of the early attempts to define the measurements of the "normal" American male and female. By basing themselves in elite colleges, "other" Americans—descendants of African slaves, North American Indians, and the many recent European migrants from Ireland, southern Europe, and eastern Europe—were effectively excluded from defining the norm. Rather, their bodies were more often the subject of racist evolutionary oriented studies concerned with "race crossing," degeneracy, and the effects of the "civilizing" process (see Blakey 1987).

Academia was not the only place where body standards were being developed. By the early part of the twentieth century industry began to make widespread commercial use of practical anthropometry: the demand for standardized measures of the "average" body manifested in everything from designs for labor-efficient workstations and kitchens to standardized sizes in the ready-to-wear clothing industry (cf. Schwartz 1986). Soon insurance companies would enter the scene. Between 1900 and 1920, the first medicoactuarial standards of weight and height began to appear. The most significant of these, the Dublin Standard Table of Heights and Weights, developed in 1908 by Louis Dublin, a student of Franz Boas and statistician for the Metropolitan Life Insurance Company, became the authoritative reference in every doctor's office (cf. Bennett and Gurin 1982:130–138). However, what began as a table of statistical averages, soon became a means of setting ideal "norms." Within a few years of its creation, the Dublin table shifted from providing a record of statistically "average" weights to becoming a guide to "desirable" weights which, interestingly enough, began to fall notably below the average weight for most adult women. Historian Joan Brumberg points to the Dublin Table, widely disseminated to doctors and published in popular magazines, together with the invention of the personal or bathroom scale, as the two devices most responsible in America for popularizing the notion that the human figure could be standardized and that abstract and often unrealistic norms could be uniformly applied (1988:232–235).

By the 1940s the search to describe the normal American male and female body in anthropometric terms was being conducted on many fronts fueled by a deepening concern about the physical fitness of the American people. Did Americans constitute a distinctive physical type? Were they physically stronger or weaker than their European ancestors? Could they defend themselves in time of war? And who did this category of "Americans" include? Questions such as these fed into an already long-standing preoccupation with defining a specifically American national character and, in 1945, led to the creation of some of the most celebrated and widely publicized life-size anthropometric statues of the century: Norm and Norma, the average American male and female. These statues, sculpted by Malvina Hoffman, were based on the composite measurements of thousands of white eighteen to twenty-five year old subjects. Both figures were put on display, but it was Norma who received the greatest media attention when the Cleveland Health Museum, which had purchased the pair, decided to sponsor a contest to find the woman in Ohio whose body most closely matched the dimensions of Norma. Under the catchy headline, "Are you Norma, Typical Woman?" the publicity surrounding this contest instructed women how to take their measurements for the contest. Within ten days, 3863 women had sent in their measurements to compete for the $100 prize in U.S. War Bonds that would go to the woman who most resembled the average American girl.

Besides bolstering the circulation of the *Cleveland Plain Dealer*, the idea behind the contest was to promote interest in physical fitness. Norma was described in the press as everything the young American woman should be in a time of war: fit, strong-bodied and at the peak of her reproductive potential. Newspaper articles emphasized that women had a national responsibility to be fit if America was to continue to excel after the war. Few contestants apparently measured up to the challenge (Shapiro 1945). Only one percent came close to Norma's proportions. Commenting on the search for Norma, Dr. Gebhard, director of the Cleveland Health Museum, was quoted in one of the many newspaper articles as saying that "if a national inventory of the female population of this country were taken there would be as many "4Fs" among the women as were revealed among the men in the draft" (Robertson 1945:4). The contest provided the occasion for many health reformers to voice their concern about the weakening of the "American stock" and to call for eugenic marital selection and breeding.

Norma and Norman were thus always more than statistical composites, they were prescriptive ideals that, like the college studies that preceded them, erased American's racial and ethnic differences. The "average American" of the post-war period was still imagined as a youthful white body. However, there were competing ideals. Health reformers, educators, and doctors who approved and promoted Norma as an ideal for American women were well aware that her sensible, strong, thick-waisted body differed significantly from the tall, slim-hipped bodies of fashion models in vogue at the time.[8] As the post-war period advanced, Norma would be overshadowed by the array of images of fashion models and pin up girls put out by advertisers, the entertainment industry, and a burgeoning consumer culture. These fashion images were becoming increasingly thin in the sixties and seventies while the "average" woman's body was in fact getting heavier.

THE ANTHROPOMETRY OF BARBIE: TURNING THE TABLES

Anthropometry, like the very notion of a "normal" body it has been used to construct, is part of an unsavory history. Nevertheless, in the contemporary cultural context where an impossibly thin image of women's bodies has become the most popular children's toy ever sold, it strikes us it might just be the power tool we need for destabilizing a fantasy spun out of control. It was with this in mind that we asked students in one of our social biology classes to measure Barbie to see how her body compared to the average measurements of young American women of the same period. Besides estimating what Barbie's dimensions would be if she were life-size, we see the experiment as an occasion to turn the anthropometric tables from disciplining the bodies of living women, to measuring the ideals by which we have come to judge ourselves and others. We also see it as an opportunity for students who have grown up under the regimes of normalizing science, students who no doubt have been measured, weighed, and compared to standards since birth, to use those very tools to unsettle a highly popular cultural ideal.

Our initial experiment involved measuring many Barbies and Kens from different decades as well as some of their friends. Here we will only report on the results for Barbie and Ken from the Glitter Beach collection, as well as Jamal and Shani, Barbie's more recent African-American friends. Mattel had marketed these latter dolls as having a more authentic African-American appearance and a "rounder more athletic" body, and we wanted to test that out.

After practicing with the calipers, discussing potential observational errors, and performing repeated trial runs, we began to record. In scaling Barbie to be life-sized, the students decided to translate her measurements using two standards: (a) If Barbie were a fashion model (5'10") and (b) if she were of average height for women in the United States (5'4"). We also decided to measure Ken, in the same way, using an average male stature, which we designated as 5'8", and the more "idealized" stature for men, 6'. We report here only the highlights of the measurements taken on the newer Barbie and newer Ken, Jamal, and Shani, scaled at the fashion-model height. For purposes of comparison, we include data on average body measurements from the standardized published tables of the 1988 Anthropometric Survey of the Army Personnel. We have dubbed these composites for the female and male recruits "Army Norma" and "Army Norm," respectively (see Table 1).

Both Barbie and Shani's measurements at 5'10" reveal the extreme thinness expected of the runway model. Both dolls have considerably smaller measurements than Army Norma *at all points*, even though they are six inches taller than her. When we scaled the dolls to

Table 1 Measurements of Glitter Beach Barbie, African-American Shani, and the Average Measurements of the 1988 U.S. Army Women Recruits.[1]

MEAS.	BARBIE	SHANI	U.S. ARMY "NORMA"
Height	5'10"	5'10"	5'4"
Chest Circum.	35"	35"	35.7"
Waist Circum.	20"	20"	31"
Hip Circum.[2]	32.50"	31.25"	38.10"
Hip Breadth	11.6"	11.0"	13.49"
Thigh Circum.	19.25"	20.00"	22.85"

[1] "Norma" is based on 2,208 army recruits, 1,140 of which were white, 922 of which were black.
[2] Hip circumference is referred to as "buttock circumference" in anthropometric parlance.

5'4"—the same as Army Norma—we can see just how skewed the dimensions are: Barbie's chest, waist, and hip measurements come out as 32"–17"–28," clinically anorectic to say the least. We also wanted to see if Mattel had physically changed the Barbie mold in making Shani. Most of the differences we could find appeared to be in the face. Shani's nose is broader and her lips are slightly larger. The only significant difference we found in the bodies was that Shani's back is arched in such a way that it tilts her buttocks up, producing the visual illusion of a higher, rounder, butt . . . Perhaps this is what Mattel was referring to in claiming that Shani has a realistic or ethnically correct body (Jones 1991).

When it came to the male dolls, we did not find the same kind of dramatic difference between them and Army Norm as we did in the female dolls. As Table 2 shows, Ken and Jamal were largely identical to each other, and they were only somewhat slimmer than the average soldier. Visually Ken and Jamal appear very tight and muscular and "bulked out," while the U.S. Army males tend to carry slightly more fat, judging from the photographs and data presented in the 1988 study.

OUR BARBIES, OUR SELVES

> I feel like Barbie; everyone calls me Barbie; I love Barbie. The main difference is she's plastic and I'm real. There isn't really any other difference.
>
> *Hayley Spicer, winner of Great Britain's Barbie-*
> *Look-Alike competition*

Our venture into anthropometry revealed that Barbie has a much more "abnormal" body than does Ken. But her hyper-thin body was by no means exceptional. Studies tracking the body measurements of Playboy magazine centerfolds and Miss America contestants show that between 1959 and 1978 the average weight and hip size for women in both of these groups has decreased steadily while the average weight of women was increasing (Wiseman, Gray, Mosimann and Ahrens 1992). A follow up study for the years 1979–1988 found this trend continuing into the eighties: approximately 69% of Playboy centerfolds and 60% of Miss America contestants were weighing in at 15% or more below their expected age and height category. In short, the majority of women presented to us in the media as having desirable feminine bodies, were, like Barbie, well on their way to qualify for anorexia nervosa.

On the surface, at least, it might seem that Barbie's signature thin body would seem at odds with the doll's seemingly endless desire for consumption and self-transformation. Being thin for most women requires repression of desire and self discipline, neither of which are traits we associate with the consummate shopper. And yet, as Susan Bordo (1990) has argued in regard to anorexia, these two phenomena—hyper thin bodies and hyper consumption—are very much linked in advanced capitalist economies which depend upon commodity excess. Bodies, says Bordo, are where the regulation of desire is played out most keenly. The imperative to manage the body and to "be all that you can be"—in fact the idea that you can *choose* the body that

Table 2   Measurements of Glitter Beach Ken, African-American Ken, and the Average Measurements of the 1988 U.S. Army Male Recruits.[1]

MEAS.	KEN	JAMAL	U.S. ARMY "NORM"
Height	6'0"	6'0"	5'9"
Chest Circum.	38.4"	38.4"	39.0"
Waist Circum.	28.8"	28.8"	33.1"
Hip Circum.[2]	36.0"	36.0"	38.7"
Hip Breadth	12.2"	12.2"	13.46"
Thigh Circum.	20.4"	20.4"	23.48"

[1] "Norm" is based on 1774 males, 1,172 of which were white and 458 of which were black.
[2] Hip circumference is referred to as "buttock circumference" in anthropometric parlance.

you want to have—is a pervasive feature of consumer culture. Keeping control of one's body, not getting too fat or flabby, in other words, conforming to gendered norms of fitness and weight, have become signs of an individual's social and moral worth. But as Bordo, Sandra Bartky (1990), and other feminist scholars have been quick to point out, not all bodies are subject to the same degree of scrutiny or the same repercussions if they fail. It is women's bodies and desires in particular where the structural contradictions—the simultaneous incitement to consume and social condemnation for overindulgence—appear to be most acutely manifested in bodily regimes of intense self-monitoring and discipline. Just as it is women's appearance which is subject to greater social scrutiny, so it is that women's desires, hunger, and appetites which are seen as most threatening and in need of control in a patriarchal society.

This cultural context is relevant to making sense of Barbie and the meaning her body holds in late consumer capitalism. In dressing and undressing Barbie, combing her hair, bathing her, turning and twisting her limbs in imaginary scenarios, children acquire a very tactile and intimate sense of Barbie's body. Barbie is presented in packaging and advertising as a role model, a best friend or older sister to little girls. Television jingles use the refrain, "I want to be just like you," while look-alike clothes and look-alike contests make it possible for girls to live out the fantasy of being Barbie. In short, there is every reason to believe that girls (or adult women) link Barbie's body shape with her popularity and glamour.

This is exactly what worries many people. As our measurements show, Barbie's body differs wildly from anything approximating "average" female body weight and proportions. Over the years her wasp-waisted body has evoked a steady stream of critique for having a negative impact on little girls' sense of self-esteem. For example, the release of a Barbie aerobics workout video for girls in 1992 was met with the following angry letter from an expert in the field of eating disorders:

I had hoped these plastic dolls with impossible proportions would have faded away in this current health-conscious period; not at all. . . . Move over Jane Fonda. Welcome again, ever smiling, breast-thrusting Barbie with your stick legs and sweat-free aerobic routines. I'm concerned about the role model message she is giving our young. Surely it's hard to accept a little cellulite when the culture tells you unrelentingly how to strive for thinness and the perfect body. [Warner 1992][9]

There is no doubt that Barbie's body contributes to what Kim Chernin (1981) has called "the tyranny of slenderness."[10] But is repression all her hyper-thin body conveys? In her work on how anorectic women see themselves, Susan Bordo writes that, "for anorectics, [the slender ideal] may have a very different meaning; it may symbolize, not so much the containment of female desire, as its liberation from a domestic, reproductive destiny" (Bordo 1990:103).

Similar observations have been made about cosmetic surgery: women often explain their experience as one of empowerment, of taking charge of their bodies and lives (Balsamo 1993; Davis 1991). What does this mean for making sense of Barbie and her long lasting appeal? We would suggest that a sub-text of agency and independence, even transgression, accompanies this pencil-thin icon of femininity. On the one hand, one can argue that Barbie's body displays conformity to dominant cultural imperatives for a disciplined body and contained feminine desires. On the other hand, however, her excessive slenderness can also signify a rebellious manifestation of will-power, a refusal of the maternal ideal, symbolized by pendulous breasts, rounded stomach and hips. Hers is a body of hard edges, distinct borders, and self control. It is literally impenetrable. While the anorectic woman becomes increasingly androgynous the more she starves herself, Barbie, in the realm of plastic fantasy, is able to remain powerfully sexualized with her large gravity-defying breasts, even while she is distinctly non-reproductive. Like the "hard bodies" in fitness advertising, Barbie's body may signify for women the pleasure of control and mastery both of which are highly valued traits in American society and both of which are predominantly associated with masculinity (Bordo 1990:105). Putting these elements together with her apparent independent wealth can make for a very different reading of Barbie than that of bimbo. To paraphrase one Barbie doll owner: she owns a Ferrari and doesn't have a husband; she must be doing something right![11]

By invoking these testimonies of anorectic women, we are not trying to suggest that playing with Barbie, or trying to become like Barbie, are paths to empowerment for little girls. Rather we want to signal the complex and contradictory meanings that her body has in contemporary American society. And we also want to underscore that our bodies, whatever the reigning ideal might be, continue to function as a vitally important stage on which gender—as well as race and class—conformity and transgression are played out.[12] It is clear that a next step we would want to take in the cultural interpretation of Barbie is an ethnographic study of Barbie doll owners.[13] It is sensible to assume that the children who play with Barbie are themselves creative users who respond variously to the messages about femininity encoded in her fashions and appearance. In the hands of their adult and child owners, Barbies have become Amazon cave warriors, drag queens, dutiful mommies, and evil axe murderers.[14] As we consider Barbie's many meanings, we should also note that the doll has become a world traveler. A product of the global assembly-line, Barbie dolls owe their existence to the internationalization of the labor market and global flows of capital and commodities that today characterize the toy industry as well as other industries in the post-war era. Designed in Los Angeles, manufactured in Taiwan or Malaysia, distributed worldwide, Barbie™ is American-made in name only. Speeding her way into an expanding global market, Barbie brings with her some of the North American cultural subtext we have outlined in this analysis. How this teenage survivor has inserted herself into the cultural landscapes of Mayan villages, Bombay high rises, and Malagasy towns is a rich topic that begs to be explored.

ACKNOWLEDGMENTS

This essay is based on a longer piece of research first published in Urla and Swedlund (1995). Follow-up research we have carried out on the ideal of the thin waist will appear in Orgel, Urla, and Swedlund (2005).

REFERENCES

Adelson, Andrea
1992   And Now, Barbie Looks Like a Billion. *New York Times.* Nov. 26. p. D3.
Balsamo, Anne
1993   On the Cutting Edge: Cosmetic Surgery and the Technological Production of the Gendered Body. *Camera Obscura* 28:207–238.
Banner, Lois W.
1983   *American Beauty.* New York, Knopf.
Bartky, Sandra Lee
1990   "Foucault, Femininity, and the Modernization of Patriarchal Power." In *Femininity and Domination: Studies in the Phenomenology of Oppression.* pp. 63–82. New York: Routledge.
Bennett, William and Joel Gurin
1982   *The Dieter's Dilemma: Eating Less and Weighing More.* New York: Basic Books.
Billyboy
1987   *Barbie, her Life and Times, and the New Theater of Fashion.* New York: Crown Publishers.
Blakey, Michael L.
1987   Skull Doctors: Instrinsic Social and Political Bias in the History of American Physical Anthropology. *Critique of Anthropology* 7(2): 7–35.
Bordo, Susan R.
1990   "Reading the Slender Body." In *Body/Politics: Women and the Discourses of Science.* M. Jacobus, E. Fox Keller, and S. Shuttleworth, eds. pp. 83–112. New York: Routledge.
Bordo, Susan R.
1991   "'Material Girl': The Effacements of Postmodern Culture." In *The Female Body: Figures, Styles, Speculations.* L.Goldstein, ed. pp. 106–130. Ann Arbor, MI: The University of Michigan Press.
Breckenridge, Carol A.
1990   Editor's Comment: On Toying with Terror. *Public Culture* 2(2):i–iii.
Brumberg, Joan Jacobs
1988   *Fasting Girls: The History of Anorexia Nervosa.* New York: New American Library.
Chernin, Kim
1981   *The Obsession: Reflections on the Tyranny of Slenderness.* New York: Harper.

Cogan, Frances B.
1989   *All-American Girl: The Ideal of Real Woman-hood in Mid-Nineteenth Century America.* Athens and London: University of Georgia Press.

Davis, Kathy
1991   Remaking the She-Devil: A Critical Look at Feminist Approaches to Beauty. *Hypatia* 6(2):21–43.

Doherty, Thomas
1988   *Teenagers and Teenpics. The Juvenilization of American Movies in the 1950's.* Boston: Unwin Hyman.

DuCille, Ann
1995   "Toy Theory: Blackface Barbie and the Deep Play of Difference." In, *The Skin Trade: Essays on Race, Gender and Merchandising of Difference.* Cambridge: Harvard University Press.

Ebersole, Lucinda and Richard Peabody, eds.
1993   *Mondo Barbie.* New York: St. Martin's Press.

Fausto-Sterling, Anne
1995   "Gender, Race and Nation: The Comparative Anatomy of "Hottentot" Women in Europe, 1815–1817." In *Deviant Bodies: Critical Perspectives on Difference in Science and Popular Culture.* J. Terry and J. Urla, eds. Bloomington: Indiana University Press.

Fee, Elizabeth
1979   Nineteenth Century Craniology: The Study of the Female Skull. *Bulletin of the History of Medicine* 53:415–433.

France, Kim
1992   "Tits 'R' Us." *Village Voice*, March 17, p. 22.

Frith, Simon
1981   *Sound Effects: Youth, Leisures, and the Politics of Rock'n'Roll.* New York: Pantheon.

Gould, Steven Jay
1981   *The Mismeasure of Man.* New York: Norton.

Hohmann, Delf Maria
1985   Jennifer and her Barbies: A Contextual Analysis of a Child Playing Barbie dolls. *Canadian Folklore Canadien* 7 (1–2):111–120.

Hooton, E. A.
1931   Up from the Ape. New York: The MacMillan Company.

Hrdlicka, Ales
1918   Physical anthropology: Its scope and aims; its history and present status in America. *American Journal of Physical Anthropology* 1(1):3–23.

1925   Relation of the Size of the Head and Skull to Capacity in the Two Sexes. *American Journal of Physical Anthropology* 8:249–250.

Hrdlicka, Ales
1939   *Practical Anthropometry.* Philadelphia: Wistar Institute of Anatomy and Biology.

Jones, Lisa
1991   Skin Trade: A Doll is Born. *Village Voice.* March 26, p. 36.

Kahn, Alice
1991   A Onetime Bimbo Becomes a Muse. *New York Times.* September 29.

Kaw, Eugenia
1993   Medicalization of Racial Features: Asian American Women and Cosmetic Surgery. *Medical Anthropology Quarterly* 7(1): 74–89.

Krause, Elizabeth
1998.   A Bead of Raw Sweat in a Field of Dainty Perspirers: Nationalism, Whiteness and the Olympic Ordeal of Tonya Harding. *Transforming Anthropology* 7(1):33–52.

Lord, M.G.
1994   *Forever Barbie: The Unauthorized Biography of a Real Doll.* New York: William Morrow.

May, Elaine Tyler
1988   *Homeward Bound: American Families in the Cold War Era.* New York: Basic Books.

Melosh, Barbara and Christina Simmons
1986   "Exhibiting Women's History." In, *Presenting the Past: Essays on History and the Public.* Susan Porter Benson, Stephen Brier, and Roy Rosenzweig eds. Philadelphia: Temple University Press.

Motz, Marilyn Ferris
1983   "'I Want to Be a Barbie Doll When I Grow Up': The Cultural Significance of the Barbie Doll." In, *The Popular Culture Reader*, 3rd ed. Christopher D. Geist and Jack Nachbar, eds. pp. 122–136. Bowling Green: Bowling Green University Popular Press.

Newsweek
1990   Finally, Barbie Dolls Go Ethnic. *Newsweek* (August 13), p. 48.

Orgel, Mary, Jacqueline Urla and Alan Swedlund
2005.   Surveying a Cultural Waist-land: Biological Poetics and Politics of the Female Body. In *Anthropology United: Challenging Bio-Social Reductivisms.* Susan McKinnon and Sydel Silverman, eds. pp. 132–156. University of Chicago Press.

Rabinowitz, Paula
1993   Accessorizing History: Girls and Popular Culture. Discussant Comments, Panel #150: "Engendering Post-war Popular Culture in Britain and America. Ninth Berkshire Conference on the History of Women. Vassar College, June 11–13, 1993.

Rand, Erica
1995.   *Barbie's Queer Accessories.* Durham and London: Duke University Press.

Robertson, Josephine
1945   Theatre Cashier, 23, Wins Title of "Norma." *Cleveland Plain Dealer.* September 21, pp. 1, 4.
Russett, Cynthia Eagle
1989   *Sexual Science: The Victorian Construction of Womanhood.* Cambridge, MA: Harvard University Press.
Schiebinger, Londa
1989   *The Mind has no Sex: Women in the Origins of Modern Science.* Cambridge: Harvard University Press.
Schiebinger, Londa
2004   *Nature's Body: Gender in the Making of Modern Science.* Rutgers University Press.
Schwartz, Hillel
1986   *Never Satisfied: A Cultural History of Diets, Fantasies and Fat.* New York: The Free Press.
Shapiro, Eben
1992   'Total Hot, Totally Cool.' Long-Haired Barbie is a Hit. *New York Times.* June 22. p. D-9.
Shapiro, Harry L.
1945   Americans: *Yesterday, Today, Tomorrow.* Man and Nature Publications. (Science Guide No. 126). New York: The American Museum of Natural History.
Spencer, Frank
1992   "Some Notes on the Attempt to Apply Photography to Anthropometry during the Second Half of the Nineteenth Century. In *Anthropology and Photography: 1860–1920.* Elizabeth Edwards, ed. pp. 99–107. New Haven, CT: Yale University Press.
Stevenson, Richard
1991   Mattel Thrives as Barbie Grows. *New York Times.* December 2.
Urla, Jacqueline and Alan Swedlund
1995.   "The Anthropometry of Barbie: Unsettling Ideals of the Feminine Body in Popular Culture." In *Deviant Bodies: Critical Perspectives on Difference in Science and Popular Culture.* J. Terry and J. Urla, eds. pp. 277–313. Bloomington: Indiana University Press.
Warner, Patricia Rosalind
1992   Letter to the Editor. *Boston Globe.* June 28.
Williams, Lena
1992   Woman's Image in a Mirror: Who Defines What She Sees? *New York Times.* February 6. A1; B7.
Willis, Susan
1991   *A Primer for Daily Life.* London and New York: Routledge.
Wilson, Elizabeth
1985   *Adorned in Dreams: Fashion and Modernity.* London: Virago.
Wiseman, C., Gray, J., Mosimann, J. and Ahrens, A.
1992   Cultural Expectations of Thinness in Women: An Update. *International Journal of Eating Disorders* 11 (1):85–89.
Wolf, Naomi
1991   *The Beauty Myth: How Images of Beauty are Used Against Women.* New York: William Morrow.

NOTES

1. The statistics and figures provided on sales reflect research carried out in the nineties.
2. While the concept of adolescence as a distinct developmental stage between puberty and adulthood was not new to the fifties, Thomas Doherty (1988) notes that it wasn't until the end of World War II that the term "teenager" became standard usage in the American language.
3. More work needs to be done on how Barbie dolls are adapted to appeal to various national markets. For example, Barbie dolls manufactured in Japan for Japanese consumption are reputed to have noticeably larger, rounder eyes than those marketed in the United States (see Billyboy 1987). For some suggestive thoughts on the cultural implications of the transnational flow of toys like Barbie dolls, TransFormers, and He-Man, see Carol Breckenridge's (1990) brief but intriguing editor's comment to *Public Culture.*
4. On Black Barbies, see DuCille 1995.
5. Though measurements of skulls, noses, facial angles for scientific comparison had been going on throughout the 19th century, it wasn't until the 1890s that any serious attempts were made to standardize anthropometric measurements of the living body. This culminated in the Monaco agreement of 1906, one of the first international meetings to standardize anthropometric measurement. For a brief review of the attempts to use and systematize photography in anthropometry see Spencer (1992).
6. Hrdlicka argued, rather fantastically, that there was more space between the brain and the cranium in women than in men. Michael Blakey refers to this as Hrdlicka's "air head" hypothesis (1987:16)
7. In her study of 18th century physical sciences, Schiebinger (2004) remarks that male bodies (skulls in particular) were routinely assumed to embody the prototype of their race in the various typologies devised by comparative anatomists of

the period. "When anthropologists did compare women across cultures, their interest centered on sexual traits—feminine beauty, redness of lips, length and style of hair, size and shape of breasts or clitorises, degree of sexual desire, fertility, and above all the size, shape, and position of the pelvis" (2004:156). In this way, the male body "remained the touchstone of human anatomy," while females were regarded as a sexual subset of the species (2004:159–60).

8. Historians have noted a long-standing conflict between the physical culture movement, eugenicists and health reformers on the one hand, and the fashion industry on the other that gave rise to competing ideals in American society of the fit and the fashionably fragile woman (e.g. Banner 1983; Cogan 1989).

9. When confronted with these kinds of accusations, Mattel and the fashion industry protest that Barbie dolls, like fashion models, are about fantasy, not reality. "We're not telling you to be that girl" writes Elizabeth Saltzman, fashion editor for *Vogue*. "We're trying to show you fashion" (France 1992:22).

10. In response to this anxiety, Cathy Meredig, an enterprising computer software designer, created the "Happy to be Me" doll. Described as a healthy alternative for little girls, "Happy to be Me" has a shorter neck, shorter legs, wider waist and larger feet, and a lot fewer clothes, designed to make her look more like the average woman ("She's No Barbie, Nor Does She Care to Be." *New York Times*, August 15, 1991, C-11).

11. "Dolls in Playland." 1992. Colleen Toomey, producer. BBC.

12. For an illuminating case study of race, class, and gender codings of the female body, see Krause 1998.

13. While not exactly ethnographic, Hohmann (1985) offers a socio-psychological study of how children experiment with social relations during play with Barbies.

14. Barbie has become a somewhat celebrated figure among avant-garde and pop artists, giving rise to a whole genre of Barbie satire known as "Barbie Noire" (Kahn 1991; Ebersole and Peabody 1993). On queer appropriations of Barbie and Ken, see Rand (1995).

VII

Gender, Property, and the State

The relationship among sexual inequality, the emergence of class structures, and the rise of the state has been an enduring interest in anthropological studies of gender. The subordination of women appears to emerge as an aspect of state formation. According to Gailey (1987: 6), "Institutionalized gender hierarchy . . . is created historically with class relations and state formative processes, whether these emerge independently, through colonization, or indirectly through capital penetration." We are led to ask what relationship class and state formation have with the oppression of women and, when gender hierarchy occurs, why women are the dominated gender. How does the state have power to penetrate and reorganize the lives of its members, whether in Sumerian legal codes decreeing monogamy for women or in welfare laws in the United States that influence household composition? Eventually, studying state formation may help us understand the origins and interrelationships of class and patriarchy and the social reproduction of inequality.

Much discussion of this subject has centered on Engels's book *The Origin of the Family, Private Property, and the State*, a nineteenth-century text in which Engels argues that the emergence of the concept of private property and its ownership by men, as well as the development of a monogamous family, led to the subordination of women. In Engels's scheme, prior to this, gender relations were egalitarian and complementary. All production was for use, and people worked together for the communal household. Thus, changes in gender relations were linked to changes in material conditions because the ownership of productive property (initially domestic animals) was concentrated in the hands of men. This thesis has been influential in many Marxist and feminist analyses of women's subordination. For example, Leacock notes, "There is sufficient evidence at hand to support in its broad outlines Engels' argument that the position of women relative to men deteriorated with the advent of class society" (1973: 30).

Following Engels, Leacock observes that in early communal society the division of labor between the sexes was reciprocal, and a wife and her children were not dependent on the husband. Further, "The distinction did not exist between a public world of men's work and a private world of women's household service. The large collective household was the community, and within it both sexes worked to produce the goods necessary for livelihood" (1973: 33). In this view the oppression of women was built on the transformation of goods for use into commodities for exchange; the exploitation of workers and of women was generated by this process, which involved the emergence of the individual family as an isolated unit, economically responsible for its members, and of women's labor as a private service in the context of the family. This led to the "world historical defeat of the female sex" (Engels 1973: 120; Silverblatt 1988: 430).

In a reanalysis of Engels, Sacks agrees that women's position declined with the elaboration of social classes but disputes Engels's emphasis on the role of private property in this process (Sacks 1982). Rather, Sacks links state formation and the decline in the centrality of kinship groups to the deterioration in women's status. She delineates two relationships defining women in noncapitalist societies: sisterhood and wifehood. "Sister" refers to women's access to resources based on membership in a kin group. This relation implies autonomy, adulthood, and possible gender symmetry. "Wife," on the other hand, refers to a relationship of dependency on the husband and his kin. Sacks suggests that the development of states undermined women's status by dismantling the kin group corporations that formed the basis for sister relations (Sacks 1982).

However, critics of Sacks's position have argued that the process of state formation may involve uneven and contradictory developments. For example, elite women in the Kingdom of Dahomey, West Africa, challenged state imperatives by means of control of marketing associations. Thus, Silverblatt rebuts Sacks's evolutionary paradigm suggesting the inevitability of the decline in women's status with state formation; instead, she suggests that we acknowledge the complex history of the emergence of elite privilege in the rise of the state. In addition, elite women such as the royalty of Dahomey may or may not share the goals of peasant women. They may instead join with the male elite in suppressing the authority and power of peasant market women. This illustrates the potential contradictions of gender affiliation, on one hand, and class position on the other.

Several anthropologists have observed that Engels lacked reliable ethnographic information and oversimplified the complexities of gender relations in kinship societies and in precapitalist states (Gailey 1987: 15). In a critique of Engels, Moore argues against his essentialist assumption that there is a "natural" division of labor in which men are concerned with productive tasks and women with domestic ones. She also disagrees that an inevitable relationship will transpire between property, paternity, and legitimacy, in which men "naturally" want to transmit property to genetic offspring (1988: 47–48).

Rayna Rapp (in this book) agrees with these criticisms, but she points out that Engels addresses many current concerns, such as the relationship between women's participation in production and female status, and the implications of the separation of the domestic–public domains for women's roles in society (see also Silverblatt 1988: 432). She warns against overgeneralizing when trying to understand the origins of the state and ignoring the history and context in which political formations change. In her view, we must examine kinship structures that were supplanted with the rise of the state and replaced by territorial and class-specific politics. Kinship domains, formerly autonomous, were subjugated to the demands of emergent elites with repercussions for gender roles and relations.

Among the processes that we need to examine are the politics of kinship, the intensification of military complexes, the impact of trade on social stratification, and the changing content and role of cosmology. For example, in stratified societies the establishment of long-distance trade and tribute systems may affect elite marriage patterns, leading to the emergence of dowry and the exchange of women to cement male political alliances. Similar alliances are forged in societies that have experienced a rise in militarism. When economies change and demand increases for a traded commodity, exploitation of labor to produce it may also increase, and marriage systems that expand trading relations may be solidified through the exchange of women. Women themselves may be important figures in trading networks, as in West Africa and in Mesoamerica, where women are active in the marketplace.

Alternatively, the extension of the state into localized communities can significantly influence gender roles and relations (Goddard 2000a). This occurs, for example, by undermining women's ritual responsibilities or by generating conflict between government policy and the respective interests of men and women. Finally, changes in political hierarchies were legitimated by cosmological explanations in early states such as those of the Inca and the Maya. For example, as Maya society became increasingly stratified, a category of elite rulers known as *ahaw* emerged. These rulers were legitimized by myths that established them as mediators between the natural and supernatural worlds and as protectors of the people. State ideology involved the celebration of both male and female forces, and the elite contained both men and women. Mothers of kings were always members of the high elite, and this class affiliation was also validated in myth (Schele and Freidel 1990; Stanley Guenter and David Freidel, in Chapter 2 of this book).

Ortner examines the process of state formation, with particular regard to its effect on gender ideology (1978; see also Goddard 2000b). She analyzes the widespread ideology that associates the purity of women with the honor and status of their families. This pattern is evident in Latin America and the Mediterranean, and in societies of the Middle East, India, and China. Broad similarities exist in these varied societies. Ortner questions why the control of female sexual purity is such a ubiquitous and important phenomenon. She notes that all modern cases of societies concerned with female purity occur in states or systems with highly developed stratification, and they bear the cultural ideologies and religions that were part of the emergence of these states. She argues that no prestate societies manifest the pattern linking female virginity and chastity to the social honor of the group. Thus, concern with the purity of women was, in Ortner's view, structurally, functionally, and symbolically linked to the historical emergence of state structures.

The rise of the state heralds a radical shift in ideology and practice, with the emergence of the patriarchal extended family in which the senior man has absolute authority over everyone in the household. Women are brought under direct control of men in their natal families and later by their husbands and affinal kin. Ideologically women are thought to be in danger, requiring male protection; they are idealized as mothers and for their purity.

One of the central questions in the analysis of the impact of state formation is the role of hypergamy (up-status marriage, usually between higher-status men and lower-status women). Ortner (1978) suggests that a significant development in stratified society involves the transformation of marriage from an essentially equal transaction to a potentially vertical one, where one's sister or daughter could presumably marry into a higher strata (wife of a nobleman, consort of a king). Hypergamy may help explain the ideal of female purity because concepts of purity and virginity may symbolize the value of a girl for a higher-status spouse. Thus "a virgin is an elite female among females, withheld, untouched, exclusive" (Ortner 1981: 32).

Hypergamous marriages often involve the exchange of significant amounts of property, particularly in the form of dowry. The relationship between dowry, inheritance, and female status has been explored in a number of societies with varying marriage patterns. Dowry has been described as a form of premortem inheritance, parallel to men's rights in property accrued through inheritance after death of parents or other legators. However, considering dowry as a form of inheritance prior to death and as part of a woman's property complex obscures an important difference between the clear legal inheritance rights that men possess and the dowry that women may or may not receive (McCreery 1976; see also Linda Stone and Caroline James in this book). Women obtain dowry at the discretion of their parents or brothers, and dowry is not based on the same rights as other forms of inheritance to which men have access.

Although dowry has been viewed as a form of inheritance for women, the dowry system in northern India has taken a pernicious turn as brides are burned to death, poisoned, or otherwise "accidentally" killed by husbands and in-laws who believe that the women have brought inadequate dowries. Conservative estimates are that at least 2,000 women die each year as a result of dowry murders (Stone and James, in this book). Legislation enacted in 1961 banning dowries, and in 1986 amending the penal code to introduce a new offense, now known as dowry death, has been ineffective, and the dowry system continues to be deeply embedded in local culture (Koman 1996). Although the bestowing of dowry in India is centuries old, dowry murders are a recent social problem. Stone and James argue that dowry deaths represent a response to a growing materialist consumerism sweeping India that has stimulated demands for larger and ever-increasing dowries. They analyze these murders in the context of a patrilineal and patrilocal society with strongly prescribed subservience of wives to husbands and in-laws, in which parents prefer to see a daughter dead rather than divorced. Women's fertility, which may once have been a source of power, is increasingly less valued. Even a woman who gives birth to sons is not protected from the risk of wife-burning. Thus women's relative lack of economic power and the loss of their one traditional source of leverage, their fertility, have heightened their vulnerability to violence.

Although the status of Indian women as reflected in the exchange of property at marriage appears to be deteriorating, in other parts of the world women's legal status and property rights have improved through state-sponsored changes in the judicial system. For example, Starr (1984) examines how in Turkey the impact of capitalistic agriculture and settled village life profoundly affected gender relations and women's access to property. These changes occurred in the cultural context of Islamic notions of male dominance and female submission and legislation giving equal rights to women.

Ottoman family law gave women rights to divorce and some protection against polygamous marriage, but inheritance practices remained constrained by Islamic law, in which women were under the authority of their husbands, had the status of a minor, received half the share of the patrimony obtained by their brothers, and had no rights to children of a marriage. According to Ataturk's secular reforms in the 1920s, women's rights were expanded to full adult status, women received equal rights to paternal inheritance, protection was granted to widows, and other legislation was enacted promoting equality for women. At first these state-initiated rights were incongruent with cultural practices, but by the late 1960s women had begun to use the courts to protect their rights to property and their reputations. Starr points out that although Engels emphasized the negative impact of private ownership on women's status, in this case law and culture played a positive counterbalancing role resulting in women's emancipation.

In her cross-cultural exploration of the political experiences of contemporary women, Josephine Caldwell Ryan (in this book) illustrates the ways in which women engage, respond to, or resist the state. She notes that women's interaction with the state may take the shape of voting, seeking political office, participating in women's movements or other forms of collective action, or acting individually in response to state policies. A global perspective on women's encounters with the state suggests that although some women have experienced an increase in formal political rights and "real" power, others have seen their gains eroded by such forces as religious fundamentalism and global economic crises. Major world religions, including Christianity, Hinduism, and Islam, have experienced an increase in religious fundamentalism in the last thirty years. Accordingly, Caldwell Ryan traces the impact of religious fundamentalism in Iran, Afghanistan, and India on the status of women in those countries. She shows that it is useful to consider the specific circumstances of national histories and identities rather than focusing solely on religious doctrine to analyze the impact of religious fundamentalism on women in particular states.

Similarly, global economic upheavals have negatively affected women's everyday lives as well as demonstrating their limited political power. Structural adjustment policies initiated by the World Bank and the International Monetary Fund, for example, have led to higher prices for food and a decline in public spending on health and social services, all leading to increased burdens for women, who have been forced to take on a greater responsibility for providing for their families in response to economic austerity measures. Caldwell Ryan's discussion underscores the links between women's political empowerment and economic autonomy. Ultimately, one catalyst for global gender equity is the emergent international feminist movement, which has succeeded in putting gender on the agenda of nearly every state. Thus such issues as girls' education, female labor, child custody, and women's inheritance and property rights have emerged as matters for national debate and political action.

If the state can shape family and gender relations directly through legislation such as that determining rights to property, it may also have more indirect impact. Anne Allison (in this book) argues that in Japan, boxed lunches (*obentō*), prepared by mothers for their children, are invested with a gendered state ideology. The state manipulates the ideological and gendered meanings associated with the box lunch as an important component of nursery school culture. Nursery schools, under state supervision, not only socialize children and mothers into the gendered roles they are expected to assume but also introduce small children to the attitudes and structures of Japanese education. The *obentō*, elaborately and artistically arranged, is intended to allow the mother to produce something of home and family to accompany the child into this new and threatening outside world. Embedded in the school's close scrutiny of *obentō* production and consumption is a message to obey rules and accept the authority of the school and, by extension, of the state. The *obentō*'s message is also that mothers sustain their children through food and support state ideology as well.

In all the works included in this chapter we see the enduring influence of the issues raised by Engels with regard to the relationship among gender, property rights, and state structures. However, cross-cultural data demonstrate that this relationship is much more complex and varied than Engels's original formulation. Equally, universal evolutionary paradigms that posit a uniform impact of the rise of the state on gender roles cannot do justice to the myriad ways in which specific cultural histories, diverse social hierarchies, and systems of stratification affect gender relations and ideology. Thus, Silverblatt (1988: 448) asks, "What of the challenges that women and men, caught in their society's contradictions, bring to the dominant order of chiefs and castes, an order they contour and subvert, even as they are contained by it? And what of the other voices, the voices that chiefs and rulers do not (or cannot or will not) express?" The complex histories of the relationship between any particular state and gender relations in it show that while state formation has contributed to the definition of womanhood, women have also contributed to the definition of states (Silverblatt 1988: 452).

REFERENCES

Engels, Frederick. 1973. *The Origin of the Family, Private Property and the State.* New York: International Publishers.

Gailey, Christine Ward. 1987. *Kinship to Kingship: Gender Hierarchy and State Formation in the Tongan Islands.* Austin: University of Texas Press.

Goddard, Victoria Ana. 2000a. "Introduction." In Victoria Ana Goddard (ed.). *Gender, Agency and Change,* pp. 1–32. London: Routledge.

Goddard, Victoria Ana. 2000b. "'The Virgin and the State.' Gender and Politics in Argentina." In Victoria Ana Goddard (ed.). *Gender, Agency and Change,* pp. 221–250. London: Routledge.

Koman, Kathleen. 1996. "India's Burning Brides." *Harvard Magazine* 98 (3): 18–19.

Leacock, Eleanor Burke. 1973. "Introduction." In Frederick Engels (ed.). *The Origin of the Family, Private Property and the State,* pp. 7–57. New York: International Publishers.

McCreery, John L. 1976. "Women's Property Rights and Dowry in China and South Asia." *Ethnology* 15: 163–174.

Moore, Henrietta L. 1988. *Feminism and Anthropology.* Minneapolis: University of Minnesota Press.

Ortner, Sherry. 1978. "The Virgin and the State." *Feminist Studies* 4 (3): 19–35.

——— 1981. "Gender and Sexuality in Hierarchical Societies: The Case of Polynesia and Some Comparative Implications." In Sherry B. Ortner and Harriet Whitehead (eds.). *Sexual Meanings: The Cultural Construction of Gender and Sexuality,* pp. 359–410. Cambridge, UK: Cambridge University Press.

Sacks, Karen. 1982. *Sisters and Wives: The Past and Future of Sexual Equality.* Urbana: University of Illinois Press.

Schele, Linda, and David Freidel. 1990. *A Forest of Kings.* New York: William Morrow.

Silverblatt, Irene. 1988. "Women in States." *Annual Review of Anthropology* 17: 427–461.

Starr, June. 1984. "The Legal and Social Transformation of Rural Women in Aegean Turkey." In Renee Hirschon (ed.). *Women and Property: Women as Property.* pp. 554–579. New York: St. Martin's Press, Inc.

Thinking about Women and the Origin of the State

Rayna Rapp

While anthropologists vary widely in their assessment of the autonomy of women in prestate societies, there seems to be a general

Revised by the editors with the permission and approval of the author.

consensus that with the rise of civilization, women as a social category were increasingly subjugated to the male heads of their households (Gailey 1987; Leacock 1978; Rohrlich 1980; Sacks 1982; Sanday 1981; Silverblatt 1988). This consensus is based, implicitly or explicitly, on a formulation developed by Frederick Engels (1973) in *The Origin of the Family, Private Property, and the State.* Engels linked the growth of private productive property to the dismantling of a system of communal kinship that existed in prestate societies. In this process, he argued, marriage grows more restrictive, legitimacy of heirs more important, and wives generally become means of reproduction to their husbands. At the same time, reciprocal relations among kin are curtailed, unequal access to strategic productive resources gradually develops, and estates or classes arise out of formerly kin-based social organizations. In this analysis, the creation of a class hierarchy is intimately linked to the creation of the patriarchal family and to restrictions on women's autonomy.

Engels' analysis provides the foundation for many themes concerning women that are currently being investigated: the relation between the economic roles of women, their control of resources, and their social status; the relation between the mode of production and the mode of reproduction;[1] and the effects of the separation or merger of domestic and public spheres of activity on the lives of women.[2] However, a thesis central to Engels' analysis—the link between class oppression and gender oppression—has remained less well examined. Drawing on a growing body of theory and data concerning state formation that has been amassed in recent years by twentieth-century archaeologists,[3] this article examines Engels' theory about the relationship between the subjugation of women, social stratification, and the rise of the state.

Most of the early theoretical work on emergence of state society was reductive, and it often condensed a multiplicity of processes into overly simplistic models. These theories ranged from a concentration on the extraction of social surplus (surplus material resources or labor beyond that needed for subsistence) via increasing division of labor and more productive technology (Childe 1950, 1952); to a focus on the emergence of central political authority to administer irrigation-based societies (Wittfogel 1955, 1957); to the effects of population pressure and warfare within circumscribed environments (Carneiro 1970; Harner 1970).

All of these theories tend to see the state as an inevitable and efficient solution to a particular set of problems. They ignore the specific historical, political, and economic contexts in which societies change.[4] Finally, they underplay the importance of kinship as a domain within which resistance to state formation is situated.[5] Not uncoincidentally, it is within the kinship domain that women's subordination appears to occur.

In recent years, a new set of theoretical and systemic formulations that are more processual have been developed. Such formulations offer fascinating hints about the role of kinship structure, and possibly women, in stratification. Some of the processes examined in state formation—the politics of kinship, the changing content and role of religious systems, the intensification of military complexes, and the role of trade in stimulating or increasing social stratification—are most pertinent to our interests here. I will discuss each of these briefly, suggesting some of the lines of inquiry they direct us to pursue.

THE POLITICS OF KINSHIP

Many anthropologists have examined the internal tensions of ranked kinship systems (Kirchoff 1959; Sahlins 1958; Fried 1967). In highly ranked kinship systems, the role of women is of crucial importance. Women not only transmit status, but may be contenders for leadership positions, either directly or through their children. This seems to be the case in Polynesia and in parts of Africa. As Gailey (1987) shows for Tonga, the existence of elite, ranked women became more problematic as stratification increased.

We need to know more about marriage patterns in such systems. In archaeology, ethnology, and Western history, we find that elite marriages may be implicated in the politics of establishing and maintaining long-distance trade and tribute systems.[6] Dowry is associated with highly stratified systems and dowered, elite women may appear as pawns in a classic case of male alliances formed via their exchange.[7] Ortner (1978) suggests that in state-organized systems, marriage may shift from horizontal alliances between individuals of similar social and economic backgrounds to vertical alliances between individuals of different backgrounds. In the latter situation there is a marked tendency toward hypergamy whereby lower-status women marry upper-status men. Ortner links these structural properties of the marriage system with ideologies requiring sexual purity and the protection of women (but not of men).

Silverblatt (1987), in a study of the Inca elite, suggests that as the Incas extended their rule, they required conquered communities to send women to Cuzco to serve in the temples, courts, and as noblemen's wives. For the conquered communities, this practice represented a loss of autonomy in marriage patterns, and a burden. At the same time, it made possible upward mobility to the specific males who sent sisters and daughters to Cuzco. The women themselves gained a great deal of prestige, but lost any control they might have had in arranging their own marriages and living within their natal communities.

CHANGING COSMOLOGIES

Both Silverblatt and Ortner draw our attention to the relationship between women and the religious systems in early states. They remind us that religious systems were the glue that cemented social relations in archaic societies. Such systems were used, as in the Inca case, to underwrite and justify changes in political hierarchies.

Tension about female status is often found within these religious systems. Eliade (1960) claims that the ritual expression of sexual antagonism and the existence of bisexual and/or androgynous gods accompanies the social organizational changes associated with the neolithic period. Male gods are often superimposed on female and androgynous gods. Evidence for this layering over of female and/or androgynous figures comes from Mesoamerica (Nash 1980), Peru (Silverblatt 1987), and is, of course, a favorite theme of classicists for early Greek society (Arthur 1976; Pomeroy 1975).

Pagels (1976), working with second-century A.D. Gnostic texts, analyzes the symbol system of sects in which the early Christian god was bisexual, and the Holy Family consisted of mother, father, and son. Such sects were organized into non-hierarchical religious communities, in which offices were rotated, and women participated in both teaching and preaching—a far cry from the ascendant Christian cosmology and practice which became the mainstream tradition. Cosmological changes are ideological precipitates of structural tensions; it is clear that their form and content have a great deal to tell us about class and gender.

INTENSIFICATION OF WARFARE

As early states became increasingly militaristic, social organization was transformed.[8] Several case histories lead us to believe that under conditions of intense warfare, men were not only burdened by conscription, but were blessed with increasing power as household heads (Muller 1987; Rohrlich 1980). Elite males may gain land, political domains, and alliance-forming wives in the process. Yet, sweeping statements about male supremacy and warfare (Divale and Harris 1976) are overgeneralized, and some evidence seems to contradict the association of warfare and an elevation of male status at the expense of female autonomy.

In the ancient West, for example, the correlation often works the other way: Spartan women held offices, controlled their own property, and had a great deal of sexual freedom, allegedly because they kept society functioning while the men were at war. Moreover, producing soldiers was considered as important as training them. In Athens, women's access to public places and roles seems to have increased a great deal during times of warfare. In Rome, during the Second Punic War, women gained in inheritance settlements and held public offices formerly closed to them (Pomeroy 1975). In the medieval Franco-Germanic world, noblewomen attained approximate parity in politics and property-management during the years of the most brutal military crisis (McNamara and Wemple 1973).

All these examples concern elite women only; we know very little about the effects of warfare on laboring women, who probably suffered then, as they do now. Nonetheless, it is not clear that warfare degrades women's status; the specific context within which military organization and practice occurs must be taken into account. Blood and gore clearly are not universal variables in theorizing about women's subordination.

TRADE

The role of trade in increasing and/or spreading stratification is an intriguing one.[9] Foreign-trade goods may be spread in many ways: by middlemen, via migrations, through central trading centers, and in marriage exchanges, to name but a few. Several studies suggest that the social relationships that surround production and distribution, and which undergird trade, may generate class and gender inequality (Adams 1974; Kohl 1975; Wiley 1974; Gailey and Patterson 1987). We need to know who produces goods, who appropriates them, and who distributes them. As demand for a trade commodity increases, exploitation of labor to produce it may arise. Marriage systems may also be intensified to expand the reproduction of trading alliances. Certainly there are numerous ethnographic examples of polygyny as a means to increase access to goods that wives produce. There are also many instances of increasing class division linked to increasing bridewealth.

But the control, ownership, and distribution of valued resources after they are produced is not exclusively a male function. In Mesoamerica and the Andes, to this day, women are active in the marketplace. Silverblatt (1978) suggests that they were important traders in early Incan times. Adams (1966) records their existence in Mesopotamia. And of course, their presence is felt in stratified groups throughout Africa and the Caribbean as well (Mintz 1971). Under what conditions does long-distance trade pass into the hands of men, and when is it possible for women to continue to perform it? When women are traders, do they constitute an elite, class-stratified group? To the extent that trade

is implicated in the intensification of production for exchange, women as producers, reproducers, and traders must be implicated too.

CONCLUSION: COLONIALISM, CAPITALIST PENETRATION, AND THE "THIRD WORLD"

As we come to identify the factors in state formation as they affect women, we must be careful to think in probabilistic rather than deterministic terms. We need to better understand the relative power of kinship and class, the interplay of household and public economic functions, the flexibility within religious systems, and the relative autonomy or subordination of women, in light of the possibilities open to each society. We should expect to find variations within state-making (and unmaking) societies over time, and between such societies, rather than one simple pattern.

Nowhere is this more evident than in analysis of the process of rapid penetration by patriarchal national states into the so-called Third World. While the history of such penetration varies from place to place and must be taken into account, certain patterns affecting the ways of life of women can be traced at a general level. Wherever women have been active horticulturalists of collective lands, the imposition of private property, taxation, labor migration, and cash cropping has had devastating effects. Their realm of productivity and expertise has been deformed and often destroyed (Blumberg 1976; Boserup 1970; Tinker 1976). Depending upon context, they may become either super-exploited, or underemployed, but always more dependent upon men.

The evidence also suggests a general pattern concerning political organization. Prior to colonial penetration, gender relations in indigenous cultures appear to have been organized along essentially parallel and complementary lines. Men and women had distinct but equally significant roles in production, distribution, and ritual activities.[10] Case histories from Africa, Asia, and the Americas suggest that patriarchal, colonizing powers rather effectively dismantled native work organizations, political structures, and ritual contexts.

Leadership and authority were assigned to male activities, while female tasks and roles were devalued or obliterated. The complementary and parallel gender relations that characterized indigenous societies were destroyed. Several authors have gone so far as to argue that women, thus divested of their social organization and collective roles, have become like underdeveloped, monocrop regions. Once they lived in a diversified world; now they have been reduced to the role of reproducing and exporting labor power for the needs of the international world economy (Bossen 1973; Boulding 1975; Deere 1976).

State formation and penetration occurs over time; its form and force are highly variable, both within and between societies. Yet it is important to remember that the processes which began millennia ago are ongoing. Cumulatively, they continue to transform the lives of the masses of people who exist under their structures. It is a long way from the Sumerian law codes declaring monogamy for women to the welfare laws of the United States which affect parental relations and household structure. But in both cases, the power of the state to penetrate and reorganize the lives of its members is clear. As we seek to understand the complex, stratified societies in which we now operate, we are led to reflect on archaic societies in which the dual and intertwined processes of hierarchy we now retrospectively label "class" and "patriarchy" took their origins.

REFERENCES

Adams, R. M. 1966. *The Evolution of Urban Society.* Chicago. Aldine.

———. 1974. "Anthropological Perspectives on Ancient Trade." *Current Anthropology* 15: 239–258.

Arthur, M. 1976. "Liberated Women: The Classical Era." In R. Bridenthal and C. Koontz (eds.). *Becoming Visible: Women in European History.* pp. 60–89. New York: Houghton and Mifflin.

Blumberg, R. 1976. "Fairy Tales and Facts: Economy, Fertility, Family and the Female." Unpublished paper.

Boserup, E. 1970. *Women's Role in Economic Development.* London: George Allen and Unwin.

Bossen, L. 1973. "Women in Modernizing Societies." *American Ethnologist* 2: 587–601.

Boulding, E. 1975. *Women, Bread, and Babies.* University of Colorado, Institute of Behavioral Sciences, Program on Research of General Social and Economic Development.

Brown, J. 1970. "A Note on the Economic Division of Labor by Sex." *American Anthropologist* 72: 1073–1078.

Brown, J. 1975. "Iroquois Women." In R. Reiter (ed.). *Toward an Anthropology of Women.* pp. 235–252. New York: Monthly Review Press.

Carneiro, R. J. 1970. "A Theory of the Origin of the State." *Science* 169: 733–738.

Childe, G. 1950. "The Urban Revolution." *Town Planning Review* 21 (3): 3–17.

Childe, G. 1952. "The Birth of Civilization." *Past and Present* 2: 1–10.

Deere, C. 1976. "Rural Women's Subsistence Production in the Capitalist Periphery." *Review of Radical Political Economics* 8: 9–18.

Diamond, S. 1951. *Dahomey: A Protostate in West Africa.* Ann Arbor: University of Michigan Press.

Diamond, S. 1974. *In Search of the Primitive: A Critique of Civilization.* New Brunswick, NJ: Transaction Books.

Divale, W., and M. Harris. 1976. "Population Warfare and the Male Supremacist Complex." *American Anthropologist* 78: 521–538.

Eliade, M. 1960. "Structures and Changes in the History of Religions." In C. Kraeling and R. Adams (eds.). *City Invincible.* pp. 331–366. Chicago: University of Chicago Press.

Engels, Frederick. 1973. *The Origin of the Family, Private Property and the State.* New York: International Publishers.

Flannery, K. 1972. "The Cultural Evolution of Civilizations." *Annual Review of Ecology and Systematics* 3: 399–426.

———. Fried, M. 1967. *The Evolution of Political Society.* New York: Random House.

Gailey, Christine Ward. 1987. *Kinship to Kingship: Gender Hierarchy and State Formation in the Tongan Islands.* Austin: University of Texas Press.

Gailey, Christine Ward, and Thomas C. Patterson. 1987. "Power Relations and State Formation." In Thomas C. Patterson and Christine W. Gailey (eds.). *Power Relations and State Formation,* pp. 1–26. Washington, DC: American Anthropological Association.

Goody, J., and S. Tambiah. 1973. *Bridewealth and Dowry.* Cambridge: Cambridge University Press.

Harner, M. 1970. "Population Pressure and Social Evolution of Agriculturalists." *Southwestern Journal of Anthropology* 26: 67–86.

Kirchoff, P. 1959. "The Principles of Clanship in Human Society." In M. Fried (ed.). *Readings in Anthropology* (Vol. 2). pp. 370–382. New York: Thomas Crowell.

Kohl, P. 1975. "The Archaeology of Trade." *Dialectical Anthropology* 1: 43–50.

Krader, L. 1968. *Formation of the State.* Englewood Cliffs: Prentice Hall.

Leacock, Eleanor. 1978. "Women's Status in Egalitarian Society: Implications for Social Evolution." *Current Anthropology* 19: 247–275.

McNamara, J., and S. Wemple. 1973. "The Power of Women through the Family in Medieval Europe: 500–1100." *Feminist Studies* 1: 126–141.

Meillassoux, C. 1975. *Femmes, greniers et capitaux.* Paris: Maspero.

Mintz, S. 1971. "Men, Women and Trade." *Comparative Studies in Society and History* 13: 247–269.

Muller, Viana. 1987. "Kin Reproduction and Elite Accumulation in the Archaic States of Northwest Europe." In Thomas C. Patterson and Christine W. Gailey (eds.). *Power Relations and State Formation.* pp. 81–97. Washington, DC: American Anthropological Association.

Nash, J. 1980. "Aztec Women: The Transition from Status to Class in Empire and Colony." In M. Etienne and E. Leacock (eds.). pp. 134–148. *Women and Colonization.* New York: Praeger.

Ortner, S. 1978. "The Virgin and the State." *Feminist Studies* 4 (3): 19–35.

Pagels, E. 1976. "What Became of God the Mother? Conflicting Images of God in Early Christianity" *Signs* 2: 293–303.

Pomeroy, S. 1975. *Goddesses, Whores, Wives and Slaves.* New York: Schoken Books.

Reiter, R. 1975. "Men and Women in the South of France." In R. Reiter (ed.). *Toward an Anthropology of Women,* pp. 252–282. New York: Monthly Review Press.

Rohrlich, Ruby. 1980. "State Formation in Sumer and the Subjugation of Women." *Feminist Studies* 6: 76–102.

Rubin, G. 1975. "The Traffic in Women." In R. Reiter (ed.). *Toward an Anthropology of Women.* pp. 157–211. New York: Monthly Review Press.

Sabloff, J., and C. C. Lamberg-Karlovsky. 1975. *Ancient Civilizations and Trade.* Albuquerque: University of New Mexico Press.

Sacks, K. 1974. "Engels Revisited." In Michelle Rosaldo and Louise Lamphere (eds.). *Woman, Culture and Society,* pp. 207–222. Stanford: Stanford University Press.

———. 1982. *Sisters and Wives: The Past and Future of Sexual Equality.* Urbana: University of Illinois Press.

Sahlins, M. 1958. *Social Stratification in Polynesia.* Seattle: University of Washington Press.

Sanday, Peggy. 1974. "Toward a Theory of the Status of Women." In Michelle Rosaldo and Louise Lamphere (eds.). *Woman, Culture and Society,* pp. 189–206. Stanford: Stanford University Press.

———. 1981. *Female Power and Male Dominance: On the Origins of Sexual Inequality.* Cambridge: Cambridge University Press.

Service, E. 1975. *Origins of the State and Civilization.* New York: Norton.

Silverblatt, Irene. 1978. "Andean Women in Inca Society." *Feminist Studies* 4 (3): 37–61.

———. 1987. *Moon, Sun, and Witches: Gender Ideologies and Class in Inca and Colonial Peru.* Princeton: Princeton University Press.

———. 1988. "Women in States." *Annual Review of Anthropology* 17: 427–461.

Siskind, J. 1978. "Kinship and Mode of Production." *American Anthropologist* 80: 860–872.

Tilly, C. 1975. "Reflections on the History of European State-Making." In C. Tilly (ed.). *The Formation of National States in Western Europe.* pp. 17–25. Princeton: Princeton University Press.

Tinker, I. 1976. "The Adverse Impact of Development on Women." In I. Tinker and M. Bramsen (eds.). *Women and World Development.* pp. 22–34. Washington, DC: Overseas Development Council.

Van Allen, J. 1972. "Sitting on a Man: Colonialism and the Lost Political Institutions of Igbo Women." *Canadian Journal of African Studies* 6: 165–181.

Webb, M. 1975. "The Flag Follows Trade." In J. Sabloff and C. C. Lamberg-Karlovsky (eds.). *Ancient Civilizations and Trade.* pp. 185–211. Albuquerque: University of New Mexico Press.

Wiley, G., 1974. "Precolumbian Urbanism." In J. Sabloff and C. C. Lamberg-Karlovsky (eds.). *Ancient Civilizations and Trade.* Albuquerque: University of New Mexico Press.

Wiley, G., and D. Shimkin. 1971. "The Collapse of the Classic Maya Civilization in the Southern Lowlands." *Southwestern Journal of Anthropology* 27: 1–18.

Wittfogel, K. 1955. "Oriental Society in Transition." *Far Eastern Quarterly* 14: 469–478.

———. 1957. *Oriental Despotism.* New Haven: Yale University Press.

NOTES

1. Productive activities are those that generate income in cash, or other valued resources. Reproduction refers, broadly, to the set of activities encompassing domestic chores and other

household activities such as childbearing, child-rearing, and cooking.

2. For analyses implicitly or explicitly influenced by Origins, see Brown 1975; Meillassoux 1975; Reiter 1975; Rubin 1975; Sacks 1974; Sanday 1974.

3. Summaries of the state formation literature may be found in Flannery 1972; Krader 1968; Service 1975; Webb 1975.

4. A less determinant and more processual perspective on stratification and state formation is set forth in Flannery 1972; Sabloff and Lamberg-Karlovsky 1975; and Tilly 1975. Such thinking also informs the corpus of Marxist historiography.

5. This has been a major thrust in Stanley Diamond's work (1951, 1974).

6. Such links are suggested in Flannery 1972; Wiley and Shimkin 1971; and by much of the literature

on stratified chiefdoms (Sahlins 1958; Kirchoff 1959; and Fried 1967). In European history, we find instances in the international royal marriage patterns. See McNamara and Wemple (1973) for some of the implications of feudal marriage patterns.

7. See Arthur 1976; Ortner 1978; Goody and Tambiah 1973.

8. The temple and military complexes figure in the state formation schemes of Adams 1966; Steward 1955; and Wiley 1974 to name but a few.

9. The archaeology of trade is discussed in Sabloff and Lamberg-Karlovsky 1975, and is critically summarized in Adams 1974 and Kohl 1975. See also Wiley 1974.

10. Parallel and interarticulating forms of gender social organization are analyzed by Brown 1970; Silverblatt 1978; Siskind 1978; and Van Allen 1972.

Dowry, Bride-Burning, and Female Power in India

Linda Stone and Caroline James

Over the last two decades, the reports from India have shocked the world: married women murdered (usually burned to death) by their husbands and/or in-laws over the issue of inadequate dowry. These recent incidents of bride-burning are a shocking example of the new forms of violence against women which are arising in modern, or modernizing, settings in many areas of the world. In India, these events are occurring alongside the growth of feminist organizations, the expansion of educational and economic opportunities for women, and some societal questioning of traditional gender roles.

This article examines the bride-burning problem in India by looking at recent changes which have occurred not only with respect to dowry transactions, but also with respect to more traditional sources of female domestic

Reprinted from *Women's Studies International Forum*, Vol 18, No 2, Stone and James, "Dowry, Bridge-Burning and Female Power in India," pp. 125–135, March/April 1995. © 1995, with permission from Elsevier.

power. It is not possible here to consider all of the complex factors which are contributing to the dowry murders in India, but we suggest, though necessarily tentatively, that along with the traditional lack of female control over family property and marriage arrangements, the problem may be further compounded by a new loss of female power in another important sphere, namely the power women could traditionally exercise through their fertility.

The article draws upon published accounts of bride-burning combined with material from interviews with a bride-burning survivor carried out by one of the authors (James). This case emerged not from research focused on bride-burning, but rather as part of a larger study of literacy programs in adult education centers in Madhya Pradesh. In this study James (1988) found that many of the women who came to the adult education centers were fleeing dowry harassment or attempted burnings. The case we present here was selected for the depth and detail of information provided by the woman involved.

Before examining dowry murders, we offer some comments on dowry in India to place the issue in a broader cross-cultural perspective.

DOWRY IN INDIA

One feature of dowry systems in general which applies strongly to India is their association with socioeconomic stratification and the concerns of kin groups with maintaining or enhancing social status through marriage. In an historical treatment of dowry, Goody (1971, 1973, 1976) argued that in Eurasia, in contrast to Africa, intensive plow agriculture created differential wealth, promoting divisions between status groups. It then became important to perpetuate these divisions over the generations to insure that control over property remained within the status group. This was achieved in part by instituting "status group endogamy" through the mechanism of dowry marriage. Thus, "status group endogamy"

> . . . is not simply a question of the absence of marriage between groups . . . but of matching like for like, or getting an even better bargain. And the usual mechanism by which this is achieved is the matching of property, often by means of the dowry. . . . (Goody, 1973, p. 593)

Dowry, then, goes hand-in hand with a class system and with maintenance of the superiority of higher groups over lower. Here marriages, at least among the upper classes, must be well-controlled and, by extension, so must courtship. The roles of matchmaker and chaperone become important in this Eurasian context, along with a high value placed on female virginity at marriage (Goody, 1976, p. 17). Women must be endowed with property in order to attract husbands of equal or higher rank, and their sexuality must be controlled in order to limit ". . . the possibility of conflicting claims on the estate in which a woman has rights" (Goody, 1976, p. 14). Schlegel (1991) has more recently confirmed the strong association between dowry transactions and cultural concerns with female premarital virginity, which, she argues, helps to prevent lower class

males from claiming wealth through impregnating higher class females. Ultimately the whole complex of cultural values centering on female "purity" and the notion that the honor of male kin groups rests on the seclusion and sexual purity of its women (see Mandelbaum, 1988) is related to the institution of dowry as an instrument in preserving and perpetuating socioeconomic classes. As we shall see, both the themes of social status and female chastity recur through accounts of dowry murders.

There is, however, another common idea about dowry systems which does not apply well in India. This is the idea that dowry is a form of female property or wealth. Thus, Goody (1973) and others (e.g., Tambiah, 1973) have seen Eurasian dowry universally as "female inheritance"—women receive a portion of the family estate at marriage, rather than upon the death of the father or mother. This portion they receive as movable property rather than land which is left to sons. But many working in India, such as Miller (1981) and Sharma (1984), have convincingly shown that whereas this may be true in many areas of the world, in India dowry is property which passes from the bride's family to that of the groom, and that even if perceived to be "women's property" (*stridhan*) by some Indians themselves, in fact a bride does not have (and historically never had) genuine control over the use and distribution of this property. Women in the Indian dowry system should be seen as vehicles of property transmission rather than as true inheritors.

Madhu Kishwar (1986), who has written several articles on dowry for the Indian feminist magazine *Manushi*, has argued that Indian dowry effectively functions to disinherit women and promote their economic dependency on men, which in her view is the real crux of the modern problem of dowry murders. Although current law permits daughters to inherit from the father's estate, more often women are upon marriage made to sign over these rights to their brothers. As for the dowry itself, Kishwar (1986) writes:

> In actuality, a woman is seldom allowed to have control even over things that are supposedly for

her personal use. Gold and other jewelry are traditionally supposed to be a woman's personal security, but, in practice, the gold usually stays in the custody of her mother-in-law or husband. It is up to them to give her what they wish for her personal use and daily wear. . . . It is fairly common for certain items of her jewelry to be incorporated into her husband's sister's dowry. (pp. 6–7)

Moreover, Kishwar points out that were the point of Indian dowry to provide a daughter with some financial security, parents would give her productive assets such as land or a shop, rather than clothing and household goods, which depreciate in value.

Defining dowry as female inheritance, Goody (1976) saw it as a kind of economic "gain" for women. But the irony, to him, was that the system also entails a "loss" of women's control over their marriages or their sexual behavior:

The positive control of marriage arrangements . . . is stricter where property is transmitted to women. It is a commentary on their lot that where they are more propertied they are initially less free as far as marital arrangements go. (Goody, 1976, p. 21)

But in the Indian context, it would appear that women lose on all counts. This context (and the whole question of sources, or lack of sources, of female power) is important to bear in mind in any discussion of dowry murders. In India dowry not only serves to promote status group endogamy (hypergamy) to maintain a class system, but it is now actively manipulated to serve new ends of status-seeking among individual families. In this modern context, women as vehicles of property transmission not only lack control over both property and marriage arrangements, as was largely the case previously, but may in fact suffer considerable harassment, physical abuse, and even murder in connection with their roles as bringers of dowry.

DOWRY MURDERS

From what is known about dowry deaths, it is possible to see some patterns, although exceptions exist in every case. They appear to be largely, though not exclusively, occurring in Northwest India, and they are largely, though no longer exclusively, among Hindu groups. They occur most often in cases of arranged marriages (the most common form of marriage in India) but have occurred in cases of a "love match," and they occur predominantly among the urban middle-class (Kumari, 1989; van Willigen & Channa, 1991). It is difficult to know how widespread the problem is, but most conservative estimates are that at least 2000 women are victims of dowry deaths per year in India (Chhabra, 1986, pp. 12–13). The area showing the greatest problem is New Delhi, with an estimated two dowry deaths per day (Bordewich, 1986, p. 21). The number of reported cases increases yearly. It is not known to what extent the increase reflects an increase in reporting rather than an increase in the crime. However, it may be that the crime is still underreported since the number of hospital cases of severe burns in young married women exceeds reports of violence against women by burning (Kumari, 1989, p. 24).

The preponderance of cases of bride-burning in North India is significant. This is also the area in which Miller (1981) finds significantly more males than females in juvenile age groups. This she attributes to neglect of female children, who are an economic liability relative to males. In the Northern region, too, dowry marriages are more common. The expense of providing dowry for daughters is one reason which Miller finds for the relatively intense preference for sons and relative neglect of female children in the North.

Sharma suggests that North Indian dowry has dramatically inflated as India has shifted to a market, cash economy over the last 50 years: ". . . dowry used to be more or less conventionally determined and many items could be made in whole or part by members of the bride's family themselves (e.g. rugs, clothing, bedding)" (Sharma, 1984, p. 70). But now, especially among the urban middle classes, expectations of televisions, motor scooters, refrigerators, large sums of cash, and so on are usual. Many observers related modern dowry and dowry deaths to the frustration of the urban middle class, caught in a new consumerism, status-seeking, and rising expectations of a life style they cannot on their own earning power quite afford (Bordewich, 1986, pp. 24–25).

Sharma's (1984) work on dowry has also cleared up one confusion, namely how it is that marriageable women appear to be in great supply (everyone is anxious to marry off a daughter and even accused dowry murderers manage to secure new brides!) even though there are far more males than females in the marriageable age groups in the North. Hypergamy (marriage of women upward into higher status groups) was traditionally common in the North and with modern dowry is becoming more so. In addition, lessening of caste restrictions in modern marriages promotes more hypergamous competition. Dowry givers are thus competing upwards for scarce grooms at the top (Sharma, 1984, p. 72).

Dowry and dowry murders continue despite the fact that dowry transactions have been illegal in India since the Dowry Prohibition Act of 1961.[1] As a result of pressure by women's organizations, subsequent amendments to the Act have even strengthened the laws against dowry and dowry harassment (Ghadially & Kumar, 1988, pp. 175–176). However, what is actually dowry can be legally claimed as "voluntary gifts" at marriage. Dowry persists not only because the law is ineffective or difficult to enforce, nor because of the pressures and demands of the groom's family, but also because the families of brides, in spite of growing public awareness of the tragic consequences, continue to give dowry. This may be due to concerns that otherwise a daughter could not be married at all (universally considered an undesirable event in India), or that the family could not secure an appropriate match. Also, parents of the bride may continue to believe that a lavish dowry will help to secure their daughter's favorable treatment in her in-laws' home, after which they may "yield to extortion out of fear for their daughter's safety . . ." (Bordewich, 1986, p. 24). Stein (1988) reports that many Indian women "still believe . . . that not only can dowry be used to overcome disadvantages in the marriage market, such as dark skin color, but it gives them dignity and status" (p. 485).

From the reported cases of dowry murders, it appears that the difficulties usually start early in the marriage. A new bride is harassed and criticized for the pitiful dowry she has brought. She is encouraged to wrangle more and more from her family, yet her in-laws remain unsatisfied until, at some point, the situation explodes into an attempt on her life. One woman ("Sita") whose husband attempted to burn her, reported the following:

> I got married when I was 23 years old to a person whose family was not as wealthy as our family. My father [a businessman] gave $8,000 cash as dowry. [He] gave me expensive clothes like 500 saris, 10 golden jewelry sets and one diamond set, all the pots and pans necessary for the house, a television set, wardrobe, freezer, cooler fan, double bed, furniture and other things he thought would be useful in the house. More than that, he used to send things from time to time, like on festivals. One year of my marriage has not passed when my in-laws and husband started giving me trouble every day for more dowry. My mother-in-law started telling my husband, "Leave this woman and we will get you another one, at least the other party will give us more and better dowry than what these people have given us. What her parents have given us is nothing. Moreover, this girl is ugly and she is dark."

Sita's reference to the relative wealth of her family and her detailed description of her lavish dowry appear to reinforce the same materialistic values which evidently lie behind dowry harassment and murders. Later she spoke with bitter resentment about her husband's new wife who ". . . is using all my things, like all my expensive saris, jewelry and other things." Her account also suggests a blatant economic motive for dowry murder—that it frees the woman's in-laws to get a new bride and an additional dowry. A similar idea reported in an article by Bordewich (1986) is expressed by the father of an allegedly murdered bride:

> . . . as soon as we agreed on the marriage they started troubling us. First they told us to buy diamond rings instead of mere gold ones. . . . Then they insisted on a sofa bed for fifteen thousand rupees, but I could only afford one that cost seven thousand. Whatever was in my means I did, but they were always displeased . . . they

demanded a stereo and tape-cassette system, and then they asked for saris for the boy's sisters . . . and then for a gas stove. I gave them . . . I had read that there were so many tortures and murders of young women over dowry and I was afraid of what might happen to [my daughter]. I told them I would pay whatever I could. . . . But they didn't even wait for the money to come. They probably realized they had gotten all they could from us. A few days later [my daughter] was dead. . . . There has never been an investigation. . . . Now they can marry their son to another girl and get another dowry. (p. 25)

The most common means of murder is soaking the bride in kerosene and setting her aflame, with a report to the police of a suicide or an accident in the kitchen. Sita describes how this was attempted on her:

[The winter my son was born] my mother-in-law started telling me not to wear so much gold jewelry at home, to remove it at night and keep it in the wardrobe. I did not understand why she was telling me this when she had not done so before. But I did what she asked. [Then] one evening my husband went into the kitchen and asked for a match box. My mother-in-law's sister-in-law gave him a match box which my husband then kept in the wardrobe very close to our bed. Then he left the house, saying he would be coming in late that night. That same evening, the electricity went off and my mother-in-law's sister-in-law came to get the match box to light a lamp. She found the match box in the wardrobe and took it. My husband came in very late that night when my son and I were sound asleep. Due to the cold, I had pulled the covers up over our heads. Suddenly I felt that the quilt was wet and cold, but I thought it was just due to being cold at night. But when I removed the quilt from my face, there was a strong smell of kerosene. I got up quickly and saw my husband getting into bed and covering himself, pretending he was sound asleep . . . he had been looking for the match box which he could not find. You can imagine that if he could have found the match box, my son and I would not have survived. We would have been burned to ashes.

One theme recurrent in many dowry murder cases is the issue of the bride's "reputation" and sexual "purity," which, as we saw in Goody's (1976) discussions of dowry, serves as a link between the institution of dowry, family concerns with status, and the perpetuation of socioeconomic classes. With respect to this issue, a woman facing dowry harassment is truly vulnerable as any suggestion of her "loose" character is an easy defense for her husband or in-laws. In the case above Sita reports that after fleeing from the bed,

I started crying loudly, then my husband and mother-in-law came and started telling me to leave the house. I told them I would not step out of the house until my parents came, because if I would have left the house, they would have told the police and everybody that I was the one who wanted to leave the husband and the house, that it was my fault and not anyone else's in the family. They would have cooked up another story that I am a bad character and that that is why I left the house at that hour of the night (3:00 a.m.).

In a dowry murder case discussed by Kumari (1989), the husband accused of burning his young wife claimed that she had committed suicide because she could not forget her own "murky past" involving previous sexual activity (p. 64). Similarly, in newspaper accounts of dowry deaths it is common to find some innuendo of lapsed sexual behavior on the part of the victim.[2] Also illustrative is the following account, taken down by Bordewich (1986), from a woman who virtually sees a dowry murder:

. . . In the house across the street we could see a man beating his wife. I went out onto the balcony and saw that the neighbors had gathered in the street to watch. . . . A moment later I heard a scream . . . and there in front of me was the woman, burning in the window. She tried to wrap herself in the curtains, but they went up in flames. I ran into the street, but none of the neighbors seemed disturbed. People were saying it was "just a domestic issue" or that the woman must have had "a loose moral character." The woman died soon afterward in the hospital. The husband was never charged. (p. 26)

Dowry, Fertility, and Female Power

Dowry murders must be viewed within the context of Indian culture, which is characterized by patrilineal descent, patrilocality, the joint family, and strongly prescribed subservience of wives to husbands and in-laws. In both the popular press and scholarly literature, discussions of dowry murders incorporate these and other elements of Indian cultural traditions and women's roles within them. Certainly the association of death, fire, and female chastity or purity has caught the attention of writers who have drawn parallels between modern bride-burning and the ancient upper caste custom of *sati*, or the burning of a widow alive on her husband's funeral pyre. This was considered a (theoretically self-willed) act of great religious merit, only to be performed by a chaste wife in a state of ritual purity (Stein, 1988, p. 464). Again, in Hindu mythology, Sita must prove her chastity to her husband, Rama, through passing unburned through fire, and in another myth Sati Devi proves her loyalty to her husband, Shiva, by leaping to her death into the ceremonial fire of her father who insulted him.

Whatever deeper meaning all this may have within the Indian consciousness, Stein (1988) rightly points out that both the ancient sati and modern bride-burning reflect one clear fact of Indian life: the unacceptability of the unmarried adult woman. Thus sati was a way to dispose of the widow, who in earlier times among high castes, could not remarry, but who could, if alive, remain in society as a threatening, uncontrolled sexual woman. In the modern context, the existence of an unmarried adult daughter, with all the same connotations of uncontrolled, dangerous sexuality, brings shame and dishonor to her parents whose duty it is to marry her off, and who receive religious merit for doing so. So great is the pressure to marry the daughter (and keep her married, a divorced woman being equally unacceptable and threatening in Indian society) that a woman's parents remain in a weak and vulnerable position with respect to dowry harassment. Stein (1988) concludes:

> . . . marriage is still seen as the only way in which Indian women can be part of their own society, can function as social beings, even at the expense of their own personalities, and occasionally their lives. (p. 485)

The situation is compounded by another deep-rooted Indian tradition: the religious and social inferiority of the bride's family to that of the groom. In Hindu tradition a bride is a religious gift (*kanyadan*, gift of the virgin) and, as such, can only be given upward to those of higher rank, those to whom one must show perpetual deference and respect. The inferior and subservient position of a wife to her husband is on another level shared by the family who gives her. Thus "the subordination and frequently oppressed position of the daughter-in-law is exacerbated by the exclusion and deference of her own kin" (Stein, 1988, p. 476).

Kishwar (1986) also refers to these relationships in her discussions of dowry deaths, highlighting the powerless position of a bride and her parents. For her, dowry harassment is but one of many techniques by which a groom and his family can humiliate a bride to "accept a subordinate position within the family and feel grateful for being allowed to survive at all in the marital home" (p. 4). She also affirms that marriage of the daughter and dowry are matters of status and family honor, so that ". . . most parents would rather see their daughters dead than have them get a divorce and return permanently to the parental home" (p. 5).

Chhabra (1986), noting the many cases of dowry deaths which involve the mother-in-law, discusses the role of the traditionally problematic relationship between a woman and her daughter-in-law in India in terms of modern dowry harassment. Participating in or encouraging dowry harassment is the mother-in-law's way of rejecting the new bride, whom she perceives as a threat to her son's support and loyalty to herself (pp. 6–10).

All of these sociocultural factors and many more are fundamental to accounting for dowry deaths and, along with the inability of police and the courts to alleviate the problem, go a long way toward explaining why these deaths persist. However, most of these cultural traditions, which have in various ways, degrees, and combinations deeply shaped Indian women's lives, have been around for centuries, whereas dowry murders are apparently quite new, becoming a recognized social issue in India in the 1970s (Kumari, 1989). The concept of "dowry death" was only legally established in India in the 1980s (van Willigen & Channa, 1991, p. 371).

What has changed in Indian society to bring about this form of violence against women? Along with the new socioeconomic issues already referred to, it is important to ask also whether women in this modern context have lost sources of power which previously gave them some leverage. Despite all the constraints on women and the general sense of powerlessness which any account of the traditional Hindu woman's life will give, it was still the case that a new bride did not endlessly suffer ill-treatment from and subservience to in-laws, but gradually transformed herself from lowly bride to respected mother, perhaps eventually to become a powerful mother-in-law herself.[3] Regardless of however lowly the position of the affinal women in this strongly patrilineal society, she was, at worst, a necessary evil since she alone held the power to reproduce the husband's lineage. In a more traditional scenario, the adept Hindu woman tried to please her husband not only to express a culturally required subservience but also in order to become pregnant, as this would ultimately be her way out of misery and toward a rising status within the husband's household. With each sign of successful fertility, and particularly with the birth of sons, her position improved. As with many areas of Asia, sons were desired to continue the patrilineage, serve as heirs, perform important funeral rituals for parents, and to provide security in old age. Economically they contributed to home-based production or could bring in cash income.

A woman's fertility was the key to what can be considered a "great transition" in her status and identity. Summarizing this for the whole of India, Mandelbaum (1970) wrote of the bride that

> . . . the real relief comes when she becomes pregnant. Her mother-in-law can afford to relax a bit in her role as taskmistress; her husband is pleased; the men of the household are glad; there is an awakened interest in seeing that she eats well and rests easily. This first burgeoning also marks her first upward move in the family status hierarchy. . . . [then with childbirth] She is no longer the lowly probationer she was at first.

If the child is a son, she has proved herself in the most important way of all and her confidence is the more secure. The son is her social redeemer and thenceforth her importance in the family tends gradually to increase. (pp. 88–89)

Raising this issue shifts the focus somewhat away from dowry, over which women evidently never had much control, and toward other sources of female power which may be changing, at least among the urban middle classes of the North. In a sense, female fertility, or the high value placed on women's successful reproduction, may have served as a "safety valve" for women in the past. But once this fertility value diminishes, women's position is indeed insecure. One startling feature of the dowry murder cases is the high number of women murdered who had already produced children, even sons. In one study 36% of the dowry murder cases involved women who had already produced children; another 11% of the women were pregnant at the time of death (Ghadially & Kumar, 1988, p. 168). Although she does not give numbers, Stein (1988) notes of dowry murder victims that ". . . a surprising number of them are pregnant when they die" (pp. 474–475).

Even victims of dowry harassment seem surprised to realize that childbirth and particularly the birth of a son does not alleviate their situation. Sita, in the case discussed earlier, remarked that after being harassed over dowry, "I gave birth to a male child. [But even with this] they did not want to keep me or the child either. They cared only for the dowry." Similarly in the case of Suman, described in the Indian feminist magazine *Manushi*, it was reported that

> . . . [the husband's] maltreatment of Suman continued to escalate. He pawned all her jewelry. Even the birth of her son did not improve the situation. When the son was a year old, Suman was once more beaten and thrown out of the house in the hope of pressuring her parents to give more dowry. (Kishwar, 1986, p. 8)

Demographic data from India supports the suggestion that the country's traditional strong value on high fertility may be changing. Fertility rates are declining and have been since the mid-1960s. An analysis of the 1981 census produced the following report:

India, the second most populous country in the world, is experiencing the early stages of fertility transition. The unprecedented acceleration in the rate of growth of India's population, sparked off by declining mortality as early as 1921, has finally been arrested. . . . It is beyond doubt that a significant contribution to this phenomenon lately has been from declining fertility, of which there is ample cumulative evidence. (Rele, 1987, p. 513)

One reason for the decline is undoubtedly urbanization, which tends to dampen fertility since the "cost" of children increases while their economic benefits decline. The above report also shows that the pace of decline is accelerating and that although the decline is occurring in both rural and urban areas, urban fertility remains much lower than rural fertility. Other studies show that fertility rates are lower and declining faster among wealthier and more educated groups (Goyal, 1989). Along with fertility declines, some studies show declines in desired number of children, again most notable among urban, educated, and wealthier groups (Jejeebhoy & Kulkami, 1989).

Could it be that changes in fertility values are taking place and that, however advantageous this may be for India's population problems, it may be a contributing factor to dowry murders? Demonstrating a significant change in fertility values (beyond merely showing a decline in fertility levels) and a definite connection with dowry murders would, of course, require much further research. Nevertheless, our inquiry into dowry murders, and discussion of the problem within the context of more traditional ways in which women acquired some domestic leverage, is suggestive. Previously through much of India a large joint family and the production of many sons was itself a source of prestige. Through successful reproduction, women could gain respect and greater security in the husband's household. In today's context, children and grandchildren, though undoubtedly still desired for all the same cultural reasons as before, become economically

less important. At the same time a new urban consumerism and concern with material displays of wealth is widely reported in India and is directly referred to in all studies of dowry deaths. We suggest that insofar as these shifts in values may be occurring, they may diminish the domestic leverage women once exercised through reproduction.

WOMEN IN PRODUCTION AND REPRODUCTION

In his study of dowry systems, Goody (1976) incorporated the work of Boserup (1970), who distinguished systems of "female farming" (shifting cultivation), where women perform the major part of agricultural work, from "male farming" (plow agriculture) where male labor predominates. The latter is associated with private land ownership, a landless class of laborers, and dowry, as opposed to bridewealth marriages. Boserup saw the development of male farming in Asia, and the later shift to male farming in Africa, as detrimental to women since the diminution of their roles in production increased their economic and social marginalization.[4]

Boserup (1970) made the important point that in regions of female farming, women are valued both as workers and as child bearers, whereas in systems of male farming, they are valued as mothers only (p. 51). Applying these ideas to modern, urban India (where the valued economic activity is income-earning), it appears that a new problem facing women, at least among the middle classes, may be that women lack value, and therefore power, either as workers or as mothers. Of course middle class Indian women can and do make important contributions to household income, increasingly so in the modern context. But, as Sharma (1984) points out, we need to look at women's work in relation to the proportion of their economic potential relative to that of men:

It might be possible to show that the expansion of dowry has been accompanied by a decline in women's capacity to contribute household income compared with that of men, even though there has been no absolute diminution of women's economic activity. New opportunities to earn cash wages in factories, in government employment and white collar occupations have expanded far more rapidly for men than for women. . . . (pp. 67–68)

Boserup's critics (Beneria & Sen, 1981) claim that one problem with her analysis is that she ignored women's roles in reproduction. Their point is that women's reproductive roles in many cases hinder their full or equal participation in wage labor or other socially valued economic activities, whereas Boserup laid the blame on sexually biased cultural values and changes in technology. In fact, however, Boserup did address women's roles in reproduction, though not quite in the way her critics would have liked to have seen. Writing before 1970, she seems to have foreseen that changes in fertility values could occur and could negatively impact women. Speaking in general of societies with male farming systems, where women have been devalued as workers but are still valued as mothers, she wrote: "There is a danger in such a community that the propaganda for birth control, if successful, may further lower the status of women both in the eyes of men and in their own eyes" (Boserup, 1970, p. 51). Whereas it is unlikely that "propaganda for birth control" alone would have this effect, it may be that in India, urbanization and the growth of the consumer economy are bringing about the same result.

CONCLUSION

Many observers of the problem of dowry murders in India have contributed to showing a powerful link between this form of violence against women and women's relative lack of economic power. With the urbanization and consumerism characterizing India today, women have not shared in access to new economic opportunities with men. We suggest that at the same time, their one traditional source of leverage, their fertility, has possibly diminished in value. Regrettably, women are valued for the dowry they will bring; but so long as

their valuation rests primarily in their being vehicles of property transmission, they will remain vulnerable to dowry harassment and murder.

REFERENCES

Beneria, Lourdes, and Sen, Gita. (1981). "Accumulation, Reproduction, and Women's Role in Economic Development: Boserup Revisited." *Signs,* 7, 279–298.

Bennett, Lynn. (1983). *Dangerous Wives and Sacred Sisters: Social and Religious Roles of High Caste Women in Nepal.* New York: Columbia University Press.

Bordewich, Fergus M. (1986). "Dowry Murders." *Atlantic Magazine,* July, pp. 21–27.

Boserup, Ester. (1970). *Women's Role in Economic Development.* London: George Allen & Unwin, Ltd.

Chhabra, Sagari. (1986). *Dowry Deaths in India: A Double Bind Perspective.* Unpublished master's thesis, Washington State University, Pullman.

Engels, Fredrich. (1884). *The Origin of the Family, Private Property, and the State.* New York: International.

Ghadially, Rehana, and Kumar, Promod. (1988). "Bride-burning: The Psycho-Social Dynamics of Dowry Deaths." In Rehana Ghadially (Ed.), *Women in Indian Society* (pp. 167–177). New Delhi: Sage Publications.

Goody, Jack. (1971). "Class and Marriage in Africa and Eurasia." *American Journal of Sociology.* 76, 585–603.

———. (1973). "Bridewealth and Dowry in Africa and Eurasia." Jack Goody and S. J. Tambiah (Eds.), *Bridewealth and Dowry* (pp. 1–58). Cambridge: Cambridge University Press.

———. (1976). *Production and Reproduction.* Cambridge: Cambridge University Press.

Goyal, R. S. (1989). "Social Inequalities and Fertility Behavior." In S. N. Singh, M. K. Premi, P. S. Bhatia, and Ashish Bose (Eds.), *Population Transition in India* (Vol. 2, pp. 153–161). New Delhi: B. R. Publishing Corporation.

James, Caroline. (1988). *People and Projects in Development Anthropology: A Literacy Project in Madhya Pradesh, India.* Unpublished Ph.D. dissertation, Washington State University, Pullman.

Jejeebhoy, Shireen J., and Sumati Kulkami. (1989). "Demand for Children and Reproductive Motivation: Empirical Observations from Rural Maharashtra." In Singh, M. K. Premi, P. S. Bhatia, and Ashish Bose (Eds.), *Population Transition in*

India (Vol. 2; pp. 107–121). New Delhi: B. R. Publishing Corporation.

Kishwar, Madhu. (1986). Dowry: "To Ensure Her Happiness or to Disinherit Her?" *Manushi*, 34, 2–13.

Kumari, Rajana. (1989). *Brides are Not for Burning: Dowry Victims in India.* London: Sangam Books Ltd.

Leacock, Eleanor, Safa, Helen, and contributors. (1986). *Women's Work, Development and the Division of Labor by Gender.* Boston: Bergin and Garvey Publishers, Inc.

Mandelbaum, David, (1970). "Society in India," Vol 1: *Continuity and Change.* Berkeley: University of California Press.

————, (1988). *Women's Seclusion and Men's Honor.* Tucson: University of Arizona Press.

Miller, Barbara. (1981). *The Endangered Sex.* Ithaca: Cornell University Press.

Rele, J. R. (1987). "Fertility Levels and Trends in India." *Population and Development Review*, 13, 513–530.

Schlegel, Alice. (1991). "Status, Property and the Value on Virginity." *American Ethnologist*, 18, 719–734.

Sharma, Ursula. (1984). "Dowry in North India: Its Consequences for Women." In Renee Hirschon (Ed.). *Women and Property—Women as Property* (pp. 62–73). New York: St. Martin's Press.

Stein, Dorothy. (1988). "Burning Widows, Burning Brides: The Perils of Daughterhood in India." *Pacific Affairs,* 61, 465–485.

Tambiah, S. J. (1973). "Dowry and Bridewealth and the Property Rights of Women in South Asia." In Jack Goody and S. J. Tambiah (Eds.), *Bridewealth and Dowry* (pp. 59–169). Cambridge, UK: Cambridge University Press.

Tiano, Susan. (1987). "Gender, Work and World Capitalism: Third World Women's Role in Development." In Beth B. Hess and Myra Marx Ferree (Eds.), *Analyzing Gender: A Handbook of Social Science Research* (pp. 216–243). Newbury Park: Sage Publications.

van Willigen, John, and V. C. Channa, (1991). "Law, Custom, and Crimes Against Women: The Problem of Dowry Death in India." *Human Organization*, 50, 369–376.

NOTES

1. In India there has been a long history of anti-dowry movements, and only recently have they concerned dowry harassment and murder issues. For discussion, see Kumari (1989).
2. This observation was made by Frank Myka (personal communication) in his review of cases of dowry murders in the *Hindustan Times* during 1989.
3. For discussion of these aspects of women's lives in Hindu Nepal, see Bennett (1983).
4. Boserup's work was an early contribution to what has become a vast literature that links female subordination to women's roles in production and women's access to property. Many of the arguments put forth in this line of research follow, with modification, Engels' (1884) treatise on the origin of the family. Important current studies can be found in Leacock and Safa (1986). Modern studies have in general emphasized that both the development of the world capitalist system and international development projects in the Third World have had adverse consequences for women. Today, different positions are taken within this framework. For a review of the literature, see Tiano (1987).

Encountering the State:
Cross-Cultural Perspectives on Women's Political Experience

Josephine Caldwell Ryan

In 1987, a Kenyan woman named Wambui Otieno became involved in a protracted legal

Original material prepared for this text. Reprinted by permission of the author

battle that pitted her against her husband's family (Nzomo 1997; Nzomo and Staudt 1994). Otieno, a Christian Kikuyu, had married a Luo man who, suspecting that his family might attempt to dispossess his wife after his death, had asked to be buried on his farm near Nairobi. The case was decided in favor of Otieno's husband's relatives, and he was buried in his natal village instead. The case had clear implications for women's rights in customary law, a fact that was not lost on Otieno. According to the *Washington Post,* she "warned Kenyan women that if she did not have the right to bury her husband, then they may not have the right to inherit their husband's property" (May 25, 1987, cited in Nzomo 1997: 242).

In Wambui Otieno's case, she did retain control over property rights, but this is not always the outcome. In sub-Saharan African countries with plural legal systems, disputes may be settled in courts of statutory law, customary law, and in some cases, Islamic law. Zambia, for example, has a dual legal system in which both customary law and statutory laws apply to inheritance. Statutory law, which gives more consideration to women's inheritance rights, is frequently ignored in favor of customary law that privileges male kinship ties over conjugal ties should the husband die intestate. The specifics of applicable customary law vary between ethnic groups, but in general, widows may be "inherited" as part of the estate or may be left destitute as a result of "property-grabbing" by the husband's family. New laws have attempted to address the problem by allowing men to designate women as heirs in their wills, but the problem persists. The Intestate Succession Act of 1989, for example, allows a woman to contest property-grabbing, yet a study by the Women in Southern Africa Research Trust found that most women do not take advantage of the law because of fear of witchcraft being worked against them by the husband's relatives (Munalula and Mwenda 1995: 99).

The first case provides an example of a woman choosing to use a legal system to fight for her rights, while the second shows the failure of law to ensure that women's rights are protected even when that is the intent. This essay draws upon data from a variety of cultural contexts to illustrate ways in which women engage, respond to, or resist the state. Depending on their circumstances, women's interaction with the state may take the shape of formal participation (i.e., electoral politics), participation in women's movements or other forms of collective action with a political intent or effect, or individual responses to state policies that directly or indirectly affect quality of life for themselves and their families.

It is understood that the term "state" is not being considered as an impersonal, homogeneous force exclusively for evil or good but rather, as Waylen has observed, "a differentiated set of institutions, agencies, and discourses, and the product of a particular historical and political conjuncture (1998: 7). The term "political engagement" is also used in a broad sense. Since the 1970s Western feminist scholars have mounted a critique of male-dominated mainstream political practice and "politics" as an area of intellectual investigation. Deconstructing the androcentric biases inherent in the language and basic concepts of political science, they have argued for a broader definition of politics, one that would include activities of women not usually considered to be within the parameters of "conventional politics" (Paxton and Hughes 2007; Phillips 1998; Randall and Waylen 1998; Silverblatt 1988; Waylen 1996). It is not the intention here to present a comprehensive survey of women's political activities or power; Silverblatt (1988: 452) is correct in her observation that "no uniform history of women in the state can account for the complex, often contradictory, histories of how women have engaged their particular political worlds."

CURRENT TRENDS AFFECTING WOMEN'S POLITICAL STATUS

In the last twenty years there has been a dramatic increase in the number of women office-holders globally, most notably as legislators. The world average percentage of women in national parliaments has reached 17.5 percent, but this aggregate figure masks the real disparity between regions such as the Arab states, where 9 percent of members of parliaments are women and the Nordic countries, where the current figure is nearly 42 percent

(Inter-parliamentary Union 2007). With a few exceptions, women in contemporary states have the legal right to vote, but this does not mean it can always be exercised.[1] For example, Patience Ndetei, an elected member the Kenyan Parliament, made the following comments regarding the 1988 elections:

> My experience in the field was that a lot of women do not have the final say, especially at home as to whom they should vote for. I had a woman who was badly beaten by her husband and she had to run away from him simply because she was going to vote for me. I confronted many other cases where women were not free (*Daily Nation*, April 30, 1988, cited in Nzomo 1997: 237).

Contemporary feminist political theorists have suggested that formal representation (legal rights) is only the first step to political gender equality. Descriptive representation addresses the question of whether legislative and executive bodies actually represent the demographic, ethnic and other characteristics of their constituents. Paxton and Hughes (2007) identify five historical pathways to increase or decline in women's descriptive representation: flat rates, consistent increases in representation, rapid and significant increases ("big jumps"), small gains, and plateaus or falling rates. In Rwanda, female representation leaped from 4.3 percent to 17.1 percent in 1997, and in 2003, changes in the Rwandan constitution resulted in even more women being elected; currently Rwanda has the highest percentage of female legislators (48.8 percent) of any nation in the world (Paxton and Hughes 2007: 75). In contrast to the "big jump" Rwanda experienced, many of the former Soviet bloc nations saw steep declines in women's representation in the 1990s.

Jane Jaquette (1997) observed that women's political participation and representation does not automatically result from having the right to vote, cannot be explained solely by cultural factors such as the degree of gender equality, and cannot be predicted by the level of economic development. For example, women's representation in the Japanese parliament was about two percent until 1986 when a wave of

women's activism known as the "Madonna Boom" led to more women winning parliament seats (Iwamoto 2001). A combination of factors, including the effects of persistent attitudes regarding proper feminine behavior and strict campaign regulations, have been suggested to explain Japan's relatively low levels political representation for women (Paxton and Hughes 2007: 249). Jaquette (1997: 27) attributed the global increase in female officeholders to three interconnected factors: the rise of a worldwide women's movement, a new willingness by parties and states to ease the constraints on women's access to politics through electoral reforms such as quotas, and a changed post–Cold War political environment, in which social issues supplanted security concerns, which in turn created opportunities for new styles of leadership.

In the first decade of the millennium significant changes in the international political landscape, especially concerns about terrorism and civil war, demand a new analysis, and increasingly powerful tools to evaluate women's political progress are permitting new insights. Using quantitative data from a cross-national survey of gender attitudes in forty six countries, Paxton and Kunovich (2003) demonstrated that gender ideology does affect the number of women in national legislatures; negative gender attitudes were a more powerful predictor of differences in women's political representation than labor force participation, education, industrialization and other social-structural variables. In the United States gender stereotyping in the political arena continues even as the number of female politicians has increased. The terrorist attacks of September 11, 2001, stimulated a national discussion about leadership in the "war against terrorism." Lawless (2004) reports compelling evidence that citizens in the United States prefer male leadership in a war time environment, believe that men more competent at dealing with issues surrounding terrorism, and are less willing to vote for a qualified woman presidential candidate than they were in previous decades.

Electoral reforms have resulted in meaningful increases in women's political participation in many countries. Today about forty countries have introduced gender quotas for parliamentary elections through constitutional amendment or changes in electoral law, and in more than fifty countries political parties have included gender quotas in their statutes (Dahlerup and Freidenvall 2004). Quotas can be a "fast track" to equal representation; in Costa Rica, for example, a 40 percent quota and strong implementation resulted in an increase from 19 to 35 percent in 2002 (Dahlerup and Freidenvall 2004: 28). As noted above, quotas were also instrumental in vaulting Rwanda to the top of the gender equality rankings. Quotas are more frequently found in proportional representation systems than plurality/majority systems such as the United States and are strongly associated with higher levels of women's political representation (Paxton and Hughes 2007). In 1992 India passed legislation reforming the structure of local government, instituting a requirement that every village council (*panchayat*) have at least 33 percent women in its membership and leadership, and mandating the inclusion of lower castes and other marginalized groups. Although more women are active in local government than before, many face resistance and even physical violence as a consequence of their participation (Staudt et al. 2001). For quota systems to be effective, they must be enforced and as in the case of India, do not eliminate other barriers to political participation such as illiteracy and poverty.

Writing in 1994, the editors of a detailed comparative study of women's political engagement in forty-three countries concluded that "in no country do women have political status, access, or influence equal to men's" (Chowdhury et al. 1994: 3). Although there have been positive changes since then, more recent work affirms the enduring truth of the statement (Burn 2007: 225). Drawing on the findings from the individual case studies, they pointed to four major trends influencing the political participation of women at the national and subnational level: the rise of religious fundamentalism, the changing nature of nationalism, international economic forces, and the growth of international feminism (1994: 4–10.)

RELIGIOUS FUNDAMENTALISM

Chowdhury et al. acknowledge an increase in religious fundamentalism in major world religions such as Christianity and Hinduism during the last three decades, but emphasize that Muslim fundamentalism has had the most significant impact (1994: 8). Two relevant examples of Muslim fundamentalism linked to political power are the 1977–1979 Revolution in Iran, led by the party of the Ayatollah Khomeini, and the fall of the modernist People's Democratic Party of Afghanistan to fundamentalist Mujahideen revolutionaries in 1992. Both events resulted in immediate and dramatic shifts in the status of women in those countries.

In Iran, women's roles were dramatically restructured through a process of Islamization after the 1979 Revolution, but as Parvin Paidar's study of gender and the political process in twentieth-century Iran shows, women were granted legal and social rights "because they were mothers or potential mothers" (1995: 260). Ayatollah Khomeini adopted a policy of women's formal participation in national processes because he believed that the new Islamic Republic would only survive if both men and women were active in society. Contrary to many expectations, the establishment of a theocratic state did not result in outright prohibition of women from social activities (Paidar 1995: 303). Policies requiring veiling and sex segregation allowed many religious women access to education and employment (Povey 2001: 46). The case of Iran continues to provoke academic debate regarding impact of Islamization on feminist consciousness and women's involvement in social change.

Valentine Moghadam's (1994) analysis shows that in Afghanistan, reform measures were introduced by the Marxist People's Democratic Party of Afghanistan (PDPA), which came to power in the Saur Revolution of 1978. These included campaigns to improve literacy rates and educational attainment for women, stop payment of bride price, the levirate, and coerced marriages, and end the exploitation of female labor. These measures met resistance because they posed a direct challenge to patriarchal values, economic practice, and the control of land. In the face of armed resistance and outside interference, the PDPA backed away from some of their original goals, and in the end the drive to raise the status of women failed. The Islamic opposition groups, known as the Mujahideen, received support from Pakistan, Saudia Arabia, Iran, and several other nations, including the United States, and the result was a protracted period of internal conflict. In 1992 the Mujahideen assumed power; this signaled the beginning of a period of reversal of gains for women. In 1996 a group of religious students, now known as the Taliban, formed an opposition army and captured the capital, Kabul, after a bloody two year campaign. Raised in refugee camps in the 1980s, the men of the Taliban espoused a particularly conservative doctrine of Islam, and according to Moghadam, had "no conception of modern governance, democratic or participatory rule, or women's rights" (1999: 180). The oppression of women in Afghanistan became a matter of world attention, partly due to efforts such the Feminist Majority Foundation's "Stop Gender Apartheid in Afghanistan" campaign (Hirschkind and Mahmood 2002).[2] In response to the September 11 terrorist attack on the United States, the United States and international allies launched Operation Enduring Freedom in Afghanistan, which resulted in the removal of the Taliban. Unfortunately, women and girls in Afghanistan still experience significant discrimination and hardship and, partly due to long-entrenched gender role expectations, are "unable to take advantage of the theoretical freedoms that are now available to them (Coursen-Neff 2003: 10).

These examples suggest that the specific circumstances of national histories and identities must be considered in comprehending the political status of women in any particular context, rather than using Islam or Islamization as the sole explanatory factor. Deniz Kandiyoti's (1988) concept of the "patriarchal bargain" is also useful in understanding why women may act in ways that maintain the status quo of patriarchy; women pay the price of a patriarchal

bargain, and in return get some degree of protection. According to Kandiyoti, different systems offer different sorts of "patriarchal bargains" to women, each with different "rules of the game and different strategies for maximizing security and optimizing their life options" (1988: 277). Gerami and Lehnerer (2001) build on Kandiyoti's work by describing how women in Iran adopted various strategies in their response to Islamization, including collaboration, acquiescence, co-optation, and subversion.

Swarup et al. (1994: 375–376) provide two singular examples of growing religious fundamentalism in India. In contrast to decades of legislative action that outlawed sati (the immolation of widows), ended child marriage, and prohibited dowry, in 1986 the Indian government introduced the Muslim Women's (Protection of Rights in Divorce) Act. This law was intended to pacify leaders of conservative factions of the Muslim community who were outraged by the outcome of the Shah Bano case, in which the Indian Supreme Court awarded alimony to the wife of a Muslim lawyer who had already married a much younger woman. The husband claimed that the Indian government was meddling in matters of Islam set forth in the Sharia. The 1986 Act affirmed the primacy of Sharia law for Muslim women and was opposed by women's rights groups and many educated Muslims. In the following year, a young widow was burned on her husband's funeral pyre. The act was condemned by women's rights organizations and intellectuals, but thousands of Hindu men and women marched in support of sati as a matter of cultural and family right. The Indian government responded by enacting the Sati Prevention Measure of 1987, but pro-Sati attitudes persist. Swarup et al. conclude:

> Thus, in the name of supporting traditional law and custom, Muslim and Hindu fundamentalists have tried to reinforce the loosening shackles of medieval paternalistic morality and preserve male supremacy. Although fundamentalists have so far been only somewhat successful, their power is increasing. This resurgence, coupled with the desire of the central government to maintain political stability at all costs, means that the

influence of progressive and secular women is likely to be less powerful on this issue than on others. (1994: 377)

Historically, religion has often been a contentious issue for global feminists. For example, untangling the relationship between patriarchy and religion and refuting stereotypic depictions of Muslim women is a central theme in the writings of Nawal El Saadawi. Trained as a physician and a gifted writer, El Saadawi's activism on behalf of women's rights and other political issues in Egypt resulted in her being fired from her post as Director of Public Health and jailed by the government of Anwar Sadat. In 1982 she founded the Arab Woman's Solidarity Foundation, whose motto is "Power of Women-Solidarity-Unveiling of the Mind" (El Saadawi 1997). A controversial figure at home and abroad, El Saadawi consistently affirms her identity as an Arab woman and a Muslim while simultaneously denouncing religious fundamentalism and its subordinating effects on women.

THE CHANGING NATURE OF NATIONALISM

Modern nationalism is complex and variable in terms of fundamental concepts and practices, and the resulting configurations have different effects on women's status and political options. Chowdhury et al. (1994: 6–8) note that the dominant themes during the period of decolonizing and rebuilding following World War II were achieving and strengthening the political power of the nation-state. In the process of state building most women in the world achieved formal (though not actual) legal equality. In addition, state secularism resulted in more opportunities for women as it weakened the power of gender hierarchy associated with religious denominations. In recent decades, however, state-focused nationalism has been challenged by the growth of ethnic, regional, and communal forces. The expansion of the European Economic Community, on the one hand, and the disintegration of the former Soviet Union,

on the other, are recent examples of the trends of universalism and particularism at work.

Nations formed through revolution, such as the former Soviet Union, or decolonization, such as many countries in sub-Saharan Africa, have had to deal with serious internal ethnic and communal conflicts, and "often with only a thin veneer of representative government to find solutions" (Chowdhury et al. 1994: 7). Another dimension of nationalism in African states is the effect of the colonial heritage on women's status. Colonialism affected women in two ways: first, colonial policies rendered women invisible and ignored any political authority they had possessed; second, the form of nationalist movements and the position of women within them and the new governments themselves reflected the colonial overlay (Staudt 1981). The new socialist governments, such as those of Angola, Ethiopia, Guinea, Mozambique, and Tanzania, were more likely to incorporate "emancipation ideology" in the state structures, explicitly mandating access to education and political participation for women, many of whom had participated in protests and guerilla movements in the nationalist cause. However, most failed to address women's roles in the domestic and subsistence spheres, which produced glaring contradictions; for example the inability of women in Tanzanian villages to access control over important resources, such as the control of land or money from crops they had farmed (Staudt 1981: 8–10). In the late 1980s and early 1990s, women's movements played an important role in the wave of electoral reform and democratization that has reconfigured the political map of Africa today. In 2006, Ellen Johnson-Sirleaf of Liberia became Africa's first democratically elected female president, signaling a permanent change in the gender dynamics of African politics (Zeleza 2006: 20).

Africa is not the only continent to be changed by democraticization, a process that has significantly altered the political map of the world. The process has varied from region to region; in Latin America, dictatorships were replaced by popular sovereignty, while many European nations shook off the mantle of

Soviet control. Women were participants in the transition in both cases, but there were differences too, as described by Jaquette and Wolchik:

> In Latin America, women organized to protest economic conditions and undermined the claims of authoritarian regimes that they were creating the necessary conditions for economic growth. In Central and Eastern Europe, women contributed to undermining support for the Communist regimes by fostering values in the home which were not approved by the Communist leadership. In Latin America these strategies of resistance resulted in the mobilization of women around gender issues, whereas the reverse was true in Central and Eastern Europe, where women's movements have been slow to organize after the transitions. There some women expressed their desire to return to the home; others voiced open skepticism about the value of equality in labor force participation and politics, the core goals of Western feminism. (1998: 4)

In summary, women's political engagement is shaped partially by the form of any particular nation-state as well as the historical circumstances that produced it. It thus both reflects and creates particular forms of gender relations and inequity (Waylen 1998: 7).

INTERNATIONAL ECONOMIC FORCES

The relationship between economic status and political power is extremely complex. Writing about the history of women and development in Africa, Snyder and Tadesse (1995) identified educational opportunities and economic empowerment as the two most pressing areas that must be addressed in Africa to improve women's status. While acknowledging the importance of women's machinery within the government to insure women's voices are heard and ultimately to transform the institution, they emphasized the idea that economic autonomy is a prerequisite for political empowerment (1995: 182–184).

It is beyond the scope of this essay to review the large body of literature on gender and economic development (see Victoria S. Lockwood, Chapter 11 of this volume). Development theories have shifted several times since World War II, both with respect to economic development in general and with respect to women in particular (Burn 2005; Kabeer 1994; Marchand and Parpart 1995; Snyder and Tadesse 1995; Staudt 1990). By the mid-1970s it was clear that both planned and unplanned economic development was not benefiting women and men equally and that in some cases women were actually losing ground (Boserup 1970; Tinker 1990). Trends and crises in the global economy in the 1970s exacerbated flawed development strategies, resulting in mounting debt, run-away inflation, and declining standards of living. These problems and others were addressed by policies introduced by the World Bank and the International Monetary Fund to promote macroeconomic stabilization and force internal structural transformation beginning in 1979. Loans were granted with conditions attached to them, which frequently created major economic upheavals as a result of mandatory devaluation of currency and belt-tightening of national budgets. Although the results varied from country to country, the overall pattern was that "structural adjustment" policies decreased public spending on education, health, and food subsidies and had the result of increasing the burden on women, who frequently had to work longer hours to absorb the cost of basic necessities, frequently in the informal sector of the economy.

In Ghana, for example, high male unemployment forced women to take on greater responsibility for providing for their families' needs. Work in the informal sector provides an important survival strategy for poor women, who gain income from subsistence farming, petty trading, food processing, and soap making, but it is complicated by social and infrastructural obstacles. Women work up to sixteen hours a day in economic activities. Whereas men are more likely to be involved in cash-cropping activities, 90 percent of women are subsistence farmers, meaning that they engage in small-scale hoe cultivation for survival needs. Women also work their husbands' farms and are responsible for transporting and marketing the farm produce of their husbands' farms. Women in rural Ghana have access to communal land through their male relatives but have low levels of production because of heavy demands on their own labor and lack of capital to invest in production. They may cooperate with other women to share labor, or join a local credit pool to obtain capital but throughout the 1980s were largely bypassed by extension agents and state resources (Okine 1993).

Okine carried out research in Ghana during the regime of Flight Lieutenant Jerry Rawlings, who came to power in 1981 via a political coup. Market women, targeted as corrupt enemies of the state, were blamed for the high price of commodities (Fallon 2003). Vending or trading without a license was illegal, and petty traders had to be wary of the police in order to avoid having their goods confiscated. Okine noted that the economic activities of Ghanaian working women could hardly be described as liberating, in contrast to the way that economic productivity has been framed in Western Europe. In fact, women's economic contributions were not recognized by policy makers or given any sort of meaningful state support. From this she concluded that the cause of the "persistent impoverishment" of Ghanaian women was not a male-dominated society, but rather "a lack of political power" (Okine 1993: 191). A decade later, Ghanaian women were actively mobilizing to improve gender rights in a democratizing state. Before democratization, women had emphasized social rights and the need to generate income to support their families, but after 1992 used the rights they had obtained as a result of political changes to lobby for more social and civil rights (Fallon 2003).

Daines and Sedden (1993) also explored the responses of women to austerity measures associated with the economic reforms of the 1980s, borrowing Scott's (1985) concept of "everyday forms of resistance" to emphasize the agency that exists even in mundane, unorganized action with clearly defined, short-term objectives. They suggest that "even defensive struggles can, in the right circumstances, develop into more extensive forms of struggle

with a greater capacity for expanding the room for maneuver and for changing the conditions within which struggle takes place" (Daines and Sedden 1993: 11). They also discuss ways in which women use networks, associations, and diverse forms of protest to respond to austerity measures. One dramatic form of collective action is illustrated by "bread riots," which often develop from street protests over concerns about cost of living and increases in staple commodities. The fact that such protests are spontaneous and based on immediate short-term objectives (economic relief) does not change the fact that they are political actions with the potential to change state policies.

Linked with democratization is a trend toward neoliberal economic reforms, not all of which have been positive for women. With reference to Africa, Zeleza writes:

> There is overwhelming evidence that the costs of privatization of services engendered by economic liberalization and deregulation have been disproportionately borne by women. The case for addressing the gender implications of macro-economic policy and incorporating gender in any national project of sustainable development is imperative indeed. (2006: 21)

WOMEN AND COLLECTIVE ACTION IN INTERNATIONAL FEMINISM

Maxine Molyneaux distinguished women's movements that are based on "practical" gender interests and address short-term, immediate concerns from those based on "strategic" interests; the latter derive "deductively from an analysis of women's subordination and from the formulation of a more satisfactory set of arrangements" (1985, cited in Waylen 1996: 20–22). Activities motivated by practical gender interests are diverse and take many forms, including bread riots, communal kitchens, human rights campaigns, urban women's centers, and the like. Feminist movements involve women coming together self-consciously as women to press gender issues and are thus based on "strategic" gender interests. There is overlap between the two categories, but the scheme assists in understanding why women's movements do not necessarily involve a feminist consciousness.

The political participation of women in Argentina provides examples of both kinds of women's movements (Feijoo 1998). Although they were not enfranchised until 1947, Argentinean women were active in trade unions, anarchist and socialist movements, and other organizations. Before the 1976 military takeover, the women in various class and ethnic categories had been exposed to and had interacted with a variety of political ideologies, including international feminism in the 1970s, which resulted in the establishment of explicitly feminist organizations. The 1976 takeover introduced a period of state terrorism aimed at eliminating all dissident forces. Students, activists, and other "leftist" elements who posed a threat of popular mobilization were kidnapped and tortured, resulting in the "disappearance" of over 30,000 people (Feijoo 1989: 31–33). In response, women, generally mothers in their forties and fifties, engaged in large public demonstrations in the Plaza de Mayo, the main government square in Buenos Aires. Because they were acting in the role of mothers looking for their children, the military did not apply the usual punishments for subversion (Waylen 1996: 109). After the transition to democracy, however, the Madres distanced themselves from active political participation. Still, their example was a model for similar movements in other Latin American dictatorships as well as for groups within Argentina seeking to cope with the difficult economic times that accompanied the transition. In the process of constitutional reorganization, a quota law was passed requiring that 30 percent of upper level positions on party tickets be filled with women candidates, dramatically increasing the formal participation of women.

Further evidence of the overlap between practical and strategic gender interests in women's organizing is provided by Scarpaci's (1993) study of poor Chilean women under the Pinochet dictatorship (1973–1990). He interviewed members of a sewing cooperative formed to provide income from sewing tapestries and appliqués to offset the costs of filing appeals on behalf of family members who had been detained by the state security forces. One finding was that the collective expanded to include literacy campaigns as well as discussion of women's issues. According to one member:

> When I began working I realized that I contribute to my household. I contribute economically and therefore I don't find it fair that my husband should get upset because I participate in the [cooperative] and that he tells me I should do the wash and other things. I get upset, damn it, because I don't think only women should do these household chores. (Scarpaci 1993: 41)

In this case, it appears that a feminist consciousness was being produced through interaction in an organization that began as a response to a "practical" gender issue.

The technological advances in information processing, storage, and communications that helped fuel democratization and a new world economic order have also contributed to the emergence of a transnational women's movement. In September 1995, some 36,000 women from 189 nations met in Beijing, China, for a United Nations Conference on Women, the fourth such conference to be held since 1975. Previous conferences had been held in Mexico City, Copenhagen, and Nairobi as part of the United Nations Decade on Women (1975–1985). In the two decades between the designation of 1975 as the Year of the Woman by the United Nations and the Beijing conference, a global institutional framework for empowering women was established, a complex process involving national governments, international agencies, nongovernmental organizations, activists, and scholars. In addition to creating the institutional structures for addressing gender issues at a global level, the process also involved reconciling a myriad of diverse national and regional identities and agendas, as well as exploring diverging conceptions of feminism.

One result of the Beijing conference was the *Declaration and Platform for Action*, a sophisticated and comprehensive document that unequivocally situated gender inequality as a matter of human rights and social justice. It outlined a plan of action to create the conditions that will result in empowered girls and women achieving gender equity in all areas of life. It called for national governments, the international community, and all segments of civil society to implement proposals and instruments from earlier conferences, such as the Convention on the Elimination of All Forms of Discrimination Against Women (CEDAW), and to take immediate action in twelve "critical areas of concern."[3] The increasing burden of poverty on women, inequality in access to equal and adequate education and training, inequality in economic structures and policies, and inequality between women and men in the sharing of power and decision making were among those so identified. In addition to putting gender issues on the global agenda, the Beijing conference was turning point in the development of the international women's movement partly because of the political implications of the Plan of Action (Lycklama a Nijeholt et al. 1998).

The impact of the Beijing conference can be measured by the events that followed. Gender mainstreaming, an approach that requires a gender analysis to ensure that gender concerns are addressed in all types of development, was embraced by development agencies by 2000 (Burn 2005; Elson 2004). In the same year, world leaders met at the Millennium Summit and formulated a list of eight specific development goals to use as a framework for coordinated action. The third Millennium Development Goal is the promotion of gender equality and the empowerment of women, with a specific target of eliminating all gender disparity in primary and secondary education by 2015 (United Nations 2007).

The Internet, then relatively new, was extensively used in the preplanning phase of the Beijing conference, and now plays an important role for local, regional, and international nongovernmental organizations and activist groups (Travers 2003). Five years before the 2001 invasion of Afghanistan, the Feminist Majority Foundation had been using the Internet to promote awareness of gender inequality under the Taliban. Today the Internet disseminates the views of organizations such as the Women's Environment and Development Organization (WEDO), which advocates for women's equality in global policy. Founded in 2000, WEDO is best known for its 50/50 campaign, which seeks to increase the percentage of women in local and national politics worldwide to 50% (Paxton and Hughes 2007: 179). However, the Internet is of little use to those who lack access, such as the lower-caste women challenging the political agenda in India (Staudt et al. 2001: 1256).

CONCLUSION: IS IT RHETORIC OR REALITY?

As the foregoing discussion indicates, there are no easy generalizations about the nature or degree of political power of women. The last 30 years have been characterized by unprecedented global social, economic, and political change. Given that many of the obstacles to women's formal political participation have been removed (on paper at least) in most of the world's nations, does it mean that real political equality is in the near future for women?

A comprehensive evaluation of the progress in gender equality since the Beijing conference concluded that while there has been some improvement, social and economic disparities will make it hard to achieve the global gender equality goals set out in 1995 (United Nations 2005). Elson (2004) points out that even as gender awareness grows in developing nations, the ability to "engender" government budgets is often hampered by the requirements of market-led globalization, and in some less developed countries, the requirements that public international financial institutions such as the World Bank and the International Monetary Fund impose constraints on decision making.

Where women are disadvantaged educationally or struggle under entrenched patriarchal world views, political empowerment has not come easily. In Zimbabwe, for example, legislation was passed in the last two decades that permitted women to vote and made both men and women legally of age at 18. It also reformed divorce law for civil marriage, although marriage under customary law, which includes traditions of succession and inheritance, is also recognized. Before the years of structural adjustment, women also benefited from literacy campaigns and public health initiatives. Some state policies are less positive, such as the "clean up" campaigns that ostensibly target prostitutes. According to Jacobs, a 1983 campaign was directed against "younger, better-off-than-average women who appeared to be beyond 'traditional' patriarchal controls; that is, women for whom some employment opportunities have opened up recently" (1989: 168). Land tenure reforms in Zimbabwe were less beneficial for women than men due to discriminatory regulations that made it more difficult for women to gain title to land (Jacobs 1998).

In Rwanda, 800,000 people died in the genocide of 1994, leaving a population that was 70 percent female. In the subsequent social reconstruction, women gained a political toehold through constitutionally mandated parliamentary gender quotas. Yet men's resistance to women in politics is strong, as many perceive recent achievements as attempts to deprive them of authority over women. Some women are also dissatisfied with the performance of some new members of parliament, viewing them as ineffective or disconnected from the concerns of their constituents (Women for Women International 2004).

This overview of trends affecting women's political engagement shows that the goals and strategies of women's political struggles are diverse and that the results of their efforts show uneven progress. It is also clear that the growth of an international feminist movement, a measurable trend to include "women's rights machinery" in national governments, and even increased numbers of female officeholders, will not bring women political power by themselves.

The international attention focused on the case of Mukhtaran Bibi, a young woman living in Pakistan, reveals both the challenge and the potential of the future. In 2002, Mukhtaran Bibi, living in a remote village in Pakistan, was raped by four men acting on order of the village council to compensate for an alleged crime her 12-year-old brother had committed. (In the investigation that followed, the accusation was found to be false.) After the legally sanctioned rape, Mukhtaran Bibi walked home nearly naked in front of several hundred people. It was assumed that she would commit suicide, the typical course of action for a dishonored woman. Instead, she took advantage of new political freedoms to testify against her accusers, and she prevailed in court. She used compensation she received from the government to start two new schools, one for boys and one for girls (Kristof 2004). In the last few years her story has been widely disseminated on the Internet, spawning petitions in her support and bringing embarrassing attention to the government of Pakistan, which has attempted to restrict her international travel (Kristof 2005). The well-publicized struggle of Mukhtaran Bibi to claim gender justice has become iconic of the need for women worldwide to be assured of civil rights and an effective political voice. At this point, it is reasonable to assume that although there is a long way to go ahead, political equality for women is not an unachievable goal.

REFERENCES

Boserup, Esther. 1970. *Women's Role in Economic Development.* New York: St. Martin's Press.

Burn, Megan Shawn. 2005. *Women Across Cultures: A Global Perspective* (2nd edition). New York: McGraw-Hill.

Chowdhury, Najma, and Barbara J. Nelson, with Kathryn A. Carver, Nancy J. Johnson, and Paula L. O'Loughlin. 1994. "Redefining Politics: Patterns of Women's Political Engagement from a Global Perspective." In Barbara J. Nelson and Najma Chowdhury (eds.), *Women and Politics Worldwide*, pp. 3–24. New Haven, CT: Yale University Press.

Coursen-Neff, Zama. 2003. "Afghan Women and Girls Still Held Hostage." *Middle East Report* 228: 8–11.

Dahlerup, Drude, and Lenita Freidenvall. 2005. "Quotas as a 'Fast Track' to Equal Representaton for Women." *International Feminist Journal of Politics* 7 (1): 26–48.

Daines, Victoria, and David Seddon. 1993. "Confronting Austerity: Women's Responses to Economic Reform." In Meredith Turshen and Briavel Holcomb (eds.). *Women's Lives and Public Policy: The International Experience*, pp. 3–32. Westport, CT: Praeger Publishers.

El Saadawi, Nawal. 1997. *The Nawal El Saadawi Reader.* London: Zed Books.

Elson, Diane. 2004. "Engendering Government Budgets in the Context of Globalization." *International Feminist Journal of Politics* 6 (4): 623–642.

Feijoo, Maria del Carmen. 1998. "Democratic Participation and Women in Argentina. In Jane S. Jaquette and Sharon L. Wolchik (eds.). *Women and Democracy: Latin America and Central and Eastern Europe*, pp. 29–46. Baltimore, MD: Johns Hopkins University Press.

Gerami, Shahin, and Melodye Lehnerer (2001). "Women's Agency and Household Diplomacy: Negotiating Fundamentalism." *Gender and Society* 15 (4): 556–573.

Hirschkind, Charles, and Saba Mahmood. 2002. "Feminism, the Taliban, and Politics of Counter-Insurgency." *Anthropological Quarterly* 75 (2): 339–354.

Iwamoto, Misako. 2001. "The Madonna Boom: The Progress of Japanese Women into Politics in the 1980's." *PS: Political Science* 34 (2): 225–226.

Jacobs, Susan. 1989. "Zimbabwe: State, Class, and Gendered Models." In Jane L. Parpart and Kathleen A. Staudt (eds.). *Women and the State in Africa*, pp. 161–184. Boulder, CO: Lynne Rienner Publishers.

———. 1998. "The Gendered Politics of Land Reform: Three Comparative Studies." In Vicky Randall and Georgina Waylen (eds.). *Gender, Politics, and the State*, pp. 121–142. London: Routledge.

Jaquette, Jane S. 1997. "Women in Power: From Tokenism to Critical Mass." *Foreign Policy*, Fall 1997, pp. 23–37.

———, and Sharon L. Wolchik. 1998 "Women and Democratization in Latin America and Central and Eastern Europe: A Comparative Introduction." In Jane S. Jacquette and Sharon L. Wolchik (eds.). *Women and Democracy: Latin America and Central and Eastern Europe*, pp. 1–28. Baltimore, MD: John Hopkins University Press.

Kabeer, Nalia. 1994. *Reversed Realities: Gender Hierarchies in Development Thought*. London: Verso.

Kandiyoti, Deniz. 1988. "Bargaining with Patriarchy." *Gender and Society* 2 (3): 274–290.

Kristof, Nicholas. 2004. "Sentenced to Be Raped." *New York Times*, September 29, p. A25.

———. 2005. "Raped, Kidnapped, and Silenced." *New York Times*, June 14, p. A23.

Lawless, Jennifer L. 2004. "Women, War, and Winning Elections: Gender Stereotyping in the Post-September 11th Era." *Political Research Quarterly* 57 (3): 479–490.

Lycklama a Nijeholt, Joke Sweibel, and Virginia Vargas. 1998. "The Global Institutional Framework: The Long March to Beijing." In Geertje Lycklama a Nijeholt, Virginia Vargas, and Saskia Wieringa (eds.). *Women's Movements and Public Policy in Europe, Latin America, and the Caribbean*, pp. 25–48. New York: Garland Publishing, Inc.

Marchand, Marianne H., and Jane L. Parpart (eds). 1995. *Feminism/Postmodernism/Development*. London: Routledge.

Moghadam, Valentine M. 1994. "Revolution, Islamist Reaction, and Women in Afghanistan." In Mary Ann Tétrault (ed.). *Women and Revolution in Africa, Asia, and the New World*, pp. 211–235. Columbia: University of South Carolina Press.

———. 1999. "Revolution, Religion, and Gender Politics: Iran and Afghanistan Compared. In *Journal of Women's History* 10 (4): 172–195.

Molyneux, M. 1985. "Mobilization Without Emancipation? Women's Interest, the State and Revolution in Nicaragua." *Feminist Studies* 11 (2): 227–254.

Munalula, Margaret Mulela, and Winnie Sithole Mwenda. 1995. "Case Study: Women and Inheritance Law in Zambia." In Margaret Jean Hay and Sharon Stichter (eds.). *African Women South of the Sahara*, pp. 93–100. New York: Longman.

Nzomo, Maria. 1997. "Kenyan Women in Politics and Public Decision-Making." In Gwendolyn Mikell (ed.). *African Feminism: The Politics of Survival in Sub-Saharan Africa*, pp. 232–254. Philadelphia: University of Pennsylvania Press.

———, and Kathleen Staudt. 1994. "Man-Made Political Machinery in Kenya: Political Space for Women?" In Barbara J. Nelson and Najma Chowdhury (eds.). *Women and Politics Worldwide*, pp. 416–433. New Haven, CT: Yale University Press.

Okine, Vicky. 1993. "The Survival Strategies of Poor Families in Ghana and the Role of Women Therein." In Joycelin Massiah (ed.). *Women in Developing Economies: Making Visible the Invisible*, pp. 167–194. Providence, RI: Berg Publishers.

Paidar, Parvin. 1995. *Women and the Political Process in Twentieth-Century Iran*. Cambridge, UK: Cambridge University Press.

Paxton, Pamela, and Melanie M. Hughes. 2007. *Women, Politics, and Power: A Global Perspective*. Los Angeles, CA: Pine Forge Press.

Paxton, Pamela, and Sheri Kunovich. 2003. "Women's Political Representation: The Importance of Ideology." *Social Forces* 82 (1): 87–113.

Phillips, Anne. Ed. 1998. *Feminism and Politics*. New York: Oxford University Press.

Povey, Elaheh Rostami. 2001. "Feminist Contestations of Institutional Domains in Iran." *Feminist Review* 69: 44–72.

Randall, Vicky, and Georgina Waylen (eds.). 1998. *Gender, Politics and the State*. London: Routledge.

Scarpaci, Joseph L. 1993. "Empowerment Strategies of Poor Urban Women under the Chilean Dictatorship." In Meredith Turshen and Brian Holcomb (eds.). *Women's Lives and Public Policy*, pp. 33–50. Westport, CT: Greenwood Press.

Scott, J. C. 1985. *Weapons of the Weak: Everyday Forms of Peasant Resistance.* New York and London: Yale University Press.

Silverblatt, Irene. 1988. "Women in States." *Annual Review of Anthropology* 17: 427–461.

Snyder, Margaret C., and Mary Tadesse. 1995. *African Women and Development: A History.* London: Zed Books.

Staudt, Kathleen. 1981. "Women's Politics in Africa." *Studies in Third World Societies* 16: 1–28. Williamsburg, VA: College of William and Mary.

——— (ed.). 1990. *Women, International Development, and Politics.* Philadelphia: Temple University Press.

Staudt, Kathleen, Shirin M. Rai, and Jane L. Parpart. 2001. "Protesting World Trade Rules: Can We Talk about Empowerment?" *Signs* 26 (4): 1251–1257.

Swarup, Hem Lata, Niroj Sinha, Chitra Ghosh, and Pam Rajput. 1994. "Women's Political Engagement in India: Some Critical Issues." In Barbara Nelson and Najma Chowdhury (eds). *Women and Politics Worldwide,* pp. 363–379. New Haven, CT: Yale University Press.

Tinker, Irene (ed.). 1990. *Persistent Inequalities: Women and World Development.* New York: Oxford University Press.

Travers, Ann. 2003. "Parallel Subaltern Feminist Counterpublics in Cyberspace." *Sociological Perspectives* 46 (2): 223–237.

United Nations. 1995. Report of the Fourth World Conference on Women, Beijing, 4–15 September 1995. A/CONF./177/20.

United Nations. 2005. *Gender Equality: Striving for Justice in an Unequal World.* Geneva: United Nations Research Institute for Social Development.

United Nations. 2007. Millenium Development Goals. http://www.un.org/millenniumgoals/goals.html. Accessed on August 1, 2007.

Waylen, Georgina. 1996. *Gender in Third World Politics.* Boulder, CO: Lynne Rienner Publishers, Inc.

———. 1998. "Gender, Feminism, and the State: An Overview." In Vicky Randall and Georgina Waylen (eds.). *Gender, Politics and the State,* pp. 1–16. London: Routledge.

Zeleza, Paul Tiyambe. 2006. "Madam President: The Changing Gender Dynamics of African Politics." *CODESRIA Bulletin* 1–2: 20–22.

NOTES

1. After a long struggle, Kuwait passed women's suffrage in 2005.
2. The Feminist Majority Foundation mounted a large-scale education and petition drive to raise global awareness of the situation in Afghanistan. See the Foundation's homepage at www.feminist.org.
3. CEDAW was adopted in 1979 by the U.N. General Assembly and is an international bill of rights for women. It defines what constitutes discrimination against women and sets up an agenda for national action to end it. An Optional Protocol to the Convention sets up procedures to make claims and to investigate cases of grave or systematic violations of women's rights is in process. (See the Web site for United Nations Division for the Advancement of Women, www.un.or/womenwatch/daw.)

Japanese Mothers and Obentōs:
The Lunch-Box as Ideological State Apparatus

Anne Allison

INTRODUCTION

Japanese nursery school children, going off to school for the first time, carry with them a

Reprinted with permission from *Anthropological Quarterly* 64: 195–208, 1991. Copyright © The Catholic University of America.

boxed lunch (*obentō*) prepared by their mothers at home. Customarily these *obentōs* are highly crafted elaborations of food: a multitude of miniature portions, artistically designed and precisely arranged, in a container that is sturdy and cute. Mothers tend to expend inordinate time and attention on these *obentōs* in efforts both to please their children and to affirm that they are good mothers. Children at nursery school are taught in turn that they must consume their entire meal according to school rituals.

Food in an *obentō* is an everyday practice of Japanese life. While its adoption at the nursery school level may seem only natural to Japanese and unremarkable to outsiders, I will argue in this article that the *obentō* is invested with a gendered state ideology. Overseen by the authorities of the nursery school, an institution which is linked to, if not directly monitored by, the state, the practice of the *obentō* situates the producer as a woman and mother, and the consumer, as a child of a mother and a student of a school. Food in this context is neither casual nor arbitrary. Eaten quickly in its entirety by the student, the *obentō* must be fashioned by the mother so as to expedite this chore for the child. Both mother and child are being watched, judged, and constructed; and it is only through their joint effort that the goal can be accomplished.

I use Althusser's concept of the Ideological State Apparatus (1971) to frame my argument. I will briefly describe how food is coded as a cultural and aesthetic apparatus in Japan, and what authority the state holds over school in Japanese society. Thus situating the parameters within which the *obentō* is regulated and structured in the nursery school setting, I will examine the practice both of making and eating *obentō* within the context of one nursery school in Tokyo. As an anthropologist and mother of a child who attended this school for fifteen months, my analysis is based on my observations, on discussions with other mothers, daily conversations and an interview with my son's teacher, examination of *obentō* magazines and cookbooks, participation in school rituals, outings, and Mothers' Association meetings, and the multifarious experiences of my son and myself as we faced the *obentō* process every day.

I conclude that *obentō* as a routine, task, and art form of nursery school culture are endowed with ideological and gendered meanings that the state indirectly manipulates. The manipulation is neither total nor totally coercive,

however, and I argue that pleasure and creativity for both mother and child are also products of the *obentō*.

CULTURAL RITUAL AND STATE IDEOLOGY

As anthropologists have long understood, not only are the worlds we inhabit symbolically constructed, but also the constructions of our cultural symbols are endowed with, or have the potential for, power. How we see reality, in other words, is also how we live it. So the conventions by which we recognize our universe are also those by which each of us assumes our place and behavior within that universe. Culture is, in this sense, doubly constructive: constructing both the world for people and people for specific worlds.

The fact that culture is not necessarily innocent, and power not necessarily transparent, has been revealed by much theoretical work conducted both inside and outside the discipline of anthropology. The scholarship of the neo-Marxist Louis Althusser (1971), for example, has encouraged the conceptualization of power as a force which operates in ways that are subtle, disguised, and accepted as everyday social practice. Althusser differentiated between two major structures of power in modern capitalist societies. The first, he called (Repressive) State Apparatus (SA), which is power that the state wields and manages primarily through the threat of force. Here the state sanctions the usage of power and repression through such legitimized mechanisms as the law and police (1971: 143–5).

Contrasted with this is a second structure of power—Ideological State Apparatus(es) (ISA). These are institutions which have some overt function other than a political and/or administrative one: mass media, education, health and welfare, for example. More numerous, disparate, and functionally polymorphous than the SA, the ISA exert power not primarily through repression but through ideology. Designed and accepted as practices with another purpose—to educate (the school system), entertain (film industry), inform (news media), the ISA serve not only their stated objective but also an unstated one—that of indoctrinating people into seeing the world a certain way and of accepting certain identities as their own within that world (1971: 143–7).

While both structures of power operate simultaneously and complementarily, it is the ISA, according to Althusser, which in capitalist societies is the more influential of the two. Disguised and screened by another operation, the power of ideology in ISA can be both more far-reaching and insidious than the SA's power of coercion. Hidden in the movies we watch, the music we hear, the liquor we drink, the textbooks we read, it is overlooked because it is protected and its protection—or its alibi (Barthes 1957: 109–111)—allows the terms and relations of ideology to spill into and infiltrate our everyday lives.

A world of commodities, gender inequalities, and power differentials is seen not therefore in these terms but as a naturalized environment, one that makes sense because it has become our experience to live it and accept it in precisely this way. This commonsense acceptance of a particular world is the work of ideology, and it works by concealing the coercive and repressive elements of our everyday routines but also by making those routines of the everyday familiar, desirable, and simply our own. This is the critical element of Althusser's notion of ideological power: ideology is so potent because it becomes not only ours but us—the terms and machinery by which we structure ourselves and identify who we are.

JAPANESE FOOD AS CULTURAL MYTH

An author in one *obentō* magazine, the type of medium-sized publication that, filled with glossy pictures of *obentōs* and ideas and recipes for successfully recreating them, sold in the bookstores across Japan, declares, ". . . the making of the *obentō* is the one most worrisome concern facing the mother of a child going off to school for the first time (*Shufunotomo* 1980: inside cover). Another *obentō* journal, this one

heftier and packaged in the encyclopedic series of the prolific women's publishing firm, *Shufunotomo*, articulates the same social fact: "First-time *obentōs* are a strain on both parent and child" ("*hajimete no obentō wa, oya mo ko mo kinchō shimasu*") (*Shufunotomo* 1981: 55).

An outside observer might ask: What is the real source of worry over *obentō*? Is it the food itself or the entrance of the young child into school for the first time? Yet, as one look at a typical child's *obentō*—a small box packaged with a five or six-course miniaturized meal whose pieces and parts are artistically arranged, perfectly cut, and neatly arranged—would immediately reveal, no food is "just" food in Japan. What is not so immediately apparent, however, is why a small child with limited appetite and perhaps scant interest in food is the recipient of a meal as elaborate and as elaborately prepared as any made for an entire family or invited guests.

Certainly, in Japan much attention is focused on the *obentō*, investing it with a significance far beyond that of the merely pragmatic, functional one of sustaining a child with nutritional foodstuffs. Since this investment beyond the pragmatic is true of any food prepared in Japan, it is helpful to examine culinary codes for food preparation that operate generally in the society before focusing on children's *obentōs*.

As has been remarked often about Japanese food, the key element is appearance. Food must be organized, re-organized, arranged, re-arranged, stylized, and re-stylized to appear in a design that is visually attractive. Presentation is critical: not to the extent that taste and nutrition are displaced, as has been sometimes attributed to Japanese food, but to the degree that how food looks is at least as important as how it tastes and how good and sustaining it is for one's body.

As Donald Richie has pointed out in his eloquent and informative book *A Taste of Japan* (1985), presentational style is the guiding principle by which food is prepared in Japan, and the style is conditioned by a number of codes. One code is for smallness, separation, and fragmentation. Nothing large is allowed, so portions are all cut to be bite-sized, served in small amounts on tiny individual dishes, and are arranged on a table (or on a tray, or in an *obentō* box) in an array of small, separate containers.[1] There is no one big dinner plate with three large portions of vegetable, starch, and meat as in American cuisine. Consequently the eye is pulled not toward one totalizing center but away to a multiplicity of de-centered parts.[2]

Visually, food substances are presented according to a structural principle not only of segmentation but also of opposition. Foods are broken or cut to make contrasts of color, texture, and shape. Foods are meant to oppose one another and clash: pink against green, roundish foods against angular ones, smooth substances next to rough ones. This oppositional code operates not only within and between the foodstuffs themselves, but also between the attributes of the food and those of the containers in or on which they are placed: a circular mound in a square dish, a bland colored food set against a bright plate, a translucent sweet in a heavily textured bowl (Richie 1985: 40–41).

The container is as important as what is contained in Japanese cuisine, but it is really the containment that is stressed, that is, how food has been (re)constructed and (re)arranged from nature to appear, in both beauty and freshness, perfectly natural. This stylizing of nature is a third code by which presentation is directed; the injunction is not only to retain, as much as possible, the innate naturalness of ingredients—shopping daily so food is fresh and leaving much of it either raw or only minimally cooked—but also to recreate in prepared food the promise and appearance of being "natural." As Richie writes, ". . . the emphasis is on presentation of the natural rather than the natural itself. It is not what nature has wrought that excites admiration but what man has wrought with what nature has wrought" (1985: 11).

This naturalization of food is rendered through two main devices. One is by constantly hinting at and appropriating the nature that comes from outside—decorating food with seasonal reminders, such as a maple leaf in the fall or a flower in the spring, serving in-season fruits and vegetables, and using season-coordinated

dishes such as glassware in the summer and heavy pottery in the winter. The other device, to some degree the inverse of the first, is to accentuate and perfect the preparation process to such an extent that the food appears not only to be natural, but more nearly perfect than nature without human intervention ever could be. This is nature made artificial. Thus, by naturalization, nature is not only taken in by Japanese cuisine, but taken over.

It is this ability both to appropriate "real" nature (the maple leaf on the tray) and to stamp the human reconstruction of that nature as "natural" that lends Japanese food its potential for cultural and ideological manipulation. It is what Barthes calls a second order myth (1957: 114–7): a language which has a function people accept as only pragmatic—the sending of roses to lovers, the consumption of wine with one's dinner, the cleaning up a mother does for her child—which is taken over by some interest or agenda to serve a different end—florists who can sell roses, liquor companies who can market wine, conservative politicians who campaign for a gendered division of labor with women kept at home. The first order of language ("language-object"), thus emptied of its original meaning, is converted into an empty form by which it can assume a new, additional, second order of signification ("metalanguage" or "second-order semiological system"). As Barthes points out however, the primary meaning is never lost. Rather, it remains and stands as an alibi, the cover under which the second, politicized meaning can hide. Roses sell better, for example, when lovers view them as a vehicle to express love rather than the means by which a company stays in business.

At one level, food is just food in Japan—the medium by which humans sustain their nature and health. Yet under and through this code of pragmatics, Japanese cuisine carries other meanings that in Barthes' terms are mythological. One of these is national identity: food being appropriated as a sign of the culture. To be Japanese is to eat Japanese food, as so many Japanese confirm when they travel to other countries and cite the greatest problem they encounter to be the absence of "real" Japanese food. Stated the other way around, rice is so symbolically central to Japanese culture (meals and *obentōs* often being assembled with rice as the core and all other dishes, multifarious as they may be, as mere compliments or side dishes) that Japanese say they can never feel full until they have consumed their rice at a particular meal or at least once during the day.[3]

Embedded within this insistence on eating Japanese food, thereby reconfirming one as a member of the culture, are the principles by which Japanese food is customarily prepared: perfection, labor, small distinguishable parts, opposing segments, beauty, and the stamp of nature. Overarching all these more detailed codings are two that guide the making and ideological appropriation of the nursery school *obentōs* most directly: (1) there is an order to the food: a right way to do things, with everything in its place and each place coordinated with every other, and (2) the one who prepares the food takes on the responsibility of producing food to the standards of perfection and exactness that Japanese cuisine demands. Food may not be casual, in other words, nor the producer casual in her production. In these two rules is a message both about social order and the role gender plays in sustaining and nourishing that order.

SCHOOL, STATE, AND SUBJECTIVITY

In addition to language and second order meanings I suggest that the rituals and routines surrounding *obentōs* in Japanese nursery schools present, as it were, a third order, manipulation. This order is a use of a currency already established—one that has already appropriated a language of utility (food feeds hunger) to express and implant cultural behaviors. State-guided schools borrow this coded apparatus: using the natural convenience and cover of food not only to code a cultural order, but also to socialize children and mothers into the gendered roles and subjectivities they are expected to assume in a political order desired and directed by the state.

In modern capitalist societies such as Japan, it is the school, according to Althusser, which assumes the primary role of ideological state apparatus. A greater segment of the population spends longer hours and more years here than in previous historical periods. Also education has not taken over from other institutions, such as religion, the pedagogical function of being the major shaper and inculcator of knowledge for the society. Concurrently, as Althusser has pointed out for capitalist modernism (1971: 152, 156), there is the gradual replacement of repression by ideology as the prime mechanism for behavior enforcement. Influenced less by the threat of force and more by the devices that present and inform us of the world we live in and the subjectivities that world demands, knowledge and ideology become fused, and education emerges as the apparatus for pedagogical and ideological indoctrination.

In practice, as school teaches children how and what to think, it also shapes them for the roles and positions they will later assume as adult members of the society. How the social order is organized through vectors of gender, power, labor, and/or class, in other words, is not only as important a lesson as the basics of reading and writing, but is transmitted through and embedded in those classroom lessons. Knowledge thus is not only socially constructed, but also differentially acquired according to who one is or will be in the political society one will enter in later years. What precisely society requires in the way of workers, citizens, and parents will be the condition determining or influencing instruction in the schools.

This latter equation, of course, depends on two factors: (1) the convergence or divergence of different interests in what is desired as subjectivities, and (2) the power any particular interest, including that of the state, has in exerting its desires for subjects on or through the system of education. In the case of Japan, the state wields enormous control over the systematization of education. Through its Ministry of Education (Monbusho), one of the most powerful and influential ministries in the government, education is centralized and managed by a state bureaucracy that regulates almost every aspect of the educational process. On any given day, for example, what is taught in every public school follows the same curriculum, adheres to the same structure, and is informed by textbooks from the prescribed list. Teachers are nationally screened, school boards uniformly appointed (rather than elected), and students institutionally exhorted to obey teachers given their legal authority, for example, to write secret reports (*naishinsho*), that may obstruct a student's entrance into high school.[4]

The role of the state in Japanese education is not limited, however, to such extensive but codified authorities granted to the Ministry of Education. Even more powerful is the principle of the "*gakureki shakkai*" (lit. academic pedigree society) by which careers of adults are determined by the schools they attend as youths. A reflection and construction of the new economic order of post-war Japan,[5] school attendance has become the single most important determinant of who will achieve the most desirable positions in industry, government, and the professions. School attendance is itself based on a single criterion: a system of entrance exams which determines entrance selection and it is to this end—preparation for exams—that school, even at the nursery school level, is increasingly oriented. Learning to follow directions, do as one is told, and "*ganbaru*" (Asanuma 1987) are social imperatives, sanctioned by the state, and taught in the schools.

NURSERY SCHOOL AND IDEOLOGICAL APPROPRIATION OF THE *OBENTŌ*

The nursery school stands outside the structure of compulsory education in Japan. Most nursery schools are private; and, though not compelled by the state, a greater proportion of the three- to six-year-old population of Japan attends preschool than in any other industrialized nation (Tobin et al.1989; Hendry 1986; Boocock 1989).

Differentiated from the *hoikuen*, another pre-school institution with longer hours which is more like daycare than school,[6] the *yochien* (nursery school) is widely perceived as

instructional, not necessarily in a formal curriculum but more in indoctrination to attitudes and structure of Japanese schooling. Children learn less about reading and writing than they do about how to become a Japanese student, and both parts of this formula—Japanese and student—are equally stressed. As Rohlen has written, "social order is generated" in the nursery school, first and foremost, by a system of routines (1989: 10, 21). Educational routines and rituals are therefore of heightened importance in *yochien,* for whereas these routines and rituals may be the format through which subjects are taught in higher grades, they are both form and subject in the *yochien.*

While the state (through its agency, the Ministry of Education) has no direct mandate over nursery school attendance, its influence is nevertheless significant. First, authority over how the *yochien* is run is in the hands of the Ministry of Education. Second, most parents and teachers see the *yochien* as the first step to the system of compulsory education that starts in the first grade and is closely controlled by Monbusho. The principal of the *yochien* my son attended, for example, stated that he saw his main duty to be preparing children to enter more easily the rigors of public education soon to come. Third, the rules and patterns of "group living" (shudanseikatsu), a Japanese social ideal that is reiterated nationwide by political leaders, corporate management, and marriage counselors, is first introduced to the child in nursery school.[7]

The entry into nursery school marks a transition both away from home and into the "real world," which is generally judged to be difficult, even traumatic, for the Japanese child (Peak 1989). The *obentō* is intended to ease a child's discomfiture and to allow a child's mother to manufacture something of herself and the home to accompany the child as s/he moves into the potentially threatening outside world. Japanese use the cultural categories of *soto* and *uchi; soto* connotes the outside, which in being distanced and other, is dirty and hostile; and *uchi* identifies as clean and comfortable what is inside and familiar. The school falls initially and, to some degree, perpetually, into a category of *soto*. What is ultimately the definition and location of *uchi,* by contrast, is the home, where family and mother reside.[8] By producing something from the home, a mother both girds and goads her child to face what is inevitable in the world that lies beyond. This is the mother's role and her gift; by giving of herself and the home (which she both symbolically represents and in reality manages).[9] The *soto* of the school is, if not transformed into the *uchi* of home, made more bearable by this sign of domestic and maternal hearth a child can bring to it.

The *obentō* is filled with the meaning of mother and home in a number of ways. The first is by sheer labor. Women spend what seems to be an inordinate amount of time on the production of this one item. As an experienced *obentō* maker, I can attest to the intense attention and energy devoted to this one chore. On the average, mothers spend 20–45 minutes every morning cooking, preparing, and assembling the contents of one *obentō* for one nursery school–aged child. In addition, the previous day they have planned, shopped, and often organized a supper meal with leftovers in mind for the next day's *obentō*. Frequently women[10] discuss *obentō* ideas with other mothers, scan *obentō* cookbooks or magazines for recipes, buy or make objects with which to decorate or contain (part of) the *obentō*, and perhaps make small food portions to freeze and retrieve for future *obentō*.[11]

Of course, effort alone does not necessarily produce a successful *obentō*. Casualness was never indulged, I observed, and even mothers with children who would eat anything prepared *obentō* as elaborate as anyone else's. Such labor is intended for the child but also the mother: it is a sign of a woman's commitment as a mother and her inspiring her child to being similarly committed as a student. The *obentō* is thus a representation of what the mother is and what the child should become. A model for school is added to what is a gift and a reminder from home.

This equation is spelled out more precisely in a nursery school rule—all of the *obentō* must be eaten. Though on the face of it this is petty and mundane, the injunction is taken very seriously by nursery school teachers and is one not easily realized by very small children. The logic is that it is time for the child to meet certain expectations. One of the main agendas of the nursery school, after all, is to introduce and indoctrinate children into the patterns and rigors of Japanese education (Rohlen 1989; Sano 1989; Lewis 1989). And Japanese education, by all accounts, is not about fun (Duke 1986).

Learning is hard work with few choices or pleasures. Even *obentōs* from home stop once the child enters first grade.[12] The meals there are institutional: largely bland, unappealing, and prepared with only nutrition in mind. To ease a youngster into these upcoming (educational, social, disciplinary, culinary) routines, *yochien obentōs* are designed to be pleasing and personal. The *obentō* is also designed, however, as a test for the child. And the double meaning is not unintentional. A structure already filled with a signification of mother and home is then emptied to provide a new form: one now also written with the ideological demands of being a member of Japanese culture as well as a viable and successful Japanese in the realms of school and later work.

The exhortation to consume one's entire *obentō*[13] is articulated and enforced by the nursery school teacher. Making high drama out of eating by, for example, singing a song; collectively thanking Buddha (in the case of Buddhist nursery schools), one's mother for making the *obentō*, and one's father for providing the means to make the *obentō*; having two assigned class helpers pour the tea, the class eats together until everyone has finished. The teacher examines the children's *obentōs*, making sure the food is all consumed, and encouraging, sometimes scolding, children who are taking too long. Slow eaters do not fare well in this ritual, because they hold up the other students, who as a peer group also monitor a child's eating. My son often complained about a child whose slowness over food meant that the others were kept inside (rather than being allowed to play on the playground) for much of the lunch period.

Ultimately and officially, it is the teacher, however, whose role and authority it is to watch over food consumption and to judge the person consuming food. Her surveillance covers both the student and the mother, who in the matter of the *obentō,* must work together. The child's job is to eat the food and the mother's to prepare it. Hence, the responsibility and execution of one's task is not only shared but conditioned by the other. My son's teacher would talk with me daily about the progress he was making finishing his *obentōs.* Although the overt subject of discussion was my child, most of what was said was directed to me; what I could do in order to get David to consume his lunch more easily.

The intensity of these talks struck me at the time as curious. We had just settled in Japan and David, a highly verbal child, was attending a foreign school in a foreign language he had not yet mastered; he was the only non-Japanese child in the school. Many of his behaviors during this time were disruptive: for example, he went up and down the line of children during morning exercises hitting each child on the head. Hamada-sensei (the teacher), however, chose to discuss the *obentōs.* I thought surely David's survival in and adjustment to this environment depended much more on other factors, such as learning Japanese. Yet it was the *obentō* that was discussed with such recall of detail ("David ate all his peas today, but not a single carrot until I asked him to do so three times") and seriousness that I assumed her attention was being misplaced. The manifest reference was to box-lunches, but was not the latent reference to something else?[14]

Of course, there was another message, for me and my child. It was an injunction to follow directions, obey rules, and accept the authority of the school system. All of the latter were embedded in and inculcated through certain rituals: the nursery school, as any school (except such non-conventional ones as Waldorf and Montessori) and practically any social or institutional practice in Japan, was so heavily ritualized and ritualistic that the very form of ritual took on a meaning and value in and of itself (Rohlen 1989: 21, 27–8). Both the school day and school year of the nursery school were organized by these rituals. The day, apart from two free periods, for example, was broken by discrete routines—morning exercises, arts and crafts, gym instruction, singing—most of which

were named and scheduled. The school year was also segmented into and marked by three annual events—sports day (*undōkai*) in the fall, winter assembly (*seikatsu happyōkai*) in December, and dance festival (*bon odori*) in the summer. Energy was galvanized by these rituals, which demanded a degree of order as well as a discipline and self-control that non-Japanese would find remarkable.

Significantly, David's teacher marked his successful integration into the school system by his mastery not of the language or other cultural skills, but of the school's daily routines—walking in line, brushing his teeth after eating, arriving at school early, eagerly participating in greeting and departure ceremonies, and completing all of his *obentō* on time. Not only had he adjusted to the school structure, but he had also become assimilated to the other children. Or restated, what once had been externally enforced now became ideologically desirable; the everyday practices had moved from being alien (*soto*) to familiar (*uchi*) to him, from, that is, being someone else's to his own. My American child had to become, in some sense, Japanese, and where his teacher recognized this Japaneseness was in the daily routines such as finishing his *obentō.* The lesson learned early, which David learned as well, is that not adhering to routines such as completing one's *obentō* on time leads to not only admonishment from the teacher, but rejection from the other students.

The nursery school system differentiates between the child who does and the child who does not manage the multifarious and constant rituals of nursery school. And for those who do not manage there is a penalty which the child learns either to avoid or wish to avoid. Seeking the acceptance of his peers, the student develops the aptitude, willingness, and in the case of my son—whose outspokenness and individuality were the characteristics most noted in this culture—even the desire to conform to the highly ordered and structured practices of nursery school life. As Althusser (1971) wrote about ideology: the mechanism works when and because ideas about the world and particular roles in that world that serve other (social, political, economic, state) agendas become familiar and one's own.

Rohlen makes a similar point: that what is taught and learned in nursery school is social order. Called *shudanseikatsu* or group life, it means organization into a group where a person's subjectivity is determined by a group membership and not "the assumption of choice and rational self-interest" (1989: 30). A child learns in nursery school to be with others, think like others, and act in tandem with others. This lesson is taught primarily through the precision and constancy of basic routines: "Order is shaped gradually by repeated practice of selected daily tasks . . . that socialize the children to high degrees of neatness and uniformity" (p. 21). Yet a feeling of coerciveness is rarely experienced by the child when three principles of nursery school instruction are in place: (1) school routines are made "desirable and pleasant" (p. 30), (2) the teacher disguises her authority by trying to make the group the voice and unit of authority, and (3) the regimentation of the school is administered by an attitude of "intimacy" on the part of the teachers and administrators (p. 30). In short, when the desires and routines of the school are made into the desires and routines of the child, they are made acceptable.

MOTHERING AS GENDERED IDEOLOGICAL STATE APPARATUS

The rituals surrounding the *obentō* consumption in the school situate what ideological meanings the *obentō* transmits to the child. The process of production within the home, by contrast, organizes its somewhat different ideological package for the mother. While the two sets of meanings are intertwined, the mother is faced with different expectations in the preparation of the *obentō* than the child is in its consumption. At a pragmatic level the child must simply eat everything in the lunch box, whereas the mother's job is far more complicated. The onus for her is getting the child to consume what she has made, and the general attitude is that this is far more the mother's responsibility (at this nursery school, transitional stage) than the child's. And this is no simple or easy task.

Much of what is written, advised, and discussed about the *obentō* has this aim explicitly in mind: that is, making food in such a way as to facilitate the child's duty to eat it. One magazine advises:

> The first day of taking *obentō* is a worrisome thing for mother and "*boku*" (child) [15] too. Put in easy-to-eat foods that your child likes and is already used to and prepare this food in small portions (*Shufunotomo* 1980: 28).

Filled with pages of recipes, hints, pictures, and ideas, the magazine codes each page with "helpful" headings:

- First off, easy-to-eat is step one.
- Next is being able to consume the *obentō* without leaving anything behind.
- Make it in such a way for the child to become proficient in the use of chopsticks.
- Decorate and fill it with cute dreams (*kawairashi yume*).
- For older classes (*nencho*), make *obentō* filled with variety.
- Once he's become used to it, balance foods your child likes with those he dislikes.
- For kids who hate vegetables. . . .
- For kids who hate fish. . . .
- For kids who hate meat. . . . (pp. 28–53)

Laced throughout cookbooks and other magazines devoted to *obentō*, the *obentō* guidelines issued by the school and sent home in the school flier every two weeks, and the words of Japanese mothers and teachers discussing *obentō*, are a number of principles: (1) food should be made easy to eat: portions cut or made small and manipulable with fingers or chopsticks, (child-size) spoons and forks, skewers, toothpicks, muffin tins, containers, (2) portions should be kept small so the *obentō* can be consumed quickly and without any left-overs, (3) food that a child does not yet like should be eventually added so as to remove fussiness (*sukikirai*) in food habits, (4) make the *obentō* pretty, cute, and visually changeable by presenting the food attractively and by adding non-food objects such as silver paper, foil, toothpick flags, paper napkins, cute handkerchiefs, and variously shaped containers for soy sauce and ketchup, and (5) design *obentō*-related items as much as possible by the mother's own hands including the *obentō* bag (*obentōfukuro*) in which the *obentō* is carried.

The strictures propounded by publications seem to be endless. In practice I found that visual appearance and appeal were stressed by the mothers. By contrast, the directive to use *obentō* as a training process—adding new foods and getting older children to use chopsticks and learn to tie the *furoshiki*[16] —was emphasized by those judging the *obentō* at the school. Where these two sets of concerns met was, of course, in the child's success or failure completing the *obentō*. Ultimately this outcome and the mother's role in it, was how the *obentō* was judged in my experience.

The aestheticization of the *obentō* is by far its most intriguing aspect for a cultural anthropologist. Aesthetic categories and codes that operate generally for Japanese cuisine are applied, though adjusted, to the nursery school format. Substances are many but petite, kept segmented and opposed, and manipulated intensively to achieve an appearance that often changes or disguises the food. As a mother insisted to me, the creation of a bear out of miniature hamburgers and rice, or a flower from an apple or peach, is meant to sustain a child's interest in the underlying food. Yet my child, at least, rarely noticed or appreciated the art I had so laboriously contrived. As for other children, I observed that even for those who ate with no obvious "fussiness," mothers' efforts to create food as style continued all year long.

Thus much of a woman's labor over *obentō* stems from some agenda other than that of getting the child to eat an entire lunch-box. The latter is certainly a consideration and it is the rationale as well as cover for women being scrutinized by the school's authority figure—the teacher. Yet two other factors are important. One is that the *obentō* is but one aspect of the far more expansive and continuous commitment a mother is expected to make for and to her child. "*Kyōiku mama*" (education mother) is the term given to a mother who executes her responsibility to oversee and manage the education of her children with excessive vigor. And yet this excess is not only demanded by the state even at the level of the nursery school; it is conventionally given by mothers. Mothers who manage the home and children, often in virtual absence of a husband/father, are considered the factor that may make or break a child as s/he advances towards that pivotal point of the entrance examinations.[17]

In this sense, just as the *obentō* is meant as a device to assist a child in the struggles of first adjusting to school, the mother's role generally is perceived as being the support, goad, and cushion for the child. She will perform endless tasks to assist in her child's study: sharpen pencils and make midnight snacks as the child studies, attend cram schools to verse herself in subjects her child is weak in, make inquiries as to what school is most appropriate for her child, and consult with her child's teachers. If the child succeeds, a mother is complimented; if the child fails, a mother is blamed.

Thus at the nursery school level, the mother starts her own preparation for this upcoming role. Yet the jobs and energies demanded of a nursery school mother are, in themselves, surprisingly consuming. Just as the mother of an entering student is given a book listing all the pre-entry tasks she must complete, for example, making various bags and containers, affixing labels to all clothes in precisely the right place and with the size exactly right, she will be continually expected thereafter to attend Mothers' Association meetings, accompany children on fieldtrips, wash the clothes and indoor shoes of her child every week, add required items to a child's bag on a day's notice, and generally be available. Few mothers at the school my son attended could afford to work in even part-time or temporary jobs. Those women who did tended either to keep their outside work a secret or be reprimanded by a teacher for insufficient devotion to their child. Motherhood, in other words, is institutionalized through the child's school and such routines as making the *obentō* as a full-time, kept-at-home job.[18]

The second factor in a woman's devotion to over-elaborating her child's lunch-box is that her experience doing this becomes a part of her and a statement, in some sense, of who she is. Marx writes that labor is the most "essential" aspect to our species-being and that the products we produce are the encapsulation of us and therefore our productivity (1970: 71–76). Likewise, women are what they are through the products they produce. An *obentō* therefore is not only a gift or test for a child, but a representation and product of the woman herself. Of course, the two ideologically converge, as has been stated already, but I would also suggest that there is a potential disjoining. I sensed that the women were laboring for themselves apart from the agenda the *obentō* was expected to fill at school. Or stated alternatively, in the role that females in Japan are highly pressured and encouraged to assume as domestic manager, mother, and wife, there is, besides the endless and onerous responsibilities, also an opportunity for play. Significantly, women find play and creativity not outside their social roles but within them.

Saying this is not to deny the constraints and surveillance under which Japanese women labor at their *obentō*. Like their children at school, they are watched by not only the teacher but each other, and perfect what they create, partially at least, so as to be confirmed as a good and dutiful mother in the eyes of other mothers. The enthusiasm with which they absorb this task then is like my son's acceptance and internalization of the nursery school routines; no longer enforced from outside it becomes adopted as one's own.

The making of the *obentō* is, I would thus argue, a double-edged sword for women. By relishing its creation (for all the intense labor expended, only once or twice did I hear a mother voice any complaint about this task), a woman is ensconcing herself in the ritualization and subjectivity (subjection) of being a mother in Japan. She is alienated in the sense that others will dictate, inspect, and manage her work. On the reverse side, however, it is precisely through this work that the woman expresses, identifies, and constitutes herself. As Althusser pointed out, ideology can never be totally abolished (1971: 170); the elaborations that women work on "natural" food produce an *obentō* which is creative and, to some degree, a fulfilling and personal statement of themselves.

Minami, an informant, revealed how both restrictive and pleasurable the daily rituals of motherhood can be. The mother of two children—one, aged three and one, a nursery school student, Minami had been a professional opera singer before marrying at the relatively late age of 32. Now, her daily schedule was organized by routines associated with her child's nursery school: for example, making the *obentō*, taking her daughter to school and picking her up, attending Mothers' Association meetings, arranging daily play dates, and keeping the school uniform clean. While Minami wished to return to singing, if only on a part-time basis, she said that the demands of motherhood, particularly those imposed by her child's attendance at nursery school, frustrated this desire. Secretly snatching only minutes out of any day to practice, Minami missed singing and told me that being a mother in Japan means the exclusion of almost anything else.[19]

Despite this frustration, however, Minami did not behave like a frustrated woman. Rather she devoted to her mothering an energy, creativity, and intelligence I found to be standard in the Japanese mothers I knew. She planned special outings for her children at least two or three times a week, organized games that she knew they would like and would teach them cognitive skills, created her own stories and designed costumes for afternoon play, and shopped daily for the meals she prepared with her children's favorite foods in mind. Minami told me often that she wished she could sing more, but never once did she complain about her children, the chores of child-raising, or being a mother. The attentiveness displayed otherwise in her mothering was exemplified most fully in Minami's *obentōs*. No two were ever alike, each had at least four or five parts, and she kept trying out new ideas for both new foods and new designs. She took pride as well as pleasure in her *obentō* handicraft; but while Minami's *obentō* creativity was impressive, it was not unusual.

Examples of such extraordinary *obentō* creations from an *obentō* magazine include: (1) ("donut *obentō*"): two donuts, two wieners cut to look like a worm, two cut pieces of apple, two small cheese rolls, one hard-boiled egg made to look like a rabbit with leaf ears and pickle eyes and set in an aluminum muffin tin, cute paper napkin added, (2) (wiener doll *obentō*): a bed of rice with two doll creations made out of wiener parts (each consists of eight pieces comprising hat, hair, head, arms, body, legs), a line of pink ginger, a line of green parsley, paper flag of France added, (3) (vegetable flower and tulip *obentō*): a bed of rice laced with chopped hard-boiled egg, three tulip flowers made out of cut wieners with spinach precisely arranged as stem and leaves, a fruit salad with two raisins, three cooked peaches, three pieces of cooked apple, (4) (sweetheart doll *obentō—abekku ningyō no obentō*): in a two-section *obentō* box there are four rice balls on one side, each with a different center, on the other side are two dolls made of quail's eggs for heads, eyes and mouth added, bodies of cucumber, arranged as if lying down with two raw carrots for the pillow, covers made of one flower—cut cooked carrot, two pieces of ham, pieces of cooked spinach, and with different colored plastic skewers holding the dolls together (*Shufunotomo* 1980: 27, 30).

The impulse to work and re-work nature in these *obentos* is most obvious perhaps in the strategies used to transform, shape, and/or disguise foods. Every mother I knew came up with her own repertoire of such techniques, and every *obentō* magazine or cookbook I examined offered a special section on these devices. It is important to keep in mind that these are treated as only flourishes: embellishments added to parts of an *obentō* composed of many parts. The following is a list from one magazine: lemon pieces made into butterflies, hard boiled eggs into *daruma* (popular Japanese legendary figure of a monk without his eyes), sausage cut into flowers, a hard-boiled egg decorated as a baby, an apple piece cut into a leaf, a radish flaked into a flower, a cucumber cut like a flower, a *mikan* (nectarine orange) piece arranged into a basket, a boat with a sail made from a cucumber, skewered sausage, radish shaped like a mushroom, a quail egg flaked into a cherry, twisted *mikan* piece, sausage cut to become a crab, a patterned cucumber, a ribboned carrot, a flowered tomato, cabbage leaf flower, a potato cut to be a worm, a carrot designed as a red shoe, an apple cut to simulate a pineapple (Shufunotomo 1980: pp. 57–60).

Nature is not only transformed but also supplemented by store-bought or mother-made objects which are precisely arranged in the *obentō*. The former come from an entire industry and commodification of the *obentō* process: complete racks or sections in stores selling *obentō* boxes, additional small containers, *obentō* bags, cups, chopstick and utensil containers (all these with various cute characters or designs on the front), cloth and paper napkins, foil, aluminum tins, colored ribbon or string, plastic skewers, toothpicks with paper flags, and paper dividers. The latter are the objects mothers are encouraged and praised for making themselves: *obentō* bags, napkins, and handkerchiefs with appliquéd designs or the child's name embroidered. These supplements to the food, the arrangement of the food, and the *obentō* box's dividing walls (removable and adjustable) furnish the order of the *obentō*. Everything appears crisp and neat with each part kept in its own place: two tiny hamburgers set firmly atop a bed of rice; vegetables in a separate compartment in the box; fruit arranged in a muffin tin.

How the specific forms of *obentō* artistry—for example, a wiener cut to look like a worm and set within a muffin tin—are encoded symbolically is a fascinating subject. Limited here by space, however, I will only offer initial suggestions. Arranging food into a scene recognizable by the child was an ideal mentioned by many mothers and cookbooks. Why those of animals, human beings, and other food forms (making a pineapple out of an apple, for example) predominate may have no other rationale than being familiar to children and easily reproduced by mothers. Yet it is also true that this tendency to use a trope of realism—casting food into realistic figures—is most prevalent in the meals Japanese prepare for their children. Mothers I knew created animals and faces in supper meals and/or *obentos* made for other outings, yet their impulse to do this seemed not only heightened in the *obentō* that were sent to school but also played down in food prepared for other age groups.

What is consistent in Japanese cooking generally, as stated earlier, are the dual principles of manipulation and order. Food is manipulated into some other form than it assumes either naturally or upon being cooked: lines are put into mashed potatoes, carrots are flaked, wieners are twisted and sliced. Also, food is ordered by some human rather than natural principle; everything must have neat boundaries and be placed precisely so those boundaries do not merge. These two structures are the ones most important in shaping the nursery school *obentō* as well, and the inclination to design realistic imagery is primarily a means by which these other culinary codes are learned by and made pleasurable for the child. The simulacrum of a pineapple recreated from an apple therefore is less about seeing the pineapple in an apple (a particular form) and more about reconstructing the apple into something else (the process of transformation).

The intense labor, management, commodification, and attentiveness that go into the making of an *obentō* laces it, however, with many and various meanings. Overarching all is the potential to aestheticize a certain social order, a social order which is coded (in cultural and culinary terms) as Japanese. Not only is a mother making food more palatable to her nursery school child, but she is creating food as a more aesthetic and pleasing social structure. The *obentō's* message is that the world is constructed very precisely and that the role of any single Japanese in that world must be carried out with the same degree of precision. Production is demanding; and the producer must both keep within the borders of her/his role and work hard.

The message is also that it is women, not men, who are not only sustaining a child through food but carrying the ideological support of the culture that this food embeds. No Japanese man I spoke with had or desired the experience of making a nursery school *obentō* even once, and few were more than peripherally engaged in their children's education. The male is assigned a position in the outside world where he labors at a job for money and is expected to be primarily identified by and committed to his place of work.[20] Helping in the management of home and raising of children has not become an obvious male concern or interest in Japan, even as more and more

women enter what was previously the male domain of work. Females have remained at and as the center of home in Japan and this message too is explicitly transmitted in both the production and consumption of entirely female-produced *obentō*.

The state accrues benefits from this arrangement. With children depending on the labor women devote to their mothering to such a degree, and women being pressured as well as pleasurized in such routine maternal productions as making the *obentō*—both effects encouraged and promoted by institutional features of the educational system heavily state-run and at least ideologically guided at even the nursery school level—a gendered division of labor is firmly set in place. Labor from males, socialized to be compliant and hard-working, is more extractable when they have wives to rely on for almost all domestic and familial management. And females become a source of cheap labor, as they are increasingly forced to enter the labor market to pay domestic costs (including those vast debts incurred in educating children) yet are increasingly constrained to low-paying part-time jobs because of the domestic duties they must also bear almost totally as mothers.

Hence, not only do females, as mothers, operate within the ideological state apparatus of Japan's school system that starts semi-officially, with the nursery school, they also operate as an ideological state apparatus unto themselves. Motherhood is state ideology, working through children at home and at school and through such mother-imprinted labor that a child carries from home to school as with the *obentō*. Hence the post–World War II conception of Japanese education as being egalitarian, democratic, and with no agenda of or for gender differentiation, does not in practice stand up. Concealed within such cultural practices as culinary style and child-focused mothering, is a worldview in which the position and behavior an adult will assume has everything to do with the anatomy she/he was born with.

At the end, however, I am left with one question. If motherhood is not only watched and manipulated by the state but made by it into a conduit for ideological indoctrination, could not women subvert the political order by redesigning *obentō*? Asking this question, a Japanese friend, upon reading this paper, recalled her own experiences. Though her mother had been conventional in most other respects, she made her children *obentōs* that did not conform to the prevailing conventions. Basic, simple, and rarely artistic, Sawa also noted, in this connection, that the lines of these *obentōs* resembled those by which she was generally raised: as gender-neutral, treated as a person not "just as a girl," and being allowed a margin to think for herself. Today she is an exceptionally independent woman who has created a life for herself in America, away from homeland and parents, almost entirely on her own. She loves Japanese food, but the plain *obentōs* her mother made for her as a child, she is newly appreciative of now, as an adult. The *obentōs* fed her, but did not keep her culturally or ideologically attached. For this, Sawa says today, she is glad.

ACKNOWLEDGMENTS

The fieldwork on which this article is based was supported by a Japan Foundation Postdoctoral Fellowship. I am grateful to Charles Piot for a thoughtful reading and useful suggestions for revision and to Jennifer Robertson for inviting my contribution to this issue. I would also like to thank Sawa Kurotani for her many ethnographic stories and input, and Phyllis Chock and two anonymous readers for the valuable contributions they made to revision of the manuscript.

REFERENCES

Althusser, Louis. 1971. *Ideology and Ideological State Apparatuses (Notes toward an investigation in Lenin and philosophy and other essays)*. New York: Monthly Review.

Asanuma, Kaoru. 1987. *"Ganbari" no Kozo (Structure of "Ganbari")*. Tokyo: Kikkawa Kobunkan.

Barthes, Roland. 1957. *Mythologies*. Trans. by Annette Lavers. New York: Noonday Press.

Boocock, Sarane Spence. 1989. Controlled diversity: An overview of the Japanese preschool system. *The Journal of Japanese Studies* 15(1): 41–65.

Chicago Tribune. 1991. Burdens of Working Wives Weigh Heavily in Japan. January 27, Section 6, p. 7.

Cummings, William K. 1980. *Education and Equality in Japan*. Princeton NJ: Princeton University Press.

Doi, Takeo, 1971. *The Anatomy of Dependence: The Key Analysis of Japanese Behavior*. Trans. by John Becker. Tokyo: Kodansha Int'l. Ltd.

Dore, Ronald P. 1965. *Education in Tokugawa Japan*. London: Routledge and Kegan Paul.

Duke, Benjamin. 1986. *The Japanese School: Lessons for Industrial America*. New York: Praeger.

Fallows, Deborah. 1990. "Japanese Women." *National Geographic* 177(4): 52–83.

Fujita, Mariko. 1989. "It's All Mother's Fault": Childcare and the Socialization of Working Mothers in Japan. *The Journal of Japanese Studies* 15(1): 67–91.

Greenbie, Barrie B. 1988. *Space and Spirit in Modern Japan*. New Haven, CT: Yale University Press.

Hendry, Joy. 1986. *Becoming Japanese: The World of the Pre-School Child*. Honolulu: University of Hawaii Press.

———. 1987. *Understanding Japanese Society*. London: Croom Helm.

Horio, Teruhisa. 1988. *Educational Thought and Ideology in Modern Japan: State Authority and Intellectual Freedom*. Trans. by Steven Platzer. Tokyo: University of Tokyo Press.

Imamura, Anne E. 1987. *Urban Japanese Housewives: At Home and in the Community*. Honolulu: University of Hawaii Press.

Juristo zōkan Sōgōtokushu. 1985. Josei no Gensai to Mirai (The present and future of women). 39.

Kadeshobo shinsha. 1981. *Hahaoya (Mother)*. Tokyo: Kadeshobo shinsha.

Kawai, Hayao. 1976. *Bosei shakai nihon no Byōri (The Pathology of the Mother Society—Japan)*. Tokyo: Chuo Koronsha.

Kondo, Dorinne K. 1990. *Crafting Selves: Power, Gender, and Discourses of Identity in a Japanese Workplace*. Chicago, IL: University of Chicago Press.

Kyūtoku, Shigemori. 1981. *Bogenbyo (Disease Rooted in Motherhood)*. Vol. II. Tokyo: Sanma Kushuppan.

Lewis, Catherine C. 1989. From Indulgence to Internalization: Social Control in the Early School Years. *Journal of Japanese Studies* 15(1): 139–157.

Lock, Margaret. 1990. Restoring Order to the House of Japan. *The Wilson Quarterly* 14(4): 42–49.

Marx, Karl, and Frederick Engels. 1970 (1947). *Economic and Philosophic Manuscripts*, ed. C. J. Arthur. New York: International Publishers.

Mirai shakan. 1979. Shufu to onna (Housewives and Women). Kunitachishi Komininkan Shimindaigaku Semina-no Kiroku. Tokyo: Miraisha.

Mouer, Ross and Yoshio Sugimoto. 1986. *Images of Japanese Society: A Study in the Social Construction of Reality.* London: Routledge and Kegan.

Nakane, Chie, 1970. *Japanese Society.* Berkeley: University of California Press.

Ohirasōri no Seifu kenkyūkai. 1980. Katei Kiban no Jujitsu (The Fullness of Family Foundations). (Ohirasōri no Seifu Kenkyūkai-3). Tokyo: Okurashō Insatsukyōku.

Peak, Lois. 1989. "Learning to Become Part of the Group: The Japanese Child's Transition to Preschool Life." *The Journal of Japanese Studies* 15(1): 93–123.

Richie, Donald. 1985. *A Taste of Japan: Food Fact and Fable, Customs and Etiquette, What the People Eat.* Tokyo: Kodansha International Ltd.

Rohlen, Thomas P. 1974. *The Harmony and Strength: Japanese White-Collar Organization in Anthropological Perspective.* Berkeley: University of California Press.

———. 1983. *Japan's High Schools.* Berkeley: University of California Press.

———. 1989. "Order in Japanese Society: Attachment, Authority and Routine." *The Journal of Japanese Studies* 15(1): 5–40.

Sano, Toshiyuki. 1989. "Methods of Social Control and Socialization in Japanese Day-Care Centers. *The Journal of Japanese Studies* 15(1):125–138.

Shufunotomo Besutoserekushon shiri-zu. 1980. Obentō 500 sen. Tokyo: Shufunotomo Co., Ltd.

Shufunotomohyakka shiri-zu. 1981. 365 nichi no *obentō* hyakka. Tokyo: Shufunotomo Co.

Sōrifu Seihonen Taisaku Honbuhen, 1981. *Nihon no kodomo to hahaoya (Japenese mothers and children): Kokusaihikaku (international comparisons).* Tokyo: Sōrifu Seishonen Taisaku Honbuhen.

Tobin, Joseph J., David Y. H. Wu, and Dana H. Davidson. 1989. *Preschool in Three Cultures: Japan, China, and the United States.* New Haven, CT: Yale University Press.

Vogel, Erza. 1963. *Japan's New Middle Class: The Salary Man and His Family in a Tokyo Suburb.* Berkeley: University of California Press.

White, Merry. 1987. *The Japanese Educational Challenge: A Commitment to Children.* New York: Free Press.

Yamamura, Yoshiaki. 1971. *Nihonjin to Haha: Bunka Toshite No Haha no Kannen Ni Tsuite no Kenkyu (The Japanese and Mother: Research on the Conceptualization of Mother as Culture).* Tokyo: Toyo-shuppansha.

NOTES

1. As Dorinne Kondo has pointed out, however, these cuisinal principles may be conditioned by factors of both class and circumstance. Her *shitamachi* (more traditional area of Tokyo) informants, for example, adhered only casually to this coding and other Japanese she knew followed them more carefully when preparing food for guests rather than family and when eating outside rather than inside the home (Kondo 1990: 61–2).

2. Rice is often, if not always, included in a meal: and it may substantially as well as symbolically constitute the core of the meal. When served at a table it is put in a large pot or electric rice maker and will be spooned into a bowl, still no bigger or predominant than the many other containers from which a person eats. In an *obentō* rice may be in one, perhaps the largest, section of a multi-sectioned *obentō* box, yet it will be arranged with a variety of other foods. In a sense rice provides the syntactic and substantial center to a meal yet the presentation of the food rarely emphasizes this core. The rice bowl is refilled rather than heaped as in the preformed *obentō* box, and in the *obentō* rice is often embroidered, supplemented, and/or covered with other foodstuffs.

3. Japanese will both endure a high price for rice at home and resist American attempts to export rice to Japan in order to stay domestically self-sufficient in this national food *qua* cultural symbol. Rice is the only foodstuff in which the Japanese have retained self-sufficient production.

4. The primary sources on education used are Horio 1988; Duke 1986; Rohlen 1983; Cummings 1980.

5. Neither the state's role in overseeing education nor a system of standardized tests is a new development in post–World War II Japan. What is new is the national standardization of tests and, in this sense, the intensified role the state has thus assumed in overseeing them. See Dore (1965) and Horio (1988).

6. Boocock (1989) differs from Tobin et al. (1989) on this point and asserts that the institutional differences are insignificant. She describes extensively how both *yochien* and *hoikuen* are administered (*yochien* are under the authority of Monbusho and *hoikuen* are under the authority of the Koseisho, the Ministry of Health and Welfare) and how both feed into the larger system of education. She emphasizes diversity:

though certain trends are common amongst preschools, differences in teaching styles and philosophies are plentiful as well.

7. According to Rohlen (1989), families are incapable of indoctrinating the child into this social pattern of *shū ndanseikatsu* by their very structure and particularly by the relationship (of indulgence and dependence) between mother and child. For this reason and the importance placed on group structures in Japan, the nursery school's primary objective, argues Rohlen, is teaching children how to assimilate into groups. For further discussion of this point, see also Peak 1989; Lewis 1989; Sano 1989; and the *Journal of Japanese Studies* issue [15(1)] devoted to Japanese preschool education in which these articles, including Boocock's, are published.

8. For a succinct anthropological discussion of these concepts, see Hendry (1987: 39–41). For an architectural study of Japan's management and organization of space in terms of such cultural categories as *uchi* and *soto,* see Greenbie (1988).

9. Endless studies, reports, surveys, and narratives document the close tie between women and home; domesticity and femininity in Japan. A recent international survey conducted for a Japanese housing construction firm, for example, polled couples with working wives in three cities, finding that 97% (of those polled) in Tokyo prepared breakfast for their families almost daily (compared with 43% in New York and 34% in London); 70% shopped for groceries on a daily basis (3% in New York, 14% in London), and that only 22% of them had husbands who assisted or were willing to assist with housework (62% in New York, 77% in London) (quoted in *Chicago Tribune* 1991). For a recent anthropological study of Japanese housewives in English, see Imamura (1987). Japanese sources include *Juristo zokan sogo tokushu* 1985; *Mirai shakan* 1979; *Ohirasōri no seifu kenkyūkai* 3.

10. My comments pertain directly, of course, to only the women I observed, interviewed, and interacted with at the one private nursery school serving middle-class families in urban Tokyo. The profusion of *obentō*-related materials in the press plus the revelations made to me by Japanese and observations made by other researchers in Japan (for example, Tobin at al. 1989; Fallows (1990), however, substantiate this as a more general phenomenon.

11. To illustrate this preoccupation and consciousness: during the time my son was not eating all his *obentō* many fellow mothers gave me suggestions, one mother lent me a magazine, his teacher gave me a full set of *obentō* cookbooks (one per season), and another mother gave me a set of small frozen food portions she had made in advance for future *obentōs*.

12. My son's teacher, Hamada-sensei, cited this explicitly as one of the reasons why the *obentō* was such an important training device for nursery school children. "Once they become *ichinensei* (first-graders) they'll be faced with a variety of food, prepared without elaboration or much spice, and will need to eat it within a delimited time period."

13. An anonymous reviewer questioned whether such emphasis placed on consumption of food in nursery school leads to food problems and anxieties in later years. Although I have heard that anorexia is a phenomenon now in Japan, I question its connection to nursery school *obentōs*. Much of the meaning of the latter practice, as I interpret it, has to do with the interface between production and consumption, and its gender linkage comes from the production end (mothers making it) rather than the consumption end (children eating it). Hence while control is taught through food, it is not a control linked primarily to females or bodily appearance, as anorexia may tend to be in this culture.

14. Fujita argues, from her experience as a working mother of a daycare (*hoikuen*) child, that the substance of these daily talks between teacher and mother is intentionally insignificant. Her interpretation is that the mother is not to be overly involved in, nor too informed about, matters of the school (1989).

15. "*Boku*" is a personal pronoun that males in Japan use as a familiar reference to themselves. Those in close relationships with males—mothers and wives, for example—can use *boku* to refer to their sons or husbands. Its use in this context is telling.

16. In the upper third grade of the nursery school (*nenchō* class; children aged five to six) my son attended, children were ordered to bring their *obentō* with chopsticks and not forks and spoons (considered easier to use) and in the traditional *furoshiki* (piece of cloth which enwraps items and is double tied to close it) instead of the easier-to-manage *obentō* bags with drawstrings. Both furoshiki and chopsticks (*o-hashi*) are considered traditionally Japanese and their usage marks not only greater effort and skills on the part of the children but their enculturation into being Japanese.

17. For the mother's role in the education of her child, see, for example, White (1987). For an

analysis, by a Japanese of the intense dependence on the mother that is created and cultivated in a child, see Doi (1971). For Japanese sources on the mother-child relationship and ideology (some say pathology) of Japanese motherhood, see Yamamura (1971); Kawai (1976); Kyūtoku (1981); *Sorifu seihonen taisaku honbuhen* (1981); *Kadeshobo shinsha* (1981). Fujita's account of the ideology of motherhood at the nursery school level is particularly interesting in this connection (1989).

18. Women are entering the labor market in increasing numbers yet the proportion to do so in the capacity of part-time workers (legally constituting as much as thirty-five hours per week but without the benefits accorded to full-time workers) has also increased. The choice of part-time over full-time employment has much to do with a woman's simultaneous and almost total responsibility for the domestic realm (*Juristo* 1985: see also Kondo 1990).

19. As Fujita (1989: 72–79) points out, its mothers are treated as a separate category of mothers, and non-working mothers are expected, by definition, to be mothers full time.

20. Nakane's much quoted text on Japanese society states this male position in structuralist terms (1970). Though dated, see also Vogel (1963) and Rohlen (1974) for descriptions of the social roles for middle-class, urban Japanese males. For a succinct recent discussion of gender roles within the family, see Lock (1990).

VIII

Gender, Household, and Kinship

The study of kinship has been central to cross-cultural research. Marriage customs, systems of descent, and patterns of residence have been described and compared in a range of societies around the world. At the heart of traditional studies of kinship is the opposition between the domestic domain, on the one hand, and the public, political, and jural domain on the other. Anthropologists, particularly those working in Africa, studied kinship in this latter domain. They delineated large corporate descent groups called lineages that managed property and resources and that were the basic building blocks of political organization (Fortes 1949, 1953). Marriage, for some kinship theorists, is a political transaction, involving the exchange of women between men who wish to form alliances (Levi-Strauss 1969; see also Ortner 1978). A woman, from this perspective, is a passive pawn with little influence over kinship transactions. She is viewed "in terms of the rights her kin have to her domestic labor, to the property she might acquire, to her children, and to her sexuality" (Lamphere 1974: 98). The dynamic, affective, and even interest-oriented aspects of women's kinship are essentially ignored in an approach that is rooted in androcentric principles: Women have the children; men impregnate the women; and men usually exercise control (Fox 1967).

Recent critiques of the traditional study of kinship have pointed out that it is "no longer adequate to view women as bringing to kinship primarily a capacity for bearing children while men bring primarily a capacity for participation in public life" (Collier and Yanagisako 1987: 7). A gendered approach to kinship takes a number of different directions but focuses on the status of men and women in different kinship systems and on the power (defined as the ability to make others conform to one's desires and wishes) that accrues to women through their manipulation of social relations (Maynes et al. 1996). Cross-cultural variations in the status of men and women have been examined in relation to rules of descent and postmarital residence (Friedl 1975; Martin and Voorhies 1975). Among horticulturalists, for example, women have higher status in societies characterized by matrilineal descent (descent through the female line from a common female ancestor) and matrilocal residence (living with the wife and her kin after marriage) than in societies characterized by patrilineal descent (descent through the male line from a common male ancestor) and patrilocal residence (living with the husband and his kin after marriage). In matrilineal systems, descent group membership, social identity, rights to land, and succession to political office are all inherited through one's mother.

When matrilineality is combined with matrilocal residence, a husband marries into a household in which a long-standing domestic coalition exists between his wife and her mother, sisters, and broader kin relations (Friedl 1975). These women cooperate with one another in work endeavors and provide mutual support. Although in a matrilineal system a man retains authority over his sisters and her children, the coalitions formed by kin-related women can provide them with power and influence both within and beyond the household (Brown 1970; Lamphere 1974; Menon 1996) and also with a degree of sexual freedom. The important issue for women's status, as Schlegel (1972: 96) has argued, is not the descent system per se but the organization of the domestic group.

In contrast to matrilineal and matrilocal systems, in patrilineal and patrilocal societies women marry in to their husband's household and family and hence do not have their own kin nearby. One of the classic examples of such a family has been the patrilineal extended Chinese family. In her essay in this volume, Monica Cable opens with a discussion of this family and its association with the concept of filial piety that is central to Confucianism. She describes the patrilineal lineages that are at the core of Han Chinese kinship and that placed women in an inferior position (also see Ruth S. Watson in Chapter 5 of this volume). A woman enters her husband's household as a stranger. She must pay homage to her husband's ancestors, obey her husband and mother-in-law, and bear children for her husband's patrilineage. According to Margery Wolf (1972: 32), who carried out research in Taiwan, "a woman can and, if she is ever to have any economic security, must provide the links in the male chain of descent, but she will never appear in anyone's genealogy as that all-important name connecting the past to the future."

Separated from her own kin, she cannot forge lateral alliances easily. However, other opportunities are open to women that enhance their power and status in patrilineal and patrilocal societies. After a Taiwanese wife gives birth to a son, her status in the household begins to change, and it improves during her life course as she forges what Wolf calls a uterine family—a family based on the powerful relationship between mothers and sons. The subordination of conjugal to intergenerational relationships that is exemplified by the Taiwanese or classic Han Chinese case, as well as the opportune ways in which women take advantage of filial ties to achieve political power within and beyond the household, are apparent in other societies around the world—for example, in sub-Saharan Africa (Potash 1986).

After discussing the classic Han family, Cable turns our attention to much greater complexity in Chinese family structure, arguing that within the majority Han culture, and among the fifty-five ethnic minority groups, there are variations in kinship, including the matrilineal Mosuo, Dai bilateral kinship, and dyadic Lahu kinship. Cable frames some of her analysis of this diversity in relation to historical changes in China after 1949, and in the process demonstrates the important relationship between the family and the state. For example, the Chinese Constitution of 1950 provided women in China with *de jure* equality and the concurrent Marriage Law outlawed concubinage. The introduction of the one-child policy in China caused further changes and has raised controversial issues surrounding technology, reproduction, gender and kinship. Clearly, this policy has slowed population growth in China. In a single generation, the birth rate in China has declined to 1.9 children per mother. Children are being brought up without siblings, something that will have a significant impact on the traditional patrilineal lineage as well as on kinship in general. Hong (1987), for example, has argued that one-child policy would result in more uxorilocal marriages (where a husband takes up residence with his wife and her family).

But perhaps most interesting is the impact on gender equality. Fong (2002), for example, has demonstrated that urban daughters who are only children have benefited from this policy since they now garner parental attention and investment that they did not have when they were part of a family with brothers. She suggests that in this context daughters have the power to defy disadvantageous gender norms. The one-child policy has also opened up educational opportunities and new career paths to young women (Veeck, Flurry, and Jiang 2003).

As suggested above, the early work on the traditional Chinese family suggested that even within a patriarchal and patrilineal system, women could manipulate kinship to their own advantage, something that Lamphere (1974: 99) has suggested gives them a measure of power. The strategic use of kinship by women has been identified in several other cultural contexts. Pioneering work by Carol Stack (1974) demonstrated how African-American families in a Midwestern town drew on kinship networks as a mechanism for economic survival. Through their domestic networks, women exchange a range of goods and services including child care. They rely on one another and through collective efforts keep one another afloat. When one member of the network achieves a degree of economic success she can choose to withdraw from kin cooperation to conserve resources. However, by reinitiating gift-giving and exchange, at some point she can easily reenter the system.

Sharon Hicks-Bartlett (in this volume) offers a more recent portrait of poor African American families in the United States who are coping with urban poverty. Her research population resides in a small black suburb outside a major Midwestern city, but they too call on family-based, helping networks to minimize risk and fulfill immediate needs. Hicks-Bartlett describes the emotionally draining and labor-intensive work of parenting in a neighborhood filled with drugs and violence. The necessity of hypervigilance means that women often call on kin to help them with their children so that they can work. Adult children also put aside self-interest to assist one parent in the care of the other. In the absence of public programs and facilities, it is the kinship networks that become the lifelines of the urban poor. It is kin who provide transportation, housing, food, and employment leads, in addition to childcare service. But, given the extent of poverty and hardship, the kin networks are often stressed and overwhelmed.

Afro-Caribbean families also confront conditions of economic uncertainty and stress. Research in the Caribbean region has generated a vigorous debate about a complex of characteristics, including female-headed households, women's control of household earnings and decision making, kinship networks linked through women, and the absence of resident men. This complex of characteristics has been referred to as matrifocality. Drawing on data from her research in Jamaica, Marsha Prior (in this book) reviews the concept of matrifocality, a concept first introduced by Raymond Smith in 1956 to describe the central position and power of the mother within the household. Rather than viewing these households as disorganized or pathological results of slavery and colonialism, anthropologists recently have stressed their adaptive advantages (Bolles and Samuels 1989) for women who are both mothers and economic providers. Furthermore, as Prior suggests, the composition of households in the Caribbean is fluid; they can be female-headed at one point in time and nuclear at another. Arguing against a widely held conception within anthropology, Prior suggests that fathers and male partners are by no means marginal to the household.

Prior points out that very little work has been done on the relations between men and women in such households because men were always assumed to be absent. One neglected aspect of male–female household relations is domestic violence.

Such violence often emerges because the expectations that women hold for men, whether they are monetary contributions to the household or fidelity, are not fulfilled. The potential for violence that can erupt when women challenge men about these unfulfilled obligations can undercut the power that women otherwise maintain within the household.

Women-centered families like those of African-Americans and Afro-Caribbeans have been described for other parts of the world (Tanner 1974). Both Brettell (1986) and Cole (1991) find such families among populations in northern Portugal and link them to a long history of male emigration. Whether in agriculture or in fishing, many women in northern Portugal must fulfill both male and female roles within the household. In this region women often inherit significant property, and there is a tendency for matrilocal residence or neolocal residence near the wife's kin. This matrilateral bias is also apparent among Japanese-American immigrants in the urban United States (Yanagisako 1977). Manifested in women-centered kin networks, this bias influences patterns of co-residence, residential proximity, mutual aid, and affective ties. Rather than stressing the economic reasons for the maintenance of kinship ties, Yanagisako draws attention to the role of women as kin keepers who foster and perpetuate channels of communication and who plan and stage elaborate family rituals.

The social and ritual importance of kinship is precisely what Micaela di Leonardo (in this book) focuses on in her discussion of the female world of cards and holidays. The Italian-American women she describes work in the labor market and at home, but they are also engaged in "kin work." Kin work is women's work and involves maintaining contact through all kinds of mechanisms with family members who are deemed important. Unlike childcare and house cleaning, it is a task that has to be carried out by the woman herself. Though it is often burdensome, women undertake kin work, according to di Leonardo, because through it they can set up a chain of valuable and long-term obligations within a wide circle of social relations.

Although di Leonardo identifies other parts of the developed world in which women have greater kin knowledge than men and work hard at maintaining kinship networks (for example, Lomnitz and Perez-Lizaur 1987), several questions are open to further empirical investigation. For example, why does kin work take on ritual significance in some societies, and why is it culturally assigned to women in some contexts and to men in others? Di Leonardo interprets the emergence of gendered kin work in association with a relative decline in importance of the domain of public male kinship that is found, for example, in African societies characterized by a powerful principle of descent. The shift, she suggests, is part of the process of capitalist development. Enloe (1990) has taken these arguments much further by demonstrating how both global politics and global economics are engendered. Without kin work, for example, Hallmark (the card manufacturer) would be out of business.

Collier and Yanagisako (1987) have argued that gender and kinship are mutually constructed and should be brought together into one analytic field (see also Stone 1997). Kinship and gender are closely allied because they are both based in, but not exclusively determined by, biology and because what it means to be a man or a woman is directly linked to the rules of marriage and sexuality that a culture constructs. As Lindenbaum (1987: 221) has observed, "Relations of kinship are in certain societies, relations of production. If kinship is understood as a system that organizes the liens we hold on the emotions and labors of others, then it must be studied in relation to gender ideologies that enmesh men and women in diverse relations of productive and reproductive work. The variable constructions of male and female that emerge in different times and places are central to an understanding of the character of kinship."

REFERENCES

Bolles, A. Lynn, and Deborah d'Amico Samuels. 1989. "Anthropological Scholarship on Gender in the English-Speaking Caribbean." In Sandra Morgen (ed.). *Gender and Anthropology*, pp. 171–188. Washington, DC: American Anthropological Association.

Brettell, Caroline B. 1986. *Men Who Migrate, Women Who Wait: Population and History in a Portuguese Parish*. Princeton, NJ: Princeton University Press.

Brown, Judith K. 1970. "Economic Organization and the Position of Women Among the Iroquois." *Ethnohistory* 17: 151–167.

Cole, Sally. 1991. *Women of the Praia: Work and Lives in a Portuguese Coastal Community*. Princeton, NJ: Princeton University Press.

Collier, Jane Fishburne, and Sylvia Junko Yanagisako. 1987. *Gender and Kinship: Essays Toward a Unified Analysis*. Stanford, CA: Stanford University Press.

Enloe, Cynthia. 1990. *Bananas, Beaches and Bases: Making Feminist Sense of International Politics*. Berkeley: University of California Press.

Fong, Vanessa. 2002. "China's One-Child Policy and the Empowerment of Urban Daughters." *American Anthropologist* 104: 1098–1109.

Fortes, Meyer. 1949. *The Web of Kinship Among the Tallensi*. London: International African Institute. New York: Oxford University Press.

———. 1953. "The Structure of Unilineal Descent Groups." *American Anthropologist* 55: 25–39.

Fox, Robin. 1967. *Kinship and Marriage: An Anthropological Perspective*. Harmondsworth, UK: Penguin.

Friedl, Ernestine. 1975. *Women and Men: An Anthropologist's View*. New York: Holt, Rinehart and Winston.

Gough, Kathleen. 1961. "Nayar: Central Kerala." In David M. Schneider and Kathleen Gough (eds.) *Matrilineal Kinship*, pp 298–384. Berkeley: University of California Press.

Hong, Lawrence K. 1987. "Potential Effects of the One-Child Policy on Gender Equality in the People's Republic of China." *Gender and Society* 1: 317–326.

Lamphere, Louise. 1974. "Strategies, Cooperation, and Conflict Among Women in Domestic Groups." In Michelle Z. Rosaldo and Louise Lamphere (eds.). *Woman, Culture, and Society*, pp. 97–112. Stanford, CA: Stanford University Press.

Levi-Strauss, Claude. 1969. *The Elementary Structures of Kinship*. Boston: Beacon Press.

Lindenbaum, Shirley, 1987. "The Mystification of Female Labors." In Jane Fishburne Collier and Sylvia Junko Yanagisako (eds.). *Gender and Kinship: Essays toward a Unified Analysis*. pp. 221–244. Stanford, CA: Stanford University Press.

Lomnitz, Larissa, and Marisol Perez-Lizaur. 1987. *A Mexican Elite Family, 1820–1980*. Princeton, NJ: Princeton University Press.

Martin, M. Kay, and Barbara Voorhies. 1975. *Female of the Species*. New York: Columbia University Press.

Maynes, Mary Jo, Ann Waltner, Birgitte Soland, and Ulrike Strasser. 1996. *Gender, Kinship, Power: A Comparative and Interdisciplinary History*. New York: Routledge.

Menon, Shanti. 1996. "Male Authority and Female Authority: A Study of the Matrilineal Nayars of Keral, South India." In Mary Jo Maynes, Ann Waltner, Birgitte Soland, and Ulrike Strasser (eds.). *Gender, Kinship, Power: A Comparative and Interdisciplinary History*, pp. 131–148. New York: Routledge.

Ortner, Sherry. 1978. "The Virgin and the State." *Feminist Studies* 4 (3): 19–35.

Potash, Betty (ed.). 1986. *Widows in African Societies*. Stanford, CA: Stanford University Press.

Schlegel, Alice. 1972. *Male Dominance and Female Autonomy: Domestic Authority in Matrilineal Societies*. New Haven, CT: Human Relations Area Files.

Smith, Raymond. 1956. *The Negro Family in British Guiana: Family Structure and Social Status in the Villages*. London: Routledge and Kegan Paul.

Stack, Carol. 1974. *All Our Kin*. New York: HarperCollins.

Stone, Linda. 1997. *Kinship and Gender: An Introduction*. Boulder, CO: Westview Press.

Tanner, Nancy. 1974. "Matrifocality in Indonesia and Africa and Among Black Americans." In Michelle Z. Rosaldo and Louise Lamphere (eds.). *Woman, Culture, and Society*, pp. 129–156. Stanford, CA: Stanford University Press.

Veeck, Ann, Laura Flurry, and Haihua Jiang. 2003. "Equal Dreams: The One Child Policy and the consumption of Education in Urban China." *Consumption Markets & Culture* 6:81–94.

Wolf, Margery. 1972. *Women and the family in rural Taiwan.* Stanford, CA: Stanford University Press.

Yanagisako, Sylvia Junko. 1977. "Women-Centered Kin Networks in Urban Bilateral Kinship." *American Ethnologist* 2: 207–226.

Beyond the "Pattern of Heaven":
Gender, Kinship and the Family in China

Monica Cable

Traditional Chinese culture, with its heavy Confucian influence, is often portrayed as an example of extreme patrilineality with women playing a nearly invisible role in the family line. However, there is a danger of oversimplifying the relationship between gender and kinship in Chinese society, especially when the focus is on the strict hierarchical relationships that seem to be the foundation of traditional Chinese culture. In her significant research on the Chinese family, Margery Wolf (1968) acknowledges that the study of the Chinese family is a popular one and cautions her readers saying, "the study of the Chinese family is a never-ending enterprise, and [readers] must be ready to revise [their] ideas on it as research of increasing sophistication is put before [them]" (Wolf 1968: xiii). This warning, coupled with Freedman's (1958) assertion a decade earlier that China is hardly a homogenous society, has served to expand the scope of Chinese gender and kinship studies, no easy task given the great difficulty and often impossibility of conducting research in mainland China between the 1940s and late 1970s.

Greater access to mainland China in the last 25 years is showing just how complex Chinese culture is and how widely it varies across the country. The majority ethnic group in China is the Han at nearly 92% of the population, with the remaining 8% (some 100 million people)

divided among 55 different minority groups. Not only is the majority Han Chinese culture not homogenous, but many of these minority ethnic groups—also considered to be "Chinese"—have traditions vastly different from those of the Han. While Han Chinese society almost certainly represents one of the most male-centric kinship systems, there are important subtleties within the Han Chinese tradition and distinctive practices among China's minority ethnic groups that deserve a closer look. In this article, I explore the interrelationship between gender, kinship and the family in what scholars have frequently termed "Chinese" culture, suggest that it be more accurately termed Han Chinese culture, and offer examples of alternative models of kinship seen in several of China's ethnic minority groups.

THE HAN CHINESE

Up until the unification projects undertaken by the Qin Dynasty (221 B.C.–206 B.C.), China consisted of smaller kingdoms that were likely home to diverse ethnic groups. Under China's first emperor Qin Shihuang, however, these groups were united and the written language (and perhaps the spoken one as well) was standardized. Han Chinese identity was formed during the Han Dynasty (206 B.C.–220 A.D.), and throughout the next 2,000 years the category of Han was marked by a unity and cohesion that transcends great ecological, physical, linguistic

Original text prepared for this book. Reprinted by permission of the author.

and subcultural diversities. Several factors unite this otherwise heterogeneous group, two of the most important ones being the Confucian tradition and patrilineal kinship.

Confucianism

Founded by Kong Fuzi (romanized as Confucius in the Western tradition) in the 6th century B.C., Confucianism is an open system, and people (namely men) may join through self-cultivation, not by birth. Unlike some forms of nationalism or racism that set up strict boundaries between "us" and "them," Confucianism defines "us" quite loosely, traditionally allowing anyone (again, typically male) who adopts its doctrine to join. One of the primary tenets of Confucianism is filial piety, and classical Chinese texts are filled with references from Confucius and his disciples extolling this virtue. One book, the *Classic of Filial Piety* written during the Han Dynasty (206 B.C.–220 A.D.), emphasizes that "Filial piety is the pattern of Heaven," and without this virtue humankind is subject to chaos and disorder (Ebrey 1981b:65).

Confucianism's emphasis on filial piety is not limited to the relationship between sons and fathers, but rather requires that children of both sexes honor their father and mother equally. On this the *Classic of Filial Piety* is quite clear, stating that scholars (those well-versed in the Classics) "serve their mothers as they serve their fathers; the love shown them is the same" (ibid.) Despite this lip-service paid to the importance of mothers, Confucian tradition is otherwise marked by an embedded sexism and double standard for men and women. Men, according to Confucianism, should strive to become *junzi* (gentlemen), acting with *ren* (compassion, benevolence) and observing *li* (propriety, ritual). Women, on the other hand, are simply encouraged to be a good wife and mother and help the men in her life (husband and sons) become *junzi*.

A second important facet of Confucianism is its emphasis on the five relationships (*wu lun*): ruler/minister, father/son, elder brother/younger brother, husband/wife, and friend/friend. These relationships, based on the idea of benevolence on the part of the superior and obedience on the part of the inferior, were the foundation of Chinese society. Through observing the five relationships and their strict hierarchy, Chinese society (including the family) could avoid conflict and achieve the goal of group harmony (Baker 1979).

Patrilineal Kinship

The Confucian emphasis on filial piety and the very limited role played by women is echoed in the Chinese practices of ancestor worship and patrilineal kinship. Patrilineal surnames provided the Han Chinese with connections to a common (albeit distant) ancestor, and family records have been kept since at least as far back as the Han Dynasty. These genealogies served to cement male hegemony as women were typically noted in family histories only as daughters, wives and mothers, not individuals. Excerpts from genealogy rules set forth by one extended family indicate that women who were widowed and then remarried, or divorced by their husband would not be recorded in the family tree "because the relationship between the husband and the wife was terminated" (Ebrey 1981a:327).

One reason for such careful record keeping is that Han Chinese kinship groups often played an important role in political and economic concerns, particularly for those highly organized corporate lineages. Opinion is divided as to whether or not this corporate aspect is a defining characteristic of the Han Chinese lineage, especially considering that this ownership of property is not a rigid criterion of several Chinese kinship terms that may be translated as lineage (Watson 1982; Cohen 1990; Wolf 1989; Faure 1989). Even if corporate ownership is not a defining factor, there is abundant evidence that many lineages did own land and maintained ancestral halls, as well as other shared entities (Baker 1979; Freedman 1970; Hsu 1948; Ruf 2000; Skinner 1977; Szonyi 2002; R. Watson 1985; Watson 1982).

Lineage organization varied widely throughout China, and could range from several hundred members to over ten thousand (Johnson 1983). Membership in these lineages was reckoned through the male line, and due to patrilocal marriage tendencies could create entire villages composed of one or two extended families. Despite some alternatives (discussed below), this extensive male network in which women may be seen as only a means to propagate the lineage is often cited as a major factor in the low status of Han Chinese women. The traditional Han Chinese patrilocal residence pattern entailed women leaving their natal families to marry outside their own community, in effect removing women from what might have otherwise been a supportive network of kin.

The Surname

The importance of the Han Chinese patriline is reflected in Chinese kinship terms and the (formerly) strict rules of surname exogamy. Kinship terms for the father's side of the family are numerous and varied, and there are distinct terms (often differing in terms of relative age) for related males from the great-great-grandfather to the more distantly related third cousin. On the mother's side, however, kinship terms were more general, and even close male relatives like mother's brother were lumped together under one term regardless of age.

All holders of a given surname were believed to have descended from a common ancestor, and marriages must be arranged outside of these broad family groups. Since descent was traced through the male line, marriage to a woman born into the group descended from the great-great-grandfather was deemed inappropriate, while marriage to one's mother's brother's daughter would be entirely acceptable. The traditional assumption that all members of a surname were related may be somewhat absurd, especially considering that the widespread nature of the surname Li is due to it being an honor conferred during the Tang Dynasty (618–907 A.D.) (Baker 1979). In addition, due to the mutually incomprehensible dialects in the Chinese language, there exist surnames written with different characters that are in some regions pronounced the same. In areas where the family names were pronounced the same, members could not intermarry; in those parts of China where the characters had different pronunciations, however, these individuals were not considered to be related.

Life Stages of the Han Chinese Woman

Han Chinese traditions placed the female in an extremely inferior position. An historical Han Dynasty (206 B.C.–220 A.D.) text entitled *Admonitions for Women*—written by a female—details the proper behavior for women in traditional Han Chinese culture.

"In ancient times, on the third day after a girl was born, people placed her at the base of the bed, gave her a pot shard to play with, and made a sacrifice to announce her birth. She was put below the bed to show that she was lowly and weak and should concentrate on humbling herself before others. Playing with a shard showed that she should get accustomed to hard work and concentrate on being diligent." (Ebrey 1981c:75)

Due to their subordinate position, women should defer to men throughout their lives: first to their fathers, then to their husbands, and upon widowhood to their sons. Even after death women continued to rely on men as the fate of their soul depended on the ancestor worship conducted by descendents of a male line (Baker 1979).

From birth, Han Chinese girls were at a disadvantage vis-à-vis their position in the family. First, there was the possibility of infanticide—poor families may be particularly reluctant to "waste" precious resources on a member who would not be able to perform as much labor on behalf of the group and ultimately marry out. One Chinese proverb goes so far as to compare raising a daughter to the watering of someone else's garden; another saying from southern China calls daughters "goods on which one loses one's capital" (Baker 1979:41).

Perhaps the most important life event for a Han Chinese woman was her marriage. While men seldom had more say in their marriage partner than women, the patrilocal residence patterns of the Han Chinese effectively removed women from whatever kin-based support network they might have. In the act of marrying into her husband's family, a Han Chinese woman in effect became the property of her husband's patriline and served the purpose of providing the family with (male) heirs and serving her new mother-in-law. Not surprisingly, the relationship between a new bride and her mother-in-law was one fraught with discord and often tyranny on the part of the elder female, who at last had someone in her household of lower status than herself.

A variation on this preferred patrilocal form of marriage was a minor form, the practice of purchasing or fostering a young girl and raising her with the idea that she would ultimately marry one of the fostering family's sons. Often referred to as *sim-pua*, this minor marriage in some ways was beneficial to both the bride's family and that of the groom. For one, the cost of raising a daughter (who often replaced the family's own daughter who was similarly fostered out) was much less than the cost of a traditional wedding and the accompanying bride price, and the new daughter-in-law would in theory already be accustomed to the ways of her husband's family. Secondly, the girl's family was spared the expense of raising a child who would leave the household almost as soon as she became a productive member. On the other hand, these marriages were often characterized by marital issues between the husband and wife, issues likely founded in the fact that the two were raised almost as siblings.

If marriages were not difficult enough on Chinese women, divorce was something even more feared and another matter in which the Han Chinese woman's position was highly precarious. While it was almost impossible for a woman to initiate the divorce process, she could be expelled from her husband's family for reasons such as barrenness, wanton conduct, and the neglect of her in-laws, among others (Baker 1979). The most feared of these three was barrenness, and only after a woman had borne a son (thus continuing the patriline) was her position in her husband's family made more secure.

Nuanced Approaches to Han Chinese Gender and Kinship

Much of the information on the conventional Han Chinese cultural practices detailed above comes from China's extensive historical record—a record that itself is male-centric. Given China's large geographic, cultural, and class differences, it is not surprising that there were many departures from the traditional theme—variations that indicate women may have been less of the pawns painted by the above discussion. It is this lack of cultural homogeneity that a number of scholars (Duara 1988; Ebrey 1981; R. Watson 1981; Wolf 1968) point to as they object to this overly andro-centric picture of Han Chinese kinship and the family and instead present viable alternative models.

Perhaps most famous is Wolf's idea of the uterine family, a mother-centered family unit that could serve to support women cut off from their natal kin networks. Before this groundbreaking research on Chinese kinship from a female's perspective, it had largely been assumed that Chinese women fit into the patriline only as wives and mothers; this is somewhat understandable as most research done on Chinese kinship in particular and culture in general had been conducted by men and relied on historical documents written by men or male informants. Wolf's research and theories on the uterine family were innovative in that they explore the previously overlooked or neglected role and perceptions of Chinese women.

According to Wolf (1972), the uterine family consisted of mothers and their children, who belonged to her husband's patriline. By focusing her energy and efforts on her uterine family, a woman may create a future source of influence and security not found in her husband's family. Whereas patrilineal bonds were often reinforced by ritual, these uterine ties were strengthened by the emotional attachments between a woman and her children. For Wolf, the Chinese family from the female perspective is not the same as the patrilineal unit of her father or husband, but rather a domestic unit that centers on herself. Unlike the patriline, the uterine family is not distinguished by lines of descent and continuity with the ancestors, but rather it is a short-lived but crucial unit held together through the resolve of the woman herself.

Uterine families should not necessarily be seen as being more egalitarian toward women, however, since they continued to depend heavily on the woman's sons. Because of the patrilocal residence patterns, a woman's daughters would marry out; her sons, however, traditionally remained in their natal home and once grown could serve to protect their mother's interests in family affairs. A Confucian element to the uterine family can be seen in the idea that the mother would need to stress the idea of filial piety. In order for a woman's investment in this mother-centric family to pay off, her son(s) would need to remain loyal to his mother—perhaps even at the cost of the patriline—in order to repay the many sacrifices made by his mother on his behalf.

Arguing that the more traditional, patrilineal kinship model neglects to account for the relationship between children and parents, Stafford (1995, 2000) presents a more inclusive kinship model focusing on the role of both parents. Using the Chinese term *yang* (to raise), Stafford posits that Han Chinese kinship is instead a complex system of mutual responsibility between parents and children. When the children are young, the parents provide for their young both in terms of food and money; when the parents are aged, the obligations are reversed and the adult children provide for and nurture the elderly. Similar to Wolf's idea of a uterine family in which adult sons are obligated to protect the interests of their mother in old age, Stafford's *yang* theory expands the obligation to include the duty of sons to care for both parents.

In the uterine family, the key relationships are between the mother and her sons, a structure that makes the daughter-in-law a potential danger to the mother. Once a daughter-in-law comes into the picture, the mother has competition for her son's attention and affection as the new bride seeks to create her own uterine support network. Stafford's *yang* cycle, however, does not pit the mother and her daughter-in-law(s) against each other; instead, the sense of responsibility felt by daughters is transferred to her in-laws, a shift influenced by the patrilineal focus of traditional Han society. This continued androcentric emphasis in Chinese kinship may change, however, as China's families are radically restructured by the one-child policy discussed below.

Post-1949 Trends

Whether the Han Chinese pattern of family connections is patrilineal, uterine, or a nurturing cycle, the intertwining relationships between kinship, gender, and the family has been affected by changes in China since the founding of the People's Republic in 1949. Despite the new revolutionary and institutional milieu created by the Communist victory that appeared to counteract the importance of kin networks, some Chinese Communist Party (CCP) policies are generally regarded as having strengthened the traditional Chinese family. For example, governmental focus on public health and centralized assistance during widespread famines reduced mortality and concurrently increased the Chinese life span, providing people with expanded networks of kin (Tu, Liang, and Li 1989). In addition, new residence laws and restrictions on internal migration bound most men (and their sons) to their natal home, serving to reinforce and fortify local patrilines and increase their ability to provide intergenerational support (Davis-Friedmann 1991).

The CCP and the Constitution of 1950 provided women in China with at least *de jure* equality. The concurrent Marriage Law outlawed the practices of child betrothal and concubinage while at the same time granting women the right to divorce. While public and familial disapproval made divorce uncommon among both Han Chinese men and women (Baker 1979), before the Marriage Law women had many fewer options if they wanted out of a union. During Imperial times, a woman who left her husband's home would be guilty of abandonment and under the legal code could be imprisoned, beaten, and even sold by her husband (Ch'ü 1965). Extensive work on the part of CCP cadres in the 1950s to raise the status of women and promote this new equality appears to have been successful. The first three years of the policy saw the granting of close to two million divorces and by the end of the decade child marriage and the concubine tradition had been all but eliminated (*Beijing Review*, Sept. 12, 1983).

The collectivization of the Chinese economy and subsequent elimination of most private property, in tandem with increasing governmental pressure to abandon "superstitious" practices like ancestor worship, did create difficulties for large kinship institutions. On the corporate side of kinship, lineage associations in many areas of China were replaced by Communist Party organizations. Under pressure from the CCP to eliminate religious and so-called superstitious practices, traditional family shrines and temples disappeared from China's rural and agrarian regions (Yang 1965).

One of the greatest recent influences on the Chinese family has been the one-child policy, first outlined by the CCP in 1979. At first, the state-implemented birth control guidelines largely restricted women to bearing one child; a second child was permissible if the first one died of a noninheritable disease or was severely handicapped. "In one stroke of the bureaucratic pen, Chinese leaders decided that henceforth only half of all families would have a son to carry on the family name, [and] that the sibling relationship would disappear" (Davis and Harrell 1993:3). In less than a decade, however, the Chinese government had modified this overly-ambitious undertaking to reduce fertility, instead mandating that many rural families and minority ethnic groups could bear a second child, as could urban couples who were both only children themselves (Feeny 1989); in some areas, if the firstborn child was a girl the couple was also allowed to have a second. In this case, the government's decision to allow couples a second child if the first is female only serves to perpetuate the "feudal" idea that girls are less desirable than boys.

China's one-child policy has, not surprisingly, greatly affected the male/female ratio in the country. In 1982, the government began a vigorous campaign against the so-called "feudal" ideas that caused families to prefer boys over girls and urged the media to publicize cases of female infanticide (Honig and Hershatter 1988). The 1982 census indicated that the 0- to 4-year old group of the Chinese population contained an unexpectedly high ratio of boys to girls (Bannister 1984), and by 1985 some rural birth ratios hovered around 110 males for every 100 females, much higher than the norm of 105 males to 100 females (Davin 1985:63).

Technology seems to play an increasing role in the growing imbalance of male and female births as couples rely on ultrasound tests to determine the sex of the fetus. While this practice is not allowed by Chinese law, the practice is common and frequently leads to the abortion of a female fetus (Hardee, Xie and Gu 2004).

There are some questions regarding the accuracy of the male/female birth ratios, and some scholars believe that female births are severely underreported (so that parents can try again for a son), causing the ratio to appear greater than it actually is (Graham, Larsen, and Xu 1998; Yi, Ping, Gu, Xu, Li, and Li 1993). Whether or not the sex ratio for male and female births is as high as it appears—1.27 males for every 1 female in some rural areas (Graham, Larsen, and Xu 1998:73)—the male/female imbalance in China has some serious implications for gender relations, marriage, and the family. There are already reports of an increase in the trafficking of women to provide men with brides (Schmetzer 1991; *China Focus* 1995; *China News Digest* 1995; Gates 1996) and if left unchecked, this gender imbalance will have tremendous repercussions as fewer men are able to find brides and continue their patriline.

The one-child policy may have already radically impacted the power of the traditional patriline as the extended family network has been greatly reduced. By now there is a generation of Chinese born without siblings; as these only children begin to have children of their own, the next generation will find themselves largely without collateral relatives, reducing the patrilineal network to direct lineal kin and effectively pruning what had been a complex family tree (Hong 1987; Chen 1985).

Despite the advantages and possibly the economic and environmental necessity of controlling population growth in China, the one-child policy may have serious social repercussions. As mentioned above, Chinese children will ideally be only children; the sole focus of parental and grandparental attention is already creating little emperors and empresses, and these children have become demanding and self-indulgent (Huang 1982).

The one-child policy may have serious consequences on social security, particularly in terms of care for the elderly in China. Since the 1950s, not only has the average number of children dropped from 6 to around 2, but life expectancy has risen from some 40 years to almost 70 (Jiang 1995:127). The implications are clear: as China's population ages, there will be an increased burden on adult children to care for their elderly parents who are living longer. The combination of a lack of siblings and the recent socio-economic reforms that have reduced welfare programs may leave couples with a heavy burden and responsibility with little opportunity for assistance or respite. In such an atmosphere, it would seem that Stafford's *yang* (to raise) cycle may become especially important as aging parents depend solely on their child for support.

ALTERNATE MODELS OF KINSHIP AND THE FAMILY IN CHINA

As mentioned above, China consists of 56 different ethnic groups with widely varying cultural traditions and as citizens of China, all of these different groups may be regarded as Chinese. Just as earlier scholars urged their readers to remember that Chinese culture is not homogenous, I argue that the time has come to take this idea one step further. No less "Chinese" than the majority Han, minority groups like the Dai, the Lahu, and the Mosuo have vastly different models of kinship and gender, and as such western scholars need to include these traditions and thus broaden the idea of the relationship between the family, gender, and kinship in China.

The Dai

The Dai, also known as the Tai-Lue (or simply Lue), are a Tai-speaking group of some 300,000 residing in the Xishuangbanna Dai Autonomous Prefecture in the People's Republic of China's southwestern province of Yunnan. Xishuangbanna, sometimes referred to in Mandarin simply as Banna, is a form of the Dai word for the region, or Sipsong Panna, "twelve rice-growing regions."

Unlike the Han, Dai kinship is bilateral, with descent reckoned through both the female and male lines. Among the Dai there are no corporate lineages—in fact, the Dai lack surnames that make lineage membership easily identifiable. Instead, Dai proper names for men all begin with the syllable Ai, and names for women begin with the syllable Yi. For example, because of my long-term fieldwork among the Xishuangbanna Dai, I have been given a Dai name that clearly identifies me as female: Yi Xiang Ga.

Another aspect that clearly sets the Dai apart from the Han is their matrilocal post-marriage residence pattern. According to tradition, husbands move into their bride's natal homes for three years, during which the men provide labor for the woman's family. At the end of the three years, the couple may remain in the woman's natal village and set up their own independent household, or they may move to the man's natal village and set up a household there.

In the case of divorce, again the Dai tradition is much different from that of the Han. Even before the legal protection afforded women in China after the Marriage Law of 1950, a divorce could occur at the request of either the husband or the wife. According to my sources, a woman only had to pack up her belongings and move back to her natal home or village for a divorce to occur; and in most cases, any children born during the marriage remained with the mother.

Perhaps the most perplexing aspect of Dai culture to outsiders (particularly the Han) is the practice of changing one's name based on the eldest child. For example, when a child is born, both parents lose their original names and become "Mother of so-and-so" or "Father of so-and-so." As Rubie Watson discusses in this volume, Han Chinese women frequently lose their given names after marriage or childbirth, but Han men may gain more names depending on their stage in the life cycle. For the Dai, however, the names of both the mother and the father change in the same manner. Once the eldest child has children of their own, most men and women are simply called *Botao* (old man) or *Mietao* (old woman) respectively.

The Lahu

The Lahu, a Tibeto-Burman speaking group (Matisoff 1988) residing in the mountainous border regions of Myanmar (Burma), Laos, Thailand, Vietnam, and China, are noted for their high degree of gender equality. As evidenced by the saying, "Chopsticks only work in pairs," the Lahu place a great deal of value on gender unity, with this ideal being traced back to their dyadic worldview in which men and women work together in teams (Du 2002).

Unlike the Han, the Lahu show no preference towards male or female children and families are run jointly by the husband and wife team. "According to [the Lahu] worldview, it is only right and natural that men and women . . . take joint roles as much as possible in all areas, including pregnancy, childbirth, childcare, domestic chores, subsistence work, and leadership" (Ibid.:1).

Whereas Han Chinese kinship is patrilineal, Lahu kinship is bilateral and the kin terms are not only based on the individual, but on the married couple. This type of "dyadic ego" (Du 2002:140) is highly unusual, and serves to take the married couple as a single entity, with the new spouse using the same kin terms as their partner had used before marriage. For example, even if a man is older than his wife's elder brother, he will use the same kinship terminology as his wife uses; for the Lahu, the married dyad is more important than the individual.

The husband and wife team is expected to share the workload both in the fields and at home, to the extent that the husband is expected to participate in all stages of his wife's pregnancy, childbirth, and the care of the child. Whereas in Han Chinese culture the pregnant woman may be assisted by a female midwife, Lahu tradition dictates that the husband plays this role, comforting and even physically supporting his wife as the baby is born (Du 2002). As the child grows, Lahu gender dynamics again differ from Han tradition where childcare falls almost exclusively on the woman (Jacka 1997). Lahu villagers interviewed by Du expressed their surprise that the Han did not share the burden of childcare, saying that Han fathers acted "as if the children were not theirs" (Du 2002:96). This is a particularly ironic statement considering that children born to the Han are virtually the property of their father's patriline.

The Mosuo

A matrilineal group living in southwest China, the Mosuo are subsumed within the officially recognized Naxi minority, a group whose kinship is also matrilineal. The formation of the family and the relationships between men and women in Mosuo culture provide another alternate form of kinship that varies from the Han Chinese, as well as both the Dai and Lahu minority groups. Also known as Moso or Na, the Mosuo practice a unique form of male/female pairing they call *tisese*, or *zouhun* in Mandarin, commonly translated as "walking marriage."

Both men and women reside in their natal households, which often are made up of three or four generations of blood relatives all linked by the matriline (Shih 2001). The *tisese*, or walking marriage, may be initiated by either the man or the women showing interest in the other. Men visit their lovers at night (and may indeed visit several in one night just as the women may have multiple visitors) and then return to their own home in the early morning. Both men and women have the right to refuse advances from the opposite sex, and the relationship may continue until the man is refused entrance to the woman's home or he stops coming. At no point in the relationship is there an economic tie between the couple; instead, the relationship exists "to fulfill their needs for procreation and sexual gratification" (Ibid.:384).

In effect, Mosuo society functions without husbands or fathers (Hua 2001). Like the Han lineage, the Mosuo female line or *lignée* may be corporate and all property held by the matriline is communal (Ibid.). Unlike the Lahu, in Mosuo culture there is a distinct sexual division of labor, although the Mosuo *lignée* does mirror the Lahu dyadic couple and is headed by a male and female pair—typically the eldest son and daughter of a generation.

Children born as a result of walking marriages are never considered illegitimate, but rather belong to the household in which they are born—in most cases their mother's. Because of the matrilineal aspect of the group, the primary male figure in a child's life is his mother's brother; in many cases, the genitor (biological father) of the child may never be known. The importance of the matriline and the lack of a formalized marriage institution is evident in Mosuo kinship terminology; based on the idea of consanguinity, there are no Mosuo kinship terms for affines (in-laws), husband, or father. While the institution of marriage does exist among the Mosuo, it is a product of cross-cultural borrowing likely during the Yuan (1279–1368 A.D.) and the Qing (1644–1911 A.D.) (Shih 2001); interestingly enough, both of these dynasties were ruled not by the Han ethnic group, but by the Mongols and the Manchus respectively.

CONCLUSION

The above examples of four different Chinese societies could not be more different. The majority Chinese, the Han, are characterized by a heavily patrilineal system in which women at first glance have no other role than to bear children for their husband's lineage. Researchers like Margery Wolf and Freedman warned against an overly simplistic interpretation of gender and kinship in Chinese society, and through a closer examination of Wolf's uterine family and Stafford's *yang* (to raise) cycle, one can see more nuanced ways in which to better interpret the relationship between gender, kinship, and the family among the Han.

While the Han and their filial piety that Confucius declared to be the "pattern of heaven" are the majority in China, the remaining 55 ethnic minority groups constitute a population of over 100 million people with diverse kinship systems and gender relationships. Among the Dai, kinship is bilateral and individuals lack a last name that would place them firmly in a patri- or matriline. Lahu culture is characterized by gender equality and the idea that men and women work together in married dyads, as "chopsticks only work in pairs." Matrilineal Mosuo families are made up of natal households, with both men and women participating equally in a "walking marriage" in which the idea of father or even husband is unrecognized.

Through this examination of the various expressions of family relationships and gender in four different cultures in China, I have provided the reader with a glimpse of the diverse traditions that fall under the category of "Chinese." By looking at the variations both within Han

Chinese culture and some of the minority traditions, it is my hope that scholars will see the need to move beyond the strict patrilineal interpretation based on the Han tradition, and instead develop a more nuanced understanding of gender, kinship, and the family in China.

REFERENCES

Baker, Hugh D. R.
1979　*Chinese Family and Kinship*. New York: Columbia University Press.
Bannister, Judith
1984　Population Policy and Trends in China 1978–83. *The China Quarterly* 100:717–741.
Beijing Review
1983　"Woman Judge Talks About Divorce". (37):5–6.
Ch'ü, T'ung-Tsu
1965　*Law and Society in Traditional China*. Paris: Mouton & Co.
Chen, Xiangming
1985　The One-child Population Policy, Modernization, and the Extended Chinese Family. *Journal of Marriage and the Family* 47(1): 193–202.
China Focus
1995　*Kidnapping of Women and Children*. 3(5):7.
China News Digest (online)
1995　*China Hammers Insidious Crimes Against Female College Students*. April 22:#10.
Cohen, Myron
1990　Lineage Organization in North China. *Journal of Asian Studies* 49(3):509–534.
Davin, Delia
1985　The Single-Child Family Policy in the Countryside. In *China's One-Child Family Policy*, Elizabeth Cross, Delia Davin and Penny Kane, eds., pp. 37–82. New York: St. Martin's Press.
Davis, Deborah and Stevan Harrell
1993　Introduction, in *Chinese Families in the Post-Mao Era*, Deborah Davis and Stevan Harrell, eds., pp. 1–22. Berkeley: University of California Press.
Davis-Friedmann, Deborah
1991　*Long Lives*, 2nd ed. Stanford: Stanford University Press.
Du, Shanshan
2002　*"Chopsticks Only Work in Pairs": Gender Unity and Gender Equality Among the Lahu of Southwest China*. New York: Columbia University Press.

Duara, Prasenjit
1988   *Culture, Power, and the State, Rural North China, 1900–1942.* Stanford: Stanford University Press.

Ebrey, Patricia B.
1981a   Women in the Kinship System of the Southern Song Upper Class. *Historical Reflections,* 8:113–128.
1981b   *Chinese Civilization and Society: A Sourcebook.* New York: Free Press.

Ebrey, Patricia B. trans.
1981c   Admonitions for Women. In *Chinese Civilization,* Patricia Ebrey, ed., pp. 75–76. New York: The Free Press.

Faure, David
1989   The Lineage as a Cultural Invention: The Case of the Pearl River Delta. *Modern China,* 15(1):4–36.

Feeny, Griffith
1989   Recent Fertility Dynamics in China. *Population and Development Review* 15(4):707–730.

Freedman, Maurice.
1958   *Lineage Organisation in Southeastern China.* London: Athlone.
1970   Ritual Aspects of Chinese Kinship and Marriage. In *Family and Kinship in Chinese Society,* Maurice Freedman, ed., pp. 163–187. Stanford: Stanford University Press.

Gates, Hill
1998   Buying Brides in China Again. *Anthropology Today* 12(4):8–11.

Gates, Hill
1995   Buying Brides in China—Again. *Anthropology Today* 12(4):8–11.

Graham, Maureen J., Ulla Larsen and Xiping Xu
1998   Son Preference in Anhui Province. *International Family Planning Perspectives* 24(2):72–77.

Hardee, Karen, Zhenming Xie and Baochang Gu
2004   Family Planning and Women's Lives in Rural China. *International Family Planning Perspectives* 30(2):68–76.

Hong, Lawrence K.
1987   Potential Effects of the One-Child Policy on Gender Equality in the People's Republic of China. *Gender & Society* 1(3):317–326.

Honig, Emily and Gail Hershatter
1988   *Personal Voices: Chinese Women in the 1980's.* Stanford: Stanford University Press.

Hsu, Francis
1948   *Under The Ancestors' Shadow: Kinship, Personality and Social Mobility in Village China.* New York: Columbia University Press.

Hua, Cai
2001   *A Society without Fathers or Husbands.* New York: Zone Books.

Huang, L. J.
(1982)   Planned fertility of one-couple/one-child policy in The People's Republic of China. *Journal of Marriage and the Family,* 44, 775–784.

Huang, Lucy Jen
1982   Planned Fertility of One-Couple/One-Child Policy in the People's Republic of China. *Journal of Marriage and the Family* 44(3):775–784.

Jacka, Tamara
1997   *Women's Work in Rural China: Change and Continuity in an Era of Reform.* Cambridge: Cambridge University Press.

Jiang, Lin
1995   Changing Kinship Structure and its Implications for Old-Age Support in Urban and Rural China. *Population Studies* 49(1):127–145.

Johnson, Kay Ann
1983   *Women, the Family, and Peasant Revolution in China.* Chicago: University of Chicago Press.

Matisoff, James A.
1988   *The Dictionary of Lahu.* Berkeley: University of California Press.

Ruf, Gregory
2000   *Cadres and Kin: Making a Socialist Village in West China, 1921–1991.* Stanford: Stanford University Press.

Schmetzer, Uli
1991   China's Slavers Willing to Murder to Cover Tracks. *Chicago Tribune,* November 21:1.

Shih, Chuan-Kang
2001   Genesis of Marriage among the Moso and Empire-Building in Late Imperial China. *The Journal of Asian Studies* 60(2):381–412.

Skinner, G. William
1977   Introduction. *The Study of Chinese Society: Essays by Maurice Freedman,* William G. Skinner, ed. Stanford: Stanford University Press.

Stafford, Charles
1995   *The Roads of Chinese Childhood: Learning and Identification in Angang.* Cambridge: Cambridge University Press.
2000   Chinese Patriliny and the Cycles of *Yang* and *Laiwang.* In *Cultures of Relatedness: New Approaches to the Study of Kinship,* Janet Carsten, ed., pp. 37–54. Cambridge: Cambridge University Press.

Szonyi, Michael
2002   *Practicing Kinship: Lineage and Descent in Late Imperial China.* Stanford: Stanford University Press.

Tu, Edward, Jersey Liang, and Shaomin Li
1989   Mortality Decline and Chinese Family Structure, *Journal of Gerontology* 44(4):157–168.

Watson, James
1982   Chinese Kinship Reconsidered: Anthropo-
       logical Perspectives on Historical Research.
       China Quarterly 92:586–622.
Watson, Rubie
1981   Class Differences and Affinal Relations in
       South China. *Man* 16:593–615.
1985   *Inequality Among Brothers: Class and Kinship
       in South China.* Cambridge: Cambridge Uni-
       versity Press.
1986   The Nameless and the Named: Gender and
       Person in Chinese Society. American Eth-
       nologist 13(4):619–631.
Wolf, Arthur
1989   The Origins and Explanations of Varia-
       tion in the Chinese Kinship System. In
       Anthropological Studies of the Taiwan Area:

Accomplishments and Prospects. Taibei:
National Taiwan University.
Wolf, Margery
1968   *The House of Lim.* New York: Appleton-
       Century-Crofts.
Wolf, Margery
1972. *Women and the family in rural Taiwan.* Stanford,
       CA: Stanford University Press.
Yang, C. K.
1965   *The Chinese Family in the Communist Revolu-
       tion.* Cambridge: MIT Press.
Zeng, Yi, Tu Ping, Baochang Gu, Yi Xu, Bohua Li,
    and Yongping Li
1993   Cases and Implications of the Recent
       Increase in the Reported Sex Ratio at Birth
       in China. *Population and Development Review*
       19(2):283–302.

Between a Rock and a Hard Place:
The Labyrinth of Working and Parenting
in a Poor Community

Sharon Hicks-Bartlett

It was a quiet summer night in Meadow View. The crisp air and blue-black sky were tranquil. Suddenly the night's stillness was pierced by screams and yells of chilling distress. Shots rang out. No one could recall how many. At times like this, people move away from windows. Someone surely summoned the police. Although the station is only two minutes from any point in the community, the police take their time showing up. Events inside Lillie's apartment stunned the occupants and made it difficult later to remember exactly what transpired that terrible night. Things happened quickly. Everyone agreed, however, that men with guns broke into the apartment, yelling, cussing, and looking for Lillie's teenage son. When the boy refused to step forward, the gunmen threatened to kill

everyone. Lillie's son finally identified himself. At this point, things spun out of control.

All the gunmen wanted was Lillie's only son. But this was more than Lillie was willing to give. A slight woman, barely five feet, three inches, Lillie leapt in front of him, shielding him, flailing her arms, screaming and pleading for them not to hurt her child. They didn't. In split-second pandemonium, they killed Lillie instead. Dead at the age of forty-two, leaving five children and one grandchild.

Few people were able to maintain their equanimity during Lillie's funeral. Many wept openly as versions of what transpired that night circulated through the large, crowded church. A self-described, longtime family friend sang a mournful rendition of Lillie's "favorite" song, *"It's So Hard to Say Goodbye to Yesterday."* The minister railed at the unsaved souls, insisting that only those who had not accepted the Lord should experience difficulty saying good-bye. His words were less a eulogy than a stern lecture to those who were "living by the sword." As

Sharon Hicks-Bartlett, "Between a Rock and a Hard Place: The Labyrinth of Working and Parenting in a Poor Community," in *Coping with Poverty The Social Contexts of Neighborhood, Work, and Family in the African American Community.* Sheldon Danziger and Ann Chih Lin, eds., pp. 27–51. Ann Arbor: University of Michigan Press, 2000 .

sounds of sobbing filled the church, the minister bellowed at those who refused to identify Lillie's killers. The woman with whom I attended the funeral pointed out Lillie's ex-husband, who evidently had come up north to pay his respects and to retrieve his son. The community denounced the father for his son's refusal to cooperate with police. But silence, the father believed, was the only way to save his son's life. Following the funeral, father and son would be heading south to live.

At the funeral people whispered about the shame of it all, how things here had gone from bad to worse, how people couldn't even be safe at home, and how they feared for the future. They talked about the possible fallout from the killing. Might there be a retaliation murder like the one that occurred years before, when one young man shot another, only to be killed later by the brother of the man he had murdered days before? Back then, the community's lone undertaker prepared the bodies of both men. For the community's viewing convenience, the bodies were placed in adjacent parlors at the same time. Even then, many years before Lillie's murder, people were horrified by what was happening to Meadow View. Today, people continue to shake their heads in dismay, declaring that "people have simply gone mad."

In Meadow View families struggle to survive. Few do so unscathed. Even for those a step or two above the poorest, living in Meadow View is a merciless challenge. As residents often remark, "stuff is always happening here." The strain of rebounding from one crisis before the next occurs depletes the body and mind. Lillie's story captures the violence that can transpire here.

In discussing how we experience place, Tony Hiss explains that whether we realize it or not, we all react "consciously and unconsciously" to where we reside and work. "[P]laces have an impact on our sense of self, our sense of safety, the kind of work we get done, the ways we interact with other people, even our ability to function as citizens in a democracy . . . the places where we spend our time affect the people we are and can become" (Hiss 1990, xi). Meadow View is one of the nation's poorest suburbs; it is isolated from jobs, quality schools, and adequate community resources. In Meadow View,

for the greatest numbers of family members to survive, space must be strategically and carefully managed, which requires a level of vigilance that burdens families and reinforces their interdependency. But despite the gloomy state of affairs here, residents are tied to this terrain and to each other in real and symbolic ways. Despite all its problems, people call this place home. The stigma attached to coming from this place engenders in many a defensive bond that strengthens intergroup relations at the same time that it threatens to rip them apart. Affective bonds are always at risk because material, social, and financial need is unremitting. Already vulnerable families struggle to fulfill each other's needs, and this very exertion reinforces a "collective ethos" that binds people together (Jones 1986, 229).

Here, people manage working and parenting by relying on loose, family-based networks that minimize risk and center on meeting immediate needs. These networks provide the only security available to families in the face of recurrent threats to their physical well-being, isolation from jobs both within and outside their neighborhoods, and meager finances. Personal sacrifices, made for the good of the family unit, strain already limited family resources. Not surprisingly, the help of relatives who are themselves poor is never enough to change one's life situation. But when "self-sufficiency" is promoted as a policy objective without attention to the central role that family members play for one another, it is easy to overlook the fact that family and community sufficiency is required for the problems of the poor to be fully addressed.

Meadow View is a small black suburb outside a major midwestern city. This chapter is based on more than nine years of fieldwork in Meadow View. The daily lives of ten women were explored with an emphasis on family, community, and work. Four of the ten women were first interviewed during an earlier project; the others were added during research for this project, which took place during an eighteen-month period beginning in the summer of 1995 and ending in December 1996. The women, all of whom are mothers, were engaged in conversations of both a general and specific nature. Most of the interviews were tape-recorded and transcribed verbatim. Formal interviews ranged from two to more than five per person. In addition, my impromptu visits to homes produced many opportunities to talk, woman to woman, about a variety of topics.

These mothers were located through old contacts in the community, a worker at a community center, and one or two key informants. I explained to all the participants that I was interested in learning about family and community life. Consent forms that proffered more information about the study were disseminated to everyone. Participation was unanimous. Initially, no mention of money was made. Upon completion of the first interview, ten dollars was given to each informant. No mention of money was made or offered thereafter.

Interviews transpired in one of two places, with the vast majority occuring in private homes. A small number of first interviews were conducted in a vacant office at the community center. Subsequent interviews took place in the mothers' homes at their convenience. In addition, I often dropped by for informal "interviews."

All of the mothers are African-American. They represent a cross section of the women I have interviewed over my many years of involvement in the community. Each mother has had work experience, which tends to be part-time and low wage. Welfare use has ranged from a few months to more than ten years. All the women acquired their first job as teens in a federally funded summer youth employment program. Two of the women later secured either part-time or full-time work as adults in the same program. The other women typically hold jobs in service, retail, or manufacturing. With the exception of Sissy, the mother with the most education and work experience in the group, the mothers often talk of desiring jobs in the care-giving fields.

A SUBURB IN NAME ONLY

Although Meadow View is a suburb situated near a once-booming industrial region, it looks like the rural south, with its unpaved roads, two outhouses, and a creek set deep in the woods. Most of its nearly forty-five hundred residents, whether employed or not, are low income and black. By 1990, 49.2 percent of the population was below poverty level. Per capita income is just over $4,500. A large stamping plant sits outside the community, but few Meadow View residents hold these skilled and semiskilled jobs. By any measure, unemployment and underemployment are pervasive, creating a community dependent on government assistance. For those sixteen and over, Meadow View's unemployment rate is 26 percent. Local officials set the "real" unemployment rate higher than 50 percent. One glance around the community on any summer day gives credence to a community perception that "almost everybody is out of work."

Meadow View has always been a poor community. But not until it became poor *and* black did it develop such intractable problems. In the shift from a poor white community to a poor black community, Meadow View became a choice locale for low-income public housing projects. Now, 65 percent of housing is government projects. Their construction in this particular suburb, as opposed to other nearby middle-class suburbs, is a prime example of the collusion among local, state, and federal agencies to perpetuate racial and class segregation within Meadow View. This small community was particularly attractive to those who preferred suburban living but could only afford it where rock-bottom housing prices and regional housing discrimination allowed them to live.

Rajah, who is married and the mother of seven boys and an infant daughter, voices her trepidation about Meadow View; she routinely checks for opportunities to move to other suburbs.

> I've been looking and looking for a house for my kids. Looking forever! I got to get away from here before I go crazy or something happens to my boys. I'm sick of the water, I'm sick of the drugs, I'm sick of living here. This is insane! Too much stuff is happening all the time, something is always going on.

Theoretically, Rajah's income and housing subsidy would permit her to leave Meadow View. But if she succeeds, she will most likely relocate to another overwhelmingly poor, black suburb. Her subsidy was once a ticket into a safer, more economically viable suburb in the area. Now, those who want to leave often find themselves blocked as a result of a political battle between county and local housing authorities that restricts the mobility of the Section 8 certificates in this region (Hicks-Bartlett forthcoming). Leaving the community is even more difficult for those with little income and no housing subsidy.

Economic stability, adequate community resources, healthy infrastructure, strong institutions, a robust tax base, fiscal viability, and effective local government are some indicators of community well-being. Meadow View falls short on every single one. Like other old black suburbs, Meadow View's local government strains to keep afloat financially (Logan 1983/ 1988). Ironically, although Meadow View provides fewer services to its residents than its nearby suburban neighbors, its per capita expenditures are higher than theirs. This is because the local government's weak property tax base is insufficient to provide adequate services or maintain its deteriorating infrastructure. Delaying needed repairs to save money often costs more in the long run. Several times, the local government has teetered on the brink of bankruptcy. On more than one occasion both the police and fire department have gone on strike, imperiling the safety of residents. Except for church, few institutional supports are available to supplement and reinforce parental efforts. Community-sanctioned outlets for youth do not exist. Local services are so inadequate (e.g., years ago the local library had to be closed due to its unsafe structure and lack of operating funds) that people must go outside the community for most things.

In the summer of 1996, more than one hundred fifty people were arrested in a series of drug busts conducted by undercover sting operations. Previous raids had done little to clean up the community's drug trade. The latest round of sweeps came on the heels of the arrest of the police chief for allegedly permitting the drug trade to flourish with impunity, which had been rumored for years. More than a decade of police "passes" have brought down not only the police chief but also six current and former police officers, all of whom now face serious charges and lengthy prison sentences. Such corruption and graft lead many parents to believe that the job of protecting children from the fallout of this destitute place is their responsibility alone.

Surviving a summer requires considerable vigilance and management of one's space. Hot homes drive people outdoors to enjoy the camaraderie on the street. At the same time, an unremitting flow of out-of-state cars scouting for drug dealers stir feelings of besiegement and spark endless discussions of safety, drugs, and violence. Drugs control certain streets, making them difficult to maneuver. Late-model, expensive automobiles, with white people at the wheel, block traffic along some streets. These outsiders are the topic of considerable community discussion, distrust, suspicion, and anger. The mother of two young children summed up her feelings regarding these invasions:

> We can't even drive through their neighborhoods. But they can come here and do whatever they want. They don't care about nothing but getting drugs, but we the one's suppose to be so bad. We the ones *they* don't want to live by.

Often communities like this become a market for all sorts of spillover vice. Women and young girls are propositioned by strangers hunting for drugs and sexual thrills. Although men of all types scout the community for willing females, white males, perhaps because of their high visibility, evoke the greatest ire.

The fear of getting caught in the crossfire of a drug shoot-out and the concern that one's child will either use, deal drugs, or be caught up in spillover crime as a victim or participant preoccupy parents. Parents assert that "you've got to watch out for your own." Meadow View has become a place where children must learn the community's alarm call: "hit the deck" or simply, "get down." Watching children here is endless, exacting work. As one mother comments:

> We ain't been doing nothing but staying inside. They been shooting the last two nights. Girl, I'm scared to look out the window. My nerves is

already bad, now they really messed up. Seems like every time I try to fall asleep, racing cars or shooting wakes me up. You gotta keep yours inside—if you want 'em safe.

During interviews, mothers habitually peek out the window. This seemingly small gesture is repeated in households throughout the community. Parents survey the landscape, tirelessly scanning the environment, monitoring slow-moving cars, scrutinizing suspicious gatherings—behavior all rooted in indisputable facts of daily life. Before venturing out, people caution each other to "be careful." Some avoid going out at night altogether for fear of getting "caught" out after dark.

Young boys risk being seduced into illegal work. A fieldnote entry describes the challenges a parent can face. Mabel, mother of eight, expressed considerable angst about her sons. Her daughters worried her less because she had more success keeping them at home. One son, a particularly quiet youth of fifteen named Mark, was approached to work as a "lookout" for a local drug dealer. Fearing his mother's wrath, the boy rebuffed the offers. Later, a rather persistent drug dealer invited himself to Mabel's house to ask permission for the youth to work for him. Mabel listened patiently to the dealer's request. When he finished, she said, "Leave my son alone.... He can't work for you. Just leave him alone!" She was dead serious and hoped her steely glare transmitted that spirit.

Fearing that Mark would eventually turn to drug work, Mabel first thought of sending him south to live with his father's family. When this proved not to be a viable option, she tried to get him into a special program where he would leave the community to work on an out-of-state farm, safe from Meadow View streets. "For three years I wouldn't have to worry about him getting killed or something," she sighed. The program seemed a perfect solution. One problem remained, however. Because her son had never been in serious trouble, he was not eligible to enter the program through normal channels. Only if she abdicated her parental rights, formally declaring herself unfit, could he be admitted. The logic that required her son to be in trouble before he could receive

help seemed inane to Mabel. She weighed her options and declared that if giving up her rights was the only way to save her son, so be it. As she explains it:

I don't care too much about giving up my rights, if it can help him. He knows I'm his momma and I know I'm his momma. No piece of paper can change that. When he gets out, I'm quite sure he'll look me up and quite naturally he'll be grown and can understand what I had to do.

Mabel escaped having to surrender her parental rights. Her son managed to avoid drug work on his own. To Mabel, what happened seemed worse in some ways. A young cousin, while showing Mark his gun, accidentally shot and seriously wounded Mark in the head. Now, for the rest of his life, he will ingest medicines to control his seizures.

To separate working and parenting from this situational context is to fail to appreciate how bound the two are. Parents in nonpoor areas expect certain community qualities and services that support parenting. There is a vast difference, however, between the communities in which the poor and nonpoor reside, particularly those in which poor minority and poor non-minority live (Wilson 1987, 1996). While protecting children is a universal parental behavior, in Meadow View it can require extreme measures; it is labor-intensive, emotionally draining work. The need to protect children and the vigilance this requires create major barriers to working and parenting, especially when the two are attempted simultaneously. The mother of four young boys reveals what transpired one day.

Girl, a boy got shot the other day. Right out here in front of my apartment. He couldn't have been no more than fifteen. They killed him right out in broad day light. I was so glad my kids wasn't outside 'cause usually they would be right out there playing. But I had just made them come in a few minutes before. It took the ambulance a long time to get here. I was so scared . . . Blood, all in the street—it's still there. I just think about my kids. Girl what if they were out there. They coulda' got kill, too.

Frightened by her experience, she immediately requested, to no avail, that the project housing authority relocate her family to a safer area. Mothers like this woman cannot but think that if they were not at home to make their children come in, their children might be the next victims. Meadow View lacks before and afterschool programs that could engage children in constructive activities while parents work. Ironically, the luxury of such programs belongs to parents who live in neighborhoods where tax dollars can support such services or to parents who can purchase whatever care they desire for their children. But in Meadow View, where the need for such programs is so much greater, parents have neither the income nor the institutional supports to establish them.

Adults and children feel the effects of this stressful environment. Meadow View mothers often complain of "nerve problems." Some children become fearful and edgy. Others obsess about danger or being shot. Like Meadow View adults, children become extremely preoccupied with the environment and its inherent dangers. "Hypervigilance" is striking, seen in the ". . . scan[ning] [of] their surroundings for danger and over-interpret[ing] the actions of others . . ." (Brownlee 1996, 72). Nightmares about being chased, hurt, or killed are common. In one family, the stress on a mother and her two children, ages six and ten, is palpable. In discussing her children's fears, the mother laments:

> I can't get them out of my bed. You know, they are too big to be sleeping with me. But they too scared to be in the room by themselves. They got good beds to sleep in, but I can't get them in them for nothing. They sleep in here real good, but now I don't get any sleep. And my back stay hurt with one on each side kicking me, and I can't get comfortable. I really don't sleep at night. I catnap in the day, when they in school.

This sleep-deprived mother frequently complains of physical ailments. The only time she rests is when her children are at school. The many implications this would have on working outside the home are obvious.

The constancy of trauma and fear in their environment causes other problems in chil-

dren. One report found that children who experience early trauma (e.g., witnessing or fearing violence) show measurable physiological and chemical changes in the body and brain (Brownlee 1996, 72). When frightened, they react in a "fight-or-flight" response. The body attempts to compensate by releasing certain stress hormones. In affected children, normal physiological and chemical reactions jump track, producing abnormal levels and imbalances in the body. The impact on learning for children in these environments has been well documented (Garbarino et al. 1992; Prothrow-Stith and Weissman 1993). Affected children have a shorter attention span; language and critical thinking suffers. High levels of these harmful chemical changes create children who are ripe for a host of learning difficulties. Children in these environments may also misconstrue normal play as aggressive and get into physical altercations.

All of these challenges influence parental decisions about work and family. This does not mean that those who face such barriers should be exempt from paid labor. When faced with objective situations that require hypervigilance (e.g., children who require extraordinary nurturing, fear management, patience, and care of chronic health problems), most mothers concentrate on performing their maternal role above all else. Those lucky enough to find others they trust to care for their children are able to work—at least on and off—because of it. Without such support, employed work is difficult and sometimes impossible to sustain. Yet money for survival is as necessary as care for children and families. The support networks that spring up to meet these challenges address this dilemma, but in ways that lessen the significance of individual achievement and self-sufficiency.

KIN MATTERS

Meadow View families depend heavily on each other. Individuals and families expect to share with others. In addition to financial support, families provide an array of essential services, without which most would not be able to work, attend school, or enroll in training programs.

All of the families discussed here are involved in extensive helping networks that can buckle under the weight of a widening circle of needy members. Just how critical to survival these networks are is exemplified by one mother's family.

Wanda once lived in a two-bedroom project apartment with her two children. It also provided temporary quarters for her two brothers and two cousins, whom her parents raised after their mother died. Although she now works as a teacher's aide, Wanda received welfare for more than ten years. Throughout much of this time, she cared for her invalid mother. On occasion, Wanda received money from her parents but this was neither regular nor expected. To avoid placing the mother in a nursing home, Wanda's father, who worked full-time at a factory in a neighboring state, sought his children's help in caring for their mother. Since Wanda had a small child to care for, she was the designated sibling to help her mother and her employed siblings who might need occasional help. Two sisters, one employed in clerical work, the other in factory work, sometimes called on Wanda for child care. Providing care to those who need it is highly valued, particularly over low-wage work that may only slightly improve the individual's life while potentially burdening and making matters worse for the extended kin network.

Known for being able to stretch her welfare check, Wanda was often called on for a loan or a meal or a place to stay for a few days. She earned extra income by operating an in-house "store," a table set up in her kitchen from which she sold soda, potato chips, and candy to neighborhood youth; at best, her efforts rarely generated more than $30 a month. Although Wanda had her own share of money worries, she rarely refused anyone in need. For unexpected emergencies, she kept twenty dollars stashed away. Wanda's only complaint was that she did not have anyone as generous on whom *she* could rely. Although she felt she gave more than she ever received, Wanda did benefit from some invaluable help from this arrangement.

During her second pregnancy, Wanda moved from her parents' home into a subsidized apartment. Soon afterward, an assortment of relatives moved in and out. Until they found jobs, they were neither asked nor expected to help financially. When two relatives acquired jobs at a rehabilitation center, through another relative, they began giving Wanda money, helping with groceries and continuing to baby-sit. Whether working or not, they baby-sat whenever needed. Not only did this allow Wanda respite from her children, it also relieved the ennui of being housebound. Wanda benefited, too, from the protection and security of having men present.

> I don't mind having them here, they are good company. Plus, I know that no one is going to come in here on me when they know that a man lives here. . . . They help out just by being here. Plus it's good for my kids to be around their uncles and cousins.

Years later, while living alone with her two children, Wanda suffered a near fatal brain aneurysm. Her family sprang into action. During her nearly six-month rehabilitation, the extended family focused on Wanda's health. At the time, Wanda's brother Donnie had been planning to go to Mississippi for a long-awaited job. Unemployed for years, he looked forward to finally getting work—even though it required a major relocation. Because the other siblings were engaged in full- or part-time work, they were less available to attend to Wanda's needs. Together, the family decided that Donnie should move into Wanda's apartment and assume primary care of her children and her personal affairs. Other relatives helped out on weekends. When asked how he felt about having to give up his job, Donnie remarked, "You can always get another job, but you can't get another sister" (see also Stack 1990).

Wanda and her family viewed her miraculous recovery as a sign from God that she should improve her life. With the help of her caseworker, she enrolled in a community college and eventually became a teacher's aide. During Wanda's course work, Donnie, still unemployed, continued to live with her and help out, without pressure from his family to get a job. Caring for Wanda was a job that everyone in the family valued. Donnie never mentioned going South again. Until she finished school and found a job, Donnie selflessly contributed his unpaid labor to the family and Wanda's dreams. Now and then, Wanda gave him money, but he did not receive regular pay. Without his help, her recovery would have been difficult; her schooling would have been impossible. His child care and household work allowed Wanda to recover fully, reach a goal sparked by her illness, and obtain a job.

Most families will respond supportively to each other in times of crisis. In this sense, Wanda and her family are not unique. What is truly notable in Meadow View families is the degree to which individuals are summoned to meet the needs of others and to suppress personal goals to do so (see also Rank 1994). A great deal of working and schooling is made possible only because of the willingness of others to set aside self-interest. Many who manage to hold jobs have kin willing to defer individual pursuits for the sake of others. Because poor families cannot purchase the care their families need, they must supply it to each other.

Exploring the complicated arrangements mothers must make to work and parent simultaneously reveals how tenuous these arrangements are and how even a slight error can trigger a full-blown, snowballing crisis in families. Children's illness is a universal barrier to working that all parents face, particularly parents of young children. According to Heymann, Earle, and Egleston (1996), fully one-fourth of all parents reported that they had no sick leave available to take care of sick relatives, including their children. But children's ailments often require them to miss school. An estimated ten million children have some sort of chronic disorder. Not surprisingly, poor children have poorer health. They have a higher incidence of chronic ailments, while their working parents have the least amount of sick leave to tend to them. Sissy, a young mother who worked in retail, tells how she finally had to quit her job because of her infant's chronic respiratory condition.

> My sister was watching him but he just kept a cold. He'd have one a couple of weeks. Then he'd be okay a couple of weeks. Then he'd get sick again. I had to keep taking off to take him back and forth to the doctor. He wasn't eating right at all. My baby was so sick! They wanted to

put tubes in his ears. When he couldn't breathe, my sister would call me at work and I had to rush home to take him to the hospital. She couldn't take him because she had to watch her own baby. So I had to quit because I was taking off a lot. I wasn't making no money. They were going to fire me because I had so many problems with the baby. I don't know if they believed me. My mother said I need to think about my baby and stay at home to take care of him myself. So I quit.

A preference for family/friend child care over other types of care derives from the conviction that only family can be depended on to deal flexibly with frequent emergencies.

In Meadow View the importance of caregiving can compete with a work ethic that values paid labor over nonpaid caring work. Anyone trying to combine simultaneous working and parenting can identify with Darla, an unemployed mother. Darla has four sons who attend school with her sister's three daughters. Her sister, a pregnant, single mother, works as a file clerk. By 7:30 A.M. the girls arrive at Darla's apartment. When it is time, they walk to school with Darla's two school-aged sons. After school, the five children return to Dalra's, where the girls remain until their mother arrives. When the mother is late, the girls stay over or are retrieved by another family member. Before and after school, Darla is in charge of seven children under the age of eleven. She prepares snacks and sometimes entire meals for the children.

During the time we were meeting, Darla was battling cervical cancer. While often in severe physical discomfort and under medication that made her somnolent and temperamental, she took care of these children. She received little money from her sister but often was rewarded with free weekends while her boys slept at their cousin's house, a respite Darla enjoyed. Occasionally, the boys received gifts of clothing or other small items. On payday, Darla's sister brought over groceries for the children. The arrangement helped both women. As Darla explained:

> I help out my sister, she's got her hands full with the girls. And she's pregnant, too! Since I got to be here anyway, I might as well take care of hers, too. You can't just leave your kids with anybody. She knows I'll do right by my nieces—I wanted

girls, she was the one wanted boys. She's not going to leave her kids with just anybody.

When Darla recovered from the cancer, she found a job at a department store. Immediately, her job altered her sister's child-care arrangements and created new child-care needs for Darla. Now her nieces spend their before-school time in the care of another aunt, who just happened to quit her job because of doctor-ordered bed rest due to pregnancy complications. The girls continue to go to Darla's after school; until she arrives home from work, the children are now in the care of Darla's new boyfriend.[1]

The strain that such child-care arrangements can place on families is also evident from Vicki's story. Vicki, mother of two teenage daughters, once worked nights at a local bar, in part so that she could take care of her young nephew during the day. Her child-care work began soon after she got home from work in the early mornings, forcing her to get by on little sleep. Although she did receive pay for caring for Tony, whose mother, Kelly, worked on a cleanup crew at a local animal shelter,[2] the pay was sporadic due to Kelly's variable work hours. But as Vicki explained, this far-from-ideal situation was still the best option that the family, as a whole, had.

> I took care of Tony' cause Kelly really didn't have anyone to watch him. She was going to get him in Head Start but someone had to get him there and go get him later. I didn't want to have to walk there and back [twice]. It was just easier to bring him over here in the morning. That way he'd be in one place all day. . . . That's why I wasn't really looking for a full-time day job then. She'd really have a hard time finding someone if I worked full-time, days.

When Vicki was unable to keep Tony because of foot surgery, another sister reluctantly used a week of her vacation time to fill in. This help was offered more out of duty to the larger family than respect for her sister. As she tells it:

> You know my sister and I don't get along at all! But that don't have nothing to do with Tony. I sure don't want to spend my vacation watching him. But somebody's got to watch him 'til Vicki gets back on her feet. My mother don't need to

be bothered with this boy, she's too old. So I just took off to take care of him.

In a community without child-care programs for young and school-age children, someone willing and able to provide such care is highly valued. Child care, essential to all working parents with dependent children, is especially critical here. Mothers all want their children to receive the best care, to develop preschool skills, and to be involved in constructive activities with other children. Middle-class parents can purchase this care with greater assurance that it will be reliable and responsive to their needs.[3] Being able to purchase child care allows parents to exercise some control over the quality of that care. Quality is desired by poor mothers also. But few are fortunate enough to be able to take advantage of a program like Head Start because it fails to serve all those who want it or need it. Moreover, such programs are typically structured around a clock that conflicts with the working schedules of full-time mothers. Thus, poor mothers take what they can get. It is important to keep this point in mind when trying to understand why significant numbers of poor families' children are cared for by relatives.

Relatives can be intrinsically good caretakers and many are. But the preference for relatives must also be understood as part of an economic reality: mothers can trust and negotiate with family and friends in ways they could not with institutions. Given a choice, it is not clear that Kelly would have chosen one sleep-deprived sister and another disapproving one to care for her son. The help they offered was better than nothing. Even if her sisters were ideal caretakers, Kelly might simply wish to avoid reliance on custodial care done out of obligation. But it is unlikely that Kelly could have found a quality child-care provider who would have allowed her to pay erratically, or one who would take her son even when doing so violated the provider's self-interest. As another mother makes clear:

> . . . Beggars can't be too choosy. I'm grateful I got family that will help out. It's better than nothing. I don't particularly like them over there, but right now I can't do no better. And for what I'm

paying, I can't be telling people how to run their house. I'm just grateful I have someone that can help me. It's better than nothing.

While limited options make one grateful for what one gets, they can place children at risk. Custodial care performed by caregivers with limited skills, poor health, little knowledge of normal child development, and unsafe homes creates anxiety for working mothers.[4] But out of a desperate need for care, mothers may pardon poor quality and disregard potentially hazardous situations. They make do, forever ready to establish new plans if absolutely necessary. High standards for the quality of child care one will accept is a luxury few Meadow View mothers can afford if they also want to work.

The symbiosis between working poor mothers and "nonworking" "welfare-taking" mothers makes it impossible to draw moral and ethical distinctions between the two. These mothers serve as lifelines to each other. A work ethic that always defines workers as more deserving than nonworkers misses this connection (Katz 1989). Given limited education, lack of job prospects, child-care needs, and inadequate transportation, these mothers recognize their dependence on others. They realize their ability to endure on low wages is possible, in large part, because of the misfortunes of other poor women whose labor helps them with their child-care needs. Those "lucky" enough to get a job realize that keeping it most often is directly related to someone else's current unemployment. And one frequently hears, "There but for the grace of God go I."

Reliance on the family can actually intensify after a job is obtained. One suddenly needs to find regular child care, to borrow money "til pay-day." to scrounge clothes to wear to work, to borrow bus fare or endlessly pursue other transportation means; these needs can ultimately weigh on everyone. Mabel, a mother who recently secured factory work, depends exclusively on her family's services. Just as the children are leaving for school, the mother is arriving home from work. When they return home, Mabel is often sleeping before departing for her graveyard shift. An older daughter who is a student at a local community college prepares the children for school in the morning and arranges her schedule to be home when the children return from school.[5] Without this help Mabel would not be able to keep her job. A parent working nights must maintain a schedule that is not conducive to rearing young children. Things are difficult, leading Mabel to wonder at times if she really is better off working. She comments on her ongoing struggles:

> You know, if it wasn't for [my family] I wouldn't make it. I'd be in the hole a lot. When I finish paying my bills, ain't much left. I like my job, especially getting paid every Friday, but it's hard to make it. I try to give a little to [her daughter] for helping with the kids. [Referring to the used car she recently purchased to get to her job]; I'm deep in the hole now 'cause of that piece of car. Seems like soon as I got it, it needed some of everything done to it and that ate up my little money. And the car still ain't right. It's bad when you work and still can't do no better. Girl, sometimes my brother has to get up out of his sleep and take me to work.

Life can be as tough for employed poor mothers as it is for welfare-receiving mothers who work within the home. Having a job may *feel* worse in some ways for employed poor mothers who see that working has made their lives more complicated and unmanageable than before. One mother comments on her attempts to make it:

> I don't expect nothing on welfare so I make do with nothing. But when I was working, I expected to make it and seem like I was worse. I couldn't really stay up on it. I needed things to wear more, I needed money to pay for getting back and forth to work, the kids needed snacks when they went over to [a relative's house] and I had to send enough for her kids too, I wasn't really paid much. . . . And I could never get regular hours and that made it hard if I had to be there before they went to school. When [youngest child] is in school full-time, I can probably work more.

Alluding to the help she requires, another "self-sufficient" working mother states:

> I'm squeezing by. This has been a good month . . . knock on wood! I'm just gonna keep my fingers crossed—that's all I can do. You know, as soon as you think you doing all right, something

happens to remind you, you not. I ain't had to ask my family for nothing this month, and I hope it stays that way. I know my family gets tired of me begging, 'cause I get tired of me begging, too.

Rarely does this mother get through a month without the help of relatives and close friends. Her mother "keeps a freezer full of meat," allowing her to borrow food when money is tight. Such borrowing, in turn, exacts a cost from those who may have a little more than their poorest relatives but are also living close to the financial edge themselves. In fact, a tension exists between the pursuit of individual goals and the needs of the family. One woman explains the pressures she felt at college:

You know I knew my family needed me. I knew they were depending on my stipend. I'd call, and they would be having problems. I felt bad being here, having all this and they were having a hard time. I decided to come home after my first year and get a job to help out my family. I can always go to college at home.

This woman never finished her four-year business degree. She did, however, manage to complete two years of junior college. Until she was twenty-seven, she lived with her mother and siblings in a crowded project apartment. When she left home, she moved to an apartment a few blocks away.

Even young women with the opportunity to make a better life for themselves relinquish it to meet pressing family obligations. The assumption that working makes one better off is not always true. For whom are things better off? In this context, it is questionable that children are better off. Without reliable, affordable, quality child care for multi-aged children, it is doubtful that these mothers, who worry incessantly about the safety of their children, feel that they are better off. It makes sense to value their children's health and safety above low-wage work. When low-wage work wins out, it is in part because these mothers want to work badly and have managed to secure the support they need from others in hopes of making work pay. Many learn that work does not always pay, and that when it does, it does so primarily because of the current non-labor-force participation of others.

Some of the problems mothers face would be more easily resolved if Meadow View residents were able to work in their neighborhood. But Meadow View suffers from a lack of jobs and little transportation to where the jobs are. Family-based networks often refer workers to jobs and provide transportation alternatives. But when nearly everyone in one's network is poor, isolated from good opportunities, or dependent upon unreliable transportation, the network can provide only minimal assistance.

FINDING WORK, REACHING WORK

One of the ironies of employment in Meadow View is that when poor mothers exchange their informal, family caretaking roles for paid, outside employment, the employment they find often involves caring for other people. In this region the demand for home health-care work is high, corresponding with a Department of Labor prediction that home health care will have the largest job growth of any industry between 1994 and 2005 (Eisler 1997). But while people everywhere must rely increasingly on purchased care, care-giving work is low paying and receives little credit for being important and necessary work (Abel and Nelson 1990; DeVault 1991; Stack 1974; Tronto 1994). These positions tend to be low wage, labor intensive, and little more than a "ghetto" for women, minorities and illegal immigrants (Eisler 1997; Statham, Miller, and Mauksch 1988). But the "soft" skills these mothers possess from years of traditional female work are usually enough to secure a job in these female-dominated fields. At least five of the ten mothers in my study have worked in nursing homes or in home health care. When asked what type of work they felt qualified for, all but one felt they could get a job in caregiving because as one mother put it, "that's mostly what I've been doing all along."

Home health care has advantages that other low-wage work does not; it allows for some flexibility in work schedules, which is especially important for single mothers (Schein 1995).

Because of high demand for these workers, mothers can enter and exit the field at will, depending on the availability of help at home. Home health care also allows for more autonomy than other types of service work. Working in private homes, women can be their own bosses. Workers also develop strong relationships with their charges and often develop a sense of loyalty to the patient. They feel positive about providing a much-needed service to those less fortunate.

Even these advantages, however, are often insufficient to compensate for the job stress and low pay. Full-time pay at some agencies is $7 per hour, a pittance for a breadwinner. Home health care remains a poorly regulated industry, whose profits depend on unskilled, poorly trained, and uncertified workers. Currently the supply of workers is high, giving agencies little incentive to invest in better training for better-qualified workers, or to share with workers the industry's considerable profits. Without better training and industry regulations, the psychological stress and backbreaking physical demands of the job ultimately take their toll. Vicki, who has worked more than once in home health care, explains:

> I stayed with old man Jones for three years. Broke my heart when he died. I told them I didn't wanna work for no one for a while. I just couldn't take it. I needed a break. I had to leave.

Maggie is married, in her fifties, and mother of two adult children. She has worked as a nurse's aide and as a home health-care worker. When asked what she does for a living, she responds, "I'm a nurse." Due to health problems, she is currently on disability. She appears clinically depressed about not being able to work and is worried about her health. She is trying to will herself back to health because she "can't afford to be sick" much longer. She comments:

> I worked in a home for years before I quit. I left 'cause it was too hard and you get so attached to those old people. I remember coming in the room and this lady I'd taken care of had died. They'd already stripped her bed and cleaned the room. Nobody told me nothing. I just didn't want to be around all that death—took me a long time

to get over that. . . . No, I will not work in the old folks homes again.

Many women suffer from the physical demands of the work:

> After awhile, moving people gets hard. That's dead weight you're trying to move, 'cause a lot of them can't move by themselves. You change diapers on grown people, clean up after them, bathe them, dress them. After awhile you just can't do it. You go home sore and hurting when you get through. I like the people and helping, but I was killing myself.

Like people everywhere, many people in Meadow View get jobs through family and friend networks. Those seeking work regularly interrogate others about job leads. But workers who sponsor relatives run the risk of damaging their own reputation if the relatives do not succeed. For instance, Wanda's brother, John, who held a respected position at a residential rehabilitation center, sponsored two cousins, a brother, and a sister for jobs. On his recommendation, all were hired, and eventually everyone quit. One resigned because he feared being fired. Because he worked a different shift than his relatives, he had to "bum" rides to and from work. Without reliable transportation, he was habitually late. The sister, who worked in the laundry, hated the drudgery of the work and claimed her supervisor was unfair and mistreated her. She left and eventually found other employment. A third quit after a disagreement with another co-worker. Of the four who terminated, one remained unemployed for more than a year. John, embarrassed, vowed never to sponsor anyone again. His sister explains why she believes things did not work out:

> They didn't really like the work. See, John has a good job there, he don't get messed over. But the rest of them . . . they caught it coming and going. And the whites kept on John about his relatives, what they did and didn't do.

On the other hand, if an employee works out well, an employer may come to view the sponsor as a reliable source for bringing responsible workers into the workplace. In Mabel's family, job sponsoring has worked out for two siblings in their early twenties.

> Both of them work at Brown's Chicken now. Ron got the job first and when his boss asked him if he knew some good workers, he told him about Juanda. Now they both are there. They're doing good, they like it. They get called in to do extra work all the time when somebody doesn't show up.

Many of the mothers I interviewed have acquired jobs through similar networks; they recognize their personal and skill limitations. They know that "good" jobs (i.e., full-time jobs that pay above minimum wage, with benefits) are not the jobs they will secure. For the most part they find jobs that are temporary, part-time, devoid of benefits, and always low paying.

The unavailability of good jobs is not the only obstacle that these mothers in Meadow View confront when they try to obtain employment. Simply getting to one's place of employment is difficult. It is widely accepted that urban communities are usually removed from suburban jobs, housing, quality schools, and other amenities. But the same isolation plagues old black suburbs. The significance of race is an indisputable fact in suburban development (Logan 1983/1988; see also Farley 1976). Decisions regarding transportation, suburban zoning codes, restrictive racial covenants in real estate investment and lending practices, redlining, and other discriminatory practices have historically been racially influenced (Massey and Denton 1993). Meadow View is not only a community that lacks industry, it is also situated in a region that is geographically isolated. Workers need to travel well beyond its borders to find work. Even though hordes of suburban workers access a highly developed transportation system that brings them to city jobs each day, traveling between suburbs in this region is much more difficult. And when Meadow View workers find jobs in the city that can be reached by public transportation, they may not be able to afford the commute. A round trip from Meadow View to the city costs almost ten dollars. To take advantage of travel discounts offered to frequent riders, one must purchase a monthly ticket, requiring a considerable outlay of money up front.

Amy, the mother of four young boys, is in her late twenties. At the age of nineteen she won custody of her five siblings after her mother died and her father abandoned them. Until recently and for ten years, she received welfare. She then got a job in a suburb not far from Meadow View and hoped that she would be able to walk the two miles from the bus to her job. The only problem she anticipated was inclement weather. When asked about arranging a daily taxi pickup from the bus, she reminded me that such luxuries were beyond her means and that the region does not have a dependable taxi service. Instead, Amy created an elaborate strategy for getting herself and her current boyfriend to and from work, which involved a carefully managed arrangement with a former boyfriend. This man, who was considerably older than Amy, considered her four children his responsibility—although he was the biological father of only the third child. Initially he agreed to drive Amy and her new boyfriend to work; if he was in a generous mood and did not have to work himself, he would even loan his car to her. But this arrangement was inherently unstable. When friends and other intimates are repeatedly called on for transportation, there is a good chance that personal mood and disposition will eventually get in the way. Amy tells of her experience calling on her former boyfriend:

> We were paying my ex-boyfriend to take Curtis (her new boyfriend) to work. No problems. Then he started getting an attitude and saying he couldn't take him. Now he knew there was no other way for him to get there. But because he was mad at me, he wanted to pull out.

Her new boyfriend worked part-time at a fast-food establishment. No bus routes went near his job and a cab was out of the question. Finally, the couple agreed to pay the ex-boyfriend more money until they could find another means of transportation. Because her plan was highly unreliable and filled with tension. Amy experienced considerable anxiety each day about getting to work.

Meadow View mothers unanimously desire work. They attempt it whenever they can. But they fail often, and not because they lack motivation or a work ethic. They fall short because the demands of simultaneous parenting and working eventually spin out of control, even with family support. They fail because the jobs for which they qualify turn out to be awful in the long run and eventually clash with family demands. They fail also because they work in job markets that discriminate against female bread-winners. In response, mothers quit. They hope to return at a more opportune time. Settings like Meadow View place considerable burdens on families, making it difficult, and often impossible, to parent and work successfully.

SUMMARY

Barriers of space and place are not unique to Meadow View. Poverty and racial segregation, conjoined with spatial isolation and disconnection from the city that it lies near, prevent this suburb from receiving many basic services. The inability to afford a quality police and fire department, for example, exacerbate many problems here. Crime and fear of random violence force parents to become hypervigilant about their children, especially because the suburb has no institutional supports—afterschool programs, day care providers—to help parents keep their children safely occupied. Parents must rely on family networks, but such networks are often strained by the demands placed on them. For people here, options are extremely limited.

Keeping children safe consumes parents and influences decisions about looking for work outside the home. Mothers, who assume much of the parenting, easily become overwhelmed by the unrelenting demands of this environment. The community is devoid of adequate resources such as a public library, youth services, and recreation programs. Poor pay tempts some police officers and firefighters to partner with the drug economy, leaving residents unprotected and vulnerable to random violence. Consequently, considerable effort is devoted to watching and protecting children.

One must be forever vigilant about keeping children near and troublemakers far, a task that is not easy.

In Meadow View, the family is key to survival. Families provide transportation, housing, food, job leads, and emotional succor. Child care, a service that every working mother with dependent children requires, is provided by relatives and friends who are outside the labor force. Because of this, mothers' work is inextricably linked to the nonwork or misfortunes of other women who may or may not be employed. Since few can afford to actually purchase the care they need, child care provided by industry chains is out of reach for these families, both financially and geographically. Although mothers appreciate the custodial care the family provides, they have limited alternatives. Head Start fails to reach all those who need it, and those who use it must make elaborate plans to retrieve children, whose school schedules do not correspond with a regular, full-time workday. Child care here is prone to disruptions and is unreliable. Unexpected illnesses interrupt work, making mothers more likely to be tardy, absent, and distracted on the job.

These family networks are not without tensions. As more and more families experience hardships, the networks become increasingly stressed. It is difficult to meet everyone's needs. In some families, substance abuse has created a need to provide shelter for children and the substance abuser. Eventually the core group of givers becomes overwhelmed, forced to make tragic choices as to who can and who cannot be salvaged.

The emphasis from both the political right and left focuses on reducing welfare dependency rather than on eliminating poverty (Schram 1995). The right, with its emphasis on the individual as the key to achievement, sees the problem as a lack of good character, behavior, and sound morals. The liberal left, with its stress on developing one's human capital (Gans 1995; Handler 1995) argues that with the proper schooling, job preparation, and skills, the poor can assimilate into the world of work and perform like other Americans. But neither understands the multiple effects of poverty on poor mothers (single or married) who live in a community context that manufactures major barriers to simultaneous working and parenting. Work does not exist in isolation from family and community (see McKnight 1995). What is missing from both camps is an understanding of the daily demands on families trapped in an economically depressed and racially segregated community that is also geographically isolated and lacks the most basic resources.

Over time, such conditions create deep and multiple needs in both people and institutions. Parenting in an impoverished, unsafe community forces parents to make decisions about employment and self-sufficiency based on how they can best protect their children and hold on to the coping strategies that have worked in the past. Being thrust into low-wage work, without substitute supports and services or a method for maintaining what has already been carved out, puts already vulnerable families and children at great risk. Parents need the security of knowing that the most vulnerable among them, their children and the elderly, will be safe, cared for, and protected.

Successful work programs will need to go beyond teaching job skills to consider community issues that program participants confront regularly. At the very least, work programs should address issues of community space, family obligation, local institutional support, and how these forces, alone and together, affect parents' ability to be productive workers and effective parents. For poor people to be simultaneously good workers and good parents, they need access to the same supports and resources that other working citizens have. Policymakers must develop a perspective that incorporates the full array of forces that go into work and parenting decisions (Dickerson 1995; McKnight 1995). Lacking this, policymakers will create policies and programs that have little relevance to the real, day-to-day world in which the poor struggle to survive.

NOTES

1. Although few talked about leaving children with boyfriends for this chapter previous fieldwork suggests that this is often done out of desperation and rarely considered an ideal situation. The risk to children left with unskilled and unwilling care-givers needs to be examined from a child safety perspective.

2. This animal shelter worker has held several nursing home jobs but found them emotionally stressful, unpleasant, and difficult to manage without a car.

3. As more middle-class families experience problems with abusive child-care workers and poorly managed child-care chains, this is less true.

4. Living conditions in Meadow View are often unsafe. Over 34 percent of Meadow View's housing is considered "substandard."

5. The daughter's need to adjust her college schedule to accommodate the child-care needs of her family could be a barrier for completing her education. The potential exists that she will leave school due to unexpressed pressures to help her family, that family needs supersede her own. An afterschool program could ease this type of child-care issue. For now, the daughter's school schedule is secondary to her family's needs.

REFERENCES

Abel, E. K., and M. K. Nelson, eds. 1990. *Circles of Care: Work and Identity in Women's Lives.* Albany: State University of New York Press.

Brownlee, S. 1996. "The Biology of Soul Murder." *U.S. News & World Report,* 11 November, 121:71–73.

DeVault, M. L. 1991. *Feeding the Family: The Social Organization of Caring as Gendered Work.* Chicago: University of Chicago Press.

Dickerson, B. J., ed. 1995. *African American Single Mothers: Understanding Their Lives and Families.* Thousand Oaks, CA: Sage.

Eisler, P. 1997. "Home Health Care: 'All the Components for Disaster.'" *USA Today,* Special Home Health Care Report 4D:Life, 18 March.

Farley, R. 1976. "Components of Suburban Population Growth." In *The Changing Face of the Suburbs,* ed. B. Schwartz. Chicago: University of Chicago Press.

Gans, H. J. 1995. *The War Against the Poor: The Underclass and Antipoverty Policy.* New York: Basic Books.

Garbarino, J., N. Dubrow, K. Kostelny, and C. Pardo, eds. 1992. *Children in Danger: Coping with The Consequences of Community Violence.* San Francisco: Jossey-Bass.

Handler, J. F. 1995. *The Poverty of Welfare Reform.* New Haven: Yale University Press.

Heymann, S. J., A. Earle, and B. Egleston. 1996. "Parental Availability for the Care of Sick Children." *Pediatrics: The Journal of the American Academy of Pediatrics* 98:226–230.

Hicks-Bartlett, S. T. Forthcoming. *Kin of Mine: Community and Family Life in a Low Income Suburb.*

Hiss, T. 1990. *The Experience of Place.* New York, Vintage Books.

Jones, J. 1986. *Labor of Love, Labor of Sorrow: Black Women, Work and the Family, From Slavery to the Present.* New York: Basic Books.

Katz, M. B. 1989. *The Underserving Poor. From the War on Poverty to the War on Welfare.* New York: Pantheon Books.

Logan, J. R. 1983/1988. "Realities of Black Suburbanization." In *New Perspectives on the American Community,* compiled by Roland L. Warren and Larry Lyon, 231–40. Homewood, IL: Dorsey Press.

Massey, D. S., and N. A. Denton. 1993. *American Apartheid: Segregation and the Making of the Underclass.* Cambridge: Harvard University Press.

McKnight, J. 1995. *The Careless Society: Community and Its Counterfeits.* New York: Basic Books.

Prothrow-Stith, D., and M. Weissman. 1993. *Deadly Consequences.* New York: HarperCollins.

Rank, M. R. 1994. *Living on the Edge: The Realities of Welfare in America.* New York: Columbia University Press.

Schein, V. E. 1995. *Working from the Margins: Voices of Mothers in Poverty.* Ithaca and London: ILR Press.

Schram, S. F. 1995. *Words of Welfare: The Poverty of Social Science and the Social Science of Poverty.* Minneapolis: University of Minnesota Press.

Stack, C. B. 1974. *All Our Kin: Strategies for Survival in a Black Community.* New York: Harper & Row.

Stack, C. B. 1990. "Different Voices, Different Visions: Gender, Culture and Moral Reasoning." In *Uncertain Terms: Negotiating Gender in American Culture,* eds. F. Ginsburg and A. L. Tsing, 19–27. Boston: Beacon Press.

Statham, A., E. M. Miller, and H. O. Mauksch, eds. 1988. *The Worth of Women's Work: A Qualitative Synthesis.* New York: State University of New York Press.

Tronto, J. C. 1994. *Moral Boundaries: A Political Argument for an Ethic of Care.* New York: Routledge.

Wilson, W. J. 1987. *The Truly Disadvantaged: The Inner City, the Underclass, and Public Policy.* Chicago: University of Chicago Press.

———. 1996. *When Work Disappears: The World of the New Urban Poor.* New York: Knopf.

Matrifocality, Power, and Gender Relations in Jamaica

Marsha Prior

Anthropologists have long recognized kinship units in which women maintain considerable control over the household earnings and decision making. While numerous studies have provided pertinent data and have contributed to the theory of social organization, the subject of female-focused kinship units has always been controversial, subject to bias, and confusing. The variations in terminology and a preoccupation with the origin of these units is responsible for much of the confusion. In addition, two biases, prevalent throughout the twentieth century, have influenced our understanding and acceptance of female-focused units. One bias has been the predominant view that nuclear families are "normal"; the other bias is the failure

Original material prepared for this text. Reprinted by permission of the author

to recognize the full extent of female roles in society. The unfortunate result of this is that very little is known about the dynamics within and between female-focused kinship units.

The term *matrifocal*, which is most commonly used to refer to households composed of a key female decision maker, was coined by R. T. Smith in 1956. Recognition of such households precedes the usage of this term, however. As early as the 1930s, scholars noted that African-American and African-Caribbean households were not composed of nuclear families as were the majority of middle-class households in the United States and Great Britain. Observers were struck by the authoritative role of women in these households and the limited role of the father in the family. Mothers controlled the earnings brought into the household and made key decisions. Fathers were either absent or did not appear to play a major role in economic contributions and in household decision making. However, attempts to address this situation reveal more the attitudes and biases prevalent at that time—many of which remain with us today—than any real insight as to the nature of such units. These *maternal families*, as they were often called during this early period, were viewed by scholars as deviant structures (Mohammed 1988). The high rate of illegitimacy and instability among mating partners was cited as proof that these families were disorganized and detrimental to the well-being of their members (Henriques 1953; Simey 1946; see also Moynihan 1965).

The bias toward nuclear family organization that dominated early studies stems from nineteenth-century evolutionists who viewed the nuclear family as a superior system of kinship organization and from Malinowski who argued that nuclear families are universal (Collier, Rosaldo, and Yanigisako 1982). Thus, societies that exhibited large numbers of nonnuclear households were considered abnormal, and it was essential that their development be explained.

Scholars naturally turned to the common characteristics of these female-focused societies, noting that they were former slave societies from Africa. One explanation, suggested by Frazier (1939), held that maternal families were an adaptive strategy to the slave system that defined slaves as individual property who could be traded to another plantation at any time. Nuclear families would have been torn apart with frequent trading of adult slaves. Plantation owners were less likely, though, to tear apart mother–child dyads, at least until the child reached adolescence. Thus, the stable unit in a slave system was a household consisting of mothers and their children. The other explanation common during this time period, argued that the maternal family stemmed from the traditional African system that survived in spite of the Africans' forced migration and subsequent integration into the slave system (Herskovits 1941). These two theories enjoyed a lively debate until the mid-1950s, when scholars moved away from historical explanations

and emphasized the role of present social or economic conditions.

M. G. Smith (1962) argued that family structure in the West Indies was determined by the already existing mating systems that vary somewhat throughout the region. Clarke (1957), R. T. Smith (1956), and Gonzalez (1960) focused more on the effect that the current economic system had on household organization. The prevalent household structure found among African descendants in the United States and the Caribbean was viewed as an adaptive strategy to poverty, unemployment, or male migration. Nuclear families with only two working adults per household are believed by some to be at risk in socioeconomic environments in which poverty conditions exist, unemployment is high, and adult men must migrate to find work (see Durant-Gonzalez 1982; Gonzalez 1970: 242). Thus, in such societies we are more likely to see households composed of a mother, a grandparent, and children; a mother and children; adult siblings and their children; or adult siblings, their children, and a grandparent.

The emphasis placed on the socioeconomic environment marked a new trend in matrifocal studies whereby the relationship between men and women took a more prominent position. However, the studies placed more emphasis on the "marginal" or absent man than on the ever-present woman and were criticized for ignoring the wide range of roles and tasks performed by women. Furthermore, Smith noted (1962: 6) specific ethnographic data were used to generalize about matrifocal societies throughout the Caribbean. This proved to be problematic in understanding matrifocal societies theoretically, and it generated confusion as scholars used different terms to refer to similar types of kinship and household organizations.

R. T. Smith used the term *matrifocal* to refer to the type of structure he originally witnessed among lower class British Guianese (1956). Taking a developmental approach, Smith noted that matrifocal households arise with time after a man and woman begin to cohabit. Early in the cycle the woman is economically dependent on the male partner. Her primary role is to provide care for the children, but as the children grow older and earn money for small tasks and labor it is the mother who controls their earnings. The father, meanwhile, has been unable to make significant contributions to the household economy due to his overall low status within a society that maintains prejudicial hiring policies. Smith's concept of matrifocality focuses on two criteria—the salience of women in their role as mothers and the marginality of men (i.e., their inability to contribute economically to the household) (1956, 1973, 1988).

The study of household structure conducted by Gonzalez on the Garifuna (Black Carib) of Guatemala was not intended, nor originally identified, as a study on matrifocality per se, but Gonzalez did note the effect that male emigration had on household structure (1960). Gonzalez observed that households were comprised of members who were related to each other consanguineally (through blood); no two members of the household were bound by marriage. These consanguineal households developed in response to a socioeconomic environment that encouraged men to migrate as they sought employment (see also Gonzalez 1984 for comments regarding the applicability of dividing households into consanguineal and affinal types).

The terms and definitions for the household structures observed by R. T. Smith and Gonzalez were created to fit specific ethnographic data. They were later applied by various scholars to other societies that exhibited similar structures, which created confusion (see Kunstadter 1963; Randolph 1964; M. G. Smith 1962: 6; and R. T. Smith 1973: 126) and was exacerbated by the use of other terms to rectify the problem (e.g., the use of matricentric or female-headed). Thus, in the literature we see these terms used interchangeably to refer to structures in which women control household earnings and decision making and men are viewed as marginal, though the impetus behind such household formation may differ from one society to the next. The whole concept became so clouded with terms and biases that Gonzalez astutely noted that depending on which scholar one is reading, matrifocality can suggest (1) that women are more important than the observer had expected, (2) that women maintain a good

deal of control over money in the household, (3) that women are the primary source of income, or (4) that there is no resident male (1970: 231–232).

Recent authors have criticized the emphasis on men's marginality and the focus on women's domestic tasks that arose in the study of matrifocality (Barrow 1988; Mohammed 1988; Tanner 1974). Concentration on women's *domestic* tasks ignores the full extent of women's networks, their access to resources, control over resources, relations with men, and relationship between household and society, all of which are important considerations when discussing matrifocality. Male marginality is problematic in part because the term is difficult to define. Does it mean that the father does not live in the household? Has he migrated out of the community? Does he contribute sporadically, or not at all, to the household economy? Is he not around to make household decisions?

As Tanner has remarked, matrifocality should not be defined in "negative terms" (i.e., by the absence of the father). Instead, we should focus on the role of women as mothers, and note that in matrifocal systems mothers have at least some control over economic resources and are involved in decision making. According to Tanner, however, matrifocality goes beyond these two criteria. To be matrifocal a society must culturally value the role of mother—though not necessarily at the expense of fathers. In matrifocal societies the woman's role as mother is central to the kinship structure, but Tanner does not limit this role to domestic tasks. As mothers women may participate in cultivation, petty marketing, wage labor, in rituals, and so forth (1974). This broader definition allows us to recognize matrifocal units within a variety of kinship systems. Matrifocal units can exist in matrilineal or patrilineal societies, within nuclear families, and in bilateral systems. In any society with an emphasis on the mother–child dyad where this unit is culturally valued and where the mother plays an effective role in the economy and decision making of the unit, that unit can be defined as matrifocal (Tanner 1974: 131–132).

Tanner's definition finally allows us to avoid some of the problems that previous studies encountered and permits us to further address issues pertinent to matrifocal units. We can examine gender relations within the context of gender hierarchies and the broader socioeconomic environment of which matrifocal households are a part. One area that has received little attention is the relationship between physical violence against women and matrifocality. Violence against women and matrifocality seem to contradict each other due to the assumptions regarding power and the authoritative role of women in matrifocal households.

Women, having access to and control over resources and authority to make household decisions, are viewed as powerful. This view has been particularly evident in studies of women in the Caribbean where a large number of matrifocal households exist (Massiah 1982). Caribbean women are frequently portrayed as powerful, autonomous individuals (Ellis 1986; Powell 1982, 1986; Safa 1986). Although Caribbean women's control and power over resources and decisions is not to be discounted, fieldwork in a low-income community in Jamaica suggests that matrifocality and physical violence against women are not mutually exclusive. To understand the relationship between these two phenomena requires knowledge of sociocultural elements that affect both gender relations and matrifocal household organization.

The community of study is a low-income urban neighborhood of approximately 0.05 square miles located in the parish of St. Andrew, Jamaica. During the time at which data were collected, 1987 to 1988, there were an estimated 210 households with a population of 1,300. The majority of the households were of wooden construction, many without electricity, and very few with running water. Some of the wealthier residents maintained houses constructed of concrete. No telephones were present in any household because telephone lines were not available.

Within the community a variety of household organizational units were observed. Nuclear families based on common-law marriage, legal marriage, or coresidency existed. There were also single female-headed households, single male-headed households, and a variety of extended and collateral arrangements. Finally, there were households whose membership included kin and nonkin (i.e., a friend or acquaintance may reside in the household). This range in domestic organization demonstrates that household membership may vary in response to economic and social conditions.

What makes these arrangements more interesting is that the households are subject to change. During the course of the fieldwork households altered their membership; thus, a nuclear arrangement would shift to single female-headed with children as the father moved out, and it might have shifted again if a grandmother or sister moved in. Regardless of the various household arrangements, matrifocality was observed. Women certainly maintained control over the economic resources and were responsible for many household decisions. Women as mothers were structurally central to the kinship units, and mothers were culturally valued as indicated by both male and female informants.

Although Caribbean women are portrayed as powerful and autonomous, male–female relations, as anywhere in the world, are based on some form of interdependence. Within this community social and economic status are intricately tied to gender relations. Both genders support the basic notion that women are to provide sexual services and domestic labor for men, and men are to provide women with money and gifts. However, the relationships are not a simple equation whereby women provide sexual services and domestic labor in exchange for money. Women often spoke of sexual activity as something that they desired and enjoyed, and men felt free to request money from women with whom they have had relations (especially the mother to any of his children). Nevertheless, there is an understanding that if a woman will not provide sexual services or domestic labor or if the man does not provide cash or gifts from time to time, the relationship will end. These expectations played key roles in understanding gender relations and the behavior of men and women.

In addition to these expectations, adult status is primarily attained by the birth of a child.

At this socioeconomic level higher educational degrees, prestigious employment, and ownership of cars and houses are out of most community members' reach. Both men and women view the birth of a child as an opportunity to announce their own adult status. Thus, children are normally desired and are a source of pride for both the mother and father.

The instability that marks male–female relationships is recognized by community members and can be related to cultural values as well as to the socioeconomic environment that encourages men and women to seek more resourceful partners. Male and female informants readily acknowledged the shifting allegiances between men and women. Men were known to keep several girlfriends at one time, and marriage, common-law or legal, was no guarantee that monogamy will follow. Women also admitted to keeping an eye out for a better partner and said they would initiate a change if they so desired. Couples tended to set up visiting relationships whereby the couple did not coreside. Children, of course, may be born from these unions. If a Jamaican woman of this socioeconomic class married at all, it was more likely to occur after the age of thirty (see Brody 1981: 253–255).

As households were observed and data collected through the course of fieldwork, it became apparent that fathers and male partners were not marginal to the households. Whether or not they resided in the same household as the woman, they could potentially be very influential. It also became clear that in certain situations female control over household issues could be jeopardized. A brief look at some of the households and the gender relations among men and women will demonstrate these points.

MARY'S HOUSEHOLD

Mary is a twenty-seven-year-old mother occupying a one-room wooden house—no electricity or running water—with four children. The two oldest children were fathered by one man; the youngest two were fathered by another. Sexual relations with the first father had ceased several years ago; however, Mary does maintain sexual relations with the younger children's father, though he keeps other girlfriends.

Mary's primary source of income stems from sporadic petty marketing. When Mary has the capital to invest in goods, she sells clothing and shoes in a downtown Kingston stall that is rented by her mother. Mary is very much involved in politics; she attends meetings, distributes literature, and talks to anyone about her party's political candidates and officials. She was able to work for a few months as an enumerator during a national campaign to register voters. Mary depends on contributions from the two fathers of her children. The first father rarely comes to visit, but he is in the National Guard, draws a steady paycheck, and consistently sends money for the children.

The father of her two youngest children, who works as a cook and a driver, is usually good about bringing money but has, on occasion, lapsed. Such lapses can be a severe stress on Mary's limited household budget and were the source of domestic violence on one occasion. Earl, the father of Mary's youngest children, had promised to bring some money. When he showed up at her doorstep she asked for the money, and he told her that he didn't have any. This made her angry so she began yelling at him, and a fight ensued. They began hitting each other with their fists, but the fight escalated when Earl picked up a shovel and hit Mary on the wrist. Mary fought back by taking a cutlass and striking him on the shoulder. Earl then left the premises, and Mary sought medical treatment for the pain in her wrist.

This was the first and only act of violence between the two in a seven-year period. Mary stated that they rarely even quarrel. Though not typical, the violence demonstrates the economic dependence of Mary on the contributions of the fathers and the stress that can surface when she is threatened by the lack of such contributions. Mary admitted that she was extremely angry when he told her that he had no money to give her because he had promised earlier that he would bring her some. She was convinced that he had the money to give but was holding out on her.

DORA'S HOUSEHOLD

Dora, twenty-eight years old, lives under similar circumstances as Mary and has had comparable experience regarding fathers and money. Dora is the mother of three children. Two live with her; one stays with relatives in the country. Dora's one-room house has neither electricity nor running water.

The father of Dora's first two children provides some money to the household. Dora is almost totally dependent on these contributions because she is confined to the house and cannot work due to a crippling disease. Ned, the father of her youngest child, provides nothing to the household, which is a continuous source of grief to Dora. Dora is quiet and normally avoids conflict. Her one attempt to address Ned's negligence resulted in violence, as had Mary's. Dora had decided that because Ned did not provide clothes or money for their son, Michael, he did not deserve to see the child. She packed up Michael's belongings and sent him over to Ned's sister's house for a short while, believing that the sister would feed Michael and buy him some clothes. When Ned arrived to take Michael for a visit to his own house, he questioned the child's whereabouts and became angry when Dora told him that he had been sent to Ned's sister's house. Ned began hitting Dora. She struck back once but relented when Ned punched her in the side and ran off. She did not see him again for several days. This incident occurred six months prior to our interview, and Dora has not asked Ned for anything since and vows that she never will.

RITA'S HOUSEHOLD

Rita lives in a household consisting of six members, including herself. Two of her four children, a granddaughter, a friend of her daughter, and Rita's boyfriend occupy a three-room apartment without electricity or running water. Rita is thirty-nine years old. Her boyfriend, Tom, is 40 and has lived with her for four years. They have no common children.

Rita runs a successful neighborhood bar, giving her control over the major portion of the household budget. She receives some financial contribution from the father of one daughter. Rita and Tom have established a reciprocal relationship regarding money. She does expect him to contribute from his earnings as a taxi driver when he is able, but she may be just as likely to provide Tom with money when he is in need. Rita is aware of Tom's other girlfriends and realizes that a good deal of his earnings go to entertaining these women. With her own successful business, Rita is less financially dependent on her male partner than other women. She does look to Tom, however, for companionship and emotional support. The time he spends with other women is reluctantly accepted, though on one occasion his infidelities did result in conflict. One night, as he came home late, Rita began cursing Tom and made derogatory remarks about Tom's other girlfriend. Tom responded by punching Rita. She fought back for a few minutes then they both simply let it go. In the past year Rita has avoided comment on Tom's affairs and is determined to put up with it, for now at least, because she is not ready to end the relationship. Rita's attitude is that most men do this, so there is little point in severing this relationship to find another boyfriend who will do the same.

HANNAH'S HOUSEHOLD

Thirty-six-year-old Hannah is an articulate and ambitious woman. She lives in a two-room house with seven other people (five of her six children live with her along with a friend her age and a friend of one of her daughters). Hannah worked as a domestic but lost her job during my stay in the community. She did have a job lined up, cleaning the office of a dentist.

Hannah's first three children were fathered by one man; her fourth child was fathered by another man; and her last two children were fathered by a third man. The first man to father her children is now sick and unable to work. He does not provide any financial support to Hannah's household. The other two fathers help out every now and then, but the support is not enough for her to rely on. She rarely sees any of her children's fathers now, but Hannah did relate an incident involving the last father, Gerald, that occurred nearly five years prior to our interview. At the time of the incident Hannah and Gerald were still intimately involved but did not coreside. Hannah had grown dissatisfied with the relationship because Gerald provided no support for herself or his children. Thus, she had decided to break off the relationship. When Gerald learned of her decision he became angry and abusive. One night after everyone had gone to bed, he came to her house, began yelling at her, and proceeded to destroy some of her belongings: He broke a lamp and smashed a small table. Another night he came to her window, tore off the screen, and began yelling at her again. He threw a bucket of water on her and the children and threw stones. Hannah, not wanting the children to get hurt, went outside to confront him, and he began physically assaulting her. Hannah managed to grab a broken bottle and cut him with it. Gerald then left the premises, never bothering her much afterward.

SUMMARY

Although women in matrifocal households often maintain control over resources and decision making within the household, the previous data indicate that the power associated with such control and authority can be compromised. Power, as defined by Adams, is the control over one's environment and the ability to control the environment of others based on access and control of resources that are of value to the other (1975: 12). In the cases cited above the interdependence between men and women and the access that men have to certain resources must be addressed to understand female power and domestic violence.

As indicated previously, both genders view women as exercising control over sexual services and domestic labor, and men have access to some (though not all) of the economic resources that women need. At this socioeconomic level men may not be able to contribute significantly to the household economy. Nevertheless, women view men as a source of monetary and material needs and feel they have the right to demand

these resources. Though women are constantly seeking ways to earn money and often don't want to rely on contributions from male partners, many, again due to the socioeconomic environment, are dependent on male contributions, no matter how small. The data suggest that while men are dependent on women, they can more easily circumvent the control that female partners have over desired resources than women can circumvent the resources that men control. In this culture it is acceptable for men to have more than one female partner. While women complain of this it is expected and negates the control that individual women can exert. Women, on the other hand, may try to circumvent male control over economic resources, but they are also subjected to an economic system that exploits the lower class for their cheap labor and that offers high unemployment. In addition to this interdependence these women are members of a culture that may value women as *mothers,* but women in general do not necessarily enjoy a high status. In other words, the *mother* role is valued, but women are overall subordinate to men (Henry and Wilson 1975). Male informants felt it was their right to physically coerce or punish women as they saw fit, but a man would almost never physically abuse his own mother.

In relating the cases cited previously the intent is not to suggest that the women were weak, powerless, and always dominated by men. Women often fought back and worked to become as independent as possible. These cases are also not intended to promote negative images of men. I recount incidences of abuse to demonstrate the extreme to which men can affect matrifocal households, but I must emphasize that male influence can also be positive and rewarding for members of the household. Fathers were observed visiting their children, taking them to the health clinic, and providing money, food, and clothing.

The data collected from this study remind us that, in spite of a long interest in matrifocality, we still have much to learn. We must rid ourselves of biases that narrow our focus. Just as it was wrong to assume that men are marginal, that women perform only domestic tasks, and that the nuclear family is "normal," we must not assume that women in matrifocal societies are *always* powerful or that they consistently enjoy a high status within that society. The power that women exert must be documented and integrated into the overall cultural context that would also note gender relations, the socioeconomic environment, the political environment, and cultural values. Only then can studies on matrifocality provide us with a better understanding of human behavior.

REFERENCES

Adams, Richard N. 1975. *Energy and Structure: A Theory of Social Power.* Austin: University of Texas Press.

Barrow, Christine. 1988. "Anthropology, the Family and Women in the Caribbean." In Patricia Mohammed and Catherine Shepherd (eds.). *Gender in Caribbean Development*, pp. 156–169. Mona, Jamaica: University of West Indies.

Brody, Eugene B. 1981. *Sex, Contraception, and Motherhood in Jamaica.* Cambridge, MA: Harvard University Press.

Clarke, Edith. 1957. *My Mother Who Fathered Me.* London: George Allen & Unwin.

Collier, Jane, Michelle Rosaldo, and Sylvia Yanagisako. 1982. "Is There a Family? New Anthropological Views." In Barrie Thorne (ed.). *Rethinking the Family: Some Feminist Questions*, pp. 25–39. New York: Longman.

Durant-Gonzalez, Victoria. 1982. "The Realm of Female Familial Responsibility." In Joycelin Massiah (ed). *Women and the Family*, pp. 1–27. Cave Hill, Barbados: University of the West Indies, Institute of Social and Economic Research.

Ellis, Pat. 1986. "Introduction: An Overview of Women in Caribbean Society." In Pat Ellis (ed.). *Women of the Caribbean*, pp. 1–24. Kingston, Jamaica: Kingston Publishers.

Frazier, E. Franklin. 1939. *The Negro Family in the United States.* Chicago: Chicago University Press.

Gonzalez, Nancie L. 1960. Household and Family in the Caribbean. *Social and Economic Studies* 9: 101–106.

———. 1970. "Toward a Definition of Matrifocality." In Norman E. Whitten, Jr. and John F. Szwed (eds.). *Afro-American Anthropology*, pp. 231–244. New York: The Free Press.

———. 1984. "Rethinking the Consanguineal Household and Matrifocality." *Ethnology* 23 (1): 1–12.

Henriques, Fernando M. 1953. *Family and Colour in Jamaica.* London: Eyre and Spottiswoode.

Henry, Frances, and Pamela Wilson. 1975. "The Status of Women in Caribbean Societies: An Overview of Their Social, Economic and Sexual Roles." *Social and Economic Studies* 24 (2): 165–198.

Herskovits, Melville J. 1941. *The Myth of the Negro Past.* New York: Harper & Brothers.

Kunstadter, Peter. 1963. "A Survey of the Consanguine or Matrifocal Family." *American Anthropologist* 65: 56–66.

Massiah, Joycelin. 1982. "Women Who Head Households." In Joycelin Massiah (ed.). *Women and the Family*, pp. 62–130. Cave Hill, Barbados: University of West Indies, Institute of Social and Economic Research.

Mohammed, Patricia. 1988. "The Caribbean Family Revisited." In Patricia Mohammed and Catherine Shepherd (eds.). *Gender in Caribbean Development*, pp. 170–182. Mona, Jamaica: University of West Indies.

Moynihan, Daniel P. 1965. *The Negro Family: The Case for National Action.* Washington, DC: U.S. Department of Labor.

Powell, Dorian. 1982. "Network Analysis: A Suggested Model for the Study of Women and the Family in the Caribbean." In Joycelin Massiah (ed.). *Women and The Family*, pp. 131–162. Cave Hill, Barbados: University of the West Indies, Institute of Social and Economic Research.

———. 1986. "Caribbean Women and Their Response to Familial Experiences." *Social and Economic Studies* 35 (2): 83–130.

Randolph, Richard R. 1964. "The 'Matrifocal Family' as a Comparative Category." *American Anthropologist* 66: 628–31.

Safa, Helen. 1986. "Economic Autonomy and Sexual Equality in Caribbean Society." *Social and Economic Studies* 35 (3): 1–21.

Simey, Thomas. 1946. *Welfare Planning in the West Indies.* Oxford, UK: Clarendon Press.

Smith, M. G. 1962. *West Indian Family Structure.* Seattle: University of Washington Press.

Smith, Raymond T. 1956. *The Negro Family in British Guiana: Family Structure and Social Status in the Villages.* London: Routledge and Kegan Paul.

———. 1973. "The Matrifocal Family." In Jack Goody (ed.). *The Character of Kinship*, pp. 121–144. London: Cambridge University Press.

———. 1988. *Kinship and Class in the West Indies: A Genealogical Study of Jamaica and Guyana.* New York: Cambridge University Press.

Tanner, Nancy. 1974. "Matrifocality in Indonesia and Africa and Among Black Americans." In Michelle Zimbalist Rosaldo and Louise Lamphere (eds.). *Woman, Culture, and Society*, pp. 129–156. Stanford, CA: Stanford University Press.

The Female World of Cards
and Holidays:
Women, Families, and the Work of Kinship

Micaela di Leonardo

Why is it that the married women of America are supposed to write all the letters and send all the cards to their husbands' families? My old man is a much better writer than I am, yet he expects me to correspond with his whole family. If I asked him to correspond with mine, he would blow a gasket.

Letter to Ann Landers

Women's place in man's life cycle has been that of nurturer, caretaker, and helpmate, the weaver of those networks of relationships on which she in turn relies.

Carol Gilligan, In a Different Voice[1]

Feminist scholars in the past fifteen years have made great strides in formulating new understandings of the relations among gender, kinship, and the larger economy. As a result of this pioneering research, women are newly visible and audible, no longer submerged within their families. We see households as loci of political struggle, inseparable parts of the larger society and economy, rather than as havens from the heartless world of industrial capitalism.[2] And historical and cultural variations in kinship and family forms have become clearer with the maturation of feminist historical and social-scientific scholarship.

Two theoretical trends have been key to this reinterpretation of women's work and family domain. The first is the elevation to visibility of women's nonmarket activities—housework, child care, the servicing of men, and the care of the elderly—and the definition of all these activities as *labor*, to be enumerated alongside

and counted as part of overall social reproduction. The second theoretical trend is the nonpejorative focus on women's domestic or kin-centered networks. We now see them as the products of conscious strategy, as crucial to the functioning of kinship systems, as sources of women's autonomous power and possible primary sites of emotional fulfillment, and, at times, as the vehicles for actual survival and/or political resistance.[3]

Recently, however, a division has developed between feminist interpreters of the "labor" and the "network" perspectives on women's lives. Those who focus on women's work tend to envision women as sentient, goal-oriented actors, while those who concern themselves with women's ties to others tend to perceive women primarily in terms of nurturance, other-orientation—altruism. The most celebrated recent example of this division is the opposing testimony of historians Alice Kessler-Harris and Rosalind Rosenberg in the Equal Employment Opportunity Commission's sex discrimination case against Sears Roebuck and Company. Kessler-Harris argued that American women historically have actively sought higher-paying jobs and have been prevented from gaining them because of sex discrimination by employers. Rosenberg argued that American women in the nineteenth century created among themselves, through their domestic networks, a "women's culture" that emphasized the nurturance of children and others and the maintenance of family life and that discouraged women from competition over or heavy emotional investment in demanding, high-paid employment.[4]

I shall not here address this specific debate but, instead, shall consider its theoretical background and implications. I shall argue that we need to fuse, rather than to oppose, the domestic network and labor perspectives. In what follows, I introduce a new concept, the work of kinship, both to aid empirical feminist research on women, work, and family and to help advance feminist theory in this arena. I believe that the boundary-crossing nature of the concept helps to confound the self-interest/altruism dichotomy, forcing us from an either-or stance to a position that includes both perspectives. I hope in this way to contribute to a more critical feminist vision of women's lives and the meaning of family in the industrial West.

In my recent field research among Italian-Americans in Northern California, I found myself considering the relations between women's kinship and economic lives. As an anthropologist, I was concerned with people's kin lives beyond conventional American nuclear family or household boundaries. To this end, I collected individual and family life histories, asking about all kin and close friends and their activities. I was also very interested in women's labor. As I sat with women and listened to their accounts of their past and present lives, I began to realize that they were involved in three types of work: housework and child care, work in the labor market, and the work of kinship.[5]

By kin work I refer to the conception, maintenance, and ritual celebration of cross-household kin ties, including visits, letters, telephone calls, presents, and cards to kin; the organization of holiday gatherings; the creation and maintenance of quasi-kin relations; decisions to neglect or to intensify particular ties; the mental work of reflection about all these activities; and the creation and communication of altering images of family and kin vis-à-vis the images of others, both folk and mass media. Kin work is a key element that has been missing in the synthesis of the "household labor" and "domestic network" perspectives. In our emphasis on individual women's responsibilities within households and on the job, we reflect the common picture of households as nuclear units, tied perhaps to the larger social and economic system, but not to *each other*. We miss the point of telephone and soft drink advertising, of women's magazines' holiday

issues, of commentators' confused nostalgia for the mythical American extended family: it is kinship contact *across households*, as much as women's work within them, that fulfills our cultural expectation of satisfying family life.

Maintaining these contacts, this sense of family, takes time, intention, and skill. We tend to think of human social and kin networks as the epiphenomena of production and reproduction: the social traces created by our material lives. Or, in the neoclassical tradition, we see them as part of leisure activities, outside an economic purview except insofar as they involve consumption behavior. But the creation and maintenance of kin and quasi-kin networks in advanced industrial societies is *work*; and, moreover, it is largely women's work.

The kin-work lens brought into focus new perspectives on my informants' family lives. First, life histories revealed that often the very existence of kin contact and holiday celebration depended on the presence of an adult woman in the household. When couples divorced or mothers died, the work of kinship was left undone; when women entered into sanctioned sexual or marital relationships with men in these situations, they reconstituted the men's kinship networks and organized gatherings and holiday celebrations. Middle-aged businessman Al Bertini, for example, recalled the death of his mother in his early adolescence: "I think that's probably one of the biggest losses in losing a family—yeah, I remember as a child when my Mom was alive . . . the holidays were treated with enthusiasm and love . . . after she died the attempt was there but it just didn't materialize." Later in life, when Al Bertini and his wife separated, his own and his son Jim's participation in extended-family contact decreased rapidly. But when Jim began a relationship with Jane Batemen, she and he moved in with Al, and Jim and Jane began to invite his kin over for holidays. Jane single-handedly planned and cooked the holiday feasts.

Kin work, then, is like housework and child care: men in the aggregate do not do it. It differs from these forms of labor in that it is harder for men to substitute hired labor to accomplish these tasks in the absence of kinswomen. Second, I found that women, as the workers in this arena, generally had much greater kin knowledge than did their husbands, often including more accurate and extensive knowledge of their husbands' families. This was true both of middle-aged and younger couples and surfaced as a phenomenon in my interviews in the form of humorous arguments and in wives' detailed additions to husbands' narratives. Nick Meraviglia, a middle-aged professional, discussed his Italian antecedents in the presence of his wife, Pina:

NICK: My grandfather was a very outspoken man, and it was reported he took off for the hills when he found out that Mussolini was in power.

PINA: And he was a very tall man; he used to have to bow his head to get inside doors.

NICK: No, that was my uncle.

PINA: Your grandfather too, I've heard your mother say.

NICK: My mother has a sister and a brother.

PINA: Two sisters!

NICK: You're right!

PINA: Maria and Angelina.

Women were also much more willing to discuss family feuds and crises and their own roles in them; men tended to repeat formulaic statements asserting family unity and respectability. (This was much less true for younger men.) Joe and Cetta Longhinotti's statements illustrate these tendencies. Joe responded to my question about kin relations: "We all get along. As a rule, relatives, you got nothing but trouble." Cetta, instead, discussed her relations with each of her grown children, their wives, her in-laws, and her own blood kin in detail. She did not hide the fact that relations were strained in several cases; she was eager to discuss the evolution of problems and to seek my opinions of her actions. Similarly, Pina Meraviglia told the following story of her fight with one of her brothers with hysterical laughter: "There was some biting and hair pulling and choking . . . it was terrible! I shouldn't even tell you. . . ." Nick, meanwhile, was concerned about maintaining an image of family unity and respectability.

Also, men waxed fluent while women were quite inarticulate in discussing their past and present occupations. When asked about their work lives, Joe Longhinotti and Nick Meraviglia, union baker and professional, respectively, gave detailed narratives of their work careers. Cetta Longhinotti and Pina Meraviglia, clerical and former clerical, respectively, offered only short descriptions focusing on factors of ambience, such as the "lovely things" sold by Cetta's firm.

These patterns are not repeated in the younger generation, especially among younger women, such as Jane Batemen, who have managed to acquire training and jobs with some prospect of mobility. These younger women, though, have *added* a professional and detailed interest in their jobs to a felt responsibility for the work of kinship.[6]

Although men rarely took on any kin-work tasks, family histories and accounts of contemporary life revealed that kinswomen often negotiated among themselves, alternating hosting, food-preparation, and gift-buying responsibilities—or sometimes ceding entire task clusters to one woman. Taking on or ceding tasks was clearly related to acquiring or divesting oneself of power within kin networks, but women varied in their interpretation of the meaning of this power. Cetta Longhinotti, for example, relied on the "family Christmas dinner" as a symbol of her central kinship role and was involved in painful negotiations with her daughter-in-law over the issue: "Last year she insisted—this is touchy. She doesn't want to spend the holiday dinner together. So last year we went there. But I still had my dinner the next day. . . . I made a big dinner on Christmas Day, regardless of who's coming—candles on the table, the whole routine. I decorate the house myself too . . . well, I just feel that the time will come when maybe I won't feel like cooking a big dinner—she should take advantage of the fact that I feel like doing it now." Pina Meraviglia, in contrast, was saddened by the centripetal force of the developmental cycle but was unworried about the power dynamics involved in her negotiations with daughters-and mother-in-law over holiday celebrations.

Kin work is not just a matter of power among women but also of the mediation of power represented by household units.[7] Women often choose to minimize status claims in their kin work and to include numbers of households under the rubric of family. Cetta Longhinotti's sister Anna, for example, is married to a professional man whose parents have considerable economic resources, while Joe and Cetta have low incomes and no other well-off kin. Cetta and Anna remain close, talk on the phone several times a week, and assist their adult children, divided by distance and economic status, in remaining united as cousins.

Finally, women perceived housework, child care, market labor, the care of the elderly, and the work of kinship as competing responsibilities. Kin work was a unique category, however, because it was unlabeled and because women felt they could either cede some tasks to kinswomen and/or could cut them back severely. Women variously cited the pressures of market labor, the needs of the elderly, and their own desires for freedom and job enrichment as reasons for cutting back Christmas card lists, organized holiday gatherings, multifamily dinners, letters, visits, and phone calls. They expressed guilt and defensiveness about this cutback process and, particularly, about their failures to keep families close through constant contact and about their failures to create perfect holiday celebrations. Cetta Longhinotti, during the period when she was visiting her elderly mother every weekend in addition to working a full-time job, said of her grown children, "I'd have the whole gang here once a month, but I've been so busy that I haven't done that for about six months." And Pina Meraviglia lamented her insufficient work on family Christmases, "I wish I had really made it traditional . . . like my sister-in-law has special stories."

Kin work, then, takes place in an arena characterized simultaneously by cooperation and competition, by guilt and gratification. Like housework and child care, it is women's work, with the same lack of clear-cut agreement concerning its proper components: How often should sheets be changed? When should children be toilet trained? Should an aunt send a niece a birthday present? Unlike housework and child care, however, kin work, taking place across the boundaries of normative households, is as yet unlabeled and has no retinue of experts prescribing its correct forms. Neither home economists nor child psychologists have much to say about nieces' birthday presents. Kin work is thus more easily cut back without social interference. On the other hand, the results of kin work—frequent kin contact and feelings of intimacy—are the subject of considerable cultural manipulation as indicators of family happiness. Thus, women in general are subject to the guilt my informants expressed over cutting back kin-work activities.

Although many of my informants referred to the results of women's kin work—cross-household kin contacts and attendant ritual gatherings—as particularly Italian-American, I suggest that in fact this phenomenon is broadly characteristic of American kinship. We think of kin-work tasks such as the preparation of ritual feasts, responsibility for holiday card lists, and gift buying as extensions of women's domestic responsibilities for cooking, consumption, and nurturance. American men in general do not take on these tasks any more than they do housework and child care—and probably less, as these tasks have not yet been the subject of intense public debate. And my informants' gender breakdown in relative articulateness on kinship and workplace themes reflects the still prevalent occupational segregation—most women cannot find jobs that provide enough pay, status, or promotion possibilities to make them worth focusing on—as well as women's perceived power within kinship networks. The common recognition of that power is reflected in Selma Greenberg's book on nonsexist child rearing. Greenberg calls mothers "press agents" who sponsor relations between their own children and other relatives; she advises a mother whose relatives treat her disrespectfully to deny those kin access to her children.[8]

Kin work is a salient concept in other parts of the developed world as well. Larissa Adler Lomnitz and Marisol Pérez Lizaur have found that "centralizing women" are responsible for these tasks and for communicating "family ideology" among upper-class families in Mexico City. Matthews Hamabata, in his study of upper-class families in Japan, has found that women's kin work involves key financial transactions. Sylvia Junko Yanagisako discovered that, among rural Japanese migrants to the United States, the maintenance of kin networks was assigned to women as the migrants adopted the American ideology of the independent nuclear family household. Maila Stivens notes that urban Australian housewives' kin ties and kin ideology "transcend women's isolation in domestic units."[9]

This is not to say that cultural conceptions of appropriate kin work do not vary, even within the United States. Carol B. Stack documents institutionalized fictive kinship and concomitant reciprocity networks among impoverished black American women. Women in populations characterized by intense feelings of ethnic identity may feel bound to emphasize particular occasions—Saint Patrick's or Columbus Day—with organized family feasts. These constructs may be mediated by religious affiliation, as in the differing emphases on Friday or Sunday family dinners among Jews and Christians. Thus the personnel involved and the amount and kind of labor considered necessary for the satisfactory performance of particular kin-work tasks are likely to be culturally constructed.[10] But while the kin and quasi-kin universes and the ritual calendar may vary among women according to race or ethnicity, their general responsibility for maintaining kin links and ritual observances does not.

As kin work is not an ethnic or racial phenomenon, neither is it linked only to one social class. Some commentators on American family life still reflect the influence of work done in England in the 1950s and 1960s (by Elizabeth Bott and by Peter Willmott and Michael Young) in their assumption that working-class families are close and extended, while the middle class substitutes friends (or anomie) for family. Others reflect the prevalent family pessimism in their presumption that neither working-nor middle-class families have extended kin contact.[11] Insofar as kin contact depends on residential proximity, the larger economy's shifts will influence particular groups' experiences. Factory workers, close to kin or not, are likely to disperse when plants shut down or relocate. Small businesspeople or independent professionals may, however, remain resident in particular areas—and thus maintain proximity to kin—for generations, while professional employees of large firms relocate at their firms' behest. This pattern obtained among my informants.

In any event, cross-household kin contact can be and is effected at long distance through letters, cards, phone calls, and holiday and vacation visits. The form and functions of contact, however, vary according to economic resources. Stack and Brett Williams offer rich accounts of kin networks among poor blacks and migrant Chicano farmworkers functioning to provide emotional support, labor, commodity, and cash exchange—a funeral visit, help with laundry, the gift of a dress or piece of furniture.[12] Far different in degree are exchanges such as the loan of a vacation home, a multi-family boating trip, or the provision of free professional services—examples from the kin networks of my wealthier informants. The point is that households, as labor- and income-pooling units, whatever their relative wealth, are somewhat porous in relation to others with whose members they share kin or quasi-kin ties. We do not really know how class differences operate in this realm; it is possible that they do so largely in terms of ideology. It may be, as David Schneider and Raymond T. Smith suggest, that the affluent and the very poor are more open in recognizing necessary economic ties to kin than are those who identify themselves as middle class.[13]

Recognizing that kin work is gender- rather than class-based allows us to see women's kin networks among all groups, not just among working-class and impoverished women in industrialized societies. This recognition in turn clarifies our understanding of the privileges and limits of women's varying access to economic resources. Affluent women can "buy out" of housework, child care—and even some kin-work responsibilities. But they, like all women, are ultimately responsible, and subject to both guilt and blame, as the administrators of home, children, and kin network. Even the wealthiest women must negotiate the timing and venue of holidays and other family rituals with their kinswomen. It may be that kin work is the core women's work category in which all women cooperate, while women's perceptions of the appropriateness of cooperation for housework, child care, and the care of the elderly varies by race, class, region, and generation.

But kin work is not necessarily an appropriate category of labor, much less gendered labor, in all societies. In many small-scale societies, kinship is the major organizing principle of all social life, and all contacts are by definition kin contacts.[14] One cannot, therefore, speak of labor that does not involve kin. In the United States, kin work as a separable category of gendered labor perhaps arose historically in concert with the ideological and material constructs of the moral mother/cult of domesticity and the privatized family during the course of industrialization in the eighteenth and nineteenth centuries. These phenomena are connected to the increase in the ubiquity of productive occupations for men that are not organized through kinship. This includes the demise of the family farm with the capitalization of agriculture and rural–urban migration; the decline of family recruitment in factories as firms grew, ended child labor, and began to assert bureaucratized forms of control; the decline of artisanal labor and of small entrepreneurial enterprises as large firms took greater and greater shares of the commodity market; the decline of the family firm as corporations— and their managerial work forces—grew beyond the capacities of individual families to provision them; and, finally, the rise of civil service bureaucracies and public pressure against nepotism.[15]

As men increasingly worked alongside of non-kin, and as the ideology of separate spheres was increasingly accepted, perhaps the responsibility for kin maintenance, like that for child rearing, became gender-focused. Ryan points out that "built into the updated family economy . . . was a new measure of voluntarism." This voluntarism, though, "perceived as the shift from patriarchal authority to domestic affection," also signaled the rise of women's moral responsibility for family life. Just as the "idea of fatherhood itself seemed almost to wither away" so did male involvement in the responsibility for kindred lapse.[16]

With postbellum economic growth and geographic movement, women's new kin burden involved increasing amounts of time and labor. The ubiquity of lengthy visits and of frequent letter-writing among nineteenth-century women attests to this. And for visitors and for those who were residentially proximate, the continuing commonalities of women's domestic labor allowed for kinds of work sharing—nursing, childkeeping, cooking, cleaning—that men, with their increasingly differentiated and controlled activities, probably could not maintain. This is not to say that some kin-related male productive work did not continue; my own data, for instance, show kin involvement among small businessmen in the present. It is, instead, to suggest a general trend in material life and a cultural shift that influenced even those whose productive and kin lives remained commingled. Yanagisako has distinguished between the realms of domestic and public kinship in order to draw attention to anthropology's relatively "thin descriptions" of the domestic (female) domain. Using her typology, we might say that kin work as gendered labor comes into existence within the domestic domain with the relative erasure of the domain of public, male kinship.[17]

Whether or not this proposed historical model bears up under further research, the question remains, Why do women do kin work? However material factors may shape activities, they do not determine how individuals may perceive them. And in considering issues of motivation, of intention, of the cultural construction of kin work, we return to the altruism-versus-self-interest dichotomy in recent feminist theory. Consider the epigraphs to this article. Are women kin workers the nurturant weavers of the Gilligan quotation, or victims, like the fed-up woman who writes to complain to Ann Landers? That is, are we to see kin work as yet another example of "women's culture" that takes the care of others as its primary desideratum? Or are we to see kin work as another way in which men, the economy, and the state extract labor from women without a fair return? And how do women themselves see their kin work and its place in their lives?

As I have indicated previously, I believe that it is the creation of the self-interest/altruism dichotomy that is itself the problem here. My women informants, like most American women, accepted their primary responsibility for housework and the care of dependent children. Despite two major waves of feminist activism in this century, the gendering of certain categories of unpaid labor is still largely unaltered. These work responsibilities clearly interfere with some women's labor force commitments at certain life-cycle stages; but, more important, women are simply discriminated against in the labor market and rarely are able to achieve wage and status parity with men of the same age, race, class, and educational background.[18]

Thus for my women informants, as for most American women, the domestic domain is not only an arena in which much unpaid labor must be undertaken but also a realm in which one may attempt to gain human satisfactions—and power—not available in the labor market. Anthropologists Jane Collier and Louise Lamphere have written compellingly on the ways in which varying kinship and economic structures may shape women's competition or cooperation with one another in domestic domains.[19] Feminists considering Western women and families have looked at the issue of power primarily in terms of husband–wife relations or psychological relations between parents and children. If we adopt Collier and Lamphere's broader canvas, though, we see that kin work is not only women's labor from which men and children benefit but also labor that women undertake in order to create obligations in men and children and to gain power over one another. Thus Cetta Longhinotti's struggle with her daughter-in-law over the venue of Christmas dinner is not just about a competition over altruism, it is also about the creation of future obligations. And thus Cetta's and Anna's sponsorship of their children's friendship with each other is both an act of nurturance and a cooperative means of gaining power over those children.

Although this was not a clear-cut distinction, those of my informants who were more explicitly antifeminist tended to be most invested in kin work. Given the overwhelming historical shift toward greater autonomy for younger generations and the withering of children's financial and labor obligations to their parents, this investment was in most cases tragically doomed. Cetta Longhinotti, for example, had repaid her own mother's devotion with extensive home nursing during the mother's last years. Given Cetta's general failure to direct her adult children in work, marital choice, religious worship, or even frequency of visits, she is unlikely to receive such care from them when she is older.

The kin-work lens thus reveals the close relations between altruism and self-interest in women's actions. As economists Nancy Folbre and Heidi Hartmann point out, we have inherited a Western intellectual tradition that both dichotomizes the domestic and public domains and associates them on exclusive axes such that we find it difficult to see self-interest in the home and altruism in the workplace.[20] But why, in fact, have women fought for better jobs if not, in part, to support their children? These dichotomies are Procrustean beds that warp our understanding of women's lives both at home and at work. "Altruism" and "self-interest" are cultural constructions that are not necessarily mutually exclusive, and we forget this to our peril.

The concept of kin work helps to bring into focus a heretofore unacknowledged array of tasks that is culturally assigned to women in industrialized societies. At the same time, this concept, embodying notions of both love and work and crossing the boundaries of households, helps us to reflect on current feminist debates on women's work, family, and community. We newly see both the interrelations of these phenomena and women's roles in creating and maintaining those interrelations. Revealing the actual labor embodied in what we culturally conceive as love and considering the political uses of this labor helps to deconstruct the self-interest/altruism dichotomy and to connect more closely women's domestic and labor-force lives.

The true value of the concept, however, remains to be tested through further historical and contemporary research on gender, kinship, and labor. We need to assess the suggestion that gendered kin work emerges in concert with the capitalist development process; to probe the historical record for women's and men's varying and changing conceptions of it; and to research the current range of its cultural constructions and material realities. We know that household boundaries are more porous than we had thought—but they are undoubtedly differentially porous, and this is what we need to specify. We need, in particular, to assess the relations of changing labor processes, residential patterns, and the use of technology to changing kin work.

Altering the values attached to this particular set of women's tasks will be as difficult as are the housework, child-care, and occupational-segregation struggles. But just as feminist research in these latter areas is complementary and cumulative, so researching kin work should help us to piece together the home, work, and public-life landscape—to see the female world of cards and holidays as it is constructed and lived within the changing political economy. How female that world is to remain, and what it would look like if it were not sex-segregated, are questions we cannot yet answer.

ACKNOWLEDGMENT

Many thanks to Cynthia Costello, Rayna Rapp, Roberta Spalter-Roth, John Willoughby, and Barbara Gelpi, Susan Johnson, and Sylvia Yanagisako of Signs for their help with this article. I wish in particular to acknowledge the influence of Rayna Rapp's work on my ideas.

Acknowledgment and gratitude to Carroll Smith-Rosenberg for my paraphrase of her title, "The Female World of Love and Ritual: Relations between Women in Nineteenth-Century America," *Signs: Journal of Women in Culture and Society* 1, no. 1 (Autumn 1975): 1–29.

NOTES

1. Ann Landers letter printed in *Washington Post* (April 15, 1983); Carol Gilligan, *In a Different Voice* (Cambridge, Mass.: Harvard University Press, 1982), 17.

2. Heidi I. Hartmann, "The Family as the Locus of Gender, Class, and Political Struggle: The Example of Housework," *Signs* 6, no. 3 (Spring 1981): 366–94; and Christopher Lasch, *Haven in a Heartless World: The Family Besieged* (New York: Basic Books, 1977).

3. Representative examples of the first trend include Joann Vanek, "Time Spent on Housework," *Scientific American* 231 (November 1974): 116–20; Ruth Schwartz Cowan, "A Case Study of Technological and Social Change: The Washing Machine and the Working Wife," in *Clio's Consciousness Raised*, ed. Mary Hartmann and Lois Banner (New York: Harper & Row, 1974), 245–53; Ann Oakley, *Women's Work: The Housewife, Past and Present* (New York: Vintage, 1974); Hartmann; and Susan Strasser, *Never Done: A History of American Housework* (New York: Pantheon Books, 1982). Key contributions to the second trend include Louise Lamphere, "Strategies, Cooperation and Conflict among Women in Domestic Groups," in *Woman, Culture and Society*, ed. Michelle Zimbalist Rosaldo and Louise Lamphere (Stanford, Calif.: Stanford University Press, 1974), 97–112; Mina Davis Caulfield, "Imperialism, the Family and the Cultures of Resistance," *Socialist Revolution* 20 (October 1974): 67–85; Smith-Rosenberg; Sylvia Junko Yanagisako, "Women-centered Kin Networks and Urban Bilateral Kinship," *American Ethnologist* 4, no. 2 (1977): 207–26; Jane Humphries, "The Working Class Family, Women's Liberation and Class Struggle: The Case of Nineteenth Century British History," *Review of Radical Political Economics* 9 (Fall 1977): 25–41; Blanche Weisen Cook, "Female Support Networks and Political Activism: Lillian Wald, Crystal Eastman, Emma Goldman," in *A Heritage of Her Own*, ed. Nancy F. Cott and Elizabeth H. Pleck (New York: Simon & Schuster, 1979); Temma Kaplan, "Female Consciousness and Collective Action: The Case of Barcelona, 1910–1918," *Signs* 7, no. 3 (Spring 1982): 545–66.

4. On this debate, see Jon Weiner, "Women's History on Trial," *Nation* 241, no. 6 (September 7, 1985): 161, 176, 178–80; Karen J. Winkler, "Two Scholars' Conflict in Sears Sex-Bias Case Sets Off War in Women's History," *Chronicle of Higher Education* (February 5, 1986), 1, 8; Rosalind Rosenberg, "What Harms Women in the Workplace," *New York Times* (February 27, 1986); Alice Kessler-Harris, "Equal Employment Opportunity Commission vs. Sears Roebuck and Company: A Personal Account," *Radical History Review* 35 (April 1986): 57–79.

5. Portions of the following analysis are reported in Micaela di Leonardo, *The Varieties of Ethnic Experience: Kinship, Class and Gender among California Italian-Americans* (Ithaca, N.Y.: Cornell University Press, 1984), Chap. 6.

6. Clearly, many women do, in fact, discuss their paid labor with willingness and clarity. The point here is that there are opposing gender tendencies in an identical interview situation, tendencies that are explicable in terms of both the material realities and current cultural constructions of gender.

7. Papanek has rightly focused on women's unacknowledged family status production, but what is conceived of as "family" shifts and varies (Hanna Papanek, "Family Status Production: The 'Work' and 'Non-Work' of Women," *Signs* 4, no. 4 [Summer 1979]: 775–81).

8. Selma Greenberg, *Right from the Start: A Guide to Nonsexist Child Rearing* (Boston: Houghton Mifflin Co., 1978), 147. Another example of indirect support for kin work's gendered existence is a recent study of university math students, which found that a major reason for women's failure to pursue careers in mathematics was the pressure of family involvement. Compare David Maines et al., *Social Processes of Sex Differentiation in Mathematics* (Washington, D.C.: National Institute of Education, 1981).

9. Larissa Adler Lomnitz and Marisol Pérez Lizaur, "The History of a Mexican Urban Family," *Journal of Family History* 3, no. 4 (1978): 392–409, esp. 398; Matthews Hamàbata, *Crested Kimono: Power and Love in the Japanese Business Family* (Ithaca, N.Y.: Cornell University Press, 1990); Sylvia Junko Yanagisako, "Two Processes of Change in Japanese-American Kinship," *Journal of Anthropological Research* 31 (1975): 196–224; Maila Stivens, "Women and Their Kin: Kin, Class and Solidarity in a Middle-Class Suburb of Sydney, Australia," in *Women United, Women Divided*, ed. Patricia Caplan and Janet M. Bujra (Bloomington: Indiana University Press, 1979), 157–84.

10. Carol B. Stack, *All Our Kin: Strategies for Survival in a Black Community* (New York: Harper & Row, 1974). These cultural constructions may, however, vary within ethnic/racial populations as well.

11. Elizabeth Bott, *Family and Social Network*, 2d ed. (New York: Free Press, 1971): Michael Young and Peter Willmott, *Family and Kinship in East London* (London: Routledge & Kegan Paul, 1957), and *Family and Class in a London Suburb* (London: Routledge & Kegan Paul, 1960). Classic studies that presume this class difference are

Herbert Gans, *The Urban Villagers: Group and Class in the Life of Italian-Americans* (New York: Free Press, 1962); and Mirra Komarovsky, *Blue-Collar Marriage* (New York: Random House, 1962). A recent example is Ilene Philipson, "Heterosexual Antagonisms and the Politics of Mothering," *Socialist Review* 12, no. 6 (November–December 1982): 55–77. Edward Shorter, *The Making of the Modern Family* (New York: Basic Books, 1975), epitomizes the pessimism of the "family sentiments" school. See also Mary Lyndon Shanley. "The History of the Family in Modern England: Review Essay," *Signs* 4, no. 4 (Summer 1979): 740–50.

12. Stack; and Brett Williams, "The Trip Takes Us: Chicano Migrants to the Prairie" (Ph.D. diss., University of Illinois at Urbana-Champaign, 1975).

13. David Schneider and Raymond T. Smith, *Class Differences and Sex Roles in American Kinship and Family Structure* (Englewood Cliffs, N.J.: Prentice-Hall, Inc., 1973), esp. 27.

14. See Nelson Graburn, ed., *Readings in Kinship and Social Structure* (New York: Harper & Row, 1971), esp. 3–4.

15. The moral mother/cult of domesticity is analyzed in Barbara Welter, "The Cult of True Womanhood, 1820–1860," *American Quarterly* 18, no. 2 (Summer 1966): 151–74; Nancy Cott, *The Bonds of Womanhood: "Women's Sphere" in New England, 1780–1835* (New Haven, Conn.: Yale University Press, 1977); and Ruth Bloch, "American Feminine Ideals in Transition: The Rise of the Moral Mother, 1785–1815," *Feminist Studies* 4, no. 2 (June 1978): 101–26. The description of the general political-economic shift in the United States is based on Harry Braverman, *Labor and Monopoly Capital: The Degradation of Work in the Twentieth Century* (New York: Monthly Review Press, 1974); Peter Dobkin Hall, "Family Structure and Economic Organization: Massachusetts Merchants, 1700–1850," in *Family and Kin in Urban Communities, 1700–1950*, ed. Tamara K. Hareven (New York: New Viewpoints, 1977), 38–61; Michael Anderson, "Family, Household and the Industrial Revolution," in *The American Family in Social-Historical Perspective*, ed. Michael Gordon (New York: St. Martin's Press, 1978), 38–50; Tamara K. Hareven, *Amoskeag: Life and Work in an American Factory City* (New York: Pantheon Books, 1978); Richard Edwards, *Contested Terrain: The Transformation of the Workplace in the Twentieth Century* (New York: Basic Books, 1979); Mary Ryan, *The Cradle of the Middle Class: The Family in Oneida County, New York, 1790–1865* (Cambridge: Cambridge University Press, 1981); Alice Kessler-Harris, *Out to*

Work: A History of Wage-earning Women in the United States (New York: Oxford University Press, 1982).

16. Ryan, 231–32.

17. Sylvia Junko Yanagisako, "Family and Household: The Analysis of Domestic Groups," *Annual Review of Anthropology* 8 (1979): 161–205.

18. See Donald J. Treiman and Heidi I. Hartmann, eds., *Women, Work and Wages: Equal Pay for Jobs of Equal Value* (Washington, D.C.: National Academy Press, 1981).

19. Lamphere (n. 4 above); Jane Fishburne Collier, "Women in Politics," in Rosaldo and Lamphere, eds. (n. 3 above), 89–96.

20. Nancy Folbre and Heidi I. Hartmann, "The Rhetoric of Self-Interest: Selfishness, Altruism, and Gender in Economic Theory," in *The Consequences of Economic Rhetoric,* ed. Arjo Klamer and Donald McCloskey (New York: Cambridge University Press, 1988).

IX

Gender, Ritual, and Religion

In many non-Western societies, women's ritual roles are central and indispensable to community cohesion and well-being. In contrast, in Anglo-European cultures, women's religious activities tend to be secondary and marginal because of the pre-eminence of men in both organizational hierarchies and doctrine. Anthropological research has long recognized that religious systems reflect, support, and carry forward patterns of social organization and central values of a society. What has not been sufficiently recognized is the interrelationships of men and women in the perpetuation of social life through religious activities and the relationship between gender stratification and gendered religious symbolism.

The study of the ritual activities of women has often been embedded in analyses of life cycle events, such as the Nkang'a girl's puberty ritual among the Ndembu of Central Africa (Turner 1968: 198) or pregnancy and childbirth rituals in Asia (Jacobson 1989; Laderman 1983). With the exception of these areas of research, the study of women and religion has often been neglected, despite the fact that women are prominent in religious activities. As a result of a renewed interest in the study of gender in various cultures, scholars have begun to explore how the religious experience of women is different from that of men; whether and how women become ritual specialists; what religious functions they perform and the degree to which these are private or public; and, finally, what implications these ritual activities have for women's prestige, status, and empowerment.

This has led, in some cultural contexts, to an attempt to formulate a more complete ethnographic picture. For example, in the literature on Australian aborigines, where there is a good deal of debate about gender roles, a number of ethnologists have asserted that the dominance of senior men is sustained by their control of sacred knowledge and that their position is recognized by both men and women in the culture (Bern 1979; Warner 1937; White 1975). This viewpoint has been challenged by Diane Bell (1981, 1983), who notes that male anthropologists have underestimated and underreported the religious life of Australian aboriginal women. She argues that "both men and women have rituals that are closed to the other, both men and women allow the other limited attendance at certain of their rituals, and, finally, there are ceremonies in which both men and women exchange knowledge and together celebrate their membership in one society and their duty to maintain the law of their ancestors" (1981: 319).

Bell focuses in particular on the love rituals of women, rituals that originally were viewed by ethnologists as magic and therefore deviant, unimportant, and marginal to the central decision-making realm of men. In contrast, Bell suggests that in the celebration of these rituals, used by women to establish and maintain marriages of their own choosing, "women clearly perceived themselves as independent operators in a domain where they exercised power and autonomy based on their dreaming affiliations with certain tracts of land. These rights are recognized and respected by the whole society" (1981: 322). The love rituals of Australian aboriginal women are, in short, by no means peripheral to the society. They are underwritten by Dreamtime Law and feared by men who are often unaware that they are being performed and unable to negate their power. Through their rituals some Australian aboriginal women have, as Hamilton (1981) suggests, a mechanism with which to challenge the ideology of male superiority that is expressed in male ritual.

Mathews (1985) provides us with another example of an important arena of religious activity—the civil–religious hierarchy or cargo system in Mesoamerica—that has long been considered a public and exclusively male arena. If women were mentioned at all in studies of the cargo system, it was for their peripheral roles in food preparation. Based on her research in the state of Oaxaca in Mexico, Mathews begins by pointing out that an application of the domestic–public model (see Section III) to an understanding of these religious ceremonies obscures the significant ritual roles of women because it places the cargo system in the public sphere of activity and fails to acknowledge the importance of the household unit. Rather than oppose men and women within a rigid domestic–public model, Mathews emphasizes the parallel and interdependent roles of men and women in the execution of cargo. Male cargo holders (mayordomos) organize and coordinate the activities of men, and female cargo holders (mayordomas) organize and coordinate the activities of women. At the end of their year of responsibility, both share in the prestige gained from service.

If Oaxacan women have an important and prestige-conferring role within the religious sphere of cargo activity, similar opportunities are denied them within the civil sphere. Thus Mathews explores the impact of the penetration of the state (see Section VII) on the lives of women. A sexual divide-and-rule state policy, she argues, makes men into social adults and women into domestic wards whose dealings with the public sphere become restricted. Prestige in local institutions is undermined by its absence in extracommunity institutions, and as civil offices assume increasing importance at the expense of cargo offices, the position of women is eroded.

In contrast to the underestimation of women's religious roles in the literature on Australian aborigines and the Mesoamerican cargo system, studies of sub-Saharan Africa have long recognized that the ritual life of women is both significant and highly elaborated. In this region, women are involved in complex ceremonies of initiation; they are engaged in witchcraft and divination (Mendonsa 1979; Ngubane 1977); they act as spirit mediums and healers (Green 1989; Sargent 1989); they lead and participate in possession cults (Berger 1976); and they form their own secret societies (MacCormack 1979).

Janice Boddy (in this book) discusses the role of women in the zar spirit possession cult of northern Sudan. In particular, she emphasizes how *zâr* serves as a cultural resource mobilized by individuals, particularly women, under certain conditions. Boddy argues that the Sudanese women in the village of Hofiriyat, where she conducted her research, view themselves in a complementary rather than inferior or subordinate position vis-à-vis men. This complementarity in gender relations is reflected in the dialectical relationship between zar and Islam. "If women are constrained by their gender from full participation in Islam, men are constrained by theirs from full participation in the zar" (Boddy 1989: 60). Zar is not, in Boddy's view, a "peripheral cult" (Lewis 1971).

In a range of cultural contexts, anthropologists have argued that women use spirit possession and trance as an outlet for the stress that results from their social and material deprivation and subordination (Broch 1985; Hamer and Hamer 1966; Lewis 1966, 1986; Morsy 1979; Pressel 1973). As Danforth (1989: 99) argues with regard to firewalking (Anastenaria) in northern Greece, "Through these rituals women seek to address the discrepancies that characterize the relationship between an official ideology of male dominance and a social reality in which women actually exercise a significant degree of power. Spirit possession . . . provides a context for the resolution of conflict often associated with gender roles and gender identity." Boddy views the zar cult in more nuanced terms. Although she acknowledges that some of her informants use *zâr* to improve their subordinate status, she emphasizes that women are more susceptible to spirit attack (as illness episode) "as a function of their femininity." *Zâr* is a form of feminist discourse for women with marital or fertility problems. Close to 50 percent of Hofriyati women who were ever or are married have succumbed to possession. "Spirits, villagers assert, rarely trouble themselves with the unwed" (Boddy 1989: 166).

Discourse, in the form of sexually explicit funerary songs and dances performed by women, is also the subject of Janet McIntosh's analysis (in this book) of death rituals among the Giriama of Kenya. McIntosh begins by noting that many ritual forms, particularly in sub-Saharan Africa, lend themselves to unruliness, turning the normative social world upside down (see also Davis 1971, 1975). But, she asks, does such ritual behavior really pose a threat to patriarchal orders and how can it be understood from an insider's perspective? Have these perceptions changed in conjunction with the arrival of Western lifestyles and tourism? McIntosh argues that in a gender-neutral sense the sexual license of funerary songs is a mechanism by which the Giriama can confront the power of death. Grief and sexual expression are assimilated such that a funeral becomes like a wedding: "the last wedding of the deceased." However, the persistence of this "tradition" occurs in a society where women's sexuality is still controlled by a set of popular expectations about female modesty and yet simultaneously challenged by the growth of a "sex safari" industry. The obscenities expressed by women in the funerary rituals are thus viewed with ambivalence—innocuous tradition on the one hand; a training ground for real sexual promiscuity and misconduct on the other. Today women are frequently derided for, if not prohibited by their husbands from participating in these unruly rituals.

The relationship between women's religion and sexuality is equally central to Laurel Kendall's discussion (in this book) of Korean shamans, but in this case she wonders whether this is an appropriate interpretation of what is going on and suggests that it is an interpretation rooted in Western culture. While she acknowledges that the belief that shamanic experience implies a sexual union between the female shaman and her guardian god "lurks in some corners of the Korean popular imagination," she emphasizes that Korean shamanistic rituals are less about repressed sexuality than they are about expressive bodily play and challenges to gender oppression.

Kendall's essay also introduces us to the concept of female religious practitioners (healers and shamans) more generally. Such women frequently transcend local cultural definitions of womanhood and are recognized as having extraordinary characteristics. Korean women who become *mansin* (shamans) stand above the social and economic constraints generally imposed on a proper Korean wife and mother. The *mansin* occupies an ambiguous status similar to that of other "glamorous but morally dubious female marginals, the actress, the female entertainer, and the prostitute" (Kendall 1985). Though not always accorded respect, the *mansin* wears the costumes and speaks with the authority of the gods. *Mansin* and their rituals are, in Kendall's view, "integral components of Korean family and village religion. Within this religious system, women and shamans perform essential ritual tasks that complement men's ritual tasks" (1985: 25). Korean housewives come to the *mansin* for therapeutic answers to a range of personal and household problems; for divinations about the future and prospects for the coming year; and for female solidarity and a "venting of the spleen" (Kendall 1985: 25). Women's rituals in Korea, like those in some other parts of the world, are both practical and expressive.

Another important area of research addresses how social, political, and economic change impacts the religious lives of men and women. For a long time scholars believed that modernization would result in secularization. Of course, this is far from true, and research has illustrated the diverse ways in which globalization and change impact religious beliefs and practices without eradicating them (Henfer 1998; Moore and Sanders 2001; Schiller 1997). Gender is not often considered in relation to this question (Bayes and Toihidi 2001) but this is precisely the issue that Susan Starr Sered (in this book) explores in her study of how modernization has affected the religious lives of elderly Jewish women of Asian origin who are now living in Israel. In their home countries, women's and men's religious lives were highly segregated, and women's religious roles focused largely on protecting the well-being of their families. Sered finds that the move to Israel has opened new religious opportunities for women. They can pursue more religious education, assume leadership roles, and expand their social networks. Further, even their traditional roles are enhanced because women become the repositories of culture—"guardians of the old ways," holders of sacred knowledge. Sered cites several examples of similar processes in other parts of the world and in other times (see also Espiritu 2003; Kurien 2003). And yet, even while they are preserving ritual and religious traditions, women are also adapting some of them to a new context, and, in some cases, abandoning some of them when the state intervenes. Women's rituals, Sered argues, are often evaluated "in light of modern knowledge and modern wisdom" and as a result often labeled as superstition. The end result, Sered concludes, is that in the face of modernization women's religion is at once "vulnerable, tenacious, and creative."

In this book, we have taken the approach that what it means to be male and female (i.e., gender) is learned and shaped within a cultural context. Religious symbols are a powerful mechanism by which culturally appropriate gender messages are transmitted. As Bynum observes, "It is no longer possible to study religious practice or religious symbols without taking gender—that is, the cultural experience of being male or female—into account" (1986: 1–2). Very often, in fact, the diverse roles of women are projected into the religious sphere. This is as characteristic of Haitian Vodou (Brown 1991) as it is of Catholic culture where the values about ideal womanhood are sanctified by the image of the Virgin Mary, who represents submission, humility, serenity, and long suffering (Stevens 1973). In Mexico, for example, Eve and the Virgin Mary are contrasting images that "encode the cycle of reproduction within the domestic group. When a woman is nursing and sexually continent she resembles the Virgin. When she submits to sex, she is more like Eve" (Ingham 1986: 76). Hindu goddesses are also multifaceted; they are mothers, mediators, and protectresses. According to Preston (1985: 13), there is a connection "between the role of women in Indian life and the special position of female deities in the Hindu pantheon. Though Indian women are supposed to be absolutely devoted to their husbands who are respected as embodiments of the deity, women may also reign supreme in their own domains as mothers of their children." In Dinaan Hinduism the Great Goddess takes several forms, some good and some evil. Babb (1975: 226) suggests that these two aspects reflect an opposition in male and female principles: "When female dominates male, the pair is sinister; when male dominates female the pair is benign."

Through participation and leadership in ritual, women may enhance or challenge their socially- or culturally-defined position. Involvement in religious activities may also generate a sense of female or community solidarity through membership in a congregation or participation in ritual functions. And in many cultures there are parallel religious traditions. If possession is more characteristic of women than it is of men it is precisely because it provides an outlet for ritual expression. This is as true in the simpler societies as it is in state societies with masculinist or patriarchal religions. Thus, Michael Lambek (1993) has described a symbiotic relationship between Islam on the one hand and the spirit possession rituals of women on the other on the island of Mayotte off the coast of Tanzania in Africa. While men are "expected and enabled to display their moral concerns in the universalistic arena provided by Islam," women, through mediumship, "can exercise their authority and play a significant role in the *mraba* (their family) and the community. This can protect or further their own interests, for example, enabling sisters to continue to lay immoral claims upon their brothers after their parents' death" (Lambek 1993: 335, 334). These symbiotic relationships are certainly worthy of further exploration.

REFERENCES

Babb, Lawrence. 1975. *The Divine Hierarchy*. New York: Columbia University Press.

Bayes, Jane H., and Nayeren Tohidi (eds.). 2001. *Globalization, Gender and Religion*. New York: Palgrave McMillan.

Bell, Diane. 1981. "Women's Business Is Hard Work: Central Australian Aboriginal Women's Love Rituals." *Signs* 7: 314–337.

———. 1983. *Daughters of the Dreaming*. London: George Allen and Unwin.

Berger, Iris. 1976. "Rebels or Status-Seekers? Women as Spirit Mediums in East Africa." In Nancy J. Hafkin and Edna G. Bay (eds.). *Women in Africa*, pp. 157–182. Stanford, CA: Stanford University Press.

Bern, J. 1979. "Ideology and Domination: Toward a Reconstruction of Australian Aboriginal Social Formation." *Oceania* 50: 118–132.

Boddy, Janice. 1989. *Wombs and Alien Spirits:Women, Men,and the Zar Cult in Northern Sudan*. Madison: University of Wisconsin Press.

Broch, Harald Meyer. 1985. "'Crazy Women Are Performing in Sombali': A Possession-Trance Ritual on Bonerate, Indonesia." *Ethos* 13: 262–282.

Brown, Karen McCarthy. 1991. Mama Lola: *A Vodou Priestess in Brooklyn*. Berkeley: University of California Press.

Bynum, Caroline Walker. 1986. "Introduction: The Complexity of Symbols." In Caroline Walker Bynum, Steven Harrell, and Paula Richman (eds.). *Gender and Religion: On the Complexity of Symbols*, pp. 1–20. Boston: Beacon.

Danforth, Loring M. 1989 *Firewalking and Religious Healing: The Anastenaria of Greece and the American Firewalking Movement*. Princeton: Princeton University Press.

Davis, Natalie Zemon. 1971. "The Reasons of Misrule: Youth Groups and Charivaris in Sixteenth-Century France." *Past and Present* 50: 41–75.

———. 1975. "Women on Top." In Natalie Zemon Davis, *Society and Culture in Early Modern France*, pp. 124–151. Stanford, CA: Stanford University Press.

Espiritu, Yen Le. 2003. "We Don't Sleep Around Like White Girls Do: Family, Culture, and Gender in Filipina American Lives." In Pierette Hondagneu-Sotelo (ed.). *Gender and U.S. Immigration*, pp. 263–284. Berkeley: University of California Press.

Green, Edward C. 1989. "Mystical Black Power: The Calling to Diviner-Mediumship in Southern Africa." In Carole Shepherd McClain (ed.). *Women as Healers: Cross-Cultural Perspectives*, pp. 186–200. New Brunswick, NJ: Rutgers University Press.

Hamer, J., and I. Hamer. 1966. "Spirit Possession and its Socio-Psychological Implications among the Sidamo of Southwest Ethiopia." *Ethnology* 5: 392–408.

Hamilton, Annette. 1981. "A Complex Strategical Situation: Gender and Power in Aboriginal Australia." In N. Grieve and P. Grimshaw (eds.). *Australian Women: Feminist Perspectives*, pp. 69–85. Melbourne: Oxford University Press.

Henfer, Robert W. 1998. "Multiple Modernities: Christianity, Islam and Hinduism in a Globalizing Age." *Annual Review of Anthropology* 27: 83–104.

Ingham, John. 1986. *Mary, Michael and Lucifer*. Austin: University of Texas Press.

Jacobson, Doranne. 1989. "Golden Handprints and Red-Painted Feet: Hindu Childbirth Rituals in Central India." In Nancy Auer Falk and Rita M. Gross (eds.). *Unspoken Worlds: Women's Religious Lives*, pp. 59–71. Belmont, CA: Wadsworth Publishing Co.

Kendall, Laurel. 1985. *Shamans, Housewives, and Other Restless Spirits: Women in Korean Ritual Life*. Honolulu: University of Hawaii Press.

Kurien, Prema. 2003. "Gendered Ethnicity: Creating a Hindu Indian Identity in the United States." In Pierette Hondagneu-Sotelo (ed.). *Gender and U.S. Immigration*, pp. 151–173. Berkeley: University of California Press.

Laderman, Carol. 1983. *Wives and Midwives: Childbirth and Nutrition in Rural Malaysia*. Berkeley: University of California Press.

Lambek, Michael. 1993. *Knowledge and Practice in Mayotte: Local Discourses of Islam, Sorcery and Spirit Possession*. Toronto: University of Toronto Press.

Lewis, L. M. 1966. "Spirit Possession and Deprivation Cults." *Man* 1: 307–329.

———. 1971. *Ecstatic Religion: An Anthropoligical Study of Spirit Possession and Shamanism*. Baltimore, MD: Penguin Books.

———. 1986. *Religion in Context: Cults and Charisma*. Cambridge, UK: Cambridge University Press.

MacCormack, Carol P. 1979. "Sande: The Public Face of a Secret Society." In Bennetta Jules-Rosette (ed.). *New Religions of Africa*, pp. 27–39. Norwood, NJ: Ablex.

Mathews, Holly F. 1985. "'We are Mayordomo': A Reinterpretation of Women's Roles in the Mexican Cargo System." *American Ethnologist* 12 (2): 285–301.

Mendonsa, Eugene L. 1979. "The Position of Women in the Sisala Divination Cult." In Bennetta Jules-Rosette (ed.). *The New Religions of Africa*, pp. 57–67. Norwood, NJ: Ablex.

Moore, Henrietta, and Todd Sanders. 2001. *Magical Interpretations, Material Realities: Modernity, Witchcraft and the Occult in Post Colonial Africa*. London and New York: Routledge.

Morsy, Soheir. 1979. "Sex Roles, Power, and Illness." *American Ethnologist* 5: 137–150.

Ngubane, H. 1977. *Body and Mind in Zulu Medicine: An Ethnography of Health and Disease In Nyuswa-Zulu Thought and Practice*. New York: Academic Press.

Pressel, Ester. 1973. "Umbanda in Sao Paulo: Religious Innovations in a Developing Society." In Erika Bourguignon (ed.). *Religion, Altered States of Consciousness and Social Change*, pp. 264–318. Columbus: Ohio State University Press.

Preston, James J. 1985. *Cult of the Goddess: Social and Religious Change in a Hindu Temple*. Prospect Heights, IL: Waveland. (Orig. pub. 1980.)

Sargent, Carolyn. 1989. "Women's Roles and Women Healers in Contemporary Rural and Urban Benin." In Carole Shepherd McClain (ed.). *Women as Healers: Cross-Cultural Perspectives*, pp. 204–218. New Brunswick, NJ: Rutgers University Press.

Schiller, Anne. 1997. *Small Sacrifices: Religious Change and Cultural Identity among the Ngaju of Indonesia*. Oxford, UK: Oxford University Press.

Stevens, Evelyn. 1973. "Marianismo: The Other Face of Machismo in Latin America." In Ann Pescatello (ed.). *Female and Male in Latin America*, pp. 89–101. Pittsburgh: University of Pittsburgh Press.

Turner, Victor. 1968. *Drums of Affliction*. Oxford, UK: Clarendon Press.

Warner, William Lloyd. 1937. *A Black Civilization: A Study of an Australian Tribe*. New York: Harper & Row.

White, I. 1975. "Sexual Conquest and Submission in the Myths of Central Australia." In L. Hiatt (ed.). *Australian Aboriginal Mythology*, pp. 123–142. Canberra: Australian Institute of Aboriginal Studies.

Spirit Possession and Gender Complementarity
Zâr in Rural Northern Sudan

Janice Boddy

July 20, 1976, 4:00 P.M. The door to my hôsh bangs open. Asia ducks beneath the lintel, lifts the water container from her head, and pours its contents into my zîr. Her face is seamed with sweat. "Allaaah!" she exclaims, "The land is hot today! Shufti, ya Janice, I've heard they are drumming in Goz. Do you want to go?"

Of course!—a zâr is on. But the walk in this heat is a long one, and my leg has been badly swollen for several days.

"Sadig is borrowing camels from his cousin. You must ride."

Moments later I am teetering sidesaddle, following the equally inexpert Sadig along a trail that hems some withered fields of maize. My camel munches lazily at each low acacia, and I am soon covered in scratches from their thorns. Prodding seems only to anger the beast, and I fear a painful bite; it would have been faster to walk. Still beyond sight of Goz we are reached by the deep bass of drumming, fitful through the sultry air. The camels perk, raise their heads, start trotting toward the sound.

Goz is a newish settlement, an odd assortment of square thatched huts, thorn corrals, and a couple of half-completed mud-brick hôshs. The drumming comes from one of these. Hofriyati[1] arriving by foot have preceded my arrival; the zâr has just begun. Ideally a zâr should take place in the room of a house,

if capacious, but because of the heat, today's has been mounted in the yard.

A litany of greetings over, I am seated near the dancing grounds an open area (mîdân) bounded on three sides by palm-fiber ground mats. Here sit several dozen chanting women: the spirit-possessed. Now and then one rises to her knees and begins to move her upper body in time with the sonorous beat. In the center of the mîdân stands the shaykha—zâr practitioner or "priestess"—a forceful, brawny woman in an electric-pink pullover, tôb[2] tied loosely at her waist. She is arguing with a woman just as brash as she, who, between expletives, puffs furiously on a cigarette. I learn that the shaykha speaks not to the woman but to her spirit, in an effort to diagnose the source of the woman's complaint. Observing from the side is a tall, very black, incongruously muscled figure clad in a tôb, large wristwatch, and hairnet— the shaykha's reputedly transvestite assistant from south of Shendi. In contrast, the ayâna—"sick woman" and focus of the ceremony—is frail, elderly. She rests quietly on a pillow next to the musicians, facing the front of the hôsh, arms and legs curled tight against her white-tôbed body.

The shaykha concludes her discussion, sits down, and starts to drum. Using only the tips of her fingers, she beats a large earthen dallûka stretched with goat hide, its whitened flanks boldly adorned with mauve geometric designs. Another dallûka responds in shifted accents, joined half a second later by the nugarishan, a tall brass mortar that rings, when struck, like a cowbell, only deeper. A fourth woman beats a complementary rhythm on

This essay is excerpted from Janice Boddy, *Women, Men and the Zâr Cult in Northern Sudan* (University of Wisconsin Press, 1989) and adapted for this volume.

an inverted aluminum washtub or tisht. The result is a complicated syncopation, its underlying pattern one long beat, three short. The sound is less soothing than cacophonous, yet endlessly repeated and accompanied by reiterative chants, the effect is indeed soporific. The chants, I learn, are called "threads"—khuyût (singular is khayt)—and when sung they are said to be "pulled."

The rhythm intensifies; the ayâna rises to dance. Now visible over her tôb is a red sash attached to a reddish waist cloth in the style of a Sam Browne belt. She is possessed, my companions say, by Khawâja (Westerner) spirits: a doctor, lawyer, and military officer—all of these at once. Yet it is the lattermost she appears to manifest in dance. Her tôb is folded cowl-like over her head, obscuring her face; she flourishes a cane—hooked, as in vaudevillian burlesque. Her dance is a slow, rhythmic walk crisscrossing a chimeric square, feet first moving side to side, then forward and back. With a leap of the imagination she is an officer of the desert corps conducting drill. Every so often she bends rigidly at the hip and, cane pressed to her forehead, bobs her torso up and down. I am told that her spirits have requested the white tôb, cane, cigarettes, "European" belt, and yet to be purchased, a radio.

The band takes up the chant of another zâr. The ayâna sits; the shaykha leaves her drum and starts to dance, tôb covering her head. Suddenly, the tôb is thrown off. She turns on her heel, goose-steps the length of the mîdân, stops before me, abruptly pulls herself to attention. She salutes me three or four times, stiffly, eyes glazed and staring, a grin playing wildly on her face. Her left hand grips a sword within its sheath; with her right she grasps my own with unusual strength and pumps it "Western style" in time to the drums. I am shaken by this treatment and by thoughts of her sword. The chant sounds like a military march: I recognize the British Pasha spirit, Abu Rîsh Ya Amîr ad-Daysh ("Owner of Feathers, O Commander of the Army"). The drums desist. At once my hand is released. The shaykha's features assume a more dignified composure and she returns to the center of the mîdân.

Evening falls. Women rise to dance—or "descend" (nazal), as the zâr step is called—throughout the night. Others respond to the spirits' chants from a kneeling position, bobbing up and down from the waist, tôbs covering their heads like so many Halloween ghosts. One who stands has mounted a zâr in

the past: she has "slaughtered" (dabahat, for dhabahat) for the spirits, thus confirming relations with those by which she is possessed. A woman who remains sitting or kneeling has yet to sacrifice; though acknowledged to be possessed, and perhaps even aware of the types of zayran that bother her, she remains somewhat uncertain of her spirits and limited to kneeling at their ceremonies until she undertakes a cure. Yet she is no less an adept for this.

In the waning, eerie light I see a woman—spirit—performing a strange pantomime with a sword, crouching low, sweeping the flat of the weapon back and forth along the ground. She dashes through these postures with skill and grace; I am reminded of a hunter flushing game, or a soldier wary of enemies lying hidden in dense vegetation.

At the start of another chant a tall older woman dressed in red lights a cigarette. She struts down the mîdân, smoking, walking stick held perpendicular to the ground at the end of an outstretched arm, pompous, indifferent, mandarinlike. Some chants later she reappears, transmogrified. Now she and the transvestite stage a sword fight closely resembling the men's dance of a nearby desert people. The combatants leap at each other with apparent abandon, landing within inches of the audience, their sharp unsheathed blades swooping dangerously from aloft. Spectators shrink in terror at their bravado. The two are possessed, I learn, by zâyran of the Arab (Nomad) species.

Occasionally during the evening's drumming, the shaykha dances around the ayâna, encircling her with her arms, coaxing a seemingly reluctant spirit to enter its host and fully reveal itself before the assembly. But the ayâna has not risen since her foray into the mîdân at the start. She sits, silently watching.

I notice at the end of each chant that several who have "descended"—standing or kneeling—begin to scratch themselves, and hiccup and burp indiscriminately. Zaineb tells me these reactions signify the spirit's departure from the body of its host, of a woman's leaving trance.

July 24, 5:30 P.M. Last day of the ceremony. The sacrificial ram is led into the mîdân, and a red and gold cloth—a garmosîs or bridal shawl—is placed over its back and head. The musicians play a chant. Incense is freshly lit, and the brazier thrust beneath the shawl. The animal is forced to inhale the smoke, then led from the mîdân and slaughtered by the ayâna's son. Blood spurting from its throat is collected in a bowl and placed before the drums. The ayâna crosses seven times over the carcass before it is dragged off to be butchered. With the others I now step forward to deposit a few piasters in the victim's congealing blood. Someone whispers an invitation to drink araki (liquor) . . . being khawâja (a westerner) I am expected to imbibe. The possessed anoint themselves with blood, some also take a sip; the shaykha daubs it on herself and the ayâna's feet and arms. Drumming and chanting recommence. Still wearing her stigmata of the zâr the ayâna rises to dance.

A woman "descends" with a prayer shawl round her neck, holding its fringed ends in her hands, rocking to and fro as she paces the mîdân. The gesture echoes that of men at a zikr, a "remembrance" ceremony of the Islamic (sûfi) fraternities from whose membership women are excluded.

Later another woman (Zaineb's cousin and sister-in-law) dances briskly wearing trousers of a European cut; she is possessed, I learn, by the Airplane Captain zâr.

Later still, an older lady performs the local "pigeon dance," concluding with a shabâl[3] to the dancer in the Mediterranean head scarf. She has been seized by Muna, Sitt ash-Shabâl, a southern prostitute zâr given to mimicking village women when appearing in their midst.

An unwed girl now rises, snatches up the bridal shawl, and flings it over her head. She shuffles forward, out of time with the chant. Onlookers gasp. This is the costume of Luliya, the Ethiopian prostitute fond of Hofriyati weddings whose thread was sung some time ago; it is unlikely that She[4] would return so soon, and uninvited. The audience tries to dissuade the girl without success. It is not right, they say, for an unmarried girl to dance so like a bride, in public. Has she no shame? Beside me a woman snaps, "That virgin is not possessed (mazûr). She just wants a husband!"

Night falls; a pressure lamp is placed on a low table near the musicians. The mîdân is a pond of light shallowing to darkness at its sides. Dancers cast weird shadows on the sand, eyes in faces lit from below appear enormous, wild. Drums throb without flagging; redolent smoke of incense clouds the evening. The atmosphere is tense, intoxicating, eerie.

A piercing cry—a uniformed schoolgirl nine or ten years old has sprawled forward into the mîdân, upheld on all four limbs, body jerking rapidly up and down from the shoulders. Immediately, she is led

off by some older women, told it is not proper for a child to behave this way at a zâr. But she does not stop. Outside the mîdân the women try to calm her. Now she is sobbing and has gone quite limp. When efforts to revive her fail she is dragged, resisting, back into the center. She balks at attempts to bring her to the shaykha and is deposited before the drums. The shaykha approaches; the girl cringes. The shaykha censes her, covers her with a white tôb, and asks, "What do you want? Who are you?" No response.

Onlookers taunt the intrusive zâr, trying vainly to garner its sympathy: "Ah, her father is poor! Her mother is blind! Her brother is ill!" The shaykha sends for the girl's father. He is brought into the mîdân and made to give his daughter's spirit ten piasters (about twenty-five cents). Still there is no word from the zâr; the girl remains limp, appearing deeply entranced.

It is getting late. Smells of cooking waft through the mîdân, and laughter from the kitchen. More drumming and dancing are called for. The shaykha requests certain threads to test for various species of zayran, hoping the presumptuous spirit will be drawn to identify itself. She blows into the schoolgirl's ears and behind her neck, she pulls at her limbs, whips her softly with a length of rope, beats her lightly with an iron spear. She censes her, rolls her head along the girl's body. She takes the girl in her arms and dances to and fro, blowing a whistle to the incessant beat. She leads the girl around the mîdân and is twice successful in getting her to move briefly of her own accord. At last the girl jogs back and forth through the open space, one arm pumping like the wheel of a locomotive, the other, raised and crooked at elbow, sounding an imagined alarm. The shaykha blows her pipe whistle in accompaniment. The troublesome spirit is identified: Basha-t-Adil the Khawâja railway engineer.

Still the episode continues. For over an hour the shaykha tries every technique in her repertoire, aiming to convince the implacable zâr to abandon his newfound host and refrain from bothering her again until she is a woman and married. Finally the shaykha guides the girl out of the mîdân and out of the hôsh. They cross the threshold, the khashm al-bayt,[5] backwards, facing the assembly; they remain in the path for several minutes, then return as they had left facing the mîdân. The girl, now calmed and weeping softly, is brought to sit near me—a human khawâja—but placed with her back to the ritual.

Soon the sacrificial meal is served and proceedings brought to a close. It is almost 2:00 A.M. The ayâna is now formally well, though tomorrow she must eat the head meat of the ram in a private ceremony followed by a procession to the Nile. Several people approach the ayâna, touch her right shoulder and say "Insha 'allâh byinf'ik, "God willing, it is benefiting you." In the company of my neighbors I return, exhausted, to Hofriyat.

ZÂR AND ZAYRAN

Smoking, wanton dancing, flailing about, burping and hiccuping, drinking blood and alcohol, wearing male clothing, publicly threatening men with swords, speaking loudly lacking due regard for etiquette: these are hardly the behaviors of Hofriyati women for whom dignity and propriety are leading concerns. But in the context of a *zâr* they are common and expected. The ceremony is rich in complex imagery and movement. Yet it has none of the solemn pageantry of a Mass, nor the predictable, repetitive manipulation of symbols which I, raised as a Catholic, might have found familiar. The tone of a zâr resembles neither the subdued formality of a Muslim Friday prayer, nor the unorchestrated ceremoniousness of life cycle rites in Hofriyat. It is closer in character to *zikrs* of the Qadriya and Khatmiya sûfî orders in Sudan, but lacks their cohesion and transcendent focus. What is singular about a *zâr* is its spontaneity, its imagination, whose basis nonetheless is a comprehensive repertoire of symbols and spirit roles—a resource on which participants draw for inspiration. Moves are lightly choreographed—improvisations on well-known themes; "players" are interchangeable, costumes readily borrowed and exchanged. But during the performance, neither players' bodies nor their costumes belong to village women—they belong, instead, to *zayran*. Zâr rituals are always fraught with tension and surprise, for at any moment a woman might be "seized" by a spirit that Hofriyati did not before know existed, or she did not know she had.

How is all of this to be understood? What is this phenomenon; who or what are these spirits that so dramatically appear in women's bodies?

THE POSSESSION CONCEPT

Zâr refers to a type of spirit, the illness such spirits can cause by possessing humans, and the rituals necessary to their pacification. The cult[6] is found throughout the northern Sudan and variations of the same name appear in Egypt, Ethiopia, Somalia, (where it is called *sâr*), Arabia, and southern Iran.[7]

In writing of spirit "possession" in Hofriyat, I am using indigenous terms. When someone is considered to be affected by a *zâr,* people say of her, *inda rih, inda zâr,* or *inda dastûr[8]*—"she has a spirit." Alternatively, they say she is *mazûr* or *madastîr*—"with spirit," possessed. *Zâr* influence, being possessed of and by a spirit, is considered an affliction and expressed as illness. A spirit causes its novice host to suffer; however initial misery should be surpassed by a more positive concern on the part of the spirit for its host's well-being as their relationship progresses. Once possessed, always possessed: zayran never wholly abandon those they have chosen as their hosts.

Someone diagnosed as *zâr* possessed is liable to be affected by her spirit(s) at any time. *Zayran* are able to infiltrate the bodies of their hosts at will, a move which villagers say always coincides with the latter's entrancement. According to Hofriyati, possession trance (*ghaybîya* or *ghaybûba*) is a state induced by the spirit's forceful entry into the body, which displaces or shifts the person's human self to another perceptual plane. It is, as Bourguignon (1973: 12–13) suggests, "a radical discontinuity of personal identity"; yet in contrast to her model, the distortion of perception this entails pertains not only to the self but to other entities as well.

Still, trance is only one manifestation of possession in Hoftiyat, for *zayran* affect their hosts in countless additional ways (see also Constantinides 1972, 1977; Cloudsley 1983:81). They are always near, or in local parlance "above" (*fôg*), their human hosts, whence they might influence people's perceptions and behaviors in the course of daily life. Further, despite the acknowledged powers of *zayran*, possession trance rarely occurs unpremeditatedly, outside of ritual contexts. Here one is not diagnosed as possessed because she becomes entranced; rather, she becomes entranced because she is possessed. Schoolgirl mishaps notwithstanding, the possessed rarely enter trance spontaneously; this is something one must learn to do in the course of a curing ceremony in order to negotiate an appropriate relationship with instrusive *zayran*. As adepts put it, one must learn how not to resist a spirit's attempts to enter the human world through the medium of her body. The implicit link to ideas about sexual intercourse in Hoftiyat is striking and reiterated in the fact that a woman should be married before she becomes possessed.

Thus trance is in no way aberrant; it is a practiced behavior which the possessed are expected to display under certain conditions. Although an integral part of possession therapy and relapse prophylaxis, it is not consistently evinced by the possessed during ceremonies, and when evinced, it is variable in apparent depth and duration from one episode or individual to the next. Since it is considered inappropriate to be entered by a spirit (or a husband) while menstruating, a woman at a *zâr* signals *zayran* of her condition by tying a knot in her braids, so constraining the spirits' activity. Moreover, because it must conform to prescribed patterns of "spiritness," trance performance requires skill and considerable control. Thus it is not, as some would assert, a spontaneous neurological manifestation of nutritional deficiency which (at least originally) is accounted for after the fact as possession (e.g., Kehoe and Giletti 1981). Such models betray their foundation in a Western rationalism which derogates any mode of consciousness other than that of critical self-awareness. In the search for reductive biological explanations as to why trance should occur, trance itself is misconstrued, parted from its cultural context. Here an essential point is missed. For villagers the system of meaning—possession—is both logically and contextually prior to the behavior—trance—through which it finds expression (cf. Lambek 1981:7).

This is not to deny that biological factors might affect the proclivity to enter trance or the ease with which the behavior is learned.

Some of the possessed initially experience difficulty in becoming lost from themselves and allowing their spirits to assume control; others do not. Here perhaps one's nutritional status plays a role. Still, it must be stressed that Hofriyati generally enter trance after having been diagnosed as possessed or, if undiagnosed, when attending a spirit ritual. And in either case, an individual's trance behavior is learned (cf. Bourguignon 1973:4–15, 1976: 37 ff.), shaped by her knowledge of *zayran* and their provenance. It may be novel and unexpected, but must be consistent with villagers' understanding of spirits to be accepted as legitimate possession and not considered dissimulation or idiosyncratic madness. The few women who do enter trance spontaneously—apparently uninduced, in nonceremonial situations—are hardly neophytes. Rather, they are long-term adepts of the *zâr* who, in the course of their possession careers, have become progressively more skilled at alternating modes of consciousness and allowing the spirits to exhibit themselves through their bodies (see also Besmer 1983:24).

According to Hofriyati, the fact that possession trance typically must be induced and is rare apart from public ritual has less to do with human ability or volition than with spirit caprice. Humans convoke *zayran* through ritual drumming and singing, and normally the spirits—for whom access to the human world is a principal motive for possession—are willing to oblige. Indeed, they regard such invitations as their due, in partial fulfillment of bargains struck with humans, and are likely to become disgruntled and dangerous when neglected or put off. If the possessed take care to mollify them, spirits ought to respond by confining their appearance to ritual contexts where they can frolic and be entertained. Yet none of this is certain. Spirits are willful, and for sport or revenge might "descend" into their hosts without benefit of prior summons. So despite the controlled nature of possession trance and spirit display, the startling possibility exists that at any moment a woman might not be who she usually is.

In Hofriyat possession is a matter of fact. Here the reality of spirits and their powers goes unchallenged, even by villagers who have no firsthand experience of them and regardless of how hotly they dispute the proper therapy for possession affliction, discussed later. Clearly, Hofriyati, like the rest of us, face doubts concerning their beliefs from time to time. But cosmological mavericks they are not. Doubts, like beliefs, are grounded in a social context. Zayran are immanent in the world of Hofriyat; sceptic and zealot, both, are canopied by their existence.

THE POSSESSED

In Hofriyat, as elsewhere in Sudan, possession activity is mainly, but not exclusively, the province of women.[9] Somewhat more than 40 percent of Hofriyati women ever married and over the age of fifteen ($N = 129$ [1977] and 135 [1984]) claim a *zâr* affliction. Marital status is a significant factor in possession illness: spirits, villagers assert, rarely trouble themselves with the unwed—with women whose fertility has yet to be activated.[10] Most affected are those between the ages of thirty-five and fifty-five, two-thirds of whom have spirits. This proportion is due to a cumulative effect: once possessed a woman is always possessed thereafter.

By contrast, only a handful of men from the entire village area are publicly acknowledged to be possessed. In Hofriyat itself only four men (about 5 percent of the resident adult male population) are considered adepts of the *zâr*; three have undergone the requisite ceremonies, one when only thirteen years of age. Two men born in the village but now living elsewhere are known to have spirits, and I obtained information concerning ten others from the vicinity, five of whom were deceased prior to fieldwork. During my six-year absence from the village, only one man had become possessed, in contrast to sixteen women. In 1984, several male acquaintances privately declared themselves to be possessed and confessed admiration for the *zâr*, but would not publicly seek to confirm their afflictions for fear of losing face.

Why is this the case? Why, assuming that possession is a public idiom for the articulation

and interpretation of experience,[11] should there exist sexual disproportion among those who acknowledge having spirits? An obvious approach is to ask whether the range of experience that possession constructs is more common to Hofriyati women than to men. This I think to be the case, mainly because possession is closely linked to fertility with which women are identified and for which they bear responsibility. I do not agree with I. M. Lewis (1971, 1986) on this issue, who, arguing from a sociological perspective, suggests that *zâr* possession is a strategy which women use in an oblique attempt to redress the effects of their subordinate social status. Lewis holds that since spirits demand desiderata which husbands must provide if their wives are to regain well-being, possession can be seen as a measure of gender conflict: it is a strategic evocation of shared beliefs by women wishing to mitigate their subordination to men.

The perspective is illuminating, but presents a number of difficulties. First, it places unwarranted emphasis on the assumed intentionality of women and thus insidiously underestimates the factuality of spirits in the Sudanese world. Words like strategy imply volition, which may certainly be present and, if so, motivated by status considerations in some cases of possession but certainly not in all. Moreover, Lewis's deprivation hypothesis appears to presume that women seek the same status held by men, which, since men have deprived them of it, was originally within their purview. Such assumptions fail to bear scrutiny in Hofriyat, where the social worlds of men and women are largely separate and distinct, a condition due not to happenstance or the prevailing wills of men, but to cultural design. Wilson's (1967) critique of the model tries to address this problem by shifting the locus of proposed status competition from intersex to intrasex relations and, in so doing, is sympathetic to the Sudanese context. However, it shares with Lewis's theory the drawback of a conflict orientation to social interaction that is firmly rooted in Western premises of individualism,[12] whose validity in non-Western cultures must be open to debate (cf. Morsy 1978; Boddy 1988). Even granting that status may be a consideration in certain episodes of possession illness, the sociological argument cannot account for the *zâr* in its entirety. It glosses over the issue of belief and is therefore unable to explain or interpret possession forms (for example, the characteristics of spirits, the nature and variety of possession symptoms) and processes (such as the reevaluation of one's past that acquiring a spirit entails). Such factors, however important to the possessed, are implicitly deemed incidental when the investigator's focus is competition.[13] The social status model is unidimensional, at once too general in application and too narrow in concern to deal adequately with the complexities of *zâr*.

It is imperative to ask why so many scholars—among them Kehoe and Giletti (1981)—are committed to viewing possession as a consequence of women's deprivation rather than their privilege, or perhaps their inclination. Such explanations consistently mislocate the question of why women should be more susceptible to possession than men. Especially in his early work, Lewis (1971:77), for example, suggests that joining a *zâr* coterie enables women to express solidarity vis-à-vis men, who are seen as their oppressors. Men have Islam, which excludes women from active participation; hence women, who are socially peripheral, must resort to the equally peripheral cult of *zâr* both to mitigate their subordination and to express religious fervor (Lewis 1971: 66–99; see also Lewis 1986:23–50, 102–5). This is a classic but unhappily androcentric portrayal of women, who are forever seen as reacting to men rather than acting for themselves within a specific cultural context.

To avoid such pitfalls, we need to examine closely how the sexes in Hofriyat conceive of their interrelations both collectively and individually. Judging from my informants, some women—by no means all or only those who are possessed—clearly feel subordinate to men, resent their positions, and are not consistently above vituperation. However, their feelings seem to derive less from their status as women than from the specific actions of individual men, notably husbands. And the problem these men pose is not that they deny women, as a class, an elevated social position, but that

they sometimes—often inadvertently—thwart individual women's legitimate attempts to achieve it. The reverse can also be said for women, who may frustrate the status aspirations of men. Both sexes are active participants in the social life of Hofriyat, bisected as it is into gender-distinct yet partially overlapping spheres. If men are central and women peripheral with respect to Islam and external relations, women are central and men peripheral when it comes to physical, social, and cultural reproduction: the worldliness of village life. Although men and women are subject to different constraints, the actions of each bear consequence for those of the other.

Indeed, whatever consciousness women have of themselves as a group is hardly one of inferiority and wholescale subordination to men, but of complementarity. As villagers see it, the sexes are engaged—not in a war—but in a dialectical relationship of qualitatively disparate yet socially equivalent parts, each commanding certain resources but reliant on the other for fulfillment. They do not conceive of themselves as locked in a struggle between classes, hierarchically understood. Although a Marxist critique might legitimately consider this to be a mystification of political realities, it cannot be ignored if we are truly concerned with the meaning of *zâr* to women and men in Hofriyat. Political relations are mystified for both within the Hofriyati universe of meaning.

When properly situated in the framework of sexual complementarity, the question of why women as a category should be more likely than men to interpret certain experiences as possession expands to two: Why women? Why not men? As Kapferer (1983:98) astutely argues with respect to women's preponderance in Sri Lankan exorcisms, such questions cannot be resolved by focusing on the possessed's motives and intentions alone, independent of the cultural constructs that inform them. We need to consider the qualities that define the sexes in Hofriyat, the typifications each sex holds of the other, the components of gender identity (see also Nelson 1971). Only then might we have a basis for deciding whether a particular incidence of possession constitutes attempted cross-sex or intrasex status manipulation, or something else—an expression of psychological or social disturbance (cf. Crapanzano 1973, 1977b, 1980; Obeyesekere 1970, 1981; Kapferer 1983, 1986), cross-sex communication (cf. Lambek 1980, 1981), religious experience (cf. Constantinides 1972, 1977; Lewis 1986), a form of play, dramatic allegory, or all of these and more. Its cultural underpinnings—idioms of the everyday world, prosaic conceptualizations of gender—empower possession as a form of social discourse.

Thus put, a focus on the articulatory potential of possession instead of on the status aspirations of individuals possessed changes the tenor of the analytic enterprise. It widens the interpretive net and does not attempt to simplify matters where simplicity belies the facts. Rather, it makes possible a variety of explanations at different levels of analysis and experience, all of them immanent in the *zâr* as a system of meaning, all of them potentially relevant to any specific episode of possession.

Returning to Hofriyati gender constructs and the *zâr*, both sexes allege that women are naturally more vulnerable to spirit attack as a function of their femininity.[14] Spirits are attracted to women—and married women in particular—for it is they who use henna, perfumes, soaps, and scented oils; wear gold jewelry and diaphanous wraps, all human finery which spirits are known to covet. The proclivities of *zayran* are symmetrical to those of Hofriyati women: both are regarded as consumers of goods provided by men.

Although many questions remain to be addressed, this goes some way toward explaining why women interpret certain experiences and illness episodes as possession. It also suggests why, in this sexually polarized community, men do not. But here more remains to be said. A common characterization of women that they do not completely share is that because they are wanting in *'agl* (reason or social sense), they lack sufficient moral strength to uphold the tenets and ideals of Islam. According to local religious authorities it is reprehensible and abhorrent—though not, strictly speaking, *haram* (forbidden)—for Muslims to traffic with spirits. They say that each individual has the responsibility to steer a proper course of spirit avoidance, something women find more difficult to do than men. Women's perceived inability to resist and so deny *zayran* access to earthly pleasures is put down to their inherent moral frailty, notwithstanding that they are more likely to encounter jinn than men. Just as the public identity of women accounts for their greater participation in the *zâr* so the public identity of men as pious Muslims accounts, in part, for their forbearance (see also Lambek 1981:62–64).

The last is solely a masculine perspective. Women see no incompatibility between the *zâr* and Islam: to them possession ritual is part of a general religious enterprise (cf. Constantinides 1972:98). Hofriyati culture therefore contains conflicting interpretations of the relationship between possession and Islam. These, in turn, have divergent implications for the handling of troublesome spirits.

EXORCISM VERSUS ACCOMMODATION

Where men hold the reputedly orthodox view that intrusive spirits can and must be dislodged from the body by force, women maintain that *zayran* cannot be got rid of at all.[15] Adepts insist that if one's illness is caused by a *zâr*, no amount of Islamic or even Western medicine will effect a cure. Attempts to exorcise the spirit serve merely to exacerbate the patient's condition. Symptom remission alone can be achieved, and only if the afflicted agrees to hold a propitiatory ceremony on behalf of the as yet unnamed *zâr*. During this ceremony, often held long after her initial illness has dissipated, the possessed enters into a contractual relationship with the spirit(s) responsible for her lapse from health. There, in response to drumming and singing chants associated with the various named *zayran*, she ideally enters trance: a spirit's chant is an invitation to "descend" (*nazal*) and enter the body of its host, where its identity can be affirmed and its demands revealed.[16] In return for certain offerings, acquisitions, and observances, the invasive spirit agrees to restore, and refrain from further jeopardizing, its host's well-being.

Henceforward, human host and possessive *zâr* are joined in continuous but unequal partnership. The spirit remains above her, able to exert its influence or infiltrate her body at will. To some extent the possessed can rely on the spirit's compliance in maintaining her health, but only so long as she regularly attends the ceremonies of others, abstains from traditional mourning behavior, associates herself with clean and sweet-smelling things, and is not given over to strong emotion. A violation of these provisions renders her vulnerable to relapse. Yet the curing rite has opened communications between the two entities, and it is hoped that any future problems can be dealt with expeditiously. From the spirit's perspective, contracts with humans are infinitely renegotiable, so if the possessed wishes to allay further attack from her *zâr*, she must take scrupulous care to mollify it. If all goes well, what begins as an uneasy truce between a willful spirit and its initially reluctant host might graduate to positive symbiosis as their relationship stabilizes and matures. Alleviating the symptoms of possession illness is a matter of establishing reciprocal obligations between spirit and host; their relationship should become, like that between partners in a marriage, one of complementarity, exchange, and mutual accommodation.

Although the majority of men denounce the propitiation of *zayran,* this is not because they deny that such spirits exist. In Hofriyat, *zayran* comprise a distinct class of *jinn,*[17] mischievous invisible beings that populate a world that is parallel to our own and contiguous with it but imperceptible to humans most of the time. Typical of their exceptional attributes, jinn can transform themselves into animals, assume human form (but incompletely so, for their feet are always hooved), or take possession of live human bodies at will. *Jinn* are mentioned in the Quran (Suras 6, 17, 18, 34, 37, 46, 55, 72, and 114); they are a constant if often low-key part of both men's and women's daily lives.

Further, should a man become ill there is a chance that the diagnosis will be possession regardless of its feminine associations. Men recognize the powers of *zayran* and acknowledge that even the most pious among them occasionally succumbs to spirit attack. But this is where their public support for the cult stops: most insist that, despite a practiced resistance, *zayran,* like other jinn, must eventually capitulate to the powerful exorcistic techniques of Islamic medicine. In the company of their fellows they decry as un-Islamic women's ceremonial attempts to assuage and socialize the spirits.

In face of such weighty opposition the *zâr* cult thrives, and its rites are attended even by the most submissive and religious of wives. For women, *zâr* falls squarely within the purview of Islam. And when arguing their position with men (something I witnessed only twice), women said that Allah expects the afflicted to seek respite from their suffering—clearly, it is better to be healthy than "broken" by spirits or overzealous efforts to dislodge them. Perhaps men are right that involvement in the cult imperils one's prospect of a pleasurable afterlife, but then, is Allah not merciful?

Men, for their part, though publicly adamant that only exorcism is correct in the eyes of Islam, are privately not so intractable (cf. Barclay 1964:206; Constantinides 1982). Often hesitant, concerned, uncertain that Islamic medications will effect a cure or fearing reprisals of a powerful spirit if it is put off, most do not interfere when their womenfolk conduct propitiatory ceremonies, and provide money to meet the spirits' demands. Here perhaps, as Lewis (1971: 88) suggests, men tacitly recognize the contradiction between the formal ideology of male supremacy and the social (and cultural) importance of women. Intriguing, too, in the light of the ethnographic situation in Hofriyat, is Lewis's more recent view that woman's participation in the *zâr* might offer men "the privilege of vicarious participation in what they ostensibly condemn as superstition and heresy. Thus, if there is a dual spiritual economy [male and female], its two branches are interdependent and complementary" (Lewis 1986:106). It seems plausible that just as men's religious devotions count also for their womenfolk (1986:106), so women's *zâr* devotions might count indirectly for their men. As noted earlier, several male informants confided in 1984 that they believe themselves incurably possessed by *zayran*. These men enjoy listening to spirit rituals from afar or watching *bi shubbak* ("through a window"), but do not openly attend for fear of ridicule. Such peripheral and vicarious participation echoes that of women at a *zikr*—the "dervish" rite of Islamic fraternities whose membership in Sudan is exclusively male.

GLOSSARY

dallûka	large pottery drum used in weddings and zâr ceremonies
hôsh	house yard and/or wall that encloses it
shabâl	woman's gesture of flicking her hair at an approaching man in the context of a wedding dance; said to confer luck
shaykha zâr	female curer of the zâr cult a type of spirit, the illness it can cause, and the ritual by which the illness is assuaged; more generally, the "cult" that surrounds such spirits
zikr	remembrance: ceremony of the Islamic fraternities
zîr	large water jar

REFERENCES

Al-Guindi, Fadwa. 1978. *The Angels of the Nile: A Theme in Nubian Ritual. In Nubian Ceremonial Life*, edited by John Kennedy, pp. 104–113. Berkeley: University of California Press.

Barclay, Harold. 1964. Buurri al-Lamaah: *A Suburban Village in Sudan*. Ithaca, N.Y.: Cornell University Press.

Besmer, Fremont E. 1983. *Horses, Musicians, and Gods: The Hausa Cult of Possession-Trance*. South Hadley, Mass.: Bergin and Garvey.

Boddy, Janice. 1988. Spirits and Selves in Northern Sudan. The Cultural Therapeutics of Possession and Trance. *American Ethnologist* 15(1): 4–27.

———. 1989. *Wombs and Alien Spirits: Women, Men and the Zâr Cult in Northern Sudan*. Madison: University of Wisconsin Press.

Bourguignon, Erika. 1973. "Introduction: A Framework for the Comparative Study of Altered States of Consciousness." In *Religion, Altered States of Consciousness, and Social Change*, edited by Erika Bourguignon, pp. 3–35. Columbus: Ohio State University Press.

———. 1976. *Possession*. San Francisco: Chandler and Sharp.

Cloudsley, Ann. 1983. *Women of Omdurman: Life, Love, and the Cult of Virginity*. London: Ethnographica.

Constantinides, Pamela. 1972. Sickness and the Spirits: A Study of the "Zâr" Spirit Possession Cult in Northern Sudan. Ph.D. dissertation, University of London.

———. 1977. "Ill at Ease and Sick at Heart": Symbolic Behavior in a Sudanese Healing Cult. In *Symbols and Sentiments*, edited by Ian M. Lewis, pp. 185–205. Bloomington: Indiana University Press.

———. 1982. Women's Spirit Possession and Urban Adaptation in the Muslim Northern Sudan. In *Women United, Women Divided: Comparative Studies of Ten Contemporary Cultures*, edited by P. Caplan and D. Bujra, pp. 141–76. New York: John Wiley.

———. 1991. "The History of Zâr in the Sudan." In I. M. Lewis, Ahmed al-Safi, and Sayyid Hurreiz, editors. *Women's Medicine: The Zâr-Bori Cult in Africa and Beyond*, pp. 83–99. Edinburgh: International African Institute, Edinburgh University Press.

Crapanzano, Vincent. 1973. *The Hamadsha: A Study in Moroccan Ethnopsychiatry*. Berkeley: University of California Press.

———. 1977a. Mohammed and Dawua: Possession in Morocco. In *Case Studies of Spirit Possession*, edited by Vincent Crapanzano and Vivian Garrison, pp. 141–76. New York: John Wiley.

———. 1977b. *Introduction to Case Studies of Spirit Possession*, edited by Vincent Crapanzano and Vivian Garrison, pp. 1–39. New York: John Wiley.

———. 1980. *Tuhami: Portrait of a Moroccan*. Chicago: University of Chicago Press.

Hillelson, S. 1930. *Sudan Arabic, English Arabic Vocabulary*. 2nd ed. London: Sudan Government.

Kapferer, Bruce. 1983. *A Celebration of Demons: Exorcism and the Aesthetics of Healing in Sri Lanka*. Bloomington: Indiana University Press.

———. 1986. Performance and the Structure of Meaning and Experience. In *The Anthropology of Experience*, edited by V. W. Turner and E. M. Bruner, pp. 188–206. Chicago: University of Illinois Press.

Kehoe, Alice B., and Dody H. Giletti. 1981. Women's Preponderance in Possession Cults: The Calcium Deficiency Hypothesis Extended. *American Anthropologist* 83(3): 549–61.

Kennedy, John G. 1978. *Nubian Ceremonial Life*, edited by John Kennedy. Berkeley: University of California Press.

Kenyon, Susan. 1991. *Five Women of Sennar*. New York: Oxford University Press.

———. 2000. "The Case of the Butcher's Wife: Illness, Possession and Power in Central Sudan." In Heike Behrend and Ute Luig, editors. *Spirit Possession, Modernity, and Power in Africa.* Madison: University of Wisconsin Press.

Lambek, Michael. 1980. Spirits and Spouses: Possession as a System of Communication among the Malagasy Speakers of Mayotte. *American Ethnologist* 7(2):318–31.

———. 1981. *Human Spirits: A Cultural Account of Trance in Mayotte.* New York: Cambridge University Press.

Leiris, Michel. 1958. *La Possession et ses aspects théâtraux chez les Ethiopiens de Gondar.* L'Homme: Cahiers d'ethnologie, de géographie et de linguistique. Paris: Plon.

Lewis, I. M. 1971. *Ecstatic Religion: An Anthropological Study of Spirit Possession and Shamanism.* Baltimore, Md.: Penguin Books.

———. 1986. *Religion In Context: Cults and Charisma.* Cambridge: University of Cambridge Press.

Modaressi, Tahgi. 1968. *The Zar Cult in South Iran. In Trance and Possession States,* edited by Raymond Prince, pp. 149–55. Montreal: R. M. Bucke Memorial Society.

Morsy, Soheir. 1978. Sex Roles, Power, and Illness in an Egyptian Village. *American Ethnologist,* 5:137–50.

Nelson, Cynthia. 1971. Self, Spirit Possession, and World-View: An Illustration from Egypt. *International Journal of Psychiatry* 17:194–209.

Obeyesekere, Gananath. 1970. The Idiom of Possession. *Social Science and Medicine* 4:97–111.

———. 1981. *Medusa's Hair: An Essay on Personal Symbols and Religious Experience.* Chigago: University of Chicago Press.

Saunders, Lucie Wood. 1977. Variants in Zar Experience in an Egyptian Village. In *Case Studies in Spirit Possession,* edited by Vincent Crapanzano and Vivian Garrison, pp. 177–91. New York: John Wiley.

Trimingham, J. Spencer. 1965. *Islam in the Sudan.* 1949. Reprint. London: Oxford University.

Vantini, Giovanni. 1981. *Christianity in the Sudan.* Bologna, Italy: EMI Press.

Wehr, Hans. 1976. *A Dictionary of Modern Written Arabic.* 3rd ed. Edited by J. Milton Cowan. Ithaca, N.Y.: Spoken Language Services.

Wilson, Peter. 1967. Status Ambiguity and Spirit Possession. *Man,* n.s. 2:366–78.

Young, Allan. 1975. Why Amhara Get Kureynya: Sickness and Possession in an Ethiopian Zar Cult. *American Ethnologist* 2(3):567–84.

Zenkovsky, Sophie. 1950. Zar and Tambura as Practiced by the Women of Omdurman. *Sudan Notes and Records.* 31(1):65–81.

NOTES

1. Hofriyat is a pseudonym for the Sudanese village where I began conducting field work in 1976. "Hofriyati" refers to the people of the village, all of whom speak Arabic and profess Islam. The village is located on the Nile, a little over 120 miles (200 km) north and east of Khartoum.

2. A woman's modesty garment, consisting of some nine meters of cloth wound around the body and covering the head.

3. A flick of the hair, a movement said to confer luck on the recipient.

4. I use an initial capital letter (e.g. He, She) when referring to a specific spirit in order to indicate its sex while distinguishing it from its human host.

5. Literally, mouth of the house.

6. For a discussion of the cult's possible origins, see Boddy 1989 and Constantinides 1991.

7. On northern Sudan, see Constantinides 1977, 1982, 1991; Kenyon 1991, 2000. On zar in Egypt, see Al-Guindi 1978; Kennedy 1978; Saunders 1977; in Ethiopia, Leiris 1958; Young 1975; in Somolia, where it is better known as *sar,* Lewis 1971, 1986; in Arabia, Trimingham 1965:258; and in southern Iran, Modarressi 1968.

8. This term literally means "statute" or "constitutional law," and colloquially, "permission" (Wehr 1976:281). In northern Sudan, however, the term also refers to a door jamb (Constantinides 1977:65–66, n. 6) or a bolt (Hillelson 1930:35). The reference to doorways is significant, and discussed in Boddy 1989.

9. See Barclay (1964:196–206); Cloudsley (1983: 67–87); Constantinides (1972, 1977); Trimingham (1965:174–77); Zenkovsky (1950).

10. For a discussion of the relationship between female fertility and possession, see Boddy 1989.

11. See Crapanzano 1977a. This point is more fully developed in Boddy 1989.

12. Although the fluctuating kinship networks of Hofriyati are individualistic, this is not to say that the individual is the focal social unit in Hofriya. Hofriyati women and men are always subordinate to a range of collective interests: family, lineage, village, religious group, etc.

13. Lewis (1971:30) certainly does not consider other factors unimportant, yet they do not figure into his analysis to the same extent as does the question of cross-sex competition.

14. See Kapferer (1983:100–110) for a similar view of the susceptibility of Sri Lankan women.

15. Interestingly, this is similar to the situations of men and women in a marriage: although men may divorce an unwanted wife at will, women must accommodate themselves to the marriage, however unhappy.
16. Spirits are hardly inanimate or genderless, as my use of the impersonal pronoun implies. But when not referring to specific spirits and possession episodes, I use the neuter form to avoid confusion between humans and *zayran*.

17. However, the classification of spirits varies somewhat from area to area in Sudan, and in some places (though not in Hofriyat or its environs) *zayran* and jinn are considered different forms of spirit being. On this issue, see Constantinides (1972:102–4) and Trimingham (1965:177 ff.).

"Tradition" and Threat
Women's Obscenity in Giriama Funerary Rituals

Janet McIntosh

INTRODUCTION

It is midday in the Giriama village outside the town of Malindi, Kenya, and women are gathering on one side of a well-swept clearing framed by mud and thatch huts. They sit with their legs stretched before them, comparing their finery—flamboyant *leso* cloths; clean, bright polyester blouses from town; and the customary bustles of grass and cotton that accentuate their hips. My black skirt and T-shirt seem dull by comparison, but as always the women greet me warmly, seating me on a woven mat on the earth next to them. We are assembling to mark the passing of a young woman who died in childbirth; her body lies in the center of the clearing, cradled by a bed of woven sisal ropes. Her mother and three elderly women flank the bed, waving small handkerchiefs in desultory motions to chase off the flies. They have not slept since the tragic night before, but some of them are capable of laughter as well as tears, and occasionally break into a low-key song and dance, swishing their handkerchiefs rhythmically. Other female kin are out of sight, gathered in a nearby hut where they will receive well-wishers during the next five days of ceremony. And at the other

side of the homestead the men carry out their tasks: six or seven take turns digging a grave, while others decide where they will buy the planks to build a coffin. Most sit on mats, drinking from small gourds of palm wine, discussing local politics, and comparing the jobs they have lost and gained in town.

Word has gone out through the neighboring communities that a funeral has begun, and the crowd swells to about two hundred as the afternoon wears on. When a male song leader arrives and positions himself near the corpse, ten or fifteen enthusiastic women gather around him. At his cue, several of them begin to jangle winnowing trays laden with broken glass, creating a silvery percussive effect. The rest break into song and dance, shuffling in a circle, shimmying their hips emphatically, and punctuating their movement now and then by falling forward and catching themselves with a well placed step. Some of their songs speak to death and decay: "Fly away, housefly. You can't land on this body, because it's covered with rashes." But many of the lyrics are teasing and a little startling: "Mother's clothes are falling off," quips one song. As the singers warm to their task, the lyrics become graphic:

May I screw you? May I screw you?
An unmarried non-virgin will be screwed

Original material prepared for this text. Reprinted by permission of the author.

A man's wife is maize meal and meat
I will die and stop screwing

One by one, women and girls from the surrounding crowd join in, and the circle widens to accommodate them. Soon they put aside the winnowing trays, clapping with enthusiasm as they sing and shuffle around the corpse and its tenders, who continue to whisk the flies away. From time to time the dancers stop in their tracks and face the center of the circle, clapping loudly. Several women leap into the middle and begin to gyrate their pelvises, inching up to the others to simulate sexual contact and intercourse. Normal decorum is abandoned; a seventy-year-old woman grinds against a thirty-year-old male song leader, while a young woman simulates sex with her mother-in-law. A woman with gray hair organizes a stunt, placing a giant wooden pestle upside down by the head of the corpse, climbing onto it and moving her pelvis in quick circles, barely keeping her balance. I turn to my neighbor, a married woman holding a baby, and remark: "I have talked to many people about your funerals, but I still wonder why the women perform these songs and dances."

"It's just our tradition," she says with a gentle smile, adding: "They are trying to distract the bereaved people from their pain." I ask why she doesn't join in. "My husband doesn't like me to," she replies, "He thinks the women who do the dances have no respect for their men." Another woman inside the circle, an unmarried forty-something, mimes a sex act with more zeal than most. A young man from the village passes me and whispers in my ear snidely: "That one is a prostitute; she keeps a lot of men happy." Another song begins:

Mr. Charo Baya knows how to screw
Finish fast; I want to get home and cook!
My husband doesn't screw me that way.
Charo Baya you've won me—Your penis is big;
my hips can't hold you.

As the dancing grows louder and more exuberant, three giggling teenagers pull me into the fray and prod me before them, daring me to perform the dance moves. An old woman glares at us from just outside the circle; like some other elders, she objects to the participation of young unmarried women, and I wonder if her ire is directed partly at me. I clap and step my way around the corpse until shyness gets the better of me and I withdraw to the margins, craning my neck to take in the scene. I can see the men still clustered on their side of the homestead, drinking, talking, and observing the grave-diggers, who sweat profusely as they struggle to complete their job before nightfall. A few young men stand on the edge of the dancing circle, looking on with small gourds of palm wine in their hands, ogling and occasionally lunging at the women they admire the most. One of the men plunges in and is set on by two women who gyrate against his side and back until he extricates himself, laughing. The circle closes again, a riot of stepping, clapping women, who seem to delight as each new song ups the ante of bawdy suggestion.

A Giriama funeral in the Malindi area is a momentous event, a protracted ritual far longer, more expensive, and better attended than any other rite in Giriama custom. Social life is magnified during these gatherings: men gain and lose prestige in displays of generosity; commerce in food, palm wine, and property quickens; old friends strike up new relations; and enemies settle their grudges, sometimes violently. Above all, women's funerary songs and dances escalate into lewd rebellions that, like the above scenario, far outstrip normal expectations for female behavior. What does this sexual performance by women signify? Is it considered mere "tradition," a benign ritual release, as the young woman above and many others wanted me to believe? Or do the currents of disapproval—her husband's denunciation of the dancing women, the passing young man's whisper, and the old woman's stare—suggest another level of interpretation, one that takes the rebellious overtones of the songs and dances more seriously?

These questions have a precedent in a broader literature that explores the relationship among gender, power, and ritual. Much of this literature emphasizes the unique opportunity that ritual offers subordinate groups, particularly women, to violate custom and express discontent. Ritual spirit possession, for example, has been heralded as a means of "[expressing] dissatisfaction with existing patterns" (Bourguignon 1973: 33), especially in cultures where other avenues of redress are not available (Lewis 1971). Possession can also open a space for violations of sexual protocol redolent of those in Giriama funerals; in Danforth's account of possession by St. Constantine among Anastenaridien Greeks, possessed women engage in "flamboyant, demonstrative, even flirtatious behavior that is considered more appropriate for men" (1989: 100). By becoming "symbolically male" through possession, Danforth says, such women garner publicity while enhancing their power and status beyond the domestic sphere (100). Whereas spirit possession partakes of its own special devices—including the appropriation of the agency and powers of the possessing spirit—other types of ritual offer women additional opportunities for misbehavior. In numerous sub-Saharan African rituals, for example, normative arrangements are turned upside-down and subordinate groups, women in particular, may temporarily take on the roles of their social superiors (Gluckman 1965). Ritual form, then, seems to lend itself to unruliness like that in Giriama women's funerary song and dance.

While it may provide a useful emotional outlet for women's frustrations, the enduring question is whether unruly ritual behavior poses a substantial threat to patriarchal orders. When there is no possessing spirit from which to borrow prestige, do the exceptional events within a ritual confer any new powers on the participants? Do ritual acts really challenge the tenets of social life once the ritual moment has passed? Social theorists have tended to address this issue in general terms. Mary Douglas, for example, sees ritual misbehavior as universally beguiling and potentially threatening to the status quo: "We seek to create order," she writes, "[yet] we do not simply condemn disorder. We recognise that it is destructive to existing patterns; also that it has potentiality. It symbolizes both danger and power" (Douglas 1966: 94). In his analysis of medieval carnivals, Mikhael Bakhtin interprets ritual bawdiness as a moment of freedom that just

might have enduring effects; a "true feast of becoming, change, and renewal" (Bakhtin 1962: 18). Although such readings credit unruly ritual with liberating potential, others doubt that it poses a genuine threat or challenge to the powers that be. According to Gluckman, a ritual of rebellion that takes place within a strong social structure is but an ineffectual gesture; a form of "instituted protest [that] in complex ways renews the unity of the system" (1954: 3).

In this essay, I approach the question of ritual power from a somewhat different angle. Rather than asking whether Giriama women's funerary songs and dances actually change the social system, I instead explore how Giriama themselves perceive them. And in a parallel to the tension between theorists like Douglas and Gluckman, I detect two conflicting interpretations of funerary obscenity among Giriama in the Malindi area. At one level, the women's performance is publicly couched as Gluckman might have predicted: a harmless "tradition" and a salubrious tool of emotional healing. Yet another, less formal discourse implies that the songs and dances threaten the sexual dignity of Giriama women. Although Douglas might locate this threat in some generic danger inherent to unruly ritual, "danger" is always construed in light of tensions specific to a given social moment. In fact, I argue, Giriama women's funerary songs have long been obscene, yet the current disapproval among Giriama in Malindi is distinctly colored by a development that is both modern and local: the arrival of Western lifestyles and tourism on the Kenya coast, and the corresponding emergence of a fraught sexual ethos in society-at-large.

GIRIAMA, PAST AND PRESENT

The Giriama are the largest of nine related Bantu groups called the Mijikenda, who live in a 5,000-square-mile strip in the coastal hinterland of eastern Kenya. According to Mijikenda oral history, their people dwelled as subsistence farmers for centuries while based in fortified villages called *kaya* that were governed by male elders and organized by sacred spaces, age-set rituals, and semisecret societies termed *mwanza*. The *kaya* dispersed in the nineteenth century, and since then Mijikenda culture has been subject to forces that threaten older ways of life. But like all self-told histories, Mijikenda accounts are both reflections of the past and "statements of what informants feel it should be" (Willis 1993: 44). *Kaya* are often invoked as part of a nostalgic call for unity and "authenticity" in moments of social, economic, and political insecurity (Mazrui 1997; Parkin 1991), yet stories of isolated life in the *kayas* obscure the fact that for centuries, coastal Mijikenda have interacted with wealthier town-dwelling Arab and Swahili Muslims in fluid economic, religious, and even kin relations. And in the colonial and postcolonial eras, Mijikenda have endured difficult integration into a multicultural coastal economy of Europeans, Asians, Arabs, Swahili, and upcountry Kenyans. Today, cash is increasingly important for the essentials of life in and near Malindi, making wage labor a virtual necessity, yet many Giriama who seek jobs are hampered by lack of training and employer prejudice. Education is perceived as a key to wealth, but school fees are out of reach for many Giriama families. Now as then, few Mijikenda own land or large businesses, and other ethnic groups on the coast regard them as a low-status, "backward" people. Such economic and ideological pressures have resulted in numerous Giriama conversions to Islam or Christianity, yet aggressive assertions of Giriama "tradition" still play a role in local and governmental politics. And rituals such as funerals remain popular despite Muslim and Christian censure.[1]

SEX AND DEATH IN FUNERARY RITUAL

The two major funerary song-and-dance types for Giriama women in the Malindi area, termed *kifudu* and *kihoma,* are considered "traditional," yet oral histories indicate that both originated outside of Giriama funerals. *Kifudu* songs are accompanied by the rhythmic shaking of shells or broken glass in a broad winnowing tray, and the dances involve much shimmying of the breasts and hips. According to Giriama elders, *kifudu* emerged from a women's fertility cult called *mwanza wa kifudu* that dates back to the *kaya* era. In the *mwanza wa kifudu,* women kept sacred clay pots that were named after their deceased former custodians and believed to have a life force of their own. Since *kifudu* pots could either protect or destroy women's health and reproductive capacities, they were supplicated at every new moon: removed from their shrines to be spoken to, sung and danced to, and "played" by blowing air over their openings. The supplicatory songs and dances were called *kifudu cha tsongo,* and, according to anthropologist Monica Udvardy, were characterized by "obscene or ludicrous" lyrics and correspondingly "suggestive movements" (Udvardy 1990b: 142). These songs were imported into the funerals of members of the *mwanza wa kifudu* but at some point, for unknown reasons, they were generalized to funerals at large. The propitiation of *kifudu* pots still takes place in some Giriama homesteads further inland, but in many areas, including Malindi, the tradition has dwindled, and the *kifudu* fertility medicines have been dispersed among and reinterpreted by individual diviner/healers (Thompson 1990).[2] Yet *Kifudu* songs endure, and some women still compose new ones that address two major themes: death and grief, and bawdy sexual antics. *Kifudu* songs are customarily sung by postmenopausal women (Udvardy 1990a: 145), but in the Malindi area the sanctions for their performance have been blurred, and young women and even pubescent girls participate, to the dismay of some elders.

The second variety of funerary song, called *kihoma,* is said to be more obscene than *kifudu.* *Kihoma* involves a slightly different dance style accompanied by vigorous clapping and, unlike *kifudu,* is totally prohibited after the corpse has been buried. Men as well as women compose these songs, and the lyrics discuss graphic sexual themes from both male and female points of view.[3] In some Giriama groups, men occasionally dance to *kihoma* songs as well, but among Giriama close to Malindi, women and girls dominate the dancing almost exclusively. Giriama informants claim that *kihoma* songs originated with another Mijikenda group, the Chonyi, and some elders suggest they have been popularized in recent years by young funeral participants who are excessively zealous about their sexual content. But while elders distinguish between *kifudu* and *kihoma* and decry the changes in funerary performance, most youth are only dimly aware of the songs' histories, and are hard-pressed to categorize individual songs as either *kifudu* or *kihoma*. I will return to the subject of how elders regard changes in funerary songs below, for their disapproval signals more holistic changes in Giriama life.

Leaving these controversies aside for the moment, I want to explore Giriama explanations for why sexual songs should be performed at funerals in the first place. Anthropologists van Gennep (1960) and Victor Turner (1967) have written at length about the "liminal" phase in rites of passage, in which normal social rules are suspended and ritual participants behave in unorthodox ways. In many sub-Saharan funerals, liminality takes the specific form of inversion: a reversal of ordinary hierarchies and taboos.[4] In Giriama funerals, the visibility of the corpse defines the boundaries of the liminal phase; Giriama say that its uncanny presence opens behavioral possibilities that are curtained off from everyday experience.[5] And, in keeping with the sub-Saharan funerary theme of inversion, *kifudu* and *kihoma* song and dance upend customary expectations with implications of female promiscuity, female sexual aggression, incest, adultery, and homosexuality.[6] Yet funerary inversions in other African cultures include all kinds of reversals, including turning clothing inside out, moving in a counterclockwise direction, and slandering local rulers. So why should sexual license be the inversion of choice for Giriama? Giriama explain that sex has an antithetical relation to death, a tension that lends sexual imagery a special emotional charge. The funerary songs and dances, they say, "mock" death by confronting its power with defiant expressions of sexual pleasure. For those who remember that *kifudu* performances emerge from a fertility cult, the songs and dances also invoke reproductive capacity, the continuation

of life even in the presence of its end. And the ecstatic and ridiculous elements of the songs and dances are said to "change the minds" of the bereaved, distracting them from their grief by presenting them with images pleasurable, extreme, and, sometimes, silly.[7] Witty double-entendres such as the line: "I'll bury something in you!" instantaneously defuse the miseries of death and burial by rhetorically transforming the death rite into a sexual encounter.

Yet there is another, more paradoxical relationship between death and sexual permissiveness at these funerals, in which they are not so much juxtaposed as aligned.[8] The dancing circle where the corpse lies is referred to as a "bad place" with negative supernatural overtones, and this "bad place," say informants, is a place in which "bad things can happen." The corpse, then, is both a signal that existential normalcy has vanished and a prompt to wreak further havoc, as the *kifudu* and *kihoma* songs and dances do with their dissolute symbolism. One Giriama man aligns the destruction of death with the disgrace of sexual abandon; when I asked him to explain *kifudu* and *kihoma* to me, he replied: "Someone has died! Things have already turned to shit, so why not let everything run to ruin?" Other informants assimilate grief and sexual expression on the emotional level, saying: "When someone has died, and your grief is so bad, what can you do but laugh and celebrate?" Such utterances surely have performative elements, as expressions of wishful thinking that might help to create the kind of celebration they describe and in so doing help the bereaved to forget their sorrow. But they also contain an implicit theory, a strange emotional geometry in which extreme grief passes beyond sorrow and travels full circle to the giddy version of joy seen in *kifudu* and *kihoma* performances. This paradox is echoed in the expression of some funeral participants: "A funeral is like a wedding; the last wedding of the deceased."

GENDER, SEXUALITY, AND CHANGE IN GIRIAMA LIFE

The sexual content of *kifudu* and *kihoma* songs and dances appears to play an important role in processing and transforming the emotions that accompany death, but it is also a pivotal site for complex and changing gender relationships among Giriama in the Malindi area. Before discussing local interpretations of women's funerary performances, I offer here a brief history of the shifting gender dynamics that underlie them. Since the nineteenth century, the patriarchal household arrangements of the *kaya* era have undergone considerable change in many Giriama communities, yet the theme of male dominance persists. Homesteads in the *kaya* model are made up of several polygynous households headed by a senior man who makes decisions about property allocation, conflicts, and patrilineal rituals. Parents and other elders oversee marital arrangements, including bride-price transactions, and women's rights to resources are severely constrained by a patrilineal inheritance system. These structures endure in some Giriama communities, but in others, economic changes and cultural contact have destabilized older ways of life. In the small villages flanking Malindi town, for example, household arrangements have an improvisational feel. Young men may split off from their father's homestead in search of economic opportunities closer to town, squatting on land owned by Muslims or upcountry Kenyans with other Mijikenda hopefuls, and building one or two huts for their wife or wives. In cases of divorce or abandonment, some women choose to live on their own, supporting themselves and their children rather than returning to their natal homestead. But shifting household arrangements have not greatly enhanced women's economic opportunities. Although men venture into town to seek wage labor, and may aspire to private investments and property ownership, women rarely accumulate capital or property of their own, tending to remain close to home as they raise children and till the family's small subsistence farm plot. For income they may sell domestic animals, firewood, thatch, deep-fried goods, and the surplus from their small farming plots, but such enterprises rarely yield a large profit. A significant number of women become professional diviner-healers, an increasingly popular choice that can lead to prestige and a limited degree of financial power (Thompson 1990). Yet even such creative pursuits do not weaken the pervasive gender ideology that limits girls' and women's prospects. Many parents prefer to spend their limited school fee money on their sons, a pattern that perpetuates both economic and ideological inequities. One man justifies the limitations on girls' education with the assertion that "our women are pure womanhood in its natural state." In Giriama discourse, this "natural state" is deemed servile, irresponsible, and capricious, while men, by contrast, are considered strong, brave, and more intellectual (McIntosh 1996; Thompson 1990).

The sexual customs that emerged from the *kaya* era have also changed in the Malindi area, yet a powerful residue of sanctions and proscriptions remains. According to *kaya* custom, sexual courtship and behavior should be highly discreet. Sex itself must be engaged in with care because it is believed to be linked to supernatural powers. Ritual sexual intercourse, for example, is said to bring prosperity and purification when performed at moments of significant social transition (Udvardy 1990a, 1990b). Termed "*mathumia*," these rites between spouses can mark the "coming out" ceremony of a newborn, the circumcision of a son, and the various training phases of a diviner-healer. They may sanction a child's marriage arrangement, or purify individuals in a compromised state (a widow, for example, should have ritual intercourse with another man if her husband dies an inauspicious death). Senior males are pivotal figures in *mathumia* rites; when an individual in a homestead dies, for example, or when a homestead relocates, the senior male must perform *mathumia* with his first wife before other homestead members can resume normal sexual relations. When a couple violates *mathumia* restrictions, their children are believed susceptible to illness and death. Udvardy suggests that *mathumia* rites underscore the "mutual dependence of the genders for the prosperous enactments of creation, recreation, and transformation" (Udvardy 1990a: 87), but, she adds, the rites often depend on the leadership of male homestead heads, and therefore re-inscribe their seniority. Meanwhile, the Giriama belief in women's "greater potential to cause disorder" (Thompson 1990) generates additional constraints for female sexuality. Unmarried girls are expected to protect their chastity, and married women (not men) who are unfaithful may inflict their children with a supernaturally borne illness termed *kirwa*.

With cultural contact and change, Giriama communities everywhere have altered some or all of these customs, yet women's sexuality is still policed by popular expectation. Christianity and Islam, of course, do not recognize *mathumia* or *kirwa* beliefs, but both portray premarital sex and overt expressions of sexuality as sinful, particularly among women. Among Giriama who do not consider themselves Muslim or Christian, *kirwa* beliefs and *mathumia* proscriptions are followed only erratically by members of the younger generation. In fact, popular expectations in Malindi operate primarily by means of secular ideologies. Whereas today's men are said to be more sexually aggressive than in the past, women are still expected to resist advances, defining their decency through modesty. In conversation this theme occasionally appears through trope of hunting: men play the role of predator, women of prey, and the ones with integrity elude capture until they can run no more. And while they may desire sex, women are constrained by an unwritten rule of silence: unlike men, women should not initiate sexual liaisons verbally. "A woman can say it [express desire] with her body," my informants tell me, "but not with her mouth." The female body's language, furthermore, should be subtle and indirect: a glance, a fleeting half-smile, or a slight, sinuous motion. The burden of sexual comportment, hence, has largely shifted from both sexes (as seen in *mathumia* proscriptions) to women and girls alone.

If sexual expectations continue their policing function, sexual behavior in Malindi town constantly threatens to violate these proscriptions. While Giriama communities everywhere are faced with sexual changes, Malindi's economic and cultural situation has created exceptional tensions. In recent decades, numerous upcountry Kenyans have moved to the coast for economic opportunities, bringing versions of modernity in tow, including nuclear family structure, consumerist aspirations, and "Western" sexual behavior with demonstrative premarital passion. The last twenty years have also brought a high volume of European and American tourists, who flock to the palm-lined beaches of the Indian Ocean in a display of wealth, hedonism, and exposed flesh. Malindi has become a popular "sex safari" destination, with visitors of both sexes searching for an exotic fling. This clientele has lured many young African men and women into hustling and prostitution in Malindi's casinos, hotels, and beaches. Even Giriama who rarely enter town are aware of the changing sexual habits in urban centers, reading about them in the newspapers, and noting the sexual lyrics of the urban-based music that pumps from young men's boom boxes. And the practice of exchanging sex for cash has filtered into the surrounding villages, where some women have begun to solicit local clients, often because of economic need. In one village on the outskirts of Malindi town, a sixty-year-old Giriama man was recently arrested for paying a thirteen-year-old girl for sex; she capitulated, she said, because her single mother had no source of income for food. Several elder women told me stories of schoolgirls selling their bodies to teachers and other students—narratives that entwine the elders' anxieties about the lures of prostitution and the perils of a Western-style education. Even Giriama women who do not sell sex are also said to be changing their sexual habits. One Giriama man in his late thirties, for example, told me that he had recently propositioned a woman for sexual relations, but was so shocked and revolted when she accepted on the spot (rather than putting him off time and again as he expected) that he withdrew the suggestion. Evidently, expectations of female modesty are alive in Giriama ideology in the Malindi area, but are constantly challenged and changed. This tension sets the stage for local interpretations of funerary songs.

WOMEN'S RITUAL LICENSE: CONFLICTING INTERPRETATIONS

On the face of it, *kifudu* and *kihoma* performances offer Giriama women a unique opportunity to express their desires and decry male power while asserting their own self-worth. At a funeral, any woman—old, young, married or single—can intone a sexual invitation ("May I screw you?") and exult in the imagined pleasures of adultery ("Charo Baya knows how to screw!"). While they flout conventions verbally, the women enact further obscenities with their bodies by dancing suggestively and simulating sexual intercourse with partners normally forbidden to them. But *kifudu* and *kihoma* performances do not simply play with expressions of desire; they also enact women's rivalry with and resentment against men. Whereas Giriama men compete with other men during funerary "prestige competitions" (Parkin 1972: 81), women bond with one another in their funerary songs, directing antagonism and rivalry outward toward men and toward women from neighboring areas. Sexual derision is a popular weapon: "My husband doesn't know how to screw me," complains one lyric. Another song mocks jealous husbands while belittling their genitalia: "A jealous husband will not grow fat/He only has thin legs and long testicles." Still another song degrades women from a rival community, then berates an elderly man for being an inept provider: "You don't clothe me or feed me, grandfather. You know, you're just yoghurt." In a way, these songs are the symbolic antithesis of *mathumia:* they desacralize sex, they flout the order of sexual custom, they put a thumb in the eye of male elders, and they stress antagonism between genders rather than interdependence. In a culture where women's power, sexual autonomy, and general worth are constrained and demeaned, these full-throated testimonies of anger, sexual agency, and pride are surely emotionally significant gestures of resistance.

But can we assume that onlookers, and the singers themselves, understand the women's words and actions as an important and enduring statement of rebellion? *Kifudu* and *kihoma* take place within a ritual frame, and like all rituals, this one sets up an extraordinary and perplexing relationship between the ritual participants and what they are saying and doing. In his exploration of this relationship, Gluckman analyses numerous rituals of rebellion that flout the existing power structure through blasphemy, humor, and obscenity

(Gluckman 1954, 1965). Using ethnographic evidence from Zulu and other African cultures, he concludes that participation in such rituals does not constitute a threat to the status quo. In fact, he argues, such rituals often emerge from a strong social order, and further solidify it:

> The acceptance of the established order as right and good, and even sacred, seems to allow unbridled license, very rituals of rebellion, for the order itself keeps this rebellion within bounds. Hence to act the conflicts, whether directly or by inversion or in other symbolical forms, emphasizes the social cohesion within which the conflicts exist. (1965: 125)

The "ritual of rebellion," then, is a kind of cage for disorder, particularly in societies where social structure is already strong. If anything, Gluckman implies, rebellion is less likely after such rituals, for rebellious impulses are restricted to a socially sanctioned time and place, and thus reminded of their impotence.

At the same time that the ritual context brackets antisocial behavior, ritual form can also defuse subversive messages by virtue of the fact that most ritual behaviors are second-hand. Anthropologist Lila Abu-Lughod makes a related observation in her account of Egyptian Bedouin women's poetry (Abu-Lughod 1986). Bedouin women recite poetry to express feelings of grief and self-pity that would normally be unacceptable because in Bedouin culture, stoicism and emotional self-control are considered essential to social dignity. Abu-Lughod suggests that a poem is an acceptable medium of expression because it offers the woman who recites it a kind of alibi: if the woman reciting the poem did not author it, she cannot be fully credited with the sentiments in the text. As a result, a woman performing poetry is exempt from normal critiques of emotional expression, being evaluated instead by a "different set of standards regarding conformity to societal ideals" (207). While Abu-Lughod's analysis does not directly concern ritual, we can extrapolate her analysis to ritual form, in which participants' acts and utterances have a prescripted, second-hand quality similar to that of poetic recitation.

If we combine Gluckman's and Abu-Lughod's accounts, we can interpret ritual as doubly qualified to defuse potentially subversive messages. First, ritual is sharply bracketed from everyday life by a special space, time, and behavioral protocol; its boundaries might be likened to quotation marks that set it off from the continuous stream of ordinary happenings. Second, the content of ritual does not spring anew from the agency and opinions of ritual participants, but instead is derivative of rituals past, and as such, resembles reported speech more than first-hand utterance. If these devices are central to local interpretations of *kifudu* and *kihoma*, we might expect the performances to pose no threat to Giriama social order, and the singers themselves to be treated no differently for participating. And indeed, this is a common account of *kifudu* and *kihoma* among Giriama near Malindi. In interviews, I asked numerous informants whether women's funerary songs are permissible given the overarching expectation of female sexual modesty, and was repeatedly told that the songs are "just tradition," and hence do not constitute a genuine rebellion against social expectations. This reassurance was often delivered in a quick and patterned fashion, rather like a stock response designed to strip the performances of any significance beyond their generic status as "tradition," and, perhaps, to preclude further inquiry by this probing outsider.[9] These stock dismissals of *kifudu* and *kihoma* may have a protective function for the Giriama community at large, for they emphasize that such behaviors are restricted to the ritual frame and hence pre-empt accusations that their non-ritual social habits are primitive and debased. And women defend their performances as "just tradition" with special alacrity, guarding their most privileged moment of expression by denying that real expression is involved at all.

But are Giriama women's funerary utterances and actions completely absolved by the ritual context? Are women really free to say and do anything in ritual without consequence? Despite the public sanction for *kifudu* and *kihoma*, unofficial currents of ambivalence and disapproval run through the Giriama communities near Malindi town. In informal contexts

such as casual conversations, gossip sessions, and whispered asides like that of the man who passed me during the funeral, men of all ages and elder women voice anxiety about *kifudu* and *kihoma* performances today. A number of young men say that although they might be tempted to sleep with a woman who enjoys performing the songs and dances, they would not marry her—implying that the free sexual expression in the performances is sexually attractive, but suggests inferior virtue. Still other men, like the husband of the woman I spoke to at the funeral above, forbid their wives to participate in the singing and dancing at all, seeming to fear either that stigma will attach to their wives, or that the performance might augur actual promiscuity. Meanwhile, older women complain that the young girls who participate in funerary songs and dances "don't respect their elders anymore" and are prone to promiscuity and prostitution. In such discussions, *kifudu* and *kihoma* are portrayed not as meaningless ritual behaviors, but instead as a kind of training ground for real sexual misconduct. Apparently, Giriama detect the seeds of genuine danger and resistance described by Douglas and Bakhtin, and fear that these might escape the ritual boundary, putting down roots in ordinary life.

Where does this tension between stock approval of funerary obscenity and informal disapproval emerge from? The moralizing forces of Islam and Christianity doubtless contribute to the discourse of danger, since both religions construe Giriama rituals as heathenistic and corrupt. But those who regard the rituals with suspicion include numerous Giriama who do not call themselves converts—in fact some of them, including some elderly women, openly despise the influence of world religions on their milieu. Although Mary Douglas might ascribe their disapproval of funerary ritual to the inherent dangers of "disorder," she may undervalue the ways in which culturally specific anxieties define "disorder" as "dangerous." Interestingly, Gluckman anticipates the importance of context in construals of unruly ritual, though he deals with it only indirectly. Where there is little threat of misconduct outside of the ritual context, he says, ritual rebellion will not affect the extant social order. But, he predicts, "where the [social] relationships involved are weak, there cannot be license in ritual" (1965: 132). Gluckman does not explain the concept of "weak relationships" in great detail, but the fraught sexual issues in the Malindi area surely bring Giriama society under this rubric. While the homestead breaks apart, women and girls are loosed from the mast, and through a kind of *bricolage* of the examples that surround them, improvise new sexual identities. Male homestead heads in the Malindi area no longer orchestrate sexual conduct through *mathumia,* and as supernatural proscriptions for sexual transgression fade, fears of adultery mount. Women's potential promiscuity spells a drop in male control over female sexuality (and, by implication, paternity), giving men reason for discomfort.[10] Meanwhile, the elders' authority is shunted to the side, making both elder men and elder women uncomfortable as they watch old hierarchies of respect and resource distribution crumble.

As these social anxieties grow, the membrane surrounding the ritual becomes permeable in two directions. Sexual threats run from the outside in, as growing numbers of girls join the obscene dancing circles—a violation of previous ritual guidelines that the elders link to their exposure to promiscuity and prostitution in daily life. In turn, the portrayal of sexual dissolution in the ritual threatens, in the popular imagination, to spill beyond its bounds and influence daily behavior. Since the acts and utterances in funerary songs and dances have begun to speak of possible rather than unlikely behavior, the ritual content is no longer totally dismissed as a benign kind of reported speech. Instead, currents of suspicion frame the ritual content as a first-hand report of the unruly desires of women participants. Thus ritual participants are caught between two interpretations of their actions: although they are partially absolved by the protective cloak of tradition, they also risk the labels of promiscuity or unmarriagability. In funerary ritual today, an expressive space for women is offered with one hand and revoked with the other.

I would like to return briefly to a subject I mentioned earlier: the elder women's claim that funerary songs are now revoltingly obscene compared to the gentler, more graceful performances of their youth. Although this complaint may have an element of truth, I do not take it entirely at face value. First, I witnessed some of the same elderly women who complain about funerary obscenity participating in the lewdest songs and dances with delight; evidently, the style was not as alien to them as they suggested. Secondly, early missionary and colonial reports of *kifudu* song and dance suggest that it was obscene long before these women were young. Ludwig Krapf, the first missionary to East Africa, mentions "immoralities and abominations" practiced at a *mwanza wa kifudu* ceremony he witnessed in 1847, noting that "[these] are well known to every one" (Krapf 1968 [1860]: 162). The colonial officer Arthur Champion, writing around 1914, describes one *kifudu* dance as "demoniacal" and "frenz[ied]" (26), and relates that "[another] dance performed by two old women over the grave was of an extremely sensual character. This unseemly dance produced great mirth amongst the mourners" (Champion 1967: 28). Although these accounts are colored by an overarching colonialist horror toward African rites, and although they do not rule out the possibility that the rituals contain more brazen material now than then, they do suggest that overtly sexual material in funerary songs and dances is not new. It is possible, then, that the elder women's complaints are about something more than obscenity within ritual. Although the obscene signifiers within funerary ritual may not have changed significantly, the social context for their interpretation has changed, lending the sexual phenomena signified in the ritual a more real and threatening cast. The elder women's nostalgia, then, may not be for another kind of song, but for another way of life altogether.

CONCLUSION

Sex is considered "appropriate" subject matter at a Giriama funeral for gender-neutral reasons.

It symbolizes the extremity of life's borders, it distracts the mourners from their misery, and it mocks the despair and the finality of death. Yet in their songs and dances, women magnify these sexual elements and direct them at male targets, giving funerary rituals acute significance for Giriama gender politics. Through these ritual moments women assert female unity and pride, vent their complaints about male power, and convey their joy in breaking through the sexual decorum normally expected of them.

Given all of this, what should we make of the original tension between Douglas' and Gluckman's accounts of ritual license? Gluckman's insistence that rituals of rebellion are benign is echoed by Giriama themselves when they attest that their funerals are "just tradition." But although the protective ritual frame may render their acts partially permissible, the women's fulminating grievances do not go unacknowledged. Douglas' suggestion that ritual disorder spells "danger" also circulates among Malindi-based Giriama as an interpretive possibility. Thus, for the ambivalent onlooker at a funeral, an archetypical expression of Giriama "tradition" threatens to encourage, if not serve as a catalyst for a transformation in the gendered order.

As I have suggested, the perceived "danger" in women's funerary songs stems not simply from the presence of disorder in the ritual, but largely from changes in the surrounding social context that influence the interpretation of that disorder. The new sexual options in Malindi both vex the patriarchal order and challenge the "official" notion that ritual can successfully contain its own subversive strains. But I don't mean to imply that Malindi is the only site of such contests over ritual meaning. Giriama everywhere interact with other cultures, creating local social tensions that could challenge the security of the ritual frame—a pattern that may reach into the past as well. Although elders idealize the virtuous sexual codes of their youth, their memories are shaped by nostalgia, raising the possibility that sexual behavior has long run up against customary expectations, and that a double discourse about women's funerary performances

has obtained for some time. We might, in fact, expand this argument outward, into a general suggestion. Perhaps Gluckman idealizes the "official" discourses of social unity in the African societies he studies, and in so doing, overlooks the changes, tensions, and fault lines elemental to all societies. If this is the case, if no society is so intact, then disorderly ritual moments are potentially as uniformly "dangerous" as Mary Douglas posits—only the degree and shape of danger will be locally construed, and presumably construed differently by various groups within a given society. The mere presence of "danger" in ritual, then, should not encourage theoreticians to leap to a universally triumphant narrative of female ritual unruliness, for such a leap would overlook the nuance and force of local interpretations of the ritual and its relationship to everyday life. In the Giriama case, such interpretations limit the practical efficacy of women's ritual gestures, for either the ritual gestures are not taken seriously or they are taken seriously and met with the sort of redress we have seen (derision or prohibition). What women can accomplish through unruly ritual, then, remains an open question that can only be addressed case by case, with close attention to the local anxieties that define the perplexing relationship between the mundane social world and the exhilarating alternatives encoded in ritual.

ACKNOWLEDGMENTS

I would like to thank Jennifer Dickinson, Rachel Heiman, Larry Hirschfeld, Penelope Papailias, and Gaye Thompson for their valuable feedback on a draft of this essay. Gaye Thompson provided rich insights into Giriama society, as did Kainga Kalume Tinga. My research assistant, Maxwell Phares Kombe, supported me with astonishing patience and intelligence, for which I will always be grateful. The people who assisted me along the way are far too numerous to name, but they include many Giriama, Swahili, and Europeans who welcomed me, talked to me, and tolerated me, often with kindness and good humor. Thanks are also due to the Malindi Museum Society and Fort Jesus Museum, Mombasa for their interest and support. This research was carried out with a grant from the Fulbright-Hays Foundation.

REFERENCES

Abu-Lughod, Lila. 1986. *Veiled Sentiments: Honor and Poetry in a Bedouin Society.* Berkeley: University of California Press.

Ardener, Edwin. 1977. "Belief and the Problem of Women." In Shirley Ardener (ed.). *Perceiving Women,* pp. 1–27. New York: John Wiley and Sons.

Bakhtin, M. M. 1962. *Rabelais and His World.* Transl. Helene Iswolsky. Cambridge, MA: MIT Press.

Bataille, Georges. 1962. *Death and Sensuality: A Study of Eroticism and the Taboo.* New York: Walker and Company.

Berglund, A. I. 1957. *Some African Funerary Inversions.* Unpublished M.A. thesis. Uppsala, Sweden: Department of Cultural Anthropology, Library of the African Research Programme.

Bourguignon, Erika (ed.). 1973. *Religion, Altered States of Consciousness, and Social Change.* Columbus: Ohio State University Press.

Champion, A. M. 1967. *The Agiriama of Kenya.* London: Royal Anthropological Institute.

Danforth, Loring M. 1989. *Firewalking and Religious Healing: The Anastenaria of Greece and the American Firewalking Movement.* Princeton, NJ: Princeton University Press.

Douglas, Mary. 1966. *Purity and Danger: An Analysis of the Concepts of Pollution and Taboo.* London: Routledge.

Gluckman, Max. 1954. *Rituals of Rebellion in South-East Africa.* Manchester, UK: Manchester University Press.

———. 1965. *Custom and Conflict in Africa.* Oxford, UK: Basil Blackwell.

Hobsbawm, Eric, and Terence Ranger. 1983. *The Invention of Tradition.* Cambridge, UK: Cambridge University Press.

Krapf, J. Lewis. 1968. *Travels, Researches, and Missionary Labors during an 18 Years' Residence in Eastern Africa.* Missionary Researches and Travels Nr. 2. London: Frank Cass and Co.

Lewis, I. M. 1971. *Ecstatic Religion: A Study of Shamanism and Spirit Possession.* London: Routledge.

Mazrui, Alamin M. 1997. *Kayas of Deprivation, Kayas of Blood: Violence, Ethnicity, and the State in Coastal Kenya.* Nairobi: Human Rights Commission.

McIntosh, Janet S. 1996. Professed Disbelief and Gender Identity on the Kenya Coast. In Natasha Warner et al. (eds.). *Gender and Belief Systems.* pp. 481–490. Berkeley, CA: Berkeley Women and Language Group, University of California.

Parkin, David J. 1972. *Palms, Wine, and Witnesses: Public Spirit and Private Gain in an African Farming Community.* London: Intertext Books.

———. 1991. *Sacred Void: Spatial Images of Work and Ritual among the Giriama of Kenya.* Cambridge, UK: Cambridge University Press.

Thompson, Sally Gaye. 1990. *Speaking "Truth" to Power: Divination as a Paradigm for Facilitating Change among Giriama in the Kenyan Hinterland.* Unpublished Doctoral dissertation in Anthropology, presented to the School of African and Oriental Studies, University of London.

Turner, Victor. 1967. *The Forest of Symbols.* Ithaca, NY: Cornell University Press.

Udvardy, Monica. 1990a. *Gender and the Culture of Fertility among the Giriama of Kenya.* Unpublished Doctoral dissertation in Anthropology, presented to the University of Uppsala, Sweden.

———. 1990b. "Kifudu: A Female Fertility Cult among the Giriama." In Anita Jacobson-Widding and Walter van Beek (eds.). *The Creative Communion: African Folk Models of Fertility and the Regeneration of Life,* pp. 137–152. Uppsala: Academiae Ubsaliensis. Distributed by Almquist and Wiksell International, Stockholm, Sweden.

van Gennep, Arnold. 1960. *The Rites of Passage.* Transl. Monika B. Vizedom and Gabrielle L. Caffee. Chicago: University of Chicago Press.

Willis, Justin. 1993. *Mombasa, the Swahili, and the Making of the Mijikenda.* Oxford, UK: Clarendon Press.

NOTES

1. Although Giriama have partially internalized the message that they are "backward," they counter it with themes of rebellion against the groups who have scorned them. A number of funerary songs, which I do not present here, are laced with expressions of defiance against Muslims, Christians, and upcountry tribes. The strategic use of a stigmatized "tradition" as a tool of vengeance has important implications for Giriama political ideology, but these are beyond the scope of this article.

2. Udvardy notes that despite their importance, the *kifudu* secret societies are "not much talked about" (1990b: 151) by comparison to men's cults, lending them a "muted" quality common

to female-dominated institutions (Ardener 1977). Perhaps this relative silence has facilitated their rapid transformation and quick disappearance from memory. Most Giriama under thirty in Malindi know *kifudu* as funerary song and dance only, not as a secret society—despite the fact that the *kifudu* society is still active several kilometers west of the town.

3. The dual narrative perspective of funerary songs is important to their significance, but it introduces complexities beyond the scope of this article. Briefly, I think that the songs' narrative volatility helps to construct the "ritual alibi" I discuss later in this article, by making the songs seem more like reported speech than first person expression. Yet, clearly, this alibi is not sufficient to defuse all suspicion toward the women who participate.

4. A survey of texts on East Africa, conducted over forty years ago, found more than 600 sources describing inversions in connection with death rituals (Berglund 1957).

5. Kihoma songs must cease the instant the corpse has been buried, suggesting that the visibility of the corpse defines the boundaries of the liminal period. This seems a fitting criterion, given that a corpse appears to embody liminality itself: the dead person is neither here nor there, for breath and mind have vanished, yet the flesh, bafflingly, remains.

6. Despite the fact that women may dance against one another in a sexually suggestive way at funerals, I found no evidence that lesbian sex is a Giriama cultural category. While they are aware that female–female sexual relations can occur among their Swahili and Arab neighbors, they have no term for it in their mother tongue. Informants tell me that if a woman loves another woman, she will sexualize the relationship not through direct contact but by arranging an affair between her husband and the female object of her affection. Homosexual sex between men, on the other hand, is acknowledged and condemned.

7. In a village about fifty kilometers Southwest of Malindi, Udvardy reports that Giriama considered funerary songs "entertainment for the departing spirit . . . the songs must be sung to accompany the spirit, so that it knows it is not alone and need not be sad" (Udvardy 1990a: 145–146). In Malindi, however, the emphasis is entirely on the emotions of those still living. This discrepancy may reflect a gradual move away from customary ancestor propitiation in Malindi; those who decline to consider the departing spirit set a precedent for neglecting the ancestral spirit as well.

8. The alignment of sex and death has been suggested too by Western avant-garde theorists such as Georges Bataille (1897–1962), who posited a fundamental kinship between sex and death in the human psyche. According to Bataille (1962), sex and death are conceptually aligned for existential reasons: both can dissolve the social self, lifting the boundary between individual subjectivity and the rest of the world. Bataille's theory emerges from a particular moment in Western history—after Renaissance writers had construed orgasm as a "small death"; after de Sade made his mark with his sex- and violence-ridden fiction; and after Freud suggested that orgasm resolves both life and death instincts—so should be applied with caution to other cultural contexts. Yet it does seem that numerous cultures have drawn some kind of symbolic equivalence between sex and death, suggesting that their sign qualities lend them to symbolic interplay.

9. The category of "tradition" has strategic dimensions in numerous colonial and postcolonial contexts. It may, for example, be used to protect or decry a given cultural practice; to sanction new forms of authority; or to confer an aura of unquestionability upon an otherwise contentious act. For more on such processes, see Hobsbawm and Ranger (1983).

10. It is worth noting that male objections to funerary songs primarily address their obscene contents, and not the contents that articulate a female–male rivalry. I suggest this discrepancy emerges from the fact that at the economic and political levels, patriarchy among Giriama remains intact and so is not threatened by the songs that express rivalry per se. Male control over female sexuality, on the other hand, is under threat. Men's disapproval of funerary performances, then, is correspondingly focused on female sexual expression.

Shamans, Bodies, and Sex
Misreading a Korean Ritual

Laurel Kendall

"But isn't it sexual?" This paper owes its genesis to the presentation of another—"Of Gods and Men: Performance, Possession, and Flirtation in Korean Shaman Ritual"—to the questions it raised, and to my bemusement when more than one respondent, on more than one occasion, insisted that sexuality "explained" the activities of female Korean shamans.[1] Speaking of the a modern, Western intellectual tradition, Michel Foucault describes sexuality as, "the general and disquieting meaning that pervades our conduct . . . a general signification, a universal secret, an omnipresent cause, a fear that never ends."[2] This chapter illustrates how this pervasive and common sense notion of sexuality gets in the way of ethnographic clarity.

The shamans who are the subjects of this paper are women. Indeed, most Korean shamans are women and the minority of male shamans dress in traditional women's clothing before donning the spirits' robes for a ritual. Shamans are chosen by the spirits; women experience this calling as frighteningly vivid dreams and visions, manic behavior, and compulsions to wander. They also experience misfortunes, both personally, and within their families, which recur until they accept their calling and are initiated. The initiation enables the shaman to call on the spirits for inspiration and visions which she will use to prognosticate both during divination sessions and when speaking in the persona of the spirits during minor and major rituals. Through her ability to make this connection with the spirits, the Korean shaman secures their favor on behalf of her clients. Ill health, problematic personal relations, and increasingly, business reverses, cause clients to seek out shamans, obtain divinations, and sponsor rituals. In addition to performing divinations, newly-initiated shamans can, with a minimum of training, perform simple prayer ceremonies for the good fortune of a client's family or business. The client makes offerings to the spirits and the shaman makes a petition on behalf of the client, then briefly manifests the spirits, offering in the voices of household gods and ancestors advice and cautions for all members of the client's family. With more training and observation of experienced shamans, the initiate learns to perform more complicated rituals for healing, business success, success in finding a marriage partner, and conceiving a child.[3]

The most elaborate, potent, and expensive ritual that Korean shamans perform is called *kut*. In *kut*, shamans wear clothing associated with the gods and ancestors and through song and dance, summon these spirits, in proper sequence, to the ritual space, manifesting them in their own bodies. In the persona of demanding gods and tearful ancestors, they scold, banter and commiserate with the clients, offer advice and prognostications, and depart with promises to help the family move toward a more optimistic future. The *kut* satisfies the appetites and demands of household gods and the worldly cravings of ancestors so that the troubling emotions they have vented toward the living family are transformed into good will and promises of future blessing and protection. Ominous forces are expelled and the path to an auspicious fortune is opened wide. The work of successful shamanship, closely bound with the successful performance of *kut*, requires a range of skills: singing, dancing, miming, playing the drum

Originally appeared in French in *Anthropologie et Societies*, Vol. 22, n. 2, 1998 as "Maisn'est-ce pas sexuel, Le lapsus derriere le regard ethnographique," and in English as "But Isn't She Sexual? The Freudian Slip Beneath the Ethnographic Gaze," in *Gender/Bodies/Religions*, edited by Sylvia Marcos, 2000. Reprinted here in English with the Permission of Anthropologie et Societies and Adler Publications.

and percussive instruments, arranging elaborate offerings, and above all, providing canny divinations and convincing spirit manifestations. How was sexuality read into my description of these activities?

THE ETHNOGRAPHIC PROBLEM: "AMBIGUOUS SEXUALITY WAFTING"

The problem was of my own making. In my earlier ethnography, I had written that "an element of ambiguous sexuality wafts about the *mansin's* (shaman's) performance."[4] "Of Gods and Men" explored the sources of that ambiguity. The presentation began with a disturbing memory from the field of a male spectator pinching the breast of a dancing shaman while he secured a thousand-*won* bill under her chest band. I used this image to approach a nagging question: why is the Korean shaman profession constructed as both disreputable and a service to the gods? I located my answer in the domain of dance. Dance, a source of pleasure and play, becomes in shaman ritual an amusement for the gods as well as the spectators, all of whom are said "to play" (*nolda*). As a gateway for the release of playful impulses and powerful emotions and as a sign and instrument of healing, dance also carries the danger of emotional abandon and disgrace. In extreme cases, the gods seize the dancing woman and claim her as a shaman.

A colleague wrote to thank me for a copy of my paper on "erotic dance." Erotic dance? What had I said?

I had included dancers' descriptions of a sense of joy, mirth, or excitement rising from the belly to the chest[5] and noted that this rising of spirited feelings (*hung, sinparam*) mapped the same trajectory as that taken by the personal body-governing gods who rise up when clients borrow shamans' costumes to dance, and by choking, potentially fatal emotions of rage and frustration that rise to the chest in "fire sickness" (*hwabyong*) when they have been held too long inside. I had written that in shaman rituals, the dance becomes a gateway for the expression of strong emotion in the idiom of spirits who, when they "play" in the person of a shaman or a client, vent their desires and appetites and attain (temporary) satisfaction. Korean shaman rituals dramatize the obverse of the Buddhist ideal of transcendence and of the Confucian injunction to controlled moderation; they deal with the consequences of worldly craving, using the dance as one idiom of both symptom and cure. I suggested that these associations, and the attendant possibility of being possessed by either spirits or compulsions and consequently disgraced, vested both dancing and the women who dance for a living with an aura of moral ambivalence (Kendall 1991).

"It must be sexual."

One respondent to an oral presentation of my paper insisted that sexual cravings necessarily explained the sensations Koreans described as rising from the belly. In a dialogue that exhausted the question-and-answer period, I was equally stubborn in my insistence that dancing Koreans did not read these experiences as sexual, that sexual desire—expressed most explicitly in the dancing compulsion—was but one of several emotions that Koreans expressed through the dancing, possessed or otherwise. Was lust more profound than the other bundled appetites and cravings that even nominal Korean Buddhists would recognize as obstacles to enlightenment or, in popular religion, as burdens weighing upon the restless dead? Is sexuality the engine that propels the dancer and runs the dance? A classic Freudian reading would have it so. Is the power that shamans claim through their danced possession by (mostly but not exclusively) male gods the regenerative power of sexuality turned to ritual ends? This is what respondents to my paper seemed to insist upon. One discussant even delicately suggested that I should "not be afraid" to give my ethnography a sexual gloss. Why hadn't I seen it? Was I "hung up?" I was challenged, aware of corroborating examples elsewhere in the world, but I maintained an abiding unease with what seemed to be a reductionistic interpretation of the Korean material.

WOMEN, BODIES, AND SEX

In the 1970s, anthropologists concerned with what were then called "sex roles" asked, "Is female to male as nature is to culture?" Sherry Ortner, who phrased the question, argued that while the symbolic relegation of women to a lower order of existence is necessarily a cultural construct, the near universality of such perceptions is grounded in "the body and the natural procreative functions specific to women alone."[6] Much subsequent anthropological writing echoed this assumption that disparate cultures constructed women within the biological "givens" of the female body.[7] While Sherry Ortner and Harriet Whitehead,[8] as well as Bryan Turner[9] all explicitly eschew a simple biological determinism, they nevertheless assume that much of the anxious life of a given society is constructed around women's bodies as instruments of sexuality and reproduction. This is the obverse and conscious rejection of an abiding but more simplistic assumption, sometimes encountered in the literature on women and spirit possession (see below) that sexual repression is a common female problem.

Michel Foucault speaks of the "hysterization of women's bodies," the notion that women's sexuality as innately problematic and that women's problems are innately sexual," as a historical development of the early modern West.[10] The publication of Foucault's *The History of Sexuality* prompted a veritable cottage industry in social and historical writings about the body as a site through which social discipline is imposed and social power is affirmed.[11] These efforts have opened the question of gender to complex historical and cultural analyses—how are different notions of "masculity" and "femininity" experienced through male and female bodies that are made to act in socially prescribed ways? A few voices of caution have been raised against the ease with which such endeavors might slide into an older tendency to define "woman" through the body, sex, and reproduction to the exclusion of other dimensions of experience.[12]

In emphasizing that the men's and women's bodily experiences are redefined through history, Foucault offered liberation from, in Gayle Rubin's words, "the traditional understanding of sexuality as a natural libido yearning to break free of social constraint."[13] Sexualities could now be seen as multiple and both culturally and historically constituted, rather than simply "natural."[14] Eroticism is thus one dimension of a larger question posed by Clifford Geertz and restated by Nancy Scheper-Hughes and Margaret Lock as, ". . . whether any expression of human emotion and feeling—whether public or private, individual or collective, whether repressed or explosively expressed is ever free of cultural shaping and cultural meaning. The most extreme statement of Geertz's position, shared by many of the newer psychological and medical anthropologists, would be that without culture we would simply not know how to feel."[15]

What does this material bring to the question, "But isn't it sexual?" First, recognizing the importance of contemporary studies that regard women, and in particular the sexuality of women, as culturally and historically constituted, it simultaneously recognizes a deep-rooted impulse in Western social science writing to approach the question of women through sexuality and reproduction, an impulse that may obscure other possible readings.[16] Second, a plea for the recognition of culturally-constituted ideologies of eroticism, or any other expression of human feeling, is a plea for ethnographic precision and imagination and an honest recognition of the profound difficulty of interpreting human motivation in the absence of confident psychobiological "givens."

And now to Korea.

IS POSSESSION EROTIC?

The idea that shamanic experience implies a sexual union between the female shaman and her guardian god does seem to lurk in some corners of the Korean popular imagination. In the film version of "Portrait of a Shaman" (*Munyodo*), released in the 1970s, but *not* in Kim Tongni's original novella, the seasoned shaman and her initiate periodically ingest a blood-red concoction of Chinese medicine, whereupon they emit orgasmic shrieks while painted images of brawny gods leer up in front of the camera. In fact, the use of hallucinogens is unknown in Korean shamanic practice. More recently, an initiate who came to the shaman profession after attending graduate school in the United States and reading Eliade, evolved a signature dance style that required her to kneel in front of the altar and bend her torso backward, gestures which Western observers readily interpreted as a sexual reception of the god. Her Korean shaman colleagues found these same movements strange and referred to her performance as the "vagina dance" (*poji chum*).[17] Both portrayals suggest the influence of foreign notions of an eroticized shamanism.

Shamans have told me that because *most* (but not all) of the gods are male, or *if* predominantly male gods possess a shaman (rather than female gods or divine couples), a shaman will have a troubled marital history. Some shamans claim that jealous gods prevent them from having marital relations with their husbands, but other *mansin* scoff at this.[18] Songjuk Mansin told me, "Male gods don't like what is between man and woman," a statement that suggested her own agreement. Similarly, Okkyong's Mother, who enjoys the most stable marriage of all of the shamans I know well, affirmed that she sleeps upstairs in her shrine while her husband sleeps on the ground floor. A shaman colleague, describing a similar arrangement, asserted that "men stink" (a literal translation).

Yongsu's Mother complained that her dead husband, installed as a guardian god in her shrine, had prevented her from marrying again after an early widowhood, but she made it clear that the god was no substitute for a flesh and blood husband, that she would have preferred not to live alone. An aged shaman, initiated while still a young woman, wept when she described her many long years without a mate. A young married shaman described the stress of periods of enforced abstinence before performing significant rituals. In sum, *mansin* may boast of their gods' jealousy as a measure of their gods' power, an attribute of the shaman's own professional success. The gods may drive living husbands away, but they do not, in most instances, replace absent husbands as sexual partners. If some shamans use the gods as a justification for avoiding sexual contact with their husbands, this seems more an expression of distaste than a divine cure for or sublimation of

repressed sexuality. This material counters what Pat Caplan has dubbed "the so-called 'hydraulic' model of sexuality,"[19] the Freudian assumption that an innate and problematic sexual drive must necessarily find expression or sublimation, if not in men, then in gods. The Korean material contains only the thinnest and most idiosyncratic suggestion that these needs might ever find expression in some Korean shamans' experience of possession.

Among the many scholars who have published on the subject of Korean shamanism, to my knowledge only Jung Young Lee has attempted to make a case for "a fundamental motive in Korean shamanism through a study of sexual repression."[20] Lee's study suffers from an excess of innuendo and inaccuracy—old men encountered in dreams are necessarily objects of sexual attraction, prayers for fertility are ultimately expressions of thwarted sexuality (rather than thwarted desires for sons), and the installation of guardian deities (who need not be male) in the initiate's shrine invariably establishes a sexual relationship between shaman and deity. The first two claims are unsubstantiated, either in the body of Lee's work or elsewhere in the literature on Korean shamanism. The third rests on the testimony of one shaman informant, possessed by a divine general, who "dreamed that she went to bed with the general."[21]

It is revealing that Lee utterly confuses the term "sexual repression"—the forcing of inexpressible sexual needs and desires into the subconscious mind—with "sexual oppression"—the systematic subjugation of women on the basis of gender.[22] This is an honest mistake insofar as psychological interpretations of female trance phenomena reveal an almost unconscious tendency to dissolve the social into the sexual. Consider, for example, psychiatrist and medical anthropologist Arthur Kleinman's field observation of a Taiwanese possession cult:

> Informants described it [possession] to me as one of the most exciting experiences they had ever witnessed or participated in. This must have been especially true for lower-class mothers and grandmothers, ordinarily trapped in the physical confines and daily routines of their homes. Cult members did not merely trance: they danced, jumped around, sang, exhibited glossolalia, gave

voice to strong emotions, and sometimes engaged in activities with strong sexual overtones. For example, men and women touched and massaged each other; they jumped around together; women rubbed the inside of their thighs and men exhibited rapid thrusting movements of the pelvis; at times the ecstatic frenzy of the trances resembled orgasmic behavior.[23]

In this passage, "orgasmic behavior" and "sexual overtones" are the judgments of a clinical observer who deems the excitement of possession "especially true for lower-class mothers and grandmothers" as a release from "the physical confines and daily routines of their homes." The passage makes a reflex link between social constraints, sexual repression, and ritual release, and again, finds a locus in the problematic bodies of women, although pelvis-thrusting men were also present. Consider also Melford Spiro's well-known description of women in Burmese *nat* cults:

> Restricting this discussion to female shamans, it will be recalled that, typically, females are possessed by a *nat* [spirit], and/or decide to marry a *nat* who had previously possessed them, either in adolescence or in or near menopause. These are females, in short, who are either first experiencing the mounting pressures of sexual desire and therefore—especially in Burma, where any physical contact with the opposite sex is prohibited—of sexual frustration, or they are females who, at menopause, are experiencing a heightening of their sex drives combined with the fear of losing their sexual attractiveness. The attendant frustration of the menopausal females is further intensified (in a large percentage of cases) by marriages with socially weak and sexually inadequate husbands. Add to this a previous observation, *viz.,* that the majority of those possessed, being of lower-class origin, are also suffering from status deprivation, and it then becomes at least plausible that one explanation for the differential effect of *nat* festivals is differential drive-intensity. That is, it is the women with the strongest frustrations (sexual, prestige, etc.) who are most susceptible to possession.[24]

By Spiro's logic, Burmese women respond to menarche and menopause with an emotional script that would not be out of place in an American women's magazine. And as in American women's magazines, "sexual attractiveness" is assumed to be at least as important to a woman's esteem as "prestige, etc." The contribution of Burmese culture to these constructions of self is that of a restrictive sluice gate, imposing sexual segregation upon the torrents of spring. The passage assumes a clinical familiarity with the subjects' "sexual frustration," "heightening of their sex drives," and "marriages with socially weak and sexually inadequate husbands," but elsewhere Spiro implies that these deductions must necessarily have been commonsensical, "When interviewed, these shamans describe the onset of possession as a highly pleasurable physical act, accompanied by deep and accelerated breathing, palpitations, and tingling of the flesh. The descriptions sounded very much like the description of sexual orgasm, but I could not pursue this line of inquiry because of *the near impossibility in Burma of discussing sexual matters with females*" (emphasis added).[25]

Spiro, at least, asked the shamans what the sensations of trance felt like. Gregory Bateson and Margaret Mead made inductive associations in their description of the Balinese trance dancer fallen backward onto the ground "writhing in some sort of orgasmic climax."[26] Perhaps possession behavior and erotic experience have so thoroughly bled together within the ethnographic gaze because, as Scheper-Hughes and Lock suggest, "It is sometimes during the experience of sickness, as in moments of deep trance or sexual transport, that mind and body, self and other become one."[27] For their part, Scheper-Hughes and Lock maintain a distinction between different kinds of experiences that may "sometimes" be equivalent in their consequences. They urge that such experiences be studied as part of an ambitious project to understand "the mindful body, as well as the self, social body, and body politic."[28] Such challenges are foreclosed when one domain of experience, "deep trance," is subordinated to the explanatory power of another, "sexual transport." The association of possession and sexual experience is compounded when the subject is a woman who dances. The Western tradition has long associated dancing with sexual expression.[29] The Korean tradition also views the dancing woman as at least potentially sexually available but in very specific contexts.

To summarize, the question "But isn't it sexual?" seems to have been provoked by strong (Western) associations. In the literature, possession experiences have sometimes been described as "erotic" or equivalent to "orgasm," a particularly tempting association where those possessed are women, socially oppressed, and consequently (it is assumed) sexually repressed. Most Korean shamans are women and most (but not all) of the gods who claim any one shaman are male. Therefore (by the logic of a flawed deduction) shamans experience possession either sexually or as sublimation. The sex question is posed primarily because Korean shamans are women.

This path of association—women, possession, dance, sex—is at least loosely "Freudian;" ultimate causes are situated in the individual subconscious, in drives that find expression, satisfaction, or sublimation through ritual participation, dance, and the experience of possession. But "Isn't it sexual?" may also indicate a different and more subtle line of interpretation. Mikhail Bakhtin's characterized aspects of medieval and renaissance folk culture as a celebration of the regenerative power of the body and bodily life." In carnivalistic portrayals of eating, drinking, copulation, and defecation, visions of a regenerated world were brought close to human experience through the body.[30] Bakhtin inverts the Freudian premise that all things come from psychobiological drives; rather, it is the body that takes the world into itself and reconstitutes it in performance."[31] Jean Comaroff describes the organizing sexual metaphors of a Tswana dance, performed to welcome male initiates after their return from the bush, as a regenerative replication of the Tswana social world. The different positions assumed by the dancing men and women and the different movements they assumed in the dance, the lateral rolling motions of the women and the vertical, or phallic movement of the upright sticks held by the men "implied not only the complementarily of male-female sexuality but the distinction between agnatic rank and matrilineality. . . . The map of the dance floor also replicated the spatial order of the social world, its organization of center and periphery, its opposed yet complementary relations between male and female."[32] Jean Comaroff postulates a widespread use of bodily metaphors in such world-defining dance forms, citing a similar emphasis on male "phallic" leaps and female lateral swaying in a fertility ritual of the Umeda people of the West Sepik District of New Guinea, described by Alfred Gell,[33] and Eric Ten Raa's description of mimed copulation in a ritual performed by the Sandawe of central Tanzania for the purpose of making the country fertile.[34] As Judith Lynn Hanna observes, dance is a particularly powerful medium for focusing awareness on the body and its associations.[35] Comaroff notes that danced celebrations of sexuality and Bakhtinean "bodily life" were precisely what provoked missionary ire in many parts of the world and, in some instances, resulted in local denials of prior practices.[36]

When an indigenous intelligentsia internalizes Western judgments, the result may be expurgated reinscriptions of custom. Frederique Marglin describes the nearly vanished devadasis of Puri, temple dancers and ritual specialists who celebrate the auspicious dimensions of female sexuality and fertility: "well-being and health or more generally . . . all that creates, promotes, and maintains life."[37] The devadasi's identity as a sexual being, as reflected in the link between temple dancing and prostitution, is central to Marglin's analysis of the devadasi's auspicious associations. To reach this understanding, Marglin first found it necessary to read through a process of historical reinterpretation. Indian reformers had attempted to retrieve Indian dance as an art form distinct from the onus of prostitution. It was claimed that the devadasi were originally chaste virgins, meant only for the gods, who were later debased by degenerate rulers and rich and powerful men, or that economic hardship had forced the devadasis into prostitution.[38]

We turn again to the Korean material with an awareness both of the expressive potential of the danced body, and of the likelihood of denials and redefinitions. Indeed, for the last twenty-five years, I have listened with amusement to emphatic denials of the existence of a living, vital, Korean shaman tradition. Over less than a decade in the 1970s, I saw elements of Bakhtinian body humor—mimed phallic display, defecation, and the unceremonious tossing away of a soiled baby—disappear from the performance of a rural masked dance tradition as it gained popularity among students and urbanites and was no longer performed as a celebration punctuating the agricultural cycle. Are the auspicious forces engendered by a Korean shaman's *kut* (her major ritual) in any sense generated by a danced and performed expression of positive sexual forces? Here, as elsewhere, the shamanic experience is realized in the performing body of the shaman.[39] Drumming and percussion inspire lively dancing and the inspiration to speak "the true words of the spirits." A successful *kut* resolves, in an atmosphere of play, the vexations (*soksanghada*) of the gods and ancestors and satisfies their tremendous appetites (*yoksim*). But are these "vexations" and "appetites," expressed through the dancing, miming, and speaking body of the shaman, innately sexual? Is there any evidence at all that this should be the cause? This passage caused some of my readers to think so:

> The *mansin* (shaman) who performs the Official's play (the segment of a shaman ritual that appeases a particularly greedy god) is . . . encouraged to dance her way to the far sidelines and coax the men into accepting an empty wine cup which she fills to the brim. . . . Her gesture is suggestive. To fill a man's cup outside the intimacy of kinship suggests the behavior of a woman paid to serve men's pleasure, the hospitality offered in a wine house . . . [during the Official's play] the *mansin* who distributes the [Official's] . . . wine encourages a spectator of either sex to dance a few bars with her in the enthusiasm of the moment.[40]

The few bars of dance described here are distinct from the jumps, accompanied by percussive drum beats, that bring on possession.[41] When shamans dance a few steps while selling the Official's wine, and when they dance a slow and graceful prelude to the jumping dance of possession, they execute the basic steps performed at Korean country celebrations, arms stretched out from the shoulders and bent slightly at the elbows to gesture rhythmically as the dancer takes slow steps with slight bends of the knee. The grace of the dancer is in her arms, her strength and flexibility in her shoulders. Women dance this way with each other, and men with men. Indeed, the women with whom I danced at a village Mother's Day picnic told me that they could not imagine how Americans had any fun at parties where, as I had told them, men and women "played together."

Such dancing, in and of itself, is neither explicitly gendered nor erotically charged. To dance at a *kut* or a country party is to "play" (*nolda*), to amuse oneself in a relatively unrestrained and pleasurable moment. Sexual expression, danced or otherwise, is euphemized as "play," but certainly as a subset and not a generative form.[42] Between women and men, dancing takes on a flirtatious cast (but can we call it "erotic"?) when a woman—a *kisaeng* or a shaman—invites a man to dance and pours him a cup of wine. In the Official's play, the gesture is ambiguous, since the shaman acts in the persona of a masculine god, a "man" dancing with a man.[43]

In her *Dance, Sex and Gender,* Judith Hanna cites selections from my 1985 ethnography to present the interactions of Korean shamans and male spectators as one among many other examples of "aphrodisiac dancing . . . which conveys the gender role of sexual object or partner."[44] The reader might never realize that this material comes from an ethnography subtitled *Women in Korean Ritual Life,* that it is the men who are marginal at Korean shaman rituals. Taken as a whole, Hanna's ethnographic overview of sexual expression through dance unravels some of the many different contexts, stakes, and consequences of such expression: in courtship, in prostitution, as an expression of union with the sacred, as a means of coping with supernatural forces, as a sex-role script, or as a sublimation. Her interpretation of dance as the gendered body's mediation of an "instinctual sexual drive," however, leads her to appropriate decontextualized data in support of a universal psychobiological "truth."

Hanna links "the sexuality of dance and its potential to excite" to her quantifiable, verifiable observation that "Dancing can lead to altered states of consciousness (with changed physiological patterns in brain wave frequency, adrenalin, and blood sugar) and hence to altered social action."[45]

My Korean data appears in Hanna's study under the heading "Seduction of Forces and Female Shamans," a section intended to illustrate that dance not only can be "performed to arouse the passion of a human lover, but it has sexual overtones in relationship to overcoming the forces of nature."[46] The selling of a cup of wine, a mildly nuanced flirtation, becomes, in this appropriation, an act of sexual arousal equivalent to a striptease. A marginal bit of business becomes the central encounter of a complex ritual process. What is assumed to happen between female shamans and male spectators "explains" what must then necessarily happen between shamans and gods.

Some representations in Korean popular culture—and, I suspect, many Korean men—assume that shamans are sexually promiscuous.[47] Recall that it was a male spectator's tweak of a shaman's breast that caused me to write about "performance, possession, and flirtation" in the first place. The stereotype is a function both of what shamans do—their public performance—and who they are (by virtue of what they do)—women who earn a livelihood outside the constraints and protections of respectable family life and who are simultaneously independent and vulnerable to harassment. Shamans whom I have known seem anxious to preserve their reputations and genuinely vexed by importunate men.[48] Is this flirtation/harassment a necessary part of the *kut*? From at least the turn of the century, some *kut* were always performed in shrines away from home, sometimes without the knowledge of the sponsor's husband, a tendency that may be even more pronounced today when *kut* are performed in commercial shrines rather than in cramped apartments where neighbors, particularly Christian neighbors, might complain about the noise of drum and symbols.[49] *Kut* were performed within the women's quarters of the palace and,[50] if we are to believe an old genre painting, in the segregated women's quarters of elite eighteenth-century homes. Thus, while shamans may, on the one hand, exploit the men's presence by selling lucky wine, and on the other, risk the men's harassment, the men's presence with its potential for play is not essential to the successful performance of a Korean shaman ritual. An efficacious, auspicious ritual does not require the energies unleashed by a brief heterosexual danced encounter. Rather it is the gods and ancestors who must play and feast to their satisfaction while spectators, particularly the sponsoring woman, are encouraged to dance to satisfy their own body-governing spirits.

Korean shaman rituals do include some more general representations of Bakhtinian "bodily life," most notably in the final send-off of wandering ghosts (*yongsil*) in which the performing shaman mimics the manner of their death, clutching her throat and rolling her eyes for the hanged, pantomiming dysentery, or simulating childbirth by dropping a metal bowl with a clatter from under her skirts.[51] In this exorcistic sequence, the shaman's play suggests not so much the celebration of a regenerative life force as a comfortingly humorous acknowledgment of the terrors of the mortal body.

Manifestations of sexual appetite are mimed in a small bit of business when a shaman seizes a dried fish, drumstick, or gong mallet, thrusts it out from the vicinity of her well-clothed genitals, and draws it up, usually pointing in the direction of the ritual's female sponsor. Sometimes the phallus (I think we can safely call it a phallus) is manipulated under the shaman's costume to suggest an erection. This is a bit of improvisational business, not a requisite element of the formal structure of the *kut* as recorded by folklorists. (So far as I know, folklorists have not bothered to record it.) The gesture is sharp and quick, always too quick for my camera. However often performed, it is almost invariably met with giggles from the spectators and an exchange of smirks among the shaman team. When Songjuk Mansin wrapped the dried fish in her costume vest and proceeded to rub it, Yongsu's mother expressed humorously exaggerated disgust, swatting with her drumstick at Songjuk's hands and at the makeshift phallus. At another *kut,* Yongsu's mother complained to Songjuk Mansin that the Spirit Warrior, manifested by a third shaman, was making too many demands of the client. To underscore her point, she improvised a phallus with a length of twisted towel, held out taught, and muttered "too much of this" as she gave it a thrust and a jerk.

What does this body play signify? The gods who receive a phallus in passing are among the most stereotypically demanding (the Official and the Spirit Warrior), not the highest gods (the Mountain God, the Heavenly King, the House Lord) whose dignified portrayals in *kut* are briefer and far less amusing to the spectators. Gods of middling rank have less shame and are consequently more active in stirring up trouble in client households. When they appear in *kut* they level outrageous and comically executed demands for food, music, and cash, and are met with equally stubborn resistance from the female spectators. The shaman's humorous portrayals make it possible for shamans and clients to engage the gods in a bargaining, bantering process of reconciliation. In caricature, the god's phallus is less an instrument of domination, or object of desire, than one more comic sign of a demanding, overbearing appetite, "too much of this." Could the gesture and the remark just possibly be a shaman's comment upon the masculine gender? When I saw a shaman, in the persona of the Official, playfully tweak a client's breast, I began to wonder.

CONCLUSION

Is it sexual? If so, then not in predictable ways. It would be difficult to read the phallic play described above as an expression of repressed sexual desire, or view these tumescent gods as idealized alternatives to mortal men. Indeed, they seem very much the opposite. If, as late twentieth century anthropological writing would have it, expressions of bodily life make statements about social relationships, then the gods' phallic exhibitionism underscores the general tenor of their dealings with mortals; they are, like lusty mortal men, bothersome and demanding. This is a measure of their power and of their obvious foibles. The "drag" act, Judith Butler suggests, is the "site of a certain ambivalence" against the order of things that can be both an expression of surrender and of insurrection,[52] but Rosalind Morris's cautions that this playful parody should not be over read as a serious act of resistance.[53]

Let us not, once again, mistake a part for the whole. That some shamans sometimes improvise phalluses adds a gloss to their portrayal of a particular category of masculine gods and gendered relationships more generally. These comic portrayals no more "explain" the sum of shamanic performance in sexual terms than does the shaman's occasional harassment by men or the selling of cups of wine. Such phenomena might, however, contribute to an analysis of gendered perceptions of a sexual Other. Performance offer a rich and subtle ground for such a project, as the work of Judith Butler, Linda Williams, Jennifer Robertson, and others suggests,[54] but this ground is also mined with booby traps. Ritual, myth, and art may, in Geertzian terms, show us "how people feel about things"[55] but interpretation comes through the reading eye, and there's the rub. The burden is on the anthropologist to provide the best and most valid reading possible, knowing that if it is worth considering, it is also worthy of contestation.

In other places, I have offered my own reading of the Korean shaman's relationship with her gods.[56] In this essay, I have been concerned with misreading, with how an observer, influenced by psychobiological interpretations of human—and particularly female—behavior could draw commonsensical but ultimately unfounded conclusions about sexual expression in Korean shaman rituals. I have also considered recent studies that regard social phenomena as "embodied," expressed by and through the body and its imagery. Specifically, I explored a possible interpretive link between those ritual dances observed elsewhere in the world that create and regenerate social worlds through their portrayal of heterosexual sexuality, encounters between female Korean shamans and male spectators, and instances of phallic play in shamanic ritual. I found this particular association weak as an overarching explanation but useful in one restricted case of performance business. A further consideration of the body and expressions of body life in Korean shaman ritual, in folk dramas, and in jokes and conversations, may offer other kinds of insights into the operation of gender and sexuality in Korean popular culture. But "Korean popular culture" is itself a moving target. The particular shamans who are the subjects of this paper inhabit a very different world of experience from that of media-savvy young Korean women who, in the 1990s, have begun to articulate totally new and unabashedly explicit discourses of sexuality.[57] The argument is for more, better, and more varied fieldwork.

This paper originally appeared in French in *Anthropologie et Societes*. vol. 22, n. 2, 1998, as "Mais n'est-ce pas seuxel, Le lapsus derriere le regard ethnographique," and in English as "'But Isn't it Sexual?' The Freudian Slip beneath the Ethnographic Gaze" in *Gender/Bodies/Religions*, edited by Sylvia Marcos., 2000.

NOTES

1. Laurel Kendall, "Of Gods and Men: Performance, Possession, and Flirtation in Korean Shaman Ritual, *Cahiers d'Extreme-Asie* (special issue on Korean Ritual, Alex Guillemoz, ed.), vol. 3 (1991/2), no. 2, pp. 185–202.

2. Michel Foucault, *The History of Sexuality, Volume I: An Introduction*, New York, Vintage Books, 1980, p. 69.

3. These are described in Laurel Kendall, *Shamans, Housewives, and Other Restless Spirits: Women in Korean Ritual Life*, Honolulu, University of Hawaii Press, 1985, p. 61.

4. Laurel Kendall, *Shamans, Housewives, and Other Restless Spirits: Women in Korean Ritual Life*, Honolulu, University of Hawaii Press, 1985, p. 61.

5. Cho Dongwha, cited in Alan C. Heyman, *Dances of the Three-Thousand-League Land*, Seoul, Dong-A Publishing Co, p. 5.

6. Sherry B. Ortner, "Is Female to Male as Nature Is to Culture?" in *Women, Culture, and Society*, M. Z. Rosaldo and L. Lamp here, eds., 1974, Stanford, Stanford University Press, pp. 67–87.

7. Judith Hock-Smith and Anita Spring, eds., *Women in Ritual and Symbolic Roles*, New York and London, Plenum Press, 1978, p. 3.

8. Sherry B. Ortner and Harriet Whitehead, eds., *Sexual Meanings: The Cultural Construction of Gender and Sexuality*, New York, Cambridge University Press, 1981, pp. 3, 19.

9. Sherry B. Ortner and Harriet Whitehead, eds., *Sexual Meanings: The Cultural Construction of Gender and Sexuality*, New York, Cambridge University Press, 1981, pp. 3, 19.

10. Foucault, *op. cit.*, especially pp. 104, 153. See also Pat Caplan, "Introduction," in *The Cultural Construction of Sexuality*, P. Caplan, ed., London and New York, Tavistock, 1987, pp. 1–30.

11. As a bellwether, in 1990 the American Ethnological Society took "the body" as the theme of its annual meeting. In this same year, the journal *History of Religions* devoted a theme issue to "the body." For a critical review of anthropological approaches to the body, see Nancy Scheper-Hughes and Margaret Lock, "The Mindful Body: A Prolegomenon to Future Work in Medical Anthropology," *Medical Anthropology Quarterly* vol. 1, no.1, 1987, pp. 6–41. For an overview of historical writing on sexuality and of anthropological thinking on this topic, see Caplan, *op. cit.*

12. See in particular Gesela Bock, "Women's History and Gender History: Aspects of an International Debate," *Gender and History*, vol. 1, no. 1, 1989, pp. 7–29; and Jane Flax, "Postmodernism and Gender Relations in Feminist Theory," *Signs: Journal of Women in Culture and Society*, vol., 12 no. 4, pp. 621–643.

13. Gayle Rubin, "Thinking Sex: Notes for a Radical Theory of the Politics of Sexuality," in *Pleasure and Danger: Exploring Female Sexuality*, C. Vance, ed., Boston, Routledge and Paul, 1984, pp. 287–319.

14. See Judith Butler, *Bodies that Matter: On the Discursive Limits of "Sex,"* New York, Routledge, 1993; Caplan, *op. cit.*, Teresa De Laruetis, ed., *Technologies of Gender*, Bloomington, University of Indiana Press, 1986; and Sherry B. Ortner, *Making Gender: The Politics and Erotics of Culture*, Boston, Beacon Press, 1996.

15. Scheper-Hughes and Lock, *op. cit.*, p. 28.

16. This tendency is not exclusively Western. Earlier generations of Japanese historians and folklorists regarded women as "mothers," a tendency that has lingering influence upon the historical study of Japanese women. See Helen Hardacre, "Sex and Gender in Women's History in Japan," paper presented to the Annual Meeting of the Association for Asian Studies, Chicago, April 8, 1990.

17. Chungmoo Choi, personal communication.

18. Youngsook Kim Harvey, *Six Korean Women: The Socialization of Shamans*, St. Paul, West Publishing Company, 1979, p. 200.

19. Caplan, *op. cit.*, p. 1.

20. Jung Young Lee, *Korean Shamanistic Rituals*, The Hague, Mouton, 1981.

21. Ibid., p. 174.

22. Ibid., pp. 167–170.

23. Arthur Kleinman, *Patients and Healers in the Context of Culture: An Exploration of the Borderland between Anthropology, Medicine, and Psychiatry*, Berkeley and Los Angeles: University of California Press, 1980. p. 315. "Sexual oppression" has been widely offered as an ultimate, and ultimately circular, explanation for the ethnographic predominance of women in spirit possession. For the most synthesized and intellectually provocative statement of this approach, see I. M. Lewis's, *Ecstatic Religion*, Harmondsworth, Penguin, 1969. The women are assumed to be manipulative, their possession a coercive strategy, although whether this is a conscious or a subconscious motivation is seldom made explicit. For a critique which, like much recent writing on religious activities, argues that possession activities should be understood through the meanings imparted to them by the participants, see Anita Spring, "Epidemiology of Spirit Possession among the Luvale of Zambia," in *Women in Ritual and Symbolic Roles*, J. Hock-Smith and A Spring, eds., New York and Longdon, Plenum Press, pp. 165–190. For a critique specific to the Korean material, see Kendall, 1985, *op. cit.*

24. Melford E. Spiro, *Burmese Supernaturalism*, Englewood Cliffs, New Jersey, Prentice-Hall, Inc., p. 223.

25. Ibid., p. 122.

26. Gregory Bateson and Margaret Mead, *Balinese Character: a Photographic Analysis*, Special Publications of the New York Academy of Sciences, vol. 2, 1942, p. 168.

27. Scheper-Hughes and Lock, *op. cit.*, p. 29.

28. Ibid.

29. Judith Lynne Hanna, *Dance, Sex, and Gender: Signs of Identity, Dominance, Defiance, and Desire*, Chicago and London, University of Chicago Press. 1988, p. 19.

30. Mikhail Bakhtin, *Rabelais and His World*, H. Isowolsky, trans., Cambridge, Mass., MIT Press, 1968 [1965], pp. 38–39.

31. Jean Comaroff, 1985, *Body of Power, Spirit of Resistance: The Culture and History of a South African People*, Chicago, University of Chicago Press, pp. 6–7.

32. Comaroff, *op. cit.*, p. 111.

33. Alfred Gell, *Metamorphosis of the Cassowaries: Umeda Society, Language, and Ritual*, New Jersey, Humanities Press Inc., 1975, p. 234.

34. Eric Ten Raa, "The Moon as a Symbol of Life and Fertility in Sandawe Throught," *Africa*, vol. 39, 1969, p. 38.

35. Hanna, 1988, *op. cit.*, p. 13.

36. Comaroff, *op. cit.*, p. 151.

37. Frederique Apffel Marglin, *Wives of the God-king: The Rituals of the Devadasis of Puri*, Delhi, Oxford University Press, 1985, p. 19.

38. Ibid., pp. 8–9. As in India, Korean dance has been recontextualized as an icon of "Korean tradition," taught to respectable young women in studios and university dance departments. Following Foucaultian logic, dancing could now be viewed as an instrument of discipline in the construction of Korean or Indian femininity.

39. Amanda Porterfield, "Shamanism: A Psychosocial Definition," *Journal of the American Academy of Religion*, vol. 55, no. 4, 1987, pp. 721–739.

40. Kendall, 1991, *op. cit.*

41. In summoning the gods, the shaman begins a slow and ordinary dance, broken by a sudden leap encouraged by a sudden burst of rapid drumbeats. The dancer continues to jump, rotating on the balls of her feet, pumping her arms up and down. When the dancer is a client who has borrowed the shaman's costume to entertain her personal spirits, this activity is sufficient. The client jumps to exhaustion, save on those rare occasions where her body-governing god chooses to gesture or speak. When the shaman stops jumping, however, she mimes, sings, and speaks in the persona of the god.

42. One can find explicit representations of sexual acts and possible erotic glosses in some more specialized Korean dances. Korean masked dance dramas seem to suggest sexual intercourse when two characters place their arms on each others' shoulders and rock from side to side, provoking humor rather than titillation. The multi-drum dance, performed as the grand finale of nearly every recital of "traditional Korean dance," has erotic overtones. The dance is said to express the Buddhist initiate's religious fervor but is also associated with the legend of a famous courtesan who performed it to the distraction of a hypocritically lustful monk, as described by Alan C. Heyman, *op. cit.* It is almost invariably performed by a woman, but is taught now at dancing schools servicing the middle class and in university dance departments.

43. As the shaman Yongsu's Mother said, after knocking an importunate male customer against the wall, "Oh, that wasn't me, it was the honorable Official [the possessing spirit] who did that." See Kendall, 1985, *op. cit.*, p. 61.

44. Hanna, *op. cit.,* pp. 46, 71–72.

45. Ibid., p. 22.

46. Ibid., p. 70.

47. Ch'oe and Chang indicate that men used to gather and amuse themselves at the home of the *mansin,* Cho Yong-ja, until her son took up residence. The *mansin* recalls the village chief's proposition as a grievous insult. See Ch'oe Kil-sÚng and Chang Chu-gun, *KyÚnggido chiyÚk musok* (Regional shaman practices of KyÚnggi Province), Seoul, Ministry of Culture, 1967, pp. 32–33, 54). In folklore circles I have heard it said that shamans used also to serve as itinerant prostitutes, but I have no corroborating evidence. The novels of Kim Tongni portray the shaman as a woman who casually enters sexual liaisons.

48. See Kendall, 1985, *op. cit.,* pp. 61–62.

49. See "Korean Mudang and Pansu," *Korea Review,* vol. 3, 1903, p. 147.

50. For descriptions of shamanic practices in dynastic times, as gleaned from old records, see Yi Nung-hwa, *ChosÚn musok ko* (Reflections on Korean shamanism), translated into modern Korean by Yi Chae-gon, Seoul, Paengnôk, 1976 [1927]. In historical references to shaman rituals on Cheju Island before the ChosÚn period (1392–1910), men and women together celebrated communal rituals "in the form of gregarious songs and dances." See Chang Chu-gun, *Kankoku no mingan sinko* (Korean Folk Beliefs), Tokyo, Kinkasha, 1973, English summary, p. 12. Chang argues that the gendered dichotomy of Confucian rites for men and folk religious practices for women was a consequence of the Confucian transformation of Korean society during the ChosÚn period. If this local example can be expanded, and if these heterosexual songs and dances can be shown as fundamental to the ritual and not the sideline activities of more recent times, then perhaps one finds the Korean equivalent of a Bakhtinian carnival undermined by the imposition of a new moral hegemony. This would be an intriguing example, innocent of missionary influence and Western-derived values.

51. Watching one such performance, I realized that the shaman had borrowed some of the lines from the childbirth scene in the Yangju Masked Dance Drama which is still, despite self-censorship, a creditably Bakhtinian celebration of bodily life. In abbreviated contemporary *kut,* the final send-off of wandering ghosts is greeted with sighs of impatience from other members of the shaman team, anxious to finish up and get home.

52. Butler, *op. cit.,* p. 124.

53. Rosalind C. Morris, " ALL MADE UP: Performance Theory and the New Anthropology of Sex and Gender," *Annual Review of Anthropology,* vol. 24, 1995, pp. 567–592.

54. Butler, *op. cit.;* Williams, *op. cit.;* and also Jennifer Robertson, "Doing and Undoing 'Female' and 'Male' in Japan: The Takarazuka Revue," in *Japanese Social Organization,* Takie Sugiyama Lebra, ed., Honolulu, University of Hawaii Press, 1992, pp. 79–107.

55. Clifford Geertz, *The Interpretation of Culture,* New York, Basic Books, 1973, p. 82.

56. Kendall 1991/2 *op. cit.*

57. For the changing sexual discourses of young Korean women, see So-Hee Lee, "The Concept of Female Sexuality in Korean Popular Culture," in *Under Construction: The Gendering of Modernity, Class, and Consumption in the Republic of Korea,* L. Kendall, ed., Unpublished ms.

Women, Religion, and Modernization
Tradition and Transformation among Elderly Jews in Israel

Susan Starr Sered

A number of studies have noted the different effects that modernization has upon the lives of women and men (Boserup 1970; Bossen 1975; Etienne and Leacock 1980; Beneria and Sen 1981; Dube, Leacock, and Ardener 1986). The bulk of the current research stresses that with the breakup of the traditional extended family and the introduction of wage labor, women may lose the power that derived from their traditional social and economic expertise, and become deprived of the cooperation and solidarity that kin- and village-based female support networks had formerly provided (for a more positive view see Obbo 1980).

In this article I examine the impact of modernization on women's religious lives. Specifically, I ask whether the models suggested by studies of women's economic and familial lives are applicable to the religious sphere, a question that has received little attention either in studies of religious change, which have focused almost exclusively upon men's lives (Deshen 1970; Douglas 1982; Geertz 1957; Kishimoto 1968; Wilson 1988), or in studies of women and modernization, which have focused primarily upon kinship and/or economic and political change. Throughout, I assume that gender issues are relevant to the study of religious experience (Bynum 1986) and that religion must be seen as "independent, yet interdependent" with social structure, rather than a mere reflection of it (Geertz 1957:53).

I conducted fieldwork during 1984 and 1985 among a group of approximately one hundred elderly Jewish women who frequented the Senior Citizens' Day Center in

Susan Starr Sered, "Women, Religion and Modernization: Tradition and Transformation Among Elderly Jews in Israel," *American Anthropologist* 92(2)m, 1990, pp. 306–318. Not for sale or further reproduction.

Jerusalem. The majority of the women were born in Kurdistan, with smaller numbers having come to Israel from Yemen, Iran, Iraq, Morocco, and Turkey approximately sixty years ago.[1] The traditional Jewish societies from which they came were highly segregated by sex, particularly in the religious sphere. Women and men frequented different sacred spaces—men met at synagogue, women met at homes and at holy tombs. They conducted different religious rituals—men spending time in study or formal Hebrew prayer, women preparing ritual foods. They emphasized different religious goals; the primary religious goal for most women was safeguarding the health and well-being of their families, a goal that was peripheral for men.

At the time of my research, the female-oriented religious tradition of these women was deeply threatened both by modern secular culture and by the institutionalized, masculine religious establishment in Israel. In light of the well-documented economic and social losses suffered by women in many developing societies (cf. Boserup 1970; Bossen 1975; Beneria and Sen 1981), I expected to find that under the attack of modernity the women's religious world was narrowing, their rituals disappearing, their opportunities for religious leadership and self-expression decreasing, and prestige for women in the religious sphere declining. In fact, I found this model insufficient for understanding either the religious experience of the women of my study or, as will be discussed below, the religious lives of women of many other cultures studied by anthropologists and historians of religion.[2]

The diverse women described here have experienced political, social, economic, or ideological upheavals that encouraged, permitted, or forced them to embrace or resist new religious modes. Because of the variety of contexts examined, I use the term "modernization" in a broad sense, indicating situations of accelerated social change (e.g., urbanization, Westernization, and colonization). Following Eisenstadt (1973:23) and Smelser (1971:354), I see the development of wide and nontraditional group identities and associations, increased social differentiation, more specialized and autonomous social units, and various kinds of social disturbances as among the relevant structural characteristics of modernization. All of these dimensions interact with women's experience of religion.

NEW OPPORTUNITIES

Modernization often results in an increase of religious choices for women: where there used to be only the traditional religious framework, a foreign framework may be introduced. In addition, new native or local religions may develop in response to modernization, the traditional all-male religious domain may open to women, and the traditional female religious domain may expand.

The Traditional Male Religion

In the wake of modernization, women sometimes find new opportunities to participate in what were traditionally men's rituals. Many Oriental women in modern Israel have begun attending synagogue and Judaica lessons, two activities that were formerly for men only. In both Yemen and Kurdistan the synagogue was a purely male domain (Katzir 1976:38; Brauer 1947:215). The women I interviewed feel fortunate that women today are able to attend synagogue; they believe that they receive divine "merit" or reward for synagogue attendance. The Judaica lessons that they attend take place three times weekly at the Day Center, and once or twice each week at local synagogues. The women are well aware that in the Jewish world knowledge translates into power. In the Judaica lessons, they learn about Jewish law, history, mythology, and philosophy in a way that their mothers and grandmothers never could. They feel that because of their new Jewish knowledge they are now better Jews, better able to carry out God's will, and better able to accumulate merit on their own behalf and on behalf of their families. Many of the women have even attended literacy classes. While most claim to be too old or "thickheaded"[3] to learn to read, they are happy to know that they can have access to literacy, which was once a male prerogative.

A new type of female religious leader has begun to develop among the Oriental women of Israel, and while as of yet they are few in number, their influence is widely felt. In Jerusalem, a middle-aged and self-educated Yemenite *rabbanit* (rabbi's wife or learned woman) teaches Judaica classes at the Day Center and at a local synagogue. Her teaching consists of reading aloud and explaining passages from the Bible, expounding on details of Jewish ritual observance, and relating miraculous stories taken from written collections. Public teaching that centers around written texts is an innovation for Oriental Jewish women; in the Old Country only men studied from books. The roles that were available in the Old Country for female religious leaders (such as midwife and expert in ceremonies aimed at averting the evil eye) did not necessitate literacy, wide knowledge of Jewish law and history, or extensive intervillage connections.

These innovations in the religious lives of the Oriental women take on greater significance when examined in light of the experiences of women of other, diverse cultures. Powers has found Oglala women on the Pine Ridge Reservation in South Dakota participating in rituals that had once been restricted to males: the Sun Dance, the Vision Quest, and the Sweat Lodge have opened to women (1986:194). In the Yucatan, women curers and chanters of Catholic prayers have now replaced male shamans and reciters (Redfield 1941; also see Silverblatt 1980:177 on 17th-century Andean society). Among the Aowin people of southwest Ghana, women now serve as head mediums, a role that traditionally belonged to men (Ebin 1982). And in modern India, Hindu women "who stay at home often perform the morning worship (*puja*) to the deity in the home shrine, especially in the urban areas, for the hours of the modern work day do not permit men time for traditional ritualism" (Young 1987:98; see Obeyesekere 1978 on Sri Lanka).

The Traditional Female Religion

Evidence shows that the traditional female religious sphere may sometimes acquire new significance or prestige. With modernization, women may come to be seen as guardians of the old ways, as experts in the traditional religion. In a number of interviews, children of the Oriental Jewish women of Jerusalem made comments such as, "My mother is closer to God than I am." "The way my mother does it [religion] is better, but I myself am not strong enough to do it like she does." Even the "modern" children and grandchildren, who consider much of the old women's religion to be "superstition," acknowledge the spiritual potency of their ancestresses and turn to them for information concerning the old ways (especially during life crises).

The elderly Oriental women see themselves, and are seen by their families, as spiritual guardians of their kin. The women are experts both at performing rituals, such as candle-lighting and pilgrimage (see Bilu 1988) on behalf of needy descendants, and at caring for ancestors through, for example, tending graves and collecting blessings in memory of the dead. The female role of spiritual guardianship has expanded in modern society; elderly women are viewed by their children and grandchildren as the most authentic repositories of the ancient traditions. Many of the children and grandchildren do not know exactly how the old women perform the rituals. The women often pray in Arabic, Kurdish, or other languages the younger generation does not know, and the youngsters generally do not accompany the old women to the holy tombs. The old women's sacred knowledge has come to be surrounded by an aura of mystery that was not connected to the rituals in the Old Country. Even the old women's cooking has taken on a new mystique: they proudly describe their traditional foods as needing special knowledge to prepare, "not just anyone can do it."

Working in a variety of contexts on almost every continent, scholars have discovered the critical role of women in preserving the old ways. Even more interesting are the studies describing situations, remarkably similar to that of the Oriental women, in which women's traditional rituals have increased in prestige.

Silverblatt writes that Andean women in the colonial period "were increasingly viewed by indigenous society as the defenders of ancient traditions and thus were encouraged to assume leading roles in the carrying out of native ritual" (1980:177). Shimony finds that nowadays among the Iroquois "the chiefs' matrons [keepers of the wampum beads] have been chosen largely on the basis of their knowledge of Iroquois traditions and their willingness to 'keep things going' " (1980:248). Besides their political roles, they are often sought out as authorities in such nonpolitical contexts as providing names from the stock of lineage or clan names for infants, commemorative feasts, medicinal rituals, and solving family problems. In addition, female faith-keepers, fortune-tellers, and dispensers of traditional herbal cures are influential in the retention of religion (Shimony 1985).

Burman, writing about European immigrant Jewish women in England, 1880–1930, notes that "while the actual [religious] practices of women have undergone relatively little alteration, the significance of these activities has changed. . . . Formerly regarded as peripheral, they now developed as key components in the transmission of a sense of Jewish identity and attachment" (1986:253). In modern Turkey the traditional ritual celebrating the birth of the Prophet Muhammed has changed significantly for men, while "the women seem to have become the repositories of spiritual values to which both women and men subscribe but which, paradoxically, only women can experience with performative immediacy because of their inferior status vis-á-vis past and present religious establishments" (Tapper and Tapper 1987:87).

Two opposing yet complementary trends to seem emerge. On the one hand, women are frequently seen as the guardians of the old ways. On the other hand, women may be ready to jump into the breach left by men who are no longer able or willing to conduct traditional male rituals.

New Religions

Modernization sometimes offers women new opportunities within frameworks of modern or conquering religions.[4] Although the Oriental women who came to Israel and confronted European Judaism and modern Zionism have not self-consciously joined a new and foreign religious framework, they have come into contact with a cultural system that is in many ways alien to both the traditional male and the traditional female religious ways. These women sometimes adopt modern rituals, subtly transforming them to make the new rituals consistent with the traditional female domain. For example, on Tu b'Shvat (the holiday celebrating the new year for trees) the women who attend the Senior Citizens' Day Center were taken on a trip to a new forest to plant saplings. As they placed the young trees in the earth, they made petitions such as, "In the merit of my planting this tree, my family should have good health, there should be peace, everything should be good." Planting trees on Tu b'Shvat is a modern, secular, Zionist act, generally performed by tourists, schoolchildren, or Scouts for the express ecological purpose of reforestation. When it is done by these groups, no accompanying blessing is recited. When the Day Center women planted trees they created a new ritual, drawing upon a traditional conception of the relationship between God and humans, and modern conceptions of forest management and civic duty (cf. Deshen 1970:266).

The women have extended their notion of kin over whom they as women must guard, to include soldiers serving in the Israeli Defense Forces. They bless the soldiers, pray for them, light candles for them, and mention the soldiers when they visit holy tombs. While the actual rituals are almost all traditional ones, the decision to expand the category of kin to include Israeli (including non-Jewish) soldiers is one that the women themselves have made—there was no rabbinical guidance in the matter. In this instance, the modern state of Israel has provided the women with a new arena for religious activity. The women feel great satisfaction in ritually caring for the soldiers: this is a communal activity in which all can participate, and it is one that the women believe is of the utmost importance for the survival of the Jewish people and state. If we can tentatively describe modern Zionism as a "new religion," the women have adopted it most wholeheartedly.

Even more dramatic are instances in which women join religions that are entirely foreign to their traditional cultures. While both intrafamily tension and conflict between the old ways and the new tend to be far more significant in these instances, we may also note remarkable similarities to the Jerusalem case.

Yung-Chung Kim, looking at the spread of both Catholic and Protestant Christianity in Korea, postulates that women especially were drawn to Christianity because it helped break down class and gender barriers, encouraged social innovations, allowed women to participate in religious ritual, provided women with opportunities for education, condemned the double standard of sexual morality, and provided a vision of an afterlife that was meaningful to women (1982:198; see also Blanchard 1975 on Navajo women and Forman 1984 on Oceania). A similar situation has been described regarding mission churches in Zululand: many more women than men attend church, women serve as local church leaders, and in some churches women may act as media for a risen Bantu Christ. Sundkler (1961) suggests several reasons for these phenomena: men feel that clothes and Christianity are "unmanly"; men prefer polygamy, forbidden by the Church; boys are busy looking after cattle and have no time to go to church school; church women's organizations that help women with loans attract many women; in traditional magic and ritual women had only minor roles, whereas in the mission churches the influence of women is enhanced (cf. Bond 1987 on Presbyterian church membership among the Yombe).

New local or native religious structures that offer women increased opportunities may be another effect of modernization. According to

Constantinides (1982), in present-day North-ern Sudan the *zaar* (spirit) cult is an urban phe-nomenon, a mechanism for helping village women adjust to life in the city by offering them opportunities to build social networks with other women, to be cured of a wide range of ailments, and to actively participate in an exciting religious ritual (see also Kennedy 1978:210). For East African women the role of spirit medium in the new spirit-possession Cwezi cults and ceremonies contrasts dramat-ically with their limited participation in pre-colonial religious activity, much of which revolved around lineage cults that represented the husband's patrilineal family (Berger 1976). In Zambia, new local cults of affliction attract mainly women and youths, and most of the adepts and leaders are women. These cults do not concern ancestors and community sym-bols; instead, members come from a number of villages and join for ritual purposes that cut across, rather than reinforce, the structure of local communities (van Binsbergen 1981).

Women are not always more attracted to conquering or new native religions than are men. However, we are able to identify a series of factors that encourage women's participa-tion in new religious frameworks. These include: enhanced ritual and leadership roles for women, especially in instances where women were excluded from significant aspects of the traditional religion (for example, where the traditional religion revolved around a patri-lineal ancestor cult); an emphasis on female education and literacy; support for female con-cerns (such as monogamy); emphasis on heal-ing; an ideology that appeals to women's needs; and improved social networks. In addi-tion, evidence suggests that in new religious movements an emphasis on personal charisma rather than on institutions allows women access to a wider variety of roles (cf. Ruether and McLaughlin 1979).

Female Solidarity

Most studies that mention women's religion in developing societies stress that when the social support networks of neighbors and kin available to women in traditional rural societies break down, women may join cults or churches as a means of creating new relationships. Indeed, Bourguignon suggests that the "appeal of novel religious groups may lie in the oppor-tunity they offer for the creation of private net-works of power, influence and authority in a nondomestic setting" (1980:340). Writing about Navajo women, Blanchard cites field data from a 1951 study and suggests that par-ticipation in the church "provided [women] new sources of involvement, relationship, and entertainment, occasional material benefits . . . , new and satisfying fictive kinship bonds, emo-tional security, and an opportunity for personal recognition and prestigious accomplishment" (1975:46; see also Bell 1983:145 on Australia, Constantinides 1982:195 on the Sudan, Stro-bel 1979 on Mombasa).

My fieldwork among the Oriental women in Jerusalem bears out the connection between religious involvement and social networks. The women of my study come together in the con-text of the Senior Citizens' Day Center. They are of diverse ethnic groups, and most had been housewives for many years, with few opportunities to meet women other than rela-tives and nearby neighbors. In recent years many of their close friends have died, and their neighborhood has become partially gentrified. The Day Center provides them with an oppor-tunity to widen their circle of female friends. Many of the women avow that they come to the Center in order to get out of the house, in order not to be alone, "because I have to do something and not sit at home alone all day."[5]

However, it must be stressed that the mem-bers of the Day Center can choose their own activities (within a budget determined by the Municipality of Jerusalem) and almost all of the activities they select are religious in nature: Judaica lessons, pilgrimage to holy tombs, and holiday celebrations. At day centers in other neighborhoods of Jerusalem the members have chosen to listen to lectures on gerontol-ogy or to hold English classes. And, while the Day Center is run by the Municipality and is open to all senior citizens, only women attend; the occasional man who wanders in looks uncomfortable and does not return. Thus it seems that the women who attend this partic-ular Day Center are actively seeking communal religious involvement in a nontraditional but all-female context. Whatever intention they may verbalize, the actual function of their Day Center involvement is a dramatic expansion of their religious world.

These elderly women have created a new type of female solidarity, but they have created it in order to pursue more active religious lives; other benefits that they receive as a result of their Center membership are by-products. The new network that the women have created by joining the Center cannot be understood as a material mutual-aid society (cf. Cucchiari 1988 on Pentecostals in Sicily).

It seems to me unnecessary reductionism to suppose that women become involved in religious organizations because of economic or social needs. My conversations with the Oriental women indicate that they join the Day Center because they are interested in expanding their religious opportunities; they specifically want the Day Center to organize pilgrimages to holy tombs, not outings to public swimming pools or museums. While not denying that there are social and sometimes economic benefits to new female religious networks, it is neither necessary nor productive to explain women's religiosity as a fallout of economic, social, or psychological factors.

VULNERABILITY OF WOMEN'S RELIGION

Modernization has a paradoxical effect upon women's religious lives, sometimes bringing in its wake a dramatic widening of religious opportunities and sometimes resulting in institutionalized attacks upon women's rituals, "normativization" of male religious structures, and the denigration of women's health and reproductive expertise.

The traditional female-oriented religion of the Oriental women in Jerusalem has suffered a number of direct and indirect attacks at the hands of modern, male-oriented society. The most striking example concerns holy tombs, where Oriental Jewish women have traditionally gone to request the assistance of righteous ancestors. Two of the most widespread and important rituals that women perform at tombs (men generally do not perform these rituals) are lighting candles on behalf of needy family members and leaving the candles to burn next to the tomb, and kissing and touching the tomb in order to establish close contact with the holy person. Because many of the women who visit the tombs are illiterate, such nonbook rituals are crucial to their religious lives.

At a number of tombs in Israel the Ministry of Religion has prohibited the lighting of candles, ostensibly because of fire hazard (although most of the tombs are in solid stone buildings), and asked the male guards at the tombs to enforce this new prohibition. In addition, at one very sacred shrine (the tombs of Shimon Bar Yochai and his son Elazar in Meron) a high metal fence has been erected around the tombs. This fence prevents pilgrims (mostly women) from touching the tomb or from lighting candles next to the tomb. For women, whose traditional religion was intensely relationship-oriented, both in terms of attempts to establish intimacy with deceased ancestors and in terms of rituals aimed at preserving the well-being of beloved descendants, prohibiting candle-lighting and building fences around tombs must be seen as a serious affront.

Cross-culturally, this is not an isolated case. Among certain of the Bari, small indigenous groups in Colombia, modernization (i.e., contact with Western capitalism) has meant a forced transition from egalitarianism to male dominance. In the ritual realm, the Bari traditionally exhibited full sexual symmetry. Their biggest ritual, *Los Cantos*, involved singing and the exchange of gifts by pairs of men and women. In recent years, women no longer participate in *Los Cantos*. Buenaventura-Posso and Brown (1980) see this as part of a constellation of changes including the artificial creation of male chiefs (formerly there were no chiefs), forced breakup of the collective living unit and its replacement by the patriarchal nuclear family with females dependent upon a wage-earning male, elimination of traditional female tasks and shift of women's work from productive to service work, and the usurpation of women's role in healing by distribution of new medicines through male healers chosen by Westerners (see also Silverblatt 1980:171 on Andean society, Bell 1983 on Australia, Forman 1984:161 on Oceania).

Similarly, Davis notes that among the Muang in northern Thailand traditional religious practice reflected a complementarity between the sexes, with male ritual power deriving from knowledge of written texts and female ritual power deriving from the tutelage of matrilineal domestic spirits. However, "In urban and commercially developed areas the importance of matriliny has significantly declined. There are no rites for matrilineal cults in Nan town. One reason for this decline was the introduction of patronymic surnames by the Siamese government" (1984:268).

A common effect of modernization is to define the male sphere as normative for the entire society. This may help explain why so many modernized women have begun participating in traditional male rituals—once the male realm is defined as normative, women may choose or be forced to abandon their traditional female practices in order to take part in the "mainstream" religion.

Women, Superstition, and [Im]modesty

In the modern Islamic world, attacks on both traditional popular Islam and pre-Islamic beliefs are common. The attack is frequently two-pronged, arising from growing secularization and/or the increase in orthodox Islamic beliefs (the result of growing literacy, especially among men, improved transportation allowing more Muslims to visit Mecca, and backlash against modernization). Women's rituals are often the targets of such attacks.

Krulfeld has found that in more modernized Indonesian villages pilgrimage to Mecca has become the most important and prestigious religious enterprise, and almost all pilgrims are male. "The religious pilgrimage was not a goal nor a means to prestige in the traditional *adat*-oriented Sasak villages. In such communities traditional rituals for girls, such as ear-piercing and tooth-filing ceremonies, counterbalanced the male circumcision ceremonies" (Krulfeld

1986: 199–200). In traditional villages there were a number of roles for female ritual experts: heads of *adat* houses, spirit mediums for particular holy places, *lontar* palm book changers, toothfilers, ear-piercing experts, weavers of holy name cloths woven at the birth of each child. "No such positions existed in the modernized villages" (Krulfeld 1986:200).[6]

Among the Nubian, "In the period just prior to . . . [Kennedy's] study the dancing of women in the *mawlid* [popular Islamic ritual on a sheikh's birthday] had been subject to a great deal of criticism because of a growing belief that it was anti-Islamic and immodest. . . . Thus in 1963 [for the first time] some men entered the dancing circle and imitated the movements of the women" (Kennedy 1978:92). McGilvray (1982) found that among Moors in Sri Lanka public observance of female puberty rituals has disappeared in major coastal settlements. She suspects that Moorish modesty about female puberty has increased in recent years because of the spread of greater pan-Islamic consciousness—Islamic respectability means more emphasis on the seclusion of women. For a Hindu variation on a similar theme, we can look at the decline of female temple dancers, the *devadasis* of Puri. With the introduction of European morality, the dancers became branded as prostitutes, and their dances have been coopted by non-*devadasis* who perform them in government-supported theaters (Marglin 1985).

More Rituals, Less Power

In the first part of this article, whenever I have pointed to widening religious opportunities for women I have in fact been looking primarily at quantity—women have more niches in the multilayered modern religious world. However, this discussion has not adequately addressed the status and power of those niches. While it seems that with modernization women may increase their ritual repertoire, it is not clear that a quantitative increase always translates into more power (spiritual or profane) or more success at thinking about and working out ultimate concerns. In fact, a frequent effect of modernization is to change the meaning of women's rituals from acts that are necessary for the well-being of the entire community, to acts that effect only the individual women themselves. Modernization may mean that women's traditional rituals are now evaluated in light of "modern" knowledge, and modern "wisdom" often labels women's religion as irrational superstition, or even witchcraft.

Rabbis and *rabbaniot* (pl. fem. form of rabbi) bombard the Oriental women of Jerusalem with admonishments to ask a (male) rabbi or (male) scholar whenever they have questions about Jewish ritual observances. These women were not accustomed to turning to a male authority in order to properly conduct their religious lives. In the Old Country, men and women did not participate jointly in most religious rituals, and women were usually in charge of female matters such as *kashrut* (food taboos), menstrual taboos, and women's mourning rituals (Brauer 1947:161–162). In modern society, much of this has been taken out of female hands. For example, nowadays the ritual baths (for immersion after menstruation and childbirth) are run by the centralized, male religious establishment, and women working at the baths are repeatedly instructed to call a male rabbi anytime a slightly unusual or unclear case comes up.

Rituals to avert the evil eye, many of which were female rituals in the Old Country, are often no longer perceived as necessary for the well-being of the community. Young couples getting married today may permit their grandmothers to smear henna on their hands (a traditional fertility ritual), they may even enjoy the ritual as a way of strengthening ethnic identity, but this smearing is no longer seen as an absolute prerequisite for the future fertility of the couple and the well-being of the community. In the Old Country the line between official required-by-Jewish-law observances, and folk, unofficial, not-required-by-Jewish-law rituals was all but nonexistent.[7] It is in modern Israel that many of the traditional female rituals have come to be seen as "old wives' tales."

Strobel describes a parallel situation in Mombasa, where female puberty rites changed when they moved to an urban environment. In the traditional rites, "the women in charge of [the Bemba] ceremony were convinced that they were causing supernatural changes to take place in the girls under their care. . . . In contrast, the Mombasa *makungwi* express little mystical or magical intent. Rather, the rites are expected to instill good manners in the adolescent through fear" (Strobel 1979:209). Strobel suggests a number of reasons for this shift, including the decline of the importance of matrilineality and tribal history in the city. And, "in an agricultural village the emphasis on fertility in puberty rites pertains to crops as well as human beings, for livelihood depends on the fertility of the soil. In an urban environment this facet of the rites is greatly diminished" (1979:210; see also Forman 1984:156–157 on Oceania).

Writing about Australia, Bell argues that "expanded possibilities for ritual displays and assertions of women's solidarity are not necessarily signs of an increase in women's status in the wider society of the Northern Territory" (1983:145). "[T]here is no way in which women can restore the responsibility they enjoyed in the past for good health, happiness and harmony, for their independent base for action has been undermined by loss of land. In the process women's confidence that they can effectively maintain good health, has been seriously shaken" (1983:151).

In many societies the decline of the midwife as a female ritual specialist with expertise both in health care and in religion has had a profound effect on women's religious power (see Paul and Paul 1975 on the role of midwife in traditional Guatemalan society; Cosminsky 1982 on the decline of Guatemalan midwives). As modern technology penetrates the traditional female reproductive sphere—a sphere that was both physical and spiritual—women may lose important specialist functions. Not only midwives, but fertility, infertility, and child health experts become replaced by modern medical personnel, and women's traditional knowledge becomes denigrated. The medicalization and resultant despiritualization of childbirth and fertility—relating to birth as a biotechnical rather than a magical-spiritual event—has, in many cases, undermined one of the most important treasuries of female religious power.

CONCLUSION

The studies cited here indicate that in response to modernization women's religion is vulnerable, tenacious, and creative. I have argued that the vulnerability stems from institutionalized attacks upon women's traditional domain, from defining the male as normative, from legitimizing only the male religious sphere, and from the devaluation of certain areas of traditional female expertise. These are all external factors. I now suggest that the tenacity stems from the very nature of women's religion: women's religion is often domestic; personal both in its structure and in its aims; hidden from the view of male missionaries, priests, politicians, and anthropologists; and above all, flexible.

Myerhoff defines the little tradition, or domestic religion, as the unsystematized, not elaborately idealized oral tradition practiced constantly and often unconsciously by ordinary people without external enforcement or interference. "Its potential for being sacred comes from its being throughly embedded in a culture. Its authority comes from its being totally internalized in peoples' psyches" (1979:256). The domestic nature of much of the religious experience of Oriental Jewish women means that women are in charge of many of the religious symbols and rituals that reach people at the basic or "gut" level of emotion and childhood memories. In particular, the role of food in religious observance should not be underestimated. Many of the second- and third-generation secular Israelis whom I interviewed declared that the one type of ritual they still find meaningful is the consumption of traditional foods; the aroma of nut cookies baking, the texture of *Shavuot* rice pudding, and the taste of the Sabbath afternoon stew are not easily eradicated. And it is women who have the specialized expertise that the preparation of these foods demands (see also Kaplan 1982 on Jewish women in Imperial Germany).

The personal nature of women's religion is another key factor in its tenacity. It may be relatively simple to convince someone that a different doctrine is "truer," or to force someone to accept a powerful ecclesiastical hierarchy.

However, the myriad of rituals performed by women to protect their babies are often private, personal rituals, performed outside of the formal, official religious structure, and filled with strong emotive power. My data from Jerusalem show that most of the daughters and granddaughters of the Day Center women have rejected most formal and legal Jewish observances (for example, they drive on the Sabbath), yet they continue to place protective amulets beneath the mattresses of their babies' cribs. Women who may be willing to risk their hypothetical happiness in the world to come would not think of taking a gamble concerning the well-being of their children.

The fact that women's religion is sometimes invisible to modern secular and religious establishments may mean that it can sometimes avoid direct attacks; missionaries can only propagandize against rituals that they know of. Rabbis may not like the almost silent invocations against the evil eye spontaneously muttered by Oriental women at all sorts of occasions, but there is no real way of preventing their whispering.

It seems likely that because women frequently stand on the fringes and sidelines of institutionalized religion, and because women often lack access to sacred texts, women can more easily both absorb new rituals and discard old rituals. The Day Center women, who cannot read, describe all religious rituals as "written in the Torah." Because they in fact cannot know exactly what is written in the Torah, they do not feel a need to consult rabbinical authorities before adding new rituals, such as tree-planting, to their repertoire.

A certain flexibility, an ability to reinterpret, seems to be a common characteristic of female religiosity (in patriarchal societies). For the Oriental women of Jerusalem, safeguarding the health and fertility of their descendants is a major religious concern. With the advent of Western medicine, the women's traditional herbal and ritual efforts on behalf of their offspring have become less valued. However, because the women's traditional approach to health and fertility allowed for the use of very eclectic means, they have been able to reinterpret and refocus their ritual activity. Mothers and grandmothers are no longer the primary dispensers of medical care, and the old women profess that if one is sick, infertile, or about to give birth it is advisable to consult a Western doctor. However, "None of it will help if God has decreed the opposite." Instead of providing direct medical assistance, the elderly women now devote a great deal of time, energy, and expertise to influencing God to grant good decrees.

When the Israeli Ministry of Religion erected metal fences around certain holy tombs and prohibited candle-lighting in the area of the tombs, Oriental women spontaneously created a new ritual. Many women began to throw unlit candles through the holes in the fences. This sort of institutionalized attack followed by female creativity may well serve as a paradigm for the ways in which women experience modernization in their religious lives. Despite the evidence for suppression and denigration of women's rituals, we frequently find women expanding their religious worlds in directions that they find satisfying and meaningful. Indeed, there is no simple, unidimensional model for understanding the impact of modernization upon women's religious lives.

NOTES

Acknowledgments. I would like to thank Daphna Izraeli, Michael Harrison, and the *American Anthropologist* editor and reviewers for their help with this article. I am also grateful to the many superb anthropologists and historians of religion whose work I have cited here.

1. The exact Center population was somewhat fluid from day to day, season to season, and activity to activity. I use the term "Oriental" (*mizrachi*) to refer to Jews of Asian origin. While stereotypes persist, the significance of ethnic differences has greatly declined in recent decades (Zenner 1965:133). There are no major studies of the religious lives of Jewish women in Asia. On Kurdish Jewry see Brauer 1947; on Yemenite Jewry see Gilad 1982; on Turkey see Garnett 1893. While my informants remember Jewish life in the Old Country, they tend to romanticize certain elements. Therefore, my picture of Old Country Jewry is drawn both from the memories of my informants and from whatever written sources are available.

2. My field study was qualitative in nature and these particular women are not meant to be seen as representative of Jewish women of other age and ethnic groups (on Ashkenazi women in modern society see Berger-Sofer 1979; Kaplan 1982). My ideas concerning women, religion, and modernization grow out of my own fieldwork and my reading of the available ethnographic and historical literature concerning women of other cultures.

3. At least half of the women had attended literacy classes at some point, but none have attained a level of functional literacy. Most of the information cited in this article was gathered at small group interviews. Quotation marks indicate my translation of a remark made in Hebrew by a particular woman. Where I have summarized a point agreed upon by a group of women I have not used quotation marks.

4. I am somewhat arbitrarily using the term "modern religion" to describe the conquering non-native religion. Most of the cases in this article involve Christianity or Islam as "conquering" religions.

5. In fact, few of the women sit home alone; children and grandchildren visit and phone daily. In Jerusalem there are other types of gathering places for senior citizens that would equally well provide them with a place to go in order to get out of the house and make new friends.

6. Almost all of the examples of modern religion enhancing opportunities for women concern Christianity as the conquering religion. Almost all of the examples of suppression of women's rituals concern Islam. However, because the data I have collected are so sporadic (this is the first study of these issues), I am at this point hesitant to draw any theological or sociological conclusions.

7. The Day Center women frequently demonstrated their ignorance of or disinterest in differentiating between rituals required by Jewish law and rituals not required by Jewish law. For example, when they are served bread for their snack at the Day Center, none of the women perform the legally required hand-washing ritual. However, they cover their arms to their wrists in synagogue "because we must." In fact, Jewish law does not require this.

REFERENCES CITED

Bell, Diane
1983 Daughters of the Dreaming. Melbourne: McPhee Gribble/George Allen and Unwin.

Beneria, Lourdes, and Gita Sen
1981 Accumulation, Reproduction, and Women's Role in Economic Development: Boserup Revisited. Signs 7:279–298.

Berger, Iris
1976 Rebels or Status-Seekers? Women as Spirit Mediums in East Africa. *In* Women in Africa. Nancy Hafkin and Edna Bay, eds. Pp. 157–181. Stanford, CA: Stanford University Press.

Berger-Sofer, Rhonda
1979 Pious Women: A Study of Women's Roles in a Hassidic and Pious Community: Mea She'arim. Ph.D. dissertation, Rutgers University.

Bilu, Yoram
1988 The Inner Limits of Communitas: A Covert Dimension of Pilgrimage Experience. Ethos 16:302–325.

Blanchard, Kendall
1975 Changing Sex Roles and Protestantism among the Navajo Women in Ramah. Journal for the Scientific Study of Religion 14:43–50.

Bond, George C.
1987 Ancestors and Protestants: Religious Coexistence in the Social Field of a Zambian Community. American Ethnologist 14:55–72.

Boserup, Esther
1970 Women's Role in Economic Development. London: George Allen and Unwin.

Bossen, Laurel
1975 Women in Modernizing Societies. American Ethnologist 2:587–601.

Bourguignon, Erika, ed.
1980 A World of Women. New York: Praeger.

Brauer, A.
1947 Jews of Kurdistan. Jerusalem: HaMaarav Press.

Buenaventura-Posso, Elisa, and Susan E. Brown
1980 Forced Transition from Egalitarianism to Male Dominance: The Bari of Colombia. *In* Women and Colonization, Anthropological Perspectives. Mona Etienne and Eleanor Leacock, eds. Pp. 109–33. New York: Praeger.

Burman, Rickie
1986 "She Looketh Well to the Ways of Her Household": The Changing Role of Jewish Women in Religious Life, c. 1880–1930. *In* Religion in the Lives of English Women, 1760–1930. Gail Malmgreen, ed. Pp. 234–259. Bloomington: Indiana University Press.

Bynum, Carol Walker
1986 Introduction: The Complexity of Symbols. *In* Gender and Religion. Carol Walker Bynum, Stevan Harrell, and Paula Richman, eds. Pp. 1–22. Boston: Beacon Press.

Constantinides, Pamela
1982 Women's Spirit Possession and Urban Adaptation in the Muslim Northern Sudan. *In* Women United, Women Divided. Patricia Caplan and Janet Bujra, eds. Pp. 185–205. Bloomington: Indiana University Press.

Cosminsky, S.
1982 Childbirth and Change: A Guatemalan Study. *In* Ethnography of Fertility and Birth. Carol MacCormack, ed. Pp. 205–229. London: Academic Press.

Cucchiari, Salvatore
1988 "Adapted for Heaven": Conversion and Culture in Western Sicily. American Ethnologist 15:417–441.

Davis, Richard
1984 Muang Matrifocality. Mankind 14:263–271.

Deshen, Shlomo
1970 On Religious Change: The Situational Analysis of Symbolic Action. Comparative Studies in Society and History 12:260–274.

Douglas, Mary
1982 The Effects of Modernization on Religious Change. Daedalus 111:1–19.

Dube, Leela, Eleanor Leacock, and Shirley Ardener, eds.
1986 Visibility and Power: Essays on Women in Society and Development. Delhi: Oxford University Press.

Ebin, V.
1982 Interpretation of Infertility: The Aowin People of South-West Ghana. *In* Ethnography of Fertility and Birth. Carol MacCormack, ed. Pp. 141–159. London: Academic Press.

Eisenstadt, S. N.
1973 Tradition, Change, and Modernity. New York: John Wiley and Sons.

Etienne, Mona, and Eleanor Leacock, eds.
1980 Women and Colonization, Anthropological Perspectives. New York: Praeger.

Forman, Charles W.
1984 "Sing to the Lord a New Song": Women in the Churches of Oceania. *In* Rethinking Women's Roles, Perspectives from the Pacific. Denise O'Brien and Sharon Tiffany, eds. Pp. 153–172. Berkeley: University of California Press.

Garnett, Lucy
1893 The Women of Turkey and Their Folklore. London: David Nutt.

Geertz, Clifford
1957 Ritual and Social Change: A Javanese Example. American Anthropologist 59:32–54.

Gilad, Lisa
1982 Yemini Jewish Women. Ph.D. dissertation, Cambridge University.

Kaplan, Marian
1982　Tradition and Transition: The Acculturation, Assimilation, and Integration of Jews
in Imperial Germany—A Gender Analysis.
Leo Baeck Institute Year Book, pp. 3–35.

Katzir, Yael
1976　The Effects of Resettlement on the Status
and Role of Yemini Women: The Case of
Ramat Oranim, Israel. Ph.D. dissertation,
University of California.

Kennedy, John G.
1978　Nubian Ceremonial Life. Berkeley/Cairo:
University of California Press/American
University in Cairo Press.

Kim, Yung-Chung
1982　Women of Korea: A History from Ancient
Times to 1945. Seoul: Ewha Woman's University Press.

Kishimoto, Hideo
1968　Urbanization and Jinja Shinto in Japan. *In*
Proceedings of the XIth International Congress of the International Association for
the History of Religions, Vol. 1. Pp.
117–126. Leiden: E. J. Brill.

Krulfeld, Ruth
1986　Sasak Attitudes Towards Polygyny and the
Changing Position of Women in Sasak Peas-
ant Villages. *In* Visibility and Power: Essays
on Women in Society and Development.
Leela Dube, Eleanor Leacock, and Shirley
Ardener, eds. Pp. 194–208. Delhi: Oxford
University Press.

Marglin, Frederique Apffel
1985　Wives of the God-King, The Rituals of the
Devadasis of Puri. Delhi: Oxford University
Press.

McGilvray, D. B.
1982　Sexual Power and Fertility in Sri Lanka: Bat-
ticaloa Tamils and Moors, *In* Ethnography
of Fertility and Birth. Carol MacCormack,
ed. Pp. 25–73. London: Academic Press.

Myerhoff, Barbara
1979　Number Our Days. New York: E. P. Dutton.

Obbo, Christine
1980　African Women: Their Struggle for Economic Independence. London: Zed Press.

Obeyesekere, Gananath
1978　The Fire-Walkers of Kataragama: The Rise
of Bhakti Religiosity in Buddhist Sri Lanka.
Journal of Asian Studies 37:457–476.

Paul, Lois, and Benjamin Paul
1975　The Maya Midwife as Sacred Specialist: A
Guatemalan Case. American Ethnologist
2:707–720.

Powers, Marla
1986　Oglala Women. Chicago: University of
Chicago Press.

Redfield, Robert
1941　Folk Culture of the Yucatan. Chicago: University of Chicago Press.

Ruether, Rosemary, and Eleanor McLaughlin, eds.
1979　Women of Spirit, Female Leadership in the
Jewish and Christian Traditions. New York:
Simon and Schuster.

Shimony, Annemarie
1980　Women of Influence and Prestige among
the Native American Iroquois. *In* Unspoken
Worlds: Women's Religious Lives in Non-
Western Cultures. Nancy Falk and Rita
Gross, eds. Pp. 243–259. San Francisco:
Harper and Row.

1985　Iroquois Religion and Women in Historical Perspective. *In* Women, Religion and
Social Change. Yvonne Yazbeck Haddad
and Ellison Banks Findly, eds. Pp. 397–418.
Albany: State University of New York Press.

Silverblatt, Irene
1980　Andean Women under Spanish Rule. *In*
Women and Colonization: Anthropological
Perspectives. Mona Etienne and Eleanor Leacock, eds. Pp. 149–185. New York: J. F. Bergin.

Smelser, Neil J.
1971　Mechanisms of Change and Adjustment to
Change. *In* Economic Development and
Social Change: The Modernization of Village Communities. George Dalton, ed. Pp.
352–374. Garden City, NY: Natural History
Press.

Strobel, Margaret
1979　Muslim Women in Mombasa 1890–1975.
New Haven, CT: Yale University Press.

Sundkler, Bengt
1961　Bantu Prophets in South Africa. London:
Oxford University Press.

Tapper, Nancy, and Richard Tapper
1987　The Birth of the Prophet: Ritual and Gender in Turkish Islam. Man 22:69–92.

van Binsbergen, Wim. M. J.
1981　Religious Change in Zambia. London:
Kegan Paul International.

Wilson, Bryan R.
1988　The Functions of Religion: A Reappraisal.
Religion 18: 199–216.

Young, Katherine K.
1987　Hinduism. *In* Women in World Religions.
Arvind Sharma, ed. Pp. 59–104. Albany:
State University of New York Press.

Zenner, Walter
1965　Syrian Jewish Identification in Israel. Ph.D.
dissertation, Columbia University.

X

Gender, Politics, and Reproduction

All human reproductive behavior is culturally patterned. This cultural patterning includes menstrual beliefs and practices; restrictions on the circumstances in which sexual activity may occur; beliefs and practices surrounding pregnancy, labor, and the postpartum period; understanding and treatment of infertility; and the significance of menopause. Although research on human biological reproduction has been dominated by medical concerns such as normal and abnormal physiological functioning, an increasing anthropological literature emphasizes the centrality of reproduction to global social, political, and economic processes (Ginsburg and Rapp 1995; Sargent and Brettell 1996). Biological reproduction refers to the production of human beings, but this process is always a social activity, leading to the perpetuation of social systems and social relations. The ways in which societies structure human reproductive behavior reflect core social values and principles, informed by changing political and economic conditions (Browner and Sargent 1990: 215).

Much of the available anthropological data on reproduction prior to 1970 is to be found within ethnographies devoted to other subjects. For example, Montagu (1949) analyzed concepts of conception and fetal development among Australian aborigines, and Malinowski (1932) wrote about reproductive concepts and practices among the Trobriand Islanders. Several surveys of ethnographic data on reproduction were compiled, such as Ford's (1964) study of customs surrounding the reproductive cycle or Spencer's (1949–1950) list of reproductive practices around the world.

In the past twenty-five years, anthropologists have sought to use cross-cultural data from preindustrial societies to help resolve women's health problems in the industrialized world (Davis-Floyd and Sargent 1997; Jordan 1978). For example, comparative research on birth practices has raised questions regarding the medicalization of childbirth in the United States. Anthropologists have also involved themselves in international public health efforts to improve maternal and child health around the world. In addition, anthropological research has helped clarify the relationship between population growth and poverty. While some analysts have held the view that overpopulation is a determinant of poverty and the poor must control their fertility to overcome impoverishment, others argue the reverse: People have many children because they are poor (Rubinstein and Lane 1991: 386).

Concern with population growth has often focused on women as the potential users of contraceptives, although women's personal desires to limit fertility may not be translated into action because of opposition from husbands, female relations, or others with influence or decision-making power. In this area of research anthropologists have an important contribution to make in examining such factors as cultural concepts regarding fertility and family size, the value of children, dynamics of decision making within the family and community, and the relationship between women's reproductive and productive roles.

Since the 1970s, anthropological interest has turned to the linkages among cultural constructions of gender, the cultural shaping of motherhood, and reproductive beliefs and practices. In many societies throughout the world the relationship between women's social positions and maternity is clear: A woman becomes adult by child-bearing, and her prestige may be greatly enhanced by bearing numerous male children (Browner and Sargent 1990: 218). Thus, in the Middle East a woman is "raised for marriage and procreation [and] acquires her own social status only by fecundity" (Vieille 1978: 456), while in parts of Africa pressures to be prolific weigh heavily on women (Sargent 1982).

In much of the world infertility is dreaded by men and women alike but is a particular burden to women (Browner and Sargent 1990: 219; Inhorn and Van Balen 2002). Such pressure to reproduce is especially intense in agrarian societies, which have a high demand for labor. However, in many hunter–gatherer and horticultural societies, motherhood and reproduction are less emphasized. As Collier and Rosaldo observe, "Contrary to our expectation that motherhood provides women everywhere with a natural source of emotional satisfaction and cultural value, we found that neither women nor men in very simple societies celebrate women as nurturers or women's unique capacity to give life" (1981: 275).

Just as beliefs and practices regarding fertility are culturally patterned, birth itself is a cultural production (Jordan 1978). As Romalis notes, "The act of giving birth to a child is never simply a physiological act but rather a performance defined by and enacted within a cultural context" (1981: 6). Even in advanced industrial societies such as the United States, childbirth experiences are molded by cultural, political, and economic processes (Martin 1987; Michaelson et al. 1988; Oakley 1980). Studying the cultural patterning of birth practices can illuminate the nature of domestic power relations and the roles of women as reproductive health specialists, and it can increase our understanding of the relations between men and women cross-culturally.

Robbie E. Davis-Floyd (in this book) illustrates how gender ideology is revealed in the management of American pregnancy and birth. Childbirth in the United States is routinized, and it is usually highly technological. Davis-Floyd argues that core beliefs in American society about science, technology, and patriarchy shape American birth. Through the normalizing of high-tech childbirth, a message is conveyed to American women that their bodies are defective machines and that they must therefore rely on more efficient machines to give birth. Drawing on centuries-old Western European notions of nature, culture, and society, today's dominant medical model regards the male body as the ideal body-machine, while the female body is considered abnormal and inherently inadequate. Hospital birth "rituals" work to transform the birthing woman into an "American mother," who has been socialized through the birth experience to accept core values of the society. Thus birth is a cultural rite of passage, in which the patriarchal status quo is reproduced and reaffirmed.

Although reproduction is culturally patterned, not all individuals in a society share reproductive goals. As Browner (1986) points out, reproductive behavior is influenced by the interests of a woman's kin, neighbors, and other members of the community, and these interests may conflict. Government policies regarding the size and distribution of population may differ from the interests of reproducing women. Women's goals in turn may not be shared by their partners or other individuals and groups in the society. Browner examines the ways in which access to power in a society determines how conflicts concerning reproduction are carried out and dealt with by analyzing population practices in a Chinantec-Spanish-speaking township in Oaxaca, Mexico.

In this community the government's policy to encourage fertility reduction was imposed on a preexisting conflict between the local community as a whole, which encouraged increased fertility, and women of the community, who sought to limit family size. Women and men manifested very different attitudes concerning fertility desires: Women sought much smaller families than men. As children increasingly attended school their economic benefits appeared slight to their mothers. Further, women viewed pregnancy as stressful and debilitating. Yet despite these negative views, women felt they could not ignore pressures to reproduce.

Such pressure came from community men, who valued a large population for the defense and well-being of the collectivity, and from women, who, while not desiring more children themselves, wanted other women to bear children in the interests of the group. In spite of the ease of obtaining government contraceptives, women rejected their use. In this cultural, political, and economic context, local women experienced conflict between personal desires to have few children, local pressures to be prolific, and national interests in reducing population growth.

State interests in shaping reproductive strategies are nowhere more evident than in the case of Romania during the Ceausescu regime, as Gail Kligman (in this book) documents in her powerful analysis of official pronatalist policies and citizens' everyday lived experiences. Romanian policy, from the mid-1960s, was one of extreme pronatalism, aimed at supporting a demographic trajectory that would build a strong socialist labor force. In this "political demography," the state engaged in coercive measures to underscore the significance of family and population growth.

As Kligman observes, the bodies of Romanian women became instruments used in the service of the state. According to state rhetoric, women occupied a position of singular value, as mothers (and thus as reproducers of the workforce) and as workers themselves. Mothers who gave birth to and raised many children were honored as socialist heroes. Yet in reality, officially obligatory childbearing in the absence of social supports (job security, childcare, maternity leaves) and in the context of a deteriorating economy generated overwhelming burdens for women and families.

State pronatalist strategies relied heavily on antiabortion legislation, penal sanctions for physicians and women, intrusive public health campaigns and required physical examinations for women of childbearing age, and lack of access to contraception. However, the surge in unwanted births led to abandonment of infants and children to the care of the state. Children institutionalized in state orphanages risked sickness, death, and generalized neglect; ultimately, such children generated an international adoption industry with mixed consequences. This period in Romania's demographic history effectively exemplifies "stratified reproduction" (Ginsburg and Rapp 1995), in which some categories of a population are encouraged to reproduce while others are not. In the Romanian case, the implications of state reproductive policies for women varied by social class, urban or rural residence, and ethnicity. Fundamentally, fertility control was the right of the state rather than that of women or families. However, personal and familial interests led to sometimes desperate measures of resistance in spite of this coercive state pronatalism.

Personal desires for children together with a pronatalist culture and advances in reproductive technology have generated consumer interests of a very different sort in the United States—a demand for surrogate motherhood, as Heléna Ragoné's innovative research details (in this book). Ragoné explores surrogates' stated motivations for becoming surrogate mothers as well as the details of their actual experiences. She describes surrogates' explanations as a cultural script reflecting widely accepted ideas about reproduction, motherhood, and family. In contrast to popular opinion, surrogates deny being motivated by financial gain. Rather, they conceptualize surrogacy as a "gift," a priceless donation to the commissioning couple. The apparent "commodification" of women's bodies represented in surrogate motherhood remains a troubling issue, however. In addition, the recent shift from traditional surrogacy (in which the surrogate contributes an ovum) to gestational surrogacy, where the surrogate gestates the couples' embryos, raises important questions about what constitutes "real" parenthood. Surrogacy challenges the Euro-American emphasis on genetic relatedness and the biological basis of kinship and creates potential conflicts surrounding the claims of different kinds of biological and nonbiological mothers and fathers. Thus surrogacy poses profound challenges to our understandings of kinship, family, and reproduction.

Advanced reproductive technologies, including fetal diagnostic testing and surveillance technologies such as amniocentesis and ultrasound imaging, continue to change values and expectations associated with conception, pregnancy, and birth (Rapp 1999). Critical feminist writings have questioned the excessive medicalization of women's reproductive processes, moving from the earlier focus on technocratic birth described by Davis-Floyd to the rapid developments in reproductive science and technology such as gestational surrogacy. These technologies, more widely available in industrialized societies, are increasingly accessible to populations in other countries as well, where they pose challenging ethical dilemmas as well as opportunities.

Women and men confronting infertility, for example, look to sophisticated medical interventions in the hope of a successful pregnancy outcome (Inhorn and Van Balen 2002; Layne 1999). Inhorn's (1994) rich account of Egyptian women's attempts to overcome infertility inaugurated the expanding anthropological literature on infertility in societies with high-technology medical systems as well as in poorer countries where low-income populations have access principally to low-technology biomedical treatment. Globally, feminists have expressed concern at the gap between the growing availability of the technology and the public understanding of its social, legal, and moral implications. The low success rates of infertility technologies, the high expense, and the physical toll on women have prompted concerns that women's bodies are objectified as sites of medical experimentation.

Ginsburg (1987) also discusses reproduction as a domain of contested moral and medical meanings, using the example of abortion in American culture. She suggests that the focus of this conflict of interests is the relationship among reproduction, nurturance, sex, and gender. Using life histories of pro-life and pro-choice activists in Fargo, North Dakota, she reveals how different historical conditions affect reproductive decisions. The activist protesters in Fargo vie for the power to define womanhood in light of a basic American cultural script in which, in the context of marriage, pregnancy results in childbirth and motherhood. Ginsburg (1987) argues that the struggle over abortion rights is a contest for control over the meanings attached to reproduction in America and suggests that "female social activism in the American context operates to mediate the construction of self and gender with larger social, political, and cultural processes."

Similarly, Whitbeck argues that controversy over abortion rights in the United States must be understood in relation to a cultural context that neglects women's experiences and the status of women as "moral individuals." Rather, American culture regards women and women's bodies as "property to be bartered, bestowed, and used by men" (Whitbeck 1983: 259). Concern with restricting access to abortions derives from the interest of the state or others in power to control women's bodies and their reproductive capacity (Whitbeck 1983: 260).

Whereas Ginsburg discusses how abortion activists seek to define American womanhood in relation to cultural ideals of motherhood and nurturance, Ellen Gruenbaum (in this book) shows that cultural expectations of marriage and motherhood in Sudan form the context for the deeply embedded practice of female genital cutting (FGC). FGC is reported to exist in at least twenty-eight countries, and current estimates are that between 200,000 and 1 million girls experience some form of genital cutting annually. Other estimates suggest that as many as 5 million children are operated on each year (Kouba and Muasher 1985; Sargent 1991; Toubia 1994). The various forms of FGC present serious risks, such as infection and hemorrhage at the time of the procedure and future risks to childbearing; therefore, social scientists, feminists and other local activists, and public health organizations have opposed the practices. However, as Gruenbaum observes, FGC remains highly valued and continues to be most strongly defended by women who carry out the practice.

Women in Sudan derive status and security as wives and mothers. Virginity is a prerequisite for marriage, and in this context clitoridectomy and infibulation, the major forms of FGC, are perceived as protecting morality. Thus, these practices persist because they are linked to the important goal of maintaining the reputation, marriageability, and long-term economic security of daughters. Forty years of policy formulated by the Sudanese government and by international health organizations emphasizing the physically dangerous dimensions of FGC and prohibiting the most extensive forms of the practice have not resulted in its elimination, although conditions seem ripe for change. For anthropologists, FGC has tested the limits of cultural relativism and generated continuing debate about how to respect cultural difference while taking a stance in accord with one's own moral positions.

Miller's discussion of female infanticide and child neglect in North India (1987) is also set in a strongly patrilineal, patriarchal society and again dramatically illustrates ethical conflicts that emerge from prevailing gender ideologies that favor sons and the associated devaluation of daughters. In North India family survival depends on the reproduction of sons for the rural labor force, and preference for male children is evident in substantial ethnographic data documenting discrimination against girls. In this region preferences for male children result in celebrations at the birth of a boy, while a girl's birth goes unremarked. Sex-selective child care and female infanticide also indicate cultural favoring of male children.

Reports of female infanticide in India have occurred since the eighteenth century. There is evidence that a few villages in North India have never raised one daughter. In spite of legislation prohibiting female infanticide, the practice has not totally disappeared, although Miller argues that direct female infanticide has been replaced by indirect infanticide or neglect of female children. Indirect female infanticide is accomplished by nutritional and health care deprivation of female children, a phenomenon also discussed by Charlton (1984). Miller argues that the strong preference for sons in rural North India is related to their economic and social functions.

The preference for male children has important repercussions in the increasing demand for abortion of female fetuses following amniocentesis. For example, in one clinic in North India, 95 percent of female fetuses were aborted following prenatal sex determination. Thus, new reproductive technologies such as amniocentesis are seen to be manipulated by patriarchal interests. Miller suggests that, ultimately, understanding the patriarchal culture of north India may help promote more effective health care and enhanced survival chances for female children.

The readings in this section illustrate the ways in which human reproductive behavior is socially constructed and influenced by global economic and political processes (Ginsburg and Rapp 1991). Rather than perceiving reproductive health in a narrow biological or purely personal framework, cross-cultural research suggests that women's health needs should be addressed in the context of their multifaceted productive, reproductive, and social roles. Consequently, decisions about such reproductive health issues as family size and composition are never left to the individual woman but are influenced by kin, community, and state interests. These interests are often contested with the introduction of new reproductive technologies enabling sophisticated prenatal testing, treatment for infertility, and surrogate mothering. As these technologies increasingly spread throughout the world, their availability will raise important questions regarding cultural definitions of family, gender ideology, and reproductive health.

REFERENCES

Browner, Carole. 1986. "The Politics of Reproduction in a Mexican Village." *Signs* 11 (4): 710–724.

Browner, Carole, and Carolyn Sargent. 1990. "Anthropology and Studies of Human Reproduction." In Thomas M. Johnson and Carolyn Sargent (eds.). *Medical Anthropology: Contemporary Theory and Method*, pp. 215–229. New York: Praeger Publishers.

Charlton, Sue Ellen M. 1984. *Women in Third World Development*. Boulder, CO: Westview Press.

Collier, Jane F., and Michelle Z. Rosaldo. 1981. "Politics and Gender in Simple Societies." In Sherry B. Ortner and Harriet Whitehead (eds.). *Sexual Meanings: The Cultural Construction of Gender and Sexuality*, pp. 275–329. Cambridge, UK: Cambridge University Press.

Davis-Floyd, Robbie, and Carolyn Sargent. 1997. "Introduction: The Anthropology of Birth." In Robbie Davis-Floyd and Carolyn Sargent (eds.). *Childbirth and Authoritative Knowledge*, pp. 1–51. Berkeley: University of California Press.

Ford, Clellan Stearns. 1964. "A Comparative Study of Human Reproduction." *Yale University Publications in Anthropology* No. 32. Human Relations Area Files Press.

Ginsburg, Faye. 1987. "Procreation Stories: Reproduction, Nurturance, and Procreation in Life Narratives of Abortion Activists." *American Ethnologist* 14 (4): 623–636.

Ginsburg, Faye, and Rayna Rapp. 1991. "The Politics of Reproduction." *Annual Review of Anthropology* 20: 311–43.

———. (eds.). 1995. *Conceiving the New World Order: The Global Politics of Reproduction*. Berkeley: University of California Press.

Inhorn, Marcia, 1994. *Quest for Conception*. Philadelphia: University of Pennsylvania Press.

Inhorn, Marcia, and Frank Van Balen. 2002. *Infertility Around the Globe*. Berkeley: University of California Press.

Jordan, Brigitte. 1978. *Birth in Four Cultures*. Montreal: Eden Press Women's Publications.

Kouba, Leonard J., and Judith Muasher. 1985. "Female Circumcision in Africa: An Overview." *African Studies Review* 28 (1): 95–110.

Layne, Linda. 1999. "I Remember the Day I Shopped for Your Layette." In L. Morgan and M. Michaels (eds.). *Fetal Subjects, Feminist Positions*, pp. 251–278. Philadelphia: University of Pennsylvania Press.

Malinowski, Bronislaw. 1932. *The Sexual Life of Savages in Northwestern Melanesia*. London: Routledge and Kegan Paul.

Martin, Emily. 1987. *The Woman in the Body: A Cultural Analysis of Reproduction*. Boston: Beacon Press.

Michaelson, Karen et al. 1988. *Childbirth in America: Anthropological Perspectives*. South Hadley, MA: Bergin and Garvey.

Miller, Barbara. 1987. "Female Infanticide and Child Neglect in Rural India." In Nancy Scheper-Hughes (ed.). *Child Survival*, pp. 95–112. Dordrecht, Holland: D. Reidel Publishing.

Montagu, M. F. Ashley. 1949. "Embryology from Antiquity to the End of the 18th Century." *Ciba Foundation Symposium* 10 (4): 994–1008.

Oakley, Ann. 1980. *Women Confined: Towards a Sociology of Childbirth.* New York: Schocken Books.

Rapp, Rayna. 1999. *Testing Women, Testing the Fetus: The Social Impact of Amniocentesis in America.* New York: Routledge.

Romalis, Shelly (ed.). 1981. *Childbirth: Alternatives to Medical Control.* Austin: University of Texas Press.

Rubinstein, Robert A., and Sandra D. Lane. 1991. "International Health and Development." In Thomas M. Johnson and Carolyn Sargent (eds.). *Medical Anthropology: Contemporary Theory and Method,* pp. 367–391. New York: Praeger Publishers.

Sargent, Carolyn. 1982. *The Cultural Context of Therapeutic Choice.* Dordrecht, Holland: D. Reidel Publishing Company.

———. 1991. "Confronting Patriarchy: The Potential for Advocacy in Medical Anthropology." *Medical Anthropology Quarterly* 5 (1): 24–25.

Sargent, Carolyn F., and Caroline B. Brettell (eds.). 1996. *Gender and Health: An International Perspective.* Upper Saddle River, NJ: Prentice Hall.

Spencer, Robert. 1949–1950. "Introduction to Primitive Obstetrics." *Ciba Foundation Symposium* 11 (3): 1158–1188.

Toubia, Nahid, M.D. 1994. "Female Circumcision as a Public Health Issue." *The New England Journal of Medicine* 331 (11): 712–716

Veille, Paul, 1978. "Iranian Women in Family Alliance and Sexual Politics" in L. Beck and N. Keddie, eds., *Women in the Muslim World* pp 459–477. Cambridge, MA: Harvard University Press.

Whitbeck, Caroline. 1983. The Moral Implication of Regarding Women as People; New Perspectives on Pregnancy and Personhood. In William B. Bondeson et al. (eds.), *Abortion and the Status of the Fetus,* pp 247–272. Dordrecht, Holland: D Reidel Publishing Co.

Gender and Ritual:
Giving Birth the American Way

Robbie E. Davis-Floyd

Although the array of new technologies that radically alter the nature of human reproduction is exponentially increasing, childbirth is still an entirely gendered phenomenon. Because only women have babies, the way a society treats pregnancy and childbirth reveals a great deal about the way that society treats women. The experience of childbirth is unique for every woman, and yet in the United States childbirth is treated in a highly standardized way. No matter how long or short, how easy or hard their labors, the vast majority of American women are hooked up to an electronic fetal monitor and an IV (intravenously administered fluids and/or medication), are encouraged to use pain-relieving drugs, receive an episiotomy (a surgical incision in the vagina to widen the birth outlet in order to prevent tearing) at the moment of birth, and are separated from their babies shortly after birth. Most women also receive doses of the synthetic hormone pitocin to speed their labors, and they give birth flat on their backs. Nearly one-quarter of babies are delivered by Cesarean section.

Many Americans, including most of the doctors and nurses who attend birth, view these procedures as medical necessities. Yet anthropologists regularly describe other, less technological ways to give birth. For example, the Mayan Indians of Highland Chiapas hold onto a rope while squatting for birth, a position that is far more beneficial than the flat-on-your-back-with-your-feet-in-stirrups (lithotomy) position. Mothers in many low-technology cultures give birth sitting, squatting, semi-reclining in their hammocks, or on their hands and knees, and are nurtured through the pain of labor by experienced midwives and supportive female relatives. What then might explain the standardization and technical elaboration of the American birthing process?

One answer emerges from the field of symbolic anthropology. Early in this century, Arnold van Gennep noticed that in many societies around the world, major life transitions are ritualized. These cultural rites of passage make it appear that society itself effects the transformation of the individual. Could this explain the standardization of American birth? I believe the answer is yes.

I came to this conclusion as a result of a study I conducted of American birth between 1983 and 1991. I interviewed over 100 mothers, as well as many of the obstetricians, nurses, childbirth educators, and midwives who attended them.[1] While poring over my interviews, I began to understand that the forces shaping American hospital birth are invisible to us because they stem from the conceptual foundations of our society. I realized that American society's deepest beliefs center on science, technology, patriarchy, and the institutions that control and disseminate them, and that there could be no better transmitter of these core values and beliefs than the hospital procedures so salient in American birth. Through these procedures, American women are repeatedly told, in dozens of visible and invisible ways, that their bodies are defective machines incapable of giving birth without the assistance of these other, male-created, more perfect machines.

RITES OF PASSAGE

A *ritual* is a patterned, repetitive, and symbolic enactment of a cultural belief or value; its primary purpose is alignment of the belief system of the individual with that of society. A *rite of passage* is a series of rituals that move individuals from one social state or status to another as, for example, from girlhood to womanhood, boyhood to manhood, or from the womb to the world of culture. Rites of passage transform both society's perception of individuals and individuals' perceptions of themselves.

Rites of passage generally consist of three stages, originally outlined by van Gennep: (1) *separation* of the individuals from their preceding social state; (2) a period of *transition* in which they are neither one thing nor the other; and (3) an *integration* phase, in which, through various rites of incorporation, they are absorbed into their new social state. In the year-long pregnancy/childbirth rite of passage in American society, the separation phase begins with the woman's first awareness of pregnancy; the transition stage lasts until several days after the birth; and the integration phase ends gradually in the newborn's first few months of life, when the new mother begins to feel that, as one woman put it, she is "mainstreaming it again."

Victor Turner, an anthropologist famous for his writings on ritual, pointed out that the most important feature of all rites of passage is that they place their participants in a transitional realm that has few of the attributes of the past or coming state. Existing in such a non-ordinary realm, he argues, facilitates the gradual psychological opening of the initiates to profound interior change. In many initiation rites involving major transitions into new social roles (such as military basic training), ritualized physical and mental hardships serve to break down initiates' belief systems, leaving them open to new learning and the construction of new cognitive categories.

Birth is an ideal candidate for ritualization of this sort, and is, in fact, used in many societies as a model for structuring other rites of passage. By making the naturally transformative process of birth into a cultural rite of passage, a society can ensure that its basic values will be transmitted to the three new members born out of the birth process: the new baby, the woman reborn into the new social role of mother, and the man reborn as father. The new mother especially must be very clear about these values, as she is generally the one primarily responsible for teaching them to her children, who will be society's new members and the guarantors of its future.

THE CHARACTERISTICS OF RITUAL

Some primary characteristics of ritual are particularly relevant to understanding how the initiatory process of cognitive restructuring is accomplished in hospital birth. We will examine each of these characteristics in order to understand (1) how ritual works; (2) how the natural process of childbirth is transformed in the United States into a cultural rite of passage; and (3) how that transformation works to cement the patriarchal status quo.

Symbolism

Above all else, ritual is symbolic. Ritual works by sending messages in the form of symbols to those who perform and those who observe it. A *symbol* is an object, idea, or action that is loaded with cultural meaning. The left hemisphere of the human brain decodes and analyzes straightforward verbal messages, enabling the recipient to either accept or reject their content. Complex ritual symbols, on the other hand, are received by the right hemisphere of the brain, where they are interpreted holistically. Instead of being analyzed intellectually, a symbol's message will be *felt* through the body and the emotions. Thus, even though recipients may be unaware of incorporating the symbol's message, its ultimate effect may be extremely powerful.

Routine obstetric procedures are highly symbolic. For example, to be seated in a wheelchair upon entering the hospital, as many laboring women are, is to receive through their bodies the symbolic message that they are disabled; to then be put to bed is to receive the symbolic message that they are sick. Although no one pronounces, "You are disabled; you are sick," such graphic demonstrations of disability and illness can be far more powerful than words. Suzanne Sampson told me:

I can remember just almost being in tears by the way they would wheel you in. I would come into

the hospital, on top of this, breathing, you know, all in control. And they slap you in a wheelchair! It made me suddenly feel like maybe I wasn't in control any more.

The intravenous drips commonly attached to the hands or arms of birthing women make a powerful symbolic statement: They are umbilical cords to the hospital. The cord connecting her body to the fluid-filled bottle places the woman in the same relation to the hospital as the baby in her womb is to her. By making her dependent on the institution for her life, the IV conveys to her one of the most profound messages of her initiation experience: In American society, we are all dependent on institutions for our lives. The message is even more compelling in her case, for *she* is the real giver of life. Society and its institutions cannot exist unless women give birth, yet the birthing woman in the hospital is shown, not that she gives life, but rather that the institution does.

A Cognitive Matrix

A *matrix* (from the Latin *mater*, mother), like a womb, is something from within which something else comes. Rituals are not arbitrary; they come from within the belief system of a group. Their primary purpose is to enact, and thereby, to transmit that belief system into the emotions, minds, and bodies of their participants. Thus, analysis of a culture's rituals can lead to a profound understanding of its belief system.

Analysis of the rituals of hospital birth reveals their cognitive matrix to be the *technocratic model* of reality which forms the philosophical basis of both Western biomedicine and American society. All cultures develop technologies. But most do not supervalue their technologies in the particular way that we do. This point is argued clearly by Peter C. Reynolds (1991) in his book *Stealing Fire: The Mythology of the Technocracy* (a *technocracy* is a hierarchical, bureaucratic society driven by an ideology of technological progress). There he discusses how we "improve upon" nature by controlling it through technology. The technocratic model is the paradigm that charters such behavior. Its early forms were originally developed in the 1600s by Descartes, Bacon, and Hobbes, among others. This model assumes that the universe is mechanistic, following predictable laws that the enlightened can discover through science and manipulate through technology, in order to decrease their dependence on nature. In this model, the human body is viewed as a machine that can be taken apart and put back together to ensure proper functioning. In the seventeenth century, the practical utility of this body-as-machine metaphor lay in its separation of body, mind, and soul. The soul could be left to religion, the mind to the philosophers, and the body could be opened up to scientific investigation.

The dominant religious belief systems of Western Europe at that time held that women were inferior to men—closer to nature and feebler both in body and intellect. Consequently, the men who developed the idea of the body-as-machine also firmly established the male body as the prototype of this machine. Insofar as it deviated from the male standard, the female body was regarded as abnormal, inherently defective, and dangerously under the influence of nature.

The metaphor of the body-as-machine and the related image of the female body as a defective machine eventually formed the philosophical foundations of modern obstetrics. Wide cultural acceptance of these metaphors accompanied the demise of the midwife and the rise of the male-attended, mechanically manipulated birth. Obstetrics was thus enjoined by its own conceptual origins to develop tools and technologies for the manipulation and improvement of the inherently defective, and therefore anomalous and dangerous, process of birth.

The rising science of obstetrics ultimately accomplished this goal by adopting the model of the assembly-line production of goods as its template for hospital birth. Accordingly, a woman's reproductive tract came to be treated like a birthing machine by skilled technicians working under semiflexible timetables to meet production and quality control demands. As one fourth-year resident observed:

> We shave 'em, we prep 'em, we hook 'em up to the IV and administer sedation. We deliver the baby, it goes to the nursery, and the mother goes to her room. There's no room for niceties around

here. We just move 'em right on through. It's hard not to see it like an assembly line.

The hospital itself is a highly sophisticated technocratic factory; the more technology the hospital has to offer, the better it is considered to be. Because it is an institution, the hospital constitutes a more significant social unit than an individual or a family. Therefore it can require that the birth process conform more to institutional than personal needs. As one resident explained,

> There is a set, established routine for doing things, usually for the convenience of the doctors and the nurses, and the laboring woman is someone you work around, rather than with.

The most desirable end-product of the birth process is the new social member, the baby; the new mother is a secondary by-product. One obstetrician commented, "It was what we were all trained to always go after—the perfect body. That's what we were trained to produce. The quality of the mother's experience—we rarely thought about that."

Repetition and Redundancy

Ritual is marked by repetition and redundancy. For maximum effectiveness, a ritual concentrates on sending one basic set of messages, repeating it over and over again in different forms. Hospital birth takes place in a series of ritual procedures, many of which convey the same message in different forms. The open and exposing hospital gown, the ID bracelet, the intravenous fluid, the bed in which she is placed—all these convey to the laboring woman that she is dependent on the institution.

She is also reminded in myriad ways of the potential defectiveness of her birthing machine. These include periodic and sometimes continuous electronic monitoring of that machine, frequent manual examinations of her cervix to make sure that it is dilating on schedule, and, if it isn't, administration of the synthetic hormone pitocin to speed up labor so that birth can take place within the required 26 hours.[2] All three of these procedures convey the same messages over and over: *Time is important, you must produce on time, and you cannot do that without technological assistance because your machine is defective.* In the technocracy, we supervalue time. It is only fitting that messages about time's importance should be repeatedly conveyed during the births of new social members.

Cognitive Reduction

In any culture, the intellectual abilities of ritual participants are likely to differ, often markedly. It is not practical for society to design different rituals for persons of different levels of intellectual ability. So ritual utilizes specific techniques, such as rhythmic repetition, to reduce all participants to the same narrower level of cognitive functioning. This low level involves thinking in either/or patterns that do not allow for consideration of options or alternative views.

Four techniques are often employed by ritual to accomplish this end. One is the *repetition* already discussed above. A second is *hazing*, which is familiar to undergraduates who undergo fraternity initiation rites but is also part of rites of passage all over the world. A third is *strange-making*—making the commonplace appear strange by juxtaposing it with the unfamiliar. Fourth is *symbolic inversion*—metaphorically turning things upside-down and inside-out to generate, in a phrase coined by Roger Abrahams (1973), "The power attendant upon confusion."

For example, in the rite of passage of military basic training, the initiate's normal patterns of action and thought are turned topsy-turvy. He is made strange to himself: His head is shaved, so that he does not even recognize himself in the mirror. He must give up his clothes, those expressions of his past individual identity and personality, and put on a uniform identical to that of the other initiates. Constant and apparently meaningless hazing, such as orders to dig six ditches and then fill them in, further breaks down his cognitive structure. Then through repetitive and highly symbolic rituals, such as sleeping with his rifle, the basic values, beliefs, and practices of the Marines are incorporated into his body and his mind.

In medical school and again in residency, the same ritual techniques that transform a youth into a Marine are employed to transform college students into physicians. Reduced from the high status of graduate to the lowly status of first-year medical student, initiates are subjected to hazing techniques of rote memorization of endless facts and formulas, absurdly long hours of work, and intellectual and sensory overload. As one physician explained:

> You go through, in a six-week course, a thousand-page book. You have pop quizzes in two or three courses every day the first year. We'd get up around 6, attend classes till 5, go home and eat, then head back to school and be in anatomy lab working with a cadaver, or something, until 1 or 2 in the morning, and then go home and get a couple of hours sleep, and then go out again.

Subjected to such a process, medical students often gradually lose any broadminded goals of "helping humanity" they had upon entering medical school. A successful rite of passage produces new professional values structured in accordance with the technocratic and scientific values of the dominant medical system. The emotional impact of this cognitive narrowing is aptly summarized by a former resident:

> Most of us went into medical school with pretty humanitarian ideals. I know I did. But the whole process of medical education makes you inhuman. . . . You forget about the rest of life. By the time you get to residency, you end up not caring about anything beyond the latest techniques and most sophisticated tests.

Likewise, the birthing woman is socialized by ritual techniques of cognitive reduction. She is made strange to herself by being dressed in a hospital gown, tagged with an ID bracelet, and by the shaving or clipping of her pubic hair, which symbolically de-sexualizes the lower portion of her body, returning it to a conceptual state of childishness. (In many cultures, sexuality and hair are symbolically linked.) Labor itself is painful, and is often rendered more so by the hazing technique of frequent and very painful insertion of someone's fingers into her vagina to see how far her cervix has dilated. This technique also functions as a strange-making device. Since almost any nurse or resident in need of practice may check her cervix, the birthing woman's most private parts are symbolically inverted into institutional property. One respondent's obstetrician observed, "It's a wonder you didn't get an infection, with so many people sticking their hands inside of you."

Cognitive Stabilization

When humans are subjected to extremes of stress and pain, they may become unreasonable and out of touch with reality. Ritual assuages this condition by giving people a conceptual handle-hold to keep them from "falling apart" or "losing it." When the airplane starts to falter, even passengers who don't go to church are likely to pray! Ritual mediates between cognition and chaos by making reality appear to conform to accepted cognitive categories. In other words, to perform a ritual in the face of chaos is to restore order to the world.

Labor subjects most women to extremes of pain, which are often intensified by the alien and often unsupportive hospital environment. They look to hospital rituals to relieve the distress resulting from their pain and fear. They utilize breathing rituals taught in hospital-sponsored childbirth education classes for cognitive stabilization. They turn to drugs for pain relief, and to the reassuring presence of medical technology for relief from fear. LeAnn Kellog expressed it this way:

> I was terrified when my daughter was born. I just knew I was going to split open and bleed to death right there on the table, but she was coming so fast, they didn't have any time to do anything to me. . . . I like Cesarean sections, because you don't have to be afraid.

When you come from within a belief system, its rituals will comfort and calm you. Accordingly, those women in my study who were in basic agreement with the technocratic model of birth before going into the hospital (70%) expressed general satisfaction with their hospital births.

Order, Formality, and a Sense of Inevitability

Its exaggerated and precise order and formality set ritual apart from other modes of social interaction, enabling it to establish an atmosphere that feels both inevitable and inviolate. To perform a series of rituals is to feel oneself locking onto a set of "cosmic gears" that will safely crank the individual through danger to safety. For example, Trobriand sea fishermen described by anthropologist Bronislaw Malinowski (1954) regularly performed an elaborate series of rituals on the beach before embarking. The fishermen believed that these rituals, when carried out with precision, would obligate the gods of the sea to do their part to bring the fishermen safely home. Likewise, obstetricians, and many birthing women, feel that correct performance of standardized procedures ought to result in a healthy baby. Such rituals generate in humans a sense of confidence that makes it easier to face the challenge and caprice of nature.

When women who have placed their faith in the technocratic model are denied its rituals, they often react with fear and a feeling of being neglected:

> My husband and I got to the hospital, and we thought they would take care of everything. I kept sending my husband out to ask them to give me something for the pain, to check me, but they were short-staffed and they just ignored me until the shift changed in the morning.

Hospital rituals such as electronic monitoring work to give the laboring woman a sense that society is using the best it has to offer—the full force of its technology—to inevitably ensure that she will have a safe birth.

However, once those "cosmic gears" have been set into motion, there is often no stopping them. The very inevitability of hospital procedures makes them almost antithetical to the possibility of normal, natural birth. A "cascade of intervention" occurs when one obstetric procedure alters the natural birthing process, causing complications, and so inexorably "necessitates" the next procedure, and the next. Many of the women in my study experienced such a "cascade" when they received some form of pain relief, such as an epidural, which slowed their labor. Then pitocin was administered through the IV to speed up the labor, but pitocin very suddenly induced longer and stronger contractions.

Unprepared for the additional pain, the women asked for more pain relief, which ultimately necessitated more pitocin. Pitocin-induced contractions, together with the fact that the mother must lie flat on her back because of the electronic monitor belts strapped around her stomach, can cause the supply of blood and oxygen to the fetus to drop, affecting the fetal heart rate. In response to the "distress" registered on the fetal monitor, an emergency Cesarean is performed.

Acting, Stylization, Staging

Ritual's set-apartness is enhanced by the fact that it is usually highly stylized and self-consciously acted, like a part in a play. Most of us can easily accept this view of the careful performances of TV evangelists, but it may come as a surprise that those who perform the rituals of hospital birth are often aware of their dramatic elements. The physician becomes the protagonist. The woman's body is the stage upon which he performs, often for an appreciative audience of medical students, residents, and nurses. Here is how one obstetrician played to a student audience observing the delivery he was performing:

> "In honest-to-God natural conditions babies were *sometimes* born without tearing the perineum and without an episiotomy, but without artificial things like anesthesia and episiotomy, the muscle is torn apart and if it is not cut, it is usually not repaired. Even today, if there is no episiotomy and repair, those women quite often develop a rectocoele and a relaxed vaginal floor. This is what I call the saggy, baggy bottom." (Laughter by the students. A student nurse asks if exercise doesn't help strengthen the perineum.) "No, exercises may be for the birds, but they're not for bottoms. . . . When the woman is bearing down, the leveator muscles of the perineum contract too. This means the baby is caught between the diaphragm and the perineum. Consequently, anesthesia and episiotomy will reduce the pressure on the head, and hopefully, produce more Republicans." (More laughter from the students) (Shaw 1974: 90)

Cognitive Transformation

The goal of most initiatory rites of passage is cognitive transformation. It occurs when the symbolic messages of ritual fuse with individual emotion and belief, and the individual's entire cognitive structure reorganizes around the newly internalized symbolic complex. The following quote from a practicing obstetrician presents the outcome for him of such transformative learning:

> I think my training was valuable. The philosophy was one of teaching one way to do it, and that was the right way. . . . I like the set hard way. I like the riverbanks that confine you in a direction. . . . You learn one thing real well, and that's the way.

For both nascent physicians and nascent mothers, cognitive transformation of the initiate occurs when reality as presented by the technocratic model, and reality as the initiate perceives it, become one and the same. This process is gradual. Routine obstetric procedures cumulatively map the technocratic model of birth onto the birthing woman's perceptions of her labor experience. They align her belief system with that of society.

Take the way many mothers come to think about the electronic fetal monitor, for example. The monitor is a machine that uses ultrasound to measure the strength of the mother's contractions and the rate of the baby's heartbeat through electrodes belted onto the mother's abdomen. This machine has become the symbol of high technology hospital birth. Observers and participants alike report that the monitor, once attached, becomes the focal point of the labor.[3] Nurses, physicians, husbands, and even the mother herself become visually and conceptually glued to the machine, which then shapes their perceptions and interpretations of the birth process. Diana Crosse described her experience this way:

> As soon as I got hooked up to the monitor, all everyone did was stare at it. The nurses didn't even look at me anymore when they came into the room—they went straight to the monitor. I got the weirdest feeling that *it* was having the baby, not me.

This statement illustrates the successful conceptual fusion between the woman's perceptions of her birth experience and the technocratic model. So thoroughly was this model mapped on to her psyche that she began to feel that the machine was having the baby, that she was a mere onlooker. Soon after the monitor was in place, she requested a Cesarean section, declaring that there was "no more point in trying."

Consider the visual and kinesthetic images that the laboring woman experiences—herself in bed, in a hospital gown, staring up at an IV pole, bag, and cord, and down at a steel bed and a huge belt encircling her waist. Her entire sensory field conveys one overwhelming message about our culture's deepest values and beliefs: Technology is supreme, and the individual is utterly dependent upon it.

Internalizing the technocratic model, women come to accept the notion that the female body is inherently defective. This notion then shapes their perceptions of the labor experience, as exemplified by Merry Simpson's story:

> It seemed as though my uterus had suddenly tired! When the nurses in attendance noted a contraction building on the recorder, they instructed me to begin pushing, not waiting for the urge to push, so that by the time the **urge** pervaded, I invariably had no strength remaining but was left gasping and dizzy. . . . I felt suddenly depressed by the fact that labor, which had progressed so uneventfully up to this point, had now become unproductive.

Note that she does not say "The nurses had me pushing too soon," but "My uterus had tired," and labor had "become unproductive." These responses reflect her internalization of the technocratic tenet that when something goes wrong, it is her body's fault.

Affectivity and Intensification

Rituals tend to intensify toward a climax. Behavioral psychologists have long understood that people are far more likely to remember, and to absorb lessons from, those events that carry an emotional charge. The order and stylization of ritual, combined with its rhythmic repetitiveness and the intensification of its messages, methodically create just the sort of highly charged emotional atmosphere that works to ensure long-term learning.

As the moment of birth approaches, the number of ritual procedures performed upon the woman will intensify toward the climax of birth, whether or not her condition warrants such intervention. For example, once the woman's cervix reaches full dilation (10 cm), the nursing staff immediately begins to exhort the woman to push with each contraction, whether or not she actually feels the urge to push. When delivery is imminent, the woman must be transported, often with a great deal of drama and haste, down the hall to the delivery room. Lest the baby be born *en route,* the laboring woman is then exhorted, with equal vigor, *not* to push. Such commands constitute a complete denial of the natural rhythms of the woman's body. They signal that her labor is a mechanical event and that she is subordinate to the institution's expectations and schedule. Similar high drama will pervade the rest of her birthing experience.

Preservation of the Status Quo

A major function of ritual is cultural preservation. Through explicit enactment of a culture's belief system, ritual works both to preserve and to transmit the culture. Preserving the culture includes perpetuating its power structure, so it is usually the case that those in positions of power will have unique control over ritual performance. They will utilize the effectiveness of ritual to reinforce both their own importance and the importance of the belief and value system that legitimizes their positions.

In spite of tremendous advances in equality for women, the United States is still a patriarchy. It is no cultural accident that 99 percent of American women give birth in hospitals, where only physicians, most of whom are male, have final authority over the performance of birth rituals—an authority that reinforces the cultural privileging of patriarchy for both mothers and their medical attendants.

Nowhere is this reality more visible than in the lithotomy position. Despite years of effort on the part of childbirth activists, including many obstetricians, the majority of American women still give birth lying flat on their backs. This position is physiologically dysfunctional. It compresses major blood vessels, lowering the mother's circulation and thus the baby's oxygen supply. It increases the need for forceps because it both narrows the pelvic outlet and ensures that the baby, who must follow the curve of the birth canal, quite literally will be born heading upward, against gravity. This lithotomy position completes the process of symbolic inversion that has been in motion ever since the woman was put into that "upside-down" hospital gown. Her normal bodily patterns are turned, quite literally, upside-down—her legs are in the air, her vagina totally exposed. As the ultimate symbolic inversion, it is ritually appropriate that this position be reserved for the peak tranformational moments of the initiation experience—the birth itself. The doctor—society's official representative—stands in control not at the mother's head nor at her side, but at her bottom, where the baby's head is beginning to emerge.

Structurally speaking, this puts the woman's vagina where her head should be. Such total inversion is perfectly appropriate from a social perspective, as the technocratic model promises us that eventually we will be able to grow babies in machines—that is, have them with our cultural heads instead of our natural bottoms. In our culture, "up" is good and "down" is bad, so the babies born of science and technology must be delivered "up" toward the positively valued cultural world, instead of down toward the negatively valued natural world. Interactionally, the obstetrician is "up" and the birthing woman is "down," an inversion that speaks eloquently to her of her powerlessness and of the power of society at the supreme moment of her own individual transformation.

The episiotomy performed by the obstetrician just before birth also powerfully enacts the status quo in American society. This procedure, performed on over 90 percent of first-time mothers as they give birth, expresses the value and importance of one of our technocratic society's most fundamental markers—the straight line. Through episiotomies, physicians can deconstruct the vagina (stretchy, flexible, part-circular and part-formless, feminine, creative, sexual, non-linear), then reconstruct it in accordance with our cultural belief and value system. Doctors are taught (incorrectly) that straight cuts heal faster than the small jagged tears that sometimes occur during birth. They learn that straight cuts will prevent such

tears, but in fact, episiotomies often cause severe tearing that would not otherwise occur (Klein 1992; Shiono et al. 1990; Thorp and Bowes 1989; Wilcox et al. 1989[4]. These teachings dramatize our Western belief in the superiority of culture over nature. Because it virtually does not exist in nature, the line is most useful in aiding us in our constant conceptual efforts to separate ourselves from nature.

Moreover, since surgery constitutes the ultimate form of manipulation of the human body-machine, it is the most highly valued form of medicine. Routinizing the episiotomy, and increasingly, the Cesarean section, has served both to legitimize and to raise the status of obstetrics as a profession, by ensuring that childbirth will be not a natural but a surgical procedure.

Effecting Social Change

Paradoxically, ritual, with all of its insistence on continuity and order, can be an important factor not only in individual transformation but also in social change. New belief and value systems are most effectively spread through new rituals designed to enact and transmit them; entrenched belief and value systems are most effectively altered through alterations in the rituals that enact them.

Nine percent of my interviewees entered the hospital determined to avoid technocratic rituals in order to have "completely natural childbirth," yet ended up with highly technocratic births. These nine women experienced extreme cognitive dissonance between their previously held self-images and those internalized in the hospital. Most of them suffered severe emotional wounding and short-term post-partum depression as a result. But 15 percent did achieve their goal of natural childbirth, thereby avoiding conceptual fusion with the technocratic model. These women were personally empowered by their birth experiences. They tended to view technology as a resource that they could choose to utilize or ignore, and often consciously subverted their socialization process by replacing technocratic symbols with self-empowering alternatives. For example, they wore their own clothes and ate their own food, rejecting the hospital gown and the IV. They walked the halls instead of going to bed. They chose perineal massage instead of episiotomy, and gave birth like "primitives," sitting up, squatting, or on their hands and knees. One of them, confronted with the wheelchair, said "I don't need this," and used it as a luggage cart. This rejection of customary ritual elements is an exceptionally powerful way to induce change, as it takes advantage of an already charged and dramatic situation.

During the 1970s and early 1980s, the conceptual hegemony of the technocratic model in the hospital was severely challenged by the natural childbirth movement which these 24 women represent. Birth activists succeeded in getting hospitals to allow fathers into labor and delivery rooms, mothers to birth consciously (without being put to sleep), and mothers and babies to room together after birth. They fought for women to have the right to birth without drugs or interventions, to walk around or even be in water during labor (in some hospitals, Jacuzzis were installed). Prospects for change away from the technocratic model of birth by the 1990s seemed bright.

Changing a society's belief and value system by changing the rituals that enact it is possible, but not easy. To counter attempts at change, individuals in positions of authority often intensify the rituals that support the status quo. Thus a response to the threat posed by the natural childbirth movement was to intensify the use of high technology in hospital birth. During the 1980s, periodic electronic monitoring of nearly all women became standard procedure, the epidural rate shot up to 80 percent, and the Cesarean rate rose to nearly 25 percent. Part of the impetus for this technocratic intensification is the increase in malpractice suits against physicians. The threat of lawsuit forces doctors to practice conservatively—that is, in strict accordance with technocratic standards. As one of them explained,

> Certainly I've changed the way I practice since malpractice became an issue. I do more C-sections . . . and more and more tests to cover myself. More expensive stuff. We don't do risky things that women ask for—we're very conservative in our approach to everything. . . . In 1970 before all this came up, my C-section rate was around 4 percent. It has gradually climbed every year since then. In 1985 it was 16 percent, then in 1986 it was 23 percent.

The money goes where the values lie. From this macro-cultural perspective, the increase in malpractice suits emerges as society's effort to make sure that its representatives, the obstetricians, perpetuate our technocratic core value system by continuing through birth rituals to transmit that system. Its perpetuation seems imperative, for in our technology we see the promise of our eventual transcendence of bodily and earthly limitations—already we replace body parts with computerized devices, grow babies in test tubes, build space stations, and continue to pollute the environment in the expectation that someone will develop the technologies to clean it up!

We are all complicitors in our technocratic system, as we have so very much invested in it. Just as that system has given us increasing control over the natural environment, so it has also given not only doctors but also women increasing control over biology and birth. Contemporary middle-class women do have much greater say over what will be done to them during birth than their mothers, most of whom gave birth during the 1950s and 1960s under general anesthesia. When what they demand is in accord with technocratic values, they have a much greater chance of getting it than their sisters have of achieving natural childbirth. Even as hospital birth still perpetuates patriarchy by treating women's bodies as defective machines, it now also reflects women's greater autonomy by allowing them conceptual separation from those defective machines.

Epidural anesthesia is administered in about 80 percent of American hospital births. So common is its use that many childbirth educators are calling the 1990s the age of the "epidural epidemic." As the epidural numbs the birthing woman, eliminating the pain of childbirth, it also graphically demonstrates to her through lived experience the truth of the Cartesian maxim that mind and body are separate, that the biological realm can be completely cut off from the realm of the intellect and the emotions. The epidural is thus the perfect technocratic tool, serving the interests of the technocratic model by transmitting it, and of women choosing to give birth under that model, by enabling them to use it to divorce themselves from their biology:

> Ultimately the decision to have the epidural and the Cesarean while I was in labor was mine. I told my doctor I'd had enough of this labor business and I'd like to . . . get it over with. So he whisked me off to the delivery room and we did it. (Elaine)

For many women, the epidural provides a means by which they can actively witness birth while avoiding "dropping into biology." Explained Joanne, "I'm not real fond of things that remind me I'm a biological creature—I prefer to think and be an intellectual emotional person." Such women tended to define their bodies as tools, vehicles for their minds. They did not enjoy "giving in to biology" to be pregnant, and were happy to be liberated from biology during birth. And they welcomed advances in birth technologies as extensions of their own ability to control nature.

In dramatic contrast, six of my interviewees (6 percent), insisting that "I am my body," rejected the technocratic model altogether. They chose to give birth at home under an alternative paradigm, the *holistic model.* This model stresses the organicity and trustworthiness of the female body, the natural rhythmicity of labor, the integrity of the family, and self-responsibility. These homebirthers see the safety of the baby and the emotional needs of the mother as one. The safest birth for the baby will be the one that provides the most nurturing environment for the mother.[5] Said Ryla,

> I got criticized for choosing a home birth, for not considering the safety of the baby. But that's exactly what I was considering! How could it possibly serve my baby for me to give birth in a place that causes my whole body to tense up in anxiety as soon as I walk in the door?

Although homebirthers constitute only about 2 percent of the American birthing population, their conceptual importance is tremendous, as through the alternative rituals of giving birth at home, they enact—and thus guarantee the existence of—a paradigm of pregnancy and birth based on the value of connection, just as the technocratic model is based on the principle of separation.

The technocratic and holistic models represent opposite ends of a spectrum of beliefs about birth and about cultural life. Their differences are mirrored on a wider scale by the ideological conflicts between biomedicine and holistic healing, and between industrialists and ecological activists. These groups are engaged in a core value struggle over the future—a struggle clearly visible in the profound differences in the rituals they daily enact.

CONCLUSION

Every society in the world has felt the need to thoroughly socialize its citizens into conformity with its norms, and citizens derive many benefits from such socialization. If a culture had to rely on policemen and make sure that everyone would obey its laws, it would disintegrate into chaos, as there would not be enough policemen to go around. It is much more practical for cultures to find ways to socialize their members from the *inside,* by making them *want* to conform to society's norms. Ritual is one major way through which such socialization can be achieved.

American obstetrical procedures can be understood as rituals that facilitate the internalization of cultural values. These procedures are patterned, repetitive, and profoundly symbolic, communicating messages concerning our culture's deepest beliefs about the necessity for cultural control of natural processes. They provide an ordered structure to the chaotic flow of the natural birth process. In so doing, they both enhance the natural affectivity of that process and create a sense of inevitability about their performance. Obstetric interventions are also transformative in intent. They attempt to contain and control the process of birth, and to transform the birthing woman into an American mother who has internalized the core values of this society. Such a mother believes in science, relies on technology, recognizes her biological inferiority (either consciously or unconsciously), and so at some level accepts the principles of patriarchy. She will tend to conform to society's dictates and meet the demands of its institutions, and will teach her children to do the same.

Yet it is important to note that human beings are not automatons. Human behavior varies widely even within the restraints imposed by particular cultures, including their rituals. As July Sanders sums it up:

> It's almost like programming you. You get to the hospital. They put you in this wheelchair. They whisk you off from your husband, and I mean just start in on you. Then they put you in another wheelchair, and send you home. And then they say, well, we need to give you something for the depression. [Laughs] Get away from me! That will help my depression!

Through hospital ritual procedures, obstetrics deconstructs birth, then inverts and reconstructs it as a technocratic process. But unlike most transformations effected by ritual, birth does *not* depend upon the performance of ritual to make it happen. The physiological process of labor itself transports the birthing woman into a naturally transitional situation that carries its own affectivity. Hospital procedures take advantage of that affectivity to transmit the core values of American society to birthing women. From society's perspective, the birth process will not be successful unless the woman and child are properly socialized during the experience, transformed as much by the rituals as by the physiology of birth. In the latter half of this century, women have made great strides in attaining equality with men on many cultural fronts. Yet, as I noted at the beginning, the cultural treatment of birth is one of the most revealing indicators about the status of women in a given society. In the United States, through their ritual transformation during birth, women learn profound lessons about the weakness and defectiveness of their bodies and the power of technology. In this way, every day in hospitals all over the country, women's status as subordinate is subtly reinforced, as is the patriarchal nature of the technocracy.

REFERENCES

Abrahams, Roger D. 1973. "Ritual for Fun and Profit (or The Ends and Outs of Celebration)." Paper delivered at the Burg Wartenstein Symposium No. 59, on "Ritual: Reconciliation in Change." New York: Wenner-Gren Foundation for Anthropological Research.

Davis-Floyd, Robbie E. 1992. *Birth as an American Rite of Passage*. Berkeley: University of California Press.

Goer, Henci. 1995. *Obstetric Myths Versus Research Realities: A Guide to the Medical Literature*. Westport, CT: Bergin and Garvey.

Jordan, Brigitte. 1993. *Birth in Four Cultures: A Cross-Cultural Investigation of Birth in Yucatan, Holland, Sweden and the United States* (4th edition revised). Prospect Heights IL: Waveland Press.

Klein, Michael et al. 1992. "Does Episiotomy Prevent Perineal Trauma and Pelvic Floor Relaxation?" *Online Journal of Current Clinical Trials* 1 (Document 10).

Leveno K. J., F. G. Cunningham, S. Nelson, M. Roark, M. L. Williams, D. Guzick, S. Dowling, C. R. Rosenfeld, A. Buckley. 1986. "A Prospective Comparison of Selective and Universal Electronic Fetal Monitoring in 34,995 Pregnancies." *New England Journal of Medicine* 315 (10): 615–619.

Malinowski, Bronislaw. 1954. (orig. pub. 1925). "Magic, Science, and Religion." In *Magic, Science and Religion and Other Essays*, pp. 17–87. New York: Doubleday/Anchor.

Prentice, A. and T. Lind. 1987. "Fetal Heart Rate Monitoring During Labor—Too Frequent Intervention, Too Little Benefit." *Lancet* 2: 1375–1877.

Reynolds, Peter C. 1991. *Stealing Fire: The Mythology of the Technocracy*. Palo Alto, CA: Iconic Anthropology Press.

Sandmire, H. F. 1990. "Whither Electronic Fetal Monitoring?" *Obstetrics and Gynecology* 76 (6): 1130–1134.

Shaw, Nancy Stoller. 1974. *Forced Labor: Maternity Care in the United States*. New York: Pergamon Press.

Shy, Kirkwood, David A. Luthy, Forrest C. Bennett, Michael Whitfield, Eric B. Larson, Gerald van Belle, James P. Hughes, Judith A. Wilson, Martin A. Stenchever. 1990. "Effects of Electronic Fetal Heart Rate Monitoring, as Compared with Periodic Auscultation, on the Neurologic Development of Premature Infants." *New England Journal of Medicine* 322 (9): 588–593.

Thorp, J. M. and W. A. Bowes. 1989. "Episiotomy: Can Its Routine Use Be Defended?" *American*

Journal of Obstetrics and Gynecology 160 (5Pt1): 1027–1030.

Turner, Victor. 1979. (orig. pub. 1964). "Betwixt and Between: The Liminal Period in Rites de Passage." In W. Lessa and E. Z. Vogt (eds.). *Reader in Comparative Religion*, pp. 234–243. 4th edition. New York: Harper and Row.

van Gennep, Arnold. 1966. (orig. pub. 1908). *The Rites of Passage*. Chicago: University of Chicago Press.

Wilcox, L. S. et al. 1989. "Episiotomy and Its Role in the Incidence of Perineal Lacerations in a Maternity Center and a Tertiary Hospital Obstetric Service." *American Journal of Obstetrics and Gynecology* 160 (5Pt1): 1047–1052.

NOTES

1. The full results of this study appear in Davis-Floyd 1992.
2. In Holland, by way of contrast, most births are attended by midwives who recognize that individual labors have individual rhythms. They can stop and start; can take a few hours or several days. If labor slows, the midwives encourage the woman to eat to keep up her strength, and then to sleep until contractions pick up again (Beatriz Smulders, personal communication, 1994; Jordan 1993).
3. As is true for most of the procedures interpreted here as rituals, there is no scientific justification for the routine use of the electronic fetal monitor: Numerous large-scale studies have shown no improvement in outcome (Leveno et al. 1986; Prentice and Lind 1987; Sandmire 1990; Shy et al. 1990). What these studies do show is that a dramatic increase in the rate of Cesarean section accompanies routine electronic monitoring. Most commonly, this increase is due both to the occasional malfunctioning of the machine, which sometimes registers fetal distress when there is none, and to the tendency of hospital staff to overreact to fluctuations on the monitor strip.
4. See Goer 1995: 274–284 for summaries and interpretations of these studies and others concerning electronic fetal monitoring.
5. For summaries of studies that demonstrate the safety of planned, midwife-attended home birth relative to hospital birth, see Davis-Floyd 1992, Chapter 4, and Goer 1995.

Political Demography:
The Banning of Abortion in Ceausescu's Romania

Gail Kligman

Rumania . . . had anticipated Gilead in the eighties by banning all forms of birth control, imposing compulsory pregnancy tests on the female population, and linking promotion and wage increases to fertility.

—MARGARET ATWOOD, *The Handmaid's Tale*

In Nicolae Ceausescu's Romania, the "marriage" between demographic concerns and nationalist politics turned women's bodies into instruments

Gail Kligman, "Political Demography: The Banning of Abortion in Ceausescu's Romania," in Faye D. Ginsberg and Rayna Rapp, eds., *Conceiving the New World Order: The Global Politics of Reproduction*, Berkeley: The University of California Press, 1995.

to be used in the service of the state. The paternalist state exercised its authority partially through the elaboration of a discourse and related set of practices centered on "the family." In that "traditional" Romanian family structure is patriarchal, the state's rhetoric about the family resonated with familiar cultural patterns (see Kligman 1988); the dependency relations created through patriarchal family organization were elevated to the level of the socialist state's "legitimate" rule over its citizens. In this chapter I explore the relationship between official rhetoric, policy, and everyday practice through an analysis of the politics of reproduction during Ceausescu's reign. Analysis of the politics of reproduction (or political demography, in regime parlance) serves partially as a focused case study of the relations between the state and its citizens. These policies brought the state directly into its citizens' bodies and their intimate relations. As such, the pronatalist policies may be viewed as indicative of the character of the polity, of how the state conceived of and represented itself. Analysis of the complex relationship between the official discourse about reproduction, the policies that translated this official rhetoric into state practices, and citizens' lived experiences of these policies in Ceausescu's Romania enables us to understand the means by which the regime was perpetuated and by which compliance and complicity were systemically structured. At the same time, analysis of this complex relationship underscores the increasing separation between the official rhetoric of the regime and the average citizen's experience; this growing disjunction ultimately contributed to the regime's downfall.

The former socialist states, driven by command economies, were actively engaged in social engineering. In theory, societal transformation incorporated all levels of life, and the population had to be mobilized accordingly. The "building of socialism" was predicated on a productionist mentality, the underlying rationale of which was the contribution of each citizen "according to his abilities." In recognition of one of women's "abilities"—childbearing—the socialist state intended to help women enter the economy by providing various forms of social assistance: guaranteed maternity leaves, job security, childcare facilities. These entitlements functioned as positive incentives and were progressive in intention if not in realization. Although gender equity was ideologically extolled in all of the formerly existing socialist states, the progressive legislation regarding women's rights as workers often came into conflict with their obligations as reproducers of the labor force—that is, with their roles as mothers. The resultant relation between state policy and demographic factors bore directly on issues of changing gender relations and underscored the often contradictory interests of the state and its citizens, especially women. Romanian policy was an "extreme case

of the generalized pronatalism" (Teitelbaum and Winter 1985: 100) that, from the mid-1960s, typified the region. Pronatalist policies, aimed at securing an adequate work force to build socialism, formed part of the modernization strategies of these states.

Following a brief summary of key ideological tenets that contributed to the shaping and implementation of the Ceausescu regime's pronatalist policies, I present an overview of the development of these political demographic policies, concentrating on their full elaboration in the 1980s. I comment on the human dramas born of the pronatalist policies: illegal abortion, child abandonment, infant AIDS among abandoned "surplus" babies, and international adoption. I next discuss the politics of reproduction in post-Ceausescu Romania. Between 1989 and 1992, two phases of policy formulation related to reproduction may be distinguished. These phases reflect the gradual formation of effective institutional procedures meant to recognize and protect the rights of individuals in society. They are indicative of the fundamental changes taking place in Romania, however traumatically.

THE PRONATALIST POLICIES

Under Ceausescu's rule, the Romanian state increasingly intruded into its citizens' intimate lives to ensure "normal demographic growth" of the labor force and the "triumph of socialism" (Resolution of the Executive Political Committee of the Central Committee of the Romanian Communist Party, March 1984). The Constitution and the Family Code laid the groundwork for active political-educational campaigns as well as for the implementation of positive incentives, augmented over the years by an increasing number of coercive measures. (See, for example, Trebici 1988.) The Constitution of the Socialist Republic of Romania (SRR) granted all citizens the right to work as well as equal pay for equal work. Measures for protection and safety at work and special measures for the protection of women's and youth's work were also established by law.

The state assumed legal responsibility for the family as a way to underscore the family's significance in the development of the "new socialist person." The family's primary contributions to the building of socialism were in the realms of reproduction of the population (and, by implication, of the work force) and of education, with respect to the "spiritual reproduction of society" and the social integration of youth into society. (See Liciu 1975: 10.) Marriage into which partners entered on the basis of "free consent" was the legal foundation of the family. Law 4/1953, Article 1, of the Family Code read: "In the SRR, the state shall protect marriage and the family; it shall support the development and strengthening of the family through economic and social measures. The state shall defend the interests of mother and child and shall display a special care for the upbringing and education of the young generation."

In the state-controlled public sphere, women, like minorities, were represented in positions of authority. An operative quota system paid lip service to the participation of women and minorities (Hungarians, Germans, Gypsies, Jews) in leadership roles. Access to power was stratified. A few women entered the ranks of the Central Committee, such as Elena Ceausescu and Lina Ciobanu, who—as workers—respectively represented chemistry and the textile industry; most women, however, generally filled positions in cultural or educational institutions or in light industry—that is, positions deemed suitable for women. Women in the labor force tended to occupy lower-status, more poorly paid job niches. Moreover, the early emphasis on heavy industrialization as a modernizing strategy often led to the feminization of agriculture. Agricultural labor was more attractive to women because of flexible work schedules. They could both work and tend to families; they were not tied strictly to the clock of industrial production.

Women's participation in the national economy and society as workers and mothers created the classic double and triple burdens: working in the state sphere, doing housework, and raising children. (These burdens increased over the decades as the double burdens of the 1960s and 1970s became triple burdens in the 1980s when childbearing became officially obligatory.) Occupational "advances" were not coupled with the production of time-saving household devices or with any emphasis on changing gender roles within the family.

The initial pronatalist measures were instituted in 1966. The birthrate in Romania had fallen to 14.3 per 1,000 from a 1960 rate of 19.1 per 1,000 (*Anuarul stâtistic al Romaniei* 1990:67). This decline was attributed, in part, to the liberal law that had legalized abortion and made it readily accessible. To remedy this situation, Law 770/1966 was introduced. This law prohibited abortions except if the pregnancy endangered the life of the woman and no other means could be taken to save it, a hereditary disease was involved, the pregnancy was the result of rape, the woman was forty-five years of age or over, or she had delivered and reared four children. The imposition of this law caught Romanians by surprise; in 1967 the birthrate dramatically shot up to 27.4. (There were 527,764 live births in 1967 compared with 273,678 in 1966; *Anuarul stâtistic al Romaniei* 1990:66.) The antiabortion law was accompanied by a series of progressive measures meant to encourage women to bear children, including financial allowances for families and child-support benefits (Decree 410/1985),[1] maternity leaves and work protection (Decision 880/1965, Articles 13–17; maternity leaves were usually fifty-two days prior to delivery and sixty days thereafter, these being interchangeable), protection for working women and children (the Work Code, especially section VII), access to medical attention throughout all phases of pregnancy and to medical care for mother and child (Law 3/1978; Decree 246/1958), and access to childcare facilities (Decree 65/1982). Similar incentives existed throughout Eastern Europe, although their particulars varied. Romania followed the spirit of this progressive legislation but had the least adequate provisions. Ultimately, as shall be seen, Ceausescu added coercive measures unparalleled elsewhere.

As in other spheres of production, mothers who bore many children were honored as "heroes of socialist labor," for which they were awarded decorations and minor privileges. To this end, State Council Decree 190/1977, Article 13, announced that:

- women who delivered and reared ten or more children were awarded the title of "Heroine Mother";
- women who had delivered and reared nine children received the first-class "Order of Maternal Glory"; those with eight children, the second-class "Order of Maternal Glory"; those with seven, the third-class award in this category;
- women who had delivered and reared six children were awarded the first-class "Medal of Maternity"; those with five, the second-class "Medal of Maternity."

The stipulations of this decree must be read carefully. A woman who bore ten children did not automatically qualify for the honor of Heroine Mother. She also had to have reared them. Given the high incidence of infant mortality, especially in rural areas, this honor was difficult to achieve. Wording is also significant in the 1966 abortion law, which states that women must have given birth to "four children and have them in her care." Children acquired through second marriages or adoption did not qualify women for medals or abortions.

The pronatalist policies introduced by Ceausescu in the 1960s were a mild version of what was later to become a draconian policy, and in the 1970s the minimum age for abortion was lowered to forty (Article 2, Instructions 27/1974). In these earlier years, Ceausescu emphasized the role of women in politics, the economy, and society. In 1971, he began promoting his wife, Elena. To legitimize this first step in the creation of "dynastic socialism,"[2] a political-educational campaign glorifying women in the labor force as workers and as mothers of future workers was inaugurated. Ceausescu opposed gender discrimination: "If we speak about the creation of conditions of full equality between the sexes, this means that we must treat all people not as men and women, but in their qualities as Party members, as citizens, for which they are exclusively judged according to their work contributions" (*Address to the Plenary Session of the Central Committee of the Romanian Communist Party* 1973). He also began stressing that "an obligation of

national interest is the protection and consolidation of the family, the development of a corresponding consciousness about the growth of an increased number of children, and the formation of healthy and robust generations profoundly devoted to the cause of socialism; in this realm women have a distinguished role and a noble mission" (*Decisions of the Plenary Session of the Central Committee of the Romanian Communist Party* 1973).

Ceausescu superficially recognized the stress created for women by their roles as mothers and workers. In 1978 he urged that particular attention be paid to the solving of these problems through the construction of childcare facilities, the production and distribution of household appliances, the sale of semi-prepared foods, so that women could use their time efficiently in their many pursuits. However these exhortations were not fulfilled, and women experienced an inverse relationship between Ceausescu's official statements about their lives and the demands of their everyday reality.

Propaganda notwithstanding, by 1983, the birthrate had again declined to the 1966 level, although there had long been no prochoice law to which this decline could be attributed, as was the case in 1966. Romanians had managed as best they could in an environment in which contraceptives were unavailable through legal means;[3] pregnancies were avoided through illegal abortions, abstinence, and coitus interruptus. The decline in the birthrate coincided with a steady deterioration in the material conditions of everyday life. In the interest of national self-determination, Ceausescu had decided that Romania's outstanding foreign debts would be repaid—at enormous cost to the quality of life. Production was targeted for export. By 1984, winters were endured with little heat or electricity; food staples were rationed.

The Orwellian reproductive politics that inspired Margaret Atwood's novel *The Handmaid's Tale* and a Romanian national tragedy were unveiled on International Women's Day, March 8, 1984: Ceausescu saluted women's importance to the nation by again exhorting them to bear four or more children in order to fulfill the national goal of increasing the population from 22.6 to 25 million by 1990. As was inevitably the case, the popular response could be gauged by jokes. One noted that people were willing to agree to the four-child plan as long as it was applied consistently with state production policy: keep one child, and export the other three. This joke also referred to the unpublicized state trade in babies for hard currency. Also in 1984, Ana Blandiana, a revered poet (and now a fêted member of the Civic Alliance social movement), wrote a poem, "Children's Crusade," criticizing such brutal policies as the legal obligation of women to bear four (later five) children:

An entire population
as yet unborn
but condemned to birth
lined up in rows, before birth
fetus beside fetus
An entire population
which doesn't see, doesn't hear, doesn't understand
but develops
through the convulsed bodies of women
through the blood of mothers
Unasked.

Amfiteatru

Blandiana's poignant words presaged the death sentence unwanted children were later to face as a consequence of the AIDS-infected transfusions given routinely to children in orphanages. Statistics on this situation were deliberately suppressed. Nonetheless, pronatalist propaganda flourished. Demographers, doctors, and women's and youth organizations were solicited to participate in the propaganda campaign. Sex education was stepped up, including premarital health counseling and checkups, lectures, and films at work locales. Competitions about "health knowledge" were promoted in magazines such as *Sanatatea*. Ideological bombast was cemented by threats of punishment which ensured widespread complicity. The women's magazine *Femeia*, found in all of the cultural centers across the country, soon ceased being a typical magazine for women. By the 1980s, articles about household concerns were limited, while those about women in the work force had increased. The

ads for clothing and household items characteristic of the 1960s had been replaced by pictures of the ruling couple, his speeches, and "patriotic" poems or stories from the national cultural festival, *Cintarea Romaniei*, the Singing of Romania. A new section on children, "the supreme joy, supreme responsibility," was introduced in 1987, in the interest again of increasing the birthrate. Motherhood—regardless of marital status—was the message.

Morality tales about good and bad mothers abounded. A young, single mother wanting to give her child up for adoption was chastised in the response to her letter of inquiry (of the "Dear Abby" sort). What kind of young woman was she? She had a job, was healthy with her whole future ahead of her. She herself had been left motherless at the age of thirteen. The thrust of the argument was that a "single mother is not to be condemned; a mother will always be respected. Perhaps for a while you won't be able to offer your child the maximum, but be certain that no one in this world can offer what you can [mother love]" (*Femeia* 12, 1988, p. 13).

Educators and activists received all manner of booklets about the relationship between health and demography, about marital harmony, care of infants and children, and the consequences of abortion. For example, one publication of the Health Ministry's Institute of Hygiene and Public Health included topics such as the methods and contents of health education in relation to the problems of demography; protection of mothers, children, and youth (including the topic of reproduction and problems related to it: fecundity, pregnancy, birth); elementary notions of infant and child care; and venereal diseases. A normal, regulated sexual life, with "normal relations of 3–4 weekly" was recommended.

The virtues of motherhood were extolled: "motherhood is itself the meaning of women's lives" was a ubiquitous formula. Articles in the state paper *Scinteia* instructed the population about the patriotic virtues of large families and the noble mission of mothers. For example, the headline for March 9, 1984, read: "Goals of extraordinary significance for the nation's future are contained in Comrade N. Ceausescu's address: Families with many children—a law of life and of human fulfillment, a noble patriotic duty." This theme was reiterated incessantly for the rest of the decade. A series of articles titled "A House with Many Children" (January to April 1986) highlighted individual families and whole villages as "heroes of socialist labor." Other headlines read: "Demographic growth—an exalted responsibility of the entire society" (April 3, 1984); "For the eternity of families, for the vigor of our people" (March 16, 1984); "The joy of being a mother" (June 4, 1987). Images of the happy maternal-child relation abounded.

Women were differentially affected by the pronatalist policies. Urban women with higher education managed to acquire black-market contraceptives or to arrange for illegal abortions performed by medical personnel. Others, such as factory workers, bore the costs, material and bodily, of these policies. It is assumed that rural women were less radically affected because of the influences of religion and local habits. Although these assumptions may generally be true, there was considerable regional variation. Many rural women participated in the seasonal migrant labor force and, as a consequence, were introduced to different practices. Some of them married outside their own region and had abortions that they might not have had in their natal villages. In an unsuccessful bid, the regime attempted to get rural women to sign contracts to produce four children in the same way that peasants signed contracts with the state to meet production quotas. "Women as cows" were castigated by village women, who questioned what would happen if they were unable to have a third or fourth child. Would they be sent to prison? What if a child died; would they be required to produce another? The "what ifs" were recounted with outrage. These same women, and their families, often expressed a desire to have more children although they were unable to support those they already had.

Also, and again undocumented by hard data, responses to these policies were differentiated by ethnicity as well as class. Physicians repeatedly pointed out that Hungarian Romanians, for example, had greater access to black-market contraceptives through their kin or ethnic networks. (Hungary was a source for contraceptives.) Moreover, many medical practitioners mentioned that Hungarian Romanians drew upon a different cultural and educational heritage, the relation between educational level and family planning being relevant. In 1983–84, as the pronatalist campaign intensified and in keeping with the ideological line, a Hungarian Romanian radio station offered a program on stimulating fertility. The editors of this show and of other Hungarian radio programs were informed that there was no need for them to offer this information. Although the pronatalist policies were formally applicable to all, there seems to have been an unstated preference to increase the birthrate of Romanians but not "hyphenated" Romanians such as Hungarians.[4]

Demographers also quietly called attention to the need to bring under control the birthrates of the Gypsy population. "Their exaggerated reproduction is determined especially by their lifestyle, the degree of their social and cultural backwardness."[5] The Gypsy natality rate created concern among Romanians, who pointed out derogatorily that Gypsies "multiply like rabbits," like people in the developing world, while the "European" birthrate—such as that of Romanians and Hungarian Romanians—mirrored West European trends (zero or declining population growth; this concern has been heightened throughout Europe). It is believed that most Gypsy women, in accordance with cultural beliefs, do not practice abortion, although this is not considered true for assimilated, urban middle-class Gypsies. It seems that, at the end of the 1970s, Gypsy women, regardless of their age or the number of children in their care, could get abortions in Arad, a city in Transylvania; whether this was a local initiative or a general policy remains unverified. In any event, the politics of reproduction in Romania had hidden dimensions to it: stringent measures could be more leniently applied in the case of ethnic "others."

When it became obvious in 1983 that the birthrate was not increasing despite the pronatalist policies already in effect, the regime resorted to a more determined strategy: coercion. On December 26, 1985, a stringent antiabortion law was passed. The age at which women became eligible for legal abortions was again raised to the 1966 limit of forty-five; the number of children "delivered and under her care" was increased to five. Also on this day, another pronatalist measure (originally signed into law in 1977) was modified, increasing the monthly "contributions of childless persons"— that is, all persons over the age of twenty-five, regardless of sex or marital status, who were childless. The sums subtracted from monthly wages varied, depending on the sector of the state economy in which one worked, those in agriculture being taxed somewhat less. To avoid this monthly fee, some quit their jobs in state enterprises to work as migrant laborers— a little-discussed adaptive strategy. One way or another, reproductive and abortion statistics had become political tools to discipline the population and were used accordingly.

The altered antiabortion law, and the "instructions" regarding its application, included provisions to punish both physicians and women. In an attempt to secure the obedience of the medical profession, medical practitioners were held responsible for rectifying the birthrate crisis, in part associated with alarming abortion and infant mortality statistics (discussed below). Health practitioners were assumed to assist in illegal abortions for personal gain. They became subject to imprisonment for any infraction of the abortion law, including failure to notify the prosecutor's office. Such notification alerted that office to cases for which doctors could be held responsible. Of course, prosecutors also had wives, sisters, and daughters who might need abortions, and so not all acted in strict accordance with the law. Others were paid off by concerned, and profit-interested, physicians. Given the penal sanctions for doctors, abortion costs were from 2,000 to 10,000 lei (then approximately $160 to $830, with basic salaries ranging between 1,500 and 2,400 lei per month).

Medical personnel were disciplined by various means, depending on their relations with legal authorities, co-workers, immediate superiors, as well as the nature of the legal infraction. Publications such as *Muncitorul Sanitar* (The Health Worker) regularly printed moralizing articles about professional responsibility.

(These were similar in form to the articles in women's magazines about good and bad mothers, discussed above. Official rhetoric was disseminated homologously in all realms.) Such articles reported cases that had come before a Disciplinary Board for Health Personnel, which existed in each administrative region of the country. These boards functioned as public, institutionalized confessionals through which medical practitioners were disciplined.

From time to time, there were show trials of doctors, midwives, and backroom-abortion practitioners. In one case, several women were convicted of having performed illegal abortions or of having been involved in arranging them. The abortionist received 500 lei plus a package of coffee and dried soup for her efforts. Her sentence was lessened, however, because of her lack of prior convictions as well as her "sincerity" (cooperation with the police). Generally, those who informed on others were not sent to prison. Their sentences often made it possible for them to remain at work on carefully scrutinized probation. Those who did not cooperate, however, received prison sentences. If they were women, they frequently left children motherless at home—hardly the "ideal conditions" for their upbringing that the Romanian state claimed to have created.

The intrusion of the state into the intimacy of the body was inescapable. In 1986, Ceausescu introduced a campaign—unique in the history of Romanian medicine—to analyze the health of the population, particularly that of women between the ages of sixteen and forty-five, the years when most women are fertile. These exams, regardless of officially professed intentions, subjected women of childbearing age to state control of their reproductive lives. Women working in or attending state institutions were given at least annual, and in some places, trimesterly gynecological exams to verify that their reproductive health was satisfactory.[6] If, in such a routine exam, a woman was discovered to be pregnant, the development of her pregnancy could then be closely followed lest there be any untoward mishap. Women who had already had abortions (legal or not) were carefully watched for "preventive reasons" and, in some cases, were confined to a hospital. For women living in rural areas, local medical personnel were expected to follow up with home visits (a practice resented by all involved).

Much was written in the official press about these exams, and the language of these stories was telling. According to them, the intent of obtaining medical histories about women of childbearing age was to have "in evidence . . . . all of the elements that might negatively influence the normal evolution of a pregnancy." While pre- and postnatal care may be commendable under normal circumstances, in the context of a coercive pronatalist policy, such prenatal care served to police the body, with doctors put in the position of aiding and abetting the interests of the state. Women were not always aware that they were deliberately being checked to see whether they were pregnant; annual exams were considered routine, another obligation. One doctor confided that among her staff, some took pleasure in "finding" a pregnant woman. Others, who were more compassionate, did not.

Despite the consequences for nonconformity with the law, many doctors—of all ranks in the party hierarchy (most doctors being party members)—became adept at manipulating both the official rhetoric and statistics. Strikingly, most people I queried offered praise for the attempts doctors made to assist women and families during these harsh years. Many doctors tried to "hide" a woman's pregnancy if she indicated that she, or she and her husband, did not want the child. As one doctor remarked: "If a woman adamantly was against having a child, there was nothing you could do about it. She would risk dying rather than bear the child. So we tried to help." Various ailments such as measles, recurrent fevers, hepatitis, tuberculosis, syphilis, malignant tumors, and diabetes qualified a woman for a legal abortion. Doctors took advantage of this rule as much as possible. Similarly, taking certain medications that are counterindicated during pregnancy (chemotherapy, antimalarial drugs, anticonvulsants) could be used as the excuse for an abortion. Given the dearth of medications available in Romania, this excuse was not easily manufactured. Nonetheless, whenever possible, most doctors seem to have done what they could to accommodate a woman's "choice."

According to a document stamped *secret de serviciu* that circulated internally in the health ministry in 1988, the number of abortions increased between 1979 and 1988, with the exception of a decline in 1948–85 (Roznatovschi 1989). A similar drop in abortion rates occurred following the original 1966 antiabortion law. Citizens needed time to learn to adapt to the intensified pronatalist campaign. The increase in abortions coincided with the previously mentioned deterioration in the conditions of everyday life. Families were unable to feed the children they had, yet were required by law to have more.

In many cases, unwanted children were abandoned to the care of the paternalist state that had demanded them. That "care," best described as systematic neglect, resulted in institutionalization of the innocent, the rise of infant AIDS, and international trafficking in babies and children through adoption. Abandoning a child was the consequence of despair combined with dependence on the state for the basics of life. Centralized production and distribution limited what families had to eat. (The rise of the second economy paralleled that of illegal abortions; these were the means through which people managed their everyday lives.) These material and psychological conditions make it possible to understand why parents gave up their children. Traditionally, peasant families unable to support another child would ask a relative to raise one; others were adopted by childless couples. During the Ceausescu years, some mothers left their infants in the hospital; others left them at orphanages or in other places where they were likely to be found. (I have not heard of infanticide as a common practice, although punitive statutes exist in the legal code—for example, Article 177.) Some parents relied upon state institutions as a temporary residence for children; they then attempted to retrieve them later when they were able to support them at home. This "pawn-shop" strategy often succeeded; in other cases, parents were unable to locate the children they had given up. Only after the fall of the regime did they—and the rest of the world—learn why: institutionalized children often died of neglect or were put up for adoption.

Women who did not comply with the pronatalist law resorted to illegal abortions. Those privileged with connections and the means could bribe medical practitioners. Those without sought the assistance of less-qualified abortionists or used the varied remedies that abortion lore and popular practice offered them. When the state punished physicians who for humanistic or economic reasons performed illegal abortions, the increase in maternal deaths or deformities due to nonmedically performed abortions was assured. Between 1965 and 1989, 9,452 women died because of complications arising from illegal abortions. As Mezei notes: "The liberation of abortion in January 1990 proves yet again the positive dependent relation between delegalization of abortion and the rise of maternal mortality rates. If, following the chronology of events, 1989 represents the year with the most elevated maternal mortality figures [545] . . . for 1990, 181 cases of maternal deaths due to illegal abortions were registered, [numbers] that had not been seen since 1968" (1991: 4).

Among those who died were women who already had three or four children but who were unable to deal with yet another cold, hungry child. Thus, the population of orphaned or abandoned children necessarily increased.[7] So great were the traumas associated with the pronatalist policies that months after the legalization of abortion, the Ministry of Health still received files of mothers who had died as a result of illegal abortions; some of these were mothers of five children who would have been eligible for legal abortions even during the Ceausescu regime.

The heartbreaking and chilling irony of Ceausescu's pronatalist policies was that illegal abortion became the predominant contraceptive method. According to Ministry of Health statistics, the greatest number of abortions—60.1 percent—were "incomplete abortions" recorded upon the arrival of a woman at the hospital for emergency treatment.[8] The decision to abort (made by the woman alone or with her husband's consent) was a rational decision based on the real conditions of daily life. Insensitive to the realities of the lives of most Romanian citizens, the regime clung to its ideological visions of everyday productive—and reproductive—life. A stringent pronatalist policy was enforced through a series of coercive legal measures even as data on the rise of infant AIDS were suppressed and as the recording of births was delayed so that infant-mortality rates would not appear too large. The consequences of legislating reproduction without regard for the material conditions of daily life meant that many women, unable to fulfill their "patriotic duties" and "noble mission" in life, gave up their lives—and, frequently, those of their children—in the service of the state.

POST-CEAUSESCU ABORTION AND INTERNATIONAL ADOPTION

The "revolution" of December 1989 liberated most women's bodies from the grip of the centralized state. The day after the execution of Ceausescu, abortion became fully legal in Romania. Legalization simultaneously kept abortion the preferred method of fertility control, other means being generally unavailable.[9] Urban and rural women alike expressed gratitude for the legalization of abortion. The fear of becoming pregnant had dramatically colored the sexual lives of women (especially), married or not. This fear compounded the basic culture of fear that had pervaded everyday life. The right to abortion granted women in Romania basic, if minimal, control over their lives again. Abortion, in this context, was understood as a fundamental aspect of the right to self-determination being articulated by republics and nationalities demanding their independence, as well as by ethnic groups clamoring for recognition and respect. Abortion was assumed to be an essential ingredient of democratic practice.

As a consequence of legalization, by the summer of 1990, the principal hospitals in Bucharest were each reporting 70 to 100 abortions daily. This rate seemed potentially problematic for women's health and future demographic trends. However, health officials and physicians (personal communications) pointed out that the legalization of abortion had quickly alleviated one of the problems from the past; they also suggested that there were more urgent concerns than these given that the country was in total disorder. In addition to finding ways to finance the development and distribution of contraceptives, the country desperately needed funds for AIDS research, treatment, and education.

By summer 1991, the skyrocketing number of abortions made attention to this issue imperative. The ratio of abortions to live births was reported at 3 to 1. (At the same time, the marked decrease in maternal mortality recorded for 1990 continued. The birthrate also declined.)[10] Doctors at one of the largest maternity wards in Bucharest stated that they had performed as many as three abortions for the same woman during the course of the year. In response, the government began to address the need for family planning and sex education. Several nongovernmental associations (NGOs) established soon after 1989 had already become active, although with limited means. NGOs hoped to maintain their politically independent identities. However, in the heightened political atmosphere in Romania, doing so has not been easy. One of the primary tasks for health workers is to educate the population. Because television remains essentially state-controlled, and the majority of newspapers have political agendas, access to and use of the mass media for education is fraught with problems that have subordinated health issues to political struggles. NGO workers have expressed concern that governmental institutions will coopt their efforts. At present, both governmental and non-governmental organizations depend on international assistance, financial and instructional. As many of the doctors with whom I spoke noted, it is difficult for them to train specialists in family planning when they themselves are not trained. Obviously, in view of the former policies, physicians and others lacked access to such training.

Furthermore, years of propaganda against the use of contraceptives must be combatted. Thus far, the Ministry of Education—unlike the Ministry of Health—has not been overly receptive to governmental or non-governmental proposals to introduce health and sex education into the high school curriculum. There has been more interest at the university level. The state-controlled media have also been reticent to engage in discussion of these issues, which are vital to the nation's health.

A similar mentality exists toward AIDS: ignore or downplay its importance. Some Romanian physicians insisted that AIDS was not a real problem in their country, claiming that the epidemic among children who received transfusions was contained within that population. By 1992, 1,557 cases of AIDS had been recorded. AIDS is likely to be on the rise because of poor hygiene in hospitals, increased drug traffic and usage, and increased prostitution without "safe sex" practices. Married women with children often become prostitutes with the full consent of their husbands so that they can obtain hard currency and increase household cash flow. One doctor interviewed who was concerned about the state of public health in Romania pointed out: "Here, people do not have respect for their own bodies." He attributed much of this attitude to the destructive effects of the former regime.

Without a concerted campaign to educate the population (including medical practitioners) about reproductive health, some physicians fear that women's health, in particular, will continue to be at risk. Most of the women factory workers I interviewed informally in 1990 mentioned often that their husbands would object to the use of contraceptives even if they were more readily available. In addition, although condoms are obtainable from tobacco shops, in general birth control devices and pills have to be obtained from pharmacies, hospital clinics, and some private medical practitioners. As several young gynecologists remarked, "People associate hospitals with illness. They will not come to the hospital to get contraceptives. It's impractical!" (This attitude also points to the problems of the medicalization of family planning. See Hord et al. 1991:237–38.) Thus, for the immediate future, abortion will remain the primary method. Women of all ages wait in endless lines for abortions performed in factory-like conditions.

In an attempt to discourage women from having abortions, the hospital price was raised from 30 to 500 lei (500 lei was equivalent to about $2.50 in the summer of 1991). Obstetrician-gynecologists expressed concern that raising the price would encourage poor women to seek cheaper abortions done by nonmedically qualified persons, thereby repeating the problems of the past. Well-to-do women were already going to doctors in private practice, where prices are significantly higher, in exchange for privacy, personal attention, and more sterile conditions. At the same time, these physicians emphasized that the current situation has to be changed; raising the price of an abortion, increasing contraceptive availability, and introducing a multifaceted educational campaign were all considered necessary. Unfortunately, it is easier to adjust prices upward than to introduce family planning and sex education or to assure the production and distribution of contraceptives. Thus, women's health, especially among the poor and less educated, remains particularly vulnerable.

The vulnerability of women and children also emerged in another context that is only partially the direct result of Ceausescu's pronatalist policies: the international adoption of Romanian children.[11] During the later years of the regime, Ceausescu authorized limited foreign adoption of Romanian babies for hard currency. This little-publicized practice was a facet of the "commerce in human flesh" that usually enabled Jews and Germans to be "bought" out of Romania. (Hungarians wanting to emigrate to Hungary were not so fortunate, the *forint* not having been convertible to hard currency.) Children began to figure among Romania's export goods, in direct contradiction to the stated ideological goals of the pronatalist policies.

When the regime fell, and the plight of Romania's orphans surfaced, international humanitarian groups moved in to help. Many institutions and individuals contributed greatly to alleviating the pain of these children.[12] As it became known that not all of the children incarcerated in orphanages were "irrecoverable" or were the victims of the infant AIDS epidemic, foreigners journeyed to Romania with hopes of adopting children.

As word spread in the international community of persons wanting to adopt, Romania became the adoption hot spot. In early 1990, to deal with the growing number of adoptions, the Romanian government formed the National Adoption Commission. Among its tasks was coordination of data about available institutionalized children. However, lack of an adequate staff or a computerized information system led to bureaucratic inefficiency. Inadvertently, rather than facilitate the adoption process, creation of the commission encouraged expansion of the private market in adoptions, or "baby trading."

Gradually, as different channels for adoption developed, the emotional rhetoric about the humanitarian rescue of children from abysmal conditions in the orphanages lost its force. In its stead, a more generalized rhetoric emerged about saving children from the difficult living conditions in Romania and giving them the opportunity for a better life in the West. By July 1991 most children no longer came from the orphanages but were acquired through private connections, a fact usually overlooked in the numerous media accounts about the baby trade in Romania. According to U.S. consular representatives, most of these children were Gypsies, or Roma. Though they are notably dark-skinned by Romanian standards, Westerners do not generally consider them markedly different in appearance.[13] Given that prejudice against the Gypsies in Romania is unlikely to be eliminated in the near future, adoption was thought to provide a humanitarian road out for some of these children, whose chances for productive lives would otherwise be slim. Many Romanians viewed the exodus of adopted Gypsy children as a legitimate means to rid the country of them at the expense of foreigners; there are others who resented the squandering of Western altruism and resources on Gypsies.

For Westerners, opting for the private adoption process was faster than going through official bureaucratic procedures; it was also more expensive, arbitrary, and led to coercion and corruption. The victims of this process were not only, as is often implied in Western media coverage, foreign adoptive parents but rather poor or single (or both) Romanian mothers, many of whom were Gypsies. Some poor women considered their bearing of children to be little more than the means of production that yielded a valuable commodity. In these cases, private adoptions contributed to the exploitation of women's reproductive labor. Husbands, brothers, and parents found compensation for their "public shame" in the money so readily obtained. With it, they purchased refrigerators, video recorders, and the like, or finished building or furnishing their homes. Given the sharp rise in prices in Romania, increasing unemployment, and depressed wages, it is not difficult to explain why people were tempted to sell their own children, as well as those of other people. Dealing in babies is also a lucrative business for intermediaries, bureaucrats, and lawyers who may be bribed to falsify papers and speed up the process.

Hence, for all of the legitimate adoptions, there were many that were not legitimate. Coercion of Romanian mothers happened in various ways. By law, a mother had fifteen days in which to change her mind about consenting to the adoption of her child. When a mother had a change of heart (or conscience), her decision was not necessarily accepted graciously by the adoptive parents or their negotiators, regardless of the law. One Romanian woman was told by the translator that she would be responsible for the costs accrued during the stay of the American adoptive parents (personal communication from an official investigator of this case). No Romanian could conceivably have covered such expenses. Whether the Americans knew of the translator's methods is not known. That the translator had much to lose if the adoption fell through *is* known, as is the fact that the American woman intended to appeal to her Congressman. Most adoptive parents in such situations chose not to know about possible coercion, even though they may have intuited that something was amiss. Because of the language barrier, lack of knowledge was easy to rationalize. To have allowed themselves to know meant that they would have had to deal with their own emotional pain at the loss of a child with whom they might already have bonded. It was (and

is) easier to believe, whatever the temporary experience, that adoption was simply for the good of the child, who would thereby escape from the hardships of Romania.

Since the fall of the Ceausescu regime, the Romanian government has embraced measures that suggest at least a minimal recognition of the fundamental significance of respecting citizens' rights. To be sure, these measures have been noticeably inadequate, particularly in the realm of ethnic rights. Nonetheless, in the midst of traumatic change, there has been some movement to redress certain of the dehumanizing policies of the past. Hence, the legalization of abortion in 1990 may be considered a necessary response to a dramatic situation fostered by the stringent political-demographic policies. At the same time, the legalization of abortion was not a policy decision made with socioeconomic and demographic aims, or long-term trends, in mind. The formation of the National Adoption Commission was similarly a practical response to circumstances—in this case, to the growing number of foreign adoptive parents. While the institutionalization of adoption procedures at that time may have been well-intentioned, it was not carefully planned, and it inadvertently contributed to the expansion of the private adoption market. Indeed, the systemic and societal confusion generated by the fall of the Ceausescu regime did not initially lead to effective policy formulation in the realm of family-related issues. This first phase of policy formulation was, in actuality, characterized by the lack of effective policy formulation and implementation.

On July 16, 1991, President Ion Iliescu signed a new adoption law meant to stop the Romanian baby trade; adoption would henceforth be done through institutional channels, thereby removing the private profit motives of all involved.[14] Among the law's provisions is the necessary institutionalization of orphaned children. This provision is meant to prevent the sale of children and to determine the legal status of children as orphans. (Children must be orphaned or abandoned; if they are under the care of a parent, then they are not legally adoptable.) Children must reside in an orphanage for six months, during which time the natal parents may change their minds or, if possible, adoptive parents may be found among Romanian citizens.[15] Only after that are foreigners legally able to adopt Romanian children.

The adoption law should be applauded for its attempt to apply the rule of law operative elsewhere in Europe. The politics of reproduction in Romania are now different from the situation in the Ceausescu period. Under Ceausescu's rule, the masses were forced to reproduce in the service of the state. Women's reproductive lives and human rights were blatantly exploited. Today, as Romania struggles with the "transition" and as Romanian society becomes more clearly class-differentiated, those who were most vulnerable—poor and single women—have often been forced to reproduce in the service of market demands. The adoption law has helped to diminish one source of abuse suffered by those women coerced into giving up their children.[16]

Moreover, this law was an important step toward the recognition and protection of citizens' rights, especially those of women and children. The political-demographic policies of the Ceausescu regime contributed significantly to the social atomization and dehumanization that remain a tragic legacy. Women's bodies were glorified as the machines that produced the future workers of the state. Celebrated in public political rhetoric, women were overwhelmed by the exigencies of daily life. Their identities as workers and mothers were ideologically dictated, but the conditions of everyday life did not make such identities attractive. The institutionalized violence of the state against its citizens resulted in the denial of women's rights in particular. The state's violence against its citizens was bolstered by a web of interdependent practices that engaged most people in the prescribed practices of the state: doctors were expected to perform gynecological exams; adults without children were taxed; those who had had an abortion were manipulated into becoming police informants. Men's and women's sexual relations were intimately affected, at great psychological cost to the population. Fertility control was proclaimed to be the right of the state, not of women or families. The loss of life (for

women and children) due to illegal abortions was evidence of societal despair and increasing dehumanization. The abandonment of children to the "care" of the paternalist state's orphanages was yet another indicator of the extremely deteriorated conditions that made the upbringing of children next to impossible for most citizens of Romania.

By 1991, life in Romania had gradually acquired more routine; the government began to function somewhat more smoothly. The Ministries of Health, Labor, and Education—which were important for the concerns addressed here: reproduction, health, and welfare—each turned to the details of restructuring; what may be viewed as the second phase of policymaking began. Foreign agencies and individuals continued to offer needed and welcome assistance, particularly with respect to scientific exchange about AIDS (testing, research, education) and problems related to the orphanages. Diverse specialists came to train Romanians to care for the handicapped and to teach Romanian health professionals about family planning. All these efforts, combined with passage of the adoption law, have pointed to a recognition that the state must participate responsibly in the protection of its citizens' rights and well-being. To what extent it shall do so remains to be seen.

IMPLICATIONS FOR REPRODUCTIVE POLICY

Romania's experience in the realm of reproductive health can guide policymakers, health administrators, and reproductive-health professionals throughout the world. "At a time when reproductive rights are increasingly threatened by conservative forces throughout central and eastern Europe and other parts of the world, the tragic elements of Romania's reproductive health experience under Ceausescu and the country's struggle to reverse that grim legacy can serve as a guide for health care professionals everywhere" (Hord et al. 1991: 238–239).

Restrictive reproductive legislation is on the agenda throughout Eastern Europe, with the notable—and understandable—exception of Romania. Similar legislation is being considered and contested in the United States, as well as elsewhere. Here, I wish to stress that the Romanian case must not be categorized as specific to the evils of the Ceausescu regime or of communism. This study enables us to focus on the social implications and human costs of restrictive reproductive legislation and policies, especially as they affect the lives of women and children.

The effects of banning abortion transcend political or religious interests. When abortion is criminalized, women resort to illegal abortions; that is a comparative as well as historical fact. Banning abortions does not stop women from having them; it simply makes abortion "invisible." Prohibiting abortion—as has always been the case—forces abortion underground and makes it the privilege of the wealthy, while further disenfranchising poor women, who generally bear the brunt of such policies. For poor women, illegal abortions are typically done by unqualified practitioners—the woman herself, backroom abortionists—and result in increased maternal deaths as well as maternal and fetal physical deformities. In Romania, the masses were poor. The tragic consequences have been detailed above.

Again, these consequences are specific neither to communism nor to Ceausescu-ism. Indeed, these consequences suggest that the Romanian case must be borne in mind by those who would ban abortion in the United States. If, as James Madison understood, a test of democracy lies in its treatment of society's most vulnerable members, among whom are women and children, then democracy in the late twentieth-century United States (and elsewhere) may fail.

NOTES

This chapter is drawn from a final grant report (Kligman 1992c) submitted to the National Council for Soviet and East European Studies, which supported the final phase of a field research project. Additional funding was granted by the American Council of Learned Societies, the International Research and Exchanges Board, and the Rockefeller Foundation. Kligman (1992a) is based on the final section of the grant report and this chapter; Kligman (1992b) is an almost complete version of the grant report. Because of space constraints, notes have been kept to a minimum. For references and commentary, refer to the above-mentioned works.

1. These allowances were adjusted according to income level, number of children, and place of residence (urban or rural). They were lower in rural areas, the rationale being that rural families were able to provide some of their food from their personal plots, although these same citizens were required to provide "barter" to receive their ration cards for staples. Rural payments were erratic. As was typical, this system functioned well only in theory.

2. Ceausescu's consolidation of power involved securing key loyalties through appointment of extended-family members. Thus, his version of communist rule was variously described as *socialism in one family* or *dynastic socialism*. See, for example, Tismaneanu (1986). That so many members of the extended family were in key positions was captured in the play on the acronym for the Romanian Communist Party: PCR. Popularly, this also meant Petrescu (Elena Ceausescu's natal family), Ceausescu, and Rudele ("relatives"). Other plays on PCR underscore the importance of personal relations and influence in this regime.

3. Contraceptives were not forbidden by law; however, they were unavailable and thus could be obtained only through illegal, black-market connections. Abortion was illegal. The distinction is worth noting.

4. According to a study prepared by the Ministry of Health in 1986, the number of live births varied by nationality. For Romanian women, the median was 1.93 children; for Hungarians, 1.73; for Germans, 1.6; and for others, 2.56. The lower German birthrate is probably due to the older population of Germans; as conditions worsened under Ceausescu, many younger Germans with relatives abroad emigrated.

5. Mesaros (1990: 29). Dr. E. Mesaros was a member of the National Commission on Demography until 1985, when he resigned. The cited article was dated October 3, 1974. The distinction between a social and a national problem was meant partially to signal the class distinctions operative in reproductive behavior. The Gypsy birthrate was considered troublesome because of their low levels of education and presumed high degree of participation in delinquent behavior.

6. The Western press did exaggerate the extent and frequency of these exams. I could not obtain any verification from women that they had been subjected to the much-heralded monthly exams. The exams were ordered; how they were done is quite another matter. The Western press had little justification for sensationalism.

7. For 1989, the number of children left orphaned because of illegal abortions was reported to be 1,193; between 1981 and 1989, 8,004 children were orphaned as a consequence of illegal abortions. See Mezei (1991: 8).

8. These numbers do not include women who died from complications prior to arrival at a hospital. In 1989 at one of Bucharest's largest maternity clinics, 3,129 women were hospitalized for complications associated with illegally performed abortions. Of these 26.6 percent needed intensive treatment for raging infections, 3.9 percent had hysterectomies, and 1.1 percent died. (See Mezei 1991.) The second highest number of abortions were among women who had five or more children and had at least five in their care (22.8 percent), followed by those with legal medical reasons (16.6 percent) and those who were of legal age (0.5 percent forty-five years or older). See Roznatovschi (1989).

9. While international contributions of contraceptives began to pour into Romania in response to this tragic situation, problems associated with distribution and lack of contraceptive education meant that perceptions and behavior did not change significantly, even though Romanians were tired of "natural" methods and their uncertainty.

10. The maternal mortality figures for 1990 were 83 deaths per 100,000 live births, with maternal deaths from abortion decreasing to 69 percent of 249 maternal cases as compared with 87 percent of 588 maternal deaths attributable to abortions in 1989. Reported in Hord et al. (1991: 234).

11. It is beyond the scope of this chapter to discuss fully the adoption of Romanian children or the situation of children in Romanian orphanages. Refer to my grant report (Kligman 1992c) as well as to Kligman (1992b) for fuller discussions and references.

12. By the summer of 1992, almost all orphanages had a foreign agency (governmental or non-governmental) working collaboratively with them.

13. Anti-Roma sentiment is widespread in Europe and, since 1989, has led to violence. Romania was the first of several countries with which Germany concluded agreements to deport illegal immigrants, among whom are many Roma.

14. Some Romanians accused the government of wanting to rob ordinary people of one of the few means by which they could make money so that the government might profit instead. Some foreigners criticized the government for preventing them from taking Romanian children to a better life. In an update to a guide written by a woman who had adopted two Romanian children, the author summarized the consequences of the new law. (See Delvecchio 1991.) Her letter closed with: "God Bless You in your efforts to rescue a little one."

The new adoption law modified Law no. 11 signed in 1990. Another law, no. 47/1933, specifies the terms by which a court may declare a child legally abandoned. The adoption of Romanian children has been a prickly issue between the United States and Romania, and has been manipulated on both sides.

15. Infertility has reportedly been on the rise in Romania as a consequence of pollution, malnutrition, and deteriorated conditions. The preferential treatment accorded Romanian citizens in adopting Romanian orphans is meant to eliminate the demographic problems posed by a declining birthrate as well as the problems that may accompany intercultural adoptions as the children grow older.

16. Virtually no public attention is given to the physical abuse of women. Here, the government and its agencies, including research institutes that might well address such issues, are sorely negligent.

REFERENCES

Anuarul statistic al Romaniei. 1990. Bucharest: Comisia Nationala Pentru Statistica.

Decisions of the Plenary Session of the Central Committee of the Romanian Communist Party, July 18–19, 1973, with Attention to the Growth of the Role of Women in the Economic, Political, and Social Life of the Country. 1973. Bucharest: Editura Politica.

Delvecchio, A.-M. 1991. "How to Adopt From Romania: A Comprehensive Step-by-Step Guide." Sebastopol, Calif.: Hearthstone Publishers.

Hord, C., H. P. David, F. Donnayi, and M. Wolf. 1991. "Reproductive Health in Romania: Reversing the Ceausescu Legacy." *Studies in Family Planning* 22 (4): 231–40.

Kligman, G. 1988. *The Wedding of the Dead: Ritual, Poetics, and Popular Culture in Transylvania.* Berkeley: University of California Press.

———. 1992a. "Abortion and International Adoption in Post-Ceausescu Romania." *Feminist Studies* 18(2): 405–20.

———. 1992b. "The Politics of Reproduction in Ceausescu's Romania: A Case Study in Political Culture." *East European Politics and Society* 6(3): 364–418.

———. 1992c. *When Abortion is Banned: The Politics of Reproduction in Ceausescu's Romania*. Washington, D.C.: National Council for Soviet and East European Studies.

Liciu, V. 1975. *Pregatirea pedagogica a adolescentiilor pentru viata de familie: Cu privire speciala asupra educatiei afectivitatii si sexualitatii*. Bucharest: Editura didactica si Pedagogica.

Mesaros, E. 1990. "Consideratii asupra politicii demografice a Romaniei." *Alternative 90* 1(4): 29.

Mezei, S. 1991. "Une analyse démo-sociologique des consequences de la politique démographique roumaine." Unpublished manuscript.

Roznatovschi, L. 1989. *Aspecte ale intreruperilor de sarcina in R. S. Romania 1988*. Bucharest: Centrul de Calcul si Statistica Sanitara, Ministerul Sanatatii.

Teitelbaum, M., and J. Winter. 1985. *The Fear of Population Decline*. New York: Academic Press.

Tismaneanu, V. 1986. "Byzantine Rites, Stalinist Follies: The Twilight of Dynastic Socialism in Romania." *Orbis* (spring): 65–91.

Trebici. 1988. "Demografie intre stiinta si actiune sociala." *Viitorul social* 81 (1): 69–78.

Surrogate Motherhood:
Rethinking Biological Models, Kinship, and Family

Heléna Ragoné

In the wake of publicity created by the Baby M Case,[1] it seems unlikely that anyone in the United States can have remained unfamiliar with surrogate motherhood or can have failed to form an opinion. The Baby M Case raised, and ultimately left unanswered, many questions about what constitutes motherhood, fatherhood, family, reproduction, and kinship. When I began my field research in 1987, surrogate mother programs and directors had already become the subject of considerable media attention, a great deal of it sensationalized and negative in character. Much of what has been written about surrogate motherhood, has, however, been largely speculative or polemic in nature. Opinions have ranged from the view that surrogate motherhood is symptomatic of the dissolution of the American family[2] and the sanctity of motherhood, to charges that it reduces or assigns women to a breeder class structurally akin to prostitution (Dworkin

Original material prepared for this text. Reprinted by permission of the author.

1978), or that it constitutes a form of commercial baby selling (Annas 1988; Neuhaus 1988).

Data for this chapter derive from nine years of ongoing ethnographic research. Twenty-eight formal interviews with traditional surrogates and twenty-six with gestational surrogates were conducted, as well as twenty-six interviews with individual members of couples (i.e., individuals who had enlisted the services of traditional as well as gestational surrogates) and five interviews with ovum donors. Aside from these formal interviews I also engaged in countless conversations with surrogates, observing them as they interacted with their families, testified before legislative committees, worked in surrogate programs, and socialized at program gatherings with directors and others. The opportunity to observe the daily workings of the surrogate mother programs provided me with invaluable data on the day-to-day operations of such programs. I attended the staff meetings of one such program on a regular basis and observed the consultations in which prospective couples and surrogates were interviewed singly by such members of the staff as the director, a psychologist, a medical coordinator, or the administrative coordinator.

In addition to these formal interviews I conducted thousands of hours of participant observation and was able to observe numerous consultations between program staff, intending couples, and prospective surrogate mothers. I have attempted, whenever possible, to select individuals from the various phases of the traditional and gestational surrogacy process: those individuals who have not yet been matched, those who are newly matched and are attempting "to get pregnant," those who have confirmed pregnancies, and those who have recently given birth, as well as those for whom several years have elapsed since the birth of their child. My decision to interview individuals in all stages of the process has been motivated by my wish to assess what, if any, shifts individuals might experience as they go through the process.

Historically there have been three profound shifts in the Western conceptualization of the categories of conception, reproduction, and parenthood. The first occurred in response to the separation of intercourse from reproduction through birth control methods (Snowden et al. 1983), a precedent that may have paved the way for surrogate motherhood in the 1980s (Andrews 1984: xiii). A second shift occurred in response to the emergence of assisted reproductive technologies (ARTs) and to the subsequent fragmentation of the unity of reproduction, when it became possible for pregnancy to occur without necessarily having been "preceded by sexual intercourse" (Snowden et al. 1983: 5). The third shift occurred in response to further advances in reproductive medicine that called into question the "organic unity of fetus and mother" (Martin 1987: 20). It was not, however, until the emergence of reproductive medicine that the fragmentation of motherhood became a reality; with that historical change what was once the "single figure of the mother is dispersed among several potential figures, as the functions of maternal procreation—aspects of her physical parenthood—become dispersed" (Strathern 1991: 32).

TRADITIONAL SURROGACY

There are two types of surrogate mother programs: "open" programs, in which surrogate and couple select one another and interact throughout the insemination and the pregnancy, and "closed" programs, in which couples select their surrogates from biographical and medical information and a photograph of the surrogate is provided to them by programs. After the child is born in a "closed" program, the couple and surrogate meet only to finalize the step-parent adoption. Due to advances in reproductive medicine and to consumer demand, there are now also two types of surrogacy: traditional surrogacy in which the surrogate contributes an ovum to the creation of the child, and gestational or in-vitro fertilization (IVF) surrogacy where the surrogate gestates the couple's embryos.

Studies of the surrogate population tend to focus, at times exclusively, on surrogates' stated motivations for becoming surrogate mothers (Parker 1983). Their stated reasons include the desire to help an infertile couple start a family, financial remuneration, and a love of pregnancy (Parker 1983: 140). Soon after I began my own research, I observed a remarkable degree of consistency or uniformity in surrogates' responses to questions about their initial motivations for becoming surrogates. It was as if they had all been given a script in which they espoused many of the motivations earlier catalogued by Parker: motivations that also, as I will show, reflect culturally accepted ideas about reproduction, motherhood, and family.

I also began to uncover several areas of conflict between professed motivations and actual experiences, discovering, for example, that although surrogates claim to experience "easy pregnancies" and "problem-free labor," it was not unusual for surrogates to have experienced miscarriages, ectopic pregnancies, and related difficulties. For example, Jeannie, age 36, divorced with one child, described the ectopic pregnancy she experienced while she was a traditional surrogate in this manner: "*I almost bled to death: I literally almost died for my couple.*" Nevertheless, she was again inseminated a second time for the same couple. As this and other cases demonstrate, even when their experiences are at odds with their stated motivations, surrogates tend not to acknowledge inconsistencies between their initially stated motivations and their subsequent experiences. This reformulation of motivations can be seen in the following instance. Fran, age 27, divorced with one child, described the difficulty of her delivery in this way: "*I had a rough delivery, a C-section, and my lung collapsed because I had the flu but it was worth every minute of it. If I were to die from childbirth, that's the best way to die. You died for a cause, a good one.*" As both these examples illustrate, some surrogates readily embrace the idea of meaningful suffering, heroism, or sacrifice, and although their stated motivations are of some interest they do not adequately account for the range of shifting motivations uncovered in my research.

One of the motivations most frequently assumed to be primary by the casual observer is remuneration and I took considerable pains in trying to evaluate the influence of monetary rewards on surrogates. In all programs, surrogates receive between $10,000 and $15,000 (for three to four months of insemination and nine months of pregnancy, on average), a fee that has changed only nominally since the early 1980s. As one program psychologist explained, the amount paid to surrogates is intentionally held at an artificially low rate so as to screen out women who might be motivated by monetary gain alone. One of the questions I sought to explore was whether surrogates were denying the significance of remuneration in order to cast their actions in the more culturally acceptable light of pure altruism, or whether they were motivated, at least in part, by remuneration and in part by other factors with the importance of remuneration decreasing as the pregnancy progressed, the version of events put forth by both program staff and surrogates.

The opinion popular among both scholars and the general population, that surrogates are motivated primarily by financial gain, has tended to result in oversimplified analyses of surrogate motivations. More typical of surrogate explanations for the connection between the initial decision to become a surrogate and the remuneration received are comments such as those expressed by Fran. "*It [surrogacy] sounded so interesting and fun. The money wasn't enough to be pregnant for nine months.*" Andrea, age 29, who was married with three children, said "*I'm not doing it for the money. Take the money: that wouldn't stop me. It wouldn't stop the majority.*" Sarah, age 27, who attended two years of college, and was married with two children, explained her feelings about remuneration in the following way: "*What's $10,000 bucks? You can't even buy a car. If it was just for the money you will want the baby. Money wasn't important. I possibly would have done it for expenses, especially for the people I did it for. My father would have given me the money not to do it.*"

The issue of remuneration proved to be of particular interest in that, although surrogates do accept monetary compensation for their reproductive work, its role is a multifaceted one. The surrogate pregnancy, unlike a traditional pregnancy, is viewed by the surrogate and her family as work; as such, it is informed by the belief that work is something that occurs only within the context of a paid occupation (Ferree 1984: 72). It is interesting to note that surrogates rarely spend the money they earn on themselves. The majority of surrogates I interviewed spent their earnings on home improvement, gifts for their husbands, a family vacation, or simply to pay off "family debts."

One of the primary reasons that most surrogates do not spend the money they earn on themselves alone appears to stem from the fact that the money serves as a buffer against and/or reward to their own families, particularly to their husbands who must make a number of compromises as a result of the surrogate arrangement. One of these compromises is obligatory abstention from sexual intercourse with their wives from the time insemination takes place until a pregnancy has been confirmed (a period that lasts on average from three to four months in length, but that may be extended for as long as one year).

The devaluation of the amount of the surrogate payment by the surrogates themselves as insufficient to compensate for "nine months of pregnancy" serves several important purposes. First, this view is representative of the cultural belief that children are "priceless" (Zelizer 1985); in this sense surrogates are merely reiterating a widely held cultural belief when they devalue the amount of remuneration they receive. For example, when the largest and one of the most well-established surrogate mother programs changed the wording of its advertising copy from "Help an Infertile Couple" to "Give the Gift of Life," the vastly increased volume of response revealed that the program had discovered a successful formula with which to reach the surrogate population. With surrogacy, the gift is conceptualized as a child, a formulation that is widely used in Euro-American culture—for example, in blood donation (Titmuss 1971) and organ donation (Fox and Swazey 1992).

The gift formulation holds particular appeal for surrogates because it reinforces the idea that having a child for someone is an act for which one cannot be compensated. As I have already mentioned, the gift of life narrative is further enhanced by some surrogates to include the near-sacrifice of their own lives in childbirth (Ragoné 1996, 1999). Fran, whose dismissal of the importance of payment I have already quoted, also offered another, even more revealing account of her decision to become a surrogate mother: "*I wanted to do the ultimate thing for somebody, to give them the ultimate gift. Nobody can beat that, nobody can do anything nicer for them.*" Stella, age 38, married with two children, noted that the commissioning couples "*consider it [the baby] a gift and I consider it a gift.*" Carolyn, age 33, married with two children, discussed her feelings about remuneration and having a surrogate child in these terms: "*It's a gift of love. I have always been a really giving person, and it's the ultimate way to give. I've always had babies so easily. It's the ultimate gift of love.*" For Euro-Americans it is "gift relations" rather than economic exchanges that characterize the family (Carrier 1990: 2). Thus, when surrogates minimize or dismiss the importance of money, they are on the one hand reiterating cultural beliefs about the pricelessness of children, and they are on the other hand suggesting that the exchange of a child for money is not a relationship of reciprocity but of kinship.

Once a surrogate enters a program, she also begins to recognize just how important having a child is to the commissioning couple. She sees with renewed clarity that no matter how much material success the couple has, their lives are emotionally impoverished because of their inability to have a child. In this way the surrogate's fertility serves as a leveling device for perceived, if unacknowledged, economic differences, and many surrogates begin to see themselves as altruistic or heroic figures who can rectify the imbalance in a couple's life. The surrogate's sense of place and her social network are greatly enlarged as she receives telephone calls from the program, rushes to keep doctor's appointments, meets with prospective couples (she may even be flown to other cities to meet couples), and later on attends (in the open programs) monthly or semimonthly surrogate support-group meetings. In some programs she may attend individual therapy sessions. She is often taken out socially by her couple, she may receive gifts from them for herself and her children, be telephoned regularly by them or receive cards and letters from them, and she attends holiday parties and other social events hosted by the program. Her sense of importance is also enhanced when she tells others about her new and unusual work. Once a surrogate meets, selects, and is selected by her couple and begins insemination—another rite of passage that confers additional status upon her—the couple becomes central to her life, adding an important steady source of social interaction and stimulation.

The entire surrogate experience serves to alter the balance of power in the surrogate's personal life, giving her entrée to a more public role and creating new and exciting demands upon her time. From the moment she places a telephone call to a surrogate mother program to the moment she delivers a child, the balance of power in a surrogate's personal life is altered radically. Her time can no longer be devoted exclusively to the care and nurture of her own family because she has entered into a legal and social contract to perform an important and economically rewarded task: helping an infertile couple to begin a family of their own. Unlike other types of employment, this activity cannot be regarded as unfeminine, selfish, or nonnurturant.

In this sense, we can see how surrogacy assists surrogates in their efforts to transcend the limitations of their domestic roles by highlighting "their differences from men . . . [b]y accepting and elaborating upon the symbols and expectations associated with their cultural definition" (Rosaldo 1974: 37), for example, motherhood. The gravity of the task provides the surrogate with an opportunity to do more than care for her family alone, and surrogates often report feeling that they are undertaking a task laden with importance, a project that fills them with a sense of pride and self-worth. Sally, age 33, married with two children and a full-time homemaker, discussed how surrogacy provided her with a feeling of unique accomplishment: *"Not everyone can do it. It's like the steelworkers who walk on beams ten floors up; not everyone can do it, not everyone can be a surrogate."*

GESTATIONAL SURROGATES

From 1987 to 1993, over 95 percent of all surrogacy arrangements were traditional. As of 1994, a profound shift occurred with 50 percent of all surrogacy arrangements gestational and as of 1999 that percentage continues to increase at the largest surrogate mother program (which is also the largest ovum donation program). With the advent of gestational surrogacy, however, reproduction is not only separated from sexual intercourse and motherhood but from pregnancy as well. In addition, gestational surrogacy creates three discernible categories of motherhood where there was previously only one: (1) the biological mother, the woman who contributes the ovum (traditionally assumed to be the "real mother"); (2) the gestational mother, the woman who gestates the embryos but who bears no genetic relationship to the child; and (3) the social mother, the woman who raises or nurtures the child.

The growing prevalence of gestational surrogacy is, in part, guided by recent legal precedents in which a surrogate who does not contribute an ovum toward the creation of a child has a significantly reduced possibility of being awarded custody in the event that she reneges on her contract and attempts to retain custody of the child. However, although legal factors have certainly contributed to the meteoric rise in the rates of gestational surrogacy, it should be remembered that for couples the ability to create a child genetically related to both parents is the primary reason that gestational surrogacy continues to grow in popularity.

But not all gestational surrogate arrangements involve the couple's embryos; numerous cases involve the combination of donor ova and the intending father's semen. Why then do couples pursue gestational surrogacy when traditional surrogacy provides them with the same degree of biogenetic linkage to the child, has a higher likelihood of being successful, and costs less? Several reasons are cited by the staff of the largest surrogate mother program. The primary reason is that many more women are willing to donate ova than are willing to serve as surrogate mothers. This surrogate program is now also the largest ovum donation program in the United States with over 300 screened donors on file. The second reason, as previously mentioned, is that the U.S. courts would, in theory, be less likely to award custody to a gestational surrogate than to a traditional surrogate who contributed her own ovum to the creation of the child.[3] But perhaps most importantly, when commissioning couples choose donor ova/gestational surrogacy, they sever the surrogate's genetic link to and/or claim to the child. By contrast, with traditional surrogacy the adoptive mother must emphasize the importance of nurturance and social parenthood, while the surrogate mother deemphasizes her biogenetic tie to the child.

An additional reason, and one of critical importance, is that couples from certain racial, ethnic and religious groups (e.g., Japanese, Taiwanese, and Jewish) could find women who were willing to donate their ova, but were rarely able to locate women who were willing to serve in the capacity of surrogate. Thus, couples from particular ethnic/racial/religious groups who are seeking donors from those groups often pursue ovum donation/gestational surrogacy.[4]

The gestational surrogate's articulated ideas about relatedness (or more accurately, the presumed lack thereof) also produce a shift in emphasis away from potentially problematic aspects of gestational surrogacy, such as race and ethnicity. Unlike traditional surrogate arrangements in which the majority of couples and surrogates are Euro-American, it is not unusual for gestational surrogates and commissioning couples to come from diverse racial, ethnic, religious and cultural backgrounds. In fact, approximately 30 percent of all gestational surrogate arrangements at the largest program now involve surrogates and couples matched from different racial, ethnic, and cultural backgrounds. I have, over the last four years, interviewed a Mexican-American gestational surrogate who was carrying a child for a Japanese couple; an African-American gestational surrogate who had attempted several embryo transfers unsuccessfully for both a Japanese couple and a Euro-American couple; a Euro-American gestational surrogate who had delivered twins for a Japanese couple; and a Taiwanese couple looking for an Asian American ovum donor and gestational surrogate.

When I questioned Carole, an African-American gestational surrogate (who at twenty-nine was single, with one child, and had yet to sustain a gestational pregnancy) about the issue of racial difference (between herself and her couple), she stated: "*I had friends who had a problem because [they thought] I should help blacks. And I told them, Don't look at the color issue. If a white person offered to help you, you wouldn't turn them down.*" However, the following statement by Carole reveals that the issue of racial difference is further nuanced as a positive factor, one that actually facilitates the surrogate/child separation process: "*My mom is happy the couple is not black because she was worried I would want to keep it [the baby]. The first couple I was going to go with was black. I don't want to raise another kid.*"

When I questioned Linda, a thirty-year old Mexican-American woman pregnant with a child for a couple from Japan, about this issue, her reasoning illustrated how beliefs concerning racial difference can be used by surrogates (and couples) to resolve any conflicting feelings about the child being related to a surrogate by virtue of having been carried in her body: "*No, I haven't [thought of the child as mine], because she's not mine, she never has been. For one*

thing, she is totally Japanese. It's a little hard for me. In a way she will always be my Japanese girl; but she is theirs." In this quote, we can see how Linda recapitulates one of the initial motivations cited by gestational surrogates, the desire to bear a child for an infertile couple while highlighting the lack of physical and racial resemblance, or biogenetic tie. "*If I was to have a child, it would only be from my husband and me. With AI [traditional surrogacy], the baby would be a part of me. I don't know if I could let a part of me. . . . AI was never for me; I never considered it.*"

Carole and Linda are aware, of course, as are other gestational surrogates, that they do not share a genetic tie with the children they produce as gestational surrogates. But concerns such as Carole's about raising an African-American couple's child reveal how racial resemblance raises certain questions about relatedness even when there is no genetic tie.[5] Although she knows that the child is not genetically hers, certain boundaries become blurred for her when an African-American couple is involved whereas with a Euro-American couple the distinction between genetic/nongenetic or self/other is clear. Cultural conceptions such as this about the connection between race and genetics deserve further exploration.

Not surprisingly, the shift from traditional to gestational surrogacy has attracted a different population of women. Overall, women who elect to become gestational surrogates tend to articulate the belief that traditional surrogacy, even though less medically complicated[6] is not an acceptable option for them because they are uncomfortable with the prospect of contributing their own ovum to the creation of a child. They also cannot readily accept the idea that a child who is genetically related to them would be raised by someone else. In other words, they explicitly articulate the opinion in traditional surrogacy (where the surrogate contributes an ovum) that the surrogate is the mother of the child, whereas in gestational surrogacy (where she does not contribute an ovum) she is not. They are nonetheless interested in participating in gestational surrogacy because it provides them with access to the world of surrogacy.[7] This often includes, interestingly enough, women who have been voluntarily sterilized (tubal ligations). For example, Barbara, age 30, married with three children, a Mormon and a two-time gestational surrogate (now planning a third pregnancy) stated: "*The baby is never mine. I am providing a needed environment for it to be born and go back to mom and dad. It's the easy kind of babysitting.*"

Oddly enough, the beliefs of IVF surrogates run contrary to current legal opinion as expressed in the findings of both Britain's Warnock Report and the Australian Waller Commission's report that "when a child is born to a woman following the donation of another's egg the woman giving birth should, for all purposes, be regarded in law as the mother of that child" (Shalev 1989: 117). It should be noted that the opinion expressed in both the Warnock Report and the Waller Commission contradicts not only the views expressed by IVF surrogates but also by commissioning couples who choose gestational surrogacy precisely because it eliminates the issue of genetic relatedness for them. It also contradicts Euro-American kinship ideology, specifically the continued emphasis on the importance of biogenetic relatedness.[8] However, this effort to expand our definition of biological relatedness, which has until recently depended on a genetic component, runs contrary to the Euro-American emphasis on biogenetic relatedness, in which genetic parents are legally and socially considered the "real" parents. This fragmentation or dispersal of parenthood, a byproduct of reproductive technologies, has resulted in what Marilyn Strathern has describes as the "claims of one kind of biological mother against other kinds of biological and nonbiological mothers" (1992: 32) and fathers.

How then to account for the gestational surrogate's motivations? Should a gestational surrogate's maternal rights be "modeled on the law of paternity, where proof of genetic parentage establishes . . . parentage, or . . . on the nine month experience of pregnancy as establishing the preponderant interest of . . . parentage" (Hull 1990: 152). It is of fundamental importance to gestational surrogates to circumvent the biogenetic tie to the child, and they do so in spite of the greatly increased degree of physical discomfort and medical risk they face in IVF procedures (as compared to

risks associated with traditional surrogacy, which are the same as those faced in traditional pregnancy.[9] Any effort, legal or ethical, to argue that pregnancy is a determining factor in parenthood not only fails to consider Euro-American kinship ideology but perhaps most importantly neglects to consider the position of the gestational surrogate and commissioning couple.

The medical procedures commonly encountered by gestational surrogates [the self-administration of hormonal medications] can cause considerable discomfort. In the following example, Barbara discussed her experience: "*After a while you dread having to do it; I had lumps from all those injections. Two times a day and twice a week, three injections a day. If you don't do it, the pregnancy would be lost. . . . You are just [as] concerned with the pregnancy as if it's your own, sometimes more.*" Vicky, age 33, Euro-American, married with three children, who had given birth three weeks earlier, explained how she was able to sustain her motivation and commitment throughout the difficult medical procedures: "*It was hard, but it needed to be done for the baby's sake. All the shots [were] on a daily basis. I didn't mind it at all, but it had to be at a certain time. It was like a curfew. Sure it was painful, but it does go away.*"

The sentiments expressed by Barbara and Vicky are similar to those expressed by traditional surrogates who have experienced difficult, sometimes life-threatening pregnancies and deliveries. Both cast these experiences in terms of meaningful or heroic suffering (Ragoné 1996). The vastly increased physical discomfort and scheduling difficulties are, however, a price that gestational surrogates are willing to endure in order to circumvent what they regard as the problematic biogenetic tie. Barbara expressed a belief shared by many gestational surrogates about their pregnancies when she stated: "*I separate AI [artificial insemination] and IVF completely, almost to the point I don't agree with AI. I feel like that person is entering into an agreement to produce a child to give to someone else. I feel it is her baby she is giving away*". In a similar fashion, Lee, age 31, married with two children, Euro-American, who was waiting for an embryo transfer, discussed the differences between traditional (AI) and gestational surrogacy. "*Yes, it's [the fetus] inside my body, but as far as I am concerned, I don't have any biological tie. The other way [AI], I would feel that there is some part of me out there."*

This view of surrogacy differs in several important ways from the one expressed by traditional surrogates, who advance the idea that the term "parent" should be applied only to individuals who actually choose to become engaged in the process of raising a child, regardless of the degree of relatedness. They achieve this perspective in part by separating motherhood into two components: biological motherhood and social motherhood. Only social motherhood is viewed by traditional surrogates as "real" motherhood; in other words, nurturance is held to be of greater importance than biological relatedness. In this respect, it is the gestational surrogate, not the traditional surrogate, who tends to subscribe to a decidedly more traditional rendering of relatedness.

It was perhaps impossible to predict with any degree of certainty that advances in reproductive medicine coupled with an increase in consumer demand would produce such a profound shift in the rates of traditional (AI) and gestational surrogacy. Assistive reproductive technologies (e.g., surrogate motherhood, ovum donation, and sperm donation), have called into question what was once understood to be the "natural" basis of parenthood. As we have seen, traditional surrogates underplay their own biological contribution in order to bring to the fore the importance of the social, nurturant role played by the adoptive mother. In this way motherhood is reinterpreted as primarily an important social role in order to sidestep problematic aspects of the surrogate's biogenetic relationship to the child and the adoptive mother's lack of a biogenetic link. For traditional surrogates nurture takes precedence and ascendancy over nature; motherhood is understood as a social construct rather than a biological phenomenon. Gestational surrogates however, interestingly remain committed to the genetic model of parenthood,[10] reasoning that "real" parenthood is in fact genetic.

Many of the early theories about the future of surrogacy focused, at times exclusively, upon its potential for exploitation, but they failed to take into consideration the fact that both fertility and infertility must be contextualized: both are embedded in a series of personal, social, historical, and cultural processes and practices. Within surrogates' statements, assessments, and questions is testimony to the plasticity and resilience of family, which in spite of these seemingly odd changes, persists.

ACKNOWLEDGMENTS

I owe a very special thank you to Dr. Sydel Silverman of the Wenner Gren Foundation for Anthropological Research for her support. An additional thank you is also owed to the University of Massachusetts–Boston for ongoing support in the form of Faculty Development Grants. I am especially indebted to the women and men who have shared their experiences with me over the last ten years; their belief in and commitment to this research has made it an engaging and rewarding experience. I would also like to extend very special and heartfelt thanks to the directors, psychologists, and surrogate program staff who have over the years generously given of their time and their expertise.

NOTES

1. A couple, Elizabeth and William Stern, contracted with a surrogate, Mary Beth Whitehead, to bear a child for them because Elizabeth Stern suffered from multiple sclerosis, a condition that can be exacerbated by pregnancy. Once the child was born, however, Whitehead refused to relinquish the child to the Sterns, and in 1987, William Stern, the biological father, filed suit against Whitehead in an effort to enforce the terms of the surrogate contract. The decision of the lower court to award custody to the biological father and to permit his wife to adopt the child was overturned by the New Jersey Supreme Court, which then awarded custody to William Stern, prohibiting Elizabeth Stern from adopting the child while granting visitation rights to Mary Beth Whitehead. These decisions mirrored public opinion about surrogacy (Hull 1990: 154).
2. See Rapp (1978: 279) and Gordon (1988: 3) for a historical analysis of the idea of the demise of the American family.

3. In June 1993, the California Supreme Court upheld the decisions of both the lower court and the court of appeals with respect to gestational surrogacy contracts. In *Anna Johnson v Mark and Crispina Calvert,* Case #SO 23721, a case involving an African-American gestational surrogate, a Filipina American mother and a Euro-American father, the gestational surrogate and commissioning couple both filed custody suits. Under California law, both of the women could, however, claim maternal rights: Johnson, by virtue of being the woman who gave birth to the child; and Calvert, who donated ovum, because she is the child's genetic mother. In rendering their decision, however, the court circumvented the issue of relatedness, instead emphasized the "intent" of the parties as the ultimate and decisive factor in any determination of parenthood. The court concluded that if the genetic and birth mother are not one and the same person then "she who intended to procreate the child—that is, she who intended to bring about the birth of a child that she intended to raise on her own—is the natural mother under California law."

4. Why women from certain cultural groups are willing to donate ova but not serve as surrogates is a subject of considerable interest. Since gestational surrogates reason that they (unlike traditional surrogates and ovum donors) do not part with any genetic material, they are able to deny that the child(ren) they produce are related to them. Given the parameters of Euro-American kinship ideology, additional research will be required to ascertain why ovum donors do not perceive their donation of genetic material as problematic.

5. During the course of the interview, I specifically asked her what her feelings and ideas were about having a child for a couple from another racial background (I also asked this question of all the surrogates who were matched with couples from different racial backgrounds).

6. Gestational surrogates often complain about the discomfort they experience as a result of having to self-inject two or three times per day for as long as three to four months of the pregnancy. They report that progesterone is especially painful, since it is oil-based and has a tendency to pool and lump under the skin. Even though the largest of the surrogate programs claims to inform gestational surrogates about the need to self-administer shots, several gestational surrogates reported that they had not anticipated either the frequency or the discomfort of the injections.

7. I have discussed elsewhere in great detail the system of rewards that makes surrogate motherhood attractive to this group of women (Ragoné 1994, 1996, 1999).

8. While there are in fact observable differences in family patterns within the United States, most notably among poor and working poor African-Americans whose alternative models of mothering/parenting may stem from "West African cultural values" as well as "functional adaptations to race and gender oppression" (Collins 1988: 119; Stack 1974), we should not lose sight of the fact that such perceived differences in family patterns do not necessarily weaken Euro-American kinship ideology. They continue to privilege the biogenetic model of family.

9. Aside from studies of the increased rates of multiple births, there are few longitudinal studies on the effects of infertility treatments. Research does, however, suggest that infertility patients have an increased risk of ovarian cancer (Jensen, Riis et al. 1987). The question remains: Although an infertile woman knowingly accepts the risks associated with infertility treatments, do surrogacy and ovum donation programs provide their populations with adequate information about the possibility of long-term risk?

10. Once a gestational surrogate has begun to develop a relationship with her couple and has experienced several unsuccessful embryo transfers, she may begin to reformulate or revise her initial beliefs concerning relatedness and family. An unsuccessful gestational surrogate may, for example, opt to become what is referred to in surrogate-mother programs as a "cross-over," someone who chose initially to participate in gestational surrogacy but then decided to become a traditional surrogate.

REFERENCES

Andrews, Lori. 1984. *New Conceptions: A Consumer's Guide to the Newest Infertility Treatments.* New York: Ballantine.

Annas, George. 1988. "Fairy Tales Surrogate Mothers Tell." In Larry Gostin (ed.). *Surrogate Motherhood: Politics and Privacy,* pp. 43–55. Bloomington: Indiana University Press.

Carrier, James. 1990. "Gifts in a World of Commodities: The Ideology of the Perfect Gift in American Society." *Social Analysis* 29:19–37.

Collins, Patricia Hill. 1988. *Black Feminist Thought: Knowledge, Consciousness and the Politics of Empowerment.* New York: Routledge.

Dworkin, Andrea. 1978. *Right-Wing Women.* New York: Perigee Books.

Ferree, Myra. 1984. "Sacrifice, Satisfaction and Social Change: Employment and the Family." In Karen Sacks and Dorothy Remy (eds.). *My Troubles are Going to Have Trouble with Me*, pp. 61–79. New Brunswick, NJ: Rutgers University Press.

Fox, Renee, and Judith Swazey. 1992. *Spare Parts: Organ Replacement in American Society*. New York and Oxford: Oxford University Press.

Gordon, Linda. 1988. *Heroes of Their Own Lives*. New York: Viking.

Hull, Richard. 1990. "Gestational Surrogacy and Surrogate Motherhood." In Richard Hull (ed.). *Ethical Issues in the New Reproductive Technologies*, pp. 150–155. Belmont, CA: Wadsworth Publishers.

Jensen, P., B. Riis, P. Rodbro, V. Stram, and C. Christiansen, 1987. "Climacteric Symptoms after Oral and Percutaneous Hormone Replacement Therapy." *Matvritas* 9: 207–215.

Martin, Emily. 1987. *The Woman in the Body: A Cultural Analysis of Reproduction*. Boston: Beacon Press.

Neuhaus, Robert. 1988. "Renting Women, Buying Babies and Class Struggles." *Society* 25 (3): 8–10.

Parker, Phillip. 1983. "Motivation of Surrogate Mothers: Initial Findings." *American Journal of Psychiatry* 140: 117–119.

Ragoné, Heléna. 1994. *Surrogate Motherhood: Conception in the Heart*. Boulder, CO, and Oxford, UK: Westview Press/Basic Books.

———. 1996. "Chasing the Blood Tie: Surrogate Mothers, Adoptive Mothers and Fathers." *American Ethnologist* 23 (2): 352–365.

———. 1998. "Incontestable Motivations." In Sarah Franklin and Heléna Ragoné (eds.). *Reproducing Reproduction: Kinship, Power, and Technological Innovation*, pp. 118–131. Philadelphia: University of Pennsylvania Press.

———. 1999. "The Gift of Life: Surrogate Motherhood, Gamete Donations and Constructions of Altruism." In Linda Layne (ed.). *Transformative Mothering: On Giving and Getting, in a Consumer Culture*, pp. 132–176. New York: New York University Press.

———. 2000. "Of Likeness and Difference: How Race Is Being Transfigured by Gestational Surrogacy." In Heléna Ragoné and France Winddance Twine, (eds.). *Ideologies and Technologies of Motherhood: Race, Class, Sexuality and Nationalism*, New York and London: Routledge.

Rapp, Rayna. 1978. "Family and Class in Contemporary America: Notes Toward an Understanding of Ideology. *Science and Technology* 42 (3): 278–300.

Rosaldo, Michelle. 1974." Woman, Culture and Society: A Theoretical Overview." In M. Rosaldo and L. Lamphere (eds.). *Woman, Culture and Society*, pp. 17–43. Stanford, CA: Stanford University Press.

Shalev, Carmel. 1989. *Birth Power: The Case for Surrogacy*. New Haven, CT: Yale University Press.

Snowden, R., G. Mitchell, and E. Snowden, 1983. *Artificial Reproduction: A Social Investigation*. London: Allen and Unwin.

Strathern, Marilyn. 1991. The Pursuit of Certainty: Investigating Kinship in the Late Twentieth Century. Distinguished Lecture. Society of the Anthropology of Europe.

———. 1992. *Reproducing the Future: Anthropology, Kinship and the New Reproductive Technologies*. Manchester, UK: Manchester University Press.

Titmuss, Richard. 1971. *The Gift Relationship: From Human Blood to Social Policy*. New York: Pantheon Books.

Zelizer, Viviana. 1985. *Pricing the Priceless Child*. New York: Basic Books.

Female Genital Cutting:
Culture and Controversy

Ellen Gruenbaum

"Get away! What's the matter with you? You kids are behaving like a bunch of animals!" an older

The Female Circumcision Controversy: An Anthropological Perspective by Ellen Gruenbaum. © 2000 University of Pennsylvania Press. Reprinted by Permission.

Sudanese woman yelled from inside the adobe brick room where the circumcision was to take place. She slapped the wire netting that screened the window and stomped outside to chase the small throng of laughing, curious children away from the window where they were peeking inside. She rounded the corner of the well-built rectangular adobe house and accosted the boys and girls at the window in a high-pitched, agitated voice, "Move on! See this switch? Let's go!" She smacked the ground threateningly with her long, thin stick, the sort commonly used to prod a wayward donkey or goat.

The children scattered. An older, more sensible boy took up a position near the window where he could keep the others away. The woman adjusted her long tobe, the over garment that covers the hair and body but not the face, and returned to the other women inside, who were preparing for the circumcisions. They had already moved one bed, made of wood and woven rope, into the center of the room where the trained midwife would have good light. The cotton mattresses on three beds where the children would recuperate were covered with clean cotton sheets and pillows. The midwife directed them to cover the bed for the surgeries with a red oilcloth over a cotton pillow and a pile of clean cloth scraps that could support a girl gently, and wash it with soap and water. They boiled water in a kettle on the charcoal fire, and the midwife prepared her instruments to be sterilized in an enamel bowl: a hypodermic, two sharp new razors, a curved suture needle, suturing thread, and a small scissors.

"Come, sit right close to me so you can see everything!" the midwife urged, motioning me to a small, low stool beside her. I hesitated, wondering if I would be able to watch the little girls experience the cutting that awaited them, known locally as "Pharaonic circumcision." But as an anthropologist doing research on rural health services and women's roles in this Sudanese village, I wanted this opportunity to observe, to be better able to understand and describe this important experience in the lives of girls. What I was about to witness was the most severe form of female genital cutting and closure (infibulation) found anywhere in Africa.

CLITORIDECTOMY, EXCISION, AND INFIBULATION

The term "female genital mutilation," or FGM, has been widely used in recent years, to describe various forms of "female circumcision" that are found in many countries. "Mutilation" is technically accurate for most variants of the practices since they entail damage to or removal of healthy tissues or organs. The provocative term, as well as the realities it conveys, has stimulated great international concern and action against the practices.

But since "mutilation" connotes intentional harm, its use is tantamount to accusing the women who do it of harmful intent. Some people, even those who favor stopping the practices, have been deeply offended by the term FGM, arguing that it is not women's intent to mutilate their daughters but to give them proper, socially expected treatment. Their intent is simply to "circumcise," or "purify." The words commonly used for female genital cutting in Arabic-speaking countries, *tahur* or *tahara*, means "purification," that is, the achievement of cleanliness through a ritual activity. "Female circumcision," however, echoes the term for the removal of the foreskin in the male, which has been considered non-mutilating (Toubia 1993:9)—at least until the recent movement to end that practice as well (see the work of the organization NOCIRC)—and is therefore rejected by many people, since it seems to trivialize the damage done and the huge scale of the practices. I prefer the term "Female Genital Cutting," or "FGC," which has become well established in international discourse: it avoids disparaging the practitioners yet does not minimize the seriousness of the issue.

There are several types of cutting and removal of tissues of genitalia of young girls and women, done to conform to social expectations in communities of many different religions and ethnicities. The form varies not only from one sociocultural context to another but even within a single village, such as the Sudanese village just described, where different ethnic groups do different types of cutting. Forms vary between families, too, with some preferring their ethnic group's traditional forms while other families seek less harmful forms. Also, trained midwives and other practitioners (including traditional birth attendants, other older women, barbers, and even medical doctors) have their own individual techniques of doing the procedures, resulting in varying amounts of tissue taken and various levels of hygiene. (In most countries, medical doctors are now strongly discouraged or forbidden by their professional organizations and governments from doing *any* form of FGC.)

In some cultural contexts, it is very young children who are cut, including infants or toddlers (Shandall 1967, Toubia 1993, 1994, Abdal Rahman 1997). Anne Jennings reported southern Egyptian girls undergoing genital cutting at age 1 or 2 (1995:48). Most commonly, it is done to young girls between the ages of 4 and 8. But in some cultural contexts (e.g. the Maasai of East Africa), cutting is delayed until a young woman is in her teens and about to be married (14–15 or even older).

In the past few years the World Health Organization has developed a comprehensive typology that technical experts use for the different types. People who practice female genital cutting have their own terms for different types in their many languages, of course, which may or may not fit well with the World Health Organization's four types. Researchers can, however, place the range of the practices into the following categories.

Clitoridectomy. The World Health Organization's Type I includes both the partial and total removal of the clitoris, called clitoridectomy, and also the less severe forms of the operations, such as the cutting away of part or all of the clitoral prepuce, or "hood," analogous to the foreskin removal of male circumcision. Removal of only the prepuce seems to be very rare, but partial removal of the clitoris is fairly common.

Clitoridectomy, whether partial or total, is often referred to by Muslims and others as "*sunna* circumcision" or "*sunna* purification." In my experience doing ethnographic research in Sudan, the term "*sunna* circumcision" was in fact applied to a wide variety of surgeries, perhaps because of the positive association between that word and Muslim religious values.

Excision. The World Health Organization's Type II is called "excision." In this type, the cutting goes further than clitoridectomy to include removal of the prepuce, the entire clitoris, and partial or total excision of the labia minora (the smaller inner lips of the vaginal opening). In Sudan this form is usually also called "*sunna*," even though it is more damaging than what some people mean by "*sunna*." They are grouped in common parlance because there are just two basic folk terms—*sunna* and pharaonic circumcision—and they use the "*sunna*" terminology for both clitoridectomy and excision. In fact, it is often applied to any circumcisions that are not "pharaonic." Imprecise terms (such as *nuss* for "half") are also used for some of the in-between forms that would be included in Type II.

Infibulation and reinfibulation. The most severe cutting occurs with Type III, or infibulation. It is the main type in Sudan, where it is commonly called "pharaonic circumcision." People think it dates back to the days of the Pharaohs. In Egypt, where this severe infibulation is rare, it is called "Sudanese circumcision." In this type, part or all of the external genitalia—prepuce, clitoris, labia minora, and all or part of the labia majora—are removed and the raw edges are infibulated (held together by stitching or thorns). When healed, infibulation leaves a perfectly smooth vulva of skin and scar tissue with only a single tiny opening for urination and menstrual flow, preserved during healing by the insertion of a small object such as a piece of straw. In a variation of infibulation that is slightly less severe, the trimmed labia minora are sewn shut but the labia majora are left alone. In either case, it is essential that a midwife be present for childbirth to make an incision in the tissue to allow the baby to be born. The new mother is then reinfibulated by the midwife, a practice that is repeated after each pregnancy. The new mother often asks the midwife to make the opening very small, "like a virgin," to enhance her husband's sexual pleasure. This is analogous to, although more severe than, what some North American obstetricians do: take an extra stitch, called "the husband's stitch," when doing an episiotomy, for the purpose of restoring tightness to the opening.

Other variations. Others that do not include tissue removal are grouped as Type IV. This includes practices such as pricking, piercing, incision, stretching of the clitoris or labia, cauterization, cuts or scrapes on the genitalia, or the use of harmful substances in the vagina. Labia stretching to pursue culturally preferred aesthetics of the body is not particularly harmful, but other variations can be painful or damaging. In some East African countries, some men's preference for "dry sex" has resulted in the introduction of dangerous or uncomfortable astringents into the vagina to dry it out before intercourse, which is included in Type IV. In Europe and North

America, the fad of labia piercing could be included as a Type IV practice.

HARMFUL EFFECTS

The harmful effects of these forms differ, but all forms—from clitoridectomy to infibulation—create risks for the girls at the time of cutting. Medical reports document cases of excess bleeding (hemorrhage), infections, blood poisoning (septicemia), retention of urine, or shock. Such complications can be life-threatening. Later on, the infibulated state sometimes results in retention of menses (if the vagina is blocked by scar tissue), difficulty in urination (if there is excess scar tissue around or over the urethra), and a high incidence of urinary tract and chronic pelvic infections. At first intercourse, the extremely small size of the opening created by infibulation presents a barrier which can make first sexual intercourse very difficult or impossible. Often the scar tissue around the opening must be painfully ruptured or is cut by the husband, a midwife, or a doctor. During childbirth, the inelastic scar tissue of infibulation must be cut by the birth attendant at the right time so labor will not be obstructed. Not only is obstructed labor dangerous to the baby, but also the mother's internal tissues can be damaged, creating a fistula (opening in the tissue separating the vagina from the urinary bladder), which can result in an embarrassing condition with constantly leaking urine (Shandall 1967, Shell-Duncan & Hernlund 2000b:14–18, Gruenbaum 2001, Toubia 1994).

The psychological effects are less well understood, not systematically researched, and no doubt differ a great deal from one situation to another. There is anecdotal evidence of adverse psychological effects, perhaps particularly if it comes without warning and seems a betrayal of trust. Yet many women simply accept the experience as just part of becoming a woman.

Damage to sexual responsiveness is suspected for many women, yet there is also data that suggests the frequency and extent of problems vary greatly. Many women do not lose sexual interest and retain the ability to achieve sexual satisfaction and orgasms, even among the infibulated (Gruenbaum 2001, chapter 5, and Lightfoot-Klein 1989). Sexual responsiveness could be affected differently depending on which tissues are cut and how, whether the surrounding or underlying tissues retain sensitivity, whether there is severe infibulation, and of course whether the emotional attachment of the partners is strong and the relationship loving and supportive. Some midwives have been careful to avoid cutting too much of the sensitive tissue (clitoris and erectile tissue) hoping to preserve sensitivity, but still make the result look like an infibulation by joining the labia across the opening.

It is therefore erroneous to assume that all women who have been cut have lost their sexual responsiveness. Similarly, although many experience very harmful medical consequences, many do not, so one cannot generalize about the effects without reference to the specific practices and circumstances.

BUT WHY?

Indeed, the world wonders how loving parents can allow their daughters to be held down and cut, usually causing fear, pain, and possible major damage to health and physical functions, immediate or long-term. It seems incongruous and shocking to imagine a six-year-old girl enduring such pain and indignity, particularly at the hands of those she trusts.

Yet current estimates are that somewhere between 200,000 and a million girls experience some form of female genital cutting each year (Yoder 2003), mostly in 28 countries in Africa, and many millions of women and girls are living with FGC's life-long effects. In addition, the practices are found in other countries where they have spread by immigration or due to adoption of genital cutting if they believe it is associated with their religion. Why do women continue to arrange for these practices to be done to their daughters?

Is it because of any particular religion? No. The practices are found in many countries and among people of widely different ethnic groups and religions, including Judaism, Christianity,

Islam, and traditional African religions. Yet it often happens that people who follow circumcision traditions often *do* associate the practices with their own religious beliefs.

For example, although many learned religious scholars have declared that infibulation has no place in Islam, and others say that no form whatsoever should be permitted, other teachers consider female circumcision as an "ennobling" act that is very proper for Muslims, so long as they don't go beyond clitoridectomy, which is usually called "*sunna* circumcision." The basic meaning of the Arabic word "*sunna*" is "tradition," which usually connotes the traditions of the Prophet Mohammed, i.e., those things that he did or advocated during his lifetime (570–622 C.E.), handed down through oral tradition and the writings know as the *Hadith.* Muslims believe the Holy Qur'an to be God's direct revelation, and the first source of guidance for righteous living, and it is silent on female circumcision. But Muslims also respect the sayings and actions attributed to the Prophet Mohammed during his lifetime as a secondary source of guidance. Although disputes remain among Muslims about which stories and quotations offer the most reliable versions of the Prophet's advice and how the sayings and stories should be interpreted, many Muslims have concluded that the Prophet Mohammed's words on the subject—"Reduce but do not destroy"—mean that only the less severe cutting is acceptable, though not required. Others believe the Prophet actually advocated it, making it either an obligation or at least a blessing to do it. Others believe Muslims should avoid female circumcision completely, since it is not mentioned in the Qur'an as a duty of the faithful. Using the term *sunna,* then, seems to imply that it is expected of Muslims, and while the term may help convince Muslims to give up infibulation, it may reinforce their continuing clitoridectomy. No doubt there will be many lively discussions among Muslim scholars in the coming years!

How about male dominance—is that the cause of this practice? Many analysts have noted that female genital cutting forms a part of the subordination of women where it is found. While of course not all strongly patriarchal societies of the world utilize female genital cutting, where it is found it is indeed embedded in the patriarchal structures of male domination of the lives of women and girls (Gruenbaum 2001, Shell-Duncan & Hernlund 2000a, Assaad 1980, Hayes 1975, El Saadawi 1980b.) That is not to say that women do not have any control or influence on the decisions, types, and timing of the cutting. And that does not mean it is always men who are pushing for it. Rather, the conditions of women's lives often encourage their participation in and celebration of the cutting, their advocacy or their tolerance of the rituals, and their willingness to endure or accept the health risks.

In analysis of several case examples, including my Sudanese research, the manifestation of male dominance is primarily in disparate economic and social circumstances of women and men. While women are usually economically productive (whether for the market economy or for subsistence), carry out important services in the domestic sphere, and have some distinctive rights in each of the different cultures of Africa, most societies nevertheless accord greater political and economic power to men, especially older and more dominant and successful men. Economic and social situations of women vary a great deal—traders/market women have their own incomes to spend and farming women may have sources of income they use to help support their families or provide for their personal needs, but in many cultures, a woman's access to economic resources is mediated by men. In Islamic law, Muslim women are entitled to own and manage property, but the inheritance rules favor men—a daughter receives half the share of a son, for example. Even then, local groups often expect daughters not to claim shares, so that their brothers can be more secure, arguing that women are entitled to rely on husbands and male kin for support and should not need separate holdings. In other cultures, women may be dependent on men for access to land, livestock, foodstuffs, a share of a husband's income, and old-age support by sons. But women are vulnerable to divorce or polygyny that might reduce their security. If economic security and socially-approved reproduction are mediated by the dominant roles of men, women clearly need to conform to whatever rules the culture requires, including varying expectations for virginity, excision, or infibulation in order to have successful marriages and child-bearing. Their enculturation process must prepare girls for their subordinate roles.

Women's consciousness regarding their positions may range from strong belief in the moral superiority of men, to wry acceptance of the role disparity, to willingness to challenge the status quo in favor of better futures. But given the power of social pressure and the rewards of acceptance of genital cutting—propriety, marriage, children, and financial support—it should not be surprising that most women have not yet jumped on the bandwagon of abandoning female genital cutting.

CULTURAL CONTEXTS
AND PEOPLE'S REASONS

The explicit reasons people give for circumcising their daughters are varied, depending on the cultural contexts in which FGC practices occur. For some, genital cutting is a rite of passage to marriageable womanhood. The Maasai of Kenya, for example, usually wait until a girl's marriage has been arranged, and she is then excised (Type II) and her head is shaved during the weeks of marriage preparations. After she has healed she goes to her husband and new home ready for womanhood.

Female genital cutting often plays a role in gender identity. Some even use terms like "male parts" for the clitoris and labia, saying removal of them results in a more feminine and aesthetically pleasing body. In many of the Nile Valley cultures of Egypt and Sudan, genital cutting helps to define feminine gender and is considered an essential prerequisite to marriage. Nile Valley girls are cut at earlier ages, so that they will be known to be virgins and ready for socially approved marriage when old enough.

The type of circumcision done sometimes defines ethnic identity. Even within a single village, such as the Sudanese village described above, different ethnic groups do different types of cutting. Thus, the Zabarma and Hausa

minorities who have immigrated to Sudan anywhere from a century ago to more recent decades have usually resisted adopting infibulation, yet some have also adopted it along with other changes as part of their cultural and linguistic acculturation to the dominant Arab-Sudanese culture.

Some practitioners in Sudan advocated genital cutting as a way to preserve virginity. Not only is cutting expected to reduce some sexual sensitivity, thought to help girls and wives resist improper sexual relationships by taming what are thought to be overly powerful female sexual impulses, but also the infibulation is an actual barrier to penetration, preventing premarital pregnancy. People have even speculated, without any confirmation, that the practice may have developed in ancient times as a measure to prevent rape by strangers passing through on trade routes.

THE BIG DAY

The morning cool was beginning to fade, and the day promised to be hot and dry, as usual. The midwife washed her hands thoroughly with soap and water, shook off the water, and let them dry. The two pretty little girls were guided through the door by their mother. Recently bathed, hair freshly plaited and dotted with some henna paste, the girls wore colorful new dresses and special ornaments known as *jirtig*, as protection against excessive blood loss or the harm that might be done by spirits (*jinn*). The family's gold jewelry was ready for them to put on during recovery. They looked proud, though a little anxious, about this first time to be treated as such special people.

Their male cousin, about 7, lay silently on a bed in the corner, his face to the wall. Earlier in the morning he had been taken by car to the small hospital in a town several kilometers away to be circumcised by a medical assistant. When he returned, he was greeted with celebratory ululations and helped into a bed in the corner of this room to recover.

As the dozen women present greeted the mother and girls with smiles and encouragement, the mother hesitated, reconsidering the wisdom of doing the younger, who looked to be only about four years old. The other was six, the best age to be able to complete healing before starting school. But there were many advantages to cutting three children the same day, since the families could share the expenses of the celebration and not have to do it again in two years for the younger one. The midwife and the others quickly overcame the mother's hesitation, urging her to do it right away. Don't worry, it will soon be over, she's already prepared, and, as the saying goes, "You grow up, you forget" (*Tekbara, tensa*). Outside, other relatives and neighbors were cooking over charcoal fires, preparing a dried meat and yogurt stew, beans, bread, tea, and sweets for the well-wishers expected to begin arriving soon. The ceremony would not be easily delayed.

So, both girls were cut, the younger first. Thankfully the midwife's methods were fairly hygienic, not like the old methods, when the cutting was done using broken glass or an unsterilized knife with thorns for sutures. This midwife's better techniques were respected, as her patients usually avoided the worst complications. The first girl was washed carefully, held by loving but firm arms of the women, and injected—painfully—with the local anesthetic xylocaine into her clitoris, prepuce, and labia to deaden the feeling. A few minutes later, she was cut carefully, avoiding major arteries. She did not feel any pain when her prepuce, clitoris, and labia minora (inner lips) were cut off with one of the sterilized razor blades. Her labia majora (outer lips) were trimmed slightly and the two sides sutured together with the curved needle so they could heal with a smooth surface, leaving just one opening for urine and future menstrual flow. The second girl was done the same way, and after each cutting, the midwife rinsed the wound with an antiseptic, sprinkled the wound with antibiotic powder, and gave the girl some aspirin. Amid celebratory ululating, each girl was moved to a side bed to recover.

As soon as the work was completed, the bed cleaned up, and bowl with the discarded tissues carried out, adult well-wishers, both men and women, began arriving. They congratulated each child and tucked a little money

under their pillows, then moved outside to share in the breakfast meal that the families had prepared. It was a joyful occasion of visiting and drinking tea. Meanwhile, as the local anesthetic wore off, the newly circumcised children endured their pain with aspirin and loving mothers.

BUT WHAT ABOUT GIRLS' AND WOMEN'S HUMAN RIGHTS?

Did these young girls consent to this cutting? They appeared to be willing. Of course in other places where girls are not informed beforehand, the practice is to surprise the girl and circumcision is carried out by force (see for example El-Saadawi for Egypt) it is obvious that such girls did not consent. But it is also quite common in Sudan and other countries for older girls to make fun of younger uncircumcised girls, teasing them with peer pressure until the younger girls' enviousness of being a big girl (i.e., circumcised) leads them to nag their mothers to let them be cut. Or suppose you grow up simply knowing that it will happen, and when your mother prepares the new dress, fusses over getting you ready, and tells you the big day has arrived, you go willingly, trusting your mother that it is for the best? Have you given your informed consent?

People concerned about the human rights of children would say no. At 5 or 6 years of age, one is by no means fully informed about the risks and consequences. A girl probably has no idea about sexual pleasure or infections or childbirth. Similarly, if you live in a culture where arranged marriages are common, and at 13 your father and mother arrange for you to get married to a groom they have selected for you, would you be able to speak up for yourself? Like so many other girls, you would probably feel you had no choice, or you would trust that your parents know best and accept the situation.

Both are violations of what have come to be understood as human rights for girls—the right to bodily integrity (that is, not to have her body permanently altered) and the right to consent to or decline to marry. Both of these clearly have not always been accepted as rights and certainly are not yet accepted in many societies. But should they be rights? The international community increasingly agrees that they should be, although there is no general agreement on what the age of consent should be: 16? 18? Most of the world's countries are signatories to agreements like the Convention on Elimination of All Forms of Discrimination Against Women, the Convention on the Rights of the Child, and other international agreements that stand against violations of girls' and women's rights, but not all enforce them.

Bodily integrity is something an adult woman can decide for herself. In the United States or Europe, it is accepted that someone over 18 is free to get tattoos or consent to having her labia pierced if she wishes. But to impose a decision on a child that will permanently alter her body, even if she is passively acquiescing, is to deny her right to make that decision when she is old enough to understand the consequences.

SO, WHAT'S BEING DONE ABOUT FEMALE GENITAL CUTTING?

As you might expect, many who learn about female genital cutting practices respond with outrage and take strong positions against the practices. Outsiders often have evoked horrible stereotypes of malicious intent, condemning the people who practice such genital cutting of girls as intending to "torture" females or "deprive women of their sexuality."

Local reformers sometimes engage in similar strongly worded condemnations in international discourse. But grassroots change agents realize that inflammatory rhetoric and "preaching" alone are not likely to change strongly held values and traditions. Reformers recognize that it may take some time to enlist local practitioners in the change process, so they have patiently promoted health education that they hope will lead people to voluntarily abandon female genital cutting. Others have introduced alternate rituals that contribute to the social goals, for example a rite of passage for maturing girls that substitutes for a traditional ritual of circumcision, but without the physical harm of cutting. Meanwhile, a large number of countries are also pursuing legal reforms and policy changes to criminalize or otherwise discourage the cutting of underage girls. (See Rahman and Toubia, 2000, for an international comparison of laws and policies on female genital cutting.)

But the first step in changing anything is to understand what it means to the people who do it. With more insight, we can better understand why people have resisted widespread change and why some are now pursuing change. Many writers, particularly social scientists and public health researchers, have tried to improve the understanding of people's reasons for genital cutting without condemning the people who have followed their traditional practices (Cloudsley 1983, Gruenbaum 1982, 1996, 2001, El Dareer 1982, Obermeyer 2003).

In the Sudanese villages I studied, female genital cutting still persists, but change is in progress. In one village in the Gezira area, over the past twenty years female circumcision has become an increasingly important topic for discussions. Some mothers have quietly arranged to have their daughters be cut less severely, moving from severe infibulation to preserving more of the tissue and not closing the opening as much. Others have gone further, dropping infibulation and doing only Type II or Type I, resisting the social pressure to conform.

A few years later, when I interviewed the midwife from the descriptions above on a return visit, she said she hoped to change over to doing only the milder *sunna*, but the vast majority of her clients still wanted infibulations. Her changing attitude was encouraged by the government trained medical assistant at their local clinic, who was taking an active role in persuading people to stop infibulating. The public health discussions that have been held separately among the women, among the men, among school boys, and among girls, have resulted in greater willingness to talk about modification, a moderate change, though not total abandonment. Throughout the country, doctors and other medical personnel have decided to actively oppose all forms of female genital cutting. A law against the severe form, dating back to 1946, had seldom been enforced, but recently, the government of Sudan is showing renewed interest in enforcement of the laws against all forms of female genital cutting.

Stated intentions, of course, are not always realized, especially when there is such opposition. Nevertheless it is encouraging that grassroots developments, education, and organized public health education are having an effect to reduce the incidence of new cases.

SOCIAL MOVEMENTS FOR CHANGE

Successful social change requires widespread support, not merely written laws and policies. How will that support be won? Reformers need to endeavor to fully understand people's reasons. As Gerry Mackie has noted, "The followers of mutilation are good people who love their children; any campaign that insinuates otherwise is doomed to provoke defensive reaction" (Mackie 1996:1015).

But remaining detached and uninvolved with this serious problem tests the ethical limits of "cultural relativism" (the respect that anthropologists use to try to understand each culture in its own terms rather than to judge it ethnocentrically by the values of another culture). The World Health Organization, the United Nations Children's Fund (UNICEF) and United Nations Population Fund issued a joint statement in 1996:

> It is unacceptable that the international community remain passive in the name of a distorted vision of multiculturalism. Human behaviours and cultural values, however senseless or destructive they may appear from the personal and cultural standpoint of others, have meaning and fulfil a function for those who practise them. However, culture is not static but it is in constant flux, adapting and reforming. People will change their behaviour when they understand the hazards and indignity of harmful practices and when they realize that it is possible to give up harmful practices without giving up meaningful aspects of their culture.

Both elements are necessary to a successful change effort aimed at a cultural practice: a deep understanding of people's reasons and motivations for keeping a practice, yet recognition of the flexibility of culture. People have demonstrated many times that cultures can adapt, and people can make changes when convinced of the need without losing cultural identity and meaning. Ultimately, it is up to them to decide when the time is ripe, but can efforts within a cultural group and efforts from outside accelerate the process?

Opinion leaders and grassroots activists, working in different ways, are vital to social change. An outspoken critic of the Islamist government of Sudan and a long-time supporter of the leftist movement there, Fatima Ibrahim challenged the government's interpretation of Islam, and argued that the Islamic religion can be used to *support* women's rights and social justice. The Medical Assistant who holds discussions about FGC in the village where he works, the doctor who studies Islamic texts to help her clarify the limits of *sunna* circumcision to the medical establishment, the midwife who tries to convince her clients to do milder forms or none at all—all of these that I observed in Sudan are helping to prepare for change.

In the past two decades organized efforts for change throughout the African countries affected have accelerated dramatically, as international and non-governmental organizations have become involved and as African women have moved into leadership positions in speaking out about female genital cutting. International organizations, such as the Inter-African Committee Against Harmful Traditional Practices, have taken a lead role in conducting public health education by organizing discussion groups in towns and villages. The World Health Organization has taken on the anti-circumcision work, as have other international organizations. Can such a message be carried forward effectively, so that female circumcision might actually be ended soon?

OBSTACLES TO CHANGE: RISK OF *NOT* CUTTING

The social conditions that act as barriers to parents taking the risk of leaving their daughters uncircumcised help to explain resistance to change (Gruenbaum 1996). No matter how clever the public health education message on the hazards of cutting or how authoritative the religious sources that say it is unnecessary, parents know that it *is* necessary if it is the prerequisite for their daughter's marriageability and long-term social and financial security. Even when the religious authorities speak against the practices and medical risks are known, these may not be sufficient reasons for parents to risk their daughters' marriageability and long-term security.

To counteract the social risks there are a number of possible directions for policy-makers and change agents to address. One is to reduce the economic dependency of women. Better educational opportunities and employment opportunities would allow young women and their families to see delayed marriage as something other than a disaster. Daughters could be encouraged more in their education and careers, secure in the knowledge that although marriage is desirable, failure to marry or loss of spouse will not necessarily result in penury and dependence on male relatives. Better support for inheritance rights of women might help.

This is indeed a part of the change process that I have observed in Sudan. The teachers, professors, public health workers, students and other activists now working on reform are, as a result of their awareness, literacy, and cosmopolitan outlook, better able to confidently state that female circumcision can be left behind, that it is both harmful to health and not Islamic. Such women are confident that they will have a say in the decision on the circumcision of daughters, and they endeavor to provide their daughters with the educational opportunities needed to be self-reliant.

But even educated and confident women cannot be certain their uncircumcised daughters will be marriageable. If the young men in the community remain committed to marrying infibulated brides, a daughter's education may preserve her from poverty, but it will not assure her of marriage and children. The risk is lessened if there are social and familial ties to progressive families where men prefer *sunna* or no circumcision.

But as this cultural debate unfolds (Gruenbaum 1996), it is encouraging that some young men do state their preference for uninfibulated brides. One educated young man I knew in Khartoum told me he had insisted that the family not infibulate his sister, and he swore he would not marry an infibulated woman, even if she were a cousin. But will he or others like him actually refuse to marry a cousin the family expects him to marry? Or would he refuse to marry the young woman who has caught his eye, simply because she is infibulated? And can young men effectively prevent their sisters' circumcisions? How do families cope with the risk that there may not be men like this for their daughters to marry?

Risk avoidance remains the most significant factor to explaining why otherwise well-informed families cling to female genital cutting practices. Gerry Mackie offered a provocative exploration of the risks involved in such social changes by comparing efforts to end infibulation and excision in Africa with the process of ending the painful, crippling footbinding of girls (i.e., tightly binding their small feet so they would not grow) practiced in China for centuries. Footbinding, which lasted until the early 20th century, was also related to making daughters marriageable (Mackie 1996).

While there had been efforts to change footbinding historically, parents were afraid to be the first to change, since men sought to marry women with tiny feet only. However, once a critical mass of people was persuaded of its harm through educational campaigns, they found they could take the risk of change when, with other parents, they pledged not to let their daughters' feet be bound nor let their sons marry women with bound feet. The movement led to wholesale abandonment of footbinding in a single generation (Mackie 1996:1001). Pledge groups do function in African societies for various purposes, so now that there is growing awareness of the risks of female genital cutting, perhaps people will develop this pledge idea for female genital cutting as well.

Thus, despite the spread of female genital cutting and its tenacity, there is no reason to conclude that it cannot change rapidly in the coming years, when people have learned enough about the issue and when they believe the risks of not doing it are not too high. The conditions are ripe for change in infibulation and excision practices in Africa. The international activism, the efforts at culturally appropriate approaches, and the emergence of, and a degree of support for, indigenous leaders of the movement make this an excellent time, if the additional resources can be mobilized, for rapid change to occur. Indeed, the World Health Organization, UNICEF, and the United Nations Population Fund have announced a joint plan to "significantly curb female genital mutilation over the next decade and completely eliminate the practice within three generations" (Reaves 1997).

To mobilize the Islamic religious arguments against infibulation—i.e., claiming only *sunna* is permitted for Muslims—often results in people favoring *sunna*, allowing them to continue to reject total abandonment of all forms. Reformers debate the wisdom of this: although abandoning infibulation constitutes a definite improvement in the health of women and girls, what public health officials have often advocated as "harm reduction," it might result in even stronger belief in the Islamic rightness of the remaining form, clitoridectomy, which might delay the demise of *all* forms.

ALTERNATIVE RITES

Even where circumcisions continue in Sudan, the celebration of it has lessened. Whether that indicates a decline in importance of the event or is due to harsh economic conditions is not clear, but even wealthy families have curtailed the celebrations. Reduction in celebrations suggests that cutting is beginning to lose its symbolic power, and might in a few years decline.

An extremely positive development in the last few years has been even more explicit changes in the way circumcision is celebrated in several areas where activists have been at work. Recognizing that circumcision is a rite of passage in many of the places where it is practiced, reformers have begun to introduce alternative ways to mark these important life transitions without involving the usual genital cutting. One good example comes from Kenya, where rural families have been adopting an alternative rite to circumcision over the last few years, known as "Circumcision Through Words" (*Ntanira na Mugambo*). As described by Malik Stan Reaves (1997), groups of families have participated in bringing together their appropriate-aged daughters to spend a week of seclusion learning their traditions concerning women's roles as adults and as future parents. The Kenyan national women's group, Maendeleo ya Wanawake Organization, worked with international collaborators to develop this program to include self-esteem and dealing with peer pressure, along with traditional values, as well as messages on personal health and hygiene, reproductive issues, and communications skills. At the end of the week of seclusion, a community celebration of feasting, singing, and dancing affirms the girls' transition to their new status.

Such approaches recognize that female circumcision has deep cultural significance, and if that significance can be preserved while the actual cutting is discontinued, there is strong hope that change can be rapid. Indeed, Reaves quotes the Chair of the Maendeleo ya Wanawake Organization, Zipporah Kittonysaid, as saying she was "overjoyed" to see the positive response and believes it was a critical achievement toward the eradication of female circumcision (Reaves 1997). This project serves as an excellent example of combining local initiative, international expertise, preparatory research and community discussion, and support from private foundations (including the Moriah Fund, Ford, Population Action International/Wallace Global Fund, and Save the Children–Canada) to accomplish a culturally sensitive alternative to female circumcision.

PUBLIC HEALTH EDUCATION

Poster campaigns, teachers on lecture tours, training for health workers, and public health announcements in the media have all been used at various times and places for several decades to spread the word on the dangers of female genital cutting. In the past two decades, the movement has accelerated, with more respectful and effective teaching tools and methods available. The Inter-African Committee, for example, uses a technique that involves sending a woman health worker into a marketplace where women are found, and striking up a discussion. She asks questions like "What do you think, is female circumcision a good tradition?" Rather than preaching, she listens to what they have to say, what their beliefs are. "Are you aware of the hazards?" leads to a discussion of the short and long term complications.

The educator encourages women to bring up their beliefs and then discusses them respectfully. For example, there is an erroneous belief in some countries that if the clitoris touches the baby's head at birth the baby will die. An educator brought the idea up in one such discussion filmed by the Inter-African Committee for their film *Female Circumcision: Beliefs and Misbeliefs* (1992), and the health worker explained that that was not possible. She also discussed other potentially harmful traditional practices such as nutritional taboos and marrying too young, encouraging the women to offer opinions and discuss their ideas with each other.

The work of national women's organizations in the countries affiliated with the Inter-African Committee is having a positive effect. Through such means as community discussions, formal classes with anatomical teaching aids, and organizing in villages willing to undergo friendly "inspections" of their baby girls, to show the success of the message, each national committee is reporting progress. The Sudan National Committee for Traditional Harmful Practices, for example, has many rural branches now, and although their efforts were met with resistance initially, their work is now better received according to the Executive Secretary, Amna Abdel Rahman Hassan (2002). Rogaia Abusharaf noted that the Sudan National Committee consistently avoids making female circumcision a separate issue, but always discusses it as one among several reproductive health issues (1999). Discussing child spacing, contraceptive use, and maternal and child health first, women are better prepared to consider

not only the anti-circumcision message but also their well-being and rights.

TAKING A STANCE?

Regardless of the emotional or moral response one may feel about these situations, it is my opinion that those who are committed to improving the lives of women and girls must channel their responses into change efforts that are culturally informed and socially contextualized if they are to be effective. Anthropologists commonly advocate using cultural relativism to encourage people to overcome their prejudicial and ethnocentric tendencies and learn to understand cultures in their own terms. People who have been raised with the values and practices of their own culture, values and practices that have developed in adaptation to their own environment and social experiences, can be expected to have great faith in their own traditions. People are usually very unwilling to be judged according to, or expected to conform to, some other culture's values. So anthropologists rely on the mental exercise and teaching tool of cultural relativism to cultivate respect for cultural difference and enhance our ability to be analytical rather than ethnocentrically judgmental.

But that does not mean that we cannot discuss cultural practices in terms of their consequences, whether apparently neutral, helpful to some (e.g., to the preservation of identity), or harmful in certain respects (e.g., resulting in increased rates of infections). Indeed, most cultural practices are contested even within a cultural group: women and men may see things differently. Calm elders and testosterone-influenced youth may differ on when to fight. Men of a culture may like the "double standard" of sexual liberty for themselves but faithfulness for their wives, while the women have a different view of this.

As our human dialogs among cultures expand among societies and we humans try to agree on health protection measures or human rights protections, each culture must stretch a little as new information, experiences, and knowledge affect them. Once we have accepted that culture is dynamic and each of us is a citizen of a multi-cultural planet, it becomes easier to engage in respectful discussion, rather than the denunciation or preaching that often results from those who take a strong, absolute position in their interactions.

What feminist does not have respect for women's voices and their process of setting their own priorities, whether it be to end a war, get clean water, or change a traditional practice they have been questioning? What humanist can refuse to listen to the voices of women telling us of *their* priorities? And often anthropologists and public health workers, aware of possible harm from a practice, conduct a respectful dialog about it with people of another culture? Many anthropologists choose to advocate respectfully for change, and that is entirely in keeping with professional work in applied anthropology. But at other times an anthropologist steps back to observe, understand, and analyze in a non-interfering fashion, knowing that could be useful both for promoting mutual understanding and for assisting change agents.

As I see it, female genital cutting practices are changing and appear to be on their way to eventual abandonment as people become more knowledgeable, have alternative options that serve the same identity goals and promote values concerning morality, and become better able to resist the risks of change. Outsiders can help most effectively by offering understanding, respect, and support for grassroots and international change efforts, not only on female genital cutting but also on the *many* issues faced by the women and children of poor countries. It's fine to take a strong position ("I think people should stop doing this!"). But it's equally important to learn respectful dialog for those who do not see it your way.

My personal view is one of respectful challenge. As an anthropologist, my first commitment is to research and promote understanding, but as a humanist, I do not recoil from engagement in fostering improvements of the human condition. Female genital cutting practices vary so much that they clearly are not equally harmful. But because they are performed on non-consenting children, the human rights stance of total opposition to all forms, based on a right to bodily integrity, is ultimately hard to refute. [That principle would also prohibit male infant circumcision and ear-piercing of babies and toddlers, perhaps even extraction of a 12-year-old's teeth for orthodontia, so there are many ethical discussions to be had!] At the same time, my cultural relativism leads me to respect the values people choose to live by, recognizing that people themselves will make their future and choose when and how to change.

Thus, for outsiders, it has little practical consequence whether one is "for it" or "against it," since it is only the practitioners themselves who are in a position to abandon female genital cutting. What really matters is that we engender the respect and understanding for dialog to take place. That requires a respectful "cultural relativist" understanding on which to build the dialog for change, but anthropologists also recognize that "culture" is always contested and changing. Change is inevitable, and the world community should offer practitioners of female genital cutting not racist or ethnocentric condemnation, but understanding and listening. The international community can foster respectful dialog, help deliver information, and offer help with alternatives and improvement of underlying conditions that perpetuate the practices. Women and children living in poverty or marginal economic circumstances without the comforts of clean water, decent housing, adequate food resources, educational opportunities, job opportunities, electricity, or immunizations and basic health services may have social change agendas for their lives that do not list ending female genital cutting as their top priority. The international community would be wise to listen to African women and offer international assistance for their highest priorities as well.

While students, policy-makers, and the general public engage in disputes about female genital cutting, listening to the ideas of those affected and including attention to questions of context, motive, perspective, and the process of persuasion can only help. Change will need deep thinkers with passionate hearts and caring words.

BIBLIOGRAPHY

Abdal Rahman, Awatif. 1997. Member of the Sudan National Committee on Harmful Traditional Practices, quoted in Reuter report, "Sudan Tackles 'Silent Issue' of Female Circumcision," Feb. 20.

Abusharaf, Rogaia. 1999. Personal communication, Nov. 18.

Assaad, Marie Bassili. 1980. "Female Circumcision in Egypt: Social Implications, Current Research, and Prospects for Change." *Studies in Family Planning* 11, No. 1:3–16.

Cloudsley, Anne. 1983. *Women of Omdurman: Life, Love, and the Cult of Virginity.* London: Ethnographia.

El Dareer, Asma. 1982. *Woman, Why Do You Weep? Circumcision and Its Consequences.* London: Zed Press.

El Sadaawi, Nawal. 1980a. "Creative Women in Changing Societies: A Personal Reflection." *Race and Class* 22, No. 2:159–82.

———. 1980b. *The Hidden Face of Eve: Women in the Arab World.* London: Zed Press.

Gruenbaum, Ellen. 1982. "The Movement Against Clitoridectomy and Infibulation in Sudan. *Medical Anthropology Newsletter* 13, no. 2:4–12. (Reissued in 1997 in *Gender in Cross-Cultural Perspective*, 2d ed., ed. Caroline Brettell and Carolyn Sargent, pp. 441–53. Upper Saddle River, N.J.: Prentice Hall.)

Gruenbaum, Ellen. 1996. "The Cultural Debate Over Female Circumcision: The Sudanese Are Arguing This One Out for Themselves." *Medical Anthropology Quarterly* 10, no. 4:455–75.

———. 2001. *The Female Circumcision Controversy: An Anthropological Perspective.* Philadelphia: University of Pennsylvania Press.

Hassan, Amna Abdal Rahman, Executive Secretary of the Sudan National Committee Against Harmful Traditional Practices, personal communication, 2002.

Jennings, Anne. 1995. *The Nubians of West Aswan: Village Women in the Midst of Change.* Boulder, CO: Lynne Rienner.

Mackie, Gerry. 1996. "Ending Footbinding and Infibulation." *American Sociological Review* 61:991–1017.

———. 2000. "Female Genital Cutting: The Beginning of the End." *In* Shell-Duncan and Hernlund 2000: 253–281.

Obermeyer, Carla Maklouf. 2003. "The Health Consequences of Female Circumcision: Science, Advocacy, and Standards of Evidence," *Medical Anthropology Quarterly.* 17(3):394–412

Rahman, Anika, and Nahid Toubia. 2000. *Female Genital Mutilation: A Guide to Worldwide Laws and Policies.* London: Zed Press.

Reaves, Stanley. 1997. "Alternative Rite to Female Circumcision Spreading in Kenya." Africa News Services. Nov. 19.

Shandall, Ahmed Abu El Futuh. 1967. "Circumcision and Infibulation of Females." *Sudan Medical Journal* 5, no. 4:178–212.

Shell-Duncan, Bettina, and Ylva Hernlund, eds. 2000a. *Female "Circumcision" in Africa: Culture, Controversy, and Change.* Boulder, CO: Lynne Rienner.

Shell-Duncan, Bettina, and Ylva Hernlund. 2000b. "Female 'Circumcision' in Africa: Dimensions of the Practice and Debates." *In* Shell-Duncan and Hernlund, eds., 2000a:1–40.

Toubia, Nahid. 1993. *Female Genital Mutilation: A Call for Global Action.* New York: Women, Ink.

———. 1994. "Female Circumcision as a Public Health Issue." *New England Journal of Medicine* 331, no. 11 (Sept. 15):712–16.

———. 1996. Interview on "Fresh Air." National Public Radio.

World Health Organization, 1996, Female Genital Mutilation: A Joint WHO/UNICEF/UNFPA Statement. Geneva. World Health Organization (www.unfpa.org/swp/1997/box16.htm

Yoder, Stan. 2003. Personal communication, July 29.

XI

Culture Contact, Development, and the Global Economy

We live today in a global world based on complex political and economic relationships. There are few places that remain untouched by international markets, the mass media, geopolitics, or economic aid. However, the global world, particularly the global economy, is not a new phenomenon. It has its roots in the sixteenth century, when the powerful countries of Western Europe began to colonize populations in Asia, Africa, and the Americas. Part of this process involved the extraction of raw materials such as gold, sugar, rubber, and coffee, and the exploitation of the labor of indigenous populations for the profit of the colonizing nations.

Although most of the colonized world achieved independence by the 1960s, the economic domination of the capitalist world system that was initiated during the colonial period has not been significantly altered. In the early twenty-first century, an imbalanced relationship between the countries of the industrial, or "developed," world and the developing, or Third World, remains. How have the men and women of the developing world experienced the continuing impact of the penetration of capitalism and the integration of their societies into the global economy?

This question has been addressed in particular with regard to women, and two opposing views have been formulated. Chaney and Schmink (1980), in a review of studies on women and modernization, describe a minority position suggesting that women in the Third World are downtrodden and that capitalist development can help them improve their situation. Those who hold this opinion emphasize that women's economic and social status can be enhanced by an increase in female labor-force participation. Another perspective, stimulated by Ester Boserup's argument that in the course of economic development women experience a decline in their relative status within agriculture (1970: 53), suggests that culture contact, colonialism and development have introduced "a structure and ideology of male domination" (Leacock 1979: 131). In many parts of the world, originally egalitarian gender relationships have been replaced by more hierarchical ones, and women have consequently been marginalized and removed from the positions of economic and political decision making that they held in the precolonial period.

Researchers have demonstrated the negative effects of colonialism and capitalist penetration in a number of different historical contexts. Silverblatt (1980: 160), for example, portrays the Spanish conquest of the Andes as a "history of the struggle between colonial forces which attempted to break down indigenous social relations and reorient them toward a market economy and the resistance of the indigenous people to these disintegrating forces." Her focus is on the impact of this struggle on the lives of Andean women.

In the pre-Inca and Inca periods, Andean women had status and power that were manifested in their customary usufruct rights to land and in their ability to organize labor. After the conquest, Spanish law came up against Andean custom with regard to the property rights of women. In addition, "The Spanish system . . . ignored the deeply embedded Andean conception of the household embodying the necessary complementarity of male and female labor" (Silverblatt 1980: 168). The result of Spanish colonialism in the Andes was the strengthening of patrilineal and patrilocal ties at the expense of matrilineal and matrilocal ties. Women became both politically and religiously disenfranchised. Indeed, women who continued to practice traditional religion were persecuted. Despite this persecution, the religious practices survived and became a very important mechanism of cultural resistance and defense (Silverblatt 1980: 179).

Etienne and Leacock (1980) have suggested that in many historical contexts women resisted colonization and acted to defend themselves. This was true, for example, of Seneca women in Pennsylvania and New York who withstood the attempts of Quakers to put agricultural production in the hands of men, to individualize land tenure, and to deny them political participation (Rothenberg 1980). A similar resistance to change has been documented for several other North American Indian groups (Grumet 1980). According to Weiner (1980: 43), the colonial period did not diminish the economic power of women in the Trobriand Islands in Melanesia "because no one ever knew that banana leaves had economic value." Women's wealth withstood a number of Western incursions and, as a result, "served to integrate new kinds of Western wealth, as well as individual economic growth, into the traditional system."

The impact of culture contact and colonialism on the lives of women in the developing world has not been uniform. Indeed, Silverblatt (1980) stresses class distinctions—elite Inca women had different experiences from peasant women. However, it is evident that one aspect of colonialism was the imposition of European and American ideas about the appropriate roles of men and women, an issue that Victoria S. Lockwood addresses in her essay in this volume. Programs designed to stimulate economic development in Third World societies continue to perpetuate culturally rooted assumptions about gender and the division of labor, particularly the definition of men as breadwinners and women as homemakers (Charlton 1984). Based on these assumptions, development planners, often with the support of local elites, direct their efforts at providing new skills and technology to men, even when women are the ones involved in subsistence production and trade (Chaney and Schmink 1980). As Schrijvers (1979: 111–112) has observed, "If women got any attention, it was as mothers and housekeepers in family-planning projects and in training programs for home economics. . . . Male-centered development programs often resulted in new divisions of labor between the sexes, by which the dependency of women on men greatly increased."

Lockwood (in this book) reviews the literature on the differential effects of the penetration of capitalism and development around the world, which sometimes work to the benefit of women and sometimes to their detriment. More specifically, she explores the relationships among gender ideology, women's control of material resources, family and kinship structures, and capitalist development. Based on a comparative analysis of two Tahitian cases where development programs were introduced in the 1960s, she argues that a gender ideology that empowers women is not sufficient to counter the increasing dependence on men that often results from developmental change. Rather, women must also control strategic resources in order to maintain status and power in both household and community in the face of capitalist penetration.

Like Lockwood, Margot Wilson-Moore (in this book) shows that under certain conditions development programs can have a positive impact on women and their families. She explores the viability of homestead gardening as an economic strategy for women in Bangladesh, where both men and women are involved in gardening but use different methods and cultivate different crops. Women's gardens can be an effective foundation for the nutritional well-being of family members and do not necessarily have to compete with those of men. Development, in Wilson-Moore's view, is as much about feeding as it is about profit, and any program that is introduced should take into account the importance of subsistence as well as cash cropping in the context of the complementary gender roles in the local social system.

Agribusiness and multinational industrial production are other forms of global capitalism that bring mixed benefits for women in developing countries. Arizpe and Aranda (1981) argue that strawberry agribusiness, although a major employer for women in Zamora, Mexico, does not enhance women's status or create viable new opportunities for women. These researchers examine why women comprise such a high proportion of the employees in this business and cite cultural factors that constrain opportunities for women and continue to define women's work as temporary and supplementary. Employers take advantage of these constraints—they permit them to keep wages low and work schedules flexible. Arizpe and Aranda's conclusions support those of other researchers who point to a range of phenomena that make a female labor force attractive to multinational business and industry. "Women's socialization, training in needlework, embroidery and other domestic crafts, and supposedly 'natural' aptitude for detailed handiwork, gives them an advantage over men in tasks requiring high levels of manual dexterity and accuracy; women are also supposedly more passive—willing to accept authority and less likely to become involved in labour conflicts. Finally, women have the added advantage of 'natural disposability'—when they leave to get married or have children, a factory temporarily cutting back on production simply freezes their post" (Brydon and Chant 1988: 172).

As with agribusiness, the internationalization of capitalist production has led to the relocation in developing countries of many labor-intensive and export-oriented manufacturing and processing plants owned by multinational corporations. Many of these have provided new opportunities for employment, primarily for women. For example, in some electronics factories in Southeast Asia, women make up 80 percent to 90 percent of the labor force (Brydon and Chant 1988). However, just as with the assessment of the impact of development schemes on the lives of women in the developing world, there are two opposing views about the effect of multinationals. Some emphasize the benefits of jobs that provide women with greater financial stability (Lim 1983), while others see multinationals perpetuating or even creating new forms of inequality as they introduce young women to a new set of individualist and consumerist values. The sexually segregated work force remains in place within paternalistic industrial contexts that encourage turnover and offer no opportunities for advancement (Nash and Fernandez-Kelly 1983).

Fernandez-Kelly (1984) analyzes workers' responses to the international political and economic system at the levels of household and factory along the Mexican side of the U.S.–Mexico border, where more than 100 assembly plants (*maquiladoras*) have been established. These industries primarily employ women. By working herself in the apparel industry, Fernandez-Kelly documented hiring practices and working conditions of factory women. Low wages, oppressive working conditions, lack of job mobility, and insecure job tenure make *maquiladoras* a precarious option, selected by women with few alternatives. Factory workers also suffer from the contradictions between idealized notions of women's roles and their actual involvement in wage labor, which causes conflict over mores and values.

M. Laetitia Cairoli (in this book) describes how young unmarried Moroccan women employed in the export garment industry in Fez, Morocco, reconcile some of the contradictions between the cultural values and role expectations for women and the reality of their industrial employment. Inspired by Aihwa Ong's (1991: 280) emphasis on the "experiential and interpretive dimensions of work relations," Cairoli discusses how these female laborers transform their workplace into an interior domestic space, operating in it as they would in their own household. "They model their position in the factory hierarchy on their role in the household and so are able not only to accept the domination of the factory, but to find in that domination their own sources of personal self-worth and power." Factory owners become like fathers who guard the virtue of their female workers. Fellow garment workers are like sisters and thus the authority of a female supervisor is akin to the authority of the eldest sister. As in the Moroccan home, female space in the factory is separated from male space.

Another result of globalization and the spread of capitalism is the movement of people, both men and women. In recent years the literature focused on the impact of migration on gender roles and gender ideologies has grown significantly (Brettell 2003; Hondagneu-Sotelo 2003; Pessar 2003). This reflects the growing number of women involved in both internal and international population flows, a phenomenon that has led some scholars to speak of the "feminization of migration." These female migrants have become domestic workers in households as far afield as Washington, DC, Los Angeles, Italy, Kuwait, and Malaysia. They have become factory workers on the global assembly lines located along the U.S.–Mexican border or throughout Asia and Southeast Asia—that is, working for multinational industries that are especially dependent on a mobile female labor force. They have become garment workers in the gateway cities of the United States. And migrant women, some of them very young, have become prostitutes in the cities of both the developed and developing world, part of the growing global sex industry.

Nicole Constable (in this book) outlines the case of Filipina domestic workers in Hong Kong. Women from the Philippines have been migrating to the United States to fill the demand for nurses (Ong and Azores 1994) and to Western Europe to serve as domestics (Parreñas 2001) since the 1970s when Ferdinand Marcos implemented a new labor export policy. Hong Kong became a major destination in the 1980s as the demand for domestic workers increased. As Constable notes, many of the Filipinas who responded to this demand had some advanced education and this created problems for their Chinese employers who began to see these women as sexually threatening—morally loose and looking for men, and hence subject to discipline and restraint. Through the clothes they wear, Filipina immigrant women mediate and negotiate these stereotypes, often appropriating the self-discipline that is imposed on them by their employers.

In the final essay in this section, Laura Zimmer-Tamakoshi explores the relationship between wage labor and the shift from household to factory industry on the one hand and gender relations on the other. She discusses the sexual politics of Papua New Guinea's educated elite, and the sexual competition among men of different tribal and national backgrounds. In a situation where men have access to cash and women have become more dependent on them, cases of domestic violence have increased. Women are experiencing a growing sense of gender oppression, and rape and violence against women have become "women's issues" largely ignored by male politicians. Those women who themselves enter the cash economy may experience more autonomy, but this too may generate domestic violence from men motivated by a fear of women's independence and their own economic uncertainty.

Although Cairoli's work, coupled with that of Ong (1987), show examples of adaptation and resistance in the face of global capitalism, in the final analysis, much of the work on women in development tends to support Leacock's (1979) rather pessimistic assessment. Real development, from her perspective, "would mean bringing an end to the system whereby the multinational corporations continue to 'underdevelop' Third World nations by consuming huge proportions of their resources and grossly underpaying their workers" (1979: 131). This will require a truly international effort. The gendered approach to culture contact, colonialism, and development has demonstrated the close relationship among capitalist penetration, patriarchal gender ideologies, and the sexual division of labor. This relationship has been present since the early days of colonialism and has been perpetuated by a global economy that has created an international division of labor often oppressing both men and women, but especially women. As Chaney and Schmink (1980: 176) put it, development policies and programs frequently lead "not only to the degradation of the physical environment but also of the social environment, as various groups are systematically excluded from the tools of progress and their benefits."

REFERENCES

Arizpe, Lourdes, and Josefina Aranda. 1981. "The 'Comparative Advantages' of Women's Disadvantages: Women Workers in the Strawberry Export Agribusiness in Mexico." *Signs* 7: 453–473.

Boserup, Esther. 1970. *Woman's Role in Economic Development.* New York: St. Martin's Press.

Brettell, Caroline B. 2003. "Gender and Migration." In Caroline B. Brettell (ed.). *Anthropology and Migration: Essays on Transnationalism, Ethnicity, and Identity*, pp. 139–151. Walnut Creek, CA: Altamira Press.

Brydon, Lynne, and Sylvia Chant. 1988. *Women in the Third World: Gender Issues in Rural and Urban Areas.* New Brunswick, NJ: Rutgers University Press.

Chaney, Elsa M., and Marianne Schmink. 1980. "Women and Modernization: Access to Tools." In June Nash and Helen I. Safa (eds.). *Sex and Class in Latin America*, pp. 160–182. South Hadley, MA: J. F. Bergin Publishers.

Charlton, Sue-Ellen M. 1984. *Women in Third World Development.* Boulder, CO: Westview Press.

Etienne, Mona, and Eleanor Leacock. 1980. "Introduction." In Mona Etienne and Eleanor Leacock (eds.). *Women and Colonization: Anthropological Perspectives*, pp. 1–24. New York: Praeger.

Fernandez-Kelly, Maria Patricia. 1984. "Maquiladoras: The View From the Inside." In Karen Brodkin Sacks and Dorothy Remy (eds.). *My Troubles are Going to Have Trouble With Me*, pp. 229–246. New Brunswick, NJ: Rutgers University Press.

Grumet, Robert Steven. 1980. "Sunksquaws, Shamans, and Tradeswomen: Middle Atlantic Coastal Algonkian Women During the 17th and 18th Centuries." In Mona Etienne and Eleanor Leacock (eds.). *Women and Colonization: Anthropological Perspectives*, pp. 43–62. New York: Praeger.

Hondagneu-Sotelo, Pierrette. 2003. *Gender and U.S. Immigration: Contemporary Trends.* Berkeley: University of California Press.

Leacock, Eleanor. 1979. "Women, Development, and Anthropological Facts and Fictions." In Gerrit Huizer and Bruce Mannheim (eds.). *The Politics of Anthropology: From Colonialism and Sexism Toward a View from Below*, pp. 131–142. The Hague: Mouton.

Lim, Linda Y. C. 1983. "Capitalism, Imperialism, and Patriarchy: The Dilemma of Third-World Women Workers in Multinational Factories." In June Nash and Maria Patricia Fernandez-Kelly (eds.). *Women, Men and the International Division of Labor*, pp. 70–91. Albany: State University of New York.

Nash, June, and Maria Patricia Fernandez-Kelly (eds.). 1983. *Women, Men and the International Division of Labor*. Albany: State University of New York.

Ong, Aihwa. 1987. *Spirits of Resistance and Capitalist Discipline: Factory Women in Malaysia*. Albany: State University of New York Press.

———. 1991. "The Gender and Labor Politics of Post-Modernity." *Annual Review of Anthropology* 20: 279–309.

Ong, Paul, and Tania Azores 1994. "The Migration and Incorporation of Filipino Nurses," In Paul Ong, Edna Bonacich and Lucie Cheng (eds.). *The New Asian Immigration in Los Angeles and Global Restructuring*, pp. 3–35. Philadelphia: Temple University Press.

Parreñas, Rhacel. 2001. *Servants of Globalization: Women, Migration, and Domestic Work*. Stanford, CA: Stanford University Press.

Pessar, Patricia. 2003. "Anthropology and the Engendering of Migration Studies," In Nancy Foner (ed.). *American Arrivals: Anthropology Engages the New Immigration*, pp. 75–98. Santa Fe, NM: School of American Research Press.

Rothenberg, Diane. 1980. "The Mothers of the Nation: Seneca Resistance to Quaker Intervention." In Mona Etienne and Eleanor Leacock (eds.). *Women and Colonization: Anthropological Perspectives*, pp. 63–87. New York: Praeger.

Schrijvers, Joke. 1979. "Viricentrism and Anthropology." In Gerrit Huizer and Bruce Mannheim (eds.). *The Politics of Anthropology: From Colonialism and Sexism Toward a View from Below*, pp. 97–115. The Hague: Mouton.

Silverblatt, Irene. 1980. "Andean Women Under Spanish Rule." In Mona Etienne and Eleanor Leacock (eds.). *Women and Colonization: Anthropological Perspectives*, pp. 149–185. New York: Praeger.

Weiner, Annette. 1980. "Stability in Banana Leaves: Colonization and Women in Kiriwina, Trobriand Islands." In Mona Etienne and Eleanor Leacock (eds.). *Women and Colonization: Anthropological Perspectives*, pp. 270–293. New York: Praeger.

The Impact of Development on Women:
The Interplay of Material Conditions and Gender Ideology

Victoria S. Lockwood

During the colonial era, European nations expanded their cultural, economic, and political hegemony over much of the non-western world (see Wolf 1982). To gain access to the material wealth of their colonies, the Europeans established conditions under which native populations had little choice but to produce crops or other commodities for markets, or to work for wages on European plantations or in mines. As these processes escalated and other western interventions intensified, capitalist relations of production began to subsume indigenous economies in most parts of the world.

Original material prepared for this text. Reprinted by permission of the author.

Since that time, capitalism has proven a versatile, dynamic, and ever-expanding political economic system. Today, even the most remote and isolated village has been touched and transformed by it. The general terms often applied to that transformation—"development" and "modernization"—describe not only the processes of market integration (and shifts to capitalist production relations), but also the dynamic restructuring of social institutions, social relations, and world view that accompanies it.

Although there is great diversity in how this structural and ideological transformation has taken place around the world, research focused on gender issues in development has identified several important themes. First, men and women rarely participate in development the same way; in other words, they do not have access to the same kinds of development-generated opportunities and choices. Second, men and women rarely share equally in the various "costs" and "benefits" of development. Indeed, a growing number of studies suggest that women's social, economic, and political position relative to that of men actually deteriorates with capitalist development, or that, at best, its effects on women are highly mixed (Afonja 1981; Boserup 1970; Bossen 1975, 1984; Caulfield 1981; Charleton 1984; Etienne and Leacock 1980; Fernandez-Kelly 1981; Nash 1977).

At the same time, a number of cases in which women's position and status have improved show that there are important exceptions to this general trend. In other words, it is clear that "the changes brought about by colonialism, or, later, capitalist productive relations, are not automatically detrimental to women" (Rapp 1979: 505, cited in di Leonardo 1991: 15). Thus, ". . . we must be wary of simplistically portraying men as the winners and women as the losers" (Moore 1988: 79). As the rapidly growing body of literature on women and development points out, the situation is much more complex than that.

The highly variable impact of development on non-western women raises a number of important questions. How, specifically, does development (capitalist integration) differentially affect men and women, and why does women's position frequently deteriorate? And, in those cases where women's position has improved, is it possible to identify particular material/structural or ideological factors that have contributed in the development process to maintaining women's position or to promoting gender equity?

My goal in this essay is twofold: first, to discuss these questions in the context of recent research; and second, to present a comparative case study of two rapidly modernizing, neighboring Tahitian islands[1] that sheds light on these issues.

VARIABILITY IN DEVELOPMENT'S IMPACT ON WOMEN

Most scholars agree that it is difficult to generalize about the impact of development on non-Western women. As Moore (1988: 74) notes, "Women are not a homogeneous category, and the circumstances and conditions of their lives in the varying regions of the world are very different." Nevertheless, it is possible to identify the factors that play a major role in shaping how women in any particular society are affected by integration into capitalist markets and production systems. These factors interact in highly complex ways to shape the choices and options—the "opportunity structures"—open to women.

But first, in order to understand how men and women—even husbands and wives in the same family—can differentially experience development, it is important to remember that families are internally stratified units and that family members do not necessarily share the same priorities or goals (see Wilk 1989). Gender and age differences structure patterns of unequal access to authority, decision-making prerogatives, and control over family activities and resources. Those that do have access—most often senior males or male heads of households—may be in a favored position to participate in new and prestigious economic activities (e.g., commercial agriculture). In contrast, other family members, such as wives, may find that "modernization" simply means working longer hours at devalued household tasks that bring in little or no money, and having less say over the affairs of their families.

Forms of Capitalist Integration

One of the key factors affecting women's position is the manner in which different communities participate in capitalist markets and are integrated into global capitalism (see Mukhopadhyay and Higgins 1988). In rural areas, previously subsistence-based families may begin producing cash crops for local or export markets, become involved in other kinds of commodity production (i.e., crafts), or seek jobs in nearby towns. If jobs are available, families may abandon agriculture wholly or in part. As they become more dependent on money and imported foods and the cost of living increases, some rural villagers leave the countryside, migrating to nearby cities in search of wage work. Sometimes the search for work ultimately takes rural migrants to foreign industrialized nations where they are absorbed into the low-skilled, low-paid urban work force.

Each of these forms of capitalist integration has different implications for men and women depending on how the sexual division of labor is renegotiated to reflect new economic conditions; that renegotiation will be shaped by ideological notions of the types of work "appropriate" for men and women. Cash-crop agriculture may be defined as the domain of men, while women continue to produce food crops. Women may specialize in the production and sale of crafts if craft production was a female activity before market integration. If men migrate to find wage jobs, women may be left at home to feed and support families. If families migrate, men may find work in the city, but women who cannot find jobs may resort to street peddling or other marginal activities in the urban informal sector.

Degree of Structural Transformation

The *degree* to which a particular society has been incorporated into capitalist relations of production also plays a role in shaping how women are affected by development. Some communities have resisted or avoided full incorporation and maintained pre-capitalist institutions and values (see, for example, Rodman 1993; Petersen 1993); this is true in many rural "peasant" communities in the Third World, where families produce for markets or hold wage jobs yet simultaneously maintain kin-based relations of production and property ownership. In other communities, pre-capitalist institutions have largely been replaced by capitalist relations of production; this is true in areas of the most extensive commercial and missionary intervention.

These structural changes include shifts from kin- or family-based systems of property ownership to individual ownership. Land and labor become commodified and production becomes oriented to market sales and making money; wealth accumulation becomes a major goal. Those who are able to accumulate capital become an elite who are in a position to concentrate control over land and the other means of production. These processes result in the formation of class structures and the promotion of individualistic, competitive, and profit-oriented value systems characteristic of capitalist societies.

The impact of development on women will, in part, be shaped by how far this structural transformation has advanced. If, for example, increasing pressure on land has caused a system of land tenure to shift from matriclan ownership to individual ownership, women may find that they have lost control over land while men who participate in cash-cropping or other market-oriented activities are increasingly gaining individual control. On the other hand, where communities have resisted this shift to individual ownership, women may find that their property rights have not diminished.

EXISTING SYSTEMS OF GENDER, FAMILY, AND SOCIAL RELATIONS

Another critical factor shaping the impact of development on women is the local system of gender and family relations, including patterns of gender stratification and ideology. There is great diversity in these systems around the world ranging from the relatively egalitarian, horticultural societies of island New Guinea (Lepowsky 1993), to the highly gender stratified and segregated Islamic societies of the Middle East (see Abu-Lughod 1986). Variability in gender structures is accompanied by fundamental differences in how different societies conceive of femaleness and maleness, and in what they perceive to be the basic mental and physical capabilities of men and women. Gender ideology, as well as family and kinship structures, will play a major role in determining the kinds of behaviors and socioeconomic roles that are considered appropriate (and consistent with family responsibilities) for women.

The Western Gender Bias in Development

Appreciating the complexity of forces that shape the options open to men and women as their communities develop explains little, however, about the frequently negative impact of development on women. If development were in fact a gender-neutral phenomenon, one would expect that the *relative* social, economic, and political position of men and women would remain the same—both men's and women's situations would either improve or deteriorate in more or less the same ways. But this rarely happens. Numerous studies now point to several important processes of gender discrimination embedded in Western-style, capitalist development, processes that have contributed to women's deteriorating position in many developing regions. In some cases, development has introduced forms of gender bias that did not previously exist in non-western communities; in others, introduced gender biases have intensified existing gender asymmetries.

Women and "Modernization"

Prior to the 1970s and the surge of scholarly interest in women's issues, it was widely (and ethnocentrically) assumed that modernization ("Westernization") promoted more egalitarian gender relations, and greater rights and freedoms for women. In an influential article, Laurel Bossen (1975) noted, "The Western industrialized nations [were] thought to be closest to an ideal of modern egalitarian treatment for women. . . . Hence modern changes that [brought] societies closer to the Western pattern and standard [were] presented as advantageous to women" (1975: 587). Evidence of women's increasing equality included legal freedoms; the right to vote, run for office, and own property; as well as greater participation in the wage labor force. The latter was thought to promote female economic independence from "traditional family structures." In contrast, women in rural developing areas were thought to be "servile, dependent, and decidedly inferior to . . . men" (1975: 587).

Bossen effectively argues that neither the egalitarian view of Western gender relations nor the servile, inferior view of Third World women reflects reality. Although Western women may possess certain legal rights, they do not enjoy full equality with men; nor are they as socially valued or esteemed as men. At the same time, research in less technologically sophisticated, non-Western cultures has shown that, in some cases, women may be highly valued and possess many of the same socioeconomic and political prerogatives as men (see Lepowsky 1993 on the Vanatinai of New Guinea; Geertz 1961 on the Javanese; Kluckhohn and Leighton 1946 on the Navajo; and Etienne and Leacock 1980). Thus, as Bossen (1975: 589) notes, ". . . it does not follow that the greater wealth and superior technology controlled by modern societies corresponds to greater equality among its members, female or otherwise."

"Modernized Patriarchy"

The gender biases that characterize Western capitalist societies—and that were more severe in the Victorian era—were first introduced in many non-western regions during the colonial era. They have continued to reappear, however, as one "subtext" of many Western-designed or Western-oriented development programs.

One of these gender biases is a structural feature of Western, capitalist relations of production in which the formal economic ("productive") and domestic/reproductive spheres are artificially distinguished, and the latter is devalued. In capitalist societies, "The concept of labor [is] reserved for activity that produces surplus value" (i.e., cash-earning activities) (Mies 1982a: 2; see also Sacks 1974). Thus, "work" becomes commodity or cash-crop production, or wage employment, activities that were typically dominated by men after their introduction; men, then, become associated with a formal, "productive" sphere that is often physically (spatially) separated from the activities of the household/domestic sphere.

Many of the typical activities of women—giving birth to and caring for children, maintaining the household and its affairs, producing for family use/consumption—are not defined as "productive" in capitalist systems because they generate nothing of monetary value, and thus women do not "work." Thus much of the work that women do perform in the domestic domain becomes "invisible." An important example of this is that agricultural development efforts in Africa and elsewhere have frequently focused on men, even though "invisible" women farmers actually produce 50 percent of the world's food for direct consumption (Escobar 1995: 172–173).

Capitalist enterprises benefit from the structural separation of the productive and domestic domains because, since women do no work, they do not have to be compensated for their labor; they also benefit in that women (and sometimes children) serve as a relatively inexpensive, available, and easily dismissed pool of labor. If the demand for labor increases in the capitalist system or families cannot support themselves on one income, women may move into wage labor, but they are typically paid less than men. The rationale of capitalist employers is that women are "temporary" (and less skilled) workers who really belong at home with the children.

This capitalist economic rationale for the devaluation and domestication of women was reinforced during the colonial era (and since) by patriarchal, Victorian-era notions of appropriate male/female activities and relations, and by notions of female inferiority (physically and intellectually). In the Society Islands, for example, English missionaries believed that cultivation (previously practiced by both Tahitian men and women) was "unsuitable to [the female] sex" and that precontact women's other economic activities were "derogatory to the female and inimical to an improvement in morals"; they decided that "men should dig, plant, and prepare the food, and the women make cloth, bonnets, and attend to the householdwork" (Ellis 1981, III: 392–393, cited in Thomas 1987). Being relegated to making bonnets at home was quite a step down, particularly for high-ranking Tahitian women, who had figured prominently in the affairs and sociopolitical machinations of their chiefdoms—and sometimes even led warriors into battle—before the arrival of the Europeans (Lockwood 1988; Oliver 1974).

The model of Christian family life advanced by missionaries and colonial officials provided a supporting ideological framework for the structural separation of the male-dominated productive domain and the devalued, female domestic domain. The Bible describes the moral and correct family as consisting of a male head of family who is father and provider, and a female wife and mother who is his helpmate and subordinate. Women's financial dependence on the male "breadwinner" is a cornerstone of their secondary status.

Western gender biases not only domesticated non-Western women, they frequently also introduced a "value structure that defines women's primary task in society as biological and social reproduction"; when this occurs in conjunction with a system—capitalism—that "allocates higher rewards to production roles in the public domain . . . men [achieve] an edge over women" (Afonja 1986: 134). That edge frequently supported patriarchal gender and family systems.

Relegation to a devalued, "nonproductive" domestic sphere was frequently accompanied in many cases by women's loss of control over productive resources and property; these were vested in the male "breadwinner" and head of the family. And that loss of control had a critical, negative impact on women's social position, authority, and status. In capitalist systems, control over the means of production (resources, capital, technology) is the material basis of differential authority and power; this is true not only in the community at large, but also in the internally stratified family. Following Schlegel

(1977), "power" can be defined as the ability to control one's own and others' persons and activities, as well as the ability to make the decisions and shape the affairs/policies of the family or social group. Where women do not participate in productive activities or control resources or income, they are not only financially dependent on men, they are also relatively powerless and politically subordinate to men (see Freidl 1975, 1991).

By introducing structures and ideologies that privilege men and "domesticate" women, Western-style development has frequently limited the options available to women and contributed to a decline in their status in the family and community.[2] In these cases, development becomes more than simply a means for promoting market integration or raising the standard of living, it becomes a vehicle for institutionalizing "modernized" patriarchy (Escobar 1995: 177).

Contemporary Negative Trends for Women

Several of the major trends in Third World development today reflect these gender biases. In rural areas, the devaluation and domestication of women has contributed to the *feminization of subsistence agriculture*. When new cash crops and technologies were introduced (during the colonial era and more recently), it was typically assumed that men were the farmers, and new opportunities, credits, and modern technology were made available to them. In many areas of Africa and Latin America where women had in fact been the major farmers, women were pushed into subsistence cultivation for family consumption. Defined as part of the "domestic" domain, subsistence production became both devalued and "invisible." As women assumed "the burden for providing for 'family' consumption" they were "often prevented from engaging in cash-crop production themselves, and the frequent bias of government schemes and incentives in favour of male farmers (and the cash crops they produce) lead to further discrimination and disadvantage for women" (Moore 1988: 75). The cost to women of the feminization of subsistence agriculture was often exacerbated by changes in

land tenure and other systems of property rights that effectively negated women's rights and institutionalized systems of individual (often male) ownership and inheritance.

Women are frequently pushed into subsistence production not only by male domination of cash-crop production (and of resources and technology), but also by male domination of most wage jobs and by male out-migration. In rural areas, where jobs are available on plantations or on commercial farms, women are typically hired as low-paid domestics, while men have access to the higher-paying and more prestigious jobs. When men migrate from rural areas to towns in search of wage work, rural women are frequently left at home with the double burden of caring for the house and children, and fulfilling familial subsistence needs.

Not only does subsistence production become devalued and invisible in the domestic domain, but women's other productive—and even cash-earning—activities frequently do as well. In many developing regions, women have found ways to earn small amounts of cash income by producing marketable crafts or other commodities (i.e., prepared foods) in their homes ("cottage industries").

In the Yucatan, for example, Mayan women weave hammocks (Littlefield 1978), and in India women make lace (Mies 1982b). But these women's situation is much like that of other poor, female commodity producers who work out of their homes. They are dependent on outside suppliers who bring them the raw materials for their craft, and they are exploited by commercial middlemen and exporters who pay them little yet reap large profits for themselves. Because women have few income-earning options outside the domestic domain and are largely bound to this domain by gender and family structures, they are unable to alter the conditions of that exploitation. Because this work is frequently defined as "domestic activity women do in their spare time," instead of as productive labor (Moore 1988: 84 citing Mies 1982b), these contributions to family livelihood are devalued and become invisible.

It is important to note that in both the cases where rural women seek wage jobs or produce commodities at home, the prevailing perception that women are domestics who make no productive contributions to the family has little to do with reality. Indeed, the entire artificial conceptualization of a female "domestic" domain in opposition to a formal, male "productive" domain is largely a myth in most developing regions (see Louise Lamphere, Chapter 3 in this volume). Nevertheless, the "myth" remains strong and western gender ideology supports it. The dual beneficiaries are men, whose dominant position as "provider" and head of the family remains intact and unthreatened, and capitalist enterprises, which hire female "domestics" cheaply.

Another major trend in Third World development has been the *feminization of the industrial labor force*. It has been estimated that 80 percent of the workers in world market factories (typically owned by Western multinational corporations) are young women (13–25 years old) (Moore 1988: 100; see also Nash and Fernandez-Kelly 1983). Young women are hired because of their ". . . apparently innate capacities for the work—'nimble fingers'— their docility, their disinclination to unionize, and the fact that women are cheap because, while men need an income to support a family, women do not" (Moore 1988: 101). Women are also paid less (as noted above), and hired at the lowest levels (skilled and management positions go to men), because they are seen as temporary workers. It appears that wage earning and financial contributions to families frequently do enhance young women's personal autonomy (see Ong 1987; Kung 1994). But often there are also significant social costs, and rarely does women's position improve in the male-dominated family.

These cases suggest that even though women's income earning is a *potential* material foundation for enhanced authority and status in the household, that potential may not be realized. Young female Taiwanese factory workers, for example, turn over their wages to their fathers, the heads of patriarchal Chinese families (Kung 1994). And in other cases, women's income may be so meager (due to low wages) or devalued that it is seen only as a "domestic supplement." Thus gender ideologies and

family structures may redefine or "mystify" women's actual productive and income contributions—effectively negating them.

MAINTAINING WOMEN'S POSITION: THE INTERPLAY OF MATERIAL CONDITIONS AND GENDER IDEOLOGY

The relatively smaller number of cases in which women's position has not deteriorated illustrates how key material factors, supported by prevailing gender ideology and family systems, have worked to enhance women's autonomy, authority, and power in the family and community. In rural Java, for example, shifts to an export agricultural economy during the Dutch colonial period (and since) were not associated with major changes in the sexual division of labor, or in women's relatively high status and economic independence (Stoler 1977). Both men and women played important roles in labor-intensive, wet rice cultivation, and women were also significantly involved in trading activities. Through agricultural wage labor and trading, women became significant income earners in the household: ". . . women clearly control family finances and dominate the decision-making process" in the domestic domain, but Stoler notes that the domestic and public domains actually merge and overlap (1977: 85). In poorer households, women's income gives them both independence and authority in the family; in wealthier households, women's earnings could become the "material basis for social power" (84); where they are able to buy land or expand lucrative trading operations, women achieved both economic and political power.

Similarly, women in male-dominated Yoruba society (Nigeria) have achieved economic independence by participating in commercial enterprises and trade, and by owning houses (Barnes 1990). In this society, where marriages are brittle and women do not inherit property from husbands, owning a house is an important form of social security for women. Income from commercial enterprises is used to purchase a house; the house then generates capital from rents. By owning the house, Yoruba women achieve the status of senior authority figure in the household. This is possible because even though Yoruba gender and family structures strongly favor men, women and men "are [seen as] equally capable of performing society's valued and essential tasks" (Barnes 1990: 255). Thus, when a woman owns a house, she is able to undermine the conditions that promote her structural subordination and achieve some social power. Female "home owners" also achieve political clout in their urban neighborhoods and sometimes become community leaders.

All the cases that have been cited in which development-related socioeconomic change did not promote women's increasing subordination have two significant characteristics in common. First, women were able to exert control over strategic productive resources (usually through ownership), and/or they were able to earn and control cash income (capital). And second, prevailing gender ideologies supported (did not redefine or negate) female participation in production and income earning, as well as female control over the products of their labor, including income. Whether women's productive efforts take place in the "formal" public domain or in the domestic domain (or in that large amorphous area where the two domains are actually one in many cases), they are socially defined as "producers," and they control key resources and income.

The cases of rural Tahitian women on the islands of Tubuai and Rurutu (Austral Islands, French Polynesia) show how different forms of market integration may have strikingly different consequences for women (even in the same society). They also show how women's control of resources and income plays a critical role in shaping their differential authority, decision making, and "power" in the household and community.

DIFFERENT OUTCOMES FOR WOMEN ON NEIGHBORING TAHITIAN ISLANDS

Rurutu and Tubuai are neighboring islands in rural French Polynesia. They are culturally similar, sharing the relatively homogeneous, Neo-Tahitian sociocultural patterns that coalesced in the region following centuries of French colonial and Christian missionary intervention. They have also both experienced the intense French government efforts to "modernize" and develop its overseas Pacific territory over the last three decades. In addition, the islands are similar in their geographic and population sizes (about 2,000 people, 300 households).

The push for regional development began in the early 1960s. In the rural outer islands, development programs were aimed at modernizing agriculture by transforming Tahitian taro farmers and fishermen into export producers for the rapidly growing Papeete market. Various heavily subsidized projects were implemented on different islands; they included copra and coffee production, European vegetable cultivation, and other kinds of commodity production (e.g., crafts).

Rural modernization also included the building of schools and clinics, rural electrification and telephone services (late 1980s), and integration of rural populations into the French family welfare and legal systems. Each rural island was designated a "municipality" and provided with a budget to employ a significant number of islanders on the government payroll (as road or maintenance workers, clerks, teachers, or secretaries). In the absence of commercial and tourist development on these remote islands, there are few other kinds of jobs. Today, about 45 percent of all families on Rurutu and Tubuai include an employed member, usually the male household head; about 25 percent of all jobs are held by women. Despite income earning from jobs or commodity production, most families continue to rely on agriculture/fishing to fulfill their subsistence needs.

Through their various cash-earning activities, as well as government social programs, many rural Tahitian families have achieved relatively high incomes and a level of material affluence unknown in many parts of the "developing" world (see discussion later in this chapter). At the same time, however, the cost of living in this import-dependent society is extremely high, and consumption standards are constantly rising. Consequently, and despite their high incomes, cash is ever-scarce and highly coveted. Most families today pursue any and all economic activities possible to generate cash income.

Premodernization Gender Relations and Stratification

Before the introduction of development programs in the 1960s, rural families on both Tubuai and Rurutu mainly cultivated gardens (taro and other root crops, coconuts, bananas) and fished to fulfill subsistence needs. Small amounts of cash were earned through copra production or vanilla cultivation, or from sporadic sales of manioc starch, fresh foods, or pandanus craft items to passing schooners. Land was owned jointly by cognatic groups of kin; both men and women inherited rights in the land owned by their parents and grandparents.

Patterns of Tahitian domestic organization and gender relations reflected French colonial and Christian missionary efforts to transform Tahitians in their own images. As noted earlier, missionaries specifically sought to bring Tahitian society more into line with Victorian-era mores and practices (Thomas 1987). In accord with those patterns, as well as with Christian precepts, men were defined as the "breadwinners," "providers," and heads of their families. Men performed most agricultural labor and fished. Women's appropriate (and moral) domain was the household, where they spent their time caring for children, doing the housework, and weaving pandanus mats (and making bonnets) (Ellis 1981, III: 392–393, cited in Thomas 1987). Islanders today sometimes describe women's domain as "interior" (household) and men's domain as "exterior," the fields and ocean.

Men dominated cash-earning opportunities where they were available. Men processed copra and planted vanilla gardens, and controlled the cash earnings (see Lockwood 1988; Oliver 1981). Although women's efforts were concentrated in the household itself, they also worked in their husbands' gardens, fished from the reef, and performed many other kinds of "productive" labor. Nevertheless, a general pattern of male authority and preeminence (and

female subordination) in the household was promoted by Christian teachings and the Bible, and by male control of increasingly coveted cash income. Although wives were usually in charge of daily expenditures for food and other necessities, husbands dispersed these monies to their wives as they saw fit.

Despite these structural changes, Tahitians somehow failed to become indoctrinated in Victorian-era attitudes about women's relative inferiority. Although Tahitians were (and are) devout believers in the familial/domestic prescriptions of the Bible, their own understandings of the nature of men and women differed substantially from those of the French and the missionaries. Most importantly, they did not have a belief in individuals' superiority or inferiority based on gender criteria.[3] This was reflected in a psychological study of Tahitian men and women conducted in the early 1960s (Levy 1973). Levy (1973: 236) concluded that in the Tahitian world view, women and men are seen to be much alike in their capabilities and talents, and to have no major personality, behavioral, or intellectual differences. He noted that Tahitians acknowledged that men's and women's lives were different—because of women's role in reproduction and because they perform different tasks—but that's all.

Indeed, one of the major themes of Tahitian gender ideology is male/female interdependence, and not hierarchy (superiority/inferiority) as in many western societies. Thus, although Tahitian women were economically and politically subordinate in the postcontact, male-dominated household, they were not (and are not today) treated as inferiors. In contemporary communities, women receive a great deal of respect and admiration from both men and other women for their roles as managers of the family and domestic domain, and for their devoted care of their children (see Langevin 1990). Despite their "domesticity," they are outspoken at community meetings and exhibit little deference to men.

Rural Development: Differing Paths for Tubuai and Rurutu

The economic profiles of Tubuai and Rurutu began to diverge in the early 1960s when government development planners charted different courses for each island. Tubuai was chosen as a major target for agricultural development, specifically European green vegetable and potato cultivation. It also became the administrative center for the five Austral Islands, and the site for the one high school in the group. A small airstrip was built to facilitate transport and contact with Tahiti.

Today, Tubuai Islanders are heavily involved in commercial agriculture, as well as other kinds of commodity production and export; these activities are largely the domain of men, although women are needed to perform substantial amounts of secondary labor in agricultural fields. Tubuai is today the regional potato producer, exporting over 1,200 tons (metric) to Papeete each year; it also exports about 550 tons of vegetables annually. The commodification of land and labor, shifts to individual land ownership (from the previous kin-based system), and the spread of new ethics of wealth accumulation and consumerism are increasingly observable. Of all of the Austral Islands, Tubuai is the most developed and affluent; in 1994, average familial income was about $2,000/month (Lockwood 1993). It is also the most Westernized as measured in the number of islanders who have attended the French-staffed high school and who aspire to a Western material lifestyle.

In the mid-1980s and despite the fact that they were not "farmers," Tubuai women began to sign up with the Agricultural Service in large numbers to plant potatoes. Women's access to land was assured by their own familial lands, and they also had access to the same financial subsidies and credits as male farmers. By the early 1990s, 43 percent of all potato farmers were women (Lockwood 1993).

Tubuai women had always earned small amounts of money from selling crafts or a few vegetables to other families, and a few held jobs as teachers, secretaries, or maintenance workers. But, for most women, potato cultivation was the first opportunity to earn significant amounts of income of their own; most women—who typically cultivate on a smaller scale than men—earn between $1,000 and $1,500 during the three-month potato season.

Because Tahitians believe that income earned by an individual belongs to that individual, wives are able to make their own independent decisions about how their money will be expended. Indeed, many female potato farmers explain that they decided to plant potatoes to have their own money to do as they like; women's money is, however, almost always used to buy food, clothes, and other items for their families.

Thus by the early 1990s, Tubuai women were adopting new "modern" socioeconomic roles and breaking down barriers in the traditional sexual division of labor that defined women as "domestics." They had also achieved a level of financial autonomy.

The Island of Rurutu

The island of Rurutu's development trajectory has been significantly different. Because of its rugged interior terrain, agricultural development projects were not promoted, although in recent years limited efforts have been made to expand the potato project and green vegetable cultivation there. (In 1990, islanders exported about 35 tons of onions and 60 tons of taro, tarua, and bananas.) A small airstrip was built on the island, and government services and jobs were created much as on Tubuai.

Most families on Rurutu earn money from the craft production of their female members and craft items are Rurutu's major export. Crafts include pandanus mats, satchels, and hats, Tahitian quilts (*tifaifai*), and shell and flower necklaces—items once made exclusively for household use. Rurutu women produce crafts as part of their domestic work in their own households, or while participating in a *pupu*, a cooperative work group of ten to twenty women who usually belong to the same church. Their reputation for fine craft production extends throughout the territory.

Rurutu women have organized cooperatives to help sell their crafts, and these are supported and subsidized by various government programs. (Craft cooperatives are present on most outer islands, but they are most highly developed on Rurutu.) Women are active agents in making arrangements to sell their items in Papeete though relatives, or if necessary, through a retailer at the central urban market. The minimal use of nonkin middlemen means that female producers retain almost all of the market price of their products. In the early 1990s, Rurutu's annual craft exports were valued at about $400,000 (one-third the value of Tubuai's potato crop).

How Rurutu women came to specialize in craft production to an extent that far exceeds that of other rural islands, however, is not clear (and informants could not explain it). As noted earlier, most rural Tahitian women weave mats and make quilts for household use. This specialization probably began to emerge in the predevelopment decades; at that time, the populations of neighboring islands earned small amounts of cash selling copra, coffee, or manioc starch. Rurutu families had little of these items to sell; they could, however, sell mats and hats to the local Chinese family-owned general stores for export to Papeete. Thus, in the absence of other significant options, it is likely that women launched themselves into commercial craft production and in so doing, they became central agents in the generation of their families' incomes.

Although Rurutu is integrated into regional markets through craft and other kinds of small-scale production, it is today less "Westernized" than Tubuai. As commercial agriculture is little developed, the traditional, family-based system of land ownership is not threatened by the kinds of changes taking place on Tubuai. Ethics of familial sharing and participation in cooperative work groups (pupus) are widespread on Rurutu, but have generally disappeared on Tubuai. Because families do not participate in potentially lucrative vegetable exports, most make significantly less money than Tubuai families (the average monthly income is $1,500). Consequently, there is less Western-style consumerism. And because until recently, Rurutu children were required to board at the Tubuai high school in order to attend it, fewer Rurutu Islanders have received as many years of formal French education as Tubuai Islanders.

And clearly, on Rurutu, there has been little change in the traditional division of labor. The division between the female's "interior" world and the male's "exterior" world is strictly maintained. Interestingly, it is women who chastise other women who violate these "proper" roles by "doing men's work" in the gardens; women are highly protective of their domain. Compared to more "modern" Tubuai women, then, Rurutu women appear to be both "traditional" and domestic.

THE GENDER CONSEQUENCES OF DIFFERENT DEVELOPMENT PATHS

Although Rurutu women may not be doing anything "new," they have achieved an important role in income generation (and control) that is unparalleled on the more modernized Tubuai.[4] Careful examination of household budgets and income on both islands revealed that women on Rurutu are indeed significant "providers." On Rurutu, women bring in more than 50 percent of all income in almost half of all families (45.5 percent). In other words, it is almost equally likely in Rurutu families that the wife/mother is the breadwinner as it is that the husband/father is the breadwinner. On Tubuai, women are the breadwinners in only 26 percent of all families[5] (see Table 1).

And in this society where women retain control of the income they generate, Rurutu women are given credit for their productivity. This was summed up by one Rurutu man who said that women today differed from those of his grandmother's generation because they helped to "provide" for the family (the male role). I had not heard Tubuai women described this way, although they are certainly involved in many productive activities. It became clear that a general ethic of women as "providers" existed on Rurutu that was not articulated on Tubuai.

Rurutu women's status as "providers" was reflected in a subtle shift away from the typical pattern of husbands as heads of families to "joint husband/wife" family heads. In 49 percent of all Rurutu families, the husband was declared head of the family, while in 41 percent, husbands and wives were joint household heads. In comparison, Tubuai had a much

TABLE 1   Comparison of Rurutu and Tubuai: Development and Gender

	RURUTU	TUBUAI
Percent of families with female breadwinners	45.5%	26%
Economic status of women	"Providers"	Not "Providers"
Degree of female financial dependence on males	Low	High
Household headship		
Male household head	49%	68%
Joint male/female heads	41%	25%
Women's household decision making	High	Moderate
Women's community political participation	Moderate	Low

higher proportion of male household heads (68 percent) and husbands and wives were "joint" heads in only 25 percent of all families.[6] Rurutu women also played a greater role than Tubuai women in decision making about household budgets and expenditures[7] (differences between the two islands are summarized in Table 1).

There were also significant differences between the two islands in how women and men were perceived and valued. Informants were asked to compare men and women in terms of various characteristics including intelligence, who worked harder, and several other personality traits. They were also asked who was "superior": men, women, or both (equal). Tubuai and Rurutu islanders generally agreed on most of the characteristics of men and women, with the exception of intelligence and superiority. On Rurutu, the majority of informants (58 percent) thought that women were more intelligent, while on Tubuai, the majority (64 percent) thought that men and women were equally intelligent.[8] (Only 29 percent of Tubuai Islanders thought that women were more intelligent.) And, on both Rurutu and Tubuai, the majority thought that men and women were "equal" (56 percent and 82 percent respectively); but on Rurutu, 23 percent of all informants thought that women were superior, whereas this was true of only 2 percent of all Tubuai informants. (It is also interesting to note that no one thought men worked hardest; both sets of islanders thought either women worked hardest, or that men and women worked equally hard.)

The higher valuation of Rurutu women can also be seen in women's greater political participation on the island. In 1994, three women served on the 16-member, island municipal council; one woman had been elected as a district mayor (the island has three districts). On Tubuai, islanders could remember no woman ever serving on the municipal council, and no woman has ever been elected mayor or district mayor.

There was also a tendency for both male and female Rurutu Islanders to extol the virtues of women to a greater extent than on Tubuai, although women were clearly held in high regard on both islands. When asked to compare the thoughts and mentality of men and women, Rurutu informants (male and female) described women as more expressive and outgoing (men were reserved), as better organizers, and generally as "seeing farther" than men. Women were described as more active in church and community groups than men, and they tended to take on the organizational roles in those activities. Both men and women described men's thoughts as centered on their taro gardens and fishing; once these tasks were successfully accomplished, men relaxed or got together with other men to drink; they were described as having "few concerns" other than farming and fishing. Women, however, were described as constantly thinking about how to make ends meet, how to generate the money that was needed for a household purchase, or how to organize the next church event. They "saw further" in that they were constantly contemplating the future needs of their families.

It should be noted that although Rurutu women's economic roles and income generation have promoted greater gender equity in familial authority and decision making and in community leadership than on Tubuai, they are not associated with other differences in family organization, fertility, or gender-based land-use patterns. On both islands, most families are nuclear in structure (about two-thirds of all families), have an average household size of five to six people, and produce approximately five children. Between 20 and 30 percent of all families reside on and cultivate the wife's land (most familial); the rest utilize the husband's land.

CONCLUSION

As the discussion has shown, many of the Western gender biases described above were introduced into Tahitian society, promoting the structural domestication of women, including their economic dependence on male "providers" and heads of families. But at the ideological level, Tahitians never accepted notions of male superiority and female inferiority, continuing to see men and women in a largely egalitarian, interdependent way that afforded mutual respect for both. Consequently, and despite other kinds of changes in their society, women never lost their rights to own and control land and other resources, they were never divested of the right to control the income they earned, and they were given credit for the productive contributions they made regardless of their "domesticity."

But because development took different courses on Rurutu and Tubuai, its impact on women has been different. On Rurutu, island women appear to be "traditional" and have continued to perform domestic roles, including craft production. Because of a lack of other major cash-earning opportunities, women's craft earnings have become a major component of total familial cash income and women are increasingly seen as family "provisioners" (the male role). As women have been credited with that status, there has been an increase in women's authority and decision making in the household and community, as evidenced mainly in the large number of families in which both husbands and wives are considered to be

joint household heads (see Table 1). Interestingly, Jennings (1995) describes a similar phenomenon among the Sudanese Baggara, an Islamic pastoral society; when Baggara women's income from selling milk and butter became a significant component of family income, they began to have greater say in important family and community decisions, including herd movement.

If one compares the situation on Rurutu to Tubuai, is appears that Tubuai women—unlike the more "domestic" Rurutu women—are performing new kinds of economic roles and making inroads into lucrative, male-dominated development projects (potato cultivation). While this is certainly true, they are actually able to earn only a small percentage of what men are able to earn. Thus, in the vast majority of families, women are not family breadwinners, as they are on Rurutu, and most women are financially dependent on husbands. Since they are not breadwinners, they are not viewed as "provisioners" (women's income continues to be a household supplement) and they have not experienced the added clout that being a family provisioner brings (increased decision making and authority). Consequently, on Tubuai, most families are led by male household heads, and not by joint teams of husbands and wives (as on Rurutu). The fact that Tubuai women are participating in a new, development-oriented activity (potatoes) while Rurutu women are performing a traditional domestic role (craft production) appears to have virtually no impact on women's evolving status; the key factors are relative contribution to familial income ("breadwinning" or not) and being credited with the status of "provisioner."

The cases of Tubuai and Rurutu highlight the interplay of both material conditions and gender ideology in shaping how capitalist development affects women. They suggest that a gender ideology that "empowers" women (i.e., Tahitian women's generally high status found on both Tubuai and Rurutu) is *not* sufficient—in and of itself—to ensure that women will not be subordinate to, and dependent on, men in developing regions of the world. The Rurutu data reinforce the conclusion drawn from other cases where women's position has not deteriorated: Women's control of strategic material resources and capital—the material basis of "power" in all capitalist systems—is a necessary condition for achieving a position of relative authority and power in both the household and community. It is important to note, however, that the extent to which women are able to control resources and capital will in part be determined by prevailing gender ideologies and family structures. Thus one can conclude that where women in developing regions are able to produce a strong material base, and where gender ideology empowers them to control it for their own ends, they will be in a position to achieve greater gender equity with men.

REFERENCES

Abu-Lughod, Lila. 1986. *Veiled Sentiments: Honor and Poetry in a Bedouin Society*. Berkeley: University of California Press.

Afonja, Simi. 1986. "Changing Modes of Production and the Sexual Division of Labor Among the Yoruba." In E. Leacock and H. Safa (eds.). *Women's Work: Development and the Division of Labor by Gender* pp. 122–139. S. Hadley: Bergin & Garvey.

Barnes, Sandra. 1990. "Women, Property and Power." In P. Sanday and R. Goodenough (eds.). *Beyond the Second Sex*, pp. 253–280. Philadelphia: University of Pennsylvania Press.

Boserup, Ester. 1970. *Women's Role in Economic Development*. London: George Allen and Unwin.

Bossen, Laurel. 1975. "Women in Modernizing Societies." *American Ethnologist* 2 (4): 587–601.

———. 1984. *The Redivision of Labor: Women and Economic Choice in Four Guatemalan Communities*. Albany: State University of New York Press.

Caulfield, Mina. 1981. "Equality, Sex, and the Mode of Production." In G. Berreman (ed.). *Social Inequality: Comparative and Developmental Approaches*, pp. 201–219. New York: Academic Press.

Charleton, Sue Ellen. 1984. *Women in Third World Development*. Boulder, CO: Westview.

Di Leonardo, Michaela, ed. 1991. *Gender at the Crossroads of Knowledge: Feminist Anthropology in the Postmodern Era*. Berkeley: University of California Press.

Escobar, Arturo. 1995. *Encountering Development: The Making and Unmaking of the Third World*. Princeton, NJ: Princeton University Press.

Etienne, M., and E. Leacock, eds. 1980. *Women and Colonization: Anthropological Perspectives*. Cambridge, MA: J. F. Bergin.

Fernandez-Kelly, Maria P. 1981. "The Sexual Division of Labor, Development, and Women's Status." *Current Anthropology* 22 (4): 414–419.

Friedl, Ernestine. 1975. *Women and Men: An Anthropologist's View*. Prospect Heights, IL: Waveland Press.

———. 1991. "Society and Sex Roles." In E. Angeloni (ed.). *Annual Editions, Anthropology 91/92*, pp. 112–116. Guilford, CT: Dushkin Publishing.

Geertz, Hildred. 1961. *The Javanese Family*. New York: Free Press.

Jennings, Anne M. 1995. *The Nubians of West Aswan*. Boulder, CO: Lynne Rienner.

Kluckhohn, C., and D. Leighton. 1946. *The Navaho*. Cambridge, MA: Harvard University Press.

Kung, Lydia. 1994. *Factory Women in Taiwan*. New York: Columbia University Press.

Langevin, Christine. 1990. *Tahitiennes de la Tradition a l'Integration Culturelle*. Paris: Editions L'Harmattan.

Lepowsky, Maria. 1993. *Fruit of the Motherland: Gender in an Egalitarian Society*. New York: Columbia University Press.

Levy, Robert. 1973. *Tahitians: Mind and Experience in the Society Islands*. Chicago: University of Chicago Press.

Littlefield, Alice. 1978. "Exploitation and the Expansion of Capitalism: The Case of the Hammock Industry of Yucatan." *American Ethnologist* 5 (3): 495–508.

Lockwood, Victoria. 1988. "Capitalist Development and the Socioeconomic Position of Tahitian Peasant Women." *Journal of Anthropological Research* 44 (3): 263–285.

———. 1993. *Tahitian Transformation: Gender and Capitalist Development in a Rural Society*. Boulder, CO: Lynne Rienner.

Mies, Maria. 1982a. "The Dynamics of the Sexual Division of Labor and the Integration of Rural Women into the World Market." In L. Beneria (ed.). *Women and Development: The Sexual Division of Labor in Rural Societies*, pp. 1–28. New York: Praeger.

———. 1982b. *The Lace Makers of Narsapur*. London: Zed Press.

Moore, Henrietta. 1988. *Feminism and Anthropology*. Minneapolis, MN: University of Minneapolis Press.

Mukhopadhyay, C., and P. Higgins. 1988. "Anthropological Studies of Womens' Status Revisited:

1977–1987." *Annual Review of Anthropology* 17: 461–495.

Nash, June. 1977. "Women and Development: Dependency and Exploitation." *Development and Change* 8: 161–182.

Nash, June and Maria Fernandez-Kelly, eds. 1983. *Women and Men and the International Division of Labor.* Albany: State University of New York Press.

Oliver, Douglas. 1974. *Ancient Tahitian Society.* (3 vols.) Honolulu: University of Hawaii Press.

———. 1981. *Two Tahitian Villages: A Study in Comparison.* Honolulu: The Institute for Polynesian Studies.

Ong, Aihwa. 1987. *Spirits of Resistance and Capitalist Discipline: Factory Women in Malaysia.* Albany: State University of New York Press.

Petersen, Glenn. 1993. "Some Pohnpei Strategies for Economic Survival." In V. Lockwood et al. (eds.). *Contemporary Pacific Societies: Studies in Development and Change,* pp. 185–196. Englewood Cliffs, NJ: Prentice Hall.

Rapp, Rayna. 1979. "Anthropology: Review Essay." *Signs* 4 (3): 497–513.

Rodman, Margaret. 1993. "Keeping Options Open: Copra and Fish in Rurual Vanuatu." In V. Lockwood et al. (eds.). *Contemporary Pacific Societies: Studies in Development and Change,* pp. 171–184. Englewood Cliffs, NJ: Prentice Hall.

Sacks, Karen. 1974. "Engels Revisited: Women, the Organization of Production and Private Property." In M. Rosaldo and L. Lamphere (eds.). *Woman, Culture and Society,* pp. 207–222. Stanford, CA: Stanford University Press.

Schlegel, Alice. 1977. *Sexual Stratification: A Cross-Cultural View.* New York: Columbia University Press.

Stoler, Ann. 1977. "Class Structure and Female Autonomy in Rural Java." *Signs* 3: 74–89.

Thomas, Nicholas. 1987. "Complementarity and History: Misrecognizing Gender in the Pacific." *Oceania* 57 (4): 261–270.

Wilk, Richard, ed. 1989. *The Household Economy: Reconsidering the Domestic Mode of Production.* Boulder, CO: Westview Press.

Wolf, Eric. 1982. *Europe and the People Without History.* Berkeley: University of California Press.

NOTES

1. In 1994–1995, a comparative study of the differential impact of capitalist development on women was undertaken on the neighboring Tahitian islands of Tubuai, Rurutu, and Raivavae. Two other anthropologists, Jeanette Dickerson-Putman and Anna Laura Jones, contributed to the project. The study was funded by a gratefully acknowledged grant from the National Science Foundation (SBR-9311414).

2. Women's relative lack of opportunity compared to men can also be seen in their strikingly lower rates of literacy and educational attainment (particularly in Latin America, the Middle East, and Africa) (see Moore 1988), as well as in higher rates of female morbidity and mortality (Charleton 1984).

3. Precontact Tahitians (both male and female) were ranked relative to one another in terms of the amount of *mana,* or supernatural power, they possessed (see Oliver 1974). *Mana,* and thus social rank, was determined by birth and genealogical distance from high-ranking chiefs; males and females were ranked in this highly stratified society by these criteria and not by gender. High-ranking women clearly dominated lower-ranking men.

4. In this comparative study, 164 Tubuai households and 181 Rurutu households were included (approximately 55–60 percent of all island households). These households were chosen to be representative of the populations at large in terms of two criteria: (1) major household economic activity/socioeconomic status (income), and (2) stage in the developmental cycle of the family (young, middle, elderly families). Informants included male and female household heads, as well as couples.

5. Tubuai households ($N = 139$): In 103 (74 percent) women earn less than half of all income; in 36 (26 percent) women earn more than half of all income. Rurutu households ($N = 134$): In 73 (54.5 percent) women earn less than half of all income; in 61 (45.5 percent) women earn more than half of all income. This is a statistically significant difference: Chi-square = 11.47; $p < .00071$; df = 1. (Families of single male or female heads were not included.)

6. For Tubuai ($N = 134$ households), husbands were declared head of the family in 91 households (68 percent), husbands and wives were joint heads in 34 households (25 percent), and wives were declared the head in 9 households (7 percent). For Rurutu ($N = 134$ households), husbands were declared head in 66 households (49 percent), husbands and wives were joint heads in 55 households (41 percent), and wives were declared the head in 13 households (10 percent). The difference between the two islands is statistically significant (Chi-square = 9.66; $p < .0079$; df = 2). (Households of single household heads were not included in the analysis.)

7. Although on both islands the predominant pattern is for either wives, or husbands and wives together, to oversee day-to-day household expenditures, this is more often true on Rurutu (82 percent of all families) than on Tubuai (74 percent). Similarly, wives contribute to decision-making about large consumer purchases in 87 percent of all Rurutu families, but in 75 percent of Tubuai families.

8. Tubuai informants ($N = 58$): Most intelligent—women (17 or 29 percent); men (4 or 2 percent), both (37 or 64 percent). Rurutu informants ($N = 33$): Most intelligent—women (19 or 58 percent), men (2 or 6 percent), both (12 or 36 percent). The difference between the two islands is statistically significant (Chi-square = 7.20, $p < .0272$; df = 2).

Doing Their Homework:
The Dilemma of Planning Women's Garden Programs in Bangladesh

Margot Wilson-Moore

Recently a number of development agencies in Bangladesh (for example, CARE, CIDA, Helen Keller International, the Mennonite Central Committee, Save the Children, UNICEF, USAID) have planned and implemented independent projects or program components directed specifically toward homestead gardening as an alternative to field crop production. For the growing cadre of marginal and landless farmers with little or no cultivable land outside of the household, homestead gardening constitutes a subsistence strategy with considerable potential for improving family nutrition and cash generation.

Traditionally a complement to field crop production, homestead gardens provide a much-needed supply of nutritious, interesting, and vitamin-rich foods for home consumption. In addition, the sale of homestead garden produce makes substantial amounts of cash available for rural farm families. The discussion that follows considers homestead gardening within the broad context of international development in Bangladesh and more particularly in relation to the burgeoning literature on the role of women in development. This discussion focuses specifically on homestead gardening as a viable development strategy for rural women.

Original material prepared for this text. Reprinted by permission of the author.

International development aid constitutes a major influence for change today. In Bangladesh millions of foreign aid dollars comprise a large proportion of the national budget. From 1974 to 1975, Bangladesh has received not less than $700 million from the United States each year in international aid, and these donations represent two-to three-and-one-half times the total revenue budget generated in-country. However, the results in terms of quantifiable improvements are relatively few, and despite these substantial foreign aid contributions Bangladesh continues to demonstrate a negative balance of payments (greater than $5 million U.S. in 1984 and 1985) and a negative balance of trade ($135 million U.S. in 1984 and 1985).

Environmental stress, population pressure, illiteracy, and historical explanations such as exploitation and isolation have been espoused as general causes for the persistent poverty in Bangladesh. Similarly, behavioral causes, such as a closely structured hierarchy and system of patronage, rugged individualism, and failure of Bangladeshis to "trust" one another and work cooperatively, have been offered as causes of the destitution and privation that characterize daily life in Bangladesh (Maloney 1986).

Whatever the causes, pervasive poverty and widespread destitution are commonplace, and in terms of standard "development" criteria, such as per capita income, literacy rate, mortality and fertility rates, economic diversification, and physical and social infrastructure, Bangladesh can only be termed a development failure. Historically, vast transfers of resources out of the area have significantly depleted the resource base while more recent problems of overpopulation, land fragmentation, and environmental disasters have drawn the attention of the international aid community.

Women's issues have received considerable attention from the international donor community in recent years, but to understand the "state of the art" of women and development research[1] in Bangladesh, it is necessary to trace its roots in broader issues of development theory and feminism. Early development theory tended to overlook the special needs of women, anticipating perhaps a "trickle-down" of benefits from men toward whom most programs are directed. Feminist critiques of development theory revolve primarily around this issue—the failure of development theory to address the problems of women directly. Women are either categorized with men or ignored altogether. Women are routinely subsumed within the rubric of more general development processes that are expected to address the issues of both men and women.

A variety of critiques of development theory exist (for an in-depth discussion, see Jaquette 1982; Barnes-McConnell and Lodwick 1983; Wilson-Moore 1990), and the ongoing dialogue among these critiques has generated a vast and critical literature addressing the issue of women and development in the Third World. The feminist critique of development theory is firmly grounded in feminist thought, and the theoretical perspectives that have emerged in feminist development theory clearly reflect theoretical underpinnings in feminist theory. Feminist theoretical models predict relationships between various spheres of women's lives[2] and generate research questions and information useful, indeed imperative, for appropriate development planning for women.

Too often, however, women and development researchers fail to incorporate feminist theory into their research designs or neglect to articulate the underlying feminist assumptions that influence their work. Theorizing is, in large part, left to feminist academicians who usually rely on ethnographic (rather than development) literature for constructing and testing their models. As a result, feminist theory, women, and development research have progressed, in recent years, along separate and divergent paths. Despite the actuating influence of feminist theory on women and development research and their common concerns with the situation of women, discourse between these two bodies of literature is remarkably scant.

Women and development research tends to be of a highly practical nature, concentrating on the immediate and pragmatic problems faced by women in developing nations. Resources and institutional support are then directed toward these identified needs. A women's component may be incorporated into existing development programs, or alternatively projects may be designed specifically and solely for women. Often, however, development programs do not meet the needs of the women for whom they are designed. Many focus on "individual solutions," such as education to improve women's opportunities for urban wage employment, increase their access to innovative technology, or improve their subsistence production skills. Too often the systemic constraints on Third World people in general and on women in particular, such as high rates of unemployment and lack of child-care facilities, are overlooked.

The role of women in socioeconomic development has been the subject of much interest in Bangladesh (cf. Hossain, Sharif, and Huq 1977; Islam 1986) and has focused the attention of the aid community on those development issues particular to women, especially those at the lowest economic levels who are often the poorest of the poor. Khan et al. (1981) have shown that in 1981 326 government and nongovernment programs for women were registered with the Ministry of Women's Affairs. The majority provide training in knitting, sewing, embroidery, handicrafts, and garment-making. Unfortunately, however, although directed toward poor and destitute women, the income-generating potential of these skills is minimal (Khan et al. 1981: 24) and the emphasis on low payment and domestic-like work only serves to perpetuate women's subordinate status and economic circumstance.

In 1986 Schaffer found that the focus of more than 100 development projects directed specifically toward women had expanded to include self-help and income generation, family planning and health, education and literacy, agriculture development projects, rural employment and industry, and female leadership training. The majority of these projects focus on integrating women into existing programs, although a few "women only" projects exist. Most donor agencies philosophically support development activities for women (Schaffer 1986: 4); however, a number of cultural attitudes toward women constrain them. The view of women's work as minimal and unimportant is compounded by the women's own perception of their work as noneconomic and therefore without value.

Beyond this, religious proscriptions that predicate family honor on women's virtue and legislate women's appropriate place as inside the household necessitate development on an outreach basis (providing inputs and training to women in their own homes), while effectively preventing agencies from recruiting female staff to provide that outreach service.

Initially, little specific information was available about women in Bangladesh, and the resulting imperative for more and better data regarding women's roles, statuses, and activities generated a predominantly descriptive focus in the early research. This is especially true in the rural areas, where early village studies (cf. Raper 1970; Zaidi 1970) provided only brief references to women's activities. Other village studies followed (cf. Arens and Van Beurden 1980; BRAC 1983; Chowdhury 1978; Hartmann and Boyce 1983; Mukherjee 1971), but still little direct reference was made to women.

More recently a number of authors have commented on the "invisibility" of women's economic contribution in Bangladesh (cf.

Chen 1986; Huq 1979; Islam 1986; Smock 1977; Wallace et al. 1987). Women's labor routinely includes postharvest processing of field crops, such as rice, jute, mustard seed, lentils, and millet; care of animals; homestead gardening; and minor household maintenance, to name only a few. Because the labor of rural women takes place primarily inside the household, it often goes unnoticed. Nevertheless, their economic contribution is substantial (Chen 1986; Wallace et al. 1987). The importance of these kinds of studies is in shifting the focus away from the view of women as dependent and helpless. Instead, they are recognized as actors, engaged in economic pursuits in both rural and urban areas. As such they cease to be "welfare cases" and become instead an appropriate target for "mainstream" development processes.

In addition to their traditional domestic roles, increasing numbers of women from landless and marginal families are being forced by economic circumstance to leave their homes to seek wage labor. At the same time technology, especially mechanized rice processing, is displacing rural women from their traditional roles in postharvest processing of field crops (Begum 1989). Cooperative programs are encouraging and supporting female entrepreneurs, but the success of these schemes often accrues from their constituting an extension of existing female roles that do not "encroach upon the traditional domain of men . . . [and are] not conceived as a threat to men's interests" (Begum 1989: 527).

Homestead gardening as a development strategy for women fits easily within these dictates because it neither encroaches on nor threatens men's traditional subsistence activities. Homestead gardening is an integral part of women's work in Bangladesh (cf. Hannan 1986; Hassan 1978; Huq 1979; Hussain and Banu 1986; Scott and Carr 1985) and provides an opportunity for women to make sizable contributions to the rural farm family in terms of nutritious food for consumption as well as income generated from the sale of excess produce.

Homestead gardening is not the exclusive purview of women, although much of the research to date suggests that it is (Chen 1986;

Huq 1979). This misconception is likely a result of research bias toward women. In Bangladesh women's issues have become a primary concern of development planners, and as a result women's roles are often considered without reference to other members of the community and to men in particular. The result is a misrepresentation of women as the principal, even exclusive, actors in certain sectors of the subsistence economy; in this case as the cultivators of homestead gardens. By contrast, data from my own research (Wilson-Moore 1989, 1990) show that both men and women are involved in vegetable cultivation, although some clear differences exist between what men and women do in the garden.

Men and women grow different crop varieties at different times of the year—men in winter, women in summer. The fact that the crops grown by women tend to be more indigenous in nature and those cultivated by men more likely to be imported varieties may be an artifact of men's more active participation in the public sphere. Because men are active in the marketplace, they may simply be exposed to new varieties of vegetables most often and are therefore more predisposed to experimentation. In a similar vein, it may be argued that women are in some sense a reservoir of traditional information and cultivation patterns, reflective of a time before imported varieties and development inputs were available.

A clear distinction also exists between male and female patterns of vegetable cultivation in which men's patterns are reminiscent of field crop production patterns characterized by monocropping and the rows and beds of European gardens. Women's gardens, by contrast, have a jumbled appearance and may represent the indigenous patterns commonly in practice prior to outside influence (for a discussion of cross-cultural gardening traditions, see Brownrigg 1985).

Women's gardens are found inside or immediately adjacent to the household. Requirements for housing, cooking, stabling of animals, and postharvest processing and storage of field crops necessitate that individual plants or small clusters of plants be scattered throughout the homestead, dotted around the central courtyard and household structures. Small plots may be located around the periphery of larger homesteads, usually immediately outside of the circle of infacing buildings.

Gourds are encouraged to grow over trellises, along the walls, and across the roofs of buildings. Other climbing plants may be trained to grow up the trunks of nearby trees. Shade-loving plants are grown under the cover of fruit and fuelwood trees, and those more tolerant of direct sun are planted in the clear places.

Plant species are highly diverse. Because there are no beds or rows, tall and medium height trees, smaller bushy shrubs, upright plants, creepers, and root crops form the horizontal layers characteristic of this type of garden. Weeding is infrequent, and it is often difficult to differentiate the homestead garden from the surrounding undergrowth. In fact an untrained observer might not recognize this type of homestead garden at all.

Husbands often fail to recognize the gardening efforts of their wives, even when the proof was crawling across the roofs and walls of the homestead and into the cooking pot at meal times. That men fail to acknowledge women's productive labor in gardens may lie partially in more general societal attitudes toward women as producers (they are not seen as such) but also in the scattered appearance of their homestead gardens, which prevents their immediate recognition by uninterested, or uninitiated, observers, be they husband, anthropologist, or development worker.

Women cultivate vegetable varieties that spring up readily, can be produced from seed preserved from the previous year, and are well adapted to the seasonal vagaries of the climate, flourishing inside and around the homestead with a minimum of care or input. Women often stagger the planting times so that everything does not mature at once. In fact, related women in separate households may coordinate their planting times, as well as the varieties planted, to maximize their production through sharing.

Vegetable gardens cultivated by women tend to have a high diversity of plant species but a small number of plants of any particular type.

Accordingly, the quantities are smaller yet more varied, and they are intended for family consumption. High diversity and low volume production is the predominant characteristic of women's gardening patterns in Bangladesh and throughout Asia, a strategy well suited to fulfilling family consumption needs.

It is no coincidence that the vegetables grown most commonly in homestead gardens are the ones villagers prefer to eat. These vegetables can be eaten on a daily basis without becoming unappetizing. Alternatively, the diversity of vegetables produced in the homestead garden also helps to offset the boredom of eating the same food every day. In fact, villagers prefer to have a variety of foods, even if that means eating something that they dislike from time to time.

In this way the garden acts as a living larder, providing fresh produce on a daily basis. As individual plants become ripe, the women harvest them and prepare them for consumption. If more vegetables become ripe than can be consumed within the household at one time, they may be given away, traded with neighbors, or sent to the market for sale.

Homestead gardening as a development strategy for women is predicated on a view of women's production as valuable and essential to the nutritional and economic welfare of the rural farm family. Furthermore, the minimal overlap between men's and women's gardening patterns ensures that as a development strategy homestead gardening also does not compete with men's traditional activities in field crop cultivation or vegetable production. Thus, homestead gardening conforms to two primary stipulations (Begum 1989; Schaffer 1986) for success and would seem an ideal development strategy for women.

Unfortunately, these stipulations do not necessarily guarantee a positive result, and outcomes of garden programming may prove surprising if the planners have not "done their homework" prior to implementation. In this regard, Brownrigg has (1985) emphasized the necessity of in-depth locally based research and observes that when such research is omitted or conducted in a cursory manner programs often fail to meet the needs of the target population.

Barnett (1953) has argued that acceptance of innovation is based on the ability of recipient populations to analyze new ideas and technologies and to identify some similarity with existing culture traits. Accordingly, the more identifiable an innovation is, the more easily it can be matched with a trait already existing in the cultural lexicon, and the more readily it will be adopted.

Social science, and anthropology in particular, has much to contribute. Participant observation is a field methodology well suited to producing detailed information about existing indigenous practices; information often not available through any other means; and information appropriate, perhaps imperative, for planners who wish to build on and enhance those existing practices. By focusing on extant patterns, planners can effectively determine which goals are attainable and which populations are most appropriately targeted.

In the context of Bangladesh, for example, homestead garden programs intended to improve family nutrition and increase consumption of vitamin-rich vegetables are most appropriately directed toward women because their production is intended, in the first instance, for home consumption. If, on the other hand, program goals include increasing family income through sale of garden produce, men may constitute a more appropriate target group because their vegetable production is traditionally intended for the market. Finally, a program goal of increased access to cash for women requires careful consideration because women's limited access to the market and ramifications of cash generation on family nutrition are two important, potentially negative, dimensions of income-generating schemes for women.

Women routinely remain secluded within the household in Bangladesh. As a result, marketing of women's garden produce constitutes something of a dilemma. Produce must be transported and sold by a male family member or neighbor. Women are able to retain control over the cash generated in this way by providing a shopping list (for household essentials such as oil or kerosene) when they turn over the produce for sale. Accordingly, the money is recycled back into the family budget on a daily basis and does not accumulate. It fails to be assigned a "value" by men or women and as a result goes unrecognized. That this particular economic contribution fails to affect women's status in any appreciable way has been discussed elsewhere (Wilson-Moore 1989).

Beyond the lack of recognition that greets women's economic enterprise in the garden, Boserup (1970) has shown that when women's economic activities become profitable (especially in terms of cash generation), men tend to take them over (see also Chaney and Schmink 1976). Male takeovers of the income-generating component of women's homestead gardening and the displacement of women from their traditional roles in vegetable production necessitates only a small shift in production activities. However, the ramifications in terms of family nutritional well-being may be far-reaching. Rural farm families depend on women's homestead production for a ready supply of varied and vitamin-rich vegetable foods, a complement nutritionally and aesthetically to the masebhate (rice and fish) mainstays of the Bangladeshi diet.

Redirecting women's vegetable production toward the market would necessitate a change in production technique, disrupting the traditional patterns of women's homestead garden production and interfering with that ready supply of vegetable foods. The traditional pattern that produces small quantities of diverse vegetable foods intended for consumption within the homestead would have to be replaced by high-output, low-diversity cropping. Furthermore, there is little evidence to suggest that rural families would use the cash earned in this way to "buy back" or replace vegetable foods in the diet. Rather, high-status processed foods such as tea, white sugar, white flour, and bread are more apt to make an appearance when cash becomes available for their purchase.

Maintaining a balance between growing vegetable crops in large volume for sale and in sufficient variety for home consumption represents a problem in terms of the space and time constraints of homestead production. However, the existing, complementary yet rarely overlapping patterns of men's and women's traditional vegetable production seems well-suited to the respective cash generation and consumption needs of the family. Accordingly, planners concerned with pervasive poverty and widespread nutritional deficiency diseases in Bangladesh may wish to consider the benefits of developing each of these gardening strategies as they mutually, yet independently, support the rural farm family.

REFERENCES

Arens, Jenneke, and Jos Van Beurden. 1980. *Jhagrapur: Poor Peasants and Women in a Village in Bangladesh.* Calcutta: Orient Longman.

Barnes-McConnell, Pat, and Dora G. Lodwick. 1983. *Working with International Development Projects: A Guide for Women-in-Development.* East Lansing: Michigan State University, Office of Women in International Development.

Barnett, Homer. 1953. *Innovation: The Basis of Culture Change.* New York: McGraw-Hill.

Begum, Kohinoor. 1989. "Participation of Rural Women in Income-Earning Activities: A Case Study of a Bangladesh Village." *Women's Studies International Forum* 12 (5): 519–528.

Boserup, Ester. 1970. *Women's Role in Economic Development.* New York: St. Martin's Press.

BRAC (Bangladesh Rural Advancement Committee). 1983. *Who Gets What and Why: Resource Allocation in a Bangladesh Village.* Dhaka: BRAC Publication.

Brownrigg, Leslie. 1985. *Home Gardening in International Development: What the Literature Shows.* Washington, DC: League for International Food Education.

Chaney, Elsa, and Marianne Schmink. 1976. "Women and Modernization: Access to Tools." In June Nash and Helen Safa (eds.). *Sex and Class in Latin America.* pp. 160–182. New York: Praeger.

Chen, Martha Alter. 1986. *A Quiet Revolution: Women in Transition in Rural Bangladesh.* Cambridge, MA: Schenkman Publishing.

Chowdhury, Anwarullah. 1978. *A Bangladesh Village: A Study of Social Stratification.* Dhaka: Centre for Social Studies.

Friedl, Ernestine. 1975. *Women and Men: An Anthropologist's View.* New York: Holt, Rinehart and Winston.

Hannan, Ferdouse H. 1986. *Past, Present and Future Activities of Women's Desk.* Comilla: Bangladesh Academy for Rural Development.

Hartmann, Betsy and James K. Boyce. 1983. *A Quiet Violence: Views from a Bangladesh Village.* London: Oxford University Press.

Hassan, Nazmul. 1978. *Spare Time of Rural Women: A Case Study.* Dhaka: University of Dacca, Institute of Nutrition and Food Science.

Hossain, Monowar, Raihan Sharif, and Jahanara Huq (eds.). 1977. *Role of Women in Socio-Economic Development in Bangladesh.* Dhaka: ABCO Press.

Huq, Jahanara. 1979. "Economic Activities of Women in Bangladesh: The Rural Situation." In Women for Women (eds.). *The Situation of Women in Bangladesh,* pp. 139–182. Dhaka: BRAC Printers.

Islam, Shamima. 1986. "Work of Rural Women in Bangladesh: An Overview of Research." Paper presented at workshop on women in agriculture. Comilla: Bangladesh Academy for Rural Development.

Jaquette, Jane S. 1982. "Women and Modernization Theory: A Decade of Feminist Criticism," *World Politics* 34 (2): 267–284.

Khan, Salma, Jowshan Rahman, Shamima Islam, and Meherunnessa Islam. 1981. *Inventory for Women's Organizations in Bangladesh.* Dhaka: UNICEF.

Maloney, Clarence. 1986. *Behavior and Poverty in Bangladesh.* Dhaka: University Press Limited.

Mukherjee, Ramkrishna. 1971. *Six Villages of Bengal.* Bombay: Popular Prakashan.

Raper, Arthur. 1970. *Rural Development in Action: The Comprehensive Experiment at Comilla, East Pakistan.* Ithaca, NY: Cornell University Press.

Sanday, Peggy. 1973. "Toward a Theory of the Status of Women." *American Anthropologist* 75(5): 1682–1700.

———. 1974. "Female Status in the Public Domain." In Michelle Z. Rosaldo and Louise Lamphere (eds.). *Woman, Culture, and Society,* pp. 189–206. Stanford, CA: Stanford University Press.

Schaffer, Teresita C. 1986. *Survey of Development Project and Activities for Women in Bangladesh.* Dhaka: Provatee Printers.

Scott, Gloria L., and Marilyn Carr. 1985. *The Impact of Technology Choice on Rural Women in Bangladesh: Problems and Opportunities.* Washington, DC: World Bank Working Paper No. 731.

Smock, Audrey Chapman. 1977. "Bangladesh: A Struggle with Tradition and Poverty." In Janet Z. Giele and Audrey C. Smock (eds.). *Women: Roles and Status in Eight Countries,* pp. 83–126. New York: John Wiley and Sons.

Wallace, Ben J., Rosie M. Ahsan, Shahnazz H. Hussain, and Ekramul Ahsan. 1987. *The Invisible Resource: Women and Work in Rural Bangladesh.* Boulder, CO: Westview Press.

Wilson-Moore, Margot. 1989. "Women's Work in Homestead Gardens: Subsistence, Patriarchy, and Status in Northwest Bangladesh." *Urban Anthropology* 18 (203): 281–297.

———. 1990. "Subsistence, Patriarchy, and Status: Women's Work in Homestead Gardens in Northwest Bangladesh." Ph.D. dissertation, Southern Methodist University, Dallas, Texas.

Zaidi, S. M. Hafeez. 1970. *The Village Culture in Transition: A Study of East Pakistan Rural Society.* Honolulu: East-West Press.

NOTES

1. Throughout this essay, the terminology women and development has been used as a generic term for women's development in an effort to avoid more specific references such as women in development (WID) or development for women. These advocate, in the first case, the incorporation of a women's component into existing programs and, in the second, separate programming by women for women (see Jaquette 1982; Barnes-McConnell and Lodkwick 1983; Wilson-Moore 1990 for a more comprehensive discussion of these terms).

2. For example, see Boserup (1970), Friedl (1975), and Sanday (1973, 1974) for models that predicate women's status on women's participation in the work force and their economic contribution to the family.

Factory as Home and Family:
Female Workers in the Moroccan Garment Industry

M. Laetitia Cairoli

My factory is better . . . because every girl in it is like a daughter of the owner.

Thus, one Fez clothing factory worker explained why she had remained at her job for four years, despite the notoriously low pay and constant overtime demanded there. In the past two decades the Moroccan garment industry has developed into one of the country's most significant export trades and Moroccan females have become the labor power for clothing manufacture. Although their role in the garment factories is widely regarded as exploitative and demeaning, the workers themselves continue to use the idiom of family to describe their relationships to factory owners, administrators, supervisors, and their fellow workers. In the course of a year of ethnographic research in the city of Fez, I began an exploration of how garment factory workers make sense of their labor on the shop floor.

Inside one Fez garment factory, where I worked during a three-month period, I observed workers as they sought to impose their own assumptions and values upon the factory system and thereby render their labor meaningful. Nearly all of Morocco's garment factory workers are female and most are unmarried.[1] They confront the factory with a set of cultural values that order their social world, central to which is their identity as kinswoman, a self-perception workers believe to be ordained by Islam. Despite their engagement with the factory, workers continue to perceive themselves first and foremost as daughters, sisters, and perhaps wives and mothers in a patriarchal family. As such, they

Reproduced by permission of the Society for Applied Anthropology from *Human Organization* vol. 57, no. 2, 1998.

presume that their rightful place is in the private sphere of the home, which is the arena of their most noble efforts. Thus, they transform the workshop floor into an interior space, recast factory staff into family, and operate in the factory as they would in the household. In this way they retain their prized identity as kinswoman, even within the factory, and they convert factory labor into work that is significant to them.[2] In doing so, however, they render themselves more amenable to the factory's exploitation.

There are, of course, limits to the workers' re-creation of the factory: for Moroccan females, the garment factory is a new kind of public space with characteristics unlike the private arena of the home. In some instances, workers find that their efforts to impose the blueprint of home and family on the factory fall short, and they confront what they recognize to be foreign work regimes and excessive domination. When this occurs, workers resist. I do not see this behavior as contradictory; rather, I assert that the workers' ability to comply with factory domination (which occurs far more frequently than does resistance) is rooted in their conversion of factory into home. Here I explore how this transformation is enacted.

THE "GLOBAL FACTORY"

Any study of Moroccan female garment workers must be set in the context of the recent literature on the phenomenon of women's participation in factory production. Over the past two decades, this scholarship has explored the effects of global capitalism on the definitions and meanings of gender. Two central questions have been posed: the first concerns the impact of women's participation in industrialization on the women themselves, on the men, on the family, and on the local culture. The second question is whether this impact—and the very participation of women in factories worldwide—is intrinsic to factory technology itself and/or capitalism, or if it results from local culture (Warren and Borque 1989). Researchers have sought to understand whether women's participation in these new forms of labor marks their liberation from local "patriarchy," or marks a new kind of enslavement to the demands of foreign capital. Those arguing the former possibility have pointed to ways in which factory work provided women an escape from the confines of home and new opportunities for personal autonomy (Lim 1983; Salaff 1981). Other researchers have emphasized, instead, the exploitation in modern production systems that is particularly detrimental to female status (Nash and Fernandez-Kelly 1983).

The literature on women and technology has demonstrated that women's entry into capitalist wage work affects the nature of gender roles and relations in complex and contradictory ways. As Nash (1981) notes, female participation in new forms of capitalist wage labor intensifies existing forms of gender subordination, while simultaneously decomposing and recomposing them. The roots of these transformations are found both in local patriarchies and in global capitalism. While the literature on women in the global factory has illuminated critical aspects of gender transformations which accompany the movement of global capital, much of the early research was limited in scope.

A particular weakness in the literature is its relative lack of detailed cultural analysis of what Ong (1991:280) calls the "experiential and interpretive dimensions of work relations." Much of the earliest research overlooked the unique ways in which workers transform capitalist work regimes and formulate their own kinds of meanings. This limitation in the literature was partly a result of the analysts' perspective on the nature of capitalism. Characterizing the capitalist system as powerful and deterministic, theorists often assumed that the methods and relations of production associated with high-tech factories would occur wherever these

factories were established (Blim 1992). Theorists would then analyze the new industrialization as an effect of a standard logic, or as the result of the intersection of capitalism and a local patriarchal system.

More recent conceptualizations of the global capitalist system stress the flexibility of capitalist processes and allow for a new interpretation of the effects of industrialization (Blim 1992; Ong 1991). Capitalism (including its associated technology) is no longer seen as a homogenizing agent that flattens local systems into replicas of each other. Instead, capitalism is now understood to merge with indigenous values and practices and thus to proliferate new kinds of labor processes and relations.

If this particular perspective on capitalism is adopted, the phenomenon of the factory, and the lives of its workers, can be studied as a cultural process linked to other local cultural forms, rather than as a consequence of capitalist production (Calagione and Nugent 1992). With this perspective, the local particulars in the worker's experience of industrialization become central; indeed, they become the focus of the study. Here, I follow this approach and discuss the Moroccan clothing factory as another expression of specifically Moroccan cultural values. Workers experience their labor according to Moroccan categories already familiar to them, and use their own cultural meanings to interpret the garment factory. The Fez garment factory is thoroughly "Moroccanized" despite imported technology and systems of production.

Inside the factory, the garment workers struggle to retain a notion of themselves as family members, specifically as daughters (or sometimes as wives) in patriarchal households. They have accepted a notion of themselves as subservient and dutiful long before they enter the garment factory. They model their position in the factory hierarchy on their role in the household and so are able not only to accept the domination of the factory, but to find in that domination their own sources of personal self-worth and power. Thus, workers transform colleagues into loyal sisters and factory owners into concerned fathers. They are able to accept the constraints that the factory imposes by assimilating the owners' dominance into other, more acceptable forms of relationships. This re-molding of relationships formed inside the factory to fit the prototypes of ties formed outside ultimately makes the workers available for increased exploitation. Persons with authority in the factory capitalize on workers' interpretations of their roles to maximize production and ultimately increase profit.

RESEARCH METHODS

I conducted the fieldwork for this study in the city of Fez from August 1994 to August 1995. The fieldwork involved intensive ethnography, which included formal interviews of Fez factory owners, formal and informal interviews of workers and their families, two random surveys carried out in separate garment factories in the city, and three months of participant observation inside one of those garment factories. The factory where I worked, which I call "Confection," employs some 150 workers and has been in operation for some six years. It is typical in size and operation of garment factories in Fez. At Confection I worked in the packaging department, where finished garments are tagged and prepared for shipment. This experience provided me a position from which to observe everyday work routines, the nature of the work process, staff hierarchies, and personal interactions inside the factory. It was through "acting like a worker" that I began to understand something of what factory work means to Moroccan factory girls.

THE ECONOMIC CONTEXT
OF GARMENT PRODUCTION

Today clothing manufacture is one of Morocco's chief export industries, and garments account for a quarter of the country's exports (Leymarie and Tripier 1992). Conservative estimates suggest that Morocco's garment factories employ close to a quarter of the country's factory workers: some 95,000 of the country's total 444,000 industrial workers produce garments. Virtually

all of these workers are female (Ministère du Commerce 1994).[3]

The importance of the garment industry to the Moroccan economy is a recent phenomenon. Before the 1980s, garment manufacture was relatively insignificant. Between 1981 and 1991 the production of garments more than quadrupled (Leymarie and Tripier 1992) and, although males had formerly predominated in the garment factories, it was females who were hired, en masse, to staff the new enterprises.[4] The boom in the Moroccan garment business, and the concomitant employment of females, was fueled by several factors. These included the government economic readjustment program, trade agreements with the European Economic Community, and the movement of European production "off-shore."

The Moroccan government economic readjustment program, instituted in 1983, was a primary catalyst of the new trend (Leymarie and Tripier 1992). Before the institution of the readjustment program, Moroccan industry consisted largely of state-owned, high-tech enterprises with little capacity for generating employment. These included such industries as phosphate mining and production of thread and cloth. The program sought to replace such industries with private, low capital, labor-intensive ones. This change in Moroccan industry marked a shift in the gender of the country's work-force. As Morocco turned to light manufacturing for export, including garment production, food processing and electronics manufacturing, females flooded into factories. This employment of female factory workers is characteristic of export-oriented industries across the globe (Nash and Fernandez-Kelly 1983; Rothstein and Blim 1992; Ong 1987, 1991; Nash 1981).

European sub-contractors (predominantly French), motivated by favorable trade conditions and the desire for "off-shore" production sites, became involved in the industry in the late 1970s. They sought out Moroccan enterprises that could supply them with low cost labor, they sent in raw materials needed for production and exported the final products. These sub-contractors encouraged the wide scale employment of females, enjoying greater profits because women would accept far lower wages than the salaries men demanded (Joekes 1982a, 1982b, 1985). Thus, the nature and structure of the Moroccan garment industry is defined by the relationship between the European contractors and private Moroccan industrialists.

Moroccan garment factories are generally small, family-owned businesses with staffs of 50 employees or less, flexible enough to respond to a foreign, somewhat volatile, market. Because of their relatively small size they can, and often do, elude government regulation. The garment factories commonly do not heed Moroccan labor law, which in part accounts for their poor working conditions. The factories open and close rapidly and unexpectedly, with fluctuations in the external market. Thus, Moroccan females labor in an industry that provides them insecure positions and relatively poor conditions (Leymarie and Tripier 1992).

Originally, Morocco's garment factory workers, like all Moroccan factory hands, were predominantly male. Before the 1980s, female garment factory workers did unskilled work on the margins of production, but they did not operate sewing machines. Today, however, women and girls fill nearly all positions in the garment factories. The wide-scale employment of females as garment factory workers takes on new meanings in the Moroccan context.

The Social Context of Garment Production

In my research I found that garment factory workers are, for the most part, unmarried young girls who live at home with their parents and unmarried siblings. This fact is widely recognized in Morocco. The workers are generally daughters of lower class households which, in comparison with others of their class, are relatively poor and suffer high rates of male unemployment. (I herein refer to the households where garment workers live as "factory households"). The vast majority of garment workers contribute all or at least part of their earnings to household support and are significant wage-earners.[5]

Despite their positions as breadwinners, factory workers retain a fierce hold on the value of the patriarchal family. Both in word and action, they revere the traditional hierarchy that establishes males as protectors and females as dependents. Garment workers speak of factory labor as a temporary aberration they must tolerate until a successful marriage places them in the position of non-working wife and mother (married workers, a minority, are often young and as yet childless; workers with children generally work because they are destitute).

In their homes, garment workers enact the rituals of subservience that confirm and reinforce their positions as daughters, or sometimes as wives, in either case female and junior members of the household. In spite of their engagement with the factory, workers strive to maintain their identity as kinswoman because this identity is more central to them than their self-perception as workers.[6]

Local ideologies of gender, to which workers adhere, reinforce the patriarchal structure of factory households. Male authority in the family is legitimized by an ideology that defines women as economically dependent, subservient, and in need of control. According to the Moroccan gender code, a woman's proper role is that of wife and mother, a position that is essentially non-economic and properly played out in the privacy of the domestic sphere. Men appropriately take the position of breadwinner and operate in the economic sphere outside the home. Thus, women are symbolically associated with the home and with private, interior domestic space. A family's honor is embedded in its ability to keep women inside and protected, thus maintaining the divide between male and female that is at once a separation between inside and outside, private and public, kin and non-kin, home and business.[7]

The favored portrayal of female activities as home-bound, kin-related and non-economic obscures the fact that Moroccan women have always been active in the economy (Beneria 1984, Davis 1983). Today, the economic participation of Moroccan females represents 36% of national economic activity (Direction de la Statistique 1994), although it goes largely unrecognized. Still, the above-described gender code retains its position as an ideal, rooted in the popular understanding of Islam. The mass entry of Fez's women into the garment factories blatantly contradicts the pervasively held Moroccan notions of family and gender. In this article, I explore how factory workers live with this contradiction.

The Factory in Fez

Fez is an ancient city, revered among Moroccans as a spiritual capital and regarded as a bulwark of Islam and Muslim society. Traditionally, Fez has been an important artisanal center. Today it is a textile town. At independence, the Moroccan government established its largest public cloth spinning and weaving factories in Fez, which were (and are today) staffed by men. During the 1980s garment manufacturing emerged as the city's principal industry and today the sewing factories of Fez employ more than a third of all Fez factory workers, nearly all of them women (Ministère du Commerce 1994). This is a vivid contrast to the situation that existed less than three decades ago, when the town's textile enterprises were the province of men.

Industrial enterprises are scattered throughout the city of Fez, although most industry is located in three industrial quarters. Small factories and artisanal workshops producing for the local market and the tourist trade are found in the ancient medina. Other modest-sized factories exist in the city's newer sections, including the Ville Nouvelle and the recently developed urban periphery. The bulk of Fez's industry, including the largest and most "modern" factories, many of which produce for export, is located in the city's industrial quarters. These include the oldest and largest, Quartier Industriel Sidi Brahim, the industrial quarter of Doukkarat, and the most recently created quarter in Ben Souda. Three-quarters of Fez's factory workers labor in these districts (Fejjal 1987).

The majority of Fez's garment factories are privately owned by a class of Moroccan elite, known as the Fassi. The term "Fassi" is used throughout the country to describe a group of influential families originally native to the city of Fez, who control much of Morocco's wealth and political power. The Fassi are at the top of the local class structure, which includes a middle level of educated bureaucrats and a lower level made up of the majority of city dwellers, who are relatively poor and uneducated. This lower class is the class with which garment workers identify.

THE LABOR PROCESS AND FACTORY STAFF

The labor process in Fez garment factories involves six separate steps, which precede and follow upon the actual sewing of the garments. They include, in sequential order: the intake and inventory of fabric and supplies imported from Europe; the cutting of the fabric; the actual sewing of the garments, carried out by workers seated in rows ("sewing lines"); the ironing of finished products; the final inspection of completed garments; and packaging and shipment. This production sequence is carried out in the same manner, using the same kind of technology, in garment factories throughout the world.

These production tasks are carried out by factory staff who labor in a hierarchy of authority. At the top of this hierarchy are the factory owners, who are either upper-class Moroccans (generally the above-described Fassi) or Europeans; in both cases, those at the top owners of the factory hierarchy are most frequently men.[8] Owners generally leave the daily direction of the factory to be handled by administrators, the garment manufacturing technicians who plan and supervise production. Like the owners, these individuals are upper-class Moroccan men (often of the owner's family) or Europeans.[9] A workshop director, generally a Moroccan man, oversees the management of all factory staff on the workshop floor. Next in the hierarchy are the workshop supervisors, who manage each particular production process; there are, for instance, one or two line supervisors for each sewing line. These supervisors are generally Moroccan males or females, of the same class as the workers. Finally, at the bottom of the factory hierarchy, are the mass of factory workers, who are Moroccan females of the lower class.

On the margins of production are the factory mechanics, transport bus drivers, secretaries and maids. The mechanics and bus drivers are Moroccan lower-class men, the former considered relatively skilled. The secretaries are Moroccan females who, because they are literate and not engaged in manual work, hold relatively high status within the factory. The maids, unskilled and impoverished females in a demeaned occupation, occupy the lowest position in the hierarchy.

Factory staff rely on familiar and valued models of relationships to interact with each other and with those who control them. I will explore how local assumptions about home and family, assumptions that are themselves infused with ideas about gender, inform the workers' attempts to transform factory relations into meaningful intercourse.

Factory as Home and Family

> I like this factory very, very much. The people here are nice, it is like a family. There are hardly any men working here . . . so it is like being in your own house. . . . If I ever left this job, I would go straight back home.

The gendering of the workshop floor as female transforms what might have been a public and immoral space into a private and acceptable one. As Emen, a seven-year employee of the Confection expressed it above, the fact that garment factories hire (nearly) only females makes the work that goes on in them somewhat more respectable. The factory is a private space, like a house, because it is a female space, a space free from the threat of illicit sexuality. Whatever transpires inside the factory is less morally questionable because the shop floor is imagined to be a private rather than a public arena. As one worker explained with pride, "one girl passes her cloth to another girl, and we are at ease, because we are all girls."

Garment factory workers are generally demeaned by Fez inhabitants for their participation in factory labor. Factory labor is in itself poorly regarded because it is manual labor, neither autonomous nor artisanal, and participation in factory work connotes a low class status.

But for females, it suggests as well a lack of family honor and the real or potential loss of personal virtue. Girls who engage in factory labor are assumed to be related to males who are unable to appropriately support and protect them. The glaring presence of factory girls on the streets of Fez is often cited as proof of the inability of families to control and monitor their daughters. In response to such deprecating images, garment workers take refuge in the fact that they work in a safe, protected, all-female environment.

The actual physical construction of the factories and the way workers approach and understand factory space expresses the notion of factory as home. The factories producing for export, situated in Fez's three industrial districts, are large, low-lying structures that look like warehouses. Rows of narrow windows parallel the factory roofs but are almost unnoticeable from outside. The windows are generally too high for a passerby to see inside and, unlike the male-staffed cement and construction factories (where metal doors are often left open and interior courtyards are visible to the outside), the garment factories in the same districts housing Moroccan girls are shut tight to the stranger's eye. They look at first glance as if they are unoccupied.

Large metal doors mark the entrance to the factories and a guardian sits directly behind these doors. The doors open into a courtyard where the trucks that transport materials to and from Europe load and unload. The factory men—the guardian, mechanics and drivers—often remain in this open, transitional space. On arrival workers file through the courtyard and directly into the workshop. This is an area separate from the courtyard, located behind it, or up a flight of stairs. Once they have arrived inside the factory, workers may not leave the building without permission (often written) from their supervisors. At the Confection factory, workers who became ill during the work day required written authorization to get past the guardian and walk out of the building. Even if a worker wished to quit the job permanently, she could not leave the premises with written permission. The factory is a private space, tightly enclosed and closely monitored.

Altogether, then, the garment factory is a concrete structure built around an open courtyard, monitored by a male guardian, in which women remain protected from view and separate from males present. This description of place is reminiscent of the traditional Fez household (Mernissi 1994), in which a male slave prevented the entrance of strangers, and where women remained protected inside, carrying out the labor specific to them. While such households may have existed only rarely and for the wealthy few, the notion of the home as a private, enclosed and specifically female space remains a Moroccan ideal. The female garment factory is modeled on this prototype.

Unlike Moroccan female bureaucrats who wear European business suits, or university students who wear western style skirts or jeans on campus,[10] garment factory workers do not don "professional" or western dress to go to work. They travel to and from the factory in the modest jellaba, a long, loose fitting robe worn in public spaces by traditional Moroccan women. Their retention of the jellaba signals identification with conventional Moroccan womanhood, as opposed to "modern" working women or with university girls (two other groups of women in transition). Inside the factories, workers are dressed in the informal clothing Moroccan women wear in the privacy of the home: baggy, pajama-like dresses or skirts or blue jeans in distinctive Moroccan combinations of style and color (in some factories workers must wear regulation smocks). Most wear plastic sandals on their bare feet, as they would at home. In summer the workshops can be stiflingly hot, and workers who take pains to dress modestly in the public arena of the streets labor in a minimum of clothing in the factory, as if confident that they are not exposed to a stranger's view.

Inside this production center imagined as domestic space, factory owners and workers alike assert that they work together "as a family"; owners claim to treat workers "as daughters." Workers identify the owners in a protective role that their fathers might hold, and assert that all fellow garment workers are "sisters."[11] Even where workers recognize the discontinuities between ties formed inside the factory and those formed at home, the analogy to family life is implicit. For example, one worker, who detested the factory, claimed she would prefer to stay at home because her mother, as she said, "would never yell at (her) the way this administrator does."

The factory is the home and family is the idiom through which factory personnel think about their relations to each other. The gendered dimension of family relationships is evident in the way female factory workers approach owners, co-workers and supervisors, male and female.

In using the metaphor of family, workers quite consciously help owners in their achievement of production goals. Despite a skill hierarchy among them, they treat each other as "sisters" and thus with relative equality. Workers vehemently assert that they support each other in the accomplishment of factory tasks. Repeatedly, I was told stories of lines of machine operators who had stayed late in order to help one of their slower members, or of individual machine operators who had fallen behind in their own tasks in order to assist an inexperienced newcomer. Workers emphasized their willingness to work well with each other, taking pride in their ability to behave in a sisterly fashion. At Confection (as at many other Fez factories) workers ate lunch together from communal plates, just as they would at home, making evident their attempts to replicate the atmosphere of the home inside the factory.

The sisterly relations among workers is perhaps most evident in the way they interact with their supervisors, particularly in their defiance of factory demands. Females are increasingly being placed in supervisory positions inside Fez factories and the majority of sewing line supervisors today are female. At Confection, workers were relatively free in directly challenging female supervisors; they seemed to fear these supervisors less than they feared supervisory males.

Disputes between workers and female supervisors were not uncommon and often took the form of loud and sudden outbursts of resistance from workers in response to unbearable production pressures. Before such exchanges became problematic, however, the defiant worker's co-workers would often intervene, attempting to assuage the stressed worker's feelings and encourage her compliance. In one such case, I watched as a put-upon worker argued with her supervisor, refusing to complete a particular task. When the other workers tried to calm this worker and urge her compliance, the worker asked, "Why should she be allowed to boss me?" In response, her colleague asserted, "If Hakima cannot boss us, then who will?" The annoyed worker ultimately complied.

Co-workers had reminded the rebellious worker of the validity of the hierarchy among them, one not foreign to the mode of control used within the family. An age-hierarchy among siblings is accepted in traditional Moroccan homes, and it is recognized that the eldest sister has the authority to lead her younger sisters in the housework. Verbalization of defiance and argument is not uncommon among siblings in a household. Neither is the eventual cooperation attained through a common acknowledgement of, and respect for, a universally recognized hierarchy, The authority of the female supervisor gains validity because it is reminiscent of the authority of the eldest sister. This argument, like others between workers and their female supervisors, is reminiscent of arguments between sisters in a household. Arguments with male supervisors take on a different tone, as discussed below. First, however, it is necessary to discuss the position of males in the factory.

Workers and workshop-level supervisors are today nearly exclusively female. Still, there are some males present inside the factories and on the workshop floor. The men may be the factory owners, high level administrators, the workshop director, supervisors, or the male service workers (who include the factory transport drivers, guardians, and mechanics). It is now rare to find men on the sewing lines; three was the greatest number of male sewing machine operators I could identify in any Fez factory, and most have none.

In general, the factory men attempt to separate themselves from the females. Factory guardians and transport drivers generally remain in the courtyard, separate from the workshop floor and the females there. The mechanics' duties compel them to be present on the workshop floor amidst the females. At Confection, they did not dally on the floor and remained in a separate room when possible. The factory men took lunch together, eating only after the mass of workers had left the lunch room. Just as men in Moroccan homes often remove themselves after meals to retreat to the all-male public cafes and street corners, men in the factory did not linger with women in a space that was clearly female.

The men present on the workshop floor are most often the workshop director and the supervisors directing the labor of the female machine operators. As noted above, the majority of line supervisors in Fez factories today are female; still, most factories retain at least several men in the position of sewing line supervisor. Almost all factories have retained men in the position of cutting supervisor (a post requiring technical training largely unavailable to lower-class Moroccan females). All the Fez factories I visited retained a male as workshop director, the position of greatest authority on the workshop floor. Workshop directors are always men, one informant explained, because "a man can make the girls afraid, but a woman cannot."

This hierarchy of gender authority on the factory floor reflects the hierarchy within the domestic sphere, where women carry out the daily labor and men retain the authority, The organization and use of space inside the factory makes explicit a gender hierarchy taken for granted. The few men who are present on the workshop floor (either administrators, supervisors or mechanics) are free to move about the factory at will. The female workers, however, are not permitted to leave their positions without authorization; a pass is required even to use the restroom. Workers must remain in place until production quotas are met and often do not know when the workday will end. Officially, they are not permitted to speak while they work.[12]

Thus, the very few males present on the workshop floor are upright figures standing and moving with relative self-control across a space in which females are fixed. It appears that males control females in an otherwise all-female space. The apparent immobilization of women in fixed places inside the factory parallels the limits placed on their freedom of movement in the culture generally. It also reiterates the local gender ideology that defines women as subservient and men as in control.

Given this presumed hierarchy of authority between male and female, the female garment workers directly confront male supervisors less often than female supervisors. In one case I observed a young packaging worker carrying heavy boxes down a staircase while the male workshop supervisor stood by, watching her without assisting. When the task was done the worker complained to her colleagues that the supervisor had done nothing to help. One colleague responded, "What business does a man have working in this factory?" and the other coworkers agreed that a man has no compelling interest in factory work. The demeaned labor in the garment factory is not worthy of a man's time or energy. It is common in Moroccan households to watch females toil while males relax, and factory families invariably defend this as natural. Just as a girl would not expect her father, or even her brother, to help her carry out her household tasks, so a garment factory worker ought not to expect assistance from males on the workshop floor. Garment factory work is degraded work and it is the work of females.

Nonetheless, workers do occasionally resist the authority of men in the factory; they are, however, sanctioned for it. In one case at Confection, a sewing line operator asked her male supervisor for permission to use the restroom. When he refused her, she stood up to leave her seat nonetheless. He slapped her and she, in return, slapped him. She was fired for her deed. In explaining to me why the worker was forced to leave, one girl said, "In Morocco a man can hit a woman but a woman must never, ever, hit a man. Even if he hits her, she must not hit him back." These customs prevail on the shop floor.

Factory owners, almost always male, are removed from everyday interactions on the shop floor, and thus are not engaged in the quotidian labor process. According to the dominant metaphor, factory owners are fathers and the mass of females who toil on the workshop floor, daughters. Cast in the role of fathers, owners take their positions as guardians of female virtue seriously. They provide transportation so that workers can travel to and from the factory in the protected space of factory vans (which are frequently all-female spaces; male workers often travel separately). In this way, owners curb the workers' wanderings on the streets of Fez, like fathers protecting their chastity.[13] In many factories, owners required the workers to remain inside while awaiting the arrival of the company vans, thereby preventing their unnecessary exposure on the street. At Confection the owner instituted a rule forbidding workers from travelling to and from the factory on public transportation and requiring all workers to commute in the company vans. The rule was put in place when the owner discovered that young men were frequenting the local streets in the early evening, hoping to socialize with workers leaving the factory.

Thus, the owners' control of workers reaches beyond service inside the factory. The owners' efforts to monitor female comportment on the streets of Fez were approved by community members and workers as well. Owners themselves used the idiom of family to characterize their relations with workers. One owner described himself as the workers' "father, brother, uncle, friend." He reported that he gave extra money to the neediest workers, and he claimed to buy many of them the rams needed for the ritual annual sacrifice. Although it was impossible to corroborate his story, owners cultivated the loyalty of workers by presenting themselves as concerned and watchful fathers.

Typically, workers verbalized feelings of fondness and respect for the factory owners. Concerning the above-mentioned transportation regulations at Confection, many workers defended the restrictions placed on their movements outside the factory, claiming that such controls helped maintain their reputations and assure the community that they were honorable girls. In a similar way, I found that

Moroccan girls who chafed at the restrictions their fathers and brothers placed upon them would nonetheless defend these men against criticism and readily portray their influence as a form of protection or an expression of concern. Thus, workers justified the owners' increased control just as they might justify the limits placed on them by male kin as the men's attempt to guard and shelter them. Workers, perceiving themselves as "daughters," were compelled by a sense of family obligation to comply with the limits imposed on them.

This rich and meaningful basis for relationship binds girls to the factory in a sort of moral obligation that many workers acknowledge. Work becomes a commitment to the father and, through fulfilling it, a worker demonstrates her high moral standing as a female, and as a member of the community. One worker at a Fez garment factory described the working of overtime as a kind of moral obligation, a burden necessary to bear. "If the boss needs us to stay and work till seven o'clock in the evening, we must stay. We have to help him keep his commitments with people overseas." She explained how a fellow worker got fired: one evening when they were working overtime, the girl just got up from her machine and said to the owner, "Just give me my money for my hours worked." She then left the factory without waiting to be certain the export truck was ready to go, unwilling to help the owner meet his deadlines. "One must not speak like that," the first worker said, criticizing the actions of her colleague. "It sounds hard, as if you do not trust that the boss will give you what he owes you." Although workers frequently see little of the factory owners, the relationship between worker and owner is phrased as highly personalized and based on trust.

Another worker described an incident that forced her to miss the seven-day naming ceremony for her sister's first-born child, which she sorely regretted. In recounting how this had come to pass, she emphasized the cooperative and dutiful quality of her own response:

On the day of the naming ceremony, I went to the director and said, "Today is the seventh-day naming ceremony for my sister's first child, I want to leave early to attend." The director pleaded with me "Please, we cannot let you go early today. Please, don't go. You understand we need you, don't you?" I answered, "Yes, no problem."

In continuing, the worker explained that she could have feigned illness in order to be released from the factory that day, but she would not do so because she was an honest and trustworthy person. Although I prompted her, the worker would express no resentment or anger at this sequence of events. According to her interpretation, she was never forbidden to leave the factory but rather was begged to stay and help. And to this appeal she responded. She missed her sister's party because she was obliged to answer a higher duty.

This worker's description of loyalty to the factory is a familiar form of discourse among workers, and it precisely parallels the way in which relations with family are described. For instance, another worker described to me her premature departure from school, which came about when her father approached her and (by her account) said, "my little daughter . . . you can see the situation we are in. Please, can you leave school and try to get work to help us?" The worker emphasized that her father had never commanded her but rather had pleaded with her. As she recounted his words, the worker imitated her father's begging voice and placed her fingertips over her mouth and kissed them, mimicking the gesture her father had used to signal a request.

Within the family, workers do not experience authority simply as a gripping hold on their liberties and personal autonomy. Instead, in submitting to authority, they perceive themselves as providing a needed response to a call for service. The assistance they provide to the owners, and to their male kin as well, is in some ways a source of personal power, for it is these females alone who can answer the males' call for assistance. They interpret their own compliance as a moral obligation, and in cooperating they display their own good character and worthiness as daughters or wives.[14]

As the worker/owner relationship gets carried out in terms of the code associated with father/daughter, parent/child or possibly husband/wife, what might appear as domination or exploitation of workers by owners often gets reconfigured into something more acceptable. By thinking in terms of the family model, workers can experience owners and administrators not as dominating, but as begging or pleading for their cooperation and assistance. In cooperating with the owner, they assert their own moral rectitude as loyal, principled individuals who understand the importance of preserving the social tie above all else.

CONCLUSION

It is young unmarried women who staff the garment factories of Morocco. Fez locals, and Moroccans generally, claim that the low pay, long hours, and unpaid overtime associated with garment factory labor are accepted by these young girls because they work "only for clothes and make-up." As daughters (or sometimes wives), workers are presumed to be supported by family males; they are believed to contribute minimally, at most, to household support. As noted above, contrary to public opinion, research indicates that garment factory workers are an important source of household support.

Nonetheless, the local understanding of women's participation in low-paid factory labor coincides with Marxist feminist explanations of female employment on the global assembly line (Elson and Pierson 1981). From both perspectives, it is women's role in reproduction, and their position as dependent daughters, wives, and/or mothers, that explains their vulnerability to and acceptance of low-wage work.

Here, I have attempted to explore how Moroccan understandings of home, family and gender render females willing workers on the garment factory shop floor. Workers transform the public space of the factory into the private space of the home in an attempt to assuage the contradiction inherent in their presence inside the factory, outside the home, in a role ideologically reserved for men. They behave inside this "home" as kinswoman, using the assumptions and practices associated with family to regulate their comportment inside factory walls. They approach owners much like fathers, and supervisors like parents or elder sisters. They treat each other like siblings. They accept factory hierarchies based on their understanding of, and reverence for, the patriarchal family and the gender order it endorses.

Local meanings and values thus mediate the workers' approach to the factory. Their transformation of factory into a home allows them to accommodate the owners' power with little resistance. They willingly accept the factory administration's power as they would accept the authority of their own fathers, in their role as daughters, or that of their husbands in the role of wife. In this way, the owners are able to appropriate labor at a low cost without risking resistance. To some extent, workers and their families are willing accomplices in the factory's exploitation, because this exploitation gets phrased in terms that are not only accepted, but revered.

REFERENCES

Abu Lughod, Lila. 1986. *Veiled Sentiments*. Berkeley: University of California Press.

Beneria, Lourdes. 1984. Women and Rural Development: Morocco. *Cultural Survival Quarterly* 8(2):30–32.

Blim, Michael L. 1992. Introduction: The Emerging Global Factory and Anthropology. In *Anthropology and the Global Factory: Studies of the New Industrialization in the Late Twentieth Century*. M.L. Blim and F.A. Rothstein, eds., pp. 1–30. New York: Bergin and Garvey.

Calagione, John and Daniel Nugent. 1992. Workers' Expressions: Beyond Accommodation and Resistance on the Margins of Capitalism. In *Worker's Expressions: Beyond Accommodation and Resistance*. J. Calagione and D. Nugent, eds., pp. 1–34. Albany: SUNY Press.

Comaroff, John L. and Jean Comaroff. 1987. The Madman and the Migrant: Work and Labor in the Historical Consciousness of a South African People. *American Ethnologist* 14(2): 191–209.

Combs-Schilling, M. Elaine. 1989. *Sacred Performances: Islam, Sexuality and Sacrifice*. New York: Columbia University Press.

Davis, Susan S. 1983. Patience and Power: *Women's Lives in a Moroccan Village*. New York: Schenkman.

Direction de la Statistique de Maroc. 1994. *Femme et Condition Feminine au Maroc*. Rabat: Les Editions Guessous.

Dwyer, Daisy H. 1978. *Images and Self-Images: Male and Female in Morocco*. New York: Columbia University Press.

Elson, Diane and Ruth Pierson. 1981. The Subordination of Women and the Internationalisation of Factory Production. In *Of Marriage and the Market: Women's Subordination in International Perspective*. Kate Yound, ed., pp. 144–166. London: CSE Books.

Fejjal, Ali. 1987. Industrie et Industrialisation à Fes. *Revenue de Geographie Marocaine Nouvelle Serie* 11(2): 55–70.

Hijab, Nadia. 1988. *Womanpower: The Arab Debate on Women at Work*. Cambridge: Cambridge University Press.

Ibrahim, Beth. 1985. "Cairo's Factory Women". *In Women and the Family in the Middle East*. Elizabeth Fernea, ed., pp. 293–299. Austin: University of Texas Press.

Joekes, Susan. 1982a. *The Multifibre Arrangement and Outward Processing: The Case of Morocco and Tunisia*. In EEC and the Third World. C. Stevens, ed., pp. 102–112. London: Hodder and Soughton.

———. 1982b. Female-led Industrialization and Women's Jobs in Third World Export Manufacturing: The Case of the Moroccan Clothing Industry. *Brighton: Institute of Development Studies Research Reports* No. 15.

———. 1985. Working for Lipstick? Male and Female Labour in the Clothing Industry in Morocco. In *Women, Work and Ideology in the Third World*. H. Afshar, ed., pp. 183–214. London: Tavistock Publications.

Leymarie, Serge and Jean Tripier. 1992. *Maroc: Le Prochain Dragon?* Casablanoa: Editions Eddif Maroc.

Lim, Linda Y.C. 1993. Capitalism, Imperialism and Patriarchy: The Dilemma of Third-World Women Workers in Multinational Factories. In *Women, Men, and the International Division of Labor*. June Nash and M.P. Fernandez-Kelly, eds., pp. 205–223. Albany: State University of New York Press.

Macleod, Arlene E. 1991. *Accommodating Protest: Working Women, the New Veiling, and Change in Cairo*. New York: Columbia University Press.

Mernissi, Fatima. 1987. *Beyond the Veil: Male-Female Dynamics in a Modern Muslim Society*. Bloomington: Indiana University Press.

———. 1994. *Dreams of Trespass: Tales of a Harem Girlhood*. New York: Addison-Wesley Publishing Company.

Ministère du Commerce de L'Industrie et de la Privatisation. 1994. Situation des Industries de Transformation. Rabat: Dèlegation de Commerce et de l'Industrie de la Wilaya de Fes.

Nash, June. 1981. Ethnographic Aspects of the World Capitalist System. *Annual Review of Anthropology* 10:393–424.

Nash, June and Maria P. Fernandez-Kelly eds., 1983. *Women, Men and the International Division of Labor*. Albany: State University of New York Press.

Ong, Aibwa. 1987. *Spirits of Resistance and Capitalist Discipline: Factory Women in Malayisia*. Albany: State University of New York Press.

———. 1991. The Gender and Labor Politics of Postmodernity. *Annual Review of Anthropology* 20: 279–309.

Peristiany, J.G. 1966. *Honor and Shame: The Values of Mediterranean Society*. Chicago: University of Chicago Press.

Rothstein, Francis A. and Michael L. Blim, eds., 1992. *Anthropology and the Global Factory: Studies of the New Industrialization in the Late Twentieth Century*. New York: Bergen and Garvey.

Sabbah, Fatna. 1984. *Woman in the Muslim Unconscious*. New York: Oxford Pergamon Press.

Salaff, Janet. 1981. *Working Daughters of Hong Kong: Filial Piety or Power in the Family?* New York: Cambridge University Press.

Wallman, Sandra, ed. 1979. *The Social Anthropology of Work*. London: Academic Press.

Warren, Kay B. and Susan C. Bourque. 1989. Women, Technology and Development Ideologies: Frameworks and Findings. In *Gender and Anthropology*. S. Morgen, ed., pp. 382–411. Washington, DC: American Anthropological Association.

White, Jenny B. 1994. *Money Makes Us Relatives: Women's Labor in Urban Turkey*. Austin: University of Texas Press.

NOTES

1. Here, the word "workers" refers to the female garment factory workers of Fez. I refer to the workers as "girls" rather than women because the vast majority of them are unmarried and thus defined, in Morocco, as girls, or *binet*. The residents of Fez, Moroccans generally, and the workers themselves refer to garment factory workers as girls.

2. Here I contrast the idea of "labor" with that of "work" as in Comaroff and Comaroff (1987) and Wallman (1979).

3. The accuracy of these numbers is questionable. The figures are based on government census

materials and reflect only the factories officially registered with the government. It is widely understood in Morocco, however, that many industrial operations are unregistered and "hidden." Factory owners prefer to keep their operations unnoticed by the government to avoid the financial and legal implications that are inherent in official recognition. Even where the factory itself is recognized by the government, many of its workers may not be. Factory owners often regard even permanent, full-time employees as seasonal workers, temporary staff, or apprentices, and thus deny them the work papers that would ensure them the benefits prescribed by law. Obviously, government data cannot account for such employees. One economist in Morocco suggested that government figures be doubled to arrive at a more accurate count of industrial workers in Fez. During one year in Fez, I met few garment workers who held work registration papers. None of the 150 workers in the factory where I worked had working papers.

4. Moroccan men were slowly replaced by women in the garment industry. Throughout the 1980s females were hired to replace departing males in existing factories and most workers hired in new factories were female. Females were frequently hired to replace males involved in labor unrest. Fez factory owners recounted that males working in Fez garment factories before the general workers strike of 1990 were replaced by females. Morocco suffers high rates of unemployment, and male joblessness has not been alleviated by the boom in the garment industry.

5. According to my survey research, 76% of workers surveyed were never-married females, 16% were married, and 8% were divorced. Nearly all of the workers surveyed (92%) were between the ages of 13 and 25. Never-married and divorced workers (84% of the total) almost invariably lived as daughters in their natal households (divorced young women return to their natal homes when possible). Married workers lived either in their husband's natal home or in a separate conjugal home. The majority of married workers were newly married women who had worked in the factory before marriage. Most of the married workers who continued working after having children were destitute women whose husbands were unable to work. Workers earned anywhere from 300 to 800 dirhams per month, and 89% of workers reported contributing some or all of their salary to the family. These salaries were considered significant in lower class households in which men found difficulty securing steady work.

6. Although I am not in any way suggesting a privileged relationship between Islam and women's subjugation to factory labor, other researchers have investigated women's participation in wage labor with focus on the Muslim context (Hijab 1988; Ibrahim 1985; Macleod 1991; Ong 1987; and White 1994).

7. Abu Lughod (1986) provides a complex exploration of the notion of honor, and an early, comprehensive collection on the notion of honor is found in Peristiany (1966). See Dwyer 1978, Mernissi 1987, Sabbah 1984, and Combs-Schilling 1989 for discussions of specifically Moroccan notions of honor as they pertain to gender and gender relations.

8. Related women—the wives and sometimes daughters of the owners—are prominent in the operation of a few Fez factories. But it is most frequently men who play the day-to-day role of factory owner and administrator.

9. It is interesting to note that many of the European technical directors are female while Moroccan technical directors are almost exclusively male.

10. There is a growing number of university students who today dress in distinctively Islamic robes, but I do not consider them here.

11. This situation is reinforced by the fact that many workers are related to each other through biological kinship. High level factory staff are often relatives of the factory owner (Fejjal 1987) so that there is a sense in each factory that this is a family enterprise. Personal ties are key in the recruitment of new workers: factory owners and administrators give the relatives and friends of trusted workers preference in hiring. It is common for sisters, cousins, even mother and daughter to work in the same factory, either at the same time or sequentially. At Confection, 10% of the workers had sisters or cousins working contemporaneously with them; others reported that their relatives had worked there previously. Nearly 20% of the workers surveyed had sisters who worked in other garment factories in Fez. Biological kin ties among the workers help contribute to making the idiom of family a reality.

12. Moroccans, men in particular, characterize women as "full of empty talk." Their propensity to be engaged in meaningless speech is prohibited on the factory floor.

13. There are economic reasons for providing transport as well: for many workers, the cost of public transportation to and from the factory would represent such a large percentage of the salary as to

make working purposeless. The father of one former worker laughed wryly when he explained that his daughter's month of factory work had actually cost the family money; the girl's salary did not cover her bus fare to and from the factory. (She was considered an apprentice, which explains her absurdly low salary.)

14. Abu Lughod (1986) explores the dimensions of the authority relationship between Bedouin men and women.

Sexuality and Discipline among Filipina Domestic Workers in Hong Kong

Nicole Constable

In January 1993 Christina, a 27-year-old unmarried Filipina, arrived in Hong Kong to begin work as a foreign domestic helper (or "FDH"). As she told me several months later, Mrs. Wong, her employer, met her at Kai Tak airport. In the car on the way home, Mrs. Wong began their conversation by reciting a list of rules: "On your day off you must be home by 8 P.M. You cannot wear dresses or skirts, only pants. You must keep your shoulders and upper arms covered at all times, and you cannot wear fingernail polish, jewelry, or perfume." Furthermore, she said that Christina's hair, which was thick and long at the time, had to be short. Mrs. Wong then proceeded directly to a barber shop where she instructed the barber to give Christina a "man's cut." Two days later Christina's contract was abruptly terminated.

I met Christina at the shelter for domestic workers where she was staying during the summer of 1993. As she described her ordeal, another Filipina interjected: "*Bruha* (witch) obviously didn't know you'd look even more beautiful with short hair!" I later described Christina's experiences to Mr. Chen, the owner and director of a successful employment agency that recruits women from the Philippines to work as "helpers" in Hong Kong. His comment was remarkably similar. He nonchalantly said, "Perhaps she was too pretty and the employer was worried about her husband."

American Ethnologist 24(3):539–558. Copyright © 1997, American Anthropological Association. Not for sale or further reproduction.

In this article I argue that Mrs. Wong's treatment of Christina represents far more than the idiosyncratic behavior of a jealous and controlling employer. Instead, Mrs. Wong's attempt to reduce Christina to a less threatening, gender-neutral (or masculine) image is representative of general anxieties about the sexuality of foreign domestic workers in Hong Kong, and the threat that they are thought to pose to Chinese women employers in particular, the Chinese family in general, and Hong Kong society at large as it makes the transition from British colony to Special Administrative Region of the People's Republic of China. As I contend in this article, the public concern about Filipinas and their sexuality is linked to broader changes in women's roles in the home and the public workforce and in the social identities of foreign domestic workers.

Criticisms of Filipinas are partly a reflection of more private concerns writ large and superimposed on a rapidly changing and soon-to-be postcolonial city. On Sundays in Hong Kong's Central District, in what decades ago was an elite and largely male territory, young, nubile, foreign women gather in the thousands on their day off, "taking over," as the locals say, the core of the city's financial region. There, on the steps of such great monuments to capitalism as the Hong Kong and Shanghai Bank, foreign maids speak in languages that the locals cannot understand, and they conduct what is generally regarded as private (indoor) rituals or business—polishing nails, giving each other haircuts, and applying makeup—in public. Some dress up and others dress "like men"— both practices being cause for concern. In contrast to locals' images or memories of the Chinese "amahs" of the past, who are said to have "known their places" and to have posed no fundamental or moral challenge to existing patterns of authority (see Constable 1996; Gaw 1991; Ooi 1992), contemporary foreign domestic workers constitute a threat and are considered to be a symbol of a moral order turned inside out. This inversion in the public spaces of Hong Kong on Sundays is locally regarded as scandalous, immoral, provocative, and threatening because, for the other six days of the week, the discourse on sexuality is negotiated in a far more covert arena. The problematic integrity of the modern Chinese family, changing gender roles, and the rapidly changing social geography of Hong Kong is, in part, what the Sunday performance of foreign workers lays bare.

The concern of Hong Kong residents over the sexuality of foreign domestic workers— which is most clearly articulated through attempts by residents to control, discipline them, constrain their sexuality, and enforce their own morality on them—is not about the actual sexual licentiousness or lax morals of foreign domestic workers. As scholars recognize, allegations of promiscuity among the working class in Victorian England say more about the middle and upper classes who made the accusations, and about the wider socioeconomic conditions of the industrial revolution, than about those who stood accused of immorality and debauchery (see Barret-Ducrocq 1991; Gallagher 1987; Gilman 1985; Laqueur 1992). Similarly, the discourse on foreign domestic workers is inextricably linked, not to any actual disproportionate immorality on their part, but to broader social issues in modern, capitalist, international Hong Kong.[1]

Over the past decade and a half, the literature on histories and discourses of sexuality has grown exponentially to include entire journals devoted to the subject. This literature has emerged largely in response to Michael Foucault's *History of Sexuality* (1990[1976]) in the form of applications, refinements, and critiques of his work (see Parker and Gagnon 1995; Stanton 1992). Historians, literary critics, feminists, and scholars in the field of cultural studies are among those who have contributed most to this body of literature and, perhaps not surprisingly, the literature focuses almost exclusively on sexuality in western Europe and the United States. Anthropologists have also contributed to this field and have paid greater attention to discourses of sexuality in non-Western locales. Their studies of non-Western societies, however, are often grounded in, or proceed from, Western colonial ideas about sexuality as they were—and often continue to be—expressed in colonial and postcolonial settings (e.g., Hansen 1989, 1990; Kelly 1991; Stoler 1989).[2]

One of my objectives in this article is to move away from an analysis of sexuality that begins with Western notions of sexuality or focuses exclusively on the history of sexuality to one that is more ethnographically grounded in present day discourses. One could justifiably argue that the analysis of sexuality in contemporary, urban Hong Kong would benefit from greater attention to history and that Western and colonial—as well as Chinese— notions of appropriate sexuality are of relevance. This can be taken for granted. The purpose of my article, by contrast, is to begin with a critical focus on the present by describing the contemporary Hong Kong Chinese discourse on the sexuality of foreign domestic workers and by analyzing the modes of discipline that are deployed. In this article, an offshoot of my historical and ethnographic study of domestic workers in Hong Kong (Constable 1996, 1997), I focus specifically on the problematic relationships among work, discipline, and sexuality.[3]

In the following sections I look at the position of Filipina domestic workers in Hong Kong, the form and content of public images of domestic workers, the ways in which domestic workers are disciplined, and the ways in which workers experience or negotiate certain stereotypes in their day-to-day lives. I have chosen to examine distinct modes of dress among Filipina domestic workers because in this forum there is invaluable opportunity to examine the interface between employers' discipline of workers, domestic workers' self-discipline, and their contestation or appropriation of particular sexual images. As Barnes and Eicher contend, "social identity expressed in dress becomes not only an answer to *who* one is, but also *how* one is, and concerns the definition of the self in relation to a moral and religious value system" (1992:2; see also Broch-Due et al. 1993; Sandborg 1993). As such, modes of dress allow us to see how Filipina domestic workers simultaneously resist and embrace the existing system of power as it is inscribed in the discourse of sex and encoded in sexuality (Abu-Lughod 1990:47).

GUEST WORKERS

Dramatic shifts in patterns of women's employment in Hong Kong are integrally related to the increasing numbers of foreign domestic workers. The proportion of women in Hong Kong's formal paid workforce rose from 21 percent in 1931 to 34 percent in 1971 (Salaff 1981:294), and stood at 49 percent in 1995 (Census and Statistics Department 1996).[4] The number of foreign domestic workers has also increased dramatically: there were a few hundred workers in the early 1970s, 38,000 in 1987, and almost four times that number—150,000—in late 1995. At that time approximately 130,000 of the domestic workers were from the Philippines and the remaining 20,000 came from Thailand, Indonesia, India, and Sri Lanka (Immigration Department, personal communication, June 1996). Currently over 90 percent of these workers are women; most are between the ages of 25 and 35; and at least three quarters of them are single. Restricted by Hong Kong immigration policies from bringing their families with them, even married foreign domestic workers are perceived as arriving in Hong Kong "unattached."

The rapid increase in the number of Filipina domestic workers is related to socioeconomic conditions in Hong Kong and to the Philippine labor export policy that was initiated by President Ferdinand Marcos during the 1970s. With the rapid growth of Hong Kong's manufacturing economy during the 1960s and

1970s, Chinese women domestic workers left their employers in favor of factory work, which they considered far less demeaning (Salaff 1981; Sankar 1978; cf. Armstrong 1990). The growth of industry was followed by an even greater boom in the service economy during the 1980s—linked in large part to the post-Mao economic liberalization on the mainland—and Hong Kong experienced a severe labor shortage. As a result many previously unemployed middle-class Chinese women were encouraged to take jobs in the service sector (Labour Department 1992). These factors, combined with the increase in numbers of nuclear households—which meant that households were less likely to have kin to share the household work and child care—led to an even greater need for alternative forms of household labor.[5] In response to this demand, the 1980s witnessed the establishment of hundreds of recruitment agencies in the Philippines and counterpart placement agencies in Hong Kong specializing in the international trade of "domestic helpers" (see Constable 1997). The Hong Kong government established special institutions and policies to control and regulate the rapidly growing number of foreign workers. Today almost ten percent of Hong Kong households—some 600,000 individuals—benefit directly from the labor of domestic workers.[6] Most employers, constituting the fastest growing group, come from the middle class. According to one government survey, the median monthly household income for employers of full-time domestic workers was $35,000 in Hong Kong dollars (U.S.$4,500) in 1993, and over 62 percent of households with a monthly income of $80,000 (U.S.$10,000) hired domestic workers (Census and Statistics Department 1995a:3).[7]

In contrast to Chinese amahs who might have stayed with the same family for decades or for life and who were reputed to uphold traditional Chinese familial values (Constable 1996; Gaw 1991; Sankar 1978), foreign domestic workers stay in Hong Kong for less than four years on average (i.e., generally two, back-to-back contracts of two years each), and are consequently less well-integrated into individual households. The class identity of Filipina domestic workers is also ambiguous. In contrast to uneducated Chinese domestic workers, Filipina domestic workers often have high levels of education and their previous "high status" occupations contradict their current identity as "servants." Indeed, surveys suggest that in 1989 almost two-thirds of Filipina domestic workers in Hong Kong had some postsecondary school education (Asian Migrant Centre 1991:15).[8] Many of the workers I interviewed were trained professionals who had previously worked in the Philippines as nurses or schoolteachers, while others had university degrees in such fields as agriculture and business. To employers, a number of whom have lower-level clerical occupations, or who have recently joined the ranks of the educated middle class, the education and class background of some of the new domestic workers come too close for comfort.[9] The ambiguous class identity of foreign domestic workers is one important factor that fuels anxiety, which is expressed in general terms as a concern over their morality and sexuality.

SEXUAL THREATS: FAMILY AND ECONOMY

That women domestic workers are perceived as posing a sexual threat is not exceptional, either in Chinese society (Jaschok 1988; McMahon 1995; Watson 1991) or in other regions of the world (e.g., Hansen 1989, 1990; Rollins 1985, 1990). In a study of domestic workers and employers in Zambia, Karen Hansen shows how European women employers in colonial Northern Rhodesia resisted employing local women as household workers because of the threat posed by their sexuality. The preference for hiring "manservants" continues in postcolonial Zambia, where black women still view women servants as threatening. As Hansen notes, Zambian women explain in troubled voices how women workers are "insolent and cheeky . . . they steal; they go through your panties and toiletries. But worst of all, before you know it they move into the bedroom and take over the house" (1990:138). The concerns about women household workers in Hong Kong strike a similar chord, although the pattern of primarily employing women to cook, clean house, and care for children has been the norm among both Chinese and Westerners in Hong Kong since at least the early 20th century (see Jaschok 1988; Sankar 1978; Watson 1991).

Foreign domestic workers are viewed as posing a challenge to the Chinese woman employer's role as both wife and mother. As Margery Wolf has argued, a woman's position within the extended Chinese household depended in large part on the creation of a "uterine family" and the maintenance of a close, affective bond with her sons (Wolf 1968, 1972; see also McMahon 1995:13). If a strong mother-child bond is still a source of women's power in the household, then a close relationship between a domestic worker and the children for whom she cares may threaten the mother's authority (see Constable 1996). In 1996 I learned of several cases of workers whose contracts were terminated because of the female employers' jealousy. In two cases, according to Chinese sources, the domestic worker was dismissed because her charge called her "mommy" and refused to address his "real" mother in this way. I heard of employers who hired workers for only one contract in order to prevent their children from becoming too attached to the workers.

Similarly, the domestic worker also poses a threat to a woman employer's role as wife and sexual partner. She is regarded as a potential seductress—as one who can both turn a man's attention away from family matters and also deplete his energy for productive and reproductive work. In Chinese literature and history, a man's sexual involvement with other women has been viewed as constituting a threat to the well-being of his wife, concubines, and other family members (Ebrey 1993; Jaschok 1988; McMahon 1995).[10] In contemporary Hong Kong, controlling a foreign domestic worker—and especially her sexuality—can be a wife's way of trying to control her husband and defend the integrity of her family unit against a potentially aggressive outsider.[11]

A connection between sexuality and work is made explicit in several studies of Victorian England. As Katherine Gallagher observes in the case of female Irish "costermongers" (street vendors) in London, their work was not viewed as "morally deleterious," yet they were still considered "fallen women" because they served as "a visible and audible emblem of the sexual and economic exploitation that . . . [went] on behind closed doors" (1987:101). If costermongers as a group were guilty of anything, it was "embodying and hence raising to the surface the consciousness of a ruthless struggle for marketplace advantage" (1987:101).

Like that of the Irish costermongers in Victorian London, the work of foreign domestic workers in Hong Kong is not itself considered immoral. It includes duties that once were, and in some cases still are, performed by a mother, wife, or daughter-in-law. Moreover, it would also be difficult to argue that bringing market relations into the household is in itself problematic for Hong Kong Chinese. Household work that is done for *another* family for a wage, however, is highly stigmatized compared with work done for no wage within one's own home; and paid household work is valued far less than most work that takes place outside the domestic sphere.[12] It is not that household work became debased in Hong Kong as it was transformed into wage labor: the status of unpaid bondservants was clearly below that of the lowliest paid servants in the past. But even today it remains true that Hong Kong women who are desperately in need of money hesitate to work as "maids" in other people's homes. Their reluctance has more to do with attitudes toward servants than with the work itself. Similarly, the sense of threat that foreign workers pose does not stem from the kind of work they do but from their reluctance to accept or enact the role of servant.

In an analysis of the ways in which sexuality and capitalism are intrinsically and inextricably linked in the discourses of the industrial revolution, Thomas Laqueur suggests that prostitutes in 19th-century England came to be viewed as "*the* social evil" (1992:212, 1990). They were deemed barren and sterile in an attempt to guard the social boundaries "between home and economy, between public and private, self and society" (1992:213). In a similar vein, following Mary Douglas, Aihwa Ong explains that "persons in an interstitial position are often symbolized as dangerous and filthy, since they suggest a

poorly articulated social system" (Ong 1991:292; see also Douglas 1970[1966]). As young women, foreigners, and outsiders whose moral position in the social system is not clearly defined, foreign domestic workers have also come to be viewed as dangerous and filthy. Laqueur's argument hinges on the notion that home provided the safeguard "against the disintegrative forces of the market" (1990:230–233). In the Chinese case, it is not the market that people view as essentially disintegrative, but those individuals who lose sight of their familial role and obligations (Harrell 1985). Foreign domestic workers pose a threat, not simply because they work for wages or because a market economy is inherently evil, but because they are foreigners who work within the intimate realm of the household and refuse to accept their debased position. Foreign workers, moreover, reputedly maintain a primary commitment to their own families abroad, not to those of their employers.

Unlike Chinese domestic workers of the past, who allegedly accepted their lowly position in the household hierarchy, Filipinas are considered unwilling to accept their humble status. Many Filipinas proudly insist on being called "workers" rather than "helpers" and reject the idea that they are "servants" or "amahs." The "foreignness" of Filipina domestic workers, their cultural differences, their ambiguous class and social status, and their disinclination to accept such a role also make it more difficult to integrate them comfortably as fictive "members of the family" (Colen and Sanjek 1990:3–4; Gaw 1991; Watson 1991). The contractual nature of their position—linked to recruitment agencies, immigration policies, labor laws, and official contracts—is also more difficult to soften or disguise with familial metaphors and fictive kinship terms than were the market relations of Chinese servants of the past.

PUBLIC IMAGES: FLIRTS, PROSTITUTES, AND MAIL-ORDER VIRGINS

Although foreign domestic workers usually labor in seclusion, the problem of their identity is far from private. An extensive public discourse on the topic of foreign domestic workers in Hong Kong generates and perpetuates certain notions and stereotypes that are openly expressed in both English- and Chinese-language newspaper editorials, in advertisements created by placement agencies, and in poems, stories, and jokes published in popular magazines. Much of this discourse is "public" in the sense that it is expressed and mediated in public spaces and fora. Local Chinese, Filipinos, and other foreigners all contribute to this discourse by espousing, contesting, or debating various aspects of the putative identity of domestic workers.

Despite the vital role that foreign domestic workers play in Hong Kong's economy, their presence has not—especially in recent years—evinced a public sense of gratitude and relief. Instead, some Chinese have characterized them as constituting an invasion, and concern and anxiety surround their presence. Among the stereotypes and popular images of foreign domestic workers are notions that they are lazy, demanding, lacking commitment to their work, or "only in it for the money." Hong Kong Chinese also label them as "apathetic" about Hong Kong, a "nuisance," "impolite guests," or ungrateful workers who make too much noise and leave litter in public places (Chan 1996; Chow 1987; Jaschok 1993; Lam 1996; Lee 1993). Many contradictory notions about domestic workers exist. They are at once criticized for acting "too much at home" and for not treating Hong Kong as home (Ong 1992). They are also characterized as poor, as being from "backward" countries, and as unsophisticated and uneducated (Chong 1985). Some view them as, on the whole, hard workers who contribute valuable labor to the colony, but others are far more critical. Filipinas are increasingly described by Hong Kong Chinese as too smart, too savvy, and too assertive to make ideal workers.

Scholars have noted that young "nubile" women in the paid workforce are often represented as bearers of a rampant or "uncontained" sexuality (e.g., Enloe 1990; Ong 1991). As Aihwa Ong notes, the large number of Malay women in international manufacturing "has occasioned negative public commentary on the conduct of female workers. . . . As new

workers, young women engage in activities that isolate traditional boundaries (spatial, economic, social, and political) in public life, forcing a redefinition of the social order" (1991:292). Filipina domestic workers in Hong Kong have evoked similar but even more volatile concerns than their industrial counterparts because they bring ambiguity and danger into a far more problematic domain: the archetypal, tightly knit, patriarchal Chinese home. Yet they are also highly visible in public places and much of the criticism of their behavior centers on the impropriety of their public behavior (see Constable 1997; Jaschok 1993).

On their Sundays off work, tens of thousands of foreign domestic workers gather in Statue Square and other areas of Central District. Their perceived flirtatiousness and friendliness in public contributes to an image that they are very different from Chinese women. Filipinas are not merely understood as friendlier or more outgoing than Chinese women—although this is certainly one part of the image. Filipinas are also characterized by local Hong Kong people as morally loose and on the lookout for men. They groom themselves in public and they drink, loiter, and gamble in public places. What Françoise Barret-Ducrocq writes of Victorian England could apply equally well to contemporary Hong Kong:

> As long as she was in a hurry, obviously busy, the woman . . . was playing her proper role; her brisk pace through the streets was the gauge of her honesty. Loitering in the street, on the other hand, hanging about for too long or without an obvious errand was seen as unnatural. . . . So any wandering about which could not be explained by shopping or some other necessary activity came to be perceived as a . . . factor or sign of doubtful morality. [1991:10]

Ideas about the sex trade in the Philippines and in Thailand also fuel stereotypes about promiscuous foreign domestic workers among the Hong Kong public. As one employment agency worker explained in 1994, the announcement of the closing of the U.S. bases in the Philippines caused numerous prospective Chinese employers to express concern that former Filipina prostitutes would come to

Hong Kong in the guise of maids. One staff member said that her agency had recently stopped recruiting women from Thailand because prospective Chinese employers were even more fearful of Thai women becoming prostitutes. Hong Kong's mass media also fortify the association between foreign domestic workers and the sex trade. Both English and Chinese newspapers often carry sensational stories about prostitution in Hong Kong, and about Filipina and Thai women who are "lured" or coerced into prostitution after entering the colony—to work, presumably, as maids or entertainers (e.g., Bociurkiw 1992a, 1992b; Laxton 1993; Mendoza and Bociurkiw 1992; *South China Morning Post* 1992; Wallis 1992; Wong 1993). Domestic workers are viewed as poor and willing to leave their families (parents, siblings, husbands, and children) in order to earn money to send home. Prostitution, in the public imagination, is thought to be far more lucrative than domestic work. Although the "immoral" aspect of prostitution is an issue of public concern for many Hong Kong people, the notion of filial piety manifested in sacrificing oneself to such a dishonorable occupation for the sake of one's family's wellbeing is not unknown to the Chinese (Wolf 1968). But the family for whom the foreign domestic worker would be putatively making the sacrifice is not the Chinese family to whom she has sold her labor power, and for whom her public image and private behavior is of critical importance.

Ideas about Filipina "mail-order brides" fuel similar images. Despite protest from the Filipino community, the Australian-made film "Filipina Dream Girls" was aired on Hong Kong television in 1993. As an article in a Hong Kong Filipino migrant worker magazine describes it, the film gives viewers advice on "how to find a 'young, obedient and virgin' Filipina wife" (*Tinig Filipino* 1993a:25). According to Filipino critics, the film shows "an obese man playing the part of an agent . . . convincing sex-starved bachelors that 'Filipinas will do anything, *anything*'" (1993a:25). The Australian film maker is quoted as saying that the top export commodity of the Philippines is "Filipina virgins" and that they are "obedient . . . and do not complain even when they are maltreated" (1993a:25). More to the point, he says, "[Filipinas] would do anything to get a foreigner for a husband to attain economic security" (1993a:25). Although the impression of most Chinese women with whom I spoke was that Filipinas "prefer Western men," there is also a pervasive fear that they would take any man they could get, including Hong Kong Chinese.

DISCIPLINE

A common view among Hong Kong Chinese is that Filipina domestic workers ought to be generally better disciplined and restrained. The perceived threat of rampant sexuality is one of several reasons for employers and the Hong Kong public to increase the control and discipline they impose on domestic workers. Many employers, members of the Hong Kong Employers of Overseas Domestic Helpers Association, and the staff at employment agencies explained that strict forms of discipline were imposed for the workers' own good. Several Chinese employers commented that domestic workers could not be trusted to behave. Many employers considered themselves responsible for helping to assure that a domestic worker "won't get herself into trouble." As one woman employer explained, "even the most well-intentioned domestic workers need a bit of help resisting [sexual temptations]."

Thus employers use the potentially rampant sexuality of foreign workers to justify the imposition of strict curfews and rules. Typically these include eight or nine o'clock curfews on the worker's day off and strict dress codes. Sleeveless shirts, tight pants, skirts above the knee, perfume, jewelry, or makeup of any sort are forbidden. The following is an excerpt from a list of rules given to prospective domestic workers by one employment agency:

- Fingernails shall be kept short, clean and not polished. No makeup is allowed at home.
- Shorts, [and] nightgowns are not allowed except within servant's quarters.
- Personal hygiene is strictly emphasized.
- No smoking or drinking alcohol is allowed.
- All the clothes of the maid should separate to wash [from] the employer [*sic*].

- During holidays [the days off], you shall be back before curfew time as prescribed by the employer. Staying overnight elsewhere is strictly forbidden.

Numerous other lists I collected, or that were custom-made or tailored by employers, emphasize similar points. One list prohibits the domestic worker from closing her door or locking it except when undressing. Another warns her to "beware of the 'bad guys' when going in or out." Yet another stipulates that she "must not go out earlier than 10:00, . . . must be back home no later than 19:00 and . . . can never stay out overnight." Many employers require domestic workers to have a regular pregnancy test.[13]

As one official of the Hong Kong employers' association explained, employers are responsible for the well-being of their domestic workers and must insure that they not get into trouble. Regardless of domestic workers' age, they are often treated like children who might be tempted to stay out late, mix with bad company, and get into trouble. Time and time again, employers reiterated the idea that domestic workers must be controlled and disciplined. Some suggested that venues for good, clean fun should be provided for foreign workers so that they would not get into trouble or simply loiter and "waste time" in public places on their days off work.[14] As an employers' association official explained, "[Filipinas] are not all bad, but they are unfamiliar with Hong Kong. They can get into trouble, and then employers have to go to the trouble and the expense of finding and training a new one."

Some employers take it for granted that a Filipina domestic worker will be willing to provide sexual favors. Minda, 30 years old, married, and with two small children in the Philippines, had only worked for her new employers for two days when her male employer asked her to help him in the bathroom. When Minda arrived at the door of the bathroom, the 40-year-old man stood there completely naked and requested that she wash him and give him a massage. Minda was horrified, left, and began to look for a new job. Rosaria, aged 20, had a similar experience, and described how her employer's teenage son repeatedly appeared in the nude to greet her when his mother was not at home.

After several weeks of "stomach pain," Louisa, a 40-year-old with a husband and children in the Philippines, decided to go for a consultation at the local public hospital. She told the doctor that fried food seemed to irritate the problem. As she explained,

> the doctor, [a young Chinese man,] recommended that I have a pregnancy test. I told him "I'm having my period! And I'm married! My husband is in the Philippines." He winked at me and said "Don't worry, we won't tell anyone." He was joking with me. The worst thing was he also wanted to test for AIDS. I said "Doctor, I'm clean. Only with my husband." That tells you what they think about us Filipinas.

The issue of prostitution is important, not because domestic workers are likely to become prostitutes, but because it articulates with a number of other concerns regarding domestic workers that often have a more substantive basis. The relatively sudden appearance of a large number of "unattached" young foreign women creates anxiety among the host population for a variety of reasons. Foreign domestic workers, like other temporary migrants, are thought, regardless of particular circumstances and the uncertainty of the 1997 transition to Chinese rule, to want to remain in Hong Kong. Although the immigration figures for early 1996 suggest that the number of Filipinas may be starting to decrease, and although many expressed to me their intention of leaving Hong Kong before July 1997, some Hong Kong locals—echoing ideas from "Filipina Dream Girls"—fear that foreign domestic workers might be willing to do almost anything in order to stay. Their alleged tactics include seducing local married men with sex in the hopes of eventually marrying them to gain legal permanent residence. Very few Filipinas intend to stay in Hong Kong permanently, and certainly not by these means. According to an Asian Migrant Centre survey, 85 percent of Filipina domestic workers would remain in the Philippines if they could earn as much there. Most go back to the Philippines after less than two contracts, citing the "discrimination" and "hostility" of the Hong Kong locals (Asian Migrant Centre 1991) and their concerns about 1997 as important factors in their decision to return home.

Yet domestic workers are still perceived as wanting to stay in Hong Kong. "Of course they would," one Chinese woman employer told me. "Why would anyone want to go back there [the Philippines], where it's so poor?" Foreign domestic workers who signed a contract in 1995 earn a monthly wage of $3,750 (U.S. $480) in addition to room and board. Most workers and employers consider this a good wage; it is more, I was told, than the workers could earn as doctors or lawyers in the Philippines. As another Chinese employer put it, her friends "are afraid that Filipinas are after whatever ugly old husband they have just to stay in Hong Kong." I had the opportunity to meet several current and former domestic workers who had married local men as a way to remain in Hong Kong. In some cases, I was told, it was "true love," but in others I learned that it was merely "convenient." Several Filipinas also joked with me, a white woman with a British passport, about whether I could introduce them to my brother. Yet far more women described their complete avoidance of local men, citing one example after another of women who had become involved with Chinese men or expatriates and were eventually deserted. This theme is especially common in poems and short stories by and about domestic workers (see Layosa and Luminarias 1992).

A Chinese social worker I interviewed offered a blunt explanation: Chinese women employers "may not feel comfortable having young attractive Filipinas living in their homes. . . . Although it would be very difficult for them to admit it, they may not entirely trust them with their husbands." As several domestic workers suggested, the mistrust that might be legitimately directed toward the husband is often directed instead at the domestic worker. The latter is in the awkward and powerless position of being a putative "seductress" in the home of the jilted wife. The domestic worker is the newcomer and in many cases has already been labeled as inherently promiscuous. Indeed, I met many women who came to the Mission for Filipino Domestic Workers (a nonprofit organization run mainly by Filipina volunteers) for legal or personal advice because male members of the household had made sexual advances and, in a few cases, had attempted rape.[15] In some instances, when domestic workers reported sexually aggressive behavior to their female employers, they were accused of having initiated the aggression. As one might expect, in cases of sexual assault reported in the local papers the employers' defense was usually that the domestic workers had initiated the sexual encounters. Many women who came to the mission for advice simply refused to speak to their female employers. They already feared the mistrust or jealousy of these women. Instead, they simply wanted advice on how to terminate their contracts.

A woman employer's jealousy is potentially dangerous. I was repeatedly told of women whose contracts were terminated on the first day, or immediately after arrival in Hong Kong, because the domestic worker was "too beautiful" and therefore posed a threat to her woman employer. A number of domestic workers told me that they thought their male employers were "much nicer" than their wives, but they went out of their way to avoid them lest they incur the woman employers' wrath and find their contracts terminated as a result.

Although the point may seem obvious, it is important to note that age, gender, menial status, and temporary legal residence place foreign domestic workers in a subordinate position. Although domestic workers are often viewed as the ones who pose a sexual threat, it is in fact they who are most vulnerable (Colen and Sanjek 1990:179). Unlike factory workers—who enjoy at least a degree of anonymity and strength in numbers—domestic workers not only work in the home, a moral and ethical crucible, but they live in separate households where they are isolated from the support of their coworkers and where they are usually outnumbered by their employers. In many cases domestic workers speak little or no Chinese and are economically vulnerable, often having acquired large debts in order to arrange to come to Hong Kong in the first place. As a result they are often unwilling to risk complaining or disobeying their employers.

MEDIATING IMAGES

Domestic workers simultaneously resist and promote discipline. On one hand they attempt to counter certain negative public images. Some workers share their employers' enthusiasm for particular restrictions and forms of self-discipline, promoting sexual and other kinds of self-control among their compatriots. This they often do for the sake of Philippine national pride. Others actively espouse ways of remaining "feminine" without appearing too "sexy." On the other hand, domestic workers sometimes adopt or manipulate certain sexual images as a means of resisting controls placed on them by employers and the wider Hong Kong public.

Filipina domestic workers are well aware of their reputation as "loose" or willing to "do almost anything" to obtain permanent foreign residence, but most Filipinas would criticize this reputation as unfounded and as based on the bad image that a few women have created for all Filipinas. Some Filipinas, for example, opposed a family planning campaign aimed at Filipina domestic workers (Greenway 1986) and openly defended "Filipino people's lofty regard for chaste womanhood" (Nubla 1986). The campaign, Filipina critics claimed, "promoted the thinking and conclusion" that Filipinas in Hong Kong "mostly single and/or married women whose husbands are not here . . . need the services of the Family Planning Association" (Nubla 1986). Like African Americans who participated in the Social Hygiene Movement (1910–40) and promoted "sexual Victorianism" (Simmons 1993), some Filipinas actively promote "social improvements" and clean and healthy recreational activities aimed at keeping foreign workers off the streets.

Filipinas in Hong Kong use the terms *barracuda* or the acronym *AB* to refer to prostitutes, or women who are "sleeping around." Barracudas, I learned, are women associated with a Philippine gang whose members "wear barracuda tattoos." These women are reputed to work as prostitutes on ships and, like the barracuda (a "man-eating fish"), they "eat the flesh of drowning sailors." AB is slang that derives from the term *akyat barco* (literally "to enter a boat"). Akyat Barco, the name of a gang in the Philippines, is also slang for women who hustle sailors. In Hong Kong both terms are used by domestic workers to refer specifically to prostitutes, or, more commonly, as an epithet to chastise and insult women whose behavior appears to be loose or immoral. One worker used both terms to describe a woman who had slept with her husband in the Philippines.

Clothing is another vehicle through which critique and mediation are expressed and identity is negotiated (see Sandborg 1993). Advice Filipinas give one another reflects a strong concern for dressing appropriately and a notion that, if women dress in certain ways, they may be asking for trouble. In the domestic worker magazine, *Tinig Filipino*, Annabelle Basabica writes that some domestic workers "complain about their bosses because of sexual molestation but sometimes we forget that it is due to our own mistakes. Could you expect a man to act like a saint when you are garbed in sexy clothes? If you want to be respected, you should choose the right clothes [to] wear in various and specific occasions, so that everyone you meet will not frown" (1993:37). Basabica's article earned many accolades from fellow domestic workers. Marivic Dacilla (1993:25) and Thelma Ventenilla (1993:28) both agreed that Filipinas should be more moderate in their style—that they should not wear too much makeup or wear their "skirts too short or too [close-] fitting" (Ventenilla 1993:28). Another *Tinig Filipino* article, entitled "Protect Yourself From Sexual Molestation," makes an explicit connection between provocative clothing and sexual abuse, cautioning women, "Do not expose yourself to the possibility of abuse by the way you dress and conduct yourself" (1993b:45).

Acosta is one domestic worker who tries to steer clear of the barracuda image but who also tries "not to go too far toward the other extreme" in an attempt to create what she considers the "right" message about her sexuality. The way she dresses and acts in public is directly related to the particular conditions of her work. One reason for her concern is that much of the domestic work she does is illegal. She does "aerobics" (part-time work), which is not permitted according to the official domestic worker contract.[16] Acosta's contract is a scam that she created together with Mr. Woo ("the one who signed my contract"). While working for her previous full-time employer, Acosta also did some part-time work for Mr. Woo, a Hong Kong-born, Canadian-educated employee of the Hong Kong government. Mrs. Zee, the employer who had signed Acosta's previous contract, did not pay her the legal minimum wage stipulated in the official contract. Instead, she "allowed" Acosta to make up the difference by illegally working on a part-time basis. After the contract was terminated (i.e., when Mrs. Zee emigrated to Canada), Acosta asked Mr. Woo if he would hire her. As Acosta explained, Mr. Woo and his wife have a large apartment and their income was more than sufficient to enable them to employ a full-time domestic worker; Acosta suspected, however, that Mrs. Woo simply did not want her around. Acosta then suggested that Mr. Woo sign the contract and pay her half of a monthly salary in exchange for half a week's work. It was agreed that Acosta would arrange for her own housing and that she would use her free time as she liked. Although she feels she does more work for the Woos than a half-time worker should, she prefers this arrangement to one full-time job because she can earn more money. She also prefers the freedom it gives her to organize and manage her own time.[17]

Although it is illegal, at least a quarter of all foreign domestic workers have at one time or another done aerobics (Mission for Filipino Migrant Workers, personal communication, June 1994). Acosta's situation is somewhat extreme, however, and involves some risk. If discovered by immigration department officials, at best she could be deported; at worst she could be fined and imprisoned. Even though her employers are also legally at fault, employers are rarely, if ever, punished for hiring part-time workers.

Acosta works in as many as eight different households a week, some for as few as four hours a week. This entails much commuting and traveling and many possibilities of encountering people who could potentially betray her to Labour or Immigration Department authorities for breach of contract. She is particularly concerned with the impression she makes on people like the Chinese building watchmen and elevator attendants, and is therefore extremely polite to them and often greets them in Cantonese.

Acosta's main objective is to dress in such a way that she is viewed as stylish and attractive enough to be mistaken for a local wife. She plays what she describes as the role of a "local Filipina lady" who, by virtue of the fact that she has a foreign (i.e., Anglo or expatriate) husband, would be legally permitted to work part-time. Although she has never become sexually or emotionally involved with a man in Hong Kong during the 15 years she has worked there (and she questioned whether something might be "wrong" with her because of her general lack of sexual desire), she wanted to project an appearance that would suggest to observers that she has a foreign husband.

Another concern, as she put it, "is that I look younger than I really am." In her early forties, she wears her hair longer and her skirts shorter than she otherwise would because she is afraid that employers may decide that she is getting too old for domestic work. But she does not want to dress so as to attract too much male attention or create the impression of being a barracuda. Thus, she wears skirts that reach above the knee, but are not too short; she wears some—but not too much—makeup; she wears nice shoes with heels but the heels that are not too high. Her jewelry and her blouses often introduce a South or Southeast Asian element such as batik or cotton print blouses and silver dangling earrings. Wearing such "ethnic clothing" was popular among both Filipina domestic workers and many Filipina "professionals" in 1993 and 1994 but was not generally associated with the style of barracudas—nor was it a style popular among Chinese women. Despite an awareness that her way of "dressing up" can be threatening to some employers, she prefers to take that risk than to wear what she calls the "DH uniform" of jeans, T-shirt, and tennis shoes that would undermine the image she wants to portray.

Because she works part-time, she must choose her employers carefully. She only works for people to whom she has been referred by friends or who are acquaintances of her current employers. In one case a new woman employer, Mrs. Cheung, reacted strongly to her appearance, asking on the first day whether she was "looking for a boyfriend" or "on the way to a disco." Acosta stood her ground and asserted her right to dress up and wear lipstick. She explained that she would change her shoes and clothes when she arrived but that she would not be seen "poorly dressed" in public. "Even in the Philippines I would not dress like that, so why should I do it here?" she recounted having told Mrs. Cheung. Eventually she stopped working for the Cheungs. Mr. Cheung made remarks about Acosta's attractiveness and teased his wife about her jealousy in Acosta's presence. Acosta decided it was better to resign than face the ultimate risk of possible deportation.

BLUE JEANS, T-SHIRTS, AND T-BIRDS

The domestic worker "uniform" of blue jeans and T-shirts to which Acosta alluded is one of the most common outfits donned by domestic workers in Hong Kong and it is also a common style of dress among female workers in the Philippines. Most female employers approve—indeed encourage—this style of dress, as long as the blue jeans "are not too tight." Both Chinese employers and domestic workers agree that such clothes are cheap, comfortable, and easy for work (except in the sweltering summer months). This uniform fits the rules of many employers: the knees and shoulders are covered and the neckline is high. Domestic workers themselves usually much prefer the blue-jean uniform to the "real" uniform: the pastel pink, baby-blue, or pale green dress with a white apron, that many are required to wear in summer, or the heavier, black, long-sleeved dress with the white apron that many are required to wear in winter or on formal occasions

in the household. Unlike the "playboy bunny" or "cocktail waitress" version of the maid's uniform, the real uniform is not short, fitted, and sexy, but is long, baggy, and matronly in appearance. As Maria explained, she is ashamed to be seen in public wearing a real uniform "because then everyone knows I'm a maid." The blue-jean uniform does not bear the same stigma as the formal uniform, which can, like other types of official uniforms, "negate the gender identity of the wearer" (Barnes and Eicher 1992:7; see also Young 1992); nor do blue jeans and T-shirts carry the connotation of sloppy clothing, as they are usually meticulously clean and carefully pressed. Like the official or formal uniform that some women must wear, however, the blue-jean uniform is nonetheless often striking for what employers and many workers regard as its asexual, "maidish" appearance. As domestic workers and agency staff explained, employers do not want to hire domestic workers who are "too attractive," nor do they want them to dress too enticingly (cf. Rollins 1990:84–85).

Mrs. Lee described how her friends and neighbors often commented on the attractiveness of her domestic worker and on the elegance of Sophia's clothes. Some of Sophia's clothes are in fact Mrs. Lee's fashionable, expensive, designer hand-me-downs. Mrs. Lee's friends disapprove of this practice. They ask her whether she is worried about having such a good-looking and well-dressed young woman around her husband. But Mrs. Lee feels secure—perhaps because, as she told me, Sophia is too fat to be really beautiful, is extremely religious, and has a boyfriend back home.

Sophia's situation is exceptional in the sense that Mrs. Lee allows her to wear whatever she wants at work and when she goes out in public. Many domestic workers must observe a strict dress code at all times. Even on their days off work they are not allowed to put on makeup or jewelry in their employers' homes, so many wait until they reach the destined park benches in Central District to do so. Others change in public lavatories or go to a friend's house to dress up each Sunday before going to town for the day.

On Sunday, the most common day off work for domestic workers, they reveal numerous styles of dress, but two patterns are especially striking. Many women take Sunday as an occasion to dress up in fancy dresses, heels, makeup, jewelry, and similar finery. Many others wear jeans and T-shirts. The first pattern—regardless of the details of the style—reflects the desire of domestic workers to escape the role of maid by which they feel confined during the rest of the work week. While dressing up follows different patterns, one concern is clearly expressed by Sophia and her church-going friends: they want to look "like ladies," not as though they were going to a bar.

The second pattern can be seen as a continuation of the workday style, but its variations carry a number of possible meanings. While most Hong Kong Chinese see T-shirts and blue jeans as simply a convenient—and sexually unthreatening—style for domestic workers, this style, taken to one extreme, can convey several other messages. One, as Acosta sees it, is that they are accommodating the demands of employers who want domestic workers to look and act like maids—that is, gender-neutral, submissive, and subordinate. Another meaning—of which domestic workers like Acosta are highly aware, but of which employers largely remained ignorant until early 1996—is the image of the "T-bird" or "tomboy."

Well before I had the opportunity to meet her, I heard Noel, an activist domestic worker, described as a T-bird. The terms *T-bird* (short for "thunderbird") or *tomboy* in Filipino slang refer to a lesbian; particularly one who adopts a masculine style of dress. A T-bird, I was told, is "a gay," but the term can also allude to a lesbian style of dress, common among Filipina workers. Noel sometimes wears jeans and T-shirts. In the summer she often wears a man's short-sleeved, button-down shirt, carefully ironed pleated pants, flat laced shoes, and a distinctive "flat top" haircut. Sometimes she also wears a baseball cap.

Several articles about lesbians and about the T-bird style were published in *Tinig Filipino* during the early 1990s (e.g., Corpuz 1993; Ferrer 1993; Saddi 1993; Torrefranca 1992). A striking feature of these articles is that while the T-bird or tomboy appears as a lesbian or as a member of a "third sex," the "Juliet," her partner, is not represented as lesbian or homosexual but as someone who is attracted to a T-bird in the same way she might be attracted to a man. In "The Modern Romeos in the Making," Lizby Eronico observes:

> If you happen to check the lesbian populace among Filipino migrant workers in Hong Kong, you will be amazed at their increasing number. Take for example Sundays and holidays. You can chop my head off if you can't find one with her "Juliet" by her side.
>
> And whether you like it or not, lesbians nowadays are going places. They have finally come out from their shells triumphant. Girls have started fighting over this new breed of "masculine women" who have become genuine lovers to the surprise of everyone. . . .
>
> In spite of being rejected by some segment of society at times, they enjoy playing a gentleman's game. Not to mention wearing men's accessories, perfumes and—hold your breath—men's underwear! With a haircut that will make Kevin Costner get envious and a perfume that makes everyone turn their heads . . . how can a very feminine woman resist?
>
> "*They're gorgeous, faithful, sympathetic, etc.* . . ." These are words from women who are too afraid of flushing their fetus down the toilet. "With a lesbian, I'm safe. . . ." Unlike men, lesbians don't regard women as their "sex objects." [1994:10]

During our first interview, Gina described her encounter in Statue Square one Sunday with Lorna, a friend from the Philippines whom she had not seen for several years. Lorna was very sad because she had just left her children and her husband back in the Philippines. When Gina ran into Lorna a few Sundays later, "the woman was transformed into a T-bird!" As Gina described, Lorna had cut off all her hair and had changed her name. She was wearing a white T-shirt with cigarettes rolled up her sleeve, blue jeans, and black leather boots and carried a leather jacket.

This T-bird style can be seen as one extreme of the blue-jean uniform. It is often considered acceptable by women employers, who usually interpret it as sexually neutral or at least as heterosexually neutral. Several Filipinas told me that this style conveys a clear message that women are not barracudas or after men. Yet many Filipinas consider dressing like a T-bird or even the milder version of the blue-jean uniform "not feminine enough." Several articles and editorials written by domestic workers in *Tinig Filipino* illustrate this point. Veronica Gamboa (1993) and Nimfa Saddi (1993) both express frustration at the fact that they are mistaken for T-birds because of the way they dress. Saddi writes that "my hairstyle and my outfit look like that of a tomboy . . . [but] I feel more comfortable in this kind of attire" (1993:24). Gamboa says that like Saddi, she is "not a 'woman in disguise,' but some of my colleagues keep calling me a T-bird. According to them they haven't seen me yet wearing a lady's outfit. I'm used to wearing jeans or trousers with matching T-shirt and a baseball cap, too. Although I hate hearing those comments from them, I still keep my cool" (1993:24). Some women, Gamboa and Saddi suggest, don this style because it is comfortable, not because they are lesbians.

The disparagement of the T-shirt, blue-jean style among some Filipina domestic workers did not appear to emerge out of a general fear of being mistaken for a lesbian or out of a condemnation of lesbian sexuality, but out of a concern for appearing inelegant, unfeminine, and unrefined. Although several articles in *Tinig Filipino* (e.g., Mommie Jingco 1991; Corpuz 1993) criticized the immorality of lesbianism from a Christian or Catholic perspective, and one letter writer expressed the fear that "T-birds will lose their jobs if they are found out" (Sombrio 1996), these were not common themes. Like Acosta, most women to whom I spoke did not think lesbians were immoral but held that there were other, more appropriate feminine images for those who were not T-birds. As Maribel Mahusay implores T-birds and those who are mistaken for them: "Why don't you try wearing women's clothes? Show them all the feminine side of yourself. . . . This does not mean that you have to wear an inch-long skirt and heavy makeup. Just follow the appropriate and modest way of wearing women's clothes" (1993:25). The opposite of appearing like a loose or promiscuous woman is not to emulate

men or to dress in a gender neutral style but to dress like "good" women.

In early 1996 employers became increasingly concerned about lesbianism when a television news documentary quoted a member of a domestic workers union who estimated that a quarter of all Filipina domestic workers were lesbians (Balagtas 1996; Wilde 1996). A hysterical letter in a local newspaper declared that employers should be alerted to the "threat posed to our children by Filipino T-birds or tomboys" (Ching 1996). According to Ching, "there are an alarming number of T-birds," and she wonders how she can explain women kissing other women to her children: "How can we explain the women the maid brings home. And how can we reason about the trousers, the rolled up sleeves, the hair cropped like a man, the men's clothes?" Ching fears, moreover, that "T-birds will bring to our homes and our children the danger of venereal and killer diseases."

CONCLUSION

Broadly speaking, foreign domestic workers are faced with several options of clothing style and self-presentation. The complicated set of choices regarding self-presentation evokes different contradictions and dimensions of power within the Hong Kong context: the women can dress in a sexually unthreatening way, as their employers demand, and can submit to their control and class expectations; they can dress up and assert their femininity and be viewed as sexual competitors who threaten class boundaries, as do Acosta and Sophia; they can dress like, or be, T-birds like Noel, aligning themselves with masculine images of power, diffusing the heterosexual threat that they might pose but arousing homophobic reactions; or they can dress like barracudas, in a sexually provocative style, and "invite" abuse and perpetuate a stereotype.

Filipinas such as Sophia and Acosta reject the barracuda as well as the T-bird image in favor of what amounts to "feminine decorum." This decorum is more in keeping with their employers' notions of appropriate sexuality. Yet in many cases a significant difference emerges between the chaste femininity deemed appropriate by an employer and that espoused by domestic workers. While both groups are critical of appearing too cheap or too sexy, many domestic workers who accommodate themselves to this criticism are nevertheless viewed as attempting to dress more like elegant professional ladies than as the domestic helpers their employers would prefer.

Each of these examples suggest ways in which domestic workers may simultaneously contest, resist, and appropriate specific sexual images. Filipina domestic workers are not unlike the Bedouin women described by Lila Abu-Lughod, following Foucault, as both resisting and embracing the existing system of power (1990:47, 1986). In their attempts to dispel the widespread notion of Filipina rampant sexuality, Filipina domestic workers often find themselves arguing in favor of, or unintentionally supporting, the forms of self-discipline that their employers impose on them.

I have tried to show how domestic workers are both complicit in, and express resistance toward, various forms of control. I have also illustrated how the image of foreign domestic workers in Hong Kong is both molded by, and reflexive of, local social and cultural concerns. Although integral to the new economy, foreign domestic workers are commonly regarded as disruptive and dangerous. The sexuality of Filipina domestic workers in Hong Kong is not an issue because they are highly sexed or lacking in self-control but because they are foreign-Asian others with an ambiguous class identity, highly visible, and intimately linked with changes occurring at the very core of Chinese households. In recent decades Chinese families in Hong Kong (as elsewhere) have seen a major shift in the role of mothers, a decrease in the importance of the extended household, and growing women's participation in wage employment. Changes in notions of romance and monogamy have also altered marital relations. In a situation where Chinese women appear to be losing the power they once derived from their role within the household, the discipline that women employers direct at controlling the sexuality of domestic workers offers them one way of continuing to exert authority. To control a domestic worker may be easier for a woman than to control her husband's fidelity, her children's affection, or the vicissitudes of her own workday experiences. Employers' discipline and control of domestic workers can also be seen as an attempt to reduce them to docile social bodies, to deprive them of full personhood, and to craft for them a less morally ambivalent—but sufficiently subordinate—position within the household.

An important lesson we may derive from the recent literature on Victorian sexuality is that the middle and upper classes were not as pious as they affected to be, nor were the working classes guilty of the sexual laxity and licentiousness attributed to them. The discovery of working-class testimonials and other historical documents (e.g., Barret-Ducrocq 1991; Peiss 1990; Peiss and Simmons 1989) suggests—and the ethnographic lesson of Hong Kong demonstrates—that the reputations of working-class women reveal more about upper-class anxieties than about working-class immorality and licentiousness (Gallagher 1987; Gilman 1985). Yet such an analysis cannot adequately account for some of the striking similarities between the images of Filipina domestic workers in Hong Kong in the 1990s and those of working-class women in 19th-century England. The underlying meanings are in all likelihood *not* the same. For one, it is foreign domestic workers who are depicted as promiscuous in Hong Kong, less so other young working women. Moreover, Hong Kong was industrialized long before the appearance of foreign domestic workers and their supposed debauchery. This suggests that foreign domestic workers are not considered dangerous because they render visible the evils of a market system—although the contractual nature of their employment is far more difficult to disguise than it was for Chinese amahs—but because they refuse to play the role of servants who willingly subordinate themselves to their employers' families. They therefore render visible broader changes in the family, gender roles, and political economy, and serve as a reminder of further changes yet to come as Hong Kong reverts to Chinese rule.

NOTES

Acknowledgments. I presented an earlier version of this article at the 1994 American Anthropological Association meeting in Atlanta, GA, as part of a panel organized by Kathleen Adams and Sara Dickey. I am grateful to them, the members of the panel, and discussant Jane Atkinson, for their comments and suggestions. I also owe a debt of thanks to Nancy Abelmann, Joseph Alter, Jeanne Bergman, Corazon Canete, Mimi Chan, Michael Herzfeld, Richard Manwui Ho, Jane Margold, Aihwa Ong, Elizabeth Sinn, Gabriele Stüzenhofecker, Maria Siu-mi Tam, Cynthia Tellez, Jun Tellez, Rubie Watson, the anonymous reviewers for *American Ethnologist*, the members of the Anthropology of Work seminar at the University of Pittsburgh, the staff and volunteers at the Mission for Filipino Migrant Workers, and numerous domestic workers and employers in Hong Kong. Research during the summer of 1993 was supported by a grant from the Western Michigan University Research and Creative Activities Support Fund, and in summer 1996 by grants from the Hewlett Foundation International Small Grants Program, and the Chinese Studies Program of the University of Pittsburgh.

1. Similar observations have been made about the sexual stereotypes of African Americans and Jews (e.g., Gilman 1994; JanMohamed 1992; Rollins 1985; Ware 1992).
2. There are exceptions; see, for example, Allison 1994, Alter 1994, Gladney 1994, Parker 1991, and the immense anthropological literature on the body. I am not, of course, alluding here to the vast anthropological literature on sex, which takes a less discursive approach to the subject.
3. I conducted research during the summer and fall of 1993, and the summers of 1994 and 1996. It included the collection of documentary materials including videotapes, newspaper and magazine articles, and editorials by and about domestic workers. Hundreds of hours of interviews were conducted with Filipina domestic workers, Chinese employers, employment agency staff, and representatives of various domestic worker and employer organizations.
4. The labor force participation rate in 1994 for women aged 25 to 29 was 81.7 percent; for those aged 30 to 34 it was 63.5 percent; and for those aged 35 to 44 it was 52.5 percent (Census and Statistics Department 1995b:18).
5. Between 1981 and 1991, nuclear households increased from 54 percent to 62 percent of the total (Census and Statistics Department 1995b:3).
6. In 1995 Hong Kong's population was 6.2 million (Census and Statistics Department 1996). Eighty percent of those with full-time, live-in domestic workers employed only one; and the average size of households employing domestic workers was 3.6 members (Census and Statistics Department 1995a:6, 8). Since many other employers hire part-time workers, this suggests that 550,000 to 600,000 people—about 150,000 households—employ domestic workers.
7. During the time of this research, $7.80 in Hong Kong dollars was worth approximately U.S.$1.00. In September 1994 a domestic worker's monthly income, on top of room and board, was officially raised from $3,500 to $3,750 (U.S.$480).
8. A 1984 study found that almost half of over 1,000 Filipina domestic workers surveyed attained a high school education, and that another 38 percent received university, college, or some sort of postsecondary education (French 1986). A 1989 study of 1,700 Filipinas found that 60 percent had a postsecondary education and that, of these, one third had obtained a college or university degree (Asian Migrant Centre 1991:15).
9. About 31 percent of the households employing full-time domestic workers in the 1993 government survey had a total household monthly income below $25,000 (U.S.$3,200) (Census and Statistics 1995a:7).
10. The competition and hostility felt by the spurned wife is graphically expressed in *Stories of the West Lake (Xihu erji)* where the wife has the maid, with whom her husband has had sexual relations, killed. She then has the maid's genitals cut off and forces her husband to wear them on his face (McMahon 1995:58).
11. Concerns about extramarital affairs may be heightened by the fact that polygyny has been illegal in Hong Kong since 1971. Although the law reinforces the exclusivity of the legal rights of the first wife, it also increases the risk that a man might divorce his wife in order to form a legal bond with another woman (see Jaschok 1988; Watson 1991).
12. Lisa Rofel explains that the distinction between "inside" and "outside" that traditionally marked appropriate activities for women in China "did not necessarily refer to the literal physical structure of the home" (1994:235). The inside/outside dichotomy did not necessarily oppose family to work. Inside work took place within a familial social sphere; outside work was done for or among strangers, outsiders, or non-kin. It was not, therefore, simply the wage that demeaned the housework of domestic workers, but the fact that it was

done for people outside the familial social sphere. The same distinction does not seem to hold for the more prestigious outside work done by many women employers in Hong Kong today.

13. In Singapore foreign domestic workers are legally required to undergo pregnancy testing every six months.

14. The middle-class concern with providing "respectable" entertainment for working-class women was also an issue in the United States (Peiss 1990) and Victorian England (Barret-Ducrocq 1991).

15. As Colen and Sanjek write,

Unlike concubines . . . female household workers do not provide sexual services as part of their role. Yet, in most if not all places studied, sexual advances from males, harassment, and rape occur in some household workplaces, and this threat or danger is widely appreciated by women household workers. [1990:181]

16. "Aerobics" is sometimes also used to refer to "sexual encounters"—and is thus the topic of many jokes—but domestic workers more often use it to refer to illegal part-time jobs.

17. Chicana domestic workers express similar preferences for the greater freedom and control to be gained by working in several part-time jobs rather than one full-time one (Romero 1992).

REFERENCES CITED

Abu-Lughod, Lila
1986   Veiled Sentiments: Honor and Poetry in a Bedouin Society. Berkeley: University of California Press.
1990   The Romance of Resistance: Tracing Transformations of Power through Bedouin Women. American Ethnologist 17:41–55.

Allison, Anne
1994   Nightwork: Sexuality, Pleasure, and Corporate Masculinity in a Tokyo Hostess Club. Chicago: University of Chicago Press.

Alter, Joseph S.
1994   Celibacy, Sexuality, and the Transformation of Gender into Nationalism in North India. Journal of Asian Studies 53:45–65.

Armstrong, M. Jocelyn
1990   Female Household Workers in Industrializing Malaysia. In At Work in Homes: Household Work in World Perspective. Roger Sanjek and Shellee Colen, eds. Pp. 146–163. Washington, DC: American Anthropological Association.

Asian Migrant Centre
1991   Foreign Domestic Workers in Hong Kong: A Baseline Study. Hong Kong: Asian Migrant Worker's Centre.

Balagtas, B.
1996   Gay Report Is Irresponsible. Eastern Express, January 19.

Barnes, Ruth, and Joanne B. Eicher
1992   Dress and Gender: Making and Meaning in Cultural Contexts. Oxford: Berg.

Barret-Ducrocq, Françoise
1991   Love in the Time of Victoria: Sexuality, Class and Gender in Nineteenth-Century London. John Howe, trans. New York: Verso.

Basabica, Annabelle
1993   The Way We Wear in Summer. Tinig Filipino, May: 37.

Bociurkiw, Michael
1992a   Letters Home Give Vital Clues to Police on Mercy Mission. Sunday Morning Post, June 28.
1992b   Philippines Urged to Act Over "Sex Slaves" in HK. Sunday Morning Post, December 27.

Broch-Due, Vigdis, Ingrid Rudie, and Tone Bleie, eds.
1993   Carved Flesh/Cast Selves: Gendered Symbols and Social Practices. Oxford: Berg.

Census and Statistics Department
1995a   Domestic Helpers. In Social Data Collected by the General Household Survey: Special Topics Report No. 12. Pp. 3–10. Hong Kong: Government Printer.
1995b   Hong Kong Social and Economic Trends. 1995 Edition. Hong Kong: Government Printer.
1996   Hong Kong in Figures. 1996 Edition. Hong Kong: Government Printer.

Chan, Stephen
1996   Honest and Hard-Working. South China Morning Post, May 15.

Ching, Linda
1996   Motives for Defence of Lesbians Questioned. Eastern Express, January 22.

Chong, M. S.
1985   Filipina Maids Are Spoiled. South China Morning Post, June 18.

Chow, M. S.
1987   The Rising Tide against Domestics. Hong Kong Standard, May 11.

Colen, Shellee, and Roger Sanjek
1990   At Work in Homes I: Orientations *and* At Work in Homes II: Directions. In At Work in Homes: Household Work in World Perspective. Roger Sanjek and Shellee Colen,

eds. pp. 1–13, 176–188. American Ethnological Society Monograph Series, Number 3. Washington, DC: American Anthropological Association.

Constable, Nicole
1996   Jealousy, Chastity, and Abuse: Chinese Maids and Foreign Helpers in Hong Kong. Modern China 22:448–479.
1997   Maid to Order in Hong Kong: Stories of Filipina Workers. Ithaca, NY: Cornell University Press.

Corpuz, Daisy
1993   Is Homosexuality Already Accepted? Tinig Filipino, April: 25.

Dacilla, Marivic
1993   Cheers to "The Way We Wear. . . ." Tinig Filipino, June: 25.

Douglas, Mary
1970[1966]   Purity and Danger. Harmondsworth, UK: Penguin.

Ebrey, Patricia Buckley
1993   The Inner Quarters: Marriage and the Lives of Chinese Women in the Sung Period. Berkeley: University of California Press.

Enloe, Cynthia
1990   Bananas, Beaches, and Bases: Making Feminist Sense of International Politics. Berkeley: University of California Press.

Eronico, Lizby G.
1994   The Modern Romeos in the Making. Tinig Filipino, February: 10.

Ferrer, Babes
1993   Women in Disguise. Tinig Filipino, February: 8.

Foucault, Michel
1990[1976]   The History of Sexuality: An Introduction, 1. New York: Vintage Books.

French, Carolyn
1986   Filipina Domestic Workers in Hong Kong. Ph.D. dissertation, University of Surrey.

Gallagher, Catherine
1987   The Body versus the Social Body in the Works of Thomas Malthus and Henry Mayhew. In The Making of the Modern Body: Sexuality and Society in the Nineteenth-Century. Catherine Gallagher and Thomas Laqueur, eds. Pp. 83–106. Berkeley: University of California Press.

Gamboa, Veronica
1993   Misunderstood Me. Tinig Filipino, June: 24

Gaw, Kenneth
1991   Superior Servants: The Legendary Amahs of the Far East. Singapore: Oxford University Press.

Gilman, Sander L.
1985   Difference and Pathology: Stereotypes of Sexuality, Race, and Madness. Ithaca, NY: Cornell University Press.
1994   Sigmund Freud and the Sexologists: A Second Reading. In Sexual Knowledge, Sexual Science: The History of Attitudes to Sexuality. Roy Porter and Kikulas Teich, eds. Pp. 323–349. New York: Cambridge University Press.

Gladney, Dru
1994   Representing Nationality in China: Refiguring Majority/Minority Identities. Journal of Asian Studies 53:92–123.

Greenway, Alice
1986   Birth Campaign Aims at Filipinos. South China Morning Post, July 28.

Hansen, Karen Tranberg
1990   Part of the Household Inventory: Men Servants in Zambia. In At Work in Homes: Household Work in World Perspective. Roger Sanjek and Shellee Colen, eds. Pp. 119–145. Washington, DC: American Anthropological Association.
1989   Distant Companions: Servants and Employers in Zambia, 1900–1985. Ithaca, NY: Cornell University Press.

Harrell, Stevan
1985   Why Do the Chinese Work So Hard: Reflections on an Entrepreneurial Ethic. Modern China 13(1):90–109.

JanMohamed, Abdul R.
1992   Sexuality on/of the Racial Border: Foucault, Wright and the Articulation of "Racialized Sexuality." In Discourses of Sexuality. Domna Stanton, ed. Pp. 94–116. Ann Arbor: University of Michigan.

Jaschok, Maria
1988   Concubines and Bondservants: A Social History. London: Zed Books.
1993   "A Public Nuisance": Reflections on the Occupation of City Spaces by Filipina Domestic Helpers in Hong Kong. Paper Presented at the International Conference on Africa and Asia. Hong Kong, August 24, 1993.

Kelly, John D.
1991   A Politics of Virtue: Hinduism, Sexuality, and Countercolonial Discourse in Fiji. Chicago: University of Chicago Press.

Labour Department
1992   Labour and Employment in Hong Kong. Hong Kong: Government Printer.

Lam, Rowena
1996   Let Unhappy Maids Return to the Philippines. South China Morning Post, May 14.

Laqueur, Thomas W.
1990   Making Sex: Body and Gender from the Greeks to Freud. Cambridge, MA: Harvard University Press.
1992   Sexual Desire and the Market Economy during the Industrial Revolution. *In* Discourses of Sexuality. Domna Stanton, ed. Pp. 185–215. Ann Arbor: University of Michigan.

Laxton, Andrew
1993   Police Hunt "Asia's Biggest Pimp." Sunday Morning Post, September 19.

Layosa, Linda, and Laura P. Luminarias
1992   Sa Pagyuko Ng Kawayan: A Collection of Short Stories by Overseas Workers. Hong Kong: AsiaPacific Publishing Company.

Lee, P. K.
1993   Tax on Maids Is Workable. South China Morning Post, February 9.

Mahusay, Maribel
1993   Judge People by the Clothes They Wear. Tinig Filipino, August: 25.

McMahon, Keith
1995   Misers, Shrews, and Polygamists: Sexuality and Male-Female Relations in Eighteenth-Century Chinese Fiction. Durham, NC: Duke University Press.

Mendoza, Alice, and Michael Bociurkiw
1992   Thousands of Illegals Work in HK Brothels. South China Morning Post, July 5.

Mommie Jingco
1991   Shocking. Tinig Filipino, April: 24–25.

Nubla, M. G.
1986   Family Planning for Filipinas. Hongkong Standard, August 11.

Ong, Aihwa
1991   The Gender and Labor Politics of Postmodernity. Annual Review of Anthropology 20:279–309.

Ong, J.
1992   No Foreigner Can Stand above the Law. South China Morning Post, December 15.

Ooi Keat Gin
1992   The Black and White Amahs of Malaya. Journal of the Malaysian Branch of the Royal Asiatic Society 65(2):69–84.

Parker, Richard G.
1991   Bodies, Pleasures, and Passions: Sexual Culture in Contemporary Brazil. Boston: Beacon Press.

Parker, Richard G., and John H. Gagnon, eds.
1995   Conceiving Sexuality: Approaches to Sex Research in a Postmodern World. New York: Routledge.

Peiss, Kathy
1990   "Charity Girls" and City Pleasures: Historical Notes on Working-Class Sexuality, 1880–1920. *In* Unequal Sisters: A Multicultural Reader in U.S. Women's History. Ellen Carol DuBois and Vicki L. Ruiz, eds. Pp. 157–166. New York: Routledge.

Peiss, Kathy, and Christina Simmons, eds., with Robert A. Padgug
1989   Passion and Power: Sexuality in History. Philadelphia: Temple University Press.

Rofel, Lisa
1994   Liberation Nostalgia and a Yearning for Modernity. *In* Engendering China: Women, Culture and the State. Christina K. Gilmartin, Gail Hershatter, Lisa Rofel, and Tyrene White, eds. Pp. 226–249. Cambridge, MA: Harvard University Press.

Rollins, Judith
1985   Between Women: Domestics and Their Employers. Philadelphia: Temple University Press.
1990   Ideology and Servitude. *In* At Work in Homes: Household Work in World Perspective. Roger Sanjek and Shellee Colen, eds. Pp. 74–88. Washington, DC: American Anthropological Association.

Romero, Mary
1992   Maid in the U.S.A. New York: Routledge.

Saddi, Nimfa
1993   I Am Not a Woman in Disguise. Tinig Filipino, May: 24.

Salaff, Janet
1981   Working Daughters of Hong Kong: Filial Piety or Power in the Family? New York: Cambridge University Press.

Sandborg, Kirsten
1993   Malay Dress Symbolism. *In* Carved Flesh/Cast Selves. Vigdis Broch-Due, Ingrid Rudie, and Tone Bleie, eds. Pp. 195–206. Oxford: Berg.

Sankar, Andrea
1978   Female Domestic Service in Hong Kong. *In* Female Servants and Economic Development. Louise Tilly, Anna Rubbo, Michael Taussig, Susan Berkowitz Luton, and Andrea Sankar, eds. Pp. 51–62. Occasional Papers in Women's Studies, No. 1. Ann Arbor: University of Michigan.

Simmons, Christina
1993   African Americans and Sexual Victorianism in the Social Hygiene Movement, 1910–40. Journal of the History of Sexuality 4:51–75.

Sombrio, Rose
1996 Don't Just Cry for the T-Birds. Eastern Express, January 22.
South China Morning Post
1992 Sordid Truth of "Girlie Bars." October 29.
Stanton, Domna C.
1992 Discourses of Sexuality: From Aristotle to AIDS. Ann Arbor: University of Michigan.
Stoler, Ann
1989 Making Empire Respectable: The Politics of Race and Sexual Morality in 20th-Century Colonial Cultures. American Ethnologist 16:634–660.
Tinig Filipino
1993a Filipina Virgins: Philippines' Top Export Commodity? Tinig Filipino, June: 24.
1993b Protect Yourself from Sexual Molestation. Tinig Filipino, December: 45
Torrefranca, Ma. Shiela S.
1992 The Man Behind the Skirt. Tinig Filipino, April: 40.
Ventenilla, Thelma S.
1993 Hot Issue: The Way We Wear. Tinig Filipino, November: 28.
Wallis, Belinda
1992 Plea to Smash Sex Syndicates As Mercy Found. South China Morning Post. July 3.

Ware, Vron
1992 Beyond the Pale: White Women, Racism and History. New York: Verso.
Watson, Rubie S.
1991 Wives, Concubines and Maids: Servitude and Kinship in the Hong Kong Region, 1900–1940. In Marriage and Inequality in Chinese Society. Rubie S. Watson and Patricia Buckley Ebrey, eds. Pp. 231–255. Berkeley: University of California Press.
Wilde, Wally
1996 "Observation" Earns Contempt. Eastern Express, January 18.
Wolf, Margery
1968 The House of Lim: A Study of a Chinese Farm Family. Englewood Cliffs, NJ: Prentice Hall.
1972 Women and the Family in Rural Taiwan. Stanford, CA: Stanford University Press.
Wong, Joe
1993 Crackdown on Fake Weddings for Prostitutes. Hongkong Standard, December 11.
Young, Malcolm
1992 Dress and Modes of Address: Structural Forms for Policewomen. In Dress and Gender. Ruth Barnes and Joanne B. Eicher, eds. Pp. 266–284. Oxford: Berg.

"Wild Pigs and Dog Men":
Rape and Domestic Violence as "Women's Issues" in Papua New Guinea

Laura Zimmer-Tamakoshi

INTRODUCTION

Male violence against women is a concern of feminists in both developed and developing countries (Counts, Brown, and Campbell 1992; Davies 1994). Leaders in many developing countries, however, have been slow in recognizing the extent and nature of the problem. This is in part because of insufficient research and cultural norms allowing for a "certain amount of wife-beating" and forced sex within

marriage (United Nations 1989). It is also the result of women's weaker political presence in developing countries and male resentment over a few women's gains in economic and social independence. Nevertheless, prompted by alarm over increased violence against women, concern over the deleterious effects of violence on women's participation in development, and negative images of Papua New Guinea in the world press, in 1982 the Papua New Guinean government directed its Law Reform Commission to begin research into domestic violence. The resulting, and for a developing country, unprecedented publications

Original material prepared for this text. Reprinted by permission of the author.

revealed that a majority of Papua New Guinean wives have been hit by their husbands, most more than once a year, with urban wives suffering a higher level of violence than their rural counterparts (Toft, ed. 1985, 1986a, 1986b; Toft and Bonnell 1985). Less systematically researched, rape is also a concern as Papua New Guinea tops the United States with a reported rate of 45 rapes per 100,000 persons versus 35 per 100,000 in the United States and well above the lower incidences of reported rapes in Japan and other industrial and nonindustrial nations (Herman 1989: 23). In 1990 there were 1,896 rapes reported in Papua New Guinea, a country with a population of less than 4 million (Dinnen 1993). Such statistics do not capture the severity of the problem, however, as most of these rapes were committed by three or more rapists (with more than 15, 20, or 40 males participating in any particular gang rape), and, as in the United States and elsewhere, many rapes are unreported, especially those committed by the victims' husbands, lovers, dates, or close relatives (Dinnen 1996; Finkelhor and Yllo 1985; Russell 1984; Toft 1985; Toft 1986a; Zimmer 1990).

This chapter examines violence against women in Papua New Guinea, reviewing past and present patterns of rape and domestic violence and adding to a multidimensional theory concerning the prevalence and increase of such violence. Although traditional attitudes toward violence contribute to its acceptance, recent research has targeted the psychological and economic pressures of development and inequality as fueling violence against women, particularly as they have different effects on the circumstances and attitudes of males and females. Josephides (n.d.), for example, argues that in Papua New Guinea, "Much of men's violence towards women is motivated by a fear that women are gaining a new kind of independence," and that men's violence is an attempt to terrify and control the women. Both Josephides and Bradley (1994), who worked at the Papua New Guinea Law Reform Commission from 1986 to 1990, see the violence as stemming not only from men's insecurities about their wives' potential independence but also their own uncertain situations and the effects of urban lifestyles (including alcohol abuse and reduced social support networks) on male–female relations. Other factors are increased eroticism and sexual conflicts as old taboos disappear and men (and sometimes women) place greater demands on their spouses and sexual partners (Jenkins 1994; Rosi and Zimmer-Tamakoshi 1993).

Supporting these arguments with cases and other material, I also develop a needed political dimension to better understand violence against women in Papua New Guinea (and elsewhere, as I discuss in the concluding section of this chapter). While individuals commit violence and it is individuals who experience the traumas and dislocations of change and development, the intersection of sex and class politics also informs and fuels sexual and domestic violence. With a small number of Papua New Guineans enjoying an elite lifestyle and under pressure from the "grass-roots" to bring about an economic miracle on their behalf, elite women have become targets of disaffection not only from men and women in the lower classes but also from men in their own class. Feeling harassed on all sides, by unsympathetic constituents and, from their perspective, "demanding" or *bikhet* (uncontrollable, conceited) wives and girlfriends, many elite males have taken the path of least resistance and higher political capital, scapegoating elite women and using violence to assert control over them (Rosi and Zimmer-Tamakoshi 1993; Zimmer-Tamakoshi 1993b and 1995). Thus, I not only contend, along with others, that (1) women's opportunities for self-expression and economic independence threaten the self-esteem and security of men who do not have such opportunities, and (2) such men use violence against women to assert or regain a sense of dominance. I also argue that (3) violence against women is rife among Papua New Guinea's elite (a fact demonstrated by the Law Reform Commission reports) even when one excludes what Josephides has referred to in person as antifeminist *rascals* (or criminals), some of whom are members of elite society (as has been reported by Dinnen 1993; Harris 1988; and Zimmer-Tamakoshi n.d.); and (4) the violence is partly motivated by class and sexual tensions that paint elite females as symbols of all that is wrong with contemporary Papua New Guinean society. Finally, violence against women does not occur in isolation from other forms of violence. Political tensions in Papua New Guinea are grounded in a weak state that is unable to ensure even basic services to its population or to control public disturbances such as tribal conflicts over land. As has been argued for Papua New Guinea (A. Strathern 1993) and other parts of the world (Riches 1986), expressions of conflict such as the resumption of tribal warfare in the New Guinean highlands have strategic value in the context of a weak state. In a weak state violence may be a rational means of social advantage when there are no higher-level powers strong enough or interested enough in interfering with lower-level clashes. In the case of violence against women, men who want to can assert their dominance over women with little fear of resistance as long as there is widespread envy or fear of those women, and state officials charged with protecting them are unable or unwilling to do so.

WILD PIGS AND DOG MEN

Rape and domestic violence are not common in every New Guinean society (see Goodale 1980 and Mitchell 1992), but, fearing violence, most Papua New Guinean women walk in groups when going to and from their gardens or to office, school, or marketplace. Because husbands and boyfriends are likely perpetrators of violence against them, women also seek the protective company of family and friends when they are at home. Women's fear of violence, especially sexual violence, is fanned with vivid stories of past attacks on women and fresh accounts in the daily press. Around village hearths in the night, women and girls listen to the hushed and often admonitory tones of older persons telling them tales (captured in early anthropological monographs) of gang rape and mutilation of women's genitals as ways men "used to" punish errant wives and daughters (Meggitt 1964: 204, 207; Newman 1964: 266; Read 1952: 14); how wife-swapping

or preying on other men's wives were tolerated as long as neither was too blatant an attack on a man's self-esteem (Berndt 1962: 160; Brown 1969: 94; Langness 1969: 45 and 1974: 204; Read 1954: 866); and how rape did and does occur in the varied contexts of women being found alone on a garden path or at work in their gardens, in war, and when a man tires of his lover, wishes to end an adulterous affair, or wants to lessen his culpability in either case by instigating a gang rape of the woman (Berndt 1962: 168). Outside the highlands, Tolai women shudder when they hear how Tolai men's cults once celebrated masculinity with the sexual abuse of widows and other women without male protection (Bradley 1982, 1985; Parkinson 1907: 473). And in West New Britain, Lakalai women do not mourn changes in the men's ceremonial season, which once included the casual rape of women in their own villages (Chowning 1985: 85).

Although many men's cults and their predations on women have died out as Christianity has taken over (Bradley 1985 and Chowning 1985), violence against women continues. Today, the contexts in which violence occurs are more but there are parallels in the circumstances of some of the victims and the motivations of their attackers. Finding a woman alone on a garden path is now varied in cases like one in 1983 in which a former rugby league star and two other assailants beat and raped a three-months-pregnant woman when they found her alone on the Daulo Pass, where she was stranded after the vehicle in which she was a passenger broke down (*PNG Post Courier* 1984a). Tiring of his lover, a young man may arrange to have her gang-raped as did a young man in the city of Lae when he forced his girlfriend to have sex with his friends after he had sex with her (*PNG Post Courier* 1984c). Another traditional form of violence—humiliating the enemy by raping their women—was echoed in the same month when a man was held by two assailants and forced to watch while a third man raped his wife in Rabaul village (*PNG Post Courier* 1984g). In the same month, a gang of about 15 youths, all under the age of 20, raped a nine-year-old girl, her mother, and another woman while the women's husbands were beaten and held at knifepoint. The gang then broke into a nearby house and stole $6,000 worth of cash and goods (*PNG Post Courier* 1984b, d, e, f, g). The gangs' actions replicated attacks against the enemies' women in warfare, but in this instance there was the added twist that some of the younger rapists were trying to prove their right to membership in the gang by raping white women (see Harris 1988 on *rascal* gang entry requirements). Echoes of using rape and beatings to punish errant wives or daughters abound in the case of "Bill and Maria" (Case 2 below), in which "Bill" (all names are pseudonyms for obvious reasons) rapes his wife in a public carpark as a means of asserting his dominance and punishing her independence.

In many traditional Papua New Guinean societies, particularly in the Highlands, violence against women was part of a sociopolitical context in which political eminence was achieved through the control and distribution of wealth, and older men and women controlled access to land and marriage, two main ingredients in the acquisition of wealth. Marriage was important for both males and females for it was through marriage that one acquired a helpmate, produced children, and paid off one's debts to society. For men of ambition, marrying several women was virtually the only means of becoming a "Big Man," as women's gardening and pig-raising activities and daughters' brideprices brought men the necessary "wealth" (pigs, yams, shells) to fund networks of supporters and to outgive competitors within and outside their clans. To marry at all required the support of older men and women, who gathered together the brideprice. The process of attracting brideprice supporters began during a man's childhood and youth, when he and his peers participated in lengthy initiations designed to test and strengthen their obedience and relationships to their supporters. During initiation, young men were told many falsehoods about women as a way of keeping them away from women until their elders were ready to support their marriages. Such fabrications included depictions of women, particularly young women, as dangerous and untrustworthy creatures who were to be feared and avoided if possible (Counts 1985; Faithorn 1976; Gelber 1986; Zimmer-Tamakoshi 1996a). Boys learned that "overindulgence in sexual relations with women depletes a man's vital energies leaving his body permanently exhausted and withered" (Meggitt 1964: 210) and that contact of any kind with women causes a man "to accumulate debilitating dirt in his body" (Newman 1964: 265). Young women's powers of seduction were portrayed as so great that young men were warned not to look at a young woman because "if you look at her, and she looks at you, then you will copulate" (Berndt 1962: 103; Read 1954: 867; Langness 1967: 165).

Part of the ideology initiates learned included notions of male superiority and dominance over women. Men's superiority was said to reside in their greater capacity for self-control. Initiates were taught that mature men do not act "like wild pigs" having sex indiscriminately or like "women" acting on whim and self-interest rather than promoting the social good (Gelber 1986, Chapter Two; Lindenbaum 1976: 56). Young men who were disrespectful of or doubted their elders' injunctions risked permanent bachelorhood as they depended on older men and women for brideprice help (Bowers 1965; Glasse 1969: 26; Waddell 1972: 46), and few prospective in-laws would allow their daughters to marry "dog men," men with inordinate desires for sex who spent their lives "sniffing" after other men's wives and destroying the village peace.

Promoting male solidarity, notions of male superiority allowed for effective regulation of access to and control over women. In most Papua New Guinean societies, the importance of female labor to men was such—and still is— that men have variously portrayed women as men's "hands" (Lindenbaum 1976: 59), "trade-stores" (M. Strathern 1972: 99), "tractors" (Langness 1967: 172), and "capital assets" (Cook 1969: 102). Several ethnographies suggest it was more young women's sexuality and labor than older women's that was at issue, as older women had rewards and reasons of their own to support their husbands' activities and to promote the well-being of their children's clans as well as their own (Counts 1985; M. Strathern 1980; Zimmer-Tamakoshi 1996a). Just as parents warned sons against the dangers of women, so too did they warn daughters against unregulated association with young men. They also taught their daughters that safety lay in cooperating with their elders to achieve fruitful marriages and honorable lives. Women—young or old—who rebelled against such beliefs or interfered with men's activities and plans, risked beatings and punitive rapes (Berndt 1962; Josephides 1985; Meggitt 1964; Read 1954; and M. Strathern 1972). Believing women to be weak-willed, husbands justified beating their wives fairly regularly as a way of getting them to fulfill their obligations to them. Also believing women to be by nature deceitful and seductive, men readily blamed rape victims for bringing the rapes on themselves. Women were thus wise to build large networks of supporters in their own and their husbands' groups who might rise to their defense in the case of rape or an overzealous wife-beater.

Today, introduced notions of women's inferiority and men's right to dominate them, men's greater access to cash incomes and women's increasing dependence on men, the weakening of parents' economic control over sons and daughters (especially those living and working in urban areas), and opportunities (primarily through education) for a few women to achieve both economic and social independence all contribute to an increasing incidence of violence against women in Papua New Guinea. Grafted onto old beliefs, the views of some Christian missions—that women be subservient to and mindful at all times of their husbands' and, much less so, their parents' wishes—and foreign media portrayals of women as erotic sex objects, docile housewives, or man-eaters further alienate young Papua New Guineans from one another as women are shrouded in further mystifications. During my first year of fieldwork with a group of Highlanders known as the Gende, an urban gang member bragged to me about his sexual exploits, which included kidnapping and raping young girls and even a married woman. In response to my shocked expression, he assured me that "They liked it! It was like it is in a James Bond movie—sexy! The woman fights with James Bond and tries to kill him and then he

forces her to have sex with him and she is his woman from then on. Sometimes he kills her if she is a really bad woman." When I asked if he had killed anyone, he said he had killed the one woman because he feared she would tell her husband that he had raped her (which he denied, insisting that it wasn't rape and that "She liked it! I'm sexy!").

In the material realm, men's control of economic resources has tightened in both village and town as the proceeds from most cash crops are controlled by men, men dominate the job market, and men's educational opportunities are greater than women's. Women's dependence on men is greatest among urban women. One result of this dependence is that urban husbands—especially prosperous ones—are more likely to fight with their wives, to cheat on them, and to abuse them both physically and sexually (Ranck and Toft 1986; Rosi and Zimmer-Tamakoshi 1993; Zimmer-Tamakoshi 1993a). Several Gende women I know left husbands who beat them, drank too much, and wasted their salaries on other women, saying they'd rather marry a village husband who worked with them in the gardens and not against them in town. In the case of low-income husbands who are less attractive to other women, a wife's threat to return to the village to find another husband is taken very seriously, and such a husband is less likely even than a villager to beat his wife (Ranck and Toft 1986; Zimmer-Tamakoshi 1996b).

The weakening of parental control over the beliefs and actions of the younger generation and its relationship to violence against women can be illustrated in the experience of another Gende woman. This young woman's husband, also Gende, grew up in Port Moresby and is more Western in his outlook on life than she is. Jealous of his womanizing and pressured by her relatives to get him to pay off the remaining brideprice he owes them, she has stayed in town, playing cards most of the time her husband is working and being the butt of his anger or lust whenever he is home. Although she usually suffers his abuse quietly, on one occasion he forced her to have sex during her period, a heinous act in the eyes of more traditional Gende. Hysterical and threatening suicide, the young woman cut off one of her fingers with an axe, thereby demonstrating her shame. A parallel experience occurred a generation before to the girl's aunt. Married to a migrant but living in the village, the aunt was forced by her young husband—on a rare visit home—to have sex during her period. Ashamed and angry, the aunt moped around the village for a day and then left for her garden house—several miles distant from the village—where she hung herself. Unsuspecting, her family did not find her until it was too late. When the women cleaned her body for burial, they discovered menstrual blood mixed with semen smeared over her lower body and skirt as well as bruises on her arms and chest where her husband had apparently held her down forcefully. Although such actions would have resulted in the young man's death in the past, the aunt's husband stayed in town, away from the girl's parents and male relatives, hiding behind the power of Australian colonial law and her parents' belief that the young man would be more useful to them if he continued working and paid them a large compensation payment for their daughter's death.

How far outside the normal realm of parental control (and protection) young persons can get is illustrated in "Violet's" case. In this case, parental pressures and absence are only part of the story. Other factors responsible for "Violet's" fate are her naive hopes for love and romance, and a sociocultural environment in which many young men no longer fear women so much as see them as sexual prey.

Case 1—"Violet"

I have written elsewhere on the motives and circumstances of young village women moving to town in the hope of attracting suitors who can pay the large brideprices expected by the women's families and fulfill women's dreams of a prosperous lifestyle (Zimmer-Tamakoshi 1993a). Living with younger kinsmen, married sisters, or even nonrelatives, these girls are poorly chaperoned and often end up victims of sexual assault and bondage. One such victim was Violet. When she first came to Port Moresby, Violet stayed with an older sister and brother-in-law in a house provided by the company her brother-in-law worked for. Violet spent her days looking after her sister's children while her sister worked as a checker in a local supermarket. Evenings, Violet attended the local movie theater with girlfriends or stayed home to watch TV with her sister's family. As soon as she moved in with her sister, Violet became the target of her brother-in-law's unwanted sexual advances. On numerous occasions, feigning illness in order to spend the day at home and threatening to kill her if she revealed what he was doing, Violet's brother-in-law had sex with Violet. When Violet became pregnant, her sister wanted to send her back to the village, but Violet feared the censure and disappointment of her parents. Violet obtained an illegal abortion and moved in with a girlfriend.

Supporting herself by prostitution and frequenting the notorious "Pink Pussycat" and other cocktail lounges, Violet continues to hope that she will one day meet and marry a "nice man" who will take her out of her misery. The types of men Violet is most likely to meet, however, are married men looking for an evening's distraction or university students preying on naive husband-hunters. The violent and sexually charged atmosphere of both the university and the city are well known to anyone who has spent time in either location. In a paper on the situations of women students at the University of Papua New Guinea (UPNG), Joan Oliver reported that "women students had a pervasive fear of attack, harassment, threats, bashings, rape and breaking into rooms by male students or strangers" (1987: 159; see also Still and Shea's report of 1976). She further reported that because of their fears many women either drop out of school or become engaged to male protectors who not infrequently soon have the women pregnant (1987: 170).

With the proportion of female students at UPNG hovering at 10 percent, male students are in keen competition with one another for the friendship of female classmates. The competition works itself out along divisions of language and region as, for example, Chimbu *wantoks* (persons who speak Chimbu) jealously attempt to guard all Chimbu girls for themselves and Papuans (from southern Papua New

Guinea) fight off any non-Papuans who might try to have a relationship with a Papuan girl. Since having sex with a female student risks reprisal from her campus *wantoks*—but not the police!—many University men satisfy their sexual desires by visiting Port Moresby's night spots and bringing back girls like Violet to the University playing fields and dorms, where they have sex with them—often forced. These escapades may also bring reprisals, of course, as happened when a gang of University students raped a young girl from a nearby squatter settlement on the University football field while her younger brother was made to watch. Class antagonism as well as ethnic outrage was evident as men and boys from the settlement stalked the campus paths and housing areas for weeks after threatening to rape female students and teachers at UPNG for what the "spoiled, *bikhet* school boys" had done.

Meri Wantok and Meri Universiti

As suggested in the previous paragraph, a broad set of factors that seems conducive to high levels of violence against women in Papua New Guinea is the extralocal politics of sexuality. This set of factors includes the intersections of elite and urban sexual politics with nationalist and class interests and rhetoric. In a paper on nationalism and sexuality in Papua New Guinea, I argued that the practice of holding educated women, or *meri universiti*, responsible for all that is wrong with contemporary Papua New Guinean society is both a political maneuver to ease class and interethnic tensions and jealousies in Papua New Guinea's culturally diverse society (Zimmer-Tamakoshi 1993b) and a satisfying fiction for the majority of Papua New Guineans who feel left out of "progress" and "development." Symbolizing privilege and, in some instances, sexual freedom (or anarchy), *meri universiti* and *skull meri* (school girls) are both envied for their perceived opportunities and hated as selfish betrayers of their cultural roots, while "grassroots" women and more circumspect elite women who show (or appear to show) greater concern for their kin and language groups are accorded respect as *meri wantok* and *meri bilong ples*.

There is as much diversity within the elite as without, particularly between educated men and women. Unlike their male counterparts, who come from all parts of the nation, Papua New Guinea's small class of educated elite women come almost entirely from coastal and off-shore island areas that have been long involved with the outside world. As a result, they are more likely than their male peers to come from educated and economically privileged backgrounds, and as a group they are more Western in demeanor and appearance than most Papua New Guinean women. Another difference between educated men and women (and between educated women and the majority of Papua New Guinea's population) is that many educated elite women come from matrilineal societies in which women's status tends to be higher relative to many patrilineal societies and women are freer in their relations with men. On one occasion, when I was having dinner at the Bird of Paradise hotel in Goroka, I was surprised to learn that the couple at the table beside me were married (but not to each other!), were traveling together throughout the Highlands on government business, and that their spouses on Bougainville Island were satisfied with the phone calls the pair made at each stop on their tour of duty. It was difficult to imagine such easy professionalism in a partnership involving a Highlands man and woman. Rumors and jealous spouses would prevent this, as Highlanders (and many other Papua New Guineans) believe it is impossible for men and women to be together for long without engaging in sex. Unusual, such behavior becomes a focus of the anger and jealousies that exist between the sexes and among class, ethnic, and racial groupings in Papua New Guinea.

Increasing the distance between elite men and themselves some elite women have opted for marriage with non–Papua New Guineans or to forgo marriage entirely. Several examples are two of the three women to ever sit as members of National Parliament and a former president of the National Council of Women, all married to or in long-term relationships with white, expatriate males. Such high-profile interracial relationships on the part of women embarrass the male leadership as the majority of Papua New Guineans see them as signs of elite immorality and weakness (e.g., elite men's inability to control their women) and collaboration of the elite with outsiders and former colonials. There have been attempts to control elite women's freedoms at all levels of Papua New Guinean society from the government down, including public censure, violence, and the refusal of full citizenship rights to foreign spouses and recurrent threats to disenfranchise the children of mixed marriages.

An example of the public scapegoating of elite or educated women is the "mini-skirt debate." The "mini-skirt debate" began back in the early 1970s—prior to Papua New Guinea's independence in 1975—with Tolai religious and political leaders in East New Britain calling for a campaign against immodest dress and claiming that school girls and young women were provoking an increasing incidence of rape and sexually transmitted diseases (STDs) in East New Britain by wearing provocative Western-style clothing and makeup. The debate entered the pages of Papua New Guinea's *Post Courier*, where it has continued off and on for years. The response of young women to men's condemnation of their dress is summed up in one early letter to the editor signed "Four Tolai Girls" (*PNG Post Courier* 1973a). As quoted in Hogan (1985: 56–57),

> [The young women] had no doubts that the banning of mini-skirts would have wider implications. For its writers, wearing mini-skirts signified that they wanted greater control over their lives. They accused the initiators of the circular of having political motivations—of using the issue of public morality for their own political purposes . . . and [of knowing] that with education women would be able to judge the decisions of men.

Three male Tolai students at the University of Papua New Guinea added their opinions to the debate by writing that the four Tolai girls were blindly following the dictates of Western culture and wanting "to keep on 'pleasing' and 'praising' the colonial administration without stopping and asking themselves a single question" (*PNG Post Courier* 1973b).

The political advantages of focusing on the behaviors of a few elite women and suggesting that they are the root cause of problems both for women and the country as a whole are the obvious appeal to the masses, the small cost of blaming persons who do not constitute a large constituency, and the ease of following a time-honored tradition of blaming women for problems that men create or holding them up as suspicious characters bent on interfering in men's relations with one another. The anti-colonial sentiment and racial undercurrents in elite men's condemnation of elite women is also a popular cause in a nation that is trying to unite a diversity of regions and language groups into one strong nation (see Lindstrom 1992).

Two cases that illustrate the sexual politics of Papua New Guinea's educated elite and the sexual competition among men of different tribal and national backgrounds are the cases of "Bill and Maria" and "Lita." Although their cases are well-known to me, I can only sketch in the barest of details here in this brief essay. Readers who wish to read more detailed cases are referred to Susan's Toft's harrowing account of marital violence of two couples living in Port Moresby (1985) and Andrew Strathern's grisly report on sadistic rape in Hagen (1985).

Case 2—"Bill and Maria"

I have written about Bill and Maria in a paper on love and marriage among the educated elite in Port Moresby (Rosi and Zimmer-Tamakoshi 1993). I described how this young couple—both Highlanders, both finishing their education at UPNG and the parents of two young children—were suffering severe pressures and tensions in their marriage, with the result that they fought often and violently. Much of the tension was caused by in-laws: Maria's father demanding a large brideprice for his educated daughter, and Bill's village-based family critical of Maria's lack of traditional skills and anxious that the couple pay most of the brideprice and childwealth payments themselves. Raised on a government station and exposed in her religious and educational experience to western ideas about appropriate and desirable marital relations, Maria was hurt and angered by Bill's drinking, his numerous infidelities, and by his toying with the idea of marrying a second wife back in the Highlands to raise pigs for exchange purposes.

What I did not discuss in that paper was the fact that Bill ended most arguments with his wife by raping her, sometimes in public places. On one occasion, after coming home drunk and disheveled in the early morning hours, Bill dragged Maria out of bed and raped her—spread-eagled over a car hood in a University parking lot—while loudly accusing her of being the cause of all his troubles, of having affairs with other men, and of dressing and behaving too provocatively to be a good wife. While there was little truth to his accusations, his use of these particular criticisms to justify his brutality reveals important contradictions in the lives of educated men, contradictions arising from the complex politics of sexuality in contemporary Papua New Guinea. On many occasions, Bill expressed pride in Maria's education and her poise in social situations involving both Papua New Guineans and expatriates. At one large garden party, for example, at which scores of University professors and students had gathered, Bill and Maria joined easily into the festivities, eating, drinking, dancing, and talking with the other guests—together and singly. As the evening progressed, however, Bill began following Maria around, demanding that she join the group of women who were sitting on woven mats on the perimeter of the night's action. These women—the wives of older and more conservative faculty and staff—were dressed modestly in *meri wantok* fashion in form-hiding *meri blouses* and ankle-length *laplaps* and spent the evening quietly talking with one another and tending small children they had brought with them to the party. Also on the fringes, but drinking heavily, were some of Bill's male relatives—several students and several older men who did maintenance work at the University. These men ogled skimpily dressed expatriate women and the more daring *meri universiti* at the same time they criticized Bill for allowing Maria to wear a short, tight skirt and form-revealing blouse.

At the University club and at parties, I many times heard men slander particular women, their clothing choices, and their alleged sexual habits. If the women were not related to the men, they would also discuss ways of going about seducing or raping the woman. Add to this the disapproving and often envious statements of men's lesser-educated kin—telling their more advantaged brothers to avoid marrying women who waste money on makeup and fancy clothes like spoiled white women at the same time as they express their desire to have sex with such women—and a situation arises in which it seems impossible for men like Bill to have it both ways—a wife who is attractive in new and sophisticated ways but one who does not attract the desire or censure of men who are her husband's associates, friends, relatives, or enemies.

Case 3—"Lita"

Further illuminating the sexual side of interethnic and interracial politics in urban Papua New Guinea, Lita's case is interesting because she is one of a small number of Papua New Guinean women who have discarded traditional relationships in order to express themselves in new and unusual ways. Pretty, bright, and poised in the presence of men of all ages and nationalities, Lita was engaged to a middle-aged expatriate when I first met her in one of the classes I was teaching at UPNG. Spurning her age-mates and vocal about her preference for white men—whom she claimed were gentler and more supportive of women's interests (for similar sentiments see the case of "Barbara" in Rosi and Zimmer-Tamakoshi 1993)—Lita accepted the gifts and attentions of her lover while at the same time playing the field at local discos and bars frequented by expatriate and Papua New Guinean businessmen and leaders.

Halfway through the semester, Lita began a secret love affair with one of her teachers at UPNG—an expatriate who was much younger than her fiance. When the affair became public knowledge and both expatriate lovers were spying on the other and attempting to engage the sympathies and help of Lita's friends, Lita's *wantoks* abducted her from her apartment, severely beat her and raped her, warning her to cease having affairs with either man and to choose someone from her own ethnic and racial background to marry. When I learned about the attack from some of Lita's classmates, I was dismayed by their lack of sympathy for her. Saying that she should not have embarrassed her *wantoks* and other Papua New Guineans by choosing white lovers over black, the majority felt she had only gotten what she deserved and that she was lucky her *wantoks* had not killed her.

Lita's social background is similar to Maria's in that both women were raised in urban or peri-urban settings by parents who are employed in the government sector and who—in their commitment to a more Western, or "modern" ethic—have raised their daughters to expect more egalitarian and open relations with men than is the norm in most parts of Papua New Guinea. Unfortunately for both young women, most of their *wantoks* do not agree and feel that the young women's "immodest" and "loose" behavior is injurious to ethnic and racial pride. Furthermore, both young women's *wantoks* are for the most part far less prosperous than either young woman's family, and there are economic and class tensions to contend with. When Lita informed her parents she was engaged to a foreigner, they at first protested it would never work. Promised a large brideprice, however, they and many of their village *wantoks* allowed that the marriage might be a good idea. Lita's *wantoks* at UPNG, however, took her engagement as an insult to them as more suitable partners, and when she compounded the insult by having affairs with two expatriates at the same time, it was too much to bear. In Maria's case, while her father and brothers have threatened to have her husband arrested for his repeated brutality, her *wantoks* side with Bill, contending that Maria is at least partly to blame for his behavior and that her husband and father should see to it that she conform to the clothing and behavioral norms of most highlanders rather than some small segment of PNG and expatriate society.

RAPE AND DOMESTIC VIOLENCE AS "WOMEN'S ISSUES"

As the foregoing suggests, violence against women has long been accepted in many Papua

New Guinean societies as a legitimate means of controlling women and expressing or affecting men's relations with other men. From studies done in the 1980s by the Law Reform Commission (Toft, ed. 1985, 1986b) and other ethnographic sources, we know that in the past both women and men agreed to men's right to chastise women with beatings and sometimes rape. Today, when some women's increased opportunities for self-expression and economic independence are perceived as threatening men's relations and the general good, many men and even many women consider violence to be an acceptable "comeuppance" for young women like Maria and Lita, and a means of preserving ethnic and national unity and pride. Nevertheless, there has been a sea change in women's attitudes toward violence against them and not only amongst elite women. Since World War II and the expansion of Papua New Guinea's towns and cities, urban dwellers have voiced their concerns over high rates of urban crime and domestic violence. Urban women have been especially concerned with the ever-present threat of pack rape and domestic violence associated with urban men's greater alcohol consumption, male sexual jealousy, and money problems (Toft 1986a: 12–14). In 1981, the National Council of Women passed a resolution stating that crimes against women seemed to be increasing and that there were inadequate controls to protect women. The Council then requested the government to investigate the problem, and on August 18, 1982, the Papua New Guinea Minister for Justice passed to the Law Reform Commission a Reference on Domestic Violence (Toft, ed. 1986a). The ensuing studies revealed many things about the nature, extent, and causes of domestic violence in Papua New Guinea as well as changing attitudes toward violence against women. Positive correlations were shown to exist, for example, between a decreasing acceptance of domestic violence and a person's sex, degree of urbanization, and levels of education and income (Toft 1986a: 23–26). Significantly, both urban low-income women and elite women are far less prepared than rural women to admit fault in failing to meet obligations to their husbands or to believe they "deserve" occasional beatings. Although the majority of urban men—especially educated men—also say it is unacceptable to hit wives, their apparent change in attitude is not reflected in their behavior.

Statistics are a weak measure of reality, however, and it is in case studies that we learn the depth of experience and motivations behind women's change of attitudes. In a study of two cases of marital violence in Port Moresby, Toft (1985) shows how men's violence against women interferes with the women's abilities, needs, and desires to function well in urban environments. One informant, "Rose," was regularly hit by her husband, who also phoned her at work in jealous piques and sometimes beat her so badly she could not work or take care of their young children. In a paper on Gende women in town, I make the point that while many urban women are technically unemployed, they fulfill many obligations to their village kin and in-laws and must be free to move about the urban environment without fear (Zimmer-Tamakoshi 1996b). Women in low-income households, for example, are almost always in town to protect their husbands' incomes from dissipation (e.g., alcohol, cards, prostitutes) and to see that their children get a better education than is always possible in the village. To achieve these ends, women meet husbands at their place of work on pay day for the handing over of the pay packet, they search the urban markets and stores for bargains to make their husbands' small incomes pay for both household and extra-household exchange demands, and they do without their school-age children's help in the daily round of collecting firewood and water for use in substandard squatter settlements at the edge of town. Such women have little patience with violent husbands whose utility to them is marginal at best. Women with more education have potentially greater opportunities to live life differently than their mothers' generation. Often, however, their desires and potential are not realized as violence, and fear of violence, keeps them out of work. Female graduates of Papua New Guinea's teachers' colleges, for example, rarely teach

for more than a year or so after graduating, even though they express, during their training, a strong desire and ability to be career teachers. A major constraint against their fulfilling their self-expectations is the threat of male violence against them, causing many to flee into early marriages and the comparative safety of compliance with men's wishes (Wormald and Crossley 1988).

Women's growing sense of gender oppression and their anger over their wasted potential reveals itself in diverse and often unusual ways. Young women like "Violet," impregnated by her brother-in-law and more or less abandoned by her family, may turn to prostitution to earn a living and make men pay for what they would otherwise take anyway. In urban contexts where women and girls have few options, "selling their bodies" to husbands or customers makes economic sense, however much self-violence it represents (see also Borrey 1994). Cases like "Donna's" (see below), in which women are packraped because they represent a threat to men's interests or, as in this case, a threat to Papua New Guinean pride, are more and more seen as deliberate assaults against women as a whole and not individual women.

Case 4—"Donna"

Donna was a successful Filipina business woman married to one of the expatriate lecturers at UPNG and living on campus in one of the homes provided for UPNG faculty and their families. Resentment against expatriate women is high in Papua New Guinea, because most expatriate women live enviable lifestyles and many fill full- or part-time positions in the work force that Papua New Guineans feel should be given to Papua New Guinean workers, especially male workers. Openly critical of what she felt were lax working habits on the part of her Papua New Guinean employees, Donna earned even more enmity than usual.

Sometime in the late 1980s, Donna and her husband were eating dinner when a gang of *rascals* broke through their dining room windows, beat the husband, and abducted Donna. Taking Donna by car to a remote location, they gang raped her and then left her, naked and badly injured. After crawling and stumbling back to the University, Donna left the country to be joined soon after by her husband. Newspapers and gossip revealed that Donna had been the victim of a payback rape for her racial slurs and her successful competition against Papua New Guinean businessmen. Although her rape shocked the University community, particularly the expatriates, many persons—expatriate and Papua New Guinean, male and female—blamed Donna for being too outspoken and too obviously successful for a female expatriate business woman.

As time went on, however, public outcry began to divide itself along sexual rather than racial lines, and all women were more fearful as they went about their daily activities. In another much-reported case in the city of Lae, several Papua New Guinean men raped and then murdered a respected and well-liked white helicopter pilot when the man she was trying to sell her car to drove her to a secluded place, where he was joined by the other men. During the trial, there were demonstrations throughout Papua New Guinea in favor of a strong penalty—"Death," "*Katim bol bilong ol*" ("cut their balls off!")—and when the defendants were let off with light sentences there was a spontaneous demonstration of several thousand women in Port Moresby protesting "men's disregard for women."

CONCLUSION

Although in the mid-1980s Papua New Guinea's male-dominated government supported the Law Reform Commission studies and a subsequent public awareness campaign on violence against women, rape and domestic violence are now "women's issues" in Papua New Guinea and no longer even a small part of male politicians' rhetoric. This shift became brutally apparent in 1987 when an all-male Parliament booed Rose Kekedo and other women from the floor when they tried to present the Law Reform Commission's interim report on domestic violence (*The Times of Papua New Guinea* 1992). In 1987 and since there have been no women in Papua New Guinea's Parliament.

Papua New Guinea has never had more than a few women in higher government positions, and at most there have been only three Papua New Guinean women in Parliament at the same time (1977–1982). Significantly, none of these women ever felt the need to run a feminist campaign, until recently, that is. Since 1987, as the numbers of female candidates and winners continues to shrink (Wormald 1992), female leaders such as former Parliamentarians Josephine Abaijah and Nahau Rooney have taken public positions on women's issues, focusing most on the concerns of "grassroots" women as crucial to Papua New Guinea's future and, of course, their own reelection. Rape and domestic violence top the list of concerns, however, as they affect all women (Waram 1992a and 1992b). Women's organizations have joined the campaign against violence with women leaders in Port Moresby choosing the theme "Violence Against Women" for their May 1993 International Women's Day Celebration (*The Times of Papua New Guinea* 1993b) and provincial women's leaders in East New Britain embarking on a campaign against violence and making plans to open a women's crisis center by 1994 (*The Times of Papua New Guinea* 1993a).

Similar situations exist in other Pacific countries, where violence against women is less prevalent but nonetheless serious and feared by women who see it destroying their families and any hopes they have for establishing new opportunities and relationships for themselves (Dominy 1990; Lateef 1990; Ralston 1993; Trask 1989; Zimmer-Tamakoshi 1993b and 1995). Women in Vanuatu and the Solomon Islands have been especially vocal, decrying the effects of colonialism and modernity on their societies (most notably alcohol abuse, consumerism, gambling, and class and sex inequalities), but, above all, the impact of male dominance on women's hopes and aspirations (see Billy, Lulei, and Sipolo 1983; Griffen 1976; Molisa 1983, 1987, 1989). Asserting what it is that women want, Vanuatu poet and feminist Grace Mera Molisa both unites and speaks for women throughout the Pacific in her poem

"Colonised People" (1987: 9–13), part of which is reprinted here:

> Women too
> have a right
> to be Free.
> Free to think
> Free to express
> Free to choose
> Free to love
> and be loved
> as Woman Vanuatu.

She does not, however, any more than my argument has, lay the blame for women's plight simply on the shoulders of men. While she blasts male leaders for scapegoating female politicians who threaten their grasp of power in "Hilda Lini" (1987: 26–27), she also condemns women for envying other women's successes and going along with men's definitions of things in "Delightful Acquiescence" (1989: 24):

> Half of Vanuatu
> is still colonized
> by her self.
> Any woman
> showing promise
> is clouted
> into acquiescence.

REFERENCES

Berndt, Ronald M. 1962. *Excess and Restraint: Social Control among a New Guinea Mountain People.* Chicago: University of Chicago Press.

Billy, A., H. Lulei, and J. Sipolo, eds. 1983. "*Mi Mere*": *Poetry and Prose by Solomon Islands Women Writers.* Honiara, Solomon Islands.

Borrey, Anou. 1994. "Youth, Unemployment, and Crime." Paper presented at the National Employment Summit, 11–12 May, Port Moresby, New Guinea.

Bowers, Nancy. 1965. "Permanent Bachelorhood in the Upper Kaugel Valley of Highland New Guinea." *Oceania* 36: 27–37.

Bradley, Christine. 1982. "Tolai Women and Development." University College of London. Unpublished Ph.D. thesis.

———. 1985. "Attitudes and Practices Relating to Marital Violence Among the Tolai of East New Britain." In Susan Toft (ed). *Domestic Violence in Papua New Guinea*, pp. 32–71. Port Moresby: Papua New Guinea Law Reform Commission Monograph No. 3.

———. 1994. "Why Male Violence Against Women Is a Development Issue: Reflections from Papua New Guinea." In Miranda Davies (ed). *Women and Violence*, pp. 10–26. London: Zed Books, Ltd.

Brown, Paula. 1969. "Marriage in Chimbu." In R. M. Glasse and M. J. Meggitt (eds.). *Pigs, Pearlshells, and Women: Marriage in the New Guinea Highlands*, pp. 77–95. Englewood Cliffs, NJ: Prentice Hall.

Chowning, Ann. 1985. "Kove Women and Violence: The Context of Wife-Beating in a West New Britain Society." In Susan Toft (ed.). *Domestic Violence in Papua New Guinea*, pp. 72–91. Port Moresby: Papua New Guinea Law Reform Commission Monograph No. 3.

Cook, E. A. 1969. "Marriage Among the Manga." In R. M. Glasse and M. J. Meggitt (eds.). *Pigs, Pearlshells, and Women: Marriage in the New Guinea Highlands*, pp. 96–116. Englewood Cliffs, NJ: Prentice Hall.

Counts, Dorothy Areyers. 1985. "Tamparonga: 'The Big Women' of Kaliai." In J. K. Brown, Virginia Kerns, and Contributors. In *Her Prime: A New View of Middle-Aged Women*, pp. 49–64. South Hadley, MA: Bergin and Garvey Publishers, Inc.

Counts, Dorothy Ayers, Judith K. Brown, and Jacquelyn C. Campbell (eds.). 1992. *Sanctions and Sanctuary: Cultural Perspectives on the Beating of Wives.* Boulder, CO: Westview Press.

Davies, Miranda (ed.). 1994. *Women and Violence: Realities and Responses Worldwide.* London: Zed Books Ltd.

Dinnen, Sinclair. 1993. "Big Men, Small Men and Invisible Women." *Australian and New Zealand Journal of Criminology* (March 1993) 26: 19–34.

———. 1996. "Law, Order, and State." In Laura Zimmer-Tamakoshi (ed.). *Modern PNG Society.* Bathurst, Australia: Crawford House Press.

Dominy, Michelle. 1990. "Maori Sovereignty: A Feminist Invention of Tradition." In J. Linnekin and L. Poyer (eds.). *Cultural Identity and Ethnicity in the Pacific*, pp. 237–257. Honolulu: University of Hawaii Press.

Faithorn, Elizabeth. 1976. "Women as Persons: Aspects of Female Life and Male-Female Relations Among the Kafe." In P. Brown and G. Buchbinder (eds.). *Man and Woman in the New Guinea Highlands*, pp. 86–95. Washington, DC: American Anthropological Association.

Finkelhor, David, and Kersti Yllo. 1985. *License to Rape: Sexual Abuse of Wives.* New York: Holt, Rinehart, and Winston.

Gelber, Marilyn G. 1986. *Gender and Society in the New Guinea Highlands: An Anthropological Perspective on Antagonism Toward Women.* Boulder, CO: Westview Press, Inc.

Glasse, R. M. 1969. "Marriage in South Fore." In R. M. Glasse and M. J. Meggitt (eds.). *Pigs, Pearlshells, and Women: Marriage in the New Guinea Highlands*, pp. 16–37. Englewood Cliffs, NJ: Prentice Hall.

Goodale, Jane C. 1980. "Gender, Sexuality, and Marriage: A Kaulong Model of Nature and Culture." In C. MacCormack and M. Strathern (eds.). *Nature, Culture and Gender*, pp. 119–142. Cambridge, UK: Cambridge University Press.

Griffen, V. (ed.). 1976. *Women Speak Out! A Report of the Pacific Women's Conference, October 27–November 2.* Suva, Fiji

Harris, Bruce. 1988. *The Rise of Rascalism—Action and Reaction in the Evolution of Rascal Gangs.* Port Moresby: Papua New Guinea Institute of Applied Social and Economic Research.

Herman, Dianne F. 1989. "The Rape Culture." In Jo Freeman (ed.). *Women: A Feminist Perspective*, pp. 20–44. Mountain View, CA: Mayfield Publishing Company.

Hogan, Evelyn. 1985. "Controlling the Bodies of Women: Reading Gender Ideologies in Papua New Guinea." In Maev O'Collins et al. (eds.). *Women in Politics in Papua New Guinea*, pp. 54–71. Working Paper No. 6. Canberra Department of Political and Social Change, Australian National University.

Jenkins, Carol (and The National Sex and Reproduction Research Team). 1994. *National Study of Sexual and Reproductive Knowledge and Behaviour in Papua New Guinea.* Papua New Guinea Institute of Medical Research Monograph 10.

Josephides, Lisette. 1985. *The Production of Inequality: Gender and Exchange Among the Kewa.* London: Tavistock.

———. n.d. "Gendered Discourses of Tradition and Change." Unpublished paper.

Langness, L. 1967. "Sexual Antagonism in the New Guinea Highlands: A Bena Bena Example." *Oceania* 37: 61–177.

———. 1969. "Marriage in Bena Bena." In R. M. Glasse and M. J. Meggitt (eds.). *Pigs, Pearlshells, and Women: Marriage in the New Guinea Highlands*, pp. 38–55. Englewood Cliffs, NJ: Prentice Hall.

———. 1974. "Ritual, Power, and Male Dominance." *Ethos* 2: 189–212.

Lateef, S. 1990. "Current and Future Implications of the Coups for Women in Fiji." *The Contemporary Pacific* 2 (1): 113–130.

Lindenbaum, Shirley. 1976. "A Wife is the Hand of Man." In P. Brown and G. Buchbinder (eds.). *Man and Woman in the New Guinea Highlands*, pp. 54–62.

Washington, DC: American Anthropological Association.

Lindstrom, Lamont. 1992. *Pasin Tumbuna: Cultural Traditions and National Identity in Papua New Guinea. Culture and Communications Working Paper.* Honolulu: Institute of Culture and Communications, East-West Center.

Meggitt, Mervyn J. 1964. "Male-Female Relationships in the Highlands of Australian New Guinea." *American Anthropologist* 66: 204–224.

Mitchell, William E. 1992. "Why Wape Men Don't Beat Their Wives: Constraints toward Domestic Tranquility in a New Guinea Society." In Dorothy Ayers Counts, Judith K. Brown, and Jacquelin C. Campbell (eds.). *Sanctions and Sanctuary: Cultural Perspectives on the Beating of Wives*, pp. 89–98. Boulder, CO: Westview Press.

Molisa, Grace Mera. 1983. *Black Stone.* Suva.

———. 1987. *Colonised People.* Port Vila, Vanuatu.

———. 1989. *Black Stone II.* Port Vila, Vanuatu.

Newman, Philip L. 1964. "Religious Belief and Ritual in a New Guinea Society." *American Anthropologist* 66: 257–272.

Oliver, Joan. 1987. "Women Students at the University of Papua New Guinea in 1985." In S. Stratigos and P.J. Hughes (eds). *The Ethics of Development: Women as Unequal Partners in Development*, pp. 156–172. Port Moresby: University of Papua New Guinea Press.

Parkinson, R. 1907. Thirty Years in the South Seas (trans. by N. C. Barry from Dreissig Jahre in der Sudsee). Stuttgart: Strecker and Schroder. Typescript in the Papua New Guinea Collection, University of Papua New Guinea.

PNG Post Courier. 1973a. "Four Tolai Girls." June 13.

———. 1973b. "Three Mataungan Students." June 28.

———. 1984a. "Gang Rapist Jailed for Seven Years." April 13, p. 9.

———. 1984b. "Pack Rape! Horror Attack on Two Families." October 4, p. 1.

———. 1984c. "Two More Attacks." October 23, p. 2.

———. 1984d. "Another Youth is Charged." October 25, p. 2.

———. 1984e. "Badili Horror: Sixth Youth Charged." October 26, p. 2.

———. 1984f. "Badili Attack Man Charged." October 30, p. 2.

———. 1984g. "Young Girl Raped." October 31, p. 2.

Ralston, Caroline. 1993. "Maori Women and the Politics of Tradition: What Roles and Power Did, Do, and Should Maori Women Exercise?" *The Contemporary Pacific* 5 (1): 23–44.

Ranck, Stephen and Susan Toft. 1986. "Domestic Violence in an Urban Context with Rural Comparisons." In S. Toft (ed.). *Domestic Violence in*

Urban Papua New Guinea, pp. 3–51. Law Reform Commission of Papua New Guinea, Occasional Paper No. 19.

Read, Kenneth E. 1952. "Nama Cult of the Central Highlands, New Guinea." *Oceania* 23: 1–25.

———. 1954. "Marriage Among the Gahuka-Gama of the Eastern Central Highlands, New Guinea." *South Pacific* 7: 864–871.

Riches, David, ed. 1986. *The Anthropology of Violence*. Oxford, UK: Basil Blackwell.

Rosi, Pamela, and Laura Zimmer-Tamakoshi. 1993. "Love and Marriage Among the Educated Elite in Port Moresby." In R. Marksbury (ed.). *The Business of Marriage: Transformations in Oceanic Matrimony*, pp. 175–204. Pittsburgh, PA: The University of Pittsburgh Press.

Russell, Diana E. H. 1984. *Sexual Exploitation*. Beverly Hills, CA: Sage Publications.

Still, K., and J. Shea. 1976. *Something's Got to be Done So We Can Survive in This Place: The Problem of Women Students at UPNG*. Education Research Unit Research Report 20. Port Moresby: University of Papua New Guinea.

Strathern, A. 1985. "Rape in Hagen." In S. Toft (ed.). *Domestic Violence in Papua New Guinea*, pp. 134–140. Law Reform Commission of Papua New Guinea Monograph No. 3.

Strathern, M. 1972. *Women in Between: Female Roles in a Male World*, Mt. Hagen, New Guinea. London: Seminar Press.

———. 1980. "No Nature, No Culture: The Hagen Case." In C. MacCormack and M. Strathern (eds.). *Nature, Culture and Gender*, pp. 174–222. Cambridge, UK: Cambridge University Press.

The Times of Papua New Guinea. 1992. "The Status of Women in Papua New Guinea." 9 January, p. 19.

———. 1993a. "East New Britain Women Embark on Campaign Against Violence." 4 March, p. 5.

———. 1993b. "Women Celebrate Their Day on Monday." 4 March, p. 2.

Toft, Susan. 1985. "Marital Violence in Port Moresby: Two Urban Case Studies." In S. Toft (ed.). *Domestic Violence in Papua New Guinea*, pp. 14–31. Papua New Guinea Law Reform Commission Monograph No. 3.

Toft, Susan (ed.). 1985. *Domestic Violence in Papua New Guinea*. Papua New Guinea Law Reform Commission Monograph No. 3.

———. 1986a. *Domestic Violence in Urban Papua New Guinea*. Papua New Guinea Law Reform Commission Occasional Paper No. 19.

———. 1986b. *Marriage in Papua New Guinea*. Papua New Guinea Law Reform Commission Monograph No. 4.

Toft, Susan, and S. Bonnell (eds.). 1985. *Marriage and Domestic Violence in Rural Papua New Guinea*.

Papua New Guinea Law Reform Commission Occasional Paper No. 18.

Trask, Haunani-Kay. 1989. "Fighting the Battle of Double Colonization: The View of an Hawaiian Feminist." *Ethnies* 8–9–10 (1): 61–67.

United Nations. 1989. *Violence Against Women in the Family*. Vienna: Centre for Social Development and Humanitarian Affairs.

Waddell, Eric. 1972. *The Mound Builders: Agricultural Practices, Environment and Society in the Central Highlands of New Guinea*. Seattle: University of Washington Press.

Waram, Ruth. 1992a. "Violence: A Crime Against Women." Papua New Guinea *Post Courier* 13 February, 24–25.

———. 1992b. "Women's Day Snubbed, While Many Centres Go Without Celebrations." Papua New Guinea *Post Courier* 26 March, 25 and 28.

Wormald, Eileen. 1992. "1992 National Election— Women Candidates in the Election." *The Times of Papua New Guinea* 28 May, 23–26.

Wormald, Eileen, and Anne Crossley, eds. 1988. *Women and Education in Papua New Guinea and the South Pacific*. Port Moresby: University of Papua New Guinea Press.

Zimmer, Laura J. 1990. "Sexual Exploitation and Male Dominance in Papua New Guinea." In a special issue on Human Sexuality. *Point* 14: 250–267.

Zimmer-Tamakoshi, Laura. 1993a. "Bachelors, Spinsters, and 'Pamuk Meris.'" In R. Marksbury (ed.). *The Business of Marriage: Transformations in Oceanic Matrimony*, pp. 83–104. Pittsburgh, PA: University of Pittsburgh Press.

———. 1993b. "Nationalism and Sexuality in Papua New Guinea." *Pacific Studies* 16 (4): 61–97.

———. 1995. "Passion, Poetry, and Cultural Politics in the South Pacific." In R. Feinberg and L. Zimmer-Tamakoshi (eds.). Politics of Culture in the Pacific Islands, special issue *Ethnology* 34 (2 & 3): 113–128.

———. 1996a. "Empowered Women." In W. Donner and J. Flanagan (eds.). *Social Organization and Cultural Aesthetics: Essays in Honor of William H. Davenport*, pp. 84–101. Pittsburgh, PA: University of Pennsylvania Press.

———. 1996b. "Papua New Guinean Women in Town: Housewives, Homemakers, and Household Managers." In L. Zimmer-Tamakoshi (ed.). *Modern PNG Society*. Bathurst, Australia: Crawford House Press.

———. n.d. "Patterns of Culture in the Tower of Babel: Letters from Port Moresby, Papua New Guinea." *Journal de la Société des Océanistes*, 103(2): 163–171.